America's History

Volume 2: Since 1865

FOURTH EDITION

America's History

Volume 2: Since 1865

James A. Henretta
University of Maryland

David Brody
University of California, Davis

Susan Ware
Radcliffe College

Marilynn S. Johnson
Boston College

Bedford / St. Martin's
Boston • New York

For Bedford/St. Martin's

Executive Editor: Katherine E. Kurzman
Senior Developmental Editor: Elizabeth M. Welch
Senior Production Editor: Shuli Traub
Senior Production Supervisor: Joe Ford
Senior Marketing Manager: Charles Cavaliere
Art Director: Lucy Krikorian
Text and Cover Design: Wanda Kossak
Advisory Editor for Cartography: Michael P. Conzen, University of Chicago
Copy Editors: Alice Vigliani/Patricia Herbst
Indexer: Melanie Belkin
Photo Research: Pembroke Herbert and Sandi Rygiel/Picture Research Consultants & Archives
Cover Art: Downtown Dallas by Robine Artline Smith. Courtesy of David Dike Fine Art, Dallas, Texas.
Composition: TSI Graphics
Printing and Binding: RR Donnelley & Sons Company

President: Charles H. Christensen
Editorial Director: Joan E. Feinberg
Director of Editing, Design, and Production: Marcia Cohen
Managing Editor: Erica T. Appel

Library of Congress Catalog Card Number: 99-62280

Manufactured in the United States of America.

5 4 3 2 1 0
f e d c

For information, write: Bedford/St. Martin's, 75 Arlington Street, Boston, MA 02116 (617-426-7440)

ISBN: 0-312-19389-0

Credits
Credits and copyrights are continued at the back of the book on pages C-1–C-2, which constitute an extension of the copyright page.

For our families

Preface for Instructors

The year 2000 is an auspicious time to be publishing the fourth edition of *America's History*. There's nothing like a new millennium to get the historical juices flowing, even in the most unsuspecting student. She is going to pause before some monumental development and say, "Whoa, wait a minute, how did that happen?" It might be the crowd of students in the library, online, peering into computer screens; or, on so many campuses, the glorious multi-ethnic, multi-racial mix of her classmates; or, on TV, news of more U.S. aid to Russia (formerly of President Reagan's Evil Empire). How did that happen?

This question is the very substance of historical inquiry. And in asking it, the student is thinking historically. In *America's History* we aspire to satisfy that student's curiosity. We try to ask the right questions—the big ones and the not-so-big ones—and then write narrative history that illuminates the answers. The story, we hope, tells not only what happened, but *why*. We exclude no student from our potential audience of readers. How could we, when we hold the conviction that every student, bar none, is curious about his or her past?

From the very inception of *America's History*, we set out to write a democratic history, one that would convey the experiences of ordinary people even as it recorded the accomplishments of the great and powerful. Throughout the book, we focus not only on the marvelous diversity of peoples who became American but also on the institutions—political, economic, social, and cultural—that forged a common national identity. And we present political and social history in an integrated way, using each perspective to make better sense of the other. In our discussion of government and politics, diplomacy and war, we show how they affected—and were affected by—ethnic groups and economic conditions, intellectual beliefs and social changes, and the religious and moral values of the times. Just as

important, we place the American experience in a global context. We trace aspects of American society to their origins in European and African cultures, consider the American Industrial Revolution within the framework of the world economy, and plot the foreign relations of the United States as part of an ever-shifting international system of imperial expansion, financial exchange, and diplomatic alliances.

In emphasizing the global context, however, we had something more in mind. We wanted to remind students that America has never existed alone in the world; that other societies have experienced developments comparable to our own; and that, knowing this, we can better understand what was distinctive and particular to the American experience. At opportune junctures, we pause along the way for a comparative discussion, as, for example, in this fourth edition, about the abolition of slavery in different nineteenth-century plantation economies. This enables us to explain why, in the universal struggle by emancipated slaves for economic freedom, the freedmen of the American South became sharecrop tenants in a market economy and not, as in the Caribbean, gang laborers or subsistence farmers. The operative word is *explain* and, insofar as we can make it so, explaining the past is what we intend *America's History* to do. The challenge is to write a text that has explanatory power and yet is immediately accessible to every student who enrolls in the survey course.

Organization

This means first of all grounding *America's History* in a clear chronology and a strong conceptual framework. Each half of the nation's history is divided into three parts, with each part corresponding to a distinct phase of development. Each part begins at a crucial turning point, such as the American Revolution or the Cold War, and emphasizes the dynamic forces that unleashed it and that symbolized the era. We want to show how people of all classes and groups make their own history, but also how people's choices are influenced and constrained by circumstances: the customs and institutions inherited from the past and the distribution of power in the present. We are writing narrative history, but harnessed to historical argument—not simply a retelling of "this happened, then that happened."

To aid student comprehension, each part begins with a two-page overview: first, a **thematic timeline** highlights the key developments in government, economy, society, culture, and diplomacy; then these themes are fleshed out in a corresponding **part essay.** Each part essay focuses on the crucial engines of historical change—in some eras, primarily economic; in others, political or diplomatic—that created new conditions of life and transformed social relations. The part organization, encapsulated in the thematic timelines and opening essays, helps students understand the major themes and periods of American history, to see that individual historical facts acquire significance as part of a larger pattern of development.

The individual chapters are similarly constructed with student comprehension in mind. A **chapter outline** gives readers an overview of the text discussion, followed by a **thematic introduction** that orients them to the main issues and ideas of the chapter. We reiterate the themes in an analytic **chapter summary,** which is paired with a **chapter timeline** that reminds students of important events. The **suggested readings** that conclude each chapter are annotated for students and, to facilitate research, divided into sections corresponding to the main sections of the chapter.

Features

The fourth edition of *America's History* contains a wealth of special features, offered not with an eye to embellishing the book but as essential components of the text's pedagogical mission. Each chapter includes two **American Voices**—excerpts from letters, diaries, autobiographies, and public testimony that convey the experiences of ordinary Americans in their own words. One-third of these personal documents are new to this edition, including Philip Fithian on "Sadism under Slavery," Black Hawk on "A Sacred Reverence for Our Lands," and Anne Moody on "'We Would Like to Be Served.'" Entirely new are the **Voices from Abroad**—first-person testimony in every chapter by a foreign visitor or observer that casts the American experience in a different light. Recognizing the centrality of technology in American life, we have doubled the number of **New Technology** essays, in which we describe key technical innovations and their impact on American history. New subjects include folk medicine, the battleship, and the biotech revolution. We retain our well-received **American Lives** feature—incisive biographies in every chapter of important, representative American figures of the time. Among the new Lives in this edition are the Shawnee prophet Tenskwatawa, the World War I propaganda chief George Creel, the black New Dealer Mary McLeod Bethune, and the architect of Cold War containment, George Kennan.

America's History has always been noted for its rich illustration program. In this edition, a new full-color design complements our special effort to enlarge many of the pictures and maps for better clarity and impact. Over one-third of the pictures are new to this edition, selected to reflect changes in the text and to underscore book themes. Ten new maps, mainly political in content, bring the number of maps to over 125, covering every aspect of American life that can be captured geographically.

Taken together, these documents and illustrations provide instructors with a trove of teaching materials, and students with a chance to enter the life of the past and see it from within.

Textual Changes

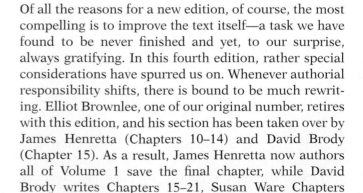

Of all the reasons for a new edition, of course, the most compelling is to improve the text itself—a task we have found to be never finished and yet, to our surprise, always gratifying. In this fourth edition, rather special considerations have spurred us on. Whenever authorial responsibility shifts, there is bound to be much rewriting. Elliot Brownlee, one of our original number, retires with this edition, and his section has been taken over by James Henretta (Chapters 10–14) and David Brody (Chapter 15). As a result, James Henretta now authors all of Volume 1 save the final chapter, while David Brody writes Chapters 15–21, Susan Ware Chapters 22–26 and 31, and Lynn Johnson Chapters 27–30.

We have also reduced the number of chapters from 33 to 31 to correspond more closely to the weeks of the academic calendar. In Part Three, former Chapters 13 (on sectionalism) and 14 (on the crisis of the Union) have been combined, with much of Chapter 13's discussion of southern society, Northeast industrialization, and the West shifted to earlier chapters. In Part Six, former Chapter 30 (on the politics of the 1960s) has been incorporated into the surrounding chapters. Structural changes of this magnitude have a bracing effect, and we are hopeful that by being forced to think hard about how to organize materials, we have come up with a stronger periodization and a clearer thematic development.

We also decided to cut text discussion by ten percent, in part to accommodate a richer array of features, but also to achieve a leaner, more sharply delineated narrative. In this, we were instructed by our experience in writing the Concise version of *America's History* that appeared in 1999. Brevity, we have learned all over again, is the best antidote to imprecise language and shoddy thinking. As textbook authors, we have always contended that if written with enough clarity and skill, the introductory survey text could be made accessible to students at all levels without simplifying the story or skimping on explanation. In this fourth edition, we have enlisted the power of brevity to get us ever closer to that goal.

The revising process is also an opportunity to incorporate new scholarship into our text. In this edition we have expanded the treatment of native Americans in the colonial era, and we have been more attentive to the appearance of a distinctive southern social order before 1820. Our treatment of the coming of the Industrial Revolution shifts the emphasis from industrialization as such to the extension of markets, in keeping with new scholarship on the Market Revolution. Chapter 11 on antebellum reform now stresses the religious roots and impulses common to communalism, women's rights, and abolitionism. We have drawn on recent Reconstruction scholarship that sees the transition from slavery to freedom in large part as a battle over labor systems, and that reveals the gender dimensions of the black struggle for racial equality, including most notably the political role of black women after disfranchisement in the late nineteenth century. We have continued our efforts to incorporate the West into the nation's historical narrative, relying on the new western history for insight into the interactions among environment, peoples, and economic development. In our coverage of the 1930s, we have linked the discussion of popular culture and movies more explicitly to the impact of the depression, and we have expanded our coverage of Mexican Americans during World War II and postwar decades. In our look at the modern era, more attention is given to the role of religion in American life and politics, and in our discussion of diplomacy our treatment of the Cold War is informed by recent scholarship drawing on hitherto closed Soviet and U.S. archives.

Finally, in deference to the new millennium, Susan Ware closes this fourth edition with the epilogue "America and the World at 2000: How Historians Interpret Contemporary Events and Their Legacy for the Future."

In seeking her own bearings at the millennium, Ware invites the student to enter the historian's world—to participate with her in the act of interpretation that lies behind every historical text, including this one.

Supplements

Readers of *America's History* often cite its ancillary package as a key to the book's success in the classroom. Hence we have revised and expanded with care our array of print and electronic ancillaries for students and teachers. We are especially pleased to welcome in the **Bedford Series in History and Culture** a new collection of potential supplements.

For Students

Documents Collection—Volume 1 by David L. Carlton (Vanderbilt University), Volume 2 by Samuel T. McSeveney (Vanderbilt University). This affordable two-volume Documents Collection offers students over 350 primary-source readings on topics covered in *America's History*, arranged to match the organization of the textbook. One-quarter of the documents in the collection are new, giving emphasis to contested issues in American history that will spark critical thinking and class discussions. Sets of documents highlight different perspectives on the same issue, while added attention has been given to America in the context of the larger world. Each document is preceded by a brief introduction and followed by questions for further thought.

Student Guide—Volume 1 by Timothy R. Mahoney (University of Nebraska); Volume 2 by Albert Berger (University of North Dakota). The two-volume Student Guide serves as a personal aid to students in their study of *America's History*, paralleling the textbook chapter by chapter to help them identify key ideas and assess their own grasp of the material. Each chapter in the Student Guide opens with all-new learning objectives that identify key themes for students to look for as they read, and a chapter summary that helps them determine whether they have mastered the primary concepts. The chapter timelines from the textbook appear with annotations, providing further framework for students' review. Newly expanded chapter glossaries include terms specific to each chapter as well as broader historical concepts that have changed in meaning over time. A set of exercises on the maps, art, and special features in the text encourage critical thinking, while identification and multiple-choice questions allow students to test their knowledge of the material. Guides to studying the part introductions (thematic timelines and corresponding part essays) in the textbook and a set of questions for each part help students understand the major themes in each period of American history. Finally, two new essays—"Doing History" and "What History Is"—set the study of *America's History* in a broader context and offer an understanding of the purpose and the techniques of the discipline.

Bedford/St. Martin's History Website—Developed by a group of scholars from Columbia University and New York University, the Bedford/St. Martin's History Website allows students to crystallize their knowledge of the themes and discussions in American history and to develop their own critical-thinking skills through a technological medium. Interactive chapter quizzes, map exercises, and primary-source research modules give students a means of reviewing what they have learned in *America's History* and of making meaningful connections between individual events in American history and larger trends. A prominently placed Research Room provides students with a collection of important documents from American history; an organized and annotated set of links to major libraries, history research centers, and American history sites; and a tutorial to help students evaluate historical sources critically for content and reliability. An unabridged online version of Scott Hovey's *Using the Bedford Series in History and Culture in the United States History Survey* can also help instructors integrate primary documents into their course syllabi, lectures, and class discussion.

The Bedford Series in History and Culture—Any of the volumes from this highly acclaimed series of brief, inexpensive, document-based supplements can be packaged with *America's History* at a reduced price. More than forty titles include *The Sovereignty and Goodness of God*, *The Interesting Narrative of the Life of Olaudah Equiano*, *The Autobiography of Benjamin Franklin*, *Narrative of the Life of Frederick Douglass*, *The Souls of Black Folk*, *Plunkitt of Tammany Hall*, and many more.

For Instructors

Instructor's Resource Manual—by Bradley T. Gericke (United States Military Academy). The *Instructor's Resource Manual*, provided free of charge with adoption of the textbook, offers an extensive collection of tools to aid both the first-time and the experienced teacher in structuring and customizing the American history course. Paralleling the textbook organization, this guide includes for each chapter in the text an all-new set of instructional objectives, a new annotated chapter outline to guide lectures, a chapter summary,

and an expanded version of the chapter timeline that gives greater detail about each entry. Lecture strategies and ideas for class discussion offer possible approaches to teaching each chapter and cover potentially difficult topics and how to present them; also included are suggestions for teaching the special boxed features in the textbook. A set of exercises for students includes questions about maps, graphs, and pictures in the textbook, and suggested writing assignments include topics involving the boxed features. The manual also reproduces the part introductions from the text and offers part instructional objectives to help instructors tie together larger sections of the book for students.

In addition to the chapter-by-chapter guidelines, the *Instructor's Resource Manual* features a set of fifteen updated historiographic essays on particular topics intended either as background for the instructor or for use with students. An expanded set of special primary-source modules on significant themes in American history allows instructors to customize their courses by emphasizing certain topics or perspectives in assignments or class discussions. Retained modules have been updated with new documents to represent more fully African Americans, Latino Americans, native Americans, women, the South, and constitutional history. All-new modules address religious history, military history, economic history, the presidency, and the West. A new essay about writing history can be photocopied and shared with students, while an updated and extensive list of suggested films is arranged by chapter and gives full detail for instructors wishing to use other media in the classroom. Finally, a new essay on using computers in the teaching of history keeps instructors abreast of the rapidly changing arena of electronic resources.

Test Bank—by James Miller. A fully updated Test Bank offers over 120 exercises for each chapter, allowing instructors to pick and choose from a collection of multiple-choice, fill-in, and map questions and short and long essay questions. To aid instructors in customizing their tests to suit their classes, every question is labeled by topic according to the chapter headings and includes a textbook page number that allows instructors to direct students to a particular page for correct answers. The multiple-choice questions are also labeled for instructors by difficulty level, and the correct answers are included. The Test Bank is available in bound paper format, with perforated pages for easy removal, or in Macintosh and Windows formats on disk.

Transparencies—A newly expanded set of over 150 full-color acetate transparencies, free to adopters, includes all maps and many tables, graphs, and images from the text.

CD-ROM with Presentation Manager Pro—For teachers who wish to use electronic media in the classroom, this new CD-ROM includes images, maps, graphs, and tables from *America's History* as well as sound recordings and a collection of supplementary images, in an easy-to-use format that allows instructors to customize their own presentations. The CD-ROM may be used with Presentation Manager Pro or with PowerPoint.

***Using* the Bedford Series in History and Culture *in the United States History Survey*—by Scott Hovey.** Recognizing that many instructors use a survey text in conjunction with supplements, Bedford/St. Martin's has made the Bedford series volumes available at a discount to adopters of *America's History*. This short guide gives practical suggestions for using more than forty volumes from the **Bedford Series in History and Culture** with a core text. The guide not only supplies links between the text and the supplements but also provides ideas for starting discussions focused on a single primary-source volume.

Acknowledgments
——★——

We are extremely grateful to the following scholars and teachers who reported on their experiences with the third edition or reviewed manuscript chapters of the fourth edition. Their comments often challenged us to rethink or justify our interpretations and always provided a check on accuracy down to the smallest detail.

Ruth M. Alexander, Colorado State University
Robin F. Bachin, University of Miami
Albert I. Berger, University of North Dakota
Neal A. Brooks, Essex Community College (Maryland)
Thomas Bryan, Alvin Community College
Markus C. Cachia-Riedl, University of California, Berkeley
Kay J. Carr, Southern Illinois University at Carbondale
Myles L. Clowers, San Diego City College
John P. Daly, Louisiana Tech University
Bradley T. Gericke, United States Military Academy
Nita S. Howard, Clovis Community College
Jen A. Huntley-Smith, University of Nevada—Reno
Davis D. Joyce, East Central University (Oklahoma)
Norman D. Love, El Paso Community College

John R. McKivigan, West Virginia University
Samuel T. McSeveney, Vanderbilt University
M. Catherine Miller, Texas Tech University
Charles K. Piehl, Mankato State University
Edwin G. Quattlebaum III, Phillips Academy
Steven D. Reschly, Truman State University
Leonard Riforgiato, Penn State University—Shenango
Howard B. Rock, Florida International University
Peter H. Shattuck, California State University—Sacramento
Emily J. Teipe, Fullerton College
Suzanne R. Thurman, Mesa State College
Ken L. Weatherbie, Del Mar College
Arthur J. Worrall, Colorado State University

As the authors of *America's History*, we know better than anyone how much of this book is the work of other hands and other minds. We are grateful to R. Jackson Wilson, who served as intellectual midwife at the project's birth, and to David Follmer, who in various guises as our editor, publisher, and agent has from the outset been a partner in our endeavors. We are equally appreciative of the help given us during our years at Worth Publishers by three very special people: Bob Worth, Paul Shensa, and our indefatigable editor, Jennifer Sutherland.

At Bedford/St. Martin's, Elizabeth Welch has held us to the highest standards of clarity and accuracy as she masterfully edited our text. Charles Christensen, Joan Feinberg, and Katherine Kurzman have been generous in providing the resources we needed to produce the fourth edition. Special thanks are due to many other individuals: Pembroke Herbert and her staff at Picture Research Associates; editor John Elliott; our senior project editor, Shuli Traub; the fine copyeditors who worked closely with us—Patricia Herbst and Alice Vigliani; editorial assistants Becky Anderson, Gretchen Boger, and Regan Park; our senior marketing manager, Charles Cavaliere; and senior production supervisor Joe Ford. We also want to express our thanks for the valuable assistance provided by John Cashman, Patricia Deveneau, Scott Hovey, and Lawrence Peskin.

From the very beginning we have considered this book as a joint intellectual venture and with each edition our collaborative effort has grown. We are proud to acknowledge our collective authorship of *America's History*.

James A. Henretta
David Brody
Susan Ware
Marilynn S. Johnson

Presenting *America's History:* An Introduction for Students

★

ITS TITLE REVEALS a lot about this book. From the very inception of *America's History*, the authors were determined to write a democratic history, one that would convey the experiences of ordinary people just as it recorded the accomplishments of the famous and powerful. They wanted to show the remarkable diversity of peoples who became American, and they wanted to show how broad historical forces and institutions—political, economic, social, and cultural—have influenced people's choices and forged a common national identity. In keeping with their inclusive vision of U.S. history, the authors sought also to place the American experience in a global context, to reveal the interactions between America and the wider world that have helped to shape the United States.

Broader in scope and richer in information and ideas than many texts, *America's History* nonetheless explains the past clearly and compellingly for all students of the U.S. survey. For explaining America's history—telling not only what happened but why it happened and why it matters—is what the authors set out to do. By reading this introduction, you will discover how they constructed their book and how to gain the most from it.

Part and Chapter Structure

There are many ways to tell the multifaceted story of America's past. Even if the basic information remains the same, historians understand causes and effects differently, consider different facts as more or less important, and—because social, cultural, and political developments often have rhythms and timelines of their own—even tell parts of the story in a different order. The authors of *America's History* intend to explain major social, cultural, and economic developments as clearly as political and diplomatic ones. Hence they have given careful thought to the structure of their book, so that its very organization might make clear all the main themes and developments of American history.

The thirty-one chapters in the text are grouped into six parts, with each part corresponding to a distinct historical period, or phase of development. Each part begins at a crucial turning point, such as the American Revolution or the Cold War, and chapters within each part explore the central historical forces—the engines of change—that shaped each period. This part organization, encapsulated in the part introductions, will help you to place individual events into historical context and to understand the major themes and periods of American history.

Part Introductions

Each part opens with a two-page overview intended to serve as a road map for the chapters ahead. First, a **thematic timeline** highlights the key developments in government, diplomacy, the economy, society, and culture that characterized the period. By reading the timelines vertically, you will see the principal developments in each of these categories over the course of the part; by reading them horizontally you will see what was happening on all those fronts at a specific time.

Second, a **part essay** that faces the timeline discusses the themes labeled in the timeline. By reading each part timeline and essay, you will gain a firm grasp on the main ideas and topics developed in the following chapters. Too, the part introductions double as useful review aids in preparation for tests and exams.

THEMATIC TIMELINE

	Government	Diplomacy	Economy	Society	Culture
	The Rise of the State	From Isolation to World Leadership	Prosperity, Depression, and War	Nativism, Migration, and Social Change	The Emergence of a Mass National Culture
1914	Wartime agencies expand power of the federal government	United States enters World War I (1917) Wilson's Fourteen Points (1918)	Shift from debtor to creditor nation Agricultural glut	Southern blacks begin migration to northern cities	Silent screen; Hollywood becomes movie capital of the world
1920	Republican ascendancy Prohibition (1920–1933) Business-government partnership	Treaty of Versailles rejected by U.S. Senate (1920) Washington Conference sets naval limits (1922)	Economic recession (1920–1921) Booming prosperity (1922–1929) Rise of welfare capitalism	Rise of nativism National Origins Act (1924) Mexican American immigration increases	Jazz Age (1920s) Advertising promotes consumer culture, supports radio and new magazines
1930	Franklin D. Roosevelt becomes president (1933)	Roosevelt's Good Neighbor Policy toward Latin America (1933)	Great Depression (1929–1941) Rise of labor movement	Farming families migrate from Dust Bowl states to California and	Documentary impulse Federal patronage of the arts

B Y 1914 INDUSTRIALIZATION, economic expansion abroad, massive immigration, and the growth of a vibrant urban culture had set the foundations for a distinctly *modern* American society. In all facets of politics, the economy, and daily life, American society was becoming more organized, more bureaucratic, and more complex. By 1945, after having fought in two world wars and weathering a dozen years of economic depression, the edifice of the new society was largely complete.

Government. First, an essential building block of modern American society was a strong national state. This state came late and haltingly to America compared with that of the industrialized countries of Western Europe. American participation in World War I called forth an unprecedented mobilization of the domestic economy,

was also the only one to possess a dangerous new weapon—the atomic bomb. Within wartime decisions and strategies lay the roots of the Cold War that followed.

Economy. Third, modern America developed a strong domestic economy. In fact, between 1914 and 1945 the nation's industrial economy was the most productive in the world. Even the Great Depression, which hit the United States harder than any other industrialized nation, did not permanently affect America's global economic standing. Indeed, American businesses successfully competed in world markets, and American financial institutions played the leading role in international economic affairs. Large-scale corporate organizations replaced smaller family-run businesses. The

Chapter Introductions

Just as the part introductions highlight central themes and topics in both graphic and narrative form, each chapter opens with two expressions of its main ideas and topics. To start, a **chapter outline** consisting of the main headings and subheadings of the chapter introduces you to subject matter and organization even before you begin to read. Next, a **thematic introduction** picks up from the outline to forecast the main issues and ideas of the chapter.

Chapter Headings

America's History contains a lot of information important for you to learn and remember. To help you navigate each chapter successfully, the authors employ three levels of headings—main headings to announce major topics and themes, subheadings to identify different aspects of the main topic, and sub-subheadings to divide subsections into related but distinct categories. The size and design of each heading indicate its level, with main headings the largest and most visually arresting and sub-subheadings the smallest and least prominent. As you read the chapter, consider the headings as signposts to main and contributing ideas and topics.

American Neutrality, 1939–1941
The Road to War
The Attack on Pearl Harbor

Organizing for Victory
Mobilizing for Defense
Mobilizing the American Fighting Force
Workers and the War Effort
Civil Rights during Wartime
Politics in Wartime

Life on the Home Front
"For the Duration"
Japanese Relocation

Fighting and Winning the War
Wartime Aims and Strategies
The War in Europe
The War in the Pacific

O N A SUNDAY night in October 1938 the actor Orson Welles's "Mercury Theater of the Air" broadcast a modern version of *The War of the Worlds* (1898) by the British writer H. G. Wells. The fictional news bulletins, interspersed with simulated on-the-spot reports, convinced many people that Martians had landed near Princeton, New Jersey, and were invading the countryside. Even though the broadcast included four announcements that the radio program was a dramatization, some people fled their homes. No one doubted the power of radio anymore.

One reason that so many people believed in Orson Welles's fictional invasion may have been that in September 1938, radio programs had been interrupted repeatedly by ominous news bulletins about a possible European war. Even the September 30 reports of the Munich agreement among Britain, France, and Germany, which prevented war for another year, did not ease people's fears of imminent catastrophe. In the late 1930s popular culture reflected America's connection to international events, an involvement that the coming of World War II would intensify. When radios announced on December 7, 1941, that the Japanese had attacked Pearl Harbor, Americans realized that this news flash was not a hoax.

---

were not uniformly grim. The depression was not on everyone's mind twenty-four hours a day. People continued their daily routine of work, family, and leisure. Literature and the arts flourished, and Hollywood movies and radio provided a welcome relief from hard times. Novelist Josephine Herbst recalled "an almost universal liveliness that countervailed universal suffering."

The Coming of the Great Depression

———★———

Since the beginning of the Industrial Revolution early in the nineteenth century the United States had experienced recessions or panics at least every twenty years. But none was as severe or lasted as long as the Great Depression. Only as the economy shifted toward war mobilization in the late 1930s did the grip of the depression finally ease.

The Causes of the Depression

The downturn began slowly and almost imperceptibly. After 1927, consumer spending declined and housing construction slowed. Inventories piled up, and in 1928 and 1929 manufacturers began to cut back on production and lay off workers; reduced incomes and buying power in turn reinforced the downturn. By the summer of 1929 the economy was clearly in a recession.

Stock Market Speculation and the Great Crash. Among the causes of the Great Depression, a flawed stock market was an important but not the dominant influence. By 1929 the market had become the symbol of the nation's prosperity and an icon of American business culture. The financier John J. Raskob captured this attitude in a *Ladies' Home Journal* article, "Everyone Ought to Be Rich." Invest $15 a month in sound common stocks, Raskob advised, and in twenty years the investment will grow to $80,000. Not everyone was playing the stock market, however. Only about 4 million Americans, representing about 10 percent of the nation's households, owned stock in 1929, and less than one-third of them had portfolios large enough to require the services of a stockbroker.

Stock prices had been rising steadily since 1921, but in 1928 and 1929 they surged forward with the

---

Chapter Conclusions

Each chapter ends with a **chapter summary** that revisits central issues and themes. A paired **chapter timeline** lists key events and dates. Together, the summary and timeline provide a quick review of the main developments discussed in the chapter and the specific events that shaped those developments.

Suggested Readings

The final page of each chapter provides a comprehensive list of Suggested Readings, each entry succinctly described by the text authors. If you want to learn more about a certain subject or need to find secondary sources for research, these up-to-date bibliographies will direct you toward interesting and important scholarship. To help you find easily works on a particular subject, the Suggested Readings are organized under headings that correspond to the main sections of the chapter.

Summary

★

A new chapter in American reform began at the start of the twentieth century. For decades the problems resulting from industrialization and urban growth had been mounting. Now, after 1900, reform began to dominate the nation's public life. The unifying element in progressivism was a common intellectual outlook, highly principled and idealistic as to goals, and confident of the human capacity to find the means.

Beyond this shared outlook, progressives broke up into diverse and often conflicting groups. Political reformers included business groups concerned chiefly with improving the efficiency of city government. Other progressives, such as Robert La Follette, opposed privilege and wanted to democratize the political process. Both groups worked to enhance their power at the expense of entrenched party machines.

T I M E L I N E

1889	Jane Addams and Ellen Gates Starr found Hull House
1893	Panic of 1893 starts depression of the 1890s
1899	National Consumers' League founded
1900	Robert M. La Follette elected Wisconsin governor
	Commission form of city government first appears, in Galveston, Texas
1901	President McKinley assassinated; Theodore Roosevelt succeeds him
1902	President Roosevelt settles national anthracite strike
1903	National Women's Trade Union League founded
1904	Supreme Court dissolves the Northern Securities Company
1905	*Lochner v. New York* overturns law restricting

Suggested Readings

★

Western history has become a bitterly contested ground in recent years. The fountainhead of the voluminous traditional scholarship is Frederick Jackson Turner's famous essay "The Significance of the Frontier in American History" (1893), reprinted in Ray A. Billington, ed., *Frontier and Section: Selected Essays of Frederick Jackson Turner* (1961). The "new" western history is critical of Turnerian scholarship for being "Eurocentric"—for seeing western history only through the eyes of frontiersmen and settlers—and for masking the rapacious and environmentally destructive underside of western settlement. Patricia N. Limerick's skillfully argued *The Legacy of Conquest: The Unbroken Past of the American West* (1987) opened the debate. Richard White, *"It's Your Misfortune and None of My Own": A New History of the American West* (1991), provides the fullest synthesis of the new scholarship. For an authoritative, balanced treatment of the main themes of western history, see the essays in Clyde A. Milner II *et al.*, *The Oxford History of the American West* (1994). On women's experience—another primary concern of the new western history—the starting point is Susan Armitage and Elizabeth Jameson, eds., *The Women's West* (1987). There are incisive environmental essays in Donald Worster, *Under Western Skies: Nature and History in the American West* (1992).

The Great Plains

The classic book, stressing the settlers' adaptation to climate and environment, is Walter P. Webb, *The Great Plains* (1931). There is an excellent chapter on the ecological history of the southern plains in Donald Worster, *The Great Plains* (1979). Robert M. Utley, *The Indian Frontier of the American West, 1846–1890* (1984), is a good introduction; Robert H. Lowie, *Indians of the Great Plains* (1954), is a classic anthropological study. On the religious life of the Plains Indians, see Howard L. Harrod, *Renewing the World: Plains Indian Religion and Morality* (1987). The assault on Indian culture is recounted in Fredrick E. Hoxie, *A Final Promise: The Campaign to Assimilate the Indians, 1880–1920* (1984). On phases of plains settlement, see Oscar Winther, *The Transportation Frontier: The Trans-Mississippi West, 1865–1890* (1964); Lewis Atherton, *The Cattle Kings* (1964); Gilbert Fite, *The Farmer's Frontier, 1865–1900* (1966); and Mary W. M. Hargreaves, *Dry-Farming in the Northern Great Plains* (1954). The ecological impact is

Illustration Program

America's History contains an unusually rich assortment of pictures, maps, graphs, and tables, all carefully chosen to extend or to reinforce the text. To help you appreciate the historical significance of each illustration, explanatory captions link the images to chapter discussion.

Quaker Oats
Like crackers, sugar, and other nonperishable foods, oatmeal had traditionally been marketed to consumers in bulk from barrels. In 1882 the grain merchant Henry P. Cowell completed the first continuous-process mill for oatmeal, cutting production costs and greatly increasing output. He also hit on the idea of selling oatmeal in boxes of standard size and weight to a national market. Broadsides showing the Quaker Oats man soon appeared in every American town, advertising a product

Pictures

Historians value the art and artifacts of a period much as they value its written documents—as primary sources, or historical evidence for what people thought and did in the past. The over 500 images in *America's History* are all contemporaneous with the period under discussion; that is, people living at that time created the art and artifacts reproduced. Thus you can examine each picture for clues to the period, much as you would study a printed historical document.

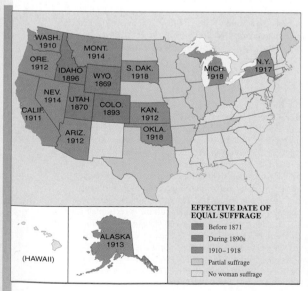

MAP 20.1
Woman Suffrage, 1869–1918
By 1909, after more than sixty years of agitation, only four lightly populated western states had granted women full voting rights. A number of other states offered partial suffrage, limited mostly to voting for school boards and such issues as taxes. Between 1910 and 1918, as the effort shifted to the struggle for a constitutional amendment, eleven states (and Alaska) joined the list granting full suffrage. The most stubborn resistance was in the South.

EFFECTIVE DATE OF EQUAL SUFFRAGE
- Before 1871
- During 1890s
- 1910–1918
- Partial suffrage
- No woman suffrage

Maps

Maps in *America's History* show much more than a visual representation of the land—each conveys information that is significantly dependent on *place*. The over 125 maps in your book cover every aspect of American life that can be captured geographically, from military campaigns and political shifts to territorial expansion and changes in ethnic and religious distribution. Study each map and its caption critically, remembering that maps extend as well as reinforce the text. (For a complete listing of maps, see p. xxxiii.)

Presenting America's History: *An Introduction for Students*

Graphs

Like maps, graphs reveal some historical patterns more clearly and vividly than words alone can. The many graphs in *America's History* show how specific data can add up to large social, economic, cultural, and political trends. Study them in conjunction with the text to understand key developments in greater depth and to learn how historians support their arguments with statistical evidence. (For a complete listing of graphs, see p. xxxiv.)

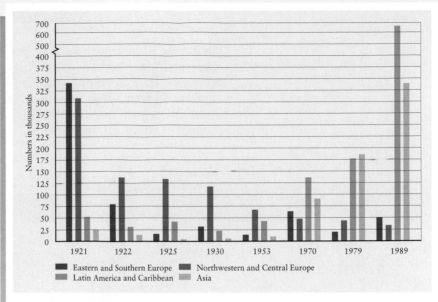

FIGURE **23.1**

American Immigration after World War I

Legislation reflecting nativism slowed the influx of immigrants after 1920, as did the dislocations brought on by depression and war in the 1930s and 1940s. Note the higher rate of non-European immigration since the 1970s.

Tables

Tables present factual information, often involving dates or quantities, in rows and columns for easy comparison. By looking at the information presented, you can usually identify an increase or decrease over time, a contrast or similarity between different places, and other progressions or developments. (For a complete listing of tables, see p. xxxiv.)

TABLE 19.1

Ten Largest Cities by Population, 1870 and 1910

	1870		1910	
City	Population	City	Population	
1. New York	942,292	New York	4,766,883	
2. Philadelphia	674,022	Chicago	2,185,283	
3. Brooklyn*	419,921	Philadelphia	1,549,008	
4. St. Louis	310,864	St. Louis	687,029	
5. Chicago	298,977	Boston	670,585	
6. Baltimore	267,354	Cleveland	560,663	
7. Boston	250,526	Baltimore	558,485	
8. Cincinnati	216,239	Pittsburgh	533,905	
9. New Orleans	191,418	Detroit	465,766	
10. San Francisco	149,473	Buffalo	423,715	

*Brooklyn was consolidated with New York in 1898.
Source: U.S. Census data.

Special Features

History is something one does, not just something one reads. Behind every historical narrative is the historian's act of interpretation, focused on questions that he or she has posed, researched, and sought to answer. In four special features, the authors of *America's History* highlight central questions and issues they have explored in their effort to write a balanced, inclusive narrative of the nation's history.

AMERICAN VOICES

ISAAC NELSON
Atomic Witness
★

Isaac Nelson, a naval veteran of World War II, returned to his hometown of Cedar City, Utah, in 1945 and went to work for a nearby hardware company. Like many other residents of southern Utah, he and his wife Oleta lived downwind from the Nevada Test Site, where the U.S. government detonated 126 atomic bombs into the atmosphere between 1951 and 1963.

After 1951 they were going to start the testing in Nevada, and everybody was really excited, and thought maybe we'd get a part to play in it and show our patriotism. We wanted to help out what little we could. My wife and I and a hundred or so residents of Cedar drove out to see the first one. We huddled up, our blankets around us because it was cold, so early in the morning before daylight, and we were chattering like chipmunks so excited! Pretty soon,

would go out and ooh and aah just like a bunch of hicks. We was never warned that there was any danger involved in going out and being under these fallout clouds all the time I lived here. . . .

Along about 1955 a cloud came over Cedar, and my wife and I, the kids and the neighbors stood outside looking at it and talking about it. Later on towards evening, my wife, her skin, her hands, arms, neck, face, legs, anything that was exposed just turned a beet red. . . . She got a severe headache, and nausea, diarrhea, really miserable. We drove out to the hospital, and the doctor said, "Well it looks like sunburn, but then it doesn't." Her headache persisted for several months, and the diarrhea and nausea for a few weeks.

Four weeks after that I was sittin' in the front room reading the paper and she'd gone into the bathroom to wash her hair. All at once she let out the most ungodly scream, and I run in there and there's about half her hair layin' in the washbasin! You can imagine a woman with beautiful, raven-black hair, so black it would glint green in the sunlight just like a raven's wing. . . . She was in a state of panic. . . . After that she kept getting weaker, and listless, and she didn't even have any desire to go out

American Voices

Each chapter contains two primary-source excerpts drawn from letters, diaries, autobiographies, public testimony, and other documents that convey the experience of ordinary Americans in their own words. Individually each feature provides a firsthand account of an event or development central to the chapter; together the excerpts reveal the rich diversity of the American people. (For a complete listing of "American Voices," see p. xxxv.)

Voices from Abroad

Despite its geographic distance from other parts of the world, America has always been influenced by events and traditions elsewhere. To illuminate what is comparable in the American experience and what is distinctive, first-person testimony in every chapter by a foreign observer casts America's history in a global perspective. (For a complete listing of "Voices from Abroad," see p. xxxvi.)

VOICES FROM ABROAD

HANOCH BARTOV
"Everyone Has a Car"
★

One of Israel's foremost writers and journalists, Hanoch Bartov spent two years in the United States working as a correspondent for the newspaper Lamerchav. As a newcomer to Los Angeles in the early 1960s, he was both fascinated and appalled by Americans' love affair with the automobile.

Our immediate decision to buy a car sprang from healthy instincts. Only later did I learn from bitter experience that in California, death was preferable to living without one. Neither the views from the plane nor the weird excursion that first evening hinted at what I would go through that first week.

Very simple—the nearest supermarket was about half a kilometer south of our apartment, the

never thought I might interpret his remark to refer to the walking distance. The moment a baby sees the light of day in Los Angeles, a car is registered in his name in Detroit. . . .

At first perhaps people relished the freedom and independence a car provided. You get in, sit down, and grab the steering wheel, your mobility exceeding that of any other generation. No wonder people refuse to live downtown, where they can hear their neighbors, smell their cooking, and suffer frayed nerves as trains pass by bedroom windows. Instead, they get a piece of the desert, far from town, at half price, drag a water hose, grow grass, flowers, and trees, and build their dream house. . . .

The result? A widely scattered city, its houses far apart, its streets stretched in all directions. Olympic Boulevard from west to east, forty kilometers. Sepulveda Boulevard, from Long Beach in the south to the edge of the desert, forty kilometers. Altogether covering 1200 square kilometers. As of now.

Why "as of now"? Because greater distances mean more commuting, and more commuting leads to more cars. More cars means problems that push people even further away from the city, which

American Lives

The authors want to show how people of all classes and groups shape their own history, but also how people's choices are influenced and constrained by circumstances: the customs and institutions inherited from the past and the distribution of power in the present. Incisive biographies in every chapter demonstrate how influential Americans confronted the major issues of their times. (For a complete listing of "American Lives," see p. xxxv.)

AMERICAN LIVES

Mary McLeod Bethune: Black Braintruster

★

THE NEW DEAL brought many remarkable people to Washington, but few had traveled as far as Mary McLeod Bethune. As the Reverend Adam Clayton Powell Sr. wrote to her in 1935 when she received the prestigious Spingarn Medal from the National Association for the Advancement of Colored People, "It is a long way from the rice and cotton fields of South Carolina to this distinguished recognition, but you have made it in such a short span of years that I am afraid you are going to be arrested for breaking the speed limit." In terms of her contributions to black history, Mary McLeod Bethune deserves to be remembered alongside such luminaries as Frederick Douglass, W. E. B. Du Bois, and Martin Luther King Jr.

Born on July 10, 1875, near Mayesville, South Carolina, Mary was the fifteenth of seventeen children born to Sam and Patsy McLeod, former slaves liberated after the Civil War. She was educated at the Scotia Seminary in Concord, North Carolina, and the Bible Institute for Home and Foreign Missions in Chicago (later the Moody Bible Institute) in preparation for her chosen career as a missionary. Turning from her original plan to go to Africa, she redirected her missionary ____ ____ ____ ____ and the field

Mary McLeod Bethune
This 1943 painting by Betsy Graves Reyneau captures the strength and dignity of one of the twentieth century's most important African Americans. Behind Bethune is a picture of the first building at the Daytona Literary and Industrial School for Training of Negro Girls, which later became Bethune-Cookman College.
National Portrait Gallery, Smithsonian Institution/Art Resource, NY.

expanded educational opportunities for Africa-

NEW TECHNOLOGY

New Technology

Recognizing the centrality of technology in American history, the authors pause twice in each part to consider revolutionary changes in technology that were central to the economic and cultural life of that period. (For a complete listing of "New Technology," see p. xxxvi.)

The Biotech Revolution

★

WAS ZACHARY TAYLOR poisoned? Did Abraham Lincoln have a rare disease called Marfan's syndrome? Were Tzar Nicholas II and his family executed during the Bolshevik Revolution in 1918? Was the Vietnam serviceman buried in Arlington Cemetery's Tomb of the Unknowns really Air Force Lieutenant Michael Blassie? Recent advances in DNA testing, part of the dramatic growth in biotechnology in the 1980s and 1990s, mean that these historical questions, plus a host of contemporary ones, can be answered. With promises of breakthroughs in medicine (gene therapy and cancer research), the environment (genetically altered microorganisms for pollution cleanup), and agriculture (genetically engineered foods), biotechnology offers the possibility not just to understand but also to manipulate the processes of life.

The essence of biotechnology is exploiting genes, a process revolutionized by the 1953 discovery of DNA by scientists James Watson and Francis Crick. DNA (deoxyribonucleic acid) is the molecule that carries the genetic blueprint of all living things; genes are DNA chains made up of hundreds or some-

Appendices

A rich collection of important documents, historical data, and research resources follows the chapters for your reference.

Documents

In addition to the complete texts of the Declaration of Independence, the Articles of Confederation, and the Constitution, this section provides annotations to the twenty-seven constitutional amendments that explain when and why each amendment was adopted. Six amendments that did not make it into the final document are discussed as well.

Amendment XXVII [1992]

No law, varying the compensation for the services of the Senators and Representatives, shall take effect, until an election of Representatives shall have intervened.

★ ★ ★

Whereas the Twenty-sixth Amendment was the most rapidly ratified amendment in U.S. history, the Twenty-seventh Amendment had the longest journey to ratification. First proposed by James Madison in 1789 as part of the package that included the Bill of Rights, this amendment had been ratified by only six states by 1791. In 1873, however, it was ratified by Ohio to protest a massive retroactive salary increase by the federal government. Unlike later proposed amendments, this one came with no time limit on ratification. In the early 1980s, Gregory D. Watson, a University of Texas economics major, discovered the "lost" amendment

The American Nation

This section includes such cornerstone facts of American political history as the admission of states into the Union, results of presidential elections, and a record of the Supreme Court justices.

Admission of States into the Union

	State	Date of Admission		State	Date of Admission		State
1.	Delaware	December 7, 1787	18.	Louisiana	April 30, 1812	35.	West '
2.	Pennsylvania	December 12, 1787	19.	Indiana	December 11, 1816	36.	Nevad
3.	New Jersey	December 18, 1787	20.	Mississippi	December 10, 1817	37.	Nebra
4.	Georgia	January 2, 1788	21.	Illinois	December 3, 1818	38.	Color
5.	Connecticut	January 9, 1788	22.	Alabama	December 14, 1819	39.	North
6.	Massachusetts	February 6, 1788	23.	Maine	March 15, 1820	40.	South
7.	Maryland	April 28, 1788	24.	Missouri	August 10, 1821	41.	Mont
8.	South Carolina	May 23, 1788	25.	Arkansas	June 15, 1836	42.	Washi
9.	New Hampshire	June 21, 1788	26.	Michigan	January 26, 1837	43.	Idaho

The American People

Numerous charts, graphs, and tables on issues such as population size, racial and ethnic composition, life expectancy, immigration trends, and changing labor patterns serve as a demographic survey of the American people.

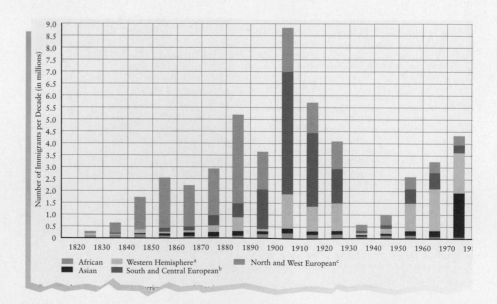

Presenting America's History: *An Introduction for Students*

Internet Resources

This section directs you to a variety of sources for further research—a list of internet sites that are major gateways to information on American history.

American Memory: Historical Collection from the National Digital Library Program. <http://rs6.loc.gov/amhome.html> An Internet site that features digitized primary source materials from the Library of Congress, among them African American pamphlets, Civil War photographs, documents from the Continental Congress and the Constitutional Convention of 1774–1790, materials on woman suffrage, and oral histories.

Decisions of the U.S. Supreme Court. <http://supct.law. cornell.edu/supct/#historic> This database can be used to search for information on various Supreme Court cases. Although the site primarily covers cases that occurred after 1990, there is information on some earlier historic cases. The justices' opinions, as originally written, are also included.

Directory of Scholarly and Professional Electronic Conferences. <http://n2h2.com/KOVAKS/> A good place to find out what electronic conversations are going on in a scholarly discipline. Includes a good search facility and instructions on how to connect to e-mail discussion lists, newsgroups, and

A central place to con native American history

Index of Resources f edu/history/index.html> sites of interest to histo eral topic. Some links information, but most a start an exploration of I

Internet Archives (tory.hanover.edu/texts.h purpose of this site is t students and faculty. A cally, and by subject, the primary-document link sources on each subject

Internet Resources (<http://www.libraries.rut A good place to begin r

Index

An unusually comprehensive index allows you to locate information in the text quickly and easily. The index, intended to double as a review aid for tests and exams, cites illustrations, maps, and figures as well as narrative discussion.

Website

In addition to the many print supplements described in the Preface, *America's History* has a website that provides further guidance to the text. Located at <http://www.bedfordstmartins.com/henretta.htm>, the website includes quizzes on each chapter with explanations of correct and incorrect answers, interactive map exercises, and exercises on how to use primary sources and to research history topics online. Use it to extend your reading of the text and your own discovery of America's history.

Contents in Brief

Contents

Maps, Figures, and Tables

Maps

Figures

Tables

Special Features

Voices from Abroad

New Technology

About the Authors

JAMES A. HENRETTA is Priscilla Alden Burke Professor of American History at the University of Maryland, College Park. He received his undergraduate education at Swarthmore College and his Ph.D. from Harvard University. He has taught at the University of Sussex, England; Princeton University; UCLA; and Boston University; as a Fulbright lecturer in Australia at the University of New England; and in 1991–1992 at Oxford University as the Harmsworth Professor of American History. His publications include *The Evolution of American Society, 1700–1815: An Interdisciplinary Analysis; "Salutary Neglect": Colonial Administration under the Duke of Newcastle; Evolution and Revolution: American Society, 1600–1820; The Origins of American Capitalism;* and important articles in early American and social history. He is currently working on a study of the *Transformation of the Liberal State in America, 1800–1970.*

DAVID BRODY is Professor Emeritus of History at the University of California, Davis. He received his B.A., M.A., and Ph.D. from Harvard University. He has taught at the University of Warwick in England, at Moscow State University in the former Soviet Union, and at Sydney University in Australia. He is the author of *Steelworkers in America; Workers in Industrial America: Essays on the 20th Century Struggle;* and *In Labor's Cause: Main Themes on the History of the American Worker.* He has been awarded fellowships from the Social Science Research Council, the Guggenheim Foundation, and the National Endowment for the Humanities. He is past president (1991–1992) of the Pacific Coast Branch of the American Historical Association. His current research is on industrial labor during the Great Depression.

SUSAN WARE specializes in twentieth-century U.S. history and the history of American women. She is affiliated with Radcliffe College, where she is editing the next volume of the noted biographical dictionary *Notable American Women.* Ware received her undergraduate degree from Wellesley College and her Ph.D. from Harvard University and from 1986 to 1995 taught in the history department at New York University. Her publications include *Beyond Suffrage: Women in the New Deal; Holding Their Own: American Women in the 1930s; Partner and I: Molly Dewson, Feminism, and New Deal Politics; Modern American Women: A Documentary History; Still Missing: Amelia Earhart and the Search for Modern Feminism;* and *Letter to the World: Seven Women Who Shaped the American Century.* She has served on the national advisory boards of the Franklin and Eleanor Roosevelt Institute and the Schlesinger Library of Radcliffe College, and has been a historical consultant to numerous documentary film projects. She is currently writing a biography of radio talk show pioneer Mary Margaret McBride.

MARILYNN S. JOHNSON is Associate Professor of History at Boston College, where she teaches U.S. social history and the history of the American West. She received her B.A. from Stanford University and her M.A. and Ph.D. from New York University. She is the author of *The Second Gold Rush: Oakland and the East Bay in World War II* and is currently working on a study of urban police violence in the late nineteenth and twentieth centuries. She has been a fellow of the American Council of Learned Societies and has served on the editorial board of *Pacific Historical Review.* Her articles and reviews have appeared in the *American Historical Review,* the *Journal of American History,* the *Journal of Urban History, Pacific Historical Review, Labor History,* and other scholarly publications.

America's History

Volume 2: Since 1865

Reconstruction,
1865–1877

I N HIS SECOND inaugural address, President Lincoln spoke of the need to "bind up the nation's wounds." No one knew better than Lincoln how daunting a task reconstruction of the Union would be. Foremost were the terms for restoring to the Union the states that had rebelled. But America's civil war had opened more fundamental questions. Slavery was finished. That much was certain. But what system of agricultural labor should replace plantation slavery? What rights should the freedmen be accorded beyond emancipation itself? How far should the federal government go to settle these questions? And who should decide? The president? Or Congress?

While the war was still on, the North began to grope for answers. Relying on his wartime powers, President Lincoln in December 1863 offered the secessionist states a chance to return to the Union on easy terms: the organization of loyal governments by 10 percent of the number of voters in 1860 who accepted Lincoln's general amnesty offer and took an oath of allegiance to the Union. Although it reflected Lincoln's conciliatory bent, his Ten Percent Plan, which only states under military occupation (Louisiana, Arkansas, and Tennessee) accepted, was really aimed at subverting the southern war effort. What it also did, however, was reveal the rocky road that lay ahead for Reconstruction. Thus, in Louisiana, sugar planters used the restored government to regain control over the freed slaves, employing curfew laws to restrict their movements and vagrancy regulations to force them back to work. But

Chloe and Sam (1882)
After the Civil War the country went through the wrenching peacemaking process known as Reconstruction. The struggle between the victorious North and the vanquished South was fought out on a political landscape, but Thomas Hovenden's warmhearted painting reminds us of the deeper meaning of Reconstruction: that Chloe and Sam, after lives spent in slavery, might end their days in the dignity of freedom.
Thomas Colville Fine Art.

the Louisiana freedmen fought right back. Led by the free-black community of New Orleans, they began to agitate for political rights. No less than their former masters, the former slaves intended to be actors in the savage drama of Reconstruction.

With Louisiana very much in mind, Republicans in Congress put forth a stricter substitute for Lincoln's Ten Percent Plan. The initiative came from the Radical wing of the party—those seeking a stern peace and full rights for the freedmen—but had broad support among more moderate Republicans. The Wade-Davis bill, passed on July 2, 1864, laid down, as conditions for the restoration of the rebellious states to the Union, the following: (1) an oath of allegiance by a majority of each state's adult white men, (2) new state governments formed and operated only by those who had never carried arms against the Union, and (3) permanent loss of voting rights by Confederate civil and military leaders. The Wade-Davis bill served notice that the congressional Republicans were not about to hand reconstruction policy over to the president.

Lincoln was not perturbed. Rather than openly challenging Congress, he executed a "pocket" veto of the Wade-Davis bill by not signing it before Congress adjourned. At the same time he initiated informal talks with congressional leaders aimed at finding common ground. Lincoln sensed that he had the upper hand. He could exploit the divisions among his fellow Republicans. And after four years of war, Americans were accustomed to strong executive leadership. The last speech Lincoln ever delivered, on April 11, 1865—two days after General Robert E. Lee's surrender at Appomattox—demonstrated his cautious realism. Reconstruction, Lincoln pleaded, had to be regarded as a practical, not a theoretical, problem. It could be solved only if Republicans remained united (even if that meant compromise) and only if the defeated South gave its consent (even if that meant forgiveness). What the speech showed, above all, was Lincoln's sense of the fluidity of events, of policy toward the South as an evolving, not a fixed, position.

What course Reconstruction might have taken had Lincoln lived is one of the unanswerable questions of American history. Three days after his speech, Lincoln was shot in the head at Ford's Theater in Washington by an unstable actor named John Wilkes Booth. (Ironically, Lincoln might have been spared if the war had dragged on longer, for Booth and his Confederate associates had originally plotted to kidnap the president to force a negotiated settlement.) Without regaining consciousness, Lincoln died on April 15. In one stroke John Wilkes Booth had sent Lincoln to martyrdom, hardened many northerners against the South, and handed the presidency to a man utterly lacking in Lincoln's moral sense and political judgment, Vice-President Andrew Johnson.

Presidential Reconstruction

At the end of the Civil War, a crucial constitutional question remained in dispute—whether, by seceding, the Confederate states had legally left the Union. If so, they were now conquered territories, and the terms of their readmission demanded the gravest consideration by Congress. If not, if even in defeat they retained their constitutional status, the initiative for restoring them to the Union might appropriately be taken by the president. This was Andrew Johnson's view, and by an accident of timing he was free to act on it: the Thirty-ninth Congress elected in November 1864 was not scheduled to convene until December 1865.

Johnson's Initiative

Andrew Johnson was a self-made man from the hills of eastern Tennessee. A Jacksonian Democrat, he saw himself as the champion of the common man. He hated what he called the "bloated, corrupt aristocracy" of the Northeast, and he was just as disdainful of the wealthy southern planters, whom he blamed for the poverty of the South's small farmers. But it was the poor *whites* that he championed; Johnson, himself a former slave-owner, had little sympathy for the slaves and was, in fact, implacably racist. His political career had taken him to the U.S. Senate, where he remained when the war broke out, loyal to the Union. After federal forces captured Nashville, Johnson became Tennessee's military governor. The Republicans nominated him for vice-president in 1864 in an effort to promote wartime political unity and to court the support of southern Unionists.

In May 1865, just a month after Lincoln's death, Johnson launched his own reconstruction plan. He offered amnesty to all southerners who took an oath of allegiance to the Union except for high-ranking Confederate officials and wealthy planters, whom Johnson held responsible for secession. Such persons could be pardoned only by presidential order. He appointed provisional governors for the southern states and laid down as conditions for their restoration only that they revoke their ordinances of secession, repudiate their Confederate debts, and ratify the Thirteenth Amendment, which abolished slavery. Within months all the former Confederate states had met Johnson's requirements and had functioning, elected governments.

At first Republicans responded favorably. The moderates among them were sympathetic to Johnson's argument that it was up to the states, not the federal government, to settle questions of the ballot and civil rights for the freedmen. Even the Radicals were optimistic. They liked the stern treatment of Confederate

Andrew Johnson
The president was not an easy man. This photograph of
Andrew Johnson (1808–1875) conveys some of the prickly
qualities that contributed so centrally to his failure to reach an
agreement with Republicans on a moderate reconstruction
program.
Library of Congress.

leaders, and they hoped that the new southern governments would respond positively to Johnson's conciliatory approach and offer the vote at least to African Americans who were literate and owned property.

Nothing of the sort happened. The South lay in ruins (see Voices from Abroad, "David Macrae: The Devastated South," p. 480). But southerners had not lost their fierce attachment to the old order. The newly seated legislatures moved to restore slavery in all but name. They enacted laws—known as Black Codes—designed to drive the freed slaves back to the plantations and to deny them elementary civil rights. The new governments had mostly been formed by southern Unionists, but when it came to racist attitudes, not a lot distinguished these loyalists from the Confederates. The latter, moreover, soon filtered back into the corridors of power. It turned out that Johnson, despite his hard words against them, forgave the former Confederate leaders easily, as long as he got the satisfaction of making them submit to his personal authority.

Stung by Republican criticism, Johnson began to rethink his political options. If the Republican establishment turned against him, then he would build a new coalition of white southerners, northern Demo-

crats, and disgruntled conservative Republicans. To retain the appearance of nonpartisanship, Johnson called his movement "National Union." The Civil War had left in disgrace the Democratic Party because it represented secession in the South and disloyalty in the North. Now Democrats realized that Johnson's gambit offered an avenue by which their discredited party could be restored to respectability. As the president warmed to Democratic applause, he granted more and more pardons to influential southerners—an average of a hundred a day in September 1865.

His perceived indulgence of their efforts to restore white supremacy emboldened the ex-Confederates. They packed the delegations to the new Congress with old comrades—nine members of the Confederate Congress, seven former officials of Confederate state governments, four generals and four colonels, and even the vice-president of the Confederacy, Alexander Stephens. For Republicans, this was the last straw.

Republican Response. Under the Constitution, Congress is "the judge of the elections, returns and qualifications of its own members" (Article 1, section 5). On this basis, the Republican majorities in both houses refused to admit the southern delegations when Congress convened in early December 1865, blocking Johnson's reconstruction program. Although relations with the president had frayed, the Republicans still assumed he would cooperate with them in formulating the new terms on which the South would be readmitted to Congress. To that end, a House-Senate committee—the Joint Committee on Reconstruction—was formed and began public hearings on conditions in the South.

In the meantime, the southern states backed away from the most flagrant of the Black Codes—those targeting one race—but in their place brought forth nonracial ordinances that were administered in the same way; they were applied to blacks, not to whites. Moreover, a wave of violence erupted across the South, intended to terrorize the freedmen into submission. In Tennessee, a Nashville paper reported that white gangs "are riding about whipping, maiming and killing all negroes who do not obey the orders of their former masters, just as if slavery existed." Listening to the vivid testimony of officials, observers, and victims, Republicans concluded that the South was trying to circumvent the Thirteenth Amendment. The only possible response was for the federal government to intervene.

Back in March 1865, the previous Congress had established the Bureau of Refugees, Freedmen and Abandoned Lands (known as the Freedmen's Bureau) to provide emergency aid to ex-slaves during the chaotic transition from war to peace. Now in early 1866, under the leadership of the moderate Republican senator Lyman Trumbull, Congress voted to extend the Freedmen's Bureau's life, gave it direct funding for the

DAVID MACRAE
The Devastated South

———————★———————

In this excerpt from The Americans at Home *(1870), an account of his tour of the United States, the Scottish clergyman David Macrae describes the war-stricken South as he found it in 1867–1868.*

I was struck with a remark made by a Southern gentleman in answer to the assertion that Jefferson Davis [the president of the Confederacy] had culpably continued the war for six months after all hope had been abandoned.

"Sir," he said, "Mr. Davis knew the temper of the South as well as any man in it. He knew if there was to be anything worth calling peace, the South must win; or, if she couldn't win, she wanted to be whipped—well whipped—thoroughly whipped." . . .

The further south I went, the oftener these remarks came back upon me. Evidence was everywhere that the South had maintained the desperate conflict until she was utterly exhausted. . . . Almost every man I met at the South, especially in North Carolina, Georgia, and Virginia, seemed to have been in the army; and it was painful to find many who had returned were mutilated, maimed, or broken in health by exposure. When I remarked this to a young Confederate officer in North Carolina, and said I was glad to see that *he* had escaped unhurt, he said, "Wait till we get to the office, sir, and I will tell you more about that." When we got there, he pulled up one leg of his trousers, and showed me that he had an iron rod there to strengthen his limb, and enable him to walk without limping, half of his foot being off. He showed me on the other leg a deep scar made by a fragment of a shell; and these were two of but seven wounds which had left their marks upon his body. When he heard me speak of relics, he said, "Try to find a North Carolina gentleman without a Yankee mark on him." . . .

Nearly three years had passed when I travelled through the country, and yet we have seen what traces the war had left in such cities as Richmond, Petersburg, and Columbia. The same spectacle met me at Charleston. Churches and houses had been battered down by heavy shot and shell hurled into the city from Federal batteries at a distance of five miles. Even the valley of desolation made by a great fire in 1861, through the very heart of the city, remained unbuilt. There, after the lapse of seven years, stood the blackened ruins of streets and houses waiting for the coming of a better day. . . . Over the country districts the prostration was equally marked. Along the track of Sherman's army especially, the devastation was fearful—farms laid waste, fences burned, bridges destroyed, houses left in ruins, plantations in many cases turned into wilderness again.

The people had shared in the general wreck, and looked poverty-stricken, careworn, and dejected. Ladies who before the war had lived in affluence, with black servants round them to attend to their every wish, were boarding together in half-furnished houses, cooking their own food and washing their own linen, some of them, I was told, so utterly destitute that they did not know when they finished one meal where they were to find the next. . . . Men who had held commanding positions during the war had fallen out of sight and were filling humble situations—struggling, many of them, to earn a bare subsistence. . . . I remember dining with three cultured Southern gentlemen, one a general, the other, I think, a captain, and the third a lieutenant. They were all living together in a plain little wooden house, such as they would formerly have provided for their servants. Two of them were engaged in a railway office, the third was seeking a situation, frequently, in his vain search, passing the large blinded house where he had lived in luxurious ease before the war.

———————

Source: Allan Nevins, ed., *America through British Eyes* (Gloucester, MA: Peter Smith, 1968), 345–347.

first time, and authorized its agents to investigate cases in which blacks were being denied the "civil rights belonging to white persons."

More extraordinary was Trumbull's proposal for a civil rights bill, declaring all persons born in the United States to be citizens and granting them—without regard to race—equal rights of contract, access to the courts, and protection of person and property. Trumbull's bill nullified all state laws depriving citizens of these rights, authorized U.S. attorneys to bring enforcement suits in the federal courts, and provided for fines and imprisonment for anyone, including public officials, found guilty of depriving a citizen of civil rights. In response to an unrepentant South, Republicans of the most moderate persuasion concluded that the federal government had to assume responsibility for securing the basic civil rights of the freedmen.

Acting on Freedom

While Congress debated, African Americans acted on their own idea of freedom. News of emancipation left them exultant and hopeful. Freedom meant many things—the reunion of separated families; the end of punishment by the lash; the ability to move around; and the opportunity to begin schools, form churches and social clubs, and, not least, engage in politics. Across the South blacks held mass meetings, paraded, and formed organizations. In the cities, where free blacks took the lead, Union Leagues and Equal Rights Leagues were formed to give the freedmen a political voice. With the encouragement of Freedmen's Bureau agents, state conventions also began to meet, passing resolutions demanding equality before the law and the right to vote—"an essential and inseparable element of self-government."

Struggling for the Land. First of all, however, came economic independence, which emancipated blacks believed was the basis for true freedom. During the Civil War they had acted on this assumption whenever Union armies drew near. During the final months of the war, when the Union directed its military operations against civilians, freedmen found greater opportunities to take control of land. Most visibly, General William T. Sherman

reserved vast tracts of coastal lands in Georgia and South Carolina—the Sea Islands and abandoned plantations within 30 miles of the coast—for liberated slaves, and settled them on 40-acre tracts. Sherman only wanted to relieve the burdens the refugees were placing on his army as it drove across the South. But freedmen took seriously the assurances of one of Sherman's generals "that they were to be put in possession of lands, upon which they might locate their families and work out for themselves a living and respectability."

As the war ended, resettlement became the responsibility of the Freedmen's Bureau, which was charged with feeding and clothing war refugees, distributing confiscated land to "loyal refugees and freedmen," and regulating labor contracts between freedmen and planters. The bureau also assisted the northern voluntary associations that were sending missionaries and teachers to work with former slaves.

Encouraged by the Freedmen's Bureau, blacks across the South occupied confiscated or abandoned land. Many families stayed on their old plantations, awaiting redistribution of the land to them after the war. One Georgia freedman offered to sell his expected share back to his former master. When the South Carolina planter Thomas Pinckney returned home, his freed slaves told him, "We ain't going nowhere. We are going to work right here on the land where we were born and what belongs to us."

Johnson's amnesty plan, entitling pardoned Confederates to recover property seized during the war, squelched these hopes. In October 1865, Johnson ordered General Oliver O. Howard, head of the Freedmen's Bureau, to tell Sea Island blacks that the land

Schoolhouse, Port Hudson, Louisiana
This was probably the first schoolhouse built for freedmen by Union forces. In front, African American soldiers from the Port Hudson "Corps d' Afrique" pose with their textbooks. It stood to reason that former slaves who had taken up arms should be first to receive the education so coveted by all freedmen.
Chicago Historical Society.

they occupied would have to be restored to the white owners. When Howard reluctantly obeyed, the dispossessed farmers protested: "Why do you take away our lands? You take them from us who have always been true, always true to the Government! You give them to our all-time enemies! That is not right!" (see American Voices, "A Plea for Land," p. 483).

In the Sea Islands and elsewhere, former slaves resisted these efforts. Often led by black veterans of the Union army, they fought pitched battles with plantation owners and bands of ex-Confederate soldiers. Landowners responded by attempting to disarm and intimidate the black veterans. One soldier wrote from Maryland: "The returned colard Solgers are in Many cases beten, and their guns taken from them, we darcent walk out of an evening. . . . They beat us badly and Sumtime Shoot us." In this warfare federal troops often backed the local whites, who generally prevailed in recapturing their former holdings.

Resisting Wage Labor.   As returning planters prepared for a new growing season, a battle began to take shape over the labor system that would replace slavery. Convinced that blacks could not work without supervision, planters insisted on retaining the gang system of plantation labor, only now paying low wages instead of the food, clothing, and shelter their slaves had once received. In this endeavor, the planters generally had the

backing of the Freedmen's Bureau. The main thing, its planners had said from the outset, was that the Union not encourage dependency "in the guise of guardianship." The ex-slave had to be "self-supporting," with no special privileges or burdens, but treated "as any other freeman." This was the message that the Bureau's agents carried into the devastated southern countryside. Rely upon your "own efforts and exertions," an agent told a crowd of freedmen in North Carolina, "make contracts with the planters," and "respect the rights of property."

This was advice given with little regard for the world in which those North Carolina freedmen lived. It was not only the unequal bargaining power between them and their former masters that they feared, or even that their former masters' real desire was to reenslave them through the coercive regulations of the Black Codes. In their eyes, the condition of wage labor was itself debasing. The rural South was not like the Yankee North, where working for wages had become the norm and qualified a man as independent. Selling one's labor to another—and in particular, selling one's labor to work another's land—implied not freedom but dependency. In the South, to be a "freeman"—a fully empowered citizen—meant heading a household, owning some property, carrying on one's own affairs.

So the issue of wage labor cut to the very core of the former slaves' struggle for freedom. Nothing had been more horrifying than the fact that as slaves, their

Wage Labor of Former Slaves
This photograph, taken in South Carolina shortly after the Civil War, shows former slaves leaving the cotton fields. Ex-slaves were organized into work crews probably not that different from earlier slave gangs, although they now worked for wages and their plug-hatted boss bears little resemblance to the slavedrivers of the past.
New-York Historical Society.

A Plea for Land

———————★———————

Following is a painfully written letter by the freedmen of Edisto Island off the coast of South Carolina to President Andrew Johnson. In it they plead for a reversal of his order that the lands they now worked be returned to their former masters.

Edisto Island S.C. Oct. 28th, 1865. To the President of these United States. We the freedmen Of Edisto Island South Carolina have learned From you through Major General O O Howard commissioner of the Freedman's Bureau, with deep sorrow and Painful hearts of the possibility of government restoring These lands to the former owners. We are well aware of the many perplexing and trying questions that burden Your mind. and do therefore pray to god (the preserver of all. and who has through our Late and beloved President [Lincoln] proclamation and the war made Us A free people) that he may guide you in making Your decision. . . . Here is where secession was born and Nurtured Here is where we have toiled nearly all Our lives as slaves and were treated like dumb Driven cattle. This is our home, we have made These lands what they are. . . . Shall not we who Are freedmen and have always been true to this Union have the same rights as enjoyed by Others? Have we broken any Law of these United States? have we forfeited our rights of property In Land?—If not then!

are not our rights as A free people and good citizens of these United States To be considered before the rights of those who were Found in rebellion against this good and just Government . . . And we who have been abused and oppressed For many long years But be subject To the will of these large Land owners. God forbid. Land monopoly is injurious to the advancement of the course of freedom, and if Government Does not make some provision by which we Freedmen can obtain A Homestead, we have Not bettered our condition.

. . . We the freedmen of this Island and the State of South Carolina—Do hereby petition to you as the President of these United States, that some provisions be made by which Every colored man can purchase land. and Hold as his own. We wish to have A home if It be but A few acres. without some provision is Made our future is sad to look upon. . . .

We pray that God will direct your heart in Making such provision for us as freedmen which Will tend to unite these states together stronger Than ever before—May God bless you in the Administration of your duties as the President of these United States is the humble prayer Of us all.—

In behalf of the Freedmen

	Henry Bram
Committee	Ishmael. Moultrie
	yates. Sampson

Source: Eileen Boris and Nelson Lichtenstein, eds., *Major Problems in the History of American Workers: Documents and Essays* (Lexington, MA: D.C. Heath, 1990), 137–139.

persons had been the property of others. In a famous oration celebrating the anniversary of emancipation, the Rev. Henry M. Turner spoke bitterly of the time when his people had "no security for domestic happiness," when "our wives were sold and husbands bought, children were begotten and enslaved by their fathers," and "we therefore were polygamists by virtue of our condition." That was why formalizing marriage was so urgent a matter after emancipation and why, when hard-pressed planters demanded that freedwomen go back into the fields, they resisted so resolutely. If the ex-slaves were to be free as white folk, then their wives could not, any more than white wives, labor for others. "I seen on some plantations," one freedman recounted, "where the white men would . . . tell colored men that their wives and children could not live on their places unless they work in the fields. The colored men

[answered that] whenever they wanted their wives to work they would tell them themselves; and if he could not rule his own domestic affairs on that place he would leave it and go someplace else."

The reader will see the irony in this definition of freedom: it assumed the wife's subordinate role and designated her labor the husband's property. But if that was the price of freedom, freedwomen were prepared to pay it. Far better to take a chance with their own men than with their former masters.

Many freedpeople voted with their feet, abandoning their old plantations and seeking better lives and more freedom in the towns and cities of the South. Those who remained in the countryside refused to work the cotton fields under the hated gang labor system or negotiated tenaciously over the terms of their labor contracts. When they could, families developed their own garden plots, guaranteeing at least a minimum level of subsistence. What was freedom all about if not to have a bit more leisure time, to labor less intensely than they had as slaves, and to work for themselves and their families?

The efforts of former slaves to control their own lives challenged deeply entrenched white attitudes. "The destiny of the black race," asserted one Texan, could be summarized "in one sentence—subordination to the white race." Southern whites, a Freedmen's Bureau official observed, could not "conceive of the negro having any rights at all." And when freedmen resisted, white retribution was swift and often terrible. The toll of murdered and beaten blacks mounted into untold thousands. The governments established under Johnson's plan only put the stamp of legality on the pervasive efforts to enforce white supremacy. Blacks "would be *just as well* off with no law at all or no Government," concluded a Freedmen's Bureau agent, as with the justice they got under the restored white rule.

In this unequal struggle, blacks turned to Washington. "We stood by the government when it wanted help," a black Mississippian wrote to President Johnson. "Now . . . will it stand by us?"

Congress versus President

Andrew Johnson was not the man to ask. In February 1866 he vetoed the Freedmen's Bureau bill, declaring it unconstitutional because Congress lacked authority to provide a "system for the support of indigent people" and because the states most directly affected by its provisions were not yet represented in Congress. The bureau, said Johnson, was an "immense patronage," showering benefits on blacks never granted to "our own people." A month later, rebuffing angry critics of his Freedmen's Bureau veto and overruling his own cabinet, Johnson vetoed Trumbull's civil rights bill, again arguing that federal protection of black civil rights constituted "a stride toward centralization." Johnson's racism, hitherto muted, now blazed forth. In his view, granting blacks the privileges of citizenship was discriminatory, operating "in favor of the colored and against the white race" and threatening all manner of evil consequences, including racial mixing.

Surprised by Johnson's attack on the civil rights bill, the Republicans were galvanized into action. They failed to override Johnson's veto of the Freedmen's Bureau bill, but in early April they got the necessary two-thirds majorities in both Houses and enacted the Civil Rights Act of 1866. This was a truly historic event, the first time Congress had prevailed over a presidential veto on a major piece of legislation. The Republican resolve was reinforced by news of mounting violence in the South, culminating in three days of rioting in Memphis. Forty-six blacks and two whites were left dead, and hundreds of black homes, churches, and schools were looted and burned. In July an angry Congress renewed the Freedmen's Bureau over a second veto by Johnson.

The Fourteenth Amendment. Anxious to consolidate their gains against Johnson, Republicans moved to enshrine black civil rights in an amendment to the Constitution. The heart of the Fourteenth Amendment was Section 1, which declared that "all persons born or naturalized in the United States" were citizens. No state could abridge "the privileges or immunities of citizens of the United States," deprive "any person of life, liberty, or property, without due process of law," or deny anyone "the equal protection of the laws." These phrases were intentionally vague, but they established the constitutionality of the Civil Rights Act and, more important, the basis on which the courts and Congress could establish an enforceable standard of equality before the law in the states.

For the moment, however, the Fourteenth Amendment was most important for its impact on national politics. With the 1866 congressional elections approaching, Johnson somehow figured he had a winning issue in the Fourteenth Amendment. He urged the states not to ratify it. Months earlier Johnson had begun to maneuver politically against the Republicans, aiming to build a coalition of white southerners, northern Democrats, and conservative Republicans under the banner of National Union. Any hope of creating a new national party, however, was shattered by Johnson's intemperate behavior and by escalating violence in the South. In New Orleans, a white mob attacked the delegates to a black convention and, aided by the local police, murdered thirty-seven blacks. A dissension-ridden National Union convention in July ended inconclusively, and Johnson's campaign against the Fourteenth Amendment became, effectively, a campaign for the Democratic Party.

Republicans responded with a scurrilous attack on the Democrats, unveiling a practice that would become known as "waving the bloody shirt." The Democrats were traitors, charged Indiana governor Oliver Morton, and their party was "a common sewer and loathesome receptacle, into which is emptied every element of treason North and South, every element of inhumanity and barbarism which has dishonored this age." In late August, Johnson embarked on a disastrous "swing around the circle"—a railroad tour from Washington to Chicago and St. Louis and back. It was unprecedented for a president to campaign personally, and Johnson made matters worse by engaging in shouting matches with hecklers and insulting members of the hostile crowds.

The 1866 congressional elections inflicted a humiliating defeat on Johnson. The Republicans won a three-to-one majority in Congress, so that, to begin with, the Republicans considered themselves "masters of the situation," free to proceed "entirely regardless of [Johnson's] opinions or wishes." As a referendum on the Fourteenth Amendment, moreover, the election registered strong popular support for the civil rights of the freedmen. The Republican Party emerged with a new sense of unity—a unity coalescing not at the center but on the left, around the program of the Radical minority.

Radical Republicans. The Radicals represented the abolitionist strain within the Republican Party. Most of them hailed from New England or from the area of the upper Midwest settled by New Englanders. In the Senate they were led by Charles Sumner of Massachusetts; in the House, by Thaddeus Stevens from Pennsylvania. For them, Reconstruction was never primarily about restoring the Union but about remaking southern society. "The foundations of their institutions . . . must be broken up and relaid," declared Stevens, "or all our blood and treasure will have been spent in vain."

Only a handful went as far as Stevens in demanding that the plantations be treated as "forfeited estates of the enemy" and broken up into small farms for the former slaves. But there was agreement about the need to guarantee the freedmen's civil rights and to grant them the suffrage. In this endeavor Radicals had no qualms about expanding the powers of the national government. "The power of the great landed aristocracy in those regions, if unrestrained by power from without, would inevitably reassert itself," warned Congressman George Julian. Radicals were aggressively partisan. They regarded the Republican Party as the instrument of the Lord, and black votes as the means by which the party could dominate the South and bring about its regeneration.

At first, in the months after the Confederacy's surrender at Appomattox, few but the Radicals themselves imagined they had any chance of putting across so extreme a program. Black suffrage especially seemed beyond reach, since the northern states themselves (except in New England) denied blacks the vote at this time. And yet, as fury mounted against the intransigent South, Republicans became ever more radicalized until, in the wake of the smashing victory of 1866, they embraced the Radicals' vision of a reconstructed South.

Radical Reconstruction

———★———

Afterward, thoughtful southerners admitted that the South had brought radical Reconstruction on itself. "We had, in 1865, a white man's government in Alabama," remarked the man who had been Johnson's provisional governor, "but we lost it." The state's "great blunder" was not to "have at once taken the negro right

Resistance in the South
This engraving, entitled *If He Is a Union Man or Freedman: Verdict, Hang the D--- Yankee and Nigger,* appeared in *Harper's Weekly* on March 23, 1857, just as the Reconstruction Act was being adopted. Thomas Nast's cartoon encapsulated the outrage at the South's murderous intransigence that led even moderate Republicans to support radical Reconstruction. Library of Congress.

under the protection of the laws." Remarkably, the South remained defiant even after the 1866 elections. Every state legislature (except, back in July, Tennessee) rejected the Fourteenth Amendment, mostly by virtual acclamation. It was as if they could not imagine that governments installed under presidential approval and fully functioning might be swept away. But that, in fact, is just what the Republicans intended to do.

Congress Takes Command

The Reconstruction Act of 1867, enacted in March by the Republican Congress, organized the South as a conquered land, dividing it (with the exception of Tennessee) into five military districts (Map 15.1), each under the command of a Union general. The price for reentering the Union involved granting the vote to the freedmen and disfranchising the South's prewar leadership class. Each military commander was ordered to register all eligible adult men (black as well as white), supervise the

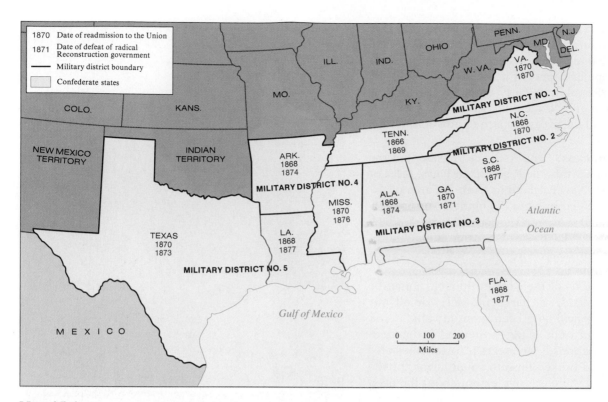

MAP 15.1
Reconstruction
The federal government organized the Confederate states into five military districts during radical Reconstruction. For each state the first date indicates when that state was readmitted to the Union; the second date shows when radical Republicans lost control of the state government. All the ex-Confederate states rejoined the Union from 1868 to 1870, but the periods of radical rule varied widely. Radicals lasted only a few months in Virginia; they held on until the end of Reconstruction in Louisiana, Florida, and South Carolina.

election of state conventions, and make certain that the new constitutions contained guarantees of black suffrage. Congress would readmit a state to the Union if its voters ratified the state constitution, if that document proved acceptable to Congress, and if the new state legislature approved the Fourteenth Amendment (thereby ensuring the needed ratification by three-fourths of the states). Johnson vetoed the Reconstruction Act, but Congress overrode the veto (Table 15.1).

The Tenure of Office Act.   Republicans also attacked President Johnson's room for maneuver. The Tenure of Office Act, a companion to the Reconstruction Act, required Senate consent for the removal of any official whose appointment had required Senate confirmation. Congress chiefly wanted to protect Secretary of War Edwin M. Stanton, a Lincoln holdover and the only member of Johnson's cabinet who favored radical Reconstruction. In his position Stanton could do much to frustrate Johnson's anticipated efforts to undermine Reconstruction. Congress also required the president to issue all orders to the army through its commanding general, Ulysses S. Grant. In effect, Congress was attempting to reconstruct the presidency as well as the South.

Seemingly defeated, Johnson appointed generals recommended by Stanton and Grant to command the five military districts in the South. But he was just biding his time. In August 1867, after Congress had adjourned, he "suspended" Stanton and replaced him with Grant, believing that the general would act like a good soldier and follow orders. Next Johnson replaced four of the commanding generals, including Philip H. Sheridan, Grant's favorite cavalry general. Johnson, however, had misjudged Grant, who publicly registered his opposition to the president's machinations. When the Senate reconvened in the fall, it overruled Stanton's suspension. Grant, now an open enemy of Johnson, resigned so that Stanton could resume his office.

Impeachment.   On February 21, 1868, Johnson formally dismissed Stanton. The feisty secretary of war, however, barricaded the door of his office and refused to admit the replacement Johnson had appointed. Three days later, House Republicans introduced articles of impeachment against the president, employing the power granted to the House of Representatives by the Constitution to charge high federal officials with "Treason, Bribery, or other high Crimes and Misde-

TABLE 15.1

Primary Reconstruction Laws and Constitutional Amendments

Law (Date of Congressional Passage)	Key Provisions
Thirteenth Amendment (January 1865*)	Prohibited slavery
Civil Rights Act of 1866 (April 1866)	Defined citizenship rights of freedmen Authorized federal authorities to bring suit against those who violated those rights
Fourteenth Amendment (June 1866†)	Established national citizenship for persons born or naturalized in the United States Prohibited the states from depriving citizens of their civil rights or equal protection under the law Reduced state representation in House of Representatives by the percentage of adult male citizens denied the vote
Reconstruction Act of 1867 (March 1867‡)	Divided the South into five military districts, each under the command of a Union general Established requirements for readmission of ex-Confederate states to the Union
Tenure of Office Act (March 1867)	Required Senate consent for removal of any federal official whose appointment had required Senate confirmation
Fifteenth Amendment (February 1869)	Forbade states to deny citizens the right to vote on the grounds of race, color, or "previous condition of servitude"
Ku Klux Klan Act (April 1871)	Authorized the president to use federal prosecutions and military force to suppress conspiracies to deprive citizens of the right to vote and enjoy the equal protection of the law

*Ratified by three-fourths of all states in December 1868.
†Ratified by three-fourths of all states in July 1868.
‡Ratified by three-fourths of all states in March 1870.

meanors." The House overwhelmingly approved eleven counts of presidential misconduct, nine of which dealt with violations of the Tenure of Office Act.

The case went to the Senate, which acts as the court in impeachment cases, with Supreme Court Chief Justice Salmon P. Chase presiding. After an eleven-week trial, thirty-five senators on May 15 voted for conviction, one vote short of the two-thirds majority required. Seven moderate Republicans had broken ranks, voting for acquittal along with twelve Democrats. The reluctant Republicans were overwhelmed by the drastic nature of the attack on Johnson; Congress had removed federal judges from office, but never a president. Even if Johnson had broken the law, they felt, the real issue was a political disagreement between Congress and the president. (In fact, the Supreme Court subsequently declared the Tenure of Office Act unconstitutional.) The vote for acquittal reflected fears that a conviction based on a policy dispute would establish a dangerous precedent and undermine the presidency—too high a price just to punish Johnson.

In any case, even without being convicted, Johnson had been defanged. For the remainder of his term he was helpless to alter the course of Reconstruction.

The Election of 1868. The impeachment controversy made Grant, already the North's most popular war hero, a Republican hero as well, and he easily won the party's presidential nomination in 1868. In the fall campaign he supported radical Reconstruction, but he also urged reconciliation between the sections. His Democratic opponent was Horatio Seymour, a former governor of New York who almost declined the nomination, certain that the Democrats could not overcome their identification with the disloyal South.

As Seymour feared, the Republicans "waved the bloody shirt," stirring up old wartime emotions against the Democrats to great effect. Seymour could only appeal lamely for a more moderate program that would permit the southern states to reorganize themselves. Grant won about the same share of the northern vote (55 percent) that Lincoln had won in 1864, and received 214 of 294 electoral votes. The Republicans also retained two-thirds majorities in both houses of Congress.

The Fifteenth Amendment. In the wake of their smashing victory, the Republicans produced the last major piece of Reconstruction legislation—the Fifteenth

"Liberty! Freedom! Tyranny is dead!
Run hence, proclaim, cry it about the street."

THE POLITICAL DEATH OF THE BOGUS CÆSAR.

"Speak to the common people, and cry out
LIBERTY, FREEDOM, and ENFRANCHISEMENT!"

Johnson's Impeachment

By including provisions for the impeachment and removal of a president, the Constitution gives Congress an orderly proceeding by which to serve the cause of justice. Perhaps inadvertently, Thomas Nast's cartoon in *Harper's Weekly*, entitled *The Political Death of the Bogus Caesar*, reveals the true nature of Johnson's impeachment. Nast's Roman senators have not concluded a judicial proceeding. They have assassinated Caesar, and that is how we must regard the Republican impeachment of Johnson, although, thanks to the Senate's acquittal, Johnson's political end was not as final as Caesar's. He served out his term, and six years later, in 1874, was elected U.S. senator from Tennessee.

Harper's Weekly, March 13, 1869.

Amendment, which forbade either the federal government or the states from denying citizens the right to vote on the basis of race, color, or "previous condition of servitude." Proponents of the amendment were aware that it left open the use of poll taxes and property or literacy tests to discourage blacks from voting. But northern states also valued such qualifications, employing them against immigrants and the "unworthy" poor. A California senator warned that in his state, with its rabidly anti-Chinese sentiment, any restriction on that power would "kill our party as dead as a stone."

Despite grumbling by Radical Republicans, the amendment passed without modification in February 1869. Congress required the unreconstructed states of Virginia, Mississippi, Texas, and Georgia to ratify it before they were readmitted to the Union. A year later the Fifteenth Amendment became part of the Constitution.

Woman Suffrage Denied. If the Fifteenth Amendment troubled some proponents of black suffrage, this was nothing as compared to the outrage felt by women's rights advocates. They had fought the good fight for so many years for the abolition of slavery, only to be abandoned when the chance finally came to get the vote for women. Leading suffragists such as Susan B. Anthony and Elizabeth Cady Stanton did not want to hear from Radical Republicans that this was "the Negro's hour" and that women would have to wait for another day. How could suffrage be granted to former slaves, Stanton demanded to know, but not to them? In her despair, Stanton lashed out in ugly racist terms against "Patrick and Sambo and Hans and Ung Tung," clueless about the Declaration of Independence yet entitled to vote, while the best and most accomplished

of American women remained voteless. In 1869 the annual meeting of the Equal Rights Association, the champion of both black and woman suffrage, broke up in acrimony, and Stanton and Anthony came out against the Fifteenth Amendment.

At this searing moment, a schism opened in the ranks of the women's movement. The majority, led by Lucy Stone and Julia Ward Howe, reconciled themselves to disappointment and accepted the priority of black suffrage. The Stanton-Anthony group, however, struck out in a new direction. Stanton declared that woman "must not put her trust in man" in fighting for her rights. The new organization that she headed, the New York–based National Woman Suffrage Association, accepted only women, focused exclusively on women's rights, and resolutely took up the battle for a federal woman suffrage amendment. It was more realistic, moderates felt, to seek piecemeal advances at the state level. Organized into the American Woman Suffrage Association, they remained allied to the Republicans in the forlorn hope that once Reconstruction had been settled, it would be time for woman suffrage.

The fracturing of the women's movement concealed the common ground the two sides shared. Both now realized that a popular constituency had to be built broader than the elite of evangelical reformers who had founded the movement. Both elevated suffrage into the preeminent women's issue. And both were energized by a shared anger not evident in earlier times. "If I were to give vent to all my pent-up wrath concerning the subordination of woman," Lydia Maria Child wrote to the Republican warhorse Charles Sumner in 1872, "I might frighten *you*. . . . Suffice it, therefore, to say, either the theory of our government is *false*, or women have a right

A Woman Suffrage Quilt
Homemade quilts provided funds and a means of persuasion for the temperance and antislavery movements. Suffragists, however, regarded quilts and needlework as symbols of the domestic subjugation of women, so woman suffrage quilts, such as this one (c. 1860–1880) depicting a women's rights lecture, were rare.
Collections of Mrs. Nancy W. Livingston and Mrs. Elizabeth Livingston Jaeger. Photo courtesy of the Los Angeles County Museum of Art.

to vote." If radical Reconstruction seemed a barren time for women's rights, in fact it had planted the seeds of the modern feminist movement.

Republican Rule in the South

Between 1868 and 1871 all the southern states met the congressional stipulations and rejoined the Union. Protected by federal troops and encouraged by northern party leaders, state Republican organizations took hold across the South and won control of the newly established Reconstruction governments. These Republican administrations remained in power for periods ranging from a few months in Virginia to nine years in South Carolina, Louisiana, and Florida (see Map 15.1). African Americans participated prominently in the Reconstruction governments. In Alabama, Florida, South Carolina, Mississippi, and Louisiana they constituted a majority of registered voters. They provided the votes for Republican victories there and in Georgia, Virginia, and North Carolina as well, where they accounted for nearly half the registered voters.

Carpetbaggers and Scalawags. Democratic ex-Confederates mocked and scorned southern whites who became Republicans as *scalawags*—an ancient

Scots-Irish term for runty, worthless animals. Whites who had come from the North they denounced as *carpetbaggers*—self-seeking interlopers who carried all their property in cheap suitcases called carpetbags. Carpetbaggers held more than half the governorships in the new Republican administrations and almost half the southern seats in Congress.

Actually, few southern Republicans conformed to the hostile stereotypes. Some carpetbaggers did come south for personal profit, but they also brought capital and skills. Union army veterans taken with the South—its climate, people, and economic opportunities—also figured heavily among the carpetbaggers. And interspersed with the self-seekers were many idealists anxious to advance the cause of emancipation.

The scalawags were even more diverse. Some had once been slaveowners, Whigs, or even Democrats, now drawn to Republicanism as the best way to attract northern capital to southern railroads, mines, and factories. In southwestern Texas the large German population was strongly Republican. They sent to Congress Edward Degener, an immigrant San Antonio grocer whom Confederate authorities had imprisoned and whose sons had been executed for treason. But most numerous among the scalawags were backcountry farmers who wanted to rid the South of its slaveholding aristocracy. Scalawags had generally fought against (or at least refused to support) the Confederacy; they believed that slavery had victimized whites as well as blacks. "Now is the time," a Georgia scalawag wrote, "for every man to come out and speak his principles publickly [*sic*] and vote for liberty as we have been in bondage long enough."

African American Leadership. The Democrats' stereotype of black political leaders as ignorant field hands who could only play at politics was just as false as the stereotypes about white Republicans. Until 1867 most African American leaders in the South came from the elite that had been free before the Civil War. With the formation of the reconstructed Republican governments in 1867, this diverse group of ministers, artisans, shopkeepers, and former soldiers reached out to the freedmen. African American speakers, some financed by the Republican Party, fanned out into the old plantation districts and recruited former slaves for political roles. Still, few of the new leaders were field hands; most had been preachers or artisans. The literacy of one former slave, Thomas Allen, who was a Baptist minister and shoemaker, helped him win election to the Georgia legislature. "In my county," he recalled, "the colored people came to me for instructions, and I gave them the best instructions I could. I took the *New York Tribune* and other papers, and in that way I found out a great deal, and I told them whatever I thought was right."

Many African American leaders who emerged in 1867 had been born in the North or had spent many

THE FIRST COLORED SENATOR AND REPRESENTATIVES.
In the 41st and 42nd Congress of the United States.

African American Congressional Delegation, 1872
This Currier and Ives lithograph celebrates one of the notable achievements of radical Reconstruction—the representation that ex-slaves won, however briefly, in the U.S. Congress. Hiram Revels of Mississippi, the Senate's first African American member, is seated at the extreme left.
Granger Collection.

years there. They moved south when radical Reconstruction offered the prospect of meaningful freedom. Like white migrants, many were veterans of the Union army. Some had fought in the antislavery crusade, some were employed by the Freedmen's Bureau or northern missionary societies, and a few came from free families and had gone north for an education. Others had escaped from slavery and were returning home. One of these was Blanche K. Bruce, who had received tutoring on the Virginia plantation of his white father. During the war Bruce escaped to Kansas from Missouri (where his father had moved) and then returned to Missouri, establishing a school for former slaves in Hannibal. He arrived in Mississippi in 1869 and entered politics; in 1874 he became the second African American elected to the Senate and the first elected to a full term.

Although never proportionate to their numbers in the population, African American officeholders held positions of importance throughout the South. Sixteen African Americans served in the U.S. House of Representatives. In 1870 Mississippi sent Hiram R. Revels, a minister born in North Carolina, to the Senate as its first African American member. In 1868 blacks constituted a majority in the lower house of the South Carolina legislature. They were heavily represented in the state's executive offices, elected to three seats in Congress, and won a seat on the state supreme court. Over the entire course of Reconstruction twenty African Americans served as governor, lieutenant governor, secretary of state, treasurer, or superintendent of education; more than six hundred served as state legislators. Almost all who became state executives had been free

before the Civil War, but in the legislatures most black members were former slaves.

The Radical Program.   The Republicans who took office had ambitious plans for a reconstructed South. They wanted to end its dependence on cotton agriculture and create an advanced economy based on manufacturing, capital investment, and skilled labor. Southern Republicans fell far short of achieving this vision, but they accomplished more of it than their critics gave them credit for.

The Republicans modernized state constitutions, eliminated property qualifications for the vote, and made more offices elective. They attended especially to the personal freedoms of the former slaves, sweeping out the shadow Black Codes enforcing labor discipline on the freedmen and controlling their movements. Women also benefited from the Republican defense of personal liberty. Nearly all the new constitutions expanded the property rights of married women, enabling them to hold property and personal earnings independent of their husbands. This was, a Georgia woman wrote, "a wonderful reform" for "the cause of Women's Rights." The Republicans' social program called for hospitals, more humane penitentiaries, and asylums for orphans and the insane. South Carolina provided medical care for the poor, and Alabama offered free legal counsel. Republican governments built roads in areas where roads had never existed. They poured money into rebuilding the region's railroad network, and they provided subsidies to attract factories. They undertook major public works programs. And they did all this without federal financing.

To pay for their ambitious programs the Republican governments copied the taxes that northern states had introduced during the Jacksonian reforms of the 1830s. These were general property taxes applying not only to real estate but to personal wealth. The Republican goal was to make planters pay their fair share of taxes and to broaden the tax base by forcing them to sell off uncultivated land. In many plantation counties, especially in South Carolina, Louisiana, and Mississippi, former slaves served as tax assessors and collectors, administering the taxation of their onetime owners.

Increasing tax revenues never managed to overtake the burgeoning obligations assumed by the Reconstruction governments. State debts mounted rapidly, and as interest payments on bonds fell into arrears, public credit collapsed. On top of that, much of the spending was wasted or ended up in the pockets of state officials. Corruption was endemic to American politics, present in the southern states before the Republicans came on the scene and rampant everywhere in this era, not least in the Grant administration itself. But there was no question that in the free-spending atmosphere of the early Republican regimes, corruption was especially widespread and damaging to the cause of radical Reconstruction.

Nothing, however, could dim the achievement in public education. Here the South had lagged woefully; only Tennessee had a system of public schooling before the Civil War. Republican state governments vowed to make up for lost time, viewing education as the foundation for a democratic order. African Americans of all ages rushed to attend the newly established schools, even when they had to pay tuition. An elderly man in Mississippi explained his desire to go to school: "Ole missus used to read the good book [the Bible] to us . . . on Sunday evenin's, but she mostly read dem places where it says, 'Servants obey your masters.' . . . Now we is free, there's heaps of tings in that old book we is just suffering to learn." By 1875 about half of all the children in Florida, Mississippi, and South Carolina were enrolled in school.

Except in New Orleans, the new schools were segregated. Most African Americans did not complain. They agreed with Frederick Douglass, the black abolitionist, that separate schools were "infinitely superior" to no schools at all. Integration was an issue for another day.

The Role of Black Churches. The building of schools was part of a larger effort by African Americans to fortify the institutions that had sustained their spirit during the days before emancipation. Religious belief had struck deep roots in nineteenth-century slave society. Now, in freedom, the African Americans buttressed their new communities by founding their own churches. They left their old white-dominated congregations, where they had been relegated to segregated balconies and denied any voice in church governance, and built churches of their own. These churches joined together to form African American versions of the Southern Methodist and Southern Baptist denominations, including, most prominently, the National Baptist Convention and the African Methodist Episcopal Church. Everywhere the robust black churches served not only as places of worship but as schools, social centers, and political meeting halls.

Black ministers were community leaders and often political officeholders. As Charles H. Pearce, a Methodist minister in Florida, declared, "A man in this State cannot do his whole duty as a minister except he looks out for the political interests of his people." Calling for the brotherhood of man and the special destiny

Freedmen's School, c. 1870
This rare photograph shows the interior of one of the 3,000 freedmen's schools established across the South after the Civil War. Although many of these schools were staffed by white missionaries, a main objective of northern educators was to prepare black women to take over the classroom. The black teacher shown here is surely one of the first.
Library of Congress.

of the former slaves as the new "Children of Israel," black ministers provided a powerful religious underpinning for the Republican politics of their congregations.

Sharecropping

In the meantime, the freedmen were locked in a great economic struggle with their former owners. In 1869 the Republican government of South Carolina had established a land commission to buy acreage and resell it on easy terms to the landless. In this way about 14,000 black families acquired farms. South Carolina's land distribution plan showed what was possible, but it was the exception, not the rule. Despite a lot of rhetoric, Republican regimes elsewhere did little to help the freedmen fulfill their dreams of becoming independent farmers. Federal efforts proved equally feeble. The Southern Homestead Act of 1866 offered 80-acre grants to settlers, limited for the first year to freedmen and southern Unionists. The advantage was strictly symbolic, however, since the public land made available to homesteaders was off the beaten track in swampy, infertile parts of the Lower South, and in any case, the freed slaves lacked the resources to get started. Only about a thousand families finally succeeded.

There was no reversing President Johnson's order restoring confiscated lands to former Confederates, even after the radical Republicans had the power to do so. Property rights, it seemed, trumped everything else, even for most champions of black rights. The Freedmen's Bureau, which had earlier championed the land claims of the ex-slaves, now devoted itself to teaching them how to be good agricultural laborers.

So, while they yearned for farms, most freedmen started out landless, and with no option but to work for their former owners. But not, they vowed, under the conditions of slavery—no gang work, no overseers, no fines or punishments, no regulation of their private lives or personal freedom. In certain parts of the agricultural South wage work became the norm—for example, on the great sugar plantations of Louisiana taken over after the war by northern investors. The problem was that cotton planters lacked the money to pay wages, at least not until the crop came in, and sometimes, in lieu of a straight wage, they offered a share of the crop. As a *wage*, this was a bad deal for the freedmen, but it opened up interesting possibilities. They soon realized that if they could be paid in shares for their work, they could pay in those same shares to rent the land they worked.

This form of land tenantry was already familiar in parts of the South among white farmers, and the freedmen now seized on it for the independence it offered them. Planters resisted, believing, as one wrote, that "wages are the only successful system of controlling hands." But in a battle of wills that broke out all across the cotton South, the planters yielded to "the inveterate

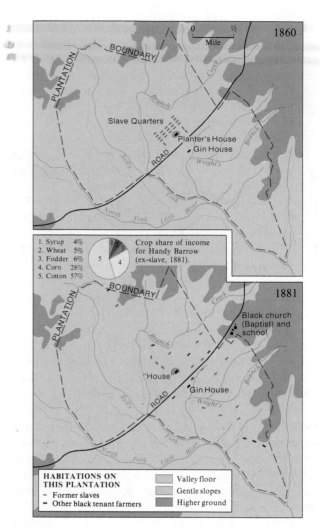

MAP 15.2
The Barrow Plantation, 1860 and 1881
Comparing the 1860 map of this central Georgia plantation with the 1881 map reveals the changing patterns of black residence and farming. In 1860 the slave quarters were clustered near the planter's house, which sat on a small hilltop. The sharecroppers of 1881 built cabins along the spurs or ridges of land between the streams, scattering their community over the plantation. A black church and school were built by this date. A typical sharecropper on the plantation earned most of his income from growing cotton.

prejudices of the freedmen, who desire to be masters of their own time."

Thus there sprang up a distinctively southern system of agricultural labor—*sharecropping*, in which the freedmen worked as renters, exchanging their labor for the use of land, house, implements, and sometimes seed and fertilizer, typically turning over half to two-thirds of their crops to the landlord (Map 15.2). The sharecropping system joined laborers and the owners of land and capital in a common sharing of risks and returns. But it was a very unequal relationship, given the force of southern law and custom on the white landowner's side, and given the dire economic circum-

Sharecroppers
This sharecropping family stands proudly in front of their new cabin and young cotton crop, which is planted nearly up to the cabin door. But the presence of the white landlord in the background casts a shadow on them, suggesting their hard struggle for economic freedom.
Brown Brothers.

stances of the sharecroppers. Starting out in poverty, they had no way of making it through the first growing season without borrowing for food and supplies.

Country storekeepers stepped in. Bankrolled by their northern suppliers, they "furnished" the sharecropper and took as collateral a *lien* on the crop, effectively assuming ownership of the cropper's share. Once indebted at one store, the sharecropper was no longer free to shop around and thus became an easy target for inflated prices, unfair interest rates, and crooked bookkeeping. As cotton prices declined during the 1870s, more and more sharecroppers fell into permanent debt. And if the merchant was also the landowner, or conspired with the landowner, the debt became a pretext for compulsory labor, or *peonage*, although evidence now suggests that sharecroppers generally managed to pull up stakes and move on once things became hopeless. Sharecroppers always thought twice about moving, however, because part of their "capital" was being known and well-reputed in their home communities. Freedmen who lacked that local standing generally found sharecropping hard going and likely ended up in the ranks of agricultural laborers.

In the face of so much adversity, black families struggled to better themselves. The fact that it enabled *family* struggle was, in truth, the saving advantage of sharecropping, because it mobilized husbands and wives in common enterprise while shielding both from personal subordination to whites. The trouble with sharecropping, one planter grumbled, was that "it makes the laborer too independent; he becomes a partner, and has to be consulted." By the end of Reconstruction, about one-quarter of sharecropping families had managed to save enough to rent with cash payments, and eventually black farmers owned about one-third of the land they cultivated—but rarely the best land and usually at a cost greater than its fertility warranted.

A Comparative Perspective. The battle between planters and freedmen over the land was by no means unique to the American South. Wherever slavery ended—in Haiti after the slave revolt of 1791, in the British Caribbean by abolition in 1833, in Cuba and Brazil by gradual emancipation during the 1880s—a fierce struggle ensued between planters seeking to restore a gang labor system and former slaves seeking to gain economic autonomy. The outcome of this universal conflict depended crucially on the ex-slaves' access to land. Where vacant land existed, as in British Guiana on the South American mainland, or where plantations could be seized, as in Haiti, the ex-slaves became subsistence farmers; and insofar as the Caribbean plantation economy survived without the ex-slaves, it did so by the importation of laborers from India and China. Where land could not be had, as in the British islands of Barbados and Antigua, the ex-slaves returned to plantation labor as wage workers, although often in some combination with customary rights to housing and garden plots. The cotton South fit neither of these broad patterns. The freedmen did not get the land, but neither did the planters get field hands. What both got was sharecropping.

The source of this exceptional outcome was ultimately political. Elsewhere, emancipation almost never meant civil or political equality for the freed slaves. Even in the British islands, where substantial self-government existed, high property qualifications effectively disfranchised the former slaves. In the United States, however, hard on the heels of emancipation came civil rights, manhood suffrage, and, for a brief era, a real measure of political power for the freedmen. Sharecropping took shape during Reconstruction, and there was no going back afterward.

For the freedmen, sharecropping was not the worst choice; it certainly beat laboring for their former owners. But for southern agriculture, the costs were devastating.

Sharecropping committed the South inflexibly to cotton, the one cash crop capable of satisfying the financial demands of landowners and furnishing merchants. Crop diversification declined, costing the South its self-sufficiency in grains and livestock. And with farms leased year-to-year, neither tenant nor owner had any incentive to improve the property. The crop-lien system lined merchants' pockets with unearned profits that might otherwise have gone into agricultural improvement. The result was a stagnant farm economy, blighting the South's future and condemning it to economic backwardness—a kind of retribution, one could say, for the fresh injustices visited on the people it had once enslaved.

The Undoing of Reconstruction

———————★———————

Ex-Confederates were blind to the benefits of radical Reconstruction. Indeed, no amount of achievement could have persuaded them that it was anything but an abomination, undertaken without their consent and intended to deny them their rightful place in southern society. Led by the planters, ex-Confederates staged a massive counterrevolution—one designed to "redeem" the South and restore them to political power under the banner of the Democratic Party. But the Redeemers could not have succeeded on their own. They needed the complicity of the North. The undoing of Reconstruction is as much about northern acquiescence as it is about southern resistance.

Counterrevolution

Insofar as they could win at the ballot box, southern Democrats took that route. They worked hard to get former Confederates restored to the rolls of registered voters, they appealed to racial solidarity and southern patriotism, and they attacked black suffrage as a threat to white supremacy. By 1869 the Democrats had enough votes to regain office in Tennessee, and a year later, in Virginia. But force was equally acceptable. Throughout the Deep South, especially where black voters were heavily concentrated, ex-Confederate planters and their supporters organized secret societies and waged campaigns of terrorism against blacks and their white allies.

The Ku Klux Klan. The most widespread of these groups, the Ku Klux Klan, first appeared in 1866 as a Tennessee social club but soon became a paramilitary force under Nathan Bedford Forrest, the Confederacy's most decorated cavalry general. (See American Lives, "Nathan Bedford Forrest: Defender of Southern Honor," pp. 496–497.)

Klan Portrait
Two armed Klansmen pose in their disguises, which they donned not only to hide their identity but also to intimidate their black neighbors. Northern audiences saw a lithograph based on this photograph in *Harper's Weekly* on December 28, 1868.
Rutherford B. Hayes Presidential Center.

By 1870 the Klan was operating almost everywhere in the South as a terrorist force serving the Democratic Party. The Klan murdered and whipped Republican politicians, burned black schools and churches, and attacked Republican Party gatherings (see American Voices, "Harriet Hernandes: The Intimidation of Black Voters," p. 498). In October 1870 a group of Klansmen assaulted a Republican rally in Eutaw, Alabama, killing four African Americans and wounding fifty-four. For three weeks in 1873 Klansmen laid siege to the small town of Colfax, Louisiana, which was defended by black Union veterans holding the county seat after a contested election. On Easter Sunday, armed with a small cannon, the whites overpowered the defenders and slaughtered fifty-two of them after they had surrendered under a white flag. Such terrorist tactics enabled the Democrats to seize power in Georgia and North Carolina in 1870 and make substantial gains elsewhere. An African American politician in North Carolina wrote, "Our former masters are fast taking the reins of government."

Congress responded by passing enforcement legislation, including the Ku Klux Klan Act of 1871, authorizing President Grant to use federal prosecutions, military force, and martial law to suppress conspiracies to deprive citizens of the right to vote, hold office, serve on juries, and enjoy equal protection under the law. For the first time, crimes by private citizens became violations of federal law. Government agents penetrated the Klan and gathered evidence that provided the basis for widespread arrests; federal grand juries indicted more than 3,000 Klansmen. In South Carolina, where the Klan was most deeply entrenched, federal troops occupied nine counties, made hundreds of arrests, and drove as many as 2,000 Klansmen from the state.

The Failure of Federal Enforcement. The Grant administration's assault on the Klan raised the spirits of southern Republicans, but it also emphasized how dependent they were on the federal government. The potency of the Ku Klux Klan Act, a Mississippi Republican wrote, "derived alone from its source" in the federal government; "no such law could be enforced by state authority, the local power being too weak." If Republicans were to prevail over ex-Confederate terrorism, they needed what one carpetbagger described as "steady, unswerving power from without."

Northern Republicans, however, grew weary of the financial costs of Reconstruction and the endless guerrilla war it seemed to produce. Prosecuting Klansmen under the enforcement laws was an uphill battle. Indeed, U.S. attorneys usually faced all-white juries, and the Justice department lacked the resources to handle the cases. After 1872, prosecutions began to drop off, and many Klansmen received hasty pardons; few served significant prison terms. Moreover, the Supreme Court undercut the enforcement legislation by ruling that the Fourteenth Amendment protected citizens from actions by the *states*, not by other citizens, so that federal prosecution of private bodies like the Klan became legally questionable.

In a kind of self-fulfilling prophesy, the unwillingness of the Grant administration to shore up Reconstruction guaranteed that it would fail. Republican governments that were denied federal help found themselves overwhelmed by ex-Confederate politicians during the day and by terrorists at night. Democrats overthrew Republican governments in Texas in 1873, in Alabama and Arkansas in 1874, and in Mississippi in 1875.

The Mississippi campaign showed all too clearly what the Republicans were up against. As elections neared in 1875, paramilitary groups such as the Rifle Clubs and Red Shirts operated openly. Often local Democrats paraded armed, as if they were militia companies. They identified black leaders in assassination lists called "dead-books," broke up Republican meetings, provoked rioting that left hundreds of African Americans dead, and threatened voters. Mississippi's

Republican governor, Adelbert Ames, appealed to President Grant for federal troops, but Grant refused. Ames then contemplated organizing a state militia but ultimately decided against it, believing that only blacks would join. Rather than escalate the fighting and turn it into a racial war, he conceded victory to the terrorists.

By 1877 Republican governments, backed by token U.S. military units, remained in only three states: Louisiana, South Carolina, and Florida. Elsewhere, the former Confederates were back in the saddle.

The Acquiescent North

At the outset, there was strong reason to believe that the North would stand fast on radical Reconstruction. The underlying ideal of equal rights inspired significant northern reform, especially in the treatment of northern blacks. This was partly because the Reconstruction amendments voided northern (as well as southern) laws denying blacks freedom to move between states and testify in court or vote. But northern states themselves moved against segregated public facilities and improved black access to education. In a typical rhetorical gesture, Michigan Republicans scorned "that political blasphemy which says, 'This is a white man's Government.' It is God's Government made for man!"

The spirit of equal rights extended to other causes—to women's rights, as already noted, and also to the labor movement. Trade unionism surged after the war. A new umbrella organization, the National Labor Union, formed in 1866 to fight "wage slavery" and advocate reforms that would bring about "the independence of the working class" and ensure "the success of our republican institutions."

The Civil War, moreover, brought into being an activist state. At the federal level, wartime Republicans legislated a national banking system, massive subsidies for interregional railroads, free homesteads for settlers, an expanded postal system, and improvements in rivers and harbors. The Republican Party sought "large and noble schemes of national advancement." The noblest of these was the U.S. Sanitary Commission, a privately funded body that started in 1861 by tending sick and wounded soldiers but ended by advancing an ambitious agenda for national betterment.

In Republican-controlled states, there was an equally dramatic increase in public programs after the war. The New York legislature established teacher-training colleges, the first state Board of Charities, a powerful Board of Health, and free public schools (in place of schools financed by parents according to the number of days their children attended). Everywhere in the North, education took pride of place, with public expenditures increasing from $19.9 million in 1860 to $61.7 million in 1870. "With free soil, free schools, a free press, and free men," a Republican journalist

Nathan Bedford Forrest: Defender of Southern Honor

★

NATHAN BEDFORD FORREST, the South's fiercest champion, as a boy had little stake in the old plantation order. His father was a blacksmith who followed the frontier to Tennessee, where Forrest, the oldest of eleven children, was born on July 13, 1821. When Forrest was only sixteen years old, his father died, leaving him as the primary breadwinner. With hardly any schooling the boy took charge of the family's rented farm; he also became an adept horsetrader. At age twenty-one, when his mother remarried, he left for Hernando, Mississippi, where his uncle ran a livery business.

Tall and physically impressive, Forrest normally spoke with great courtesy, but he had a violent temper. When four men attacked his uncle, Forrest leapt to his defense. The uncle died from a bullet meant for his nephew, but the young Forrest had shown his mettle. Admiring his raw courage, Hernando citizens rewarded Forrest by electing him town constable. Equally implacable in love, in 1845 Forrest so insistently wooed a young lady from a well-connected local family that at their third meeting she agreed to marry him.

For a hard-driving young man like Forrest, the booming cotton economy offered much opportunity. He took over his uncle's business, ran a stagecoach service, and traded livestock and—in due course—slaves as well. In 1851 ambition took him and his family to nearby Memphis, Tennessee, where he became a well-known slave trader. With his profits he purchased a large plantation in Mississippi. By now he had become a man of substance, a leading Memphis citizen. In the sectional crisis that was brewing at the time, Forrest was not a firebrand secessionist but fiercely championed southern rights and, of course, slavery.

When war broke out in 1861 he immediately organized a Tennessee cavalry regiment. In April 1862 he distinguished himself at the bloody Battle of Shiloh, although he was badly wounded during the retreat. Promoted to brigadier general, he began a brilliant career as a cavalry raider, mostly fighting behind Union lines. His aggressive spirit often carried him into the thick of battle, oblivious to the fact that he was a general and not a trooper.

Nathan Bedford Forrest, c. 1866
Tennessee State Museum.

That same explosiveness ignited one of the war's worst atrocities, the slaughter of black troops at Fort Pillow, Tennessee, on April 12, 1864, evidently because of rumors that the Fort Pillow garrison had been harassing local whites who were loyal to the Confederacy.

The Fort Pillow massacre foreshadowed the civil strife that would consume Tennessee for the next half-decade, especially after the Republican William G. Brownlow was elected governor in March 1865. A former Confederate prisoner, Brownlow was not shy about calling his enemies to account. Under his governorship the disfranchisement of former Confederates, hitherto partial, became general, leaving political power in the hands of a minority of Unionist whites and freed slaves. When racial tensions exploded into a bloody riot against blacks in Memphis in May 1866, Brownlow at once intervened, transferring the responsibility for maintaining order from local police to a commission appointed by him. Former Confederates around the state concluded that they could regain power only by waging a secret campaign of terror against Brownlow's base of support in the black community. This was the genesis, among other things, of the first "den" of the Ku Klux Klan in Pulaski, Tennessee, sometime in late 1865 or early 1866.

Home safe from the war, Forrest was absorbed by his own damaged fortunes. The wealth represented by his slaves had been wiped out by emancipation, and his Mississippi plantation was left heavily encumbered by his wartime debts. With the aid of the Freedmen's Bureau he managed to put his former slaves back to work. But flooding (probably caused by war-damaged levies) destroyed his cotton crop; in August 1866 he gave up, surrendering the plantation to his creditors. He then turned to other enterprises: a commission merchant firm, a fire and life insurance company, partnership in a Memphis street-paving firm, labor contracting for the Memphis & Little Rock Railroad. Forrest finally declared personal bankruptcy, having been swept down, like so many others, by the war-devastated economy. In desperation, he considered leading an expedition of former Confederate comrades to seize the riches of Mexico.

A more promising avenue for Forrest's energies, however, had by now opened up. From its obscure beginnings after the war, the Ku Klux Klan proliferated wildly across Tennessee and into neighboring states. What the Klan needed was a tough, respected figure able to impose order on the Invisible Empire and prevent it from spinning out of control—none other than Nathan Bedford Forrest. At a clandestine meeting in Nashville sometime in late 1866, he accepted the job and donned the robes of Grand Wizard, the Klan's highest office. Forrest's activities are mostly unknown because he worked in secrecy, but there is no mystery about why he gravitated to the Klan. For him, the Klan was politics by other means, the vehicle by which disfranchised former Confederates like himself might strike a blow against the despised Republicans who ran Tennessee.

In many towns, including Memphis, the Klan became virtually identical to the Democratic clubs; in fact, Klan members—including Forrest—dominated the state's delegation to the Democratic national convention of 1868. On the ground the Klan unleashed a murderous campaign of terror against Republican sympathizers. Governor Brownlow responded resolutely, threatening to mobilize the state militia and root out the Klan. If Brownlow tried, answered Forrest (for once emerging from secrecy), "there will be war, and a bloodier one than we have ever witnessed. . . . If the militia attack us, we will resist to the last; and, if necessary, I think I could raise 40,000 men in five days, ready for the field."

For many months, Tennessee endured a high state of tension. In September 1868 a new law identified membership in the Klan as a felony, and in the following February martial law was declared in nine Klan-ridden counties. But it was the Republicans, not the Klan, that cracked. In March 1869 the redoubtable Brownlow retreated to the U.S. Senate. The Democrats were on their way back to power, and the Klan, having served its purpose, was officially disbanded in Tennessee.

Like many other Confederate heroes, Forrest might now have anticipated a comfortable life in politics. But he had too much blood on his hands. He was among the very last to be pardoned by President Johnson. His appearance at the Democratic convention in 1868 brought forth bitter Republican denunciations against "the Fort Pillow Butcher." Physical violence, moreover, still dogged his life, including the killing (he claimed self-defense) of a sharecropper on his plantation. What sealed Forrest's political fate, however, was the Ku Klux Klan. This was, to some degree, undeserved. Forrest had regarded the Klan's mission in strictly political terms, its violence calibrated to the task of driving the Republicans from power. In this Forrest only reflected what conservative southerners generally favored. But he could not personally curb the senseless brutality against blacks done in the Klan's name. Any ruffian, he complained, could put on a white sheet and go after his neighbors. But Forrest was the Grand Wizard, and even after he resigned (probably late in 1869) his name could not be dissociated from Klan savagery. Celebrated though he might have been, when it came to supporting him for political office responsible Democrats kept their distance.

So Forrest had to cash in his chips elsewhere, which he did as president and chief promoter of the Memphis & Selma Railroad. Beginning in 1869 he worked tirelessly hawking bonds to communities along the proposed right of way, lobbying for state and county subsidies, and expending his considerable reputation to carry forward an ambitious project linking Memphis by rail to northern Alabama and eastern Mississippi. All in vain. The unfinished Memphis & Selma finally collapsed after the panic of 1873, and Forrest was left with nothing. Resilient to the end, he contracted with Selby County for convicts to work 1,700 acres of land he had rented on President's Island, four miles from Memphis. Leasing convicts was a practice that was notorious for horrendous abuses, but none were reported on President's Island. As a master Forrest had always been well reputed, even in the slave days. The swamp-ridden island, however, proved hard on him; he contracted a debilitating intestinal illness that ultimately proved fatal. After so many setbacks, his luck turned at least in this regard: against all odds, Nathan Bedford Forrest died peacefully in his bed on October 29, 1877.

HARRIET HERNANDES

The Intimidation of Black Voters

———★———

The following testimony was given in 1871 by Harriet Hernandes, a black resident of Spartanburg, South Carolina, to the Joint Congressional Select Committee investigating conditions in the South. The terrorizing of black women through rape and other forms of physical violence was among the means of oppression used by the Ku Klux Klan.

Question: How old are you?
Answer: Going on thirty-four years. . . .
Q: Are you married or single?
A: Married.
Q: Did the Ku-Klux come to your house at any time?
A: Yes, sir; twice. . . .
Q: Go on to the second time. . . .
A: They came in; I was lying in bed. Says he, "Come out here, sir; come out here, sir!" They took me out of bed; they would not let me get out, but they took me up in their arms and toted me out—me and my daughter Lucy. He struck me on the forehead with a pistol, and here is the scar above my eye now. Says he, "Damn you, fall." I fell. Says he, "Damn you, get up." I got up. Says he, "Damn you, get over this fence!" and he kicked me over when I went to get over; and then he went on to a brush pile, and they laid us right down there, both together. They laid us down twenty yards apart, I reckon. They had dragged and beat us along. They struck me right on top of my head, and I thought they had killed me;

and I said, "Lord o'mercy, don't, don't kill my child!" He gave me a lick on the head, and it liked to have killed me; I saw stars. He threw my arm over my head so I could not do anything with it for three weeks, and there are great knots on my wrist now.
Q: What did they say this was for?
A: They said, "You can tell your husband that when we see him we are going to kill him. . . ."
Q: Did they say why they wanted to kill him?
A: They said, "He voted the radical ticket [slate of candidates], didn't he?" I said, "Yes," that very way.

. . .

Q: When did [your husband] get back home after this whipping? He was not at home, was he?
A: He was lying out; he couldn't stay at home, bless your soul! . . .
Q: Has he been afraid for any length of time?
A: He has been afraid ever since last October. He has been lying out. He has not laid in the house ten nights since October.
Q: Is that the situation of the colored people down there to any extent?
A: That is the way they all have to do—men and women both.
Q: What are they afraid of?
A: Of being killed or whipped to death.
Q: What has made them afraid?
A: Because men that voted radical tickets they took the spite out on the women when they could get at them.
Q: How many colored people have been whipped in that neighborhood?
A: It is all of them, mighty near.

———

Source: Report of the Joint Congressional Select Committee to Inquire into the Condition of Affairs in the Late Insurrectionary States, House Reports, 42d Cong., 2d sess. (Washington, DC: U.S. Government Printing Office, 1972), vol. 5, South Carolina, December 19, 1871.

---

boasted, "the future is full of hope and promise." It was in this spirit of reform that the North approved the use of federal power to defend radical Reconstruction.

The Civil War, finally, fueled an economic boom in the North. Industrial production increased 75 percent between 1865 and 1873, and 3 million immigrants entered the country. Investment shifted toward iron and steel production, machine tools, and coal mining, laying the basis for an advanced industrial economy. Corporate enterprise was beginning to emerge, especially the railroads, where building went forward at a frantic pace.

The North had entered the industrial age. It was an economic giant compared to the South, and amply able to bear the costs of seeing Reconstruction through.

The North's Loss of Faith. Yet the business sector was where enthusiasm flagged most quickly. Northern entrepreneurs complained that the turmoil of Reconstruction retarded the South's economic recovery and harmed their investment opportunities. A similar calculation led to trouble between Republicans and their allies in the National Labor Union. The break came over the eight-hour workday, which labor theorists saw as the key reform that would end wage slavery and complete the equal-rights revolution inaugurated by the Civil War. This grand theory did not much trouble Republicans, but the economic cost of the eight-hour workday did, and inevitably they sided with their business allies, driving the National Labor Union out of the party and into independent politics.

Sympathy for the freedmen also began to wane. The North was flooded with one-sided, often racist reports, such as James S. Pike's *The Prostrate State* (1873), describing extravagant, corrupt Republican rule and a South in the grip of "a mass of black barbarism." The impact of this propaganda could be seen in the fate of the Civil Rights bill, which Charles Sumner introduced in 1870 at the height of radical Reconstruction. Sumner's bill was a remarkable application of federal power against discrimination in the country, guaranteeing citizens equal access to public accommodation, schools, churches, and jury service. By the time the bill passed in 1875, it had been stripped of its key provisions and was of little account as a weapon against discriminatory treatment of African Americans. The Supreme Court finished the demolition job when it declared the remnant Civil Rights Act unconstitutional in 1883.

The political cynicism that overtook the Civil Rights Act signaled the Republican Party's reversion to the practical politics of earlier days. In many states a second generation took over the party—men like Senator Roscoe Conkling of New York, who treated the Manhattan Customs House, with its regiment of political appointees, as an auxiliary of his machine; or Simon Cameron, senator from Pennsylvania, who was in the pocket of the Pennsylvania Railroad. Politicos such as Conkling or Cameron had little enthusiasm for Reconstruction, except as it benefited the Republican Party, and as the party lost headway in the South, they abandoned any interest in the battle for black rights. In Washington, President Grant presided benignly over this transformation of his party, turning a blind eye on corruption even as it began to lap against the White House.

The Liberal Republicans. As Grant's administration lapsed into cronyism, a revolt took shape inside the Republican Party. Anti-Grant factions of many stripes accepted the leadership of an influential collection of intellectuals, journalists, and reform-minded businessmen who resented the dominance of professional politicians in the party's affairs. The first order of business for them was civil-service reform that would replace corrupt patronage with a merit-based system of appointments. The reformers also, however, disliked the thrust of government activism spawned by the Civil War crisis. They regarded themselves as classical liberals—believers in free trade, market competition, and limited government. Government activity was "by nature wasteful, cor-

rupt, and dangerous." And, with unabashed elitism, they spoke out against universal suffrage, which "can only mean in plain English the government of ignorance and vice." So it followed that liberal reformers would have little patience with the former slaves. Although mostly veterans of the anti-slavery movement, they now became strident critics of radical Reconstruction.

The Election of 1872. Unable to deny Grant renomination for a second term, the dissidents broke away and formed a new party under the name Liberal Republican. Their candidate was Horace Greeley, longtime editor and publisher of the New York *Tribune* and a warhorse of American reform in all its variety, including antislavery. The Democratic Party, still in disarray, also nominated Greeley, despite the fierce animus he had always shown for Democrats: "murderers, adulterers, drunkards, cowards, liars, thieves." An ineffective campaigner, Greeley was assailed so bitterly during the campaign that, as he said, "I hardly knew whether I was running for President or the penitentiary."

Grant won overwhelmingly, capturing 56 percent of the popular vote and every electoral vote. Yet the Liberal Republicans had managed to shift the terms of political debate in the country. The new agenda they had established—civil-service reform, limited government, reconciliation with the South—was now adopted by the Democrats as they shed their treasonous reputation and reclaimed their place as a legitimate American party. In the 1874 elections, the Democrats dealt the Republicans a crushing blow, gaining control of the House of Representatives for the first time since secession and triumphing in seven normally Republican northern states.

Scandal and Depression. Charges of Republican corruption, mounting ever since Grant's reelection, came to a head in 1875. The scandal involved the Whiskey Ring, a network of liquor distillers and Treasury agents who defrauded the Treasury of millions of dollars of excise taxes on whiskey. The ring was organized by a former Union general, John A. McDonald, whom Grant had appointed supervisor of internal revenue in St. Louis. Grant's private secretary, Orville Babcock, kept a protective eye on McDonald's activities and funneled some of the spoils into the campaign coffers of the Republican Party. In 1875, however, Grant's secretary of the Treasury, Benjamin Bristow, exposed the ring and prosecuted more than 350 distillers and government officials. Many of them, including McDonald, went to prison, but Grant stood by Babcock, possibly perjuring himself to save his secretary from jail. The stench of scandal, however, had engulfed the White House.

On top of this, the economy had fallen into a severe depression after 1873. The precipitating event was the bankruptcy of the Northern Pacific Railroad and its main investor, Jay Cooke. Both Cooke's privileged role as

"Grantism"
Grant was lampooned on both sides of the Atlantic for the behavior of his scandal-ridden administration. The British magazine *Puck* shows Grant only barely defying gravity to keep his corrupt subordinates aloft and out of jail. Despite the scandals, the British public welcomed Grant with admiration on his triumphant foreign tour in 1877.
Stock Montage.

a financier of the Civil War and the generous federal subsidies to the Northern Pacific (and other railroads) suggested to many suffering Americans that Republican financial manipulations had caused the depression. Grant's administration responded ineffectually, rebuffing the pleas of debtors for relief by increasing the money supply (see Chapter 18). In 1874 Democrats gained enough support from Republicans to push through Congress a bill that would have increased the volume of currency in circulation and eased the money pinch. But President Grant vetoed it, fueling Democratic charges that Republicans served only the interests of capitalists.

Among the casualties of the depression was the Freedman's Savings and Trust Company, which held the small deposits of thousands of former slaves. When the bank failed in 1874, Congress refused to compensate the depositors, and many lost their life savings. In denying their pleas for compensation, Congress was also signaling that Reconstruction had lost its moral claim on the country. National politics had moved on, and other concerns absorbed the voter as another presidential election approached in 1876.

The Political Crisis of 1877

Abandoning Grant, the Republicans nominated Rutherford B. Hayes, governor of Ohio. He was a colorless figure but untainted by corruption or by strong convictions—in a word, a safe man. His Democratic opponent was Samuel J. Tilden, governor of New York—a wealthy lawyer with ties to Wall Street and a reform reputation for helping to break the grip of the thieving Tweed Ring on New York City politics. The Democrat Tilden favored "home rule" for the South, but so did the Republican Hayes, though more discreetly. Reconstruction did not actually figure prominently in the campaign and was mostly subsumed under broader Democratic charges of "corrupt centralism" and "incapacity, waste, and fraud." By now, Republicans had written off the South and scarcely campaigned there. Not a lot was said about the states still ruled by Reconstruction governments—Florida, South Carolina, and Louisiana.

Once the returns started coming in on election night, however, those three states began to loom very large indeed. Tilden led in the popular vote, and being victorious in key northern states, he seemed headed for the White House. But sleepless politicians at Republican headquarters realized that if they kept Florida, South Carolina, and Louisiana, Hayes would win by a single electoral vote. The campaigns in those states had been bitterly fought, replicating the Democratic assaults on blacks that had overturned Republican regimes everywhere else in the South. But Republicans still controlled the election machinery in those states, and citing Democratic fraud and intimidation, they could certify Republican victories. Late on election night the audacious announcement came forth from Republican headquarters: Hayes had carried the three southern states and won the election. But newly elected Democratic officials in the three states also sent in electoral votes for Tilden, and when Congress met in early 1877, it faced two sets of electoral votes from those states.

The Constitution does not provide for this contingency. All it says is that the president of the Senate (in 1877, a Republican) opens the electoral certificates before the House (Democratic) and the Senate (Republican) and that "The votes shall then be counted." Ever since the November 1876 election, an air of crisis had gripped the country. There was talk of inside deals, of a new election, even of a violent coup and civil war. Just in case, the commander of the army, General William T. Sherman, deployed four artillery companies in Washington. Finally, Congress decided to appoint an electoral commission to settle the question. The commission included seven Republicans, seven Democrats, and, as the deciding member, David Davis, a Supreme Court justice not known to have fixed party loyalties. But Davis disqualified himself by accepting an Illinois seat in the Senate. He was replaced by Republican Justice Joseph P. Bradley, and by a vote of 8 to 7 the commission awarded the disputed votes to Hayes (Map 15.3).

Outraged Democrats had one more trick up their sleeves. They controlled the House, and they set about stalling a final count of the electoral votes so as to prevent Hayes's inauguration on March 4. But a week earlier, secret talks had begun in Washington between southern Democrats and Ohio Republicans representing Hayes. Other issues may have been on the table, but the main thing was the situation in South Carolina and Louisiana, where Republican governors physically occupied the statehouses, protected by Union troops. If not for the disputed federal election, ironically, the military would not have intervened, and the Redeemers would already have seized power. Exactly what deal was struck, or how involved Hayes himself was, will probably never be known, but on March 1 the House Democrats suddenly ended their filibuster, the ceremonial counting of votes went forward, and Hayes was inaugurated on schedule. He soon ordered the Union troops back to their barracks, and the Republican regimes in South Carolina and Louisiana fell. Reconstruction had ended.

In 1877 political leaders on all sides seemed ready to say that what Lincoln had called "the work" was complete. But for the freedmen, the work had only begun. Reconstruction turned out to have been a magnificent aberration, a leap beyond what most white Americans actually felt was due their black fellow citizens. Redemption represented a sad falling back to the norm. Still, something real had been achieved—three rights-defining amendments to the Constitution, some elbow room to advance economically, and, not least, a stubborn confidence among blacks that by their own efforts they could lift themselves up. Things would, in fact, get worse before they got better, but the work of Reconstruction was imperishable and could never be erased.

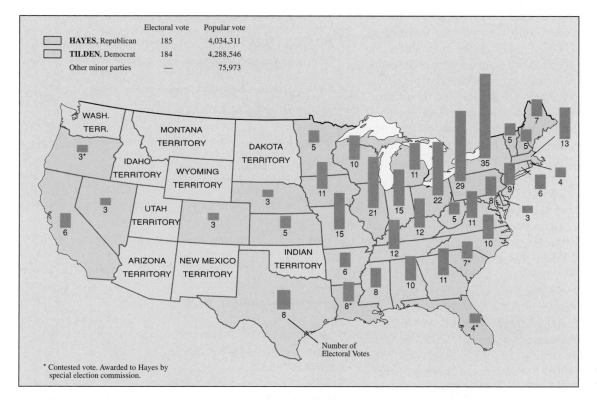

Map 15.3
The Election of 1876
In this presidential election, the closest and most contested in U.S. history, the Republican Rutherford B. Hayes won only with the disputed votes of three states in the Deep South. (Hayes also needed to defeat the efforts of the governor of Oregon to replace a Republican elector from that state with a Democrat.)

Summary
★

When the Civil War ended in 1865, no one could have foreseen the course of Reconstruction. The slaves had been emancipated, but there was no consensus about their future status as citizens. The South had been defeated, but there was no consensus about its restoration to the Union. Had Abraham Lincoln lived, these questions might have been settled peaceably and with justice for all. But with his assassination, they were left to the mercy of unfolding events.

Without consulting Congress, Lincoln's successor, Andrew Johnson, offered the South easy terms for reentering the Union. This might have succeeded had the South responded with restraint, but instead former Confederates were welcomed back into leadership and a concerted effort was made to reenslave the freedmen through the Black Codes. Infuriated by southern intransigence, congressional Republicans closed ranks behind the Radicals, embraced the freedmen's demand for full equality, placed the South under military rule in 1867, and inaugurated radical Reconstruction.

Politically empowered freedmen participated on nearly equal terms with their white allies in the new Republican state governments that undertook to reconstruct the South through ambitious programs of economic and educational improvement. No amount of accomplishment, however, could have reconciled the ex-Confederates to Republican rule, and they staged a violent counterrevolution in the name of white supremacy and "redemption." But in the meantime, before the political balance shifted against them, freedmen prevailed in the battle of wills with their former masters over a postslavery labor system. Sharecropping had many disadvantages, but it was better than the gang labor that the planters wanted.

Despite an initially stern response, the Grant administration had no stomach for a protracted guerrilla war in the South. Northern politics moved on, increasingly absorbed by Republican scandals and, after depression hit in 1873, by the nation's economic problems. Grant's reform critics, the Liberal Republicans, fatally weakened the doctrinal underpinnings of radical Reconstruction in governmental activism and equal rights. By allying with the Liberal Republicans in 1872, the discredited Democrats scrambled back into the political mainstream and began to compete on even terms with the Republicans. So close was the presidential election of 1876 that both parties claimed victory. The constitutional crisis was resolved only by the Democrats' agreement to accept the Republican Hayes as president in exchange for an end to Republican rule in South Carolina and Louisiana, thereby signaling the conclusion of Reconstruction.

TIMELINE

1863 Lincoln announces his Ten Percent Plan

1864 Wade-Davis bill passed by Congress
Lincoln gives Wade-Davis bill a "pocket" veto

1865 Freedmen's Bureau established
Lincoln assassinated; Andrew Johnson succeeds as president
Johnson implements his restoration plan
Joint Committee on Reconstruction formed

1866 Civil Rights Act passes over Johnson's veto
Memphis riots
Johnson makes disastrous "swing around the circle"
Johnson defeated in Congressional elections

1867 Reconstruction Acts
Tenure of Office Act

1868 Impeachment crisis
Fourteenth Amendment ratified
Ulysses S. Grant elected president

1870 Ku Klux Klan at peak of power
Fifteenth Amendment ratified

1871 Ku Klux Klan Act passed by Congress

1872 Grant's reelection as president

1873 Panic of 1873 ushers in depression of 1873–1877

1874 Democrats win majority in House of Representatives

1875 Whiskey Ring scandal undermines Grant administration

1877 Compromise of 1877
Rutherford B. Hayes becomes president
Reconstruction ends

Suggested Readings

———————★———————

The starting point for the study of Reconstruction is Eric Foner's synthesis, *Reconstruction: America's Unfinished Revolution, 1863–1877* (1988), which is also available in a shorter version. Two older surveys that provide useful introductions are John Hope Franklin, *Reconstruction: After the Civil War* (1961), and Kenneth M. Stampp, *The Era of Reconstruction* (1965). *Black Reconstruction in America* (1935), by the black activist and scholar W. E. B. Du Bois, deserves attention as the first book to challenge traditional interpretations that discounted the struggle of the emancipated slaves for full freedom.

Presidential Reconstruction

For important studies of presidential efforts to rebuild the Union, see the books on Abraham Lincoln listed in Chapter 14 and the following works on Andrew Johnson: Albert Castel, *The Presidency of Andrew Johnson* (1979); Eric L. McKitrick, *Andrew Johnson and Reconstruction* (1960); and James Sefton, *Andrew Johnson and the Uses of Constitutional Power* (1979). On the Radical resistance to presidential Reconstruction, see James M. McPherson, *The Struggle for Equality: Abolitionists and the Negro in the Civil War and Reconstruction* (1965).

Books that focus on Congress include LaWanda Cox and John H. Cox, *Politics, Principle, and Prejudice, 1865–1867* (1963); David Donald, *The Politics of Reconstruction, 1863–1867* (1965); and William R. Brock, *An American Crisis: Congress and Reconstruction, 1865–1867* (1963). For insight into developments in the South, see Dan T. Carter, *When the War Was Over: The Failure of Self-Reconstruction in the South, 1865–1867* (1985). Michael Perman, *Reunion without Compromise: The South and Reconstruction, 1865–1868* (1973), stresses the South's relations with President Andrew Johnson.

On the freedmen, see Willie Lee Rose, *Rehearsal for Reconstruction: The Port Royal Experiment* (1964); Peter Kolchin, *First Freedom: The Responses of Alabama's Blacks to Emancipation and Reconstruction* (1972); and Leon F. Litwack, *Been in the Storm So Long: The Aftermath of Slavery* (1979). More recent emancipation studies emphasize slavery as a labor system: Barbara Fields, *Slavery and Freedom on the Middle Ground: Maryland during the Nineteenth Century* (1985); Julie Saville, *The Work of Reconstruction: From Slave to Wage Laborer in South Carolina, 1860–1870* (1994); and Ira Berlin et al., *Slaves No More: Three Essays on Emancipation and the Civil War* (1992), incorporating the introductory essays in the initial volumes of a monumental edition of the emancipation records in the National Archives by Ira Berlin et al., *Freedom: A Documentary History of Emancipation, 1861–1867* (1985–). Eric Foner, *Nothing But Freedom: Emancipation and Its Legacy* (1983), places emancipation in a comparative context. Jacqueline Jones, *Labor of Love, Labor of Sorrow: Black Women, Work, and the Family from Slavery to the Present* (1985), is a pioneering work on the impact of emancipation on black women. An important new case study is Leslie A. Schwalm, *A Hard Fight for We: Women's Transition from Slavery to Freedom in South Carolina* (1997).

Radical Reconstruction

For Congress's role in radical Reconstruction, see Michael Les Benedict, *A Compromise of Principle: Congressional Republicans and Reconstruction* (1974), and Hans L. Trefousse, *Impeachment of a President: Andrew Johnson, the Blacks, and Reconstruction* (1975). William S. McFeely, *Grant: A Biography* (1981), explains the politics of Reconstruction. Also helpful is Brooks D. Simpson, *Let Us Have Peace: Ulysses S. Grant and the Politics of War and Reconstruction, 1861–1868* (1991). State studies of Reconstruction include Richard Lowe, *Republicans and Reconstruction in Virginia, 1856–1870* (1991), and Otto Olsen, ed., *Reconstruction and Redemption in the South* (1980). The best account of carpetbaggers is Richard N. Current, *Those Terrible Carpetbaggers: A Reinterpretation* (1988).

On blacks during radical Reconstruction, see Joel Williamson, *After Slavery: The Negro in South Carolina during Reconstruction, 1861–1877* (1965); Robert Cruden, *The Negro in Reconstruction* (1969); John Blassingame, *Black New Orleans, 1860–1880* (1973); Thomas Holt, *Black over White: Negro Political Leadership in South Carolina during Reconstruction* (1977); and Barry A. Crouch, *The Freedmen's Bureau and Black Texans* (1992). The emergence of the sharecropping system is explored in Roger L. Ransom and Richard Sutch, *One Kind of Freedom: The Economic Consequences of Emancipation* (1977); Jay Mandle, *The Roots of Black Poverty: The Southern Plantation Economy after the Civil War* (1978); Gavin Wright, *Old South, New South: Revolutions in the Southern Economy since the Civil War* (1986); Edward Royce, *The Origins of Southern Sharecropping* (1993); and Harold Woodman, *New South, New Law: The Legal Foundations of Credit and Labor Relations in the Postbellum Agricultural South* (1995).

The Undoing of Reconstruction

The most thorough study of the Ku Klux Klan is Allen W. Trelease, *White Terror: The Ku Klux Klan Conspiracy and Southern Reconstruction* (1972); on its leader, see Brian S. Wills, *A Battle from the Start: The Life of Nathan Bedford Forrest* (1992). To survey Reconstruction politics in the South, consult Michael Perman, *The Road to Redemption: Southern Politics, 1869–1879* (1984). On politics in the North, see James Mohr, ed., *The Radical Republicans in the North: State Politics during Reconstruction* (1976), and William Gillette, *Retreat from Reconstruction, 1863–1879* (1979). Laura F. Edwards, *Gendered Strife and Confusion: The Political Culture of Reconstruction* (1997), is an innovative study that explores the gendered dimension of reconstruction politics in a North Carolina county. Equally illuminating as a more traditional political narrative is Jonathan M. Bryant, *How Curious a Land: Conflict and Change in Greene County, Georgia, 1850–1885* (1996).

For the impact of Reconstruction on the national state, see Morton Keller, *Affairs of State: Public Life in Late Nineteenth-Century America* (1977), and Richard F. Bensel, *Yankee Leviathan: The Origins of Central State Authority in America, 1859–1877* (1990). On political corruption, see Mark W. Summers, *The Era of Good Stealings* (1993). On the contested election of 1876, see C. Vann Woodward's classic *Reunion and Reaction* (1956), and K. I. Polakoff, *The Politics of Inertia: The Election of 1876 and the End of Reconstruction* (1973).

Part Four

★

A Maturing Industrial Society, *1877–1914*

THEMATIC TIMELINE

	Economy	Society	Culture	Government	Diplomacy
	The Triumph of Industrialization	**Racial, Ethnic, and Gender Divisions**	**The Rise of the City**	**From Inaction to Progressive Reform**	**An Emerging World Power**
1877	Carnegie launches modern steel industry Knights of Labor becomes national movement (1878)	Defeat of the struggle for black equality End of nomadic Indian life	National League founded (1876) Dwight L. Moody pioneers urban revivalism	Election of Rutherford B. Hayes ends Reconstruction	United States becomes a net exporter
1880	Gustavus Swift pioneers vertically integrated firm American Federation of Labor founded (1886)	Chinese Exclusion Act (1882) Dawes Severalty Act divides tribal lands (1887)	Electrification transforms city life First *Social Register* defines high society (1888)	Ethnocultural issues dominate state and local politics Civil service reform (1883)	Diplomacy of inaction Naval buildup begins
1890	United States surpasses Britain in iron and steel output Economic depression (1893–1897) Era of farm prosperity begins	Black disfranchisement and racial segregation in the South Immigration from southeastern Europe rises sharply	Settlement houses spread progressive ideas to cities Hearst's *New York Journal* pioneers yellow journalism	Populist Party founded (1892) William McKinley wins presidency; defeats Bryan's free silver crusade (1896)	Social Darwinism and Anglo-Saxonism promote expansionism Spanish-American War (1898–1899); conquest of the Philippines
1900	Great merger movement Immigrants dominate factory work Industrial Workers of the World founded (1905)	Women take leading roles in social reform Revival of the struggle for civil rights Immigration restriction movement launched	Muckraking journalism Movies begin to overtake vaudeville	Progressivism in national politics Theodore Roosevelt attacks the trusts Hepburn Act enforces government's regulation of railroads (1906)	Panama cedes Canal Zone to United States (1903) Roosevelt Corollary to Monroe Doctrine (1904) Root-Takahira agreement (1908)
1910	Ford builds first automobile assembly line	NAACP founded (1910) Women win the right to vote in western states World War I ends the great European migration	Urban liberalism	Election of Woodrow Wilson (1912) New Freedom legislation creates Federal Reserve, FTC	Taft's dollar diplomacy promotes American business Woodrow Wilson proclaims U.S. neutrality in World War I

WHILE THE NATION'S attention was focused on the political drama of Reconstruction, few people noticed an equally momentous watershed in American economic life. For the first time, as the decade of the 1870s passed, farmers no longer constituted a majority of working Americans. Henceforth, America's future would be linked irrevocably to its development as an industrial society.

Economy. The effects of accelerating industrialization were felt, first of all, on the manufacturing sector itself. As heavy industry emerged and the railroad system was completed, the modern techniques of industrial management took shape, and big nationwide firms began to dominate American enterprise. The modern labor movement became firmly established, and as immigration surged, the foreign-born and their children became America's workers. What had been partial and limited changes became general and widespread as America became a land of factories, great corporate enterprise, and restless workers.

The West. Second, the demands of industrialism largely drove the final surge of settlement across the Great Plains and the Rockies. Cities called for new sources of food, and industry needed the Far West's mineral resources. In the struggle for their way of life, western Indians were ultimately defeated not so much by the rifles of army troopers as by events taking place far away in the nation's industries and cities. These same economic forces set in motion the Asian, Mexican, and European migrations that made for a multiethnic western society. Rural America was likewise locked into the advancing Industrial Revolution. The distress American farmers experienced during this period resulted from their imperfect integration into the modern industrial order. They remained small-scale operators in an economic world increasingly dominated by far-flung railroads and giant corporations.

Culture. Third, industrialization transformed the physical and human makeup of the nation's cities. By 1900 one in five Americans lived in cities. That was where the jobs were—as workers in factories; as clerks and salespeople in offices and department stores; as members of a new salaried middle class of managers, engineers, and professionals; and, at the apex, as a wealthy elite of property owners and entrepreneurs. But the city was more than just a place to make a living. It provided a setting for an urban way of life unlike anything seen before in the United States.

Government. Fourth, politics marched in step with the industrial order. In the years of unprecedented economic expansion between 1877 and 1893 there seemed little need for government intervention. The major parties were robust and active, but their vitality stemmed from a political culture of popular participation, from ethnocultural conflicts linked to party loyalties, and from the informal functions political parties performed as highly organized machines. Economic crisis during the 1890s triggered a serious challenge to the political status quo, first by distressed farmers active in the Populist Party and then, as economic troubles spread, by the divisive campaign for free silver. The election of 1896 turned back that challenge. Still unresolved, however, was another economic concern: the enormous concentration of business power that had accompanied the nation's corporate development. This issue dominated national politics during the Progressive Era. In those years, too, the nation belatedly began to address its social ills. Women progressives took the lead in the struggle to make life better for America's urban masses. African Americans, victimized by disfranchisement and segregation, found allies among white progressives and launched a new drive for racial equality.

Diplomacy. Fifth, the dynamism of America's economic development forced a decisive shift in the country's foreign relations. In the decades after the Civil War, America had been inward-looking, its indifference to global affairs reflected in an inactive diplomacy and a neglected navy. The economic crisis of the 1890s, however, brought home to American leaders the need for secure access to overseas markets for the nation's surplus products. In short order the United States fought a brief war with Spain, acquired an overseas empire, and asserted its national interests in Latin America and Asia. There was no mistaking America's standing as a Great Power and, as World War I approached, no evading the responsibilities and entanglements that came with that elevated status.

Chapter 16

The American West

DURING THE LAST decades of the nineteenth century, America seemed like two nations. One was an advanced industrial society, the America of great factories and sprawling cities. The other still seemed to be frontier country, with pioneers streaming onto the Great Plains, repeating the dramas of "settlement" they had been performing ever since Europeans had first set foot on the continent. Not until 1890 did the U.S. Census declare that a "frontier of settlement" no longer existed: the country's "unsettled area has been so broken into . . . that there can hardly be said to be a frontier line."

In that same year the country surpassed Great Britain in the production of iron and steel. Newspapers reported Indian wars and labor strikes in the same edition. The last tragic episode in the war against the Sioux, the massacre at Wounded Knee, South Dakota, occurred only eighteen months before the great Homestead steel strike of 1892. This conjunction of events from the distant worlds of factory and frontier was not accidental. The final surge of settlement across the Great Plains and the Far West was powered primarily by American industrialism.

The Industrial Revolution likewise shaped the history of agricultural America in these years. Farmers had one foot in the agrarian past and the other in the industrial age. They remained small-scale operators in an economic world dominated by far-flung railroads and giant corporations. They were thinking as family farmers but producing for international markets. Rural America could no longer be understood on its own terms. Its history had become linked ever more tightly to the larger industrial society.

The Yo-Hamite Falls (1855)
This detail of one of the earliest artistic renderings of Yosemite Valley and its great waterfall was drawn, in fact, before the place came to be called Yosemite. The scale of the waterfall, which falls 2,300 feet to the valley below, is dramatized by the inclusion of the artist's (Thomas A. Ayres) companions in the foreground. In this romantic lithograph, one can already see the grandeur of the West that Yosemite came to represent for Americans.
University of California at Berkeley, Bancroft Library, Honeyman Collection.

The Great Plains

During the 1860s agricultural settlement reached the western margins of the tall-grass prairie. Beyond, roughly from the 98th meridian, stretched vast dry country uninviting to farmers accustomed to woodlands and ample rainfall (Map 16.1). They saw it much as did the New York publisher Horace Greeley on his way to California in 1859: "a land of starvation," "a treeless desert" with a "terrible" climate of baking heat in the daytime and "chill and piercing" cold at night.

Greeley was describing the Great Plains. The geologic event creating this wide, dry expanse occurred 60 million years ago when the Rocky Mountains arose out of the ocean covering western North America. With no outlet, the shallow inland sea to the east dried up, forming a hard pan on which sediment washing down from the mountains built up a loose, featureless surface layer. The mountain barrier also made for a dry climate because moisture-laden winds from the Pacific spent themselves on the western slopes. Only vegetation capable of withstanding the bitter winters and periodic cycles of severe drought could take hold on the plains. The short gramma (buffalo) grass, the linchpin of this fragile ecosystem, matted the easily blown soil into place and sustained a rich wildlife dominated by grazing pronghorn antelope and buffalo. What the dry, short-grass country had not sustained, until the past few centuries, was human settlement.

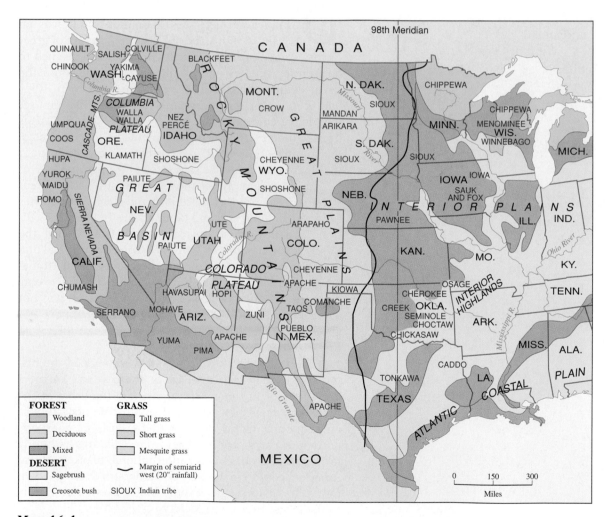

MAP 16.1
The Natural Environment of the West
As settlers pushed into the Great Plains beyond the line of semiaridity, they sensed the overwhelming power of the natural environment. In a landscape without trees for fences and barns, and without adequate rainfall, ranchers and farmers had to relearn their business. The native Americans peopling the plains and mountains had in time learned to live in this environment, but this knowledge counted for little against the ruthless pressure of the settlers to domesticate the West.

Indians of the Great Plains

Probably a hundred thousand native Americans lived on the Great Plains at mid-nineteenth century. They were a diverse people, divided into six linguistic families and at least thirty tribal groupings. The Mandan, Arikara, and Pawnee were mostly agriculturalists, planting maize and beans and living in permanent villages. Relatively concentrated and sedentary, these tribes were ravaged during the nineteenth century by smallpox and measles brought by Europeans. Less vulnerable to epidemics were the hunting tribes that had migrated onto the Great Plains since the seventeenth century: Kiowa and Comanche in the southwest; Arapaho and Cheyenne on the central plains; and, to the north, Blackfeet, Crow, Cheyenne, and the great Sioux nation (see Map 16.1).

The Teton Sioux. Originally the Sioux had occupied semipermanent settlements in the lake country of northern Minnesota. With fish and game dwindling, some Sioux tribes drifted westward during the early eighteenth century. Around 1760 they began to cross the Missouri River into the vast short-grass country. These Sioux became nomadic, living in portable skin tepees and relying on the hunt for survival. From tribes to the south and west, they acquired horses. Now mounted, the Sioux became splendid hunters and formidable fighters, claiming the entire Great Plains north of the Arkansas River as their hunting grounds and driving out or subjugating longer-settled tribes.

The westernmost Sioux—they called themselves the Teton people, or Lakotas (meaning "allies")—made up a loose confederation of seven tribes. In the winter months the tribes broke up into small bands, but each spring the bands assembled and prepared for the summer hunt. Summer was also the season for making war. Mostly, raiding parties of thirty or forty warriors rode forth, intent on capturing horses and taking scalps, but occasionally larger, well-organized territorial campaigns were mounted against rival tribes.

A society that celebrates the heroic virtues of hunting and war is likely to define gender roles sharply. But before the Sioux got horses, chasing down the buffalo had involved the entire community: women and men worked collectively to construct a "pound" and to channel the herds in the right direction. With the arrival of horses, however, the men rode off to the hunt while the women stayed behind to prepare the mounting piles of buffalo skins. This was laborious, painstaking work. Fanny Kelly, who had been a Sioux captive, considered the women's lives "a servitude"; but she noticed also that they were "very rebellious, often displaying ungovernable and violent temper." Subordination to the men was not how Sioux women understood their unrelenting labor; this was their allotted share in a partnership on which the proud, nomadic life of the Teton depended.

Teton Culture. Living so close to wild nature, depending on its bounty for survival, the Sioux saw sacred meaning in every manifestation of the natural world.

Tepee Liner
For the Plains Indians, tribal life revolved around the buffalo hunt and the battleground. These were the themes with which an unknown Indian artist decorated this dewcloth, which was hung inside a tepee to shield the occupants and provide some insulation from the cold.
American Hurrah, New York City.

Unlike Europeans, they conceived of God not as a supreme being but, in the words of ethnologist Clark Wissler, as a "series of powers pervading the universe"— Wi, the sun; Skan, the sky; Maka, the earth; Inyan, the rock. Below these came the moon, wind, buffalo—down through a hierarchy embodying the entire natural order.

By prayer and fasting in some isolated place, young Sioux prepared themselves for a vision of those mysterious powers. Medicine men provided instruction, but the religious experience was essentially personal and open to both sexes. The vision, when a supplicant achieved it, attached itself to some object—a feather, an animal skin, or a shell—that was tied into a sacred bundle and became that person's lifelong talisman, or charm. For the tribe as a whole, Sacred Pipe bundles served as the symbolic and ceremonial core of Sioux religion. In the annual Sun Dance, the entire tribe engaged in the rites of coming of age, fertility, the hunt, and combat, followed by four days of fasting and dancing in supplication to Wi, the sun.

The world of the Teton Sioux was not self-contained. All along they had been traders, exchanging pelts and buffalo robes for the agricultural products of other Plains Indians. These exchanges expanded to the white traders who had appeared on the upper Missouri River during the eighteenth century, and a substantial commerce in furs developed. Although the buffalo provided most of the essentials of life—not only food but clothing, shelter, fuel, carrying bags, and a variety of bone implements—the Sioux came to rely as well on the traders' pots, kettles, blankets, knives, and firearms. The trade system they had entered was linked to the Euro-American economy, yet it was also integrated into the traditional Sioux way of life. Everything depended on the survival of the Great Plains as the Sioux had found it—wild grassland on which the antelope and buffalo ranged free.

Intruders

On first encounter, settlers themselves saw no better use for the Great Plains. After exploring a drought-stricken stretch in 1820, Major Stephen H. Long declared it "almost wholly unfit for cultivation, and of course uninhabitable by a people depending upon agriculture for their subsistence."

For years thereafter, maps marked the plains region as the Great American Desert. And with that notion in mind, Congress formally designated the Great Plains in 1834 as permanent Indian country. The army general in charge, Edmund Gaines, wanted the border forts, stretching from Lake Superior to Fort Worth, Texas, to be constructed of stone because they would be there forever. Trade with the Indians—now closely supervised and licensed by the federal government—would continue with the Indian country otherwise off-limits to white intrusion.

Events swiftly overtook the nation's solemn commitment to the native Americans. During the 1840s settlers began a massive movement westward to Oregon and California. Indian country became a bridge to the Pacific. The first wagon train headed west for Oregon from Missouri in 1842. Over the next three decades, thousands of emigrants traveled the Oregon Trail to the Willamette Valley or, cutting south beyond Fort Hall, down into California. Approaching Fort Hall in 1859, it seemed to Horace Greeley as if "the white coverings of the many emigrant and transport wagons dott[ing] the landscape" gave "the trail the appearance of a river running through great meadows, with many ships sailing on its bosom." Only these "ships" left behind not a trailing wake of foam but a rutted landscape devoid of grass and game, and littered with abandoned wagons and rotting garbage.

The Railroads.   Talk about the need for a railroad to the Pacific soon began to be heard in Washington. How else could the distant territories stretching to the Pacific Ocean be firmly linked to the Union? Settlers bound for California and Oregon clamored for relief from the ordeal of the overland journey by wagon train. For nearly twenty years, however, the project languished while North and South argued over the eastern terminus for the route. Meanwhile, Indian country was crisscrossed by overland freight lines and Pony Express riders and, in 1861, by the telegraph lines that brought San Francisco into instant communication with the East. In the next year, with the South in rebellion, the federal government finally moved forward with the transcontinental rail project.

No private company could be expected to foot the bill by itself. The construction costs were staggering and, in the short run, not much demand for rail service existed in the thinly populated interior of the West. So the federal government offered generous land grants along the right-of-way, plus millions of dollars in public loans, to the two companies that undertook the transcontinental project.

The Union Pacific, building westward from Omaha, made little headway until the Civil War ended but then advanced rapidly across Indian country, reaching Cheyenne, Wyoming, in November 1867. It took the Central Pacific nearly that long moving eastward from Sacramento, California, to cross the crest of the Sierra Nevada. Both then worked furiously—since the government subsidy was based on miles of track built—until, to great fanfare, the tracks met at Promontory, Utah, in 1869. The transcontinental link was actually a pretty rickety affair, capable of moving people but not a lot of freight. It would eventually have to be wholly rebuilt. None of the other railroads following other westward routes made it as far as the Rockies before the Panic of 1873 hit, throwing them into bankruptcy and bringing work to an abrupt halt.

By then, however, railroad tycoons had changed their minds about the Great Plains. No longer did they see it through the eyes of the Oregon-bound settlers—as a place to be gotten through en route to the Pacific. Rail transportation, they realized, was laying the basis for the economic exploitation of the Great Plains. This calculation spurred the railroad boom that followed economic recovery in 1878. Construction soared. During the 1880s, 40,000 miles of track were laid west of the Mississippi, including links from southern California via the Southern Pacific to New Orleans and via the Santa Fe to Kansas City, and from the Northwest via the Northern Pacific to St. Paul, Minnesota.

The Cattle Kingdom. Of all the opportunities beckoning on the Great Plains, most obvious was cattle raising. The grazing buffalo made it easy to imagine the plains as cow country. But first, the buffalo had to go. A small market for buffalo robes had existed for years. And buffalo hunters like the famous William F. Cody (see American Lives, "Buffalo Bill and the Wild West," pp. 512–513) made a good living providing meat for labor gangs and army posts, and leading parties of sportsmen. Then, in the early 1870s, eastern tanneries discovered how to cure the hides, and a huge demand developed among shoe and harness manufacturers. Parties of professional hunters with high-powered rifles swept across the plains and began a systematic slaughter of the buffalo. The great herds, already diminished by disease and shrinking pasturage, almost vanished within ten years. Many people spoke out against this mass killing, but no way existed to stop people bent on making a quick dollar. Besides, as General Philip H. Sheridan pointed out, exterminating the buffalo would starve the Indians into submission and open up the feeding grounds for cattle.

About 5 million head of longhorn cattle roamed the ranches of south Texas in 1865, hardly worth bothering about because they could not be profitably marketed. In that year, however, the Missouri Pacific Railroad reached Sedalia, Missouri, far enough west to be accessible across open land to Texas cattle. At the Sedalia terminus, which connected to hungry eastern markets, a $3 longhorn might command $40. With this incentive, Texas ranchers inaugurated the famous Long Drive. Cowboys began to herd the longhorn cattle hundreds of miles north to the railroads that were pushing west across Kansas.

At Abilene, Ellsworth, and Dodge City, ranchers sold their cattle, and trail-weary cowboys went on a binge. These wide-open cattle towns captured the nation's imagination as symbols of the Wild West. The reality was much more ordinary. The cowboys, many of them blacks and Hispanics, were in fact farmhands on horseback, working long hours under harsh conditions for small pay. Colorful though it seemed, the Long Drive was actually a makeshift method of bridging a gap in the developing

Killing the Buffalo
This woodcut shows passengers shooting buffalo from a Kansas Pacific Railroad train—a small thrill added to the modern convenience of traveling west by rail.
North Wind Picture Archives.

transportation system. As soon as railroads reached the Texas range country during the 1870s, ranchers abandoned the hazardous and wasteful Long Drive.

In Texas, ranchers owned or leased the grazing land they used, sometimes in huge tracts. North of Texas, where the land was in the public domain, cattlemen simply helped themselves. Hopeful ranchers would spot a likely area along a creek and claim as much land as they could qualify for as settlers under federal homesteading laws, plus what might be added by the fraudulent claims taken out by one or two ranch hands. By a common usage that quickly became established, ranchers had a "range right" to all the adjacent land rising up to the divide—the point where the land sloped down to the next creek.

News of easy money traveled fast. Calves cost $5, and steers sold for maybe $60 on the Chicago market. Rail connections were in place or coming in. And the grass was free. Profits of 40 percent per year were a sure thing. The rush was on, drawing from as far away as Europe both hardheaded investors and romantics (like the recent Harvard graduate Teddy Roosevelt) eager for a taste of the Wild West. By the early 1880s the plains overflowed with cattle—as many as 7.5 million head, decimating the grass and trampling the water holes.

A cycle of good weather only postponed the inevitable disaster. When it came—a hard winter in 1885, a severe drought the following summer, then record blizzards and bitter cold—cattle died by the hundreds of thousands. An awful scene of rotting carcasses greeted the cowhands riding out onto the range the following spring. The recent slaughter of buffalo had produced equally ghastly sights, only no one owned the buffalo (and horror at their fate was therefore

Buffalo Bill and the Wild West

———★———

SCOTT COUNTY, IOWA, was still frontier country when William F. Cody was born there on February 26, 1846. Kansas, where his family moved in 1854, was even wilder, for it was not only frontier country but racked by bloody conflict between proslavery and free-soil settlers. Bill's father, Isaac Cody, was active on the free-soil side, serving in the Topeka legislature and frequently in harm's way from neighboring southern sympathizers and marauding Border Ruffians. One of Bill's first exploits was a wild gallop, with proslavery men in hot pursuit, to warn his father of a trap set for him near the family farm. Isaac Cody, however, was less an idealist than a typical enterprising westerner on the lookout for the main chance. He had been an Indian trader, a farm manager, a stagecoach operator, and, in Kansas, a land speculator around Grasshopper Falls. When he died suddenly in 1857, Cody left the family with a pile of land titles but little money.

Bill, never much for schooling anyway, had to find work. Only eleven, he was taken on by Majors and Waddell, the firm that transported goods from Fort Leavenworth to army posts west of the Missouri River. Bill worked as a messenger boy, livestock herder, and teamster helper on the freight wagons. When his employers organized the short-lived Pony Express in 1860, Cody became a stocktender and occasional rider in the Colorado-Nebraska division. Most of this was hard and tedious labor, but there were flashes of excitement—scrapes with Indians and with bandits (at fifteen, Bill killed one), buffalo stampedes, and brief encounters with Wild Bill Hickok and other tough western characters on whom Bill could model himself. In the early part of the Civil War Cody was at loose ends. Among other things, he engaged in horse thieving disguised as guerrilla activity in Missouri, and he became a heavy drinker. After a stint in the Seventh Kansas Cavalry and a halfhearted effort to settle down after the war

(in what turned out to be an unhappy marriage), Cody got his lucky break in 1867.

The Kansas Pacific Railroad was building a line through Indian country to Sheridan, Kansas. To provision the work crews, the contractors hired Cody at $500 a month—excellent pay—to supply the cooks with buffalo meat. Cody was a crack shot and an excellent horseman, and he knew buffalo hunting. This assignment was duck soup for him, and the aplomb with which he carried it off soon gave him the name "Buffalo Bill."

The next summer, 1868, Indian war broke out in Kansas, and Cody got his second claim to fame. He was hired as chief scout for the U.S. Fifth Cavalry. Cody knew the Kansas landscape intimately, seemed to have a remarkable instinct for following a trail, and was intrepid in the face of danger. At the height of the fighting in 1868–1869 Cody saw repeated action. In the climactic Battle of Summit Springs, his scouting played a decisive role, and he himself shot the Cheyenne chief Tall Bull. Although the legends later built up around Buffalo Bill (and the claims of others) have inclined scholars to be skeptical, Buffalo Bill was in fact an authentic hero. Perhaps the best testimony was the extra $100 awarded him by the normally tight-fisted army "for extraordinarily good services as a trailer and fighter in the pursuit of hostile Indians."

Out of these promising materials there began to emerge a mythic figure. In July 1869 the dime novelist Ned Buntline (Edward Zane Carroll Judson) came through Kansas, met Cody, and, after returning to New York, wrote *Buffalo Bill, the King of the Border Men*—the first of some seventeen hundred potboilers to feature Cody's name and exploits. Then there were the buffalo-hunting parties of the rich and famous that Cody periodically led, including a royal hunt in 1872 with Grand Duke Alexis of Russia that had the entire country agog. With his white horse, buckskin suit, crimson shirt, and broad sombrero, Buffalo Bill began to play his part to the hilt. "He realized to perfection the bold hunter and gallant sportsman of the plains," wrote one appreciative participant. In 1872 Cody was persuaded to appear as himself in a play Ned Buntline proposed to put on in New York. Buntline was said to have dashed off *The Scouts of the Prairie* in four hours, and critics pronounced it "execrable." But Buffalo Bill, who mostly ad-libbed, was a

Buffalo Bill's Wild West Show
The Wild West Show had worldwide appeal. This poster celebrates one of Buffalo Bill's
European tours.
Buffalo Bill Historical Center, Cody, Wyoming. Gift of The Coe Foundation.

great hit, and so was the production. Cody was launched on his career as a showman.

From then on, the lines between reality and make-believe began to blur. Not only did Buffalo Bill draw on his past exploits when he went on stage, but he had the stage in mind when he returned to the real world. During the Sioux wars of 1875–1876 Cody was again out in the field as an army scout. (Fortunately, the fighting took place during the theatrical off-seasons in the East.) Shortly after the annihilation of Custer's troops at Little Big Horn, Cody gained a measure of vengeance in a famous skirmish in which he killed and scalped a Sioux chief named Yellow Hand. Cody rode into that engagement wearing his stage vaquero outfit—black velvet and scarlet with lace—so that when he reenacted the mayhem on stage, he could say he was wearing the very clothes in which he had seen action. Over time, with some help from Cody, the fight with Yellow Hand assumed legendary proportions, becoming a formal duel, with a challenge laid down by the Indian chief and troopers and

Indian warriors lined up on opposing sides watching Buffalo Bill and Yellow Hand fight it out.

The mythic West that Cody was creating became full blown in his Wild West Show, first staged in 1883. Taking the circus and rodeo as his model, Cody put on an open-air extravaganza with displays of horsemanship, sharpshooting by Little Annie Oakley, real Indians (in one season Chief Sitting Bull toured with the company), and reenactments of stagecoach robberies and great events such as Custer's Last Stand. The Wild West Show toured the country every year and was a smashing success in Europe as well.

Buffalo Bill had been keen enough to see the hunger of city people for a legendary West. He traded on his talents as a showman, but he relied as well on his grasp of the authentic world behind the make-believe. When Cody died in 1917, that world was long gone, but his Wild West Show kept it alive in legend, where it still remains in the mythic figures of cowboys and Indians that populate our movies and television screens.

The Cowboy at Work
The cowboy, celebrated in dime novels, was really a farmhand on horseback, with the skills to work on the range, including the ability to stay glued to his saddle while lassoing a steer. He earned twenty-five dollars a month, plus meals and a bed in the bunkhouse, in return for long hours of lonesome, grueling work. But one can see in Charles Russell's vivid painting, *Jerked Down* (1907), why the cowhand could so readily be converted into a western hero.
Thomas Gilcrease Institute of American History and Art.

regarded as "sentimental"). Every dead steer, however, represented some rancher's investment. On top of these losses, beef prices collapsed when hard-pressed ranchers dumped the surviving cattle on the market. The boom had turned into a spectacular bust, and investors fled, leaving behind a more enduring ecological catastrophe: the native grasses never recovered from the relentless overgrazing in the drought cycle.

The ranchers who remained fenced their land and planted hay for the winter. No longer would cattle be left to fend for themselves on the open range. Elsewhere, Hispanic grazers from New Mexico brought in sheep to feed on the weeds and woody plants that had replaced the native grasses. Sheep raising, previously scorned by ranchers as unmanly and resisted as a threat to cattle, became a major enterprise in the sparser high country. Some ranchers even sold out to the despised "nesters"—those who wanted to try farming the Great Plains.

Homesteaders. Potential settlers, of course, needed first of all to be persuaded that crops would grow in that dry country. Powerful interests devoted themselves to overcoming the popular notion that the plains was a Great American Desert. Foremost were the railroads, eager to sell off the public land they had been granted—180 million acres of it—and develop traffic for their routes. They aggressively advertised, offered cut-rate tickets, and sold off their landholdings at bargain prices. Land speculators, transatlantic steamship lines, and the western states and territories did all they could to encourage settlement of the Great Plains. And so did the federal government, with its offer under the Homestead Act (1862) of 160 acres of public land to settlers.

"Why emigrate to Kansas?" asked a testimonial in *Western Trail*, the Rock Island Railroad's gazette. "Because it is the garden spot of the world. Because it will grow anything that any other country will grow, and with less work. Because it rains here more than any other place, and at just the right time." Too boastful, a prospective settler might think, but surely holding a grain of truth. Besides, the climate might improve. "Why may we not suppose that the genial influences of civilization—that extensive cultivation of the earth—might contribute to the multiplication of showers?" asked Josiah Gregg, an early traveler on the plains. Might not "these sterile regions . . . be thus revived and fertilized, and their surface covered one day by flourishing settlements to the Rocky Mountains?"

Over time Gregg's vision became an article of faith among boosters of the plains. As if to confirm the optimists, an exceptionally wet cycle occurred between 1878 and 1886. "As the plains are settled up we hear less and less of drouth, hot winds, alkali and other bugbears that used to hold back the adventurous," remarked one Nebraska man. Some settlers attributed the increased rainfall to soil cultivation and tree planting. Others credited God. As a settler on the southern plains remarked, "The Lord just knowed we needed more land an' He's gone and changed the climate."

No amount of optimism, however, could dispel the emptiness of the treeless land. "Such an air of desolation," wrote a Nebraska-bound woman; and from another woman in Texas, "such a lonely country." One old hand likened these despairing feelings to an illness. "A stranger travelling on the prairie would get his hopes up, expecting to see something different on making the next rise." But all he found was "grass and then more grass—the monotonous, endless prairie! . . . To him the disappointment and monotony were terrible. 'He's got loneliness,' we would say of such a man." For a Swedish emigrant like Ida Lindgren (see American Voices, "Ida Lindgren: Swedish Emigrant in Frontier Kansas,"

IDA LINDGREN

Swedish Emigrant in Frontier Kansas

———————★———————

Like many emigrants, Ida Lindgren did not find it easy to adjust to the harsh new life on the frontier. Her diary entries and letters home show that the adjustment for the first generation was never complete.

May 15, 1870 [Lake Sibley, Nebraska]

What shall I say? Why has the lord brought us here? Oh, I feel so oppressed, so unhappy! Two whole days it took us to get here and they were not the least trying part of our travels. We sat on boards in the work-wagon packed in so tightly that we could not move a foot, and we drove across endless, endless prairies, on narrow roads; no, no, not roads, tracks like those in the fields at home when they harvested grain. No forest but only a few trees which grow along the rivers and creeks. And then here and there you see a homestead and pass a little settlement. The Indians are not so far away from here, I can understand, and all the men you see coming by, riding or driving wagons, are armed with revolvers and long carbines, and look like highway robbers.

No date [probably written July 1870]

Claus and his wife lost their youngest child at Lake Sibley and it was very sad in many ways. There was no real cemetery but out on the prairie stood a large, solitary tree, and around it they bury their dead, without tolling of bells, without a pastor, and some-times without any coffin. A coffin was made here for their child, it was not painted black, but we lined it with flowers and one of the men read the funeral service, and then there was a hymn, and that was all.

August 25, 1874 [Manhattan, Kansas]

It has been a long time since I have written, hasn't it? . . . When one never has anything fun to write about, it is no fun to write. . . . We have not had rain since the beginning of June, and then with this heat and often strong winds as well, you can imagine how everything has dried out. There has also been a general lamentation and fear for the coming year. We are glad we have the oats (for many don't have any and must feed wheat to the stock) and had hoped to have the corn leaves to add to the fodder. But then one fine day there came millions, trillions of grasshoppers in great clouds, hiding the sun, and coming down into the fields, eating up everything that was still there, the leaves on the trees, peaches, grapes, cucumbers, onions, cabbage, everything, everything. Only the peach stones still hung on the trees, showing what had once been there.

July 1, 1877 [Manhattan, Kansas]

. . . It seems so strange to me when I think that more than seven years have passed since I have seen you all. . . . I can see so clearly that last glimpse I had of Mamma, standing alone amid all the tracks of Eslov station. Oliva I last saw sitting on her sofa in her red and black dress, holding little Brita, one month old, on her lap. And Wilhelm I last saw in Lund at the station, as he rolled away with the train, waving his last farewell to me. . . .

————————

Source: H. Arnold Barton, ed., *Letters from the Promised Land* (Minneapolis: University of Minnesota Press, 1975), 143–145, 150–156.

above), no place could have seemed so far from home and loved ones, and offered so little hope of seeing home and family again. Emigrants, indeed, had always taken parting as a kind of death, with reunion unlikely "on this side of the dark river."

For many women, this hard experience had a liberating side. Prescribed gender roles broke down as women shouldered men's work on new farms and gained a heightened sense of self-reliance. When husbands died or gave up, wives operated farms on their own. Other women started out alone. Under the Homestead Act, which accorded widows and single women the same rights as men, women filed 10 percent of the claims. "People afraid of coyotes and work and loneliness had better leave ranching alone," advised one woman homesteader. "At the same time, any woman who can stand her own company . . . and is willing to put in as much time at careful labor as she does at the washtub, will certainly succeed; will have independence, plenty to eat all the time, and a home of her own in the end."

Buffalo Chips
With no trees around for firewood, settlers on the plains had to make do with dried cow and buffalo droppings. Gathering the "buffalo chips" must have been a regular chore for Ada McColl and her daughter on her homestead near Lakin, Kansas (1893). Kansas State Historical Society.

The vision of new land to be farmed drove people onto the plains. By the 1870s, Illinois, Wisconsin, and other midwestern states had filled up, and farmers looked hungrily westward. "Hardly anything else was talked about," recalled short-story writer Hamlin Garland about his Iowa neighbors. "Every man who could sell out had gone west or was going. . . . Farmer after farmer joined the march to Kansas, Nebraska, and Dakota. . . . The movement . . . had . . . become an exodus, a stampede."

The same excitement took hold in northern Europe, as Norwegians, Swedes, and Russians for the first time joined the older German migration. At the peak of the "American fever" in 1882, over 105,000 Scandinavians immigrated to the United States. Swedish and Norwegian became the primary languages in parts of Minnesota and the Dakotas. Roughly a third of the farmers on the northern plains were foreign-born (Map 16.2).

The motivation for most settlers, American or European, was to better themselves economically. But for some southern blacks, Kansas briefly represented something more precious—the modern Promised Land of racial freedom. In the spring of 1879, with Reconstruction over and federal protection withdrawn, black communities fearful of white vengeance were swept by religious enthusiasm for Kansas. Within a month or so, some 6,000 blacks left Mississippi and Louisiana, most of them with nothing more than the clothes on their backs and faith in the Lord. They called themselves Exodusters, members of the exodus to the dry prairie. The 1880 census reported

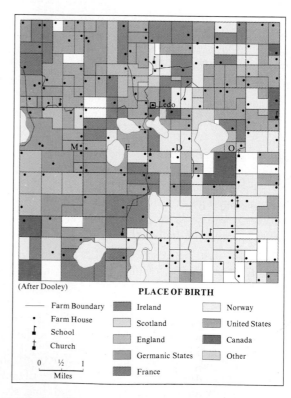

PLACE OF BIRTH

(After Dooley)

— Farm Boundary   Ireland   Norway
• Farm House   Scotland   United States
School   England   Canada
Church   Germanic States   Other
   France

0   ½   1
Miles

MAP 16.2
The Rural Ethnic Mosaic: Blue Earth County, Minnesota, 1880
What could have been more natural for emigrants such as Ida Lindgren (see American Voices, p. 515) than to settle next to others sharing common ties to a homeland? This map of Medo Township reveals that in rural America, no less than in the cities, ethnicity strongly influenced where people lived.

Exodusters
Driven from their homes by terror raids, these southern blacks camped out on a Mississippi levee on the way to Kansas.
Library of Congress.

40,000 blacks in Kansas, by far the largest African American concentration in the West aside from Texas, whose expanding cotton frontier attracted hundreds of thousands of black migrants during the 1870s and 1880s.

Farming the Plains. No matter where they came from, homesteaders found the plains a harsh place. A cloud of grasshoppers might destroy a crop in a day; a brush fire or hailstorm could do the job in an hour. What forested land had always provided—springs for water, lumber for cabins and fencing, ample firewood—was absent. For shelter, settlers often cut dugouts into hillsides and, after a season or two, erected houses made of turf cut from the ground.

The absence of trees, however, meant far less labor clearing the land. New technology and better seed overcame obstacles once thought insurmountable: steel plows enabled homesteaders to break the tightly matted ground; barbed wire, invented in 1874 by Joseph F. Glidden, an Illinois farmer, provided cheap, effective fencing against roaming cattle; and strains of hard-kernel wheat tolerant of the extreme temperatures of the plains came in from northern Europe and Russia's Crimea. The open, level land was ideal for raising grain. Homesteaders had good crops while the wet cycle held, and they began to anticipate the wood-frame house, deep well, and full coal bin that might make life on the plains tolerable.

Then, in the later 1880s, the dry years came and wrecked those hopeful calculations. "From day to day," reported the budding novelist Stephen Crane from Nebraska, "a wind hot as an oven's fury . . . raged like a pestilence," destroying the crops and leaving farmers "helpless, with no weapon against this terrible and inscrutable wrath of nature." Land only recently settled emptied out as homesteaders fled. The Dakotas

lost 50,000 settlers between 1885 and 1890, and comparable departures occurred up and down the drought-stricken plains.

Other settlers held on grimly. Stripped of the illusion that "rain follows the plow," the survivors came to terms with the semiarid climate prevailing west of the 98th meridian. The answer lay in dry-farming methods, which involved deep planting to bring subsoil moisture to the roots, and quick harrowing after rainfalls to turn over a dry mulch that slowed evaporation. Producing a low yield per acre, dry farming developed most fully on the corporate farms that covered up to 100,000 acres in the Red River Valley in North Dakota. But family farms, which remained the norm elsewhere, could not operate with less than 300 acres of grain crops. Congress came to the rescue in 1873 by amending the Homestead legislation to enable settlers to qualify for an additional 160 acres if they planted trees on a quarter of the land. No one, however, could hope to survive without machinery for plowing, planting, and harvesting. Dry farming was not for the unequipped homesteader.

By the turn of the century the Great Plains had fully submitted to agricultural development. About half of the nation's cattle and sheep, a third of its cereal crops—and nearly three-fifths of its wheat—came from the newly settled lands. This process displayed little of the "pioneering" that Americans associated with the westward movement. The railroads preceded the settlers, eastern capital financed the ranching bonanza, and agriculture depended on sophisticated dry-farming techniques and modern machinery.

And where was the economic capital of the Great Plains? Far off in Chicago. There, at the hub of the nation's rail system, the wheat pit traded western grain and consigned it to world markets, and great packing houses slaughtered western livestock and supplied the nation with sausage, bacon, and sides of beef. In return, western ranchers and farmers got lumber, barbed wire, McCormick reapers, and Sears Roebuck catalogues. Chicago was truly, as historian William Cronon has called it, "nature's metropolis."

The Fate of the Indians

What of the native Americans who had inhabited the Great Plains? Basically, their future has been told in the foregoing account of western settlement. "The white children have surrounded me and have left me nothing but an island," lamented the great Sioux chief Red Cloud in 1870, the year after the completion of the transcontinental railroad. "When we first had all this land we were strong; now we are all melting like snow on a hillside, while you are grown like spring grass."

No matter that provision for a permanent Indian country had been written into federal law and ratified by treaties with various tribes. As incursions into their lands increased from the late 1850s onward, the Indians struck back all along the frontier: the Apache in the Southwest, the Cheyenne and Arapaho in Colorado, the Sioux in the Wyoming and Dakota territories. Fighting ferociously between 1865 and 1867, the Sioux prevented a wagon road from being built through their prized Powder River hunting grounds to the booming mining town of Bozeman, Montana. The Indians hoped that if they resisted stubbornly enough, the whites would tire of the struggle and leave them in peace. This seemed not altogether fanciful, given the country's exhaustion after the Civil War. But the federal government did not give up; instead, it formulated a new policy for dealing with the western Indians.

The Reservation Solution. Few whites questioned the necessity of moving the native Americans out of the path of settlement. That, indeed, had been the fate of the eastern Indians. Now, however, Indian removal was linked to something new: a planned approach for weaning the Indians from their tribal way of life. In early 1867, Congress adopted a law "for establishing peace with certain Indian tribes now at war with the United States." To this end, a peace commission was appointed, charged especially with negotiating a settlement based on the removal of the western tribes to reservations, where, under the guidance of the Office of Indian Affairs, they would be wards of the government until they learned "to walk on the white man's road."

The government set aside two extensive areas for the Indians. It allocated the southwestern quarter of the Dakota Territory—present-day South Dakota west of the Missouri River—to the northern Plains tribes. The Indians on the southern plains were assigned to Oklahoma, where the Five Civilized Tribes—the Choctaw, Cherokee, Chickasaw, Creek, and Seminole—and other

eastern Indians had already been resettled. Scattered reservations went to the Apache, Navajo, and Ute in the Southwest and to the mountain Indians in the Rockies and beyond (Map 16.3).

As in the past, the transfer of land went through the legal process of treaty making. And, as in the past, the whites bribed and tricked the Indian chiefs and in the end forced them to accept what they could not prevent. In 1868 the western Sioux tribes signed a treaty ceding all their land outside the Dakota reservation but explicitly retaining their hunting grounds in the Powder River country. "We have now selected and provided reservations for all, off the great road," concluded the western commanding general that year. "All who cling to their old hunting-grounds are hostile and will remain so till killed off." That they would resist was inevitable. "You might as well expect the rivers to run backward as that any man who was born a free man should be contented when penned up and denied liberty to go where he pleases," said Chief Joseph of the Nez Percé. With that conviction, Joseph in 1877 led his tribe, including women and children, on an epic 1,500-mile march from eastern Oregon to escape confinement in a small reservation. In a series of heroic engagements, the Nez Percé fought off the pursuing U.S. Army until, after four months of extraordinary hardship, the remnants of the tribe were finally cornered and forced to surrender in Montana near the Canadian border.

The U.S. Army was thinly spread, having been cut back after the Civil War to a total force of 27,000. But these were veteran troops, including 2,000 black cavalrymen of the Ninth and Tenth regiments, whom Indians called, with grim respect, "buffalo soldiers." Technology also favored the army. Telegraph communications and railroads enabled the troopers to be quickly concentrated; repeating rifles and Gatling guns increased their firepower. As fighting intensified in the mid-1870s, a reluctant Congress made appropriations to augment the western troopers. Tribal rivalries meant that the army always had Indian allies. Worst of all for the Indians, however, beyond the formidable U.S. Army or their own disunity, was the overwhelming impact of white settlement.

Resisting the reservation solution, the Indians fought on for years—in Kansas in 1868–1869, in the Red River Valley of Texas in 1874, sporadically in Arizona among the Apache, who refused to be contained in the small reservation to which they had been removed in the mid-1870s. For more than a decade, bands of these fierce desert warriors made life miserable for white settlers in the Southwest until Geronimo—their wily chief—was finally captured in 1886 and began a lifetime of captivity. On the northern plains the crisis came in 1875, when the Indian Office—despite the treaty of

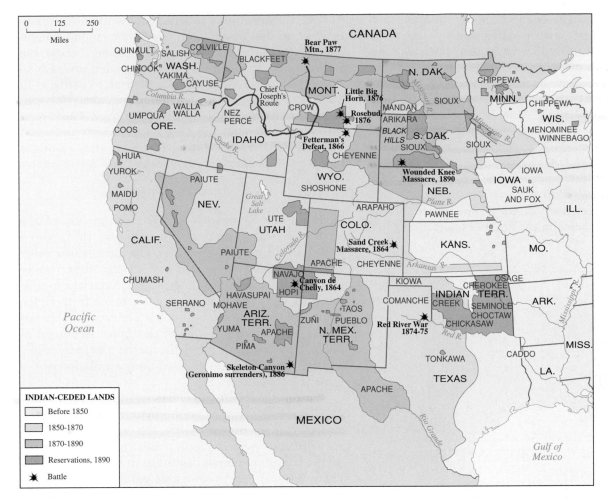

MAP 16.3
The Indian Frontier, to 1890
As settlement pushed onto the Great Plains after the Civil War, the Indians put up bitter resistance, but ultimately to no avail. Over a period of decades they ceded most of their lands to the federal government, and by 1890 they were confined to scattered reservations where the most they could expect was an impoverished and alien way of life.

1868—ordered the Sioux to vacate their Powder River hunting grounds and withdraw to the reservation.

Led by Sitting Bull, Sioux and Cheyenne warriors gathered on the Little Big Horn River to the west of the Powder River country. In a typical concentrating maneuver, army columns from widely separated forts converged on the Little Big Horn. The Seventh Cavalry, commanded by Colonel George A. Custer, famous as a Civil War cavalryman, came upon the Sioux encampment on June 25, 1876. Disregarding orders, the reckless Custer sought out battle on his own. He attacked from three sides, hoping to capitalize on the element of surprise. But his forces were spread too thin. The other two army contingents fell back with heavy losses to defensive positions, but Custer's own force of 256 men was surrounded and annihilated by Crazy Horse's Sioux warriors.

The victory was great but not decisive; it merely postponed the day of reckoning. Weakened by unrelenting military pressure and increasing physical privation, the Sioux bands one by one gave up and moved onto the reservation. Last to come in were Sitting Bull's followers. They had retreated to Canada, but in 1881, after five hard years, they recrossed the border and surrendered at Fort Buford, Montana.

By then the open plains were no more. Homesick bands of southern Cheyenne learned this bitter truth in 1878 when they escaped from their reservation in the Indian Territory of Oklahoma. Along the route to their native grounds in the Wyoming Territory lay three railroads, numerous telegraph lines, and ranchers and homesteaders eager to report the Cheyenne's movements. When the army eventually captured them, the survivors declared that they preferred death to returning to the reservation. The government relented and permitted them to stay on their native land.

In the end, not Indian resistance but relentless white pressure wrecked the reservation solution. In the mid-1870s prospectors began to dig for gold in the Black Hills, sacred land to the Sioux and entirely inside their Dakota reservation. Unable to hold back the prospectors or to buy out the Sioux, the government opened up the Black Hills to gold seekers at their own risk and in 1877, after Sioux resistance had crumbled, forced the native Americans to cede the western third of their reservation (Map 16.4).

The Indian Territory of Oklahoma met the same fate. Two million acres in the heart of the territory had not been assigned to any tribe, and white homesteaders coveted that fertile land. The "Boomer" movement, stirred up initially by railroads running across the Indian Territory during the 1880s, agitated tirelessly to open this so-called Oklahoma District to settlers. In 1889 the government gave in and placed the Oklahoma District under the Homestead Act. On April 22, 1889, a horde of claimants rushed in and staked out the entire district within a few hours. Two tent cities—Guthrie with 15,000 people and Oklahoma City with 10,000— were in full swing by nightfall.

Dividing the Reservations. The completion of the land grab was hastened, ironically, by the avowed friends of the native Americans. The Indians had never lacked sympathizers—especially in the East, where reformers created the Indian Rights Association after the Civil War. The movement got a boost from Helen Hunt Jackson's influential book *A Century of Dishonor* (1881), which told the story of the unjust treatment of the Indians. With little sympathy for the tribal way of life, however, the reformers favored the assimilation of the Indians into white society.

During the 1870s the Office of Indian Affairs had developed a program to train Indian children for farming work and prepare them for citizenship. Some attended reservation schools, while the less lucky were sent to boarding schools distant from family and home. The reformers approved of this educational program. They also favored efforts by the Indian Office to undercut tribal authority. In particular, they highly esteemed private property as a "civilizing" force. They felt, moreover, that defense of Indian lands against white encroachment was hopeless until the Indians became, individually, property owners.

The resulting policy was called *severalty*—the division of reservation lands into individually owned parcels. With the blessing of the reformers, the Dawes Severalty Act of 1887 authorized the president to divide tribal lands, giving 160 acres to each family head and smaller parcels to other individuals. The land would be held in trust by the government for twenty-five years, and the recipients would become U.S. citizens. Remaining reservation lands would be sold off and the proceeds placed in an Indian education fund.

The Last Battle: Wounded Knee. The Sioux were among the first to bear the brunt of the Dawes Act. The federal government, announcing it had gained the Sioux's approval, opened their "surplus" land to white settlement on February 10, 1890. But no surveys had been made of the reservation boundaries, nor had any provision been made for land allotments for the Indians living in the ceded areas. On top of these signs of bad faith by the whites, drought wiped out the Sioux's crops that summer.

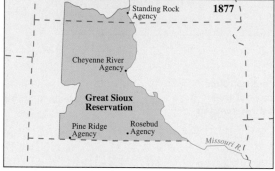

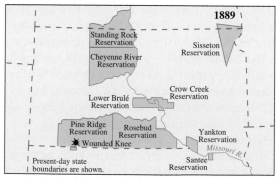

MAP 16.4

The Sioux Reservations in South Dakota, 1868–1889
In 1868, when they bent to the demand that they move onto the reservation, the Sioux thought they had gained secure rights to a substantial part of their ancestral hunting grounds. But as they learned to their sorrow, fixed boundary lines only increased their vulnerability to the land hunger of the whites and sped up the process of expropriation.

Indian School
In this photograph at the Riverside Indian School in Anadarko, Oklahoma Territory, the pupils have been shorn of their braids and dressed in laced shoes, Mother Hubbard dresses, and shirts and trousers—one step on the journey into the mainstream of white American society. Children as young as five were separated from their families and sent to Indian schools like this one that taught them new skills while encouraging them to abandon traditional Indian ways.
University of Oklahoma, Western History Collections.

It seemed beyond endurance. They had lost their ancestral lands. They faced a future as sedentary farmers that was alien to all their traditions. And immediately confronting them was a winter of starvation.

But news of salvation had also come. An Indian messiah, a holy man who called himself Wovoka, was preaching a new religion on a Paiute reservation in Nevada. In a vision, Wovoka had gone to heaven and received God's word that the world would be regenerated: the whites would disappear, all the Indians of past generations would return to earth, and life on the Great Plains would go back to the time of the roaming buffalo. All this would come to pass in the spring of 1891. Awaiting that great day, the Indians should follow Wovoka's commandments and practice the Ghost Dance. Wovoka's teachings were nonviolent, but among his Sioux adherents the new religion took a belligerent and increasingly threatening tone against white settlers. As the frenzy of the Ghost Dance swept through some Sioux encampments in the fall of 1890, resident whites became alarmed and called for army intervention.

When Indian police backed by federal troops tried to arrest Sitting Bull on December 14, a gun battle broke out, killing the old chief and at least twelve others. Worse was to come. Among the Minneconjou, the medicine man Yellow Bird had stirred up a fervent Ghost Dance following. But their chief, Big Foot, had fallen desperately ill with pneumonia, and the Minneconjou had agreed to come in under military escort to an encampment at Wounded Knee Creek on December 28. The next morning, when the soldiers attempted to disarm the Indians, a battle exploded in the encampment. In American Voices ("Black Elk: Wounded Knee: Something Terrible Happened . . . ," p. 522), Black Elk describes what happened. Among the U.S. troopers, 25 died; among the Indians, 146 men, women, and children perished, many of them shot down as they fled.

The Aftermath.   Wounded Knee was the final episode in the war against the Plains Indians, but not the end of their story. The process of severalty now proceeded without hindrance. On the Dakota lands the Teton Sioux fared relatively well, and many of the younger generation settled down as small farmers and stock grazers. Ironically, the more fortunate tribes were probably those occupying reservation lands that did not attract white settlement and thus were bypassed by the severalty process. The flood of whites into South Dakota and Oklahoma, in contrast, left the Indians as small minorities in lands once wholly theirs—20,000 Sioux in a South Dakotan population of 400,000 in 1900, 70,000 members of various tribes in a population of a million when Oklahoma became a state in 1907.

Even so, tribal life survived until, with the restoration of the reservation policy in 1934, it once again rested on a communal territorial basis. All along, native American cultures had been adaptive, changing in the face of adversity and even absorbing features of white society including, in some cases, developing written languages. This cultural resilience persisted—in religion, in tribal structure, in crafts—but the fostering native American world was gone: swept away, as an Oklahoma editor put it in the year of statehood, by "the onward march of empire."

The Far West

On the western edge of the Great Plains, the Rocky Mountains rise up to form a great barrier between the mostly flat eastern two-thirds of the country and the rugged Far West (see Map 16.1). Beyond the Rockies lie two vast plateaus: in the north the Columbia plateau,

BLACK ELK

Wounded Knee: Something Terrible Happened . . .

——★——

Black Elk, an Oglala Sioux holy man, was at Wounded Knee when the killing occurred on December 29, 1890. This is his account, as he recollected the event forty years later.

It was in the evening when we heard that the Big Foots were camped over there with the soldiers. . . . The [next] morning I went out after my horses, and while I was out I heard shooting off toward the east, and I knew from the sound that it must be wagon-guns [cannons] going off. The sounds went right through my body, and I felt that something terrible would happen. . . .

A little way ahead of us, just below the head of the dry gulch, there were some women and children who were huddled under a clay bank, and some cavalrymen were there pointing guns at them. . . .

I had no gun, and when we were charging, I just held the sacred bow out in front of me with my right hand. The bullets did not hit us at all. . . .

After the soldiers marched away, I heard from my friend, Dog Chief, how the trouble started, and he was right there by Yellow Bird when it happened. This is the way it was:

In the morning the soldiers began to take all the guns away from the Big Foots. Soldiers were on the little hill and all around, and there were soldiers across the dry gulch to the south and over east along Wounded Knee Creek too. The people were nearly surrounded, and the wagon-guns were pointing at them.

Some had not yet given up their guns, and so the soldiers were searching all the tepees, throwing things around and poking into everything. There was a man called Yellow Bird, and he and another man were standing in front of the tepee where Big Foot was lying sick. They had white sheets around and over them, with eyeholes to look through, and they had guns under these. An officer came to search them. He took the other man's gun, and then started to take Yellow Bird's. But Yellow Bird would not let go. He wrestled with the officer, and while they were wrestling, the gun went off and killed the officer. As soon as the gun went off, Dog Chief told me, an officer shot and killed Big Foot who was lying sick inside the tepee.

Then suddenly nobody knew what was happening, except that the soldiers were all shooting and the wagon-guns began going off right in among the people.

Many were shot down right there. The women and children ran into the gulch and up west, dropping all the time, for the soldiers shot them as they ran. There were only a hundred warriors and there were nearly five hundred soldiers. The warriors rushed to where they had piled their guns and knives. They fought soldiers with only their hands until they got their guns. . . .

It was a good winter day when all this happened. The sun was shining. But after the soldiers marched away from their dirty work, a heavy snow began to fall. The wind came up in the night. There was a big blizzard, and it grew very cold. The snow drifted deep in the crooked gulch, and it was one long grave of butchered women and children and babies, who had never done any harm and were only trying to run away.

———

Source: John G. Neihardt, ed., *Black Elk Speaks: The Legendary "Book of Visions" of an American Indian* (1932; rpt. New York: Washington Square Press, 1971), 216–223.

extending into eastern Oregon and Washington, and, flanking the southern Rockies, the Colorado plateau. Where they break off, the plateaus open to the desert-like Great Basin, which covers western Utah and all of Nevada. To the southeast the Great Basin gives way to plains and mountain ridges that are equally dry but are drained by the rivers of lower Arizona and New Mexico.

Separating this arid interior from the Pacific are two great mountain ranges—the Sierra Nevada and, to the north, the Cascades. Beyond these mountains lies a coastal region, the Pacific slope, cool and rainy in the north but increasingly dry as one proceeds southward, until in southern California rainfall becomes almost as sparse as in the interior.

The Dead at Wounded Knee

In December 1890 U.S. soldiers massacred 146 Sioux men, women, and children in the
Battle of Wounded Knee in South Dakota. It was the last big fight on the northern
plains between the Indians and the whites. Black Elk, a Sioux holy man, related that
"after the soldiers marched away from their dirty work, a heavy snow began to fall. . . .
and it grew very cold." The body of Yellow Bird lay frozen where it had fallen.

National Anthropological Archives, Smithsonian Institution, Washington, DC.

What most impressed white Americans about the far western country was its inhospitability. "Who are to go there?" asked Senator George McDuffie in 1843 when the nation was preparing to seize this land from Mexico. "The territory consists of mountains almost inaccessible, and low lands . . . where rain never falls, except during spring. . . . Why, sir, sir, of what use will this be for agricultural purposes? I would not, for that purpose, give a pinch of snuff for the whole territory."

The senator's assessment was too grim, perhaps, but contained enough truth to explain why the Far West could not be occupied in the familiar way—that is, by a multitude of settlers moving westward along a broad front, blanketing the land, and bringing it under cultivation homestead by homestead. The wagon trains moving to Oregon's Willamette Valley revealed an entirely different strategy of occupation—the planting of distant oases in a vast, mostly barren landscape. This had been the strategy of Spanish colonizers ever since they had sent the first wagon trains 700 miles northward from Mexico into the upper Rio Grande Valley in 1598.

When the Southwest was taken from Mexico by the United States 250 years later, in 1848, major Hispanic settlements existed in New Mexico and California, and smaller ones were scattered along the borderlands into south Texas. At that time, aside from Oregon, the only significant settlement of non-Hispanic whites was around the Great Salt Lake in Utah, where Mormons had moved to escape persecution and plant a New Zion.

Fewer than 100,000 people of European ancestry—roughly 75,000 of them Hispanic—lived in the entire Far West in 1848.

The Mining Frontier

More emigrants would be coming in, certainly, but Senator McDuffie's slight valuation of the nation's newly acquired western territory seemed about right. California was "hilly and mountainous," commented a U.S. naval officer in 1849, too dry for farming, and surely not "susceptible of supporting a very large population." He had not taken account of the recent discovery of gold in the Sierra foothills, however. California would indeed support a very large population, drawn not by the lure of arable land but by dreams of gold.

Extraction of mineral wealth became the basis for the Far West's development (Map 16.5). This meant, first of all, explosive growth. By 1860, when the Great Plains was still Indian country, California was a booming state with 300,000 residents. Overnight San Francisco became a bustling metropolis—it had 57,000 residents by 1860—and was the hub of a mining empire that stretched to the Rockies. Similarly, Denver mushroomed into the metropolis for the mining camps on the eastern slope.

In its swift urbanization, the Far West resembled Australia, whose gold rush began in 1851, much more than it resembled the American Midwest; like San Francisco, Melbourne was a city incongruously grand

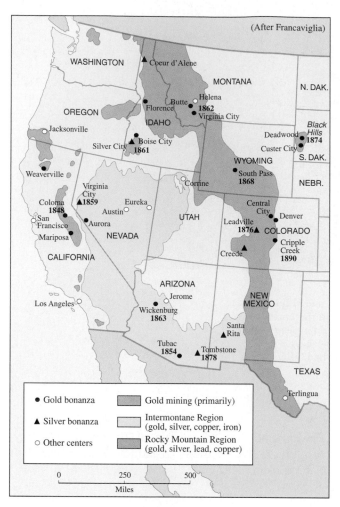

MAP 16.5

The Mining Frontier, 1848–1890

The Far West was America's gold country because of its geological history. Veins of gold and silver form when molten material from the earth's core is forced up into fissures caused by the tectonic movements that create mountain ranges, such as the ones that dominate the far western landscape. It was these veins, the product of mountain-forming activity many thousands of years earlier, that prospectors began to discover after 1848 and furiously exploit. Although widely dispersed across the Far West, the lodes that they found followed the mountain ranges, bisecting the region and bypassing the great plateaus not shaped by the ancient tectonic activity.

and along the Fraser River in British Columbia. New strikes of gold and silver occurred in Montana and Wyoming during the 1860s, in the Black Hills of South Dakota a decade later, and in the Coeur d'Alene region of Idaho during the 1880s.

As the news of each discovery spread, a wild, remote area turned almost overnight into a mob scene of prospectors, traders, gamblers, prostitutes, and saloon keepers. At least a hundred thousand fortune seekers flocked to the Pike's Peak area of Colorado in the spring of 1859. Trespassers on government or Indian land, the prospectors made their own law. The mining codes devised at community meetings limited the size of a mining claim to what a person could reasonably work. This kind of informal lawmaking also became an instrument for excluding or discriminating against Mexicans, Chinese, and African Americans in the gold fields. And it turned into hangman's justice for the many outlaws who infested the mining camps. Supplying these camps, especially in advance of the railroads, was a small industry in itself, dotting the far western interior with rough trading depots like Corinne, Utah (see Voices from Abroad, "Baron Joseph Alexander von Hübner: A Western Boom Town," p. 525).

The heyday of the prospectors was always brief. They were equipped only to skim gold from the surface of the earth and from stream beds. Extracting the metal locked in underground lodes required mine shafts and crushing mills, which called for capital, technology, and business organization. The original claim holders quickly sold out after exhausting the surface gold or when a generous bidder came along. At every gold-rush site the prospector soon gave way to entrepreneurial development and large-scale mining. Rough mining camps turned into big towns.

amid the empty spaces and rough mining camps of the Australian "outback." Finally, the distinctive pattern of isolated settlement persisted, driven now, however, by a proliferation of mining sites and by people moving not east to west but coming mainly from California and moving west to east.

By the mid-1850s, as easy pickings in the California gold country diminished, disappointed prospectors began to pull out and spread across the West in hopes of striking it rich elsewhere. Gold was discovered on the Nevada side of the Sierra, in the Colorado Rockies,

Virginia City. Nevada's Virginia City started out as a ramshackle mining camp. But once the Comstock silver lode came into production in 1859, Virginia City was rapidly transformed into a real urban center, boasting a stock exchange, five newspapers, and, in short order, ostentatious mansions for the mining kings, fancy hotels, opera, even Shakespearean theater. Virginia City was a magnet for job seekers of both sexes: the men laboring as miners below ground for $4 a day, many of the women becoming dance-hall entertainers and prostitutes because that was the best chance offered them by Virginia City's bonanza economy. In 1870 the ratio of men to women was two to one; children made up only 10 percent of the population. There were a hundred saloons, and brothels lined D Street.

Even so, when James Galloway arrived looking for work on February 4, 1875, he brought his family with him, and so did many other miners. By 1880 there were as many women and children as men in Virginia City.

BARON JOSEPH ALEXANDER VON HÜBNER

A Western Boom Town

———————★———————

During a leisurely trip around the world, Baron von Hübner, a distinguished Austrian diplomat, traveled across the United States, taking advantage of the newly completed transcontinental railroad to see the Wild West. After observing Mormon life in Salt Lake City, he went northward to Corinne, Utah, near the juncture where the Central and Union Pacific railroads met. He was struck not only by the crudeness of Corinne (see Map 16.5) but also by the tough "rowdies" inhabiting the place.

Corinne has only existed for four years. Sprung out of the earth as if by enchantment, this town now contains upwards of 2,000 inhabitants, and every day increases in importance. It is a victualing center for the advanced posts of the [miners] in Idaho and Montana. A coach runs twice a week to Virginia City and to Helena, 350 and 500 miles to the north. Despite the serious dangers and the terrible fatigue of the journeys, these diligences are always full of passengers. Various articles of consumption and dry goods of all sorts are sent in wagons. The "high road" is but a rough track in the soil left by the wheels of the previous vehicles.

The streets of Corinne are full of white men armed to the teeth, miserable looking Indians dressed in the ragged shirts and trousers furnished by the federal government, and yellow Chinese with a business-like air and hard, intelligent faces. No town in the Far West gave me so good an idea as this little place of what is meant by *border life*, the struggle between civilization and savage men and things. . . .

All commercial business centers in Main Street. The houses on both sides are nothing but boarded huts. I have seen some with only canvas partitions. . . . The lanes alongside of the huts, which are generally the resort of Chinese women of bad character, lead into the desert, which begins at the doors of the last houses. . . .

To have on your conscience a number of man-slaughters committed in full day, under the eyes of your fellow citizens; to have escaped the reach of justice by craft, audacity, or bribery; to have earned a reputation for being "sharp," that is, for knowing how to cheat all the world without being caught—those are the attributes of the true rowdy in the Far West. . . . Endowed as they often are with really fine qualities—courage, energy, and intellectual and physical strength—they might in another sphere and with the moral sense which they now lack, have become valuable members of society. But such as they are, these adventurers have a reason for being, a providential mission to fulfill. The qualities needed to struggle with and conquer savage nature have naturally their corresponding defects. Look back, and you will see the cradles of all civilization surrounded with giants of Herculean strength ready to run every risk and to shrink from neither danger nor crime to attain their ends. It is only by the peculiar temper of the time and place that we can distinguish them from the backwoodsman and rowdy of the United States.

Source: Oscar Handlin, ed., *This Was America* (Cambridge, MA: Harvard University Press, 1949), 313–315.

Galloway's diary describes a family life that was entirely ordinary—church going, picnics, the purchase of a lot for a small house. But Galloway was infected by Virginia City's pervasive gambling fever: he speculated regularly in mining stock and always lost money. In the end, he fell victim to the extraordinary hazards of hard-rock mining. He was killed when his sleeve got caught in the gears of a mine machine. He might have survived had he permitted rescuers to hack off his arm, but he took a long chance on being cut loose and coming out whole, and lost.

Industrialization of Western Mining. In its final stage the mining frontier passed into the industrial world. At some sites gold and silver proved less important than the more common metals—copper, lead, zinc—for which there was a huge demand in eastern manufacturing. Beginning in the 1870s, copper mining thrived in the Butte district of Montana, especially after the opening of the fabulous Anaconda mine, and also flourished in the Globe and Copper Queen fields of New Mexico and Arizona. In the 1890s, Idaho's Coeur d'Alene silver district became the nation's main source of lead and zinc.

Hydraulic Mining
When surface veins of gold were played out, miners turned to hydraulic mining, which
was invented in California in 1853. The technology was simple; it used high-pressure
streams of water to wash away hillsides of gold-bearing soil. Although building the
reservoirs, piping systems, and sluices cost money, the profits from hydraulic mining
helped transform western mining into big business. But, as this daguerreotype suggests, hydraulic mining wreaked havoc on the environment.
Collection of Matthew Isenburg.

Entrepreneurs raised capital, built rail connections, devised the technology for treating the lower-grade copper deposits, constructed smelting facilities, and recruited a labor force. As elsewhere in American industry, trade-union organization appeared among the miners (see Chapter 17). And as elsewhere in corporate America, the western metal industries went through a process of consolidation. The Anaconda Copper Mining Company and other Montana mining firms came under the control of the Amalgamated Copper Company in 1899. Also in that year, the American Smelting and Refining Company brought together the bulk of the nation's lead-mining and copper-refining properties.

Blackfeet and Crow country in the 1860s, the Butte copper district was a center of industrial capitalism barely thirty years later.

The Pacific Slope. If the Far West had lacked mineral wealth, the history of California, Oregon, and Washington State would certainly have been very different. Before the discovery of gold in 1848, Oregon's Willamette Valley—not dry California—attracted most westward-bound settlers. And, but for the gold rush, California would likely have remained like the Willamette Valley—an agricultural backwater lacking markets for its products and slow to build population.

In 1860, Oregon, already a state, had scarcely 25,000 inhabitants, and its principal city, Portland, was little more than a village. Over the next few decades, however, booming California pulled Oregon from the doldrums by creating a market for the state's produce and timber. North of Oregon—territory very thinly settled during the 1870s—the arrival of rail transportation in the early 1880s had an equally tonic effect. On the coastal side, Washington's development was much like Oregon's, but east of the Cascades, on the fertile, semiarid Columbia plateau, a rich grain-producing region also sprang up.

Oregon and Washington (which became a state in 1889) grew prodigiously. Where scarcely a hundred thousand settlers had lived twenty years earlier, there were by 1890 nearly three-quarters of a million (Map 16.6). Portland and, even more dramatically, Seattle blossomed into important commercial centers, both prospering from a mixed economy of farming, ranching, logging, and fishing.

California's fertile Central Valley and forested north coast experienced a comparable development, and so did the irrigated valleys of Utah, which by 1890 had over 200,000 inhabitants. At a certain point, especially as railroads opened up eastern markets, this diversified growth became self-sustaining. But what had triggered it, what had provided the first markets and underwritten the service infrastructure, was the bonanza mining economy, at the hub of which stood San Francisco, metropolis for the entire Far West.

Hispanics, Chinese, Anglos

California was the anchor of two distinct far western regions. First, with Oregon and Washington it formed the Pacific slope. Second, by climate and Hispanic heritage, California was linked to the Southwest, which today includes Arizona, New Mexico, and Texas.

The Hispanic Southwest. Along a 1,500-mile borderland, settlements planted over two centuries earlier by the Spanish viceroys formed, after the 1821 revolution, the northernmost provinces of independent Mexico. Most populous were the settlements along the upper Rio Grande Valley in New Mexico; Santa Fe, the main town and over 200 years old, contained 4,635 residents in 1860. Farther down the Rio Grande were El Paso, nearly as old but much smaller, and, as the Rio Grande emptied into the Gulf of Mexico, newer towns such as Laredo. To the north lay San Antonio, founded to establish Spain's claim to central Texas. At the other end of this Hispanic crescent, in California, a Hispanic population was spread thinly in the old *presidio*, or garrison, towns along the coast, and on a patchwork of great ranches.

The economy of the Hispanic Southwest was pastoral, consisting primarily of cattle and sheep ranching. In south Texas there were family-run ranches. Everywhere else the social order was highly stratified. At the top stood an elite, the ranching dons, who were beneficiaries of royal land grants, proudly Spanish, and devoted to the traditional life of a landed aristocracy. Below them, with little in between, was a laboring class of servants, artisans, *vaqueros* (cowboys), and farmworkers. In New Mexico there was also a large *mestizo* population, a peasantry of mixed Hispanic and Pueblo Indian blood, who were Spanish-speaking and Catholic but who, in their village life and farming methods, were faithful to their Pueblo heritage.

Pueblo Indians, though long past the golden age of their civilization, still occupied much of the Rio Grande Valley, living in the old ways in adobe villages and

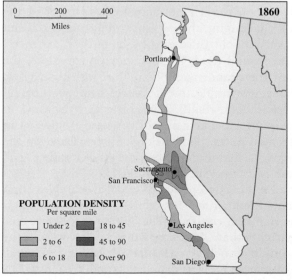

MAP 16.6
The Settlement of the Pacific Slope, 1860–1890
In 1860 the settlement of the Pacific slope was remarkably uneven—fully under way in northern California, scarcely begun anywhere else. By 1890 a new pattern had begun to emerge, with the swift growth of southern California foreshadowed and the settlement of the Pacific Northwest well launched.

Vaqueros *in a Corral*
On California cattle ranches owners relied on Mexican cowhands—*vaqueros*—whose
skills as riders and rope handlers were unexcelled. This striking painting was done in
1877 by James Walker, who came from New York City but had a special enthusiasm
for southwestern scenes.
Thomas Gilcrease Institute of American History and Art.

making the New Mexico countryside a patchwork of
Hispanic and Pueblo settlements. To the north a vibrant
new people, the Navajo, had appeared, warriors like the
Apache from whom they descended but also skilled
craft workers and sheep raisers.

New Mexico was one place where European and
native American cultures managed a successful, if
uneasy, coexistence and where the Indian inhabitants
were equipped to hold their own against the Anglo
challenge. In California, by contrast, the Hispanic
occupation had been harder on the native American
peoples, undermining their tribal structure, forcing
them to abandon hunting and gathering for compulsory labor, and making them easy prey for the aggressive Anglo miners and settlers, who, in short order,
nearly wiped out California's once numerous Indian
population.

Anglo-Hispanic Conflict. The fate of the Hispanic
Southwest after its incorporation into the United
States in 1848 depended on the rate of Anglo immigration. In New Mexico, which remained off the beaten
track even after the arrival of railroads in the 1880s,
the Santa Fe elite more than held its own, incorporat-

ing the Anglo newcomers into Hispanic society
through intermarriage and business partnerships. In
California, by contrast, aggressive Anglos grabbed
most of the great ranches even though the peace treaty
with Mexico had recognized the property rights of the
Californios and had made them U.S. citizens. The fact
that the ranch proprietors actually won most of the
lawsuits challenging their Mexican land titles did not
matter very much. Burdened by huge legal expenses,
rising taxes, and the costs of removing squatters, the
dons saw their lands auctioned off or lost in swindles
by Yankees swarming in with business deals. Around
San Francisco the great ranches disappeared almost in
a puff of smoke. Farther south, where Anglos were
slow to arrive, the dons held on longer, but by the
1880s just a handful of the original families still
retained their Mexican land holdings.

The New Mexico peasants found themselves similarly embattled. Crucial to their livelihood were their
grazing rights on communal lands. But these were customary rights that could not withstand legal challenge
when Anglo ranchers established title and began
putting up fences. The peasants responded as best they
could. Traditionally, women had raised much of the

family food in small gardens, bartered in the village markets, made the clothes, and plastered the adobe houses. With the loss of the communal lands, the men began to leave the villages seasonally to work on the railroads or in the Colorado mines and sugar-beet fields, earning crucial dollars while leaving the village economy in their wives' hands.

Elsewhere, hard-pressed Hispanics struck back for what they considered rightfully theirs. In El Paso, the inhabitants rose in unsuccessful revolt when title to their communal salt beds passed into private hands in 1879. After Anglo ranchers began to fence in communal lands in San Miguel County, the New Mexicans long settled there, *los pobres* (the poor ones), organized themselves into masked night-riding raiders and in 1889 and 1890 mounted an effective campaign of harassment against the interlopers. After 1900, when Anglo farmers swarmed into south Texas bent on exploiting new irrigation methods, the displaced *Tejano* ranchers responded with sporadic but persistent night-riding attacks. Much of the raiding by Mexican "bandits" from across the border in the years before World War I was really more in the nature of a civil war by embittered *Tejanos* who had lived north of the Rio Grande for generations.

In the long run, however, these *Tejanos*, like the New Mexico villagers who became seasonal wage laborers, could not avoid being driven into the ranks of a Mexican American working class as the Anglo economy developed. This same development also began to attract increasing numbers of immigrants from Old Mexico.

Mexican Migrants. All along the Southwest borderlands economic activity was picking up in the late nineteenth century. Railroads were being built, copper mines were opening in Arizona, and commercial agriculture was developing in south Texas (cotton and vegetable crops) and in southern California (fruit). There is no way of knowing how many people migrated to the work thus created, since the borders were open until 1917 and few bothered to register when they entered the United States. In Texas the Hispanic population increased from about 20,000 in 1850 to 165,000 in 1900. Some came as contract workers for railway track gangs and as harvest labor; virtually all were relegated to the lowest-paying and most backbreaking work; and everywhere they were discriminated against and reviled by Anglo workers.

Mostly the Mexicans came as short-term and casual workers—not as permanent settlers—but some remained and swelled the numbers and resources of established Mexican American communities. In Tucson, originally an isolated *presidio* planted in Apache country, a Mexican elite dominated the expanding local economy. But most Mexican urban dwellers were poor laboring people segregated in what was already identifiably the *barrio*—the Mexican ghetto—of the Southwest borderland cities.

What stimulated the Mexican migration was the enormous demand for workers by the region's explosive economic development—hence the exceptionally high numbers of immigrants to California. Between 1860 and 1890 roughly one-third of the state's residents were

Mexican Miners
When large-scale mining began to develop in Arizona and New Mexico in the late nineteenth century, Mexicans crossed the border to earn Yankee dollars. In this unidentified photograph from the 1890s, the men are wearing traditional clothing, indicating perhaps that they are recent arrivals at the mine.
Division of Cultural Resource, Wyoming Department of Commerce.

foreign-born, more than twice the level for the country as a whole. Many came from Europe. Most numerous were the Irish, followed by the Germans and British. But there was also another group that was unique to the West—the Chinese.

The Chinese Migration. Attracted first by the California gold rush of 1849, 200,000 Chinese came to the United States over the next three decades. In those years they constituted a considerable minority of California's population, nearly 10 percent. Because virtually all were actively employed, they represented a much larger proportion of the state's labor force, probably a quarter. Elsewhere in the West, at the crest of mining activity, their presence could surge remarkably, to over 25 percent of Idaho's population in 1870, for example.

The coming of the Chinese to North America was part of a worldwide Asian migration that began in the mid-nineteenth century. Driven by poverty from their overpopulated lands, the Chinese went to Australia, Hawaii, and Latin America; Indians to Fiji and South Africa; and Javanese to Dutch colonies in the Caribbean. Most of these Asians migrated under the system of indentured servitude, which in effect made them the property of others. In America indentured servitude was no longer lawful, so the Chinese came as free workers. Their passage was financed by a *credit-ticket system*, by which they were able to borrow passage money from a broker while retaining their personal freedom and their right to choose their employers.

Once in America, Chinese immigrants normally entered the orbit of the Six Companies, a powerful confederation of Chinese merchants in San Francisco's Chinatown. Most of the arrivals were young unmarried men eager to earn a stake and return to their native villages. The Six Companies not only acted as an employment agency but provided them with the social and commercial services they needed to survive in an alien world. The few Chinese women—the male/female ratio was thirteen to one—worked mostly as servants and prostitutes, sad victims of the desperate poverty that drove the Chinese to America. Some were sold by impoverished parents; others had been enticed into fraudulent marriages or kidnapped by procurers and transported to America.

Until the early 1860s, when surface mining played out, Chinese men labored mainly in the California goldfields—as prospectors where white miners permitted it, as laborers and cooks where they did not. Then, when construction began on the transcontinental railroad, the Central Pacific hired Chinese workers. Eventually they constituted four-fifths of the railroad's labor force, doing most of the pick-and-shovel work of laying the track across the Sierra. Many were recruited from around Canton by labor agents and worked in labor gangs under the control of "China bosses," who not only supervised but fed, housed, paid, and often cheated them.

When the transcontinental railroad was completed in 1869, the Chinese scattered. Some continued to work in railroad construction gangs, while others labored on swamp-drainage and irrigation projects in California's Central Valley and then became agricultural workers and, if they were lucky, small farmers and orchardists. The mining districts of Idaho, Montana, and Colorado also attracted large numbers of Chinese, but according to the 1880 census, nearly three-quarters remained in California. In San Francisco many of them became factory workers. The Chinese were excluded from higher-wage trades, but they soon dominated certain industries—such as cigar making—that competed with eastern products and could survive only with cheap labor. "Wherever we put them, we found them good," remarked Charles Crocker, one of the promoters of the Central Pacific. From the standpoint of employers, "their orderly and industrious habits make them a very desirable class of immigrants."

Anti-Chinese Agitation. White workers, however, did not share this enthusiasm for Chinese labor. Why they should have taken so venomous a view of the Chinese has never been easy to explain. It involved, most certainly, a sense of unfair competition that pitted them against "Chinamen's wages." But the hatred clearly went deeper. In other parts of the country, racism was directed against African Americans; in California, where there were few blacks, it found a target in the Chinese. They were "an infusible element" who could not be assimilated into American society, wrote the young journalist Henry George in a 1869 letter that made his reputation as a spokesman for California labor. "They practice all the unnameable vices of the East. [They are] utter heathens, treacherous, sensual, cowardly and cruel." Sadly, this vicious racism was intertwined with labor's republican ideals. The Chinese, argued George, would "make nabobs and princes of our capitalists, and crush our working classes into the dust . . . substitut[ing] . . . a population of serfs and their masters for that population of intelligent freemen who are our glory and our strength."

The anti-Chinese frenzy climaxed in San Francisco in the late 1870s when mobs ruled the streets, at one point threatening to burn the docks of the Pacific Mail Steamship Company at which the Chinese immigrants landed. The fiercest agitator, an Irish teamster named Denis Kearney, quickly became a dominant figure in the California labor movement. Under the slogan "The Chinese Must Go!" Kearney led a workingmen's party that strongly challenged the state's major parties. Democrats and Republicans, however, jumped on the bandwagon, joining together in 1879 to write a new state constitution replete with anti-Chinese provisions and pressuring Washington to take up the issue. Finally, after renegotiating the Burlingame Treaty (1868) with China, Congress in 1882 passed the Chinese Exclusion Act, which barred the further entry of Chinese laborers into the country. The injustice of this law—the United States remained totally open to every other nationality—rankled the Chinese. Why us, protested one woman to a federal agent, and not the Irish, "who were always drunk and fighting"? Merchants and American-born Chinese, who were free to come and go, routinely registered a newly born son after each trip, enabling many an unrelated "paper son" to enter the country. In this and other ways the Chinese were resourceful in evading the exclusion law, but the flow of immigrants nevertheless slowed to a trickle.

But the job opportunities that had attracted the Chinese to America did not subside. If anything, the West's agricultural development intensified the demand for cheap labor, especially in California, which was shifting from wheat, the state's first great cash crop, to fruits and vegetables. This intensive agriculture required lots of workers: stoop labor, meagerly paid, and mostly seasonal. This was not, as one San Francisco journalist put it, "white men's work." That ugly phrase serves as a touchstone for California agricultural labor as it would thereafter develop—a kind of caste labor system, always including some downtrodden, footloose whites, yet basically defined along color lines.

But if not the Chinese, then who? First, Japanese immigrants came in increasing numbers, and by the early twentieth century constituted half of the state's agricultural labor force. Then, when anti-Japanese agitation closed off that population flow in 1908, Mexico became the next, essentially permanent, provider of migratory workers for California's booming commercial agriculture.

The irony of the state's social evolution is painful to behold. Here was California, a land of limitless opportunity, boastful of its democratic egalitarianism. Yet simultaneously, and from its very birth, it was a racially torn society, at once exploiting and despising the Hispanic and Asian minorities whose hard labor helped make California the enviable land it was.

Golden California

Life in California contained all that the modern world of 1890 had to offer—a great cosmopolitan city, comfortable travel, a high living standard, colleges and universities, even accomplished painters and writers. By 1890 California counted over a million residents, a quarter of them in San Francisco. Yet California was still remote from the rest of America, still a long journey

Building the Central Pacific
Chinese laborers in 1867 at work on the great trestle spanning the canyon at Secrettown in the Sierra Nevada.
Huntington Library/Superstock.

away, and, of course, differently and spectacularly endowed by nature. Location, environment, and history all conspired to set California somewhat apart from the American nation. And so, in certain ways, did the Californians.

Creating a California Culture. What Californians yearned for was a cultural tradition of their own. Closest to hand was the bonanza era of the gold rush. California had the great good fortune of attracting to its parts one Samuel Clemens. He arrived in the Nevada Territory in 1861, did a bit of prospecting, worked as a reporter, and adopted the pen name Mark Twain. In 1864 he left for San Francisco and became a newspaper columnist, writing about what he pronounced "the livest, heartiest community on our continent."

Listening to the old miners in Angel's Camp in 1865, Twain jotted one tale down in his notebook, as follows:

Coleman with his jumping frog—bet stranger $50— stranger had no frog, and C. got him one:—in the meantime stranger filled C's frog full of shot and he couldn't jump. The stranger's frog won.

Market Scene, Sansome Street
This exuberant painting by William Hahn captures downtown San Francisco as he
saw it in 1872—a veritable boiling pot of races (note the black woman at left and the
Chinese group at right) and classes (note, in the middle of the market bustle, the
proper lady at far left with her Lord Fauntleroy son). It was its role as metropolis
for the entire Far West that gave San Francisco the great vitality conveyed in this
painting.
Crocker Art Museum.

In Twain's hands, this fragment was transformed into
a tall tale that caught the imagination of the country
and made his reputation as a humorist. What "The
Celebrated Jumping Frog of Calaveras County" had
somehow encapsulated was the entire world of make-
or-break optimism in the mining camps.

In such short stories as "The Luck of Roaring
Camp" and "The Outcasts of Poker Flat," Twain's fellow
San Franciscan Bret Harte developed this theme in a
more literary fashion and firmly implanted it in California's memory. But this past was too raw, too suggestive of the tattered beginnings of so many of the state's
leading citizens—in short, too disreputable for an up-
and-coming society.

Then, in 1884, Helen Hunt Jackson published her
novel *Ramona*. In this story of a half-Indian girl caught
between two cultures, Jackson intended to advance the
cause of the native Americans, but she placed her tale in
the evocative setting of Old California, and that rang a
bell. By then, the chain of Spanish missions planted by
the Catholic Church had been long abandoned. The
padres were wholly forgotten, their Indian converts scattered and in dire poverty. Now that lost world of "sun,
silence and adobe" became all the rage. Sentimental
novels and histories appeared in abundance. There was

a movement to restore the missions. The Spanish Mexican dons of the great *ranchos* became larger in death
than they had ever been in life. Many communities
began to stage Spanish *fiestas*, and the mission style of
architecture enjoyed a great vogue among developers.

In its Spanish past California found the cultural
traditions it needed. Elsewhere in the Southwest the
same kind of discovery was taking place, although in
Santa Fe and Taos there really were live Hispanic roots
to celebrate.

Land of Sunshine.   All this enthusiasm was strongly
tinged with commercialism. And so was a second distinctive feature of California's development. The southern part of the state was neglected, thinly populated,
and too dry for anything but grazing and some chancy
wheat growing. What it did have, however, was an
abundance of sunshine. At the beginning of the 1880s
there burst upon the country amazing news of the
charms of southern California: "There is not any
malaria, hay fever, loss of appetite, or languor in the air;
nor any thunder, lightning, mad dogs . . . or cold snaps."
This publicity was mostly the work of the Southern
Pacific Railroad, which had reached Los Angeles in
1876 and was eager for business.

When the Santa Fe arrived in 1885, a furious fare war broke out, and it became possible to travel by train from Chicago or St. Louis to Los Angeles for $25 or less. Thousands of people, mostly midwesterners, poured in; a dizzying real estate boom developed, along with the frantic building of such resort hotels as San Diego's opulent Hotel del Coronado. Los Angeles County, which had less than 3 percent of the state's population in 1870, had 12 percent by 1900 (see Map 16.6). By then southern California had firmly established itself as the land of sunshine and orange groves. It had found a way to translate climate into riches.

The Great Outdoors. That California was specially favored by nature some Californians knew even as the great stands of redwoods and sugar pine were being hacked down, the soil depleted by the relentless cycle of wheat crops, the streams polluted, and the hills torn apart by reckless mining techniques. Back in 1864 influential Americans who had seen it prevailed on Congress to grant to the state of California "the Cleft, or Gorge in the granite peak of the Sierra Nevada Mountain, known as Yosemite Valley," which would be reserved "for public pleasuring, resort, and recreation." When the young naturalist John Muir arrived in California four years later, he headed straight for Yosemite. Its "grandeur . . . comes as an endless revelation," he wrote. Muir, and others like him, became devoted to studying the High Sierra and protecting the mountains from "despoiling gain-seekers . . . eagerly trying to make everything immediately and selfishly commercial." One result was the creation of California's national parks in 1890—Yosemite, Sequoia, and King's Canyon. Another was the formation in 1892 of the Sierra Club, which became a powerful voice for the defenders of California's wilderness.

Champions of California's wild lands won some battles and lost some. Advocates of water-resource development insisted that California's irrigated agriculture and thirsty cities could not grow without tapping the abundant snowpack of the Sierra. By the turn of the century, Los Angeles faced a water crisis that threatened its growth. The answer was a 238-mile aqueduct to the southern Sierra, tapping the waters of the Owens River. Local residents and preservationists protested but could not prevent the damming up of the beautiful Owens Valley. More painful was the defeat suffered by John Muir and his allies in their battle to save the Hetch Hetchy gorge north of Yosemite National Park. In 1913, after years of controversy, the federal government approved the damming of Hetch Hetchy to serve the water needs of San Francisco.

When the development stakes became high enough, nature lovers like John Muir generally came out on the short end. Even so, something original and distinctive had been added to California's heritage—the linking of a society's well-being with the preservation of its natural environment.

Kitty Tatch and Friend on Glacier Point, Yosemite
From the time the Yosemite Valley was set aside in 1864 as a place "for public pleasuring, resort, and recreation," it attracted a stream of tourists eager to experience the grandeur of the American West. As is suggested by this photograph taken sometime in the 1890s, the magic of Yosemite was enough to set even staid young ladies dancing.
The Yosemite Museum.

The Farmers' World

With the settlement of the Great Plains and the Pacific slope, the regional patterns of American agriculture became well defined (Map 16.7). Wheat growing, which had shifted steadily westward with the frontier, finally settled on the Great Plains, where hardy European strains produced a better bread flour than the soft-kernel

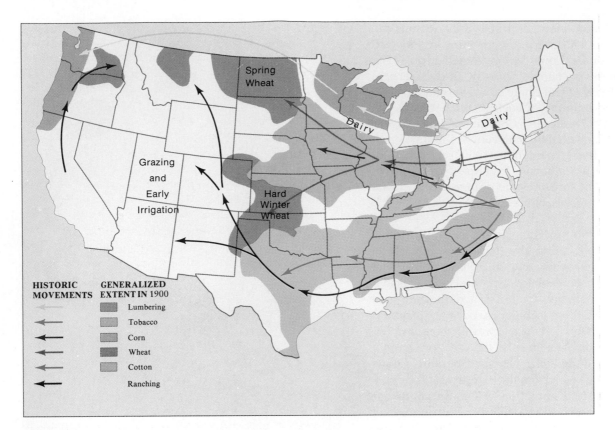

MAP 16.7
Agricultural Regions, 1900
The development of agricultural regions reflected the commercial bent of American agri-
culture—that is, farmers raised crops for market rather than for home consumption.
Regional specialization matched climate and soil to the most suitable crops. The west-
ward movement carried crops westward, of course. Wheat, generally a first crop choice in
frontier areas, was finally concentrated in the northern and central plains and in the
Northwest. By 1900 the basic pattern of crop specialization was well established in the
United States.

wheat of milder regions. On the wheat-producing
Columbia plateau in the Northwest, Spanish and Australian varieties did best. In the Midwest the main crop
was corn—feed for the nation's livestock. North of the
corn belt, dairy farming stretched from Minnesota eastward to New York and New England. In California
wheat growing had given way by 1900 to orange groves,
vineyards, and vegetable crops. Cotton dominated southern agriculture, spreading westward during the last third
of the nineteenth century from the old Cotton Kingdom
into Texas, Oklahoma, and Arkansas.

The Business of Agriculture

In certain grain-growing areas, such as California's Central Valley until the 1890s, farmers might be large-scale
and even corporate operators. In the South after Reconstruction, the typical farmer was a tenant or sharecropper. Elsewhere, and most commonly, farmers owned
their land. Deeply rooted in American tradition, Thomas
Jefferson's ideal of a country of independent, family

farmers was enshrined in the national policy of providing land from the public domain for homesteaders. In an
age of corporations and other large-scale enterprises,
farmers succeeded as did no other group in retaining the
forms of economic independence. But their *functions*
took them far from the self-sufficiency of Jeffersonian
America. They were not yeoman farmers but commodity
producers in the modern economic order.

General farming, in which no crop represented as
much as 40 percent of a farm's total production, was
still common; and so was subsistence farming in the
hilly and infertile areas of New England and the southern Appalachians. But a cash crop was what farmers
wanted, and that preference led to the remarkable
regional specialization of American agriculture. "The
old rule that a farmer should produce all he required is
part of the past," remarked one farm journal. "Agriculture, like all other business, is better for its subdivisions, each one growing that which is best suited for his
soil, skill, climate and market, and with its proceeds
purchasing his other needs."

Specialization in cash crops was one sign of the commercial leanings of American farmers. Another was their attitude toward land. Americans had little of the passionate identification with the soil that tied European peasants to their inherited plots. In 1910 more than half of all American farmers had moved within the previous five years. Farmers saw their acreage as a commodity. In frontier areas, where the value of newly developed land increased rapidly, they anticipated as much profit, if not more, from the land's value as from the crops it produced. Nor were farmers averse to borrowing money. In boom times they rushed into debt to buy more land and better farm equipment. They relished the innovations of the industrial age, especially the railroad, and supported whatever incentives might be necessary, such as the public purchase of railway bonds, to lure a line to their towns. All these enthusiasms—for cash crops, for land speculation, for borrowed money, for new technology—bore witness to the conviction that farming was a business "like all other business."

The bedrock of farmers' commercial identity was the knowledge that they stood at the center of a vast and complex network of trade and industry. A sophisticated array of commodity exchanges determined prices and found buyers throughout the country and beyond. Vast processing industries turned wheat into flour, livestock into dressed meat, and fruits and vegetables into canned goods. Entire rail systems, port facilities, and fleets of ships were devoted to moving the products of American farmers. All this activity gave farmers access to the expanding urban markets in the United States and overseas; about 20 percent of American agricultural production went abroad during the late nineteenth century. American farmers were likewise abundantly supplied with modern goods and services. The capital they needed came, via mortgage companies and banks, from distant eastern and European lenders.

No one could deny that the result was an agricultural system of amazing abundance; farm output more than tripled between 1860 and 1900. To an Austrian observer reflecting on the scarcity that had always been humankind's lot, the surplus produced by American agriculture seemed "the greatest event of modern times."

Farmers in Distress

Somehow, this triumph of American agriculture as a productive system did not translate into good times for farmers. On the contrary, the late nineteenth century was a time of deep agrarian discontent.

Farm Life. The grievances of farmers stemmed partly from the harshness of rural life. No one labored longer or harder. Farmers worked an average of sixty-eight hours a week in 1900, twelve hours longer than industrial workers. Mechanization did not reduce the workload on farms, as it generally did in factories. Crop acreage tended to increase in step with more efficient planting and harvesting machinery. Most other chores remained on the farmer's shoulders.

For women, too, farming demanded unrelenting labor. Like other work in America, farmwork was sex-typed. Except under dire necessity, northern farm women did not labor in the fields after the pioneering days. Substantial numbers of widows and single women did run farms on their own—300,000 were recorded in the 1900 census—but the evidence suggests that these women mostly relied on hired hands for the heavy fieldwork. In the South, especially among poor tenant farmers, it was different; wives, both black and white, commonly went into the fields, doing "whatever the occasion demands—plowing, hoeing, chopping, putting down fertilizer, picking cotton."

Even without working in the fields, however, farm women contributed crucially to the family enterprise. Farming could be thought of as a "dual economy," in which men's labor brought in the big payment at season's end and women's labor in the garden and barn provisioned the family day by day and produced a steady bit of money for groceries. And if the crop failed, it was women's income that carried the family through. No wonder rural society placed a high premium on marriage: a mere 2.4 percent of Nebraska women in 1900 had never married. The western farmer was well advised to take a wife for the "pecuniary advantage in the domestic economy of his household."

Throughout rural America children, too, pitched in with the farm chores and fieldwork. "Many a time a shudder has passed through the mother heart of me," said a Missouri woman, "at the sight of some little fellow struggling with the handles of a plow, jerking and stumbling over cloddy ground from daylight till dark. Boys 'making a full hand,' 'helping Pa.'" Farm children in 1900 attended school only two-thirds as many days as did city children, and they left school at an earlier age. In an era of rapidly advancing urban education, farm children still attended gloomy, ungraded one-room schools—hardly the little red schoolhouses of popular mythology.

Farm families may have accepted how hard they labored, how wives and husbands were worn out, how childhoods were sacrificed, for the living they wrested from the soil. Harder to swallow was the widening gap between life in the country and city. At the close of the nineteenth century, electricity, indoor plumbing, and paved roads were still rarities in rural areas. Work in the kitchen remained almost unaffected by appliances already commonplace in many urban homes. Laundry was "the most trying" of all household chores, long hours spent lugging and boiling water, bent over washtubs

Rural Schooling
In one-room schoolhouses such as this one, probably in Colorado, farm children got the rudiments of an education. Teaching offered one of the few opportunities for rural women to support themselves and obtain a paying job, albeit for very skimpy wages. Note the pictures cut from a fashion magazine decorating the plain log walls.
Denver Public Library, Western History Division.

and rubbing boards. Even on well-equipped farms, one Michigan woman observed, "the women must still do the work much as their mothers did before."

Hardest to bear was the sense of isolation. On the Great Plains, with its cruel winters and long, empty distances, loneliness was hard on everyone but especially on Scandinavian immigrants accustomed to neighborly living in rural communities. "Think for a moment how great the change must be from the white-walled, red roofed village on a Norway fiord . . . to an isolated cabin on a Dakota prairie," wrote one critic of dispersed American farming practices in 1893, "and say if it is not any wonder that so many Scandinavians lose their mental balance." Farm life everywhere, however, tended to be narrow and circumscribed. Rural neighborhoods, even in long-settled areas, totaled 3 or 4 square miles, where perhaps a dozen families lived. As one writer remarked, "the end of the neighborhood was almost the end of the world." Hamlin Garland and other authors of the late nineteenth century wrote powerfully about the dullness of the countryside and the lure of the city. "I hate farm life," grumbled one of Garland's heroines. "It's nothing but fret, fret and work the whole time, never going any place, never seeing anybody but a lot of neighbors just as big fools as you are. I spend my time fighting flies and washing dishes and churning. I'm sick of it all."

Understandably, when farmers formed organizations, they provided for social activity first of all. The National Grange of the Patrons of Husbandry, whose local granges spread by the thousands across rural America in the early 1870s, became the social center for farm families through its fraternal ceremonies and its dances, picnics, and lectures. Oliver H. Kelley, the government clerk who founded the Grange in 1867, hoped that participation by "the young folks of both sexes . . . will have a tendency to instill in their minds a fondness of rural life, and prevent in great measure so many of them flocking to the cities."

Economic Problems. The hunger for social activity cemented organizational ties, but what drove agrarian movements was the farmers' economic grievances. The basic problem was that farmers remained individual operators in a economic world that was becoming highly organized. And they were, in certain ways, acutely aware of their predicament. They understood, for example, the disadvantages they faced in dealing with the big businesses that supplied them with machinery, arranged their credit, and marketed their products.

One answer was cooperation. Cooperatives had first appeared before the Civil War, mostly as stores and creameries. The Grange took up the cooperative idea in a big way by purchasing in bulk from suppliers and by setting up cooperative banks, insurance companies, grain elevators, and processing plants. The Iowa Grange even started to manufacture farm implements in 1873. But private business fought back hard and generally got the better of the poorly managed and underfinanced Grange cooperatives. Most of them eventually failed. The cooperative idea, however, was highly resilient and would be revived by every successive farmers' movement. The farmers' hostility to middlemen also left as a legacy the great mail-order house of Montgomery Ward, which had been founded in 1872 to serve Grange members. As a solution to the organizational weakness of the farmer in the marketplace, however, the cooperative had to be accounted a failure.

The power of government might also be enlisted to do for farmers what they could not do for themselves. The Grange in the early 1870s encouraged independent political parties that ran on antimonopoly platforms. In a number of prairie states these agrarian parties pushed through so-called Granger laws regulating grain elevators, fixing maximum railroad rates, and prohibiting discriminatory practices against small and short-haul shippers. Constitutional difficulties arose, however, over the question of whether the states were exceeding their police powers when they tried to regulate interstate commerce. In *Wabash v. Illinois* (1886), the Supreme Court decided that they were, voiding an Illinois railroad law and putting the Granger agenda in jeopardy. By then, however, a movement had started for federal regulation of the railroads. The Interstate Commerce Act (1887) created the Interstate Commerce Commission—the first federal regulatory agency—and made railroad regulation a permanent part of national public policy, although, for the next twenty years, without much practical effect.

Farmers turned to cooperatives and government regulation out of a deep sense of organizational disadvantage. But that disadvantage, tangible as it was, did not really account for the unprofitability of farming in this period. Manufacturers and banks lacked the degree of market control ascribed to them by angry farmers. The much-maligned mortgage companies actually could not rig credit markets in the western states; their interest rates matched those in the rest of the country. Nor, for the period 1865–1890, could manufacturers establish a relative price advantage over agriculture. In fact, the wholesale prices of all commodities fell at a slightly faster rate than did farm prices during those years. And on the railroads, freight rates fell steadily and East-West differentials narrowed as improved technology reduced operating costs and the volume of western traffic increased (Table 16.1).

The impact of the general fall in prices, or *deflation*, did have dire consequences for certain kinds of farmers, however. The crops of cotton and wheat farmers were subject to the wider, more unpredictable price swings of the international commodities markets. Also at risk in deflationary periods were farmers in debt, for falling prices forced them to pay back more in real terms than they had borrowed. Who was most deeply in debt? The same two groups: cotton and wheat farmers.

In the 1870s the major wheat-growing states had been Illinois, Wisconsin, and Minnesota. These states had been at the center of the Granger agitation of that decade. By the 1880s wheat had moved onto the Great Plains. Among the indebted wheat farmers of Kansas, Nebraska, and the Dakotas, along with the cotton farmers of the South, the deflationary economy of the 1880s made for stubbornly hard times. All that was needed to bring on a real crisis was a sharp drop in world prices for wheat and cotton.

TABLE 16.1

Freight Rates for Transporting Nebraska Crops

Grand Island to Omaha (150 miles)				*Grand Island to Chicago (650 miles)*			
Date Effective	*Corn*	*Wheat* (in cents per hundredweight)	*Oats*	*Date Effective*	*Corn*	*Wheat* (in cents per hundredweight)	*Oats*
January 1, 1883	18	19½	18	January 7, 1880	32	45	32
April 16, 1883	15	16½	15	September 15, 1882	38	43	38
January 10, 1884	18	19½	18	April 5, 1887	34	39	34
March 1, 1884	17	19½	17	November 1, 1887	25	30	25
August 25, 1884	20	20	20	March 21, 1890	22½	30	25
April 5, 1887	10	16	10	October 22, 1890	22	26	22
November 1, 1887	10	12	10	January 15, 1891	23	28	25

Source: Sigmund Diamond, ed., *The Nation Transformed* (New York: George Braziller, 1963), 352.

Summary

★

In 1860 the Great Plains was still ancestral home to nomadic Indian tribes with a vibrant society based on the horse and buffalo. By 1890 the Indians were crowded onto reservations and forced to abandon their tribal way of life. With railroads leading the way, cattle ranchers and homesteaders in short order displaced the Indians and domesticated the Great Plains. Beyond the Rockies, the pattern of settlement was different. Because so much of this region was arid and uninhabitable, occupation occurred in oases of settlement rather than as the progressive force moving along the broad frontier that had prevailed east of the Rockies. And while arable land had been the lure for settlers up to that point, what drove settlement beyond the Rockies was the discovery of mineral wealth. The pace of occupation of the entire trans-Mississippi West was accelerated by the nation's economic development. Industry needed the West's mineral resources; the cities demanded agricultural products; and, from railroads to barbed wire, the industrial economy provided the means for a swift and decisive conquest of the West.

By population, economy, and strategic position, California was the regional power dominating the Far West in the late nineteenth century. It was the anchor both of a crescent of Hispanic settlement to the Southwest and of the Pacific slope region stretching up to the Canadian border. The discovery of gold had set off a huge migration that overwhelmed the thinly spread Hispanic inhabitants and swiftly transformed California into a populous state with a large urban sector. California developed a distinctive culture that capitalized on its rediscovered Hispanic heritage and its climate and natural environment. The treatment of the Chinese, Japanese, and Mexicans who provided the state's cheap labor, however, infused a dark streak of racism into California society.

The settlement of the West completed a national agricultural development characterized by regional crop specialization. American farming became integrated into the modern industrial order. However, that integration was imperfect—in particular because farming remained a family operation in an economy dominated by large-scale enterprise. Most aggrieved, and most prepared to protest, were the cotton farmers of the South and the wheat farmers of the Great Plains.

T I M E L I N E

1849	California gold rush
	Chinese migration begins
1862	Homestead Act
1864	Yosemite Valley reserved as public park
1865	Long Drive of Texas longhorns begins
1867	Patrons of Husbandry (the Grange) founded
	U.S. government adopts reservation policy for Plains Indians
1868	Indian treaty confirms Sioux rights to Powder River hunting grounds
1869	Union Pacific–Central Pacific transcontinental railroad completed
1874	Barbed wire invented
1875	Sioux ordered to vacate Powder River hunting grounds; war breaks out
1876	Battle of Little Big Horn
1877	San Francisco anti-Chinese riots
1879	Exoduster migration to Kansas
1882	Chinese Exclusion Act
1884	Helen Hunt Jackson's novel *Ramona*
1886	Dry cycle begins on the Great Plains
	Wabash v. Illinois
1887	Dawes Severalty Act
	Interstate Commerce Act
1889	Oklahoma opened to white settlement
1890	Indian massacre at Wounded Knee, South Dakota
	U.S. Census declares end of the frontier

Suggested Readings

———————★———————

Western history has become a bitterly contested ground in recent years. The fountainhead of the voluminous traditional scholarship is Frederick Jackson Turner's famous essay "The Significance of the Frontier in American History" (1893), reprinted in Ray A. Billington, ed., *Frontier and Section: Selected Essays of Frederick Jackson Turner* (1961). The "new" western history is critical of Turnerian scholarship for being "Eurocentric"—for seeing western history only through the eyes of frontiersmen and settlers—and for masking the rapacious and environmentally destructive underside of western settlement. Patricia N. Limerick's skillfully argued *The Legacy of Conquest: The Unbroken Past of the American West* (1987) opened the debate. Richard White, *"It's Your Misfortune and None of My Own": A New History of the American West* (1991), provides the fullest synthesis of the new scholarship. For an authoritative, balanced treatment of the main themes of western history, see the essays in Clyde A. Milner II *et al.*, *The Oxford History of the American West* (1994). On women's experience—another primary concern of the new western history—the starting point is Susan Armitage and Elizabeth Jameson, eds., *The Women's West* (1987). There are incisive environmental essays in Donald Worster, *Under Western Skies: Nature and History in the American West* (1992).

The Great Plains

The classic book, stressing the settlers' adaptation to climate and environment, is Walter P. Webb, *The Great Plains* (1931). There is an excellent chapter on the ecological history of the southern plains in Donald Worster, *The Great Plains* (1979). Robert M. Utley, *The Indian Frontier of the American West, 1846–1890* (1984), is a good introduction; Robert H. Lowie, *Indians of the Great Plains* (1954), is a classic anthropological study. On the religious life of the Plains Indians, see Howard L. Harrod, *Renewing the World: Plains Indian Religion and Morality* (1987). The assault on Indian culture is recounted in Fredrick E. Hoxie, *A Final Promise: The Campaign to Assimilate the Indians, 1880–1920* (1984). On phases of plains settlement, see Oscar Winther, *The Transportation Frontier: The Trans-Mississippi West, 1865–1890* (1964); Lewis Atherton, *The Cattle Kings* (1964); Gilbert Fite, *The Farmer's Frontier, 1865–1900* (1966); and Mary W. M. Hargreaves, *Dry-Farming in the Northern Great Plains* (1954). The ecological impact is subtly probed in Frieda Knobloch, *The Culture of Wilderness: Agriculture as Colonization in the American West* (1996). The peopling of the plains can be explored in Craig Miner, *West of Wichita: Settling the High Plains of Kansas, 1865–1890* (1986); Frederick C. Luebke, ed., *Ethnicity and the Great Plains* (1980); Nell Irvin Painter, *Exodusters: Black Migration to Kansas after Reconstruction* (1976); Julie Roy Jeffrey, *Frontier Women: The Trans-Mississippi West, 1840–1880* (1979); Deborah Fink, *Agrarian Women: Wives and Mothers in Rural Nebraska, 1880–1940* (1992); and Elaine Lindgren, *Land in Her Own Name: Women as Homesteaders in North Dakota* (1991). On the integration of the plains economy with the wider world, an especially rich book is William Cronon,

Nature's Metropolis: Chicago and the Great West (1991). Richard Slotkin, *The Fatal Environment: The Myth of the Frontier in the Age of Industrialization, 1800–1890* (1985), deals with the process by which Americans translated the hard realities of conquering the West into a national mythology.

The Far West

The best book on western mining is Rodman Paul, *Mining Frontiers of the Far West: 1848–1880* (1963). A valuable case study of women in a mining town is Paula Petrik, *Women and Family on the Rocky Mountain Frontier: Helena, Montana, 1865–1900* (1987). On western miners, the standard book is Mark Wyman, *Hard Rock Epic: Western Miners and the Industrial Revolution, 1860–1910* (1979). Two valuable regional histories are Carlos A. Schwantes, *The Pacific Northwest: An Interpretive History* (1989), and David Alan Johnson, *Founding the Far West: California, Oregon, and Nevada* (1992). A very imaginative recent treatment of the New Mexico peasantry is Sarah Deutsch, *No Separate Refuge* (1987). On Hispanic Texas, an important book is David Montejano, *Anglos and Mexicans in the Making of Texas* (1987). Important local studies of laboring Hispanics and their communities are Mario T. Garcia, *Desert Immigrants: The Mexicans of El Paso, 1880–1920* (1981), and Richard Griswold del Castillo, *The Los Angeles Barrio, 1850–1890* (1979). On the Asian migration to America, the best introduction is Ronald Takaki, *Strangers from a Different Shore: A History of Asian Americans* (1989), which can be supplemented with Gunther Barth, *Bitter Strength: A History of the Chinese in the United States, 1850–1870* (1964); Sucheng Chan, *This Bittersweet Soil: The Chinese in California Agriculture, 1860–1910* (1986); and, on the impact of the exclusion laws, Lucy E. Salyer, *Laws Harsh as Tigers: Chinese Immigrants and the Shaping of Modern Immigration Law* (1995). Labor's opposition to the Chinese is skillfully treated in Alexander Saxton, *The Indispensable Enemy: Labor and the Anti-Chinese Movement in California* (1971). Kevin Starr, *California and the American Dream, 1850–1915* (1973), provides a comprehensive account of the emergence of a distinctive California culture. On John Muir and the California wilderness, see Michael L. Smith, *Pacific Visions: California Scientists and the Environment, 1850–1915* (1987), and on water, with special emphasis on California, Donald J. Pisani, *Water, Land, and Law in the West: The Limits of Public Policy, 1850–1920* (1996).

The Farmers' World

The standard works are Fred A. Shannon, *The Farmer's Last Frontier, 1860–1887* (1945), and Allan G. Bogue, *From Prairie to Corn Belt: Farming on the Illinois and Iowa Prairies* (1963). On farm women, see Deborah Fink, *Agrarian Women: Wives and Mothers in Rural Nebraska, 1880–1940* (1992), and on immigration and ethnic settlement, Jon Gjerde, *The Minds of the West: Ethnocultural Evolution in the Rural Middle West, 1830–1917* (1997). The flavor of farm life can best be captured in fiction: Hamlin Garland, *Main-Travelled Roads* (1891); Willa Cather, *My Antonia* (1918); and Ole E. Rolvaag, *Giants in the Earth* (1927).

Chapter 17

Capital and Labor in the Age of Enterprise, *1877–1900*

THE YEAR THAT Reconstruction ended, 1877, also marked the end of the first great crisis of America's emerging system of industrial capitalism. In 1873, four years earlier, a severe depression had set in, bankrupting forty-seven thousand firms and driving wholesale prices down about 30 percent. Railroad building ground to a halt. Orders for industrial products disappeared. Hundreds of thousands of workers lost their jobs, and suffering was widespread. Across the country workers demanded "bread for the needy, clothing for the naked, and houses for the homeless." Before long the foundations of the social order began to shake.

On July 16, 1877, railroad workers went on strike against the Baltimore and Ohio system to protest wage cuts. In towns along the B&O tracks crowds cheered as the strikers attacked company property and prevented trains from running. The strike spread across the country. In Pittsburgh the Pennsylvania Railroad roundhouse and Union Depot went up in flames, and at many rail centers rioters and looters roamed freely. President Rutherford B. Hayes called up the National Guard, which gradually restored order. On August 15, the president wrote in his diary: "The strikers have been put down *by force.*" The Great Strike of 1877 had been crushed. But never had the nation edged so close to social revolution.

And then recovery came. Within months the economy was booming again. In the next fifteen years, the output of manufactured goods increased over 150 percent. America's confidence in its industrial future

The H. C. Frick Coke Company
Coke, a processed form of coal, is an essential ingredient in iron and steel making. The richest coking coal deposits in the country happened to be in Connellsville, Pennsylvania, not far south of Pittsburgh. The Connellsville coke industry contributed mightily to Pittsburgh's industrial preeminence as well as to H. C. Frick's millions. The men depicted in the center of this print are baking coke in beehive ovens. Once processed, the coke will be dispersed across America by train. As this picture (c. 1880) suggests, the coal industry forever altered Pennsylvania's pastoral landscape.
Library of Congress.

rebounded. "Upon [material progress] is founded all other progress," asserted a railroad president in 1888. "Can there be any doubt that cheapening the cost of necessaries and conveniences of life is the most powerful agent of civilization and progress?"

Industrial Capitalism Triumphant

★

Economic historians speak of the late nineteenth century as the age of the Great Deflation. Prices fell steadily, not only in the United States but worldwide. Normally, falling prices signal economic stagnation: there is not enough demand for the available goods and services. For England, a mature industrial power, the Great Deflation did indeed signal economic decline. But in the United States industrial expansion went into high gear during the Great Deflation (Figure 17.1). Because of increasing manufacturing efficiencies, American firms could cut prices and yet earn profits for financing still better equipment. And this achievement in turn meant a sustained upward trend in average real income, which rose for nonagricultural employees (in constant 1914 dollars) from $388 in 1877 to $573 in 1900—an increase of nearly 50 percent in scarcely a quarter of a century.

Growth of the Industrial Base

By the 1870s manufacturing was long established in America. But the early factories had really been appendages of the agricultural economy. What they produced—textiles, boots and shoes, paper and furniture—were *consumer* goods, which used familiar materials and mostly replaced things made at home or by individual artisans. Gradually, however, a different kind of demand developed. Railroads needed locomotives; new factories needed machinery; and the expanding cities needed trolley lines, sanitation systems, and commercial buildings. Locomotives, machinery, and construction materials were *capital* goods—that is, goods that themselves added to the productive capacity of the economy. Although consumer goods remained very important, it was the manufacture of capital goods that became the core of America's industrial economy.

From Iron to Steel.   Central to the development of the capital-goods sector was a new technology for manufacturing steel. The country already produced large quantities of wrought iron, whose malleability made it ideally suited for use by country blacksmiths and farmers. But wrought iron was expensive—it was produced in small batches by skilled puddlers and rollers—and did not stand up under heavy use as railway track. In 1856 the British inventor Henry Bessemer designed a furnace—the Bessemer converter—that required little labor and refined raw pig iron into an essentially new product, steel, that was harder and more durable than wrought iron (see New Technology, "Iron and Steel," pp. 544–545). Others adopted Bessemer's invention, but it was Andrew Carnegie who demonstrated its revolutionary importance.

Carnegie arrived from Scotland in 1848 at the age of twelve with his poverty-stricken family. He became a telegraph operator, then went to work for the Pennsylvania Railroad and rapidly climbed the managerial ladder. In 1865, having amassed a fortune in wartime speculation, Carnegie struck out on his own as an iron manufacturer. His main customers were his former associates in the railroad business.

In 1872 Carnegie erected a massive steel mill outside Pittsburgh, designed to take maximum advantage of Bessemer's process. Named the Edgar Thomson

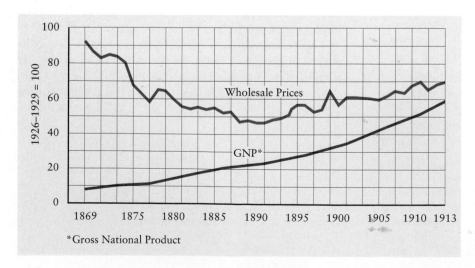

*Gross National Product

FIGURE 17.1
Business Activity and Wholesale Prices, 1869–1913
This graph shows the key feature of the performance of the late nineteenth-century economy: while output was booming, the price of goods was falling.

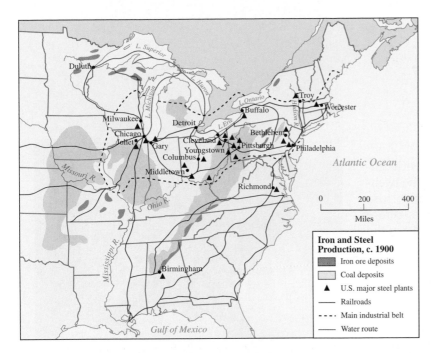

MAP 17.1

The Westward Movement of Iron and Steel Production, to 1900

Before the Civil War, the iron industry was concentrated in eastern Pennsylvania and northern New Jersey. With the shift to steel and the westward movement of population and industry, production moved first to western Pennsylvania and then to Ohio, Indiana, and Illinois, and southward into Alabama. The specific locations—Pittsburgh, Youngstown, Chicago, Birmingham—were dictated by the rail network, new sources of coal and iron ore, and markets for steel.

Works after Carnegie's admired boss at the Pennsylvania Railroad, the mill brought together all the stages of production—smelting, refining, and rolling—into a single coordinated operation. Iron ore entered the blast furnaces at one end and, with no break in operations, came out the other end as finished steel rails. Hugely profitable, the Edgar Thomson Works became a model for the modern steel industry. Large, integrated steel plants swiftly replaced the small iron mills that had once dotted western Pennsylvania.

Steel rails made up nearly three-quarters of the industry's output in 1885. But thereafter, as railroad building slowed, the demand became more diversified. More and more steel went into bridges, skyscrapers, machinery, and a host of other industrial uses, such as pipes and tubing, sheet steel and wire, and armor for the nation's new navy.

Minerals and Energy. The technological breakthrough in steel spurred the intensive exploitation of the country's mineral resources. Major discoveries of iron ore deposits occurred from the 1850s onward, first in upper Michigan and then in the huge Mesabi Range of northern Minnesota. The Mesabi ore, shipped down the Great Lakes, gave the lakeshore sites, such as South Chicago and Gary, Indiana, a competitive advantage over Pittsburgh and contributed to the westward shift of the industry (Map 17.1).

Coal mining, a minor enterprise before 1850, grew rapidly, first in the anthracite (hard coal) region of eastern Pennsylvania and then in the bituminous (soft coal) fields of western Pennsylvania and Ohio. The production of bituminous coal, the primary industrial fuel, doubled every decade between 1870 and 1910 (Table 17.1).

The Corliss Engine

The symbol of the Philadelphia Centennial in 1876 was the great Corliss engine, which towered over Machinery Hall and powered all the equipment on exhibit there. Yet the Corliss engine also signified the incomplete nature of American industrialism at that time; it soon became obsolete. Westinghouse turbines generating electricity would be the power source for the nation's next great World's Fair in Chicago in 1893.
Culver Pictures.

Iron and Steel

★

IRON WAS NOT a product new to the nineteenth century in the way that plastic was new to the twentieth century. Early Europeans had made iron tools and weapons at least a thousand years before Christ, and in the years since those remote times the underlying processes did not change, for they are dictated by the nature of iron metallurgy. What did change were the techniques for carrying out those processes.

The first break from ancient methods came when blast furnaces appeared in Belgium around 1340. Ore was melted in a charcoal-burning furnace to which limestone had been added. A blast of air then set off a combustion process that combined carbon from the charcoal with the molten iron while the impurities combined with the limestone to form a slag. The slag was drawn off from the top while the molten iron was tapped from the bottom into sand forms resembling piglets feeding from a sow—hence the term "pig iron."

Bessemer Converter, Bethlehem Works, Steelton, Pennsylvania, 1885
Workers for Bethlehem Steel in Steelton, Pennsylvania, pose for this 1885 photograph with a Bessemer converter. The late nineteenth century in America came to be known as "America's Age of Steel," thanks to the increased steel production that the Bessemer converter helped generate.
Hagley Museum and Library.

As steam engines became the nation's primary energy source, railroads and factories began to consume enormous amounts of coal. Industries previously dependent on water power converted rapidly to steam-driven machinery. By 1900, water wheels were disappearing, providing less than a sixth of the nation's industrial energy. The steam turbine, a further innovation introduced in the 1880s, provided still more power and efficiency by utilizing continuous rotation rather than the back-and-forth motion of conventional steam engines. With the coupling of the steam turbine to the electric generator, the nation's energy revolution was completed, and after 1900 factories began a massive conversion to electric power.

Thus, in the decades after the Civil War, the modern steel industry was established, the nation's mineral resources came under intensive exploitation, and energy was harnessed to the manufacturing system. All these basic elements of modern industrialism—steel, coal, and energy output—grew after 1870 at rates far exceeding that of manufacturing production itself.

The Railroads

Before the Civil War, most goods moved quite efficiently by water. But from the first appearance of primitive locomotives on iron tracks in the 1830s, Americans fell

By the late eighteenth century Great Britain was running out of wood for charcoal. The substitution of coke, made by superheating coal, saved the industry and gave Britain the competitive edge it needed to launch the Industrial Revolution. Endowed with ample forests, the United States was slow to adopt coke-using furnaces, but by 1860 it had caught up with Britain's technologically.

The search for a metal harder and more durable than wrought iron resulted in the invention in 1856 of an entirely different refining process by the Englishman Henry Bessemer. The Bessemer converter was a pear-shaped vessel that was open at the top and had a bottom perforated with many holes. Molten pig iron flowed into the top while the converter was tilted on its side. Air was blasted through the perforated bottom with great force, and the converter then swung back to its upright position. The resulting combustion set off a spectacular display of flame and smoke. Within fifteen minutes, the impurities in the molten iron burned off and the flames died down. The converter was again tilted on its side, and after manganese and other chemicals had been added, the purified iron was emptied into ingot molds. The refined metal, called steel, was ideally suited for use as railroad track.

Bessemer's device, though invented primarily with the aim of gaining a more durable metal, also proved vastly more efficient than the hand-operated puddling furnaces that produced wrought iron. The Bessemer converter turned out great quantities of steel with virtually no labor, and this forced changes up and down the line. To feed the converters' appetite for pig iron, blast furnaces were built larger and, with the introduction of the hot blast, became much faster. To handle the flow of steel from the converters, rolling mills became increasingly mechanized and automatic. Finally, blast furnaces, convertors, and rolling mills were brought together and linked into a single processing operation. The integrated steel plant of 1900—capable of producing 2,500 tons or more a day—became a voracious consumer of ore and coal.

The commanding lead the United States had built up by 1900 rested on the world's best reserves of coking coal in western Pennsylvania and the vast ore deposits in Minnesota's Mesabi Range, northern Michigan's older fields, and Alabama. The geographical face of American industrialism changed as the places best located in relation to raw materials, transportation, and markets—Pittsburgh, the steel towns along the Great Lakes, and Birmingham, Alabama—became the great centers of steel production. American cities relied on steel for the construction of skyscrapers, trolley lines, subways, and the vast underground complexes of pipe that supplied the urban millions with water and gas, and carried away their sewage. Without steel, the emerging automobile industry would not have grown, nor would a host of other industries.

It is no wonder that historians have called the last decades of the nineteenth century America's Age of Steel. What was overlooked at the time and for long afterward was the fact that the nation's natural resources were not inexhaustible. It is the exhaustion of the great Mesabi Range that has leveled the playing field among global competitors and helped trigger the recent decline of the American steel industry.

in love with railroads. They were impatient for the year-round, on-time service that canal barges and riverboats could not provide. By 1860, with a network of tracks already covering the states east of the Mississippi, the railroad clearly was on the way to being industrial America's mode of transportation (Map 17.2).

Constructing the Railroads. The question was, Who would pay for it? Railroads could be state enterprises, as most of the canals built before the Civil War had been. Or, alternatively, they could be financed by investors trying to make money. Unlike most European countries, which regarded railroads as a state responsibility, the United States left railroad building to private enterprise. Even so, government played a big role. Many states provided financial aid, mostly by buying railroad bonds but also, as in Texas and Maine, by offering state-owned land to railroad companies. Land grants were the principal means by which the federal government encouraged interregional railroads; huge tracts went to the transcontinental railroads because of the national interest in tying the Far West to the rest of the country.

The most important boost that government gave the railroads, however, was not money or land but a legal form of organization—the *corporation*—that enabled them to raise private capital in prodigious

TABLE 17.1

Increasing Output of Heavy Industry, 1870–1910

	Bituminous Coal (thousands of tons)	Rolled Iron and Steel (thousands of tons)	Copper (tons)	Industrial Machinery (millions of dollars)
1870	20,471	850*	14,112	110.4[†]
1880	50,757	3,301	30,240	98.6[‡]
1890	111,302	6,746	129,882	185.6
1900	212,318	10,626	303,059	347.6
1910	417,111	24,216	544,119	512.4

*Approximate total.
[†]Data for 1869.
[‡]Data for 1874.

amounts. Investors who bought stock in the railroads and thus became their legal owners enjoyed *limited liability:* they risked only the money they had invested and were not personally liable for the corporation's debts. A corporation also could borrow money by issuing interest-bearing bonds, which was how the railroads raised most of the money they needed.

The actual responsibility for railroad building was handed over to a construction company, which, despite the name, was really another part of the elaborate financing system. Hiring the contractors and suppliers often involved persuading them to accept the railroad's bonds as payment and, when that failed, wheeling and dealing to raise cash by selling or borrowing on the bonds. Since the promoters of the railroad and the owners of the construction company were one and the same, the opportunities for plunder were enormous. The most notorious of the construction companies, the Union Pacific's Crédit Mobilier, siphoned into the pockets of the promoters probably half of the money it paid out.

Railroad promotion was not for the faint of heart. Most successful were promoters with the best access to capital—their own or others'. John Murray Forbes, a great Boston merchant in the China trade, recruited New England money to develop the Chicago, Burlington and Quincy Railroad into the preeminent midwestern system. Cornelius Vanderbilt started with the fortune he had made in the steamboat business. He consolidated previously independent lines up the Hudson River and across New York State, and ultimately he developed the New York Central into an interregional trunk line connecting New York City to Chicago. James J. Hill, who without federal subsidy made the Great Northern into the best constructed of all the transcontinental railroads, was certainly the nation's champion railroad builder. In contrast, Jay Gould, who at one time or another controlled the Erie, Wabash, Union

Pacific, and Missouri Pacific systems, always remained a stock-market speculator at heart. Whether he was a *robber baron*—someone who loots commerce and gives nothing in return—can only be answered by closer inspection of his career (see American Lives, "Jay Gould: Robber Baron?" pp. 548–549).

Railroad development in the United States was often sordid, fiercely competitive, and subject to boom and bust. But vast sums of capital were raised—well over $10 billion, probably a quarter of it attracted from Europe—and a network was built whose track mileage exceeded that of the rest of the world combined. By 1900 virtually no corner of the country lacked rail service.

The Railway System. The railroads became increasingly efficient. Built by competing local companies, the early system was a jumble of discontinuous segments. Gauges of track—the width between the rails—varied widely, so at many points railroads were not physically connected. Moreover, each railroad company reserved its track exclusively for its own equipment. As late as 1880 goods could not be shipped through from Massachusetts to South Carolina. Eight times along the way, freight cars had to be emptied, and their contents loaded onto other cars across a river or at the other side of a city.

During the Civil War years, however, pressure increased for the physical integration of the railroads. Track was hastily laid through Philadelphia, Richmond, and other cities to speed the shipment of troops and equipment. The postwar economy, as it grew more complex and interdependent, demanded a better-organized rail system. Much railroad integration resulted from the expansion of great trunk lines, such as the New York Central, the Pennsylvania, and the Illinois Central, connecting different regions of the country. By the end of the 1880s a standard track gauge (4 feet, 8½ inches) had been adopted across the country. In 1883 the railroads rebelled

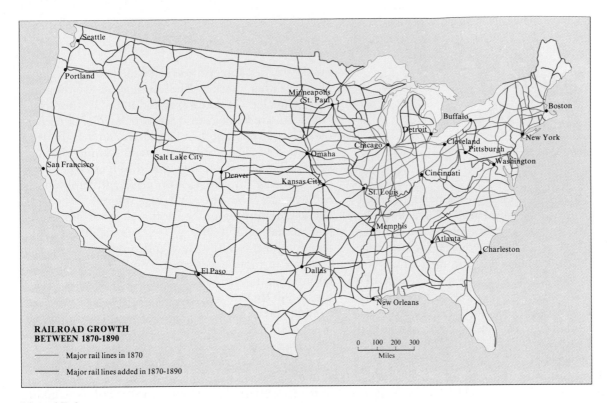

RAILROAD GROWTH
BETWEEN 1870-1890

——— Major rail lines in 1870

——— Major rail lines added in 1870-1890

0   100   200   300
Miles

Map 17.2

The Expansion of the Railroad System, 1870–1890

In 1870, the nation had 53,000 miles of rail track; in 1890, 167,000 miles. That burst of construction essentially completed the nation's rail network, although there would be additional expansion for the next two decades. The main areas of growth were in the South and west of the Mississippi. The Great Plains and the Far West accounted for over 40 percent of all railroad construction in this period.

against the confusion of local times that made scheduling a nightmare and, acting on their own, divided the country into the four standard time zones that we still use. Fast-freight firms and standard accounting procedures enabled shippers to use the railroad network as if it were a single unit, moving goods without the breaks in transit, transfers between cars, or other delays that had once bedeviled them.

At the same time, railroad technology was advancing. Durable steel rails permitted heavier traffic. The redesign of steam engines culminated in the Consolidation-type locomotive, with four sets of driving wheels and nearly triple the pulling power of its predecessors. To control the great mass and length of the new freight trains, the inventor George Westinghouse perfected the automatic coupler, the air brake, and the friction gear for starting and stopping a long line of cars. Costs per ton-mile fell by 50 percent between 1870 and 1890, resulting in a steady drop in freight rates for shippers.

The railroads brilliantly met the transportation needs of the maturing industrial economy. For investors, however, the costs of freewheeling competition and unrestrained growth were painfully high. On many routes there were too many railroads, and competitors fought for the available traffic by cutting rates to the bone. Many railroads were saddled with huge debt from bonds issued during the extravagant construction years; a fifth of these bonds failed to pay interest even in a pretty good year like 1889. So it was no wonder that when the economy turned bad, there were wholesale bankruptcies. A third of the industry went into receivership after the Panic of 1893.

Out of the rubble, however, came a major railroad reorganization. This was primarily the handiwork of Wall Street investment banks such as J. P. Morgan & Co. and Kuhn, Loeb & Co., whose main role had been to market railroad stocks and bonds. When railroads fell into bankruptcy, the investment bankers stepped in to pick up the pieces. They persuaded investors to help out by accepting lower interest rates or by putting up more money. And they eased the competitive pressures on the railroads by consolidating rivals. By the early twentieth century, half a dozen great regional systems had emerged, and the nerve center of American railroading had shifted to Wall Street.

Jay Gould: Robber Baron?

———————★———————

JAY GOULD WAS an operator pure and simple, although, in a general way of speaking, he was as far as possible from pure and as far as possible from simple. . . . It would be at least very difficult to show that the Nation as a whole is a dollar richer by the existence of JAY GOULD, while he himself has become the richer . . . from the expansion of the city and the Nation. He has simply absorbed what would have been made in spite of him.

Thus did the *New York Times* bid farewell to Jay Gould at his death on December 3, 1892. There was a name for the kind of businessman the *Times* thought Gould was: robber baron. In the Middle Ages the term described renegade knights who exacted tribute from all who passed by; by extension to Gould's time the term referred to capitalists who extracted riches from the economic system while adding nothing to it. By that definition, was Gould a robber baron? Yes, said historians for many years, following the thesis first advanced by Matthew Josephson in his book *The Robber Barons* (1934). Today historians are no longer so sure.

Jay Gould was born on May 27, 1836, in Roxbury, New York, in the mountainous Catskill region. John Gould wanted Jay, his only son, to take over the family farm, but the boy was small and sickly and detested farmwork. At sixteen he became a surveyor, at nineteen he wrote a flowery history of Delaware County, New York, for the money, and then at twenty he got a big break. An eccentric but wealthy tanner, Zadock Pratt, befriended Gould, taking him as a partner to set up a tannery in Pennsylvania, where Gould had located a rich new source of tanning bark. The venture succeeded thanks to Pratt's money and Gould's hard work, but after two years there was a falling-out and Pratt proposed terminating the partnership. He would buy Gould's share for $10,000 or sell out to the young man for $60,000. Gould found backers among the leather merchants who marketed the tannery's output and bought out the surprised Pratt. This was a typical Gould maneuver—bold, unexpected, and decisive. The new partnership quickly turned sour, primarily because of the collapse of the leather market. The damage to well-reputed merchants left Gould discredited in the leather trade. He had made money amid the wreckage of other people's businesses, another Gould trademark. In 1860 he settled in New York, bent on satisfying what had become his obsession: he wanted to be rich.

Enlisting in the Union army probably never occurred to him. The Civil War offered too good a chance for turning quick profits; and besides, Gould had no taste for fighting. In 1863 he married the daughter of a wealthy New York merchant, sired six children in rapid succession, and became a devoted family man. These were, above all, schooling years for Gould. He learned about the railroads from a controlling interest he gained in a small Vermont railroad. And—no one knows exactly how—he developed a consummate mastery of the intricacies of Wall Street finance. Few could have been aware of this in 1867 when Gould was elected to the executive board of the Erie Railroad just as a titanic battle was taking shape for control of the Erie.

The aggressor was Cornelius Vanderbilt, who wanted to ally the Erie with his emerging New York Central system. Vanderbilt began secretly buying up Erie stock, a maneuver that had gained him control of other key railroad properties. This time, however, Erie stock mysteriously kept entering the market even though no more could legally be issued by the railroad. Gould was exploiting a dubious loophole: freshly minted convertible bonds that could immediately be converted to stock. Vanderbilt countered with court injunctions, forcing Gould and his confederates to decamp to New Jersey, while in Albany Vanderbilt lobbied to prevent legalization of the convertible-bond gambit. A bidding war began for legislators' votes, which, with the Erie dollars overflowing his satchel, Gould finally won. To settle things, however, Vanderbilt and his allies had to be compensated for their losses, which Gould ingeniously arranged by spending $9 million from the Erie Railroad treasury to buy back their stock at inflated prices. The railroad was effectively bankrupted, but it was now firmly in Gould's hands.

Gould proceeded to show how money—lots of it—could be made from control of a large enterprise that was itself unprofitable and badly managed. The trick was to manipulate stock prices, buying and selling with an insider's advance knowledge. For example, Gould announced that he was replacing the United States Express Company, which operated on the Erie line, with a new company that he intended to form.

Jay Gould
Culver Pictures.

United's stock dropped from 60 to 16, at which point Gould bought, renewed the contract, and sold on the stock's rebound. He walked away with a cool $3 million. Under Gould's rule, the Erie never earned enough even to service its debt. Long-suffering European stockholders finally rebelled, forcing him out in March 1872.

Gould was never able to shed the unsavory reputation he acquired during the Erie years. But even in that buccaneering period there was another side to him as a railroad man. Indifferent to day-to-day operations, Gould had a brilliant strategic sense for how railroads should grow. The key, he knew, was integrated development, with trunk-line service between major centers. Right off Gould moved to take over the local roads west of Pittsburgh and Buffalo, in hopes of making the Erie the dominant system linking the Atlantic seaboard and the Midwest. But he lacked the resources, and the Pennsylvania and the New York Central, spurred by his challenge, beat him out, capturing the key western lines and leaving the Erie a weak secondary system.

Yet the vision had been Gould's, and ten years later he found, in the area west of St. Louis and southward into Texas, greener fields for his strategic talents. The railroads in this region were a tangle of incomplete, disconnected lines when Gould came on the scene in 1879. He began buying control, finishing the lines, and linking them into a regional system operating more than 5,000 miles of track under his parent company, the Missouri Pacific. He also moved aggressively in other parts of the country, challenging established railroads and cutting rates ruthlessly to take traffic from them. By 1882 he controlled 15 percent of the nation's entire trackage, and Western Union and the New York Elevated besides.

The economic boom that fostered this empire building did not last, however, and after 1881 Gould found himself on the wrong side of the stock market, overextended in holdings that were falling in value. On the verge of ruin in early 1884, he managed to get a "corner" on the stock of the Missouri Pacific, forcing up its price and thus saving himself. But Gould was not the same man after that. He lost his iron nerve, and his health began to fail. He swore off speculation. His business dealings, while still far-flung, became more cautious and defensive. But to the end he remained a tough customer, never justifying himself, never cloaking himself in religious piety, not even seeking to make amends by a show of philanthropy. In death he thumbed his nose at the world: his entire fortune—$75 million—went in trust to his family.

A century later historians can perhaps appreciate better than Gould's obituarists the positive side of his amazing business career. The nation's railroad network bore in some considerable degree Gould's mark by virtue of his own system building and the spur he gave to others. Moreover, his forays into the territory of other railroads broke open monopoly markets and drove shipping prices down. Railroads might have made less money, but shippers and consumers benefited from cheaper transportation costs. Even Gould's purely speculative ventures may have contributed to the nation's economic growth. Economists say that money made in speculation is an especially efficient source of fresh capital, which is what Gould's winnings were to America's capital-hungry railroads.

Let us suppose that Gould never understood this. Let us suppose further that he was motivated by greed, that his methods were as unscrupulous as they needed to be, and that, had he lived at a later time, he probably would have ended up in prison. Are we justified in calling him a robber baron?

Union Pacific's Engine No. 149
The railroads invoked a new notion of time. How fast could a person cross the continent? In 1876, a troupe of actors, scheduled to present Shakespeare's *Henry V* in San Francisco, made the trip from New York City in eighty-four hours—a record. The Union Pacific's crack engine No. 149 carried them at open throttle on the last leg from Ogden, Utah. Union Pacific Museum Collection.

The Managerial Revolution

At one time, recalled a railroad expert in 1896, it had been thought "practically impossible to manage a great railway effectively." On the early railroads "management had been personal and autocratic; the superintendent, a man gifted with energy and clearness of perception, moulded the property to his own will. But as the properties grew, he found himself unable to give his personal attention to everything. Undaunted, he sought to do everything and do it well. He ended by doing nothing."

It is not hard to understand the mistake of that early railroad superintendent. In a world of small businesses, where could he find a model for running an enterprise that was too big for personal and direct control?

In 1856 Daniel C. McCallum, an Erie Railroad official, had come to grips with the problem. On a 50-mile railroad, McCallum noted, the superintendent could personally attend to every detail, "and any system, however imperfect, may prove comparatively successful." But not on 500-mile railroads: "I am fully convinced that in the want of a system lies the true secret of their failure." Thus McCallum identified the need for a *system*—a formal administrative structure—for the successful operation of large-scale, complex enterprises. He knew he was working in the dark: "We have no precedent or experience upon which we can fully rely."

Railroads were the most complex form of nineteenth-century enterprise. They had to raise huge amounts of capital, and their properties stretched over ever-greater distances. They employed armies of workers—nearly fifty thousand on the Pennsylvania system by 1890. And, unlike the leisurely traffic on canals, trains had to be precisely scheduled and closely coordinated. Even with the use of telegraphic communication, train accidents took a heavy toll.

Step by step, always under the prod of necessity, the early trunk lines pioneered the main elements of modern business administration. They separated overall management from day-to-day operations and created departments along functional lines—maintenance of way, rolling stock, and traffic. Then they carefully defined the lines of communication from the operating divisions upward to the central office. When Albert Fink perfected his cost-accounting system for the Louisville and Nashville Railroad after the Civil War, managers at last had precise data with which to assess performance. By the end of the 1870s the managerial crisis on the railroads had been resolved.

As industrial enterprises became comparably complex, they confronted the same kind of managerial problems. However, manufacturers benefited from the experience of the railroads. Andrew Carnegie, for example, drew on his early career with the Pennsylvania Railroad. Whether by learning from the railroads or through trial and error, large companies moved toward a modern management structure and solved the problems of administering far-flung business empires.

Mass Markets and Large-Scale Enterprise

The railroads sparked a revolution in marketing as well as management. Until well into the industrial age, all but a few manufacturers operated on a small scale, producing goods mainly for nearby markets. They left the marketing to wholesale merchants and commission agents. Products normally passed through numerous hands on their way from the factory to the consumer.

Then, after the Civil War, the scale of economic activity began to grow dramatically. "Combinations of capital on a scale hitherto wholly unprecedented constitute one of the remarkable features of modern business methods," the economist David A. Wells wrote in 1889. He could see "no other way in which the work of production and distribution can be prosecuted." What was there about the nation's economy that led to Wells's sense of inevitability?

The key to large-scale enterprise lay in the American market. Immigration and a very high birth rate swelled the population from 40 million to over 60 million between 1870 and 1890. People flocked to the cities. The railroads brought these dense consuming markets within the reach of distant producers. The telegraph, fully operational by the Civil War, created instant communication across the country. Unlike Europe, with its many nation-states, the American market was unified; no political frontiers impeded the flow of goods across the continent. Meanwhile, high tariffs protected American industry from foreign competition. Nowhere else did manufacturers have so vast and accessible an internal market for their products.

Gustavus Swift and Vertical Integration. The meatpacking industry was a case in point. Before the Civil War, Cincinnati and Chicago had become great processors of preserved products such as salt pork and smoked beef. But fresh meat remained the province of local butchers, whose practices had scarcely changed since the preindustrial era. Fresh meat was a luxury item, and the diet of city dwellers, especially the poor, depended heavily on salt pork.

The coming of the railroads brought big changes to the fresh-meat business (Map 17.3). Cattle raising shifted to the grazing ranges of the Great Plains. With the opening of Union Stock Yards in 1865, Chicago became the main cattle market for the country. Livestock coming in by rail from the Great Plains was auctioned off at the Chicago stockyards and then shipped to eastern cities, where, as before, the animals were slaughtered in local "butchertowns." Such an arrangement—with distribution nationalized but processing still local—adequately met the demand of an exploding urban population indefinitely. In Europe no further development ever did occur.

But Gustavus F. Swift, a shrewd Massachusetts cattle dealer who settled in Chicago in 1875, saw the future differently. He recognized that livestock in cattle cars deteriorated en route to the East, and that small, local slaughterhouses could not utilize waste by-products and cut labor costs. If dressed beef could be kept fresh in transit, he could concentrate processing in

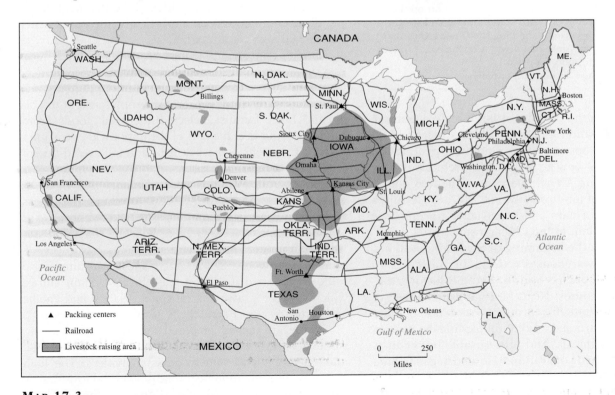

Map 17.3

The Dressed Meat Industry, 1900

The meatpacking industry clearly shows how transportation, supply, and demand combined to foster the growth of the American industrial economy. The main centers of beef production in 1900—Chicago, St. Paul, Kansas City, Fort Worth—were rail hubs with connections westward to the cattle regions and eastward to cities hungry for cheap supplies of meat. Vertically integrated enterprises sprang from these elements, linked together by an efficient and comprehensive railroad network.

Quaker Oats
Like crackers, sugar, and other nonperishable foods, oatmeal had traditionally been marketed to consumers in bulk from barrels. In 1882 the grain merchant Henry P. Cowell completed the first continuous-process mill for oatmeal, cutting production costs and greatly increasing output. He also hit on the idea of selling oatmeal in boxes of standard size and weight to a national market. Broadsides showing the Quaker Oats man soon appeared in every American town, advertising a product of reliable quality and uniform price.
Division of Political History, Smithsonian Institution.

Chicago and reap the benefits of large-scale operation. Primitive refrigeration already enabled Chicago pork-packing plants to operate year-round during the 1860s. The problem was how to apply this technology to a railroad freight car. After his engineers figured out an effective system of air circulation in 1877, Swift built a fleet of refrigerator cars and constructed an immense beef-processing plant at the Chicago stockyards.

This was only the beginning of Swift's innovations. No refrigerated warehouses existed in the cities to which he shipped chilled beef, so he built his own network of branch houses. Next, he established a fleet of wagons to distribute his products to retail butcher shops. Swift constructed additional facilities to process the fertilizer, chemicals, and other usable by-products from his slaughtering operations. He also began to handle other perishable commodities, including dairy products, so that he could fully utilize his refrigerator cars and branch houses. As the demand grew, Swift built more packing houses in other stockyard centers, including Kansas City, Fort Worth, and Omaha.

Step by step, Swift created a new kind of enterprise, the *vertically integrated* firm—that is, a national company capable of handling within its own structure all the func-

tions of an industry. In effect, Swift & Co. replaced a large number of small specialized firms with one multifunctional national firm. Swift's lead was followed by several big Chicago pork packers, of which Armour & Co. was the most prominent. By the end of the 1890s five firms, all of them nationally organized and vertically integrated, produced nearly 90 percent of the meat shipped in interstate commerce. The entire geography of the meat industry had changed (see Map 17.3).

The Birth of Mass Marketing. The refrigerator car had made all this possible in the fresh-meat trade. In most other fields no single invention was so decisive. But other manufacturers did share Swift's insight that the essential step was to identify a mass market and then develop a national enterprise capable of serving it. In the petroleum industry John D. Rockefeller during the 1870s built the Standard Oil Company partly by taking over rival firms, but he also developed a national distribution system to reach the enormous market for kerosene as a fuel for lighting and heating homes. The Singer Sewing Machine Company formed its own sales organization, using both retail stores and door-to-door salesmen. Through such distribution systems, manufacturers provided technical information, credit, and repair facilities for their products. Like the meat packers, these companies became vertically integrated firms that served a national market.

To gain the benefits of mass distribution, retail business went through comparable changes. Montgomery Ward and Sears, Roebuck developed into national mail-order houses for rural consumers. From Vermont to California, farm families selected identical goods from catalogues and became part of the nationwide consumer market. In the cities, mass distribution followed different strategies. Department stores, a form of retailing pioneered by John Wanamaker in Philadelphia in 1875, spread to every large city. The most important innovators in this field were Jewish families such as the Strauses of New York, the Lazaruses of Columbus, Ohio, and the Mays of Colorado, most of whose founders had started as peddlers or owners of dry-goods shops. An alternative route to urban distribution was through chain stores, which was the strategy of the Great Atlantic and Pacific Tea Company (A & P) and the F. W. Woolworth Company.

American society prepared its citizens to be consumers of the standardized goods produced by national manufacturers and sold by mass marketers. The high rate of geographic mobility broke down local loyalties, so strong in Europe. Social class in America, though by no means absent, was blurred at the edges and did not, for example, call for distinguishing ways of dressing. Foreign visitors often noted that ready-made clothing made it difficult to tell salesgirls from debutantes on city streets.

The American consumer's receptivity to standardized goods should not be exaggerated. Gustavus Swift, for

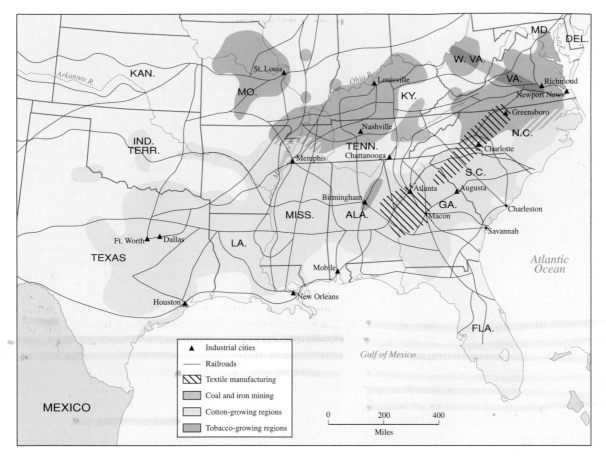

MAP 17.4
The New South, 1900
The economy of the Old South focused on raising staple crops, especially cotton and tobacco. In the New South staple agriculture continued to dominate, but there was marked industrial development as well. Industrial regions developed, producing textiles, coal and iron, and wood products. By 1900 the South's industrial pattern was well defined.

example, encountered great resistance to his Chicago beef: how could it be wholesome weeks later in Boston or Philadelphia? Cheap prices helped, but advertising mattered more. Modern advertising was born in the late nineteenth century, cluttering the urban landscape with billboards and signs. By 1900 advertisers were spending upwards of $90 million a year for space in newspapers and magazines. Advertisements urged readers to bathe with Pears' soap, eat Uneeda biscuits, sew on a Singer machine, and snap pictures with a Kodak camera. The active molding of demand for brand-name products became a major function of American business.

The New South

"Shall we dethrone our idols?" This was a question southerners had to ask themselves as they enviously observed the burst of economic activity in the North. For many, the answer was a resounding yes. Nostalgia

for the Old South, with its leisurely plantation ways, became the chief target of the advocates of southern economic development. The South, they argued, had always given "the places of trust and honor" to "warriors and orators," forgetting that "what it would most need was the practical wisdom of businessmen." Led by Henry W. Grady, editor of the Atlanta *Constitution*, an influential group of publicists made the "practical wisdom of businessmen" the credo of a "New South."

Catching up with the North was no easy task. The plantation economy of the Old South had strongly impeded industrial development. The slave states had few cities, a primitive distribution system, and not much manufacturing. This modest infrastructure was quickly restored after the Civil War. In 1877, with both Reconstruction and economic depression ended, a railroad boom developed. Track mileage doubled in the next decade and, at least by that measure, the South became nearly competitive with the rest of the country (Map 17.4).

The Industrial South
No development so raised the hopes of New South proponents as the success of the region's textile industry. After 1877 new mills sprang up in South Carolina, North Carolina, and Georgia. Investors received a high rate of return—average profits ran at 22 percent in 1882—and publicists boasted that new jobs were being created for "the necessitous masses of poor whites." This 1887 engraving of a "model" mill at Augusta, Georgia, conveys the South's sense of pride in its new industrial prowess.
Newberry Library.

But the South remained overwhelmingly agricultural; two of every three persons lived on the land. Farming and poverty are not necessarily linked, but in the South they were. Sharecropping, which required a cash crop (see Chapter 15), committed the South to cotton despite soil depletion, low productivity, and unprofitable prices. At a time of rapid technological advances in northern agriculture, cotton growing remained tied to the mule, the plow, and the hoe. Wages for southern farm labor fell steadily, dropping to scarcely half of the national average by the 1890s—roughly 75 cents a day without board.

Southern Industry. From this low agricultural wage, surprisingly, sprang the South's hopes for industrialization. Consider, for example, how southern textile mills got started in the Piedmont upcountry of North Carolina, South Carolina, and Georgia in the mid-1870s. Capital was raised locally, subscribed in large amounts and small under a drumbeat of boosterism. The mills recruited workers mostly from the surrounding hill farms, where people struggled to make ends meet. To attract them, mill wages had to be higher than farm earnings, but not much higher. Paying rock-bottom wages, the new mills had a great competitive advantage over the long-established New England industry—as much as 40 percent in labor costs in 1897.

The labor system that evolved likewise reflected southern agrarian society. To begin with, it involved hiring whole families. "Papa decided he would come because he didn't have nothing much but girls and they had to get out and work like men," recalled one woman. It was not Papa, in fact, but his girls whom the mills wanted, for work as spinners and loom tenders. But they could not be recruited individually: no right-thinking parent would have permitted that. There was, however, no objection to hiring by families; after all, on

the farm everyone had been expected to work. And so the family system of textile labor developed, in which half or more of the mill operatives were female and the work force was very young. In the 1880s, a quarter of all southern textile workers were under fifteen years of age; three-quarters were twenty-four or younger.

The hours were long—twelve hours a day—but life in the mill villages was, in the words of one historian, "like a family." Employers tended to be highly paternalistic, providing company housing and a variety of services. The mill workers themselves built close-knit, supportive communities—but for whites only. Although blacks sometimes worked as day laborers and janitors, they hardly ever got jobs as operatives in the mills.

Cheap, abundant labor might have been termed the South's most valuable natural resource. But the South was also well endowed with other natural resources. From its rich soil came tobacco—after cotton, the region's largest cash crop. When cigarettes became fashionable in the 1880s, the young North Carolina entrepreneur James B. Duke seized the new market by taking advantage of a southern invention—James A. Bonsack's machine for producing cigarettes automatically. Blacks stemmed and stripped the tobacco leaf, as they always had, but Duke followed the textile example and restricted machine tending to white women.

Lumbering, by contrast, was largely racially integrated, with a labor force evenly divided between black and white men. The extensive pine forests of the South were rapidly exploited in the post-Reconstruction years. Alabama's rich coal and iron ore deposits also attracted investors; by 1890 the Birmingham district was producing nearly a million tons of pig iron a year.

Economic Retardation. Despite the South's high hopes, this burst of industrial development did not lift the region out of poverty. Industrial output increased

TABLE 17.2

Comparison of Value Added per Worker, South and Non-South, 1910 (in dollars)

Type of Industry	South	Non-South
Lumber and timber products	820	1020
Cotton goods	544	764
Cars and general shop construction by steam railroad companies	657	746
Turpentine and resin	516	—
Tobacco manufactures	1615	1394
Foundry and machine-shop products	1075	1307
Printing and publishing	1760	2100
Cottonseed oil	1715	—
Hosiery and knit goods	461	724
Furniture and refrigerators	732	1052
Iron and steel	1182*	1433
Fertilizer	1833	1947

This table reveals the consistency with which northern industries (except tobacco manufactures) controlled the more skilled—and hence more value-creating—processes of production.
*Partially estimated.
Source: Gavin Wright, *Old South, New South: Revolutions in the Southern Economy since the Civil War* (New York: Basic Books, 1986), 163.

more rapidly than in the North but not rapidly enough to make much headway against the dominant agricultural sector. In 1900 two-thirds of all southerners made their living from the soil, just as they had in 1870. Moreover, most of the industries that did develop produced raw materials (forestry and mining) or engaged in the low-tech processing of coarse products. Industry by industry, the key economic statistic—the value added by manufacturing—showed the South consistently lagging behind the North (Table 17.2).

Southerners tended to blame the North: the South was a "colonial" economy controlled by New York and Chicago. There was some truth to this charge. Much of the capital—by no means all—did come from the North. And the integrating processes of the economy did subordinate regional to national interests. When the railway network moved to a uniform gauge in 1886, the southern railroads had to convert to the northern standard. Nor did northern interests hesitate to use their muscle to maintain the interregional status quo. Railroads, for example, varied freight rates so that it was cheap for southern cotton and timber to flow out and for northern manufactured goods to flow in.

Yet in the end the South's economic backwardness was mostly of its own making. The great advantage of the South—its cheap labor—actually kept it from becoming a more technologically advanced economy. First, low wages discouraged employers from replacing workers with machinery. Second, low wages attracted labor-intensive industry, such as textiles. Third, a cheap labor market inhibited investment in education because of the likelihood that better-educated workers would flee to higher-wage markets and the investment in them would be lost.

What distinguished the southern labor market was that it was *insulated* from the rest of the country. Why northern workers and arriving immigrants steered clear of the South is not hard to explain: wages were too low, attractive jobs were too scarce. Harder to understand is why so few southerners, black or white, left for the higher-wage North prior to World War I. At its core, the explanation has to do with the fact that the South was a place apart, with social and racial mores that discouraged all but its most resourceful inhabitants from seeking economic opportunity elsewhere. The result was that a normal flow of workers back and forth did not occur, and wage differentials did not narrow. So long as this condition persisted, the South would remain a tributary economy, a supplier on unequal terms to the advanced industrial heartland of the North.

The World of Work

In a free-enterprise system, profit drives the entrepreneur. But the industrial order is not populated only by profit makers. It includes—in vastly larger numbers—wage earners. What is done for profit always affects those who work for wages, but never so profoundly as in the late nineteenth century.

Labor Recruits

Wherever industrialism took hold, it set people in motion. Farm folk migrated to cities. Artisans moved into factories. An industrial labor force emerged. This happened in the United States just as it did in European countries, but with a difference: the United States could not rely primarily on its own population for a supply of workers.

The demand for labor was enormous. American industry required nearly three times more workers in 1900 than it had needed in 1870 (Figure 17.2). Rural Americans were highly mobile in the late nineteenth century, and half of those who moved ended up in cities. But the desirable factory jobs—puddlers, rollers, molders, and machinists—required industrial skills not held by rural Americans. Except in the South, moreover, native-born whites no longer wanted factory work. They had a basic education; they could read and calculate, and they understood American institutions and ways of doing things. City-bound white Americans found their opportunities in the multiplying white-collar jobs in offices and retail stores.

Modest numbers of blacks began to migrate northward and westward—roughly 80,000 between 1870 and 1890 and another 200,000 from 1890 to 1910. Most of them settled in cities, where the men were restricted to casual labor and janitorial work, the women to domestic service. Only 7 percent of all African American men held factory jobs in 1890. Employers turned black applicants away from the factory gates because immigrant workers were already supplying them with as much cheap labor as they needed.

Immigrant Workers. The great migration from the Old World started in the 1840s, when over a million Irish peasants fled the potato famine. In the following years, as European agriculture became increasingly commercialized, expanding peasant populations outstripped the available land. The peasant economy failed first in Germany and Scandinavia and then, later in the nineteenth century, across Austria-Hungary, Russia, Italy, and the Balkans. In the industrial districts of Europe, the forces of economic change also cut loose many workers in the declining artisan trades and in obsolete occupations such as hand-loom weaving.

Ethnic origin largely determined the kind of work that the immigrants found in their new country. Skilled artisans generally sought the types of jobs they had held in the Old World. The Welsh labored as tin-plate workers, the English as miners, the Germans as machinists and traditional artisans (for example, bakers and carpenters), the Belgians as glass workers, and the Scandinavians as seamen on the Great Lakes. For common labor, employers counted on the brawn of Irish rural immigrants.

As technology advanced, American employers had less need for European craft skills, while the demand for unskilled workers skyrocketed. The sources of

Ironworkers—Noontime
The qualities of the nineteenth-century craft worker—dignity, "unselfish brotherhood," a "manly" bearing—shine through in this painting by Thomas P. Anschutz.
Ironworkers—Noontime became a popular painting when it was reproduced as an engraving in *Harper's Weekly* in 1884.
Fine Arts Museum of San Francisco.

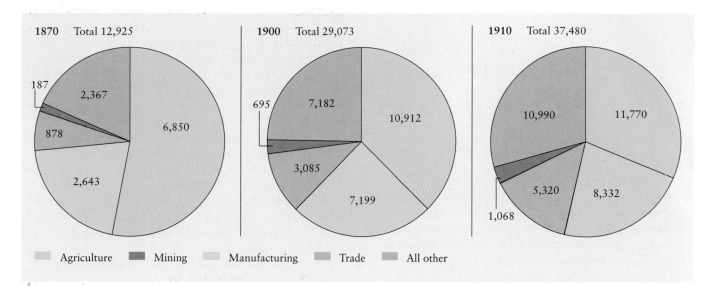

FIGURE 17.2
Changes in the Labor Force, 1870–1910
The numbers represent thousands of people (for example, 12,925 = 12,925,000 workers). They reveal both the enormous increase in the labor force between 1870 and 1910 and the dramatic shift from agriculture to industry and other nonagricultural jobs.

immigration began to shift during the 1880s, and by the early twentieth century arrivals from eastern and southern Europe far outstripped immigration from northern Europe (Figure 17.3). Slavic immigrants without job skills flooded into the lowest rungs of American industry. Heavy, low-paid factory labor became the domain of the recent immigrants (see Voices from Abroad, "Count Vay de Vaya und Luskod: Pittsburgh Inferno," p. 558). Blast-furnace jobs, one job seeker heard, were "Hunky work," not suitable for him or any other native-born whites. The derogatory term refers to Hungarian workers, but it was applied indiscriminately to Poles, Slovaks, and all the other Slavic groups arriving in America's industrial districts.

Not only skill determined where immigrants ended up in American industry. The newcomers, though generally traveling on their own, moved within well-defined networks, following relatives or fellow villagers already in America, joining their households as family members or boarders, and relying on them to land a job. A high degree of ethnic clustering resulted, even within a single factory. At the Jones and Laughlin steelworks in Pittsburgh, for example, the carpentry shop was German, the hammer shop Polish, and the blooming (ingot-reducing) mill Serbian. Immigrants also had different job preferences. Men from Italy, for example, preferred outdoor work to factory labor, often laboring in gangs under a *padrone* (boss), much as they had in Italy.

Immigrants entered a modern industrial order, but they saw their surroundings through peasant eyes. With the disruption of the traditional rural economies of eastern and southern Europe, many had lost their lands and fallen into the class of dependent, propertyless servants.

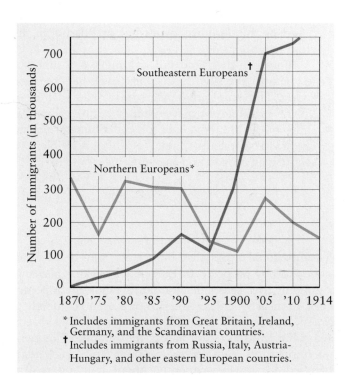

FIGURE 17.3
American Immigration, 1870–1914
This graph shows the surge of European immigration in the late nineteenth century. While northern Europe continued to send substantial numbers, it was overshadowed after 1895 by southern Europeans pouring into America to work in mines and factories.

COUNT VAY DE VAYA UND LUSKOD
Pittsburgh Inferno
———★———

*C*ount Vay de Vaya und Luskod, a Hungarian nobleman and high functionary in the Catholic Church, crossed the United States several times between 1903 and 1906 en route to his post as the Vatican's representative to Asia. In a book about his travels, he expresses his distress at the plight of his countrymen laboring in the mills of the Pittsburgh steel district.

The bells are tolling for a funeral. The modest train of mourners is just setting out for the little church-yard on the hill. Everything is shrouded in gloom, even the coffin lying upon the bier and the people who stand on each side in threadbare clothes and with heads bent. Such is my sad reception at the Hungarian workingmen's colony at McKeesport. Everyone who has been in the United States has heard of this famous town, and of Pittsburgh, its close neighbor. . . .

Fourteen-thousand tall chimneys are silhouetted against the sky . . . discharg[ing] their burning sparks and smok[ing] incessantly. The realms of Vulcan could not be more somber or filthy than this valley of the Monongahela. On every hand are burning fires and spurting flames. Nothing is visible save the forging of iron and the smelting of metal. . . .

And this fearful place affects us very closely, for thousands of immigrants wander here from year to year. Here they fondly seek the realization of their cherished hopes, and here they suffer till they are swallowed up by the inferno. He whom we are now burying is the latest victim. Yesterday he was in full vigor and at work at the foundry, toiling, struggling, hoping—a chain broke, and he was killed. . . .

This is scarcely work for *mankind*. Americans will hardly take anything of the sort; only immigrants rendered desperate by circumstances . . . and thus he is at the mercy of the tyrannous Trust, which gathers him into its clutches and transforms him into a regular slave.

This is one of the saddest features of the Hungarian emigration. In making a tour of these prisons, wherever the heat is most insupportable, the flames most scorching, the smoke and soot most choking, there we are certain to find compatriots bent and wasted with toil. Their thin, wrinkled, wan faces seem to show that in America the newcomers are of no use except to help fill the moneybags of the insatiable millionaires. . . . In this realm of Mammon and Moloch everything has a value—except human life. . . . Why? Because human life is a commodity the supply of which exceeds the demand. There are always fresh recruits to supply the place of those who have fallen in battle; and the steamships are constantly arriving at the neighboring ports, discharging their living human cargo still further to swell the phalanx of the instruments of cupidity.

Source: Oscar Handlin, ed., *This Was America* (Cambridge, MA: Harvard University Press, 1949), 407–410.

Peasants could avoid that bitter fate only if they had money to buy property. In Europe job-seeking peasants commonly tried seasonal agricultural labor or temporary work in nearby cities. America represented merely a larger leap, made possible by cheap and speedy steamship transportation across the Atlantic. The peasant immigrants, most of them young and male, never intended to stay permanently. About half did return, departing from America in great numbers during depression years. No one knows how many left because they had saved enough money and how many left for lack of work. For American employers, it scarcely mattered. What mattered was that the immigrants took the worst jobs and melted away when the jobs dried up. For the new industrial order, they made an ideal labor supply.

Railroading and a few other fields employed mostly native-born workers. Overall, however, immigrants manned American industry, constituting well over half of the labor force of the nation's principal manufacturing and mining industries after the turn of the century.

Working Women. Between 1870 and 1900 the number of wage-earning women grew by almost two-thirds. Women made up a quarter of the labor force in 1900 and were essential to America's economy. Their gender shaped their role as workers. Contemporary beliefs about womanhood determined which women entered the work force and how they were treated once they became wage earners.

Immigrant Workers
Many native-born Americans resented the influx of peasant immigrants from eastern and southern Europe that began in the 1880s. In fact, the newcomers provided most of the heavy labor on which the nation's industrial economy depended. They were Europe's gift—its most vigorous and hardworking people. In this photograph new arrivals are boarding a ferry at Ellis Island, the fabled immigration station in New York harbor, to be taken to the Battery, at the southern tip of Manhattan, from where they will scatter to factories and mines across America.
State Historical Society of Wisconsin.

Wives were not supposed to work outside the home, and in fact less than 5 percent did so in 1890. Only among African Americans did many married women, above 30 percent, work for wages. Among whites, the typical working woman at that time was under twenty-four and unmarried. In most working-class households, daughters had no choice but to work, because their families needed their earnings. When older women worked, remarked one observer, it "was usually a sign that something had gone wrong"—their husbands had died, deserted, or stopped working.

Since women were held to be inherently different from men, it followed that they should not be permitted to do "men's work." Nor, regardless of the value of their labor, could they be paid a man's wage. The dominant view was that a woman did not require a "living wage" because, as one investigator reported, "it is expected that she has men to support her." Moreover, the occupation that served as the baseline for all women's jobs was domestic service, which was always very poorly paid or, in a woman's own home, not paid at all.

At the turn of the century women workers fell into three categories. One third worked as maids or other types of domestic servants. Another third held "female" white-collar jobs in teaching, nursing, sales, and office work. The remaining third worked in industry, heavily concentrated in the garment trades and textile mills but present also in many other industries as inspectors, packers, and assemblers, and in other "light" occupations. Few worked as supervisors, fewer in the crafts, and nearly none as day laborers.

Just how jobs came to be defined as male or female—in sociological lingo, the *sex-typing* of occupations—is not easy to explain. Jobs as telephone operators and store clerks, originally held by men, had by the 1890s been taken over by women. Once women dominated an occupation, people came to think of it as having feminine attributes, even though very similar or even identical work elsewhere was done by men. Jobs identified as women's work became unsuitable for men. There were no male telephone operators by 1900.

The sex-typing of work was legitimized by the sentimental view of women as the weaker sex, but powerful interests also played a role. Craft workers protected their male domain, and employers profited from cut-rate work. Wherever they worked, women earned less than the lowest-paid males. At the turn of the century the weekly wage of women factory workers came to roughly $7, $3 less than that of unskilled men and $5 below the average for all industrial employees.

As with male workers, ethnicity and race played a big part in the distribution of women's jobs among particular groups. Exclusion from all but the most menial jobs applied as rigidly to black women as it did to black men. White-collar jobs were reserved for the native-born, which in the cities increasingly included the second-generation daughters of immigrants. And as with men, ethnicity created clustering patterns in the jobs held by wage-earning women or, in the case of Italian families, restricted them to sewing and other subcontracting tasks that could be done at home.

The Family Economy.   Disapproval of wives working
outside the home, though expressed in sentimental and
moral terms, was based on solid necessity for working-
class families. From the standpoint of the labor market,
the basic economic unit consisted of the individual
employee. For workers, however, the family was the
economic unit, and the wife's contribution to it was
crucial. Cooking, cleaning, and tending the children
were not income-producing activities or reckoned in
terms of money. But everyone knew that the family
household could not function without the wife's contribution. Therefore, her place was in the home.

Working-class families, however, found the going
hard on a single income. Only among highly skilled
workers, wrote an investigator of the family budgets of
miners and iron workers, "was it possible for the husband unaided to support his family." The rockiest
period came during the child-bearing years, when there
were many mouths to feed and only the earnings of the
father to provide the food. Thereafter, as the children
grew old enough to work, the family income began to
increase. Not only older unmarried sons and daughters
but the younger children as well contributed their
share. In 1900 one of every five children under sixteen
worked for wages, including probably a quarter of a
million younger than ten. "When the people own
houses," remarked a printer from Fall River, Massachusetts, "you will generally find that it is a large family all
working together."

By the 1890s all the northern industrial states had
passed laws prohibiting child labor and regulating
work hours for teenagers. Most of those states also
required children under fourteen to attend school for a
certain number of weeks each year. Working-class families continued to need more than one income, but this
money came increasingly from the wives. After 1890
the proportion of married women who worked crept
steadily upward; about a fifth of the wives of unskilled
and semiskilled men in Chicago held jobs in 1920.
Wage-earning wives and mothers were on their way to
becoming a primary part of America's labor force.

Autonomous Labor

No one supervised the nineteenth-century coal miner
(see American Voices, "John Brophy: A Miner's Son,"
p. 561). He was a tonnage worker, paid for the amount
of coal he produced. He provided his own tools, worked
at his own pace, and knocked off early when he chose.
Such autonomous craft workers—almost all of them
men—flourished in many branches of nineteenth-
century industry. They were mule spinners in cotton
mills, puddlers and rollers in ironworks, molders in
stove making, and machinists, glassblowers, and skilled
workers of many other types.

In the shop they abided by the *stint*, a limit placed by
themselves on the amount they would produce each day.
This informal system of limiting output infuriated
efficiency-minded engineers. But to the worker it signified personal dignity and "unselfish brotherhood" with
fellow employees. The male craft worker took pride in a
"manly" bearing toward both his fellows and the boss.
One day a shop in Lowell, Massachusetts, posted regulations requiring all employees to be at their posts in work

JOHN BROPHY

A Miner's Son

———★———

John Brophy (1883–1963), an important mine union official, recalls in an oral history what mining was like in his boyhood, a time when mining was strictly pick-and-shovel work and machinery had not yet eroded the prized skills of the miner.

I got a thrill at the thought of having an opportunity to go and work in the mine, to go and work along side my father. After . . . I got experience and some strength, and the ability to work with a little skill, I was conscious of the fact that my father was a good workman; that he had pride in his calling. . . . It was a great satisfaction to me that my father was a skilled, clean workman with everything kept in shape, and the timbering done well—all of these things: the rib side, the roadway, the timbering, the fact that you kept the loose coal clean rather than cluttered all over the workplace, the skill with which you undercut the vein, the judgment in drilling the coal after it had been undercut and placing the exact amount of explosive so that it would do an effective job of breaking the coal from the solid— indicated the quality of his work. . . .

It was skill in handling the pick and the shovel, the placing of timbers, and understanding the vagaries of the workplace—which is subject to certain pressures from the overhanging strata as you advance into the seam. It's an awareness of roof conditions. And it's something else too. Under the older conditions of mining under which I went to work with my father, the miner exercised considerable freedom in his working place in determining his pace of work and the selection of the order of time in the different work operations. Judgment was everywhere along the line, and there was also necessary skill. It was the feel of all this. You know that another workman in another place was a good miner, a passable miner, or an indifferent one. . . . I think that was one of the great satisfactions that a

miner had—that he was his own boss within his workplace. . . .

The miner is always aware of danger, that he lives under dangerous conditions in the workplace, because he's constantly uncovering new conditions as he advances in the workingplace, exposing new areas of roof, discovering some weakened condition or break which may bring some special danger. There is also the danger that comes from a piece of coal slipping off the fast and falling on the worker as he lays prone on the bottom doing his cutting. The worker has got to be aware of all these conditions that may be in the coal, that may be in the roof. . . .

Then there is the further fact that the miners by and large lived in purely mining communities which were often isolated. They developed a group loyalty under all these circumstances. They were both individualists and they were group conscious. . . . It made them an extraordinary body of workers, these miners, because of these very special conditions, because involved in it was not only earning a living, but a matter of health and safety, life and death were involved in every way. You find time and again miners, in an effort to rescue their fellow workers, taking chances which quite often meant death for themselves. . . .

Along with that is a sense of justice. There was the very fact the miner was a tonnage worker and that he could be short weighed and cheated in various ways, and that the only safeguard against it was [union] organization. In that case it was important to have a representative of the miners to see that the weight was properly done and properly credited to the individual miner. There was the whole complex of circumstances that had been in the mining industry for generations which had been their experience. The miner in my day in the United States was aware that all knowledge didn't start with his generation. . . . At least on one side of my family there are at least four generations of [British] miners, and I say this with a sense of pride; very much so. I'm very proud of the fact that there is this long tradition of miners who have struggled with the elements.

———

Source: Jerold S. Auerbach, ed., *American Labor: The Twentieth Century* (Indianapolis: Bobbs-Merrill, 1969), 44–48.

Breaker Boys
In the anthracite districts of eastern Pennsylvania, giant machines called breakers processed the coal as it came out of the mines, crushing it and sorting it by size for sale as domestic fuel. The boys shown in this photograph had the job of picking out the slate and refuse as the processed coal came down the chutes, working long hours in a constant cloud of coal dust for less than a dollar a day. Breaker boy was the first job, often begun before the age of ten, in a lifetime in the mines. The photograph does not show any old men, but sick and disabled miners often ended their careers as breaker boys—hence the saying among coal diggers, "Twice a boy and once a man is the poor miner's life."
Library of Congress.

clothes at the opening bell and remain, with the shop door locked, until the dismissal bell. A machinist promptly packed his tools and quit, declaring that he had not "been brought up under such a system of slavery."

Underlying this ethical code was a keen sense of the craft group, each with its own history and customs. Hatters—masters of the art of applying fur felting to top hats and bowlers—had a language of their own. When a hatter was hired, he was "shopped"; if fired, he was "bagged"; when he quit work, he "cried off"; and when he took an apprentice, the boy was "under teach." The hatters, most of whom worked in Danbury, Connecticut, or Orange, New Jersey, formed a distinctive, self-contained community.

Women workers found much the same kind of social meaning in their jobs. Department store clerks, for example, developed a work culture and language just as robust as that of any male craft group. The most important fact about wage-earning women, however, was their youth. The first job freed many of them from family discipline. It was an opportunity to be independent; to form friendships with other young women; and to experience, however briefly, a fun-loving time of nice clothes, dancing, and other "cheap amusements." Young male workers, by contrast, underwent a process of job socialization presided over by seasoned, older co-workers. Being young mattered to male workers, certainly, but did not define work experience for them as it did for women.

To some degree, youthful preoccupations made it easier for working women to overlook or accept the miserable terms under which many of them labored. But this did not mean that they lacked a sense of group solidarity and self-respect. Pretty clothes might appear frivolous to the casual observer, but they also conveyed the message that the working girl considered herself as good as anyone. Rebellious youth culture sometimes united with job grievances to produce astonishing strike movements in the early twentieth century, as, for example, by the Jewish garment workers of New York and the Irish American telephone operators of Boston.

Rarely, however, did women workers wield the kind of authority that the male craft worker commonly enjoyed. In many factories, he hired his own helpers, supervised their work, and paid them from his earnings. In the late nineteenth century, when the scale of production was expanding, craft workers relieved their employers of the mounting burden of shop-floor management. Many factory managers deliberately shifted this responsibility to their employees. In metal-fabricating firms that did precise machining and complex assembling, for example, a system of inside contracting developed, in which skilled employees bid for a production run, hiring and paying their own workers, taking full responsibility for the operation, and pocketing the profits.

Foremen enjoyed a similar degree of authority over the labor of unskilled workers. A multitude of laborers had been needed to dig canals, lay railroad tracks, and build cities. They were equally important in heavy industry, where until the last years of the century virtually all hauling of materials was done by hand. In the steel mills, a third or more of the workers shoveled coal and iron ore from freight cars, loaded the furnaces, and handled the tons of hot metal that passed through the mill daily. They worked in gangs, completely under the charge of the foreman or gang boss. He hired them, told them what to do, and disciplined and fired them.

Dispersal of authority was thus characteristic of nineteenth-century industry. The aristocracy of the workers—the craftsmen, inside contractors, and foremen—had a high degree of autonomy. However, their subordinates often paid dearly for that independence. Opportunities for abuse were endless. Any worker who paid his helpers from his own pocket might be tempted to exploit them. In the Pittsburgh area, foremen known as "pushers" were notorious for driving their gangs mercilessly. At the same time, industrial labor in the nineteenth century was still on a human scale. People dealt with each other face to face and often developed cohesive ties within the shop. Striking craft workers commonly received the support of helpers and laborers, and labor gangs sometimes walked out on behalf of a popular foreman.

Systems of Control

As technology advanced and modern management emerged, controls over the work process intensified. Despite fierce resistance, workers increasingly lost the proud independence that had characterized nineteenth-century craft work.

When mine owners introduced undercutting machines in the 1880s, they deprived coal miners of the pick work that was their most prized skill. "Anyone with a weak head and a strong back can load machine coal," grumbled one Kentucky miner. "But a man has to think and study every day like you was studying a book if he is going to get the best of the coal when he uses only a pick." Similar complaints came from many other craft workers as their skills fell victim to machinery—from hand-loom weavers early in the nineteenth century to glassblowers a hundred years later.

One main source of this de-skilling process was a new system of production—Henry Ford called it *mass production*—that turned out standardized, high-volume products. Agricultural implements, sewing machines, typewriters, bicycles, and, after 1900, automobiles were assembled from standardized, interchangeable parts. The machine tools that cut, drilled, and ground these metal parts were first operated by skilled machinists. But because they produced long runs of a single item, these machine tools became more specialized; they became *dedicated* machines—machines set up to do the same job over and over—and the need for skilled operatives disappeared. "A man never learns the machinist's trade now," John Morison, a machinist, complained in 1883 to a Senate investigating committee. In the manufacture of sewing machines "the trade is so subdivided that a man is not considered a machinist at all. One man may make just a particular part of a machine and may not know anything whatever about another part of the same machine." Such a worker, noted an observer, "cannot be master of a craft, but only master of a fragment."

Meatpacking did not become a mechanized industry, yet it also experienced the mass-production revolution. The key innovation in the Chicago packing houses was a shift from the traditional reliance on skilled butchers to a highly specialized division of labor. At the Armour plant, workers performed seventy-eight distinct jobs, working efficiently and at high speed as the carcasses moved along, hooked to overhead conveyors. In a ten-hour day a gang of 157 workers could handle 1,050 head of cattle, many more per employee than if one skilled butcher did everything. "If you need to turn out a little more," boasted a superintendent at Swift & Co., "you speed up the conveyor a little and the men speed up to keep pace." Complaints about speedups were a sure sign of workers' loss of control over their jobs.

Frederick W. Taylor and Scientific Management. Employers were attracted to dedicated machinery and conveyor belts because these innovations increased output; the impact on workers was not uppermost in their minds. Employers recognized that mechanization made it easier to discipline workers, but that was only an incidental benefit of the efficiencies coming from the machinery itself. Gradually, however, the idea took hold that managing workers might itself be a way to reduce the cost of production.

The pioneer in this field was Frederick W. Taylor. An expert on metal-cutting methods, Taylor believed that the same engineer's approach might be applied to managing workers, hence the name for his method: *scientific management*. To get the maximum work from the individual worker, Taylor suggested two basic reforms. The first would eliminate the brain work from manual labor. Managers would assume "the burden of gathering together all of the traditional knowledge which in the past has been possessed by the workmen and then of classifying, tabulating, and reducing this knowledge to rules, laws, and formulae." The second reform, a logical consequence of the first, would deprive workers of the authority they had been exercising on the shop floor. Workers would "do what they are told promptly and without asking questions or making suggestions. . . . The duty of enforcing . . . rests with the management alone."

Once managers had the knowledge and the power, they would put labor on a "scientific" basis. This meant subjecting each task to a *time-and-motion study* by an engineer who would analyze and time each job with a stopwatch. A personnel office would hire and train the right person for each job. Workers would be paid at a differential rate—that is, a certain amount if they met the stopwatch standard and a higher rate for additional output. Taylor claimed that his techniques would guarantee the optimum level of worker efficiency. His assumption was that only money mattered to workers and that they would automatically respond to the lure of higher earnings.

Scientific management, in practice, was not a roaring success. Implementing it called for a total restruc-

The Killing Floor
To the modern eye, the labor process depicted in this 1882 engraving of a Chicago meatpacking plant seems primitive and inefficient, but it contains the seeds of America's mass-production revolution. At the far left the steer has already been stunned by one specialist, killed by a second, and attached to a chain that will lift it onto the overhead conveyor. The division of labor is already in place (each of the workers on the line does a single repetitive task), and the process is continuous. It would be only a small step from the killing floors of the Chicago packing plants to Henry Ford's assembly line.
Library of Congress.

turing of factory administration. No company ever adopted Taylor's entire system, and the few that tried paid dearly for the effort. His method of job analysis, which was widely used, met stubborn resistance from workers. "It looks to me like slavery to have a man stand over you with a stopwatch," complained one iron molder. A union leader insisted that "this system is wrong, because we want our heads left on us." Far from solving the labor problem, as Taylor claimed it would, scientific management embittered relations on the shop floor.

Yet Taylor achieved something of fundamental importance. He was a brilliant publicist, and his teachings spread throughout American industry. Taylor's disciples moved beyond his simplistic economic psychology, creating the new professions of personnel administration and industrial psychology, which purported to know how to extract more and better labor from workers. A threshold had been crossed into the modern era of labor management.

So the circle closed on American workers. With each advance, the quest for efficiency cut deeper into their cherished autonomy. Mechanization, scientific management, and the growing scale of industrial activity diminished workers and cut them down to fit the production system. The process occurred unevenly. For textile workers the loss had come early. Miners and iron workers felt it much more slowly. Others, such as craft workers in the building trades, escaped the process almost entirely. But increasing numbers of workers found themselves in an environment that crushed any sense of mastery or even understanding.

The Labor Movement

Wherever industrialization has taken hold, workers have organized and responded collectively. However, the movements they built have varied from one industrial society to another. In the United States, workers were especially uncertain about the path they wanted to take. Only in the 1880s did the American labor movement settle into a fixed course.

Reformers and Unionists

Thomas B. McGuire, a New York wagon driver, was ambitious. He had saved $300 from his wages "so that I might become something of a capitalist eventually." But his venture as a cab driver in the early 1880s soon failed:

> *Corporations usually take that business themselves. They can manage to get men, at starvation wages, and put them on a hack [hired carriage], and put a livery on them with a gold band and brass buttons, to show that they are slaves—I beg pardon; I did not intend to use the word slaves; there are no slaves in this country now—to show that they are merely servants.*

Slave or liveried servant, the symbolic meaning was the same to McGuire. He was speaking of the crushed aspirations of the independent American worker.

Labor Reform and the Knights of Labor. What would satisfy the Thomas McGuires of the nineteenth century? Only the restoration of an egalitarian society, one in which all citizens were equals and everyone might hope to become independent. This republican goal did not require returning to the agrarian past, but rather moving beyond the existing industrial order to a juster system that did not distinguish between capitalists and workers. All would be "producers" laboring together in what was commonly called the "cooperative commonwealth." This ideal inspired the Noble and Holy Order of the Knights of Labor.

Founded in 1869 as a secret society of Philadelphia garment cutters, the Knights of Labor gradually spread to other cities and in 1878 became a national movement. Led by Grand Master Workman Terence V. Powderly, the Knights boasted an elaborate ritual and ceremony calculated to appeal to the fraternal spirit of nineteenth-century workers. From the Knights of Labor they got a sense of belonging very much like that offered by the Masons or Odd Fellows. The Knights, however, harnessed fraternalism to labor-reform advocacy. Their goal was to "give voice to that grand undercurrent of mighty thought, which is today [1880] crystallizing in the hearts of men, and urging them on to perfect organization through which to gain the power to make labor emancipation possible."

But how was "emancipation" to be achieved? Through cooperation, the Knights argued. Funds would be raised to set up cooperative factories and shops owned and run by the employees. As these cooperatives flourished and spread, American society would be transformed into a cooperative commonwealth. But little was actually done. Instead, the Knights concentrated mainly on "education." Terence V. Powderly regarded the organization as a vast labor lyceum open to almost anyone (except lawyers and saloonkeepers). The cooperative commonwealth would arrive in some mysterious way as more and more "producers" became members and learned the group's message from lectures, discussions, and publications. Social evil would not end in a day but "must await the gradual development of educational enlightenment."

Trade Unionism.   The labor reformers expressed the higher aspirations of American workers. Another kind of organization—the trade union—tended to their day-to-day needs. Unions had long been central in the lives of craft workers. Apprenticeship rules regulated entry into a trade, and the *closed shop*—by reserving all jobs for union members—kept out lower-wage and incompetent workers. Union rules specified the terms of work, sometimes in minute detail. Above all, trade unionism defended the craft worker's traditional skills and rights.

The trade union also expressed the social identity of a craft. Hatters took pride in their drinking prowess, an on-the-job privilege that was jealously guarded, and their unions sometimes resembled drinking clubs. More often, however, craft unions had an uplifting character. A Birmingham iron puddler claimed that his union's "main object was to educate mechanics up to a standard of morality and temperance, and good workmanship." Because operating trains was a high-risk occupation, the railroad brotherhoods stressed mutual aid, providing accident and death benefits and encouraging members to assist one another. On the job and off, the unions played a big part in the lives of craft workers.

The earliest unions organized local workers in the same craft, which, especially among German workers, was sometimes limited to a single ethnic group. As expanding markets broke down the insularity of these unions, they began to form national organizations. The first of them was the International Typographical

Terence V. Powderly, Labor Peacemaker
The Knights of Labor, unlike their trade-union rivals, in principle opposed strikes. In this cartoon from *Puck*, dated April 7, 1886, the little man depicted in the middle is Master Workman Powderly, leader of the Knights of Labor. The cartoon shows Powderly offering Capital and Labor the Knights' proposal for the peaceful settlement of labor disputes by means of "arbitration," which in those days meant mediation and negotiation rather than resolution by a third party. Powderly's judicious stance, however, could not keep the two sides from each other's throats, and in the national strikes soon to break out, Powderly's own members joined the picket lines.
Puck, April 17, 1886.

A Railroad Brotherhood
Locomotive firemen, who fed the boilers on nineteenth-century steam engines, ranked below locomotive engineers but still considered theirs a privileged occupation. This union certificate conveys the respectable values to which locomotive firemen adhered and, as depicted in the scenes on the right-hand side, the need they felt to protect their families (through the affordable insurance provided by their union) in the event of accidents that were so much a part of the dangerous trade they followed.
Library of Congress.

Union, in 1852. By the 1870s molders, iron workers, bricklayers, and about thirty other trades had formed national unions.

The practical job interests that trade unions espoused might have seemed a far cry from the reform idealism of the Knights of Labor. But both kinds of motives arose from a single workers' culture. Seeing no conflict, many workers carried membership cards in both the Knights of Labor and a trade union. The careers of many labor leaders, including Powderly, likewise embraced both kinds of activity. For many years even the functional lines were indistinct. At the local level, little separated a trade assembly of the Knights from a local trade union; both engaged in fraternal and job-oriented activities.

Trade unions generally barred women, and so did the Knights until, in 1881, women shoe workers in Philadelphia struck in support of their male co-workers and won the right to form their own local assembly. By 1886 probably fifty thousand women belonged to the Knights of Labor. Their courage on the picket line prompted Powderly's rueful remark that women "are the best men in the Order." For a handful of women, such as hosiery worker Leonora M. Barry, the Knights provided a rare chance to take up leadership roles as organizers and officials. For many others the liberation was more modest but very real: "timid young girls—girls who have been overworked from their cradle—stand[ing] up bravely . . . swayed . . . by the wrongs heaped upon their comrades, talk[ing] nobly and beautifully of the hope of redress to be found in organization."

Similarly, the Knights of Labor grudgingly expanded the opportunity for black workers to join, because of the need for solidarity and, just as important, in deference to the Order's egalitarian principles. The Knights could rightly boast that their "great work has been to organize labor which was previously unorganized."

The Triumph of "Pure and Simple" Unionism

In the early 1880s the Knights began to rival the trade unions. Boycott campaigns against the products of "unfair" employers achieved impressive results. With the economy booming and workers in short supply, the Knights began to win strikes, including a major victory against Jay Gould's Southwestern railway system in 1885. Workers flocked into the organization, and its membership jumped from 100,000 to perhaps 700,000 in less than a year. For a brief time the Knights stood poised as a potential industrial-union movement capable of bringing all workers into its fold.

The rapid growth of the Knights of Labor frightened the national trade unions. They tried to keep their local branches away from the Knights, but without success. The unions then began to insist on a clear separation of roles, with the Knights confined to the field of labor reform. This was partly a battle over turf, but it also reflected a deepening divergence of labor philosophies.

Samuel Gompers, a cigar maker from New York City, led the ideological assault on the Knights. Gompers hammered out the philosophical position that would become known as "pure and simple" unionism. His starting point was that grand theories and schemes such as those that excited the Knights should be avoided like the plague. Unions, Gompers believed, should focus instead strictly on concrete, achievable gains, and they should organize workers not as an undifferentiated mass of "producers" but by craft and occupation. The battleground should be where workers could mobilize their power, which was where they worked—not in the quicksands of politics. Gompers developed these views as general propositions, but they were grounded in the hard experience of unionists such as Abraham Bisno, who tried to organize his fellow workers and bargain collectively with employers (see American Voices, "Abraham Bisno: Trade Unionist," p. 568). Bisno would have nodded in agreement with Gompers's assertion that "no matter how just . . . unless the cause is backed up with power to enforce it, it is going to be crushed and annihilated."

The struggle for the eight-hour workday crystal-lized the tensions between the rival movements. Both of them favored a shorter workday, but for different reasons. To the Knights, more leisure was desirable because workers had duties "to perform as American citizens and members of society": a shorter workday was a precondition for a healthy republican society. Trade unionists took a more hard-boiled view of the eight-hour day: it would spread the available jobs among more workers, protect them against overwork, and (like higher wages) give them a better life. When the trade unions set May 1, 1886, as the deadline for achieving the eight-hour day, the Knights objected. But workers everywhere responded enthusiastically, and as the deadline approached, a wave of strikes and demon-strations broke out across the country.

The Haymarket Square Riot. At one such eight-hour strike, at the McCormick agricultural-implement works in Chicago, a battle erupted on May 3, leaving four strikers dead. Chicago was a hotbed of American *anarchism*—the revolutionary advocacy of a stateless society—and local anarchists, most of them German immigrants, called a protest meeting the next evening at Haymarket Square. The meeting went off peacefully, but when police moved in at the end to break it up, someone threw a bomb at the police, who responded with wild gunfire. Most of the casualties, including some police, came from police bullets.

The anarchist sponsors of the rally, some of them not even present, were arrested and charged wih crim-inal conspiracy, a legal doctrine so broad that no direct involvement in the bombing was required to justify a verdict of guilt. There was in fact no evidence linking them to the bombing. Four men were executed, one committed suicide, and the others received long prison sentences. They were victims of one of the great mis-carriages of American justice.

Seizing on the anti-union hysteria set off by the Haymarket affair, employers took the offensive against the campaign for an eight-hour workday. They broke strikes violently, compiled blacklists of strikers, and forced others to sign *yellow-dog contracts* guaranteeing that, as a condition of employment, they would not join a union. If trade unionists needed any further confir-mation of the tough world in which they lived, they found it in Haymarket and its aftermath.

In December 1886, having failed to persuade the Knights of Labor to desist from union activity, the national trade unions formed the American Federation of Labor (AFL), with Samuel Gompers as president. The AFL embodied the belief of the national unions that they constituted a distinctive movement. The fed-eration in effect locked into place the trade-union struc-ture as it had evolved by the 1880s. Underlying this structure was the conviction that workers had to take the world as it was, not as they dreamed it might be. At this point, the American movement's development defi-nitely diverged from that of its European counterparts, for fundamental to Gompers's AFL was rejection of a separate political party for workers.

Samuel Gompers
This is a photograph of the labor leader in his forties taken when he was visiting striking miners in West Virginia, an area where mine operators resisted unions with special fierceness. The photograph was taken by a company detective.
George Meany Memorial Archives.

ABRAHAM BISNO

Trade Unionist

Repeated strikes in Chicago caused a government commission to come to that city in 1900 to investigate the reasons for the labor troubles. Bisno, a garment worker and "walking delegate"—a local union agent—gives the trade-union side of the story.

Q. Present occupation.
A. Collecting fares on the loop here for the Union Elevated Railway Company.
Q. Former occupation.
A. I am a cloak maker by trade—made cloaks for some years—and I have had several occupations within the last few years. I have been walking delegate for our union.
Q. What union is that?
A. The Chicago Cloak Makers' Union. . . .

Q. Is the union to which you belong still in existence?
A. It is lately organized again; it was broken up after the defeat of the strike 2 years ago. . . .
Q. Are you a believer in the union of labor?
A. Yes. . . . Unless a firm recognizes the union and agrees to employ nobody except members of the union, the union cannot exist. In my own trade, when our union was weak, our best men were victimized, and were out of a job most of the time; I mean our most intelligent men—men who do not want to put up with abuse easily. . . . So when these men demand that the union be recognized to the extent of not employing other people except members of their union, this is essential to the very existence of the organization. It is a life-and-death question with them. . . .

Q. You recognize that the strike is a coercive measure—an act of war and an interference with the civil rights of a concern?
A. . . . Yes; but then the reduction in wages, or failing to raise the wages when conditions warrant, are acts of war and interference with my civil rights in a time of peace. It is the same thing. . . .
Q. What are the steps of persuasion brought into use to influence a man who has failed to yield to argument and has gone to work?
A. Well several. For instance, in one case we have alienated a man from the affections of his co-church members.
Q. That you call persuasion?
A. Yes; we went into the church and denounced the fellow as a traitor to our interests, cutting our throats, sort of sinning against the religious laws, inflicting damage on so many families.
Q. That is one step?
A. That was one of the means; called him scab.
Q. Called him scab?
A. Yes; on the streets.
Q. To his face?
A. Yes. As I told you, it depends upon the temperament of the man. We would go after him in a hundred and one ways, if we can, to drive him out of the community.
Q. That you call persuasion?
A. Within the law; and I think under certain conditions it is right for a person to violate the law and take the consequences. Supposing I am fined for calling a man a scab. I am put into a fine, say, of $10 and have to go to jail for 20 days. The abuse I am suffering may be so great that I would take my medicine. I would tell a man he was a scab, and take my medicine for it and go to jail. . . .

Source: Report of the U.S. Industrial Commission, VIII (Washington, DC: U.S. Government Printing Office, 1901), 53–58, 79–82.

The Knights of Labor never recovered from the employer counteroffensive after the Haymarket affair. Powderly retreated to the rhetoric of labor reform, but wage earners had lost interest, and he was unable to formulate a workable new strategy. By the mid-1890s, the Knights of Labor had faded away. In the meantime, the trade unions experienced steady growth, justifying Gompers's confidence that he had found the correct formula for the American labor movement.

Industrial War

The trade unions were conservative: they accepted the economic order, and all they wanted was a larger share for working people. But it was precisely that claim against business profits that made American employers so opposed to collective bargaining. In the 1890s they unleashed a fierce counterattack on the trade-union movement.

The Homestead Strike.   Skilled workers in Homestead, Pennsylvania, site of one of Andrew Carnegie's great steel mills, thought themselves safe from that threat. They earned good wages, lived comfortably, and generally owned their own homes. The town was very much their community, with a municipal government elected from their ranks. And they had faith in Carnegie. For had not Good Old Andy said in a famous magazine article that workers had as sacred a right to combine as did capitalists, and that workers had a moral claim on their jobs that forbade the use of strikebreakers by employers?

Espousing high-toned principles made Carnegie feel good, but a strong bottom line made him feel even better. He decided that collective bargaining had become too expensive, and he was confident that his skilled workers could be replaced by the advanced machinery he was installing. Lacking the stomach for the hard battle ahead, Carnegie hid himself in a remote estate in Scotland, leaving behind a second-in-command well qualified for the job at hand. This was Henry Clay Frick, a former coal baron and a veteran of labor wars in the coal fields.

After a brief pretense of bargaining, Frick announced that as of July 1, 1892, the company would no longer deal with the Amalgamated Association of Iron and Steel Workers. If the employees wanted to work, they would have to return on an individual basis. The plant had already been fortified so that strikebreakers could be brought in to resume operations and defeat the union. At stake now was not just wage cuts but the defense of a way of life. Town authorities—members of the union—turned away the county sheriff when he tried to take possession of the plant. The entire community—women no less than men—mobilized in defense of the union.

At dawn on July 6 two barges were seen approaching Homestead up the Monongahela River. On the barges were armed guards hired by the Pinkerton Detective Agency to take control of the steelworks on behalf of the company. Behind hastily erected barricades, the strikers opened fire, and a bloody battle ensued. When the Pinkertons finally surrendered, the enraged women of Homestead mercilessly pummeled them as they retreated to the railway station. Frick appealed to the governor of Pennsylvania, who called out state National Guard units and placed Homestead under martial law. The great steelworks was taken over and opened to strikebreakers, while strike leaders and town officials were arrested on charges of riot, murder, and treason.

The defeat at Homestead marked the beginning of the end for trade unionism in the iron and steel industry. Ended too were any lingering illusions about the sanctity of workers' communities such as Homestead. "Men talk like anarchists or lunatics when they insist that the workmen of Homestead have done right," asserted one conservative journal. Nothing could be permitted to interfere with private property or threaten law and order.

The Homestead strike ushered in an era of strife in which working people faced not only the formidable power of corporate industry but the even more formidable power of their own government.

The Great Pullman Boycott.   The fullest demonstration of that hard reality came at a place that seemed an even less likely site for class warfare than Homestead. Pullman, Illinois, was a model factory town, famous for the amenities it offered to workers and the beauty of its landscaping and city plan. The town was named for its creator, George M. Pullman—inventor of the Pullman sleeping car, which brought comfort and luxury to railway travel. When the Panic of 1893 struck, business fell off and the Pullman Company cut wages but did not cut the rents for company housing. For many workers take-home pay shrank to pitiful levels. When a workers' committee finally complained to Pullman in May 1894, he responded that he saw no connection between his roles as employer and landlord. As for the committee members who had approached him, they were fired.

The strike that ensued would have been no more than a footnote in American labor history but for the fact that the Pullman workers belonged to the American Railway Union (ARU), a rapidly growing industrial union of railroad workers. Its leader, Eugene V. Debs, directed ARU members not to handle Pullman sleeping cars, which, though operated by the railroads, were owned and serviced by the Pullman Company. This action was a *secondary labor boycott*: force was applied at a secondary point (the railroads) to bring pressure on the primary target (Pullman).

Railroad officials, already fearful of the growing power of the ARU, saw the Pullman boycott as their chance to break the union. The General Managers' Association, which represented the railroads serving Chicago, insisted on running the Pullman cars. Since ARU members refused to operate trains with Pullman cars, a strike soon spread across the country and threatened to disrupt the entire economy.

Quite deliberately, the railroad managers maneuvered to bring the federal government into the dispute. Their hook was U.S. mail cars, which they attached to every train hauling Pullman cars. When strikers stopped these trains, the General Managers' Association appealed to President Grover Cleveland to send in troops to protect the U.S. mail and halt the growing violence. Richard Olney, Cleveland's attorney general, was a former railroad lawyer who unabashedly sided with his former employers. Disregarding the protests of Illinois governor John P. Altgeld, President Cleveland dispatched the U.S. Army. When federal troops failed to get the trains running again, Olney obtained court injunctions

The Pullman Strike

Chicago was the hub of the railway network and the strategic center of the battle between the Pullman boycotters and the trunk line railroads. For the strikers, the crucial thing was to prevent those trains with Pullman cars attached from running; for the railroads, it was to get the trains through at any cost. The arrival of federal troops meant that the trains would move and that the strikers would be defeated. *Harper's Weekly,* July 21, 1894.

prohibiting ARU leaders from conducting the strike. Debs and his subordinates refused to obey, were held in contempt of court, and were jailed. Now leaderless and uncoordinated, the strike quickly disintegrated.

No one could doubt why the great Pullman boycott had failed: it had been crushed by the naked use of government power on behalf of the railroad companies.

American Radicalism in the Making

Oppression does not radicalize all its victims, but it does radicalize some of them. And when social injustice is most painfully felt, when the underlying power realities stand openly revealed, the process of radicalization speeds up. Such was the case during the depression of the 1890s. Out of the industrial strife of that decade emerged the main forces of twentieth-century American radicalism.

Eugene Debs and American Socialism. Very little in Eugene Debs's background suggested that he would one day become the nation's leading socialist. Born in 1855 to

middle-class French Alsatian parents, Debs grew up believing in the essential goodness of American society, as he found it in his hometown of Terre Haute, Indiana—a prosperous midwestern railroad center. A popular young man-about-town, Debs considered a career in politics or business. Instead, he returned to the railway yards where he had worked as a boy, got involved in the local labor movement, and in 1880, at the age of twenty-five, was elected national secretary-treasurer of the Brotherhood of Locomotive Firemen, one of the craft unions that represented the skilled operating trades on the railroads.

These unions were conservative, opposed to strikes, and indifferent to the well-being of low-paid track and yard laborers. Troubled by this, Debs left his comfortable union post in 1892 to devote himself to a new organization, the American Railway Union, that would organize all railroad workers irrespective of skill—that is, an *industrial union*.

The Pullman boycott visibly changed Debs. He declared it "a contest between the producing classes and the money power of the country." And he went to jail for his convictions. Debs was sentenced to six months in the federal penitentiary not for violating any law but for refusing to obey a court order he knew to be trumped-up and prejudicial. He came out of jail an avowed radical committed to a lifelong struggle against a system that enabled employers to enlist the powers of government to enforce their arbitrary rule over working people. At first Debs identified himself as a Populist (see Chapter 18), but he quickly gravitated toward the socialist camp.

German refugees had brought the ideas of Karl Marx, the German radical philosopher, to America after the failed 1848 revolutions in Europe. Marx's prescription for revolution through class struggle inspired the most durable radical movements in the industrial world. Though little noticed in most parts of American society, Marxist socialism struck deep roots in the growing German American communities of Chicago and New York. In 1877 the Socialist Labor Party was formed, and from that time on Marxist socialism maintained a continuing, if narrowly based, presence in American politics.

When Eugene Debs appeared in their midst in 1897, the socialists were in a state of crisis. Although the economic hardship of the depression had just ended, they had failed to make much headway. Many blamed the party head, Daniel De Leon—an ideological purist not greatly interested in attracting voters. Debs joined the revolt against the dogmatic De Leon and helped found the rival Socialist Party of America in 1901, with the aim of building a broad-based political movement.

A spellbinding campaigner, Debs attracted a devoted national following. He talked socialism in an American idiom, making Marxism understandable and persuasive to many ordinary Americans. Under him the new party began to break down ethnic barriers and attract American-born voters. Many trade unionists, disillusioned as Debs himself had been by the events of the 1890s, went through the same kind of radical evolution and joined in large numbers. In Texas, Oklahoma, and Minnesota socialism exerted a powerful appeal among cotton and wheat farmers. The party was also highly successful at attracting women activists. Inside of a decade, with a national network of branches and state organizations, the Socialist Party had become a force to be reckoned with in American politics.

Western Radicalism. In the meantime, a different brand of American radicalism was taking shape in the West. After many years of mostly friendly labor relations, the situation in the western mining camps turned ugly during the 1890s. Powerful new corporations were taking over, and they wanted to be rid of the miners' union, the Western Federation of Miners (WFM). Moreover, silver and copper prices began to drop in the early 1890s, bringing pressure to cut miners' wages. When strikes resulted, they took a particularly violent turn.

In 1892 at Coeur d'Alene, a silver-mining district in northern Idaho, striking miners engaged in gun battles with company guards, sent a car of explosive powder careering into the Frisco mine, and threatened to blow up processing plants. Martial law was declared, federal troops came in, the strikers were crowded into "bullpens" (enclosed stockades), and the strike was broken. Equally violent strikes took place at Cripple Creek, Colorado, in 1894; at Leadville, Colorado, in 1896; and again in Coeur d'Alene in 1899.

In these western strikes, government intervention was particularly naked and unrestrained. This was partly in response to the level of violence, but it stemmed also from the character of politics in the lightly settled western states: either the miners would dominate state politics—as they did in coalition with the Populists during their successful strike at Cripple Creek—or, as was increasingly true, the mine owners would dominate, with disastrous consequences for the miners.

In 1897 WFM president Ed Boyce called on all union members to arm themselves with rifles, and his rhetoric—he called the wage system "slavery in its worst form"—had a hard edge. Any lingering faith in the political process died in the Colorado state elections of 1904, after bitterly fought strikes across the state in the previous two years. The miners thought they had defeated their archenemy, Republican governor James H. Peabody, only to have the Colorado Supreme Court overturn the election results and reinstall Peabody (who, by prearrangement, resigned in favor of his lieutenant governor).

In 1905 the Western Federation of Miners led the way in creating a new radical labor movement, the Industrial Workers of the World (IWW). Although the IWW initially had links to the Socialist Party, it soon repudiated political action and settled on its own radical course. The Wobblies, as IWW members were called, fervently supported the Marxist class struggle—but strictly in the industrial field. By action at the point of production and by an unending struggle against employers—ultimately by means of a general strike—they believed that the workers themselves would bring about a revolution. A workers' society would emerge, run directly by the workers through their industrial unions. The term *syndicalism* describes this brand of workers' radicalism.

In both of its major forms—the politically oriented Socialist Party and the syndicalist IWW—American radicalism flourished after the crisis of the 1890s, but only within certain limits. Socialists and Wobblies lived, in a sense, on the tolerance of society. They would later be crushed without ceremony. Nevertheless, they served a larger purpose. American radicalism, by its sheer vitality, bore witness to what was exploitative and unjust in the new industrial order.

Summary

★

American industrialism took its modern shape during the last decades of the nineteenth century. Central to this development were the shift from iron making to the manufacture of steel, the great expansion of coal mining, and the technology for generating steam and electrical power. These advances made possible the production of the capital goods and energy required by an expanding manufacturing economy. An efficient railway system provided access to national markets. A managerial revolution enabled entrepreneurs to master the complex business organizations they were building. The scale of enterprise grew very large, and the vertically integrated firm became the predominant form of business organization. Only in the South did prevailing conditions—in particular, the insulated, low-wage labor market—retard the growth of an advanced industrial economy.

In the North the enormous demand for labor led to a great influx of immigrants, making ethnic diversity a distinctive feature of the American working class. Gender likewise defined occupational opportunity. Women joined the labor force in growing numbers, but almost universally they were subjected to a sex-typing process that relegated them to "women's work," always at wage rates below those of men. Mass production—the high-volume output of standardized products—vastly improved the productivity of American manufacturing but also de-skilled workers and mechanized their jobs. Scientific management, the brainchild of Frederick W. Taylor, cut further into the traditional autonomy of American workers by systematizing the labor process and shifting control into the hands of supervisors.

The late nineteenth century gave rise to the American labor movement in its modern form. In the Knights of Labor, anticapitalist labor reform enjoyed one final surge during the mid-1880s and then succumbed to the "pure and simple" unionism of the American Federation of Labor. The AFL was conservative, in that it accepted the economic order, but its insistence on a larger share of the benefits for working people guaranteed that employers would fiercely resist the trade-union movement. The result was a series of bitter strikes: Homestead in 1892, the Pullman boycott of 1894, and, the most violent, the cycle of metal miners' strikes in the Far West. The industrial warfare of the 1890s stirred new radical impulses, leading on the one hand to the political socialism of Eugene Debs and on the other to the industrial radicalism of the IWW.

T I M E L I N E

1869   Knights of Labor founded in Philadelphia

1872   Montgomery Ward, first U.S. mail-order house, founded

Andrew Carnegie starts construction of Edgar Thomson steelworks near Pittsburgh

1873   Panic of 1873 ushers in economic depression

1875   John Wanamaker establishes first department store, in Philadelphia

1876   Philadelphia Centennial Exhibition showcases Corliss steam engine

1877   Baltimore and Ohio workers initiate nationwide railroad strike

1878   Gustavus Swift introduces refrigerator car

1879   Jay Gould begins to build Missouri Pacific railway system

1883   Railroads establish national time zones

1886   Haymarket Square bombing in Chicago

American Federation of Labor (AFL) founded

1892   Homestead steel strike crushed

1893   Panic of 1893 leads to national depression

Wave of railroad bankruptcies; reorganization by investment bankers begins

1894   President Cleveland sends troops to break Pullman boycott

1895   Southeastern European immigration exceeds northern European immigration for the first time

1901   Eugene V. Debs helps found Socialist Party of America

1905   Industrial Workers of the World (IWW) launched

Suggested Readings

The most useful introduction to the economic history of this period is Edward C. Kirkland, *Industry Comes of Age, 1860–1897* (1961). A more sophisticated analysis can be found in W. Elliot Brownlee, *Dynamics of Ascent* (rev. ed., 1979). For essays on many of the topics covered in this chapter, consult Glenn Porter, ed., *Encyclopedia of American Economic History* (3 vols., 1980).

Industrial Capitalism Triumphant

On railroads a convenient introduction is John F. Stover, *American Railroads* (1970). The growth of the railroads as an integrated system has been treated in George R. Taylor and Irene D. Neu, *The American Railway Network, 1861–1890* (1956). Julius Grodinsky, *Jay Gould: His Business Career, 1867–1892* (1957), is a complex study demonstrating the contributions this railroad buccaneer made to the transportation system. Books such as Grodinsky's have gone a long way to resurrect Gilded Age businessmen from the debunking tradition first set forth with great power in Matthew Josephson, *Robber Barons: Great American Fortunes* (1934). Peter Temin, *Iron and Steel in the Nineteenth Century* (1964), is the best treatment of that industry. Joseph F. Wall, *Andrew Carnegie* (1970), is the definitive biography of the great steel maker. On the development of mass production the key book is David A. Hounsell, *From the American System to Mass Production, 1800–1932* (1984). Alfred D. Chandler, *The Visible Hand: The Managerial Revolution in American Business* (1977), is not an easy book but will amply repay the labors of interested students.

On the New South the standard work has long been C. Vann Woodward, *Origins of the New South, 1877–1913* (1951). Equally essential as a modern reconsideration is Edward L. Ayers, *The Promise of the New South: Life after Reconstruction* (1992). A brilliant reinterpretation of the causes of the South's economic retardation is Gavin Wright, *Old South, New South* (1986). Jacqueline Jones, *The Dispossessed: America's Underclasses from the Civil War to the Present (1992)*, contains an excellent treatment of southern labor.

The World of Work

For an understanding of the impact of industrialism on American workers, three collections of essays make the best starting points: Herbert G. Gutman, *Work, Culture and Society in Industrializing America* (1976); Michael S. Frisch and Daniel J. Walkowitz, eds., *Working-Class America: Essays on Labor, Community and American Society* (1983); and Leon Fink, *In Search of the Working Class* (1994). On the introduction of Taylorism, the most useful book is Daniel Nelson, *Managers and Workers: Origins of the New Factory System* (2nd ed., 1995). The impact of Taylorism on American workers is treated with insight in David Montgomery, *The Fall of the House of Labor: The Workplace, the State, and American Labor Activism, 1865–1925* (1987).

Two valuable collections of essays on immigrant workers are Richard Ehrlich, ed., *Immigrants in Industrial America* (1977), and Dirk Hoerder, ed., *American Labor and Immigration History, 1877–1920: Recent European Research* (1983). John Bodnar, *Immigration and Industrialization: Ethnicity in an American Mill Town* (1977), is an important case study of a single community. On women workers the best introduction is Alice Kessler-Harris, *Out to Work* (1982). Ava Baron, ed., *Work Engendered: Toward a New History of American Labor* (1991), is a rich collection of essays that apply gender analysis to the history of working people. Two excellent case studies in this vein are Mary Blewett, *Men, Women, and Work: Class, Gender, and Protest in the New England Shoe Industry, 1780–1910* (1988), and Stephen H. Norwood, *Labor's Flaming Youth: Telephone Operators and Worker Militancy, 1878–1923* (1990). On black workers, useful introductions are William H. Harris, *The Harder We Run: Black Workers since the Civil War* (1982), and Philip S. Foner, *Organized Labor and the Black Worker* (1974). Walter Licht, *Getting Work: Philadelphia, 1840–1950* (1992), is a pioneering history of a labor market in operation.

The Labor Movement

The standard book on the struggle between labor reform and trade unionism is Gerald N. Grob, *Workers and Utopia, 1865–1900* (1961). For the Knights of Labor, it should be supplemented by Leon Fink, *Workingmen's Democracy: The Knights of Labor and American Politics* (1983), which captures the cultural dimensions of labor reform not seen by earlier historians. Labor's place in the political environment is the subject of David Montgomery, *Citizen Worker* (1993). On the emergence of a political strategy, see Julie Greene, *Pure and Simple Politics: The American Federation of Labor, 1881–1915* (1997). Paul Krause, *The Battle for Homestead, 1880–1892* (1992), puts the great strike in a larger social context. The most recent survey, incorporating much of the latest scholarship, is Bruce Laurie, *Artisans into Workers: Labor in Nineteenth Century America* (1989).

The founder of the AFL is the subject of a lively brief biography by Harold Livesay, *Samuel Gompers and Organized Labor in America* (1978). Among the many books on individual unions, Robert Christie, *Empire in Wood* (1956), best reveals the way pure and simple unionism worked out in practice. On industrial conflict, the most vivid book is Robert V. Bruce, *1877: Year of Violence* (1959). On western miners, the standard work is Mark Wyman, *Hard-Rock Epic: Western Miners and the Industrial Revolution, 1860–1910* (1979). On the western labor movement, important new interpretations are David Brundage, *The Making of Western Working-Class Radicalism: Denver's Organized Workers, 1878–1905* (1994), and Elizabeth Jameson, *All That Glitters: Class, Conflict, and Community in Cripple Creek* (1998). The best book on the IWW is Melvyn Dubofsky, *We Shall Be All* (1969). On socialism, David Shannon, *The Socialist Party of America* (1955), remains the standard account. There is, however, a fine biography of that party's leader that supersedes previous studies: Nick Salvatore, *Eugene V. Debs: Citizen and Socialist* (1982). A dimension of American radicalism long neglected receives sensitive attention in Mari Jo Buhle, *Women and American Socialism, 1870–1920* (1982).

Chapter 18

The Politics of Late Nineteenth-Century America

E VER SINCE THE founding of the republic, foreign visitors had been coming to America to study its political system. Most famous of the early observers was the French aristocrat Alexis de Tocqueville, who had written *Democracy in America* in 1832. When an equally brilliant visitor, the Englishman James Bryce, sat down to write his own account fifty years later, he decided that Tocqueville's great book could not serve as his model. For Tocqueville, Bryce noted, "America was primarily a democracy, the ideal democracy, fraught with lessons for Europe." In his own book, *The American Commonwealth* (1888), Bryce was much less rhapsodic. The robust democracy celebrated by Tocqueville had devolved half a century later into the dreary machine politics of the industrial age.

Bryce was anxious, however, that European readers not misunderstand him. Europeans would find in his book "much that is sordid, much that will provoke unfavourable comment." But they needed to be aware of "the existence in the American people of a reserve of force and patriotism more than sufficient to sweep away all the evils now tolerated, and to make a politics of the country worthy of its material grandeur and of the private virtues of its inhabitants." Bryce was ultimately an optimist: "A hundred times in writing this book have I been disheartened by the facts I was stating: a hundred times has the recollection of the abounding strength and vitality of the nation chased away these tremours."

Just what it was that Bryce found so disheartening in the practice of American politics is this chapter's first subject; the second is the underlying vitality that Bryce

Bandanna, 1888 Election
During the late nineteenth century, politics became a vibrant part of America's culture. Party paraphernalia, such as this colorful bandanna depicting the Democratic presidential nominee Grover Cleveland and his running mate, A. G. Thurman, flooded the country.
Collection of Janice L. and David J. Frent.

sensed, and how it reemerged and began to reinvigorate the nation's politics by the century's end.

The Politics of the Status Quo, 1877–1893

——————★——————

In times of national ferment, as a rule, public life
becomes magnified. Leaders emerge. Electoral campaigns debate great issues. The powers of government
expand. All this was true of the Civil War era, when, in
the crises of Union and Reconstruction, the nation's
political structure was most severely tested. The final
crisis, the contested election of 1876, rocked the constitutional foundations of presidential succession. In
1877, with the Republican Rutherford B. Hayes safely
settled in the White House, the era of sectional strife
finally ended.

Political life went on, but drained of its earlier
drama. In the 1880s there were no Lincolns, no great
national debates. Where defenders of the Union had
once envisioned a social order and an economic system
reshaped by an activist state, now, in the 1880s, the
nation's political leaders retreated to a more modest
conception of state power. There remained an irre-
ducible core of public functions, and even, as on the
question of railroad regulation, a grudging acceptance
of new governmental responsibilities. But the dominant rhetoric celebrated the government that governed
least, and as compared to the Civil War era, American
government did govern less.

The Passive Presidency

There were five presidents from 1877 to 1893: Rutherford B. Hayes (Republican, 1877–1881), James A.
Garfield (Republican, 1881), Chester A. Arthur (Republican, 1881–1885), Grover Cleveland (Democrat,
1885–1889), and Benjamin Harrison (Republican,
1889–1893). All were estimable men. Hayes, Garfield,
and Harrison boasted distinguished war records. Hayes
had served effectively as governor of Ohio for three
terms, and Garfield had done well as a congressional
leader. Arthur, despite his reputation as a hack politician, had shown fine administrative skills as head of
the New York City customs house. Cleveland had an
enviable reputation as a reform mayor of Buffalo and
governor of New York. None was a charismatic leader,
but circumstances, more than personal qualities,
explain why these presidents did not make a larger
mark on history.

The president's biggest job was to dispense political
patronage. Under the spoils system, government

PUCK.

"WHERE IS HE?"

Where Is He?
This *Puck* cartoon, which appeared two weeks after Benjamin
Harrison's defeat for reelection at Grover Cleveland's hands in
1892, is a commentary on Harrison's insignificance as president. The hat in Uncle Sam's hands belonged to Benjamin
Harrison's grandfather, President William Henry Harrison.
Puck started using the hat as a trademark for Benjamin
Harrison after he had been elected in 1888. As his term progressed, the hat grew progressively larger, and the president
progressively smaller. By the time of his defeat, just the hat is
left and Harrison has disappeared altogether.
Bancroft Library, University of California at Berkeley. *Puck*, November 16,
1892.

appointments were treated as rewards for those who
had served the victorious party. Reform of this system
became an urgent issue after President Garfield was
killed in 1881. His assassin, Charles Guiteau, was a
deranged religious fanatic, but advocates of civil-
service reform managed to blame Garfield's death on
the poisonous atmosphere of the spoils system that left
many disappointed in the scramble for government
jobs. The resulting Pendleton Civil Service Act of 1883

created a list of civil-service jobs to be filled on the basis of examinations administered by the new Civil Service Commission. The list originally included only 10 percent of all federal jobs, however, and patronage remained a preoccupation in the White House. When the Democrats won the presidency in 1884 for the first time in nearly thirty years, the pent-up hunger for jobs among the party faithful nearly overwhelmed Grover Cleveland. He was known to complain bitterly about the "damned, everlasting clatter for office." The standards of public administration did rise measurably, but there was no American counterpart to the elite professional civil services taking shape in Britain and Germany in these years.

The executive branch, in any event, had very modest functions. As late as 1897 the White House staff consisted of half a dozen assistants plus a few clerks, doorkeepers, and messengers. Budgetary matters were not the president's province but Congress's; federal agencies accordingly paid more heed to Capitol Hill and the key money-dispensing committees than to the White House. Of the 100,000 federal employees in 1880, 56 percent worked for the U.S. Post Office. During the 1880s even the important government departments—Treasury, State, War, Navy, Interior—were sleepy places carrying on largely routine duties. Virtually all federal income came from customs duties and the excise tax on liquor and tobacco. These sources produced more money than the government spent. The question of how to reduce the federal surplus ranked as one of the most troublesome issues of the 1880s.

As for setting a national agenda, this was—unlike in Lincoln's day—not to be looked for from the White House. "The office of President is essentially executive in nature," Cleveland insisted, not policy making. In fact, as a Democratic president facing a hostile Republican Senate, Cleveland did begin to assert himself on policy matters, but in a mostly negative way: in his first term he vetoed a record number of bills.

Party Politics

On matters of national policy the president took a back seat to Congress. But Congress functioned badly. Procedural rules frequently stymied legislative business. Neither party ever stayed in power long enough to push through a coherent legislative program, and in any case congressional leaders lacked the power to keep party members in line.

Historically, Democrats and Republicans represented somewhat different traditions. The Democrats favored states' rights and limited government; the Republicans were heirs to the Whig enthusiasm for federally assisted economic development. After Reconstruction, however, the Republicans backed away from that activist position and, in truth, party differences became muddy. On most leading issues of the day—civil-service reform, the currency, and regulation of the railroads—the divisions occurred within the parties, not between them.

The Tariff Question. Only free trade remained a real fighting issue. From Lincoln's day onward, high duties had protected American industry against imported goods. It was an article of Republican faith, as President Harrison said in 1892, that "the protective system . . . has been a mighty instrument for the development of the national wealth." The Democrats, free-traders by tradition, regularly attacked Republican protectionism. In practice, however, the tariff was a negotiable issue like any other. Congressmen voted their constituents' interests, regardless of party rhetoric. As a result, every tariff bill was a patchwork of bargains among special interests.

In 1887 President Cleveland cast off his reluctance to lead the nation and took up the tariff issue. Ardently opposed to protectionism, Cleveland devoted his entire annual message to Congress to tariff reform and campaigned on that basis for reelection in 1888. His narrow defeat seemed to confirm the political wisdom of evading big issues. "They told me it would hurt the party," he later wrote. "Perhaps I made a mistake from the party standpoint; but damn it, it was right. I had at least that satisfaction."

Campaign Politics. Issues were treated gingerly partly because the parties were so equally balanced. The Democrats, in retreat immediately after the Civil War, quickly regrouped and by the end of Reconstruction stood on virtually equal terms with the Republicans. Every presidential election from 1876 to 1892 was decided by a thin margin, and neither party gained command of Congress. Political caution seemed wise; any false move on national issues might tip the scales to the other side.

James Bryce, accustomed to the ideological divisions between Tories and Liberals in Britain, grumbled about the pragmatism of American politics. "Neither party has any principles, any distinctive tenets," he wrote. Perhaps Bryce exaggerated when he added, "All has been lost, except office or the hope of it."

The weakening of principled politics was evident in the Republicans' retreat from their Civil War legacy. The major unfinished business after 1877 involved the plight of the former slaves. The Republican agenda called for federal funding to combat illiteracy and, even more threatening to the South, federal protection for black voters in southern congressional elections. Neither measure ever managed to make it through Congress. With little mileage left in Reconstruction politics, the Republicans backpedaled on the race issue and gradually abandoned the blacks to their fate.

That did not stop the Republicans from "waving the bloody shirt" against the "treasonous" Democrats. Service in the Union army gave candidates a strong claim to public office, and veterans' benefits always stood high on the Republican agenda. The Democrats played the same game in the South as the defenders of the Lost Cause. Bryce rightly criticized American politicians for "clinging too long to outworn issues and neglecting the problems . . . which now perplex the country."

Alternatively, campaigns could descend into comedy. In the hard-fought election of 1884, for example, the Democrat Cleveland burst on the scene as a reformer, fresh from his victories over corrupt machine politics in New York State. The Kansas editor William Allen White saw Cleveland as the champion of a people "sick with politics" and "nauseated at all politicians." But years earlier Cleveland, a bachelor, had fathered an illegitimate child, and throughout the campaign he was dogged by the chant "Maw, Maw, where's my Paw?" (after election day, Cleveland's supporters gleefully responded, "He's in the White House, haw-haw-haw"). Cleveland's opponent, James G. Blaine, already on the defensive for taking favors from the railroads, got tangled up in the scandalous charge by a too ardent Republican supporter that the Democrats were the party of "Rum, Romanism and Rebellion." In a twinkling, he had insulted Catholic voters who might have cast their votes for Blaine. In the midst of all the mudslinging, the issues got lost.

The characteristics of public life in the 1880s—the inactivity of the federal government, the evasiveness of the political parties, and the absorption in politics for its own sake—derived ultimately from the conviction that little was at stake in public affairs. In 1887 Cleveland vetoed a small appropriation for drought-stricken Texas farmers with the remark that "though the people support the Government, the Government should not support the people." Governmental activity was itself considered a bad thing. All that the state can do, said Republican senator Roscoe Conkling of New York, "is to clear the way of impediments and dangers, and leave every class and every individual free and safe in the exertions and pursuits of life." Conkling was expressing the political corollary to the doctrine of *laissez faire*—the belief that the government was best which governed least.

The Ideology of Individualism

At the peak of the labor strife of the 1880s, the cotton manufacturer Edward Atkinson gave a talk to the textile workers of Providence, Rhode Island. They had, he told them, no cause for discontent. "There is always plenty of room on the front seats in every profession, every trade, every art, every industry. . . . There are men in this audience who will fill some of those seats, but they won't be boosted into them from behind." (There were certainly women as well in the audience—at least half of the Rhode Island labor force was female—but, as was characteristic of the times, Atkinson assumed that economic opportunity was of interest only to men.) Every man, Atkinson continued, got what he deserved. For example, Cornelius Vanderbilt had amassed a fortune of $200 million by building the New York Central Railroad. Atkinson made some rapid calculations. Every person in the audience consumed about a barrel of flour a year. In 1865 it had cost $3.45 to ship that barrel from Chicago to Providence. In 1885, the New York Central carried it for 68 cents, taking 14 cents as profit while the workingman saved nearly $3.00. "Wasn't Vanderbilt a cheap man for you to employ as a teamster?" Atkinson asked. "Do you grudge him the fourteen cents?"

Atkinson's homely talk went to the roots of conservative American thought: any man, however humble, could rise as far as his talents would carry him; every person received his just reward, great or small; and the success of the individual, so encouraged, contributed to the progress of the whole. How persuasive the workers listening to Atkinson found his message we have no way of knowing. But the confidence with which Atkinson presented his case is evidence of the continuing appeal of the ideology of individualism in the age of industrial expansion.

A wide variety of popular writings trumpeted the individualist creed, from the rags-to-riches tales of Horatio Alger to the stream of success manuals with such titles as *Thoughts for the Young Men of America, or a Few Practical Words of Advice to Those Born in Poverty and Destined to Be Reared in Orphanages* (1871). It was a lesson celebrated in the lives of such self-made men as Andrew Carnegie, whose book *Triumphant Democracy* (1886) paid homage to a nation that had enabled a penniless Scottish child to rise from bobbin boy to steel magnate.

The Gospel of Wealth. From the pulpit came the assurances of the Episcopal bishop William Lawrence of Massachusetts that "Godliness is in league with riches." Bishop Lawrence was voicing a tradition in American Protestantism that went back to the Puritans: success in one's earthly calling signified the promise of eternal salvation. It was all too easy for a conservative ministry to make morally reassuring the furious acquisitiveness of industrial America. "To secure wealth is an honorable ambition," intoned the Baptist minister Russell H. Conwell in his lecture "Acres of Diamonds." "Money is power. Every good man and woman ought to strive for power, to do good with it when obtained." Conwell's lecture—its notion of wealth as stewardship—served as a text for what became known as the Gospel of Wealth. Its leading exemplar, Andrew Carnegie, argued that the rich had a duty to put their money to social use. They should not coddle the less

FACING THE WORLD

ALGER

Facing the World
The cover of this Horatio Alger novel (1893) captures the myth of opportunity that Edward Atkinson extolled to his audience of textile workers. Our hero, Harry Vane, is a poor but earnest lad, ready to make his way in the world and, despite the many obstacles thrown in his path, sure to succeed. In some 135 books Horatio Alger repeated this story, with minor variations, for an eager reading public that numbered in the millions.
Frank and Marie-Therese Wood Print Collections, Alexandria, Virginia.

privileged, Carnegie said, but provide the libraries, education, and cultural and scientific institutions by which the worthy poor might prepare themselves for life's challenges.

Social Darwinism. American individualism drew strong intellectual support from science. In *The Origin of Species* (1859) the British naturalist Charles Darwin had developed a bold hypothesis to explain the evolution of plants and animals. In nature, Darwin wrote, all living things struggle and compete. Individual members of a species are born with characteristics that help them survive in their particular environment: camouflage coloring for a bird, for example, or resistance to

thirst in a desert animal. Because these survival characteristics are genetic, they are transmitted to future generations and become dominant in the species. This view of evolution, which Darwin called *natural selection*, created a revolution in biological science.

Drawing on Darwin, the British philosopher Herbert Spencer developed an elaborate analysis of how human society evolved through constant competition and "survival of the fittest." Social Darwinism, as Spencer's ideas became known, was championed in America by William Graham Sumner, a sociology professor at Yale. Competition, said Sumner, is a law of nature that "can no more be done away with than gravitation." And who are the fittest? "The millionaires. . . . They may fairly be regarded as the naturally selected agents of society. They get high wages and live in luxury, but the bargain is a good one for society."

Social Darwinists regarded with horror any government interference with social processes. "The great stream of time and earthly things will sweep on just the same in spite of us," Sumner wrote in a famous essay, "The Absurd Attempt to Make the World Over" (1894). "That is why it is the greatest folly of which a man can be capable to sit down with a slate and pencil to plan out a new social world." As for the government, it had "at bottom . . . two chief things . . . with which to deal. They are the property of men and the honor of women. These it has to defend against crime."

The Supremacy of the Courts

Suspicion of activist government not only paralyzed political initiative; it also shifted power away from the executive and legislative branches. "The task of constitutional government," declared Sumner, "is to devise institutions which shall come into play at critical periods to prevent the abusive control of the powers of a state by the controlling classes in it." Sumner meant the judiciary. From the 1870s onward the courts increasingly accepted the role that he assigned to them, becoming the guardians of the rights of private property.

Under the federal system as it was understood in the late nineteenth century, the states retained primary responsibility for social welfare and economic regulation. They were responsible for exercising their *police powers* to ensure the health, safety, and morals of their citizens. The leading contemporary question in American law was where to strike the balance between state responsibility for the general welfare and the liberty of individuals to pursue their private interests. Most states, caught up in the conservative ethos of the day, were themselves cutting back on expenditures and public services. Even so, there were more than enough state initiatives to alarm vigilant judges. Thus, in the landmark case *In Re Jacobs* (1885), the New York Supreme Court struck down a state law prohibiting cigar making in sweatshop tenements on the grounds that such regulation exceeded the police powers of the state. The high courts of the states declared unconstitutional a record number of laws during the 1880s.

Increasingly, however, it was federal judges who took up the battle against state activism. The Supreme Court's crucial weapon in this campaign was the Fourteenth Amendment (1868), which prohibited the states from depriving "any person of life, liberty, or property, without due process of law." The due-process clause had been adopted during Reconstruction to protect the civil rights of the former slaves. But due process protected the property rights and contractual liberty of any "person," and legally, corporations counted as persons. So interpreted, the Fourteenth Amendment became by the turn of the century a powerful means of restraining the states in the use of their police powers to regulate private business.

The Supreme Court similarly hamstrung the federal government by a narrow reading of its constitutional powers. In 1895 the Court ruled that the federal power to regulate interstate commerce did not cover manufacturing and struck down a federal income tax law. And in areas where federal power was undeniable—such as the regulation of railroads—the Supreme Court watched like a hawk for undue interferences with the rights of property.

The preeminent conservative jurist of the day, Stephen J. Field, made no bones about the dangers he saw in the nation's headlong industrial development. "As population and wealth increase—as the inequalities in the conditions of men become more and more marked and disturbing—as . . . angry menaces against order find vent in loud denunciations—it becomes more and more the imperative duty of the court to enforce with a firm hand every guarantee of the Constitution."

Power conferred status. The law, not politics, attracted the ablest people and held the public's esteem. A Wisconsin judge boasted: "The bench symbolizes on earth the throne of divine justice. . . . Law in its highest sense is the will of God." Judicial supremacy reflected how dominant the ideology of individualism had become in industrial America, and also how low American politicians had fallen in the esteem of their countrymen.

Sources of Popular Participation

★

For all the criticism leveled against it, politics figured centrally in the nation's life. Proportionately more voters turned out in presidential elections from 1876 to

1892 than at any other time in American history. People voted Democratic or Republican for a lifetime. Many actively participated. In New York City, a fourth of all Republican voters were dues-paying party members. National conventions attracted huge crowds. "The excitement, the mental and physical strains," remarked an Indiana Republican after the 1888 convention, "are surpassed only by prolonged battle in actual warfare, as I have been told by officers of the Civil War who later engaged in convention struggles." The convention he described had nominated the colorless Benjamin Harrison on a routine platform. What was all the excitement about?

Cultural Politics: Party, Religion, and Ethnicity

In the late nineteenth century, politics was a vibrant part of the nation's culture. The journalist George M. Towle told a British audience that America "is a land of conventions and assemblies, where it is the most natural thing in the world for people to get together in meetings, where almost every event is the occasion for speechmaking." Spellbinding orators such as Herbert G. Ingersoll held forth at Republican rallies. During the election season, the party faithful marched in impressive torchlight parades. Party paraphernalia flooded the country—handkerchiefs, mugs, posters, and buttons emblazoned with the Democratic donkey or the Republican elephant, symbols that had been adopted in the 1870s. In 1888 the presidential hopefuls were pictured on cards—like baseball players—packed into Honest Long Cut tobacco. Campaigns had the suspense of baseball pennant races plus the excitement of the circus coming to town. In an age before movies and radio, politics ranked as one of the great American forms of entertainment.

Party loyalty was a deadly serious matter, however. Long after the Civil War, emotions ran high. Among family friends in Cleveland, recalled urban reformer Brand Whitlock, the Republican Party was "a synonym for patriotism, another name for the nation. It was inconceivable that any self-respecting person should be a Democrat." Or, among southerners, that any self-respecting person could be a Republican.

Beyond these sectional differences, the most important determinants of party loyalty were religion and ethnicity. Statistically, northern Democrats tended to be foreign-born and Catholic, while Republicans tended to be native-born and Protestant. (The South, which received few immigrants, had a cultural politics driven by race rather than by ethnicity.) Among Protestants, the more *pietistic* a person's faith was—that is, the more personal and direct the believer's relationship to God—the more likely he or she was to be a Republican, and to favor using the powers of the state to legislate public morality and regulate individual behavior. Northern Democrats, in contrast, favored "the largest individual liberty consistent with public order."

During the 1880s ethnic tensions began to build up in many cities. Education became an arena of bitter conflict. One issue was whether instruction would be in English in the schools. Immigrant groups often wanted their children taught in their native languages. In response, native-born Americans passed laws making English the language of instruction. In St. Louis, a heavily German city, the longstanding policy of teaching German to the entire student body was overturned after a bitter campaign.

Religion was an even more explosive educational issue. Catholics fought a losing battle over public funding of parochial schools. By 1900 such aid had been prohibited by twenty-three states. In Boston a furious controversy broke out in 1888 over the use of an anti-Catholic history textbook. When the school board withdrew the offending book, angry Protestants mounted a campaign, threw the moderates off the board, and returned the text to the curriculum.

Then there was the regulation of public morals. In many states, so-called blue laws restricted activity on Sundays. When Nebraska banned Sunday baseball, the state supreme court approved the law as a blow struck in "the contest between Christianity and wrong." But German and Irish Catholics, who saw nothing evil in a bit of fun on Sunday, considered blue laws a violation of their personal freedom.

Ethnocultural conflict also flared over the liquor question. In a speech introducing the first attempt at national prohibition in 1876, Senator Henry W. Blair of New Hampshire laid down a challenge to his immigrant critics: "Upon discussion of this issue Irishman and German will in due time demonstrate that they are Americans." Although the Blair constitutional amendment languished, many states adopted strict licensing and local-option laws governing the sale and consumption of alcoholic beverages. Indiana permitted drinking, but only joylessly in rooms containing "no devices for amusement or music . . . of any kind."

Because the hottest social issues of the day—education, the liquor question, and observance of the Sabbath—were also party issues, they lent deep significance to party affiliation (Figure 18.1). And because these issues were fought out mostly at the state and local levels, they hit very close to home. Crusading Methodists thought of the Republican Party as the party of morality. Embattled Irish and German Catholics saw the Democratic Party as the defender of their freedoms.

Organizational Politics

Political life was also important because of the remarkable organizational activity it generated. By the 1870s both major parties had evolved formal, well-organized

The Presidential B.B. Club (1888)
On the left, Grover Cleveland is the baseman; at center Benjamin Harrison is at bat; and on the right, Cleveland tags Harrison out—not, alas, the right prediction, since Harrison won the 1888 election.
Collection of Janice L. and David J. Frent.

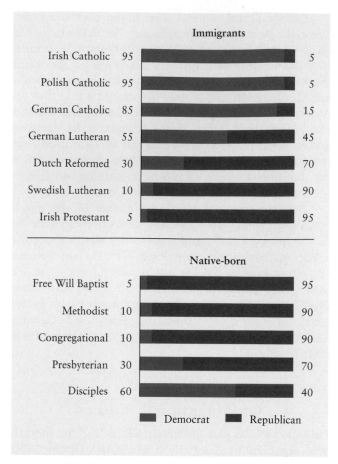

Immigrants

Irish Catholic	95	5
Polish Catholic	95	5
German Catholic	85	15
German Lutheran	55	45
Dutch Reformed	30	70
Swedish Lutheran	10	90
Irish Protestant	5	95

Native-born

Free Will Baptist	5	95
Methodist	10	90
Congregational	10	90
Presbyterian	30	70
Disciples	60	40

■ Democrat   ■ Republican

FIGURE 18.1
Ethnocultural Voting Patterns in the Midwest, 1870–1892
These figures demonstrate how voting patterns among mid-
westerners reflected ethnicity and religion in the late nineteenth century. Especially striking is the overwhelming
preference by immigrant Catholics for the Democratic Party.
Among Protestants there was an equally strong preference
for the Republican Party by certain groups of immigrants
(Swedish Lutherans and Irish Protestants) and native-born
(Free Will Baptists, Methodists, and Congregationalists), but
other Protestant groups were more evenly divided in their
party preferences.

structures. At the base lay the precinct or ward, whose
meetings could be attended by all party members.
County, state, and national committees ran the ongoing
business of the parties. Conventions determined party
rules, adopted platforms, and selected each party's candidates for public office.

At election time the party's main job was to get out
the vote. Wherever elections were close and hard
fought, the parties mounted intensive efforts organized
down to the individual voter. In Indiana, for example,
the Republicans appointed 10,000 "district men" in
1884, each responsible for turning out a designated
group of voters. The Pennsylvania Republican Party
maintained a list of 800,000 voters classified by degree
of voting reliability.

Only professionals could manage such a highly
organized political system. The German sociologist
Max Weber remarked that Americans regarded politics
as a "vocation." This factor, above all else, gave American politics its special character. The distinguishing
trait of American politicians, James Bryce observed,
was "that their whole time is more frequently given to
political work, that most of them draw an income from
politics . . . that they . . . are proficient in the arts of
popular oratory, of electioneering, and of party management." The party system required professionals, and
professionalism created careers. Politics, like professional sports and trade unionism, served as an avenue
of upward mobility for the many whose ethnic or class
background barred them from the opportunities open
to other Americans.

Machine Politics. Party administration seemed, on
its face, highly democratic, since in theory all power
derived from the party members in the precincts and
wards. In practice, however, the parties were run by
unofficial internal organizations—*machines*—that consisted of insiders willing to accept discipline and do
party work in exchange for getting on the public payroll
or pocketing bribes and other forms of "graft." The
machines tended toward one-man rule, although the
"boss" ruled more by the consent of the secondary leaders than by his own absolute power.

Absorbed in the tasks of power brokerage,
machine bosses treated public issues as somewhat
irrelevant. The high stakes of money, jobs, and influence made for intense factionalism. In New York,
Manhattan's Tammany Hall was always at odds with
the upstate Democratic machine run by Senator
David B. Hill. At the national level, Republicans
fought bitterly among themselves after Ulysses S.
Grant left the White House in 1877. For the next six
years the party was divided into two warring factions—the Stalwarts, who followed Senator Roscoe
Conkling of New York, and the Halfbreeds, led by
James G. Blaine of Maine. The split was sparked by a
personal feud between Conkling and Blaine, but it
persisted because of a furious struggle over patronage. The Halfbreeds represented a newer Republican
generation that was more inclined to pay lip service
to political reform and was less committed to the old
Civil War issues. But issues were secondary in the war
between Stalwarts and Halfbreeds. They were really
fighting over the spoils of party politics.

And yet the record was not wholly negative.
Machine politics raised the standards of government in
certain ways. Disciplined professionals, veterans of
machine politics, improved the performance of state
legislatures and the Congress because they were more
experienced in the give-and-take of politics. More
important, party machines filled a void in the nation's

The Levi P. Morton Association
The top-hatted gentlemen in this photograph constituted the local Republican Party
organization of Newport, Rhode Island, named in honor of Levi P. Morton, Republican
leader and vice-president during the Benjamin Harrison administration (1889–1893).
The maleness of party politics leaps from the photograph and asserts more clearly
than a thousand words why the suffragist demand for the right to vote was met with
ridicule and disbelief.
Newport Historical Society.

public life. They did informally much of what the government left undone in this era, especially in the cities (see Chapter 19).

The Mugwumps. But machine politics never managed to win the respect of the general public. Many of the nation's social elite—intellectuals, well-to-do businessmen, and old-line families—resented a politics that excluded people like themselves, the "best men." There was, too, a genuine clash of values. Political reformers called for "disinterestedness" and "independence"—the opposite of the self-serving careerism and party regularity fostered by the machine system. Many of them had earned their spurs as Liberal Republicans who had broken from the party and fought President Grant's reelection in 1872.

In 1884 Carl Schurz, Edwin L. Godkin, and Charles Francis Adams Jr. again left the Republican Party because they associated its presidential candidate, James G. Blaine, with corrupt politics. Mainly from New York and Massachusetts, these Republicans became known as Mugwumps—a derisive bit of contemporary slang, supposedly of Indian origin, referring to pompous or self-important persons. The Mugwumps threw their support to the Democrat Grover Cleveland and may have ensured his victory by giving him the margin for carrying New York State.

After the 1884 election, the enthusiasm for reform spilled over into local politics, spawning good-government campaigns across the country. Although they won some municipal victories, the Mugwumps were more effective at molding public opinion. Controlling the influential newspapers and journals read by the educated middle class, the Mugwumps defined the terms of debate and denied the machine system public legitimacy.

The Mugwumps registered their biggest success in the campaign for the secret ballot, which had been pioneered in Australia. Under this reform, citizens, in the privacy of a voting booth, would mark an official ballot listing the candidates of all the parties instead of submitting a party-supplied ticket in public view at the polling place. Adopted throughout the United States in the early 1890s, the Australian ballot freed voters from party surveillance as they exercised the right to vote.

The Mugwumps were reformers, but not on behalf of social justice. The problems of working people did not evoke their sympathy, nor did they favor using the powers of the state to ease the suffering of the poor. As far as the Mugwumps were concerned, that government was best which governed least. Theirs was the brand of "reform" perfectly in keeping with a politics of the status quo.

Women's Political Culture

The young Theodore Roosevelt, an up-and-coming Republican state politician in 1884, referred to the Mugwumps contemptuously as "man-milliners." The sexual slur was not accidental. In attacking organizational politics, the Mugwumps were challenging one of the bastions of male society. At party meetings and conventions, men carried on not only the business of politics but also the satisfying rituals of male sociability amid cigar smoke and whiskey. Politics was identified with manliness. It was competitive. It dealt in the commerce of power. It was frankly self-aggrandizing. Party politics, in short, was no place for a woman.

So, naturally, the woman suffrage movement met with fierce opposition. Blocked in their efforts to get a constitutional amendment introduced in Congress, suffragists concentrated on state campaigns. But except in Wyoming, Idaho, Colorado, and Utah, the most they could win in the late nineteenth century was the right to vote for school boards or on tax issues. "Men are ordained to govern in all forceful and material things, because they are men," asserted an antisuffrage resolution, "while women, by the same decree of God and nature, are equally fitted to bear rule in a higher and more spiritual realm, where the strong frame and the weighty brain count for less"—that is to say, not in politics.

Yet this invocation of the doctrine of "separate spheres"—that men and women had different natures, and that women's nature fitted them for "a higher and more spiritual realm"—did open a channel for women to enter public life. "Women's place is Home," acknowledged the journalist Retha Childe Dorr. "But Home is not contained within the four walls of an individual house. Home is the community. The city full of people is the Family. . . . And badly do the Home and Family need their mother." Indeed, women since the early nineteenth century had engaged in charitable and reform activities. Women's organizations fought prostitution, assisted the poor, agitated for the reform of women's prisons, and tried to improve educational and job opportunities for women. Since many of these goals required state intervention, women's organizations of necessity became politically active, but not, they stressed, out of any desire to participate in partisan politics or to gain the ballot. Quite the contrary: women were bent on creating their own political sphere.

Thus in 1869, Sorosis, a women's professional club in New York City, convened a Women's Parliament in the hope of launching a parallel government responsible for public matters of concern to women. Nothing came of the Women's Parliament, but it did indicate the degree to which women's sphere could take a political form. If not a parallel government, the social activism of women certainly gave rise to a female political cul-

Colorado Women Are Citizens
Colorado was one of four western states to grant women full voting rights before 1900—and the first to do so by referendum. The next day, November 9, 1893, the *Denver Republican* congratulated "the men of Colorado who showed the world yesterday that they were neither afraid nor ashamed to give their women equal rights with themselves." It would be twenty-seven more years before other men of the country showed similar gumption by ratifying the Nineteenth Amendment (1920), granting women the right to vote.
Denver Public Library, Western History Division.

ture that made itself felt in the public life of late nineteenth-century America.

No issue joined home and politics more poignantly than did the liquor question. Just before Christmas in 1873 the women of Hillsboro, Ohio, began to hold vigils and prayer meetings in front of the town's saloons, pleading with the owners to close down and end the suffering of families of hard-drinking fathers. Thus began a spontaneous uprising of women that spread across the country and closed an estimated 3,000 saloons. From this agitation came the Woman's Christian Temperance Union (WCTU), which after its formation in 1874 rapidly blossomed into the largest organization of women in the country.

Because it excluded men, the WCTU was the spawning ground for a new generation of women leaders. Under the guidance of Frances Willard, who

OUT OF WORK—
And the reason why.

Wanted, Sober Men

This drawing appeared in a magazine in 1899, twenty-five years after the women of Hillsboro, Ohio, rose in revolt against the town's saloonkeepers and launched the Woman's Christian Temperance Union (WCTU). But the emotion it expresses had not changed—that the saloon was the enemy of the family.
Culver Pictures.

became president in 1879, the WCTU moved beyond temperance and adopted a "Do-Everything" policy. Alcoholism, women recognized, was not simply a personal failing; it stemmed from larger social evils afflicting men. Willard also wanted to attract women who had no particular interest in the liquor question. Local bodies were encouraged to undertake causes that were important in their own communities. By 1889 the WCTU had thirty-nine departments concerned with such issues as labor, prostitution, health, and international peace.

Most important, the WCTU was drawn to woman suffrage. This was necessary, Willard argued, "because the liquor traffic is entrenched in law, and law grows out of the will of majorities, and majorities of women are against the liquor traffic." The WCTU began by stressing moral persuasion and personal discipline— hence the word "temperance" in its name—but

expanded its attack on liquor to include prohibition by law. Women needed the vote, said Willard, to fulfill their social responsibilities *as women* (see American Voices, "Helen Potter: The Case for Women's Political Rights," p. 586). This was very different from the claim made by the suffragists—that voting was an inherent right of all citizens as individuals—and was less threatening to masculine pride.

Not much changed in the short run. The WCTU was internally divided on the suffrage issue and did not become a major participant in the later struggles for women's right to vote. But by linking women's social concerns and women's political participation, the WCTU helped lay the groundwork for a fresh, broader-based attack on male electoral politics in the early twentieth century. And in the meantime, even without the vote, the WCTU demonstrated how potent a voice women could find in the public realm, and how vibrant a political culture they could build.

The Crisis of American Politics: The 1890s

Benjamin Harrison's election to the presidency in 1888 was the last of the cliff-hanger victories: the Democrat Grover Cleveland actually got a larger popular vote. Over the next few years, the tide went heavily against the Republicans. In 1890 Democrats took the House of Representatives decisively, capturing 235 seats to the Republicans' 88, and won a number of governorships in normally Republican states. These losses can partly be explained by the lackluster performance of the Harrison administration and by the success of the Democrats at tarring the protectionist McKinley Tariff of 1890 as a giveaway for the vested interests. Less visible but more ominous for the Republicans was an erosion of grass-roots support. The Prohibition Party, which had first appeared in national elections in 1876, made inroads among evangelical Protestants, while the Democrats gained among moderates in local battles over education and public morality. In 1892 Cleveland regained the presidency by the largest margin in twenty years.

Had everything else remained equal, the events of 1890 and 1892 might have inaugurated a long period of Democratic supremacy. But everything else did not remain equal. By the time of Cleveland's inauguration, rising farm foreclosures and railroad bankruptcies signaled economic trouble. On May 3, 1893, the stock market crashed. By year's end, 16,000 firms and hundreds of banks had failed. In Chicago 100,000 jobless

HELEN POTTER

The Case for Women's Political Rights

———————★———————

In 1883 Helen Potter, a New York educator, testified before the Senate Committee on Education and Labor. She meant to speak about the sanitary conditions of the poor in New York City, but in the course of her testimony she delivered a powerful indictment of the unequal treatment of women that spoke volumes about the evolving women's political culture of the late nineteenth century.

The Witness. It is really an important question—this of the condition of women in our community. When I was a young girl I had some ambition, and when I heard a good speaker, or when I read something written by a good writer, I had an ambition to do something of that kind myself. I was exceedingly anxious to preach, but the churches would not have me; why, they said that a woman must not be heard. . . .

Q. I suppose you have an idea that women might abolish some of the tricks of the politician's trade?

A. Well, sir, it would take them a long time to learn to dare to do those things that men do in the way of politics—to sell and buy votes. . . .

Q. What would be the effect of conferring suffrage upon women? Would not the effect be injurious to the moral character and high influence of woman, if she should devote herself to the tricks of the politician's trade, which you very properly criticize so severely?

A. . . . I certainly think it would clean our streets, and I think it would purify politics, at least for the next two hundred years. It would take about that time to get women to understand the tricks of politi-cians as at present practiced. I do not think that women would be injured by it. . . . This Government is based upon the will of the people—women are "people," yet we have not a word to say about the laws. You will hear women in the course of your acquaintance say they wish they were men; I never heard a man say he wished he was a woman. . . .

Q. Why do you think that the suffrage is not extended to women by men—what is the true reason, the radical reason, why men do not give up one half their political power to women?

A. Well, it may arise from a false notion of gallantry. I think most men feel like taking care of, and protecting the ladies. . . . It would be all very well, perhaps, if all women had representatives, and if all had a generous, straightforward honorable man to represent them. But take the case of a good woman who has a drunken husband; how can he represent her? He votes for liquor and for everything he may happen to want, even though it may ruin her and turn her out of doors, and even though it may ruin her children. If the husband is a bad man would it not be better for that woman to represent herself?

Q. What effect do you think the extension of the suffrage to women would have upon their material condition, their wage-earning power and the like?

A. They would get equal pay for equal work of equal value. I do not think a woman ought to be paid the price of an expert, when she is not herself an expert, but I believe there would be a stimulus for a woman to fit herself for the very best work. What stimulus is there for woman to fit herself properly, if she never can attain the highest pay, no matter what sort of work she does? If women had a vote I think larger avenues of livelihood would be opened for them and they would be more respected by the governmental powers.

———————

Source: U.S. Senate, Committee on Education and Labor, *Report upon Relations between Labor and Capital,* II (1885), 627, 629–632.

workers walked the streets; nationwide, the unemployment rate soared to over 20 percent. As always in hard times, suffering and unrest mounted alarmingly.

As the economic crisis of the 1890s set in, which party would prevail—and on what platform—became an open question. The first challenge to the political status quo arrived from the West and South, where the grievances of farmers had begun to crystallize into the radical program of the Populist Party.

The Populist Revolt

Farmers were of necessity joiners. They needed organization to overcome their social isolation and to obtain crucial economic services—hence the enormous appeal of the Patrons of Husbandry (see Chapter 16), which had spread across the Midwest after 1867, and, after the Grange's decline, of the farmers' alliances that began to spring up among southern and western farmers. From diffuse organizational beginnings, two dominant organizations emerged. One was the Farmers' Alliance of the Northwest, which was confined mainly to the midwestern states. More dynamic was the National (or Southern) Farmers' Alliance, which in the mid-1880s spread rapidly from Texas onto the Great Plains and eastward into the cotton South, as "travelling lecturers" extolled the virtues of cooperative activity and reminded farmers of "their obligation to stand as a great conservative body against the encroachments of monopolies and . . . the growing corruption of wealth and power." While thus recapitulating Granger resentment against railroads and merchants that had fueled earlier third-party movements, the alliances conceived of themselves as agents of social and economic reform rather than as new political parties.

The Texas alliance established a massive cooperative, the Texas Exchange, that marketed the crops of cotton farmers and provided them with cheap credit. When cotton prices fell sharply in 1891, the Texas Exchange failed. The Texas alliance then proposed a new scheme: a subtreasury system that would enable farmers to store their crops in public warehouses. Farmers would be able to borrow against those crops from a federally supplied fund at low interest rates until prices rose enough so that their cotton could be profitably marketed. The subtreasury plan would provide the same credit and marketing functions as had the defunct Texas Exchange, but with a crucial difference: the federal government would play the key role. When the Democratic Party declared the subtreasury plan too radical, the Texas alliance decided to strike out in politics independently.

These events in Texas revealed, with special clarity, a process of politicization that went on throughout the alliance movement. Rebuffed by the established parties, alliancemen more or less reluctantly abandoned their Democratic and Republican allegiances. Across the South and West, as state alliances grew stronger

and more impatient, they began to field independent slates. In 1890 third parties won control of the Nebraska and Kansas legislatures and in the South captured several governorships and eight state legislatures. These successes led to the formation of the national People's (Populist) Party. In the 1892 election, with the veteran antimonopoly campaigner James B. Weaver as their presidential candidate, the Populists captured a million votes and carried four western states (Map 18.1). For the first time agrarian protest truly challenged the national two-party system.

Populism was distinguished also by the many women in the movement. In the established parties, the grass-roots organizations—the local political clubs—were for men only. Populism, in contrast, arose from a network of suballiances that had formed for largely social purposes and that welcomed women. "The Alliance has come to redeem woman from her enslaved condition," proclaimed a female member from Texas. "She is admitted into the organization as an equal to her brother" and is free of "the ostracism which has impeded her intellectual progress in the past."

Although women participated actively and served prominently as speakers and lecturers, only a handful achieved high office in the alliances, and their role diminished once the Populist Party entered politics. In

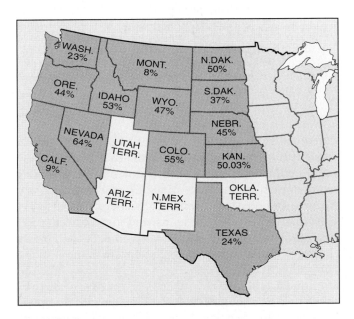

MAP 18.1
The Heyday of Western Populism, 1892
This map shows the percentage of the popular vote won by James B. Weaver, the People's Party candidate, in the presidential election of 1892. Except in California and Montana, the Populists won broad support across the West and genuinely threatened the established parties in that region.

Mary Elizabeth Lease

As a political movement, the Populists were short on cash and organization, but long on rank-and-file zeal and tub-thumping oratory. No one was more rousing on the stump than Mary Elizabeth Lease, who came from a Kansas homestead and pulled no punches. "What you farmers need to do," she proclaimed in her speeches, "is to raise less corn and more *Hell!*" Kansas State Historical Society.

deference to the southern wing, the Populist platform was silent on woman suffrage. Still, neither Democrats nor Republicans would have countenanced a spokeswoman such as the fiery Mary Elizabeth Lease, who became famous for calling on farmers "to raise less corn and more hell." Lease insisted just as strenuously on Populism's "grand and holy mission . . . to place the mothers of this nation on an equality with the fathers."

Populist Ideology.　Populism was driven as much by ideology as by the quest for political power. The problems afflicting farmers, Populists felt, could stem only from some basic evil. They identified this evil as the control of the "money power" over the levers of the economic system. "There are but two sides," proclaimed a Populist manifesto. "On the one side are the allied hosts of monopolies, the money power, great trusts and railroad corporations. . . . On the other are

the farmers, laborers, merchants and all the people who produce wealth. . . . Between these two there is no middle ground."

By this reasoning, farmers and workers formed a single producer class. Thus the Southern Farmers' Alliance renamed itself in 1889 the National Farmers' Alliance and Industrial Union. The title was not merely rhetorical. Organized in Knights of Labor assemblies, Texas railroad workers and Colorado miners cooperated with the farmers' alliances, got their support in strikes, and actively participated in forming state Populist parties. The platform of the national party contained strong labor planks, and party leaders earnestly sought the support of the labor movement. In its explicit class appeal—in recognizing that "the irrepressible conflict between capital and labor is upon us"—Populism parted company from the two mainstream parties.

In an age dominated by laissez-faire doctrine, what most distinguished Populism from the major parties was its positive attitude toward the state (see American Voices, "Datus E. Meyer: Angry Farmers," p. 590). The Populist platform declared: "We believe that the powers of government—in other words, of the people—should be expanded as rapidly and as far as the good sense of an intelligent people and the teachings of experience shall justify, to the end that oppression, injustice and poverty should eventually cease in the land." Populists such as Lorenzo Dow Lewelling, governor of Kansas, considered it to be "the business of the Government to make it possible for me to live and sustain the life of my family."

The Omaha platform, adopted at the founding convention of 1892, called for nationalization of the railroads and communications; protection of the land, including natural resources, from monopoly and foreign ownership; a graduated income tax; the creation of postal savings banks; the Texas alliance's subtreasury plan; and "the free and unlimited coinage of silver." From this array of issues, free silver emerged as the overriding demand of the Populist Party.

Free Silver.　Cotton and grain farmers were especially vulnerable to falling commodity prices (see Chapter 16). In the early 1890s rock-bottom prices wreaked havoc among cotton, wheat, and corn growers. Under this pressure, farmers turned to free silver, which they hoped, by increasing the money supply, would raise farm prices and enable them to pay back their debts with cheaper dollars. In addition, free silver would bring in hefty contributions to the Populist Party from silver-mining interests. These mine operators, scornful though they might be of Populist radicalism, yearned for the day when the government would buy at a premium price all the silver they could produce, and to that end they were prepared to support the Populists.

En Route to a Populist Rally, Dickinson County, Kansas
Farm people traveled miles to rallies and meetings for the chance to voice their grievances and socialize with like-minded folks. This tradition infused Populism with a special fervor. Gatherings such as the one these Kansans were heading to were a visible sign of what Populism meant—a movement of the "people."
Kansas State Historical Society.

Free silver was opposed by urban social reformers such as Henry Demarest Lloyd of Chicago and by agrarian radicals such as Georgia's Tom Watson. They argued that free silver would undercut the broader Populist program and drive away wage earners, who had no enthusiasm for inflationary measures. Any chance of a farmer-labor alliance that might transform Populism into an American version of the social democratic parties of Europe would be doomed. As Lloyd complained, free silver was "the cowbird of reform," stealing in and taking over the nest that others had built.

Despite the fierce debate within the party, the outcome was never in doubt. The political appeal of free silver was simply too great. But once Populists made that choice, they fatally compromised their party's capacity to maintain an independent existence. For free silver was not an issue over which the Populists held a monopoly. Free silver was, on the contrary, a question at the very center of mainstream politics in the 1890s.

Money and Politics

In a rapidly developing economy such as nineteenth-century America's, the money supply is bound to be a big political issue. Money has to increase rapidly enough to meet the economy's needs or growth will be stifled. How fast the money supply should grow, however, is a question that creates sharp divisions. Inflationists—debtors and producers of goods—want a larger money supply: more money in circulation raises prices and reduces the real cost of borrowing. The "sound-money" people—creditors, individuals on fixed incomes, those in the slower-growing sectors of the economy—have an opposite interest.

Before the Civil War the main source of the nation's money supply had been the banknotes circulated by several thousand state banks. Although more or less subject to state regulation, these banks issued notes in their private role as providers of credit to their customers. The banknotes they gave to borrowers circulated as money until presented to the banks for redemption. The burgeoning economy's need for money was amply met by the state banks, although the goodness of the banknotes—the ability of the issuing banks to stand behind their notes and redeem them at face value—was always uncertain. During the Civil War this freewheeling system came to an end. The Banking Act of 1863 sharply curtailed the freedom of the state banks to create money. They could still issue banknotes, but only insofar as these notes were backed by U.S. government bonds.

The economic impact of this nationalizing action was not immediately felt because the Lincoln administration itself was printing large amounts of paper money—greenbacks, so called—to finance the Civil War. After the war, however, the sound money interests lobbied powerfully for a return to the bimetallic policy prevailing ever since the founding of the republic, which was to base the federal currency on the *specie*—gold and silver—held by the U.S. Treasury. The issue was hotly debated for a decade, but in 1875 the inflationists were defeated, and the circulation of greenbacks as legal tender—that is, backed by nothing more than the good faith of the federal government—came to an end. With the state banknotes also in short supply, the country entered an era of chronic deflation and tight credit.

This was the context out of which the silver question emerged. The country had always operated on a

DATUS E. MEYER
Angry Farmers

———— ★ ————

*I*n his testimony before a Senate committee, Datus Meyer, a Minnesota farmer, details farmers' grievances against the railroads. Underlying his remarks is his sense of farmers as victims of powers beyond their control—hence the demand for government intervention, one of the hallmarks of Populism.

St. Paul, Minnesota, June 25, 1885

Mr. Meyer. There is very great discontent among the smaller farmers of the State in regard to [the railroads], arising both from discrimination and what they consider extortion. To illustrate what I mean by that, I can produce for you freight receipts that will show where car-loads of stuff have been brought from Springfield, Ohio, to Saint Paul at a charge of $65, a distance of about 800 miles, and carried to Saint Vincent, a distance of about 400 miles, and charged $155. . . . The plan of discriminating, and charging more for a short than for a long haul near competing points, is almost universal. . . . Then there were discriminations [that] proved they absolutely refused to allow a small farmer to have a car at all, in which to load his corn and ship it away, unless he put it through that elevator system . . . on account of having given the exclusive privilege to those elevator lines. . . . Another thing that was practiced . . . was this: They have what they call a transit-rate system in the southern part of the State. If I wanted to ship grain to Milwaukee I would have to pay the rate clear through to Chicago before they would allow me to ship at all. Then they would give me a ticket for the difference between Milwaukee and Chicago, and I would have to sell that ticket for whatever I could get for it. These abuses have caused the farmers to think that they are very much abused in the matter.

You know how hard farmers are to organize; and yet there are over three hundred secret organizations in this State, organized for the purpose of obtaining redress. . . . They think they ought to have protection; and they look to Congress to give them some relief in these matters. . . . I tell you that the feeling through the country among the small farmers and dealers, who suffer, is much greater than you think. . . . If you could get a rule laid down by which the small farmer believed he was getting justice he would be contented; but as soon as he feels that he is not getting justice there is great discontent, and that discontent will grow. . . .

The Chairman. They have a right now to go into court and sue if they are charged an unreasonable rate?

Mr. Meyer. That is true. But suppose a farmer sues under the common law. The railroads have their attorneys hired and paid for all the time, and they can carry that suit on until an ordinary farmer is ruined. He cannot contend with the railroads.

The Chairman. What would you have done?

Mr. Meyer. I would put a commission between the farmer and the railroads that would see that he obtains justice. That is what I would have done, and what the farmers desire shall be done. You can depend on that.

———

Source: U.S. Senate, Select Committee on Interstate Commerce, *Report*, 49th Cong., 1st sess. (1886), Part 2, 1335–1337; reprinted in Stanley I. Kutler, ed., *Looking for America*, vol. 2, 2nd ed. (New York: Norton, 1975), 171–174.

---

bimetallic standard, but the supply of silver had gradually tightened, and as silver became more valuable as metal than as money, silver coins disappeared from circulation. In 1873 silver was officially dropped as a medium of exchange. Soon afterward, great silver discoveries occurred in the West, and silver prices fell. Inflationists began to agitate for a resumption of the traditional bimetallic policy: if the government resumed buying silver at the fixed ratio prevailing before 1873—16 ounces of silver equaling 1 ounce of gold—silver would flow into the Treasury and greatly expand the volume of currency.

With so much at stake for so many people, the currency question became one of the staple issues of post-Reconstruction politics. Twice the prosilver coalition in Congress won modest victories. First, the Bland-Allison Act of 1878 required the U.S. Treasury to purchase and coin between $2 million and $4 million worth of silver each month. Then, the more sweeping Sherman Silver Purchase Act of 1890 required 4.5 million ounces of silver bullion to be purchased monthly to serve as the basis for new issues of U.S. Treasury notes.

These legislative battles, though hard fought, cut across party lines in the characteristic fashion of post-Reconstruction politics. But in the early 1890s, silver suddenly became a defining issue between the parties; in particular, it had a radicalizing effect on the Democratic Party.

The Cleveland Administration and the Silver Question. When the crash of 1893 hit, the Democrats held power in Washington. The party in office usually gets blamed if the economy falters, but President Cleveland made things worse for the Democrats. When jobless marchers—known as Coxey's Army—arrived in Washington in 1894 to appeal for federal relief, Cleveland's response was to disperse them forcibly and arrest their leader, Jacob S. Coxey. Cleveland's brutal handling of the Pullman strike (see Chapter 17) further alienated the labor vote. Nor was he able to deliver on his campaign promise of tariff reform. Cleveland lost control of the battle when the unpopular McKinley Tariff of 1890 came up for revision in Congress. The resulting Wilson-Gorman Tariff of 1894, which Cleveland allowed to pass into law without his signature, caved in to special interests and left the most important rates mostly unchanged.

Most disastrous, however, was Cleveland's rigidity on the silver question. A committed sound-money man, Cleveland had repeatedly denounced "the dangerous and reckless experiment of free, unlimited, and independent silver coinage." Nothing that happened after the depression set in—not collapsing prices, not the suffering of farmers, not the groundswell for free silver within his own party—budged Cleveland from his opposition to free silver.

Economic pressures, in fact, soon pushed him to abandon altogether a silver-based currency. The problem was a persistent drain on U.S. gold reserves held by the Treasury, caused partly by transfers of gold overseas to cover an unfavorable balance of international payments, and partly by redemptions of gold by holders of U.S. Treasury notes. To help preserve the government's gold reserves, Cleveland persuaded Congress in 1893 to repeal the Sherman Silver Purchase Act, effectively sacrificing the country's painfully crafted effort at maintaining a partial bimetallic standard.

As his administration's difficulties deepened, Cleveland turned in 1895 to a syndicate of private bankers led by J. P. Morgan to finance the gold purchases needed to replenish the Treasury's depleted reserves. The administration's secret negotiations with Wall Street, once discovered, enraged Democrats and completed Cleveland's isolation from his party.

William Jennings Bryan and the Election of 1896. At their national convention in Chicago in 1896, the Democrats repudiated Cleveland and turned left. The leader of the triumphant silver Democrats was William Jennings Bryan of Nebraska. Only thirty-six years old, Bryan had already served two terms in Congress and become a passionate advocate of free silver. He was a consummate politician and, no less important, an inspiring public speaker. Bryan, remarked the journalist Frederic Howe, was "pre-eminently an evangelist," whose zeal sprang from "the Western self-righteous missionary mind." With biblical fervor, Bryan swept up his audiences when he joined the debate on free silver at the Democratic convention. He had been quietly building up delegate support while distancing himself from convention politicking. Bryan locked up the presidential nomination with a stirring attack on the gold

Lawyers March for the Gold Standard
Presidential campaigns of the late nineteenth century were always hard fought, none more so than the 1896 election. Big issues were at stake: would the country stay on the gold standard or drastically expand the money supply through the free coinage of silver? Lawyers paraded in the streets of New York City to demonstrate their conviction that the nation's fate hung on sound money and the election of the Republican William McKinley.
New-York Historical Society.

The Candidates, 1896
The 1896 presidential campaign marked one small step in the technology of electioneering—the introduction of the celluloid campaign button, which a party supporter
could pin on his lapel. It is doubtful, however, that this innovation made any difference in the outcome of the election.
Collection of Janice L. and David J. Frent.

standard: "You shall not press down upon the brow of
labor this crown of thorns, you shall not crucify
mankind on a cross of gold."

Bryan's nomination meant that the Democrats had
become the party of free silver; his "cross of gold"
speech meant that the money question would turn into
a national crusade. No one could be neutral on this
defining issue. Silver Republicans bolted their party;
gold Democrats went for a splinter Democratic ticket or
supported the Republican Party; even the Prohibition
Party split into gold and silver wings. The Populists,
meeting after the Democratic convention, accepted
Bryan as their candidate. The free-silver issue had
become so vital that they could not do otherwise.
Although they nominated their own vice-presidential
candidate, Tom Watson of Georgia, the Populists found
themselves for all practical purposes absorbed into the
Democratic silver crusade.

The Republicans took up the challenge. Their key
party leader was Mark Hanna, a wealthy Cleveland iron
maker, a brilliant political manager, and an exponent of
the new industrial capitalism. He orchestrated an
unprecedented money-raising campaign among America's corporate interests. Hanna's candidate, William
McKinley of Ohio, personified the virtues of Republi-

canism, standing solidly for prosperity, high tariffs, and
sound money. While Bryan broke with tradition and
crisscrossed the country in a furious whistle-stop campaign, the dignified McKinley received delegations at
his home in Canton, Ohio. As Bryan orated with passionate moral fervor, McKinley talked of industrial
progress and a full dinner pail.

Not since 1860 had the United States witnessed
such a hard-fought election over such high stakes. For
the middle class, sound money stood symbolically for
the soundness of the social order. With jobless workers
tramping the streets and bankrupt farmers up in arms,
Bryan's fervent assault on the gold standard struck fear
in many hearts. Republicans denounced the Democratic platform as "revolutionary and anarchistic."
They called Bryan's supporters "social misfits who have
almost nothing in common but opposition to the existing order and institutions."

Though little noticed at the time, ethnocultural
issues also figured strongly in the campaign. The
Republicans, the party of morality, beat a strategic
retreat from temperance and Sunday laws. McKinley
himself had represented an ethnically mixed district of
northeastern Ohio in Congress. In appealing to his
immigrant and working-class constituents, he had

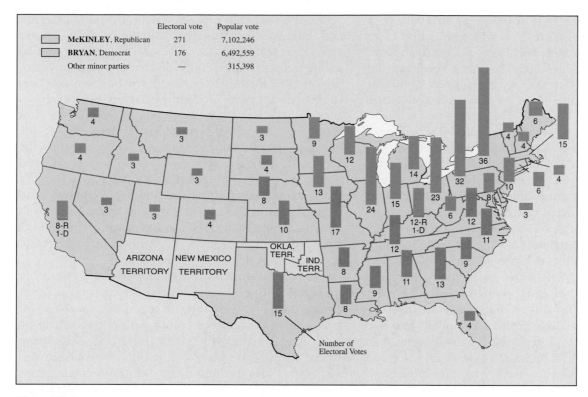

	Electoral vote	Popular vote
McKINLEY, Republican	271	7,102,246
BRYAN, Democrat	176	6,492,559
Other minor parties	—	315,398

MAP 18.2
The Election of 1896
The 1896 election was one of the truly decisive elections in American history. The Republican Party won by its largest margin since 1872. More important, the Republicans established a firm grip on the key midwestern and Middle Atlantic states—especially New York, Indiana, Ohio, and Illinois—that had been the decisive states in every national election since Reconstruction. The 1896 election broke a party stalemate of twenty years' duration and began a period of Republican domination that would last until 1932.

learned the art of easy tolerance, as expressed in his phrase "live and let live." Of the two candidates, the prairie orator Bryan, with his biblical rhetoric and moral righteousness, presented the more alien image to traditional Democratic voters in the big cities.

McKinley won handily, with 271 electoral votes to Bryan's 176 (Map 18.2). He kept the Republican ground that had been regained in the 1894 midterm elections and pushed into Democratic strongholds, especially in the cities. Boston, New York, Chicago, and Minneapolis, all taken by Cleveland in 1892, went for McKinley in 1896. Bryan ran strongly only in the South, in silver-mining states, and in the Populist West. The gains his evangelical style brought him in some Republican rural areas did not compensate for his losses in traditionally Democratic urban districts.

The paralyzing equilibrium of American politics ended in 1896. The Republicans had skillfully handled both the economic and the cultural challenges. They persuaded the nation that they were the party of pros-

perity and shifted some of the burdens of morality politics onto the Democrats. In 1896, too, electoral politics regained its place as an arena for national debate, setting the stage for the reform politics of the Progressive Era.

The Decline of Agrarian Radicalism

As for Populism, it simply faded away. Fusion with the Democrats in 1896 deprived the People's Party of its identity and undermined its organizational structure. After the election, the issue on which Populism had staked its fate—free silver—vanished. During the 1890s gold was discovered in South Africa, Colorado, and the Yukon, and the new cyanide refining method greatly increased ore yields. The newly abundant gold supply took the sting out of the lost battle for free silver. In 1897, moreover, the world market for agricultural commodities turned favorable. Wheat went from

72 cents a bushel in 1896 to 98 cents in 1909, corn from 27 cents a bushel to 57 cents, and cotton from 6 cents a pound to 14 cents. Farm prices rose faster than prices of other products, and as a result, so did the real income of farmers. A new spirit of optimism took hold in the "golden age" of American agriculture before World War I.

The farmers' sense of inferiority and deprivation—that they were "rubes" and "hicks" and that life was inherently better in the city—began to subside after 1900. The new prosperity meant that more farmers could afford labor-saving home appliances and farm machinery. Other inventions eased the isolation and monotony of rural life. The telephone became commonplace, not so much because of the spread of commercial service but through the determined efforts of farmers themselves. Telephone cooperatives were the most common type of farm cooperative in the early twentieth century. The automobile, especially the Ford Model T, gave rural Americans a mobility they had never before known. The Country Life Commission, formed in 1908, took an optimistic view of farm society: "There has never been a time when the American farmer was as well off as he is today, when we consider not only his earning powers but the comforts and advantages he may secure."

In an agrarian nation, the distress of farmers could readily be regarded as a disorder of the entire country. Pushed far enough, farmers might mobilize to seize political power. In short, they could become Populists. But by the opening of the twentieth century farmers no longer constituted a majority of the population. In 1900 scarcely a third of the labor force earned a living from the soil; the proportion doing so would shrink in each succeeding census until, in our own time, less than 3 percent of the labor force is engaged in agriculture (see the Appendix, p. A-10).

There would be times in the twentieth century when distressed farmers would turn again to insurgent politics, but never with the potency generated by the Populist Party. It would be as an organized interest group, not as a political movement, that farmers in the future would advance their cause.

Agriculture had long been at the heart of American life. In the twentieth century agriculture became just one more economic interest—important but subordinate in the larger scheme of the modern industrial order.

Race and Politics in the South

When Reconstruction ended in 1877, so did the hopes of African Americans that they would enjoy the equal rights of citizenship promised them by the Fourteenth and Fifteenth amendments. Southern schools were strictly segregated. Access to jobs, to justice, and to social welfare was racially determined and unequal. And in 1883 the Supreme Court struck down the Civil Rights Act of 1875, declaring that private citizens—owners of restaurants, theaters, hotels—were not subject to the antidiscriminatory provisions of the Fourteenth Amendment. But segregation in public accommodations was not yet legally required, and practices varied a good deal across the South. Only on the railroads, as rail travel became more common, did whites begin to demand that blacks be excluded from first-class cars. As a result, southern railroads became after 1887 the first public accommodation subject to segregation laws.

In politics, the situation in the early 1880s was even more fluid. Blacks had not been driven from politics. On the contrary, their turnout at elections was not far from that of whites. But blacks did not participate on equal terms with whites. In the Black Belt—areas where African Americans were heavily concentrated and sometimes outnumbered whites—whites gerrymandered the districts to ensure that while blacks got some electoral representation, political control remained in white hands. Blacks, moreover, were routinely intimidated during political campaigns—hence the large numbers whose votes were recorded as Democratic in those years. Even so, an impressive majority remained staunchly Republican, refusing, as the last black congressman from Mississippi told his House colleagues in 1882, "to surrender their honest convictions, even upon the altar of their personal necessities."

Whatever hope blacks entertained for better days, however, faded during the 1880s and then, in the next decade, expired in a terrible burst of racist terrorism. What made this outcome so tragic was that it coincided with a positive effort to overcome racial divisions. Black disfranchisement and rigid segregation stemmed directly from the crisis of the 1890s and, in particular, from a political upheaval that briefly challenged Democratic Party rule in the South.

The Triumph of White Conservatism

No democratic society can survive if it does not enable competing economic and social interests to be heard. In the United States the two-party system performs that role. The Civil War crisis severely tested the two-party system because, in both the North and the South, political opposition came to be seen as treasonous. In the victorious North, despite the best efforts of the Republicans, the Democrats shed their disgrace and reclaimed their status as a major party. In the defeated South, however, the scars of war cut deep, and Recon-

Disfranchisement
This political drawing that appeared in *Judge* magazine on July 30, 1892, shows members of the Ku Klux Klan barring black voters from the polls. By 1892, in fact, this drawing was behind the times. Literacy tests and poll taxes were beginning to disfranchise blacks with less menace and more likelihood of evading the constitutional requirement (note the sign behind the Ku Kluxers) under the Fifteenth Amendment that the right to vote not be denied "on account of race, color, or previous condition of servitude."
Museum of American Political Life.

struction cut even deeper. The struggle for "home rule" empowered the Democrats. They had "redeemed" the South from black Republican domination—hence the name that southern Democrats adopted: Redeemers. Cloaked in the mantle of the Lost Cause, the Redeemers claimed a monopoly on political legitimacy.

The Republican Party did not fold up, however. On the contrary, it soldiered on, sustained by stubborn black loyalty, by a hard core of white supporters, by patronage from Republican national administrations, and by a key Democratic vulnerability. This was the gap between the universality the Democrats claimed as the party of Redemption and the reality that the Democratic Party was controlled by an economic elite indifferent to the plight of poor whites.

Class antagonism, though often muted by sectional patriotism, was never absent from southern society. The Civil War had brought out long-smoldering differences between planters and hill-country farmers, who had little to gain from the slaveholding system they were called on to defend. Fresh sources of conflict now

arose from the sharecropping system—which increasingly included whites as well as blacks—and from an emerging industrial working class. Unable to loosen the grip of the conservative elite, economically distressed white southerners broke with the Democratic Party in the early 1880s and mounted independent movements across the South. Most successful were the Readjusters, who briefly gained power in Virginia by opposing full repayment of Reconstruction debts, which would enrich bond-holding speculators while leaving the state destitute. Elsewhere, conservative Democrats also faced substantial challenges from disaffected farmers organized in Granges and acting through Independent or Greenback parties or, as in Tennessee, Louisiana, and Arkansas, by utilizing the Republican Party. After subsiding briefly, this agrarian discontent revived in the mid-1880s with a vengeance, welling out of the farmers' alliances that sprang up across the South, and spawning the formidable Populist challenge to Democratic rule. Refusing to accept any opposition as legitimate, the ruling Democrats stuffed ballot boxes, intimidated black voters, murdered opponents, and stirred up racial animosity by shouting "Negro domination!"

If opposition was illegitimate, moreover, did it not follow that the incurably disloyal should be excluded from politics altogether? Exclusion had been the purpose behind the cumulative poll tax—a tax for the privilege of voting—adopted by Georgia in 1877 and South Carolina's "eight-box" law (1882), which made voting a nightmare for uneducated voters. It was clear, too, which voters these disfranchising measures mainly targeted: the blacks, whose political participation everywhere insulted southern white sensibilities and, in black-belt districts, made rule by white Democrats perpetually uneasy (see Voices from Abroad, "Charles Boissevain: Touring the South, 1880," p. 597).

But Populists themselves were uneasy about black participation. Racism cut through southern white society and, so some thought, most infected the lowest rungs. "The white laboring classes here," wrote an Alabaman in 1886, "are separated from the Negroes, working all day side by side with them, by an innate consciousness of race superiority," which "excites a sentiment of sympathy and equality with the classes above them, and in this way becomes a healthy social leaven." Yet when times got bad enough, hard-pressed whites could also see blacks as fellow victims. "They are in the ditch just like we are," asserted one white Texan. Southern Populists never fully reconciled these contradictory impulses. They never questioned the conventions of social inequality: blacks had not been admitted to the suballiances. Nor were the economic interests of white landowning farmers and black tenants and laborers always in concert. But once agrarian protest turned political, the logic of racial solidarity became hard to deny.

Kept out of the Southern Farmers' Alliance, black farmers had organized separately into the Colored Farmers' Alliance, thereby gaining a certain amount of leverage with the emerging Populist movement. The Knights of Labor, which accepted blacks, also argued for interracial unity. The realities of partisan politics, once the alliances had taken that step, clinched the argument. Where the Populists fused with the Republican Party, such as in North Carolina and Tennessee, they automatically became allies of black leaders and gained a black constituency. Where fusion did not happen and the Populists fielded independent tickets, they needed to appeal to black voters. "The accident of color can make no difference in the interest of farmers, croppers, and laborers," argued the Populist leader Tom Watson. "You are kept apart that you may be separately fleeced of your earnings." By making this interracial appeal, even if not always wholeheartedly, the Populists put at risk the foundations of conservative southern politics.

In the face of this challenge, conservative Democrats played the race card to the hilt, parading as the "white man's party" while denouncing the Populists for courting "Negro rule." Yet at the same time they shamelessly competed for the black vote. In this, they had many advantages: money; control of the local power structures; a paternalistic relationship to the black community. When all else failed, mischief at the polls enabled the Democrats to beat back the Populists. Thus the Mississippian Frank Burkitt's bitter attack on the conservatives: they were "a class of corrupt office-seekers" who had "hypocritically raised the howl of white supremacy while they debauched the ballot boxes . . . disregarded the rights of the blacks . . . and actually dominated the will of the white people through the instrumentality of the stolen negro vote."

Black Disfranchisement. In the midst of these deadly struggles the Democrats decided to settle matters once and for all. Disfranchising the blacks, hitherto pursued hesitantly, now turned into a potent movement throughout the South (Map 18.3). In 1890, Mississippi adopted a literacy test that effectively drove the blacks out of politics. The motives behind it were cynical, but the literacy test could be dressed up as a reform for Mississippians tired of electoral fraud and violence. Their children and grandchildren, argued one influential figure, should not be left "with shotguns in their hands, a lie in their mouths and perjury on their lips in order to defeat the negroes." Better, a Mississippi journalist wrote, to devise "some legal defensible substitute for the abhorrent and evil methods on which white supremacy lies." This argument even persuaded some weary Populists: Frank Burkitt, for example, was arguing *for* the Mississippi literacy test in the words quoted in the previous paragraph. Other disfranchising methods—registration laws, property qualifications, the secret ballot (which demanded some basic literacy), the already familiar poll tax—were also widely enacted during the 1890s, but none matched the literacy test as a flexible and efficient instrument for driving blacks from the polls.

The race issue had helped to bring down the Populists; now it helped reconcile them to defeat. Embittered poor whites, deeply ambivalent all along about interracial cooperation, turned their fury on the blacks. Insofar as disfranchising measures asserted militant white supremacy, poor whites approved. It was important, of course, that their own vulnerability be partially protected by lenient enforcement and by exemptions. The literacy test, for instance, was softened by Mississippi's understanding clause, which permitted illiterate voters to explain a constitutional passage that was read to them, and by Louisiana's grandfather clause, which exempted from the test

CHARLES BOISSEVAIN

Touring the South, 1880

——————★——————

*In 1880, as the South was emerging from Recon-
struction, the Dutch journalist Charles Boissevain
toured the region. Like many visitors, Boissevain
was captivated by the romance of the antebellum
South, but he was not blind to the evils of slavery or
the plantation system. Echoing his southern hosts in
his disdain for the freedmen as voters, he also reflected
a home-grown racism: if there was any contemporary
equal in the world to American slavery, it was the
relentless Dutch oppression of the blacks of South
Africa. A decade ahead of his hosts, Boissevain came
up with the solution they would eventually embrace—
constitutional disfranchisement of southern blacks.*

I visited an old-fashioned plantation and spoke with
some intelligent whites, and with free Negroes who
had once been slaves. Walking through the cotton
fields in the thick red clay mud, a great deal out of
the past and present became clearer than before. . . .
The aristocracy of Virginia, which once gave
America a Washington, was more and more degraded
through the accursed system of slavery. The gentlemen became no more than overseers and slave drivers. It was a masterful, luxurious, merry life that
they lived; and walking about here I wished, despite
myself, that I might once have been the guest of one
of the old masters of the land on his plantation. . . .

I have spoken with several old slaveholders who
acknowledge that slavery was properly abolished
and that free labor is more profitable than they had
ever thought. But they complain bitterly because
the government went too far in giving the right to
vote to the emancipated Negroes, and thereby
ruined both the land and the people. . . . The worst
disservice that could have been done for the freedmen was to throw them, unprepared, into the
American political battle, an enticing prey for the
hungry adventurers from the North who received
the picturesque name of carpetbaggers from the
suitcase which was their only luggage when they
came down the Mississippi. . . .

Now the carpetbagger instead of the slave
owner is the master of the Negro, for the idea that
the blacks in the South or elsewhere are able to govern whites is laughable. The white must remain the
older brother, the leader; this can no more be resisted than can a law of nature. . . .

The Ku-Klux Klan is at present as good as sup-
pressed, but the Negroes are in no better position to
make free use of the right to vote. In addition to the
fact that many employers make renunciation of the
privilege a condition of employment, the colored
people are directly prevented from voting for
whomever they wish through trickery and through
open frauds at the ballot box. . . . In other parts of
the country not even that much attention is paid to
the forms; the votes of the Negroes are simply not
counted.

. . . All honest and thoughtful people, all those
who recognize the sovereignty of the law and
approve no low deception, must together protest
against the frauds at the ballot box. . . . The Negro's
lack of fitness for the exercise of the ballot can be
the basis for a movement for amending the
Constitution, but the defenders of a regime who
know no better means that deceit at the polls will
earn the confidence of no one. To rule by falsified
rolls and by ballot boxes with double bottoms is
worse than a military dictatorship.

———————

Source: Oscar Handlin, ed., *This Was America* (Cambridge,
MA: Harvard University Press, 1949), 337–342.

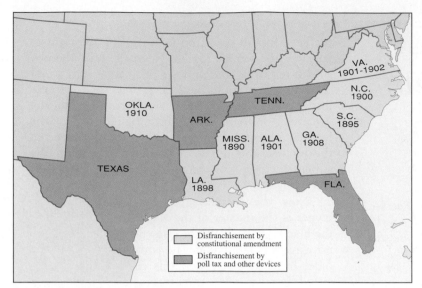

MAP 18.3
Disfranchisement in the South
In the midst of the Populist challenge to Democratic one-party rule in the South, a movement to deprive blacks of the right to vote spread from Mississippi across the South. By 1910 every state in the region except Tennessee, Arkansas, Texas, and Florida had made constitutional changes designed to prevent blacks from voting, and these four states accomplished much the same result through poll taxes and other exclusionary methods. For the next half-century the political process in the South would be for whites only.

those entitled to vote on January 1, 1867, together with their sons and grandsons. But poor whites were not protected from property and poll-tax requirements, and many stopped voting.

Poor whites might have objected more had their spokesmen not been given a voice within the Democratic Party. A new brand of southern politician came forward to speak for them, appealing not to their class interests but to their racial prejudices. Tom Watson, the fiery Georgia Populist, rebuilt his political career as a brilliant practitioner of race baiting. Starting in the early 1900s, he and other racial demagogues thrived throughout the South.

The Ascendancy of Jim Crow. With the collapse of Populism, a brand of white supremacy emerged that was more virulent than anything blacks had faced since Emancipation. The color line, hitherto incomplete, became rigid and comprehensive. Segregated seating in trains, already in force generally since first being enacted by Florida in 1887, provided a precedent for the legal separation of the races. The enforcing legislation, known as Jim Crow laws, soon applied to every type of public facility—restaurants, hotels, streetcars, even cemeteries. In the 1890s the South became for the first time a society fully segregated by law.

The Supreme Court of the United States soon ratified the South's decision. In the case of *Plessy v. Ferguson* (1896) the Court ruled that segregation was not discriminatory—that is, it did not violate black civil rights under the Fourteenth Amendment—provided that blacks had accommodations equal to those of whites. The "separate but equal" doctrine of course had little regard for the realities of southern life: segregated

facilities were rarely if ever "equal" in any material sense, and segregation itself was intended to underscore the inferiority of blacks. With a similar disregard for reality, the Supreme Court in *Williams v. Mississippi* (1898) validated the disfranchising devices of the southern states: so long as race was not a specified criterion for disfranchisement, the Fifteenth Amendment was not being violated, even though the practical effect was the virtual exclusion of blacks from politics in the South.

Race hatred became an accepted part of southern life, manifested in a wave of lynchings and race riots and in the public abuse of blacks. For example, Benjamin R. Tillman, governor of South Carolina and after 1895 a senator, excoriated blacks as "an ignorant and debased and debauched race." This ugly racism came from several sources, including intensified competition between whites and blacks for jobs during the depression of the 1890s and white anger against a less submissive black generation born after slavery. Recent scholarship also suggests more deep-seated psychological causes: the rage against blacks served as a way of reasserting a traditional sense of southern "manhood" that was under assault by rapid social and economic change. Lynching, moreover, occurred most frequently in developing areas such as the Gulf plain and in new cotton country where the population was thinly spread, community ties were weak, and blacks and whites were strangers to one another.

But what had triggered the antiblack offensive was the crisis in the South over Populism. From then on, white supremacy propped up the one-party system that the Redeemers had been fighting for ever since Reconstruction. If the southern elite had to share political

Frank J. Farrell, Black Delegate
In this illustration from a popular weekly, Farrell is introducing Master Workman Powderly to the Knights of Labor convention in Richmond, Virginia. It would be hard to exaggerate the fortitude it took for a black man to appear on such a podium in the South in 1886. By this display of interracial unity, the Knights intended to convey the message that class unity trumped racial prejudice. The Southern Farmers' Alliance, allies of the Knights, took this message to heart, at least for a while.
Library of Congress.

power with demagogic poor white leaders such as Tom Watson and James K. Vardaman, this sharing would be on terms agreeable to them—the exclusion from the political arena of any serious challenge to the economic status quo.

The Case of Grimes County. In 1890 African Americans composed more than half of the population of Grimes County, a cotton-growing area of east Texas. They had kept the local Republican Party going after Reconstruction and regularly sent black representatives to the Texas legislature during the 1870s and 1880s. More remarkably, the local Populist Party that appeared in 1892 among white farmers proved immune to the Democrats' taunts of "black rule." A Populist-

Republican coalition swept the county elections in 1896 and 1898, surviving well after the collapse of the national Populist movement.

In 1899 defeated Democratic office seekers and prominent citizens of Grimes County organized the secret White Man's Union. Armed men prevented blacks from voting in town elections that year. The two most important black leaders were shot down in cold blood. Night riders terrorized both white Populists and black Republicans.

When the Populist sheriff proved incapable of enforcing the law, the game was up. The White Man's Union, now out in the open, became the county Democratic Party in a new guise. The Democrats won Grimes County by an overwhelming vote in 1900. The day after the election, members of the Union laid siege to the Populist sheriff's office. They killed his brother and a friend and drove the sheriff, badly wounded, out of the county forever.

The White Man's Union ruled Grimes County for the next fifty years. The whole episode was the handiwork of the county's "best citizens," suggesting how respectable the use of terror had become in the service of white supremacy. The Union intended, as one of its leaders said, to "force the African to keep his place." After 1900 blacks could survive in Grimes County only if they tended to their own business and stayed out of trouble with whites.

Forms of Black Resistance

Like the blacks of Grimes County, southern blacks in many places resisted white oppression as best they could. When Georgia adopted the first Jim Crow law applying to streetcars in 1891, Atlanta blacks declared a boycott, and over the next fifteen years there were boycotts against segregated streetcars in at least twenty-five cities. "Do not trample on our pride by being 'jim crowed,'" the Savannah *Tribune* urged its readers: "Walk!" Ida Wells-Barnett emerged as the most outspoken black crusader against lynching, so enraging Memphis whites by the editorials in her newspaper *Free Speech* that she was forced in 1892 to leave the city. And individual blacks, such as Robert Charles, struck back, some of them sacrificing their own lives (see American Lives, "Robert Charles: Black Militant," pp. 600–601).

Like Charles, some were drawn to the back-to-Africa movement. It was a sign of their despair that Africa was again seen as the place of black salvation. But emigration was not a real choice, and like the blacks of Grimes County, African Americans everywhere had to bend to the raging forces of racism and find a way to survive.

Robert Charles: Black Militant

————————★————————

THE TROUBLE BEGAN in an ordinary way. The two black men were sitting quietly on the steps of a house on Dryades Street in New Orleans, between Washington and 6th streets. It was Monday evening, July 24, 1900. One was nineteen-year-old Leonard Pierce; the other was an older man named Robert Charles. They were waiting for a friend of Charles's, Virginia Banks, and her roommate to return from a day at Baton Rouge. Around 11 P.M. three policemen approached Pierce and Charles and began to question them roughly. When Charles stood up, Officer Mora grabbed him. A scuffle followed, and Mora began to beat Charles about the head with his billy club. Charles, a big man, broke away. There was an exchange of gunfire, wounding both in the thigh, Officer Mora more seriously. In a hail of bullets, Charles ran off.

"In any law-abiding community Charles would have been justified in delivering himself up immediately to the properly constituted authorities and asking for a trial by a jury of his peers," wrote the antilynching crusader Ida Wells-Barnett in her pamphlet on what followed. "Charles knew that his arrest in New Orleans, even for defending his life, meant nothing short of a long term in the penitentiary, and still more probable death by lynching at the hands of a cowardly mob." Those must have been Charles's thoughts. He made his way back to the room he shared with Pierce on 4th Street, took down his Winchester rifle, and got ready to fight.

In the meantime Pierce had been brought to the police station, where Charles's name and address were soon "sweated" out of him. Captain John T. Day, a local hero who had rescued fourteen people from a hotel fire, led a squad to bring Charles in. The entrance to Charles's room was along an alley. When the police arrived, Charles swung open the door, shot Day through the heart, then turned and fatally wounded a second officer. The other two policemen cowered along the wall and slipped into another house, where they hid in the dark. The officers on the street refused to enter the unlit alley. When reinforcements arrived at 5 A.M., Charles had slipped away, and the manhunt commenced.

The New Orleans newspapers labeled Charles a "fiend incarnate." No one who had known him would have said so. Robert Charles was one of thousands of rural blacks who had sought to escape from grinding poverty by migrating to southern cities. Robert Charles was born just after the end of slavery, in 1865 or 1866, in Copiah County, Mississippi. His parents were sharecroppers, and he was one of ten children. He worked as a day laborer on the railroads and, after arriving in New Orleans around 1894, at a variety of odd jobs. In July 1900 he was unemployed. Charles was unmarried and rather stylish in his dress, favoring a brown derby hat. Acquaintances remembered him as quiet and intelligent. He had received little education, but his room contained the well-thumbed books and papers of a studious man. One other thing about Charles: he ardently believed that blacks should return to Africa.

The back-to-Africa movement, which enjoyed a revival in these hard years, reflected the despair that poor blacks like Robert Charles felt about life in America. Africa was their only salvation, preached Bishop Henry M. Turner, the combative leader of the movement. "I see no other shelter from the stormy blast, from the red tide of persecution, from the horrors of American prejudice." Charles was a reader of Bishop Turner's fiery paper *Voice of Missions,* and in 1899 he began to sell subscriptions. He also became a local agent for the International Migration Society, working on commission to sign up members who would secure transportation to Liberia by contributing a dollar a month for forty months.

Recent events had fortified Charles's conviction that blacks had no hope in America. He was said to have been infuriated by the most infamous lynching of the era, the burning and dismemberment of Sam Hose in Georgia in 1899. In Louisiana, moreover, blacks had been disfranchised in 1898, and a crisis was brewing in state politics. As the elections of 1900 approached, the Democrats vowed that on no account would they allow the Republicans and Populists to emerge as winners. In Charles's pocket was a newspaper clipping about an opposition leader who had called on his supporters to "oil up their Winchesters and prepare to fight" if Democrats tried to steal the election. In *Voice of Missions* there was a similarly desperate message: in one editorial Bishop Turner had urged that "Negroes Get Guns" in self-defense.

Charles, in fact, habitually carried a Colt .38 revolver; it was in his belt when Officer Mora accosted

MOB RULE
IN
NEW ORLEANS.

Robert Charles.

ROBERT CHARLES
AND
His Fight to the Death.

◎◎◎◎◎◎◎

THE STORY OF HIS LIFE.
BURNING HUMAN BEINGS ALIVE.
OTHER LYNCHING STATISTICS.

IDA B. WELLS-BARNETT,
CHICAGO.

PRICE 25 CENTS.

Robert Charles
This is the only known picture of Charles, an engraving done for the cover of Ida Wells-Barnett's pamphlet on Charles's slaying.
Miriam and Ira D. Wallach Division of Art, Prints and Photographs, The New York Public Library. Astor, Lenox and Tilden Foundations.

him. There is no knowing what went through his mind when he chose not to submit to the policeman's abuse. But by drawing his gun, Charles had stepped across the line. From then until his inevitable death, he was making a political statement.

That was how the whites of New Orleans saw Charles, too: he was challenging the white power structure. As a leader of the mob that gathered in the streets on Wednesday put it:

The only way you can teach these niggers a lesson and put them in their place is to go out and lynch a few of them as an object lesson. String up a few of them, and the others will trouble you no more. . . . On to the Parish Prison and lynch Pierce!

The mob couldn't get at Pierce, but they took their fury out on any other unfortunate black they encountered as they surged through the city. In the next two days at least six people were killed and dozens of others brutally beaten. Only late on Thursday did the police and militia restore a semblance of law and order to New Orleans. But Charles remained at large. Then, on Friday afternoon, July 27, the police got a tip that he was hiding in a small house on Saratoga Street.

Springing from a back closet, Charles shot down the two police officers who came to investigate and then made his way up to the second story. A great crowd soon surrounded the house, peppering it with bullets. Dodging from window to window, Charles returned the fire for nearly two hours. In grudging admiration, one reporter wrote of his "diabolical coolness" and "wonderful marksmanship [that] never failed him for a moment." More than twenty of his attackers were hit, three fatally. As dusk began to fall, the building was set ablaze, and Charles was forced out. Still defiant, he almost made it across the courtyard when he was stopped by a bullet and went down. The crowd was at him in an instant, firing dozens of shots into him, stomping on his head. His body was carried off in a police wagon, his battered head hanging grotesquely from the back. Later that night the mob broke loose again, burning buildings and murderously attacking six more blacks.

No New Orleans black would have dared say out loud that Robert Charles had done right. But Ida Wells-Barnett, writing from the safety of Chicago, insisted that he had. "The white people of this country may charge that he was a desperado, but to the people of his own race Robert Charles will always be regarded as the hero of New Orleans." Five weeks after Charles's burial, a neighbor of Fred Clark's on South Rampart Street came up behind Clark, put a gun to his head, and shot him dead. Fred Clark was the black man who had given away Charles's hiding place to the police.

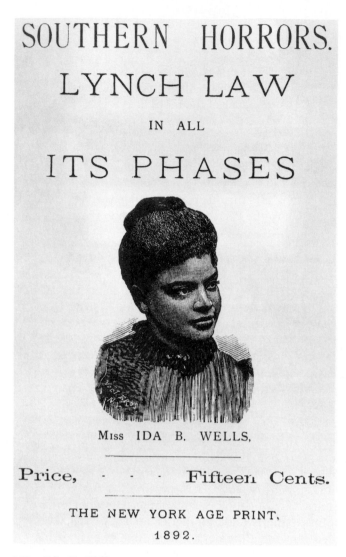

MISS IDA B. WELLS,

Price, - - - - Fifteen Cents.

THE NEW YORK AGE PRINT,
1892.

Miss Ida B. Wells

In 1887 Ida Wells (Wells-Barnett after she married in 1895) was thrown bodily from a train in Tennessee for refusing to vacate her seat in a section reserved for whites, launching her into a lifetime crusade for racial justice. Her mission was to expose the evil of lynching in the South. This portrait is from the title page of a pamphlet she published in 1892 entitled, "Southern Horrors. Lynch Law in All Its Phases."
Miriam and Ira D. Wallach Division of Art, Prints and Photographs, The New York Public Library. Astor, Lenox and Tilden Foundations.

Booker T. Washington

In an age of severe racial oppression, Washington emerged as the acknowledged leader of black people in the United States. He was remarkable for both his ability as spokesman to white Americans and his deep understanding of the aspirations of black Americans. Born a slave, Washington suffered the indignities experienced by all blacks after Emancipation. But having been befriended by several whites as he grew to manhood, he also understood what it took to gain white support—and maneuver around white hostility—in the black struggle for equality.
Library of Congress.

The Atlanta Compromise. Booker T. Washington, the foremost black leader of his day, marked the path in a speech in Atlanta in 1895. Washington retreated from the defiant stand of an older generation of black abolitionists exemplified by Frederick Douglass, who died the same year that the Atlanta speech launched Washington into national prominence. Washington was conciliatory toward the South; it was a society that blacks understood and loved. He considered "the agi-

tation of the question of social equality the extremest folly." Washington accepted segregation, provided that blacks had equal facilities. He accepted educational and property qualifications for the vote, provided that they applied equally to blacks and whites.

Washington's doctrine came to be known as the Atlanta Compromise. His approach was "accommodationist," in the sense that it avoided a direct assault on white supremacy. Despite the humble face he put on before white audiences, however, Washington did not concede the struggle. Behind the scenes he did his best to resist Jim Crow laws and disfranchisement. More important, his Atlanta Compromise, while abandoning the field of political protest, opened up a second front of economic struggle.

Booker T. Washington sought to capitalize on a southern dilemma about the economic role of the black population. Racist dogma dictated that blacks be kept down and conform to their image as lazy, shiftless workers. But to prosper, the South needed an efficient labor force. Washington made this need the target of his efforts. As founder of the Tuskegee Institute in Alabama in 1881, Washington advocated *industrial education*—manual and agricultural training. He preached the virtues of thrift, hard work, and property ownership. Washington's industrial education program won generous support from northern philanthropists and businessmen and, following his Atlanta speech, applause from progressive supporters of the New South.

Washington assumed that black economic progress would be the key to winning political and civil rights. He regarded members of the white southern elite as crucial allies, because ultimately only they had the power to change the South. More important, they could see "the close connection between labor, industry, education, and political institutions." When it was in their economic interest, when they had grown dependent on black labor and black enterprise, white men of business and property would recognize the justice of black rights. As Washington put it, "There is little race prejudice in the American dollar."

The Limits of Self-Help. Do the facts suggest that Washington was right? Or, to put the question as an economist might: was it the impersonal market or race prejudice that most determined the economic treatment of blacks? For southern industry the answer seems mixed. Employers did not discriminate very much over wage rates—that is, they did not pay whites higher wages than they paid blacks for the same work. But racial barriers certainly prevented blacks from moving into better-paid and more highly skilled jobs. This hard truth is made graphically clear in the comparative wage distributions of whites and blacks shown in Figure 18.2. In agriculture, too, the picture was mixed. The opportunity for black farmers to advance themselves clearly did exist. The proportion who became landowners inched slowly upward to roughly 25 percent by 1900. But the racial gap remained very wide, with whites almost three times as likely as blacks to be landowners.

To what extent black self-help—hard work, industrial education, the husbanding of small resources—might counterbalance race prejudice was the nub of Booker T. Washington's problem. Where the almighty dollar reigned, there was some hope of progress. Elsewhere, as Washington saw it, there was none.

For twenty years after his Atlanta address, Washington dominated the organized African American community. In an age of severe racial oppression, no black dealt more skillfully with the leaders of white

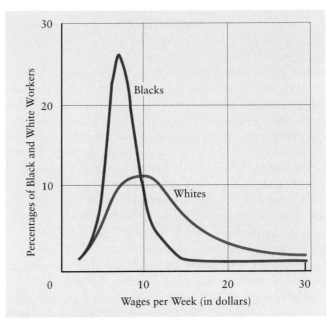

Source: Gavin Wright, *Old South, New South: Revolutions in the Southern Economy since the Civil War* (New York: Basic Books, 1986), 184.

FIGURE 18.2
Distributions of Weekly Wages for Black and White Workers in Virginia, 1907
This graph reveals that wages for common labor in the South were nondiscriminatory (otherwise no or few whites would have been bunched at the low end of the wage scale) but that discrimination denied blacks entry into higher-paying jobs.

America or wielded greater political influence than did Washington. Black leaders knew him as a hard taskmaster. Intensely jealous of his authority, he did not take opposition kindly. Black politicians, educators, and editors stood up to him at their peril.

Even so, opposition surfaced after 1900, especially among younger educated blacks. They thought Washington was conceding too much. He instilled black pride, but of a narrowly middle-class and utilitarian kind. What about the special genius of blacks that W. E. B. Du Bois, a Harvard-trained African American sociologist, celebrated in his collection of essays, *The Souls of Black Folk* (1903)? And what of the "talented tenth" of the black population, whose promise could only be stifled by manual education? Blacks also became increasingly impatient with Washington's silence on segregation and lynching. By the time of his death in 1915, Washington's approach had been superseded by a strategy that relied on the courts and political leverage, not on black self-help and accommodation.

Summary

★

When Reconstruction ended in 1877, national politics became less issue oriented and, as a formal process, less important in American life. This situation resulted from weaknesses in governmental institutions, from the prevailing philosophy of laissez faire, and from the paralysis of evenly matched political parties. Yet the politics of the years after 1877 had great vigor, as can be seen in the high levels of popular participation. For one thing, politics was the arena in which the nation's ethnic and religious conflicts were largely fought out. Equally important, the party machines were powerful and performed crucial functions that properly belonged to, but were still beyond the capacity of, governmental institutions. Finally, despite the slow headway made toward woman suffrage, women's organizations carved out for themselves a broadening public sphere of social reform activity.

During the 1890s national politics again became an important arena. Threatened by the rise of Populism, the Democratic Party committed itself to free silver and made the election of 1896 a contest over issues of real significance. The Republicans won decisively, ending a paralyzing party stalemate that had lasted for twenty years and assuring themselves of political dominance for the next thirty years. At the same time, the 1890s saw, in the failure of Populism, the last great challenge to the mainstream two-party system. And in the South the Populist failure turned into a grim reaction that disfranchised African Americans, completed a rigid segregation system, and let loose a terrible cycle of racial hatred and violence. Blacks resisted but had to bend to overwhelming white power. The accommodationist philosophy of Booker T. Washington seemed to be the best strategy for black survival in an age of extreme racism.

TIMELINE

1874 Woman's Christian Temperance Union founded

1877 Rutherford B. Hayes inaugurated as president, marking the end of Reconstruction

1881 President James A. Garfield assassinated

1883 Pendleton Civil Service Act

Supreme Court strikes down Civil Rights Act of 1875

1884 Mugwump reformers leave the Republican Party to support Grover Cleveland, first Democrat elected president since 1856

1887 Florida adopts first law segregating railroad travel

1888 James Bryce's *The American Commonwealth*

1890 McKinley Tariff

Democrats sweep congressional elections, inaugurating brief era of Democratic Party dominance

Mississippi becomes first state to adopt literacy test to disfranchise blacks

1892 People's (Populist) Party founded

1893 Panic of 1893 leads to national depression

Repeal of Sherman Silver Purchase Act (1890)

1894 "Coxey's Army" of unemployed fails to win federal relief

1895 Booker T. Washington sets out Atlanta Compromise

1896 Election of Republican president William McKinley; free-silver campaign crushed

Plessy v. Ferguson upholds constitutionality of "separate but equal" facilities

1897 Economic depression ends; era of agricultural prosperity begins

Suggested Readings

————————★————————

The best introductions to American politics in the late nineteenth century are John A. Garraty, *The New Commonwealth, 1877–1890* (1968), and R. Hal Williams, *Years of Decision: American Politics in the 1890s* (1978). More detailed and comprehensive is Morton Keller, *Affairs of State: Public Life in Late Nineteenth-Century America* (1977). Joel L. Silbey, *The American Political Nation, 1838–1893* (1991), focuses on the party system and political behavior.

The Politics of the Status Quo, 1877–1893

Various aspects of national politics are discussed in Robert D. Marcus, *Grand Old Party: Political Structure in the Gilded Age* (1971); J. Rogers Hollingsworth, *The Whirligig of Politics: The Democracy of Cleveland and Bryan* (1963); H. Wayne Morgan, *From Hayes to McKinley: National Party Politics, 1877–1896* (1969); and David J. Rothman, *Politics and Power: The Senate, 1869–1901* (1966). On the development of public administration, see Leonard D. White, *The Republican Era, 1869–1901* (1958), and Stephen Skowronek, *Building a New American State: The Expansion of National Administrative Capacities* (1982). The ideological basis for conservative national politics is fully treated in Sidney Fine, *Laissez Faire and the General Welfare State, 1865–1901* (1956), and Robert G. McCloskey, *American Conservatism in the Age of Enterprise* (1951). A useful introduction to the legal history of this era is Morton J. Horwitz, *The Transformation of American Law, 1870–1960* (1992).

Sources of Popular Participation

On popular participation in politics see especially Michael E. McGerr, *The Decline of Popular Politics: The American North, 1865–1928* (1986), and Paul Kleppner, *The Third Electoral Party System, 1853–1892: Parties, Voters, and Political Cultures* (1979). On the Mugwump reformers see John G. Sproat, *The "Best Men": Liberal Reformers in the Gilded Age* (1965), and Ari Hoogenboom, *Outlawing the Spoils: The Civil Service Reform Movement, 1865–1883* (1961). The existence of a women's political culture in the late nineteenth century can be traced in Carl N. Degler, *At Odds: Women and the Family from the Revolution to the Present* (1979). A valuable book setting the stage is Ellen Carol DuBois, *Feminism and Suffrage: The Emergence of an Independent Women's Movement in America, 1848–1869* (1978). The political role of the WCTU is one of the themes of Suzanne M. Marilley, *Woman Suffrage and the Origins of Liberal Feminism in the United States* (1997).

The Crisis of American Politics: The 1890s

The most recent synthesis on Populism is Robert C. McMath, *American Populism* (1993). Richard D. Hofstadter, *The Age of Reform* (1955), stresses the darker side of Populism, in which intolerance and paranoia figure heavily. Hofstadter's thesis once dominated debate among historians but has given way to a much more positive assessment. The key book here is Lawrence Goodwyn, *Democratic Promise: The Populist Moment in America* (1976), which argues that Populism was a broadly based radical response to industrial capitalism. Peter H. Argesinger, *The Limits of Agrarian Radicalism: Western Politics and American Politics* (1995), stresses the capacity of the political status quo to frustrate western Populism. Two stimulating books that follow the history of Populism into the twentieth century are Grant McConnell, *The Decline of Agrarian Democracy* (1953), which focuses on farm organizations, and Michael Kazin, *The Populist Persuasion* (1995), which describes how the language of Populism entered the discourse of mainstream American politics.

The money question is elucidated in Allan Weinstein, *Prelude to Populism: Origins of the Silver Issue* (1970), and, in the most recent and sophisticated account, Gretchen Ritter, *Goldbugs and Greenbacks: The Anti-Monopoly Tradition and the Politics of Finance in America, 1865–1896* (1997). On the politics of the 1890s see especially Robert F. Durden, *Climax of Populism: The Election of 1896* (1965), and Paul W. Glad, *McKinley, Bryan, and the People* (1964).

Race and Politics in the South

On southern politics the seminal book for the post-Reconstruction period is C. Vann Woodward, *Origins of the New South, 1877–1913* (1951), which still defines the terms of discussion among historians. The most far-reaching revision is Edward L. Ayers, *The Promise of the New South* (1992). Complementary books on the social basis of southern politics are Dwight B. Billings, *Planters and the Making of the "New South": North Carolina, 1865–1900* (1979), and Paul Escott, *Many Excellent People: Power and Privilege in North Carolina, 1850–1900* (1985).

The classic book on segregation is C. Vann Woodward, *The Strange Career of Jim Crow* (2nd ed., 1968), but it should be supplemented by Howard N. Rabinowitz, *Race Relations in the Urban South, 1865–1890* (1978). A powerful analysis of southern racism, stressing its psychosocial roots, is Joel Williamson, *A Rage for Order: Black/White Relations in the American South since Emancipation* (1986). Disfranchisement is treated with great analytic sophistication in J. Morgan Kousser, *The Shaping of Southern Politics: Suffrage Restriction and the Establishment of the One-Party South, 1880–1910* (1974). August Meier, *Negro Thought in America, 1880–1915* (1963), is a key analysis of black accommodation and protest. The preeminent exponent of accommodation is the subject of a superb two-volume biography by Louis B. Harlan, *Booker T. Washington: The Making of a Black Leader* (1973) and *Wizard of Tuskegee* (1983); and equally fine on Washington's main critic is David Levering Lewis, *W. E. B. Du Bois: Biography of a Race, 1868–1919* (1993).

Chapter 19

---★---

The Rise of the City

VISITING HIS FIANCÉE'S Missouri farm home in 1894, Theodore Dreiser was struck by "the spirit of rural America, its idealism, its dreams." But this was an "American tradition in which I, alas!, could not share." Said Dreiser, "I had seen Pittsburgh. I had seen Lithuanians and Hungarians in their 'courts' and hovels. I had seen the girls of the city—walking the streets at night." Only twenty-three at the time, Dreiser would go on six years later to publish one of the great American urban novels—*Sister Carrie*—about one young woman in the army of small-town Americans flocking to the Big City in the late nineteenth century. But Dreiser, a member of that army, already knew that between rural America and Pittsburgh an unbridgeable chasm had opened up.

In 1820, after 200 years of settlement, fewer than one American in twenty had lived in a city with a population of 10,000. After that, decade by decade, the urban population swelled until, by 1900, one of every five Americans lived in cities of over 100,000 residents. The same process was happening in Europe, but at a slower pace. During the nineteenth century, the percentage of Europeans living in cities tripled while in the United States the increase was sevenfold, with the greatest growth taking place in the metropolitan centers. In 1900 nearly a tenth of the nation—6.5 million persons—lived in just three cities: New York, Chicago, and Philadelphia. The late nineteenth century, an economist remarked in 1899, was "not only the age of cities, but the age of great cities."

The city was the arena of America's vibrant economic life. Here the factories went up, and here the

Mulberry Street, New York City, c. 1900
The influx of southern and eastern Europeans created teeming ghettos in the heart of New York City and other major American cities. The view is of Mulberry Street, with its pushcarts, street peddlers, and bustling traffic. The inhabitants are mostly Italians, and some of them, noticing the photographer preparing his camera, have gathered to be in the picture.
Library of Congress.

multitudes of working people settled. New immigrants swelled the ranks of the working class: at the turn of the century upwards of 30 percent of the residents of major American cities were foreign-born. Here, too, lived the millionaires and a growing white-collar middle class. For all these people the city was more than a place to make a living; it provided the setting for an urban culture unlike anything seen before in the United States. City people, though differing vastly among themselves, became distinctively and recognizably urban.

Urbanization

————★————

The march to the cities seemed inevitable to nineteenth-century Americans (Map 19.1). "The greater part of our population must live in cities—cities much greater than the world has yet known," declared Congregational minister Josiah Strong in 1898. "In due time we shall be a nation of cities." There was "no

resisting the trend," said another writer. Urbanization became inevitable because of its link to another inevitability of American life—industrialization.

Industrial Sources of City Growth

Until the Civil War, cities were centers of commerce, not industry. They were the places where merchants bought and sold goods for distribution into the interior of the country or shipment out to the world market. Early industrialism sprang up in the countryside. Mills and factories needed water power from streams and rivers, access to sources of fuel and raw materials, and workers drawn from the surplus farm population. Of the nation's fifteen largest cities in 1860, only five reported as much as 10 percent of the labor force engaged in manufacturing activity.

After midcentury, industry began to abandon the countryside. Once steam engines came along, mill operators no longer needed to locate along streams. In the iron industry, coal replaced charcoal as the primary fuel, so iron makers did not have to be near forests. Improved transportation, especially the railroads, gave

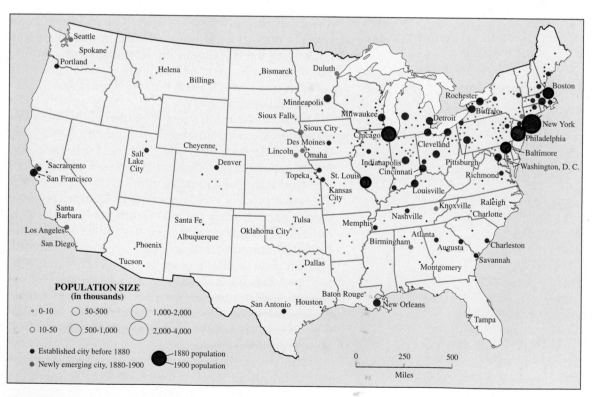

MAP 19.1
The Growth of America's Cities, 1880–1900
The number of Americans living in urban places more than doubled between 1880 and 1900. The most dramatic increases occurred in the largest metropolitan centers. New York grew from 1.2 million to 3.4 million, Chicago from 500,000 to 1.7 million. Notable among newly emerging cities—places that had been small towns or minor cities in 1880—were Los Angeles, Seattle, Birmingham, Omaha, and Atlanta.

TABLE **19.1**

Ten Largest Cities by Population, 1870 and 1910

	1870		1910	
City	*Population*	*City*	*Population*	
1. New York	942,292	New York	4,766,883	
2. Philadelphia	674,022	Chicago	2,185,283	
3. Brooklyn*	419,921	Philadelphia	1,549,008	
4. St. Louis	310,864	St. Louis	687,029	
5. Chicago	298,977	Boston	670,585	
6. Baltimore	267,354	Cleveland	560,663	
7. Boston	250,526	Baltimore	558,485	
8. Cincinnati	216,239	Pittsburgh	533,905	
9. New Orleans	191,418	Detroit	465,766	
10. San Francisco	149,473	Buffalo	423,715	

*Brooklyn was consolidated with New York in 1898.
Source: U.S. Census data.

entrepreneurs greater latitude in selecting the best sites in relation to supplies and markets. The result was a geographic concentration of industry. Iron makers gravitated to Pittsburgh because of its access not only to coal and iron ore but also to markets for iron and steel products. Chicago, ideally located between western livestock suppliers and eastern consuming markets, became a great meatpacking center in the 1870s (see Map 17.3).

Many smaller cities became one-industry towns. Youngstown, Ohio, and Johnstown, Pennsylvania, specialized in iron and steel; Brockton and Haverhill, Massachusetts, in boots and shoes; Troy, New York, in collars and cuffs; East Liverpool, Ohio, in pottery. Other cities processed the raw materials of their regions. Sacramento canned fruits and vegetables, Richmond made cigarettes, Minneapolis milled grain, and Memphis handled lumber and produced cottonseed oil.

As factories became bigger, their size contributed to urban growth. A plant that employed thousands of workers instantly created a small city in its vicinity, sometimes a company town like Aliquippa, Pennsylvania, which became body and soul the property of the Jones and Laughlin Steel Company. Many firms set up their plants near a large city so they could draw on its labor supply and transportation facilities, as George Pullman did in 1880 when he located his sleeping-car works and model town southwest of Chicago.

Sometimes the nearby metropolis spread and absorbed the smaller city, which was the fate of Pullman's town. Elsewhere, as in northern New Jersey or along Lake Michigan south of Chicago, the lines

between industrial towns blurred and an extended urban-industrial area emerged. The same process could be seen in Europe, where industrial regions were emerging in northeastern France around Lille and in Germany's Ruhr Valley.

The established commercial cities also became more industrial. Warehouse districts could readily be converted to small-scale manufacturing; a distribution network and transportation facilities were right at hand. In addition, as gateways for immigrants, port cities offered abundant cheap labor. Boston, Philadelphia, Baltimore, and San Francisco became hives of small-scale, labor-intensive industrial activity. An enormous pool of immigrant workers made New York a magnet for the garment trades, cigar making, and diversified light industry. Preeminent as a city of trade and finance, New York also ranked in the late nineteenth century as the nation's largest manufacturing center.

By 1870, a core industrial region had formed from New England down through the Middle Atlantic states to Maryland. In this region the percentage of people living in urban areas was twice the national average. Forty years later, in 1910, the original industrial core was nearly three-quarters urbanized. It had also thrust westward to include the Great Lakes states, which became America's industrial heartland. Important new centers for steel making, manufacturing, and food processing sprang up in this region. Pittsburgh, Cleveland, Detroit, Milwaukee, Minneapolis—all of them small cities or modest commercial centers in 1870—had by 1910 grown into major industrial cities with from 300,000 to well over half a million inhabitants (Table 19.1).

City Building

The commercial cities of the early nineteenth century had been compact places, densely settled around a harbor or along a river. As late as 1850, when it had 565,000 people, greater Philadelphia covered only 10 square miles. From the foot of Chestnut Street on the Delaware River a person could walk almost anywhere in the city within forty-five minutes. Thereafter, however, Philadelphia—and indeed all American cities—tended to spread out as they developed.

A downtown area emerged, usually in what had been the original commercial city. Downtown in turn broke up into shopping, financial, warehousing, manufacturing, hotel and entertainment, and red-light districts. Somewhat fluid at their edges, all these districts were well-defined areas of specialized activity. Moving out from the center, industrial development tended to follow the arteries of transportation—railroads, canals, and rivers—and, at the city's outskirts, to spread out into complexes of heavy industry. At the same time the middle class in large numbers moved out to new suburban areas.

Urban development was markedly different in continental Europe, where even cities growing rapidly in population remained physically compact, with built-up areas ending abruptly at the surrounding countryside. In America cities constantly expanded, spilling beyond their formal boundaries and forming what the federal census began to designate in 1910 as metropolitan areas. While American cities were highly congested at the center, their population density was actually much below that of European cities: 22 persons per acre for fifteen American cities in the 1890s, for example, versus 157.6 for a comparable group of German cities. Given this difference, the development of efficient urban transportation had a much higher priority in the United States than in Europe.

"The only trouble about this town," wrote Mark Twain on arriving in New York in 1867, "is that it is too large. You cannot accomplish anything in the way of business, you cannot even pay a friendly call, without devoting a whole day to it. . . . The distances are too great." Finding ways of moving nearly a million New Yorkers around was not as hopeless as Twain thought, but it did pose a challenge to city builders. The city demanded innovation no less than industry itself did and, in the end, compiled an equally impressive record of technological achievement.

Mass Transit.   The first innovation, dating back to the 1820s, had been the omnibus, an elongated version of the horse-drawn coach. The omnibus was a convenience but did not do much to relieve congestion; downtown, people could walk just as fast. Much more efficient was the horsecar, which ran on iron tracks, enabling the cars to carry more passengers, move them at a faster clip through congested city streets, and reach out into the residential areas. All this happened because of a modest but crucial refinement in railroad track design in 1852—a grooved rail that was flush with the pavement. From the 1850s onward, horsecars were the mainstay of urban transit across America, accounting for 70 percent of the traffic.

Then came the electric trolley car. Its development was primarily the work of Frank J. Sprague, an electrical engineer once employed by the great inventor Thomas A. Edison. In 1887 Sprague designed an electricity-driven system for Richmond, Virginia: a "trolley" carriage running along an overhead power line was attached by cable to streetcars equipped with an electric motor—hence the name trolley car. After Sprague's success, the electric trolley swiftly displaced the horsecar and by 1900 became the primary means of public transportation in most American cities.

Traffic Jam in Downtown Chicago, 1905
The purpose of urban transit systems was to move masses of people rapidly and efficiently through the city. However, better transportation brought more congestion as well, as this scene of gridlock at Dearborn and Randolph streets in Chicago shows.
Curt Teich Postcard Archives.

In the great metropolitan centers, however, mounting congestion led to demands that public transit be moved off the streets. Affluent suburbanites had long used the railroad to commute to the city. The problem was how to harness railway technology to the needs of ordinary city dwellers. In 1879 the first elevated lines went into operation on Sixth and Ninth avenues in New York City. Powered at first by steam engine, the "els" converted to electricity following Sprague's success with the trolley. Chicago developed elevated transit most fully (Map 19.2). New York, meanwhile, turned to the subway. Boston opened a short underground line in 1897, but it was the completion in 1904 of a subway running the length of Manhattan that demonstrated the full potential of underground mass transit. Thinly settled areas of northern Manhattan and the Bronx, predicted the *New York Times*, would soon boast "a population of ten millions . . . housed comfortably, healthfully and relatively cheaply." The subway would especially delight "all who travel with the sole purpose of 'getting there' in the least time possible." Mass transit had become *rapid* transit.

In 1890 the number of passengers carried on American street railways was more than 2 billion per year, over twice that of the rest of the world combined. Berlin, which boasted the best system in Europe, had a per capita usage that was exceeded by twenty-one American cities. In Great Britain the horsecar remained dominant long after it had disappeared from American streets. In Tokyo, the biggest Asian city, the horsecar was not even introduced until 1882, and electric streetcars first appeared there in 1903.

City Structures: Bridges, Skyscrapers, Terminals. Rivers, in earlier times the city's lifeline of trade, now became barriers that interrupted rail traffic and hindered urban expansion. Hundreds of iron and steel bridges went up in the second half of the nineteenth century. Some from this great age of bridge construction—among them the Eads Bridge (1873), spanning the Mississippi River at St. Louis, and the Brooklyn Bridge (1883), over New York's East River—are still in use. Linking Brooklyn and Manhattan, the Brooklyn Bridge took fifteen years to build. A giant suspension structure, it was not only an engineering marvel but the symbol of the new industrial era—"the first product of the age of coal and iron to achieve completeness of expression," wrote the twentieth-century architectural critic Lewis Mumford.

If urban transit evolved in response to the geographic expansion of the American city, the need for more space in the downtown business districts drove advances in building construction. New materials made it possible to construct commercial buildings of greater height, interior space, and fire resistance. With the availability by the 1880s of steel girders, mass-produced durable plate glass, and the passenger elevator, a wholly new way of construction opened up. A steel skeleton would support the building, and the walls, previously weight bearing, would serve as curtains enclosing the structure. The sky, so to speak, became the limit.

The first "skyscraper" to be built on this principle was William Jenney's ten-story Home Insurance Building (1885) in Chicago. Although this pioneering effort was itself conventional in appearance—it looked just like the other commercial buildings in the downtown

The Chicago Elevated, 1900
This is Wabash Avenue, looking north from Adams Street. For Americans from farms and small towns, this photograph by William Henry Jackson captured something of the peculiarity of the urban scene. What could be stranger than a railroad suspended above the streets in the midst of people's lives?
KEA Publishing Services Ltd.

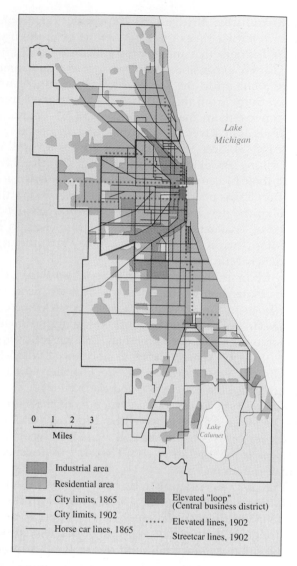

MAP 19.2

The Expansion of Chicago, 1865–1902

In 1865 Chicagoans depended on horsecar lines to get around town. By 1900 the city limits had expanded enormously, accompanied by an equally dramatic extension of streetcar service, by then electrified. Elevated trains also helped ease congestion in the urban core. New streetcar lines, some extending beyond the city limits, were important to suburban development in the coming years.

Legend:
- Industrial area
- Residential area
- City limits, 1865
- City limits, 1902
- Horse car lines, 1865
- Elevated "loop" (Central business district)
- Elevated lines, 1902
- Streetcar lines, 1902

of the fifty-five story Woolworth Building. Aptly called the Cathedral of Commerce, the Woolworth Building towered over its neighbors and marked the beginning of the modern Manhattan skyline.

By contrast, the magnificent rail terminals that graced the great cities tried to mask their function. Reflecting the architectural forms of ages past, the terminals were marvels of structural design in their soaring interiors and use of steel, glass, and stone. New York's Grand Central Station (1913), built in the French baroque style, was completely electrified. It made superb use of underground space and had a loop system that enabled trains to turn around without reversing course.

The Electric City. For ordinary citizens the electric lights that dispelled the gloom of the city at night probably offered the most dramatic evidence that times had changed. The mainstay of city lighting since the early nineteenth century had been gaslight—illuminating gas produced from coal—but, at 12 candlepower, gaslight was too dim to brighten the downtown streets and public spaces of the modern city. The first use of electricity, when generating technology made it commercially feasible, was for better city lighting. Charles F. Brush's electric arc lamps, installed in the windows of the Wanamaker department store in Philadelphia in 1878, threw a brilliant light and soon replaced gas lamps in stores and hotel lobbies and on city streets across the country. The following year Thomas Edison created the first practical incandescent light bulb, which brought electric lighting into American homes. Edison's motto—"Let there be light!"—truly described the experience of the modern city. Before electricity had any significant effect on industry, it gave the city its modern tempo, lifting and lowering elevators, powering streetcars and subway trains, turning night into day.

Meanwhile the telephone, patented by Alexander Graham Bell in 1876, speeded up communication beyond anything imagined previously. Twain's complaint of 1867 that it was impossible to carry on business in New York had been answered: all he needed to do was pick up the phone.

The City as Private Enterprise

City building was very much an exercise in private enterprise. The lure of profit spurred the great innovations—the trolley car, electric lighting, the skyscraper, the elevator, the telephone—and drove urban real-estate development. The investment opportunities looked so tempting that new cities sprang up almost overnight from the ruins of the Chicago fire of 1871 and the San Francisco earthquake of 1906. Real-estate interests, eager to develop subdivisions, were often instrumental in pushing streetcar lines outward from the central districts of cities.

district—the steel-girdered structure swiftly liberated the aesthetic perceptions of American architects. A Chicago school sprang up, dedicated to the design of buildings whose form expressed, rather than masked, their structure and function. The masterpiece of the Chicago school was Louis Sullivan's Carson, Pirie, Scott and Company department store (1904).

Chicago pioneered skyscraper construction, but the island of Manhattan, with its unrelenting need for prime downtown space, took the lead after the mid-1890s. The climax of New York's turn-of-the-century construction surge came with the completion in 1913

Thomas Edison's Laboratories in Menlo Park, New Jersey, c. 1880
Thomas Edison's dream of illuminating the world is illustrated by this fanciful drawing
of his laboratories in Menlo Park, New Jersey. For the time being, however, it was the
American home that was the primary beneficiary of Edison's wonderful lightbulb, since
electricity was slow to arrive in many parts of the world.
U.S. Department of the Interior, National Park Service, Edison National Historic Site.

Urban transit became big business. In the early 1880s Peter A. B. Widener and William L. Elkins teamed up to unite much of Philadelphia's streetcar system in the Philadelphia Traction Company. They did the same in alliance with Charles T. Yerkes in Chicago and with William C. Whitney and Thomas Fortune Ryan in New York. By 1900 their syndicate controlled streetcar systems in more than a hundred cities, as well as utilities supplying gas and electricity to urban customers. The city, like industry, became an arena for enterprise and profit.

Providing services privately, however, was a political choice. Under state laws cities had extensive powers of self-development. In authorizing a municipally owned subway in New York City in 1897, for example, the state courts reaffirmed the right of cities to carry out their responsibilities as they saw fit. Even the use of privately owned land was subject to whatever regulations the city might impose. Thus the skylines of Chicago and Boston did not resemble Manhattan's partly because of the limits those cities imposed on the heights of buildings.

But, as compared to Europe, American cities used their broad powers sparingly. America produced what the urban historian Sam Bass Warner has called the "private city"—one shaped primarily by the actions of many private individuals. All these persons pursued their own goals and tried to maximize their own profit. The prevailing belief was that the sum of such private activity would far exceed what the community could accomplish through public effort. This meant that the city itself handled only functions that could not be undertaken efficiently or profitably by private enterprise.

Despite that limitation, American cities actually compiled an impressive record in the late nineteenth century. Though by no means free of the corruption and wastefulness of earlier days, city governments in these years became more centralized, better administered, and, above all, more expansive in the functions they undertook. Nowhere in the world were there more massive public projects: aqueducts, sewage systems, street paving, bridge building, extensive park systems.

The Urban Environment. Yet streets, mainly a matter of convenience for the people, were often filthy. "Three or four days of warm spring weather," remarked a New York journalist, would turn Manhattan's garbage-strewn, snow-clogged streets into "veritable mud rivers." The environment likewise suffered. A visitor to Pittsburgh noted "the heavy pall of smoke which constantly overhangs her . . . until the very sun looks coppery through the sooty haze." As for the lovely hills rising from the rivers, "they have been leveled down, cut into, sliced off, and ruthlessly marred and mutilated, until not a trace of their original outlines remains." Pittsburgh presented "all that is unsightly and forbidding in appearance, the original beauties of nature having been ruthlessly sacrificed to utility."

It was not that America lacked an urban vision. On the contrary, an abiding rural ideal had exerted a powerful influence on American cities for many years. Frederick Law Olmsted, who designed New York's Central Park, wanted cities that exposed people to the beauties of nature. One of Olmsted's projects, the Chicago World's Fair of 1893, gave rise to the influential "City Beautiful" movement. The results included larger park systems, broad boulevards and parkways, and, after the turn of the century, zoning laws and planned suburbs.

But cities usually heeded urban planners too little and far too late. "Fifteen or twenty years ago a plan might have been adopted that would have made this one of the most beautiful cities in the world," Kansas City's park commissioners reported in 1893. At that time, however, "such a policy could not be fully appreciated." Nor, the commissioners concluded, even if Kansas City had foreseen its future, would it have shouldered the "heavy burden" of trying to shape its development. The American city had placed its faith in the operations of the marketplace, not the restraints of a planned future.

Even with planning, the city's dynamism often confounded efforts to meet the needs of the people. When completed in 1842, New York's Croton aqueduct was hailed as "more akin in magnificence to the ancient and Roman aqueducts [than anything]

achieved in our times." Yet less than a decade later water consumption was exceeding the capacity of the aqueduct. In 1885 New York started to build a second and larger aqueduct. That one also failed to meet the city's needs, so New York built still another aqueduct a hundred miles away in the Catskill Mountains. Each new facility and innovation seemed to fall short, not merely outstripped by the rising demand but also contributing to that demand. This occurred with urban transportation, high-rise buildings, and modern sanitation systems. They attracted more users, created new needs, and caused additional crowding and shortages.

Congested Housing. Hardest hit by urban growth were the poor. In earlier times low-income city residents had lived in makeshift wooden structures in alleys and back streets or in the subdivided homes of more prosperous families who had fled to better neighborhoods. When rising land values after the Civil War made this practice unprofitable, speculators began to build housing specifically designed for the urban masses. In New York City, the dreadful result was the "dumbbell" tenement, shaped to utilize nearly all the standard lot of 25 by 100 feet. A five-story building of this type could house twenty families in cramped, airless apartments (Figure 19.1). In New York's Eleventh Ward an average of 986 persons occupied each acre, a density matched only by Bombay, India. In other cities crowding was not as severe. Chicago, Boston, and St. Louis relied on two- and three-story buildings for low-income housing, while Philadelphia and Baltimore made do with dingy row houses.

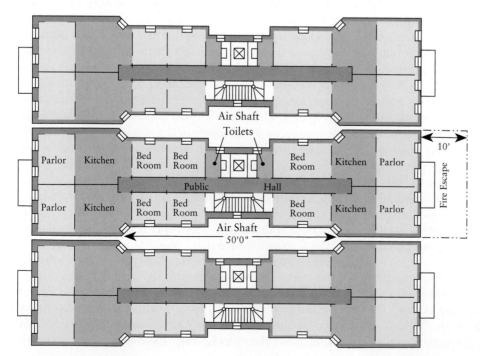

FIGURE 19.1
Floor Plan of a Dumbbell Tenement
In a contest for a design that met an 1879 requirement that every room have a window, the dumbbell tenement won. The interior indentation, which created an airshaft between adjoining buildings, gave the tenement its "dumbbell" shape. What was touted as a "model" tenement demonstrated instead the futility of trying to reconcile maximum land usage with decent housing. Each floor contained four apartments of three or four rooms, the largest only 10 by 11 feet. The two toilets in the hall became filthy or broke down under the daily use by forty or more people. The narrow airshaft provided almost no light for the interior rooms and served mainly as a dumping ground for garbage. So deplorable were these tenements that they became the stimulus for the next wave of New York housing reform.

Civic-minded people everywhere considered these districts to be blights on the city. Here is how one investigator described Chicago's Halsted Street in 1896:

The filthy and rotten tenements, the dingy courts and tumble-down sheds, the foul stables and dilapidated outhouses, the broken sewer pipes, the piles of garbage fairly alive with diseased odors, and . . . children filling every nook, working and playing in every room, eating and sleeping in every windowsill, pouring in and out of every door, and seeming literally to pave every scrap of "yard."

Reformers recognized the problem but seemed unable to solve it. Some favored model tenements financed by public-spirited citizens willing to accept a limited return on their investment. When private philanthropy failed to make much of a dent in the problem, cities turned to housing codes. The most advanced of these was New York's Tenement House Law of 1901, which required interior courts, indoor toilets, and fire safeguards for new housing, but did little about existing housing stock. Commercial development pushed up land values in downtown areas. Only high-density, cheaply built housing could earn a sufficient profit for the landlords of the poor. This economic fact defied nineteenth-century solutions.

A Balance Sheet: Chicago and Berlin. Chicago and Berlin had virtually equal populations in 1900. Their histories, however, were profoundly different. Seventy years earlier, when Chicago was just a muddy frontier outpost, Berlin was a city of 250,000 and the capital of the kingdom of Prussia.

With Prussia's unification of the German Empire in 1871, the Hohenzollern rulers rebuilt Berlin on a grander scale. "A capital city is essential for the state, to act as a pivot for its culture," proclaimed Prussian historian Heinrich von Treitschke. Berlin served that national purpose—"a center where Germany's political, intellectual, and material life is concentrated, and its people can feel united." Chicago had no such pretensions. It was strictly a place of business, made great by virtue of its strategic grip on the commerce of America's industrial heartland. Nothing in Chicago evoked the grandeur of Berlin's boulevards or its monumental palaces and public buildings, nor were Chicagoans ever witness to the pomp and ceremony of the imperial parades through the Brandenburg Gate and up broad, tree-lined Unter den Linden to the national cathedral.

Yet as a functioning city Chicago was in many ways superior to Berlin. Chicago's waterworks pumped 500 million gallons of water a day, providing 139 gallons of water per person, while Berliners had to make do with 18 gallons. Flush toilets, a rarity in Berlin in 1900, could be found in 60 percent of Chicago's homes. Its streets were lit by electricity while Berlin still relied mostly on gaslight. Chicago had a much more extensive streetcar system, twice as much acreage devoted to parks, and a public library containing many more volumes than Berlin's. And Chicago had just completed an amazing sanitation project, reversing the course of the Chicago River so that its waters—and the city's sewage—would flow away from Lake Michigan and southward down into the Illinois and Mississippi rivers.

Giant sanitation projects were one thing; an inspiring urban environment was something else. For well-traveled Americans admiring of things European, the sense of inferiority was palpable. "We are enormously rich," admitted the journalist Edwin L. Godkin, "but . . . what have we got to show? Almost nothing. Ugliness from an artistic point of view is the mark of all our cities." Thus the urban balance sheet: a utilitarian infrastructure that was superb by nineteenth-century standards but "no municipal splendors of any description, nothing but population and hotels."

City People

With its soaring skyscrapers, jostling traffic, and hum of business activity, the city symbolized energy and enterprise. When the budding writer Hamlin Garland and his brother arrived in Chicago from rural Iowa in 1881, they knew immediately that they had entered a new world: "Everything interested us. . . . Nothing was commonplace, nothing was ugly to us." In one way or another every city-bound migrant, whether from the American countryside or from a foreign land, experienced something of this exhilaration and wonder.

Newcomers

With the opportunity and boundless variety came disorder and uncertainty. The urban world was utterly unlike the rural communities the newcomers had left. In the countryside every person had been known to his or her neighbors. Mark Twain found New York "a splendid desert, where a stranger is lonely in the midst of a million of his race. A man walks his tedious miles through the same interminable streets every day, yet never seeing a familiar face, and never seeing a strange one the second time. . . . Every man rushes, rushes, rushes, and never has time to be companionable— never has any time at his disposal to fool away on matters which do not involve dollars and duty and business." If rural roles and obligations had been well understood, in the city the only predictable relationships were those dictated by the marketplace.

Italian Bread Peddlers, New York City
Because of crowded conditions in East Side tenements, immigrant life spilled out onto the streets, which offered a bit of fresh air, a chance to socialize with neighbors, and a place to shop for food, including bread.
KEA Publishing Services Ltd.

The newcomers could never re-create in the city the worlds they had left behind. But they found ways to gain a sense of belonging, they built a multitude of new institutions, and they learned how to function in an impersonal, heterogeneous environment. An urban culture emerged, and through it there developed a new breed of American who was entirely at home in the modern city.

Immigrants. At the turn of the century, upwards of 30 percent of the residents of New York, Chicago, Boston, Cleveland, Minneapolis, and San Francisco were foreign-born. The dominant groups still represented mainly the older migration from northern Europe. The biggest ethnic group in Boston was Irish; in Minneapolis, Swedish; in most other northern cities, German. But by 1910 the influx from southern and eastern Europe had changed the ethnic complexion of many of these cities. The experience of Philadelphia is shown in Table 19.2. In Chicago, Poles took the lead; in New York, eastern European Jews; in San Francisco, Italians.

All these immigrants—old and new—brought with them homeland experiences and customs that shaped their lives in the New World. But for the later arrivals from southern and eastern Europe there was less intermingling with the resident populations than in the earlier "walking cities." Beginning in the 1880s, observers invariably reported that only foreign-born people lived in the poorer downtown areas. "One may find for the asking an Italian, a German, a French, African, Spanish, Bohemian, Russian, Scandinavian, Jewish, and Chinese colony," remarked the Danish American journalist Jacob Riis in his study of New York in 1890. "The one thing you shall vainly ask for in the chief city of America is a distinctively American community."

The later arrivals from southern and eastern Europe had little choice about where they lived; they needed to be near their jobs and to find cheap housing. Some gravitated to the outlying factory districts; others

settled in the congested downtown ghettos. The immigrants did not settle randomly in these districts, however. Even where this seemed to happen, as in Philadelphia, closer study revealed that ethnic groups clustered in certain houses and portions of blocks. More commonly, as Riis discovered, an ethnic group took over an entire neighborhood. In New York City, Italians crowded into the formerly Irish neighborhoods west of Broadway, and Russian and Polish Jews pushed the Germans out of the Lower East Side (Map 19.3). A colony of Hungarians lived around Houston Street, and Bohemians occupied stretches of the Upper East Side between Fiftieth and Seventy-sixth streets.

Within ethnic groups, one could also spot clusters of people from the same province or even village. Among New York Italians, for example, Neapolitans and Calabrians populated the Mulberry Bend district, while Genoese lived on Baxter Street. Other northern

TABLE 19.2

Foreign-Born Population of Philadelphia, 1870 and 1910

	1870	1910
Irish	96,698	83,196
German	50,746	61,480
Austrian	519	19,860
Italian	516	45,308
Russian	94	90,697
Hungarian	52	12,495
Foreign-born population	183,624	384,707
Total population	674,022	1,549,008

Source: Allen F. Davis and Mark Haller, *The Peoples of Philadelphia* (Philadelphia: Temple University Press, 1973), 205.

Italians occupied the Eighth and Fifteenth wards west of Broadway, while southern Italians moved into "Little Italy" far uptown in Harlem. In 1903, along a short stretch of Elizabeth Street there lived several hundred families from a single Sicilian fishing town, Sciacca, and Sciacca's patron saint was celebrated on Elizabeth Street, as in Sicily.

Capitalizing on the fellow-feeling that drew ethnic groups together, a variety of institutions sprang up to meet the immigrants' needs. Wherever substantial numbers lived, newspapers appeared. In 1911 the twenty thousand Poles in Buffalo, New York, supported two Polish-language daily papers. Immigrants throughout the country avidly read *Il Progresso Italo-Americano* and the Yiddish-language *Jewish Daily Forward*, both published in New York City (see American Voices, "Anonymous: Bintel Brief," p. 619). Companionship could always be found on streetcorners, in barbershops and club rooms, and in saloons. Italians marched in saint's-day parades, Bohemians gathered in singing societies, and New York Jews patronized a lively Yiddish theater. To provide help in times of sickness and death, the immigrants organized mutual-aid societies. The Italians of Chicago had sixty-six of these organizations in 1903, composed mainly of people from particular provinces and towns. Immigrants built a rich and functional institutional life in urban America, to an extent unimagined in their native villages.

Urban Blacks. The vast majority of African Americans—85 percent in 1880—lived in the rural South. In the ensuing years some of them migrated to the modestly growing southern cities. By 1900 blacks constituted roughly a third of the South's urban population, ranging from 20 percent in Louisville and Dallas to majorities in Memphis and Charleston.

The great African American migration to northern cities was just beginning. The black population of New York increased by 30,000 to 91,000 between 1900 and 1910, making New York second only to Washington, D.C. Blacks in New York in 1910 still represented less than 2 percent of that population, which was roughly their percentage in Chicago and Cleveland as well.

Despite their relatively small numbers, urban blacks could not escape discrimination. They retreated from the scattered black neighborhoods of older times into concentrated ghettos—Chicago's black belt on the South Side, for example, or the early outlines of New York's Harlem. Race prejudice likewise cut down job opportunities. Twenty-six percent of Cleveland's blacks had been skilled workers in 1870, but only 12 percent were by 1890, and entire occupations such as barbering (except for a black clientele) disappeared. Two-thirds of Cleveland's blacks in 1910 worked as domestics and day laborers, with little hope of moving up the job ladder.

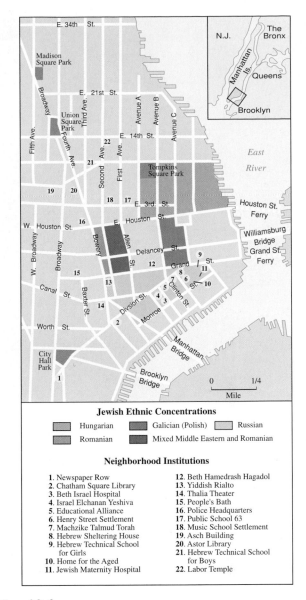

MAP 19.3
The Lower East Side, New York City, in 1900
As this map shows, the Jewish immigrants dominating Manhattan's Lower East Side preferred living in neighborhoods populated by those from their home regions of eastern Europe. Their sense of a common identity made for a remarkable flowering of educational, cultural, and social institutions on the Jewish East Side.

In the face of pervasive discrimination, urban blacks built their own communities. They created a flourishing press, fraternal orders, a vast array of women's organizations, and a middle class of doctors, lawyers, and small entrepreneurs who catered to their needs. Above all, there were the black churches—twenty-five in Chicago in 1905, mainly Methodist and Baptist. More than any other institution, remarked one scholar in 1913, it was the church "which the Negro may call his own. . . . A new church may be built . . . and . . . all the machinery set in motion without ever con-

The Economy of the Ghetto
Downtown immigrant neighborhoods would not have struck
the casual observer as industrial districts, but tucked away in
the tenements were commercial lofts and small workshops.
An entire ready-made clothing industry flourished within the
ghettos of large cities, drawing especially on the young women
of the neighborhood to perform the low-paid sewing tasks in
often dangerous conditions.
Brown Brothers.

The Cherry Family, 1906
Wiley and Fannie Cherry migrated in 1893 from North Carolina to Chicago, settling in the small African American community on the West Side. The Cherrys apparently prospered,
and by 1906, when this family portrait was taken, had entered
the black middle class. When migration intensified after 1900,
longer-settled urban blacks like the Cherrys became uncomfortable, and relations with the needy, rural newcomers were
often tense.
Courtesy Lorraine Heflin/Chicago Historical Society.

sulting any white person. . . . [It] more than anything
else represents the real life of the race." As in the southern countryside, the church was the central institution
for city blacks, and the preacher the most important
local citizen. Manhattan's Union Baptist Church,
housed like many others in a storefront, attracted the
"very recent residents of this new, disturbing city" and,
ringing with spirituals and fervent prayer, made Christianity come "alive Sunday mornings."

Ward Politics

Race and ethnicity tended to divide newcomers to the
city and turn them in on themselves. Politics, in contrast,
acted as a powerful instrument for integrating them into
the larger urban society. Every migrant to an American
city automatically became a ward resident and, by living
on a particular street, immediately acquired a spokesman
at city hall in the form of an alderman.

In earlier days aldermen had been the dominant figures in urban politics, but that was no longer the case in
the late nineteenth century. Power had largely passed to

the mayor's office and various city administrative agencies. But the city council still represented the parochial
interests of the wards, and immigrants learned very
quickly that if they needed anything from city hall, the
alderman was the person to see. That was how streets got
paved, or water mains extended, or a variance granted—
so that, for example, in 1888 Vito Fortounescere could
"place and keep a stand for the sale of fruit, inside the
stoop-line, in front of the northeast corner of Twenty-
eighth Street and Fourth Avenue" in Manhattan, and the
parishioners of Saint Maria of Mount Carmel could set
off fireworks at their Fourth of July picnic.

Machine control of political parties, present at
every level, flourished most luxuriantly in the big cities.
Urban machines depended on a loyal grass-roots con-

ANONYMOUS

Bintel Brief

★

In Yiddish bintel brief *means "bundle of letters." That was the name of the famous section of the Jewish Daily* Forward *devoted to letters from immigrant readers about their trials and tribulations in America.*

I am a girl sixteen years old. I live together with my parents and my two old sisters. Last year I met a young man. We love one another. He is a very respectable man, and makes a fine living. My sisters have no fiances. I know that should I marry they will never talk to me. My parents are also strongly against it since I am the youngest child. I do not want to lose my parents' love, and neither do I want to lose my lover because that would break my heart. Give me some advice, dear Editor!

I was born in a small town in Russia, and until I was sixteen I studied in *Talmud Torahs* and *yeshivas,* but when I came to America I developed spiritually and became a freethinker. Yet every year when the time of *Rosh Hashana* and *Yom Kippur* comes around I become very gloomy. . . . So strong are my feelings that I enter the synagogue, not in order to pray to God but to heal and refresh my aching soul by sitting among *landsleit* [countrymen] and listening to the cantor's sweet melodies. The members of my Progressive Society don't understand. They say I am a hypocrite. . . . What do you think? *Answer.* No one can tell another what to do with himself on *Yom Kippur.*

I am a Russian revolutionist and a freethinker. Here in America I became acquainted with a girl who is also a freethinker. We decided to marry, but the problem is that she has Orthodox parents, and if we refuse a religious ceremony we will be cut off from them forever. I don't know what to do. Therefore, I ask you to advise me how to act. *Answer.* There are times when it is better to be kind in order not to grieve old parents.

To a man everything is permissible, to a woman nothing. A man is king over us and may do his will. When I argue that morality is more demanding on women, my husband gets angry and denies it with all his might. There is no such thing as a man with a bad name, but just let one spot fall upon a woman. . . . Why?!

I am in favor of giving women full rights, but most of my friends are against it. They argue that the woman would then no longer be the housewife, the mother to her children, the wife to her husband—in a word, everything would be destroyed. I do not agree because a woman is a human being just like a man, and if women are recognized as human beings, they must be granted all the rights of human beings. *Answer.* Justice can reign among people only when they all have equal rights.

Why do the police favor the clothing stores on Canal Street which remain open seven days a week? . . . Where else in the world do people sell their lives to make a living with no holidays and no rest? I am one of the corpses who works seven days a week in one of those electric-lit graves on Canal Street.

I am a young man of twenty-five, and I recently met a fine girl. She has a flaw, however—a dimple in her chin. It is said that people who have this lose their first husband or wife. I love her very much. But I'm afraid to marry her lest I die because of the dimple. *Answer.* The tragedy is not that the girl has a dimple in her chin but that some people have a screw loose in their heads.

Source: Irving Howe and Kenneth Libo, eds., *How We Lived* (New York: New American Library, 1979), 88–90.

stituency, so each ward was divided into election districts of a few blocks. The district captain reported to the ward boss, who was likely also to be the alderman. The main job of these functionaries was to be accessible and, as best they could, to serve the needs of the party faithful.

The machine similarly served the business community. Contractors sought city business; gas companies and streetcar lines wanted licenses and privileges; manufacturers needed services and not-too-nosy inspectors; and the liquor trade and numbers racket relied on a tolerant police force. All of them turned to the machine boss and his lieutenants. In addition to these everyday functions, the machine continuously mediated among conflicting interests and oiled the wheels of city government.

The machines filled a void in the public life of the nineteenth-century city. They did informally much of what the municipal system left undone. "Nowhere else in the world," remarked journalist Henry Jones Ford, "has party organization had to cope with such enormous tasks . . . and its efficiency in dealing with them is the true glory of our political system."

Of course, the machine exacted a price for these services. The tenement dweller gave his vote. The businessman wrote a check. Corruption permeated this informal system. Some of the money that changed hands inevitably ended up in the pockets of machine politicians. This "boodle" could take the form of outright corruption—kickbacks by contractors; protection money from gamblers, saloonkeepers, and prostitutes; payoffs from gas and trolley companies. The Tammany Ward boss George Washington Plunkitt, however, insisted that he had no need for kickbacks and bribes. He favored what he called "honest graft," the easy profits that came to savvy insiders. Plunkitt made most of his money building wharves on Manhattan's waterfront. Tim Sullivan used his contacts to build a vaudeville empire. One way or another, legally or otherwise, machine politics rewarded its supporters (see American Lives, "Big Tim Sullivan: Tammany Politician," pp. 622–623).

For ambitious young immigrants and blacks, this was reason enough to favor the machine system. In the mid-1870s, over half of Chicago's forty aldermen were foreign-born, sixteen of them Irish immigrants. The first Italian was elected to the board in 1885 and the first Pole in 1888. Blacks did not manage to get on Chicago's board of aldermen until after 1900; but in Baltimore an African American represented the Eleventh Ward from 1890 onward, and Philadelphia had three black aldermen by 1899. As a ladder for social mobility, machine politics (like professional sports, entertainment, and organized crime) was the most democratic of American institutions.

For the ordinary tenement dweller, however, the machine had a more modest value. It acted as a rough-and-ready social service agency, providing jobs for the jobless, a helping hand for a bereaved family, and intercession with an unfeeling city bureaucracy. As a Boston ward boss remarked, "There's got to be in every ward somebody that any bloke can come to—no matter what he's done—and get help. *Help, you understand; none of your law and justice, but help.*" The Tammany Ward boss Plunkitt had a "regular system" when fires broke out in his district. He arranged for clothing and shelter, to "fix them up till they get things runnin' again. It's philanthropy, but it's politics, too—mighty good politics."

Plunkitt was an Irishman, and so were most of the ward politicians controlling Tammany Hall. But by the 1890s Plunkitt's Fifteenth District was filling up with Italians and eastern European Jews. In general the New York Irish had no love for these newer immigrants, but Plunkitt played no favorites. On any given day (as he recorded in his diary) he might attend an Italian funeral in the afternoon and a Jewish wedding in the evening, and he probably paid his respects with a few Italian words and a bit of Yiddish. In an era when so many forces acted to isolate ghetto communities, politics served an *integrating* function, cutting across ethnic lines and giving immigrants and blacks a stake in the larger urban order.

Religion in the City

For African Americans, as we have seen, the church was a central institution of urban life. This was true for many other city dwellers as well. But the city was also difficult ground for religious practice, with much that had once seemed settled now contested. All the great faiths present in late nineteenth-century America—Judaism, Catholicism, Protestantism—had to scramble to reconcile how they practiced their beliefs with the secular demands of the new urban world.

Judaism: The Challenge to Orthodoxy. About 250,000 Jews, mostly of German origin, were living in America when the eastern European Jews began to arrive in the 1880s. Well established and prosperous, the German Jews had embraced Reform Judaism, abandoning religious practices—from keeping a kosher kitchen to conducting services in Hebrew—"not adapted to the views and habits of modern civilization." Anxious to preserve their traditional piety, Yiddish-speaking immigrants from eastern Europe founded their own Orthodox synagogues, often in vacant stores and ramshackle buildings, and practiced Judaism in the old way.

In the villages of eastern Europe, however, Judaism had stood not only for worship and belief but for an entire way of life. Insular though it might be, ghetto life in America could not re-create the communal environment on which strict religious observance depended. "The very clothes I wore and the very food I ate had a fatal effect on my religious habits," confessed the hero of Abraham Cahan's novel *The Rise of David Levinsky* (1917). "If you . . . attempt to bend your religion to the spirit of your surroundings, it breaks. It falls to pieces." Levinsky shaved off his beard and plunged into the Manhattan clothing business. Orthodox Judaism survived this shattering of faith, but only by sharply reducing its claims on the lives of the faithful.

"Americanism" and the Catholic Church. Catholics faced much the same problem. The issue, explicitly defined within the Roman Catholic Church as "Americanism," turned on the degree to which Catholicism

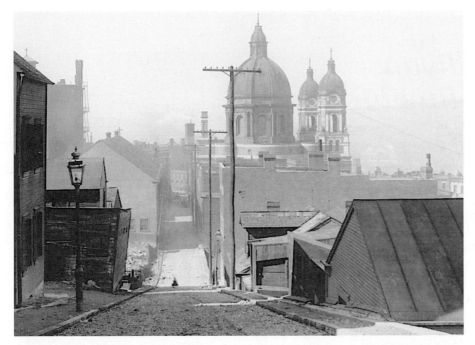

Immaculate Heart of Mary Church, 1908
In crowded immigrant neighborhoods the church rose from undistinguished surroundings to assert the centrality of religious belief in the life of the community. This photograph is a view of Immaculate Heart of Mary Church, taken from Polish Hill in Pittsburgh in 1908.
Archives of Industrial Society, University Library System, University of Pittsburgh.

should adapt to American society, with its Protestant majority and sharp separation of church and state. Should Catholic children attend parochial or public schools? Should they intermarry with non-Catholics? Should the traditional education for the clergy be changed? Bishop John Ireland of St. Paul, Minnesota, felt that "the principles of the Church are in harmony with the interests of the Republic." But traditionalists, led by Archbishop Michael A. Corrigan of New York, denied the possibility of such harmony and argued in effect for insulating the Church from the threatening American environment.

In 1895 Pope Leo XIII announced his support of the traditionalists, pronouncing America a country that did not afford "the most desirable status of the Church." The pope regretted the absence of state support for Catholicism and urged communicants "to prefer to associate with Catholics, a course which will be very conducive to the safeguarding of their faith."

Immigrant Catholics generally supported the Church's conservatism because they wanted to preserve their religion as they had known it in Europe. But their concerns were not purely religious; church life also had to express their ethnic identities. Newly arrived Catholics wanted their own parishes where they could celebrate their own customs and holidays, speak their own languages, and educate their children in their own parochial schools. When they became numerous enough, they also demanded their own bishops.

The Church had difficulty responding. The demands of immigrant congregations seemed to challenge the Catholic hierarchy, which was dominated by Irish Catholics, and even the integrity of the Church itself. The desire for ethnic parishes led to demands for local control of Church property. Moreover, if the Church appointed bishops with jurisdiction over specific ethnic groups, that would mean disrupting the diocesan structure that unified the Church.

The severity of the challenge depended partly on the religious convictions of each ethnic group. Italian men, for example, were known for religious apathy, and many Italians harbored strong anticlerical feelings, much strengthened by the papacy's stand against the unification of Italy. But the Church played such an important part in the lives of Polish immigrants that they resented any interference by the Catholic hierarchy. In 1907 fifty parishes formed the Polish National Catholic Church of America, which adhered to Catholic ritual without recognizing the pope's authority.

On the whole, the Church managed to satisfy the immigrant faithful. It met their demand for representation in the hierarchy by appointing immigrant priests as auxiliary bishops within existing dioceses. Ethnic parishes also flourished. Before World War I American Catholics worshiped in more than two thousand foreign-language churches and in many others that were bilingual. Not without strain, the Catholic Church made itself a central institution for the expression of ethnic identity in urban America.

Protestantism: Regaining Lost Ground. Protestantism was the dominant faith of the nation, but by 1890 the total church membership was only about 14 million, compared to 8 million practicing Catholics. The city posed the greatest challenge to Protestant

Big Tim Sullivan: Tammany Politician

———————★———————

Big Tim Sullivan
Culver Pictures.

TIMOTHY D. SULLIVAN was born on July 23, 1863, near the Hudson River docks in lower Manhattan. His parents were Irish immigrants, part of the mass migration of potato famine victims who flooded into New York in the 1840s. Four years later Tim's father died, leaving his young widow, Catherine Connelly Sullivan, with four small children. Soon after, Catherine married Lawrence Mulligan, an Irish laborer, and the family moved to the notorious Five Points district on the Lower East Side. There the 1870 census found them, a household of ten (including three boarders) living in an overcrowded tenement at 25 Baxter Street (see Map 19.3 for the urban geography of Sullivan's career).

Tim had a harsh childhood. His stepfather drank heavily and beat his wife and children regularly. To make ends meet, Catherine took in washing and Tim went to work at age seven bundling papers for $1.50 a week on Newspaper Row across from City Hall. Tim got through grammar school, but his family needed his earnings too much for him to go on to high school. "Free as it was," he later remarked, "it was not free enough for me to go there." Instead—Horatio Alger style—he made his way up in the newspaper business and by age eighteen was well established as a wholesale newspaper dealer. He soon became the proprietor of two saloons and in his early twenties was ready for politics. A handsome fellow, over six feet tall, Sullivan was quick with his fists. He gained a local reputation by thrashing a tough he had encountered on the street beating up a woman. True or not, the story helped him win the Democratic nomination at age twenty-three for the New York State Assembly from the Second District.

In 1889 Sullivan opposed a bill granting Manhattan's police virtually unlimited powers to detain people with jail records. The champion of the bill was Thomas F. Byrnes, chief inspector of the New York Police Department and the most celebrated detective in the country. Byrnes did not take kindly to opposition from small-time politicians. He raided Sullivan's saloons, arrested two barkeepers for excise tax violations, and denounced Sullivan as a consorter with criminals. Against the advice of friends, Sullivan took the assembly floor to answer the charge.

In tearful tones Sullivan cast himself as an "honest Bowery boy," describing his impoverished childhood, his saintly mother, his struggle to rise in the world. "When, at the conclusion [so a reporter recorded], he asked if he had any time or money to spend with thieves, there was a 'No' on nearly every member's lips." The performance was the making of the obscure assemblyman. Although he gained notoriety with uptown New Yorkers that would dog him throughout his career, he won the hearts of his own constituents, who reveled in the success story of one of their own. They thought "Big Tim" a fine fellow, and so did the Tammany leaders.

When the Tammany machine swept into power in the 1892 elections, Boss Richard Croker tapped Sullivan to run the new Third Assembly District centering on the Bowery. Sullivan swiftly consolidated his power. His inner circle was all Irish, but for election district captains he appointed Jews, Italians, and Germans who were well connected in the immigrant communities that populated his fiefdom. Sullivan became famous for his summer "chowders,"

The Bowery at Night, 1895
This painting by W. Louis Sonntag Jr. shows Big Tim's stomping ground—the Bowery—crowded with shoppers and pleasure seekers. It was during this time that the Bowery gained its raffish reputation.
Museum of the City of New York.

when he transported his constituents by riverboat to the country for a rowdy day of picnicking. At Christmas there was a fine dinner for all who were in need. And in February Sullivan handed out wool socks and shoes—always with the sentimental tale of how a teacher had given him free shoes one cold winter.

Big Tim also attended assiduously to the nitty-gritty business of running a political machine. He got jobs for his supporters, visited the jails regularly to offer bail and other aid to the inmates, and on election day made sure his strong-arm crews patrolled the polling places. Sullivan's district became the best organized in the city, and Tammany hailed him as "the most popular man on the East Side."

In the meantime, Sullivan was making his fortune. His particular form of "honest graft" was commercial entertainment. Big Tim knew instinctively how important a good time was to city people. Besides, the main street of his district, the Bowery, was the gaudy center of low-life entertainment for the entire city, lined with burlesque houses, concert saloons, restaurants, and cheap hotels. In the mid-1890s Sullivan formed a partnership with two theatrical producers and began to invest in vaudeville houses. He contributed not only money and a shrewd head but the political contacts that ensured lax enforcement of building codes and easy access to liquor licenses. Sullivan also became involved in pro-

fessional boxing, horse racing, and, more illicitly, the gambling dens that dotted his district.

Sullivan was accused of trafficking in East Side prostitution, but this he indignantly denied: "Nobody who knows me well will believe I would take a penny from any woman, much less from the poor creatures who are more to be pitied than any other human beings on earth. I'd be afraid to take a cent from a poor woman of the streets for fear my old mother would see me. I'd a good deal rather break into a bank and rob the safe. That would be a more manly and decent way of getting money."

When Boss Croker resigned in 1902, Sullivan might have succeeded him, but Big Tim preferred his own district and threw his support to Charles F. Murphy, who ruled Tammany for the next twenty-two years. Sullivan served briefly in Congress, made a lot more money investing in the early movie industry and in vaudeville syndicates across the country, and in the final phase of his career became a champion of progressive social legislation in the New York Senate. In 1912 Sullivan suffered a severe mental breakdown, possibly caused by tertiary syphilis. A year later he died under the wheels of a freight train after running off from his brother's house outside New York. His funeral procession down the Bowery was one of the largest in memory and brought out an immense crowd from every stratum of New York society, from statesmen to prizefighters to scrubwomen.

churches. They had to find ways of attracting, or reaffiliating, the great numbers of native-born Americans flocking into the cities in the late nineteenth century from the nation's farms and small towns. At the same time, they had to keep up with congregations scattering into the suburbs as European immigrants occupied the older residential neighborhoods. Many formerly prosperous churches found themselves stranded in the squalid new ghettos. Seventeen Protestant churches moved out of lower Manhattan during the twenty years after 1868 as the area below Fourteenth Street filled up with immigrants.

Every major city retained great downtown churches where wealthy Protestants worshiped. Some of these churches, richly endowed, took pride in nationally prominent pastors, including Henry Ward Beecher of Plymouth Congregational Church in Brooklyn and Phillips Brooks of Trinity Episcopal Church in Boston. But the eminence of these churches, with their fashionable congregations and imposing edifices, could not disguise the growing remoteness of Protestantism from much of its urban constituency. "Where is the city in which the Sabbath day is not losing ground?" lamented a minister in 1887. The families of businessmen, lawyers, and doctors could be seen in any church on Sunday morning, he noted, "but the workingmen and their families are not there."

To counter this decline, the Protestant churches responded in two ways. They evangelized among the unchurched and indifferent, for example, through the Sunday-school movement. Protestants also made their churches instruments of social uplift. Starting in the 1880s, many city churches provided reading rooms, day nurseries, clubhouses, and vocational classes. Some churches linked evangelism and social uplift. The Salvation Army, which arrived from Great Britain in 1879, spread the gospel of repentance among the urban poor and built an assistance program that ranged from soup kitchens to homes for former prostitutes. When all else failed, the down-and-outers of American cities knew they could count on the Salvation Army.

For young single people new to the cities, there were the Young Men's and Women's Christian Associations, which had been transplanted from Britain before the Civil War. By the mid-1880s virtually all large cities had YMCAs equipped with gymnasiums, auditoriums, and dormitories. Housing for single women was an especially important mission of the YWCAs. No other organizations so effectively combined activities for young adults with an evangelizing appeal in the form of Bible classes, nondenominational worship, and a religious atmosphere.

The social meaning that urban Protestants sought in religion explained the enormous popularity of a book called *In His Steps* (1896). The author, the Congregational minister Charles M. Sheldon, told the story of a congregation that resolved to live by Christ's precepts for one year. "If the church members were all doing as Jesus would do," Sheldon asked, "could it remain true that armies of men would walk the streets for jobs, and hundreds of them curse the church, and thousands of them find in the saloon their best friend?"

The most potent form of urban evangelism—revivalism—said little about social uplift. From its beginnings in the eighteenth century, revivalism had steadfastly focused on individual redemption. The resolution of earthly problems, revivalists believed, would follow the conversion of the people to Christ. Beginning in the mid-1870s, revival meetings swept through the cities.

The pioneering figure was Dwight L. Moody, a former Chicago shoe salesman and YMCA official. After preaching in Britain for two years, Moody returned to America in 1875. With his talented chorister and hymn writer, Ira D. Sankey, Moody staged revival meetings that drew thousands. He preached an optimistic, uncomplicated, nondenominational message. Eternal life could be had for the asking, Moody shouted as he held up his Bible. His listeners needed only "to come forward and take, TAKE!"

Many other preachers followed in Moody's path. The most notable was Billy (William Ashley) Sunday, a hard-drinking former outfielder for the Chicago White Stockings who mended his ways and found religion. Like Moody and other city revivalists, Sunday was a farm boy. His rip-snorting attacks on fashionable ministers and the "booze traffic" carried the ring of rustic America. By realizing that many people remained villagers at heart, revivalists found a key for bringing city dwellers back into the church.

In a larger sense, however, revivalism was expressive of a more general fundamentalist movement that sought to preserve old-time religion against the increasing complacency and doctrinal liberalism of mainstream Protestantism. Just as Methodism had arisen against the Church of England in the eighteenth century, so now in the late nineteenth century new churches arose against Methodism. The Holiness evangelical movement was at first nondenominational but then began to spawn such new denominations as the Church of the Nazarene (1908). Out of the Holiness Revival came the more radical Pentecostal movement, which by 1914 had brought together many local bodies into the Assemblies of God.

Leisure in the City

City people compartmentalized life's activities, setting workplace apart from home and working time apart from free time. "Going out" became a necessity, demanded not only as relief from a day of hard work but as proof that life was better in the New World than

José Martí
Coney Island, 1881
——————★——————

José Martí, a Cuban patriot and revolutionary (p. 680), was by profession a journalist. In exile from 1880 to 1895, he spent most of his time in New York City, reporting to his Latin American readers on the customs of the Yankees. Martí took special pleasure in observing Americans at play.

From all parts of the United States, legions of intrepid ladies and Sunday-best farmers arrive to admire the splendid sights, the unexampled wealth, the dizzying variety, the herculean surge, the striking appearance of Coney Island, the now famous island, four years ago an abandoned sand bank, that today is a spacious amusement area providing relaxation and recreation for hundreds of thousands of New Yorkers who throng to its pleasant beaches every day. . . .

Other nations—ourselves among them—live devoured by a sublime demon within that drives us to the tireless pursuit of an ideal of love or glory. . . . Not so with these tranquil souls, stimulated only by a desire for gain. One scans those shimmering beaches . . . one views the throngs seated in comfortable chairs along the seashore, filling their lungs with the fresh, invigorating air. But it is said that

those from our lands who remain here long are overcome with melancholy . . . because this great nation is void of spirit.

But what coming and going! What torrents of money! What facilities for every pleasure! What absolute absence of any outward sadness or poverty! Everything in the open air: the animated groups, the immense dining rooms, the peculiar courtship of North Americans, which is virtually devoid of the elements that compose the shy, tender, elevated love in our lands, the theatre, the photographers' booth, the bathhouses! Some weigh themselves, for North Americans are greatly elated, or really concerned, if they find they have gained or lost a pound. . . .

This spending, this uproar, these crowds, the activity of this amazing ant hill never slackens from June to October, from morning 'til night. . . . Then, like a monster that vomits its contents into the hungry maw of another monster, that colossal crowd, that straining, crushing mass, forces its way onto the trains, which speed across wastes, groaning under their burden, until they surrender it to the tremendous steamers, enlivened by the sound of harps and violins, convey it to the piers, and debouch the weary merrymakers into the thousand trolleys that pursue the thousand tracks that spread through slumbering New York like veins of steel.

———————

Source: Juan de Onís, trans., *The America of José Martí: Selected Writings* (New York: Noonday Press, 1954), 103–110.

---

in the Old. "He who can enjoy and does not enjoy commits a sin," a Yiddish-language paper told its readers. And enjoyment now meant buying a ticket and being entertained.

Public Entertainment. Amusement parks went up at the ends of trolley lines in cities across the country. Most glittering was Luna Park at New York's Coney Island—"an enchanted, storybook land of trellises, columns, domes, minarets, lagoons, and lofty aerial flights. . . . It was a world removed—shut away from the sordid clatter and turmoil of the streets." In fact, that escape from everyday urban life explains the appeal of amusement parks (see Voices from Abroad, "José Martí: Coney Island, 1881," above). The creators of Luna Park intended it to be "a different world—a dream world . . . where all is bizarre and fantastic . . . gayer and more different from the everyday world."

The theater likewise attracted huge audiences. Chicago had six vaudeville houses in 1896 and twenty-two in 1910. Evolving from cheap variety and minstrel shows, vaudeville moved from boisterous beer halls into grand theaters. Vaudeville cleaned up its routines, making them suitable for the entire family, and turned into thoroughly professional entertainment handled by national booking agencies. With its standard program of nine acts of singing, dancing, and comedy, vaudeville attained enormous popularity just as the movies arrived. The first primitive films, a minute or so of humor or glimpses of famous people, appeared in 1896 in penny arcades and as filler in vaudeville shows. Within a decade millions of city people were watching story films of increasing length and artistry at nickelodeons (named after the five-cent admission charge) across the country.

For young unmarried workers the leisure activities of the city created a new social space. "I want a good

625

Amusement Park, Long Beach, California
The origins of the roller coaster go back to LaMarcus Thompson's Switchback Railway, installed at Coney Island in 1884 and featuring gentle dips and curves. By 1900,
when Long Beach's Jack Rabbit Race was constructed, the goal was to create the
biggest possible thrill. Angelenos journeyed out by trolley to Long Beach not only to
take a dip in the ocean but to ride the new roller coaster. The Airplane Ride in the
foreground is a further wrinkle on the peculiarly modern notion that the way to have
fun is to be scared to death.
Curt Teich Postcard Archives.

time," a New York clothing operator remarked. "And
there is no . . . way a girl can get it on $8 a week. I guess
if anyone wants to take me to a dance he won't have to
ask me twice." Hence the widespread ritual among the
urban working class of "treating." The girls spent what
money they had on dressing up; their beaus were
expected to pay for the fun. Parental control over
courtship broke down, and amid the bright lights and
lively music of the dance hall and amusement park
working-class youth forged a more easygoing culture of
sexual interaction and pleasure seeking.

The geography of the big city carved out ample
space for commercialized sex. Prostitution was not new
to urban life, but in the late nineteenth century it
became less closeted and more intermingled with other
forms of public entertainment. In New York the most
famous sex district in this period was the Tenderloin,
running northward from Twenty-third Street between
Fifth and Eighth avenues and eventually up to Times
Square and beyond. This was also the locale of the city's
fanciest restaurants, the best hotels, and the theater
district. On the side streets many of the brownstone

row houses, abandoned by their well-to-do owners for
the quieter parts of town, were taken over by brothels.
The nearby concert saloons—the forerunners of the
nightclub—featured not only stage shows and bar-
tenders but also well-dressed prostitutes working the
premises.

The Tenderloin and the Bowery district farther
downtown were also the sites of a robust gay subculture. The long-held notion that homosexual life was
covert, in the closet, in Victorian America appears not to
be true, at least not in the country's premier city. Homosexual activity was illegal, but as with prostitution, the
law was mostly a dead letter. In certain corners of the
city a gay world flourished, with a full array of saloons,
meeting places, and drag balls, which were widely
known and often patronized by uptown "slummers."

Baseball. Of all forms of (mostly) male diversion
none was more specific to the city, or so spectacularly
successful, as professional baseball. The game's promoters decreed that baseball had been created in 1839
by Abner Doubleday in the village of Cooperstown, New

York. Actually, baseball was neither of American origin—it developed from the British game of rounders—nor a product of rural life.

Organized play began in the early 1840s in New York City, where a group of gentlemen enthusiasts competed on an empty lot. During the next twenty years the aristocratic tone of baseball disappeared. Clubs sprang up across the country, and intercity competition developed on a scheduled basis. In 1868 baseball became openly professional, as other teams followed the example of the Cincinnati Red Stockings in signing players to contracts at a negotiated salary for the season.

Big-time commercial baseball came into its own with the launching of the National League in 1876. The team owners were profit-minded businessmen who carefully shaped the sport to please the fans. Wooden grandstands gave way to the concrete and steel stadiums of the early twentieth century, such as Fenway Park in Boston, Forbes Field in Pittsburgh, and Shibe Park in Philadelphia.

For the urban multitudes baseball grew into something more than an occasional afternoon at the ballpark. By rooting for the home team, fans found a way of identifying with the city they lived in. Amid the diversity and anonymity of urban life, baseball acted as a bridge among strangers.

Students of the game have suggested that baseball was peculiarly attuned to city life. It followed strict, precise rules, which suggested an underlying order to the chaotic city. Far from respecting the rules, however, the players tried to get away with whatever they could in order to win. Did this not match the competitive scramble of urban life? The blue-coated umpire, the symbol of authority, was scorned by players and derided by fans. What better substitute for the resentment against the powers-that-be who ruled the lives of city people? Baseball, like many other emerging urban institutions, served as a mechanism for inducting people into the life of the modern city.

Newspapers. Most efficient at this task, however, was the newspaper. James Gordon Bennett, founder of the *New York Herald* in 1835, wanted "to record the facts . . . for the great masses of the community." The news was everything that interested city readers, starting with crime, scandal, and sensational events. After the Civil War Charles A. Dana of the *New York Sun* added the human-interest story, which made news of ordinary, insignificant happenings. Newspapers also targeted specific audiences. A women's page offered recipes and fashion news, separate sections covered sports and high society, and the Sunday supplement helped fill the weekend hours.

When Joseph Pulitzer, the owner of the *St. Louis Post-Dispatch*, invaded New York in 1883 by buying the *New York World*, a furious circulation war broke out. In 1895 William Randolph Hearst, who owned the *San Francisco Examiner*, bought the *New York Journal* and challenged the *World* (see Chapter 21, American Lives, "William Randolph Hearst: Jingo," pp. 682–683). Hearst developed a sensational style of newspaper reporting and writing that became known as *yellow journalism*. The term, linked to the first comic strip to appear in color, "The Yellow Kid" (1895), referred to a type of reporting that treated accuracy as secondary to a good story.

"He who is without a newspaper," said the great circus showman P. T. Barnum, "is cut off from his species." Barnum was speaking of city people and their hunger for information. By meeting this need, newspapers revealed their sensitivity to the public they served.

The World of the Urban Elite

In the midst of this popular ferment, other institutions of culture were taking shape under the sponsorship of a new social and economic elite. A hunger for the cultivated life was not, of course, specifically urban or upper class. Before the Civil War the lyceum movement had sent lecturers to the remotest towns, bearing messages of culture and learning. The Chautauqua movement, founded in upstate New York in 1874, carried on this work of cultural dissemination in the last decades of the nineteenth century. However, great institutions such as museums, public libraries, opera companies, and symphony orchestras could flourish only in metropolitan centers and with the financial support of wealthy patrons.

Creating High Culture

The nation's first major art museum, the Corcoran Gallery of Art, opened in Washington, D.C., in 1869. New York's Metropolitan Museum of Art started in rented quarters two years later. In 1880 the museum moved to its permanent site in Central Park and launched an ambitious program of art acquisition. J. P. Morgan became chairman of the board in 1905, assuring the Metropolitan's preeminence. The Boston Museum of Fine Arts was founded in 1876, Chicago's Art Institute in 1879. By 1914 virtually every major city and about three-fifths of all cities above the size of 100,000 people had an art museum.

Top-flight orchestras also appeared, first in New York under the conductors Theodore Thomas and Leopold Damrosch in the 1870s, then in Boston and Chicago during the next decade. National tours by these leading orchestras planted the seeds for orchestral societies in many other cities. Public libraries grew from modest collections (in 1870 only seven had as

OPENING GAME
BOSTON BASE-BALL CLUB.

The National Pastime
This lithograph celebrates the opening game of the 1889 season, with the Boston Base-Ball Club taking on the New York Base-Ball Club. The National League was then scarcely twelve years old. The fielders played barehanded, but otherwise the game today is much as the artist pictured it a century ago, down to the umpire's characteristic stance.
Stock Montage.

many as 50,000 books) into major urban institutions. The greatest library benefactor was Andrew Carnegie, who announced in 1881 that he would build a library in any city that was prepared to maintain it. By 1907 Carnegie had spent more than $32.7 million to establish about a thousand libraries throughout the country.

The late nineteenth century was the great age not only of moneymaking but also of money *giving*. Surplus private wealth flowed in many directions, including to universities. These schools included Vanderbilt, Tulane, and Johns Hopkins universities, all named for their chief benefactors, and the University of Chicago, founded by John D. Rockefeller in 1892. The new millionaires also richly patronized the arts, partly out of a sense of civic duty, partly as a means to establish themselves in society, as in the founding of the Metropolitan Opera in New York (see p. 629). But museums and opera houses also received generous support as an expression of national pride.

"In America there is no culture," pronounced the English critic G. Lowes Dickinson in 1909. Science and the practical arts, yes, "every possible application of life to purposes and ends," but "no life for life's sake." Such condescending remarks received a respectful hearing in the United States because of a deep sense of cultural inferiority to the Old World. In 1873 Mark Twain and Charles Dudley Warner published a novel, *The Gilded Age*, satirizing America as a land of money-grubbers and speculators. This enormously popular book touched a nerve in the American psyche. Its title has in fact been appropriated by historians to characterize the late nineteenth century—America's "Gilded Age"—as an age of materialism and cultural shallowness.

Some members of the upper class, like the novelist Henry James, despaired of the country and moved to Europe. Others spent their lives in the kind of perpetual alienation that Henry Adams, descendant of U.S. presidents John and John Quincy Adams, described in his ironic memoir *The Education of Henry Adams* (1907).

The more common response was to try to raise the nation's cultural level. The newly rich had a hard time of it. With few exceptions, they did not have much opportunity to cultivate a taste for art, and a great deal of what they collected was mediocre and garish. One exception was George W. Vanderbilt, grandson of the rough-hewn Cornelius Vanderbilt, who became a patron of the Art Students League in New York and an early champion of French Impressionism. Another was the coal and steel baron Henry Clay Frick, who built a brilliant art collection that remains housed as a public museum in his mansion in New York City. The enthusiasm of moneyed Americans—not always well directed—largely fueled the great cultural institutions that arose in many cities during the Gilded Age.

A deeply conservative idea of culture sustained this generous patronage. The aim was to embellish urban life, not to probe or reveal its meaning. "Art," says the hero of Reverend Henry Ward Beecher's sentimental novel *Norwood* (1867), "attempts to work out its end solely by the use of the beautiful, and the artist is to select out only such things as are beautiful." The idea of culture also took on an elitist cast: Shakespeare, once a staple of popular stage entertainment (in various bowdlerized versions), was appropriated into the domain of "serious" theater.

Culture also became firmly linked to femininity. In America, remarked one observer, culture was "left entirely to women. . . . It is they, as a general rule, who have opinions about music, or drama, or literature, or philosophy. . . . Husbands or sons rarely share in those interests." Men represented the "force principle," said the clergyman Horace Bushnell, and women symbolized the "beauty principle."

The treatment of life, the eminent editor and novelist William Dean Howells wrote, "must be tinged with sufficient idealism to make it all of a truly uplifting character. We cannot admit stories which deal with false or immoral relations. . . . The finer side of things—the idealistic—is the answer for us." The *genteel tradition*, as this literary school came to be called, dominated such American cultural agencies as universities and publishers from the 1860s onward.

The New Millionaires

In the compact city of the early nineteenth century, class distinctions had been expressed by the way men and women dressed, how they behaved, and the deference they demanded from or granted to others. As the industrial city grew, these interpersonal marks of class began to lose their force. In the anonymity of a large city, recognition and deference no longer served as mechanisms for conferring status. Instead, the rich began to rely on external signs: conspicuous display of wealth, exclusive association in clubs and similar social organizations, and, above all, choice of neighborhood.

For the poor, place of residence depended, as it always had, on the location of their work. For higher-income urbanites, where to live became a matter of personal means and social preference.

Life-Styles of the Rich. As early as the 1840s Boston merchants took advantage of the new railway service to move out of the congested central city. Fine rural estates appeared in Milton, Newton, and other outlying towns. By 1848 roughly 20 percent of Boston's businessmen were making the long trip from the countryside to their downtown offices. Ferries that plied the harbor between Manhattan and Brooklyn or New Jersey served the same purpose for New Yorkers.

As commercial development engulfed downtown residential areas and as transportation services improved, the exodus from cities by the well-to-do spread across America. In Cincinnati wealthy families settled on the scenic hills rimming the crowded, humid tableland that ran down to the Ohio River. On those hillsides, a traveler noted in 1883, "the homes of Cincinnati's merchant princes and millionaires are found . . . elegant cottages, tasteful villas, and substantial mansions, surrounded by a paradise of grass, gardens, lawns, and tree-shaded roads." Residents of the area, called Hilltop, founded several country clubs, the Cincinnati Riding Club, the New England Society, five downtown gentlemen's clubs, and many other institutions that ensured an exclusive social life for Cincinnati's elite.

Despite the temptations of country life, many of the very richest people preferred the heart of the city. Chicago boasted its Gold Coast; San Francisco, Nob Hill; Denver, Quality Hill; and Manhattan, Fifth Avenue. The New York novelist Edith Wharton recalled how the comfortable midcentury brownstones gave way to the "'new' millionaire houses," which spread northward beyond Fifty-ninth Street and up Fifth Avenue along Central Park. Great mansions, emulating the homes of the European aristocracy, lined Fifth Avenue at the turn of the century.

But great fortunes did not automatically confer high social standing. An established elite stood astride the social heights even in such relatively raw cities as San Francisco and Denver. It had taken only a generation—and sometimes less—for money made in commerce or real estate to shed its tarnish and become "old" and genteel. In older cities such as Boston, wealth passed intact through several generations, creating a closely knit tribe of old-line families that kept moneyed newcomers at bay. Elsewhere urban elites tended to be more open, but only to the socially ambitious who were prepared to make visible and energetic use of their money.

New York's Metropolitan Opera was one of the products of this ongoing struggle among the wealthy. The Academy of Music, home to the city's opera since 1854, was controlled by the Livingstons, the Bayards, the Beekmans, and other old New York families. Frustrated in their efforts to purchase boxes at the Academy, the Vanderbilts and their allies decided to sponsor a rival opera house. In 1883, with its glittering opening to the strains of Gounod's *Faust*, the Metropolitan proclaimed its ascendancy in the opera world and in due course won the patronage of even the Beekmans and Bayards. During this battle of the opera houses the Vanderbilt circle achieved social recognition.

"High Society." New York became the home of a national elite as the most ambitious people gravitated to this preeminent center of American economic and cultural life. Manhattan's extraordinary vitality in turn kept the city's high society fluid and relatively open. In Theodore Dreiser's novel *The Titan* (1914), tycoon Frank Cowperwood reassures his unhappy wife that if Chicago society will not accept them, "there are other cities. Money will arrange matters in New York—that I know. We can build a real place there, and go in on equal terms, if we have money enough." New York thus came to be a magnet for millionaires. The city attracted them not only because of its importance as a financial center, but also because of the opportunities it offered for display and social recognition.

From Manhattan an extravagant life of leisure radiated outward to resorts such as Saratoga Springs, New York; Palm Beach, Florida; and Newport, Rhode Island, with its grand array of summer "cottages." To these

Going to the Opera, 1873
In this painting by Seymour J. Guy, William H. Vanderbilt, eldest son and successor of
the railroad tycoon Cornelius Vanderbilt, has gathered with his family and friends
preparatory to attending the opera. It was the sponsorship of New York's Metropolitan Opera that helped the Vanderbilts achieve social recognition among the older,
more established moneyed families of New York City.
Courtesy of Biltmore Estate, Asheville, North Carolina.

resorts, the affluent traveled in great comfort by private
railway car. Entertaining was on a grand scale; luxurious restaurants like Delmonico's and Sherry's sprang
up, catering to the rich. "Our forefathers would have
been staggered at the cost of hospitality these days,"
remarked one New Yorker.

This infusion of wealth shattered the older elite
society of New York. Seeking to be assimilated into the
upper class, the flood of moneyed newcomers simply
overwhelmed it. There followed a curious process of
reconstruction, a deliberate effort to define the rules of
conduct and identify those who properly "belonged" in
New York society.

The key figure in this process was Ward McAllister, a
southern-born lawyer who made a quick fortune in gold-
rush San Francisco and then devoted himself to a second
career as the arbiter of New York society. In 1888 McAllister compiled the first *Social Register*, which announced
that it would serve as a "record of society, comprising an
accurate and careful list" of all those deemed acceptable
to participate in New York society. McAllister instructed
the socially ambitious on how to select guests, set a
proper table, arrange a ball, and launch a young lady into

society. He presided over an ordered round of assemblies,
balls, and dinners that defined the boundaries of an elite
society. At the apex stood "the Four Hundred"—the true
cream of New York society. McAllister's list corresponded
to the list of guests invited to Mrs. William Astor's great
ball of February 1, 1892.

Social registers, coming-out balls for debutantes,
and lesser versions of Ward McAllister soon popped up
in cities throughout the country. In this fashion, the
socially ambitious struggled to master the fluidity at
the height of the social order.

Americans were adept at making money, noted the
journalist Edwin L. Godkin in 1896, but they lacked the
European traditions for spending it. "Great wealth has
not yet entered our manners," Godkin remarked. "No
rules have yet been drawn to guide wealthy Americans in
their manner of life." In their struggle to find the rules
and establish the manners, the moneyed elite made an
indelible mark on urban life. If there was magnificence in
the American city, it was mainly their handiwork. And if
there was conspicuous waste and vulgarity, it was also
their doing. In a democratic society wealth finds no easier outlet than through public display.

The Urban Middle Class

★

From colonial times onward, the American economy spawned a robust middle class of lawyers, merchants, doctors, and ship captains. What most distinguished this group was the independence that came with self-employment. This older middle class remained important, but in the late nineteenth century it was joined by a new salaried middle class brought forth by the emerging corporate economy.

Bureaucratic organizations required managers, accountants, and clerks. Advancing technologies called for engineers, chemists, and designers. The distribution system sought salesmen, advertising executives, and buyers. These salaried ranks increased sevenfold between 1870 and 1910—at a much faster rate than any other occupational group. Nearly 9 million people held white-collar jobs in 1910—more than a fourth of all nonagricultural employees.

The middle class left a smaller imprint than the rich on the public and cultural faces of urban society. Its members, unlike the wealthy, preferred privacy and retreated into the domesticity of suburban comfort and family life.

Expanding Suburbs

The American middle class, particularly its salaried ranks, was an urban population. Some of its members lived within the city, in the row houses of Baltimore or Boston or the comfortable apartment houses of New York and other metropolitan centers. But far more preferred to escape from the clamor and congestion of the city. They were attracted by a persisting "rural ideal." They agreed with landscape architect Andrew Jackson Downing, who thought that "nature and domestic life are better than the society and manners of town." With the extension of trolley service from the city center, middle-class Americans followed the wealthy into the countryside. All sought what a Chicago developer promised for his North Shore subdivision in 1875—"qualities of which the city is in a large degree bereft, namely, its pure air, peacefulness, quietude, and natural scenery."

No major American city escaped rapid suburbanization during the last third of the nineteenth century. City limits everywhere expanded rapidly, but even so, much of the suburban growth took place beyond city limits. By 1900 more than half of Boston's people lived in "streetcar suburbs" outside Boston proper; and nationwide, according to the 1910 census, about 25 percent of the urban population lived in such independent suburbs.

Cincinnati Suburb
The lives of the people inhabiting these neat homes along this tree-lined street were woven into the dynamic capitalism of a major industrial metropolis, including the children lounging on the corner, who were most certainly being educated for service in the new economic order. Looking at the bucolic setting of this Cincinnati street, no one would have thought so, and that was just the illusion that the suburb was intended to create: that Americans still partook of a rural ideal and could hold at bay the modern industrial order of which they were now a part.
Cincinnati Historical Society.

On the European continent, by contrast, cities remained highly concentrated; and when expansion did occur, it was the poor, not the well-to-do, who inhabited the margins. Unlike its American counterpart, the European middle class was not attracted (except in Britain) to the rural ideal and valued urban life for its own sake. The preconditions for suburbanization were likewise much weaker in Europe: mass transit developed more slowly; traditional beam-and-post house construction did not give way to the cheaper balloon-frame techniques; and there was little of the freewheeling real-estate development that spurred American suburbanization. Finally, because European cities were ethnically more homogeneous, the middle class was not driven, as was its American counterpart, to flee the diverse masses populating the city centers.

The geography of the American suburbs was truly a map of class structure, because where a family lived told where it ranked. The farther the distance from the center of the city, the finer were the houses and the larger the lots. Affluent businessmen and professionals had the leisure and flexible schedules to travel a long distance into town. People closer in wanted transit lines that went straight into the city center and carried them quickly between home and office. Lower-income suburbanites were more likely to have more than one wage earner in the family, less secure employment, and jobs requiring movement around the city. It was better for them to live closer to the city center, because they then had easy access to the cross-town lines that gave them the mobility they needed for their work.

Location on the suburban map, though always a precise measure of economic ranking, never became rigid. Working-class residents of the city center who wanted to better their lives moved to the cheapest suburbs. Those already settled there fled from these newcomers, in turn pushing the next higher group farther out in search of space and greenery.

Suburbanization was the sum of countless individual decisions. Each move represented an advance in living standards—not only more light, air, and quiet but also better housing than the city afforded. Suburban houses had more space and better design. They came equipped with indoor toilets, hot water, central heating, and, by the turn of the century, electricity. Even people in the inner suburbs soon regarded these amenities as necessities.

The suburbs also restored a basic opportunity that rural Americans thought they had sacrificed when they moved to the city. In the suburbs home ownership again became the norm. "A man is not really a true man until he owns his home," propounded Reverend Russell H. Conwell in "Acres of Diamonds," his famous sermon on the virtues of making money,

The small town of the rural past had fostered community life. Not so the suburbs. The grid street pattern, efficient for laying out lots and providing utilities, offered no natural focus for group life. Nor did the stores and services that lay scattered along the trolley-car streets. Not even schools and churches were located where they could become centers of community life. Suburban development conformed to the economics of real estate and transportation, and so did the thinking of middle-class home seekers entering the suburbs. They wanted a house that gave them good value and convenience to the trolley line.

The need for community had lost some of its force for middle-class Americans. Two other attachments assumed greater importance: work and family.

Middle-Class Families

In the preindustrial economy farmers, merchants, and artisans had carried on their work within family units, which counted as members not only blood relatives but all others living and working in the household. As industrialism progressed, production gradually moved out of the household. For the middle class in particular, the family became dissociated from economic activity. The father left the home to earn a living, and children

spent more years in school. Clothing was bought ready-made; food came increasingly in cans and packages. Middle-class families became smaller, excluding all but nuclear members and consisting typically by 1900 of husband, wife, and three children.

Within this family circle relationships became intense and affectionate. "Home was the most expressive experience in life," recalled literary critic Henry Seidel Canby of his growing up in the 1890s. "Though the family might quarrel and nag, the home held them all, protecting them against the outside world." In a sense, the family served as a refuge from the competitive, impersonal business world. The suburbs provided a fit setting for such middle-class families. The quiet, tree-lined streets created a domestic world insulated from the hurly-burly of commerce and enterprise.

The Wife's Role.   The burdens of this domesticity fell heavily on the wife. It was nearly unheard of for her to seek an outside career; that was her husband's role. Her job was to manage the household. "The woman who could not make a home, like the man who could not support one, was condemned," Canby remembered. But with better household technology, greater reliance on purchased goods, and fewer children, the wife's workload declined. Moreover, servants still played an important part in middle-class households. In 1910 there were about 2 million domestic servants, the largest job category for women.

As the physical burdens of household work eased, higher-quality homemaking became the new ideal. This was the message of Catharine Beecher's best-selling book *The American Woman's Home* (1869) and of such magazines as *Ladies' Home Journal* and *Good Housekeeping*, which first appeared during the 1880s. This advice literature told women that in their domestic duties, they had the higher calling of bringing sensibility, beauty, and love to the household. "We owe to women the charm and beauty of life," wrote one educator. "For the love that rests, strengthens and inspires, we look to women." In this idealized view, the wife made the home a refuge for her husband and a place of nurture for their children.

Womanly virtue, even if a happy marriage depended on it, by no means put wives on equal terms with their husbands. Although the legal status of married women—the right to own property, control separate earnings, make contracts and bring suit, and get a divorce—improved markedly during the nineteenth century, sufficient legal discrimination remained to establish their subordinate role within the family. More important, custom dictated a wife's submission to her husband. She relied on his ability as the family breadwinner and, despite her superior virtues and graces, ranked as his inferior in vigor and intellect. Her mind could be employed "but little and in trivial matters," wrote one prominent physician, and her proper place was as "the companion or ornamental appendage to

Middle-Class Domesticity
For middle-class Americans the home was a place of nurture, a refuge from the world
of competitive commerce. Perhaps that explains why their residences were so heavily
draped and cluttered with bric-a-brac. All of it emphasized privacy and pride of
possession.
Culver Pictures.

man" (see American Voices, "M. Carey Thomas: 'We Did
Not Know . . . Whether Women's Health Could Stand
the Strain of College Education,'" p. 634).

No wonder that bright, independent-minded
women rebelled against marriage. The marriage rate in
the United States fell to its lowest point during the last
forty years of the nineteenth century. More than 10 percent of women of marriageable age remained single,
and the rate was much higher among college graduates
and professionals. Only half of the Mount Holyoke College class of 1902 married. "I know that something perhaps, humanly speaking, supremely precious has passed
me by," remarked the writer Vida Scudder. "But . . . how
much it would have excluded!" Married life "looks to me
often as I watch it terribly impoverished, for women."

The strains of marriage were manifest in the number of middle-class families that broke up. The national
divorce rate increased from 1.2 per 1,000 marriages in
1860 to 7.7 in 1900. Most domestic failures, however,
went unrecorded because of the stigma attached to
divorce. In a Chicago suburb in the 1880s, at a time
when divorce was virtually unknown there, about
10 percent of households had an absent spouse.

Even harder to document were the other ways
women responded to marriages that denied their

autonomy and downplayed their sexuality. Middle-class
women became the principal victims of neurasthenia, a
disorder whose symptoms included depression and
general disability. Some unhappy housewives found
"silent friends" in opium and alcohol, which often were
dispensed in well-laced patent medicines.

A healthier release came through the companionship of other women. In an age that defined separate
spheres for men and women, close ties commonly
formed between schoolmates, cousins, and mothers and
daughters. The intimacy and intensity of such attachments can be sensed in the letters of separated friends.
Such enduring female ties yielded an emotional gratification not often found in marriage. Husbands, absorbed
in business, frequently played a secondary and remote
role in the lives of their wives. Women's own sphere
often filled that emotional vacuum.

Changing Views of Sexuality.   In earlier times sexuality
and reproduction had been more or less in harmony. A
large family was considered a good thing, and the heavy
toll of repeated pregnancies on the wife was accepted as
God's will. In lower-class families this fatalism persisted,
but not among middle-class couples, who increasingly
wanted to limit their families. Birth control, however, was

M. CAREY THOMAS

"We Did Not Know ... Whether Women's Health Could Stand the Strain of College Education"

★

President of Bryn Mawr College for many years, M. Carey Thomas (1857–1935) recalls in a retrospective essay her dreams of college as a girl growing up in Baltimore in the 1870s.

The passionate desire of women of my generation for higher education was accompanied thruout its course by the awful doubt, felt by women themselves as well as by men, as to whether women as a sex were physically and mentally fit for it. . . . I was always wondering whether it could be really true, as everyone always said, that boys were cleverer than girls. . . . I often remember praying about it, and begging God that if it were true that because I was a girl I could not successfully master Greek and go to college and understand things to kill me at once, as I could not bear to live in such an unjust world. When I was a little older I read the Bible entirely thru with passionate eagerness because I had heard it said that it proved that women were inferior to men. . . . To this day I can never read many parts of the Pauline epistles without feeling again the sinking of the heart with which I used to hurry over the verses referring to women's keeping silence in the churches and asking their husbands at home. . . .

It was not to be wondered at that we were uncertain in those old days as to the ultimate result of women's education. We did not know when we began whether women's health could stand the strain of college education. We were haunted in those early days by the clanging chains of that gloomy little specter, Dr. Edward H. Clarke's *Sex in Education*. With trepidation of spirit I made my mother read it, and was much cheered by her remark that, as neither she, nor any of the women she knew, had ever seen girls or women of the kind described in Dr. Clarke's book, we might as well act as if they did not exist. Still, we did not *know* whether college might not produce a crop of just such invalids. . . .

Before I myself went to college I had never seen but one college woman. I had heard that such a woman was staying at the house of an acquaintance. I went to see her with fear. Even if she had appeared in hoofs and horns I was determined to go to college all the same. But it was a relief to find this Vassar graduate tall and handsome and dressed like other women. When, five years later, I went to Leipzig to study after graduating from Cornell, my mother used to write me that my name was never mentioned to her by the women of her acquaintance. I was thought by them to be as much a disgrace to my family as if I had eloped with the coachman. . . .

We are now [1908] living in the midst of great and, I believe on the whole beneficent, social changes which are preparing the way for the coming economic independence of women. . . . The passionate desire of the women of my generation for a college education seems, as we study it now in the light of coming events, to have been part of this greater movement.

Source: Linda K. Kerber and Jane De Hart-Mathews, eds., *Women's America: Refocusing the Past,* 2nd ed. (New York: Oxford University Press, 1987), 263–265.

---

not an easy matter. From the 1830s onward information about contraception became widely available, as did an array of commercial devices—condoms, diaphragms, sponges, douches. But the knowledge purveyed was imperfect or, like advice about the rhythm method, absolutely wrong (doctors thought women were most fertile around the menstrual period). And the devices for the most part were not very effective or, as in the case of the condom, were stigmatized by association with the brothel.

Before these barriers could be surmounted, birth control was swept up in the social-purity campaign championed by Anthony Comstock. From the 1870s onward contraceptive devices and birth-control information were legally classified as obscene, barred from the mails, and criminalized in many states. Abortion, long protected by common law, became illegal except to save the mother's life. Although the practice of abortion probably remained widespread, it was expensive and dangerous—and considered shameful besides.

Around 1890 a change set in. Although the birth rate continued to decline, more young people married, and at an earlier age. These developments reflected the beginnings of a sexual revolution in the American middle-class family. Despite the Comstock laws, contraception became more acceptable and more reliable. Experts began to abandon the notion, put forth by one popular medical text, that "the majority of women (happily for society) are not very much troubled by sexual feeling of any kind." In succeeding editions of his book *Plain Home Talk on Love, Marriage, and Parentage,* physician Edward Bliss Foote began to favor a healthy sexuality that gave pleasure to both women and men.

During the 1890s the artist Charles Dana Gibson created the image of the "new woman" in his drawings for *Life* magazine. The Gibson girl was tall, spirited, athletic, and chastely sexual. Constrictive clothing such as bustles, hoop skirts, and hourglass corsets gave way to shirtwaists and other natural styles that did not hide or disguise the female form. In the city, women's sphere began to take on a more public character. Among the new urban institutions catering to women, the most important was the department store, which became a temple for their emerging role as consumers.

Attitudes toward Children. The children of the middle class went through their own revolution. In the past, American children had been regarded as an economic asset— added hands for the family farm, shop, or countinghouse. That no longer held true for the urban middle class. Parents stopped treating their children as working members of the family. In the old days, Ralph Waldo Emerson remarked in 1880, "children had been repressed and kept in the background; now they were considered, cosseted, and pampered." There was such a thing as "the juvenile mind," lectured Jacob Abbott in his book *Gentle Measures in the Management and Training of the Young* (1871). The family was responsible for providing a nurturing environment in which the young personality could grow and mature.

Preparation for adulthood became increasingly linked to formal education. School enrollment went up 150 percent between 1870 and 1900. High school attendance, while still encompassing only a small percentage of teenagers, increased at the fastest rate. As the years between childhood and adulthood began to stretch out, a new stage of life—adolescence—emerged. While rooted in an extended period of dependency on the family, adolescence shifted much of the socializing role from parents to peer group. A youth culture—one of the hallmarks of American life in the twentieth century—was starting to take shape.

The New Woman

John Singer Sargent's painting *Mr. and Mrs. Isaac Newton Phelps Stokes* (1897) captures on canvas the essence of the "new woman" of the 1890s. Nothing about Mrs. Stokes, neither how she is dressed nor how she presents herself, suggests physical weakness or demure passivity. She confidently occupies center stage, a fit partner for her husband, who is relegated to the shadows of the picture.

The Metropolitan Museum of Art, New York. Bequest of Edith Minturn Phelps Stokes (Mrs. I. N.), 1938 (38.104).

Summary

★

America, an agrarian society since its birth, became increasingly urbanized after the Civil War. By 1900 about 20 percent of the population was living in cities with 100,000 or more people. City growth stemmed primarily from industrialization—the concentration of industry at key points, the increasingly large scale of production, and the need for commercial and administrative services that were best located in urban centers. A burst of innovation, including mass transit systems, steel-frame buildings, the telephone, and electric lighting, solved the problems arising from the concentration of large populations in a confined area. Although amply endowed with regulatory powers, American cities left decision making as much as possible in the hands of private interests. The result was dramatic growth but not much attention to the impact of growth on the urban environment.

In the cities geography defined the social order of the population. The poor were found in the city centers and the factory districts, the middle class spread out into the suburbs, and the rich lived insulated in exclusive central sections of the cities or beyond the suburbs. A distinctive urban culture emerged, drawing heavily on ethnic social institutions and new leisure activities, enabling city dwellers to accommodate themselves to the urban world. The great American cities became the sites of high culture, including art museums, opera companies, symphony orchestras, and libraries.

For the wealthy, an elite society emerged, stressing an opulent life-style and exclusive social organizations. The middle class, in contrast, withdrew into the private world of the family. For middle-class wives, the cult of domesticity reigned, but its more repressive features began to relax as a new attitude toward female sexuality took hold. Child nurture persisted, but as the years of dependent childhood lengthened, a new phase—adolescence—began to emerge that would draw teenagers out of the family orbit.

TIMELINE

1869   Corcoran Gallery of Art, the nation's first major art museum, opens in Washington, D.C.

1871   Chicago fire

1873   Mark Twain and Charles Dudley Warner publish *The Gilded Age*

1875   Dwight L. Moody launches urban revivalist movement

1876   Alexander Graham Bell patents the telephone

National Baseball League founded

1878   Electric arc-light system installed in Philadelphia

1879   Thomas Edison creates a practical incandescent lightbulb

Salvation Army arrives from Britain

1881   Andrew Carnegie offers to build a library for every American city that will maintain it

1883   New York City's Metropolitan Opera founded

Brooklyn Bridge opens

Joseph Pulitzer purchases the *New York World*

1885   William Jenney builds first steel-frame structure, Chicago's Home Insurance Building

1887   First electric trolley line constructed in Richmond, Virginia

1892   John D. Rockefeller founds University of Chicago

1893   Chicago World's Fair

"City Beautiful" movement

1895   William Randolph Hearst enters New York journalism

The comic strip "The Yellow Kid" appears

1897   Boston builds first American subway

1900   Theodore Dreiser publishes *Sister Carrie*

1901   New York Tenement House Law

1904   New York subway system opens

1906   San Francisco earthquake

1913   Fifty-five-floor Woolworth Building opens in New York City

Suggested Readings

★

Useful introductions to urban history are Charles N. Glaab and A. Theodore Brown, *A History of Urban America* (1967), and Raymond A. Mohl, ed., *The Making of Urban America* (1997). Arthur M. Schlesinger, *The Rise of the City* (1936), is a pioneering study. A sampling of the innovative scholarship that opened new historical paths can be found in Stephan Thernstrom and Richard Sennett, eds., *Nineteenth-Century Cities: Essays in the New Urban History* (1969).

Urbanization

Allan Pred, *Spatial Dynamics of U.S. Urban Growth, 1800–1914* (1971), traces the patterns in which cities grew. On the revolution in urban transit, see the pioneering book by Sam B. Warner, *Streetcar Suburbs: The Process of Growth in Boston, 1870–1900* (1962). In a subsequent work, *The Private City: Philadelphia in Three Periods* (1968), Warner broadened his analysis to show how private decision making shaped the character of the American city. Innovations in urban construction are treated in Carl Condit, *American Building Art: Nineteenth Century* (1969) and *Rise of the New York Skyscraper, 1865–1913* (1996); Robert C. Twombly, *Louis Sullivan* (1986); Alan Trachtenberg, *The Brooklyn Bridge* (1965); Harold L. Platt, *The Electric City: Energy and the Growth of the Chicago Area, 1880–1930* (1991); and Mark H. Rose, *Cities of Light and Heat: Domesticating Gas and Electricity in Urban America* (1995). The problems of meeting basic human needs are treated in Jon C. Teaford, *The Unheralded Triumph: City Government in America, 1870–1900* (1984); and David B. Tyack, *The One Best System: A History of American Urban Education* (1974). The struggle to reshape the chaotic nineteenth-century city can be explored in John D. Fairchild, *The Mysteries of the Great City: The Politics of Urban Design, 1877–1937* (1993); James Machor, *Pastoral Cities: Urban Ideals and the Symbolic Landscape of America* (1987); and David Schuyler, *The New Urban Landscape: The Redefinition of City Form in Nineteenth-Century America* (1986).

City People

A useful introduction to American immigration history is John Bodnar, *The Transplanted* (1986). Among the leading monographs are Moses Rischin, *The Promised City: New York's Jews, 1870–1914* (1962); Joseph Barton, *Peasants and Strangers: Italians, Rumanians, and Slovaks in an American City, 1890–1950* (1975); and Robert A. Orsi, *The Madonna of 115th Street: Faith and Community in Italian Harlem, 1880–1950* (1985). On blacks in the city see Gilbert Osofsky, *Harlem: The Making of a Ghetto, 1890–1930* (1966); Allan H. Spear, *Black Chicago, 1860–1920* (1966); and Kenneth L. Kusmer, *A Ghetto Takes Shape: Black Cleveland, 1870–1930* (1976). David C. Hammack, *Power and Society: Greater New York at the Turn of the Century* (1982), is a sophisticated treatment that places the party machine in the larger context of municipal power politics. The encounter of Protestantism with the city is treated in Henry F. May, *Protestant Churches and Urban America* (1949);

William G. McLoughlin, *Modern Revivalism* (1959); and Paul Boyer, *Urban Masses and Moral Order in America, 1820–1920* (1978). On the Catholic Church, see Robert D. Cross, *Liberal Catholicism in America* (1958). Aspects of an emerging city culture are studied in Gunther Barth, *City People: The Rise of Modern City Culture in Nineteenth-Century America* (1982); Susan Porter Benson, *Counter Cultures: Saleswomen, Managers, and Customers in American Department Stores, 1890–1940* (1986); Timothy J. Gilfoyle, *City of Eros: New York City, Prostitution and the Commercialization of Sex, 1790–1920* (1991); Kathy Peiss, *Cheap Amusements: Working Women and Leisure in Turn-of-the-Century New York* (1986); Robert W. Snyder, *The Voice of the City, Vaudeville and Popular Culture in New York City, 1880–1930* (1990); and David Nasaw, *Going Out: The Rise and Fall of Public Amusements* (1993). George Chauncey, *Gay New York: Gender, Urban Culture, and the Making of the Gay New York World, 1890–1940* (1994), reveals terrain hitherto invisible to the historian.

The World of the Urban Elite

On the fostering of high culture in the American city, see Daniel M. Fox, *Engines of Culture: Philanthropy and Art Museums* (1963). The best introduction to intellectual currents in the emerging urban society is Alan Trachtenberg, *The Incorporation of America: Culture and Society, 1865–1893* (1983). On the social elite see Frederic C. Jaher, *The Urban Establishment: Upper Strata in Boston, New York, Charleston, Chicago, and Los Angeles* (1982).

The Urban Middle Class

Urban social mobility is the focus of Stephan Thernstrom, *The Other Bostonians: Poverty and Progress in an American City, 1880–1970* (1973), which also contains a useful summary of mobility research on other cities. Two recent books greatly advance our understanding of the urban middle class: Stuart S. Blumin, *The Emergence of the Middle Class: Social Experience in the American City, 1760–1900* (1989), and Olivier Zunz, *Making Corporate America, 1870–1920* (1990). Aspects of middle-class life are revealed in Margaret Marsh, *Suburban Lives* (1990); Michael A. Ebner, *Creating Chicago's North Shore: A Suburban History* (1988); Gwendolyn Wright, *Moralism and the Model Home: Domestic Architecture and Cultural Conflict in Chicago, 1873–1913* (1980); Susan Strasser, *Never Done: A History of American Housework* (1983); and John F. Kasson, *Rudeness and Civility: Manners in Nineteenth-Century America* (1990). Contemporary notions of sexuality are skillfully captured in John S. Haller and Robin M. Haller, *The Physician and Sexuality in Victorian America* (1980). Whether those views actually applied to the private world of the middle class is strongly questioned in Karen Lystra, *The Searching Heart: Women, Men, and Romantic Love in Nineteenth-Century America* (1989). Control over reproduction is fully explored in Janet Farrell Brodie, *Contraception and Abortion in Nineteenth-Century America* (1994). A good introduction to family development, including childhood, is Steven Mintz and Susan Kellog, *Domestic Revolutions: A Social History of the American Family* (1988).

Collier's

THE NATIONAL WEEKLY

AGAIN!!

VOL XLIX NO 8

MAY 11 1912

Chapter 20

★

The Progressive Era

ON THE FACE of it, the political ferment of the 1890s ended after the election of 1896. The bitter struggle over free silver left the victorious Republicans with no stomach for political crusades. William McKinley's administration devoted itself to maintaining business confidence: sound money and high tariffs were the order of the day. The main thing, as party chief Mark Hanna said, was to "stand pat and continue Republican prosperity."

Yet beneath the surface a deep uneasiness had set in. The depression of the 1890s had unveiled harsh truths not acknowledged in better days. The fury of the decade's labor strikes, for example, revealed a frightening chasm opening between America's social classes. The outbreak of the great Pullman strike of 1894, declared Richard Olney, brought the country "to the ragged edge of anarchy." As Cleveland's attorney-general at the time, it was Olney's job to crush the strike, and he had done so with ruthless efficiency (see Chapter 17). But Olney took little satisfaction from his success. He asked himself what might be done in the future to avoid such one-sided state intervention. Olney advocated federal legislation, first expressed in the Erdman Mediation Act of 1898, that would regulate labor relations on the railroads and prevent "the evils and perils" of crippling rail strikes. In such ways did the crisis of the 1890s turn the nation's thinking to reform.

The problems themselves, however, were of much older origin. For half a century, Americans had been absorbed in developing their nation. At the beginning of the twentieth century they paused, looked around, and began to add up the costs. With industrialization

Again!
The Pure Food and Drug Act of 1906 was a monument to the muckraking journalism of the Progressive Era.
Collier's, *which had done the heavy work on this reform, revisited the patent-medicine scene in 1912 and found the villains alive and kicking. Vigilance seemed to be the price of permanent reform.*
Boston Athenaeum.

had come a frightening concentration of corporate economic power and, equally troubling, a rebellious working class. The cities had spawned widespread misery and corrupt machine politics. The heritage of an earlier America seemed to be succumbing to the demands of the new industrial order.

Now, with the crisis of the 1890s over, reform became an absorbing concern of many Americans. It was as if social awareness had reached a critical mass around 1900 and set reform activity in motion as a major, self-sustaining phenomenon. For this reason the years from 1900 to World War I have come to be known as the Progressive Era.

The Intellectual Roots of Progressivism

———————★———————

Intellectual climates change. Why they change is usually hard to explain, but it is not so difficult to tell when new ideas are taking hold. That new ideas were taking hold was altogether evident as the twentieth century began. An intellectual style emerged that can be called "progressive."

A Sense of Mastery

The Progressive Era was an age of scientific investigation. The federal government conducted massive statistical studies of immigration, women's and children's labor, and working conditions in many industries. Vice commissions studied prostitution, gambling, and other moral ills of American cities. Among private investigations the most notable was the Pittsburgh Survey (1911–1914). Financed by New York City philanthropists, a team of investigators recorded in great detail living and working conditions in Pittsburgh's steel district.

The facts were important because they formed the basis for corrective action. When the young journalist Walter Lippmann wrote *Drift and Mastery* (1914), he asserted the progressives' confidence in people's ability to act purposefully and constructively. This sense of mastery expressed itself in many ways—for example, in the faith people had in academic experts. In Wisconsin the state university became a key resource for Governor Robert M. La Follette's progressive administration. "The close intimacy of the university with public affairs explains the democracy, the thoroughness, and the scientific accuracy of the state in its legislation," boasted one La Follette supporter. Similarly, progressives were strongly attracted to scientific management, which had

originally been intended to rationalize work in factories (see Chapter 17). But its founder, Frederick W. Taylor, argued that his basic approach—the "scientific" analysis of human activity—offered solutions to waste and inefficiency in municipal government, schools and hospitals, and even homes and churches. Scientific management, Taylor insisted, could solve all the social ills that arise "through such of our acts as are blundering, ill-directed, or inefficient."

Attacking Nineteenth-Century Formalism. The essential thing, in the progressive view, was to resist intellectual formulations that denied people this sense of mastery, as did the Social Darwinian writings of the British philosopher Herbert Spencer and his many American disciples (see Chapter 18). Spencer argued that society develops according to fixed laws that cannot be changed. Spencer's intellectual approach was *formalistic*—that is, it proceeded from unproven general principles rather than from factual investigation.

Critics of Spencer denied that the evolution of society is guided by absolute and unvarying rules. "It is folly," protested the Harvard philosopher William James, "to speak of the 'laws of history,' as of something inevitable, which science only has to discover, and which any one can then foretell and observe, but do nothing to alter or avert." Man could "shape environmental forces to his own advantage," the sociologist Lester F. Ward argued. Society could advance through "rational planning" and "social engineering."

In the law, too, formalism had dominated. The courts treated legal rights as if these were eternal principles not rooted in—or to be tested by—social reality. Thus in the *Lochner v. New York* decision (1905) the Supreme Court invalidated a law limiting the long working hours of bakers in New York State on the grounds that such regulation violated the contractual liberty of both employers and workers. Justice Oliver Wendell Holmes, the leading critic of legal formalism, dissented; in his view, the *Lochner* decision was based on a fictional equality. If the choice was between working and starving, could it really be said that bakers freely accepted jobs requiring that they labor fourteen hours a day or that limiting their working hours violated their liberty of contract?

Holmes had earlier asserted the essence of progressive legal reasoning: "The life of the law has not been logic; it has been experience. The felt necessities of the time, even the prejudices which judges share with their fellow-men, have had a good deal more to do than logic in determining the rules by which men shall be governed." "Sociological jurisprudence," as Dean Roscoe Pound of the Harvard Law School termed it, called for "the adjustment of principles and doctrines to the human conditions they are to govern rather than assumed first principles." The law, moreover, should not claim a false neutrality; on the contrary, as Pound's student Felix Frankfurter argued, law should be "a vital agency for human betterment."

The Academic Critique. The assault against formalism took place in many scholarly disciplines. In classical economics, for example, scholars assumed that markets were perfectly competitive and thus perfectly responsive to the laws of supply and demand. Such a system left no room for reform, which would only disrupt what could not be improved. Critics of classical economics—they called themselves "institutional economists"—denied that the market ever operated so perfectly. They conducted field research to determine how institutions and power relationships influenced the marketplace. In his *Theory of the Leisure Class* (1899) and *The Instinct of Workmanship* (1914) the economist Thorstein Veblen lampooned the classical economists' abstract image of "economic man." In the real world, Veblen contended, people acted not out of pure economic calculation but from complex motives ranging from vanity to pride in their work.

In philosophy, it was William James who led the assault on formalism as an intellectual system. James denied the existence of absolute truths. In his philosophy of *pragmatism*, ideas were judged by their consequences; ideas served as guides to action that produced desired results. Philosophy should be concerned with solving problems, argued James, not with contemplating ultimate ends.

James's most important disciple was John Dewey. Like James, Dewey had a great interest in psychology, whose insights he applied to education. In his Laboratory School at the University of Chicago Dewey broke from the rigid curriculum of traditional education and instead stressed problem solving and practical activity as the keys to children's personal growth. His pupils were encouraged to explore and discover for themselves rather than learning lessons by rote. Nowhere could the intellectual bent of progressivism in action be better seen than in Dewey's experiments, which, fittingly, came to be known as progressive education.

Sources of Progressive Idealism

The reformers prided themselves on being tough-minded, on being expert at making things happen. But they were not indifferent to the purposes of effective action. On the contrary, progressives were unabashed idealists. The progressive cause, pronounced Theodore Roosevelt, "is based on the eternal principles of righteousness."

Much of this idealism came from the American past. No American hero loomed larger for progressives than Abraham Lincoln. Lincoln's example, in particular, inspired the battle for political reform. "Go back to the first principles of democracy; go back to the people," Robert La Follette told his audience when he launched his attack on the Republican machine in Wisconsin. Political reformers typically described their work as political restoration, frequently confessing that they had converted to reform after discovering how far party politics had drifted from the ideals of representative government.

Progressive idealism also derived from American radical traditions. Many progressives traced their conversion to Henry George's *Progress and Poverty* (1879), which asked why, in the midst of fabulous wealth, so many Americans lived in poverty. George's answer—that private control of land siphoned the community's wealth into the hands of nonproductive landlords—led to a Single Tax movement that served as a school for many budding progressives. Others traced their awakening to Edward Bellamy's novel *Looking Backward* (1888), with its utopian vision of an ordered, affluent American socialism, or to the Chicago social democrat Henry Demarest Lloyd's *Wealth against Commonwealth* (1894), with its powerful indictment of the Standard Oil trust. In later years this radical tradition was transmitted mainly through the Socialist Party, which flourished after 1900 under the leadership of Eugene V. Debs (see Chapter 17). Walter Lippmann and many other young reformers passed through socialism on their way to progressivism, while others, such as Charlotte Perkins Gilman, never left the socialist camp.

The most important source of progressive idealism, especially among social reformers, was religion. Protestant churches had long been concerned with the plight of the urban poor (see Chapter 19). Now this concern blossomed into a major school of religious thought—the Social Gospel. The Baptist cleric Walter Rauschenbusch, its most influential exponent, had been deeply affected by his ministry near the squalid Hell's Kitchen section of New York City. Rauschenbusch fought for more playgrounds and better housing in slum neighborhoods. The churches had to reassert the "social aims of Jesus," he argued. The "Kingdom of God on Earth" would be achieved not by striving for personal salvation but by struggling for social justice. To coordinate that effort, reform-minded clerical leaders formed the Federal Council of Churches in 1908. The council aimed at "promoting the application of the law of Christ in every relation to human life."

The Social Gospel was an explicitly religious movement, but secular progressivism was also infused with a strong element of faith. Progressive leaders characteristically grew up in families imbued with evangelical piety. Many went through a religious crisis and, having failed to experience a conversion, settled on careers in social work, education, journalism, or politics, where they could translate inherited religious belief into modern secular action. Jane Addams, for example, had taken up settlement-house work with this intention. She believed that by uplifting the poor in tenement districts, settlement workers themselves would be uplifted: they would experience "the joy of finding Christ" by acting "in fellowship" with the needy. Similarly, the philosopher John Dewey called democracy "a spiritual fact" and the "means by which the revelation of truth is carried on." At the Progressive Party national convention in 1912, Theodore Roosevelt's supporters marched around the hall singing "Onward Christian Soldiers."

The Muckrakers

The progressive mode of thought—idealistic in intent and tough-minded in approach—nurtured a new style of reform journalism. During the 1890s magazines such as *McClure's* and *Collier's* had found a wide audience of urban readers. Unlike the highbrow *Atlantic Monthly* or *Harper's*, these bright new journals, which sold for only 10 cents, specialized in lively and informative reporting. Almost by accident—Lincoln Steffens's article "Tweed Days in St. Louis" in the October 1902 issue of *McClure's* is credited with getting things started—

editors discovered that what most interested readers, and most lifted circulation, was the exposure of corruption in American life. Investigative reporters such as Charles Edward Russell fanned out on the trail of evil-doers (see American Voices, "Charles Edward Russell: Muckraking," p. 643).

In a series of powerful articles, Steffens wrote about "the shame of the cities"—the corrupt ties between business and political machines. Ida M. Tarbell attacked Standard Oil, and David Graham Phillips told how money controlled the Senate. William Hard exposed industrial accidents in "Making Steel and Killing Men" (1907) and child labor in "De Kid Wot Works at Night" (1908). Hardly a sordid corner of American life escaped the scrutiny of these tireless reporters. They were moralists as well, infusing their factual accounts with a powerful spirit of personal indignation. "The sights I saw," wrote the slum investigator Jacob Riis, "gripped my heart until I felt I must tell of them, or burst, or turn anarchist."

President Roosevelt, among many others, thought these journalists went too far. In a 1906 speech he compared them to the man with the muckrake in *Pilgrim's Progress*, by the seventeenth-century English preacher John Bunyan. The man was too absorbed with raking the filth on the floor to look up and accept a celestial

Ida Tarbell Takes on Rockefeller
A popular biographer of Napoleon and Lincoln in the 1890s, Ida Tarbell turned her journalistic talents to muckraking. Her first installment of "The History of the Standard Oil Company" appeared in *McClure's* in November 1902. John D. Rockefeller, she wrote, "was willing to strain every nerve to obtain for himself special and illegal privileges from the railroads which were bound to ruin every man in the oil business not sharing them with him." As Tarbell built her case, criticism rained down on Rockefeller. A more sympathetic cartoon in the magazine *Judge* pleads with Rockefeller's critics: "Boys, don't you think you have bothered the old man just about enough?"
Ida M. Tarbell Collection, Reis Library, Allegheny College, Meadville, Pennsylvania; Culver Pictures.

CHARLES EDWARD RUSSELL
Muckraking

———★———

*I*n this autobiographical account newspaperman *Charles Russell describes how he got into muck-raking journalism and what he thought it was all about. He never did, by the way, get back to writing music.*

All America had been accustomed to laud and bepraise the makers of great fortunes. . . . Money had become the touchstone and perfect measure of worth. . . . Now, of a sudden, men began to discover that these great and adored fortunes had been gathered in ways that not only grazed the prison gate but imposed burdens and disadvantages upon the rest of the community; that vast hoards for one man meant much less for others. In the shock of this discovery, a literature of exposition arose and daily the magazine editors looked for new dark, malodorous corners of money-grabbing upon which the spotlight could be turned.

Pure accident cast me, without the least desire, into the pursuit of this fashion. I had finally withdrawn from the newspaper business, and having enough money to live modestly I was bent upon carrying out a purpose long cherished in quite a different line. [I had concluded] that what we call the separate arts of music and poetry are really but one, and I now conceived that with a piano, my Swinburne, and some sheets of music paper I could demonstrate this priceless fact to a palpitating world. Upon this task I was intent when the whole business was upset with a single telegram.

One day, Mr. J. W. Midgley, who was a famous expert on railroad rates and conditions . . . let loose a flood of startling facts about the impositions practised by the owners and operators of refrigerator cars. My friend, Mr. Erman J. Ridgway . . . of *Everybody's Magazine* wired asking me to see Mr. Midgley and get him to write for *Everybody's* an article along the lines of his testimony. I conferred accordingly and Mr. Midgley positively refused all offers to become an exposé writer. [So] Ridgway wire[d] asking me to furnish the article *Everybody's* wanted. I had not the least disposition to do so, except only that Ridgway was my friend. . . . The next thing I knew a muck-rake was put into my hand and I was plunged into the midst of the game. . . .

I wrote two or three articles on the refrigerator car scandal and then went on to write a series on the methods of the Beef Trust and was not in the least astonished to find that I was become an unmitigated scoundrel, a hired assassin of character, a libeller of good men, an enemy of society and of the government, and probably an Anarchist in disguise. . . . We were all up and away, full of the pleasures of the chase . . . and all that business about poetry and music sheets forgotten. It was exhilarating sport, hunting the money octopus.

Source: Charles Edward Russell, *Bare Hands and Stone Walls* (New York: Charles Scribner's Sons, 1933), 135–139.

---

crown. Thus the term *muckraker* became attached to journalists who exposed the underside of American life. Their efforts were in fact health giving. More than any other group, the muckrakers called the people to arms.

The Many Faces of Reform

———★———

Historians have sometimes spoken of a progressive "movement." But progressivism was not a movement in any meaningful sense. There was no single progressive constituency, no agreed-upon agenda, and no unifying organization or leadership. At different times and places, different social groups became active. People who were reformers on one issue might be conservative on another. The term *progressivism* embraces a widespread, many-sided effort after 1900 to build a better society.

Political Reformers

One realm that cried out for reform was American politics. Like the Mugwumps of the Gilded Age, twentieth-century reformers denounced the boss rule of the party system, but the progressives' attack was much more skilled and aggressive. Indeed, because politics was about power, in this realm the motives of the progressives were always mixed, with the ideals of civic betterment elbowing uneasily with the drive for self-aggrandizement.

City Government. In many cities the demand for good government came from local businessmen. Taxes went up, they complained, but needed services always lagged. There had to be an end, as one manufacturer said, to "the inefficiency, the sloth, the carelessness, the injustice and the graft of city administrations." The solution, argued John Patterson of National Cash Register Company, lay in putting "municipal affairs on a strict business basis." Cities should be run "not by partisans, either Republican or Democratic, but by men who are skilled in business management and social service."

In 1900 a hurricane devastated Galveston, Texas, drowning five thousand people and destroying the municipal port. Local businessmen took over and, in the course of rebuilding the city, replaced the mayor and board of aldermen with a five-member commission. The Galveston plan, though widely copied, had a serious flaw: it concentrated too much power in the city commission. Dayton, Ohio, resolved this problem by assigning policy matters to a nonpartisan body and administrative functions to an appointed city manager. The commission-manager system, which aimed at running the American city "in exactly the same way as a private business corporation," was chiefly the work of the business community.

It was also a way of grabbing power. By making elections city-wide and professionalizing city administration, municipal reformers attacked the ward politics that had favored ethnic and working-class groups, shifting political power to the urban middle class. In fact, municipal reform contained a decidedly antidemocratic bias. "Ignorance should be excluded from control," said former Mayor Abram Hewitt of New York in 1901. "City business should be carried on by trained experts selected upon some other principle than popular suffrage."

Other urban progressives, however, opposed such elitism. Mayor Brand Whitlock of Toledo, Ohio, believed "that the cure for the ills of democracy was not less democracy . . . but more democracy." Whitlock's administration not only attacked municipal corruption and inefficiency but also concerned itself with providing better schools, cleaner streets, and more social services for Toledo's working people. An increasing number of cities came under the leadership of such progressive mayors, including Tom Johnson in Cleveland and Mark Fagan in Jersey City. By combining popular programs and campaign magic, they won over the urban masses and challenged the rule of the machines.

Robert M. La Follette

La Follette was transformed into a political reformer when a Wisconsin Republican boss attempted to bribe him in 1891 to influence a judge in a railway case. As he described it in his *Autobiography*, "Out of this awful ordeal came understanding; and out of understanding came resolution. I determined that the power of this corrupt influence . . . should be broken." This photograph captures La Follette at the top of his form, taking his case in 1897 to the people of Cumberland, Wisconsin. State Historical Society of Wisconsin.

State Politics. The major battleground for democratic reform, however, was not the cities but the states. Robert M. La Follette of Wisconsin led the way. Born in 1855, La Follette had followed a conventional party career as a lawyer, district attorney, and then congressman for three terms before breaking with the Wisconsin Republican machine in 1891, allegedly because of an attempt by the top party boss to bribe him. La Follette became a tireless exponent of political reform, battling the Republican old guard for a decade before finally winning the governorship in 1900 on a platform of higher taxes for corporations, stricter utility and railroad regulation, and political reform.

La Follette's key proposal was a direct primary law requiring political parties to choose candidates by means of popular election rather than in machine-run conventions. Enacted in 1903, this democratic reform not only expressed La Follette's ideals but suited his particular political talents. Republican Party regulars opposing him were insiders, more comfortable in the caucus room than out on the hustings. But on the hustings was where La Follette, a superb campaigner, excelled. The direct primary gave him an iron grip on the Republican Party in Wisconsin that he did not relinquish until his death twenty-five years later.

What was true of La Follette was more or less true of all successful progressive politicians. Albert B. Cummins of Iowa, Harold U'Ren of Oregon, and Hiram Johnson of California all espoused democratic ideals, and all skillfully used the direct primary as the stepping-stone to political power and reform. If they were newcomers—as Woodrow Wilson was when he left academic life to enter New Jersey politics in 1910—they showed a quick aptitude for politics and gained a solid mastery of the trade. They practiced a new kind of popular politics, which in a reform age could be a more effective route to power than the back-room techniques of the old-fashioned machine politicians.

Even the most democratizing of progressive reforms—the initiative, the referendum, and the recall—were really exercises in power politics. The *initiative* let ordinary citizens place issues of interest to them on the ballot. The *referendum* enabled voters to decide big legislative issues (including propositions arising from the initiative) by popular vote. The *recall* empowered citizens to remove from office politicians who had lost the public's confidence. It soon became clear, however, that direct democracy did not supplant organized politics. Initiative, referendum, and recall campaigns put a premium on organization, money, and expertise, and these were attributes not of the people at large but of well-organized special interests. Like the direct primary, the initiative, referendum, and recall had as much to do with power relations as with democratic idealism.

The Woman Progressive

Reform movements arise through a process of recruitment. Why do people enlist in a great cause? Each mobilized group—the progressive politicians just described, for example—is linked in some personal way to the evil crying out for correction. For middle-class women of the Progressive Era, the link was through their long-established identity as "social housekeepers": it was women's duty to tend to the social well-being of their communities (see Chapter 18).

Middle-class women had long borne the burden of humanitarian work in American cities. They did most of the legwork for the charity-organization societies coordinating citywide private relief after the 1870s. As voluntary investigators, women visited needy families, assessed their problems, and referred them to relief agencies.

After many years of such dedicated charity work, Josephine Shaw Lowell of New York City concluded that it was not enough to give assistance to the poor. "If the working people had all they ought to have, we should not have the paupers and criminals," she declared. "It is better to save them before they go under, than to spend your life fishing them out afterward." Lowell founded the New York Consumers' League in

1890. Her goal was to improve the wages and working conditions of female clerks in the city's stores by issuing a "White List"—a very short one at first—of cooperating shops.

From these modest beginnings the league spread to other cities and blossomed into the National Consumers' League in 1899. By then the women who ran the league had lost faith in voluntary action; only the state could rescue poor urban families. Under the crusading leadership of Florence Kelley, formerly a chief factory inspector in Illinois, the Consumers' League became a powerful lobby for protective legislation for women and children.

Among its achievements, none was more important than the *Muller v. Oregon* decision (1908), which upheld an Oregon law limiting to ten hours the workday of women workers. The Consumers' League recruited the brilliant Boston lawyer Louis D. Brandeis to defend the Oregon law before the U.S. Supreme Court. In his brief, Brandeis devoted only two pages to the narrow constitutional issue—whether, under its police powers, Oregon had the right to regulate women's working hours. Instead Brandeis rested his case on data gathered by the Consumers' League showing how long hours damaged women's health and family roles. The *Muller* decision, which accepted Brandeis's reasoning, was a victory for the new "sociological jurisprudence" and cleared the way for a wave of protective laws across the country (Table 20.1).

Women's organizations became a mighty lobbying voice on behalf of women and children (see American Lives, "Frances Kellor: Woman Progressive," pp. 646–647). Their victories included the first law providing public assistance for mothers with dependent children, in Illinois in 1911; the first minimum wage law for women, in Massachusetts in 1912; more effective child labor laws, in many states; and, at the federal level, the Children's and Women's bureaus in the Labor department, in 1912 and 1920, respectively. The welfare state, insofar as it arrived in America in these years, was what women progressives made it; they erected a "maternalist" welfare system.

Settlement Houses. Meanwhile, other women were launching the settlement-house movement. In 1889, inspired by Toynbee Hall in the slums of London, two young American women, Jane Addams and Ellen Gates Starr, established Hull House on Chicago's West Side. During the next fifteen years, scores of settlement houses sprang up in the slum neighborhoods of the nation's cities. The settlement houses served as community centers run by middle-class residents, who acted as amateur social workers for the surrounding immigrant communities. Hull House had meeting rooms, an art gallery, clubs for children and adults, and a kindergarten. Addams herself led battles for garbage

Frances Kellor: Woman Progressive

★

FROM THE DAY its doors opened in 1892, the University of Chicago was a major center of American learning. Financed by John D. Rockefeller, the university modeled itself on the great German research universities and, unlike Yale and Harvard, concentrated on graduate education. At Chicago and other American universities, modern social science was taking shape, breaking from its nineteenth-century moral foundations and seeking a scientific basis for the study of society. Economics, political science, and sociology demanded a rigorous course of study certified by the granting of the Ph.D. But if the social sciences were becoming professional, their guiding purpose was not yet disinterested research but the improvement of society. The University of Chicago saw the city surrounding it as a great laboratory for social betterment. Its students were being prepared, whether they knew it or not, to be in service to the American progressivism of the next decade. The University of Chicago, moreover, was receptive to the admission of women, and for them in particular, graduate education was a breeding ground for careers as social reformers.

Among the women entering in 1898 was Frances Alice Kellor, a recent graduate of Cornell University. Kellor was born in Columbus, Ohio, in 1873. Her father abandoned the family before she was two, and her mother made a hard living as a domestic and laundress. This was not the kind of privileged background from which most woman progressives sprang, but Kellor's experience came closer to the norm than her threadbare circumstances might have suggested. In 1875 her family moved to Coldwater, Michigan, a former abolitionist center (and station on the underground railroad) and a stronghold of Yankee culture. From the Coldwater community, with its high moral standards and strong educational institutions, Kellor received the reformist values that other budding progressives learned from their families. Kellor, moreover, had a remarkable talent for finding patrons, gaining by her wits the financial means her fellow progressives were born to. Her first patrons were the well-to-do librarians of Coldwater, Mary and Frances Eddy, who befriended her and took her into their home. Born Alice, Kellor began to call herself "Frances" as a sign that she considered herself adopted by the Eddy sisters. She graduated from high school, became a reporter for the *Coldwater Republican*, and then, with the backing of the Eddys, enrolled at Cornell in 1895. Highly athletic, Kellor made her first mark as a fighter for equal rights on a sports issue: she led the campaign for a women's crew. She got a solid education in the social sciences at Cornell and decided to become a criminologist.

When Frances Kellor arrived in Chicago in 1898, sociology was an infant discipline, with little in the way of systematic theory and an emphasis on high-minded investigations of social problems. Kellor's interest in crime was encouraged by the Chicago faculty. The prevailing theory of the time, advanced by the Italian Cesare Lombroso, was that criminality was an inherited trait—that criminals were born criminal and that this tendency was manifest in their physical features. Skeptical, Kellor conducted a study of the female inmates of five midwestern prisons. Comparing them with a control group of college women, she could find no physical differences. Kellor concluded that not heredity but social environment, economic disadvantage, and poverty produced criminality. Kellor also rejected "the prevailing opinion that when women are criminal they are more degraded and more abandoned than men." People thought so, she asserted, only because of "the difference in the standards which we set for the two sexes."

A second project on criminality among southern blacks likewise rejected heredity and stressed environmental factors, but Kellor's conclusions were pessimistic and racially conservative: centuries of slavery and indolent southern life had left blacks so morally weakened that "the Negro at present has neither the perceptions nor the solidity of character that would enable him to lead his race." She considered the southern restrictions on blacks' legal and political rights unfortunate but necessary, and she believed that "the free intermingling of the two races is impossible, at least for many generations." In drawing these illiberal conclusions, Kellor was echoing the views of her teachers and indeed of most white progressives of her generation.

Frances Kellor
This photograph of Kellor was taken in her early twenties, when she was a student at Cornell University.

Despite her precocious record, Kellor left the university in 1902 without a degree. The reasons are not altogether clear but doubtless had something to do with a painful truth of which Kellor must have been aware: the University of Chicago almost never placed its female graduate students in university teaching jobs. To be a professor, it seemed, was still a male prerogative. There was, however, a positive side to Kellor's decision. Like many of her fellow students, she had fallen under the spell of Jane Addams. Kellor lived periodically at Hull House, joined the circle of social reformers that congregated there, and began to see her future out among the disadvantaged rather than in the university. When she left Chicago, it was to do social research for New York's College Settlement Association.

Her first project was a study of unemployment. Kellor rejected the prevailing notion that being jobless was a sign of personal weakness. She was among the first investigators to see that unemployment was an economic problem, the result not primarily of individual shiftlessness or incompetence but of the impersonal operations of the labor market. Her book *Out of Work* (1904) was a pioneering investigation, paving the way for the modern study of unemployment. Kellor was especially concerned with the plight of jobless women and their exploitation by commercial employment agencies. Representing the Women's Municipal League of New York, Kellor lobbied successfully for state regulation of these agencies. Kellor thus employed her research to bring about social change. The combination of professional investigation and robust political advocacy became the hallmark of Kellor's progressivism. Her next study, on the problems of immigrants in New York, led to the establishment of the New York State Bureau of Industries and Immigration in 1910. Kellor was chosen to be its head, the first woman to hold so high a post in New York's state government.

The high point of Kellor's career came two years later, when Theodore Roosevelt launched the Progressive Party. Convinced that social reform required strong government, Kellor was drawn to the New Nationalism. She linked it with her own fervent advocacy of women's political rights. Always a fighter, she was entirely at ease in the rough-and-tumble of partisan politics. After Roosevelt's defeat in 1912, the Progressive Party set up the National Progressive Service, a kind of think tank to study social problems and formulate legislative proposals. The idea was mainly Kellor's, and she was tapped to chair the Service. This was truly a pinnacle for a woman in American politics at a time when women in most states could not vote in national elections. Unfortunately, Kellor's emphasis on scientific investigation put her at odds with the practical politicians, and she was forced out in early 1914. Hers was a brief run in national politics, exhilarating while it lasted and unique for a woman of her generation.

Kellor never married. Like many other woman progressives, including Jane Addams, she found personal fulfillment in an enduring relationship with another woman. This was Mary Dreier, one of two wealthy sisters who played leading roles in New York progressivism. From the time Kellor moved into the Dreier home in Brooklyn Heights in 1904 until her death almost fifty years later, she and Mary were constant companions. Kellor's later professional life was devoted to a distinguished career with the American Arbitration Association.

TABLE 20.1

Progressive Legislation and Supreme Court Decisions

State Laws	Federal Laws	Supreme Court Decisions
1903 Wisconsin primary law; Oregon ten-hour law for women	1898 Erdman Railway Mediation Act	1895 *U.S. v. E.C. Knight* shelters manufacturing from antitrust law
1910 New York Bureau of Industries and Immigration; Washington State adopts woman suffrage	1902 Newlands Reclamation Act; 1903 U.S. Bureau of Corporations; Elkins Act	1897 *U.S. v. Trans-Missouri* quashes "rule of reason" in antitrust suits
1911 Illinois law providing aid for mothers with dependent children; New York State Factory Commission	1906 Hepburn Railway Act; Pure Food and Drug Act; Meat Inspection Act	1904 *U.S. v. Northern Securities* orders dissolution of a company ruled a monopoly under the Sherman Act
1912 Massachusetts minimum-wage law for women and children	1909 Payne-Aldrich Tariff Act; 1913 Underwood Tariff Act; Federal Reserve Act; 1914 Federal Trade Commission Act; Clayton Antitrust Act; 1916 Seamen's Act; Federal Farm Loan Act	1905 *Lochner v. New York* invalidates a state law limiting hours of bakers; 1908 *Muller v. Oregon* approves a state law limiting working hours of women; *Loewe v. Lawlor* (Danbury Hatters case) finds a labor boycott to be a conspiracy in restraint of trade; 1911 *U.S. v. Standard Oil* restores rule of reason as guiding principle in antitrust cases

removal, better street lighting, and police protection. At the Henry Street Settlement in New York City, Lillian D. Wald made visiting nursing a major service. Mary McDowell, head of the University of Chicago Settlement, installed a bathhouse, a playground, and a citizenship school for immigrants.

Besides the modest good they did in slum neighborhoods, settlement houses also satisfied the hunger of their middle-class residents for meaningful lives. In a famous essay, Jane Addams spoke of the "subjective necessity" of the settlement house. She meant that it was as much a response to the desire of educated young men and women to serve as it was a response to the needs of slum dwellers. Addams herself was a case in point. Born in 1860 in Cedarville, Illinois, she grew up in a comfortable middle-class family and graduated from Rockford College. Then Addams faced an empty future—as an ornamental wife if she married, as a sheltered spinster if she did not. Hull House became her salvation, enabling her to "begin with however small a group to accomplish and to live." At least half of the women residents went on to careers in social service. Settlement houses thus contributed significantly to the emerging profession of social work. To a remarkable degree, the leaders of social reform—both men and women—served apprenticeships in settlement houses.

Revival of the Suffrage Movement. Almost imperceptibly, women activists such as Jane Addams and Florence Kelley breathed new life into the suffrage movement. Why, they asked, should a woman who was capable of running a settlement house or lobbying a bill be denied the right to vote? If women had the right to vote, moreover, they would demand more enlightened legislation and better government. Finally, by encouraging working-class women to help themselves, women progressives got a whole new class interested in fighting for suffrage.

In 1903 social reformers founded the National Women's Trade Union League. Financed and led by wealthy supporters, the league organized women workers, played a considerable role in their strikes, and, perhaps most important, helped to develop working-class leaders. Rose Schneiderman became a union organizer among garment workers in New York City, and Agnes Nestor led women glove workers in Illinois; both were also lobbyists for protective legislation. Athough they often resented the patronizing ways of their well-to-do sponsors, such trade-union women identified their cause with the broader struggle for women's rights. When New York State held referenda on woman suffrage in 1915 and 1917, strong support came from the Jewish and Italian precincts inhabited by unionized garment workers.

Saving the Children
In the early years at Hull House, Jane Addams recalled, toddlers sometimes arrived for kindergarten tipsy from a breakfast of bread soaked in wine. To settlement-house workers, the answer to such ignorance was in child-care education, and so began the program to send visiting nurses into immigrant homes. They taught mothers the proper methods of caring for children—including, as this photograph shows, the daily infant bath, given in a dishpan if necessary.
Chicago Historical Society.

Suffrage activity began to revive nationwide. Women won the right to vote in the state of Washington in 1910, in California in 1911, and in four more western states during the next three years (Map 20.1). Women also altered their tactics. In Britain suffragists had begun to picket Parliament, assault politicians, and go on hunger strikes in jail. Following their lead, Alice Paul, a young Quaker who had lived in Britain, applied these confrontational tactics to the American battle for woman suffrage. Rejecting the slower route of enfranchisement by the states, Paul advocated a constitutional amendment that in one stroke would give women across the country the right to vote. In 1916 she organized the militant National Woman's Party.

The National American Woman Suffrage Association (NAWSA), from which Paul had split off, was also rejuvenated. Carrie Chapman Catt, a skilled political organizer from the New York movement, took over as national leader in 1915. Under her guidance, NAWSA brought a broad-based organization to the campaign for a federal amendment.

Birth of Feminism. In the midst of this suffrage struggle something new and more fundamental began to happen. A new generation of college-educated women, out in the world and self-supporting, refused to be hemmed in by the social constraints of women's "separate sphere." "Breaking into the Human Race"

Rose Schneiderman, 1913
In their battles for better conditions, women garment workers produced their own leaders, and none was more devoted to their cause or more fiery on the platform than Rose Schneiderman. The daughter of a widowed immigrant woman, Schneiderman went to work at thirteen, quickly got caught up in union activities, and fashioned for herself a lifetime career as a trade unionist, including becoming president of the National Women's Trade Union League.
Brown Brothers.

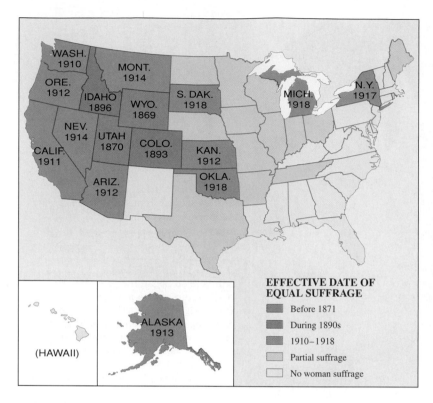

MAP 20.1
Woman Suffrage, 1869–1918
By 1909, after more than sixty years of agitation, only four lightly populated western states had granted women full voting rights. A number of other states offered partial suffrage, limited mostly to voting for school boards and such issues as taxes. Between 1910 and 1918, as the effort shifted to the struggle for a constitutional amendment, eleven states (and Alaska) joined the list granting full suffrage. The most stubborn resistance was in the South.

was the intention they proclaimed at a mass meeting in New York in 1914. "We intend simply to be ourselves," declared the chair Marie Jenny Howe, "not just our little female selves, but our whole big human selves."

The women at this meeting called themselves *feminists*, a term that was just coming into use. In this, its first incarnation, *feminism* meant freedom for full personal development, which in its specifics covered many things—freedom to follow a career, freedom from the double standard in sexual morality, freedom from social convention—but in a larger sense it meant freedom from the stifling stereotypes of women's separate sphere. Thus did Charlotte Perkins Gilman, famous for her advocacy of communal kitchens as a means of liberating women from homemaking, imagine the new woman: "Here she comes, running, out of prison and off pedestal; chains off, crown off, halo off, just a live woman."

Feminists were militantly prosuffrage, but unlike their more traditional suffragist sisters, they did not stake their claim on any presumed uplifting effect of the women's vote on American politics. Rather, they demanded the right to vote because they considered themselves fully equal to men. At the point that the suffrage movement was about to triumph, it was overtaken by a larger revolution that redefined the struggle for women's rights as a battle against all the constraints that prevented women from achieving their potential as human beings.

Feminism brought forth a new and more radical type of woman progressive: Margaret Sanger. As a public health nurse in New York, Sanger had been repeatedly asked by immigrant women the "secret" of how to avoid having more babies. When one of her patients died of a botched abortion, Sanger decided to devote herself to teaching poor immigrant women about birth control. This brought her up against the Comstock laws, which outlawed contraceptive literature and devices as obscene materials (see Chapter 19). While it was easy enough for the educated middle class to evade these laws, birth control could reach the poor only by an open campaign of education. Undeterred by police raids or public disapproval, Sanger gave speeches, published the pamphlet *Family Limitation*, and in 1916 opened the first birth-control clinic in the United States. If her ends were not different from Jane Addams's—both wanted to uplift the downtrodden—the means that Sanger used posed a more provocative challenge to the status quo.

Urban Liberalism

When Hiram Johnson first ran for governor of California on the Republican ticket in 1910, he was the reform candidate of the urban middle class and the farming community. Famous as prosecutor of the corrupt San Francisco boss Abe Ruef, Johnson pledged to purify California politics and curb the Southern Pacific Rail-

Suffragists on Parade, 1912
After 1910 the suffrage movement went into
high gear. Suffragist leaders decided to
demand a constitutional amendment rather
than rely on gaining the vote state by state. In
1912 they served notice on both parties that
they meant business and, as shown in this suffragist parade in New York, made their
demands a visible part of the presidential
campaign.
Corbis-Bettmann.

road—the dominating power in the state's economic
and political life. By his second term Johnson was
championing social and labor legislation. His original
base in the middle class had eroded and been replaced
by an immigrant working-class vote that made him an
invincible power in California for years.

Johnson's career illustrated an enduring achievement of progressivism: the activation of America's
working people as a force in reform politics. The elements in this achievement were, first, the emergence of
committed leaders, like Hiram Johnson; second, the
crafting of a reform program keyed to the needs of the
urban masses; and, perhaps most important, a rising
level of popular engagement by these immigrant working people. This last development crucially altered the
composition of progressivism, which had begun as a
movement of the middle class but then took on board
America's working people. The effect was a brand of
reform politics that historians have labeled *urban liberalism*. To understand this phenomenon, we need to
begin with city boss politics.

Machine Politicians as Reformers. Thirty minutes
before quitting time on Saturday afternoon, March 25,
1911, fire broke out at the Triangle Shirtwaist Company
in downtown New York City. The flames trapped the
workers, mostly young immigrant women. Forty-seven
leapt to their deaths; another ninety-nine never made it
to the windows (see American Voices, "Pauline Newman:
Working for the Triangle Shirtwaist Company," p. 652).
The tragedy caused a national furor and led to the creation of the New York State Factory Commission.

Over the next four years the commission developed a remarkable program of labor reform: fifty-six

laws dealing with fire hazards, unsafe machines,
homework, and wages and hours for women and children. The chairman of the commission was Robert F.
Wagner; the vice-chairman, Alfred E. Smith. Both
were Tammany Hall politicians, Democratic Party
leaders in the state legislature. They established the
commission, participated fully in its work, and mar-
shaled the party regulars to pass the proposals into
law. All this Wagner and Smith did with the approval
of the Tammany machine.

Tammany's reform role reflected something new in
urban politics. Party machines increasingly recognized
their limitations as social agencies in the modern
industrial age. Only the state could prevent future Triangle fires or cope with the evils of factory work and
city life. A new generation had entered machine politics. Al Smith and Robert Wagner, men of social vision,
absorbed the lessons of the Triangle investigation. They
formed durable ties with such middle-class progressives as the social worker Frances Perkins, who sat on
the commission as the representative of the New York
Consumers' League.

For all their organizational muscle, the urban
machines could not ignore the will of the people. In the
successes of such progressive politicians as Jersey City's
Mark Fagan and Cleveland's Tom Johnson, the machines
saw the appeal of reform programs in working-class
wards. They faced a threat from the left as well. The
Socialist Party was making headway in the cities, electing
Milwaukee's Victor Berger as the nation's first socialist
congressman in 1910 and winning municipal elections in
towns and cities across the country. The political universe
of the urban machines had changed, and they had to pay
more attention to opinion in the precincts.

PAULINE NEWMAN
Working for the Triangle Shirtwaist Company

———————★———————

Pauline Newman was an organizer and educational director for the International Ladies Garment Workers Union until her death in 1986. As a child she had worked at the notorious Triangle Shirtwaist factory in New York.

A cousin of mine worked for the Triangle Shirtwaist Company and she got me on there in October of 1901. It was probably the largest shirtwaist factory in the city of New York then. They had more than two hundred operators, cutters, examiners, finishers. Altogether more than four hundred people on two floors. . . . We started work at seven-thirty in the morning, and during the busy season we worked until nine in the evening. They didn't pay you any overtime and they didn't give you anything for supper money. . . . What I had to do was not really very difficult. It was just monotonous. When the shirtwaists were finished at the machine there were some threads that were left, and all the youngsters— we had a corner on the floor that resembled a kindergarten—we were given little scissors to cut the threads off. It wasn't heavy work, but it was monotonous, because you did the same thing from seven-thirty in the morning until nine at night.

Well, of course, there were [child labor] laws on the books, but no one bothered to enforce them. The employers were always tipped off if there was going to be an inspection. "Quick," they'd say, "into the boxes!" And we children would climb into the big boxes the finished shirts were stored in. Then some shirts were piled on top of us, and when the inspector came—no children. The factory always got an okay from the inspector, and I suppose someone at City Hall got a little something, too.

The employers didn't recognize anyone working for them as a human being. . . . If you went to the toilet and you were there longer than the floor lady thought you should be, you would be laid off for half a day and sent home. And, of course, that meant no pay. You were not allowed to have your lunch on the fire escape in the summertime. The door was locked to keep us in. That's why so many people were trapped when the fire broke out. . . .

I stopped working at the Triangle Factory during the strike in 1909 and I didn't go back. The union sent me out to raise money for the strikers. I apparently was able to articulate my feelings and opinions about the criminal conditions, and they didn't have anyone else who could do better so they assigned me. . . .

After the 1909 strike I worked with the union, organizing in Philadelphia and Cleveland and other places, so I wasn't at the Triangle Shirtwaist Factory when the fire broke out, but a lot of my friends were. . . . It's very difficult to describe the feeling because I knew the place and I knew so many of the girls. The thing that bothered me was the employers got a lawyer. . . . One hundred and forty-six people were sacrificed, and the judge fined Blank and Harris seventy-five dollars!

Conditions were dreadful in those days. But . . . even when things were terrible, I always had that faith. . . . Only now, I'm a little discouraged sometimes when I see the workers spending their free hours watching television—trash. We fought so hard for those hours and they waste them. We used to read Tolstoy, Dickens, Shelley, by candlelight, and they watch the "Hollywood Squares." Well, they're free to do what they want. That's what we fought for.

———————

Source: Joan Morrison and Charlotte Fox Zabusky, eds., *American Mosaic: The Immigrant Experience in the Words of Those Who Lived It* (New York: E. P. Dutton, 1980), 9–14. Copyright © 1980 by Joan Morrison and Charlotte Fox Zabusky. Reprinted by permission.

The Labor Movement. City machines, always pragmatic, adopted urban liberalism without much of an ideological struggle. The same could not be said of trade unions, the other institution that spoke for American working people. During its early years the American Federation of Labor (AFL) had strongly opposed state interference in labor's affairs. Samuel Gompers preached that workers should not seek from government what they could accomplish through their own economic power and self-help. Voluntarism, as trade unionists called this doctrine, did not die out, but it weakened substantially during the progressive years.

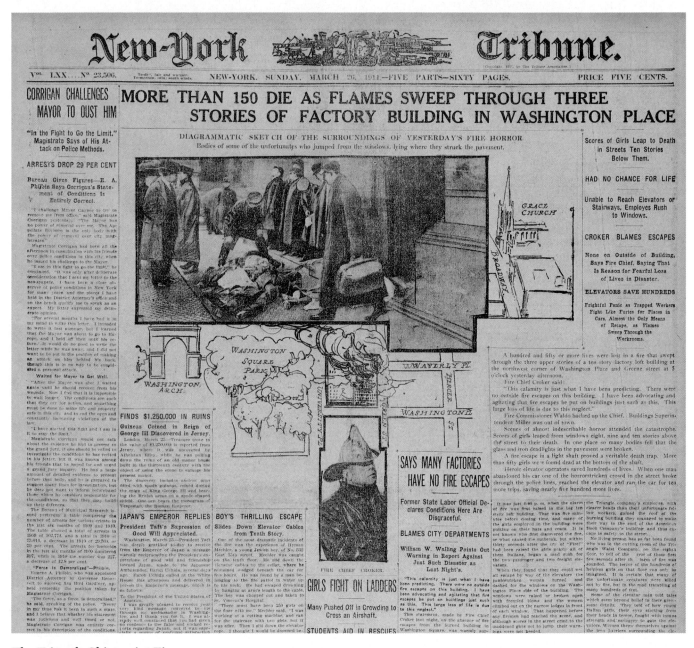

The Triangle Shirtwaist Fire
The doors were the problem. Most were locked (to keep the working girls from leaving early); the few that were open became jammed by bodies as the flames spread. When the fire trucks finally came, the ladders were too short. Compared with those caught inside, the girls who leapt to their deaths were the lucky ones. "As I looked up I saw a love affair in the midst of all the horror," a reporter wrote. A young man was helping girls leap from a window. The fourth "put her arms about him and kiss[ed] him. Then he held her out into space and dropped her." He immediately followed. "Thud—dead, Thud—dead . . . I saw his face before they covered it. . . . He was a real man. He had done his best."
The New York Tribune, March 26, 1911.

In the early twentieth century the labor movement came under severe attack by the courts. In the Danbury Hatters case (1908), the U.S. Supreme Court found a labor boycott—a call by the Hatters' Union for people not to patronize the anti-union D. E. Loewe & Company—to be a conspiracy in restraint of trade under the Sherman Antitrust Act and awarded triple damages to the company. Hundreds of union members stood to lose their homes and life savings until the labor movement raised the money to pay the fines. Even worse was the willingness of many judges to grant employers labor injunctions—court orders—prohibiting a union from carrying on a strike or boycott. The justification was to prevent "irreparable damage" to an employer while the legality of a union's acts was being adjudicated. But the effect of this "temporary" measure was to immobilize and defeat the union, as had happened, for example, to the American Railway Union in the great Pullman strike of 1894 (see Chapter 17).

Only a political response could blunt these assaults on labor's economic weapons. In its "Bill of Grievances" of 1906 the AFL demanded that Congress grant unions immunity from court attack. Rebuffed by Congress, the unions became more politically active, entering campaigns and giving nonpartisan support to candidates who favored their program. The AFL intended to "reward our friends and punish our enemies." In principle, this was "nonpartisan" politics, but in practice, labor became allied to the Democratic Party, which was more responsive than the Republican Party to labor's pleas for a curb on the courts.

Once into politics, the labor movement had difficulty denying the case for social legislation. The AFL, after all, claimed to speak for the entire working class. When muckrakers exposed exploitation of workers and middle-class progressives came forward with solutions, how could the labor movement fail to respond? Gompers served on the Triangle factory commission, and if—according to Frances Perkins—he was a less eager student than the Tammanyite members, learn he did. In state after state, organized labor joined the battle for progressive legislation and increasingly became its strongest advocate.

Conservative labor leaders offered the excuse that protective laws were for women and children, who could not defend themselves. In practice, however, trade unions became more flexible about legislative protection for men as well, and on the issue of workers' compensation they took the lead.

Social Insurance Deferred. Accidents took an awful toll in American factories and mines. Two thousand coal miners were killed every year, dying from cave-ins and explosions at a rate 50 percent higher than in German mines. Liability laws, which were still governed by common-law principles, so heavily favored the employer that victims of industrial accidents rarely got compensation. Nothing cried out more for reform than the plight of maimed workers and penniless widows. Citing state-funded accident insurance in Germany and Britain, the unions demanded comparable protections for American workers, although they were willing to compromise with the insurance industry and employers on a funding system based on accident rates. Between 1910 and 1917 workers' compensation on this basis went into effect in all the industrial states.

Compared to Europe, however, the United States was slow to protect workers against the hazards of

Maimed Factory Worker
Lewis Hine, a great photographer of immigrant life, took this undated picture of a disabled factory worker. Two of his four children are in the background. How was he to support them? If his accident occurred before the passage of workers' compensation laws in 1910, they were probably out of luck.
George Eastman House.

modern industrial life. Health insurance and unemployment compensation, familiar in Europe, scarcely made it onto the American political agenda. Old-age pensions, which Britain adopted in 1908, got a serious hearing, only to come up against the fact that the United States already had a pension system of a kind, for Civil War veterans: as many as half of all native-born white men over sixty-four or their survivors were receiving veterans' pensions in the early twentieth century. It did not help, moreover, that the Republican Party had shamelessly exploited veterans' pensions as a campaign issue, or that administration of the program was notoriously corrupt and laced with patronage, or, finally, that easy access to veterans' benefits often reinforced fears of state-induced dependency. Clarence J. Hicks, an industrial-relations expert, recalled Civil War pensioners idling away the hours around the wood stove in the grocery store in his Wisconsin town. They had decided "that the country owed them a living," lost their initiative, and "retreated from the battle of life."

Not until a later generation experienced the Great Depression of the 1930s would the country be ready for social insurance. A secure old age, unemployment compensation, health insurance—these human needs of a modern industrial order were beyond the reach of urban liberals in the Progressive Era.

Cultural Pluralism Embattled. Urban liberalism was driven not only by the plight of the economically downtrodden but also by a sharpening attack on immigrants. Old-stock evangelical Protestants had long agitated for laws that would impose their moral and cultural norms on American society. After 1900 this impulse again beat strongly, expressing, in fact, one strand of progressive reform. The Anti-Saloon League, which called itself "the Protestant church in action," became a formidable force for prohibition in many states. Outlawing the sale of liquor was related to other reform targets: the saloon made for dirty politics, poverty, and bad labor conditions. Like progressives on other fronts, prohibitionists pronounced their movement the "Revolt of Decent Citizens."

The moral-reform agenda expanded to include a new goal: restricting the immigration of southern and eastern Europeans into the United States. "No intelligent patriot," pronounced M.I.T. president Francis A. Walker, can observe "the entrance . . . of such vast masses of peasantry, degraded below our utmost concepts . . . without the gravest apprehension and alarm." La Follette's close advisor, Edward A. Ross of the University of Wisconsin, denounced the "pigsty mode of life" of immigrants. The danger, respected social scientists argued, was that the nation's Anglo-Saxon population would be "mongrelized" and its civilization swamped by "inferior" Mediterranean and Slavic cultures. Feeding on this fear, the Immigration Restriction League spearheaded a movement to end America's historic open-door policy. Like prohibition, immigration restriction was considered by its proponents to be a progressive reform.

Urban liberals thought otherwise. They denounced prohibition and immigration restriction as attacks on the personal liberty and worthiness of urban immigrants. Prohibition, protested one Catholic academic, was "despotic and hypocritical domination." The Tammany politician Martin McCue accused the Protestant ministry of "seeking to substitute the policeman's nightstick for the Bible."

Urban liberal leaders championed both the economic needs of city dwellers and their religious and cultural freedom. In many ways, certainly until the Great Depression, the second issue provided the stronger basis for urban liberal politics. And because their party cultivated the immigrant vote, the Democrats became the beneficiaries of the rise of urban liberalism. The rapid growth of this city vote destined the Democrats to become the majority party. The shift from Republican domination, though not completed until the 1930s, began during the Progressive Era.

Racism in an Age of Reform

The direct primary was the flagship of progressive politics—the crucial reform, as La Follette said, for defeating the party bosses and returning politics to "the people." The primary originated not in Wisconsin, however, but in the South, and by the time La Follette got his primary law in 1903, it was already operating in seven southern states. As in the North, the direct primary in the South was celebrated as a democratizing reform and frequently set the stage for bringing reform state administrations into power.

The southern primary, however, sprang from the furious political battles of the 1890s (see Chapter 18). In the course of those battles, as the challenge to Democratic rule failed, one of the devices that emerged for driving blacks out of politics was the primary. In the South the Democratic primary was a *white* primary. Since the Democratic nomination was tantamount to election, excluding African Americans from the nominating process effectively disfranchised them. The southern primary was dressed up as an attack on back-room party rule, but it served also to drive blacks out of politics.

White Supremacy in the Progressive Vein. How could democratic reform and white supremacy be united in this fashion? Because of the racism of the age. In a 1902 book on Reconstruction, Professor John W. Burgess of Columbia University denounced the Fifteenth Amendment. Granting the vote to the freedmen after the Civil War was a "monstrous thing," wrote Burgess. "A black skin means membership in a race of men which has never of itself succeeded to reason." Burgess was southern-born, but he was confident that his northern audience saw the "vast differences in political capacity" between blacks and whites and approved of black disfranchisement. Not even the Republican Party offered a rebuttal. Indeed, as president-elect in 1908, William Howard Taft applauded the southern laws as necessary to "prevent entirely the possibility of domination by . . . an ignorant electorate" and reassured southerners that "the federal government has nothing to do with social equality."

In the North, racial tensions were on the rise. Over 200,000 blacks migrated from the South between 1900 and 1910. Their arrival in northern cities invariably sparked white resentment. Attacks on blacks became widespread, capped by a bloody race riot in Springfield, Illinois, in 1908. Equally reflective of racist sentiment was the huge success of D. W. Griffith's epic film *Birth of a Nation* (1915), which depicted Reconstruction as a moral struggle between rampaging blacks and a chivalrous Ku Klux Klan. Woodrow Wilson found the film's history "all so terribly true." His Democratic administration marked a low point for the federal government as the ultimate guarantor of equal rights: during Wilson's tenure, segregation of the U.S. civil service would have gone into effect had there not been an outcry among black leaders and a handful of influential white allies.

Revival of the Civil Rights Struggle.   In these bleak years a core of young black professionals, mostly northern-born, began to fight back. The key figure was William Monroe Trotter, the pugnacious editor of the *Boston Guardian* and an outspoken critic of Booker T. Washington (see Chapter 18). "The policy of compromise has failed," Trotter argued. "The policy of resistance and aggression deserves a trial." In this endeavor, Trotter was joined by W. E. B. Du Bois, whose *The Souls of Black Folk* (1903) had challenged Washington's accommodationism for "practically accept[ing] the alleged inferiority of the Negro." In 1906 the two of them, having broken with Washington, called a meeting of twenty-nine supporters at Niagara Falls—in Canada, because no hotel on the U.S. side would admit blacks. The Niagara Movement, which resulted from that meeting, had an impact far beyond the scattering of members and local bodies it organized. The principles it affirmed would define the struggle for the rights of African Americans: first, encouragement of black pride by all possible means; second, an uncompromising demand for full political and civil equality; and above all, a resolute denial "that the Negro-American assents to inferiority, is submissive under oppression and apologetic before insults."

Going against the grain, a handful of white reformers rallied to the African American cause. Among the most devoted was Mary White Ovington, who grew up in an abolitionist family. Like Jane Addams, Ovington became a settlement-house worker, but among blacks in New York City rather than in an immigrant Chicago neighborhood. News of the Springfield race riot of 1908 changed her life. Convinced that her duty was to fight racism, Ovington called a meeting of sympathetic white progressives, which led to the formation of the National Association for the Advancement of Colored People (NAACP) in 1909.

Torn by internal disagreements, the Niagara Movement was breaking up, and most of the black activists joined the NAACP. Whites dominated the organization's leadership, with one crucial exception: Du Bois became editor of the NAACP's journal, *The Crisis*. With a passion that only an African American voice could provide, Du Bois used that platform to proclaim the demand for black equality.

In social welfare, the National Urban League became the lead organization, uniting in 1911 the many groups serving black migrants arriving in northern cities. Like the NAACP, the Urban League was interracial, including white reformers such as Ovington and

W. E. B. Du Bois
No activity undertaken by the NAACP in the early years was more important than the publication of its journal, *The Crisis*, which under the brilliant editorship of W. E. B. Du Bois became the strongest voice for equal rights and black pride in the country. In this photograph, Du Bois is pictured at his desk at the magazine's editorial office.
Schomburg Center for Research in Black Culture, New York Public Library.

black welfare activists such as William Lewis Bulkley, a New York school principal who was the main architect of the Urban League. In the South, social welfare was very much the province of black women, whose civic activities to some extent filled the vacuum left by the disfranchisement of black men. African American women's progressivism sprang organizationally from the churches and schools, but also from the southern affiliates of the National Association of Colored Women's Clubs, which had started in 1896. And because their activities seemed unthreatening to white supremacy, black women were able to reach across the color line and find allies and supporters among white women in the South.

Progressivism was a house of many chambers. Most were infected by the respectable racism of the age, but not all. A saving remnant of white progressives rallied to the cause of African Americans. In the interracial NAACP and Urban League, and in such black organizations as the National Association of Colored Women's Clubs, national institutions were formed that would lead the black struggle for a better life over the next half-century.

Colored Women's League of Washington, D.C.

At a time when black men were being driven from politics in the South, their wives and sisters organized themselves and became an alternative voice of black conscience. Sara Iredell Fleetwood, superintendent of the Freedman's Hospital Training School for Nurses, founded the Colored Women's League of Washington, D.C., in 1892 for purposes of "racial uplift." This picture of the League was taken on the steps of Frederick Douglass's home in Anacostia, Washington. Mrs. Fleetwood is seated at the far right, third row from the bottom. The notations are by someone seeking to identify the other members, a modest effort to save for posterity these women, mostly teachers, who did their best for the good of the race.

Library of Congress.

Progressivism and National Politics

——————★——————

The gathering forces of progressivism reached the national scene slowly. Reformers had been spurred by immediate and visible problems. Washington seemed distant from the battles they were waging in their cities and states. But in 1906 Robert La Follette left the governor's office in Wisconsin for the U.S. Senate. Other seasoned progressives, also ambitious for a wider stage, made the same move. By 1910 a highly vocal progressive Republican bloc was making itself heard in both houses of Congress.

Progressivism came to national politics not from Congress, however, but by way of the presidency. This was partly because the White House provided a "bully pulpit"—to use Theodore Roosevelt's phrase—for mobilizing national opinion. But just as important was the twist of fate that brought Roosevelt to the White House on September 14, 1901.

T. R.: The Making of a Progressive President

Except for his aristocratic background, Theodore Roosevelt was cut from much the same cloth as other progressive politicians. Born in 1858, he came from a wealthy old-line New York family, attended Harvard, and might have chosen the life of a leisured man of letters. Instead, scarcely out of college, he plunged into Republican politics and in 1882 entered the New York State legislature. Like many other budding progressives, he was motivated by a moralistic, Christian upbringing. Roosevelt always identified himself—loudly—with the cause of righteousness. But he did not scorn power and its uses. He showed contempt for the amateurism of the Mugwumps, and much preferred the company of party professionals. Roosevelt rose in the New York party because he skillfully translated his moral fervor into broad popular support and thus forced himself on reluctant state Republican bosses.

After returning from the Spanish-American War as the hero of San Juan Hill (see Chapter 21), Roosevelt won the New York governorship in 1898. During his single term he clearly signaled his reformist inclinations by pushing through civil-service reform and a tax on corporate franchises. He discharged the corrupt superintendent of insurance over the Republican Party's objections and asserted his confidence in the government's capacity to improve the life of the people.

Hoping to neutralize him, the party bosses promoted Roosevelt in 1900 to what seemed a dead-end job, as William McKinley's vice-president. Roosevelt

Theodore Roosevelt at Yellowstone National Park, 1903
President Roosevelt, a devoted conservationist, is pictured here about to enter Yellowstone, the first of America's national parks and a favorite of his. The photograph of him on horseback must have delighted Roosevelt. It showed him as he liked to be seen—as a great outdoorsman.
Picture Research Consultants & Archives.

accepted reluctantly. But on September 6, 1901, an anarchist named Leon F. Czolgosz shot the president. When McKinley died eight days later, Roosevelt became president. It was a sure bet, groaned Republican boss Mark Hanna, that "that damn cowboy" would make trouble in the White House.

Roosevelt in fact moved cautiously, attending first of all to politics. He understood the power of the conservative Republican bloc in Congress and treated the Senate leader, Nelson W. Aldrich of Rhode Island, with kid gloves while consolidating his position. He adroitly used the patronage powers of the presidency to gain control of the Republican Party. But Roosevelt was also restrained by uncertainty about what reform role the federal government ought to play. At first the new president might have been described as a progressive without a cause.

First Steps: Conservation and the Coal Strike. Even so, Roosevelt displayed his activist bent. An ardent outdoorsman, he devoted part of his first annual message to Congress to conservation. Unlike John Muir (see Chapter 16), Roosevelt was not a preservationist broadly opposed to exploitation of the nation's wilderness. Rather, he wanted to conserve the country's resources.

He was not against commercial development as long as it was regulated and mindful of the public interest. The Forest Reserve Act of 1891 had begun the process of withdrawing timberland from unregulated private use. Roosevelt added more than 125 million acres to the national forests and brought mineral lands and water power sites into the reserve system. In 1902 he backed the Newlands Reclamation Act, which designated the proceeds from public land sales for irrigation in arid regions. His administration upgraded the management of public lands and, to the chagrin of some Republicans, energetically prosecuted violators of federal land laws. In the cause of conservation Roosevelt showed his enthusiasm for exercising executive authority and his disdain for those who sought profit "by betraying the public."

The same inclinations influenced Roosevelt's handling of the anthracite miners' strike of 1902. Hard coal (anthracite) was the main fuel for home heating in those days. As cold weather approached with no settlement in sight, the government faced a national emergency. The United Mine Workers, led by John Mitchell, were willing to submit to arbitration, but the coal operators adamantly opposed recognizing the union. Roosevelt's advisors told him there was no legal basis for federal intervention. Nevertheless, the president called both sides to the White House on October 1, 1902. When the conference failed, Roosevelt threatened the operators with a government takeover of the mines. He also persuaded the financier John Pierpont Morgan to use his considerable influence with them. At that point the coal operators caved in. The strike ended with the appointment by Roosevelt of an arbitration commission to rule on the issues, another unprecedented step. While not especially supportive of organized labor, Roosevelt became positively livid at the "arrogant stupidity" of the mine owners.

"Of all the forms of tyranny the least attractive and the most vulgar is the tyranny of mere wealth," Roosevelt wrote in his autobiography. He was prepared to deploy all his presidential authority against the "tyranny" of irresponsible business.

The Problem of the Trusts. The economic issue that most concerned Roosevelt was the assault on the competitive market by big business. The drift toward large-scale enterprise had been under way for many years, as entrepreneurs sought the efficiencies of nationwide, vertically integrated firms (see Chapter 17). But they knew that creating bigger businesses also meant gaining power to control markets. This was the motive behind the scramble to merge rival firms in the aftermath of the depression of the 1890s. These mergers—*trusts,* as they were called—greatly increased the degree of business concentration in the economy. Of the 73 largest industrial companies in 1900, 53 had not existed

three years earlier. By 1910, 1 percent of the nation's manufacturers accounted for 44 percent of the nation's industrial output (see Voices from Abroad, "James Bryce: America in 1905: 'Business Is King,'" p. 660).

Most of these new combines were heavily watered—that is, the stocks and bonds they issued greatly exceeded the real value of the properties they controlled. For their underwriting services in launching the new trusts, moreover, investment bankers such as J. P. Morgan charged huge fees. Worse yet, financiers did not relinquish control over the combines they had fathered, for they sat on the boards of directors of the new firms and exerted a back-room influence on the

Jack and the Wall Street Giants
In this vivid cartoon from the humor magazine *Puck,* Jack (Theodore Roosevelt) has come to slay the giants of Wall Street. To the country, trust-busting took on the mythic qualities of the fairy tale—with about the same amount of awe for the fearsome Wall Street giants and hope in the prowess of the intrepid Roosevelt. J. P. Morgan is the giant leering at front right.
Library of Congress.

JAMES BRYCE

America in 1905: "Business Is King"

───────── ★ ─────────

James Bryce, British author of The American Commonwealth *(1888), a great treatise on American politics, visited the United States regularly over many years. In an essay published in 1905, Lord Bryce took stock of the changes he had seen during the previous quarter century. What most struck him, beyond the sheer growth of material wealth, was the loss of individualism and the intensifying concentration of corporate power. In this, he was at one with his old friend Theodore Roosevelt, who at that very time was gearing up to do battle with the trusts.*

That which most strikes the visitor to America today is its prodigious material development. Industrial growth, swift thirty or forty years ago, advances more swiftly now. The rural districts are being studded with villages, the villages are growing into cities, the cities are stretching out long arms of suburbs, which follow the lines of road and railway in every direction. The increase of wealth, even more remarkable than the increase of population, impresses the European more than ever before because the contrast with Europe is greater. The huge fortunes, the fortunes of those whose income reaches or exceeds a million dollars a year, are of course far more numerous than in any other country. . . . With this extraordinary material development it is natural that in the United States, business, that is to say, industry, commerce, and finance, should have more and more come to overshadow and dwarf all other interests, all other occupations. . . . Business is king.

Commerce and industry themselves have developed new features. Twenty-two years ago there were no trusts. . . . Even then, however, corporations had covered a larger proportion of the whole field of industry and commerce in America than in Europe, and their structure was more flexible and efficient. Today this is still more the case; while as for trusts, they have become one of the most salient phenomena of the country. They fix the attention, they excite the alarm of economists and politicians as well as of traders in the Old World, while they exercise and baffle the ingenuity of American legislators. Workingmen follow, though hitherto with unequal steps, the efforts at combination which the lords of production and distribution have been making. The consumer stands, if not with folded hands, yet so far with no clear view of the steps he may make for his own protection. Perhaps his prosperity—for he is prosperous—helps him to be quiescent.

The example of the United States, the land in which individualism has been most conspicuously vigorous, may seem to suggest that the world is passing out of the stage of individualism and returning to that earlier stage in which groups of men formed the units of society. The bond of association was, in those early days, kinship, real or supposed, and a servile or quasi-servile dependence of the weak upon the strong. Now it is the power of wealth which enables the few to combine so as to gain command of the sources of wealth. . . . Is it a paradox to observe that it is because the Americans have been the most individualistic of peoples that they are now the people among whom the art of combination has reached its maximum? The amazing keenness and energy, which were stimulated by the commercial conditions of the country, have evoked and ripened a brilliant talent for organization. This talent has applied new methods to production and distribution and has enabled wealth, gathered into a small number of hands, to dominate even the enormous market of America.

───────────

Source: Allan Nevins, ed., *America through British Eyes* (Gloucester, MA: Peter Smith, 1968), 384–387.

operating executives. Almost overnight a "money power"—a cabal of Wall Street bankers—seemed to have gained a stranglehold on the American economy.

Roosevelt's sense of the nation's uneasiness became evident as early as his first annual message, in which he referred to the "real and grave evils" of economic concentration. But what weapons could the president use in response?

The basic legal principles upholding free competition were already firmly established. Under common law—the body of judge-made legal precedents that America had inherited from Britain—it was illegal for anyone to restrain or monopolize trade. Persons who were economically injured by such actions could sue for damages. These common-law rights had been enacted into statute law in many states during the

1880s and then, because the problem went beyond state jurisdictions, had been incorporated into the Sherman Antitrust Act of 1890 and become part of federal law.

Neither the Cleveland administration nor the McKinley administration had been much inclined to enforce the Sherman Act. But the law was there to be used. Its potential rested above all on the fact that it incorporated common-law principles of unimpeachable validity. In the right hands, the Sherman Act could be a strong weapon against the abuse of economic power.

Trust-Busting. Roosevelt made his opening move in 1903 by establishing the Bureau of Corporations, empowered to investigate business practices. On the basis of facts gathered by the bureau, the Department of Justice was enabled to mount antitrust suits. The department had already filed such a suit in 1902 against the Northern Securities Company, a combination of the railroad systems of the Northwest. In a landmark decision, the Supreme Court ordered Northern Securities dissolved in 1904.

In the presidential election that year, Roosevelt handily defeated a weak conservative Democratic candidate, Judge Alton B. Parker. Now president in his own right, Roosevelt stepped up the attack on the trusts. He took on forty-five of the nation's giant firms, including Standard Oil, American Tobacco, and Du Pont. His rhetoric rising, Roosevelt became the nation's trust-buster, a crusader against "predatory wealth."

But Roosevelt was not antibusiness. He regarded large-scale enterprise as a natural result of modern industrialism. Only firms that abused their power deserved punishment. But how would those companies be identified? Under the Sherman Act, following common-law doctrine, the courts decided whether an act in restraint of trade was "unreasonable"—that is, actually harmed the public interest—and the courts thus had the discretion to evaluate the actions of corporations on a case-by-case basis. In the *Trans-Missouri* decision of 1897, however, the Supreme Court repudiated this "rule of reason." As a result, after 1897, actions that restrained or monopolized trade automatically put a firm in violation of the Sherman Act, regardless of their impact on the public interest.

Little-noticed when it was first decided, *Trans-Missouri* placed Roosevelt in an awkward position. He had no desire to hamstring legitimate business activity, but he could not rely on the courts to distinguish between "good" and "bad" trusts. The only solution was for Roosevelt to assume that responsibility. This the president could do because it was up to him—or to his attorney general—to decide whether to initiate antitrust prosecutions in the first place.

In November 1904, with an antitrust suit looming, the United States Steel Corporation's chairman, Elbert

J. Pierpont Morgan
J. P. Morgan was a giant among American financiers. He had served an apprenticeship in investment banking under his father, a leading Anglo-American banker in London. A gruff man of few words, Morgan had a genius for instilling trust and the strength of will to persuade others to follow his lead and do his bidding—qualities the great photographer Edward Steichen captured in this portrait.
George Eastman House.

H. Gary, approached Roosevelt and proposed a deal: cooperation in exchange for preferential treatment. The company would open its books to the Bureau of Corporations; if the bureau found evidence of wrongdoing, the company would be warned privately and given a chance to set matters right. Roosevelt accepted this "gentlemen's agreement," as well as a similar one with International Harvester the next year. J. P. Morgan controlled both firms, and from Morgan's standpoint the arrangement seemed entirely sensible. Two great powers, one political and the other economic, would meet as equals and settle matters between them. For Roosevelt, the gentlemen's agreements solved a serious dilemma: he could accommodate the realities of the modern industrial order while maintaining his public image as champion against the trusts.

Railroad Regulation. The railroads posed a different kind of problem for Roosevelt. As quasi-public enterprises, the railroads had always been subject to public regulation. Initially, this had been the responsibility of the states, but with the passage of the Interstate Commerce Act of 1887, the federal government had entered the field, establishing in the Interstate Commerce

Commission (ICC) the nation's first federal regulatory agency. Nevertheless, like the Sherman Act, railroad regulation remained pretty much a dead letter in its early years. Convinced, however, that the railroads needed firm regulation, Roosevelt pushed through the Elkins Act of 1903, which prohibited discriminatory rebates—that is, reductions on published rates for preferred or powerful customers. Then, with the 1904 election behind him, Roosevelt launched the drive for real railroad regulation.

The central issue was government rate-setting, which the conservative Republican bloc in Congress firmly opposed. In 1906, after nearly two years of wrangling, Congress passed the Hepburn Railway Act, which empowered the ICC to set maximum rates upon complaint of a shipper and to prescribe uniform methods of bookkeeping. But as a concession to conservatives, the courts retained broad powers to review the ICC's rate decisions.

The Hepburn Act was a triumph of Roosevelt's skills as a political operator. He had maneuvered brilliantly against determined opposition and come away with the essentials of what he wanted. Despite grumbling by Senate progressives critical of any compromise, Roosevelt was satisfied. He had achieved a landmark expansion of the government's regulatory powers over business.

Consumer Protection.   The regulation of consumer products, another hallmark of progressive reform, was very much the handiwork of muckraking journalists. In 1905 Samuel Hopkins Adams published a series of articles on the patent-medicine business in *Collier's*. The first paragraph opened with these riveting words:

> *Gullible America will spend this year some seventy-five millions of dollars in the purchase of patent medicines. In consideration of this sum it will swallow huge quantities of alcohol, an appalling amount of opiates and narcotics, a wide assortment of varied drugs ranging from powerful and dangerous heart depressants to insidious liver stimulants; and, far in excess of all other ingredients, undiluted fraud. For fraud, exploited by the skillfullest of advertising bunco men, is the basis of the trade.*

For a time, industry lobbies stymied food and drug regulation. Then, in 1906, Upton Sinclair's novel *The Jungle* appeared. Sinclair had meant to expose labor exploitation in Chicago meatpacking plants, but his graphic descriptions of rotten meat and filthy conditions excited—and sickened—the nation. President Roosevelt, previously not greatly concerned about consumer issues, weighed into the legislative battle, initiating a federal investigation of the stockyards. The Pure Food and Drug Act and the Meat Inspection Act passed within months, and another administrative agency was added to the federal bureaucratic structure Roosevelt was building: the Food and Drug Administration.

The Square Deal.   During the 1904 presidential campaign Roosevelt had taken to calling his program the Square Deal. This kind of labeling was new to American politics, introducing a political style that dramatized issues, mobilized public opinion, and asserted leadership. But the label identified something of substance as well. After many years of passivity, the federal government was reclaiming the activist role it had abandoned after the Civil War. Now, however, the target was the new economic order. When companies misused corporate power, the government had the responsibility to intercede and assure ordinary Americans a "square deal."

During his two terms as president Theodore Roosevelt struggled to bring a modern corporate economy under regulatory control. He was well aware, however, that his Square Deal was built on nineteenth-century foundations; in particular, antitrust doctrine, which aimed at enforcing competition, seemed inadequate in the face of a large-scale industrial order. Better, Roosevelt felt, to give the federal government administrative powers to regulate big business than to try to

Campaigning for the Square Deal
When William McKinley ran for president in 1896, he sat on his front porch in Canton, Ohio, and received delegations of voters. That was not Theodore Roosevelt's way. He considered the presidency a "bully pulpit," and he used the office brilliantly to mobilize public opinion and to assert his leadership. The preeminence of the presidency in American public life begins with Roosevelt's administration. Here, at the height of his crusading power, he stumps for the Square Deal in the 1904 election.
Library of Congress.

break it up. Roosevelt's final presidential speeches dwelt on the need for a reform agenda for the twentieth century. This was the task he bequeathed to his chosen successor, William Howard Taft.

The Fracturing of Republican Progressivism

William Howard Taft was an estimable man in many ways. An able jurist and a superb administrator, he had served Roosevelt loyally and well as governor general of the Philippines and as secretary of war. He was an avowed Square Dealer. But he was not by nature a progressive politician. Taft was incapable of dramatizing issues or stirring the people. He disliked the give-and-take of politics, he distrusted power, and he generally deferred to Congress. In fundamental ways, moreover, Taft was deeply conservative. After years as a federal judge, Taft sanctified property rights, revered the processes of the law, and, unlike Roosevelt, found it hard to trim his means to fit his ends.

Taft's Democratic opponent in the 1908 campaign was William Jennings Bryan. This was Bryan's last hurrah, his third attempt at the presidency, and he made the most of it. Eloquent as ever, Bryan showed again why he was known as the Commoner, the voice of the people. He attacked the Republicans as the party of the "plutocrats," and he outdid them in urging tougher antitrust legislation, lower tariffs, stricter railway regulation, and advanced labor legislation. So favorable was Bryan to the unions that despite its formal nonpartisanship, the AFL endorsed him. Bryan's campaign moved the Democratic Party into the mainstream of national progressive politics, but that was not enough to offset Taft's advantages as Roosevelt's candidate.

Taft won comfortably, if by a smaller margin than Roosevelt's smashing 1904 victory, and he entered the White House with a mandate to pick up where Roosevelt had left off. That, alas, was not to be.

Taft's Troubles. By 1909 the ferment of reform had unsettled the Republican Party. On the right, the conservatives were bracing themselves against further losses. Led by the formidable Senator Nelson W. Aldrich, they were still a force to be reckoned with. On the left, progressive Republicans were rebellious. They had broad popular support—especially in the Midwest—and, in Robert La Follette, a fiery leader. They felt that Roosevelt had been too easy on business, and with him gone from the White House, the congressional progressives were determined to make up for lost time. Reconciling these conflicting forces within the Republican Party would have been a daunting task for the most accomplished politician. For Taft, it spelled disaster.

First there was the tariff. Progressives considered protective tariffs a major reason why competition had declined and the trusts had sprung up. Although Taft had campaigned for tariff reform, he was won over by the conservative Republican bloc during the prolonged drafting process and gave his approval for the protectionist Payne-Aldrich Tariff Act of 1909, which sheltered eastern industry from foreign competition.

Next came the Pinchot-Ballinger affair. U.S. Chief Forester Gifford Pinchot, an ardent conservationist and a chum of Roosevelt, accused Secretary of the Interior Richard A. Ballinger of conspiring to transfer Alaskan public land—rich in natural resources—to a private syndicate. When Pinchot made the charges public in January 1910, Taft fired him for insubordination. Despite Taft's strong conservationist credentials, in the eyes of the progressives the Pinchot-Ballinger affair marked him for life as a friend of the "interests" bent on plundering the nation's resources.

Solemnly pledged to carry on in Roosevelt's tradition, Taft found himself propelled into the conservative Republican camp, an ally of "Uncle Joe" Cannon, the dictatorial Speaker of the House of Representatives. When a House revolt finally broke Cannon's power in 1910, it was regarded as a defeat for the president as well. Largely in reaction to Taft, the reformers in the Republican Party turned into a distinct, organized faction. By 1910 they were calling themselves "Progressives" or, in more belligerent moments, "Insurgents." Taft answered by backing their conservative foes in the Republican primaries that year. This vendetta climaxed Taft's record of clumsy leadership.

The agents of historical change sometimes take strange forms. A person out of tune with the times can, by the sheer friction he or she generates, serve as the catalyst for great events. Such was the fate of President Taft.

The Taft-Roosevelt Split. The progressives emerged from the 1910 elections stronger and angrier. In January 1911 they formed the National Progressive Republican League and began a drive to take over the Republican Party. La Follette was the progressives' leader and designated presidential candidate, but they knew that their best chance to win lay with Theodore Roosevelt.

Home from a year-long safari in Africa, Roosevelt yearned to reenter the political fray. He would have been troublesome for Taft under any circumstances. As it was, the president's handling of the progressives fed Roosevelt's mounting sense of outrage. But Roosevelt was too loyal a party member to defy the Republican establishment and too astute a politician not to recognize that a party split would benefit the Democrats. He could be spurred into rebellion only by the discovery of a true clash of principles. On the question of the trusts, just such a clash materialized.

By distinguishing between good and bad trusts, Roosevelt had managed to reconcile public policy (the Sherman Act) and economic reality (the inevitable tendency toward corporate concentration). But this was a makeshift solution that depended on a president who was willing to stretch his powers to the limit. Taft had no such inclination. His legalistic mind rebelled at the notion that he as president should decide which trusts should be prosecuted. The Sherman Act was on the books. "We are going to enforce that law or die in the attempt," Taft promised grimly.

In its *Standard Oil* decision (1911) the Supreme Court eased Taft's problem by reasserting the common-law principle of the "rule of reason," which meant that, once again, the courts themselves would distinguish between good and bad trusts. With that burden lifted from the executive branch, Attorney General George W. Wickersham picked up the pace of antitrust actions.

United States Steel Corporation became an immediate target. Among the charges against the steel trust was that it had violated the antimonopoly provision of the Sherman Act by acquiring the Tennessee Coal and Iron Company in 1907. The purchase had been made from a banking house that had fallen into trouble and urgently needed to sell its Tennessee Coal and Iron stock to raise capital. As president, Roosevelt had personally approved the acquisition as a necessary step—as United States Steel representatives had explained it to him—to prevent a financial collapse on Wall Street. Taft's suit against United States Steel thus amounted to an attack on Roosevelt. Nothing was better calculated to propel Roosevelt into action than an issue that was both an affair of personal honor and a question of broad principle.

The New Nationalism.   Ever since leaving the White House, Roosevelt had been pondering the trust problem. There was, he concluded, a third way between breaking up big business and submitting to corporate rule. The federal government could be empowered to oversee the nation's industrial corporations to make sure they acted in the public interest. They could be regulated by a federal trade commission, with powers comparable to those exerted by the Interstate Commerce Commission over the railroads or by state commissions over public utilities. In the modern age, Roosevelt was suggesting, industrial corporations were becoming, like railroads and utilities, "natural" monopolies and therefore were subject to the same degree of public oversight.

In a speech at Osawatomie, Kansas, in August 1910 Roosevelt made the case for what he now called the New Nationalism. The central issue, Roosevelt argued, was human welfare versus property rights. In modern society, property had to be controlled "to whatever degree the public welfare may require it." The govern-

ment would become "the steward of the public welfare."

This formulation removed the restraints from Roosevelt's thinking. Ultimately, after breaking with Taft, he went so far as to embrace government price-fixing for corporate industry. He took up the cause of social justice, adding to his program a federal child labor law, regulation of labor relations, and a national minimum wage for women. Most radical, perhaps, was Roosevelt's attack on the legal system. Insisting that the courts should not be making social policy, Roosevelt proposed sharp curbs on their powers, even raising the possibility of popular recall of court decisions.

Beyond these specifics, the New Nationalism advanced a distinctive political philosophy. The key source was a book by the journalist Herbert Croly, *The Promise of American Life* (1909), which called for a uniting of rival strains in the American political tradition. From Alexander Hamilton's federalism Croly drew his emphasis on strong national government; from Thomas Jefferson's republicanism came Croly's enthusiasm for democracy and the primacy of the interests of the common citizen. The result, however, was a genuine break from America's political past. To the problem of corporate power the New Nationalism offered a statist solution—an enormous expansion of the role of the federal government.

Early in 1912 Roosevelt announced his candidacy for the presidency and immediately swept the progressive Republicans into his camp. A bitter party battle ensued. Taft proved to be a tenacious opponent. Roosevelt won the states that held primary elections, but Taft controlled the party organizations elsewhere. Dominated by the party regulars, the Republican convention chose Taft.

Considering himself cheated out of the nomination, Roosevelt led his followers into a new Progressive Party, soon nicknamed the "Bull Moose" Party. In a crusading campaign Roosevelt offered the New Nationalism to the people.

Woodrow Wilson and the New Freedom

While the Republicans battled among themselves, the Democrats were on the move. The scars caused by the free-silver campaign of 1896 had faded (see Chapter 18), and in the 1908 campaign William Jennings Bryan had established the rejuvenated party's progressive credentials. The Democrats made dramatic gains in 1910, taking over the House of Representatives for the first time since 1892, winning ten Senate seats, and capturing a number of traditionally Republican governorships. After fourteen years as the party's standard-bearer, Bryan reluctantly made way for a new generation of leaders.

HARPER'S WEEKLY

EDITED BY GEORGE HARVEY

July 13 1912   THE NEW RIDER   Price 10 Cents

On to the White House
At the Democratic convention of 1912 Woodrow Wilson only narrowly defeated the front-runner, Champ Clark of Missouri. *Harper's Weekly* triumphantly depicted Wilson immediately after his nomination—the scholar turned politician riding off on the Democratic donkey, with his running mate, Thomas R. Marshall, hanging on behind. The magazine's editor, George Harvey, had identified Wilson as presidential timber back in 1906, long before the Princeton president had thought of politics, and had worked on his behalf from then on.
Newberry Library.

The ablest was Woodrow Wilson of New Jersey, a noted political scientist who, as university president, had brought Princeton into the front rank of American universities. In 1910, with no political experience, he accepted the Democratic nomination for governor of New Jersey and won. Wilson compiled a brilliant record: he cleaned up the boss system and passed a direct-primary law, workers' compensation, and stronger regulation of railroads and utilities. With these credentials as a reformer, Wilson went on to win the Democratic presidential nomination in 1912 in a bruising battle.

Forging the New Freedom. Wilson possessed, to a fault, the moral certainty that characterized the progressive politician. A brilliant speaker, he instinctively assumed the mantle of righteousness and showed little tolerance for the views of his critics. Only gradually, however, did Wilson hammer out, in reaction to Roosevelt's New Nationalism, a coherent reform program, which he called the New Freedom.

Wilson actually had much in common with Roosevelt. "The old time of individual competition is probably gone by," Wilson stressed. "We will do business henceforth, when we do it on a great and successful scale, by means of corporations." Like Roosevelt, Wilson opposed not bigness but the abuse of economic power. Nor did Wilson think that the abuse of power could be prevented without a strong federal government. He parted company from Roosevelt over *how* government should restrain private power.

As he warmed to the debate, Wilson cast the issue in the fundamental terms of slavery and freedom. "This is a struggle for emancipation," he proclaimed in October 1912. "If America is not to have free enterprise, then she can have freedom of no sort whatever." Wilson also scorned Roosevelt's social program. Welfare might be benevolent, he declared, but it also would be paternalistic and contrary to the traditions of a free people. The New Nationalism meant collectivism, Wilson warned, whereas the New Freedom would preserve political and economic liberty.

How, then, did Wilson propose to deal with the problem of corporate power? Court enforcement of the Sherman Act was Wilson's basic answer. His task was to figure out how to make that long-established antitrust approach work better. In this effort Wilson relied heavily on a new advisor—Louis D. Brandeis, famous as the "people's lawyer" for his public service in many progressive causes (including the landmark *Muller* case).

An expert on regulatory matters, Brandeis understood that an all-powerful trade commission was likely to end up not as defender of the public interest but in a cozy relationship with the industries it was supposed to regulate. Nor did Brandeis believe that bigness meant efficiency. On the contrary, he argued that trusts were wasteful compared with firms that vigorously competed in a free market. The main thing was to prevent the trusts from unfairly using their power to curb free competition. It should be the aim of public policy "so [to] restrict the wrong use of competition that the right use of competition will destroy monopoly."

The Election of 1912. Despite the rhetoric of the campaign, the election itself fell short of being a referendum on the New Nationalism versus the New Freedom. The outcome turned on a more humdrum reality: Wilson was elected because he kept the traditional Democratic vote while the Republicans split between Roosevelt and Taft (Map 20.2). Although he won by a landslide in the electoral college, Wilson received only 42 percent of the popular vote, 115,000 fewer votes than Bryan had amassed

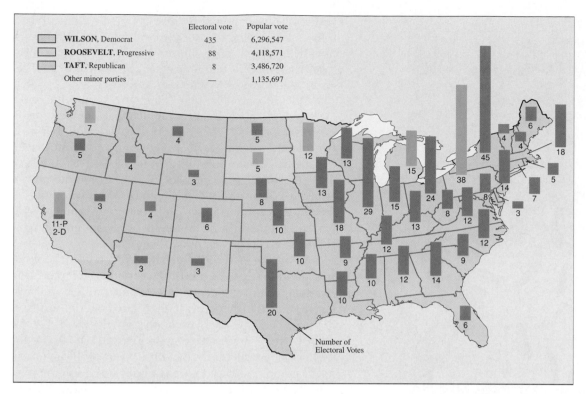

		Electoral vote	Popular vote
	WILSON, Democrat	435	6,296,547
	ROOSEVELT, Progressive	88	4,118,571
	TAFT, Republican	8	3,486,720
	Other minor parties	—	1,135,697

Number of Electoral Votes

MAP 20.2
The Election of 1912

The 1912 election reveals why the two-party system is so strongly rooted in American politics. The Democrats, though a minority party, won an electoral landslide because the Republicans divided their vote between Roosevelt and Taft. This result indicates what is at stake when major parties splinter. The Socialists, despite a record vote of 900,000, got no electoral votes. To vote Socialist in 1912 meant in effect to throw away one's vote.

against Taft in 1908. If there was a beneficiary of the reform ferment sparked by the presidential campaign, it was not Wilson but the Socialist candidate, Eugene V. Debs, who captured 900,000 votes, 6 percent of the total. At best it could be said that the 1912 election signified that the American public was in the mood for reform: only 23 percent, after all, had voted for the one candidate who stood for the status quo, President Taft. Woodrow Wilson's own reform program, however, had not received a mandate from the people.

Yet the 1912 election proved to be decisive in the history of national reform. The debate between Roosevelt and Wilson had brought forth, in the New Freedom, a program capable of finally resolving the crisis over corporate power that had gripped the nation for a decade. Just as important, the election created a rare legislative opportunity in Washington. Wilson became president with the Democrats in firm control of both houses of Congress and united in their eagerness to get on with the New Freedom.

The First Phase: Tariff Reform and the Federal Reserve. Upon entering the White House, Wilson chose a flanking attack on the problem of economic power. So long out of office, the Democrats were hun-

gry for tariff reform. From the prevailing average of 40 percent, the Underwood Tariff Act of 1913 pared rates down to an average of 25 percent. Targeting especially the trust-dominated industries, Democrats confidently expected the Underwood Tariff Act to spur competition and reduce prices for consumers by opening protected American markets to foreign products.

Wilson's administration then turned to the nation's banking system, whose key weakness was the absence of a central bank. The main function of a central bank at that time was to regulate commercial banks and back them up in case they could not meet their obligations to depositors. In practice, in the United States this role had been assumed by the great New York banks, which handled the accounts of outlying banks and assisted them when they came under pressure. However, if the New York banks weakened, the entire system could collapse. This had nearly happened in 1907, when the Knickerbocker Trust Company failed and panic swept through the nation's financial markets.

The need for a reserve system became widely accepted, but the form it should take was hotly debated. Wall Street wanted a centralized system controlled by the bankers. Rural Democrats and their spokesman, Senator Carter Glass of Virginia, preferred a decentralized network of reserve banks. Progressives in both parties agreed that the essential feature should be public control over the reserve system. The bankers, whose practices were already under scrutiny by Congress, were on the defensive in this contest.

President Wilson, no expert to begin with, learned quickly and reconciled the reformers and bankers. The monumental Federal Reserve Act of 1913 gave the nation a banking system that was resistant to financial panic. The act delegated reserve functions to twelve district reserve banks, which would be controlled by their member banks. The Federal Reserve Board imposed public regulation on this regional structure. In one stroke the act strengthened the banking system and placed a measure of restraint on the "money trust."

Settling the Trust Question. Having dealt with tariff and banking reform, Wilson turned to the big question of how to curb the trusts. During the presidential campaign, Wilson had championed a strengthened Sherman Act, but the strategy he proposed—defining with precision what constituted illegal practices that shut out competition—proved unexpectedly hard to implement. Was it feasible to state precisely when interlocking directorates, discriminatory pricing, or exclusive contracts became illegal? Wilson's advisor Louis D. Brandeis finally decided that it was not, and the president assented. In the Clayton Antitrust Act of 1914, amending the Sherman Act, the definition of unlawful practices was left flexible, subject to the test of whether the effect "substantially lessen[ed] competition or tend[ed] to create a monopoly in any line of commerce."

Brandeis realized that this retreat from a definitive antitrust prescription meant that a federal trade commission would be needed to aid the executive branch in enforcing the Sherman and Clayton acts. Wilson was understandably hesitant, given his principled opposition to Roosevelt's conception of a powerful trade commission overseeing American business. At first Wilson wanted only an advisory, information-gathering agency. But ultimately, under the 1914 law establishing it, the Federal Trade Commission (FTC) received broader powers to investigate companies and issue "cease and desist" orders against unfair trade practices that violated antitrust law. FTC decisions, however, were subject to court review, so that Wilson's entire program was situated within the original conception of antitrust enforcement. As before, the courts would ultimately decide which business practices were illegal.

Despite a good deal of commotion, this arduous legislative process was actually an exercise in consensus building. Wilson himself had opened the debate in a conciliatory way. "The antagonism between business and government is over," he said, and the time was ripe for a program representing the "best business judgment in America." Afterward, Wilson felt he had brought the long controversy over corporate power to a successful conclusion, and in fact he had. Steering a course between Taft's conservatism and Roosevelt's radicalism, Wilson carved out a middle way that brought to bear the powers of government without threatening the constitutional order, and that curbed abuse of corporate power without threatening the capitalist system.

What few Americans recognized, in the midst of this protracted struggle, was how very odd it seemed from a European standpoint. Neither of America's industrial rivals—Britain nor Germany—made such a fuss over competitive markets. It was true that the fundamental concept—restraint of trade—originated in English common law, but the British, free-traders and export oriented, lacked the opportunity to engage in market-controlling behavior and hence found no need for antitrust legislation. Germany, by contrast, was a veritable hotbed of conspiracies in restraint of trade, only they were called "cartels"—trade associations that divided the market and rigged prices, and operated with the approval of the imperial government.

Wilson's Social Program. On social policy, as with antitrust policy, President Wilson carved out a middle way. Having denounced the New Nationalism as paternalistic, he at first was unreceptive to what he saw as special-interest demands of labor and farm organizations. On the leading issue—that they be exempted from antitrust prosecution—the most Wilson was willing to accept was cosmetic language in the Clayton Act that did not give them the immunity they sought.

The labor vote had grown increasingly important to the Democratic Party, however. As his second presidential campaign drew near, Wilson lost some of his scruples about prolabor legislation. In 1915 and 1916 he championed a host of bills beneficial to American workers: a model federal workers' compensation law, a child labor law, the Adamson eight-hour law for railroad workers, and the landmark Seamen's Act, which eliminated age-old abuses of sailors aboard ship and granted them the individual rights held by other workers. Likewise, after earlier resistance, in 1916 Wilson approved the Federal Farm Loan Act, which provided the low-interest rural credit system long demanded by farmers.

Wilson encountered the same dilemma that confronted all successful progressives: the claims of moral principle versus the unyielding realities of political and economic life. Progressives were high-minded but not radical. They saw evils in the system, but they did not consider the system itself evil. They also prided themselves on being realists as well as moralists. So it stood to reason that Wilson, like other progressives who achieved power, would find his place at the center.

Summary

★

A new chapter in American reform began at the start of the twentieth century. For decades the problems resulting from industrialization and urban growth had been mounting. Now, after 1900, reform began to dominate the nation's public life. The unifying element in progressivism was a common intellectual outlook, highly principled and idealistic as to goals, and confident of the human capacity to find the means.

Beyond this shared outlook, progressives broke up into diverse and often conflicting groups. Political reformers included business groups concerned chiefly with improving the efficiency of city government. Other progressives, such as Robert La Follette, opposed privilege and wanted to democratize the political process. Both groups worked to enhance their power at the expense of entrenched party machines.

Social welfare became the province of American women, and that effort reinvigorated the struggle for women's rights. In the cities, working people and immigrants also became reform minded and set in motion a new political force—urban liberalism. While progressivism was infected by the endemic racism in American life, there was a reform wing that joined with black activists to forge the major institutions of black protest and uplift of the twentieth century: the National Association for the Advancement of Colored People, and the Urban League.

At the national level, progressives focused primarily on controlling the economic power of corporate business. This overriding problem led to Theodore Roosevelt's Square Deal, then to his New Nationalism, and finally to Woodrow Wilson's New Freedom. The role of the federal government expanded dramatically, but in service to a cautious and pragmatic approach to the problems of the country.

TIMELINE

1889   Jane Addams and Ellen Gates Starr found Hull House

1893   Panic of 1893 starts depression of the 1890s

1899   National Consumers' League founded

1900   Robert M. La Follette elected Wisconsin governor

Commission form of city government first appears, in Galveston, Texas

1901   President McKinley assassinated; Theodore Roosevelt succeeds him

1902   President Roosevelt settles national anthracite strike

1903   National Women's Trade Union League founded

1904   Supreme Court dissolves the Northern Securities Company

1905   *Lochner v. New York* overturns law restricting length of the workday

1906   Upton Sinclair's *The Jungle*

Hepburn Railway Act

AFL adopts "Bill of Grievances"

1908   *Muller v. Oregon* upholds regulation of working hours for women

Federal Council of Churches founded

William Howard Taft elected president

1909   NAACP formed

Herbert Croly's *Promise of American Life*

1910   Roosevelt announces the New Nationalism

Woman suffrage movement revives; suffrage victory in Washington State

1911   *Standard Oil* decision restores "rule of reason"

Triangle Shirtwaist fire

1912   Progressive Party formed

Woodrow Wilson elected president

1913   Federal Reserve Act

Underwood Tariff Act

1914   Clayton Antitrust Act

Suggested Readings

The most recent survey of the Progressive Era is John Milton Cooper, *Pivotal Decades: The United States, 1900–1920* (1990). A highly influential interpretation of progressive reform that is worth reading despite its disputed central arguments is Richard Hofstadter, *Age of Reform* (1955). Robert H. Wiebe, *The Search for Order, 1877–1920* (1967), places progressive reform in a broader context of organizational development. On the debate over progressivism as a movement see Daniel Rodgers, "In Search of Progressivism," *Reviews in American History* 10 (1982).

The Intellectual Roots of Progressivism

The progressive mind has been studied from many different angles. The religious underpinnings are stressed in Robert M. Crunden, *Ministers of Reform: The Progressives' Achievement in American Civilization, 1889–1920* (1982). In *The New Radicalism in America, 1889–1963* (1965), Christopher Lasch sees progressivism as a form of cultural revolt. Most useful on political thinkers is Charles Forcey, *The Crossroads of Liberalism: Croly, Weyl, Lippmann, and the Progressive Era* (1961). A provocative study set in an international context is James T. Kloppenberg, *Uncertain Victory: Social Democracy and Progressivism in European and American Thought, 1870–1920* (1986). On the journalists see David M. Chalmers, *The Social and Political Ideas of the Muckrakers* (1964), and Harold S. Wilson, *"McClure's" Magazine and the Muckrakers* (1970).

The Many Faces of Reform

Political reform has been the subject of a voluminous literature. Wisconsin progressivism can be studied in David P. Thelen, *The New Citizenship: Origins of Progressivism in Wisconsin, 1885–1900* (1972). Important progressives are discussed in Spencer C. Olin, *California's Prodigal Son: Hiram Johnson and the Progressive Movement* (1968), and Richard Lowitt, *George W. Norris: The Making of a Progressive* (1963). On city reform see Bradley R. Rice, *Progressive Cities: The Commission Government Movement* (1972); Jack Tager, *The Intellectual as Urban Reformer: Brand Whitlock and the Progressive Movement* (1968); and Melvin G. Holli, *Reform in Detroit: Hazen S. Pingree and Urban Politics* (1969).

The best treatment of the settlement-house movement is Allen F. Davis, *Spearheads of Reform* (1967). Allen F. Davis, *American Heroine: Jane Addams* (1973); George Martin, *Madame Secretary: Frances Perkins* (1976); and Kathryn Kish Sklar, *Florence Kelley and the Nation's Work: The Rise of Women's Political Culture* (1995), deal with leading woman progressives. The connection to working women is effectively treated in Nancy S. Dye, *As Equals and Sisters: Feminism, the Labor Movement, and the Women's Trade Union League of New York* (1980). Women garment workers, the key labor constituency for women progressives, are studied with great skill and insight in Susan A. Glenn, *Daughters of the Shtetl: Life and Labor in the Immigrant Generation* (1990). Two path-breaking books on the origins of American feminism are Rosalind Rosenberg, *Beyond Separate Spheres: The Intellectual Origins of Modern Feminism* (1982), and Nancy F. Cott, *The Grounding of Modern Feminism* (1987). The most recent study of the battle for the vote, Sara Hunter Graham, *Woman Suffrage and the New Democracy* (1996), treats it as a precocious exercise of the single-issue pressure politics of our own times. The leading social reformer to spring from feminism is treated in Ellen Chesler, *Woman of Valor: Margaret Sanger and the Birth Control Movement* (1992).

On urban liberalism the standard book is John D. Buenker, *Urban Liberalism and Progressive Reform* (1973). Two important recent books by historical sociologists treat the halting progress toward the welfare state: Theda Skocpol, *Protecting Soldiers and Mothers* (1992), and, in a comparison of the United States with Canada and Britain, Ann Shola Orloff, *The Politics of Pensions* (1993). Linda Gordon, *Pitied but Not Entitled: Single Mothers and the History of Welfare, 1890–1935* (1994), brilliantly uses the current crisis over welfare reform as a lens for probing the tangled history of this central concern of social progressives. The most comprehensive survey is Morton Keller, *Regulating a New Society: Public Policy and Social Change in America, 1900–1933* (1994). On the South see Jack Temple Kirby, *Darkness at the Dawning: Race and Reform in the Progressive South* (1972), and Dewey Grantham, *Southern Progressivism* (1983); on southern black women as social reformers, Glenda Elizabeth Gilmore, *Gender and Jim Crow: Women and the Politics of White Supremacy in North Carolina, 1869–1920* (1996); and on the racial conservatism of social progressives, Elizabeth Lasch-Quinn, *Black Neighbors: Race and the Limits of Reform in the American Settlement-House Movement* (1993). The revival of black protest is vigorously described in Stephen R. Fox, *The Guardian of Boston: William Monroe Trotter* (1971), and David Levering Lewis, *W. E. B. Du Bois: Biography of a Race, 1868–1919* (1993).

Progressivism and National Politics

National progressivism is best approached through its leading figures. John Milton Cooper, *The Warrior and the Priest* (1983), is a provocative joint biography of Roosevelt and Wilson that emphasizes their shared world view. Lewis S. Gould, *The Presidency of Theodore Roosevelt* (1991), provides a useful synthesis. Aspects of national progressive politics can be followed in James Penick, *Progressive Politics and Conservation: The Ballinger-Pinchot Affair* (1968); James Holt, *Congressional Insurgents and the Party System* (1969); and David Sarasohn, *The Party of Reform: The Democrats in the Progressive Era* (1989). Naomi Lamoreaux, *The Great Merger Movement in American Business, 1895–1904* (1985), offers a sophisticated modern analysis of trust activity; Thomas K. McCraw, ed., *Regulation in Perspective* (1981), contains valuable interpretative essays on the problems of trust regulation; and James Livingston, *Origins of the Federal Reserve System: Money, Class, and Corporate Capitalism, 1890–1913* (1986), treats banking reform. A comprehensive rethinking of the progressive struggle to fashion a regulatory policy for big business is offered in Martin J. Sklar, *The Corporate Reconstruction of American Capitalism, 1890–1916: The Market, the Law, and Politics* (1988).

An Emerging World Power,
1877–1914

IN 1881 GREAT BRITAIN sent a new envoy to Washington. He was Sir Lionel Sackville-West, son of an earl, brother-in-law of Tory Party leader Lord Denby, but otherwise distinguished only as the lover of a celebrated Spanish dancer. His well-connected friends wanted to park Sir Lionel somewhere comfortable but out of harm's way. So they made him minister to the United States.

Twenty years later such an appointment would have been unthinkable. All the major European powers had by then elevated their missions in Washington to embassies and staffed them with top-of-the-line ambassadors. And they treated the United States, without question, as a fellow Great Power.

In Sir Lionel's day, the United States scarcely cast a shadow on the world stage. As a military power the United States was puny, even comical. Its army was smaller than Bulgaria's; its navy ranked thirteenth in the world and was a threat mainly to the crews of its unseaworthy ships. By 1900, however, the United States was flexing its muscles. It had just made short work of Spain in a brief but decisive war, and acquired for itself an empire stretching from Puerto Rico to the Philippines. America's standing as a rising naval power was manifest, and so was its aggressive assertion of national interest in the Caribbean and the Pacific.

In practice, the United States still acted as a regional power, but Europeans were keenly aware of its capacity to cut a wider swath when it chose to do so. "Are we to be confronted by an American peril . . . before which the Old World is to go down to irretrievable defeat?" wondered a former French foreign minister. The notion of an "American peril" became a lively topic after 1900 among

Battle of Santiago de Cuba, 1898
James G. Tyler's dramatic painting of the final sea battle of the Spanish-American War (detail)
showcased America's newest weapon of war, the battleship.
Franklin D. Roosevelt Library.

Europeans surveying the industrial and military potential of the United States. No one could be sure what America's role would be, since the United States retained its traditional policy of nonintervention in European affairs. But by 1914, when a great world war engulfed Europe, one could be sure that the United States would have a big role to play. How the United States emerged onto the world stage in the decades before World War I is the subject of this chapter.

The Roots of Expansionism

★

In 1880 the United States had a population of 50 million, and by that measure ranked with the great European powers. It was the world's leading producer of wheat and cotton. In industrial production the United States was second only to Britain and was rapidly closing the gap. Anyone who doubted the military prowess of the Americans needed only to recall the ferocity with which they had fought one another in the Civil War. The great campaigns of Lee, Sherman, and Grant had entered the military textbooks and were closely studied by army strategists everywhere.

And when its vital interests were at stake, the United States had not shown itself to be lacking in diplomatic vigor. The Civil War had put the United States at odds with both France and Britain. The issue with France involved the establishment in Mexico of a French-sponsored regime under Archduke Maximilian, a move regarded by the United States as a threat to its security in the Southwest. When American troops under General Philip Sheridan began to mass on the Mexican border in 1867, the French military withdrew, abandoning Maximilian to a Mexican firing squad.

With Britain, the issue involved damages done to Union shipping by the *Alabama* and other Confederate sea raiders operating from English ports. American hopes of achieving the annexation of Canada out of this dispute were dashed by Britain's grant of dominion status to Canada in 1867. But four years later, after lengthy negotiations, Britain expressed regret for its unneutral acts against the Union and agreed to the arbitration of the *Alabama* claims, settling to America's satisfaction the last outstanding diplomatic issue of the Civil War.

Diplomacy in the Gilded Age

In the years that followed, the United States lapsed into diplomatic isolation, not out of weakness but for lack of any clear national purpose in world affairs. George Washington's warning against entangling alliances with foreign countries seemed as pertinent as it had when

America was a thinly populated land of farmers. The business of building the nation's industrial economy absorbed Americans and turned their attention inward. And while the new international telegraphic cables provided the country with swift overseas communication after the 1860s, wide oceans still kept the world at a distance and gave Americans a sense of isolation and security.

Nor did European power politics, which centered on Franco-German rivalry and on nationalistic conflict in the Balkans, seem to matter very much. As far as President Grover Cleveland's secretary of state, Thomas F. Bayard, was concerned, "we have not the slightest share or interest [in] the small politics and backstage intrigues of Europe . . . upon which we look with impatience and contempt."

As for the empires that the European powers were avidly building by the 1880s in Africa and Asia, this expression of national prowess did not tempt the United States. Even so ardent an American nationalist as the young Theodore Roosevelt saw the folly of overseas expansion. "We want no unwilling citizens to enter our Union," he wrote in 1886. "European nations war for the possession of thickly settled districts which, if conquered, will for centuries remain alien and hostile to the conquerors; we, wiser in our generation, have seized the waste solitudes that lay near us."

In these circumstances, with no external threat to be seen, what was the point of maintaining a big navy? After the Civil War, the fleet gradually deteriorated. Of the 125 ships on the navy's active list in the 1870s, only about 25 were seaworthy at any one time. No effort was made to keep up with European advances in weaponry or battleship design; the American fleet consisted mainly of sailing ships and obsolete ironclad ships like the *Monitor* and *Merrimack* of Civil War fame.

During the administration of Chester A. Arthur (1881–1885), the navy began a modest upgrading program, commissioning new ships, raising standards for the officer corps, and founding the Naval War College. But the fleet remained small, lacked a unified naval command, and had little more to do than maintain coastal defenses and a modest cruising fleet whose task in wartime would be to harass enemy commerce. An expenditure of 1 percent of the gross domestic product for the entire military establishment seemed entirely adequate in the 1880s.

The conduct of diplomacy was likewise of little account. Appointment to the foreign service was mostly made through the spoils system. American envoys and consular officers were a mixed lot, with many idlers and drunkards among the hardworking and competent. Domestic politics, moreover, made it difficult to develop a coherent foreign policy. Although diplomacy was a presidential responsibility, the U.S. Senate jealously guarded its constitutional right to give "advice and consent" on treaties and diplomatic appointments. Partisan

Sugarcane Plantation, Hawaii
Over 300,000 Asians from China, Japan, Korea, and the Philippines came to work in the Hawaiian cane fields between 1850 and 1920. The hardships they endured are reflected in plantation work songs, such as this one by Japanese laborers:

> *Hawaii, Hawaii*
> *But when I came what I saw was Hell*
> *The boss was Satan*
> *The lunas [overseers] his helpers.*

George Bacon Collection, Hawaii State Archives.

squabbling between Democrats and Republicans left the White House even less room for maneuver. For its part the State department tended to be inactive, exerting little control either over policy or over its missions abroad. Remarkably often, ministers and naval officers set policy in the field, only to see their actions repudiated or ignored by the State department. In remote areas, the American presence was likely to be religious: intrepid missionaries eager to Christianize the native populations of Asia, Africa, and the Pacific islands.

Latin American Diplomacy. In the Caribbean the United States remained the dominant power, but the expansionist enthusiasms of the Civil War era subsided. Nothing came of the grandiose plans of William H. Seward, Andrew Johnson's secretary of state, for an American empire reaching into Latin America and across the Pacific, or of President Grant's efforts to purchase Santo Domingo (the future Dominican Republic) in 1870; and the Senate regularly blocked later moves to acquire bases in Haiti, Cuba, and Venezuela (see Map 21.3). The long-cherished interest in an interoceanic canal across Central America also faded. Despite its claims of exclusive building rights, the United States stood by when a French company headed by the builder of the Suez Canal, Ferdinand de Lesseps, started to dig across the Panama isthmus in 1880. That project failed after a decade, but the reason was bankruptcy, not American opposition.

Diplomatic activity quickened when James G. Blaine became secretary of state in 1881. He got involved in a

border dispute between Mexico and Guatemala, tried to settle a war Chile was waging against Peru and Bolivia, and called the first Pan-American conference of the Western Hemisphere countries. Blaine's interventions in Latin American disputes went badly, however, and his successor canceled the Pan-American conference after Blaine left office in late 1881. This was a characteristic instance of Gilded Age diplomacy, driven partly by partisan politics and carried out without any clear sense of national purpose.

Pan-Americanism—the notion of a community of American states—took root, however, and Blaine, on returning in 1889 for a second stint at the State department, took up the plans of the outgoing Cleveland administration for a new Pan-American conference. But little came of it, except for an agency in Washington that was later named the Pan-American Union. Any Latin American goodwill won by Blaine's efforts was soon blasted by the humiliation the United States visited upon Chile because of a riot against American sailors in the port of Valparaiso in 1891. Threatened with war, Chile was forced to apologize to the United States and pay an indemnity of $75,000.

Pacific Episodes. American interest in the Pacific centered on Hawaii, where American missionaries had long been proselytizing among the islanders. With a climate ideal for raising sugarcane, Hawaii had also attracted American planters and investors. Nominally an independent monarchy, Hawaii fell increasingly under American control. In an 1875 treaty, Hawaiian sugar gained duty-free entry to the American market, and the islands were declared off-limits to other powers. A second treaty in 1887 granted the United States the right to establish a naval base at Pearl Harbor.

When Hawaii's favored access to the American market was abruptly canceled by the McKinley Tariff of 1890, sugar planters began to plot an American takeover of Hawaii. Aided by the U.S. minister to Hawaii and with American sailors conspicuously present, the planters revolted in January 1893 against Queen Liliuokalani and quickly negotiated a treaty of annexation with the administration of President Benjamin Harrison. Before the Senate could approve annexation, however, Grover Cleveland returned to the presidency and, after an investigation of the Hawaiian episode, withdrew the treaty. To annex Hawaii, he declared, would violate both America's "honor and morality" and its "unbroken tradition" against acquiring territory far from the nation's shores.

Meanwhile, the American presence elsewhere in the Pacific was growing. The 1867 purchase of Alaska from imperial Russia gave the United States not only a huge territory with vast natural resources but an unlooked-for presence stretching across the northern Pacific. And far to the south, with even less forethought, the United States had become involved in the remote Samoan Islands (see Map 21.2).

In 1878 the United States secured the right to a coaling station in Pago Pago harbor—a key link on the route to Australia—and in exchange promised local Polynesian leaders to assist in Samoa's relations with other foreign powers. An informal protectorate resulted. In the mid-1880s Germany began to press its claims to the islands, and the United States, stung by German arrogance, responded with equal fervor. In 1889 naval warfare might have broken out but for a hurricane that wrecked the German and American fleets. At that point, agreement on a three-power protectorate (the third country was Britain) averted further strife and preserved American rights in Pago Pago.

American diplomacy in these years has been characterized as a series of incidents, not the pursuit of a foreign policy. Many things happened but intermittently and without a plan, driven by individuals and pressure groups—not by any well-founded and coherent conception of national objectives. This was possible because, as Englishman James Bryce remarked in 1888, America still sailed "upon a summer sea." In the stormier waters that lay ahead, a different kind of American diplomacy would be required.

Economic Sources of Expansionism

"A policy of isolation did well enough when we were an embryo nation," remarked Senator Orville Platt of Connecticut in 1893. "But today things are different. . . . We are 65 million people, the most advanced and powerful on earth, and regard to our future welfare demands an abandonment of the doctrines of isolation." What especially demanded that Americans look outward was their enormously productive economy.

The Search for Foreign Markets. America's gross domestic product—the total value of all goods and services produced annually—quadrupled between 1870 and 1900, and industrial output quintupled. But were there markets big enough to absorb the staggering volume of goods flowing from America's farms and factories? Over 90 percent of American output in the late nineteenth century was consumed at home. Even so, foreign markets were important. Roughly a fifth of the nation's agricultural output was exported, and the proportion of major staple crops—cotton, wheat, tobacco—was much higher, up to 80 percent, for example, in the case of cotton.

As the industrial economy expanded, so did factory exports. Between 1880 and 1900, the industrial share of total exports jumped from 15 percent to over 30 percent. Although only 9 percent of manufactured output went overseas in 1900, the export share in key industries was much larger: 57 percent for petroleum products, 50 percent for copper, 25 percent for sewing machines, 15 percent for iron and steel.

Major American firms began to establish themselves overseas. As early as 1868, the Singer Sewing Machine Company established its first foreign plant in Glasgow, Scotland. The giant among American firms doing business abroad was Standard Oil. Starting with the Anglo-American Oil Company in 1888, Rockefeller's firm created European affiliates to operate its oil tankers and market its kerosene across the continent. In Asia, Standard Oil kerosene cans, converted into utensils and roofing tin, became a visible sign of American market penetration. Brand names such as Kodak (cameras), McCormick (agricultural equipment), and later Ford (the Model T) became household words around the world.

Foreign trade was important partly for reasons of international finance. As a developing economy, the United States attracted a lot of foreign investment capital but sent relatively little abroad—scarcely 1 percent of all the money Americans invested in the late nineteenth century. The result was a heavy outflow of dollars from the United States in the form of interest and dividend payments to foreign investors. To balance this account, the United States needed to export more goods than it imported. In fact, a favorable import-export balance was achieved in 1876 (Figure 21.1). But because of its dependence on foreign capital, America would have to be constantly vigilant about its foreign trade.

Even more important, however, was the relationship that many Americans perceived between foreign

The Singer Sewing Machine
The sewing machine was an American invention that swiftly found markets abroad. The Singer Company, the dominant firm, not only exported large quantities but produced 200,000 machines annually at a Scottish plant that employed 6,000 workers. Singer's advertising rightly boasted of its prowess as an international company and of a product that was "The Universal Machine."
New-York Historical Society.

markets and the nation's social stability. In hard times, farmers took up radical politics, and workers became militant strikers. The problem, many thought, was that the nation's capacity to produce was outrunning its capacity to consume. And when the economy slowed and domestic demand fell, the impact on farmers and workers was devastating, driving down farm prices and wages and causing layoffs and farm foreclosures across the country. The answer was to make sure that there would always be enough buyers for America's surplus products, and this meant, more than anything else, ensuring access to foreign markets.

Overseas Trade and Foreign Policy. How did these concerns about foreign markets link up to America's foreign policy? The bulk of American exports in the late nineteenth century—over 80 percent—went to Canada and Europe (Table 21.1). In those countries the normal instruments of diplomacy sufficed. In Europe, for example, a major issue during the 1880s was restrictions placed on imports of American pork, allegedly for health reasons. The United States protested vigorously, threatened to embargo the imports of countries that discriminated against American meat products, and in 1891 negotiated a satisfactory settlement.

But in Asia, Latin America, and other regions that Americans considered "backward," a tougher brand of American intervention seemed necessary because there the United States was competing with other industrial powers. Asia and Latin America represented only a modest part of America's export trade—roughly an eighth of the total in the late nineteenth century. Still, this trade was growing—it was worth $200 million in 1900—and parts of it mattered a great deal to specific industries, for example, the China market for American textiles manufacturers. The real importance of these non-Western markets, however, was not so much their current value as their future promise. China, with its

enormous population of potential customers, exerted a powerful hold on the American mercantile imagination. Many felt that the China trade, though quite small, would one day be the key to American prosperity. Therefore, China and other beckoning markets must not be closed to the United States.

In the mid-1880s, the pace of imperialist activity picked up. After the Berlin Conference of 1884, the European powers rapidly colonized Africa. In a burst of modernizing energy, Japan transformed itself into a major power and began to challenge China's claims to Korea. In the Sino-Japanese War of 1894–1895, Japan won an easy victory and started a scramble among the Great Powers, including Russia, to carve China into spheres of influence. In Latin America, Britain, France, and Germany began to challenge U.S. interests more aggressively. On the European continent, moreover, the free-trade liberalism of earlier years gave way after the 1870s to protectionism, threatening established European markets for American goods just as empire building was closing off new markets elsewhere.

On top of all this came the Panic of 1893, setting in motion industrial strikes and agrarian protests that many Americans, such as Cleveland's secretary of state, Walter Q. Gresham, took to be "symptoms of revolution." With the nation's social stability seemingly at stake, securing the markets of Latin America and Asia took on new urgency, inspiring the expansionist diplomacy of the 1890s.

Creating an Expansionist Foreign Policy

"Whether they will or no, Americans must now begin to look outward. The growing production of the country requires it." So wrote Captain Alfred T. Mahan, America's leading naval strategist, in his book *The Influence of Seapower upon History* (1890). While serving aboard

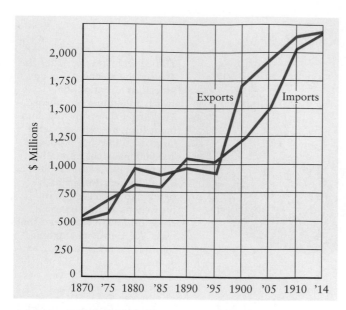

FIGURE 21.1
Balance of U.S. Imports, 1870–1914
By 1876 the United States had become a net exporting nation.
The brief reversal after 1888 aroused fears that the United
States was losing its foreign markets and helped fuel the
expansionist drive of the 1890s.

a warship cruising the coast of Latin America, Mahan
had spent his spare time reading history. In a library in
Lima, Peru, he hit upon the idea that the key to imperial power was control of the seas. From this insight
Mahan developed a naval analysis that became the cornerstone of American strategic thinking.

A Global Strategy.   "When a question arises of control
over distant regions . . . it must ultimately be decided by
naval power," Mahan advised. The United States should
regard the oceans not as barriers but as "a great high-

way . . . over which men pass in all directions." Travers-
ing that highway required a robust merchant marine
(America's had fallen on hard times since its heyday in
the 1850s), a powerful navy to protect American commerce, and strategic overseas bases. Here technology
played a role because, having converted from sails to
steam, navies required coaling stations far from home.
Without such stations, Mahan warned, warships were
"like land birds, unable to fly far from their own shores."

Mahan called for a canal across Central America to
connect the Atlantic and Pacific oceans. Such a canal
would enable the eastern United States to "compete
with Europe, on equal terms as to distance, for the markets of East Asia." The canal's approaches would need
to be guarded by bases in the Caribbean Sea. And
Hawaii would have to be annexed to extend American
power into the Pacific, a step Mahan considered "natural, necessary, irrepressible." What Mahan envisioned
was a form of colonialism different from Europe's.
Mahan aspired not to U.S. rule over large territories
and native populations but to U.S. control over strategic bases for the defense of America's trading interests.

Mahan was offering the United States a *coherent* foreign policy: first, foreign markets secured for the nation's
surplus products; second, the nation's development as a
naval power; and third, to sustain both of those goals, an
expansionist strategy anchored on an interoceanic canal
and bases in the Caribbean and the Pacific.

Other advocates of a powerful America flocked to
Captain Mahan, including such up-and-coming politicians as Theodore Roosevelt and Henry Cabot Lodge.
The influence of these men, few in number but strategically placed, increased during the 1890s. They pushed
steadily for what Lodge called a "large policy." But mainstream politicians also accepted Mahan's underlying
logic, and from the inauguration of Benjamin Harrison
in 1889 onward, a surprising consistency began to
emerge in the conduct of American foreign policy.

TABLE 21.1

*Exports to Canada and Europe Compared with Exports to Asia
and Latin America, 1875–1900*

Year	Exports to Canada and Europe ($)	Percentage of Total	Exports to Asia and Latin America ($)	Percentage of Total
1875	494,000,000	86.1	72,000,000	12.5
1885	637,000,000	85.8	87,000,000	11.7
1895	681,000,000	84.3	108,000,000	13.4
1900	1,135,000,000	81.4	200,000,000	14.3

Source: Compiled from information in *Historical Statistics of the United States,* 1960;
U.S. Department of Commerce, *Long Term Growth, 1860–1965,* 1966; National Bureau
of Economic Research, *Trends in the American Economy in the Nineteenth Century,* 1960.

Alfred T. Mahan
Mahan's theory about the influence of sea power on history came to him while he was killing time on a tour of naval duty reading Roman history in a library in Lima, Peru, in 1885. His insight was personal as well as intellectual: embarrassed by the decrepit ships on which he served, Mahan thought the United States should have a modern fleet in which officers like himself could serve with pride (and with some hope of professional advancement).
U.S. Naval Historical Foundation.

Rebuilding the Navy. Mahan argued strongly for a battleship fleet capable of roaming the high seas and striking a decisive first blow against an enemy. In 1890 Congress appropriated funds for the first three battleships in the two-ocean fleet envisioned by Benjamin F. Tracy, Harrison's ambitious secretary of the navy. Battleships might be expensive, said Tracy, but they were "the premium paid by the United States for the insurance of its acquired wealth and its growing industries." The battleship took on a special aura for those—like the young Roosevelt—who had grand dreams for the United States: "Oh, Lord! if only the people who are ignorant about our Navy could see those great warships in all their majesty and beauty, and could realize how [well fitted they are] to uphold the honor of America!" (see New Technology, "The Battleship," pp. 678–679.)

The incoming Cleveland administration was less spread-eagled and established its antiexpansionist credentials by canceling Harrison's scheme for annexing

Hawaii. But after hesitating briefly, Cleveland picked up the naval program of his Republican predecessor, pressing Congress just as forcefully for additional battleships (five were authorized) and making the same basic argument. The nation's commercial vitality—"free access to all markets," in the words of Cleveland's second secretary of state, Richard Olney—depended on its naval power.

While rejecting the colonialist aspects of Mahan's thinking, Cleveland absorbed the underlying strategic arguments about where America's vital interests lay. This explains the remarkable crisis that suddenly blew up in 1895 with Great Britain over Venezuela.

The Venezuela Crisis.   For years a border dispute had simmered between Venezuela and British Guiana. Now the United States demanded that it be resolved. The Europeans were carving up Africa and Asia in this period. How could the United States be sure that Europe did not have similar designs on Latin America? Indeed, prompted by President Cleveland, Secretary of State Olney made that point in a bristling note to London on July 25, 1895, demanding that Britain accept arbitration or face the consequences.

Invoking the Monroe Doctrine, Olney warned that the United States could not tolerate any European attempt to intimidate or overthrow nations in the Western Hemisphere. "Today the United States is practically sovereign upon this continent, and its fiat is law upon the subjects to which it confines its interposition." Olney intended to convey a clear message that the United States would brook no challenge to its vital interests in the Caribbean. These vital interests were strictly America's, not Venezuela's; Venezuela was not consulted during the entire dispute.

Despite its suddenness, the tough stand of the Cleveland administration was not an aberration but a logical step in the new American foreign policy. Once the British realized that Cleveland meant business, they backed off and agreed to arbitration of the boundary dispute. Afterward, Olney remarked with satisfaction that as a great industrial nation, the United States needed "to accept [its] commanding position" and take its place "among the Powers of the earth." Other countries would have to accommodate the American need for access to "more markets and larger markets for the consumption and products of the industry and inventive genius of the American people."

The Ideology of Expansionism.   As policy makers hammered out the new foreign policy, it was receiving strong ideological support from a variety of sources. One was the social Darwinist theory that dominated the political thought of this era (see Chapter 18). If, as Charles Darwin had shown, animals and plants evolved through the survival of the fittest, so did nations. "Nothing under the sun is stationary," warned the

The Battleship

———— ★ ————

IN THE ANNALS of naval warfare, ancient gave way to modern when sea battles ceased to be combat between shipborne soldiers. We can date that fault line quite precisely. It occurred at the defeat of the Spanish Armada in 1588, when the lumbering Spanish vessels of Philip II were pounded by the guns of the English ships without ever managing to board their troops on Elizabeth's nimble galleons. Ever since, the objective of naval combat has been to sink enemy ships. The tactical division of labor, as it evolved, called for sailing ships of many types—frigates, sloops-of-war, and smaller boats. But for a nation aspiring to command the seas, the essential weapon was the *capital* ship, carrying the biggest guns and heaviest armament. A superb example was the *Victory*, Lord Horatio Nelson's flagship at the battle against the Napoleonic fleet at Trafalgar in 1805. The *Victory* carried one hundred guns on three decks, and was among the most formidable fighting ships of her time. Because these capital ships entered battle in a line, guns blazing against the enemy fleet, they were called ships of the line or line-of-battle ships—hence the name for the next generation of capital ships: *battleships*.

In this drama of capital ships the United States figured not at all. Indeed, Trafalgar confirmed the nation's early policy against challenging Britain's command of the seas. In the War of 1812, the American fleet contained no ships of the line. At the time, this strategy was recommended by the country's few naval resources, but even after the United States developed the means for challenging Britain, geography and aspirations argued against doing so. As long as the United States defined itself as a continental nation, the mission of the U.S. Navy could be limited to coastal defense and harassing enemy commerce. The ship of the line, glorious though it was, had no place in American naval doctrine.

Even so, given America's industrial prowess, the United States contributed to the battleship's emergence as the capital ship of the age of steam and iron. The first steam-powered vessel in any navy was the U.S.S. *Fulton* (1815), and another American warship, the *Princeton* (1844), first demonstrated the superiority of the screw propeller over paddle wheels. The Civil War taught the world that wooden warships were finished. In a celebrated battle on March 8, 1862, the Confederacy's ironclad *Merrimack* rammed a sloop-of-war, sank a frigate with its

U.S.S. Atlanta
Pictured at its launching in 1884, the cruiser *Atlanta* was the first step in the navy's modernization program. The ship's transitional nature is suggested by the sailors manning the yardarms, which were there to support the sails assisting the *Atlanta*'s engines.
United States Naval Institute.

U.S.S. Oregon
Launched twelve years after the *Atlanta*, the *Oregon* was in an altogether different league, not only because of heavier tonnage and weaponry but because this vessel had left the age of sail behind and was recognizably a modern battleship.
U.S. Naval History Center.

guns, and might have destroyed the entire Union fleet blockading the Chesapeake but for the arrival of the ironclad U.S.S. *Monitor*. Unlike its European predecessors or the *Merrimack*, the *Monitor* was not a converted man-of-war. Here was an entirely new design, a ship with a low, flat deck, a dominating turret mounting two cannons, and no auxiliary sails—a prototype of the modern battleship, in fact, but in miniature, since the *Monitor* was only a shallow-draft gunboat (soon fated to founder in high seas).

Though it had helped create these technological advances, the United States had little to do with incorporating them into the battleship. The first example, completed in late 1861, was Britain's 9,210-ton *Warrior*, with a speed of 14 knots, a crew of 707, and eight 7-inch guns. Over the next twenty-five years, all the essential features of battleship design fell into place: in weaponry, rifled guns mounted on revolving turrets (the H.M.S. *Monarch*, 1869); in motive power, steam engines exclusively (H.M.S. *Devastation*, 1873); in construction, all-steel hulls and superstructures (H.M.S. *Colossus*, 1886).

Only after the battleship was an accomplished fact did the United States, heeding Captain Alfred T. Mahan's advice, shed its small-navy doctrine and build capital ships. The *Indiana*, *Massachusetts*, and *Oregon*, authorized in 1890, were, at 11,700 tons, world-class battleships, but they had some flaws.

They listed when the big guns pointed abeam; and the 8-inch turrets suffered blast effects from the 13-inch guns. Even so, these first American battleships proved more than adequate against the Spanish fleet in 1898, and the shipbuilding program then went into high gear, producing by 1914 the world's third most formidable battleship fleet, after Britain's and Germany's.

This achievement brought the United States into the front rank of twentieth-century sea powers; the battleship was Theodore Roosevelt's "big stick," and he took much pride in the Great White Fleet that circumnavigated the globe at the close of his administration. Yet after 1898 the American battleship's war record proved to be scant. By 1917, when the United States entered World War I, the German fleet had already been defeated, leaving for the U.S. Navy only convoy and blockading duties. By World War II, battleships verged on obsolescence. Like the ships of the Spanish Armada, they were vessels of great power but incapable of closing with an elusive opponent—in this instance, the aircraft carrier, which launched its planes from one hundred miles off and hoped never to see the enemy's ships. Thus, the Japanese attack on Pearl Harbor on December 7, 1941, meant little strategically because only the U.S. battleship fleet was at anchor on that Sunday morning; the U.S. aircraft carriers, safely at sea, were unscathed.

American social theorist Brooks Adams in *The Law of Civilization and Decay* (1895). "Not to advance is to recede." By this criterion, the United States had no choice; if it wanted to survive, it had to expand.

Linked to social Darwinism was a spreading belief in the inherent superiority of the Anglo-Saxon "race." In the late nineteenth century, Great Britain basked in the glory of its representative institutions, industrial prosperity, and far-flung empire—all ascribed to the supposed racial superiority of its people and, by extension, of their American cousins as well. On both sides of the Atlantic, Anglo-Saxonism was in vogue. John Fiske, an American philosopher and historian, lectured the nation on its future responsibilities: "The work which the English race began when it colonized North America is destined to go on until every land on the earth's surface that is not already the seat of an old civilization shall become English in its language, in its religion, in its political habits, and to a predominant extent in the blood of its people."

Fiske titled his lecture "Manifest Destiny." A half-century earlier this term had been used to express Americans' sense of their national mission to sweep aside the native American peoples and occupy the continent. In his widely read book *The Winning of the West* (1896), Theodore Roosevelt drew a parallel between the expansionism of his own time and the suppression of the Indians. To Roosevelt, what happened to "backward peoples" mattered little because their conquest was "for the benefit of civilization and in the interests of mankind. It is indeed a warped, perverse and silly morality which would forbid a course of conquest that has turned whole continents into the seats of mighty and flourishing civilized nations." More than historical parallels, however, linked the Manifest Destiny of the past and present.

In 1890 the U.S. Census reported the end of the westward movement on the North American continent: there was no longer a frontier line beyond which land remained to be conquered. The psychological impact of that news on Americans was profound, spawning among other things a new historical interpretation that stressed the importance of the frontier in shaping the nation's character. In a landmark essay setting out this thesis—"The Significance of the Frontier in American History" (1893)—the young historian Frederick Jackson Turner suggested a link between the closing of the frontier and overseas expansion. "He would be a rash prophet who should assert that the expansive character of American life has now entirely ceased," Turner wrote. "Movement has been its dominant fact, and, unless this training has no effect upon a people, the American energy will continually demand a wider field for its exercise." As Turner predicted, Manifest Destiny did turn outward.

Thus a strong current of ideas, deeply rooted in American experience and ideology, justified the new diplomacy of expansionism. The United States was eager to step onto the world stage. All it needed was the right occasion.

An American Empire

After Spain lost its South American empire in the early nineteenth century, Cubans yearned to join their mainland brothers and sisters in freedom. Independence movements sprang up repeatedly, most recently in a rebellion that had lasted from 1868 to 1878. In February 1895, inspired by the poet José Martí, Cuban patriots again rebelled against Spanish rule. Although Martí died in an early skirmish and no mass uprising occurred, the rebels built up substantial fighting forces and mounted a guerrilla war against the Spaniards. A standoff developed; the Spaniards controlled the towns, the insurgents held much of the countryside. Then, in early 1896, the newly appointed Spanish captain general, Valeriano Weyler, adopted the harsh policy of *reconcentration*. The Spaniards forced entire populations into armed camps and treated any Cubans on the outside as rebels. Because reconcentration was not followed by aggressive pursuit, it only inconvenienced the guerrilla fighters. The toll on civilians, however, was brutal. Out of a population of 1,600,000, as many as 200,000 may have died of starvation, exposure, or dysentery.

The Cuban Crisis

Rebel leaders shrewdly saw that their best hope was not military but political: they had to draw the United States into their struggle. Some Cubans lived there, mostly in Florida, where Cuban cigar makers taxed themselves heavily for the cause of independence. But the nerve center of the United States was New York City, and it was there that a key group of exiles—the *junta*—set up shop to make the case for *Cuba Libre*.

By itself, their cause would not have stirred much interest. The Spaniards were behaving no more dishonorably than any other colonial power in similar circumstances; nor were atrocities in short supply elsewhere in the world. The Cuban exiles, however, came on the scene at a critical juncture in American sensationalist journalism. William Randolph Hearst had just purchased the nearly moribund *New York Journal* and was in a hurry to build circulation (see American Lives, "William Randolph Hearst: Jingo," pp. 682–683). Cuba was ideal for his purposes. Locked in a furious circulation war, Hearst's *Journal* and Joseph Pulitzer's *New York World* elevated Cuba's agony into flaming front-page headlines.

THE DUTY OF THE HOUR:—TO SAVE HER NOT ONLY FROM SPAIN BUT FROM A WORSE FATE.

Free Cuba?
Independence for Cuba was not an unalloyed good for many Americans, including this cartoonist. Here he depicts Cuba as a woman about to jump from the frying pan (Spanish misrule) into the fire (anarchy). Hence the revealing caption: "The Duty of the Hour—To Save Her Not Only from Spain but from a Worse Fate."
Granger Collection.

Across the country powerful sentiments stirred: humanitarian concern for the Cubans, sympathy with their aspirations for freedom, and a superpatriotism that became known as *jingoism*. Congress began calling for Cuban independence.

Presidential Politics. Grover Cleveland, still in office when the rebellion broke out, took a cooler view of the situation. His concern was America's vital interests, which, he told Congress, were "by no means of a wholly sentimental or philanthropic character." The Cuban civil war was disrupting the sizable trade between the two countries and destroying profitable American investments, especially in Cuban sugar plantations. Of course, it was the rebels who were burning the crops, but Spain was accountable for not maintaining security. The president was also worried that Spain's troubles might draw other European powers into the situation. A chronically unstable Cuba was not compatible with America's increasing strategic interests in the region, especially its plans for an interoceanic canal whose approaches would have to be safeguarded. If Spain could put down the rebellion, that was fine with Cleveland. But as Spain's impotence became clear, he urged the Spanish government to make reforms and resolve the crisis.

Taking over in March 1897, the McKinley administration adopted much the same line. Like Cleveland, William McKinley considered the United States to be the dominant Caribbean power, with vital interests that had to be defended. But McKinley was inclined to be tougher on the Spaniards. He was appalled by Spain's "uncivilized and inhumane conduct" in Cuba and more sympathetic than his predecessor to the aspirations of the rebels. In addition, McKinley had to contend with the jingoism in the Republican Party, manifest at the 1896 national convention in a bristling platform calling for Cuban independence and proclaiming a new American imperialism. But the notion, long held by historians, that McKinley was swept along against his better judgment by popular opinion and by a Republican war faction led by Theodore Roosevelt, Henry Cabot Lodge, and other aggressive advocates of a "large policy" was not true. McKinley was very much his own man. A skilled politician and a canny if undramatic president, he would not proceed until he sensed a broad national consensus for war. In particular, McKinley was sensitive to business interests fearful of disruption to an economy just recovering from depression.

The Road to War. On September 18, 1897, the American minister in Madrid asked the Spanish government

William Randolph Hearst: Jingo

★

WILLIAM RANDOLPH HEARST, born in San Francisco on April 29, 1863, was no Horatio Alger hero. His father, George Hearst, had struck it rich in Nevada's Comstock lode, and Willie grew up in the lap of luxury: grand houses, trips to Europe, private tutors, Harvard. His mother, Phoebe, doted on him, at once indulging and smothering her only child. From these unpromising beginnings sprang a strappingly handsome young man of remarkable contradictions, beginning with his voice, which was incongruously thin and high pitched. Hearst was painfully shy but simultaneously hell-bent on mischief; his pranks at Harvard (which finally got him expelled) were legendary. He was outwardly diffident but had to dominate everyone around him. He was sentimental and generous but also without scruples. When he wanted something, he really wanted it, and he was known late into his life to throw tantrums when he was denied. All this would be of no historical moment—doubtless there were others like him among the progeny of the new millionaires—except for one thing: Hearst did not end up a dissipated alcoholic or, as was known to happen, even a quietly exemplary citizen. Hearst became a great newspaperman and, driven by his inner demons, cut a swath through American history.

His father happened to own the *San Francisco Examiner*, a money-loser that served as the elder Hearst's political organ. At Harvard the son took to reading the *Examiner* and decided that he wanted to run it. His inspiration was Joseph Pulitzer, who a few years earlier had taken over the moribund *New York World* and transformed it into a hugely successful daily. While still a college junior, Hearst wrote a remarkable letter to his father outlining his plans for the paper, which, like the *World*, would be "of that class which appeals to the people and which depends for its success upon enterprise, energy and a certain startling originality and not upon the wisdom of its political opinions or the lofty style of its editorials." The elder Hearst was unimpressed. He was thinking about unloading the paper, not pouring more money into it. Supposing it became a great success, he asked the business manager, how much might it make?

Maybe $100,000 a year, came the answer. "Hell!" snorted Hearst. "That ain't no money." But the son wasn't interested in the money; he was interested in the *circulation* and the delight he would take from orchestrating the emotions—and maybe even the actions—of thousands upon thousands of readers.

In early 1887 the young Hearst, not yet twenty-four, finally got his wish and, on taking command, immediately pronounced the sleepy *Examiner* "Monarch of the Dailies." It would be "THE LARGEST, BRIGHTEST AND BEST NEWSPAPER ON THE PACIFIC COAST," providing readers with the best news and "THE LATEST AND MOST ORIGINAL SENSATIONS." Sensation was what Hearst was after—copy that would arouse, in his editor's words, "the gee-whiz emotion." For example, were any grizzly bears left in California? Hearst dispatched an intrepid newsman to the Tehachapi Mountains, where after three months of arduous trapping he caught a grizzly. The beast was chained in a beer wagon, paraded with great fanfare around San Francisco, and given a home in Golden Gate Park. Naturally, it was named Monarch. All this the *Examiner* reported in exhaustive detail, building suspense as the search progressed and ending triumphantly with the carnival display of the unfortunate bear. There was much more of the same: rescues, murders, scandal, sob stories, anything that might give readers the "gee-whiz emotion." The other string in Hearst's bow was that he became a champion of "the people." The *Examiner* embarked on a series of noisy crusades—against the water trust, and got rates cut by 15 percent; against a city charter crafted by venal politicos and their business cronies, and got it defeated; and, on many fronts, against the rapacious Southern Pacific Railroad.

By the early 1890s the *Examiner*'s circulation was soaring and Hearst was making money. Looking around for greener fields, his eye fixed on New York City. The *Journal* was for sale, and Hearst got it cheaply. It was an anemic paper, close to folding, but Hearst didn't care. He intended to transform it, pouring money in as he had with the *Examiner* and applying everything he had learned in San Francisco. He was going to war against Pulitzer's *New York World*.

When Hearst took over the *Journal* in October 1895, the Cuban insurrection had already begun. Until then Hearst had shown no interest in foreign affairs, but he genuinely felt for the underdog Cubans and, more to the point, saw in their cause just what he needed to drive his circulation war against Pulitzer. Not much actual news could be gotten out of Cuba, for the sporadic fighting took place in the remote interior, beyond the reach of Hearst's

William Randolph Hearst
Archive Photos.

correspondents in Havana. It did not matter. Rebel claims were good enough for Hearst, and a drumbeat of superheated articles began to appear about mostly nonexistent battles and about Spanish atrocities. When General Valeriano Weyler took command, the *Journal* immediately dubbed him the "Butcher":

> Weyler the brute, the devastator of haciendas, the destroyer of families and the outrager of women. . . . Pitiless, cold, an exterminator of men . . . inventing tortures and infamies of bloody debauchery. . . .

Weyler's reconcentration program soon put meat into the *Journal*'s wild charges, and American public opinion began to harden against the Spanish.

The *Journal* was stridently for war. Hearst's jingoism sounded very much like his old crusade against the San Francisco water trust: it was the people versus the interests all over again, the freedom-loving masses against the peace-at-any-price plutocrats. President McKinley was Wall Street's puppet, with the nefarious Senator Hanna pulling the strings. When the *Maine* went down, the *Journal* was ablaze with fiery headlines charging Spanish treachery. That week circulation passed a million. Impatient for action, Hearst found ammunition even in the suicide of poor Mrs. Mary Wayt:

GRIEVED OVER OUR DELAY

"The Government May Live
in Dishonor," Said She,
"I Cannot."

The next day, April 19, the Senate passed the war resolution, and hostilities commenced. The news from Manila Bay got this screaming headline: "VICTORY . . . Complete! . . . Glorious! . . . THE MAINE IS AVENGED." A few days later, the front page asked readers: "HOW DO YOU LIKE THE JOURNAL'S WAR?"

Was it true? Had Hearst caused the war? For many years historians thought so. Now, with a better understanding of McKinley's administration, they are more inclined to stress the country's endangered strategic interests. Yet there is no denying Hearst's contribution. The war hysteria he nurtured was like a ticking bomb, forcing the president's hand because, as New York's Senator Platt noted, McKinley knew "that the people of the United States will not tolerate much longer the war in Cuba." There were also longer-term consequences. For one, public opinion became a weightier factor in the conduct of American foreign policy; whether democracy and diplomacy are compatible has been debated ever since Hearst's time. Second, Hearst introduced and never let go of a superpatriotism—"Americanism," he called it—that became a permanent, if volatile, element of the nation's political debate.

As for the war with Spain, Hearst had a grand time of it. He hired a boat, took a crew of newsmen down to Cuba, came under fire at El Caney, wrote some creditable dispatches when his star reporter was wounded, rounded up Spanish survivors of the Santiago naval battle, and returned to New York feeling that the world was his oyster.

At that time Hearst was thirty-five, with another fifty-three years to live. The news business, ultimately a huge empire, remained the core of his being. But he also entered New York politics in a quixotic quest for the presidency. He plunged into Hollywood moviemaking and formed a permanent liaison with one of his creations, the movie star Marion Davies. He built a castle at San Simeon, California, and extravagantly entertained the rich and famous. All the while he became more enigmatic, more dictatorial, more alone.

In the end Hearst gained immortality in an utterly modern way: he became the inspiration for Orson Welles's great movie *Citizen Kane* (1941). Ordinarily, we do not look to the movies for historical insight, but Welles captured something about Hearst. The plot turns on Kane's dying word, *rosebud*, which proves to be only the name of a sled remembered from his childhood.

"whether the time has not arrived when Spain . . . will put a stop to this destructive war." If Spain could not ensure an "early and certain peace," the United States would take whatever steps it "should deem necessary to procure this result." The American pressure on Spain at first seemed to pay off. The conservative regime fell, and a liberal government, upon taking office in October 1897, moderated its Cuban policy. Spain recalled Weyler, limited reconcentration, and adopted an autonomy plan granting Cuba a degree of self-rule but not independence. Madrid's incapacity soon became clear, however. In January 1898, Spanish loyalists in Havana rioted against the offer of autonomy. Cuban rebels, encouraged by the prospect of American intervention, demanded full independence.

On February 9, 1898, the *New York Journal* published a private letter written by Dupuy de Lôme, Spanish minister to the United States. In it de Lôme called President McKinley "weak" and "a bidder for the admiration of the crowd." Worse, the letter suggested that the Spanish government was not taking the American demands for reform seriously. De Lôme immediately resigned, but the damage had been done.

A week later the U.S. battleship *Maine* blew up and sank in Havana harbor, with the loss of 260 seamen. "Whole Country Thrills with the War Fever," proclaimed Hearst's *New York Journal*. From that moment on, popular passions against Spain became a major factor in the march toward war.

President McKinley kept his head. He assumed that the sinking was accidental: what motive could the Spanish have had for attacking the *Maine*? An American naval board of inquiry, however, submitted a damaging report. Disagreeing with a separate Spanish inquiry, the American board concluded that the sinking was caused by a mine, not—as the latest studies find just as likely— by an accidental explosion aboard the *Maine*. (A 1976 naval inquiry faulted the ship's design, which located the ship's explosives too close to coal bunkers prone to spontaneous fires.) No evidence linked the Spanish to the purported mine. But if a mine did in fact sink the ship, then the Spanish were at least at fault for not protecting an American vessel within their jurisdiction.

The impression that Spanish control over Cuba had broken down was reinforced by a memorable speech by Senator Redfield Proctor of Vermont after a visit to Cuba. The account by this anti-imperialist senior Republican of the devastation in the Cuban countryside convinced even the skeptical that Spain had lost its claim to Cuba.

President McKinley had no enthusiasm for the martial spirit engulfing the country. He was not swept along by calls to avenge the sinking of the *Maine*. But he did have to pay attention to an aroused public opinion. Business leaders now also became impatient for the dispute with Spain to end. War was preferable to the unresolved Cuban crisis. On March 27 McKinley cabled Madrid what was in effect an ultimatum: an immediate armistice for six months, abandonment of reconcentration, and, with the United States as mediator, peace negotiations with the rebels. A telegram the next day added that only Cuban independence would be regarded as a satisfactory outcome to the negotiations. Spain categorically rejected these humiliating demands, although, as a final concession, it unilaterally declared on April 9 an armistice whose duration would be at the discretion of the Spanish military.

On April 11 McKinley sent a message to Congress asking for authority to intervene to end the fighting in Cuba. His motives were as he described them: "In the name of humanity, in the name of civilization, in behalf of endangered American interests which give us the right and the duty to speak and to act, the war in Cuba must stop." The War Hawks in Congress—a mixture of Republicans and western Democrats—were impatient with McKinley's cautious progress. But the president did not lose control, and he defeated the War Hawks on the crucial issue of recognizing the rebel republican government, which would have greatly reduced the administration's freedom of action in dealing with Spain.

The resolutions authorizing intervention in Cuba contained an amendment by Senator Henry M. Teller of Colorado disclaiming any intention by the United States of taking possession of Cuba. No European government should say that "when we go out to make battle for the liberty and freedom of Cuban patriots, that we are doing it for the purpose of aggrandizement for ourselves or the increasing of our territorial holdings." This policy had to be made clear with regard to Cuba, "whatever," Senator Teller added, "we may do as to some other islands."

Did McKinley have in mind "some other islands"? Was this really a war of aggression, secretly motivated by a desire to seize strategic territory from Spain? In a strict sense, almost certainly no. It was not *because* of expansionist ambitions that McKinley forced Spain into a corner. But once war came, McKinley saw it as an opportunity. As he wrote privately after hostilities began: "While we are conducting war and until its conclusion, we must keep all we get; when the war is over we must keep what we want." Precisely what would be forthcoming, of course, would depend on the fortunes of battle.

The Spoils of War

Hostilities formally began when Spain declared war on April 24, 1898. Across the United States volunteer regiments began to form up. Theodore Roosevelt immediately resigned as assistant secretary of the navy, ordered a fancy uniform, and was commissioned lieutenant colonel in a volunteer cavalry regiment that became known as the Rough Riders. Raw recruits poured into makeshift bases around Tampa, Florida. Confusion

"*Remember the* Maine!"
In late January 1898 the *Maine* entered Havana harbor on a courtesy call. On the evening of February 15 a mysterious blast sent the U.S. battleship to the bottom. This dramatic lithograph conveys something of the impact of that event on American public opinion. Although no evidence ever linked the Spanish authorities to the explosion, the sinking of the *Maine* fed the emotional fires that prepared the nation for war with Spain.
Granger Collection.

reigned. Tropical uniforms did not arrive; the food was bad, the sanitation worse; and rifles were in short supply. No provision had been made for getting the troops to Cuba; the government hastily began to collect a fleet of yachts, lake steamers, and commercial boats. Fortunately, the small regular army was a disciplined, highly professional force, and its seasoned 28,000 troops provided a nucleus for the 200,000 civilians who had to be turned into soldiers inside of a few weeks.

The navy was in much better shape. Spain had nothing to match America's seven battleships and armored cruisers, and the ships Spain did have were undermanned and ill prepared for battle. The Spanish admiral Pascual Cervera gloomily expected that his navy would "like Don Quixote go out to fight windmills and come back with a broken head."

On April 23, acting on plans already drawn up, Commodore George Dewey's small Pacific fleet set sail from Hong Kong for the Philippines. There, at this Spanish possession in the far Pacific, not in Cuba, the decisive engagement of the war took place. On May 1 American ships cornered the Spanish fleet in Manila Bay and destroyed it (Map 21.1). The victory produced euphoria in the United States. Immediately, part of the army being trained for the Cuban campaign was diverted to the Philippines. Manila, the Philippine capital, fell on August 13, 1898.

With Dewey's naval victory, American strategic thinking clicked into place. "We hold the other side of the Pacific and the value to this country is almost beyond imagination," declared Senator Lodge. "We must on no account let the [Philippine] Islands go." President McKinley agreed, and so did his key advisors. An anchorage in the western Pacific had long been coveted by naval strategists. At this time, too, the Great Powers were carving China into spheres of influence. If American commerce wanted a place in that glittering market, the power of the United States would have to be projected into Asia. "With a strong foothold in the Philippine Islands, we can and will take a large slice of the commerce of Asia," Senator Mark Hanna asserted. "That is what we want . . . and it is better to strike while the iron is hot."

Once the decision for a Philippine base had been made, other decisions followed almost automatically. The question of Hawaii was quickly resolved. After stalling the previous year, in July 1898 Hawaiian annexation went through Congress by joint resolution. Hawaii had acquired a crucial strategic value: it was a halfway station on the way to the Philippines. The navy pressed for a coaling base in the central Pacific; that meant Guam, a Spanish island in the Marianas. There was need also for a strategically located base in the Caribbean; that meant Puerto Rico. By July, before the assault on Cuba, the full scope of McKinley's war aims

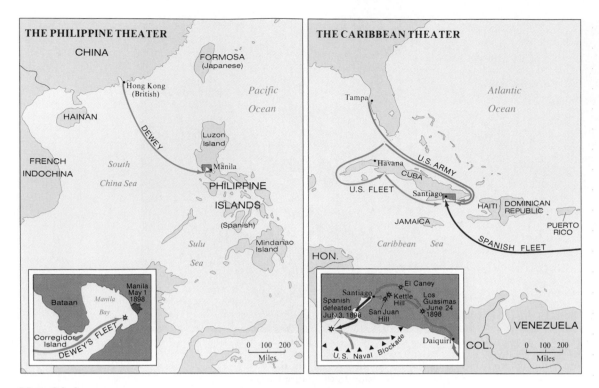

MAP 21.1
The Spanish-American War of 1898
The swift American victory in the Spanish-American War resulted from overwhelming naval
superiority. Dewey's destruction of the Spanish fleet in Manila harbor doomed the Spaniards
in the Philippines. In Cuba, American ground forces won a hard victory on San Juan Hill,
for they were ill equipped and poorly supplied. With the United States in control of the seas,
the Spaniards saw no choice but to give up the battle for Cuba.

had taken shape. The American people were vocifer-
ously behind him. In the wake of Dewey's victory,
enthusiasm for colonial annexations swept the country
and, as one close reader of the nation's press reported,
was "getting so strong it will mean the political death of
any man to oppose it pretty soon."

The campaign in Cuba was something of an anti-
climax. The Spanish fleet was bottled up in Santiago
harbor, and the city itself became the strategic key to
the military campaign. Half trained and ill equipped,
the American forces moving on Santiago might have
been checked by a determined opponent. The Spaniards
fought to maintain their honor but had no stomach for
a real war against the Americans.

The main battle, on July 1, occurred near Santiago
on the heights of San Juan Hill. On foot because there
had been no room for horses on the transports,
Roosevelt's Rough Riders seized Kettle Hill. Then a
frontal assault against the San Juan heights began.
Four black regiments took the brunt of the fighting.
White observers grudgingly credited much of the victory to the "superb gallantry" of the black soldiers (see
American Voices, "George W. Prioleau: Black Soldiers
in a White Man's War," p. 688). In fact, it was not quite
a victory. The Spaniards, driven from their forward

positions, retreated to a well-fortified second line. The
Americans had suffered heavy casualties and were
exhausted by the heat; whether they could mount a
second assault was questionable. They were spared
this test, however, by the Spanish. On July 3 Cervera's
fleet in Santiago harbor made a suicidal daylight
attempt to run the American blockade and was
destroyed. A few days later, convinced that Santiago
could not be saved, Spanish forces surrendered.

The two nations signed an armistice in which
Spain agreed to give up Cuba and cede Puerto Rico and
Guam to the United States. American forces occupied
Manila pending a peace treaty.

The Imperial Experiment

The big question was the Philippines, an archipelago of
over 7,000 islands populated—as William R. Day,
McKinley's secretary of state, put it in the racist language
of that era—by "eight or nine millions of absolutely ignorant and many degraded people." Not even the most avid
American expansionists had advocated colonial rule over
such a population—that was European-style imperialism, not the acquisition of strategic bases that Mahan
and his followers had in mind. Both Mahan and Lodge

The Battle of San Juan Hill
On July 1, 1898, the key battle for Cuba took place on heights overlooking Santiago.
African American troops bore the brunt of the fighting. Although generally overlooked,
the black role in the San Juan battle is done justice in this contemporary lithograph,
without the demeaning stereotypes by which blacks were normally depicted in an age
of intensifying racism. Even so, the racial hierarchy is maintained. The blacks are the
foot soldiers; their officers are white.
Library of Congress.

initially advocated keeping only Manila. It gradually became clear, however, that Manila was not defensible without U.S. control of the whole of Luzon, the large island on which the city is located.

Taking the Philippines. McKinley and his advisors surveyed the options. One possibility was to return most of the islands to Spain, but the reputed evils of Spanish rule made that a "cowardly and dishonorable" solution. Another possibility was to partition the Philippines with one or more of the other Great Powers. But as McKinley observed, to turn over valuable territory to "our commercial rivals in the Orient—that would have been bad business and discreditable."

Most plausible was the option of granting the Philippines independence. As in Cuba, Spanish rule had already stirred up a rebellion, led by the fiery patriot Emilio Aguinaldo. An arrangement might have been possible like the one being negotiated with the Cubans: the lease of a naval base to the Americans as the price for freedom. But after some hesitation McKinley was persuaded that "we could not leave [the

Filipinos] to themselves—they were unfit for self-rule—and they would soon have anarchy and misrule over there worse than Spain's was."

In October 1898, while the peace negotiations were in progress, McKinley made a two-week speaking tour of the Midwest to get a reading on public opinion. What he heard from the crowds confirmed his own belief that the United States would have to take the entire archipelago. On October 26 he cabled instructions to that effect to the American delegation in Paris. He had concluded that the United States "cannot let go."

As for the Spaniards, they had little choice against what they considered "the immoderate demands of a conqueror." In the Treaty of Paris they ceded the Philippines to the United States for a payment of $20 million. The treaty encountered harder going at home and was ratified by the Senate (requiring a two-thirds majority) on February 6, 1899, with only a single vote to spare.

The Anti-Imperialists. The narrowness of the administration's victory signaled the revival of an anti-expansionist tradition that had been briefly silenced by

GEORGE W. PRIOLEAU
Black Soldiers in a White Man's War

————————★————————

The chaplain of the Ninth Cavalry regiment expresses his bitterness toward the racism experienced by black troopers in the South on their way to battle in Cuba.

Hon. H. C. Smith
Editor, Gazette

Dear Sir:
The Ninth Cavalry left Chickamauga on the 30th of April for Tampa, Fla. We arrived here (nine miles from Tampa) on May 3. From this port the army will sail for Cuba. We have in this camp here and at Tampa between 7,000 and 8,000 soldiers, artillery, one regiment of cavalry (the famous fighting Ninth) and the Twenty-fourth and Twenty-fifth infantries. The Ninth Cavalry's bravery and their skillfulness with weapons of war . . . is well known by all who have read the history of the last Indian war. . . .

Yesterday, May 12, the Ninth was ordered to be ready to embark at a moment's notice for Cuba. . . . These men are anxious to go. The country will then hear and know of the bravery of these sable sons of Ham.

The American Negro is always ready and willing to take up arms, to fight and to lay down his life in defense of his country's flag and honor. All the way from northwest Nebraska this regiment was greeted with cheers and hurrahs. At places where we stopped the people assembled by the thousands. While the Ninth Cavalry band would play some national air the people would raise their hats, men, women and children would wave their handkerchiefs, and the heavens would resound with their hearty cheers. The white hand shaking the black hand. The hearty "goodbyes," "God bless you," and other expressions aroused the patriotism of our boys. . . . These demonstrations, so enthusiastically given, greeted us all the way until we reached Nashville. At this point we arrived about 12:30 A.M. There were about 6,000 colored people there to greet us (very few white people) but not a man was allowed by the railroad officials to approach the cars. From there until we reached Chattanooga there was not a cheer given us, the people living in gross ignorance, rags and dirt. Both white and colored seemed amazed; they looked at us in wonder. Don't think they have intelligence enough to know that Andrew Jackson is dead. . . .

The prejudice against the Negro soldier and the Negro was great, but it was of heavenly origin to what it is in this part of Florida, and I suppose that what is true here is true in other parts of the state. Here, the Negro is not allowed to purchase over the same counter in some stores that the white man purchases over. The southerners have made their laws and the Negroes know and obey them. They never stop to ask a white man a question. He (Negro) never thinks of disobeying. You talk about freedom, liberty, etc. Why sir, the Negro of this country is a freeman and yet a slave. Talk about fighting and freeing poor Cuba and of Spain's brutality; of Cuba's murdered thousands, and starving reconcentradoes. Is America any better than Spain? Has she not subjects in her very midst who are murdered daily without a trial of judge or jury? Has she not subjects in her own borders whose children are half-fed and half-clothed, because their father's skin is black. . . . Yet the Negro is loyal to his country's flag. . . .

The four Negro regiments are going to help free Cuba, and they will return to their homes, some then mustered out and begin again to fight the battle of American prejudice. . . .

Yours truly,
Geo. W. Prioleau
Chaplain, Ninth Cavalry

Source: Cleveland *Gazette* (May 13, 1898), reprinted in Willard B. Gatewood, *"Smoked Yankees" and the Struggle for Empire, 1898–1902* (Urbana: University of Illinois Press, 1971), 27–29.

the patriotic passions of a nation at war. In the Senate, opponents of the treaty invoked the country's republican principles. Under the Constitution, argued conservative Republican George F. Hoar, "no power is given to the Federal Government to acquire territory to be held and governed permanently as colonies" or "to conquer alien people and hold them in subjugation." Hoar rejected "the fundamental idea [of the European imperial powers] that the people of immense areas of territory can be held as subjects, never to become citizens."

But making 8 million Filipinos eligible for citizenship was equally objectionable to the anti-imperialists, who were no more champions of "these savage people" than were the expansionists who denigrated the self-governing capacity of the Filipinos.

Leading citizens enlisted in the anti-imperialist cause, including Andrew Carnegie, who offered a check for $20 million to purchase the independence of the Philippines; Samuel Gompers, who feared the competition of cheap Filipino labor; and Jane Addams, who believed that women should stand for peace. The key group, however, was a social elite of old-line Mugwump reformers including Carl Schurz, Charles Eliot Norton, and Charles Francis Adams. In November 1898 a Boston group formed the first Anti-Imperialist League, from which blossomed a national movement over the next year.

Although skillful at publicizing their cause, the anti-imperialists never managed to build a truly popular

Emilio Aguinaldo
At the start of the war with Spain, U.S. military leaders brought the Filipino patriot Aguinaldo back from Singapore because they thought he would stir up a popular uprising that would help defeat the Spaniards. Aguinaldo came because he thought the Americans favored an independent Philippines. These differing intentions—it has remained a matter of dispute what assurances Aguinaldo received—were the root cause of the Filipino insurrection that proved far costlier in American and Filipino lives than the war with Spain that preceded it.
Corbis-Bettmann.

Hurrah for Imperialism!
Amid the patriotic frenzy over Dewey's naval victory, cooler heads wondered whether the United States knew what it was getting into with all the talk about creating an American empire. Here, *Life* magazine, often a skeptical commentator on American public life, pictures a blindfolded Uncle Sam stepping off a cliff.
LIFE, 1898, Newbury Library.

movement. They shared little but their anti-imperialism and, within the Mugwump core, lacked the common touch. Nor was anti-imperialism easily translated into a viable political cause, because the Democrats, once the treaty was adopted, waffled on the issue. Although an outspoken anti-imperialist, William Jennings Bryan, the Democratic standard-bearer, provided confused leadership. He confounded his friends by favoring ratification of the treaty and afterward hesitated to stake his party's future on a crusade against a national policy that he privately believed to be irreversible. Still, if it was an accomplished fact, Philippine annexation lost the moral high ground because of grim events that began to unfold in the Philippines.

War in the Philippines. On February 4, 1899, two days before the Senate ratified the treaty, fighting broke out between American and Filipino patrols on the edge of Manila. Confronted by American annexation, Aguinaldo asserted his nation's independence and turned his guns on the occupying American forces. The ensuing conflict far exceeded in ferocity the war just concluded with Spain.

Fighting tenacious guerrillas, the U.S. Army resorted to the reconcentration tactics the Spaniards had used in Cuba, moving people into towns, carrying out indiscriminate attacks beyond the perimeters, and burning crops and villages (see American Voices, "Robert P. Hughes and Richard T. O'Brien: Subduing the Filipinos—The Realities," p. 691). Atrocities became commonplace on both sides. In three years of warfare 4,200 Americans and thousands more Filipinos died. The fighting ended in 1902, and Judge William Howard Taft, who had been appointed governor general, set up a civilian administration. He intended to make the Philippines a model of American road building and sanitary engineering.

McKinley's convincing victory over Bryan in the 1900 election, though by no means a referendum on American expansionism, suggested popular satisfaction with the country's overseas adventure. Yet a strong undercurrent of misgivings was evident. Americans had not anticipated the brutal methods needed to subdue the Filipino guerrillas. "We are destroying these islanders by the thousands, their villages and cities," protested the philosopher William James. "No life shall you have, we say, except as a gift from our philanthropy after your unconditional surrender to our will. . . . Could there be any more damning indictment of that whole bloated ideal termed 'modern civilization'?" And when the fighting ended, it was not apparent just what the United States had achieved.

There were, moreover, disturbing constitutional issues to be resolved. Did the U.S. Constitution extend to the acquired territories? Did their inhabitants automatically become U.S. citizens? In 1901 the Supreme Court ruled negatively on both questions; these were matters for Congress to decide. A special commission appointed by McKinley recommended independence for the Philippines after an indefinite period of U.S. rule, during which the Filipinos would be prepared for self-government. In 1916 the Jones Act formally committed the United States to granting Philippine independence but set no date.

The ugly business in the Philippines rubbed off some of the moralizing gloss but left undimmed America's global aspirations. In a few years the United States had acquired the makings of a strategic overseas empire: Hawaii, Puerto Rico, Guam, the Philippines, and finally, in 1900, several of the Samoan islands that had been jointly administered with Germany and Britain. The United States, remarked the legal scholar John Bassett Moore in 1899, had moved "from a posi-

Fighting the Filipinos, 1899
The United States went to war against Spain in 1898 partly out of sympathy with the Cuban struggle for independence. Yet the United States found it necessary to use the same brutal tactics against the Filipino insurrectionists that the Spaniards had employed against the Cubans. Here U.S. troops man a defensive perimeter near Pasay in 1899 against an elusive foe. California Museum of Photography.

tion of comparative freedom from entanglements into a position of what is commonly called a world power."

Onto the World Stage

———————★———————

In Europe the flexing of America's muscles caused some consternation. The assault on Spain seemed, in the words of the French envoy to Washington, "ignorant, brutal, and quite capable of destroying the complicated European structure." At the instigation of Kaiser Wilhelm II of Germany, the major powers had tried before war broke out to intercede on Spain's behalf—but tentatively, because no one was looking for trouble with the Americans. President McKinley had listened politely to the presentations of their envoys on April 6, 1898, then proceeded with his war.

ROBERT P. HUGHES AND
RICHARD T. O'BRIEN

Subduing the Filipinos—The Realities

———★———

When Arthur MacArthur, the commanding general of U.S. forces in the Philippines, appeared in 1902 before a Senate committee investigating conditions there he boasted of "planting the best traditions, the best characteristics of Americanism . . . down deep in that fertile soil."

Brigadier General Hughes offered the Senate committee a different picture of the implanting of American ideals in Filipino soil.

Sen. Rawlins: . . . [In] burning towns, what would you do? Would the entire town be destroyed by fire or would only offending portions of the town be burned?
Gen. Hughes: I do not know that we have ever had a case of burning what you would call a town in this country, but probably a barrio or a sitio; probably half a dozen houses, native shacks, where the insurrectos would go in and be concealed, and if they caught a detachment passing they would kill some of them.
Sen. Rawlins: What did I understand you to say would be the consequences of that?
Gen. Hughes: They usually burned the village.
Sen. Rawlins: All the houses in the village?
Gen. Hughes: Yes, every one of them.
Sen. Rawlins: What would become of the inhabitants?

Gen. Hughes: That was their lookout. . . .
Sen. Rawlins: If these shacks were of no consequence what was the utility of their destruction?
Gen. Hughes: The destruction was as a punishment. They permitted these people to come in there and conceal themselves and they gave no sign. It is always—
Sen. Rawlins: The punishment in that case would fall, not upon the men, who could go elsewhere, but mainly upon the women and little children.
Gen. Hughes: The women and children are part of the family, and where you wish to inflict punishment you can punish the man probably worse in that way than in any other.
Sen. Rawlins: But is that within the ordinary rules of civilized warfare? . . .
Gen. Hughes: These people are not civilized.

Richard T. O'Brien, of M Company, 26th Infantry Volunteers, U.S. Army, gave this account to the Senate committee.

[How] the order started and who gave it I don't know, but the town was fired on. I saw an old fellow come to the door, and he looked out: he got a shot in the abdomen and fell to his knees and turned around and died. . . .

After that two old men came out, hand in hand. I should think they were over 50 years old, probably between 50 and 70 years old. They had a white flag. They were shot down. At the other end of the town we heard screams, and there was a woman there; she was burned up, and in her arms was a baby, and on the floor was another child. The baby was at her breast, the one in her arms, and this child on the floor was, I should judge, about 3 years of age. They were burned. Whether she was demoralized or driven insane I don't know. She stayed in the house.

———

Source: U.S. Senate, Committee on the Philippines, *Hearings,* 57th Congress, 1st Session (1902).

The decisive outcome confirmed what the Europeans already suspected. After Dewey's naval victory the semiofficial French paper *Le Temps* observed that "what passes before our eyes is the appearance of a new power of the first order." And in a long editorial the London *Times* concluded: "This war must . . . effect a profound change in the whole attitude and policy of the United States. In the future America will play a part in the general affairs of the world such as she has never played before" (see Voices from Abroad, "James Bryce, Jean Hess, and Émile Zola: On American Expansionism," p. 692).

A Power among Powers

The politician most ardently agreeing with the London *Times*'s vision of America's future was the man who,

James Bryce, Jean Hess, Émile Zola

On American Expansionism

———————★———————

*A*merica's emergence as an imperial power provoked much anxious comment abroad. Not surprisingly, this commentary tended to mirror the concerns of the commentators. What was unexpected, as the following excerpts suggest, was how seriously Europeans had taken America's high estimate of itself. If U.S. actions violated professed ideals and traditions, Europeans were not averse to calling the United States to account.

As the debate over Hawaiian annexation raged in late 1897, James Bryce, the renowned British observer, reminded America of the wisdom of the Founding Fathers.

What have the United States to gain by territorial extension? . . . The United States has already a great and splendid mission in building up between the oceans a free, happy, and prosperous nation of two hundred millions of people. And one of the noblest parts of her mission in the world has been to show the older peoples and states an example of abstention from the quarrels and wars and conquests that make up so large and so lamentable a part of the annals of Europe. Her remote position and her immense power have, as I have said, delivered her from that burden of military and naval armaments which presses with crushing weight upon the peoples of Europe. It would be, for her, a descent from what may be called the pedestal of wise and pacific detachment on which she now stands, were she to yield to that earth hunger which has been raging among the European states, and to imitate the aggressive methods which some of them have pursued. The policy of creating great armaments and of annexing territories beyond the sea would be, if a stranger may venture to say so, an

un-American policy, and a complete departure from the maxims—approved by long experience—of the illustrious founders of the republic.

Jean Hess, a Frenchman well traveled in East Asia, questioned in 1899 American motives for intervening in the Philippines.

Nowhere, in my opinion, better than in the Philippines, has it been shown that modern wars are simply "deals." The American intervention in the struggle engaged in by the revolutionary Tagals [Filipinos] against the Spanish government has turned out to be nothing but a speculation of "business men," and not the generous effort of a people paying a debt in procuring for others the liberty that it concedes belongs to all. . . . Back of all these battles, this devastation and mourning, in spite of the newly-born Yankee imperialism, there was only, there is only, what the people of the Bourse [stock market] call a deal.

Writing in 1900, Émile Zola, the great French novelist, feared that America's military adventurism was dealing a blow to the cause of world peace.

I know that, for belief in peace and future disarmament, the time is scarcely auspicious, as we are now beholding an alarming recrudescence of militarism. Nations which till now seem to have held aloof from the contagion, to have escaped this madness so prevalent in Europe, now appear to be attacked. Thus, since the Spanish war, the United States seems to have become a victim of the war fever. . . . I can see in that great nation a dangerous inclination toward war. I can detect the generation of vague ideas of future conquest. Until the present time that country wisely occupied itself with its domestic affairs and let Europe severely alone, but now it is donning plumes and epaulets, and will be dreaming of possible campaigns and be carried away with the idea of military glory—notions so perilous as to have been responsible for the downfall of nations.

———————————

Source: Philip S. Foner and Robert C. Winchester, eds., *The Anti-Imperialist Reader: A Documentary History of Anti-Imperialism in the United States* (New York: Holmes and Meier Publishers, 1984), vol. 1: 98–99, 417–418.

with the assassination of William McKinley, became president on September 14, 1901: Theodore Roosevelt. An avid student of foreign affairs, Roosevelt had widely traveled abroad and was acquainted with many of the European leaders. He had no doubt about America's role in the world.

It was important, first of all, to uphold the country's honor in the community of nations. "I am not hostile to any European power in the abstract," Roosevelt once wrote. "I am simply American first and last, and therefore hostile to any power which wrongs us." Nor should the country ever shrink from righteous battle. "All the great masterful races have been fighting races," Roosevelt declared. But when he spoke of war, Roosevelt had in mind actions by the "civilized" nations against "backward peoples" (such as the Filipinos, whose struggle for freedom was being subdued when he entered the White House). Roosevelt felt "it incumbent on all civilized and orderly powers to insist on the proper policing of the world." That was why he sympathized with European imperialism and how he justified American dominance over the Caribbean states.

As for the "civilized and orderly" policemen of the world, the worst thing that could happen was for them to fall to fighting among themselves. Roosevelt had an acute sense of the fragility of world peace, and he was farsighted about the likelihood—in this he was truly exceptional among Americans—of a catastrophic world war. He believed in American responsibility for helping to maintain the balance of power.

Anglo-American Amity. After the Spanish-American War, the European powers had been uncertain about how to deal with the victor. Germany toyed briefly with the notion of an American alliance, but only Great Britain had a clear view of what it wanted from the United States. In the late nineteenth century Britain's position in Europe was steadily worsening in the face of industrial and military challenges by a unified Germany. Clashing expansionist ambitions in North Africa and across Asia soured Britain's relations with France and Russia. And there was general European hostility toward British imperial policy in South Africa, a policy that resulted in the Boer War against the independent-minded Dutch settlers at the end of the 1890s. In its growing isolation Britain turned to the United States. This explains why Britain bowed to American demands in the Venezuela dispute of 1895. From that time onward, after a century of cool relations (or worse) with its former colonies in North America, Britain strove for *rapprochement* (literally, a "coming together") with the United States.

In the Hay-Pauncefote Agreement of 1901 Britain gave up its treaty rights to joint participation in any Central American canal project, clearing the way for a canal exclusively under U.S. control. And two years later the last of the vexing U.S.–Canadian border disputes—this one involving British Columbia and Alaska—was settled, again to American satisfaction. The lone British member of the U.S.–Canadian tribunal cast the deciding vote, awarding to the United States the Pacific inlets and ports that provided the only convenient access to the Klondike goldfields of the Canadian Yukon.

No formal alliance was forthcoming, but Anglo-American friendship was so firm that British planners after 1901 based their war plans on the assumption that America was "a kindred state with whom we shall never have a parricidal war." Roosevelt heartily agreed: "Eng-land and the United States, beyond any other two powers, should be friendly." In his unflagging efforts to maintain a global balance of power, the cornerstone of Roosevelt's policy was the British relationship.

The Big Stick. Among nations, however, what counted was strength, not merely goodwill. Roosevelt wanted "to make all foreign powers understand that when we have adopted a line of policy we have adopted it definitely, and with the intention of backing it up with deeds as well as words." As Roosevelt famously said: "Speak softly and carry a big stick." By a "big stick," he meant above all naval power.

Under Roosevelt, the battleship program (see New Technology, pp. 678–679) went on apace. By 1904 the U.S. Navy stood fifth in the world, and by 1907 it was third. At the top of Roosevelt's agenda, however, was a canal across Central America. Indeed, the Spanish-American War had demonstrated that strategic need in the most graphic way: the entire country had waited breathlessly while the battleship *Oregon* steamed at full speed from the Pacific around the tip of South America to join the final action against the Spanish fleet in Cuba.

The Panama Canal. After Britain's surrender of its joint rights in 1901, Roosevelt proceeded to the more troublesome task of leasing from Colombia the needed strip of land across Panama, which was a Colombian province. To this end, the United States had purchased from the New Panama Canal Company the assets of de Lesseps's earlier project. The Colombian legislature, however, voted down the proposed treaty, partly because the company's rights were about to expire and the lease to the United States could then be renegotiated on terms more favorable to Colombia. Furious over what seemed to him a breach of faith, Roosevelt contemplated outright seizure of Panama but settled on a more devious solution.

The key intermediary in the sale of the de Lesseps assets, an engineer named Philippe Bunau-Varilla, let Roosevelt know that an independence movement was brewing in Panama. The United States in turn informed Bunau-Varilla that American ships were steaming toward Panama. The idea was that the Americans would covertly assist the expected uprising. But when the cruiser *Nashville* arrived at Colón, on Panama's northern coast, there was a mix-up and the American commander failed to prevent the landing of 400 troops sent by the Colombian government to hold the province. Using their wits, the conspirators managed to keep these troops from proceeding to Panama City, where the bloodless revolution against Colombian rule went off on schedule. On November 7, 1903, the United States recognized Panama. Less than two weeks later, with Bunau-Varilla serving as the representative of the new republic, Panama signed a treaty that granted the

The Panama Canal

The Canal Zone was acquired through devious means from which Americans could take little pride (and which led in 1978 to the Senate's decision to restore the property to Panama). But the building of the Panama Canal itself was a triumph of American ingenuity and drive. Dr. William C. Gorgas cleaned out the malarial mosquitoes that had earlier stymied the French. Under Colonel George W. Goethals, the U.S. Army overcame formidable obstacles in a mighty feat of engineering. This photograph shows the massive effort underway in December 1904 to excavate the Culebra Cut so that oceangoing ships would be able to pass through.
Corbis-Bettmann.

United States a perpetually renewable lease on a canal zone. Roosevelt never regretted the victimization of Colombia, although the United States, as a kind of conscience money, paid Colombia $25 million in 1922.

Building the canal was one of the heroic engineering feats of the twentieth century, involving a swamp-clearing project to rid the area of malaria and yellow fever, the construction of a series of great locks, and the excavation of 240 million cubic yards of earth. It took the U.S. Army Corps of Engineers eight years to finish the huge project. When the Panama Canal opened in 1914, it gave the United States a commanding commercial and strategic position in the Western Hemisphere (Map 21.2).

Policeman of the Caribbean.   Next came the task of making the Caribbean basin secure. The countries there, said Secretary of State Elihu Root, had been placed "in the front yard of the United States" by the Panama Canal. Therefore, as Roosevelt put it, they had to "behave themselves."

In the case of Cuba, good behavior was readily managed in the settlement that followed the Spanish-American War. Before the United States withdrew from Cuba in 1902, it reorganized Cuban finances and concluded a swamp-clearing program that eliminated yellow fever, a disease that had ravaged Cuba for many years (and had killed probably 4,000 of the occupying U.S. troops). As a condition for gaining independence, Cuba was required to include in its constitution a proviso called the Platt amendment, which gave the United States the right to intervene if Cuban independence was threatened or if Cuba failed to maintain internal order. Cuba also granted the United States a lease on Guantánamo Bay, where the U.S. Navy built a large base.

Roosevelt believed that instability in the Caribbean invited the intervention of European powers. For example, Britain and Germany blockaded Venezuela in 1902–1903 for failing to meet its debt payments. In 1904 Roosevelt announced that the United States would act as "policeman" of the region, stepping in

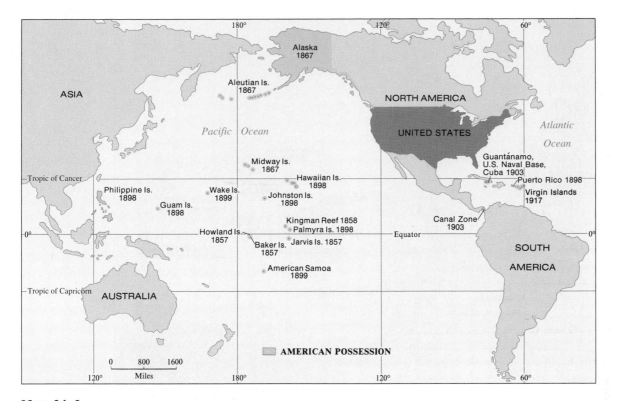

MAP 21.2

The American Empire

In 1890 Alfred T. Mahan wrote that the United States should regard the oceans as "a great highway" across which America would carry on world trade. That was precisely what resulted from the empire the United States acquired after the Spanish-American War. The Caribbean possessions, the strategically located Pacific islands, and, in 1903, the Panama Canal Zone gave the United States commercial and naval access to a wider world.

"however reluctantly, in flagrant cases . . . of wrong doing or impotence." This policy became known as the Roosevelt Corollary to the Monroe Doctrine, transforming that doctrine's broad principle of opposition to European interference in Latin America into the unrestricted right of the United States to regulate Caribbean affairs. The Roosevelt Corollary was not a treaty with other states; it was a unilateral declaration sanctioned only by American power and national interest.

Citing the Roosevelt Corollary, the United States intervened regularly in the internal affairs of Caribbean states. In 1905 American authorities took over the customs and debt management of the Dominican Republic, and similar financial supervision was imposed on Nicaragua in 1911 and on Haiti in 1916. When internal order broke down, the United States did not hesitate to send in the marines. Cuba was occupied in 1906, Nicaragua in 1909, Haiti and the Dominican Republic in later years (Map 21.3).

Roosevelt's thinking was primarily strategic; his successor, William Howard Taft, took a more commercial view. American investments in the Caribbean region grew dramatically after 1900. United Fruit Company owned about 160,000 acres in Central America by 1913, and U.S.

investments in Cuban sugar plantations quadrupled in fifteen years. Taft quickly intervened when disorder threatened American property. But he also regarded business investment as a force for stability in underdeveloped areas. Taft spoke for *dollar diplomacy*—the aggressive coupling of American diplomatic and economic interests abroad.

The Open Door in Asia

Commercial interests dominated American policy in East Asia, especially the prospect of the huge China market. But by the late 1890s Japan, Russia, Germany, France, and Britain had all carved out spheres of influence in China and instituted discriminatory trade practices in their zones. Fearful that the United States was being frozen out, Secretary of State John Hay in 1899 sent them an "open-door" note advancing the right of equal trade access—an open door—for all nations that wanted to do business in China. Despite U.S. control of the Philippines, the United States lacked real leverage and received no better than ambiguous and noncommittal responses from the occupying powers. But Hay chose to interpret them as accepting the American open-door position.

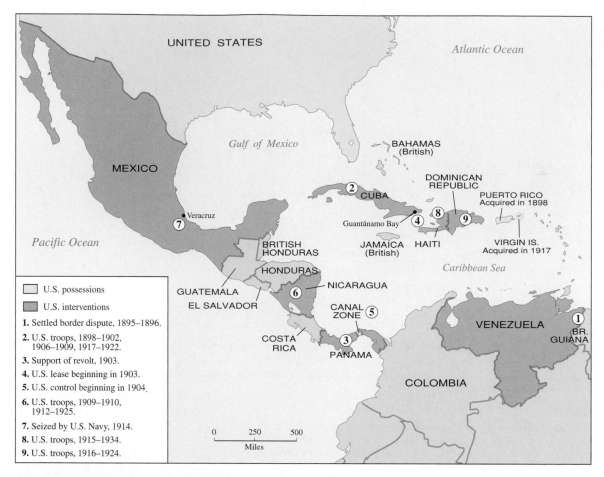

MAP 21.3
Policeman of the Caribbean
After the Spanish-American War the United States vigorously asserted its interest in the affairs of its neighbors to the south. As the record of interventions shows, the United States truly became the "policeman" of the Caribbean.

When a secret society of Chinese nationalists, the Boxers, rebelled against the foreigners in 1900, the United States sent 5,000 troops from the Philippines and joined the multinational campaign to raise the siege of the diplomatic missions in Peking (Beijing). America took this opportunity to assert a second principle of the open door: that China would be preserved as a "territorial and administrative entity." As long as the legal fiction of an independent China survived, so would American claims to equal access to the China market.

The European powers had acceded to American claims to preeminence in the Caribbean. But Britain, Germany, France, and Russia were strongly entrenched in East Asia and not inclined to defer to American interests. The United States also confronted a powerful Asian nation—Japan—that had its own vital interests. Although the open-door policy was important to him, Roosevelt quickly saw in the Pacific a deadlier game that called for American involvement.

Japan had unveiled its military strength in the Sino-Japanese War of 1894–1895, which began the dis-

memberment of China. With the formation of the Anglo-Japanese Alliance in 1902, the strategic advantage in East Asia shifted to Japan, emboldening Japan to confront Russia over their rival claims in Manchuria and Korea. In 1904, provoked by Russian demands for a military withdrawal from northern Korea, Japan suddenly attacked the Russian fleet at Port Arthur, Russia's leased port in China. In a series of brilliant victories the Japanese smashed the Russian military forces in Asia. Eager to restore some semblance of a balance of power, Roosevelt mediated a settlement of the Russo-Japanese War at Portsmouth, New Hampshire, in 1905. Japan emerged as the predominant power in East Asia.

Contemptuous of other Asian nations, Roosevelt admired the Japanese—"a wonderful and civilized people . . . entitled to stand in absolute equality with all the other peoples of the civilized world." He conceded that Japan had "a paramount interest in what surrounds the Yellow Sea, just as the United States has a paramount interest in what surrounds the Caribbean." But American strategic and commercial interests in the

The Japanese in California
The Japanese who flocked into California from 1890 onward made a mighty contribution to the state's agriculture, and through tireless labor many of them became independent and highly productive farmers. But the prejudice against them was unrelenting, and when San Francisco's school board sought to segregate Japanese children in 1906, an international incident occurred. President Roosevelt got the segregation order rescinded, and Japan voluntarily agreed to limit immigration to the United States. Despite this so-called Gentlemen's Agreement, a festering wound had been opened in the relations between the two countries.
Pat Hathaway Collection of California Views.

Pacific had to be accommodated. In exchange for Japanese acceptance of American sovereignty over the Philippines, the United States approved of Japan's protectorate over Korea in 1905 and then of its claim of full sovereignty six years later. However, a surge of anti-Asian feeling in California complicated Roosevelt's efforts. In 1906 San Francisco's school board placed all Asian students in a segregated school, infuriating Japan. In 1907 a "Gentlemen's Agreement" in which Japan agreed to restrict immigration to the United States smoothed matters over, but periodic resurgences of racism in California led to continuing tensions with the Japanese.

Roosevelt meanwhile moved to balance Japan's military power by increasing American naval strength in the Pacific. American battleships visited Japan in 1908 and then made a global tour in an impressive display of sea power. Late that year, near the end of his administration, Roosevelt achieved a formal accommodation with Japan. The Root-Takahira Agreement confirmed the status quo in the Pacific as well as the principles of free oceanic commerce and equal trade opportunity in China.

William Howard Taft, however, entered the White House in 1909 convinced that the United States had been shortchanged. He pressed for a larger role for American bankers and investors in East Asia, especially in the railroad construction going on in China. An exponent of dollar diplomacy, Taft hoped that American capital would counterbalance Japanese power and pave the way for increased commercial opportunities. When the Chinese Revolution of 1911 toppled the ruling Manchu dynasty, Taft supported the Chinese Nationalists as a counterforce to the Japanese. The United States thus entered a long-term rivalry with Japan that would end in war thirty years later.

The United States had become embroiled in a distant struggle that promised many future liabilities but few of the fabulous profits that had lured Americans to Asia.

Woodrow Wilson and Mexico

When Woodrow Wilson became president in 1913, he was bent on reform in American foreign policy no less than in domestic politics. Wilson did not really differ with his predecessors on the importance of economic development overseas. He applauded the "tides of commerce" that would arise from the Panama Canal. But he opposed dollar diplomacy, which bullied weaker countries into inequitable financial relationships and gave undue advantage to American business. It seemed to Wilson "a very perilous thing to determine the foreign policy of a nation in terms of material interest."

Within two weeks of taking office, Wilson demonstrated what he had in mind. American banks had joined an international consortium to provide a loan to China. When the investment banker J. P. Morgan sought Wilson's approval, the president refused on the grounds that the terms of the loan threatened the independence of the Chinese government. The plan "was obnoxious to the principles upon which the government of our people rests."

The United States, Wilson insisted, should conduct its foreign policy in conformity with its democratic principles. He intended to foster the "development of constitutional liberty in the world" and, above all, to extend it to the nation's neighbors in Latin America. In a major policy speech in October 1913 Wilson promised those nations that the United States would "never again seek one additional foot of territory by conquest." The president committed himself to advancing "human rights, national integrity, and opportunity" in Latin America. To do otherwise would make "ourselves untrue to our own traditions." Guided by such a moral policy, future generations would arrive at "those great heights where there shines unobstructed the light of the justice of God."

Mexico became the primary object of Wilson's ministrations. A cycle of revolutions had begun there in 1911. The dictator Porfirio Díaz was overthrown by Francisco Madero, who spoke much as Wilson did about liberty and constitutionalism. But before Madero got very far with his reforms, he was deposed and murdered in February 1913 by one of his generals, Victoriano Huerta. Other powers quickly recognized Huerta's provisional government, but the United States did not, despite America's longstanding tradition of granting quick recognition to new governments. Wilson abhorred Huerta, called him a murderer, and pledged "to force him out."

Wilson also subjected Mexico to other pressures, including the threatened use of force. By intervening in this way, Wilson insisted, "we act in the interest of Mexico alone. . . . We are seeking to counsel Mexico for its own good." Wilson meant that he intended to put the Mexican Revolution back on the constitutional path started by Madero. Wilson was not deterred by the fact that American business interests, with enormous investments in Mexico, favored Huerta. On the contrary, that seemed to spur Wilson on.

The emergence of armed opposition to Huerta in northern Mexico under Venustiano Carranza strengthened Wilson's hand. Carranza's Constitutionalist movement gave Wilson some grounds for denying recognition to Huerta, whose government did not fully control the country. More important, Carranza signified to Wilson the vitality of the reformist politics he wanted to foster in Mexico.

But the Constitutionalists, ardent nationalists, had no desire for American intervention in Mexican affairs. Carranza angrily rebuffed Wilson's efforts to bring about elections through a compromise between the rebels and the Huerta government. He also promised to resist by force any intrusion of U.S. troops into his country. All he wanted from Wilson, Carranza asserted, was recognition of the Constitutionalists' belligerent status, so that they could purchase arms in the United States. In exchange for vague promises to respect property rights and "fair" foreign concessions, Carranza finally got his way in 1914. American weapons began to flow to his troops.

When it became clear that Huerta was not about to fall, the United States threw its own forces into the conflict. On the pretext of a minor insult to the U.S. Navy at Tampico, Wilson ordered the occupation of the major port of Veracruz on April 21, 1914, at the cost of 19 American and 126 Mexican lives. At that point the Huerta regime began to crumble. Carranza nevertheless condemned the United States, and his forces came close to engaging the Americans. When he entered Mexico City in triumph in August 1914, Carranza had some cause to thank the Yankees. But if any sense of gratitude existed, it was overshadowed by the anti-Americanism inspired by Wilson's insensitivity to Mexican pride and revolutionary zeal.

The later phases of the Mexican Revolution dragged the United States ever more deeply into the morass of interventionism. No sooner had the Constitutionalists triumphed than Carranza was challenged by his northern general, Pancho Villa, who was encouraged by some American interests in Mexico. Defeated and driven northward, Villa began to stir up trouble along the border, in January 1916 killing sixteen American civilians taken from a train and two months later attacking the town of Columbus, New Mexico. Wilson sent troops led by General John J. Pershing into Mexico after the elusive Villa. Soon Pershing's force resembled an army of occupation rather than a punitive expedition. Mexican public opinion demanded that Pershing withdraw, and armed clashes with Mexican troops began. At the brink of war, the two governments backed off, and U.S. forces began to leave in early 1917. Soon after, with a new constitution ratified and elections completed, the Carranza government finally received official recognition from Washington.

The Gathering Storm in Europe

In the meantime, Europe had begun to drift toward world war. There were two main sources of tension. One was the deadly rivalry between Germany, the new military and economic superpower of Europe, and the European states threatened by its might—above all France, which had been humiliated in the Franco-Prussian War of 1870 and forced to cede the Alsace-Lorraine provinces to Germany. The second danger zone was the Balkans, where the Ottoman Empire was disintegrating and where, in the midst of explosive ethnic rivalries, Austria-Hungary and Russia were maneuvering for dominance. Out of these conflicts an alliance system had emerged: Germany, Austria-Hungary, and Italy (the Triple Alliance) were on one side, France and Russia (the Dual Alliance) on the other.

The tensions in Europe were partially released by European imperial adventures, especially by France in Africa and by Russia in Asia. These activities placed France and Russia in opposition to imperial Britain, effectively excluding Britain from the European alliance system. Fearful of Germany, however, Britain in 1904 resolved its differences with France, and the two countries reached a friendly understanding, or *entente*. In 1907 Britain came to a similar understanding with Russia, and the basis was laid for the Triple Entente. A deadly confrontation between two great European power blocs became possible.

In these European quarrels Americans had no obvious stake nor any inclination, in the words of a cau-

In Pursuit of Pancho Villa
Pancho Villa's attacks on American citizens prompted General Pershing's punitive expedition into Mexico in 1916. U.S. troops captured some of Villa's followers, but he and his main force escaped. It was an early lesson about the difficulties Great Powers have against a guerrilla foe able to melt away into a larger civilian society.
Corbis-Bettmann.

tionary Senate resolution, "to depart from the traditional American foreign policy which forbids participation . . . [in] political questions which are entirely European in scope." But on becoming president, Theodore Roosevelt took a lively interest in European affairs and was eager, as the head of a Great Power, to make a contribution to the cause of peace in Europe. In 1905 he got his chance.

The Moroccan Crisis. The Anglo-French entente of the previous year was based partly on an agreement over spheres of influence in North Africa: the Sudan was conceded to Britain, Morocco to France. Then Germany suddenly challenged France over Morocco—a disastrous move, conflicting with Germany's self-interest in keeping France's attention diverted from Europe. The German ruler, Kaiser Wilhelm, turned to Roosevelt for help. Finding in an obscure commercial treaty with Morocco the basis for American involvement, Roosevelt persuaded France to attend an international conference, which was held in January 1906 at Algeciras, Spain. With U.S. diplomats playing a key role, the crisis was defused. Germany got a few token concessions, but France's dominance over Morocco was sustained.

Algeciras marked an ominous turning point—the first time the power blocs that would become locked in battle in 1914 squared off against one another. But in 1906 the outcome of the conference seemed a diplomatic triumph, and Roosevelt's secretary of state, Elihu Root, boasted of America's success in "preserv[ing] world peace because of the power of our detachment."

Root's words prefigured how the United States would define its role among the Great Powers: it would be the apostle of peace, distinguished by its "detachment," by its lack of selfish interests in European affairs. Opposing this internationalist impulse, however, was America's strongly held isolationism.

The Peace Movement. Americans had applauded the international peace movement launched by the Hague Peace Conference of 1899. The Permanent Court of Arbitration created by the Hague conference offered new hope for the peaceful settlement of international disputes. Both the Roosevelt and the Taft administrations negotiated arbitration treaties with other countries, pledging to submit disputes to the Hague Court, only to see the treaties emasculated by a Senate unwilling to compromise the nation's sovereignty. Nor was there any sequel to Roosevelt's initiative at Algeciras. It was coolly received in the Senate and by the nation's press. Roosevelt's successor, William Howard Taft, was not inclined to challenge the doctrine of nonentanglement.

When Wilson became president, he chose William Jennings Bryan to be secretary of state. A great apostle of world peace, Bryan devoted himself to negotiating a series of "cooling off" treaties with other countries—so called because the parties agreed to wait for one year before taking other measures while disputed issues were submitted to a conciliation process. Though admirable, these bilateral agreements had no bearing on the explosive power politics of Europe. As tensions there reached the breaking point in 1914, the United States remained effectively on the sidelines.

Yet at Algeciras Roosevelt had correctly anticipated what the future would demand of America. So did the French writer Andre Tardieu, who remarked in 1908:

> The United States is . . . a world power. . . . Its power creates for it . . . a duty—to pronounce upon all those questions that hitherto have been arranged by agreement only among European powers. These powers themselves, at critical times, turn toward the United States, anxious to know its opinion. . . . The United States . . . is seated at the table where the great game is played, and it cannot leave it.

Summary

In 1877 the United States was, by any economic or population measure, already a great power. But America was inward-looking. The lax conduct of its foreign policy and the neglect of its naval power reflected the absence of significant overseas concerns. America's rapid economic development, however, began to force the country to look outward, in particular because of the felt need for outlets for its surplus products. By the early 1890s a new strategic outlook had taken hold, best expressed in the writings of Alfred Thayer Mahan. Mahan called for a battleship navy, an interoceanic canal, and overseas bases from which American naval power could be projected to ensure access to markets in Latin America and Asia. Supporting this new expansionism were arguments drawn from social Darwinism, Anglo-Saxon racism, and America's earlier tradition of Manifest Destiny.

The Spanish-American War created an opportunity for acting on these imperialist impulses. Swift victory enabled the United States to seize from Spain the key possessions it wanted, while wartime patriotism briefly silenced America's traditional antiexpansionism. In taking the Philippines, however, the United States overstepped the bounds of the limited kind of colonialism palatable to the country—overseas bases, not dominance over alien populations. The result was a resurgence of anti-imperialist sentiment that was deepened by Filipino resistance to American rule. Even so, the McKinley administration achieved the strategic goals it had set, and the United States entered the twentieth century poised to fulfill its destiny as a Great Power.

In Europe the immediate consequences were few. Only in its *rapprochement* with Britain and in Roosevelt's involvement in the Moroccan crisis did the United States begin to depart from its traditional policy of avoiding European entanglements. But in the Caribbean and Asia, where it had strong regional interests, the United States moved more decisively, building the Panama Canal, asserting its dominance over the nearby states, and pressing for the open door in China. In Japan, however, the United States encountered a formidable opponent whose interests were not easily reconciled with America's. When Woodrow Wilson became president, he tried to bring the conduct of America's foreign policy into closer conformity with the nation's political ideals, only to have the limitations of that approach driven home by his intervention in the Mexican Revolution. As world war engulfed Europe in 1914, Wilson's idealism was about to receive a much harder test.

TIMELINE

1875	Treaty brings Hawaii within U.S. orbit
1876	United States achieves favorable balance of trade
1881	Secretary of State James G. Blaine inaugurates Pan-Americanism
1889	Conflict with Germany in Samoa
1890	Alfred Thayer Mahan's *The Influence of Seapower upon History*
1893	Annexation of Hawaii fails
	Frederick Jackson Turner's "The Significance of the Frontier in American History"
	Panic of 1893 ushers in economic depression (until 1897)
1894	Sino-Japanese War begins breakup of China into spheres of influence
1895	Venezuela crisis
	Cuban civil war
1898	Outbreak of Spanish-American War
	Hawaii annexed
	Anti-imperialist movement launched
1899	Treaty of Paris
	Guerrilla war in the Philippines
	Open-door policy in China
1901	Theodore Roosevelt becomes president; diplomacy of the "big stick"
	Hay-Pauncefote Agreement
1902	U.S. withdraws from Cuba; Platt amendment gives United States right of intervention
1903	U.S. recognizes Panama and receives grant of Canal Zone
1904	Roosevelt Corollary
1906	U.S. mediates Franco-German crisis over Morocco at Algeciras
1907	Gentlemen's Agreement with Japan
1908	Root-Takahira Agreement
1909	Taft becomes president; dollar diplomacy
1913	Wilson asserts new principles for American diplomacy
	Intervention in the Mexican Revolution
1914	Panama Canal opens
	World War I begins

Suggested Readings

Two useful surveys of late nineteenth-century diplomatic history are Charles S. Campbell, *The Transformation of American Foreign Relations, 1865–1900* (1976), and Walter LaFeber, *The American Search for Opportunity, 1865–1913* (vol. 2, *The Cambridge History of American Foreign Relations*, 1993). Invaluable as a historiographical guide is Robert L. Beisner, *From the Old Diplomacy to the New, 1865–1900* (2nd ed., 1986).

The Roots of Expansionism

Standard works on the preexpansionist era are David M. Pletcher, *The Awkward Years: American Foreign Relations under Garfield and Arthur* (1963), and Milton Plesur, *America's Outward Thrust: Approaches to American Foreign Affairs, 1865–1890* (1971). Walter LaFeber's highly influential *The New Empire, 1860–1898* (1963) places economic interest—especially the need for overseas markets—at the center of scholarly debate over the sources of American expansionism. On American business overseas the definitive work is Myra Wilkins, *The Emergence of the Multinational Enterprise: American Business Abroad from the Colonial Era to 1914* (1970). Other important books dealing with aspects of American expansionism are David Healy, *U.S. Expansionism: The Imperialist Urge in the 1890s* (1970); Robert Seager, *Alfred Thayer Mahan* (1977); Emily S. Rosenberg, *Spreading the American Dream: American Economic and Cultural Expansionism* (1982); Michael Hunt, *Ideology and U.S. Foreign Policy* (1987); Mark R. Shulman, *Navalism and the Emergence of American Sea Power, 1882–1893* (1995); and Kenneth J. Hagan, *This People's Navy: The Making of American Seapower* (1991).

An American Empire

On the war with Spain the liveliest narrative is still Frank Freidel, *A Splendid little War* (1958). For fuller treatments see John Offner, *An Unwanted War: The Diplomacy of the United States and Spain over Cuba, 1895–1898* (1988); David S. Trask, *The War with Spain in 1898* (1981); Ivan Musicant, *Empire by Default* (1998); and Lewis Gould, *The Spanish-American War and President McKinley* (1982), which emphasizes McKinley's strong leadership. Ernest R. May, *Imperial Democracy: The Emergence of America as a Great Power* (1961), exemplifies the earlier view that McKinley was a weak figure driven to war by jingoistic pressures. On the Philippines see Richard E. Welch, *Response to Imperialism: The United States and the Philippine-American War, 1898–1903* (1979), and, for the subsequent history, Peter Stanley, *A Nation in the Making: The Philippines and the United States, 1899–1921* (1974). Robert L. Beisner, *Twelve against Empire: The Anti-Imperialists, 1898–1900* (1968), remains the best book on that subject.

Onto the World Stage

On the European context a useful introduction can be found in the early chapters of Felix Gilbert, *The End of the European Era, 1890 to the Present* (4th ed., 1991). For a stimulating interpretation see L. C. B. Seaman, *From Vienna to Versailles* (1955). On American relations with Britain the standard work is Bradford Perkins, *The Great Rapprochement: England and the United States, 1895–1914* (1968). On Roosevelt's diplomacy the starting point remains Howard K. Beale, *Theodore Roosevelt and the Rise of America to World Power* (1956). There are keen insights into the diplomatic views of both Roosevelt and Wilson in John Milton Cooper, *The Warrior and the Priest* (1983). On the thrust into the Caribbean see Walter LaFeber, *The Panama Canal* (1979); Richard Lael, *Arrogant Diplomacy: U.S. Policy toward Colombia, 1903–1922* (1987); David Healy, *Drive to Hegemony: the United States in the Caribbean, 1898–1917* (1988); and Thomas D. Schoonover, *The United States in Central America, 1860–1911* (1991). America's Asian involvements are treated in Thomas J. McCormick, *China Market: America's Quest for Informal Empire, 1893–1901* (1967); Michael H. Hunt, *The Making of a Special Relationship: The United States and China to 1914* (1983); and Akira Iriye, *Pacific Estrangement: Japanese and American Expansion, 1897–1911* (1972). On the Mexican involvement see John S. D. Eisenhower, *Intervention! The United States and the Mexican Revolution* (1993). There is a lively and critical analysis of Wilson's misguided policies in Robert E. Quirk, *An Affair of Honor: Woodrow Wilson and the Occupation of Veracruz* (1962). The revolution as experienced by the Mexicans is brilliantly depicted in John Womack, *Zapata and the Mexican Revolution* (1968). The standard work on the American peace movement is Roland Marchand, *The American Peace Movement and Social Reform, 1898–1918* (1973).

Part Five

★

The Modern State and Society, 1914–1945

THEMATIC TIMELINE

	Government	Diplomacy	Economy	Society	Culture
	The Rise of the State	From Isolation to World Leadership	Prosperity, Depression, and War	Nativism, Migration, and Social Change	The Emergence of a Mass National Culture
1914	Wartime agencies expand power of the federal government	United States enters World War I (1917) Wilson's Fourteen Points (1918)	Shift from debtor to creditor nation Agricultural glut	Southern blacks begin migration to northern cities	Silent screen; Hollywood becomes movie capital of the world
1920	Republican ascendancy Prohibition (1920–1933) Business-government partnership	Treaty of Versailles rejected by U.S. Senate (1920) Washington Conference sets naval limits (1922)	Economic recession (1920–1921) Booming prosperity (1922–1929) Rise of welfare capitalism	Rise of nativism National Origins Act (1924) Mexican American immigration increases	Jazz Age (1920s) Advertising promotes consumer culture, supports radio and new magazines
1930	Franklin D. Roosevelt becomes president (1933) The New Deal: unprecedented government intervention in economy, social welfare, arts	Roosevelt's Good Neighbor Policy toward Latin America (1933) Abraham Lincoln Brigade fights in Spanish Civil War U.S. neutrality proclaimed (1939)	Great Depression (1929–1941) Rise of labor movement	Farming families migrate from Dust Bowl states to California and the West Indian New Deal	Documentary impulse Federal patronage of the arts
1940	Government mobilizes industry for war production and rationing	United States enters World War II (1941) Allies defeat Axis powers; bombing of Hiroshima (1945)	War mobilization ends depression	Rural whites and blacks migrate to war jobs in cities Civil rights movement revitalized	Film industry enlisted to aid war effort

By 1914 INDUSTRIALIZATION, economic expansion abroad, massive immigration, and the growth of a vibrant urban culture had set the foundations for a distinctly *modern* American society. In all facets of politics, the economy, and daily life, American society was becoming more organized, more bureaucratic, and more complex. By 1945, after having fought in two world wars and weathering a dozen years of economic depression, the edifice of the new society was largely complete.

Government. First, an essential building block of modern American society was a strong national state. This state came late and haltingly to America compared with that of the industrialized countries of Western Europe. American participation in World War I called forth an unprecedented mobilization of the domestic economy, but policy makers quickly dismantled the centralized wartime bureaucracies in 1919. During the 1920s the Harding and Coolidge administrations embraced a philosophy of business-government partnership, believing that unrestricted corporate capitalism would provide for the welfare of the American people. Ultimately the Great Depression, with its uncounted business failures and unprecedented levels of unemployment, overthrew that long-cherished idea. Franklin D. Roosevelt's New Deal dramatically expanded federal responsibility for the economy and the welfare of ordinary citizens. An even greater expansion of the national state resulted from the massive mobilization necessitated by America's entry into World War II. Unlike the experience after World War I, the new state apparatus remained in place when the war ended.

Diplomacy. Second, America was slowly and somewhat reluctantly drawn into a position of world leadership, which it continues to hold today. World War I provided the major impetus: before 1914 the world had been dominated by Europe, but from that point on the United States increasingly dominated the world. In 1918 American troops provided the margin of victory for the Allies, and President Wilson helped shape the treaties that ended the war. The United States, however, refused to join the League of Nations. America's dominant economic position guaranteed an active role in world affairs in the 1920s and 1930s nonetheless. The globalization of America accelerated in 1941, when the nation threw all its energies into a second world war that had its roots in the imperfect settlement of the first one. Of all the powers that participated in this most devastating of global conflagrations, only America emerged physically unscathed from World War II. The country was also the only one to possess a dangerous new weapon—the atomic bomb. Within wartime decisions and strategies lay the roots of the Cold War that followed.

Economy. Third, modern America developed a strong domestic economy. In fact, between 1914 and 1945 the nation's industrial economy was the most productive in the world. Even the Great Depression, which hit the United States harder than any other industrialized nation, did not permanently affect America's global economic standing. Indeed, American businesses successfully competed in world markets, and American financial institutions played the leading role in international economic affairs. Large-scale corporate organizations replaced smaller family-run businesses. The automobile industry symbolized the ascendancy of mass-production techniques. Many workers shared in the general prosperity but also bore the brunt of economic downturns. These uncertainties fueled the dramatic growth of the labor movement in the 1930s.

Society. Fourth, American society was transformed by the great wave of European immigration and the movement from farms to cities. The growth of metropolitan areas gave the nation an increasingly urban tone, and geographical mobility broke down regional differences. Many old-stock white Americans viewed these processes with alarm; in 1924 nativists succeeded in all but eliminating immigration except from within the Western Hemisphere, where migration across the border from Mexico continued to shape the West and Southwest. In other ways internal migration changed the face of America as African Americans moved north and west to take factory jobs, and Dust Bowl farmers in the 1930s moved to the Far West to find better livelihoods. World War II accelerated these migration patterns even more.

Culture. Fifth, modern America saw the emergence of a mass national culture. By the 1920s Americans were increasingly drawn into a web of interlocking cultural experiences. Advertising and the new entertainment media—movies, radio, and magazines—disseminated the new values of consumerism; the movies exported this vision of the American experience worldwide. Not even the Great Depression could divert Americans from their desire for leisure, self-fulfillment, and consumer goods. The emphasis on consumption and a quest for a rising standard of living would define the American experience for the rest of the twentieth century.

SEPT 29th 1917

Price 10 Cents
In Canada, 15 Cents

Leslie's

Illust____ ___kly Newspaper

Notice to Reader

When you finish reading this magazine place a one cent stamp alongside of this notice, hand same to any postal employe and it will be placed in the hands of our soldiers or sailors at the front.

No wrapping—no address.

A. S. BURLESON,
Postmaster-General

Paul Stahr

Be Patriotic
sign your country's pledge to s ve the food

★

War and the American State,
1914–1920

"IT WOULD BE the irony of fate if my administration had to deal chiefly with foreign affairs," Woodrow Wilson told a friend early in his first term as president. But the United States was no longer just a regional power—it was seated at the table of what the president called the "great game" of international politics. Wilson responded to World War I with the same idealism he had brought to domestic concerns during the Progressive Era (see Chapter 20). In the first major U.S. intervention in Great Power politics, Wilson aimed for a new international order based on democratic ideals.

The American decision to enter the conflict in 1917 confirmed one of the most important shifts of power in the twentieth century. The pre–World War I world had been dominated by Europe; the postwar world was increasingly dominated by the United States. The historian Akira Iriye calls this broad transformation the "globalization" of America: the United States increasingly became "involved in security, economic, and cultural affairs in all parts of the world." This process, which is usually thought to begin with World War II and its aftermath, actually started in 1917.

Victory in a modern, global war involved more than armies. New federal bureaucracies had to be created to coordinate the efforts of business, labor, and agriculture, a process that hastened the emergence of a national administrative state. The federal government became an increased presence in the lives of Americans in everything from conscription to taxation to food conservation. War meant new opportunities, albeit temporary, for women and for blacks and other racial and ethnic minorities. The wartime experience united the nation behind a common goal of military victory, but in the

America and the War Effort
Popular magazines like Leslie's Illustrated Weekly Newspaper *teamed up with the federal government to promote food conservation. If a patriotic reader affixed a 1 cent stamp to the cover's top right corner, the magazine would be sent to soldiers or sailors at the front.*
Leslie's, *September 29, 1917/Picture Research Consultants & Archives.*

process it spawned new divisions among Americans and new hatreds—first of Germans and Austrians, and then of "Bolshevik" Reds. When the war ended, the United States was forced to confront the deep class, racial, and ethnic divisions that had surfaced during wartime mobilization in the Red Scare of 1919.

The Great War, 1914–1918

—★—

When war erupted in August 1914, most Americans saw no reason to get involved in a struggle among Europe's imperialistic powers. No vital American interests were at stake; indeed, the United States had good relationships with both sides. But a combination of factors—economic interests, violations of neutral rights, cultural ties with Great Britain and France, and German miscalculations—drew the United States into the war on the Allied side in 1917.

War in Europe

Almost from the moment France, Russia, and Britain formed the Triple Entente in 1907 to counter the Triple Alliance of Germany, Austria-Hungary, and Italy (see Chapter 21), European leaders began to prepare for what they saw as an inevitable conflict. The spark that ignited war came in Europe's perpetual tinderbox—the Balkans—where Austria-Hungary and Russia competed for power and influence. Austria's seizure of the provinces of Bosnia and Herzegovina in 1908 had enraged Russia and its client, the independent state of Serbia. Serbian terrorists responded by recruiting Bosnians to agitate against Austrian rule. On June 28, 1914, a nineteen-year-old Bosnian student assassinated Franz Ferdinand, the heir to the Austro-Hungarian throne, and his wife in Sarajevo.

After the assassination the complex European system of alliances that had for years maintained a fragile peace pulled all the major powers into war. Austria-Hungary, blaming Serbia for the assassination, declared war on that country on July 28. Russia, which had a secret treaty with Serbia, mobilized its armies; Germany responded by declaring war on Russia and its ally, France, and by invading neutral Belgium. The brutality of the invasion, as well as Britain's commitment to Belgian neutrality, prompted Great Britain to declare war on Germany on August 4. Within a few days all the major European powers had formally entered the conflict.

The combatants were divided into two rival blocs. The Allied Powers—Great Britain, France, Japan, Russia, and, in 1915, Italy—were pitted against the Central Powers: Germany, Austria-Hungary, and Turkey, joined by Bulgaria in 1915 (Map 22.1). Because of the alliance system, the conflict spread to parts of the world far beyond Europe, making this a truly global war. The Austrians and Germans faced the Russians on the Eastern

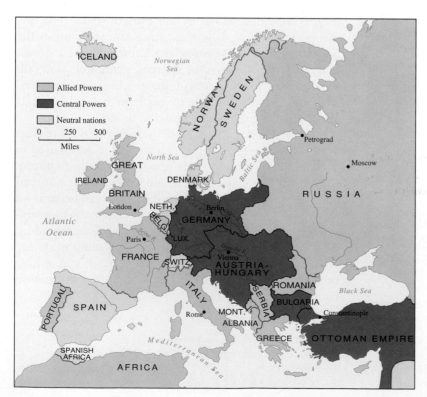

MAP 22.1
Europe at the Start of World War I
In early August 1914 a complex set of interlocking alliances drew the major European powers into war. At first the United States avoided the conflict. Not until April 1917 did America enter the war on the Allied side.

The Landscape of War
World War I devastated the countryside: this was the battleground at Ypres in western
Belgium in 1915. The carnage of trench warfare also scarred the soldiers who served
in these surreal settings, causing "gas neurosis," "burial-alive neurosis," and "soldiers'
heart"—all symptoms of shell shock.
Imperial War Museum, London.

Front; Turkey squared off against Russian and British troops in the Middle East and Mesopotamia; and the British, French, and Japanese seized German territories in Africa, China, and the South Pacific. The worldwide scope of the conflict and the staggering number of resulting casualties caused it to be known as the Great War or, later, World War I. It was also the first modern war in which extensive harm was done to civilian populations.

Modern wars drew on increasingly destructive military technology. Since the American Civil War and the Franco-Prussian War in 1870, massive industrialization and an escalating arms race among the Great Powers had transformed the technology of war. Every soldier in World War I carried a long-range, high-velocity rifle that could hit a target at 1,000 yards, a vast improvement over the 300-yard range of the rifle-musket used in the American Civil War. Significantly, the mass production of rifles in Europe relied on the adoption of technology developed in the United States. Another innovation, the machine gun, also had American roots. Its American inventor,

Hiram Maxim, had heeded a friend's advice when he moved to Great Britain in the 1880s: "If you want to make your fortune, invent something which will allow those fool Europeans to kill each other more quickly."

The concentrated fire of rifles and machine guns gave a tremendous advantage to troops in defensive positions. For four bloody years, between 1914 and 1918, the Allies and the Central Powers faced each other on the Western Front, a narrow swath of territory in Belgium and northern France crisscrossed by 25,000 miles of heavily fortified trenches, enough to circle the globe. (Barbed wire, invented to fence the western range in America, became a devastating weapon of war when coiled above the trenches: if soldiers tried to climb over the barrier or cut the barbed wire, they suffered cuts and lacerations, as well as exposed themselves to enemy sharpshooters, an often deadly situation.) Trench warfare produced unprecedented numbers of casualties. If one side tried to break the stalemate by venturing into the "no-man's land" between the trenches, its soldiers were mowed down by artillery fire or poison gas, first used by the Germans at the Belgian border town of Ypres in April 1915. Between February and December 1916 the French suffered 550,000 casualties and the Germans 450,000 as Germany tried to break through the French lines at Verdun. The front did not move.

The Perils of Neutrality

As the bloody stalemate continued, the United States grappled with its role in the international conflagration. Two weeks after the outbreak of war in Europe, President Wilson had made the American position clear. In a message widely printed in the newspapers, the president called on Americans to be "neutral in fact as well as in name, impartial in thought as well as in action."

Wilson wanted to keep out of war in order to play a larger, not a smaller, role in world affairs. The child of a Presbyterian minister, Wilson approached foreign affairs with missionary zeal. He never doubted the superiority of the Christian values he had learned as a boy or questioned the widely held belief that the United States was better than the rest of the world. Only if he kept America aloof from the European quarrel, Wilson reasoned, could he impartially arbitrate—and influence—its ultimate settlement.

The nation's divided loyalties also influenced Wilson's policy. Many Americans, including Wilson, felt deep cultural ties to the Allies, especially Britain and France. Yet most Irish Americans resented the centuries-long British occupation of their home country and the deferral of Irish home rule, authorized by Parliament in 1914, for the duration of the war. Also, the 10 million immigrants from Germany and Austria-Hungary made up one of the largest and best-established ethnic groups in the United States. Many aspects of German culture, including classical music and Germany's university system, were widely admired. It would not have been easy for Wilson to rally Americans to the Allied side in 1914.

Many isolationist Americans had no sympathy for either side. Pacifist sentiment was diffuse but broad. Progressive Republicans such as Senators Robert La Follette of Wisconsin and George Norris of Nebraska vehemently opposed American participation in the European conflict. Progressive Democrats, including Secretary of State William Jennings Bryan, and many western and southern progressives felt the same. Newly formed pacifist groups, among them the American Union against Militarism and the Women's Peace Party, both founded in 1915, also mobilized popular opposition. Practically the entire political left, led principally by Eugene Debs and the Socialist Party, condemned the war as imperialism, whereas African American leaders such as A. Philip Randolph identified it as a conflict of the white race only. Prominent industrialists, notably Andrew Carnegie and Henry Ford,

bankrolled antiwar activities. In December 1915 Ford spent almost half a million dollars to send more than a hundred men and women to Europe on a "peace ship" to negotiate an end to the war.

Conflict on the High Seas.   With no stake in the territorial struggles among the European powers, the United States might well have remained neutral if the conflict had not spread to a new theater—the high seas. Here the United States initially had as many arguments with Britain as with Germany. The most troublesome issue concerned freedom of the seas and neutrality rights— the freedom to trade with nations on both sides of a conflict. By the end of August 1914 the British had imposed a naval blockade on the Central Powers, hoping to cut off military supplies and starve the German people into submission. But their actions also prevented neutral nations such as the United States from trading with Germany and its allies. The United States chafed at this infringement of its neutrality rights but chose to do little besides complain, largely because the spectacular increase in trade with the Allies more than made up for the lost trade with the Central Powers. American trade with Britain and France grew from $824 million in 1914 to $3.2 billion in 1916, and by 1917 U.S. bankers had lent the Allies $2.5 billion. In contrast, American trade with and loans to Germany in 1917 totaled only $29 million and $27 million, respectively.

To challenge British control of the seas, the German navy launched a devastating new weapon—the U-boat, short for *Unterseeboot* (undersea boat, or submarine). In February 1915, Germany announced a naval blockade of Great Britain: German submarines would attack any ship transporting military supplies to the British Isles. Traditional rules of naval warfare required submarine commanders to warn and search a ship before sinking it. If a submarine surfaced to do this, however, it would lose its greatest advantage—surprise—and leave itself vulnerable to attack. The Germans began sinking enemy ships without warning.

What if a U-boat attacked a neutral trading vessel or unarmed passenger ship by mistake? This situation occurred when the Germans sank a British luxury liner, the *Lusitania*, off the Irish coast on May 7, 1915, killing 1,198 people, including 128 Americans. The attack on the unarmed passenger ship incensed Americans— newspapers branded it a "mass murder"—and prompted President Wilson to send a series of strongly worded protests to Germany.

The *Lusitania* crisis divided Wilson's government into pro- and anti-British factions. Secretary of State William Jennings Bryan resigned in protest, unable to support Wilson's harsh criticism of Germany's violation of neutrality rights while the president remained silent about Britain's violation of American rights with its blockade. The crisis continued until September 1915, when Germany announced that submarine commanders would not attack passenger ships without warning. A temporary lull set into the naval war.

Throughout 1915 and 1916, Wilson tried at several points to mediate an end to the European conflict through his aide, Colonel Edward House. But House concluded that neither side was seriously interested in peace negotiations. Worsening tensions with Germany in turn caused Wilson to rethink his earlier opposition to preparedness. In the fall of 1915 he endorsed a $1 billion buildup of the army and navy, and by 1916 rearmament was well under way.

The 1916 Election. The presidential election of 1916 did not serve as a referendum on the American stance toward the war. The Republican Party passed over the belligerently prowar Theodore Roosevelt in favor of Supreme Court Justice Charles Evans Hughes, a former governor of New York. The Democrats renominated Woodrow Wilson, whose campaign emphasized the progressive reform record he had accomplished during his first term (see Chapter 20). The Democrats also gained votes with their widely circulated campaign slogan, "He kept us out of war." They won a narrow victory over a Republican Party reunited after its 1912 split. Despite getting 3 million more votes than he had in 1912, Wilson defeated Hughes by only about 600,000 votes and by 277 to 254 in the electoral college. That slender margin limited Wilson's options in mobilizing the nation for war and planning the postwar peace.

Toward War. The events of early 1917 further diminished Wilson's hopes of staying out of the conflict. On January 31 Germany, frustrated by the impasse in the land war, announced the resumption of unrestricted submarine attacks. In response, Wilson broke off diplomatic relations with Germany on February 3. A few weeks later the release of the "Zimmermann telegram"

The 1916 Campaign
This campaign van sponsored by the Women's Bureau of the Democratic National Committee linked Woodrow Wilson to the themes of progressivism, prosperity, and preparedness. Note the variation on the popular slogan, "He kept us out of war."
Corbis-Bettmann.

moved the country closer to war. Newspapers published an intercepted communication from Germany's foreign secretary, Arthur Zimmermann, to the German minister in Mexico City, in which Zimmermann urged Mexico to join the Central Powers in the war. In return, Germany promised to help Mexico recover "the lost territory of Texas, New Mexico, and Arizona." When the telegram was made public on February 27, this threat to the territorial integrity of the United States jolted both congressional and public opinion—especially in the West, where support for the war had lagged. Combined with the resumption of unrestricted submarine warfare, the telegram inflamed anti-German sentiment.

Throughout March, U-boats attacked American shipping vessels without warning, sinking three ships on March 18 alone. On April 2, 1917, after consulting his cabinet, Wilson appeared before a special session of Congress to ask for a declaration of war. "It is a fearful thing to lead this great peaceful people into war," Wilson declared. It was a conflict that had already proved extremely costly—millions of Europeans killed, their landscapes and social structures destroyed. America had no selfish aims, he told the country: "We desire no conquest, no dominion. We seek no indemnities for ourselves, no material compensation for the sacrifices we shall freely make. We are but one of the champions of the rights of mankind." In a memorable phrase intended to ennoble America's role, Wilson proposed that U.S. participation in the war would make the world "safe for democracy."

Four days later, on April 6, 1917, the United States declared war on Germany. Reflecting the divided feelings of the country as a whole, the congressional vote was far from unanimous. Six senators and fifty members of the House voted against the action, including Representative Jeannette Rankin of Montana, the first woman elected to Congress. "I want to stand by my country," she declared, "but I cannot vote for war."

Over There

To native-born Americans, Europe seemed a great distance away—literally "over there," as the lyrics of George M. Cohan's popular song described it. After the declaration of war many citizens were surprised to learn that the United States planned to send troops to Europe, optimistically having assumed that the nation's participation could be limited to military and economic aid.

In May 1917 General John J. Pershing, recently returned from the unsuccessful pursuit of Pancho Villa in Mexico (see Chapter 21), traveled to London and Paris to determine how America could best support the war effort. The answer, as Marshal Joseph Joffre of France put it, was clear: "Men, men, and more men." The problem was that the United States had never maintained a large standing army in peacetime. Only about 200,000 soldiers, mostly lifetime volunteers, were on active duty in early 1917. To field a fighting force large enough to enter a global war, the government turned to conscription.

The First Woman in Congress
In 1916, Jeannette Rankin, a former suffrage organizer, became the first woman elected to Congress. Her vote against U.S. entry into World War I cost her a chance for election to the Senate in 1918. In 1940 Rankin again won election to Congress from Montana. True to her lifelong pacifism, she cast the only vote against American entry into World War II.
Corbis-Bettmann.

Conscription. The passage of the Selective Service Act in May 1917 demonstrated the increasing impact of the state on ordinary citizens. Unlike the resistance to the draft during the Civil War, no major riots occurred. The selective service system worked in part because it combined central direction from Washington with local administration and civilian control, and thus did not tread too heavily on the tradition of individual freedom and local autonomy. Draft registration also demonstrated the potential bureaucratic capacity of the American state. On a single day, June 5, 1917, more than 9.5 million men between the ages of twenty-one and thirty registered for military service in their local voting precincts.

Although compliance was not universal, most male citizens went along with the draft's premise of *service*—

WWI Pillow Cover
The three stars on this pillow cover indicated that three family members were fighting in the war. The images in the frames are of President Woodrow Wilson and General John J. Pershing.

a key progressive word—as a responsibility of modern citizenship. By the end of the war almost 4 million men, plus several thousand female navy clerks and army nurses, were in uniform. Another 300,000 men—known as slackers—evaded the draft, and 4,000 were classified as conscientious objectors.

Wilson chose General Pershing to head the American Expeditionary Force (AEF), but the newly raised army did not have an immediate impact on the fighting. The new recruits had to be trained and outfitted, and then they had to wait for one of the few available transport ships to take them across the submarine-infested Atlantic. By June 1917 only 15,000 AEF troops had arrived in France.

At first the main American contribution was to secure the safety of the seas. When the United States entered the war, German submarines were sinking Allied ships at a rate of about 900,000 tons a month and threatening the transport of American troops to the European front. Adopting a plan that aimed for safety in numbers, the government began sending armed convoys across the Atlantic. The plan worked: no American soldiers were killed on the way to Europe, and Allied shipping losses were cut dramatically.

Meanwhile, trench warfare continued its deadly grind on the Western Front. Allied commanders pleaded for American reinforcements for their units, but Pershing was reluctant to put his independent fighting unit under foreign commanders. Because the AEF was not ready as a fighting force until May 1918, the brunt of the fighting continued to fall on the French and British.

The Russian Revolution and the Collapse of the Eastern Front. On the Eastern Front the strain of fighting the Germans had exposed the weaknesses of the Russian government of Tsar Nicholas II, and a general mutiny of the troops led to the overthrow of the monarchy in March 1917. The new provisional government, which Woodrow Wilson supported, promised democratic reforms but insisted on continuing the war.

Russian workers and peasants saw no end in sight to the seemingly endless food shortages at home and the horrendous casualties at the front. Conditions were ripe for a second, more sweeping, revolution.

The communist theorist and political activist Vladimir Ilych Lenin, who had been living in exile in Switzerland when the March revolution took place, saw his chance. Lenin was a follower of German political philosopher Karl Marx and anticipated that a period of "dictatorship of the proletariat" (workers) would be necessary to root out capitalism before an ideal, classless society could emerge. The Germans, hoping to promote internal strife in Russia, cannily arranged Lenin's safe passage home in a sealed railroad car. Lenin and members of the Russian Social Democratic Workers' Party, or Bolsheviks, arrived in Petrograd (later renamed Leningrad and now St. Petersburg) in April 1917 and began to agitate against the provisional government. On November 6 Lenin directed a Bolshevik-led coup and quickly consolidated his control by promising "peace, land, and bread" to the long-suffering masses.

The new Bolshevik government kept the first part of its promise: Russia agreed to a cease-fire with Germany and Austria-Hungary on December 15, 1917, and signed the Treaty of Brest-Litovsk on March 3, 1918. In return for an end to hostilities, the Bolsheviks surrendered about one-third of Russia's territories, including Russian Poland, Ukraine, the Baltic provinces, and Finland. Yet instead of peace the Russian people got three more years of a devastating civil war.

Allied Victory in the West.   The civil war in the new Soviet state would command the Allies' attention only after the end of World War I. No longer facing a hostile Russia, Germany launched a major offensive on March 21, 1918, designed to break the stalemate on the Western Front. By May the German army had advanced to the Marne River, within 50 miles of Paris. Allied leaders intensified their calls for American troops, and Pershing, who was under orders to keep the AEF a separate fighting unit, relented a bit to help the Allies bolster their defenses. About 60,000 American soldiers helped the French repel the Germans in the battles of Château-Thierry and Belleau Wood in May and June. During the fighting, the AEF encountered firsthand the terrible effects of poison gas (see American Voices, "Frederick Pottle: Mustard Gas," p. 713).

American reinforcements soon began to arrive in large numbers. Fresh troops flooded the ports of Liverpool in Britain and Brest and Saint Nazaire in France—245,000 in May 1918, 278,000 in June, an additional 306,000 in July. From there they slowly worked their way to the front along the clogged French transportation system. Augmented by 85,000 American troops, the Allied force brought the German offensive to a halt in mid-July. The counteroffensive began with a successful campaign to drive the Germans back from the Marne (Map 22.2). In mid-September 1918 American and French troops led by General Pershing forced the Germans to retreat from Saint-Mihiel. On September 26 Pershing launched the last major assault of the war, which pitted over a million American soldiers

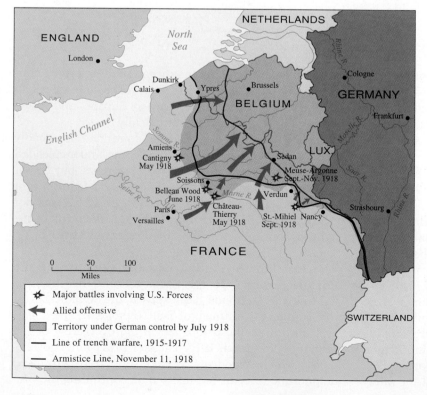

MAP 22.2
U.S. Participation on the Western Front, 1918
When American troops reached the European front in significant numbers in 1918, the Allied and Central Powers had been grinding each other down in a war of attrition for almost four years. The influx of American troops and supplies broke the stalemate. Successful offensive maneuvers by the American Expeditionary Force included those at Belleau Wood and Château-Thierry, and the Meuse-Argonne campaign.

FREDERICK POTTLE

Mustard Gas

★

Frederick Pottle volunteered for service as an enlisted man in the Medical Corps. He describes here the effects of mustard gas during the battles of Belleau Wood and Château-Thierry in June 1918.

Indeed, those dreadful mustard-gas cases were probably the most painful we had to witness in all our service. As a matter of fact, the majority were in much less serious plight than the wounded men. Mustard gas (it has nothing to do with mustard) is a heavy liquid, which, though fairly volatile, will remain for some time clinging to grass and undergrowth, and will burn any flesh with which it comes in contact. It is especially adapted for use by a retreating army. By soaking down with mustard gas the area through which the pursuing American troops had to advance, the Germans made sure that a large number of the advancing force would be incapacitated. The soldier's clothing soon becomes impregnated with the stuff as he brushes through the undergrowth, and the burns develop through the help of moisture. Those parts of the body subject to excessive perspiration are especially affected. The burns are extremely painful, but in general not fatal unless the gas has been inhaled, or (as with other surface burns) a third or more of the total skin area has been affected. A bad feature of mustard gas, however, is that it almost invariably produces temporary, but complete, blindness. Nothing demoralizes a man so much as the fear of losing his sight, and telling him that he will see again in a day or two generally fails to reassure him. The gas cases began to arrive at Juilly as early as June 12. Since most of them were immediately evacuable, we made temporary wards for them in the great cloisters which ran around two sides of the court in front of Wards F and G—the children's dormitories. By the sixteenth there were nearly seven hundred gassed men there, just out of the glare of the sunny court, lying fully dressed on blanket-covered cots, some of them badly gassed in the lungs and fighting horribly for breath, which could be a little prolonged by giving them oxygen; nearly all blinded, many delirious, all crying, moaning, tossing about. For most of the patients there was nothing to do but renew frequently the wet dressings which relieved somewhat the smart of the burns, and to try to restore their lost morale. For those who had been gassed worst, nothing effectual could be done. They were spared much by being in general delirious, but it required the constant attention of several orderlies to keep some of them in bed. Later on, the hospital service was so organized that the gas cases were handled by special gas hospitals. After we left Juilly we almost never received gas victims unless they were also wounded.

Source: Frederick A. Pottle, *Stretchers: The Story of a Hospital Unit on the Western Front* (New Haven: Yale University Press, 1929), 117–118.

against vastly outnumbered and exhausted German troops. The Meuse-Argonne campaign, the main American military contribution to the fighting, pushed the enemy back across the Selle River near Verdun and broke the German defenses at a cost of over 26,000 American lives.

World War I ended on November 11, 1918, when German and Allied representatives signed an armistice in the railway car of Marshal Ferdinand Foch of France. The flood of American troops and supplies during the last six months of the war helped provide the Allied margin of victory. In many ways this contribution was emblematic of the shift in international power as European diplomatic and economic dominance declined and the United States emerged as a world leader.

The American Fighting Force

About 2 million American soldiers were in France when the war ended. Two-thirds of them had seen at least brief action on the Western Front, but most American "doughboys" had escaped the horrors of sustained trench warfare that had sapped the morale of Allied and German troops. (The origin of the nickname *doughboy* is unclear, but it may involve the buttons on the uniforms of American infantrymen, which resembled dumplings made of dough.) During the eighteen months in which the United States fought, 48,000 American servicemen were killed in action or died from wounds. Another 27,000 died from other causes, mainly the influenza epidemic that swept the world in 1918–1919.

Fighting the Flu
The influenza epidemic of 1918–1919 strained the resources of a public health system
already fully mobilized for the war effort. Here doctors, army officers, and reporters
don surgical masks and gowns before touring hospitals that treat influenza patients.
Note the patriotic poster entreating citizens to buy bonds on the wall behind them.
Corbis-Bettmann.

But these casualties were minimal compared with the
8 million soldiers lost by the Allies and the Central Powers. The French lost far more soldiers in the siege of Verdun than the United States did during the entire war.

Although individual bravery was increasingly
anachronistic in modern warfare, the war generated its
share of American heroes. Sergeant Alvin York single-
handedly killed 25 Germans and took 132 prisoners at
the battle of Châtel-Chéhéry in the Meuse-Argonne
campaign. Although air power played only a minor role
in the conduct of the war, it captivated the popular
imagination. One of America's best-known aces (the
word coined for pilots who destroyed five or more
enemy aircraft) was the former professional race car
driver Eddie Rickenbacker, known as the "American

Ace of Aces" for shooting down more enemy aircraft
than any other pilot. The aerial exploits of daredevil
pilots, often fighting in single combat like medieval
knights, provided a thrill that contrasted with the
monotony of trench warfare. The popular fascination
with York and Rickenbacker suggests a deep-seated
need on the part of the American public to anoint
heroes in what had become an increasingly depersonal-
ized and mechanized pursuit of war.

Military Morality. Another characteristic of World
War I was the growing influence of the state—in this
case, army officials—over the private lives of American
soldiers. The high ideals of progressivism set the tone
for military service. Reformers urged the adoption of

Flying Aces
One of America's best-known aces was former professional race car driver Eddie Rickenbacker (middle) of the 94th Aero Pursuit Squadron. Note the insignia on the plane. The 94th was known as the hat-in-the-ring squadron for the American custom of throwing a hat into the ring as an invitation to fight.
Corbis-Bettmann.

progressive solutions to the "vices" of alcohol and sex, and government and military officials agreed. Reflecting the antiliquor fever taking hold in America, Secretary of the Navy Josephus Daniels declared navy ships dry. The army banned drinking by soldiers in uniform and prohibited the sale or consumption of liquor on army bases and in the surrounding localities.

The army also mounted an ambitious program of sex education. In an era when people rarely discussed sex in public, the army brought the subject into the open. Concerned that venereal disease (VD) might sap the strength of the fighting men (antibiotics had not yet been developed), the army launched an anti-VD campaign. Posters proclaimed "A German bullet is cleaner than a whore" and "How could you look the flag in the face if you were dirty with gonorrhea?" In France the army continued its campaign for moral purity, although it could not entirely stop American soldiers from patronizing French prostitutes. Army-issue condoms and safety razors, a novelty that changed the

shaving habits of future generations of men, were two of the souvenirs that American soldiers brought home from France.

World War I also marked the first time that homosexuality emerged as a major social issue. Urban reformers were concerned that military recruits would fall prey to the "urban degeneracy" of "male perversion" while passing through embarkation points such as New York City. As they cracked down on prostitution, they also attempted to curb the city's thriving gay subculture. The military also targeted male homosexuality as part of its campaign against vice. At the Newport (Rhode Island) Naval Training Station in 1919, the navy undertook an extensive undercover operation against suspected "sexual perverts" that led to more than twenty arrests.

Racism in the Armed Forces. Reformers expressed high hopes for democratization and education in the military services, yet the army reflected the divisions in American society. About one-fifth of the American soldiers had been born in another country, leading some people to call the AEF the American Foreign Legion. Army censors had to be able to read forty-nine languages to check letters written home by American doughboys.

To sort its conscripts, the army used the newly developed Stanford-Binet intelligence test, putting the progressive belief in social science at the service of wartime needs. Army psychologists, who administered the test to all recruits, expressed shock at the level of illiteracy among draftees—as high as 25 percent. Racial and ethnic variations in the test scores reinforced stereotypes about the supposed intellectual inferiority of blacks and immigrants, although in fact their lower

scores stemmed from the cultural and environmental biases of the tests. (How many recent immigrants or rural blacks knew the importance of the French painter Rosa Bonheur?) The army dropped the test in 1919, but revised versions of intelligence tests soon became a standard part of assessment measures in the American educational system.

The "Americanization" of the army remained imperfect at best, with African American soldiers receiving the worst treatment. Blacks were organized into rigidly segregated units, almost always under the control of white officers. In addition, blacks were assigned to the most menial tasks, working as stevedores (workers who loaded and unloaded the ships) and messboys (workers who cleaned up kitchen and dining facilities). Although the policy of segregation minimized contact between black and white recruits, racial violence erupted at several camps. The worst incident occurred in Houston in August 1917, when black members of the Twenty-fourth Infantry's Third Battalion killed fifteen white soldiers and police officers in retaliation for a string of racial incidents, including the beating of a black woman by a white police officer. Sixty-four soldiers were tried in military courts, and nineteen were hanged. The army quickly disbanded the battalion, but the legacy of racial mistrust lingered throughout the rest of the war.

Racial equality had never been a central concern on the progressive agenda, and the black experience in World War I reflected the persistent gap between democratic rhetoric and reality. Over 400,000 black men served in the military, accounting for 13 percent of the armed forces; 92 percent were draftees, a far higher rate than that of whites. Black soldiers often found the French more willing to socialize with them on an equal basis than white American soldiers. Despite documented cases of extreme heroism, no black received the Congressional Medal of Honor, the nation's highest military award, even though they had been so honored in the Civil War and the Spanish-American War. The French, however, had no qualms about awarding the Croix de Guerre (Legion of Honor) to several hundred African American soldiers (see Voices from Abroad, "A German Propaganda Appeal to Black Soldiers," p. 717).

Portrait of a Corporal
Black soldiers such as this corporal in the 15th New York Infantry received segregated and unequal treatment at every level of military service. Yet their pride in serving their country remained strong, as this 1918 painting by Raymond Desvarraus suggests.
West Point Museum, United States Military Academy, West Point, NY.

Demobilization.   Just as it had taken months to get American troops to Europe to join the fighting, similar delays slowed demobilization at the war's end. June 1919 was the peak month for returns, with 368,000 men—plus the women who had served in France as telephone operators, canteen workers, and nurses—coming home to begin the process of readjusting to civilian life. When their ships sailed into New York harbor, many mouthed the old vaudeville saying: "If the Statue of Liberty wants to see my face again, she'll have to turn around."

A German Propaganda Appeal to Black Soldiers

————★————

I n an effort to undermine enemy morale, each side distributed propaganda tracts behind the lines. This piece of German propaganda was specifically directed toward black soldiers in France. According to Charles Williams—who, with the cooperation of the secretary of war, the Federal Council of Churches, and the Phelps-Stokes Fund, investigated conditions for black soldiers—the reaction of soldiers who read the propaganda was clear: "We know what they say is true, but don't worry; we're not going over."

"To the Colored Soldiers of the U.S. Army,
            September, 1918, Vosges Mountains.
    "Hello, boys, what are you doing over there? Fighting the Germans? Why? Have they ever done you any harm? Of course, some white folks and the lying English-American papers told you that the Germans ought to be wiped out for the sake of humanity and democracy. What is democracy? Personal freedom, all citizens enjoying the same rights socially and before the law. Do you enjoy the same rights as the white people do in America, the land of freedom and democracy? Or aren't you rather rated over there as second class citizens? Can you go to a restaurant where white people dine, can you get a seat in a theatre where white people sit, can you get a pullman seat or berth in a railroad car, or can you ride in the South in the same street car with white people? And how about the law? Is lynching and the most horrible cruelties connected therewith a lawful proceeding in a democratic country?

    "Now all of this is entirely different in Germany, where they do like colored people, where they do treat them as gentlemen and not as second class citizens. They enjoy exactly the same social privileges as every white man, and quite a number of colored people have mighty fine positions in Berlin and other big German cities.

    "Why, then, fight the Germans only for the benefit of the Wall Street robbers to protect the millions they have lent to the English, French, and Italians? You have been made the tool of the egotistic and rapacious rich in England and America, and there is nothing in the whole game for you but broken bones, horrible wounds, broken health or—death. No satisfaction whatever will you get out of this unjust war. You have never seen Germany; so you are fools if you allow people to teach you to hate it. Come over and see for yourself. Let those do the fighting who make profit out of this war; don't allow them to use you as cannon food. To carry the gun in their defense is not an honor but a shame. Throw it away and come over to the German lines. You will find friends who will help you along."

Source: Charles H. Williams, *Sidelights on Negro Soldiers* (Boston: B. J. Brimmer Co., 1923), 70–71.

After the armistice the war lived on in the minds of the men and women who had gone "over there." Spared the horror of sustained battle, many members of the AEF had experienced the war more as tourists than as soldiers. Before joining the army, most recruits had barely traveled beyond their hometowns, and for them the journey across the ocean to Europe was a monumental, once-in-a-lifetime event. In 1919 a group of former AEF officers formed the American Legion "to preserve the memories and incidents of our association in the great war." The word *legion* perfectly captured the romantic, almost chivalric memories that many veterans held of their wartime service. Only later did disillusionment set in over the contested legacy of World War I.

War on the Home Front

————★————

The fighting of World War I required extraordinary economic mobilization on the home front: business, the work force, and the public all cooperated. At the height of mobilization fully one-fourth of the gross national product went for war production. Business and government proved especially congenial partners, a collaboration that typified the pattern of state building in America. Similarly, the rapid dismantling of that apparatus when the war ended reflected the unease that Americans felt about a strong bureaucratic state.

Mobilizing Industry and the Economy

Even before the formal declaration of war the United States had geared up as the arsenal for the Allied Powers. As hundreds of tons of American grain and military supplies crossed the Atlantic and the Allies paid for their purchases in gold, the United States reversed its historical position as a debtor and became a leading creditor. In addition, U.S. financial institutions increasingly provided capital for investment in the world market once British financial reserves started to be diverted to the war effort. This shift from debtor to creditor status, which would last until the 1980s, guaranteed the nation a major role in international financial affairs after the war and confirmed the new role of the United States as a world power.

Paying for the War. The monetary cost to the United States of World War I reached $33 billion, a huge sum for a government unaccustomed to large expenditures. The disruption in international trade after the outbreak of war in 1914 had reduced the money raised by tariffs, ordinarily a major source of federal revenues. Wilson's Treasury secretary, William McAdoo, had two options: to impose a national sales tax, or to increase income taxes. (The Sixteenth Amendment to the Constitution, which instituted a federal income tax, had been approved in 1913.) Wilson and McAdoo, in conjunction with progressive Democratic leaders in Congress, chose the second option.

The resulting War Revenue bills of 1917 and 1918 transformed the previously limited income tax into the foremost instrument of federal taxation, one of the lasting legacies of World War I. And the Wilson administration did this along lines influenced by progressivism: following the lead of the steeply graduated Revenue Act of 1916, it rejected a tax on all wages and salaries in favor of placing the burden on corporations and wealthy individuals. The corporate excess-profits tax contained in the 1917 law signaled a direct and unprecedented intrusion of the state into the workings of corporate capitalism. By 1918 U.S. corporations were paying over $2.5 billion in excess-profits taxes per year, more than half of all federal taxes.

In all, the United States raised about one-third of the cost of the war through taxes; the rest came from loans, especially the popular Liberty bonds, which encouraged public support for the war effort. The government also paid for the war by using the Federal Reserve System to expand the money supply, making it easier to borrow money. Even so, the federal debt increased from $1 billion in 1915 to $20 billion in 1920. Federal expenditures never again dropped to their prewar levels, but by 1920 the federal budget was posting a surplus.

Wartime Economic Regulation. In addition to financing the war, mobilization required the coordination of economic production. The government never seriously considered exercising total control over the economy, but the war sped up the creation of a centralized national administrative structure that ultimately would match the consolidated power of the business and banking communities. The government also created an added incentive for business cooperation by suspending antitrust laws, which ordinarily outlawed business practices that restrained or monopolized trade. For economic expertise the government turned primarily to those who knew the capacities of the economy best—the nation's business leaders. Executives flocked to Washington, regarding war work as both a duty and an opportunity for professional advancement.

A series of boards and agencies tried to rationalize and coordinate the economy. The Overman Act of 1918 granted the president control over these agencies, a significant milestone in the growth of presidential power. A network of industrial committees linked war agencies to organizations in private industry, and government leaders used a combination of public and private power to enforce their decisions. This semivoluntarist approach represented an attempt to find a middle ground between total state control of the economy and letting business operate without direction. Like most compromises, it had mixed results.

The Fuel Administration, directed by Harry Garfield, the president of Williams College, allocated the coal needed for operation of the nation's railroads and factories. Its task became more difficult during the severe winter of 1917–1918, when there were coal shortages in major cities and industries of the Northeast. At one point Garfield ordered all factories east of the Mississippi River to shut down for four days. By raising the price of coal to artificially high levels, the Fuel Administration stimulated the production of coal from previously unprofitable mines to meet the nation's energy needs.

The Railroad War Board, under Secretary of the Treasury McAdoo, coordinated the nation's sprawling transportation system. Because the army needed trains to move its troops, the board took over the railroads in December 1917. In return it guaranteed railroad owners a "standard return" equal to their average earnings between 1915 and 1917, and promised that the carriers would be returned to private control no later than twenty-one months after the war.

Perhaps the most successful government agency was the Food Administration, created in August 1917 and led by Stanford University–trained engineer Herbert Hoover. Using the slogan "Food will win the war," Hoover encouraged the expansion of domestic production of wheat and other grains from 45 million acres in

1917 to 75 million in 1919. The increased output not only fed the large domestic market but also allowed a threefold rise in food exports to war-torn Europe. At no time did the government contemplate domestic food rationing. "Wheatless" Mondays, "meatless" Tuesdays, and "porkless" Thursdays and Saturdays resulted in substantial voluntary conservation of food resources, as consumers patriotically responded to snappy jingles like "If U fast U beat U boats—if U feast U boats beat U." Hoover emerged from the war as one of the nation's most admired public figures.

The War Industries Board. The central agency for mobilizing wartime industry was the War Industries Board (WIB), which was established in July 1917. After a fumbling start that showed the limits of voluntarism in a national emergency, in March 1918 the Wilson administration reorganized the board under the centralized control of Bernard Baruch, a Wall Street financier. The WIB reflected the ambivalent attitude of Americans toward government intervention in the economy. Although Wilson recognized the need for central authority in wartime, he always saw the WIB as a temporary expedient. Baruch organized the WIB around specific commodities and industries, whose administrators then negotiated issues such as market allocation with their equivalents in private industry. This frequent consultation blurred the lines between the needs of business and those of government and often left patterns of private power undisturbed.

The WIB produced an unparalleled expansion of the economic powers of the federal government: it allocated scarce resources, gathered economic data and statistics, controlled the flow of raw materials, ordered the conversion of factories to war production, set prices, imposed efficiency and standardization procedures, and coordinated purchasing. The board had the authority to compel compliance, but Baruch preferred to win voluntary acceptance from industry, often through personal intervention. Business generally supported this governmental expansion because federal growth coincided with its own interests. Despite higher taxes, corporate profits soared, aided by the suspension of antitrust laws and guaranteed prices for war work. War profits produced an economic boom that continued without interruption until 1920.

With the signing of the armistice in November 1918, the United States scrambled to dismantle wartime controls. Wilson, determined to "take the harness off," disbanded the WIB effective January 1, 1919, resisting suggestions from economists and reformers that keeping the board in place would help stabilize the economy during demobilization. Like most Americans, he could tolerate putting planning power in the hands of the government during an emergency but not as a permanent feature of the economy.

Although U.S. participation in the war lasted only eighteen months, it left an important legacy for the modern bureaucratic state. Entire industries had been organized as never before, linked to a maze of government agencies and executive departments. A modern system of income taxation had been established, with the potential for vastly increasing federal reserves. Finally, the collaboration between business and government had been

ON THE JOB FOR VICTORY

UNITED STATES SHIPPING BOARD   EMERGENCY FLEET CORPORATION

On the Job for Victory
Shipping was a critical area of war mobilization because troops and supplies had to be transported back and forth to Europe. This poster by the United States Shipping Board highlights the bustling activity at a shipyard of the Emergency Fleet Corporation.
Library of Congress.

mutually beneficial, a lesson that both partners would put to use in the state building that occurred in the 1920s and thereafter.

Mobilizing American Workers

Modern wars are never won solely by armies and business and government leaders. Farmers, factory workers, and other civilians play crucial roles. However, World War I produced fewer rewards for workers than it did for owners and managers.

Organized Labor. Labor's position improved during the war, although it remained a junior partner to business and government. Samuel Gompers, leader of the American Federation of Labor (AFL), traded labor's support of the war for a voice in government policy, specifically a spot on the National Defense Advisory Commission. That bargain proved acceptable to government and business leaders concerned with averting crippling strikes. The War Labor Policies Board headed by Felix Frankfurter, a Harvard law professor, coordinated labor and welfare programs in government and industry, while the United States Employment Service placed 4 million workers in war jobs.

Far more important to workers, however, was the April 1918 establishment of the National War Labor Board (NWLB), which arbitrated labor disputes. Composed of representatives of labor, management, and the public, the NWLB was chaired by former president William Howard Taft, spokesperson for management, and Frank P. Walsh, a labor lawyer. The board's decisions favored labor more often than management, giving important federal support to the goals of the labor movement. During the eighteen months of the NWLB's existence it arbitrated approximately 1,250 cases. The board established an eight-hour day for war workers, with time and a half for overtime, and endorsed equal pay for women workers. Workers were not allowed to disrupt war production through strikes or other disturbances; in return, the NWLB supported their right to organize unions and required employers to deal with shop committees representing workers in the workplace. The NWLB had ample power to enforce its decisions and intervene in disputes. For example, when the Smith and Wesson arms plant in Springfield, Massachusetts, flouted NWLB rules by discriminating against union employees, the federal government took over the firm.

After years of federal hostility toward labor, the actions of the NWLB improved labor's status and power and demonstrated the wisdom of labor's decision to support the war effort to advance its own interests. From 1916 to 1919 AFL membership grew by almost a million workers, reaching over 3 million at the end of the war. Few of the wartime gains lasted, however. Wartime inflation ate up most of the wage hikes, and a virulent postwar anti-union movement caused a rapid decline in union membership that lasted into the 1930s. The labor movement did not yet have enough power to bargain on an equal basis with business and government.

Black and Mexican American Workers. When soldiers go to war, jobs open up for workers who normally are excluded from them. Black men, for example, found jobs in northern defense industries that would not have hired them in peacetime. The magnet of industrial jobs and escape from the southern agricultural system lured between 400,000 and 450,000 African Americans to northern and midwestern cities such as St. Louis, Chicago, Cleveland, and Detroit during the war. This "Great Migration," which began around 1910 and continued until the 1970s, was one of the largest population shifts of the twentieth century (see American Voices, "Southern Migrants," p. 721).

Mexican Americans in California, Texas, New Mexico, and Arizona also found new opportunities during the war. When urban growth in the Southwest made the wartime labor shortage more severe, many Mexican Americans left farm labor for new industrial opportunities. Continuing political instability in Mexico following the revolution there caused many Mexicans to relocate, temporarily or permanently, across the border, a process facilitated by newly opened railroad lines. At least 100,000 Mexican Americans entered the United States between 1917 and 1920, often settling in segregated neighborhoods (*barrios*) in urban areas, where they met discrimination similar to that experienced by African Americans.

Women and the War Effort. Women were the largest group that took advantage of new wartime opportunities. White women and, to a lesser degree, black and Mexican American women found that factory jobs formerly reserved for men were now open to them. About 1 million women joined the labor force for the first time. In addition, many of the nation's 8 million women who already held jobs switched from low-paying work such as domestic service to higher-paying industrial work. Americans soon got used to the sight of female streetcar conductors, train engineers, and defense workers. But everyone—including the working women—expected that those jobs would return to men after the war ended.

Professional women also found opportunities in government service. Mary Van Kleeck, an industrial sociologist and an expert on the problems of woman workers, joined the Department of Labor to lobby for equal pay and better working conditions for woman workers. Pauline Goldmark, a social reformer from the National Consumers' League, acted as a women's rights advocate at the Railroad Administration. Mary Anderson, a trade unionist who had been Van Kleeck's assistant, became

Southern Migrants

⎯⎯⎯★⎯⎯⎯

The Great Migration of southern African Americans to the cities of the North disrupted communities and families, but the migrants kept in touch with friends and kin through letters and visits. Cities like Chicago offered new opportunities and experiences, as these letters suggest, and migrants eagerly promoted their promise to the folks back home.

CHICAGO, ILLINOIS.

My dear Sister: I was agreeably surprised to hear from you and to hear from home. I am well and thankful to say I am doing well. The weather and everything else was a surprise to me when I came. I got here in time to attend one of the greatest revivals in the history of my life—over 500 people joined the church. We had a Holy Ghost shower. You know I like to have run wild. It was snowing some nights and if you didnt hurry you could not get standing room. Please remember me kindly to any who ask of me. The people are rushing here by the thousands and I know if you come and rent a big house you can get all the roomers you want. You write me exactly when you are coming. I am not keeping house yet I am living with my brother and his wife. My sone is in California but will be home soon. He spends his winter in California. I can get a nice place for you to stop until you can look around and see what you want. I am quite busy. I work in Swifts packing Co. in the sausage department. My daughter and I work for the same company—We get $1.50 a day and we pack so many sausages we dont have much time to play but it is a matter of a dollar with

me and I feel that God made the path and I am walking therein.

Tell your husband work is plentiful here and he wont have to loaf if he want to work. . . . Well goodbye from your sister in Christ.

CHICAGO, ILLINOIS, 11/13/17.

Mr. H⎯⎯
Hattiesburg, Miss.

Dear M⎯⎯: Yours received sometime ago and found all well and doing well. hope you and family are well.

I got my things alright the other day and they were in good condition. I am all fixed now and living well. I certainly appreciate what you done for us and I will remember you in the near future.

M⎯⎯, old boy, I was promoted on the first of the month I was made first assistant to the head carpenter when he is out of the place I take everything in charge and was raised to $95. a month. You know I know my stuff.

Whats the news generally around H'burg? I should have been here 20 years ago. I just begin to feel like a man. It's a great deal of pleasure in knowing that you have got some privilege My children are going to the same school with the whites and I dont have to umble to no one. I have registered—Will vote the next election and there isnt any "yes sir" and "no sir"—its all yes and no and Sam and Bill.

Florine says hello and would like very much to see you.

All joins me in sending love to you and family. How is times there now? Answer soon, from your friend and bro.

⎯⎯⎯⎯⎯

Source: Journal of Negro History 4, no. 4 (1919): 457, 458–459.

the first director of the Women's Bureau established by the Labor department in 1920.

World War I proved especially liberating for middle-class women outside the work force. Women's clubs and groups turned much of their organizational energy to the war effort. Suffragist leaders such as Anna Howard Shaw mobilized women's support for the war through the Women's Committee of the Council of National Defense. Housewives played a crucial role in the success of Herbert Hoover's Food Administration. Other groups, including the American Red Cross and

the Young Women's Christian Association (YWCA), sent volunteers to France to organize relief work and recreational activities in conjunction with the AEF.

Suffrage Victory. The war especially affected the battle for woman suffrage. The main suffrage organization, the National American Woman Suffrage Association (NAWSA), threw the support of its 2 million members behind the Wilson administration. Carrie Chapman Catt, president of the organization, argued that women had to prove their patriotism to avoid jeopardizing the suffrage

Wartime Opportunities
Women took on new jobs during the war, working as mail carriers, police officers, drill-press operators, and farm laborers attached to the Women's Land Army. These Newark, New Jersey, women, decked out in snazzy uniforms, clearly enjoyed their work as dispatch riders for local munitions plants and shipyards. When the war ended, women usually lost such employment.
National Archives.

movement. At the same time, NAWSA continued to lobby for the proposed woman suffrage amendment to the Constitution. The suffragists posed a simple but effective moral challenge: How could the United States fight to make the world safe for democracy while denying half its citizens the right to vote?

Alice Paul and the National Woman's Party (NWP) took a more militant and confrontational tack, widening the split in the suffrage movement that had occurred after 1914 (see Chapter 20). To the dismay of NAWSA leaders, suffrage militants led by the NWP began picketing in front of the White House in July 1917 to protest their lack of the vote. Arrested and sentenced to seven months in jail, an unusually harsh sentence, Paul and other women prisoners went on a hunger strike. Prison authorities responded by force-feeding the suffragists, which involved inserting a 20-inch-long tube through the nostril to the stomach, a process that was excruciatingly painful as well as demeaning. Public shock at their treatment caused them to be regarded as martyrs. Suffragist Rose Winslow stated forcefully, "God knows we don't want other women ever to have to do this over again."

In the end it took both suffrage militancy and the NAWSA's policy of patient persuasion to break the logjam. In January 1918 Woodrow Wilson withdrew his opposition to a federal woman suffrage amendment. The constitutional amendment quickly passed the House but took eighteen months to get through the Senate. Then came another year of hard work for ratification by the states. Finally, on August 26, 1920, Tennessee gave the Nineteenth Amendment the last vote it needed. The goal that had first been declared at the Seneca Falls convention in 1848 was finally reached seventy-two years later, its enactment spurred by women's contributions to the war effort.

Promoting National Unity

The course of American participation in World War I was fundamentally shaped by the progressive period that preceded the war. Reformers eagerly embraced American involvement as an opportunity to put progressive ideals into practice. The educator and philosopher John Dewey, a staunch supporter of the war, argued that wars represented a "plastic juncture" in which societies became more open to reason and new ideas. Dewey's optimistic view matched the spirit of the times. But the dissenting observation voiced by Randolph Bourne, an outspoken pacifist and intellectual who had once been a pupil of Dewey's, came closer to reality. "If the war is too strong for you to prevent," Bourne asked, "how is it going to be weak enough for you to control and mould to your liberal purposes?"

Although the enactment of woman suffrage confirmed Dewey's prediction that social progress could occur in a war context, the excesses committed in the name of building national unity supported Bourne's warning. Woodrow Wilson shared that foreboding: "Once lead this people into war, and they'll forget there ever was such a thing as tolerance." But the president also realized the need to manufacture support for the war: "It is not an army we must shape and train for war, it is a nation."

Wartime Propaganda. In April 1917 Wilson formed the Committee on Public Information (CPI) to promote public backing for the war, a critical task given the lack of a strong national consensus on American participation. This government propaganda agency, headed by the journalist George Creel (see American Lives, "George Creel: Holding Fast the Inner Lines," pp. 724–725), acted as a magnet for progressive reformers and muckraking journalists such as Ida Tarbell (see Chapter 20). Professing lofty goals such as educating citizens about democracy, promoting national unity, Americanizing immigrants, and breaking down the isolation of rural life, the committee also indirectly acted as a nationalizing force by promoting the development of a common ideology.

The CPI touched the life of practically every American during World War I. It distributed 75 million pieces of patriotic literature. At local movie theaters before the feature presentation (which sometimes was a CPI-supported film such as *The Hun Within* or *Pershing's Crusaders*), a volunteer called a "four-minute man" made a short speech supporting the war. (The name, a reference to Revolutionary War heroes, also reassured audiences and theater owners that the featured entertainment would be delayed only briefly.) Those speeches reached an audience estimated at more than 300 million—three times the population of the United States at the time. But the CPI sometimes went too far. In early 1918, for example, it encouraged speakers to use inflammatory stories of alleged German atrocities, such as rapes and murders of innocent citizens, to build support for the war effort.

A Climate of Suspicion. As is often true during wartime, a spirit of conformity pervaded the home front and many Americans found themselves targets of suspicion. Posters such as "Spies and Lies" warned that "German agents are everywhere." Local businesses paid for newspaper and magazine ads that asked citizens to report to the Justice department "the man who spreads pessimistic stories, cries for peace, or belittles our efforts to win the war." And quasi-vigilante groups such as the American Protective League mobilized approximately 250,000 self-appointed "agents," furnished with badges issued by the Justice department, to spy on neighbors and co-workers.

The CPI also urged ethnic groups to give up their Old World customs in the spirit of "One Hundred Percent Americanism." All new immigrants were the target of this Americanization campaign, but German Americans bore the brunt of it because of questions about their loyalty and the anti-German sentiments stirred up by the CPI propaganda. Suddenly everything German became suspect. German music and opera were banished from concert halls, publishers removed pro-German references from textbooks, and many communities banned the teaching of the German language. Sauerkraut was renamed "liberty cabbage," and hamburgers were transformed into "liberty sandwiches." Even the German measles became "liberty measles." Although anti-German hysteria dissipated when the war ended, uncertainty and hostility toward "hyphenated" Americans survived, spurring a rise of nativism in the 1920s.

Woman Suffrage Triumphant
This 1919 poster celebrating the passage of the Nineteenth Amendment by Congress promised that woman suffrage was coming, but it took still another year of intense lobbying to win the necessary ratification by the states. Then, finally, the woman's hour struck.
Poster Collection, US5084, Hoover Institution Archives, Stanford University, CA.

Curbing Dissent. Law enforcement officials tolerated little criticism of established values and institutions in wartime, as the militant suffragists picketing the White House had discovered. The main legal tools for curbing dissent were the Espionage Act of 1917 and the Sedition Act of 1918. The espionage law imposed stiff penalties for antiwar activities and allowed the federal government to ban treasonous material from being sent through the mails. The definition of treason was left to the postmaster general. The sedition law went further, punishing anyone who might "utter, print, write, or publish any disloyal, profane, scurrilous, or abusive language about the form of government of the United States, . . . or the uniform of the Army or the Navy."

George Creel: Holding Fast the Inner Lines

———★———

WOODROW WILSON CALLED George Creel, his choice to lead the Committee on Public Information, a man with a "passion for adjectives." The forty-one-year-old Creel had already made a name for himself as a muckraking journalist and unabashed progressive, picking up a number of detractors along the way for his impetuous and flamboyant style. "A little shrimp of a man with burning dark eyes set in an ugly face under a shock of curly black hair" was how one critic described him; another called him "a fascinating talker who looked like a gargoyle." Whether it concerned his appearance or his politics, no one was neutral about George Creel.

George Creel was born on December 1, 1876, in Lafayette County, Missouri, the son of a Confederate officer who had moved west from Virginia after the Civil War. His mother, who ran a boardinghouse while his father brooded and drank, made sure that her son heard the Southern version of the War Between the States. "The battle of Antietam, indeed!" she exclaimed after he recounted one history lesson from school. "Why, honey, it was the battle of Sharpsburg, and we *whipped* them." The young boy concluded about his upbringing, "The open mind was no part of my inheritance. I took in prejudice with mother's milk, and was weaned on partisanship."

Quitting high school after one year, Creel worked briefly on a Kansas City newspaper before hopping on a cattle train to New York City to try his luck as a writer and freelance journalist. By 1900 he was back in the Midwest to found the Kansas City *Independent*, a weekly paper whose slogan was "A Clean, Clever Paper for Intelligent People." With zeal shared by early twentieth-century urban progressives all around the country, he lead battles to clean up municipal government, pass laws to protect workers, and stop prostitution.

In 1909 Creel moved to Denver, a hotbed of progressive activity. When reformers won a majority in the 1912 city elections, he became police commissioner but was fired from the job a year later when his

George Creel
George Creel in 1917, at the time of his appointment as head of the Committee on Public Information.
Corbis-Bettmann.

campaigns to dismiss political holdovers and rehabilitate criminals went too far even for his fellow progressives. Freed from the straitjacket of public office, he intensified his muckraking activities, exposing, for example, the glowing personal endorsements that often accompanied advertisements for quack medical remedies by printing the death dates of these supposedly cured patients. He was an ardent woman suffragist, and he coauthored a book on child labor with Edwin Markham and Denver's crusading judge, Ben Lindsey. Along the way he married Hollywood actress Blanche Bates, star of *The Darling of the Gods* and other films, and starred in a cowboy movie himself. He also boxed professionally. Who says progressive reformers have to be dull?

Creel had been impressed by Woodrow Wilson's idealism as far back as 1905, and he became an enthusiastic backer of Wilson's presidential ambitions in 1912. In the 1916 campaign Creel wrote an influential pamphlet called *Wilson and the Issues*, which stressed Wilson's reform record and endorsed his stand of neutrality toward the European war. In return the reelected president offered him a position in Washington, but Creel declined. When America was on the verge of entering the war in the spring of 1917, Creel had a change of heart. If there was going to be someone in charge of public opinion, he told a Wilson aide, he wanted "to be *it*."

Reaction to Creel's appointment was decidedly mixed. Many newspapers, including the *New York Times*, saw him as "a radical writer" and questioned whether such an outspoken and thin-skinned figure would be able to work effectively with the press. Creel brushed these criticisms aside and promptly got down to work.

The jurisdiction of the Committee on Public Information was "everything related to public opinion, both at home and abroad," and Creel enlisted the cooperation of journalists, movie makers, advertising executives, and others in the common battle of "holding fast the inner lines" of American public opinion during wartime. His goal was affirmative propaganda, not rank appeals to emotion—to "inspire, not inflame." So confident was he of "the absolute justice of America's cause, the absolute selflessness of America's aims," that he believed "no other argument was needed than the simple, straightforward presentation of the facts." "Words evaporate," he said repeatedly, but "facts remain."

Creel later called the CPI "the world's greatest adventure in advertising." In the days before radio, printed publicity played a crucial role in reaching, and then binding together, a diverse nation. By the end of 1917 the CPI was sending each newspaper in California an average of six pounds of publicity copy a day. One unintended by-product of this government-sponsored media campaign was the stimulation of the advertising industry, which became a major force in shaping patterns of consumption in the 1920s. The war also stimulated the nascent film industry, which cooperated wholeheartedly with CPI efforts.

George Creel quickly demonstrated that he aimed not just to shape the minds of American citizens but to "fight for the mind of mankind" worldwide. The foreign section of the CPI exported ideas about American life and values to three target audiences: neutral nations, America's allies, and the civilian populations of the Central Powers. German and Austrian citizens were bombarded with propaganda leaflets dropped from balloons and airplanes or smuggled behind enemy lines. And in the newly formed Soviet Union, the CPI distributed a million pamphlets, "sounding alarms against typhus as well as against Lenin and Trotsky." Propaganda became part of a global network.

At war's end, the CPI was quickly dismantled and Creel returned to journalism. Always the publicist, he wrote a book about his CPI experiences entitled *How We Advertised America* (1920) in which he took great delight in settling old scores with his opponents, especially Republican members of Congress. He also ardently defended, to no avail, the Treaty of Versailles out of loyalty to his friend Woodrow Wilson. In 1926 he and his family moved to San Francisco, where he continued to write for national publications such as *Collier's* magazine, as well as publish books of popular history and biography.

The upheavals of the 1930s and 1940s drew Creel back into public life. He warmly supported Franklin Roosevelt's efforts to end the Great Depression and served on a variety of New Deal advisory boards. He was far more critical, however, of the administration's conduct of World War II, especially the "blundering" (in his words) propaganda efforts undertaken by the Office of War Information. With his usual inflated pride and self-justification, he commented, "A full twenty organizations now spend more than $130,000,000 a year to do the work that I did with $2,500,000 a year." By the 1940s he was moving away from his former progressive belief in reform, fearing that the federal government had gotten so big that it was stifling individual initiative. Creel died in 1951, having spent the last years of his life battling what he saw as a huge international conspiracy of communists and their sympathizers.

George Creel always thought of himself as a "rebel at large," the title he chose for his 1947 autobiography. Reflecting on the changes that had occurred in America during his lifetime, he concluded, "At twenty, when I enlisted in the progressive movement, I was appalled at the magnitude of the task of reform. Today, at seventy, I am amazed at the swiftness of our approach to equal justice." Despite his ideological journey away from progressivism toward the end of his life, Creel never deviated from his wartime creed: "Democracy is a religion with me, and throughout my adult life I have preached America as the hope of the world."

More than a thousand people were convicted under these broad restrictions on freedom of speech.

The Justice department also targeted the radical Industrial Workers of the World (IWW), or Wobblies (see Chapter 17), who passionately argued that war benefited the capitalist class at the expense of workers. When Wobblies threatened to disrupt war production in the western lumber and copper industries, the Justice department arrested 113 IWW leaders in September 1917. Vigilante groups contributed their own reprisals: a mob in Butte, Montana, dragged IWW organizer Frank Little through the streets and hanged him from a railroad trestle. By the end of the war the Wobblies had been decimated.

Socialists encountered similar reprisals for criticizing the war and the draft. In 1919 party leader Eugene Debs was sentenced to ten years in federal prison for a speech in which he stated that the master classes declared wars while the subject classes fought the battles. (He was pardoned by President Warren G. Harding in 1921.) Victor Berger, a Milwaukee socialist, was twice prevented from taking his seat in the U.S. House of Representatives because he had been jailed under the Espionage Act for his antiwar views. The Supreme Court reversed Berger's conviction in 1921, and he served in the House again from 1923 to 1929.

The reversal in the Berger case was an exception, however. The Supreme Court rarely overturned these cases of wartime excesses. In *Schenck v. United States* (1919), the justices upheld the conviction of the general secretary of the Socialist Party, Charles T. Schenck, who had mailed pamphlets urging draftees to resist induction. In a unanimous decision Justice Oliver Wendell Holmes wrote, "When a nation is at war many things that might be said in time of peace are such a hindrance to its effort that their utterances will not be endured." Therefore, an act of speech uttered under circumstances that would "create a clear and present danger to the safety of the country" could be constitutionally restricted. In *Abrams v. United States* (1919), the Court upheld the conviction for sedition of Jacob Abrams, a Russian anarchist and recent immigrant who had dumped from tenement windows in New York many Yiddish and English pamphlets denouncing American military intervention in Russia. Holmes dissented in this case, seeing no clear threat to the conduct of the war. He and Justice Louis Brandeis made up the minority in the 7-to-2 decision. Because of the national war emergency, the Court upheld limits on freedom of speech that would not have been acceptable in peacetime.

The Eighteenth Amendment. The century-old campaign for Prohibition was also affected by the wartime climate. In early twentieth-century America, Prohibition was viewed as a progressive reform, not a denial of individual freedom. Urban reformers, concerned about good government, urban poverty, and public morality, supported a nationwide ban on drinking. Among the Progressive Era leaders who supported Prohibition were William Jennings Bryan, Supreme Court Justice Louis Brandeis, former presidents William Howard Taft and Theodore Roosevelt, and settlement-house leader Jane Addams. On the eve of World War I, nineteen states had passed Prohibition laws and many more allowed communities to regulate liquor sales and consumption (Map 22.3).

The drive for Prohibition also had substantial backing in rural communities. Many people equated liquor with the sins of the city: prostitution, crime, machine politics, and public disorder. In addition, the churches with the greatest strength in rural areas, such as the Methodists, Baptists, and Mormons, strongly condemned drinking. Protestants from rural areas dominated the membership of the Anti-Saloon League, which in the 1910s supplanted the Woman's Christian Temperance Union as the leading proponent of Prohibition.

Support for the right to drink existed primarily in heavily urbanized states with large immigrant populations, such as New York, Massachusetts, Rhode Island, Illinois, and California. Alcoholic beverages, especially beer and whiskey, played an important role in certain ethnic cultures, especially those of German Americans and Irish Americans. Many saloons were in working-class neighborhoods and served as gathering places for workers; machine politicians conducted much of their business in bars. Many immigrant and working-class people rightly interpreted Prohibition as an imposition of middle-class cultural values on them.

During World War I those who supported a constitutional amendment to prohibit drinking gained political momentum. One spur was the intense anti-German hysteria of the war years. Because several major breweries (Pabst and Busch, for example) had German names, beer drinking became unpatriotic in many people's minds. To conserve food, Congress prohibited the use of foodstuffs such as hops and barley to make distilled beverages. Finally, in December 1917, Congress passed the proposed Eighteenth Amendment, which prohibited the "manufacture, transport, and sale of intoxicating liquors." Among its few exceptions were alcohol prescribed for medicinal reasons and wine consumed for sacramental purposes.

Ratified in 1919 and made effective on January 16, 1920, the Eighteenth Amendment was another example of how "progressive" solutions to issues of purity, poverty, and public safety were adopted in wartime. It also demonstrated the widening influence of the state on matters of personal behavior. Yet the ethnic and urban-rural clashes over Prohibition also foreshadowed the political and cultural debates of the 1920s.

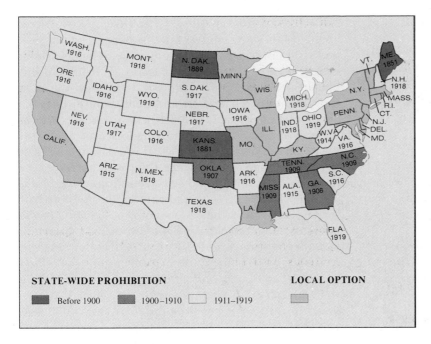

MAP 22.3
Prohibition on the Eve of the Eighteenth Amendment
Prohibition had already made headway in the states before the adoption of the Eighteenth Amendment in 1919. States such as Maine, North Dakota, and Kansas had been dry since the nineteenth century; by 1919 two-thirds of the states had passed laws banning liquor. Most states that resisted the trend were industrial centers or had large immigrant populations.

Unlike woman suffrage, the other constitutional amendment that won passage at this time, Prohibition would never gain general acceptance.

An Unsettled Peace, 1919–1920

In January 1917 Woodrow Wilson had proposed a "peace without victory," since only a "peace among equals" could last. His goal was "not a balance of power, but a community of power; not organized rivalries, but an organized common peace." With victory achieved, Wilson confronted the task of constructing this new moral international order, whose keystone was a permanent league of nations. But he would first have to win over a Senate that was controlled by Republicans and deeply divided over the peace treaty. At the same time, ethnic and racial tensions that had smoldered during the war erupted in controversy and strife, and fears of domestic radicalism boiled over in the Red Scare.

The Treaty of Versailles

Wilson scored an early victory when the Allies accepted his Fourteen Points as the basis for the peace negotiations that began in January 1919. First put forward in a speech to Congress in early 1918, the Fourteen Points represented Wilson's clearest articulation of his blueprint for the postwar world. The president called for open diplomacy, "absolute freedom of navigation upon the seas," arms reduction, the removal of trade barriers, and an international commitment to territorial integrity and national self-determination. Essential to Wilson's vision was the creation of a multinational organization "for the purpose of affording mutual guarantees of political independence and territorial integrity to great and small States alike." This League of Nations became Wilson's obsession.

The Fourteen Points matched the spirit of progressivism. Widely distributed as propaganda during the final months of the war, Wilson's declaration proposed to extend the benefits of the American way of life—democracy, freedom, and peaceful economic expansion—to the rest of the world. The League of Nations, acting as a kind of Federal Trade Commission for the world, would supervise disarmament and, according to the crucial Article X of its covenant, curb unilateralism (the tendency to conduct foreign affairs with minimal consultation with other countries or even allies) in favor of collective military action. More grandiosely, Wilson anticipated that the league would mediate disputes between nations, prevent future wars, and thereby ensure that the Great War would be "the war to end all wars." By emphasizing such lofty goals, Wilson courted disappointment: his ideals for world reformation proved too far-reaching to be practical or attainable.

The U.S. peace delegation sailed for Europe in December 1918. Wilson toured the major European capitals and received a tumultuous welcome: in Paris 2 million people lined the Champs-Élysées to pay tribute to "Wilson the Just." This reception encouraged Wilson to press ahead with his plan to dominate the peace conference. Twenty-seven countries sent representatives to the peace conference in Versailles, near Paris, although the Big Four—Wilson, Prime Minister David Lloyd George of Great Britain, Premier Georges Clemenceau of France, and Prime Minister Vittorio Orlando of Italy—did most of the negotiating. Neither Germany nor the Soviet Union were invited.

The exclusion of the Soviet Union from the Versailles negotiations was the result of the Allies' profound unease about the ideological direction of the new Soviet state. Lenin's calls for a proletarian revolution to liberate the world from capitalism and imperialism posed a direct challenge to the Wilsonian concept of international order represented by the League of Nations. Not only did Wilson refuse to recognize Lenin's legitimacy, but the Allies also took steps to topple the Bolshevik regime. Using the excuse of helping 60,000 trapped Czechoslovakians return west to fight the Germans, Wilson deployed 2,000 American troops to Vladivostok in eastern Russia in June 1918 and sent an additional 3,000 troops to northwestern Russia in July. Britain and Japan also sent troops. The unstated purpose of this military maneuver was to support anti-Bolshevik forces within Russia. American troops remained on Soviet soil until the spring of 1920, leaving a bitter legacy for American-Soviet relations.

Negotiating the Treaties. The Big Four concurred about excluding Lenin from the peace negotiations, but in other respects the three European heads of state sought a peace that differed radically from Wilson's plan. Specifically they wanted to punish Germany through heavy reparations and treat themselves to the spoils of war. In fact, before the war ended, Britain, France, and Italy had already made secret treaties to divide up the German colonies. It is a tribute to Wilson that he managed to influence the peace agreement as much as he did. National self-determination, a fundamental principle of Wilson's Fourteen Points, bore fruit in the creation of the independent states of Austria, Hungary, Poland, Yugoslavia, and Czechoslovakia from the defeated empires of the Central Powers (Map 22.4). The establishment of the new nations of Finland, Estonia, Lithuania, and Latvia not only upheld the principle of self-determination but also served Wilson's (and the Allies') determination to isolate the Soviet Union from the rest of Europe. Wilson was also able to soften some of the harshest demands for reprisals against Germany.

He had less success in achieving other goals. Certain topics, such as freedom of the seas and free trade, never made the agenda because of Allied resistance. The old central and eastern European empires were dismantled, but instead of becoming independent

MAP 22.4
Europe after World War I
World War I and its aftermath dramatically altered the landscape of Europe, most notable with the creation of new countries such as Poland, Yugoslavia, and Czechoslovakia from territory of the defeated powers of Germany and Russia. Twenty years later, these new countries were the battlegrounds of the next world war.

The Peace at Versailles
This painting by Sir William Orpen of the signing of the peace treaty in the Hall of
Mirrors at Versailles in June 1919 captures the solemnity of the occasion and the
grandeur of the surroundings. Wilson was justifiably proud of his role in the peace
negotiations, but he faced strong opposition in the Senate.
Imperial War Museum, London.

countries, the colonies were assigned to victorious
Allied nations to administer as trustees. The transfer of
Germany's colonies to imperialist powers such as
Britain and Japan hardly constituted national self-
determination. More troubling, economic issues were
not faced as squarely as were territorial ones. Wilson
yielded to French and British demands for a "war guilt"
clause, which provided justification for the restitution
demanded from Germany. The final figure, set in 1921,
was a staggering $33 billion.

In the face of his many disappointments, Wilson
consoled himself with the negotiators' commitment to
his proposed League of Nations. He acknowledged that
the treaty had defects but expressed confidence that
they could be resolved by a permanent international
organization dedicated to the peaceful resolution of
disputes. The American public seemed enthusiastic
about a league of nations, at least in principle. Major
newspapers and the Federal Council of Churches in
Christ of America supported the treaty; even a declared
opponent, Senator Henry Cabot Lodge, acknowledged
that "the people of the country are very naturally fascinated by the idea of eternal preservation of the world's
peace."

On June 28, 1919, representatives gathered in the
Hall of Mirrors in the Palace of Versailles to sign the
peace treaty. Wilson sailed for home immediately after
the ceremony and presented it to the Senate on July 10.
The treaty was already in trouble, however, with support in the Senate being far short of the two-thirds vote
necessary for ratification. Wilson had failed to pay
attention to political realities, neglecting, for example,
to include a prominent Republican in the American
commission that represented the United States at Versailles. When the Senate balked at ratification, Wilson
adamantly refused to compromise. "I shall consent to
nothing," he told the French ambassador. "The Senate
must take its medicine."

The Battle for Ratification.   Opposition to the treaty
came from several sources. One group, called the
"irreconcilables," consisted of western progressive senators such as William E. Borah of Idaho, Hiram W.
Johnson of California, and Robert M. La Follette of
Wisconsin, who disagreed fundamentally with the
premise of permanent U.S. participation in European
affairs. Moreover, they were horrified at the harshness
of the treaty toward Germany. Less dogmatic but more

influential was a group of Republicans led by Senator Lodge of Massachusetts. Lodge's Republicans proposed a list of amendments centered around Article X, the section of the covenant that called for collective security measures if a member nation should be attacked. Lodge argued that this provision restricted Congress's constitutional authority to declare war. More important, Lodge and many other senators felt that the treaty imposed unacceptable restrictions on the freedom of the United States to pursue a unilateral foreign policy.

Wilson refused to budge—especially to placate Lodge, his hated political rival. Hoping to mobilize support for the treaty, in September 1919 the president launched an extensive speaking tour in a last great effort to take his case directly to the American people. In three weeks he traveled 10,000 miles by train and gave forty speeches, sometimes to tens of thousands of people, without the aid of public address systems. He brought large audiences to tears with his impassioned defense of the treaty, but the strain proved too much for the ailing sixty-two-year-old president, who collapsed in Pueblo, Colorado, in late September. The tour had to be cut short. One week later in Washington, Wilson suffered a severe stroke.

Defeat.   We will never know whether a healthy Wilson could have mobilized public support for the League of Nations and gained Senate ratification. If he had allowed the Democrats to compromise, the treaty might have been saved. From his sickbed, however, Wilson ordered Democratic senators to vote against all Republican amendments. The treaty came up for a vote in November 1919 and was not ratified. When another attempt in March 1920 fell seven votes short of approval, the issue was dead.

While the president's wife—Edith Bolling Galt Wilson—his physician, and the various cabinet heads oversaw the routine business of government, Wilson slowly recovered but was never the same. He had delusions of making the 1920 election campaign "a great and solemn referendum" on the League of Nations and even briefly hoped to run for a third term. Neither dream was a serious possibility. Wilson died in 1924, "as much a victim of the war," David Lloyd George noted, "as any soldier who died in the trenches."

United States never ratified the Versailles treaty or joined the League of Nations. Many wartime issues remained only partially resolved, notably Germany's future, the fate of colonial empires, and rising nationalist demands for self-determination. These unsolved problems would play a major role in the coming of World War II, and some, like competing nationalisms in the Balkans, would remain unresolved for the rest of the century.

Racial Strife and Labor Unrest

Wilson spent only ten days in the United States between December 1918 and June 1919. Totally preoccupied with the peacemaking process at Versailles, for more than six months he was practically an absentee president. Unfortunately, many urgent domestic problems demanded his attention.

The war years and the immediate postwar period brought a severe decline in race relations throughout the country. The volatile mix of black migration and raised black expectations as a result of service in World War I combined to worsen white racism. In the South the number of lynchings rose from forty-eight in 1917 to seventy-eight in 1919, and several African American men were lynched in their military uniforms. In the North race riots broke out in more than twenty-five cities, with one of the first and most deadly occurring in 1917 in East St. Louis, Illinois, where nine whites and more than forty blacks died in a conflict sparked by competition over jobs at a defense plant.

Chicago Race Riot
Racial violence exploded in Chicago during the summer of 1919, and photographer Jun Fujita was on the scene to capture it. As one of the few Japanese immigrants in Chicago at the time, Fujita was probably no stranger to racism, but it took personal courage to put himself in the midst of the escalating violence. When the riot finally ended, thirty-eight people were dead and more than five hundred injured.
Chicago Historical Society, photo by Jun Fujita.

Riots in Chicago. By the summer of 1919, the death toll from racial violence had reached 120. One of the worst race riots in American history took place in Chicago that July. It began at a Lake Michigan beach when a black teenager named Eugene Williams swam into an area customarily reserved for whites. Someone threw a rock that hit him on the head, and he drowned. The incident touched off five days of rioting in which twenty-three blacks and fifteen whites died.

Chicago on the eve of the riot was ready to ignite. The arrival of 50,000 black newcomers during the war years had strained the city's social fabric. In politics black voters often determined the winners of close elections. (Unlike in the South, northern blacks generally were not prevented from voting.) Blacks and whites competed for jobs, and the more heavily unionized white population deeply resented blacks who became strikebreakers; white stockyard workers considered the words *Negro* and *scab* to be synonymous. Blacks and whites competed for scarce housing as well, and blacks soon overflowed the racially segregated South Side and moved into Chicago's intensely ethnic neighborhoods. Even before that sultry July afternoon at the beach, tensions had led to bombing of black homes and other forms of harassment.

Chicago blacks did not sit meekly by as whites destroyed their neighborhoods. They fought back both in self-defense and for their rights as citizens. World War I had an indirect effect on their actions, since many blacks had served in the armed forces. The rhetoric about democracy and self-determination raised their expectations, too.

1919—A Year of Strikes. Workers harbored similar hopes for a better life after the war. The war years had brought many industrial employees higher pay, shorter hours, and better working conditions. Yet many native-born Americans continued to identify unions with radicals and foreigners, and after the armistice many employers resumed their attacks on union activity. In addition, rapidly rising inflation—in 1919 the cost of living was 77 percent higher than its prewar level—threatened to wipe out workers' wage increases. Nevertheless workers hoped to keep, perhaps even expand, their wartime gains.

The result of workers' determination and employers' resistance was a dramatic wave of strikes. More than 4 million workers—one in every five—went on strike in 1919, a proportion never before or since equaled. The year began with a walkout by shipyard workers in Seattle, a strong union town. Their action spread into a general strike that crippled the city. In the fall the Boston police force went on strike. The idea of public employees trying to unionize shocked many Americans. Declaring "there is no right to strike against the public safety by anybody, anywhere, any time," Governor Calvin Coolidge of Massachusetts fired the entire police force, and the strike failed. The public supported this harsh reprisal, and Coolidge was rewarded with the Republican vice-presidential nomination in 1920.

The most extensive labor disruption in 1919 was the hard-fought steel strike in which more than 350,000 steelworkers across the country walked off the job in late September. The main issue was union recognition,

General Strike in Seattle
Seattle was a strong union town and 110 local unions took part in the 1919 general strike that paralyzed the city. Although the strike was peaceful, city officials deputized local citizens for police duty, such as this ragtag group of volunteers being issued guns.
Museum of History and Industry, Seattle, Washington.

but the strikers were also protesting twelve-hour shifts and seven-day workweeks. Elbert H. Gary, chair of the United States Steel Corporation, refused even to meet with representatives of the steelworkers' union to discuss their demands. The company hired Mexicans and blacks to break the strike and maintained steel production at about 60 percent of the normal level. This high production rate doomed the strike. Striker solidarity began to slacken as winter approached, and in January the strike collapsed. The union charged that U.S. Steel's "arbitrary and ruthless misuse of power" had crushed the strike, but just as important was the lack of public support for the goals of organized labor. Unions had made important gains during the war, but they were unable to hold on to them.

The Red Scare

Underlying many of the social and political tensions in the aftermath of World War I was the fear of radicalism. Wartime hatred of the German Hun was quickly replaced by postwar hostility toward the Bolshevik Red. The Bolshevik Revolution of 1917 and the founding of the Third International (or Comintern) in 1919 to export revolution throughout the world set those fears in motion. Ironically, as public concern about domestic Bolshevism mounted, American radicalism rapidly lost supporters and political influence. No more than 70,000 Americans belonged to the fledgling U.S. Communist Party or the Communist Labor Party in 1919, and the IWW and the Socialist Party had been gravely weakened by wartime repression and internal dissension. Yet the public and the press continued to blame almost every disturbance, especially labor conflicts, on radicals. "REDS DIRECTING SEATTLE STRIKE—TO TEST CHANCE FOR REVOLUTION," warned a typical newspaper headline.

Then a series of bombings shocked the nation in the early spring. "The word 'radical' in 1919," the historian Robert Murray observed, "automatically carried with it the implication of dynamite." Thirty-four mail bombs addressed to prominent government officials were discovered by postal workers before they exploded. Many people suspected that the intended bombings had been timed to coincide with the communist celebration of International Labor Day on May 1. In June a bomb exploded outside the Washington townhouse of the recently appointed attorney general, A. Mitchell Palmer. His family escaped unharmed, but the bomber was blown to bits. President Wilson's debilitating stroke prevented him from providing decisive leadership as hysteria mounted in the fall of 1919, but Attorney General Palmer seized the moment. Angling for the presidential nomination, Palmer rode the crest of public fears about domestic radicalism into 1920.

The Palmer Raids. One aspect of the wartime expansion of state power was increased surveillance of citizens and repression of dissent. Palmer set up an antiradicalism division in the Justice department, appointing as its director a young government attorney named J. Edgar Hoover. In November 1919, on the second anniversary of the Bolshevik Revolution, the attorney general staged the first of what became known as "Palmer raids." Federal agents stormed the headquarters of radical organizations and captured such supposedly revolutionary booty as a set of drawings that turned out to be blueprints for a phonograph, at first thought to be sketches for a bomb. The dragnet pulled in thousands of alien residents who had committed no crime but were suspect because of their anarchist or revolutionary beliefs or their immigrant background. Lacking the protection of U.S. citizenship, these aliens faced deportation without formal trial or indictment. In December 1919 the U.S.S. *Buford*, nicknamed the "Soviet Ark," embarked for Finland and the Soviet state with a cargo of 294 deported radicals. Its passengers included two famous anarchists, Emma Goldman and Alexander Berkman.

The peak of Palmer's power came with his New Year's raids in January 1920. In one night, with the greatest possible newspaper publicity, Palmer rounded up 6,000 radicals. Agents invaded private homes, union headquarters, and meeting halls, holding citizens and aliens without specific charges and denying them legal counsel, a violation of their civil liberties. But then Palmer overstepped himself, predicting that on May Day 1920 an unnamed conspiracy would attempt to overthrow the U.S. government. State militia units and police went on twenty-four-hour alert to guard the nation against the threat of revolutionary violence, but not a single incident occurred. The hysteria of the Red Scare began to abate as the summer of 1920 passed without major labor strikes or renewed bombings.

The Sacco-Vanzetti Case. One dramatic episode kept the wartime legacy of antiradicalism alive well into the next decade. In May 1920, at the height of the Red Scare, Nicola Sacco, a shoemaker, and Bartolomeo Vanzetti, a fish peddler, were arrested for the robbery and murder of a shoe company's paymaster in South Braintree, Massachusetts. Sacco and Vanzetti were self-proclaimed anarchists and Italian aliens who had evaded the draft; both were armed at the time of their arrest.

Convicted in 1921, Sacco and Vanzetti sat on death row for six years while supporters appealed their verdicts. Although new evidence suggesting their innocence surfaced, Judge Webster Thayer denied a motion for a new trial. Scholars still debate the question of their guilt, but most agree that they did not receive a

Awaiting Their Fate
As the executions of Nicola Sacco and Bartolomeo Vanzetti approached in 1927, they
sparked protests from around the world. This painting by Ben Shahn shows the two
handcuffed together as they wait to hear whether their verdicts will be overturned. The
judicial system declined to reopen the case.
Ben Shahn, *Bartolomeo Vanzetti and Nicola Sacco*, 1931–1932. Estate of Ben Shahn/Licensed by VAGA,
New York, NY.

fair trial. Shortly before his execution in the electric
chair on August 23, 1927, Vanzetti claimed triumph:

> *If it had not been for these thing, I might have live
> out my life among scorning men. I might have die,
> unmarked, unknown, a failure. Now we are not a
> failure. This is our career and our triumph. Never in
> our full life can we hope to do such work for toler-
> ance, for justice, for man's understanding of man, as
> now we do by an accident.*

This often-quoted elegy captures the eloquence and tolerance of a person caught in the last spasm of antiradicalism and fear that capped America's participation in
World War I.

That participation left other legacies as well. World
War I did not have the catastrophic effect on the United
States that it did on European countries. With relatively
few casualties and no physical destruction at home,
America emerged from the conflict stronger than ever
before. Consolidating developments that had begun
with the Spanish-American War, the United States
became a major international power, both economically and politically. Increased efficiency and technological advancements fostered exceptional industrial
productivity that made the United States the envy of the
rest of the world in the postwar decade. And though
mobilization was accompanied by an insistence on as
much voluntarism as possible, the war emergency did
leave a legacy of a stronger federal government and an
enlarged bureaucracy. Finally, the war—especially the
nationalism that accompanied it—contributed to a climate that was inhospitable to liberal social reforms, a
climate that would persist until the crisis of the Great
Depression.

Summary

★

American participation in World War I set in motion one of the most important shifts in international power in the twentieth century, as the United States emerged from the war as a dominant world power. The outbreak of the Great War in 1914 initially posed a great challenge to American diplomacy. For more than two years President Wilson attempted to use American power and prestige to mediate between the two sides. The United States finally entered the war in 1917 because of violations of its neutral rights at sea but, more broadly, because the country's foreign policy reflected the same moral concerns that animated the domestic reform movement. On April 6, 1917, Congress declared war on Germany.

American participation in the war was brief but decisive. Two million freshly recruited "doughboys" helped to turn the tide for the Allies on the Western Front in 1918. Flush with victory, Wilson sought to bring about a peace that would reflect his vision of a new world order. Yet the Versailles treaty only partially reflected the president's hopes for freedom of the seas, peaceful economic expansion, and national self-determination. His postwar plans suffered a worse blow when the U.S. Senate refused to ratify the treaty, which included American participation in the League of Nations.

As the Wilson administration put the nation on a war footing, progressive reform energies were largely diverted to the war effort. An army had to be created almost from scratch, American agriculture and manufacturing had to be federally coordinated to produce for the Allies as well as for the home market, and American workers had to be recruited for war work and kept on the job. All this absorbed the energies of a new group of professional-experts-turned-government-bureaucrats. World War I thus helped create the tools of the modern bureaucratic state, which (though laid aside temporarily at the war's end) would be taken up again during the nation's worst peacetime crisis, the Great Depression.

The government tried to mobilize the minds of the American people as well but succeeded mainly in inflaming passions. Certain groups, such as woman suffragists, found success during the war. But others became targets of repression, including blacks who migrated to northern cities, labor activists, and socialists and other radicals who criticized the government. Domestic tensions erupted in race riots in many northern cities, widespread labor strikes in 1919, and the Red Scare of 1919–1920. The story of U.S. involvement in World War I, then, is a story of battles and diplomacy abroad, and mobilization and strife at home—all of which ultimately had a lasting impact on the nation's future.

TIMELINE

1914	Outbreak of war in Europe
	United States declares neutrality
1915	German submarine sinks British ship *Lusitania*
1916	Wilson reelected president
	Revenue Act of 1916
1917	United States enters World War I
	War Revenue bill passed
	Selective Service Act passed
	War Industries Board established
	Suffrage militancy
	East St. Louis race riot
	Espionage Act
	Bolshevik Revolution
	Committee on Public Information established
1918	Wilson proposes Fourteen Points peace plan
	Meuse-Argonne campaign
	Socialist Eugene Debs imprisoned under Sedition Act
	Armistice ends war
	U.S. troops intervene in Russia
1919	Treaty of Versailles signed, ending World War I
	Chicago race riot
	Steel strike
	Red Scare and Palmer raids
	Schenck v. United States
	American Legion founded
	League of Nations defeated in U.S. Senate
	Eighteenth Amendment (Prohibition) ratified
	War Industries Board disbanded
1920	Nineteenth Amendment (woman suffrage) ratified
1924	Woodrow Wilson dies

Suggested Readings

———————⋆———————

Ronald Schaffer, *America in the Great War: The Rise of the War Welfare State* (1991), and David M. Kennedy, *Over Here: The First World War and American Society* (1980), provide comprehensive overviews of the period. See also Meirion Harries and Susie Harries, *The Last Days of Innocence: America at War, 1917–1918* (1997). On the links between the Progressive Era and the war, see Neil A. Wynn, *From Progressivism to Prosperity: World War I and American Society* (1986); John A. Thompson, *Reformers and War* (1987); and Robert M. Crunden, *Ministers of Reform* (1982). Ellis W. Hawley, *The Great War and the Search for a Modern Order, 1917–1933* (1979), stresses the continuities between the war years and the 1920s.

The Great War, 1914–1918

On America's entry into World War I, see John Coogan, *The End to Neutrality* (1981); Ross Gregory, *The Origins of American Intervention in the First World War* (1971); and Thomas A. Bailey and Paul Ryan, *The Lusitania Disaster* (1975). Studies of Wilson include August Hecksher, *Woodrow Wilson* (1991); Kendrick Clements, *The Presidency of Woodrow Wilson* (1992); Robert Ferrell, *Woodrow Wilson and World War I* (1985); and John Milton Cooper Jr., *The Warrior and the Priest: Woodrow Wilson and Theodore Roosevelt* (1983). See also David Steigerwald, *Wilsonian Idealism in America* (1994).

For American participation in the war, Russell Weigley, *The American Way of War* (1973), and Edward M. Coffman, *The War to End All Wars* (1968), provide useful introductions. They can be supplemented by David F. Trask, *The AEF and Coalition War-Making, 1917–1918* (1993); and A. E. Barbeau and Florette Henri, *The Unknown Soldiers: Black Troops in World War I* (1974). John Whiteclay Chambers II, *To Raise an Army* (1987), covers the draft. Allan Brandt, *No Magic Bullet* (1985), discusses anti–venereal disease campaigns, and Mary E. Odem, *Delinquent Daughters* (1995), looks at attempts to control sexuality during the war years. Paul Chapman, *Schools as Sorters* (1988), describes the intelligence-testing movement.

War on the Home Front

Robert D. Cuff, *The War Industries Board: Business-Government Relations during World War I* (1973), provides an excellent case study of mobilization for war. See also Stephen Skowronek, *Building a New American State: The Expansion of National Administrative Capacities, 1877–1920* (1982). Valerie Jean Conner, *The National War Labor Board* (1983), and Melvyn Dubofsky, *The State and Labor in Modern America* (1994), cover federal policies toward labor. Jordan Schwarz, *The Speculator* (1981), is an insightful biography of Bernard Baruch.

Maurine Greenwald, *Women, War, and Work* (1980), and Barbara Steinson, *American Women's Activism in World War I* (1982), provide good overviews of women's wartime experiences. Ellen Carol DuBois, *Harriet Stanton Blatch and the Winning of Woman's Suffrage* (1997); and Christine A. Lunardini, *From Equal Suffrage to Equal Rights: Alice Paul and the National Woman's Party, 1910–1928* (1986), cover the final stages of the woman suffrage campaign. On the peace movement, see C. Roland Marchand, *The American Peace Movement and Social Reform, 1898–1918* (1973); Charles Chatfield, *For Peace and Justice: Pacifism in America, 1914–1941* (1971); and Charles DeBenedetti, *Origins of the Modern Peace Movement* (1978).

Efforts to promote national unity are covered in Stephen Vaughan, *Holding Fast the Inner Lines: Democracy, Nationalism, and the CPI* (1980). For George Creel's story, see his *How We Advertised America* (1920) and *Rebel at Large* (1947). On free speech, see Richard Polenberg, *Fighting Faiths: The Abrams Case, the Supreme Court, and Free Speech* (1987). For the experiences of Mexican Americans, see David C. Gutierrez, *Walls and Mirrors: Mexican Americans, Mexican Immigrants and the Politics of Ethnicity* (1995); and George Sanchez, *Becoming Mexican American* (1993).

An Unsettled Peace, 1919–1920

On Wilson's diplomacy, see Thomas Knock, *To End All Wars: Woodrow Wilson and the Quest for a New World Order* (1992); Lloyd Ambrosius, *Woodrow Wilson and the American Diplomatic Tradition* (1987); Arthur Walworth, *Wilson and the Peacemakers* (1986); and N. Gordon Levin Jr., *Woodrow Wilson and World Politics* (1968). For more on Versailles and the League of Nations, see Ralph A. Stone, *The Irreconcilables: The Fight against the League of Nations* (1970), and Arno J. Mayer, *Politics and Diplomacy of Peacemaking: Containment and Counter Revolution at Versailles* (1967). See also William Widenor, *Henry Cabot Lodge and the Search for an American Foreign Policy* (1980), and Ronald Steel, *Walter Lippmann and the American Century* (1980). On American intervention in Russia, see David Foglesong, *America's Secret War against Bolshevism: U.S. Intervention in the Russian Civil War, 1917–1920* (1995); John L. Gaddis, *Russia, the Soviet Union, and the United States* (1978); and Peter Filene, *Americans and the Soviet Experiment, 1917–1933* (1967).

Robert K. Murray, *The Red Scare* (1955), summarizes the antiradicalism of the postwar period. See also John Higham, *Strangers in the Land* (1955); Burl Noggle, *Into the Twenties* (1974); and William D. Miller, *Pretty Bubbles in the Air: America in 1919* (1991). David Brody, *Labor in Crisis* (1965), describes the steel strike of 1919. On race relations, see Joe William Trotter Jr., ed., *The Great Migration in Historical Perspective* (1991); James R. Grossman, *Land of Hope: Chicago, Black Southerners, and the Great Migration* (1989); William M. Tuttle Jr., *Race Riot: Chicago in the Red Summer of 1919* (1970); Robert V. Haynes, *A Night of Violence: The Houston Riot of 1917* (1976); and Elliot M. Rudwick, *Race Riot at East St. Louis, July 2, 1917* (1964). For an introduction to the Sacco and Vanzetti case, see Louis Joughin and Edmund Morgan, *The Legacy of Sacco and Vanzetti* (1948), and Roberta Strauss Feuerlicht, *Justice Crucified* (1977).

LOOK WHO'S HERE!

WORDS BY
HAROLD ADAMSO
MUSIC BY
BURTON LAN

25¢

Famous Music
CORPORATION
719 SEVENTH AVENUE · · · NEW YORK

MADE IN U S A

Modern Times: The 1920s

IN 1924 THE sociologists Robert Lynd and Helen Merrell Lynd arrived in Muncie, Indiana, to study the life of a small American city. They observed how the citizens of Middletown (the fictional name they gave the city, which they chose for its middle-of-the-road quality) made their living, maintained their homes, educated their children, practiced religion, organized community activities, and spent their leisure time. As the Lynds' fieldwork proceeded, they were struck by how much had changed over the past thirty-five years—the actual lifetime of many Middletown residents. When *Middletown* was published in 1929, this "study in modern American culture" became an unexpected best seller. Americans wanted to better understand the forces that were transforming their society.

The transformation to a modern society had begun with World War I. Participation in the war had made the United States a major player in the world economy, and the foundations of large-scale corporate enterprise and a modern state had been firmly established. The 1920s, rather than World War I, however, were the watershed in the development of a mass national culture. Only then did the Protestant work ethic and the traditional values of self-denial and frugality begin to give way to a fascination with consumption, leisure, and self-realization that is the essence of modern American culture. Despite ambivalence toward these changes, the patterns that appeared during the "new era" of the 1920s quickly became part of American life. In economic organization, political outlook, and cultural values, the 1920s have more in common with the United States today than with the industrializing America of the late nineteenth century.

"Look Who's Here!"
This sheet music from the 1920s depicts the flapper, prosperity, and big-time athletics—all central images of the decade called the Roaring Twenties.
Picture Research Consultants & Archives.

As movies, radio, advertising, and mass production industries helped to transform the country into a modern, cosmopolitan nation, many Americans welcomed these changes as exciting evidence of progress. But others were uneasy. Flappers dancing to jazz, youthful sexual experimentation in the backseat of a Ford, hints of a decline in religious values—these harbingers of a new era worried more tradition-minded folk. In the nation's cities, the powerful presence of immigrants and African Americans suggested the waning of white Protestant cultural dominance. Beneath the clichéd images of the "Roaring Twenties" were deeply felt tensions that surfaced in conflicts over immigration, religion, Prohibition, and race relations.

The Business-Government Partnership of the 1920s

⎯⎯⎯ ★ ⎯⎯⎯

The business-government partnership accelerated by World War I continued to expand on an informal basis throughout the 1920s. As the *Wall Street Journal* enthusiastically proclaimed, "Never before, here or anywhere else, has a government been so completely fused with business." From 1922 to 1929 the nation's prosperity seemed to confirm the economy's ability to regulate itself with minimal government intervention. Gone, or at least submerged, was the reform impulse of the Progressive Era. Business leaders were no longer seen as villains but as respected public figures. President Warren Harding captured the prevailing political mood when he offered the American public "not heroics but healing, not nostrums but normalcy."

The Economy

America's transition from a wartime to a peacetime economy was not smooth. The worst problem was runaway inflation: prices jumped by one-third in 1919, accompanied by feverish economic activity. Federal efforts to halt inflation through spending cuts and a contraction of the supply of credit produced the recession of 1920–1921, the sharpest short-term downturn the United States had ever faced. Unemployment reached 10 percent, and foreign trade dropped by almost half as European nations resumed production after the disruptions of war. Prices fell so dramatically—by more than 20 percent—that much of the inflation of World War I was wiped out.

The recession lasted only a short time. By 1922 the economy began a recovery that continued with only brief interruptions until 1929. Unemployment hovered around 3 or 4 percent, and inflation stayed low. Between

1922 and 1929 the gross national product grew from $74.1 billion to $103.1 billion, approximately 40 percent. Per capita income rose from $641 in 1921 to $847 in 1929, giving the United States the highest standard of living in the world. Soon the federal government was recording a budget surplus. This economic expansion provided the backdrop for the partnership between business and government that flourished in the 1920s.

An abundance of new consumer products, particularly the automobile, stimulated recovery and prosperity. Manufacturing output expanded by 64 percent, as industries churned out cars, appliances, chemicals,

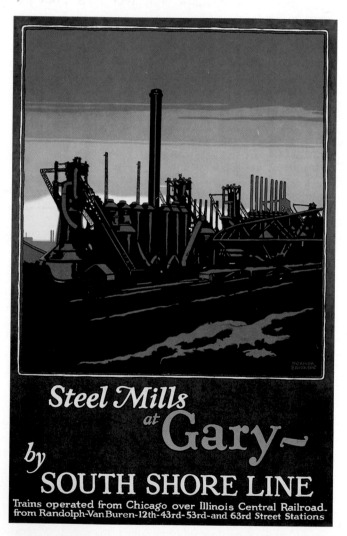

Steel Mills at Gary—by SOUTH SHORE LINE

Trains operated from Chicago over Illinois Central Railroad. from Randolph-Van Buren-12th-43rd-53rd-and 63rd Street Stations

Modern Industry
This highly stylized 1928 poster promotes the steel mills of Gary, Indiana, as a tourist attraction on par with Yellowstone or Yosemite. The Gary that steelworkers experienced was more likely to be full of soot, grime, and hard work than recreation or beauty. The sky in Gary was often similar in color to that eerie shade of orange shown in the poster due to the high levels of pollution generated by the steel mills.
Chicago Historical Society.

electricity, radios, aircraft, and movies. The value of new construction increased from $6 billion in 1921 to $12 billion in 1927. Behind the growth lay new management and mass-production techniques, many of which had been developed during the war years, which resulted in a 40 percent increase in workers' productivity. High employment rates combined with low inflation enhanced the spending power of many American consumers, especially skilled workers and members of the middle class.

The booming economy, however, had some weaknesses. Income distribution reflected significant disparity: 5 percent of the nation's families received one-third of all income. In addition, not all industries were healthy. Agriculture never fully recovered from the recession of 1920–1921. During the inflationary period of 1914–1920, farmers had borrowed heavily to finance mortgages and equipment in response to government incentives, increased demand, and rising prices. When the war ended, European countries resumed agricultural production, glutting the world market. The price of wheat dropped 40 percent as the government withdrew wartime price supports. Corn prices fell 32 percent and hog prices 50 percent. Farmers' share of national income plummeted from 16 percent in 1919 to 8.8 percent at the end of the 1920s.

Farmers were not the only ones whose income plunged: certain "sick industries," such as coal and textiles, missed out on the prosperity of the 1920s. These industries, which had expanded in response to wartime demands, now faced overcapacity or unprofitability and grew sluggishly, if at all, during the 1920s. This underside of economic life would play a role in the coming of the Great Depression of the 1930s.

The Republican Ascendancy

Except for Woodrow Wilson's two terms, the presidency had been controlled by the Republican Party since 1896. When Wilson's progressive coalition floundered in 1918, the Republicans had a chance to regain the White House. With the ailing Wilson out of the picture, in 1920 the Democrats nominated Governor James M. Cox of Ohio, with Assistant Secretary of the Navy Franklin D. Roosevelt as the candidate for vice-president. The Democratic platform called for ratification of U.S. participation in the League of Nations and a continuation of Wilsonian progressivism. The Republicans, led by Warren G. Harding and Calvin Coolidge, promised a return to "normalcy," which meant a strong probusiness stance and conservative cultural values. Hardly a towering national figure, Harding had built an uninspiring record in Ohio politics before winning election to the U.S. Senate in 1914. With a Republican victory almost a certainty in 1920, party leaders wanted a candidate they could dominate. Genial, loyal, and

mediocre, "Uncle Warren" filled the bill. Harding and Coolidge won in a landslide, marking the beginning of a Republican dominance that would last until 1932.

Central to what Republicans termed the *New Era* was business-government cooperation. Although Republican administrations generally opposed expanding state power to promote progressive reforms, they did use federal policy and power to assist corporations. Thus, Harding's secretary of the Treasury, financier Andrew W. Mellon, engineered a tax cut that undercut the wartime Revenue Acts, benefiting wealthy individuals and corporations. The Republican-dominated Federal Trade Commission (FTC) for the most part ignored antitrust laws rather than using federal power to police industry. In this the FTC followed the lead of the Supreme Court, which in 1920 had dismissed the long-pending antitrust case against U.S. Steel, ruling that bigness in business was not against the law as long as some competition remained.

Perhaps the best example of government-business cooperation emerged in the Department of Commerce, headed by Herbert Hoover, a firm believer in what historian Ellis Hawley has called the "associative state." Hoover thought that with government assistance, businessmen would work in behalf of the public interest, thereby benefiting the entire country. Under Hoover the Commerce department expanded dramatically, offering new services like the compilation and distribution of trade and production statistics to American business. It also assisted private trade associations, which brought together leading business executives from a single industry such as mining or railroads, in their efforts to make business and commerce more efficient, such as through product standardization and wage and price controls.

Unfortunately, not all government-business cooperation was as high-minded as Hoover had anticipated. Harding was an honest man, but some of his political associates had low ethical standards. When Harding died suddenly in San Francisco in August 1923 of a heart attack, evidence of widespread fraud and corruption in his administration had just started to come to light. A particularly damaging scandal concerned the government's secret leasing of oil reserves in Teapot Dome, Wyoming, and Elk Hills, California, to private companies without prior competitive bidding. Secretary of the Interior Albert Fall was eventually convicted of taking $300,000 in bribes, and became the first cabinet officer in American history to serve a prison sentence.

After Harding's death the taciturn vice-president, Calvin Coolidge, moved into the White House. In contrast to his predecessor's political cronyism and outgoing style, Coolidge personified moral rectitude. As vice-president, "Silent Cal" often sat through official functions without uttering a word. A dinner partner once challenged him by saying, "Mr. Coolidge, I've made a rather sizable bet with my friends that I can get you to speak three words this evening." Responded Coolidge icily, "You lose." Like Harding, Coolidge backed business and believed in limited government; he was said to perform all his presidential duties in four hours a day. Coolidge's image of unimpeachable morality reassured voters in the wake of the Harding scandals, and he soon announced that he would run for president in 1924.

The 1924 Election. When the Democrats gathered that July in the sweltering heat of New York City, they faced a divided party. The party drew its support mainly from the South and from northern urban political machines like Tammany Hall in New York, and the two constituencies' interests often collided. In 1924 the main disagreements were over Prohibition, immigration restriction, and, most serious, the mounting power of the Ku Klux Klan. The resolutions committee deadlocked over whether the party should condemn the racist and anti-immigrant Klan, eventually reaching a weak compromise that affirmed its general opposition to "any effort to arouse religious or racial dissension."

The convention was the first to be broadcast live on national radio, and it lasted seventeen days, prompting the humorist Will Rogers to say, "This thing has got to come to an end. New York invited you people here as guests, not to live." The convention became hopelessly deadlocked between Alfred E. Smith of New York, who had the support of northern urban politicians, and William G. McAdoo of California, Wilson's secretary of the Treasury (and son-in-law), the western and southern choice. McAdoo also had the backing of a large faction of Klan members, causing opponents to jeer "Ku, Ku, McAdoo." After 103 ballots the delegates compromised on John W. Davis, a Wall Street lawyer who had served as a West Virginia congressman and an ambassador to Great Britain. To attract rural voters the Democrats chose as their vice-presidential candidate Governor Charles W. Bryan of Nebraska, the brother of three-time presidential candidate William Jennings Bryan.

The 1924 campaign also featured a third-party challenge by Senator Robert M. La Follette of Wisconsin, who ran on the Progressive Party ticket. La Follette's candidacy mobilized reformers and labor leaders as well as disgruntled farmers in an effort to reinvigorate the reform movement both parties had abandoned. The Progressive Party platform called for nationalization of railroads, public ownership of utilities, and the right of Congress to overrule Supreme Court decisions. It also favored the election of the president directly by the voters rather than by means of the electoral college.

The Republicans won an impressive victory, with Coolidge receiving 15.7 million popular votes to 8.4 million for Davis and winning decisively in the electoral college. La Follette got almost 5 million popular votes but carried only Wisconsin in the electoral college. In the end the Democrats were unable to mount an effective challenge to their more popular and better-financed Republican rivals, whose strength came chiefly from the native-born Protestant middle class, augmented by small business people, skilled workers, farmers, northern blacks, and wealthy industrialists. Until the Democrats could overcome their sectional and cultural divisions and build an effective national organization to rival that of the Republicans, they would remain a minority party.

Perhaps an even more significant aspect of the 1924 election than its outcome was the low voter turnout. Only 52 percent of the electorate voted, compared with the more than 70 percent who had regularly voted in presidential elections in the late nineteenth century. The nation's newly enfranchised women were not to blame, however: the long-term drop in voting by men, not apathy among women, was responsible for the decline.

Women in Politics. Instead of resting after their suffrage victory, women increased their political activism in the 1920s. African American women struggled for voting rights in the Jim Crow South and pushed unsuccessfully for a federal anti-lynching law. Many women tried to break into party politics, but Republicans and Democrats granted them only token positions on party committees. Political officeholding

The Election of 1924
President Coolidge had a reputation for being a man of few words, but evidently he found enough to fill this 78-rpm phonograph record, which was distributed during his campaign.
Collection of Janice L. and David J. Frent.

remained a "widow's game": about two-thirds of the women in Congress had been appointed to finish their late husbands' terms.

Women were more influential as lobbyists. The Women's Joint Congressional Committee, a Washington-based coalition of ten major women's organizations including the newly formed League of Women Voters, lobbied for reform legislation. Its major accomplishment was the passage in 1921 of the Sheppard-Towner Federal Maternity and Infancy Act, the nation's first federally funded health care program. In an attempt to reduce the high rate of death associated with childbirth, Congress appropriated $1.25 million for well-baby clinics, educational programs, and visiting-nurse projects. Rural women were especially grateful for this government aid and eagerly sought information from government agencies such as the Children's Bureau, which administered the program (see American Voices, "Women Write the Children's Bureau," p. 742).

The Sheppard-Towner bill had passed in part because politicians feared that if it didn't, women would vote them out of office. As one supporter noted, "If the members could have voted in the cloak room, it would have been killed." Once politicians realized that women did not vote as a bloc, they stopped listening so intently to the women's lobby. Instead they listened to other powerful lobbying groups, such as the American Medical Association, which had strenuously objected to the state being involved in health care at all. In 1929 Congress cut off Sheppard-Towner's funding.

The roadblocks that women activists faced were part of a broader public antipathy to ambitious reform. Although some states—such as New York, where an urban liberalism was coalescing under leaders like Al Smith—did enact legislation that promoted workmen's compensation, public health, and conservation, on the national level reforms that would have strengthened federal power made little headway. After years of progressive reforms and an expanded presence in World War I, many Americans were unenthusiastic about increased taxation or more governmental bureaucracy. The Red Scare had given ammunition to opponents of reform by making it easy to claim that legislation calling for governmental activism was the first step toward Bolshevism. Finally, the general prosperity of the 1920s hampered the reform spirit. With a strong economy, the Republican policy of an informal partnership between business and government seemed to work and made reforms regulating corporations and the economy seem unnecessary and even potentially harmful.

Corporate Capitalism

The 1920s saw the triumph of the management revolution that had been reshaping American business since the late nineteenth century (see Chapter 17). Large-scale corporate organizations with bureaucratic structures of authority replaced family-run businesses. There were more mergers in the 1920s than at any time since the heyday of combinations in the 1880s and 1890s; the largest number occurred in rapidly growing industries such as chemicals, electrical appliances and machinery, and automobiles. By 1930 the 200 largest corporations controlled almost half the nonbanking corporate wealth in the United States. It was rare for one corporation to monopolize an entire industry; instead, *oligopolies* (in which a few large producers controlled an industry) became the norm, such as in auto manufacturing, oil refining, and steelmaking. The nation's financial institutions expanded and consolidated along with its corporations. Total bank assets rose dramatically as mergers between Wall Street banks enhanced New York's role as the financial center of the world. In 1929 almost half the nation's banking resources were controlled by 1 percent, or 250, of American banks.

By 1920 many American industries, especially in manufacturing, had modern organizational structures. The multi-unit enterprise coordinated production and distribution through divisions organized by functions, such as sales, operations, and investment. Alfred P. Sloan Jr., an engineer and midlevel manager at General Motors in the 1920s, refined this structure by relieving top management of the day-to-day control of production. This shift in responsibility freed management to concentrate on long-range planning while autonomous, integrated divisions met short-range production goals. General Motors' innovative structure set the pattern for large American companies in the 1920s and 1930s and was later adopted by companies worldwide. In addition, corporations greatly increased their commitment to research and development, using current earnings to create future profits. By 1927 more than a thousand corporations had set up independent research programs, among them Bell Laboratories, the research arm of the American Telephone and Telegraph Company, which was formally incorporated in 1925.

These huge modern corporate structures called for a new breed of employee, the professional manager (nearly always a man, as women found few opportunities in the corporate hierarchy until the 1970s). Increasingly, corporations relied on elite graduate schools of business, such as Wharton and Harvard, to produce managers, consultants, and executives, many of whom had engineering training. The chief executives at General Motors, General Electric, Singer, Du Pont, and Goodyear had all been engineering classmates at the Massachusetts Institute of Technology.

Business leaders enjoyed enormous popularity and respect in the 1920s, their reputations often surpassing those of the era's lackluster politicians. Many politicians and commentators drew parallels between

Women Write the Children's Bureau

———————★———————

The Children's Bureau in the Department of Labor was in charge of administering the Sheppard-Towner Act from 1921 to 1929. In addition to setting up clinics and offering correspondence courses, the staff answered letters from anxious mothers, such as the two excerpted here—yet another example of how the state was becoming part of everyday life.

Dear Doctor Sherbon:

You can not imagine how much I have enjoyed the Course. As soon as I received it I lay down and never stopped until I read it through. It is splendid, and if every woman could follow each lesson to the letter there would be less suffering. But how are we going to convince our families that such care is necessary? Of course the children can be taught these things, but the husbands and our mothers think it is foolishness to take such care of ourselves.

Do you think it proper to explain to children where they come from and the science of life? I have told my stepson, age 18, all of these things and how he should take care of himself, and also how he should treat girls and how much suffering there was to childbirth, and I was very much criticized by some of the family.

I must close. I am taking up your valuable time and am losing much time of my own. Thank you for all the help and the good you are doing, not only for myself but others.

Dear Madam:

I took your correspondence course last winter and enjoyed it very much although I have been a mother three times and expect to be again as [I] am pregnant three months now. Maybe you have something for me or that might help me in some way, so [I] thot that I would drop you a line.

We are a poor family and live in western Kansas and [are] heavily in debt, so this ordeal is hard for me at present. But what I would like to ask you is if a poor mother can get any county or state aid. My teeth are badly in need of dental work, and [I have] no money to pay the bill and the doctor bill worries me too. The doctor we have gone to is so high I don't see how we can afford it. We owe $125 in doctor bills in another county . . . and I dread any more until back ones are paid.

Isn't there a law in Kansas that unless a confinement case is obstetrical the limit charge is $15 and if obstetrical the limit is $25? He says he charges $25 for a confinement case and $1.00 mileage which would make a total of $37 for us for doctor bill, besides a nurse or lady to nurse and do the work too. But if you know anything about such things you know that mother and babe are sadly neglected if the nurse has all the house work to do too. . . .

Does the county doctor tend to such cases and look to the community for his money? It looks like we ought to be able to do and care for such things without asking for help, but you know there are just lots and lots of mothers in my fix that just drag along and worry because they have no way of buying the most needy things at such a time and are too proud to find out if there is any way to get help. My husband thinks it's awful to get help in any way besides paying for it, but when I know he is not financially able to help, I don't see why I should suffer if there is any way to help me, as any mother or doctor knows at that time a mother needs the best of care in every way. And it's because I have always had to work too soon after childbirth that I am broken down now.

I will see what I hear from you before going into details any more. Hoping you will not think it too trifling a matter to interest you and will answer me as soon as possible. Yours truly.

———————

Source: Molly Ladd-Taylor, *Raising a Baby the Government Way: Mothers' Letters to the Children's Bureau, 1915–1932* (New Brunswick, NJ: Rutgers University Press, 1986), 131–132, 136–138.

religious activity and business leadership. President Coolidge solemnly declared, "The man who builds a factory builds a temple. The man who works there worships there." The glorification of business reached a new height in a book called *The Man Nobody Knows* (1924), by the advertising executive Bruce Barton.

The man of the title is Jesus Christ, whom Barton portrays as the founder of modern business: Christ "picked up twelve men from the bottom ranks of business and forged them into an organization that conquered the world." Barton's parable was an instant best seller.

The most respected businessman of the decade was Henry Ford, whose rise from poor farm boy to corporate giant symbolized the values of rural society and American individualism in a rapidly changing world. Ford's automobile factories, especially the gigantic River Rouge plant in suburban Detroit, represented the triumph of mass production. Ironically, this American capitalist hero achieved great popularity in the Soviet Union. At a time when the United States and the Soviet Union had no formal diplomatic relations, Ford sold the Russians 25,000 tractors between 1920 and 1926.

Labor and Welfare Capitalism

Workers shared in the good times of the 1920s, although unskilled African Americans, Mexican Americans, and immigrants participated less fully in the prosperity of the decade. Most members of the working class enjoyed higher wages and a better standard of living. With a shorter workweek (five full days and a half day on Saturday), many workers had more leisure time; large firms such as International Harvester offered employees two weeks of paid vacation a year. But scientific management techniques, such as time-and-motion studies to increase worker efficiency, reduced workers' control over their labor and the work environment. First put forth in 1895 by Frederick W. Taylor, these techniques were not widely implemented until the 1920s.

The 1920s was the heyday of "welfare capitalism," a system of labor relations that stressed management's responsibility for the well-being of its employees. Though tinged with paternalism, this system provided benefits to workers at a time when unemployment compensation and retirement pensions did not exist. Employee security was not, however, the primary concern of those corporate programs, which were established mainly to deter the formation of unions.

Welfare capitalism appeared primarily in the largest, most prosperous firms, such as General Electric, Bethlehem Steel, Goodyear, and International Harvester, which meant that its benefits reached only a minority of American workers. Industrial workers could increase their stake in the company by buying stock below the market price, though only a small minority could actually afford to do so. Some firms subsidized mortgages or contributed to employees' savings funds; others set up insurance and pension plans. Many adopted programs for consultation between management and elected representatives of the workers. These employee representation schemes, another device to avert unionization, were called the *American Plan* in order to establish the idea that unions were un-American. Management's long-term goals included control over the workplace, an open shop (where only nonunion members were employed), and worker loyalty.

Welfare capitalism represented a form of labor relations that was squarely in keeping with the conservative values of the 1920s. It placed the responsibility for economic welfare in the private sector rather than the public sector, avoiding the possibility of government interference. It also satisfied management's desire to reverse the tide of unionization: union membership dropped from 5.1 million in 1920 to 3.6 million in 1929, about 10 percent of the nonagricultural work force. The number of strikes also fell dramatically from the level in 1919. Welfare capitalism seemed to represent the wave of the future in industrial relations.

Economic Expansion Abroad

The power of American corporations also emerged in the international arena. During the 1920s the United States was the most productive country in the world, with an enormous capacity to compete in foreign markets that eagerly desired American consumer products such as radios, telephones, automobiles, and sewing machines. The demand for U.S. capital was just as great. American investment abroad more than doubled between 1919 and 1930; by the end of the 1920s American corporations had invested $15.2 billion in foreign companies. Soon the United States became the world's largest creditor nation, reversing its pre–World War I status and causing a dramatic shift of power in world capital markets away from Europe and toward North America. This American capital sustained the international economic system in the 1920s.

Manufacturers led the way in foreign investment. Electric companies, including General Electric, built new plants in Latin America, China, Japan, and Australia. Ford had major facilities throughout the British Empire, and General Motors took over established automakers such as Vauxhall in England and Opel in Germany. The International Telephone and Telegraph Corporation, founded in 1920, employed 95,000 workers outside the country, more than did any other U.S. company.

Other American companies invested internationally during the 1920s to take advantage of lower production costs or to procure raw materials and supplies, concentrating mainly on Latin America. The three major American meat packers—Swift, Armour, and Wilson—built plants in Argentina to capitalize on low livestock prices there. Fruit growers such as the United Fruit Company established plantations in Costa Rica, Honduras, and Guatemala. American capital ran sugar plantations in Cuba and rubber plantations in the Philippines, Sumatra, and Malaya. The Anaconda Copper Corporation owned Chile's largest copper mine, and Standard Oil of New Jersey led American oil companies in acquiring oil reserves in

Bananas

... a good mixer
with every fruit that grows

Oranges, apples, grapefruit, pineapples, pears, melons, grapes—all these and many others—blend perfectly with bananas. The distinctive flavor of the banana, when added to a fruit cup, a fruit salad, or any fruit combination, brings out the flavor of the other fruits and makes them taste better.

"EAT plenty of fresh fruits" is now an accepted principle of diet—and the mere sight of mellow, luscious bananas is an invitation to serve many delicious and nourishing fruit combinations.

All year round from the tropics . . . Easter, Fourth of July, Thanksgiving, Christmas—every season, every day—bananas are available. Thanks to the nearness and all-year-round productiveness of the tropics, they always can be had at your grocery or fruit store.

Children crave the temptingly flavored banana instinctively. And it is well that they do, for bananas are one of the most important energy-producing foods. Doctors and dietitians consider the banana not only one of the most *valuable* foods, but also one of the most *easily digested* . . . as beneficial for grown-ups as for children.

Serve bananas with other fruits, with cereals, with milk or cream . . . or serve them plain. But always be sure they are fully ripe (generously flecked with brown spots). If they are not at the proper stage of ripeness when you buy them, let them ripen at room temperature. Never place them in the ice-box.

UNIFRUIT   BANANAS
Reg. U. S. Pat. Off.
A United Fruit Company Product
Imported and Distributed by Fruit Dispatch Company
17 Battery Place, New York, N. Y.

"Ripe bananas are good for little children."

American Companies Abroad
United Fruit was one of the many American companies that found opportunities for investment in South America in the 1920s. Bananas were such a new and exotic fruit that advertisements had to tell consumers such facts as how to tell when bananas are ripe and never to put them in the icebox.
Duke University Library, Special Collections.

Mexico and Venezuela. (American involvement in the oil-rich Persian Gulf became significant only after World War II.)

American banks supported U.S. enterprises abroad, especially in Europe. European countries, particularly Germany, needed private American capital to finance economic recovery after World War I. Germany had to rebuild its economy and pay reparations to the Allies; Britain and France had to repay wartime loans. As late as 1930 the Allies still owed the United States $4.3 billion. American political leaders, responding to voters' disenchantment with the cost of the nation's participation in the war, rigidly demanded payment. Referring to the European nations, President Coolidge scoffed, "They hired the money, didn't they?"

European countries had trouble repaying their debts in part because the United States maintained high protective tariffs against foreign-made goods. The Fordney-McCumber Tariff of 1922 and the Hawley-Smoot Tariff of 1930 advanced the long-standing Republican policy of protectionism and economic

nationalism. Most American manufacturers favored those high tariffs because they believed that foreign competition would reduce their profits. But the difficulty of selling goods in the United States made it harder for European nations to pay off their debts in dollars.

In 1924, at the prodding of the United States, the nations of France, Great Britain, and Germany joined with the United States in a plan to improve and promote European financial stability. The Dawes Plan (named for Charles G. Dawes, a Chicago banker who negotiated the agreement) offered substantial loans to Germany and a reduction in the amount of reparations owed to the Allies. But the Dawes Plan did not provide a permanent solution. The international economic system was inherently unstable. It depended on the flow of American capital to Germany, reparations payments from Germany to the Allies, and the repayment of debts to the United States. If the flow of capital from the United States were to slow or stop, the world financial structure might collapse.

Foreign Policy in the 1920s

American efforts to stabilize the international economy belie the common view of U.S. foreign affairs in the interwar period as isolationist—as representing a time when the United States, disillusioned after World War I, willfully retreated from involvement in the rest of the world. In fact, the United States played an active role in global affairs during this period. Economic expansion into new markets was a major component of the prosperity of the 1920s, and the United States ardently sought a peaceful and stable world order to facilitate American investments in Latin American, European, and Pacific Rim markets. This expansion abroad, which was a continuation of Taft's policy of Dollar Diplomacy (see Chapter 21), was warmly supported by the appropriate agencies of the federal government, such as the State and Commerce departments. There was little popular or political support, however, for entangling diplomatic commitments to allies, European or otherwise.

In the 1920s the United States continued its quest for peaceful ways to dominate the Western Hemisphere economically and diplomatically, but it retreated slightly from military intervention in Latin America. The United States withdrew troops from the Dominican Republic in 1924 but maintained military forces in Nicaragua almost continuously from 1912 to 1933. American troops also occupied Haiti from 1915 to 1934. Relations with Mexico remained tense as a legacy of U.S. intervention during the Mexican Revolution.

Since the United States never joined the League of Nations or the Court of International Justice (the World Court), international cooperation had to come through other forums. The Washington Conference of 1921 represented a milestone in the history of disarmament and the fulfillment of one of Woodrow Wilson's goals. By placing limits on naval expansion, policy makers hoped to encourage stability in areas such as East Asia and to protect the fragile postwar world economy from excessive spending on arms. A hidden agenda was to contain Japan, whose expansionist tendencies were already regarded as threatening two decades before the outbreak of World War II.

Led by Secretary of State Charles Evans Hughes, the three leading naval powers—Britain, the United States, and Japan—joined other countries in agreeing to halt construction of large battleships for ten years and maintain current tonnage among Britain, the United States, Japan, Italy, and France. The conferees even agreed to scrap some existing warships, leading one commentator to exclaim that in a thirty-five-minute speech the secretary of state had sunk "more ships than all the admirals of the world have sunk in a cycle of centuries." Not until the 1980s would the world see another such concerted effort to disarm.

In a similar spirit of international cooperation, the United States joined other nations in condemning militarism through the Kellogg-Briand Pact, named for its main drafters: the French foreign minister, Aristide Briand, and Coolidge's secretary of state, Frank Kellogg. Fifteen nations signed the pact in Paris in 1928, with forty-eight more approving it later. Peace groups in the United States such as the Women's International League for Peace and Freedom and the Conference on the Cause and Cure of War enthusiastically supported the pact, and the U.S. Senate ratified it 85 to 1. Yet critics claimed that it lacked enforcement machinery, calling it little more than an "international kiss." For many who abhorred war, however, the pact's broad moral statement was an important contribution to the maintenance of peace.

In the end, fervent hopes and pious declarations were no cure for the massive economic, political, and territorial problems that World War I had left in its wake. The United States vacillated, as it would in the 1930s, between wanting to play a larger role in world affairs and fearing that treaties and responsibilities would limit its ability to act unilaterally or draw the country into another world war. Diplomatic efforts ultimately proved inadequate to resolve the mounting crises of the interwar years; but rather than criticize such initiatives as naive or misguided, it is better to see them as honest but ultimately inadequate efforts to find a will to peace.

A New National Culture

The 1920s represented an important watershed in the development of a mass national culture. A new emphasis on leisure, consumption, and amusement characterized the modern era, although its benefits remained most accessible to the white middle class. Automobiles, paved roads, the parcel post service, movies, radios, telephones, mass-circulation magazines, brand names, and chain stores—all these linked mill towns in the southern Piedmont, rural outposts on the Oklahoma plains, and ethnic enclaves on the coasts in an expanding web of national experience. In fact, with the exportation of automobiles, radios, and movies to consumers throughout the world, the American experience became a global model.

Consumption and Advertising

In homes across the country in the 1920s, Americans sat down to a breakfast of Kellogg's corn flakes and toast from a General Electric toaster. They got into a Ford Model T to go about their business, perhaps shopping

Victrola
REG. U.S. PAT. OFF.

Will there be a Victrola in your home this Christmas?

If any one thing more than another can add to the joys of Christmas, it is music—and the Victrola can bring into your home, any music you may wish to hear.

The Victrola is the one instrument to which the greatest artists have entrusted their art—an unanswerable acknowledgment of its artistic achievements. Moreover, the Victrola is the only instrument specially made to play the records which these great artists have made.

Christmas day and any other day through all the years to come, the best or the newest of all the world's music may be yours to enjoy.

By all means get a Victrola this Christmas, but be sure it is a Victrola and not some other instrument made in imitation. $25 to $1500. Victor dealers everywhere.

Victor Talking Machine Company
Camden, New Jersey

"HIS MASTER'S VOICE"
REG. U.S. PAT. OFF.

This trademark and the trademarked word "Victrola" identify all our products. Look under the lid! Look on the label! VICTOR TALKING MACHINE CO. Camden, N. J.

The Amazing Talking Machine
The Victrola, or phonograph, brought music and entertainment into the homes of many Americans in the 1920s. Italian tenor Enrico Caruso was one of the first opera singers to master this new medium, broadening his appeal beyond opera houses and concert halls through his extensive recordings.
Leslie's, December 18, 1920/Picture Research Consultants & Archives.

at one of the chain stores, such as Safeway and A & P, that had sprung up across the country. In the evening the family gathered to listen to radio programs such as "Great Moments in History" and "True Story" or to read the latest issue of the *Saturday Evening Post, Reader's Digest,* or *Collier's.* On weekends they might hop in the car to see the latest Charlie Chaplin film at the local movie theater. Millions of Americans, in other words, now shared the same daily experiences.

The 1920s was a critical decade in the development of the American consumer society. Although not every family participated in the new life-style, consumption became a cultural ideal for most of the middle class, often providing the criterion for judging self-worth that had once been supplied by character, religion, and social standing. Spending money on more and better possessions became a form of self-fulfillment, a gratification of personal needs. Yet participation in commercial mass culture did not necessarily mean a total conversion to American middle-class values. For example, buying a Victrola or a radio on credit could have been a way for Italian immigrants to keep their culture alive by listening to the opera singer Enrico Caruso. The historian Lizabeth Cohen concluded that "Chicago's ethnic workers were not transformed into more Americanized, middle-class people by the objects they consumed. Buying an electric vacuum cleaner did not turn Josef Dobrowolski into *True Story's* Jim Smith."

The unequal distribution of income limited many consumers' ability to buy the enticing new products, however. At the height of prosperity in the 1920s, about 65 percent of America's families had an income of less than $2,000 a year, which barely supported a decent living standard. The average family income in the bottom 40 percent of the population was $725. Of that amount, a family spent about $290 a year for food, $190 for housing, and $110 for clothing, leaving only $135 for everything else, including medical expenses and emergencies.

Retailers and automobile manufacturers addressed this situation by selling on the installment plan. In those days, "buy now, pay later" was a revolutionary concept. Before World War I most urban families paid cash for everything except a house, but in the 1920s the automobile became such an object of desire that consumers put aside their fears of buying "on time." In 1927 two-thirds of the cars in the United States were being paid for on the installment plan. Once people saw how easy it was to finance a car, they bought radios, refrigerators, and sewing machines on credit. "A dollar down and a dollar forever," a cynic remarked. By 1929 banks, finance companies, credit unions, and other institutions were lending consumers over $7 billion a year, and consumer lending had become the tenth largest business in the United States.

Many of the new products were household appliances, made feasible by the rapid electrification that had reached 85 percent of American nonfarm households by 1930. Irons and vacuum cleaners were the most popular appliances, followed by phonographs, sewing machines, and washing machines. Radios, whose production increased twenty-five-fold in the 1920s, sold for around $75. One of the most expensive items was a refrigerator, which cost $900 at the beginning of the decade. Technological improvements soon brought the price down to $180, but many families still had to make do with an old-fashioned icebox, which supplied cooling through blocks of ice delivered to the house.

Because much of the new technology was concentrated in the home, it had a dramatic impact on women's lives. Despite enfranchisement and participation in the work force, the primary role for most women remained that of housewife. Electric appliances made housewives' chores less arduous: plugging in an electric iron was far easier than heating an iron on the stove; using a vacuum cleaner was quicker and easier than wielding a broom and a rug beater. Paradoxically, however, the time women spent on housework did not decline. More middle-class women began to do their own housework and laundry as electric servants replaced human ones. Technology also raised standards of cleanliness so that a man could wear a clean shirt every day instead of just on Sunday, and a house could be vacuumed daily rather than swept weekly.

Few of the new consumer products could be considered necessities, so the advertising industry spent billions of dollars (in 1929 an average of $15 annually on every man, woman, and child in the United States) to entice consumers to buy automobiles, cigarettes, radios, and refrigerators. Advertisements appealed to people's social aspirations by projecting images of successful and elegant sophisticates who smoked a certain brand of cigarettes or drove a recognizable make of car. Ad writers also sold products by preying on people's insecurities, coming up with a variety of socially unacceptable "diseases," including "office hips," "ashtray breath," and the dreaded "BO" (body odor). After the term *halitosis* was discovered in a British medical journal, many consumers rushed out to buy Listerine mouthwash. Advertising became a big business in the 1920s, accounting for 3 percent of the gross national product, comparable to its share after World War II. Yet American consumers were not passive victims of advertisers who manipulated their every whim: America gloried in its role as the world's first mass-consumption economy.

Many of these cultural images were embodied in the flapper, the media version of the emancipated woman of the 1920s. (The term originated with

The Flapper
The flapper phenomenon was not limited to Anglos. This 1921 photograph of a young Mexican American woman named Luisa Ronstadt Espinel shows how American fads and fashions reached into Latino communities across the country.
Arizona Historical Society.

women's fad of leaving galoshes unbuckled, which made them flap.) With her slim, boyish figure, bobbed hair, short skirt, and rolled-down silk stockings, the flapper symbolized the personal freedom trumpeted by movies, advertisements, and other elements of the emerging mass culture. Neither maternal nor wifely, the flapper wore makeup (previously assumed to be a sign of sexual availability in lower-class women) and lit up cigarettes in public, a shocking affront to ladylike decency. Like so many cultural icons, the flapper represented only a tiny minority of women. Yet the image mass-marketed the belief in women's postsuffrage emancipation.

The Automobile Culture

No possession typified the new consumer culture of the 1920s better than the automobile. "Why on earth do you need to study what's changing this country?" a resident of Muncie, Indiana, asked the sociologists Robert and Helen Lynd. "I can tell you what's happening in just four letters: A-U-T-O!" Another Middletowner volunteered, "We'd rather do without clothes than give up the car."

The showpiece of modern capitalism and the ultimate consumer toy, the automobile revolutionized the way Americans spent their money and leisure time. The isolation of rural life broke down in the wake of the automobile. New phrases such as "filling station" (or, as they were known west of the Rockies, "service stations") entered the nation's vocabulary. The automobile even affected crime, providing gangsters with a "getaway car" and the possibility of "taking someone for a ride." Cars touched so many aspects of American life that the word *automobility* was coined to describe their impact on production methods, the landscape, and American values.

The mass production of cars helped to stimulate the prosperity of the 1920s. Before the introduction of the moving assembly line in 1913, it took Ford workers twelve and a half hours to assemble one auto; it took only ninety-three minutes on an assembly line. In 1927 Ford produced a car every twenty-four seconds. Car sales climbed from 1.5 million in 1921 to 5 million in 1929, when Americans spent $2.58 billion on new and used cars. By the end of the decade Americans owned about 80 percent of all the automobiles in the entire world, an average of one car for every five people.

The success of the auto industry had a ripple effect on the American economy. In 1929, 3.7 million workers directly or indirectly owed their jobs to the automobile. Auto production stimulated the steel, petroleum, chemical, rubber, and glass industries. Total U.S. demand for oil, mainly in the form of gaso-

All in a Day's Work
Parked in the testing ground at Ford's huge River Rouge plant in Dearborn, Michigan, sit 1,000 assembled chassis, a single day's production.
Henry Ford Museum and Greenfield Village.

line, multiplied two and a half times between 1919 and 1929, and domestic oil production expanded to meet the need. (The United States was the world's chief supplier of oil in the 1920s.) The advertising industry grew along with the automobile; cars and cigarettes were two of the most heavily marketed products of the decade. Highway construction became a billion-dollar-a-year enterprise financed by federal subsidies and state gasoline taxes. Car ownership also spurred the growth of suburbs, contributed to real estate speculation, and spawned the first shopping center, Country Club Plaza, in Kansas City in 1924. Not even the deaths of 25,000 people a year in traffic accidents, 70 percent of them pedestrians, could dampen America's passion for the automobile.

Nowhere was this more obvious than in the way Americans spent their leisure time. They took to the roads, becoming a nation of tourists. The American Automobile Association, founded in 1902, reported that

Fourth of July at the Beach
Nantasket Beach became a favorite outing for Bostonians during the 1920s, and one of
the most popular ways to get there was by car. After a day lounging at the beach and
sampling the nearby amusements, families must have had trouble remembering where
they parked their cars when they first arrived.
Archive Photos/Hirz.

in 1929 about 45 million people—almost one-third of the population—took vacations by automobile. People preferred the freedom of automobiles to the rigid timetables and predetermined routes of trains. With improved roads, motorists could average more than 45 miles an hour on their way to the "autocamps" and tourist cabins that were the forerunners of motels.

Like movies and other products of the new mass culture, cars changed the dating patterns of young Americans. Contrary to many parents' views, premarital sex was not invented in the backseat of a Ford, but the Model T did indeed offer more privacy and comfort than did the family living room or the front porch. City elders in Muncie overreacted by calling automobiles "prostitution on wheels."

The Model T was the most popular car of the decade. The Ford Motor Company manufactured over 15 million Model T's between 1908 and 1927. A "Tin Lizzie," as these dependable cars were called, required a mechanically inclined driver. The motorist had to hand crank the car to start it, and keep one hand on the accelerator and the other on the wheel while driving. There was no gas gauge, and as late as 1919 only about 10 percent of cars had roofs. As for color, Henry Ford intoned, "The customer can have a Ford any color he wants—so long as it's black." By the late 1920s a new Model T, which had cost $1,000 in 1908, sold for only $295.

Consumers eventually became discontented with the plain Model T, and Ford faced stiff competition from General Motors (GM). GM's five automobile divisions turned out cars for specialized markets and introduced the concept of "trading up." The luxury Cadillac cost the most and had the lowest volume of sales; the Chevrolet cost the least and had the highest volume of sales; Oldsmobile, Pontiac, and Buick were geared to incomes in between. GM cars also featured self-starters and foot accelerators. Henry Ford finally bowed to consumer demands when he introduced the Model A in 1927. More than a million New Yorkers visited the Ford showroom during the five days after the new model was unveiled. At prices ranging from $495 to $570, the Model A fulfilled consumers' demands for different styles, more colors, and greater comfort, and helped make the automobile a permanent part of American culture.

The Movies and Mass Culture

The movie industry, whose growth coincided with America's transformation into a predominantly urban, industrial society, probably did more than anything else to disseminate common values and attitudes throughout the United States. In contrast to Europe, where cinema developed as an avant-garde, highbrow art form, American movies were part of popular culture almost from the start, a mass-entertainment industry that was both democratic and highly lucrative.

The Silent Era. Movies began around the turn of the century in nickelodeons, or theaters where for a nickel the mostly working-class audience could see a one-reel silent film such as *What Demoralized the Barbershop* (1901) and the spectacularly successful *The Great Train Robbery* (1903). Because the films, mostly comedies and melodramas, were silent, they could be understood by immigrants who did not speak English. The new medium grew in popularity and profitability.

During the first years of the twentieth century most films were made in New York City or nearby Fort Lee, New Jersey. After 1910 moviemakers such as D. W. Griffith and Cecil B. De Mille flocked to southern California, which had cheap land, plenty of sunshine, and varied scenery—mountains, deserts, cities, and the Pacific Ocean—within easy reach. Another attraction was Los Angeles's reputation as an anti-union town. Actors flocked to California as well, especially to Hollywood, a rapidly growing suburb of Los Angeles. The early movie stars—the comedians Buster Keaton, Charlie Chaplin, and Harold Lloyd; Mary Pickford (though born in Canada, "America's Sweetheart"); and dashing leading men Douglas Fairbanks, Wallace Reid, and John Gilbert—became national idols. So did Clara Bow, one of the biggest stars, male or female, of the decade (see American Lives, "Clara Bow: The 'It' Girl," pp. 752–753).

"The One and Only"

Charlie Chaplin
His Signature

In his First Million Dollar Picture
"A DOG'S LIFE"
A "First National" Attraction

The Tramp
Charlie Chaplin did not invent the tragicomic figure of the tramp, but it soon became his screen persona. Chaplin grew up poor in the London slums, but the movies brought him wealth and fame. In 1919 he joined Douglas Fairbanks, Mary Pickford, and D. W. Griffith to form United Artists.
Archive Photos.

Movies quickly outgrew their working-class origins and reached middle-class audiences. D. W. Griffith's epic *Birth of a Nation* (1915), which glorified the Reconstruction-era Ku Klux Klan, helped establish the feature film as popular entertainment. The outbreak of World War I in Europe eliminated competition from Italian and French moviemakers, in part because the chemicals used to produce celluloid for film were needed for the manufacture of gunpowder. By the war's end the United States was making 90 percent of the world's films. For the next several decades Hollywood reigned as the world movie capital, with foreign distribution of Hollywood films stimulating the market for the American material culture so lavishly displayed on the screen.

Movies fed the desires of a mass-consumption economy and set national trends in clothing and hairstyles. They also served as a form of sex education. Rudolph Valentino, best known as the romantic hero of *The Sheik* (1921), epitomized sexual passion on the screen, and the message was not wasted on the nation's youth. "It was directly through the movies that I learned to kiss a girl on her ears, neck, and cheeks, as well as on the mouth," confessed one boy. The sociologist Edward Alsworth Ross concluded that movies made young people more "sex-wise, sex-excited, and sex-absorbed" than they'd been in any previous generation. The impact of the movies on sexual attitudes and morality has remained strong ever since.

The Coming of Sound. Movies were a big business. Power was concentrated in large studios such as United Artists, Paramount, and Metro-Goldwyn-Mayer, which were controlled mainly by Eastern European Jewish immigrants such as Adolph Zukor and Samuel Goldfish (later Goldwyn) who believed deeply in the American dream and used their studios to reinforce core American values. Though most movies were made in Hollywood, the studios were financed by eastern banks, which were more interested (as were the studio heads) in maximum profitability than in artistic expression or creativity. In 1926 the movie industry grossed $1.5 billion a year. The studios controlled distribution as tightly as they did production by establishing chains of theaters, thereby achieving complete vertical integration of the movie industry.

In the late 1920s the major studios borrowed close to $300 million to convert from silent production to "talkies," but the overwhelming success of the new films quickly paid back the investment. Warner Brothers' *The Jazz Singer* (1927), starring Al Jolson, was the first feature-length film to offer sound, and by 1929 all the major studios had completed the changeover to talkies. Although no one had thought of movies as silent until talkies took their place, silent films soon became obsolete.

By the end of the 1920s the nation had almost 23,000 movie theaters, including elaborate palaces built by the studios in major cities. Movie attendance rose from 60 million in 1927 to 90 million in 1930. In two short decades movies had become thoroughly entrenched as the most popular—and probably the most influential—form of the new urban-based mass media.

Jazz. It is perhaps no coincidence that the first talkie was *The Jazz Singer*. Jazz was such a popular part of the new mass culture that the 1920s are often called the Jazz Age. An improvisational style whose notes were (and are still) rarely written down, jazz originated in the dance halls and bordellos of New Orleans's Sto-

ryville quarter around the turn of the century. A synthesis of earlier African American music, such as ragtime and the blues, it also drew on African and European styles. With roots in urban culture, jazz gave black people an outlet for expressing dissent and opposition to mainstream white values, but it also appealed to whites. Phonograph records capturing the spontaneity of jazz were so popular that they boosted the infant recording industry. The interracial appeal of jazz suggested the close, symbiotic relationship between African American and American culture in the 1920s and beyond, and jazz remains one of the most distinctly American art forms.

Most of the early jazz musicians were black. As they left the South, they took jazz to Chicago, New York, Kansas City, Los Angeles, and other cities. Some of the best known were the composer-pianist Ferdinand "Jelly Roll" Morton, the trumpeter Louis Armstrong, the singer Bessie Smith (the "Empress of the Blues"), and composer-bandleader Edward "Duke" Ellington. Soon this uniquely American art form had caught on in Europe, especially in France.

Journalism and Radio. Besides movies and sound recordings, other forms of mass media helped establish national standards of taste and behavior. In 1922 ten magazines claimed a circulation of at least 2.5 million, including the *Saturday Evening Post*, the *Ladies' Home Journal*, and *Good Housekeeping*. Moreover, *Reader's Digest*, *Time*, and the *New Yorker*—still found today in homes across the country—all started publication in the 1920s. Thanks to syndicated columns and features in newspapers, people could read the same articles anywhere in the United States. They could also read the same books, preselected by a board of expert judges for the Book of the Month Club, which was founded in 1926.

Tabloid newspapers—sometimes called jazz journalism—also became part of the national scene. In 1919, just two days before the signing of the Versailles treaty, publisher Joseph Medill Patterson introduced the *New York Illustrated Daily News*. Half the size of a regular newspaper, with bold headlines, large photographs, and short, sensational stories, tabloids were meant to be read quickly—for instance, while riding the subway to work. All the major cities had at least one tabloid by 1932.

The newest instrument of mass culture was truly a child of the 1920s. On November 2, 1920, professional radio broadcasting began when station KDKA in Pittsburgh carried the presidential election returns. By 1929 about 40 percent of the nation's households had a radio. More than 800 stations—most affiliated with the Columbia Broadcasting Service (CBS), formed in 1928, or the National Broadcasting Company (NBC), started in 1926—were on the air. (These corporations would

Clara Bow: The "It" Girl

———————★———————

WHEN CLARA BOW, the "It" Girl of the 1920s, was asked to define what "it" meant, she replied, "I ain't real sure." To most fans, "it" was synonymous with sex appeal, but Elinor Glyn, the British writer who coined the phrase, had a more nuanced definition: "To have 'It' the fortunate possessor must have that strange magnetism which attracts both sexes. 'It' is a purely virile quality belonging to a strong character. . . . There must be physical attraction, but beauty is unnecessary. Conceit or selfconsciousness destroys 'It' immediately." Whatever "it" was, when Paramount released a movie in 1927 based on the Elinor Glyn novella of the same name and starring Clara Bow, the film grossed $1 million. Soon Bow was receiving almost 35,000 fan letters a month, many addressed simply to "The 'It' Girl, Hollywood U.S.A." In 1927 she was all of twenty-two years old.

The thin plot of the film hardly seems capable of launching a national obsession. Bow played a department store clerk named Betty Lou Spense who is out to catch her rich, handsome boss. He too is smitten, and when he calls on her in her modest home, he

Twenties Sex Symbol
Clara Bow was not the girl next door, as this seductive film still from *Her Wedding Night* (1930) confirms.
Culver Pictures.

finds her minding a friend's baby. However, he jumps to the mistaken conclusion that she is an unmarried mother and propositions her. She is indignant at the insult, but after several plot twists they resolve their differences. In the final scene they kiss on the store owner's yacht, *Itola*, with the embrace obscuring all but the first two letters of the yacht's name. That's right—IT!

"It" was typical of Hollywood's fascination with flapper themes in the 1920s. On screen and off, the flapper was emancipated, urban, and young, befitting the worship of youth that was characteristic of the 1920s. The flapper was a working girl with money to spend, time on her hands, and a wardrobe of mass-produced fashions, especially short skirts suitable for dancing and dating. On screen she was sensual but not promiscuous, often marrying the male lead at the film's end. The Hollywood stars Colleen Moore and Louise Brooks also played flapper roles.

Before Bow became indelibly known as the "It" Girl, her studio had tried to promote her as the "Brooklyn Bonfire." The name never stuck, but it revealed her background. Clara Bow was born on July 29, 1905, into an extremely poor family in Brooklyn, New York; her mother was mentally unstable, and her father was often unemployed. She dropped out of school during the eighth grade. The only place she found refuge from her grim family life was at the movies. Like many other young girls, Bow decided that she wanted to be an actress.

Her break came when she won a 1921 "Fame and Fortune" beauty contest sponsored by three movie magazines, which helped her land a bit part in *Beyond the Rainbow* (1922). Her scenes ended up on the cutting room floor, but they were restored after she became a star. In 1923 Bow won a Hollywood contract, and by 1924 she had made thirteen films, none memorable. Her roles improved when she signed with Paramount in 1925; her performances in *Dancing Mothers* (1926) and *Mantrap* (1926), two movies with Jazz Age themes, led Elinor Glyn to pronounce that Bow had "it" on the screen.

Clara Bow had an amazing screen presence. On screen she never seemed to stay still. Studio executive B. P. Schulberg called her "the hottest jazz baby in films." A young man who first saw her at age seventeen observed, "I've never taken dope, but it was like a shot of dope when you looked at this girl." The *New York Times* wrote of her performance in *Mantrap*, "She could flirt with a grizzly bear." She had a boyish figure and what one reviewer called "flirts' eyes." She was especially known for her shock of red hair. In the 1920s redheads were thought to be highly sexed. Just as the vamp of the 1910s had dark hair and the typical star of the 1930s was a platinum blonde, the 1920s was the decade of the redhead.

Yet Bow's career lasted less than five years after the success of *It*. Somewhat unstable emotionally, she had several nervous breakdowns. As she once said, "A sex symbol is a heavy load to carry when one is tired, hurt, and bewildered." She was also hurt by scandals in her personal life, including widely publicized affairs with actor Gary Cooper and director Victor Fleming and a legal dispute with a former secretary. Furthermore, like many silent stars, she found the transition to talkies difficult. It was not just her Brooklyn accent—voice lessons could have smoothed that out. But her whole style of acting, which was very emotional and involved constant movement around the set, was not suited to the early days of sound recording, when an actor had to stay close to a stationary microphone to speak dialogue.

In 1931 Bow announced that she was leaving Hollywood to live with Rex Bell, a Nevada rancher whom she married later that year. She returned briefly to make two films before declaring "I've had enough" in 1933. She devoted her time to marriage and the two sons she and Bell had in 1934 and 1938, but her emotional instability made it hard for her to find happiness, and she and Bell eventually separated. She died in Los Angeles in 1965, long before her films had become cult classics. On seeing *It* for the first time in 1987, sixty years after its release, her son said, "If I ever saw Mother, I saw her in that movie. The tremendous facial expression. . . . It brought back so vividly what she was like." But it also reinforced the deep gulf between the on-screen charisma of the "It" Girl and Bow's fragile off-screen persona.

Toward the end of her life Bow reflected on the differences between Hollywood in the 1920s and the 1960s in a way that makes clear where her sympathies lay: "We had individuality. We did as we pleased. We stayed up late. We dressed the way we wanted. Today, stars are sensible and end up with better health. But we had more fun."

CRAZY BLUES

By PERRY BRADFORD

MAMIE SMITH AND HER JAZZ HOUNDS

Get this number for your phonograph on Okeh Record No. 4169

PUBLISHED BY
PERRY BRADFORD
MUSIC PUB. CO.
1547 BROADWAY, N. Y. C.

All That Jazz
The phonograph dramatically expanded the popularity and market for jazz recordings like this one by Mamie Smith and her Jazz Hounds. The success of "Crazy Blues" convinced record companies that there was a market to be tapped in black communities for what were called "race records," and Mamie Smith skyrocketed to fame with this 1920 recording.
Division of Political History, Smithsonian Institution, Washington, DC.

dominate the next leap forward in mass communication: television.) Unlike European networks, which were government monopolies, American radio stations operated for profit. Though the federal government licensed the stations, their revenue came primarily from advertisers and corporate sponsors.

Americans fell in love with radio. They listened avidly to the World Series and other sports events and to variety entertainment shows featuring performers such as the Lucky Strike Orchestra and the A & P Gypsies, sponsored (not surprisingly) by advertisers of those brand-name products or companies. One of the most popular radio shows of all time, "Amos 'n' Andy," premiered on NBC in 1928, featuring two white actors playing stereotypical black characters. Soon fractured phrases from "Amos 'n' Andy," such as "check and double check," became part of everyday speech. So many

people "tuned in" (another new phrase of the 1920s) that the country seemed to come to a halt during popular programs—a striking example of the pervasiveness of mass media.

New Patterns of Leisure

One of the most significant developments in modern life has been the growing freedom of workers from constant physical toil. As the workweek shrank and some workers won the right to paid vacations, Americans had more time—and energy—to spend on leisure. Like so much else in the 1920s, leisure became increasingly tied to consumption and mass culture.

Public recreation flourished in the 1920s as cities and suburbs built baseball diamonds, tennis courts, swimming pools, and golf courses. In the New York met-

Boxing Heroes
George Bellows (1882–1925) often painted boxing scenes. *Dempsey and Firpo* (1924) depicts a heavyweight fight between Jack Dempsey, the "Manassa Mauler," and challenger Luis Firpo, the "Wild Bull of the Pampas." Dempsey is the one being unceremoniously knocked out of the ring. Boxing was one of the most popular sports in the sports-crazy 1920s.
Whitney Museum of American Art, NY.

ropolitan area the city planner Robert Moses masterminded a vast system of parks, playgrounds, and picnic areas. His greatest achievement was Jones Beach on Long Island. Moses not only created the state park but built limited-access highways to it. Any New Yorker with a car—an important limit on freedom of consumption—could escape to a public beach in less than forty minutes.

People not only played sports but had the time and money to watch them. Newspapers, especially the tabloids, capitalized on popular interest; fans could also listen to contests on the radio or see highlights in a newsreel at a movie theater. Baseball continued to be the national pastime, drawing as many as 10 million fans a year to the ballpark. Tarnished in 1919 by the "Black Sox" scandal, in which gamblers bribed Chicago White Sox players to throw the World Series, baseball bounced back with the rise of heroes such as Babe Ruth of the New York Yankees, nicknamed the "Sultan of Swat." African Americans, however, had different heroes. Excluded from white teams, black athletes like Satchel Paige played in Negro leagues formed during the 1920s.

Thanks to media coverage, the popularity of sports figures rivaled that of movie stars. In football Red Grange of the University of Illinois was a major star, and Jack Dempsey and Gene Tunney attracted loyal followings in boxing. Bobby Jones helped to popularize golf. Bill Tilden dominated men's tennis, and Helen Wills and Suzanne Lenglen reigned in the women's game. The decade's best-known swimmer, male or female, was Gertrude Ederle, who swam the English Channel in 1926 in just over fourteen hours.

The decade's most popular hero was neither an athlete nor a movie star. On May 20, 1927, Charles Lindbergh made the first successful solo nonstop flight between New York and Paris in his plane, the *Spirit of St. Louis* (see New Technology, "Aviation," pp. 756–757). For the 3,610-mile flight that lasted 33½ hours, the pilot took only five sandwiches and one day's worth of tinned rations, saying, "If I get to Paris, I won't need any more, and if I don't get to Paris, I won't need any more either." Returning home to ticker-tape parades and effusive celebrations, Lindbergh captivated the nation because he combined the mastery of new technology (the airplane) with the traditional American virtues of individualism, self-reliance, and hard work. His charm and boyish good looks contributed further to his appeal. He was twenty-five years old at the time of his flight, and in 1928 *Time* magazine chose him as its first Man of the Year.

Dissenting Values and Cultural Conflict

——————★——————

Despite the attractions of modern times, many Americans were deeply disturbed by the new secular values of the 1920s. Cultural and political conflict broke out over issues such as immigration restriction, Prohibition, and race relations. Tension between city and country played

Aviation

★

CHARLES LINDBERGH CAPTIVATED an American public that was already captivated by aviation. In the 1910s and 1920s many Americans embraced this new technology, investing in the airplane almost utopian hopes for a new world order. There was something about seeing an airplane for the first time that called forth these feelings—it was so different from anything that anyone had ever seen before that they could only describe it in miraculous, almost mystical, terms. As a Chicago minister said of his first experience at an airshow, "Never have I seen such a look of wonder in the faces of a multitude. From the gray-haired man to the child, everyone seemed to feel that it was a new day in their lives."

World War I acted as a great accelerator to the aviation industry in both its commercial and its military applications. When the war ended, a glut of

Lucky Lindy
Charles Lindbergh stands beside the *Spirit of St. Louis*, the plane he flew solo nonstop across the Atlantic in 1927 on his way to becoming the most popular hero of the 1920s. His plane—named in honor of St. Louis, Missouri, investors and aviation enthusiasts who backed his venture—is permanently on display at the National Air and Space Museum in Washington, D.C.
Hulton Getty/Liaison.

a part in all those conflicts, but fear of and resistance to change, and ambivalence about modernity—feelings that transcended the urban-rural polarity—probably had a greater influence.

The Rise of Nativism

The cultural conflicts of the 1920s occurred in part because both rural and urban dwellers realized how far they had already strayed from previous values—especially devotion to a traditional way of life rooted in small towns and farming communities. As farmers struggled with severe economic problems, rural communities lost residents to the cities at an alarming rate. When the 1920 census revealed for the first time that city dwellers outnumbered rural people, Americans realized that a dramatic change had taken place, rivaling the closing of the frontier in 1890. In 1920 a full

inexpensive training planes became available, and these craft became the vehicles of choice for the barnstorming pilots of the 1920s. With their open cockpits, canvas wings, and rudimentary controls, these planes were tricky and often dangerous to fly, but that didn't stop the pilots from spreading the "winged gospel" through stunts, shows, and air races. These "birdmen"—and a fair number of "birdwomen"—brought aviation to towns and hamlets all across America. Said Amelia Earhart, who learned to fly in 1921, "Not to have had a ride in an airplane today is like not having heard the radio."

Hollywood discovered aviation in the 1920s, cranking out dozens of aviation-related films whose plots, often on World War I themes, featured production thrillers like dogfights and fiery crashes. Flying became a popular hobby for Hollywood celebrities like Cecil De Mille and Colleen Moore, which further added to its allure. In newspapers and tabloids across the country, aviation was front-page news precisely because aviation stories, especially crashes (of which there were many, given the technologically unsophisticated equipment of the time), sold papers. So did coverage of long-distance record-setting flights. When Admiral Richard Byrd became the first person to fly over the North Pole in 1926, he became a national hero.

It took railroads half a century to complete a cycle of pioneering, merger, regulation, and stabilization; the airlines did it in just over a decade, culminating in the 1938 Civil Aeronautics Act. An important milestone was the 1925 Contract Air Mail Act, whereby the federal government awarded contracts for airmail delivery on a competitive basis. These contracts were essential to the emergence of modern airlines, because they offered a guaranteed profit at a time when neither the technology nor the demand existed for commercial transport of passengers. Charles Lindbergh had been both a stunt pilot and an airmail pilot in Minnesota before his record-breaking flight.

Lindbergh's transatlantic solo set off a boom—often called the Lindbergh boom—that saw the number of airlines expand from sixteen in 1927 to forty-seven in 1930. But commercial air travel was still very much in its infancy. In 1929 Lindbergh joined other investors to found TAT (Transcontinental Air Transport), which promised passengers coast-to-coast passage in forty-eight hours by flying during the day and taking the train at night. (Night flying, especially over mountainous regions, was considered too dangerous a risk to paying customers.) TAT was not that much more efficient than the fastest train, however, and was much more expensive, so it never turned much of a profit despite its nickname of "the Lindbergh line." The airline was soon absorbed into TWA. In fact, by the early 1930s the outlines of the other major airline dynasties, including United, Eastern, and Northwest, were firmly in place. These companies would dominate the domestic and, in the case of Pan American, the international markets until airline deregulation in the 1970s.

Aviation technology took a quantum leap forward with the introduction in 1936 of the DC-3. With its seating capacity of twenty-one passengers, the DC-3 offered airlines the possibility of generating profits through passenger travel rather than being dependent on airmail contracts. The DC-3, manufactured by the Douglas Aircraft Company, proved to be the most influential piece of aircraft in history, as well as one of the most dependable. Hundreds of its models are still flying today.

52 percent of the population lived in urban areas, compared with 28 percent in 1870.

Though the 1920 census exaggerated the extent of urbanization—its guidelines classified towns with as few as 2,500 people as cities—there was no mistaking the trend (Map 23.1). By 1929, ninety-three cities had a population of over 100,000. During the 1920s New York City exceeded 7 million inhabitants, Chicago had close to 3 million, and the population of Los Angeles doubled to more than 1.2 million. Outside the major cities, growth was even more impressive. As a result of the availability of cheap land and better transportation—notably the automobile—expanded metropolitan areas and suburbs sprang up. This trend started long before the post–World War II suburban boom.

The mass media generally reflected the cosmopolitan values of these urban centers, and many old-stock Americans worried that the cities, and the immigrants

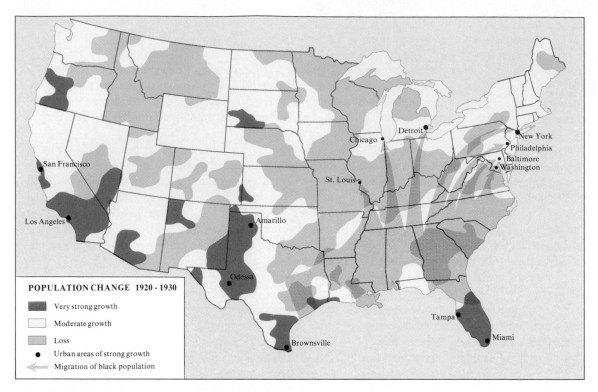

MAP 23.1
The Shift from Rural to Urban Population, 1920–1930
Despite the increasingly urban tone of modern America after 1920, regional patterns of population growth and decline were far from uniform. Cities in the South and West grew most dramatically as southern farmers moved to more promising areas with familiar climates. An important factor in the growth of northern cities, such as New York and Chicago, was the migration of southern blacks set in motion by World War I.

who clustered there, would soon dominate the culture. Yet polarities between city and country should not be overstated. The lives of rural people had been affected by the same forces that influenced urban life. Much of the new technology—especially electricity and automobiles—enhanced rural life. Indeed, rural people, like their urban counterparts, were tempted by the new materialistic values proclaimed by radio programs, magazines, and movies. Moreover, urban Americans were far from monolithic: many urban residents—immigrant Catholics, for example—were just as alarmed about declining moral standards as rural Protestants were. A simplified urban-rural duality misrepresents the complexity of the decade's cultural conflicts.

Immigration Restriction.   These conflicts often centered on the question of growing racial and ethnic pluralism. When native-born white Protestant Americans—both rural and city dwellers—looked at their communities in 1920, they saw a nation that had changed vastly in only forty years. During that time more than 23 million immigrants had come to America,

many of them Catholics or Jews, most from peasant stock. Senator William Bruce of Maryland called them "indigestible lumps" in the "national stomach," implying that the nation would be unable to absorb their large numbers and different customs. Such sentiments, which were widely shared, came to be known as nativism.

Nativist animosity fueled a new drive against immigration. The Chinese had been totally excluded in 1882, and Theodore Roosevelt had negotiated a "gentlemen's agreement" to limit Japanese immigration in 1908. Yet efforts to restrict European immigration did not meet with much success until after World War I, which had heightened suspicion of "hyphenated" Americans. During the Red Scare, nativists had played up the supposed association of immigrants with radicalism and labor unrest, charging that southern and eastern European Catholics and Jews were incapable of becoming true Americans.

In response Congress passed an emergency bill in 1921, limiting the number of immigrants to 3 percent of each national group as counted in the 1910 census.

KAZUO KAWAI

A Foreigner in America

———————★———————

Before the 1920s, the laws regulating immigration from Asia contained more loopholes for the Japanese than the Chinese. As a result, there were approximately 110,000 Japanese living in the United States in 1920. Asian immigrants' experience of prejudice was much sharper than that of Europeans; in California, for example, the Alien Land Law of 1913 barred foreign-born Japanese from purchasing land or leasing it for more than three years. At the same time, the experiences of Japanese immigrants such as Kazuo Kawai echoed the problems that many young ethnic Americans faced in the 1920s as they recognized that they did not belong in the old country but were not accepted as "One Hundred Percent Americans."

But it hurt because I couldn't say: "This is my own, my native land." What was my native land? Japan?

True, I was born there. But it had seemed a queer, foreign land to me when I visited it. America? I had, until now, thought so. I had even told my father once that even in case of war between Japan and America, I would consider America as my country. In language, in thought, in ideals, in custom, in everything, I was American. But America wouldn't have me. She wouldn't recognize me in high school. She put the pictures of those of my race at the tail end of the year book. (I was a commencement speaker, so they had to put my picture near the front.) She won't let me play tennis on the courts in the city parks of Los Angeles, by city ordinance. She won't give me service when I go to a barber's shop. She won't let me own a house to live in. She won't give me a job, unless it is a menial one that no American wants. I thought I was American, but America wouldn't have me. Once I was American, but America made a foreigner out of me—Not a Japanese, but a foreigner—a foreigner to any country, for I am just as much a foreigner to Japan as to America.

_____

Source: Stanford Survey of Race Relations (Stanford, CA: Stanford University, 1924), Hoover Institute Archives.

President Wilson refused to sign it, but the bill was reintroduced and passed during Warren Harding's administration. The new law produced immediate results. In the twelve-month period ending in June 1921, 805,228 immigrants had entered the United States; over the next twelve months, the number dropped to 309,556. In 1924 a more restrictive measure, the National Origins Act, reduced immigration through 1927 to 2 percent of each nationality as reflected in the 1890 census—which included relatively small numbers of people from southeastern Europe and Russia. After 1927 the law set a cap of 150,000 immigrants per year and continued to tie admission to a quota system that intentionally limited immigration from those regions. Japanese and Chinese immigrants were excluded entirely (see American Voices, "Kazuo Kawai: A Foreigner in America," above).

Puerto Rico provided a different source of immigration. After the Jones Act of 1917 conferred U.S. citizenship on Puerto Ricans, they could go to and from the mainland without restriction. Most of the movement was to New York, which was only a four-day sea voyage away. Thriving Puerto Rican communities, or *colonias*, sprang up in East Harlem and the Greenpoint section of Brooklyn. As it was for other migrants, the lure of New York City was primarily economic, and Puerto Ricans took jobs that had previously gone to European immigrants. But when hard times hit in the 1930s, the flow of Puerto Ricans stopped temporarily.

One remaining loophole permitted unrestricted immigration from countries in the Western Hemisphere. This source became increasingly significant over the years as Mexicans and Central and Latin Americans crossed the border to fill jobs made available by the cutoff of immigrants from Europe and Asia (Figure 23.1). Over 1 million Mexicans entered the United States between 1900 and 1930, including a wave who crossed the border after the Mexican Revolution of 1910 and another who entered during the labor shortages of World War I. Nativists and representatives of organized labor, who viewed Mexican immigrants as unwanted competition, lobbied Congress to close the loophole but met with strong

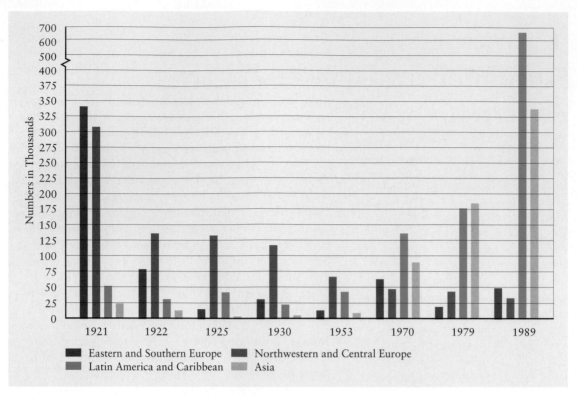

FIGURE 23.1
American Immigration after World War I
Legislation reflecting nativism slowed the influx of immigrants after 1920, as did the
dislocations brought on by depression and war in the 1930s and 1940s. Note the
higher rate of non-European immigration since the 1970s.

resistance until the 1930s and the economic devastation of the Great Depression.

Nativism took other forms during the 1920s. Many elite colleges instituted quotas to limit the enrollment of Jewish students, and many law firms refused to hire Jewish lawyers. Henry Ford spoke for many Americans when he warned of the menace of the "International Jew," referring to the supposed Jewish domination of international finance. Ford became so closely identified with anti-Semitism that decades passed before some Jewish families could bring themselves to buy his company's cars.

The New Klan. The most striking example of nativism in the 1920s was the revival of the Ku Klux Klan (KKK). Shortly after the 1915 premiere of *Birth of a Nation*, a group of southerners gathered on Stone Mountain outside Atlanta to revive the racist organization. Taking as its motto "Native, white, Protestant supremacy," the modern Klan appealed to both urban and rural folk, though its largest "klaverns" were found in urban areas. Spreading out from its southern base and encouraged by the superpatriotism of the war years, it found significant support in the Far West, the

Southwest, and the Midwest—especially Indiana, Oklahoma, and Oregon. Unlike its earlier incarnation after the Civil War, the Klan of the 1920s did not limit its harassment to blacks; Catholics and Jewish immigrants were just as likely to be its targets. Its tactics, however, remained the same: arson, physical intimidation, and economic boycotts directed at Klan targets. The new Klan also turned to politics, succeeding in electing hundreds of Klansmen to public office and emerging as a significant force in the Democratic Party.

At the height of its power in 1925 the Klan had over 3 million members, including a strong contingent of women who pursued their own distinctive political agenda combining racism, nativism, and a commitment to equal rights for white Protestant women. But after mid-decade the Klan declined rapidly. Battles between rival factions and disclosures of rampant corruption hurt its image. Especially damaging was the revelation that Grand Dragon David Stephenson, the Klan's national leader, had kidnapped and sexually assaulted his former secretary, driving her to commit suicide. And the passage of the 1924 immigration act reduced the nativist fervor that was a legacy of World War I, robbing the Klan of its most potent issue.

Patrolling the Texas Border
These Border Patrol officers in Laredo, Texas, in 1926 were deputized to stop illegal
immigration from Mexico. Their guns, military uniforms, and stern expressions did
not present a warm welcome to immigrants arriving from south of the border.
University of Texas at Austin.

Religious Fundamentalism

Other cultural tensions erupted over religion. The
debate between modernist and fundamentalist Protestants, which had been simmering since the 1890s (see
Chapter 20), came to a boil in the 1920s. Modernists
tried to reconcile religion with scientific discoveries
such as Darwin's theory of evolution and the avalanche
of recent technological and scientific discoveries. Fundamentalists favored a literal interpretation of the Bible

that could not be reconciled with science. Most major
Protestant denominations, especially the Baptists and
the Presbyterians, had heated internal conflicts in the
1920s, with the losers frequently splitting off to form
their own churches. The most conspicuous evangelical
figures, however, were outside the established denominations. Popular preachers like Billy Sunday and Aimee
Semple McPherson used revivals, storefront churches,
and open-air preaching to popularize their own brands
of charismatic fundamentalism and traditional values.

Women of the Klan
The Ku Klux Klan was so well integrated
into the daily life of white Protestants
that one woman from rural Indiana
remembered her time in the KKK in the
1920s as "just a celebration . . . a way of
growing up." Perhaps as many as
500,000 women joined the Women of the
Ku Klux Klan (WKKK) in the 1920s,
including these Indiana Klanswomen in
August 1924.
W. A. Swift Collection, A. M. Bracken Library,
Ball State University, Muncie, IN.

Religious controversy soon entered the political arena when fundamentalists, worried about declining morality and increasing secularism, turned to the law to shore up their vision of a righteous Protestant nation. Some states enacted legislation to prevent the teaching of evolution in schools. In 1925, for example, Tennessee passed a law declaring that "it shall be unlawful . . . to teach any theory that denies the story of the Divine creation of man as taught in the Bible, and to teach instead that man has descended from a lower order of animals." In a test case involving John T. Scopes, a high school biology teacher in Dayton, Tennessee, the recently formed American Civil Liberties Union (ACLU) challenged the constitutionality of that law. Clarence Darrow, a famous criminal lawyer, defended Scopes. William Jennings Bryan, a spellbinding orator and ardent fundamentalist, was the most prominent member of the prosecution team.

The Scopes trial came to be known as the "monkey trial," referring both to Darwin's theory that human beings and other primate species share a common ancestor and to the circus atmosphere that prevailed in the courtroom. In July 1925 more than a hundred journalists crowded the sweltering courthouse, and the Chicago radio station WGN broadcast the proceedings live. The trial quickly turned to volatile questions of faith and scientific theory. The judge rebuffed defense efforts to call expert scientific witnesses on evolution, dismissing such testimony as hearsay because the scientists had not been present when lower forms of life had evolved. Darrow countered by calling Bryan to the stand as an expert on the Bible. Under oath, Bryan asserted his belief that a "big fish" had swallowed Jonah, that Eve had been created from Adam's rib, and that God had created the world in six days. He hedged, however, about whether the "days" were literally twenty-four hours long, an inconsistency that Darrow ruthlessly exploited.

Even so, the jury took only eight minutes to find Scopes guilty. Though the Tennessee Supreme Court overturned the conviction on a technicality, the reversal prevented further appeal of the case and the controversial law remained on the books for more than thirty years. Historically the trial symbolizes the conflict between the two competing value systems, scientific and religious, that clashed in the 1920s. It suggests that despite the period's image as frivolous and decadent, religion continued to matter deeply to many Americans.

Prohibition

The most notorious cultural debate of the 1920s was the battle over the Eighteenth Amendment, which took effect on January 20, 1920 (see Chapter 22). More than any other issue, Prohibition gave the decade its reputation as the Roaring Twenties. In major cities, whose ethnic populations had always opposed Prohibition, noncompliance was widespread. Illegal saloons called speakeasies sprang up—more than 30,000 in New York City alone. People who preferred to drink at home imitated rural moonshiners by learning to distill "bathtub gin." Liquor smugglers operated with ease along borders and coastlines. Organized crime, already a factor in major cities, supplied a ready-made distribution network for bootleg liquor, and gangsters used the "noble experiment" of Prohibition to entrench themselves more deeply in city politics. Said the decade's most notorious gangster, Chicago's Al Capone, "Everybody calls me a racketeer. I call myself a businessman. When I sell liquor, it's bootlegging. When my patrons serve it on a silver tray on Lake Shore Drive, it's hospitality."

By the middle of the decade Prohibition was clearly failing. Government appropriations for its enforcement were woefully inadequate, and the few highly publicized raids hardly made a dent in the liquor trade. In 1929 Attorney General William D. Mitchell conceded that liquor could be bought "at almost any hour of the day or night, either in rural districts, the smaller towns, or the cities." A committee appointed by President Hoover in 1931 to study Prohibition only weakly recommended that it be retained.

But Prohibition was not just the law—it was part of the Constitution. So the forces for repeal—the "wets," as opposed to the "drys," who continued to support the Eighteenth Amendment—began the long process of gaining the necessary majorities in Congress and state legislatures to amend the Constitution again. The Women's Organization for National Prohibition Repeal, headed by Pauline Sabin, a wealthy New York Republican, lobbied Congress and mobilized support from other national organizations. The onset of the Great Depression hastened the repeal process. People argued that liquor production would create jobs and prop up the faltering economy. On December 5, 1933, the Eighteenth Amendment was repealed. Ironically, drinking became more socially acceptable, although not necessarily more widespread, than it had been before the Prohibition experiment began its rocky course.

Intellectual Crosscurrents

The most articulate and embittered dissenters in the 1920s were writers and intellectuals who were disillusioned by the horrors of World War I and the crass materialism of the new American consumer culture. Some artists felt so at odds with what they saw as the complacent, anti-intellectual, moralistic tone of American life that they settled in Europe—some temporarily, such as the novelists Ernest Hemingway and F. Scott Fitzgerald, and others permanently, such as the writer Gertrude Stein. (The strong dollar, another legacy of

Ignoring Prohibition
Despite their popularity, speakeasies were rarely drawn or photographed; after all, they were supposed to be private clubs tucked away beyond the reach of the law. Fancy hotels were unable to compete with speakeasies once their bars were shut down, and many went out of business in the 1920s. But John Sloan's 1928 painting shows the rich enjoying themselves at New York's posh Lafayette Hotel. It is likely that these gentlemen and ladies had flasks concealed somewhere in their evening finery.
John Sloan, *The Lafayette*, 1928, Metropolitan Museum of Art, New York. Gift of Friends of John Sloan, 1929 (28.18).

World War I, made this a cheap and attractive way to leave American materialism behind.) African Americans such as the dancer Josephine Baker, the writer Langston Hughes, and the painter Henry O. Tanner also sought a temporary escape from racism by moving to France. The poet T. S. Eliot, who left the United States before the war, became a British citizen. His despairing poem *The Waste Land* (1922), with its images of a fragmented civilization in ruins after the war, influenced a generation of writers.

Other writers also made powerful statements against war and contemporary culture, including John Dos Passos, whose first novel, *The Three Soldiers* (1921), was inspired by the war, and whose *1919* (1932), the second volume in his *USA* trilogy, railed against the obscenity of "Mr. Wilson's war." Ernest Hemingway described the dehumanizing consequences and futility of the war in *In Our Time* (1924), *The Sun Also Rises* (1926), and *A Farewell to Arms* (1929), which drew on his experience as an ambulance driver in Italy. In 1925 F. Scott Fitzgerald published *The Great Gatsby*, which showed the corrosive consequences of the mindless pursuit of wealth.

But the artists and writers who migrated to Europe, particularly to Paris, were not just a "Lost Generation" fleeing America; they were also drawn to Paris as the cultural and artistic capital of the world. Paris, as Gertrude Stein put it, was "where the twentieth century was happening." Indeed, the *modernist movement*, the term for the deliberate departure from tradition and the use of experimental forms in many styles of twentieth-century literature, art, and music, invigorated American writing abroad and at home.

In the 1920s the business culture and corruption of the Harding years caused intellectuals to cast a more critical eye on American society. One of the sharpest critics, the Baltimore journalist H. L. Mencken, directed his mordant wit against mass culture, small-town America, and the "booboisie," his contemptuous term for the middle class. In the *American Mercury*, the journal he founded in 1922, Mencken championed writers such as Sherwood Anderson, Sinclair Lewis, and Theodore Dreiser, who satirized the provincialism of American society.

The literature of the 1920s was varied and rich. Poetry enjoyed a renaissance in the works of Robert Frost, Wallace Stevens, Marianne Moore, and William Carlos Williams. Edith Wharton won a Pulitzer Prize for *The Age of Innocence* (1920), the first woman to be so honored. Influenced by Freudian psychology, the novelist William Faulkner achieved his first critical success with *The Sound and the Fury* (1929), set in the fictional Mississippi county of Yoknapatawpha, where inhabitants cling to the old values of the agrarian South as they try to adjust to modern industrial capitalism. The dramatist Eugene O'Neill also showed the influence of Freudian psychology in his experimental plays, including *The Hairy Ape* (1922) and *Desire under the Elms* (1924). Although Faulkner and O'Neill went on to produce major works in the 1930s, on the whole the creative energy of the literary renaissance of the 1920s did not survive into the next decade. The Great Depression, social and ideological unrest, and the rise of totalitarianism would reshape the intellectual landscape.

Harlem Renaissance. A different kind of cultural affirmation took place in the black community of Harlem in the 1920s. In the words of the Reverend Adam Clayton Powell Sr., pastor of the influential Abyssinian Baptist Church, Harlem loomed as "the symbol of liberty and the Promised Land to Negroes everywhere." One aspect of this hope was the Harlem Renaissance, an artistic movement of young writers and artists who broke with the older, genteel traditions of black literature to reclaim a cultural identity with African roots. Alain Locke, editor of the influential anthology *The New Negro* (1926), summed up the movement when he stated that, through art, "Negro life is seizing its first chances for group expression and self-determination."

The Harlem Renaissance championed racial pride and cultural identity in the midst of white society. The poet Langston Hughes, who became a leading exponent of the Harlem Renaissance, captured its affirmative spirit when he asserted, "I am a Negro—and beautiful." Authors such as Claude McKay, Jean Toomer, Jessie Fauset, and Zora Neale Hurston explored the black experience and represented the "New Negro" in fiction. Countee Cullen and Langston Hughes turned to poetry, and Augusta Savage used sculpture to draw attention to black accomplishments. Their outpouring of literary work showed the ongoing African American struggle to find a way, as W. E. B. Du Bois put it, "to be both a Negro and an American."

The artistic outpouring encouraged a wide range of creative expression. Jean Toomer, a writer passionately committed to black self-expression, wrote the influen-

The Harlem Renaissance
The Crisis, edited by W. E. B. Du Bois, was the magazine of the National Association for the Advancement of Colored People (NAACP). This 1929 cover suggests the cultural and political awakenings associated with the Harlem Renaissance.
Henry Lee Moon Library and Civil Rights Archive, NAACP, Washington, DC.

tial novel *Cane* in 1923. With its poems, sketches, and stories about a northern black's discovery of the rural black South, it inspired other African American artists and writers. Langston Hughes drew on the black artistic forms of blues and jazz in *The Weary Blues* (1926), a groundbreaking collection of poems. Considered the most original black poet and the most representative African American writer of the time, Hughes also wrote novels, plays, and essays. Zora Neale Hurston, born in Florida to a family of poor tenant farmers, attended Howard University in Washington, D.C., and won a scholarship to study anthropology at Barnard College in New York City. She spent a decade collecting folklore in the South and the Caribbean and incorporated that material into her short stories and novels. Her genius for storytelling won her acclaim.

The vitality of the Harlem Renaissance was short-lived. Although the NAACP's magazine *The Crisis* was a forum for the Harlem writers, the black middle class and the intellectual elite in Harlem were relatively small and could not support the group's efforts. Its main audience consisted of white intellectuals and philanthropists, and many writers were ambivalent about depending on white patronage as they struggled to attain an authentic voice in their fiction. Langston Hughes became disillusioned with his white patron when she withdrew support as he began to write about common black people in Kansas and New York rather than keeping with African themes.

During the Jazz Age, when Harlem was in vogue, the publishing industry courted its writers, but the stock market crash of 1929 brought that interest to a sudden end. The movement waned in the 1930s as the depression deepened. Nonetheless, the writers of the Harlem Renaissance would influence a future generation of black writers when their works were rediscovered by black intellectuals during the civil rights movement of the 1960s.

Marcus Garvey and the UNIA. Although the Harlem Renaissance was mainly an artistic movement, other African American movements sought to challenge white political and cultural hegemony. The most successful was the Universal Negro Improvement Association (UNIA), which championed black separatism under the leadership of the Jamaican-born Marcus Garvey. Based in Harlem, the UNIA was the black working class's first mass movement. At its height it claimed 4 million followers, many of whom were recent migrants to northern cities. Garvey's wife, Amy Jacques Garvey, appealed to black women by combining black nationalism with an emphasis on women's contributions to culture and politics. Like several nineteenth-century reformers, Marcus Garvey urged blacks to return to Africa because, he said, blacks would never be treated justly in countries ruled by whites. Although he did not anticipate a mass migration, he did envision that a strong black Africa could use its power to protect blacks everywhere.

The UNIA grew rapidly in the early 1920s. It published a newspaper called *Negro World*, and it opened "liberty halls" in New York, Chicago, Detroit, New Orleans, Mobile, Jacksonville, and other cities. The UNIA also undertook business ventures to support black capitalism. Its most ambitious project was the Black Star Line steamship company, which was supposed to ferry cargo between the West Indies and the United States and take African Americans back to Africa. The Black Star Line caused the downfall of the UNIA. Irregularities in fundraising led to Garvey's conviction for mail fraud in 1925, and he was sentenced to five years in prison. President Coolidge paroled him in 1927, and Garvey was deported to Jamaica. Without his charismatic leadership the organization collapsed, but his ideas remained influential even after his death in 1940.

The 1928 Election

The works of the Lost Generation and the Harlem Renaissance touched only a small minority of Americans in the 1920s, but emotionally charged issues such as Prohibition, religious fundamentalism, and nativism spilled over into national politics. The Democratic Party, which drew on Protestant rural supporters in the South and West as well as ethnic voters in northern cities, was especially vulnerable to the urban-rural conflicts of the time (see Voices from Abroad, "Li Gongpu: The Presidential Election of 1928," p. 766).

Alfred E. Smith. In 1924 the Democratic National Convention had revealed an intensely polarized party, split between the urban machines and its rural wing. In 1928 the urban wing held sway and succeeded in nominating New York's governor, Alfred E. Smith, on the first ballot. Al Smith, the grandson of Irish immigrants and a Catholic, was the first presidential candidate to reflect the aspirations of the urban working classes. Proud of his urban background, he adopted "The Sidewalks of New York" as his campaign song. Democrats hoped Smith would attract recent immigrants and workers who traditionally voted Republican. Belle Moskowitz, a New York social worker who served as Smith's political advisor, helped him appeal to women and liberal urban Jews.

But Smith had liabilities. He spoke in a heavy New York accent, sprinkling his speeches with "ain't" and "he don't," which did not play well on the radio. His early career in Tammany Hall troubled many voters, suggesting—incorrectly—that he was little more than a cog in a political machine. Smith's stand on Prohibition alienated even more voters. Although he promised to enforce Prohibition, he made no secret of his support for repeal. Smith chose John J. Raskob, a wealthy entrepreneur and one of the nation's most ardent "wets," as head of the Democratic National Committee.

By far the most damaging handicap to Smith's campaign was his Catholicism. In the midst of the heightened nativism of the decade, most Protestant Americans were not ready for a Roman Catholic president in 1928. Although Smith insisted that his religion would not interfere with his duties as president, being Catholic cost him support from Democrats and Republicans alike. Protestant clergymen, who already opposed Smith because he supported the repeal of Prohibition, led the drive against him. "No Governor can kiss the papal ring and get within gunshot of the White House," declared a Methodist bishop from Buffalo.

Herbert Hoover. Just as Smith marked a new kind of presidential candidate for the Democrats, so did Herbert Hoover for the Republicans. Coolidge's unexpected decision not to run for reelection in 1928 opened the

LI GONGPU

The Presidential Election of 1928

———————★———————

In 1927 Li Gongpu (1902–1946) came to America as an exchange student at Reed College in Oregon. As a Chinese intellectual and political activist, he was especially interested in the workings of the American electoral system. His description of going to a polling place on November 6, 1928, with a Reed classmate drew comparisons between the American system and China's ongoing struggle to live up to the promise of the 1911 revolution.

A week before the election I made preparations to go to a polling place on election day to watch the excitement and to observe the attitude of the people of this country at the time of the election. Who would have imagined that when I went with my schoolmate Cane on the afternoon of the sixth, the so-called polling place turned out to be nothing more than a little house! A small sign outside the door stated that this was Municipal Electoral Polling Place No. 137. In one half of the ground floor sat a ballot issuer, a checker, a ballot receiver, and four overseers; in the other half was room for ten people to fill out ballots. While Cane did his, I asked in detail about the procedures for filling out a ballot, and I also received an explanation of the ballot from the lady who was issuing them.

Lastly, after getting permission from the chairman of the polling place, I went upstairs and observed how the ballots were counted. Four people were counting the votes, one calling them out and three recording them. Each ballot had on it not only the presidential candidates of the various parties but also important state officials whose terms had expired, the city's mayor, and a number of important state referendum questions, such as whether to increase firemen's disability benefits and old-age pensions, whether to increase the automobile gasoline tax, and so on, with detailed rationales included, to be decided by the opinion of the majority of the people. The poll workers were deputed by a state administrative organ; each precinct has no more than three or four hundred voters registered in it, and there was not the slightest crowding or clamor. Election regulations require that the parties stop all propaganda activities on election day, so

that day was unusually peaceful everywhere. I watched two workers and an old lady fill out their ballots with extraordinary care. Such an atmosphere is truly worthy of our respect! It is extremely discouraging to compare this with our own former elections for provincial assemblymen and national assemblymen, which were confused and disorganized, without the slightest order, even to the point of knives and guns, beheadings, and bloodletting!

But if we carry our examination of the American electoral system and its true nature a bit further, the conclusion will be that the democratic form of government in the United States has so far only taken the first step and not yet reached perfection. In political matters the people are still completely manipulated by the two parties. Before an election, promises are made: if elected, this will be done or that will be carried out. Once the election period is past, the party that has gained power exercises its authority in any way it wishes. The policies and matters they had promised are for the most part treated only perfunctorily, and there is nothing that the people can do. In this respect, the external expression and inner strength of America's so-called democratic spirit are not as great as those of the English people.

As for the election of state government officials and city mayors, most are controlled by political parties, and the majority of the people do not know about the record of experience or character of nine out of ten people on the ballot and just mark any name when voting. This is a fact admitted by many of my schoolmates and professors of government. Of the personnel employed in various organs of state government and so on, more than half are mediocrities interested only in making a living, as was declared by a Democratic senator in a public speech in the city.

If people at the level of Americans still have politics that are so imperfect, then it is clear that the realization of "democracy" is not an easy matter. At the same time we should also be aware that if from now on the Nationalist government actively devotes itself to constructive work, strengthening the five-branch organization of the government, and at the same time education and the economy suddenly develop and spread, then after twenty years the progress of our politics, industry, and commerce could easily be equal to that of England and the United States. It all depends on the wisdom and hard work of us Chinese.

Source: R. David Arkush and Leo O. Lee, eds. and trans., *Land without Ghosts: Chinese Impressions of America from the Mid-Nineteenth Century to the Present* (Berkeley: University of California Press, 1989), 140–141.

field, and Hoover led from the start. As a professional administrator and engineer, Hoover embodied the new managerial and technological elite that was restructuring the economic order. He had never been elected to political office. During his campaign, in which he gave only seven speeches, Hoover promised that his vision of individualism and cooperative endeavor would banish poverty from the United States. That rhetoric, as well as his reputation for organizing humanitarian relief during the war, caused many voters to consider him more progressive than Smith.

Hoover won a stunning victory, receiving 58 percent of the popular vote to Smith's 41 percent, and 444 electoral votes to 87 for Smith (Map 23.2). For the first time since Reconstruction a Republican candidate carried Virginia, Texas, and North Carolina, largely because many Democrats refused to vote for a Catholic. The strong economy also aided the Republicans. The voter turnout rose from 52 percent in 1924 to 56.9 percent in 1928, partly as a result of extensive education campaigns undertaken by the League of Women Voters. Also, the transfer of polling places to schools and churches from their former locations in saloons made women feel more comfortable with

their new role as voters. Many Catholic and immigrant women voted for Smith, but even more native-born Republican women supported Herbert Hoover.

The 1928 election reflected important underlying political changes. Despite the party's overwhelming loss, the Democratic turnout increased substantially in urban areas. Smith won the industrialized states of Massachusetts and Rhode Island and carried the nation's twelve largest cities. The Democrats were on their way to forging a new identity as the party of the urban masses, including ethnic voters—a reorientation that the New Deal completed in the 1930s.

It is unlikely that any Democratic candidate, let alone a Catholic, could have won the presidency in 1928. With a seemingly prosperous economy, a national consensus on foreign policy, and strong support from the business community, the Republicans were unbeatable. Ironically, Herbert Hoover's victory put him in the unenviable position of leading the United States when the Great Depression struck in 1929. Having claimed credit for the prosperity of the 1920s, the Republicans found it difficult to escape blame for the depression. Twenty-four years would pass before a Republican won the presidency again.

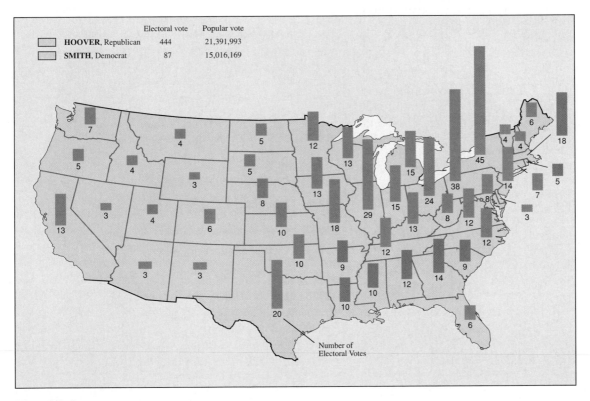

MAP 23.2
The Election of 1928
Historians still debate the extent to which 1928 was a critical election—that is, one that produced a significant realignment in voting behavior. Although the Republican Herbert Hoover swept the electoral college, Democrats were heartened by the fact that Alfred E. Smith won the heavily industrialized states of Rhode Island and Massachusetts. For the first time, the Democratic ticket carried the nation's twelve largest cities, garnering strong support from immigrants and urban dwellers.

Summary

By the 1920s modern America had arrived, a transformation that had begun with World War I. The Republican Party controlled the national government and cemented the partnership between business and government that had been accelerated by the war and that characterized the pattern of state building during the era. In foreign policy the United States promoted disarmament and the reduction of German war reparations but otherwise generally steered clear of European political affairs. The chief U.S. interest was to ensure a stable environment for economic expansion abroad, especially in the Western Hemisphere. With the exception of the 1920–1921 recession the economy performed well, although agriculture never recovered from the postwar slump, and some industries remained overextended after their wartime expansion. The automobile industry typified the new mass-production techniques that dominated economic life in the United States and revolutionized American society.

During the 1920s a national culture began to develop. It was characterized by new ways of spending leisure time, a heightened emphasis on consumption and advertising, and the wide diffusion of new, more secular ideas and values through movies, radio, and other mass media. The new life-styles of the decade, often called the Roaring Twenties or the Jazz Age, captured the popular imagination but were limited to a minority of the population. Families needed a middle-class income to buy cars, radios, vacuum cleaners, and toasters. Those left outside the circle of prosperity included farmers, blacks, and Mexican Americans.

Not everyone welcomed the new secular values of the 1920s. Conflicts arose over Prohibition, religion, race, and immigration. Those cultural disputes spilled over into politics, disrupting the already fractured Democratic Party. The 1928 election showed that the nation could not yet accept a Catholic as president. The Republican ascendancy continued under Herbert Hoover, who looked forward to a term filled with even greater prosperity and progress.

The advances of the New Era, and the expectation that the nation would continue to be vigorous and powerful at home and abroad, made the harsh realities of the Great Depression that would follow all the more shocking.

TIMELINE

1920	First commercial radio broadcast
	Warren G. Harding elected president
	Census reveals shift in population from farms to cities
	Sinclair Lewis, *Main Street*
	Edith Wharton, *The Age of Innocence*
1920–1921	National economic recession
1921	Sheppard-Towner Act
	Congress limits immigration
	Washington Conference supports naval disarmament
1922	Fordney-McCumber Tariff
	T. S. Eliot, *The Waste Land*
1923	Calvin Coolidge succeeds Harding as president
	Time magazine founded
	Jean Toomer, *Cane*
1924	Dawes Plan reduces German reparation payments
	Bruce Barton, *The Man Nobody Knows*
	Teapot Dome scandal
	U.S. troops withdraw from Dominican Republic
	National Origins Act
1925	F. Scott Fitzgerald, *The Great Gatsby*
	Height of Ku Klux Klan
	Scopes ("monkey") trial
1926	Alain Locke, *The New Negro* anthology
1927	First "talkies"
	Charles Lindbergh's solo flight
	Ford's Model A car
1928	Herbert Hoover elected president
	Kellogg-Briand Pact signed
1929	*Middletown* published
	Ernest Hemingway, *A Farewell to Arms*
	William Faulkner, *The Sound and the Fury*

Suggested Readings

───────────────★───────────────

General overviews of the 1920s are provided by Lynn Dumenil, *Modern Temper* (1995); Ellis Hawley, *The Great War and the Search for a Modern Order, 1917–1933* (1979); William Leuchtenburg, *The Perils of Prosperity*, 2nd ed. (1995); and Ann Douglas, *Terrible Honesty: Mongrel Manhattan in the 1920s* (1995). Robert S. Lynd and Helen Merrell Lynd, *Middletown: A Study in Modern American Culture* (1929), remains a superb study of American life in the 1920s.

The Business-Government Partnership of the 1920s

Discussion of corporate developments can be found in Alfred Chandler, *The Visible Hand* (1977), and Robert Himmelberg, *The Origins of the National Recovery Administration: Business, Government, and the Trade Association Ideal, 1921–1933* (1976). On labor developments, see Irving Bernstein, *The Lean Years* (1960); David Brody, *Workers in Industrial America* (1980); and David Montgomery, *The Fall of the House of Labor* (1987).

The domestic and international aspects of the economy are treated in Jim Potter, *The American Economy between the Wars* (1974), and Emily Rosenberg, *Spreading the American Dream* (1982). Interpretations of foreign policy include Akira Iriye, *The Globalizing of America, 1913–1945* (1993); Warren Cohen, *Empire without Tears* (1987); William Appleman Williams, *The Tragedy of American Diplomacy* (1962); and Walter LaFeber, *Inevitable Revolutions* (1983).

General introductions to politics in the 1920s can be found in David Burner, *The Politics of Provincialism* (1967); Robert Murray, *The Politics of Normalcy* (1973); and Alan Dawley, *Struggles for Justice* (1991). Biographies of the decade's major political figures include Donald McCoy, *Calvin Coolidge* (1967); David Burner, *Herbert Hoover* (1979); and Paula Elder, *Governor Alfred E. Smith: The Politician as Reformer* (1983). On women in politics, see Nancy Cott, *The Grounding of Modern Feminism* (1987); Elisabeth Israels Perry, *Belle Moskowitz* (1987); and Molly Ladd-Taylor, *Mother-Work: Women, Child Welfare and the State, 1890–1930* (1994).

A New National Culture

Daniel Boorstin, *The Americans: The Democratic Experience* (1973), and David Nasaw, *Going Out: The Rise and Fall of Public Amusements* (1993), introduce the emerging mass culture. On movies, see Steven J. Ross, *Working-Class Hollywood: Silent Film and the Shaping of Class in America* (1998); Robert Sklar, *Movie-Made America*, 2nd ed. (1987); Larry May, *Screening Out the Past* (1980). Material on Clara Bow can be found in David Stenn, *Clara Bow, Runnin' Wild* (1988). Erik Barnouw, *A Tower in Babel* (1966), and Susan Douglas, *Inventing American Broadcasting* (1987), discuss radio. See also Melvin Patrick Ely, *The Adventures of Amos 'n' Andy: A Social History of an American Phenomenon* (1991). On adver-tising, see Roland Marchand, *Advertising the American Dream* (1985), and T. J. Jackson Lears, *Fables of Abundance* (1994). Paula Fass, *The Damned and the Beautiful* (1977), and Beth L. Bailey, *From Front Porch to Back Seat* (1988), cover youth, and Susan Strasser, *Never Done* (1982), and Ruth Schwartz Cowan, *More Work for Mother* (1983), discuss the lives of white middle-class women. Lizabeth Cohen, *Making a New Deal: Industrial Workers in Chicago, 1919–1939* (1990), suggests how working-class communities adapted mass culture for their purposes. Joan Shelley Rubin describes the middle class in *The Making of Middlebrow Culture* (1992).

The impact of the automobile on modern American life is amply documented by James Flink, *The Car Culture* (1975) and *The Automobile Age* (1988); on women and the automobile, see Virginia Scharff, *Taking the Wheel* (1991). For sports, see Allen Guttmann, *A Whole New Ball Game* (1988); Harvey Green, *Fit for America* (1986); and Susan Cahn, *Coming on Strong: Gender and Sexuality in 20th Century Women's Sport* (1994). The Negro Leagues are covered in Robert W. Peterson, *Only the Ball Was White* (1970), and Donn Rogosin, *Invisible Men* (1985).

Dissenting Values and Cultural Conflict

Paul Carter, *Another Part of the Twenties* (1977), outlines the decade's deeply felt cultural controversies. Background on rural and urban life is provided by Don Kirschner, *City and Country: Rural Responses to Urbanization in the 1920s* (1970); Zane Miller, *The Urbanization of America* (1973); and Jon Teaford, *The Twentieth-Century American City* (1986). John Higham, *Strangers in the Land* (1955), describes immigration restriction and nativism. Richard K. Tucker, *The Dragon and the Cross* (1991), and Leonard Moore, *Citizen Klansmen* (1991), cover the Klan's rise and fall, and Kathleen M. Blee, *Women of the Klan* (1991), and Nancy MacLean, *Behind the Mask of Chivalry* (1994), offer a provocative discussion of racism and gender in the 1920s. George M. Marsden, *Fundamentalism and American Culture* (1980), and William G. McLoughlin, *Fundamentalism in American Culture* (1983), cover religion; Edward J. Larson, *Summer of the Gods* (1997), treats the Scopes trial. On intellectual development, see Robert Crunden, *From Self to Society, 1919–1941* (1972); Roderick Nash, *The Nervous Generation: American Thought, 1917–1930* (1969); and Daniel Singal, ed., *Modernist Culture in America* (1991). Virginia Sanchez Korrol, *From Colonia to Community* (1983), covers the history of Puerto Ricans in New York City. On the Harlem Renaissance, see George Hutchinson, *The Harlem Renaissance in Black and White* (1995); David Levering Lewis, *When Harlem Was in Vogue* (1981); Nathan Huggins, *Harlem Renaissance* (1971); and Cheryl A. Wall, *Women of the Harlem Renaissance* (1995). For jazz and blues, see Burton Peretti, *The Creation of Jazz* (1992), and Angela Y. Davis, *Blues Legacies and Black Feminism* (1998). Judith Stein, *The World of Marcus Garvey* (1985), describes the reformer. On Prohibition, see Andrew Sinclair, *Prohibition: The Era of Excess* (1962), and Norman Clark, *Deliver Us from Evil* (1976). The 1928 election is covered in Oscar Handlin, *Al Smith and His America* (1958); Kristi Andersen, *The Creation of a Democratic Majority, 1928–1936* (1979); and Allan J. Lichtman's quantitative study, *Prejudice and the Old Politics* (1979).

The Great Depression

FOR MOST AMERICANS, the year 1929 means only one thing—the stock market crash that touched off the Great Depression. By 1932, more than one-fourth of the nation's workers were unemployed and industrial production had fallen to barely half the 1929 level. President Herbert Hoover, formerly the symbol of business prosperity, had become the scapegoat for the depression. Images from the 1920s of flappers and movie stars, admen and stockbrokers, were replaced by depression-era images of hoboes standing in breadlines, unemployed men selling apples on city street corners, and displaced farm families piling into dilapidated jalopies to head west to California.

Did the country really go from unprecedented prosperity to the poorhouse overnight? Of course not. The extreme contrast between the flush times of the 1920s and the hard times of the 1930s is too stark. The vaunted prosperity of the 1920s was never as widespread or as deeply rooted as many believed at the time. Although America's mass-consumption economy was the envy of the world, many people lived on its margins. This unequal distribution of wealth was one of the main causes of the depression. Nor was every American devastated by the depression. Those with a secure job or a fixed income survived the economic downturn in relatively good shape, and some people even managed to get rich. Yet few could escape the depression's wide-ranging social, political, and cultural effects. Although not every event of the 1930s should be viewed through the lens of the depression, the great economic contraction unifies the history of the decade more than any other factor.

Looking for Work
This detail of Moses Soyer's painting Employment Agency (1940) *captures the despair and bleak resignation of a victim of the Great Depression—a white male, down on his luck but still trying to keep up appearances and hope.*
Collection of Philip J. and Suzanne Schiller.

Almost all our impressions of the 1930s are black and white, in part because widely distributed photographs taken by Farm Security Administration photographers etched this stark visual image of depression America on the popular consciousness. Yet conditions were not uniformly grim. The depression was not on everyone's mind twenty-four hours a day. People continued their daily routine of work, family, and leisure. Literature and the arts flourished, and Hollywood movies and radio provided a welcome relief from hard times. Novelist Josephine Herbst recalled "an almost universal liveliness that countervailed universal suffering."

The Coming of the Great Depression

———————★———————

Since the beginning of the Industrial Revolution early in the nineteenth century the United States had experienced recessions or panics at least every twenty years. But none was as severe or lasted as long as the Great Depression. Only as the economy shifted toward war mobilization in the late 1930s did the grip of the depression finally ease.

The Causes of the Depression

The downturn began slowly and almost imperceptibly. After 1927, consumer spending declined and housing construction slowed. Inventories piled up, and in 1928 and 1929 manufacturers began to cut back on production and lay off workers; reduced incomes and buying power in turn reinforced the downturn. By the summer of 1929 the economy was clearly in a recession.

Stock Market Speculation and the Great Crash. Among the causes of the Great Depression, a flawed stock market was an important but not the dominant influence. By 1929 the market had become the symbol of the nation's prosperity and an icon of American business culture. The financier John J. Raskob captured this attitude in a *Ladies' Home Journal* article, "Everyone Ought to Be Rich." Invest $15 a month in sound common stocks, Raskob advised, and in twenty years the investment will grow to $80,000. Not everyone was playing the stock market, however. Only about 4 million Americans, representing about 10 percent of the nation's households, owned stock in 1929, and less than one-third of them had portfolios large enough to require the services of a stockbroker.

Stock prices had been rising steadily since 1921, but in 1928 and 1929 they surged forward, with the average price of stocks rising over 40 percent. All this economic activity was essentially unregulated. Margin buying in particular proceeded at a feverish pace as customers borrowed up to 75 percent of the purchase price of stocks. That easy credit lured more speculators and less creditworthy investors into the market. The Federal Reserve Board warned member banks not to lend money for stock speculation—if prices dropped, many investors would not be able to repay their debts— but no one listened. As long as prices continued to soar, everyone felt like a winner. A noted economist proclaimed in mid-October 1929 that "stock prices have reached what looks like a permanently high plateau."

The stock market began sliding in early September, but people ignored the warning. Then on "Black Thursday" (October 24, 1929) and again on "Black Tuesday" (October 29, 1929) the bubble burst. More than 28 million shares changed hands in frantic trading. Overextended investors, suddenly finding themselves heavily in debt, began to sell their stocks. Waves of panic selling ensued, during which many stocks found no buyers. Practically overnight, stock values fell from a peak of $87 billion (at least on paper) to $55 billion.

The precipitous decline of stock prices became known as the Great Crash, and its impact was felt far beyond the trading floors of Wall Street. Speculators who had borrowed from banks to buy their stocks could not repay the loans because they could not sell the stocks. These defaults in turn caused bank failures. Since bank deposits were uninsured before the 1930s, a bank failure meant that all the depositors' money was lost. This sudden loss of their life savings was a tremendous shock to members of the middle class, many of whom had no other resources with which to cope with the crisis.

The stock market crash intensified the course of the Great Depression in several ways. Besides wiping out the savings of thousands of Americans, it hurt commercial banks that had invested heavily in corporate stocks. Less tangibly, it destroyed the optimism of people who had regarded the stock market as the crowning symbol of American prosperity, causing a crisis of confidence that prolonged the depression.

Structural Weaknesses. Although the stock market crash and its immediate consequences contributed to the Great Depression, longstanding weaknesses in the American economy accounted for its length and severity, especially the deep plunge between 1931 and 1933. Agriculture, in particular, had never recovered from the recession of 1920–1921. Farmers faced high fixed costs for equipment and mortgages incurred during the inflationary war years. At the same time prices fell because of overproduction, forcing farmers to default on mortgage payments and risk foreclosure. In 1929 the yearly income of a farmer averaged only $273, compared with $750 in other occupations. Because farmers accounted

Wall Street, October 1929
Crowds gather in front of the New York Stock Exchange on October 25, 1929, the day
after "Black Thursday." The mood would be even darker after "Black Tuesday," October 29, the day the bubble burst.
Corbis-Bettmann.

for about one-fourth of the nation's gainfully employed workers in 1929, their difficulties weakened the general economic structure.

Certain basic industries also had experienced economic setbacks during the prosperous 1920s. Textile manufacturers, facing a steady market decline after the war, abandoned New England for cheaper labor markets in the South but continued to suffer from decreased demand and overproduction. Mining and lumbering, which had expanded in response to wartime demands, experienced the same problem. Coal mining was especially battered by overexpansion, outdated technology, and competition from new energy sources, including hydroelectric power, fuel oil, and natural gas, as well as a legacy of bitter labor struggles. And the railroad industry, damaged by stiff competition from truck transportation on publicly subsidized roads, faced shrinking passenger revenues and stagnant freight levels. While these older sectors of the economy faltered, newer and more successful consumer-based industries, such as chemicals, appliances, and food processing, proved not yet strong enough to lead the way to recovery.

Unequal Distribution of Wealth. The country's unequal distribution of wealth also contributed to the severity of the depression. During the 1920s the share of national income going to families in the upper- and middle-income brackets increased. The tax policies of Secretary of the Treasury Andrew Mellon contributed to that concentration of wealth by lowering personal income tax rates, eliminating the wartime excess-profits tax, and increasing deductions that favored affluent individuals and corporations. In 1929, the poorest 40 percent of the population received only 12.5 percent of aggregate family personal income, whereas the wealthiest 5 percent of the population received 30 percent. Once the depression began, this skewed income distribution prevented people from spending the amounts of money necessary to revive the economy.

The Deepening Economic Crisis

The Great Depression became self-perpetuating. The more the American economy contracted, the longer people expected the depression to last; and the longer they expected it to last, the more afraid they were to spend or invest their money, if they had any—and spending and investing was exactly what was needed to stimulate economic recovery. The economy showed some improvement in the summer of 1931 when low prices encouraged consumption, but it plunged again late in the fall.

At that point the chronically depressed agricultural sector put pressure on the commercial banking system, worsening the economic contraction. The nation's banks had already been weakened by the stock market crash. When agricultural prices and incomes fell more steeply than usual in 1930, many farmers went bankrupt, causing rural banks to fail in alarming numbers. By December 1930 so many rural banks had defaulted on their obligations that urban banks also began to fail. The wave of bank failures frightened depositors into withdrawing their savings, further deepening the crisis.

A change in the nation's monetary policy in 1931 added to the banking problems. During the first phase of the depression the Federal Reserve System had reacted cautiously. But in October 1931 the Federal Reserve Bank of New York significantly increased the discount rate—the interest rate it charged on loans to member banks—and cut back the amount of money placed in circulation through purchase of government securities. This miscalculation squeezed the money supply, forcing prices down and depriving businesses of funds for investment. By March 1933, when the economy reached its lowest point, the money supply had fallen by about one-third from its August 1929 level.

In the face of that money shortage, the country could have been pulled out of the depression only if the American people spent at a higher rate. But because of falling prices, rising unemployment, and a troubled banking system, Americans preferred to hold on to their dollars, stashing them under the mattress rather than depositing them in the bank. Economic stagnation set in.

The Worldwide Depression

President Hoover later blamed the severity of the depression on the international economic situation. Although domestic factors far outweighed international causes of America's protracted economic decline, Hoover was correct in surmising that economic problems in the rest of the world affected the United States, and vice versa. Indeed, the international economic system had been out of kilter since World War I. It functioned only as long as American banks exported enough capital to allow European countries to repay their debts and continue to buy American manufactured goods and agricultural products. By the late 1920s European economies were staggering under the weight of large debts and trade imbalances with the United States, which undercut the recovery that had seemed possible earlier in the decade. By 1931 most European economies had collapsed.

In an interdependent world, the downturn of the American economy had enormous repercussions. When U.S. companies cut back production, they also cut back their purchases of raw materials and supplies from abroad, and this devastated many foreign economies. When American financiers sharply reduced foreign investment and consumers bought fewer European goods, debt repayment became even more difficult. As European economic conditions worsened,

the stock market crash in 1929 to the depths of the depression in 1932–1933, the U.S. gross national product was cut almost in half, declining from $103.1 billion to $58 billion in 1932. Consumption expenditures dropped by 18 percent, construction fell by 78 percent, private investment plummeted by 88 percent, and farm income, already low, was more than cut in half. During this period 9,000 banks went bankrupt or closed their doors, and 100,000 businesses failed. The consumer price index declined by 25 percent, and corporate profits fell from $10 billion to $1 billion.

Most telling, unemployment rose from 3.2 percent in 1929 to 24.9 percent in 1933, affecting approximately 12 million workers (Figure 24.2). Statistical measures at that time were fairly crude, and it is likely that unemployment was even higher. At least one in four workers was out of a job. Even those who had jobs faced wage cutbacks or the possibility of being laid off. Their stories put a human face on the almost incomprehensible dimensions of this economic downturn.

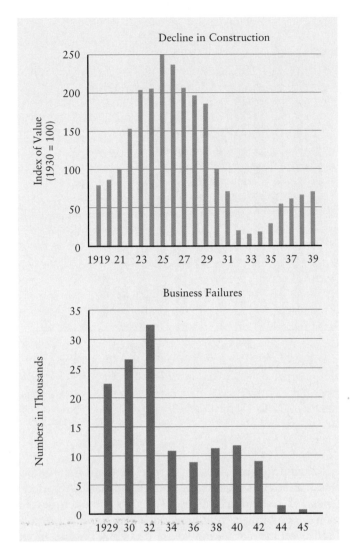

FIGURE 24.1
Statistics of the Depression
The top graph shows the decline in construction, as reflected in the value of new building permits; the bottom graph shows the numbers of business failures.
Source: Historical Statistics of the United States, Colonial Times to 1970 (Washington, DC: U.S. Government Printing Office, 1975), 626, 912.

Hard Times

★

"We didn't go hungry, but we lived lean." That statement sums up the experiences of many American families during the Great Depression. The vast majority were neither very rich nor very poor. For most, the depression did not mean losing thousands of dollars in the stock market or pulling children out of a fancy boarding school, nor did it mean going on relief or living in a shantytown. In a typical family in the 1930s, the husband still had a job and the wife was still a homemaker. Life was not easy, but it usually consisted of "making do" rather than suffering stark deprivation.

demand for American exports fell dramatically; this strained the gold standard, which provided a fixed standard against which the value of currencies could be pegged. Finally, when the Hawley-Smoot Tariff of 1930 (see Chapter 23) raised rates to all-time highs, foreign governments retaliated by imposing their own trade restrictions, further limiting the market for American goods—especially agricultural products. All these factors deepened the worldwide depression.

By 1933 the world economy was showing signs of recovery, although progress remained uneven. No other major trading nation was hit as hard as the United States, however. The statistics paint a stark picture (Figure 24.1). From the height of the prosperity before

Making Do

"You could feel the depression deepen," recalled the writer Caroline Bird, "but you could not look out the window and see it." Many people never saw a breadline or entered a soup kitchen. The depression caused a private kind of despair that often simmered behind closed doors. "I've lived in cities for many months broke, without help, too timid to get in breadlines," the writer Meridel LeSueur remembered. "I've known many women to live like this until they simply faint on the street from privations, without saying a word to anyone. A woman will shut herself up in a room until it is taken away from her, and eat a cracker a day and be as quiet as a mouse." (See Voices from Abroad, "Mary Agnes Hamilton: Breadlines and Beggars," p. 777.)

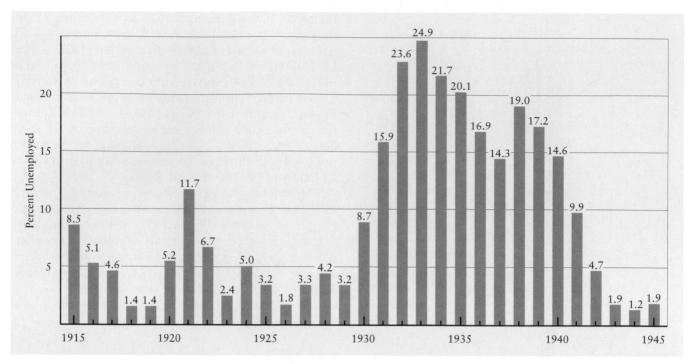

FIGURE 24.2
Unemployment, 1915–1945
As this graph shows, the historically low unemployment levels of the 1920s began to
rise in 1930. By 1933 one in four American workers was out of a job.

"Mass unemployment is both a statistic and an empty feeling in the stomach," observed the writer Cabell Phillips. "To fully comprehend it, you have to both see the figures and feel the emptiness." The victims of the depression were a varied group. The depression did not create poverty; it merely publicized the conditions of the poor. People who had always been poor were joined by the newly poor. Those formerly solid working-class and middle-class families strongly believed in the Horatio Alger ethic of upward mobility through hard work but suddenly found themselves floundering in a society that no longer had a place for them. They were proud people who felt humiliated by their plight, and many blamed themselves for their misfortune. "What is going to become of us?" asked a man in Arizona. "I've lost twelve and a half pounds this last month, just thinking. You can't sleep, you know. You wake up at 2 A.M. and you lie and think."

Hard times weighed heavily on senior citizens, many of whom faced utter destitution after losing their savings in bank failures. In a cartoon from the 1930s a squirrel asks a man on a park bench why he did not save for a rainy day. "I did," the man replies listlessly. Children, by contrast, often escaped the sense of bitterness and failure that gripped their elders; some youngsters thought it was fun to stand in a soup line. Yet hard times made children grow up fast.

Downward mobility was especially hard for middle-class Americans because it challenged basic American tenets of individualism and success. An unemployed man in Pittsburgh told the journalist Lorena Hickok, "Lady, you just can't know what it's like to have to move your family out of the nice house you had in the suburbs, part paid for, down into an apartment, down into another apartment, smaller and in a worse neighborhood, down, down, down, until finally you end up in the slums." Before a laid-off chauffeur started a relief construction job, he spent the day watching how the other men handled their picks and shovels so he could "get the hang of it and not feel so awkward." A woman broke into tears when her husband, formerly a white-collar worker, put on his first pair of overalls to go to work.

The key to surviving the depression was to maintain one's self-respect. One man spent two years painting his father's house (in fact, he painted it twice). Keeping up appearances, keeping life as close to normal as possible, was an essential strategy. Camaraderie and cooperation helped many families and communities survive as people found that they were all in the same boat. When a driver "accidentally" dumped a load of oranges or coal off the back of his truck, he was contributing to the welfare of the neighborhood. Hoboes developed an elaborate system of sidewalk chalk marks to tell one another at which back doors they could get a meal, an old coat, or some spare change.

MARY AGNES HAMILTON
Breadlines and Beggars

——————★——————

British writer and Labor Party activist Mary Agnes Hamilton arrived in the United States on a gloomy morning in December 1931 for a lecture tour that eventually took her as far west as Nebraska and as far south as Virginia. Her observations of conditions in New York during that grim winter confirm the devastation and despair gripping urban America.

One does not need to be long in New York (or for that matter in Chicago, in Cleveland, in Detroit, in Kansas, or in Buffalo) to see that there are plenty of real tragedies, as well as plenty of not-so-real ones. If those who have turned in the second or third car talk the most, the others talk—when they get the chance. In New York, one has only to pass outside the central island bounded by Lexington and Sixth Avenues to see hardship, misery, and degradation, accentuated by the shoddy grimness of the shabby houses and broken pavements. Look down from the Elevated, and there are long queues of dreary-looking men and women standing in "breadlines" outside the relief offices and the various church and other charitable institutions. Times Square, at any hour of the day and late into the evening, offers an exhibit for the edification of the theater-goer, for it is packed with shabby, utterly dumb and apathetic-looking men, who stand there, waiting for the advent of the coffee wagon run by Mr. W. R. Hearst of the New York *American*. Nowhere, in New York or any other city, can one escape from the visible presence of those who with perhaps unconscious cruelty are called "the idle." At every street corner, and wherever taxi or car has to pause, men try to sell one apples, oranges, or picture papers. Not matches—matches, in book form, are given away with every fifteen-cent package of cigarettes, lie on every restaurant table, litter the street, half used, and exemplify how little, as yet, the depression has done to overcome the national habit of easy-going wastefulness. On a fine day, men will press on one gardenias at fifteen cents apiece; on any day, rows of them line every relatively open space, eager to shine one's shoes. It is perhaps because so many people are doing without this "shine," or attempting with unfamiliar hands and a sense of deep indignity to shine their own, that the streets look shabby and the persons on them so much less well-groomed than of yore. The well-shod feet of the States struck me forcibly on my first visit; the ill-cleaned feet of New York struck me as forcibly in January and April 1932. In 1930 an English friend, long domesticated in New England, told me that she hesitated to bring her children to London, since the sight of beggars would make so painful an impression on them; in 1932 there are more beggars to be met with in New York than in London. Yes, distress is there; the idle are there. How many, no one really knows. Ten million or more in the country; a million and a half in New York are reported. They are there; as is, admittedly a dark undergrowth of horrid suffering that is certainly more degraded and degrading than anything Britain or Germany knows. Their immense presence makes a grim background to the talk of depression: there is an obscure alarm as to what they may do "if this goes on," and the charitable relief funds (about which more later) dry up, as they are in many centers already doing; their existence, in numbers that grow instead of diminishing, constitutes the fact that largely justifies the feeling of gloom. . . .

The American people, unfamiliar with suffering, with none of that long history of catastrophe and calamity behind it which makes the experience of European nations, is outraged and baffled by misfortune. Depression blocks its view: it cannot see round it. Misled in the onset by leaders who assured it, in every soothing term and tone, that reverse was to last but for a little while; that it was the preliminary to recovery; that American institutions were immune to the ills that had laid the countries of the rest of the world upon their backs; that prosperity was native to the soil of the Union, and all that was needed was to wait till the clouds, blown up by the wickedness of other lands, rolled by, as they were bound to do, and that speedily; the nation now suffers from a despair of any and every kind of leadership. Every institution is assailed; even the sacred foundations of democracy are being undermined. The defeatism that has been so lamentably evidenced in Congress is not peculiar to Congressmen, any more than is the crude individualism of their reactions. It lies like a pall over the spirit of the nation. It is felt by most people to be, in fact, the greatest obstacle to recovery, to that restoration of confidence for which everybody pleads, which everybody sees as necessary. But how to break it nobody knows.

Source: Mary Agnes Hamilton, *In America Today* (1932), in Allan Nevins, ed., *America through British Eyes* (Gloucester, MA: Peter Smith, 1968), 443–444.

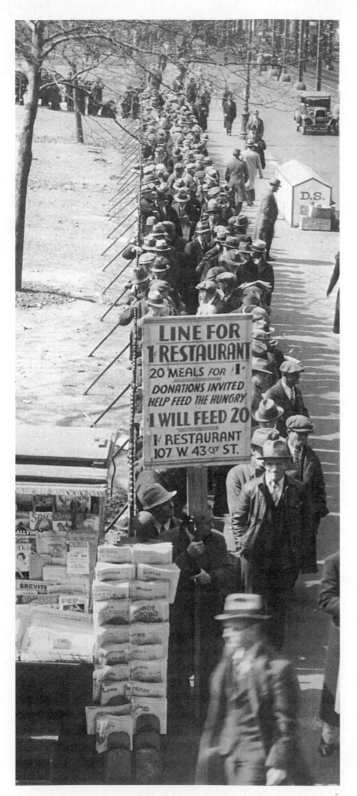

The Breadline
Some of the most vivid images from the depression were breadlines and men selling apples on street corners. Note that all the people in this breadline are men. Women rarely appeared in breadlines, often preferring to endure private deprivation rather than violate standards of respectable behavior by appearing in public to ask for help.
Franklin D. Roosevelt Library, Hyde Park, NY.

After their savings and credit had been exhausted, many families faced the humiliation of going on relief. Seeking aid from state or local governments hurt people's pride and disrupted the traditional pattern of turning to relatives, neighbors, churches, and mutual-aid societies in times of need. Even if families survived the demeaning process of being certified for state or local relief, the amount they received was a pittance. In New York State, for example, where benefits were among the highest in the nation, a family received only $2.39 a week.

Such hardships left deep wounds—Caroline Bird called it an "invisible scar." One elderly civil servant bought a plot of land outside Washington so that if the depression recurred, she would have the means to live. The labor organizer Larry Van Dusen described a common reaction: "The depression left a legacy of fear, but also a desire for acquisition—property, security. I now have twenty times more shirts than I need, because all during that time, shirts were something I never had" (see American Voices, "Larry Van Dusen: A Working-Class Family Encounters the Great Depression," p. 779). Virginia Durr, a white civil rights activist from Alabama, concurred: "The great majority reacted by thinking money is the most important thing in the world. Get yours. And get it for your children. Nothing else matters. Not having that stark terror come at you again." For many Americans, "that stark terror" of losing control over their lives summed up the Great Depression.

Families Face the Great Depression

Sociologists who studied family life during the 1930s found that the depression generally intensified existing behavior. If a family had been stable and cohesive before the depression, it pulled together to overcome the new obstacles. However, if a family had shown signs of disintegration, the depression made the situation worse. On the whole, researchers thought that far more families hung together than broke apart.

Men and women experienced the Great Depression differently, partly because of the traditional gender roles that governed behavior in the 1930s. Men had been trained from childhood to be breadwinners and considered themselves failures if they could no longer support their families. Women, however, felt their self-importance increase as they struggled to keep their families afloat. The sociologists Robert and Helen Lynd noticed this phenomenon in their follow-up study of Middletown (Muncie, Indiana), published in 1937: "The men, cut adrift from their usual routine, lost much of their sense of time and dawdled helplessly and dully about the streets; while in the homes the women's world remained largely intact and the round of cooking, housecleaning, and mending became if anything more absorbing." Even if a wife took a job when her husband lost his, she retained almost total responsibility for housework and child care.

LARRY VAN DUSEN
A Working-Class Family Encounters the Great Depression

———— ★ ————

Although many families endured the privations of the Great Depression with equanimity, others, like Larry Van Dusen's family, experienced tremendous strains. In this passage from his oral history account to journalist Studs Terkel, he describes the pressures on male wage earners and their children.

One of the most common things—and it certainly happened to me—was this feeling of your father's failure. That somehow he hadn't beaten the rap. Sure things were tough, but why should I be the kid who had to put a piece of cardboard into the sole of my shoe to go to school? It was not a thing coupled with resentment against my father. It was simply this feeling of regret, that somehow he hadn't done better, that he hadn't gotten the breaks. Also a feeling of uneasiness about my father's rage against the way things are.

My father was very much of an individualist, as craftsmen usually are. He would get jobs he considered beneath his status during this period. Something would happen: he'd quarrel with the foreman, he'd have a fight with the boss. He was a carpenter. He couldn't be happy fixing a roadbed or driving a cab or something like that. He was a skilled tradesman and this whole thing had him beat. I think it bugged the family a lot.

Remember, too, the shock, the confusion, the hurt that many kids felt about their fathers not being able to provide for them. This reflected itself very often in bitter quarrels between father and son. I recall I had one. I was the oldest of six children. I think there was a special feeling between the father and the oldest son. . . .

My father led a rough life: he drank. During the Depression, he drank more. There was more conflict in the home. A lot of fathers—mine, among them—had a habit of taking off. They'd go to Chicago to look for work. To Topeka. This left the family at home, waiting and hoping that the old man would find something. And there was always the Saturday night ordeal as to whether or not the old man would get home with his paycheck. Everything was sharpened and hurt more by the Depression.

Heaven would break out once in a while, and the old man would get a week's work. I remember he'd come home at night, and he'd come down the path through the trees. He always rode a bicycle. He'd stop and sometimes say hello, or give me a hug. And that smell of fresh sawdust on those carpenter overalls, and the fact that Dad was home, and there was a week's wages—well, this is something you remember, too. That's the good you remember.

And then there was always the bad part. That's when you'd see your father coming home with the toolbox on his shoulder. Or carrying it. That meant the job was over. The tools were home now, and we were back on the treadmill again.

I remember coming back home, many years afterwards. Things were better. It was after the Depression, after the war. To me, it was hardly the same house. My father turned into an angel. They weren't wealthy, but they were making it. They didn't have the acid and the recriminations and the bitterness that I had felt as a child.

———————

Source: Studs Terkel, *Hard Times* (New York: Pantheon Books, 1986), 107–108.

Despite the hard times, Americans maintained a fairly high level of consumption. As in the 1920s, households in the middle-income range—the 50.2 percent of American families with an income of $500 to $1,500 in 1935—did much of the buying. Several factors enabled those families more or less to maintain their former standard of living despite pay cuts or unemployment—especially the deflation that lowered the cost of living by almost 20 percent between 1929 and 1935. For example, milk sold for 10 cents a quart, bread for 7 cents a loaf, and butter for 23 cents a pound. Families also spent their reduced income differently. Telephone use and clothing sales dropped sharply, but cigarettes, movies, radio, and newspapers, once considered luxuries, now became necessities. The automobile proved to be one of the most depression-proof items in the family budget. Though sales of new cars dropped, gasoline sales were stable, suggesting that people bought used cars or kept their old models running longer.

Some families maintained their life-styles in the 1930s through "deficit living"—that is, using installment payments and credit to stretch their income. By 1936 consumer credit in the United States had increased by 20 percent over 1929 levels. A Middletown resident summed up the prevailing attitude toward installment buying: "Most of the families I know are after the same things today that they were after before the Depression, and they'll get them in the same way—on credit."

To maintain their families' life-styles, housewives substituted their own labor for goods and services they had formerly purchased. Women sewed their own clothes and canned fruits and vegetables. They practiced small economies such as buying day-old bread and heating several dishes in the oven at once to save fuel; two friends who often bought hamburger together split 2 pounds for 25 cents and took turns keeping the extra penny. Women who had formerly employed servants now did their own housework. Those economies helped pay for cars and trips to the movies. Women generally accepted their new work stoically. "We had no choice," remembered one housewife. "We just did what had to be done one day at a time."

Another way for families to make ends meet in the 1930s was to send an additional member of the household to work. At the turn of the century that additional family worker was often a child or a young unmarried adult; in the 1930s it was increasingly a married woman. Instead of expelling women from the work force, the depression solidified their position in it. The 1940 census reported almost 11 million women in the work force, approximately one-fourth of the nation's workers and a small increase over 1930. The number of married women employed outside the home rose 50 percent.

Working women, especially married ones, encountered sharp resentment and outright discrimination when they entered the depression workplace. After calculating that the number of employed women roughly equaled the 1939 unemployment total, the editor Norman Cousins suggested this tongue-in-cheek remedy: "Simply fire the women, who shouldn't be working anyway, and hire the men. Presto! No unemployment. No relief rolls. No depression." A 1936 Gallup poll asked whether wives should work when their husbands had jobs, and 82 percent of the people interviewed said no. From 1932 to 1937 the federal government would not allow a husband and wife to hold government jobs at the same time, and many states adopted laws that prohibited married women from working, especially in the field of education.

The attempt to make women scapegoats for the depression rested on shaky moral and economic grounds. Most women worked because they had to. A sizable minority were the sole support of their families

Women Face the Depression
Most information for the 1930 census, conducted just as the depression gripped the nation, was gathered in personal interviews. This well-dressed census taker, Marie Cioffi, was probably lucky to get the job. The woman she is interviewing on East 112th Street in New York City, Margaret Napolitana, was likely a homemaker and, from her attire and expression, a struggling one. Meanwhile her daughter is not quite sure what to make of the two women's conversation.
Corbis-Bettmann.

because their husbands had left home or lost their jobs. Single, divorced, deserted, or widowed women had no husbands to support them. Moreover, women rarely took jobs away from men. "Few of the people who oppose married women's employment," observed one feminist in 1940, "seem to realize that a coal miner or steel worker cannot very well fill the jobs of nurse-maids, cleaning women, or the factory and clerical jobs now filled by women." Custom, rather than law or economics, made crossovers rare.

The division of the work force by gender gave women a small edge during the depression. Many fields with large numbers of female employees, including clerical, sales, and service and trade occupations, suffered less from economic contraction than did the steel industry, mining, and manufacturing, which employed men almost exclusively. As a result, unemployment rates for women, although extremely high, were somewhat lower than those for men. This small bonus came at a high price, however. The jobs women held reinforced the traditional stereotypes of women's work. When the depression ended, women found themselves even more concentrated in low-paying, dead-end jobs than when it began.

The depression workplace also benefited white women at the expense of nonwhite women. To make ends meet, white women willingly took jobs usually held by blacks or minority workers—domestic service, for example. White men also took jobs previously held by minority group men. In both cases employers were quick to act on their preference for a white work force.

During the Great Depression there were few feminist demands for equal rights at home or on the job. On an individual basis, women's self-esteem probably rose because of their importance to family survival. Most men and women, however, continued to believe that the two sexes should have fundamentally different roles and responsibilities and that a woman's life cycle should be shaped by marriage, child rearing, and her husband's career. The substantial contributions made by women in the 1930s actually reinforced their overall identification with the home, laying the foundation for the so-called feminine mystique of the 1950s.

Demographic Trends

Another measure of the impact of the depression on family life was the change in demographic trends during the 1930s. The marriage rate fell from 10.14 per thousand persons in 1929 to 7.87 in 1932. The divorce rate dropped as well because people could not afford the legal expenses of dissolving failed marriages. Although marriage and divorce rates rebounded after 1933, postponement of marriage sometimes became permanent. Elsa Ponselle, a Chicago schoolteacher who later became the principal of one of that city's largest elementary schools, recalled her experience:

> *Do you realize how many people in my generation are not married? . . . It wasn't that we didn't have a chance. I was going with someone when the Depression hit. We probably would have gotten married. He was a commercial artist and had been doing very well. . . . Suddenly he was laid off. It hit him like a ton of bricks. And he just disappeared.*

The birth rate was the demographic factor most affected by the depression. The birth rate had fallen steadily since 1800, but from 1930 to 1933 it dropped from 21.3 live births per thousand population to 18.4, a 14 percent decrease. The 1933 level, if maintained, would have led to a population decline. The birth rate rose slightly after 1934, but by the end of the decade it had reached only 18.8. In contrast, at the height of the baby boom following World War II, the birth rate was 25 per thousand population.

The 1930s marked a significant stage in the long history of the birth control movement in America. In 1936, in *United States v. One Package of Japanese Pessaries*, a federal court struck down all federal restrictions on the dissemination of contraceptive information. Doctors now had wide discretion in prescribing birth control for married couples, which became legal in all states except Massachusetts and Connecticut. Public support for contraception increased: in a 1936 Gallup poll, 63 percent of those interviewed favored making birth control information more widely available. These changing attitudes meant thriving business for the makers of diaphragms and condoms, the most common forms of birth control at that time.

Margaret Sanger played a major role in encouraging the availability and popular acceptance of birth control. As a public health nurse in the slums of New York in the 1910s, she had fielded questions from anxious immigrant women eager to know the "secret" of how to avoid having more babies. When a patient who had been referred to her died after a botched abortion, Sanger dedicated her life to expanding access to birth control. At first she joined forces with socialist movements aimed at the working class. In the 1920s and 1930s, however, she appealed to the middle class for support, identifying this segment of the population as the key to the movement's success. Sanger also courted the medical profession, pioneering the establishment of birth control clinics staffed by doctors, and winning the American Medical Association's endorsement of contraception in 1937. Birth control became less a feminist demand and more a medical issue.

Contraception had long been a private matter between individuals. Its public acceptance increased greatly during the 1930s because of the widespread desire to limit family size for economic reasons. In 1942 the American Birth Control League, which Sanger had founded in 1921, became Planned Parenthood, an organization that remains active today.

Hard Times for Youth

The depression hit the nation's 21 million young people especially hard. Although children only dimly glimpsed the sacrifices made in the 1930s, adolescents knew that making do usually meant doing without. The writer Maxine Davis, who traveled 10,000 miles in 1936 interviewing the nation's youth, described them as "runners, delayed at the gun." She added, "The depression years have left us with a generation robbed of time and

American Youth in the 1930s
Farm Security Administration photographer Russell Lee took this photograph of a soda jerk in Corpus Christi, Texas, in 1939. A job at the local drugstore as a soda jerk (the name came from the machine handles used to make ice-cream sodas and shakes) was a great way for a teenage boy to make a little extra cash in the depression, plus show off for his peers.
Library of Congress.

opportunity just as the Great War left the world its heritage of a lost generation." Studies of social mobility confirm that the young men who entered adulthood during the depression era had less successful careers than did those before or since. About 250,000 young people became so demoralized that they took to the road as hoboes and "sisters of the road," as female tramps were called.

Because job prospects were so dim, some young people chose to stay in school longer. Public schools were free and were warm in the winter. In 1930 less than half the nation's youth attended high school, compared with three-fourths in 1940 at the end of the depression. This was partly due to increased attendance by boys, who had traditionally dropped out of school to work at an earlier age than did girls. College, however, remained the privilege of a distinct minority. With times so rough, the "college of hard knocks" was about all most depression-era youths could expect. About 1.2 million young people, or 7.5 percent of the population between the ages of eighteen and twenty-four, attended college in the 1930s, 40 percent of them women. After 1935 college became a little more affordable because of the National Youth Administration (NYA), which provided part-time employment to more than 2 million college and high school students. This

government agency also provided work for 2.6 million out-of-school youths.

Financial sacrifices contributed to the seriousness of purpose among college students in the 1930s. The influence of fraternities and sororities declined during the depression, and many students became involved in political movements. Fueled by disillusionment with World War I, thousands took the "Oxford Pledge" never to support a war in which the United States might be involved. In 1936 the Student Strike against War drew support from several hundred thousand students across the country.

Despite the economic sacrifices demanded by the depression, adolescence became increasingly institutionalized in the 1930s. Through high school and college attendance, organized athletics, and extracurricular activities, young people developed their own values and patterns of behavior. Peers, rather than parents, influenced their values and tastes. Magazines and movies promoted a youth culture that was closely tied to an ethos of consumption. Teenagers throughout the country read the same comics, wore the same style of clothes, and saw the same movies. They also experimented with necking, petting, and dating rituals that shocked their elders. By now the youth culture first noticed in the 1920s had became a permanent feature of modern life.

Dancing Cheek to Cheek
During the Great Depression, Americans turned to inexpensive recreational activities such as listening to the radio and going to the movies. One of the most popular attractions in Hollywood movies was the dance team of Fred Astaire and Ginger Rogers, who starred together in ten movies.
Steve Schapiro.

The Grapes of Wrath
John Steinbeck's best-selling 1939 novel became one of the top movies of the 1940s. Ma Joad, played by Jane Darwell, expressed the central message of both the book and the film: "We're the people that live. They ain't gonna wipe us out. Why, we're the people—we go on."
Steve Schapiro.

Popular Culture

Americans turned to popular culture to alleviate some of the worst trauma of the depression. The mass culture that grew so dramatically in the 1920s flourished in the decade that followed, offering not just entertainment but commentary on the problems that beset the nation. Movies and radio served as a forum for criticizing the system—especially politicians and bankers—as well as vehicles for reaffirming traditional ideals.

Movies. Despite the closing of one-third of the country's theaters by 1933, the movie industry and its studio system prospered. More than 60 percent of Americans saw at least one movie a week, with weekly attendance ranging from 60 million to 75 million. One of the most popular (and highly paid) stars was Mae West, who titillated—or shocked—moviegoers with sexual innuendos like "I used to be Snow White, but I drifted" and "It's not the men in my life, but the life in my men that counts." In response to public outcry by the Catholic Legion of Decency and other religious groups that were against supposed immorality in the early talkies, the industry set up the Production Code Administration in 1934. Committing themselves to a form of self-censorship, studios agreed to banish explicit sex, immorality, and violence from the screen. The new standards were so strict that censors barely permitted Rhett Butler to utter the famous last line of *Gone with the Wind*: "Frankly, my dear, I don't give a damn."

Hollywood movies offered more than just escape from hard times. Many of the 5,000 movies produced during the depression decade contained complex messages that reflected a real sense of the societal crisis that engulfed the nation. The cultural historian Lawrence W. Levine has argued that depression-era films were "deeply grounded in the realities and intricacies of the Depression" and thus offer a wealth of information about the period. Even if they did not deal specifically with the economic or political crisis, many films reaffirmed traditional values such as democracy, individualism, and egalitarianism. They also contained criticisms—suggestions that the system was not working, or that law and order had broken down. Thus, popular gangster movies—such as *Public Enemy* (1931), with James Cagney, or *Little Caesar* (1930), starring Edward G. Robinson—can be seen as perverse Horatio Alger tales in which the main character struggles to succeed in a harsh environment. Often these movies suggested that incompetent or corrupt politicians, police, and business leaders were as much to blame for organized crime as the gangsters themselves.

Depression-era films repeatedly portrayed politicians as cynical and corrupt. In *Washington Merry-Go-Round* (1932), lobbyists manipulated weak congressmen to undermine democratic rule. The Marx Brothers' irreverent comedies criticized authority and most everything else. In *Duck Soup* (1933), Groucho Marx played Rufus T. Firefly, president of the mythical nation of Freedonia, who sings gleefully:

The last man nearly ruined this place,
He didn't know what to do with it.
If you think this country's bad off now,
Just wait till I get through with it.

Few filmmakers left more of a mark on the decade than Frank Capra. An Italian immigrant who personified the possibilities of success the United States offered, Capra made films that spoke to Americans' idealism. In movies like *Mr. Deeds Goes to Town* (1936) and *Mr. Smith Goes to Washington* (1939), he pitted the virtuous small-town hero against corrupt urban shysters—business leaders, lobbyists, and newspaper publishers—whose schemes subverted the nation's ideals. Though the hero usually prevailed, Capra was realistic enough to suggest that the victory was not necessarily permanent, that the problems the nation faced were very serious.

At the height of the depression, movies continued to influence consumers. One of the decade's top box-office stars was a curly-headed little girl named Shirley Temple, who made twenty-one films by 1941. Shirley Temple dolls, books, and clothes flooded the market. Similarly, because of the popularity of glamorous blondes such as Jean Harlow, Carole Lombard, and Mae West, sales of peroxide hair rinse skyrocketed. Sales of undershirts fell drastically after Clark Gable, a leading sex symbol of the 1930s, took off his shirt in *It Happened One Night* and revealed his bare chest.

Radio Days.   Radio occupied an increasingly important place in popular culture during the 1930s (Map 24.1). At the beginning of the decade 13 million households had a radio set; by the end of the decade, 27.5 million owned one. Listeners tuned in to daytime serials such as "Ma Perkins" or picked up useful household hints on "The Betty Crocker Hour." Variety shows featured Jack Benny, George Burns and Gracie Allen, and the ventriloquist Edgar Bergen and his impudent dummy, Charlie McCarthy. Millions of listeners followed the adventures of the Lone Ranger (with his trademark cry, "Hi-Ho Silver"), Superman, and detective Dick Tracy.

Radio also brought music to depression-era audiences. Classical music devotees could listen to live Saturday afternoon performances of New York's Metropolitan Opera (begun in 1931 and still being broadcast) or the NBC Symphony Orchestra under the baton of Arturo Toscanini. On the lighter side, people loved the new Big Band "swing" music of Benny Goodman, Duke Ellington, and Tommy Dorsey—an outgrowth of the jazz craze of the 1920s—and Cole Porter songs such as "Begin the Beguine" and "Night and Day" from Broadway shows. Radio increased the consumer market for 78-rpm. phonograph records of classical music, swing, and Broadway show tunes.

Like the movies, radio offered Americans more than escape. A running gag in comedian Jack Benny's show was his stinginess: audiences could certainly identify with an unwillingness, or inability, to spend money. Even more relevant was Benny's distrust of banks. He kept his money in an underground vault guarded by a polar bear named Carmichael—presumably a more reliable place than the nation's financial institutions.

The radio program "Amos 'n' Andy" is remembered primarily for its racial stereotyping (see Chapter 23), but the popular show also dealt with hard times, often referring explicitly to the depression. A central theme of the program was the contrast between Amos's hard work and Andy's more carefree approach to life. As the historian Arthur Frank Wertheim notes, "The way that the characters' hopes for monetary success were turned into business failures mirrored the lives of many Americans."

Not all leisure time was filled by commercial entertainment. In a resurgence of traditional values, attendance at religious services rose. The home once again became a center of leisure activity, with an evening by the radio providing an inexpensive form of family entertainment. Amateur photography and stamp collecting enjoyed tremendous vogue (President Franklin Roosevelt was an avid stamp collector), as did board games like Monopoly. Reading aloud from books borrowed from the public library was another affordable diversion. But Americans bought books too, taking advantage of new manufacturing techniques that made books less expensive. Readers made best sellers of Margaret Mitchell's *Gone with the Wind* (1936), Dale Carnegie's *How to Win Friends and Influence People* (1936), Pearl Buck's *The Good Earth* (1932), and James Hilton's *Lost Horizon* (1933). Columnist Russell Baker

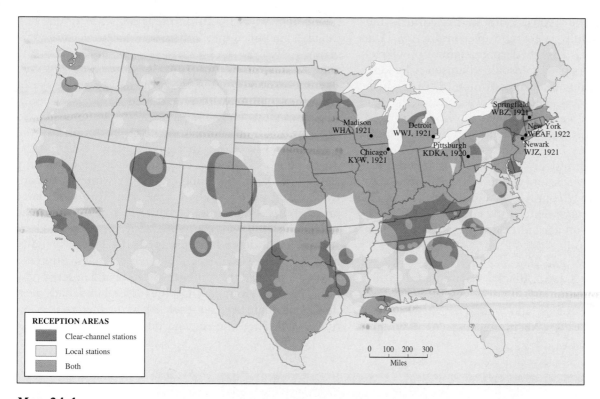

MAP 24.1
The Spread of Radio
In 1938 more than 26 million American households, or about three-quarters of the population, had a radio. Four national networks dominated the field, broadcasting news and entertainment across the country. Powerful clear-channel stations reached listeners hundreds of miles away. By 1939 only a few sparsely populated areas were beyond radio's reach.

recalled an activity everyone could afford: "Talking was the Great Depression pastime. Unlike the movies, talk was free."

Harder Times

★

Much writing about the 1930s has focused on white working-class or middle-class families that were caught in a spiral of downward social mobility. For such groups as African Americans, farmers, and Mexican Americans, times had always been hard, and during the 1930s they just got harder. As the poet Langston Hughes noted, "The depression brought everybody down a peg or two. And the Negroes had but few pegs to fall."

Blacks in the Depression

African Americans had always known discrimination and limited opportunity, so they viewed the depression differently than most whites did. "It didn't mean too much to him, the Great American Depression, as you call it," one man remarked. "There was no such thing. The best he could be is a janitor or a porter or shoeshine boy. It only became official when it hit the white man." The novelist and poet Maya Angelou, who grew up in Stamps, Arkansas, recalled, "The country had been in the throes of the Depression for two years before the Negroes in Stamps knew it. I think that everyone thought the Depression, like everything else, was for the white folks."

Despite the black migration to northern cities that had begun before World War I, as late as 1940 more than 75 percent of African Americans still lived in the South. Nearly all the farmers who were black lived in the South, their condition scarcely better than it had been at the end of Reconstruction. Only 20 percent of black farmers owned their own land; the rest toiled at the bottom of the exploitative southern agricultural system as tenant farmers, farmhands, and sharecroppers. During the 1930s African Americans rarely earned more than $200 a year, and in one Louisiana parish black women averaged only $41.67 a year picking cotton.

Throughout the 1920s southern agriculture had suffered from falling prices and overproduction. The depression made an already desperate situation worse. Some black farmers tried to protect themselves by joining the Southern Tenant Farmers Union (STFU), which was founded in 1934. The STFU was one of the few southern groups that welcomed both blacks and whites. "The same chain that holds you holds my people, too," an elderly black farmer reminded whites on the organizing committee. Landowners, however, had a stake in keeping black and white sharecroppers from organizing, and they countered the union's efforts with repression and harassment. In the end the STFU could do little to reform an agricultural system dependent on a single crop—cotton.

The Scottsboro Case. Blacks encountered other forms of discrimination and harassment, often violent, in the 1930s. Lynchings and miscarriages of justice increased, with twenty blacks lynched in 1930 and twenty-four in 1933. In a celebrated case in 1931, a freight train pulled into Scottsboro, Alabama, carrying a number of hoboes and transients who had caught a free ride. Acting on a tip from the conductor, sheriff's deputies arrested nine black men, all under the age of twenty, for fighting with some of the white hoboes. Suddenly two white women wearing men's clothing stepped off the boxcar and claimed they had been raped by the black men. The officers accepted without question the accusations of the women, Victoria Price and Ruby Bates, and barely restrained an angry white mob from lynching the accused men on the spot. Two weeks later juries composed entirely of white men found the nine defendants guilty of rape and sentenced eight of them to death. (One defendant escaped the death penalty because he was a minor.) Though the U.S. Supreme Court overturned the sentences in 1932 and ordered new trials on the grounds that the defendants had been denied adequate legal counsel, five of the men were eventually reconvicted and sentenced to long prison terms.

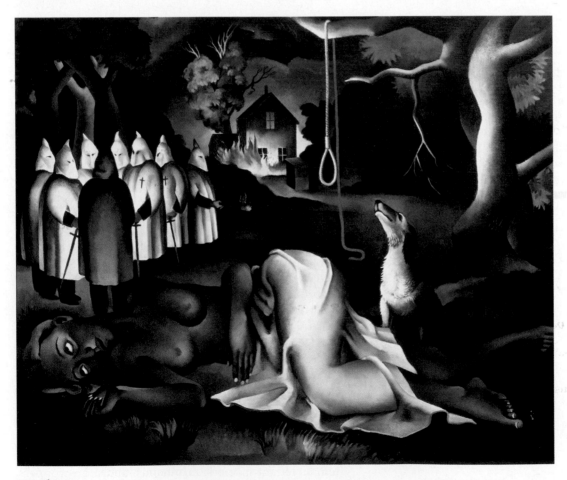

Lynching
The threat of lynching remained a terrifying part of life for African Americans in the 1930s, and not just in the South. Artist Joe Jones set this canvas in 1933, perhaps influenced by the fact that twenty-four blacks were lynched that year. He gave it the ironic title of *American Justice, 1933 (White Justice).*
Collection of Philip J. and Suzanne Schiller.

The youth of the Scottsboro defendants, their hasty trials, and the harsh sentences stirred public protest, prompting the International Labor Defense (ILD), a labor organization closely tied to the American Communist Party, to take over their defense. The Communist Party had targeted the struggle against racism as a priority in the early 1930s but was making little headway in its recruitment of blacks. "It's bad enough being black, why be red?" was a common reaction. White southerners resented the interference of those radicals as well as the fact that almost all those involved in the Scottsboro defense were northerners and Jews. In the words of a local solicitor, "Alabama justice cannot be bought and sold with Jew money from New York."

The case was complicated by the southern myth of the inviolate honor and chastity of white womanhood. The stories of the two women contained many inconsistencies, and Ruby Bates later recanted. However, when a white southern woman claimed to have been raped by a black man, she was taken at her word. As a court observer remarked, Victoria Price "might be a fallen woman, but by God she is a white woman."

The Scottsboro case received wide coverage in black communities across the country. Along with the increase in lynching in the early 1930s, it provided black Americans with a strong incentive to head for northern and midwestern cities. However, the lure of the North was offset by the lack of economic opportunities caused by the depression. About 400,000 black men and women left the South during the 1930s, only about half the number that had departed in the 1920s. Nevertheless, by 1935 eleven northern cities were home to more than 100,000 African Americans. Two of the most popular destinations were the South Side of Chicago and Harlem in New York City.

Harlem in the 1930s. Harlem's housing facilities and community services had already been strained by the enormous influx of African Americans in the 1920s, and the depression aggravated the situation. Residential segregation kept blacks from moving elsewhere, so African Americans paid excessive rents to live in deteriorating buildings. Crowded living conditions caused disease and death rates to climb, and tuberculosis became a leading cause of death in Harlem. As whites clamored for jobs traditionally held by blacks—waiters, domestic servants, elevator operators, and garbage collectors—unemployment in Harlem rose to 50 percent, twice the national rate. At the height of the depression, shelters and soup kitchens staffed by the Divine Peace Mission, under the leadership of the charismatic black religious leader Father Divine, provided 3,000 meals a day for Harlem's destitute.

In March 1935 Harlem exploded in the nation's only major race riot of the decade. Anger about the lack of jobs, a slowdown in relief services, and the economic exploitation of the black community had been building for years. Although white store owners depended entirely on black trade, they would not employ blacks. The arrest of a teenage black shoplifter, followed by rumors that he had been severely beaten by white police officers, triggered the riot. False reports of his death fueled the panic, and the city mobilized 500 police officers in response. Four blacks were killed, and property damage totaled $2 million.

The picture was not totally bleak for African Americans in the 1930s, however. The New Deal under President Franklin Delano Roosevelt would channel significant amounts of relief money toward blacks outside the South, partly in response to the 1935 riot but mainly in return for growing black allegiance to the Democratic Party (see Chapter 25). The National Association for the Advancement of Colored People continued to publicly challenge the status quo of race relations. And although calls for racial justice went largely unheeded during the depression, World War II and its aftermath would further the struggle for black equality.

Dust Bowl Migrations

Distressed conditions in agriculture had been one of the causes of the Great Depression. In the 1930s things only got worse for farmers, especially those living on the Great Plains. The decade became known as the "Dirty Thirties" because of dust storms caused by a drought, the worst in the country's history, that began in 1930 and lasted until 1941. Throughout the decade the three words most often uttered by farmers were "if it rains."

Farmers who moved onto the semiarid Great Plains after the 1870s had always risked the ravages of drought (see Chapter 16). Even in wet years the average rainfall was 20 inches or less—barely enough to raise grain crops. But low rainfall alone did not create the Dust Bowl. National and international market forces, such as the demand for wheat during World War I, had caused farmers to push the farming frontier beyond its natural limits by working increasingly marginal land to capture a profit. After that land had been stripped of its natural vegetation, the delicate ecological balance of the plains was destroyed, leaving nothing to hold the soil when the rains dried up and the winds came.

Dust became a plague of everyday life throughout the Great Plains but especially in Oklahoma, Texas, New Mexico, Colorado, Arkansas, and Kansas (Map 24.2). When the clouds of dust rolled in, streetlights blinked on as if night had fallen. Dust seeped into houses and "blackened the pillow around one's head, the dinner plates on the table, the bread dough on the back of the stove." The dust storms were not confined to the plains.

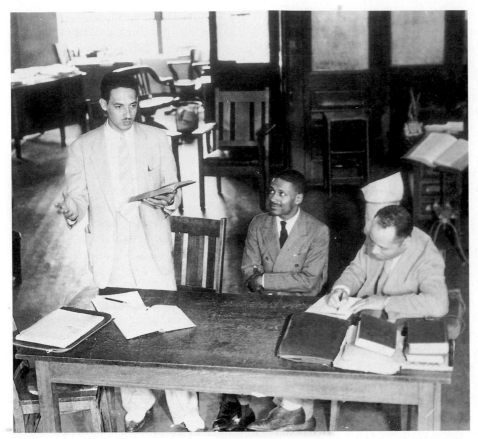

Litigating Civil Rights
In 1935 the NAACP represented Donald Gaines Murray (middle), a black Amherst College graduate who had been refused admission to the University of Maryland law school. NAACP attorneys Thurgood Marshall (left) and Charles H. Houston (right) won the case, setting an important legal precedent for later challenges to racial discrimination in education. In 1967 Thurgood Marshall became the first black to be appointed to the Supreme Court.
Library of Congress.

In May 1934 the wind took dust clouds to Chicago, where filth fell like snow, dumping the equivalent of 4 pounds of debris per person on the city. Several days later the same clouds blackened the skies and dirtied the streets of Buffalo, Boston, New York, and Washington. That winter, red snow fell on New England.

This ecological disaster caused a mass exodus from the land. Their crops ruined, their lands barren and dry, their homes foreclosed for debts they could not pay, thousands of farm families loaded their belongings into beat-up Fords and headed west along Route 66 to the promised land of California. The migrants were called "Okies," whether or not they were from Oklahoma. John Steinbeck's novel *The Grapes of Wrath* (1939) immortalized them and their journey. In the novel the Joads abandon their land not only because of drought but also as a result of the economic forces changing American agriculture. Large-scale commercialized farming was spreading to the plains. After the bank forecloses on the Joads' farm, a gasoline-engine tractor, the symbol of mechanized farming, plows under their crops and demolishes their house.

Although it is a powerful work of fiction, *The Grapes of Wrath* did not convey the diversity of the westward migration, which was both a response to hard times and part of the larger migration out of the nation's agricultural heartland that had begun around World War I and continued through the 1970s. Not all Okies were destitute dirt farmers; approximately one in six was a professional, a business proprietor, or a white-collar worker. Many were participating in chain migrations, that is, following family members or friends to a specific place. For most the drive west was fairly easy, not the life-and-death saga portrayed in Steinbeck's book. Route 66 was a paved two-lane road, and in a decent car it took just three to four days to make it from Oklahoma or Texas to California.

Before the 1930s, California had already pioneered a type of agriculture different from that practiced by southwestern and midwestern farmers. Agriculture in California was large-scale, intensive, and diversified. The state's wealth came primarily from specialty crops such as citruses, grapes, and potatoes, whose staggered harvests required a great deal of transient labor for short picking seasons. The steady supply of cheap migrant labor provided by Chinese, Mexicans, Okies, and, briefly, East Indians made such farming economically feasible. Journalist Carey McWilliams, whose nonfiction book *Factories in the Field* (1939) focused national attention on migrant workers, noted that California agriculture was basically industrial in nature:

Ownership is represented not by physical possession of the land, but by ownership of corporate stock;

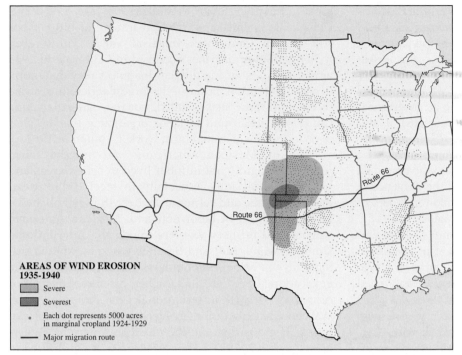

MAP 24.2
The Dust Bowl
A U.S. Weather Bureau scientist called the drought of the 1930s "the worst in the climatological history of the country." Conditions were especially severe in the southern plains, where the dramatic increases in farming on marginal land had strained production even before the drought struck. Many farm families saw no choice but to follow Route 66, the highway that went west through Missouri, Oklahoma, and north Texas, to California, the promised land.

AREAS OF WIND EROSION
1935-1940
■ Severe
■ Severest
• Each dot represents 5000 acres in marginal cropland 1924-1929
— Major migration route

farm labor, no longer pastoral in character, punches a time clock, works at piece or hourly wage rates, and lives in a shack or company barracks, and lacks all contact with the real owners of the farm factory on which it is employed.

Encouraged by handbills promising good jobs in California, at least 350,000 southwesterners headed west in the 1930s. Some went to metropolitan areas, but about half settled in rural areas. White, native-born Americans had made up about 20 percent of the migratory farm labor force before the depression, but their proportion increased to more than 85 percent in the late 1930s. Since growers needed only 175,000 workers at the peak of the picking season, this surplus ensured them a cheap supply of labor, usually docile and willing to work at any price. That price was incredibly low in the 1930s. The average yearly family income of migrant farm workers in California ranged from $350 to $450, less than one-third of the subsistence level. Yet what they earned in California was more than what they had left behind.

Those migrants had a lasting impact on California culture. At first they met outright hostility from old-time Californians, a demoralizing experience for white, native-born Protestants who were ashamed of the negative Okie stereotype. But they stayed, filling important roles in the expanding California economy. Soon communities in the rich agricultural region of central California's San Joaquin Valley—Bakersfield, Fresno, Merced, Modesto, Stockton—took on a distinctly Okie cast, identifiable by southern-influenced evangelical religion and the growing popularity of country music.

Mexican American Communities

The Mexican American experience in the West differed from that of Dust Bowl refugees. In the depths of the depression, with American fears about competition from foreign workers at a peak, perhaps one-third of the Mexican American population, most of them immigrants, returned to Mexico. A formal deportation policy instituted by the U.S. government was partly responsible for the exodus, but many more Mexicans left "voluntarily" when work ran out and local relief agencies refused to extend assistance to them. Pervasive racism, coupled with the proximity of Mexico, made Mexicans the only immigrants targeted for deportation during the depression.

The deportation of Mexican Americans was not a response to the arrival of migrants from the Dust Bowl. The largest number of deportations occurred during the Hoover administration, well before the Dust Bowl exodus reached its peak. Most occurred in California and Texas, but Indiana, Illinois, Michigan, and Colorado also deported unwanted workers. In 1932, a one-way train ticket cost the equivalent of a week's relief allotment, and officials in many southwestern and western communities realized that it was cheaper to send migrant workers back to Mexico than to support them during the winter, when there were no crops to pick.

In 1930 Los Angeles was home to 150,000 Mexican Americans, giving it the largest concentration of Mexicans outside Mexico. Mexican Americans spilled out of the downtown area, known as "Sonoratown," into neighborhoods, or *colonias*, in Belvedere and East Los Angeles, where mutual-aid societies (*mutalistas*), Spanish-language newspapers, and the Catholic Church fostered a sense of community. But Los Angeles's loss of approximately one-third of its Mexican population during the repatriation drives of the 1930s caused profound social dislocations. Although the free trip home at government expense was the source of some *chistes* (jokes), it also caused family separations, disruptions of schooling for children, and extreme financial hardships during the worst years of the depression. And for those who remained in America, the threat of deportation and the virulence of anti-Mexican sentiment were unmistakable reminders of their inferior status in the eyes of most Anglos.

Mexican migration to the United States—legal and illegal—increased steadily throughout the twentieth century. The first *bracero* (day laborer) program promoting Mexican immigration had been established during World War I to meet labor shortages. (*Bracero* comes from *brazo*, which means "arm" in Spanish; *braceros* are hired hands, those who work with their arms.) The importation of cheap Mexican labor continued throughout the 1920s. After being deported during the depression, Mexican workers were coaxed back again when World War II caused another labor shortage. Ultimately the influx of Spanish-speaking migrants with their own culture helped shape the patterns of life and work in the Southwest and the West.

Discrimination and exploitation were omnipresent in Mexican communities. The harsh experiences of César Chávez's family as migrant workers during the 1930s influenced him to become one of the twentieth century's most influential labor organizers. In the mid-1930s Chávez's father became involved in several bitter labor struggles in California's Imperial Valley. Thirty-seven major agricultural strikes occurred in California in 1933 alone, including one in the San Joaquin Valley that mobilized 18,000 cotton pickers—the largest agricultural strike to date. All these strikes failed, but they gave the young Chávez a background in labor organizing that he later used to found a national farm workers' union in 1962.

Not all Mexican Americans were migrant farm workers. A significant number lived in urban areas and held industrial jobs, especially in steel mills, meat-packing plants, and refineries, where they established a strong tradition of labor activism. Mexican American smelter and refinery workers joined the International Union of Mine, Mill and Smelter Workers (known colloquially as "Mine-Mill") in large numbers and became key leaders. Bert Corona launched his career as a labor organizer with the International Longshoremen's and Warehousemen's Union in Los Angeles (see American Lives, "Bert Corona and the Mexican American Generation," pp. 792–793). Labor activism was not limited to men, however. Mexican American women made up 75 percent of the dressmakers who toiled in Los Angeles's sweatshops, many for less than $5 a week. In 1933 Rose Pesotta, a Polish immigrant labor organizer for the International Ladies' Garment Workers Union (ILGWU), used bilingual appeals to lead a four-week strike in which Mexican American women were the most active participants.

In California, Mexican Americans also found employment in fruit and vegetable processing plants,

A Bitter Harvest
In the early 1930s California was rocked by strikes, and one of the largest was the cotton-pickers' strike of 1933. Demanding higher wages and better working conditions, the predominantly Mexican American work force set up camps for the duration of the strike. As usual, it was the women who bore most of the responsibility for cooking, cleaning, and child care. Bancroft Library, University of California, Berkeley.

especially young single women who preferred the higher wages of cannery work to domestic service, needlework, and farm labor. Corporate giants such as Del Monte dominated California's food-processing industry. In those plants Mexican American women earned around $2.50 a day, whereas their male counterparts earned $3.50 to $4.50. So pervasive was the "cannery culture" that workers could say, "We met in spinach, fell in love in peaches, and married in tomatoes," and their friends would know they were referring to the harvests of March, August, and October. In 1939 labor unions came to the canneries in the form of the United Cannery, Agricultural, Packing, and Allied Workers of America—an unusually democratic union in which women, who formed a majority of the rank-and-file workers, played a leading role.

This activism of the 1930s, both in the fields and in the factories, demonstrated how the second generation of Mexican immigrants, born in the United States, increasingly turned its orientation toward issues of political and economic justice in the United States, rather than retaining primary allegiance to Mexico. According to historian George Sanchez, they were creating "their own version of Americanism without abandoning Mexican culture." Joining American labor unions and becoming more involved in American politics were thus important steps in the creation of a distinct Mexican American ethnic identity.

Herbert Hoover and the Great Depression

During the presidential campaign of 1928 Herbert Hoover predicted that "the poorhouse is vanishing from among us" and stated that America was "nearer to the final triumph over poverty than ever before in the history of any land." Once elected, Hoover promised, he would preside over an era of Republican prosperity and governmental restraint. Even after the stock market crash in 1929, he stubbornly insisted that the downturn was only temporary. He greeted a business delegation in June 1930 with these words: "Gentlemen, you have come sixty days too late. The Depression is over." In 1931 and 1932, as the country hit rock bottom, Hoover finally acted, but by then it was too little, too late.

The Republican Response

In 1932 the journalist William Allen White wrote an article about the outgoing president entitled "Herbert Hoover—The Last of the Old Presidents, or the First of the New?" White concluded that Hoover had been a

little of both, as have historians ever since. Hoover's early efforts to fight the depression are now seen as predecessors of many New Deal programs, and his reputation among historians has risen steadily over the years. Hoover, who lived until 1964, offered a simple explanation for the improvement in his historical stature, telling Chief Justice Earl Warren of the Supreme Court that he had simply managed "to outlive the bastards."

Hoover's approach to the Great Depression was shaped by his priorities as secretary of commerce: he turned to the business community for leadership in overcoming the economic downturn. Hoover asked business to maintain wages voluntarily, keep up production, and work with the government to build confidence in the system.

Fiscal Policy. Hoover did not rely solely on public pronouncements but also used public funds and federal action to encourage recovery. Soon after the stock market crash he cut federal taxes and called on state and local governments to increase capital spending in the "energetic yet prudent pursuit" of public construction. The 1929 Agricultural Marketing Act gave the federal government its largest role to date in a program of agricultural stabilization and farm relief. In 1930 and the first half of 1931 Hoover raised the federal public-works budget to $423 million, a dramatic increase in an area not traditionally considered to be the federal government's responsibility. Hoover also eased the international crisis by declaring a moratorium on the payment of Allied debts and reparations early in the summer of 1931. The federal government's efforts to stimulate business activity were moderately effective, but the depression continued.

By 1931 more drastic action was required, but Hoover faced a cruel dilemma that had been created by the Federal Reserve's contraction of the money supply. If he embraced deficit financing and encouraged recovery through increased government spending, interest rates would remain high, since the federal government would be competing for borrowed capital with corporations and private investors. Hoover decided that significantly higher interest rates posed the greater danger to recovery, so in December 1931 he asked Congress for a 33 percent tax increase to balance the budget. The Revenue Act of 1932 represented the largest peacetime tax increase in the nation's history. Like monetary restriction, higher taxes choked both consumption and investment and contributed significantly to the severity of the Great Depression.

Not all the steps taken by the Hoover administration were so ill conceived. The president pushed Congress to create a system of government home-loan banks in 1932 and supported the Glass-Steagall Banking Act of 1932, which made government securities available to guarantee

Bert Corona and the Mexican American Generation

★

BERT CORONA ALWAYS considered himself a child of the revolution—the Mexican Revolution. His father, Noe Corona, had crossed the border from Mexico to the United States around 1915 or 1916, seeking safety after being wounded while fighting in Pancho Villa's army. Settling temporarily in El Paso, he married Margarita Escápite Salayandia, and they had four children, including Humberto (his Anglo teachers later Americanized his name to Bert), who was born in 1918.

The border is an apt metaphor for Mexican American life, capturing the fluidity of crossing back and forth between two countries and two cultures. Bert's family returned to Mexico in 1922, where two years later Noe Corona was assassinated by unknown assailants, presumably political enemies. This loss had a profound effect on Noe's six-year-old son: "The Revolution, my father's role in it, and his martyrdom symbolized the struggle for social justice. This would be the same struggle I would later pursue."

Strong female role models influenced Bert as well. The Corona family resettled in El Paso, where Bert's mother secured a job at the Mexican customs house on the El Paso–Ciudad Juarez border, and his grandmother, a doctor, pursued her practice of medicine and midwifery. The El Paso school system provided a searing introduction to the discrimination and unequal treatment that Mexican immigrants in the Southwest faced. Corona's segregated "Mexican" school in the barrio, geared primarily toward vocational education, was far inferior to white schools. Although he attended an integrated high school with a good academic reputation, racism and discrimination remained very much a part of his education, both in daily encounters with his Anglo teachers and classmates and in the general lack of respect for Mexican history and culture in the curriculum. His grandmother said tartly, "Well, you have to understand that the United States writes its history to its own convenience. It always has, and these people always will."

Bert Corona
Bert Corona addresses a press conference at the National Chicano Political Caucus in 1972.
Bert Corona.

When Bert graduated from high school in 1934 at age sixteen, it was the height of the Great Depression, and El Paso was hard hit. Fortunately, his mother kept her job at the Juarez customs house, but hard times forced many Mexicans to leave. El Paso was a major border crossing for *los repatriados* (those returning to their old country), as they fled the depression and the threat of deportation, but Mexicans were not the only group on the move. The Corona backyard faced the train tracks, and Bert vividly remembered the thousands of Dust Bowl migrants traveling through El Paso on their way west. A hundred-car freight train could carry a thousand Dust Bowlers, and there were three trains in the morning and three in the evening. "It was like the population of a small town coming in every day," he later recalled.

After working for two years in El Paso, Bert headed to the University of Southern California, where he hoped to play basketball and continue his education on an athletic scholarship. But an injury cut short his sports career, and he soon found new interests that took him away from his studies, although he later regretted not getting a college degree. What took precedence over his family's strong belief in education? Participating in the revitalized labor movement and fostering Mexican American political consciousness—the two causes that shaped the rest of Corona's life.

The Congress of Industrial Organizations, or CIO (see Chapter 25), became his vehicle for labor activism: "I had a sense of the historical importance of the CIO, and I viewed the CIO as a movement whose time had come. Nothing could stop it, and— for a time—nothing did." In the 1930s many labor activists focused on organizing Mexican American migrant workers in the fields, but Corona concentrated on recruiting Los Angeles industrial workers into the newly constituted International Longshoremen's and Warehousemen's Union (ILWU). His organizing was not restricted to Mexican workers, however. Like the CIO, he wanted the entire working class to join unions to work for social change in the workplace and in society as a whole. While organizing at an aviation plant in 1941 he met his future wife, Blanche Taff. The daughter of Polish Jewish immigrants, she shared his commitment to progressive social change. Their marriage fit right in with the interracial and interethnic culture of the CIO. So great was their commitment to organized labor that they gave up their honeymoon to participate in a major CIO organizing drive.

In addition to labor organizing, Bert Corona felt a deep commitment to the political mobilization of Spanish-speaking peoples throughout the United States. In 1939 he joined El Congreso Nacional del Pueblo de Habla Español (the National Congress of Spanish-Speaking Peoples), a militant organization founded to fight for the rights of Mexican Americans and other Latinos as part of the larger struggle against racial and class oppression. There he worked with noted activists such as Luisa Moreno, a Guatemalan-born CIO organizer who had been active in the cannery industry, and Josefina Fierro, a radical young Mexican American married to the screenwriter John Bright, who was part of Hollywood's leftist community. Their activist agenda was far to the left of that of organizations such as the League of United Latin American Citizens (LULAC), founded in 1929, which focused on assimilation and citizenship from a distinctly middle-class perspective.

After serving in the armed forces during World War II, Corona continued to be a labor and community activist. In the 1960s he became involved in the Mexican-American Political Association, or MAPA, which mobilized Latino political power to force the Kennedy and Johnson administrations to do more for those constituencies. Since then he has been involved in community organizing, especially of undocumented Mexican workers, arguing that they have just as legitimate claims to live, work, and be protected by the basic guarantees of American law as any other workers.

Bert Corona exemplifies what the historian Mario Garcia has called the "Mexican-American Generation." These men and women, who were born and raised in the United States, came of political age between the 1930s and the 1950s. They filled the leadership vacuum created when *los repatriados*, mainly older and Mexican-born, returned permanently to that country in the 1930s. Even before terms such as *Mexican American*, *Hispanic*, and *Latino* were widely used, this generation had the "double consciousness" that W. E. B. Du Bois described in African Americans: a sense of being both *mexicanos* and American citizens. Many members of the Mexican-American Generation shared Corona's commitment to organizing for social change—in their communities, on the job, and in the wider political arena. Tracing their political activism over the years provides a window on the changing character of Mexican American communities in the United States.

Since the 1930s Bert Corona has seen a dramatic expansion of Latino empowerment, but he remains modest about his role in this story. "It's hard for me to think how I would like to be remembered by history," he told Mario Garcia as they collaborated on a book about his life. "I never planned my life. It just happened the way it did. . . . If my life has meant anything, I would say that it shows that you can organize workers and poor people if you work hard, are persistent, remain optimistic, and reach out to involve as many people as possible. . . . But my life is not over yet, and I continue *la lucha*, the struggle." For Bert Corona, that commitment to *la lucha* had its roots in his Mexican heritage, but it first began to flower during the turbulent 1930s.

Federal Reserve notes and thus temporarily propped up the ailing banking system. The federal government under Hoover also spent $700 million—an unprecedented sum for the time—on public works.

The Reconstruction Finance Corporation.   The centerpiece of Hoover's new initiative to combat the depression was the Reconstruction Finance Corporation (RFC), which Congress approved in January 1932. Modeled on the War Finance Corporation of World War I and developed in collaboration with the business and banking communities, the RFC was the first federal institution created to intervene directly in the economy during peacetime. To alleviate the credit crunch for business, the RFC would provide federal loans to railroads, financial institutions, banks, and insurance companies in a strategy that has been called *pump priming*. In theory, money lent at the top of the economic structure would stimulate production, which in turn would create new jobs and increase consumer spending. Benefits would thus "trickle down" to the rest of the economy.

Congress allocated $500 million for the RFC, but the agency's cautiousness in lending money limited its influence. In July 1932 Congress doubled that amount and authorized loans to the states for relief and public works. Once again the RFC acted far too cautiously, lending only $30 million by the end of 1932 and spending only 20 percent of the $1.5 billion appropriated for public works projects.

The RFC was a watershed in American political history and the rise of the state. When voluntary cooperation failed, the president turned to federal action to stimulate the economy. Yet Hoover's break with the past had clear limits. In many ways his support of the RFC was just another attempt to encourage business confidence. Compared with previous presidents, and in contrast to his image as a "do-nothing" president, Hoover responded to the national emergency on an unprecedented scale. But the nation's needs during the Great Depression were also unprecedented, and Hoover's initiatives failed to meet them.

In particular, federal programs fell far short of helping the growing ranks of the unemployed. Hoover

Hoovervilles
By 1930 shantytowns had sprung up in most of the nation's cities. In New York City squatters camped out along the Hudson River railroad tracks, built makeshift homes in Central Park, or lived in the city dump. This scene from the old reservoir in Central Park looks east toward the fancy apartment buildings of Fifth Avenue and the Metropolitan Museum of Art, at left.
Grant Smith/Corbis.

The Despair of the Unemployed

★

In 1931 an unemployed tool and dye designer wrote to the director of the President's Organization for Unemployment Relief (POUR), but his letter drew only this penciled response: "no use answering."

Detroit, Mich.
September 29, 1931

Mr. Walter Gifford
Dear Sir:

You and Pres. Hoover shows at times about the same degree of intelligence as Andy [of the "Amos 'n' Andy" radio show] does. The other night Andy was going to send a fellow a letter to find out his address.

You have told us to spend to end the slump, but you did not tell us what to use for money, after being out of work for two years you tell us this, Pres. Hoover on the other hand tells the working man to build homes, and in face of the fact nearly every working man has had his home taken off him, "some more intelligence." This is a radical letter but the time is here to be radical. when an average of two a day has to take their own life right in the City of Detroit because they can not see their way out. right in the city where one of the worlds riches men lives who made last year 259 000 000 dollars. where hundreds of peoples are starving to death. . . . Mr. Gifford why not come clean . . . remember you have the all seeing eye of God over you. Tell us the reason of the depression is the greed of Bankers and Industrialist who are taking too great of amount of profits. . . . The other day our Pres. Hoover came to Detroit and kidded the soldier boys out of their bonus. Pres Hoover a millionaire worth about 12 000 000 dollars drawing a salary of 75 000 per year from the government asking some boys to forgo their bonus some of them have not 12 dollars of their own "Some more nerve."

Am I right when I say you and he shows the same degree of intelligence as Andy.

J.B.

Source: Quoted in Robert S. McElvaine, *Down and Out in the Great Depression* (Chapel Hill: University of North Carolina Press, 1983), 46–47.

---

remained adamant in his refusal to consider any plan for direct federal relief for unemployed Americans. Throughout his career he had believed that private organized charities were sufficient to meet social welfare needs. During World War I Hoover had headed the Commission for Relief of Belgium, a private group that distributed 5 million tons of food to relieve the suffering of Europe's civilian population. In 1927 he coordinated a rescue and cleanup operation after a devastating Mississippi River flood left 16.5 million acres of land under water in seven states. This effort involved private charities, including the Red Cross and the Rockefeller Foundation, as well as government agencies such as the U.S. Public Health Service and the National Guard. The success of these and other predominantly voluntary responses to public emergencies confirmed Hoover's belief that private charity, not federal aid, was the "American way" of solving social problems. Unfortunately, evidence from across the country supported a different conclusion: charities and state and local relief agencies could not meet the growing needs of the unemployed.

Rising Discontent

As the depression deepened, many citizens came to hate Herbert Hoover. Formerly the symbol of business prosperity, he became the scapegoat for the depression. "In Hoover we trusted, now we are busted" read hand-lettered signs carried by the down and out. New terms entered the vocabulary: *Hoovervilles* (shantytowns where people lived in packing crates and other makeshift shelters), *Hoover flags* (empty pockets turned inside out), and *Hoover blankets* (newspapers). The president's declarations that no one was starving and that hoboes were better fed than ever before seemed cruel and insensitive, and his apparent willingness to bail out business and banks while leaving individuals to fend for themselves added to his reputation for cold-heartedness (see American Voices, "The Despair of the Unemployed," above).

In 1932, as the country entered its fourth year of the depression, signs of rising discontent and rebellion began to emerge. Farmers were among the most vocal groups, banding together to harass the bank agents and government officers who enforced evictions and farm foreclosures and to protest the low prices they received for their crops. Midwestern farmers had watched the price of wheat fall from $3 a bushel in 1920 to barely 30 cents in 1932. Now they formed the Farm Holiday Association under the charismatic leadership of Milo Reno, the sixty-four-year-old former president of the Iowa Farmers' Union. Farmers barricaded local roads and dumped milk, vegetables, and other farm produce because the prices they would fetch on the market would not cover the farmers' costs. Nothing better captured the cruel irony of underconsumption and maldistribution than farmers dumping food at a time when so many people were hungry.

Protest was not confined to rural America. Bitter labor strikes occurred during the depths of the depression, despite the threat that strikers would lose their jobs. In Harlan County, Kentucky, miners struck in 1931 over a 10 percent wage cut, only to see their union crushed by the mine owners and the National Guard. In 1932, at Ford's River Rouge factory outside Detroit, a demonstration provoked violence from police and Ford security forces; three demonstrators were killed, and fifty were seriously injured. Some 40,000 people viewed the coffins under a banner charging that "Ford Gave Bullets for Bread."

In 1931 and 1932 violence broke out in the nation's cities. Groups of unemployed citizens battled local authorities over inadequate relief; people staged rent riots and hunger marches. Some of these urban actions were organized by the Communist Party, such as "unemployment councils" that agitated for jobs and food and coordinated a hunger march on Washington, D.C., in 1931. The marches were well attended and often got results from local and federal authorities, but they did not necessarily win converts to communism. In the early 1930s the American Communist Party was still a tiny organization with only 12,000 members, although it would grow dramatically later in the decade.

It was not radicals but veterans who staged the most publicized—and tragic—protest. In the summer of 1932 the "Bonus Army," a ragtag group of about 15,000 unemployed World War I veterans, hitchhiked to Washington from throughout the nation to demand immediate payment of their bonuses, originally scheduled for distribution in 1945. While their leaders unsuccessfully lobbied Congress, members of the "Bonus Expeditionary Force" (parodying the wartime American Expeditionary Force) camped out in the capital, a visible reminder of the plight of the unemployed. "We were heroes in 1917, but we're bums now," one veteran remarked bitterly. When the marchers refused to leave their camp, Hoover called out riot troops to clear the area. Led by General Douglas MacArthur, assisted by Majors Dwight D. Eisenhower and George S. Patton, the troops burned the encampment to the ground. In the fight that followed, more than a hundred marchers were injured. Newsreel footage captured the deeply disturbing spectacle of the U.S. Army firing on its own veterans, and Hoover's popularity plunged even further.

The 1932 Election

Despite evidence of discontent, the nation was not in a revolutionary mood as it approached the 1932 election. Despair and apathy, not anger, characterized the feelings of most citizens. The Republicans, who could find no credible way to abandon an incumbent president, unenthusiastically renominated Hoover. The Democrats turned to Governor Franklin Delano Roosevelt of New York, who capitalized on that state's innovative relief and unemployment programs to win the nomination.

Roosevelt's route to the presidential nomination began on a Hudson River estate north of New York City. Born into a wealthy family in 1882, he attended the Groton School (in Connecticut), Harvard College, and Columbia Law School. He had served in the New York State legislature and as assistant secretary of the navy in the Wilson administration, a post that earned him the vice-presidential nomination on the losing Democratic ticket in 1920. Except for his allegiance to Democratic rather than Republican Party ideology, he consciously modeled his career on that of his distant cousin Theodore Roosevelt, whose niece Eleanor he married in 1905.

Franklin Roosevelt was sidetracked from his path to the White House in 1921 by an attack of polio that left both his legs paralyzed for the rest of his life. Roosevelt fought back from his infirmity, emerging from the ordeal a stronger, more resilient man. "If you had spent two years in bed trying to wiggle your toe,

1932 Campaign Memorabilia
Mechanical buttons of the 1932 campaign gave voters a choice between a Republican elephant rearing its trunk to bring back prosperity and a Democratic donkey that kicked out the depression by kicking an elephant. All you had to do was pull the string.
Collection of David J. and Janice L. Frent.

after that anything would seem easy," he said. Eleanor Roosevelt strongly supported her husband's return to public life and helped to mastermind his successful campaign for the New York governorship in 1928.

The 1932 campaign foreshadowed little of the governmental activism that would characterize the New Deal. Roosevelt hinted at new approaches to the depression but stated his goals in vague terms: "The country needs and, unless I mistake its temper, the country demands bold, persistent experimentation." Roosevelt won easily, receiving 22.8 million votes to Hoover's 15.7 million. Despite the economic collapse, Americans remained firmly committed to the two-party system. The Socialist Party candidate, Norman Thomas, got fewer than a million votes. The Communist Party drew only 100,000 votes for its candidate, party leader William Z. Foster (Map 24.3).

The 1932 election marked a turning point in American politics—the emergence of a Democratic coalition that would dominate political life for the next four decades. In 1932 Roosevelt won with the support of the Solid South, which returned to the Democratic fold after defecting in 1928 because of Al Smith's religion and views on Prohibition. Roosevelt also drew substantial support in the West and in the cities, continuing a trend first noticed in the 1928 election when the Democrats successfully appealed to recent immigrants and urban ethnic groups. Roosevelt's election was

hardly a mandate to reshape American political and economic institutions, however. Many people voted as much against Hoover as for Roosevelt.

Having spoken, the voters had to wait until March 1933 before Roosevelt could put his ideas into action. (Inauguration Day was moved up to January 20 by the Twentieth Amendment in 1933.) In the worst winter of the depression, Americans could do little but hope that things would get better. According to the most conservative estimates, unemployment stood at 20 to 25 percent. The rate was as high as 50 percent in Cleveland, 60 percent in Akron, and 80 percent in Toledo—cities dependent on manufacturing jobs in industries that had essentially shut down. The nation's banking system was so close to collapse that many state governors temporarily closed banks to avoid further panic.

By the winter of 1932–1933 the depression had totally overwhelmed public welfare institutions. Private charity and local public relief, whose expenditures had risen dramatically, still reached only a fraction of the needy. Hunger haunted cities and rural areas alike. When a teacher tried to send a coal miner's daughter home from school because she was weak from hunger, the girl replied, "It won't do any good . . . because this is sister's day to eat." In New York City, hospitals reported ninety-five deaths from starvation. This was the America that Roosevelt inherited when he took the oath of office on March 4, 1933.

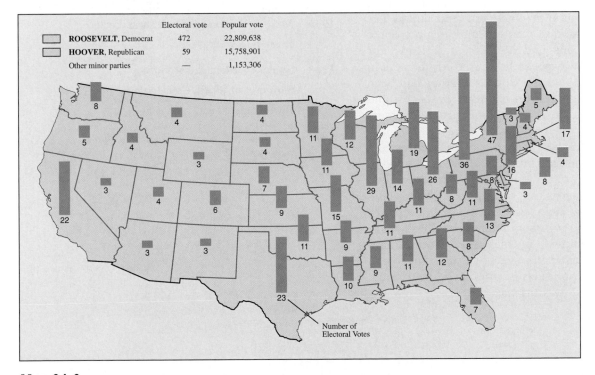

	Electoral vote	Popular vote
ROOSEVELT, Democrat	472	22,809,638
HOOVER, Republican	59	15,758,901
Other minor parties	—	1,153,306

Number of Electoral Votes

MAP 24.3
The Election of 1932
Franklin Roosevelt's convincing electoral victory over Herbert Hoover in 1932 resulted from a political realignment and dissatisfaction with the incumbent president. Even in the midst of the gravest crisis capitalism had ever faced, candidates of the Communist and Socialist Parties received fewer than 1 million votes out of almost 40 million cast.

Summary

★

The Great Depression of the 1930s was the longest and most severe economic downturn the United States had ever faced, and it had wide-ranging social, political, and cultural effects. The economic prosperity of the 1920s had rested on shaky ground. After the stock market crash of 1929 the economy entered a downward spiral that did not bottom out until 1932–1933. In addition to the collapse of the stock market, the main causes of the depression were underconsumption, an unequal distribution of wealth, an unstable international financial situation, a legacy of "sick industries" and agricultural distress from the 1920s, and the flawed monetary policies of the Federal Reserve System. At first President Hoover did not want to intervene in the economy because of his reliance on private charities and his adamant stance on maintaining a balanced budget. Then in 1932 the Hoover administration authorized the first direct federal intervention in the economy during peacetime, the Reconstruction Finance Corporation, to win business and public confidence. Though unprecedented, such measures did not end the Great Depression. In 1932 the nation turned to Franklin D. Roosevelt and the Democrats.

The Great Depression left an invisible scar on many people who lived through the 1930s, especially white middle-class Americans. Those who wanted to work blamed themselves if they could not find a job. The impact of the depression was especially catastrophic for African Americans and Mexican Americans, for whom times had always been hard. And for farmers in the Midwest, things got even worse than they had been in the 1920s. Misguided agricultural practices and drought created the Dust Bowl, forcing many farmers off their land.

Despite the devastating impact of the depression, many aspects of American life and culture continued to conform to traditional patterns. Families pulled together, with women taking on expanded roles—and often new jobs—to help support their households. Young people stayed in school longer. Families sought relief in popular culture, especially movies and radio programs, which played an especially important role in reaffirming—and obliquely criticizing—traditional American ideals and institutions.

TIMELINE

1929	Stock market crash
	Agricultural Marketing Act
1930	Midwestern drought begins
	Hawley-Smoot Tariff
1931	Scottsboro case
	Hoover declares moratorium on Allied war debts
	Miners strike in Harlan County, Kentucky
1932	Reconstruction Finance Corporation created
	Bonus Army rebuffed by Congress
	Height of deportation of Mexican migrant workers
	Strike at Ford's River Rouge plant in Michigan
	Communist-led hunger marches
1933	Unemployment rises to highest level
	Franklin Delano Roosevelt becomes president
	Birth rate drops to lowest level due to depression
	The Marx Brothers in *Duck Soup*
1934	Southern Tenant Farmers Union founded
	It Happened One Night sweeps Oscars
1935	National Youth Administration created
	Harlem race riot
1936	Student Strike against War
	Margaret Mitchell, *Gone with the Wind*
	Birth control legalized
1939	John Steinbeck, *The Grapes of Wrath*
	Frank Capra, *Mr. Smith Goes to Washington*

Suggested Readings

————————★————————

Useful overviews of the Great Depression are T. H. Watkins, *The Great Depression: America in the 1930s* (1993); John A. Garraty, *The Great Depression* (1987); and Robert S. McElvaine, *The Great Depression, 1929–1941* (1984).

The Coming of the Great Depression

Historians and economists continue to debate the causes of the Great Depression. See John Kenneth Galbraith, *The Great Crash* (1954); Milton Friedman and Anna Schwartz, *The Great Contraction, 1929–1933* (1965); Charles Kindleberger, *The World in Depression* (1974); Peter Temin, *Did Monetary Forces Cause the Great Depression?* (1976); and Michael Bernstein, *The Great Depression: Delayed Recovery and Economic Change in America, 1929–1939* (1988). Irving Bernstein, *The Lean Years* (1960), offers a compelling portrait of hard times during the Hoover years.

Hard Times

A wealth of material brings the voices of the 1930s to life. The Federal Writers' Project, *These Are Our Lives* (1939); Tom Terrill and Jerrold Hirsch, eds., *Such as Us: Southern Voices of the Thirties* (1978); and Ann Banks, ed., *First-Person America* (1980), all draw on oral histories collected by the Works Progress Administration during the 1930s. See also Robert S. McElvaine, ed., *Down and Out in the Great Depression* (1983). Evocative secondary sources include Studs Terkel, *Hard Times: An Oral History of the Great Depression* (1970), and Caroline Bird, *The Invisible Scar* (1966).

Descriptions of family life in the 1930s include Robert and Helen Lynd, *Middletown in Transition* (1937); Mirra Komarovsky, *The Unemployed Man and His Family* (1940); and Roger Angell, *The Family Encounters the Depression* (1936). Russell Baker's autobiography, *Growing Up* (1982), provides an often humorous description of family life in the 1930s. Glen H. Elder Jr., *Children of the Great Depression* (1974), and John A. Clausen, *American Lives: Looking Back at the Children of the Great Depression* (1993), consider the long-term effects. For more on youth, see Maxine Davis, *The Lost Generation* (1936); Eileen Eagan, *Class, Culture, and the Classroom* (1981); and John Modell, *Into One's Own: From Youth to Adulthood, 1920–1975* (1989).

Frederick Lewis Allen, *Since Yesterday* (1939), provides an impressionistic overview of popular culture in the 1930s. See also the essays in Lawrence W. Levine, *The Unpredictable Past* (1993), and Michael Denning, *Cultural Front: The Laboring of American Culture in the Twentieth Century* (1996). Specific studies of movies and Hollywood include Andrew Bergman, *We're in the Money* (1971); Molly Haskell, *From Reverence to Rape: The Treatment of Women in the Movies* (2d ed., 1987); and Thomas Schatz, *The Genius of the System: Hollywood Film Making in the Studio Era* (1988). On radio, see Arthur Frank Wertheim, *Radio Comedy* (1979).

Material on women in the 1930s can be found in Susan Ware, *Holding Their Own* (1982); Winifred Wandersee, *Women's Work and Family Values, 1920–1940* (1981); and Lois Scharf, *To Work and to Wed* (1981). For the special dimensions of white rural women's lives, see Margaret Hagood, *Mothers of the South* (1939). Jeane Westin, *Making Do: How Women Survived the '30s* (1976), is a lively account drawn from interviews. The birth control movement is surveyed in Linda Gordon, *Woman's Body, Woman's Right* (2d ed., 1990); Estelle Freedman and John D'Emilio, *Intimate Matters: A History of Sexuality in America* (1988); and Ellen Chesler, *Woman of Valor: Margaret Sanger and the Birth Control Movement in America* (1992).

Harder Times

Developments in the black community during the 1930s are covered in Cheryl Lyn Greenberg, *"Or Does It Explode?" Harlem in the Great Depression* (1991); Jervis Anderson, *This Was Harlem, 1900–1950* (1982); and Robert Weisbrot, *Father Divine and the Struggle for Racial Equality* (1983). James Goodman, *Stories of Scottsboro* (1994), and Dan T. Carter, *Scottsboro* (1969), discuss that case. Donald Grubbs, *Cry from Cotton* (1971), tells the story of the Southern Tenant Farmers Union. Robin D. G. Kelley, *Hammer and Hoe* (1990), is an excellent account of Alabama communists during the Great Depression. Donald Worster, *Dust Bowl* (1979), evokes the plains during the "Dirty Thirties." James N. Gregory, *American Exodus: The Dust Bowl Migration and Okie Culture in California* (1989), treats the experiences of migrants and their impact on California culture and the economy. See also Kevin Starr, *Endangered Dreams: The Great Depression in California* (1996).

On the experiences of Mexican Americans during the 1930s, see Mario T. Garcia, *Mexican Americans: Leadership, Ideology, and Identity, 1930–1960* (1989), and *Memories of Chicano History: The Life and Narrative of Bert Corona* (1994). George J. Sanchez, *Becoming Mexican American* (1993), examines Chicano Los Angeles from 1900 to 1945; and David Gutierrez, *Walls and Mirrors* (1995), looks at Mexican immigration and the politics of ethnicity. See also Richard A. Garcia, *The Rise of the Mexican-American Middle Class* (1990). For Mexican American women's lives in the twentieth century, see Vicki Ruiz's overview, *From Out of the Shadows* (1998), as well as her *Cannery Women, Cannery Lives* (1987), and Patricia Zavella, *Women's Work and Chicano Families* (1987).

Herbert Hoover and the Great Depression

Hoover's response to the depression is chronicled in Alfred Romasco, *The Poverty of Abundance* (1965), and Jordan Schwartz, *The Interregnum of Despair* (1970). Eliot Rosen, *Hoover, Roosevelt, and the Brain Trust* (1977), treats the transition between the two administrations, as does Frank Freidel, *Launching the New Deal* (1973). On the 1932 election and the beginnings of the New Deal coalition, see David Burner, *The Politics of Provincialism* (1967); Samuel Lubell, *The Future of American Politics* (1952); and John Allswang, *The New Deal in American Politics* (1978).

The New Deal,
1933–1939

IN HIS BOLD inaugural address on March 4, 1933, President Franklin Delano Roosevelt declared, "The only thing we have to fear is fear itself." That memorable phrase rallied a nation that had already endured almost four years of the worst economic contraction in its history, with no end in sight.

With his demeanor grim and purposeful, Roosevelt preached his first inaugural address like a sermon. Only in the most general terms did he speak of the economic and social problems that the nation faced, and their possible solutions. Promising "a leadership of frankness and vigor," Roosevelt issued ringing declarations of his vision of governmental activism: "This Nation asks for action, and action now." Roosevelt repeatedly compared combating the depression to fighting a war. The most explicit parallel was his willingness to ask Congress for "broad Executive power to wage a war against the emergency, as great as the power that would be given to me if we were in fact invaded by a foreign foe." This conception of presidential leadership was well suited to Roosevelt's self-confident personality and pragmatic political style.

In the end, however, Roosevelt intended not to scare the American people but to reassure them. The democratic system was basically sound, he told them, and hard times could be overcome, but only if a dispirited nation chose not to wallow in lethargy. On that cold March day in 1933 Roosevelt urged his fellow citizens to return to the values of hard work, cooperation, and sacrifice that had made the country great. Roosevelt's restoration of hope and confidence was likely his greatest contribution to American life during the Great Depression.

The CCC
The Civilian Conservation Corps (CCC) was one of the most popular New Deal programs. Over ten years, it enrolled 2.75 million young Americans who worked for $1 a day on projects such as soil conservation, disaster relief, reforestation, and flood control. The CCC was limited to men, although a few camps employed out-of-work young women.
Library of Congress.

The federal government dominated political and economic life so thoroughly during the 1930s that the term *New Deal* is often used as a synonym for that decade. In a time of deep crisis, the New Deal was meant to relieve suffering and conserve the nation's political and economic institutions through unprecedented activity on the part of the national government. Its legacy would be an expanded federal presence in the economy and the lives of ordinary citizens. By the late 1930s, however, Roosevelt became increasingly preoccupied with international relations, as Europe moved toward war and Japan flexed its muscles in East Asia. As war mobilization finally began to pull the country out of its decade-long depression, calls for further social reform stalemated.

The New Deal Takes Over, 1933–1935

★

Franklin Roosevelt first used the term *New Deal* in his acceptance speech at the Democratic National Convention in 1932. Plucked from deep within the speech by the newspaper cartoonist Rollin Kirby, the term came to stand for the Roosevelt administration's complex set of responses to the depression. The New Deal was not a carefully formulated plan. Its ideology contained many contradictions, but it provided a measure of economic security against the worst depression in U.S. history.

The Roosevelt Style of Leadership

Although the New Deal represented many things to many people, one unifying factor was the personality of its master architect, Franklin Delano Roosevelt. Every president since the 1930s has lived in the shadow of FDR, although few of his successors have matched his raw political talent and none have had to face and surmount the twin crises of depression and war. "I have no expectation of making a hit every time I come to bat," Roosevelt disarmingly told his critics. "What I seek is the highest possible batting average." Roosevelt parlayed that experimental tone into a highly effective political and governmental style.

The New Deal was "a very personal enterprise," and President Roosevelt established an unusually close rapport with the American people. "Mr. Roosevelt is the only man we ever had in the White House who would understand that my boss is a son of a bitch," remarked one worker. Many ordinary citizens credited him with the positive changes in their lives, saying, "He gave me a job" or "He saved my home." Roosevelt's masterful use of the new medium of radio, typified by the sixteen "fireside chats" he broadcast during his first two terms, fostered this personal identification. More than 450,000 letters poured into the White House in the week after

FDR
President Franklin Delano Roosevelt was a consummate politician who loved the adulation of a crowd, such as this one greeting him in Warm Springs, Georgia, in 1933. He consciously adopted a cheerful mien to keep people from feeling sorry for him because of his infirmity, knowing that he could not be a successful politician if the public pitied him.
Corbis-Bettmann.

the inauguration, and an average of 5,000 to 8,000 arrived weekly for the rest of the decade. One person had handled public correspondence during the Hoover administration, but it took a staff of fifty under Roosevelt. He also became the first president to hire a press secretary.

Franklin Roosevelt's personal charisma and political talent allowed him to continue the expansion of presidential power begun during the administrations of Theodore Roosevelt and Woodrow Wilson. From the beginning Roosevelt centralized decision making in the White House; in doing so, he dramatically expanded the role of the executive branch in initiating policy and helped to create the modern presidency. During the interregnum (the period between election and inauguration) he relied so heavily on the advice of Columbia University professors Raymond Moley, Rexford Tugwell, and Adolph A. Berle Jr. that the press dubbed them the "Brains Trust." Once in the White House, for policy formulation he turned to his talented cabinet, which included Interior Secretary Harold Ickes, Frances Perkins at Labor, Henry A. Wallace at Agriculture, and an old friend, Henry Morgenthau Jr., at the Treasury.

When searching for new ideas and fresh faces, Roosevelt was just as likely to turn to advisors and administrators scattered throughout the New Deal bureaucracy. Eager young people flocked to Washington to join the New Deal—"men with long hair and women with short hair," wags quipped (see American Voices, "Joe Marcus: A New Deal Activist," p. 804). Lawyers in their mid-twenties fresh out of Harvard found themselves drafting legislation or being called to the White House for strategy sessions with the president. Paul Freund, a Harvard Law School professor who worked in the Department of Justice, remembered, "It was a glorious time for obscure people." Many young New Dealers who went on to distinguished careers in government or public service later recalled that nothing could match the excitement of the early New Deal.

The Hundred Days

The first problem that the new president confronted was the collapse of the banking system, which, far more than the stock market crash, had brought the depression home to the middle class. On the eve of Roosevelt's inauguration thirty-eight states had closed their banks, and banks operated on a restricted basis in the rest. On March 5, 1933, the day after his inauguration, the president declared a national "bank holiday" (a euphemism for closing all the banks) and called Congress into special session. Four days later Congress passed Roosevelt's proposed emergency banking bill, which permitted banks to reopen beginning on March 13, but only if a Treasury department inspection showed that they had sufficient cash reserves. The House approved the plan after only thirty-eight minutes of debate.

The Emergency Banking Act. The Emergency Banking Act, which Roosevelt developed in consultation with banking leaders, was such a conservative document that it could have been proposed by Herbert Hoover. The difference was the public's reaction. On the Sunday evening before the banks reopened Roosevelt gave his first "fireside chat" to a radio audience estimated at 60 million. In simple terms he reassured the people that the banks were now safe, and Americans believed him. When the banks reopened on Monday morning, deposits exceeded withdrawals. "Capitalism was saved in eight days," observed Raymond Moley, who had served as Roosevelt's speech writer during the 1932 campaign. The banking bill did its job: more than 4,000 banks failed in 1933 (the vast majority in the months before the law took effect), but only 61 closed their doors in 1934 (Table 25.1).

TABLE 25.1

American Banks and Bank Failures, 1920–1940

Year	Total Number of Banks	Total Assets ($ billion)	Bank Failures
1920	30,909	53.1	168
1929	25,568	72.3	659
1931	22,242	70.1	2,294
1933	14,771	51.4	4,004
1934	15,913	55.9	61
1940	15,076	79.7	48

Source: Historical Statistics of the United States: Colonial Times to 1970 (Washington, DC: U.S. Government Printing Office, 1975), 1019, 1038–1039.

JOE MARCUS
A New Deal Activist

─────────★─────────

As an economist working for Harry Hopkins, Joe Marcus was one of thousands who formed the growing New Deal bureaucracy. Marcus's account, as told to Studs Terkel, captures some of the excitement that the New Deal generated. Marcus also suggests the way in which Roosevelt's administration expanded opportunities for Jews and other "outsiders."

I graduated college in '35. I went down to Washington and started to work in the spring of '36. The New Deal was a young man's world. Young people, if they showed any ability, got an opportu-nity. I was a kid, twenty-two or twenty-three. In a few months I was made head of the department. We had a meeting with hot shots: What's to be done? I pointed out some problems: let's define what we're looking for. They immediately had me take over. I had to set up the organization and hire seventy-five people. Given a chance as a youngster to try out ideas, I learned a fan-tastic amount. The challenge itself was great.

It was the idea of being asked big questions. The technical problems were small. These you had to solve by yourself. But the context was broad: Where was society going? Your statistical questions became questions of full employment. You were not prepared for it in school. If you wanted new answers, you needed a new kind of people. This is what was exciting.

Ordinarily, I might have had a job at the university, marking papers or helping a professor. All of a sudden, I'm doing original research and asking basic questions about how our society works. What makes a Depression? What makes for pulling out of it? Once you start thinking in these terms, you're in a different ball game.

The climate was exciting. You were part of a society that was on the move. You were involved in something that could make a difference. Laws could be changed. So could the conditions of people.

The idea of bring involved close to the center of political life was unthinkable, just two or three years before all this happened. Unthinkable for someone like me, of lower middle-class, close to ghetto, Jewish life. Suddenly you were a significant member of society. It was not the kind of closed society you had lived in before.

. . . You were really part of something, changes could be made. Bringing *immediate* results to people who were starving. You could do something about it: that was the most important thing. This you felt.

A feeling that if you had something to say, it would get to the top. As I look back now, memo-randa I had written reached the White House, one way or another. The biggest thrill of my life was hearing a speech of Roosevelt's, using a selection from a memorandum I had written.

Everybody was searching for ideas. A lot of guys were opportunists, some were crackpots. But there was a search, a sense of values . . . that would make a difference in the lives of people.

We weren't thinking of remaking society. That wasn't it. I didn't buy this dream stuff. What was happening was a complete change in social atti-tudes at the central government level. The question was: How can you do it within this system? People working in all the New Deal agencies were domi-nated by this spirit. . . .

It was an exciting community, where we lived in Washington. The basic feeling—and I don't think this is just nostalgia—was one of excitement, of achievement, of happiness. Life was important, life was significant.

───────────

Source: Studs Terkel, *Hard Times* (New York: Pantheon Books, 1986), 265–266.

The Banking Act was the first of fifteen pieces of major legislation enacted by Congress in the opening months of the Roosevelt administration. This legislative session, which came to be called the Hundred Days, remains one of the most productive ever. Congress cre-ated the Home Owners Loan Corporation to refinance home mortgages threatened by foreclosure; a full 20 percent of the nation's homeowners took advantage of it. A second banking law, the Glass-Steagall Act, curbed speculation by separating investment banking from commercial banking and also created the Federal Deposit Insurance Corporation (FDIC), which insured bank deposits up to $2,500. Another act created the Civilian Conservation Corps (CCC), through which 250,000 young men went to live in camps where they did reforestation and conservation work. The Tennessee

Valley Authority (TVA) received legislative approval for its innovative plan of government-sponsored regional development and public energy. And in a move that lifted public spirits immeasurably, Roosevelt legalized beer in April. Full repeal of Prohibition came eight months later, in December 1933.

The Agricultural Adjustment Act. The Roosevelt administration targeted three pressing problems for immediate attention: agricultural overproduction, business failures, and unemployment. Roosevelt considered a farm bill "the key to recovery." The Agricultural Adjustment Act (AAA) was developed by Secretary of Agriculture Henry A. Wallace, Assistant Secretary Rexford Tugwell, and the agricultural economist M. L. Wilson in close collaboration with the leaders of major farmers' organizations. The AAA established a domestic allotment system for seven commodities (wheat, cotton, corn, hogs, rice, tobacco, and dairy products), with cash subsidies to farmers who cut production—a pattern of federal subsidies that continues to the present. Those benefits were financed by a tax on processing (such as the milling of wheat), which was passed on to consumers. New Deal planners hoped prices would rise in response to the federally subsidized scarcity, halting the steep deflation and thus spurring a more general recovery.

The AAA stabilized the agricultural situation, but its benefits were distributed unevenly. Subsidies for reducing production went primarily to the owners of large and medium-size farms, who often cut production by reducing their renters' and sharecroppers' acreage rather than their own. In the South, where many sharecroppers were black and the landowners and government administrators were white, that strategy had racial overtones, displacing as many as 200,000 black tenant farmers from their land. New Deal agricultural policies thus fostered the migration of small farmers in the South and Midwest to northern cities and California, and consolidated the economic and political clout of larger landholders.

The National Recovery Administration. The New Deal attacked the problem of economic recovery with the National Industrial Recovery Act (NIRA), which created the National Recovery Administration (NRA). The NRA, which drew on the World War I experience of Bernard Baruch's War Industries Board, set up a system of industrial self-government to handle the problems of overproduction, cutthroat competition, and price instability. For each industry a code of prices and production quotas, similar to those for farm products, was established. In effect, those legally enforceable agreements suspended the antitrust laws. The codes also established minimum wages and maximum hours and outlawed child labor. One of the most far-reaching

provisions, Section 7(a), guaranteed workers the right to organize and bargain collectively "through representatives of their own choosing." These union rights dramatically spurred the growth of the labor movement in the 1930s.

General Hugh Johnson, a colorful though erratic administrator, headed the NRA. He supervised negotiations for more than 600 NRA codes, ranging from large industries such as coal, cotton, and steel to dog food, costume jewelry, and even burlesque theaters. The negotiating process theoretically took into account equal input from management, labor, and consumers; but trade associations, controlled by large companies, tended to dominate the code-drafting process, thereby solidifying the power of large businesses at the expense of smaller enterprises. Labor had little input, and consumer interests had almost none. To sell the program to skeptical consumers and businesspeople, the NRA launched an extensive public relations campaign, complete with plugs in Hollywood films and stickers with the NRA slogan, "We Do Our Part."

Unemployment Legislation. The early New Deal also addressed the critical problem of unemployment. In the fourth year of the depression, the total exhaustion of private and local sources of charity made it essential to provide some form of federal relief. Roosevelt was basically a fiscal conservative, fearful of large federal deficits, and he moved reluctantly toward federal responsibility for the unemployed. The Federal Emergency Relief Administration (FERA), set up in May 1933 under the direction of Harry Hopkins, a New York social worker, offered federal money to the states for relief programs. FERA was designed to keep people from starving until other recovery measures took hold. In his first two hours in office, Hopkins distributed $5 million. When told that some of the projects he had authorized might not be sound in the long run, Hopkins replied, "People don't eat in the long run—they eat every day." During its two-year existence FERA spent $1 billion.

Roosevelt always maintained a strong distaste for the dole. Wherever possible, New Deal administrators promoted work relief over cash subsidies; they also consistently favored relief jobs that did not compete directly with the private sector. When the Public Works Administration (PWA), under Secretary of the Interior Harold L. Ickes, received a $3.3 billion appropriation in 1933, Ickes's cautiousness in initiating projects limited the agency's effectiveness. In November 1933 Roosevelt assigned $400 million in PWA funds to a new agency, the Civil Works Administration (CWA), headed by Harry Hopkins. Within thirty days the CWA put 2.6 million men and women to work; at its peak in January 1934 it employed 4 million. CWA workers received $15 a week for jobs such as repairing bridges, building highways, constructing public buildings, and setting up community projects. The CWA, regarded as a stopgap measure to get the country through the winter of 1933–1934, lapsed the following spring after exhausting all its funds.

Many of these early emergency measures were deliberately inflationary; that is, they were designed to trigger price rises that were thought necessary to halt the steep deflation and thus stimulate recovery. Another element of this strategy was Roosevelt's executive order on April 18, 1933, to abandon the gold standard and let gold rise in value like any other commodity. As the price of gold rose, administrators hoped, so too would the price of manufactured and agricultural goods. Although abandoning the gold standard did not have much of an impact on the domestic economy, it did allow the Federal Reserve System to manipulate the value of the dollar in response to economic conditions, an important shift in economic power from the private to the public sector.

When an exhausted Congress recessed in June 1933, much had been accomplished. Rarely had a president so dominated a legislative session. A mass of "alphabet agencies," as the New Deal programs came to be known, flowed from Washington, and for the first time since 1929 Americans saw a ray of hope. In April 1933, at the height of the excitement over the Hundred Days, Walt Disney released a cartoon film called *The Three Little Pigs*. Echoing FDR's assertion that they had nothing to fear but fear itself, many people hummed the film's theme song, "Who's Afraid of the Big Bad Wolf?" as they started down the road toward renewed confidence.

If the measures taken during the Hundred Days had cured the Great Depression, the rest of the New Deal probably would not have occurred. But despite a slight upturn in the economy, the depression stubbornly persisted. FDR and the Seventy-third Congress now turned to more far-reaching structural changes to replace the emergency recovery measures of 1933. The reform of business practices, they argued, would be crucial to preventing future depressions.

One obvious target was Wall Street, where insider trading, fraud, and other abuses had contributed to the 1929 crash. In 1934 Congress established the Securities and Exchange Commission (SEC) to regulate the stock market. The commission had the power to regulate the purchase of stocks on credit, or margin buying, and to restrict speculation by those with inside information on corporate plans. The banking system also came under scrutiny. The Banking Act of 1935 enhanced the federal government's role in controlling the economy and business. The act authorized the president to appoint a new Board of Governors of the Federal Reserve System, placing control of interest rates and other money market policies at the federal level rather than with regional banks. By requiring all large state banks to join the Federal Reserve System by 1942 in order to take advantage of the federal deposit insurance system, the law further encouraged centralization of the nation's banking system.

"Gulliver's Travels"
So many new agencies flooded out of Washington in the 1930s that one almost needed a scorecard to keep them straight. Here a July 1935 *Vanity Fair* cartoon by William Gropper substitutes Uncle Sam for Captain Lemuel Gulliver, tied to the ground by Lilliputians, in a parody of Jonathan Swift's *Gulliver's Travels*.
Courtesy Vanity Fair. © 1935 (renewed 1963) by The Conde Nast Publications, Inc.

The New Deal under Attack

As Congress and the president consolidated the early New Deal, their work came under attack from several quarters. Although Roosevelt billed himself as the savior of capitalism, noting that "to preserve we had to reform," his actions provoked strong hostility from many Americans. To the wealthy, Roosevelt became simply "That Man," a traitor to his class. Business leaders and conservative Democrats formed the Liberty League in 1934 to lobby against the New Deal and its "reckless spending" and "socialist" reforms.

The conservative majority on the Supreme Court also disagreed with the direction of the New Deal. On "Black Monday," May 27, 1935, the Supreme Court struck down the NRA, Roosevelt's business recovery plan. In the case of *Schecter v. United States*, the Court unanimously ruled that the National Industrial Recovery Act represented an unconstitutional delegation of legislative power to the executive branch. The so-called sick-chicken case concerned a Brooklyn, New York, firm convicted of violating NRA codes by selling diseased poultry. In its decision the Court ruled that the NRA regulated commerce *within* states, whereas the Constitution limited federal regulation to *interstate* commerce. Roosevelt protested that the Court's narrow interpretation would return the Constitution "to the horse-and-buggy definition of interstate commerce" and worried privately that the Court might invalidate the entire New Deal.

Other citizens thought the New Deal had not gone far enough. Francis Townsend, a physician from Long Beach, California, spoke for the nation's elderly. Many Americans feared poverty in old age because few had pension plans and many had lost their life savings in bank failures. In 1933 Townsend proposed an Old Age Revolving Pension Plan that would give $200 a month (a considerable sum at the time) to citizens over the age of sixty. To receive payments, people would have to retire from their jobs, thereby opening their positions to others, and agree to spend the money within a month, thereby pumping cash into the economy. The plan was never enacted, but Townsend Clubs soon sprang up across the country, particularly in the West.

Father Charles Coughlin also challenged Roosevelt's leadership and attracted a large following, especially in the Midwest. Coughlin, a parish priest in the Detroit suburb of Royal Oak, had turned to the radio in the mid-1920s to increase membership in his pastorate. In 1933 about 40 million Americans listened regularly to the "Radio Priest." At first Coughlin supported the New Deal, but he soon broke with Roosevelt over the president's refusal to support nationalization of the banking system and expansion of the money supply. In 1935 Coughlin organized the National Union for Social Justice to promote his views as an alternative to

The Kingfish
Huey Long, the Louisiana governor and senator, was one of the most controversial figures in American political history. He took his nickname "Kingfish" from a character in the popular radio show "Amos 'n' Andy." Long inspired one of the most powerful political novels of all time, Robert Penn Warren's *All the King's Men*, which won a Pulitzer Prize in 1946.
Corbis-Bettmann.

"Franklin Double-Crossing Roosevelt." Because he was Canadian-born and a Catholic priest, Coughlin could not run for president, but his rapidly growing constituency threatened to become a factor in the 1936 election.

The most direct threat to Roosevelt came from Democratic senator Huey Long. In a single term as governor of Louisiana, the flamboyant Long had achieved stunning popularity. He had increased the share of taxes paid by corporations and embarked on an ambitious program of public works, which included the construction of new highways, bridges, hospitals, and schools. But Long's accomplishments came at a price: to push through his reforms he seized almost dictatorial control of the state government, and he maintained that control even after his election to the U.S. Senate in 1930. Although he supported Roosevelt in 1932, Long made no secret of his own presidential ambitions.

In 1934 Senator Long broke with the New Deal, arguing that its programs did not go far enough. Like Coughlin, he established his own national movement, the Share Our Wealth Society, which had over 4 million followers in 1935. Arguing that the unequal distribution of wealth in the United States was the fundamental cause of the depression, Long advocated taxing 100 percent of all incomes over $1 million, and all inheritances over $5 million, and distributing the money to the rest of the population. Every family would be guaranteed about $2,000 annually, he promised, even though he secretly knew his plan was unworkable. "When they figure that out," he confided privately, "I'll have something new for them." Long's rapid rise in popularity suggested the potential depth of public dissatisfaction with the Roosevelt administration. The president's strategists feared that Long might join forces with Coughlin and Townsend to form a third party, enabling the Republicans to win the 1936 election.

The Second New Deal, 1935–1938

──────── ★ ────────

By 1935 Roosevelt had abandoned his hope of building a classless coalition of rich and poor, workers and farmers, and rural and urban dwellers. Pushed from the left to do more, and bitterly criticized by the right for what he had already done, the president had no choice but to abandon the middle ground. For both political and ideological reasons, and with an eye fixed firmly on the 1936 election, Roosevelt moved dramatically to the left. Historians use the term *Second New Deal* to describe the outpouring of legislation that followed.

Legislative Accomplishments

The first beneficiary of Roosevelt's change of direction was the labor movement. The rising number of strikes in 1934, about 1,800 involving a total of 1.5 million workers, reflected the dramatic growth of rank-and-file militancy. After the Supreme Court declared the NIRA unconstitutional in 1935, invalidating Section 7(a), labor representatives demanded legislation that would protect the right to organize and bargain collectively.

The Wagner Act. Democratic senator Robert F. Wagner of New York, one of labor's staunchest supporters in Congress, had introduced similar legislation even before the Supreme Court decision of 1935. Roosevelt

was at best a lukewarm supporter of the labor movement, but he realized the importance of organized labor to the Democratic Party and his own political future. Only when Congress was on the verge of passing Wagner's bill did Roosevelt reluctantly support the legislation, signing the National Labor Relations Act, also known as the Wagner Act, on July 5, 1935.

The Wagner Act placed the weight of the federal government on labor's side in the struggle to organize. Most important, it upheld the right of industrial workers to join a union (farm workers were not covered) and outlawed many unfair labor practices used by employers to squelch unions, such as firing or blacklisting workers because of their union activities. The act also established the nonpartisan National Labor Relations

General Strike, San Francisco, 1934
A general strike in San Francisco began with the longshoremen and soon spread to almost every union member (and some middle-class supporters as well) in the city. This striker has been shot in the head during an altercation with police. On July 19, union leaders voted to accept government arbitration, and the strike ended.
Corbis-Bettmann.

Board (NLRB) to protect workers from employer coercion, supervise representation elections, and enforce the guarantee of collective bargaining. If a union won a majority of the votes in a secret election, usually conducted by the NLRB, it was entitled to recognition as the sole bargaining agent for all the employees in a factory or other appropriate bargaining unit. The NLRB had the authority to force employers to comply.

Social Security. The Social Security Act signed by Roosevelt on August 14, 1935, was the second major piece of legislation in this phase of the New Deal. The law was partly a response to the political mobilization of the nation's elderly through the Townsend and Long movements, but it also reflected the prodding of social reformers such as Grace Abbott, head of the Children's Bureau, and Secretary of Labor Frances Perkins. The Social Security Act provided pensions for most workers in the private sector, although originally agricultural workers and domestics were not covered. The pensions were paid out of a federal-state pension fund to which both employers and employees contributed. The act also established a joint federal-state system of unemployment compensation, funded by an unemployment tax on employers and employees.

The Social Security Act was a milestone in the creation of the modern welfare state. With this law, the United States joined industrialized countries such as Great Britain and Germany in providing old-age pensions and unemployment compensation to its citizens. (The Roosevelt administration chose not to push for national health insurance, even though most other industrialized nations offered such protection.) The law also mandated categorical assistance, such as aid to the blind, deaf, and disabled and to dependent children. Those recipients were the so-called deserving poor, people who could not support themselves through no fault of their own. The categorical assistance programs, which formed a small part of the New Deal, gradually expanded over the years until they became the mainstay of the American welfare system.

The Works Progress Administration. Roosevelt was never enthusiastic about large expenditures for social welfare programs. As he said in January 1935, the government "must and shall quit this business of relief." But in the sixth year of the depression 10 million Americans were still out of work, a pressing political and moral issue for FDR and the Democrats. Under the direction of Harry Hopkins, the Works Progress Administration (WPA) became the main federal relief agency for the rest of the depression. Whereas the FERA had supplied grants to the states for relief programs, the WPA put relief workers on the federal payroll. Between 1935 and 1943 the WPA employed 8.5 million Americans and spent $10.5 billion. The agency constructed

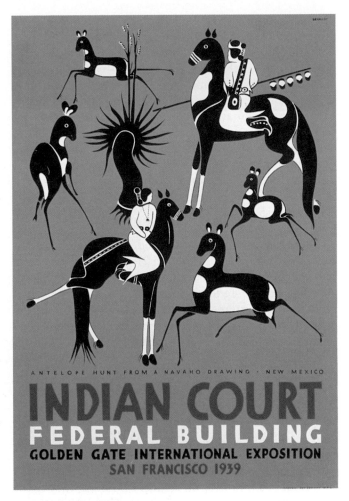

Posters of the WPA
During its eight-year existence the WPA produced 2 million posters from 35,000 designs. WPA posters—such as this one designed to promote the Indian Court at the Golden Gate International Exposition in San Francisco in 1939—spotlight the vitality of American graphic design in the 1930s.
Library of Congress.

651,087 miles of roads, 125,110 public buildings, 8,192 parks, and 853 airports, and built or repaired 124,087 bridges.

The WPA, although an extravagant operation by the standards of the 1930s (it inspired nicknames such as "We Putter Around" and "We Poke Along"), never reached more than one-third of the nation's unemployed. Its average wage of $55 a month, well below the government-defined subsistence level of $100 a month, enabled workers to eke out only a bare living. The government cut back the program severely in 1941 and ended it in 1943, when the WPA was no longer deemed necessary in the full-employment economy that resulted from World War II.

The Revenue Act of 1935 showed Roosevelt's willingness to push for reforms that were considered too controversial earlier in his presidency. Much of the business community had already turned violently against Roosevelt in reaction to the NRA, the Wagner Act, and the Social Security Act. Wealthy conservatives quickly labeled this tax reform bill—which included federal inheritance and gift taxes, higher personal income tax rates in the top brackets, and increased corporate taxes—an attempt to "soak the rich." Roosevelt, seeking to defuse the popularity of Huey Long's Share Our Wealth plan, was just as interested in the political mileage of the tax bill as in its actual results, which increased federal revenues by only $250 million a year.

The 1936 Election

As the 1936 election approached, the broad range of New Deal programs (Table 25.2) brought new voters into the Democratic coalition. Many had been personally helped by federal programs; others benefited because their interests had found new support in the expanded functions of the government. Roosevelt could count on an impressive urban-based coalition of workers, organized labor, northern blacks, white ethnic groups, Catholics, Jews, liberals, intellectuals, progressive Republicans, and middle-class families concerned about old-age dependence and unemployment. The Democrats also held on, though with some difficulty, to their traditional strength among white southerners.

The Republicans realized that they could not compete directly with Roosevelt's popularity and the potent New Deal coalition. To run against Roosevelt, they chose the progressive governor of Kansas, Alfred M. Landon, who accepted the general precepts of the New Deal. But Landon and the Republicans stridently criticized the inefficiency and expense of many New Deal programs and accused FDR of harboring dictatorial ambitions.

Roosevelt's victory in 1936 was one of the biggest landslides in American history. The assassination of Huey Long in September 1935 by a Baton Rouge doctor whose motives were never explained had deflated the threat of a serious third-party challenge; the candidate of the combined Long-Townsend-Coughlin camp, Congressman William Lemke of North Dakota, garnered fewer than 900,000 votes (1.9 percent) for the Union Party ticket. Roosevelt received 60.8 percent of the popular vote and carried every state except Maine and Vermont; Landon received 36.5 percent. Landon fought such an uphill battle that the columnist Dorothy Thompson quipped, "If Landon had given one more speech, Roosevelt would have carried Canada."

Stalemate

"I see one-third of a nation ill-housed, ill-clad, ill-nourished," the president declared in his second inaugural address in January 1937. Roosevelt's appraisal suggested that he was considering further expansion of

TABLE 25.2

Major New Deal Legislation

Agriculture

1933	Agricultural Adjustment Act (AAA)
1935	Resettlement Administration (RA)
	Rural Electrification Administration
1937	Farm Security Administration (FSA)
1938	Agricultural Adjustment Act of 1938

Business and Industry

1933	Emergency Banking Act
	Glass-Steagall Act (FDIC)
	National Industrial Recovery Act (NIRA)
1934	Securities and Exchange Commission (SEC)
1935	Banking Act of 1935
	Revenue Act (wealth tax)

Conservation and the Environment

1933	Tennessee Valley Authority (TVA)
	Civilian Conservation Corps (CCC)
1936	Soil Conservation and Domestic Allotment Act

Labor and Social Welfare

1933	Section 7(a) of NIRA
1935	National Labor Relations Act (Wagner Act)
	National Labor Relations Board (NLRB)
	Social Security Act
1937	National Housing Act
1938	Fair Labor Standards Act (FLSA)

Relief

1933	Federal Emergency Relief Administration (FERA)
	Civil Works Administration (CWA)
	Public Works Administration (PWA)
1935	Works Progress Administration (WPA)
	National Youth Administration (NYA)

the welfare state that had begun to form late in his first term. However, retrenchment, controversy, and stalemate—not further reform—marked the second term.

The Supreme Court Fight.   Only two weeks after his inauguration Roosevelt stunned Congress and the nation by asking for fundamental changes in the structure of the Supreme Court. Shortly after finding the NIRA unconstitutional in *Schecter v. United States* (1935), the Court had struck down the Agricultural Adjustment Act, a coal conservation act, and New York State's minimum wage law. With the Wagner Act, the TVA, and Social Security coming up on appeal, the future of New Deal reform legislation appeared in doubt.

In response, Roosevelt proposed adding one new justice to the Court for each currently sitting justice over the age of seventy. That scheme, which Roosevelt tried to promote as a way to reduce the workload of the elderly justices, would have increased the number of justices from nine to fifteen. Roosevelt's opponents quickly accused him of trying to "pack" the Court with justices favorable to the New Deal. The president's proposal was also regarded as an assault on the principle of separation of powers. The issue became moot when the Supreme Court, in what journalists tagged "a switch in time that saved nine," upheld several key pieces of New Deal legislation, including the Social Security Act, Washington State's minimum wage law, and the Wagner Act. A timely series of resignations allowed Roosevelt to reshape the Supreme Court with seven new appointments over the next four years, including Hugo Black, Felix Frankfurter, Stanley F. Reed, and William O. Douglas. Yet his handling of this issue was a costly blunder at a time when he was vulnerable to the lame-duck syndrome that often afflicts second-term administrations. No one yet suspected that FDR would break with tradition by seeking a third term.

Congressional Opposition. Congressional conservatives had long opposed the direction of the New Deal, but the Court-packing episode galvanized the conservatives by demonstrating that Roosevelt was no longer politically invincible. Throughout Roosevelt's second term a conservative coalition, composed mainly of southern Democrats and Republicans from rural areas, blocked or impeded social legislation. Two pieces of reform legislation that did win passage were the National Housing Act of 1937, which mandated the construction of low-cost public housing, and the Fair Labor Standards Act of 1938, which made permanent the minimum wage, maximum hours, and anti–child labor provisions in the NRA codes.

Roosevelt's attempts to reorganize the executive branch met a different fate. In both 1937 and 1938 Congress refused to consider a plan that would have consolidated all independent agencies into cabinet-rank departments, extended the civil service system, and created the new position of auditor general. Conservatives effectively played on lawmakers' fears that centralized executive management would dramatically reduce congressional power and linked the plan to popular fears of fascism and dictatorship abroad, fears fanned by Hitler's rise to power in Germany. Roosevelt settled for a weak bill in 1939 that allowed him to create the Executive Office of the President and name six administrative assistants to the White House staff. The White House also took control of the all-important budget process by moving the Bureau of the Budget to the Executive Office from its old home in the Treasury department.

The Roosevelt Recession. The "Roosevelt recession" of 1937–1938 dealt the most devastating blow to the president's political standing in the second term. Until that point the economy had made steady progress. From 1933 to 1937 the gross national product grew at a yearly rate of about 10 percent, and industrial output finally regained 1929 levels in 1937, as did real income. Unemployment declined from 25 percent to 14 percent, which meant that almost half the people without a job in 1933 had found one by 1937. Many Americans agreed with Senator James F. Byrnes of South Carolina that "the emergency has passed."

The steady improvement cheered Roosevelt, who had never overcome his dislike of large federal expenditures and the resulting deficits. Accordingly, Roosevelt slashed the federal budget in 1937. Between January and August, Congress cut the WPA's funding in half, causing layoffs of about 1.5 million workers. Moreover, the $2 billion withheld from workers' paychecks to initiate the new Social Security system further reduced purchasing power. The Federal Reserve, fearing inflation, tightened credit, causing a sharp drop in the stock market. Unemployment soared to 19 percent, which translated into more than 10 million workers without jobs. At this point Roosevelt found himself in the same situation that had confounded Hoover. Having taken credit for the recovery between 1933 and 1937, he now had to take the blame for the recession.

Shifting gears, Roosevelt spent his way out of the downturn. Large WPA appropriations and a resumption of public works projects poured enough money into the economy to lift it out of the recession by early 1938. Roosevelt and his economic advisors were groping toward the general theories advanced by John Maynard Keynes, a British economist. Keynes proposed that governments use deficit spending (the spending of public funds obtained by borrowing rather than through taxation) to stimulate the economy when private spending proved insufficient. But Keynes's theory would not be widely accepted until a dramatic increase in federal defense spending for World War II finally ended the Great Depression.

Still struggling with attacks on the New Deal, Roosevelt decided to "purge" some of his most conservative opponents from the Democratic Party as the 1938 election approached. In the spring primaries he campaigned against members of his own party who had been hostile or unsympathetic to New Deal initiatives. The effort failed abysmally and widened the liberal-conservative rift in the Democratic Party. In the general election of 1938, Republicans capitalized on the Roosevelt recession and the Court-packing backlash to pick up 8 seats in the Senate and 81 in the House. The Republicans also gained 13 governorships.

By 1938 the New Deal had basically run out of steam. For six years Roosevelt had inspired confidence that hard times could be overcome, skillfully balancing demands for more government programs with his own assessment of what was politically feasible. However, the president always set clear limits on how far he was willing to go. His instincts were basically conservative, not revolutionary—he wanted only to save the capitalist economic system by reforming it. This new activism was a major step beyond the informal and one-sided business-government partnership of the previous decade, but only because the emergency of the depression pushed Roosevelt in that direction. Under normal circumstances, he would have served out his second term and a new president would have been elected in 1940. Roosevelt won a third term (and eventually a fourth) primarily because the outbreak of World War II in Europe in 1939 made Americans reluctant to risk a change in leadership during such perilous times.

The New Deal's Impact on American Society

——————★——————

The New Deal was "somehow more than the sum of its parts." To understand its impact on society, one must look beyond the federal programs that poured out of Washington and consider broader changes in American political and social life. The New Deal set in motion dramatic growth in the federal bureaucracy and opened unprecedented opportunities for new constituencies to participate in public life. Its programs and priorities had an enormous impact on the public landscape and the arts, and it laid the groundwork for the welfare system that lasted until the 1990s. Its main legacy was an expanded federal presence in the economy and in the lives of ordinary citizens.

New Deal Constituencies and the Broker State

The New Deal accelerated the expansion of the federal bureaucracy that had been under way since the turn of the century. In one decade, the number of civilian government employees increased by 80 percent; the number of federal employees who worked in Washington grew at an even more rapid rate, doubling between 1929 and 1940. Power was increasingly centered in the nation's capital, not in the states. In 1939 a British observer summed up the new orientation: "Just as in 1929 the whole country was 'Wall Street conscious,' now it is 'Washington conscious.'"

The new bureaucrats administered federal budgets of unprecedented size. In 1930 the Hoover administra-

tion had spent $3.1 billion and had run a surplus of almost $1 billion. With the increase in federal programs to fight the depression, federal expenditures grew steadily to $4.8 billion in 1932, $6.5 billion in 1934, and $7.6 billion in 1936. In 1939, the last year before war mobilization affected the federal budget, expenditures reached $9.4 billion. Government spending outstripped receipts throughout this period, producing yearly deficits of about $3 billion. Roosevelt had come close to balancing the budget in 1938 but had triggered a major recession. The deficit climbed toward $3 billion again in the following year.

The beginnings of big government and bureaucracy are often associated with the Roosevelt years, but many of the problems commonly ascribed to the New Deal belong to later eras. The real step toward expanded government spending came during World War II, not during the depression. Federal outlays routinely surpassed $95 billion in the 1940s, and deficits grew to $50 billion. Although the deficit declined in the postwar era, government expenditures never returned to pre–World War II levels.

The growth of the federal government increased the potential impact of its decisions (and spending) on various constituencies. And the New Deal included a broader spectrum of the population in the political process, especially those people who organized themselves into pressure groups. During the 1930s the federal government operated as a *broker state*—that is, as a mediator between contending groups seeking power and influence. Democrats realized the importance of satisfying certain blocs of voters in order to cement their allegiance to the party. Even before the depression, they had begun to build a coalition based on urban political machines and white ethnic voters. In the 1930s, organized labor, women, African Americans, and other groups joined that coalition, receiving more attention from the Democrats and the federal government they controlled.

Organized Labor.   During the 1930s, labor relations became a legitimate arena for federal action and intervention, and organized labor claimed a place in national political life. Labor's dramatic growth in the 1930s was one of the most important social and economic changes of the decade, an enormous contrast to its demoralized state at the end of the 1920s. Several factors encouraged the growth of the labor movement: the inadequacy of welfare capitalism in the face of the depression, New Deal legislation such as the Wagner Act, the rise of the Congress of Industrial Organizations (CIO), and the growing militancy of rank-and-file workers. By the end of the decade the number of unionized workers had tripled to almost 9 million, or 23 percent of the nonfarm work force. Organized labor won the battle not only for union recognition but also for higher wages, seniority systems, and grievance procedures.

The CIO served as the cutting edge of the union movement by promoting industrial unionism, that is, by organizing all the workers in an industry, both skilled and unskilled, into a single union. John L. Lewis, the leader of the United Mine Workers and a founder of the CIO, was the leading exponent of industrial unionism. His philosophy put him at odds with the American Federation of Labor (AFL), which favored organizing workers on a craft-by-craft basis. Lewis began to detach himself from the AFL in 1935, and the break was complete by 1938. Although the CIO generated much of the excitement on the labor front in the 1930s, the AFL gained more than a million new members between 1935 and 1940.

The CIO scored its first major victory in the automobile industry. On December 31, 1936, General Motors workers in Flint, Michigan, staged a sit-down strike, vowing to stay at their machines until management agreed to bargain collectively. The workers lived in the factories and machine shops for forty-four days before General Motors recognized the United Automobile Workers (UAW). The CIO soon won another major victory at the U.S. Steel Corporation. Despite a long history of bitter opposition to unionization (as demonstrated in the 1919 steel strike), "Big Steel" capitulated without a fight and recognized the Steel Workers Organizing Committee (SWOC) on March 2, 1937.

The victory in the steel industry was not complete, however. A group of companies known as "Little Steel" chose not to follow the lead of U.S. Steel in making peace with the CIO, causing steelworkers to strike the Republic Steel Corporation plant in South Chicago. On Memorial Day, May 31, 1937, strikers and their families gathered for a holiday picnic and rally outside the plant's gates. Tension mounted, rocks were thrown, and the police fired on the crowd, killing ten protesters. All were shot in the back. A newsreel photographer recorded the scene, but Paramount Pictures considered the film of the "Memorial Day Massacre" too inflammatory for distribution. Workers in Little Steel did not win union recognition until 1941. The road to recognition for labor, even with New Deal protections, was still long and violent.

The 1930s constituted one of the most active periods of labor solidarity in American history. The sit-down tactic spread rapidly. In March 1937, a total of 167,210 workers staged 170 sit-down strikes. Labor unions called for nearly 5,000 strikes that year and won favorable terms in 80 percent of them. Yet large numbers of middle-class Americans felt alienated by sit-down strikes, which they considered attacks on private property. The Supreme Court agreed and in 1939 upheld a law that banned the practice.

Meanwhile, the CIO attracted new groups to the union movement. Mexican Americans and blacks found the CIO's commitment to racial justice a strong

Organize
The Steel Workers Organizing Committee was one of the most vital labor organizations contributing to the rise of the CIO. Note that the artist Ben Shahn chose a male figure to represent the American labor movement in this poster from the late 1930s. Such iconography reinforced the notion that the typical worker was male, despite the large number of women who joined the CIO.
Library of Congress.

contrast to the AFL's long-established patterns of exclusion and segregation. About 800,000 women workers also found a limited welcome in the CIO. Women participated in major CIO strikes and served as union organizers, especially in textile organizing drives in the South. Few blacks, Mexican Americans, or women held leadership positions, however.

Women found other ways to participate in the labor movement. During the Flint sit-down strike in 1937 the Women's Emergency Brigade, a group of wives, sisters, and girlfriends of striking workers, supplied food and first aid. Wearing distinctive red berets and armbands, they picketed, demonstrated, and occasionally resorted to tactics such as breaking windows to disperse the tear gas used against the strikers (see American Voices, "Genora Johnson Dollinger: Labor Militancy," p. 814). After the strike, however, UAW leaders politely but firmly told the women to go back home where they supposedly belonged.

Genora Johnson Dollinger
Labor Militancy

★

*D*uring the Flint, Michigan, sit-down strike Genora Johnson Dollinger, the wife of a General Motors striker and the mother of two small children, organized the Women's Emergency Brigade. Women like Dollinger played a major role in the Flint victory.

I was twenty-three years old on December 30, 1936, when the strike started. It lasted forty-four days, a very dramatic forty-four days, until February 11, 1937.

It was New Year's Eve when I realized women had to organize and join in the fight. I was on the picket lines when the men's wives came down. They didn't know why their husbands were sitting inside the plant. Living in a company town, you see, they got only company propaganda through the press and radio. So when they came down on New Year's Eve, many were threatening to divorce their striking husbands if they didn't quit and get back to work to bring home a paycheck.

I knew then that union women must organize on their own in order to talk with these wives. . . .

This was an independent move. It was not under the direction of the union or its administrators—I just talked it over with a few women—the active ones—and told them this is what we had to do.

Women might, after all, be called upon to give their lives. That was exactly the appeal I made while we were forming the brigade—I told the women, "Don't sign up for this unless you are prepared. If you are prone to hysteria or anything like that you'd only be in our way." I told them they'd be linking arms and withstanding the onslaughts of the police and if one of our sisters went down shot in cold blood there'd be no time for hysteria.

Around 500 women answered that call. We bought red berets and made arm bands with the white letters "EB" for Emergency Brigade. It was a kind of military uniform, yes, but it was mainly identification. We wore them all the time so we'd know who to call on to give help in an emergency. I had five lieutenants—three were factory women. I chose them because they could be called out of bed at any hour, if necessary, or sleep on a cot at the union hall. Mothers with children couldn't answer calls like that—although they did sign up for the brigade. Even a few grandmothers became brigadiers and, I remember, one young girl only sixteen.

We had no communication system to speak of. Very few people had telephones so we had to call one woman who was responsible for getting the messages through to many others.

We organized a first aid station and child care center—the women who had small children to tend and couldn't join the EB took care of these jobs.

Listen, I met some of the finest women I have every come across in my life. When the occasion demands it of a woman and once she understands that she's standing in defense of her family—well, God, *don't fool around with that woman then.* . . .

It's a measure of the strength of those women of the Red Berets that they could perform so courageously in an atmosphere that was often hostile to them. We organized on our own without the benefit of professional leadership, and yet, we played a role, second to none, in the birth of a union and in changing working families' lives forever.

Source: Genora Johnson Dollinger, quoted in Jeane Westin, *Making Do* (Chicago: Follett Publishing, 1976), 223, 225–226, 229.

Labor's new vitality spilled over into political action. The AFL had always stood aloof from partisan politics, but the CIO quickly allied itself with the Democratic Party, giving $770,000 to Democratic campaigns in 1936 through Labor's Non-Partisan League. Labor also provided one of the few solid lobbies behind Roosevelt's plan to reorganize the Supreme Court. In the 1940s the CIO would become a major contributor to the Democratic war chest.

Yet despite the breakthroughs of the New Deal, the labor movement never developed into the dominant force in American life that had seemed possible in the heyday of the late 1930s. Roosevelt never made the growth of the labor movement a high priority, and many workers remained indifferent or hostile to unionization. Although the Wagner Act guaranteed unions a permanent place in American industrial relations, it did not revolutionize working conditions. The right to collective bargaining granted labor a measure of legitimacy, but it did not redistribute power in American industry. Management even found that unions could be a useful buffer against rank-and-file militancy. New Deal social welfare programs also diffused some of the pre-1937 radical spirit by channeling economic benefits to workers whether they belonged to unions or not. During the 1940s the labor movement entered a period of consolidation and then stagnation that continued for several decades.

Women and the New Deal. In the experimental climate of the New Deal unprecedented numbers of women were offered positions in the Roosevelt administration, both as policy makers and as middle-level bureaucrats. Frances Perkins served as secretary of labor throughout all four terms, the first woman named to a cabinet post. Molly Dewson, a social reformer turned politician, headed the Women's Division of the Democratic National Committee, where she promoted an issue-oriented program that supported New Deal reforms. Roosevelt's appointments of women included the first woman director of the mint, the head of a major WPA division, and a judge on the circuit court of appeals. Many of those women were close friends as well as professional colleagues and cooperated in an informal network to advance feminist and reform causes.

Eleanor Roosevelt exemplified the growing prominence of women in public life. In the 1920s she had worked closely with other reformers to increase women's clout in political parties, labor unions, and education—an invaluable apprenticeship for her White House years. Franklin and Eleanor's marriage represented one of the most successful political partnerships of all time. He was the pragmatic politician, always aware of what could be done; she was the idealist, always pushing him—and the New Deal—to do more. Indeed, Eleanor Roosevelt served as the conscience of the New Deal.

Although Franklin Roosevelt's expansion of the personalized presidency had roots in the administrations of Theodore Roosevelt and Woodrow Wilson, the nation had never seen a first lady like Eleanor Roosevelt. She held press conferences for women journalists, wrote a popular syndicated column called "My Day," and traveled extensively throughout the country. Some people wondered why the first lady did not stay home at the White House like a good wife, but in a Gallup poll in January 1939, 67 percent approved of her conduct, a higher approval rating than the president's at that time. In 1938 *Life* magazine hailed her as the greatest American woman alive.

Despite the vocal support of prominent women such as Eleanor Roosevelt, Molly Dewson, and the rest of the female political network, grave flaws still marred the treatment of women in New Deal programs. For

A First Lady without Precedent
Reflecting Eleanor Roosevelt's tendency to turn up in odd places, a famous 1933 *New Yorker* cartoon has one coal miner saying to another, "For gosh sakes, here comes Mrs. Roosevelt." Life soon imitated art. Here the first lady emerges from a coal mine in Dellaire, Ohio, still carrying her miner's cap in her left hand, while speaking with Joseph Bainbridge on May 22, 1935.
Wide World Photos, Inc.

example, one-fourth of the NRA codes set a lower minimum wage for women than for men performing the same jobs. New Deal agencies such as the Civil Works Administration and the Public Works Administration gave jobs almost exclusively to men, mainly because construction work was considered unsuitable for women. The Social Security and the Fair Labor Standards Acts did not cover major areas of traditional employment for women, such as domestic service. And the CCC excluded women entirely, leaving critics to ask, "Where is the 'she-she-she'?"

Women fared somewhat better under the Works Progress Administration. At the WPA's peak, 405,000 women were on its rolls. The Women's and Professional Projects Division of the WPA, headed by Ellen Sullivan Woodward, a Mississippi social worker, created hundreds of programs to put women to work, although these job assignments—most women were sent to work on sewing projects, which became a sort of dumping group for unemployed women—tended to reinforce gender and racial attitudes. African American and Mexican American women, if they had access to work relief at all, often found themselves shunted into training as domestics. For the most part, progress for women did not come from specific attempts to single them out as a group but occurred as part of a broader effort to improve the economic security of all Americans.

Blacks and the New Deal. Just as the New Deal did not seriously challenge gender inequities, it did little to battle racial discrimination. In the 1930s, the vast majority of the American people did not regard civil rights as a legitimate area for federal intervention. Indeed, many New Deal programs reflected prevailing racist attitudes. CCC camps segregated blacks, and many NRA codes did not protect black workers. Most telling, Franklin Roosevelt repeatedly refused to support legislation making lynching a federal crime, claiming that it would antagonize southern members of Congress whose support he needed to pass New Deal measures.

Nevertheless, blacks did receive enormous benefits from New Deal relief programs directed toward poor Americans, regardless of race or ethnicity. Blacks made up about 18 percent of the WPA's recipients although they constituted only 10 percent of the population. Public works projects channeled funds into black communities. The Resettlement Administration—established in 1935 to aid in the resettlement of sharecroppers and tenant farmers onto more productive land by helping small farmers buy property—fought for the rights of black tenant farmers in the South—that is, until angry southerners in Congress cut its appropriation. Nevertheless, many blacks reasoned that the tangible aid coming from Washington outweighed the discrimination that marred many federal programs.

African Americans were also pleased to see blacks appointed to federal office. Mary McLeod Bethune, an educator who ran the Office of Minority Affairs of the National Youth Administration, headed the "Black Cabinet" (see American Lives, "Mary McLeod Bethune: Black Braintruster," pp. 818–819). This informal network worked for fairer treatment of blacks by New Deal agencies in the same way that the women's network advocated feminist causes. Both groups benefited greatly from the support of Eleanor Roosevelt. The first lady's promotion of equal treatment for blacks ranks as one of her greatest legacies.

Help from the WPA and other New Deal programs and a belief that the White House—at least Eleanor Roosevelt—cared about their plight caused a dramatic change in blacks' voting behavior. Since the Civil War blacks had voted Republican, a loyalty resulting from Abraham Lincoln's freeing of the slaves and radical Reconstruction, as well as the Democratic Party's off-and-on associations with the Ku Klux Klan. As late as 1932 black voters in northern cities overwhelmingly supported Republican candidates. Then, in less than four years, blacks turned Lincoln's portrait to the wall and substituted that of Franklin Roosevelt. Because of the harshness of the depression, national politics assumed a new relevance for black Americans outside the South, who gave Roosevelt 71 percent of their votes in 1936. In Harlem, where relief dollars increased dramatically in the wake of the 1935 riot (see Chapter 24), the support was an extraordinary 81.3 percent. Black voters have remained overwhelmingly Democratic ever since.

Mexican Americans and the New Deal. The election of Franklin Roosevelt had an immediate effect on Mexican American communities demoralized by the depression and the deportations of the Hoover years. In cities such as Los Angeles and El Paso, Mexican Americans found it easier to qualify for relief under New Deal guidelines, and there was more relief to go around. Even though New Deal guidelines prohibited discrimination on the basis of an immigrant's legal status, the new climate encouraged a marked rise in requests for naturalization papers, the first step toward citizenship. Inspired by New Deal rhetoric about economic recovery and social progress through cooperation, Mexican Americans increasingly identified their future with the United States, not Mexico. This shift was especially evident among members of Bert Corona's "Mexican American generation"—the American-born children of Mexican immigrants who filled the leadership vacuum created by the deportations in the early 1930s (see Chapter 24). Mexican Americans supported and benefited from the New Deal's labor policies, such as Section 7(a) of the NIRA and the Wagner Act, which fostered an upsurge in labor organizing. For many Mexican Americans, joining the CIO was an important step in becoming an American.

Many Mexican Americans felt a personal connection to President Roosevelt, and participating in the political system increasingly became a part of Mexican American life. Los Angeles activist Beatrice Griffith noted, "Franklin D. Roosevelt's name was the spark that started thousands of Spanish-speaking persons to the polls." In 1939 El Congreso Nacional del Pueblo de Habla Español, the first national civil rights conference for Spanish-speaking peoples, called on its members to become American citizens and vote. The New Deal made it clear that it welcomed the votes of Mexican Americans and considered them to be an important part of the New Deal coalition. This politicalization was well under way before World War II, and it provided additional spurs to political activism.

Native Americans and the New Deal. But what about groups that were not politically mobilized or that were not recognized as key components of the New

Deal coalition? The New Deal's impact on those groups and communities often depended on whether sympathetic government administrators in Washington undertook to promote their interests. Native Americans were one of the nation's most disadvantaged and powerless minorities. The annual individual income of a native American in 1934 was only $48, and the unemployment rate of native Americans was three times the national average. Concerned New Deal administrators such as Secretary of the Interior Harold Ickes and Commissioner of the Bureau of Indian Affairs John Collier tried to correct some of those inequities. The Indian Section of the Civilian Conservation Corps brought needed money and projects to reservations throughout the West. Indians also received benefits from FERA and CWA work relief projects.

Of far greater significance was the Indian Reorganization Act of 1934, sometimes called the Indian New Deal. That law reversed the Dawes Severalty Act of 1887 (see Chapter 16) by promoting more extensive self-government through tribal councils and constitutions. The government also abandoned the attempt to force native Americans to assimilate into mainstream society in favor of promoting cultural pluralism. The New Deal pledged to help preserve Indian languages, arts, and traditions. The problems of native Americans were so severe, however, that these changes in federal policy did little to improve their lives or reinvigorate tribal communities.

The New Deal and the Land

Concern with the land was one of the dominant motifs of the New Deal, and the shaping of the public landscape is among its most visible legacies. Roosevelt brought to the presidency a love of forestry and a conservation ethic nurtured from childhood on his Hudson River estate. The expansion of federal responsibilities in the 1930s, especially the need to put the unemployed to work on public projects, created a climate conducive to action, as did public concern heightened by dramatic images of the drought and devastation of the Dust Bowl. The resulting national resources policy stressed scientific management of the land, conservation instead of commercial development, and the aggressive use of public authority to safeguard both private and public holdings.

The most extensive New Deal environmental undertaking was the Tennessee Valley Authority (TVA). The need for dams to control flooding and erosion in the Tennessee River Basin, a seven-state area with some of the country's heaviest rainfall, had been recognized since World War I. During the 1920s progressives led by Senator George Norris of Nebraska pushed for a public corporation to control flooding and to create a cheap source of electric power on the Tennessee River, but utility companies blocked the project. In 1933 the Tennessee Valley

A New Deal for Indians
John Collier, the New Deal's Commissioner for Indian Affairs, was a former social worker who had become interested in native American tribal cultures in the 1920s. Here Collier speaks with Chief Richard of the Blackfoot Nation, one of the Indian chiefs attending the Four Nation celebration at historic Old Fort Niagara, New York, in 1934.
Corbis-Bettmann.

Authority won approval to develop the region's resources under public control (Map 25.1). The TVA integrated flood control, reforestation, and agricultural and industrial development, including the production of chemical fertilizers. A hydroelectric grid provided inexpensive electric power for the valley's residents. Admired worldwide, the Tennessee Valley became one of the most popular destinations for visitors to the United States (see Voices from Abroad, "Odette Keun: A Foreigner Looks at the Tennessee Valley Authority," p. 821).

The Dust Bowl helped to focus attention on land management and ecological balance as well. Agents from the Soil Conservation Service in the Department of Agriculture taught farmers the proper technique for tilling hillsides. Government agronomists (experts in the science of agriculture) also tried to remove marginally productive land from cultivation and prevent soil erosion through better agricultural practices. One of their most widely publicized programs was the creation of the Shelterbelts, which involved planting a line of 220 million trees running northward roughly along the 99th meridian from Abilene, Texas, to the Canadian border. Planted as a windbreak, the trees also prevented soil erosion. The Shelterbelt program was a personal favorite of Franklin Roosevelt.

Sometimes political reality dictated specific legislation affecting the environment, such as the Soil Conservation and Domestic Allotment Act of 1936, which

Mary McLeod Bethune: Black Braintruster

★

THE NEW DEAL brought many remarkable people to Washington, but few had traveled as far as Mary McLeod Bethune. As the Reverend Adam Clayton Powell Sr. wrote to her in 1935 when she received the prestigious Spingarn Medal from the National Association for the Advancement of Colored People, "It is a long way from the rice and cotton fields of South Carolina to this distinguished recognition, but you have made it in such a short span of years that I am afraid you are going to be arrested for breaking the speed limit." In terms of her contributions to black history, Mary McLeod Bethune deserves to be remembered alongside such luminaries as Frederick Douglass, W. E. B. Du Bois, and Martin Luther King Jr.

Born on July 10, 1875, near Mayesville, South Carolina, Mary was the fifteenth of seventeen children born to Sam and Patsy McLeod, former slaves liberated after the Civil War. She was educated at the Scotia Seminary in Concord, North Carolina, and the Bible Institute for Home and Foreign Missions in Chicago (later the Moody Bible Institute) in preparation for her chosen career as a missionary. Turning from her original plan to go to Africa, she redirected her missionary zeal to the United States and the field of education and racial uplift. In 1898 she married Albertus Bethune, and their only child, Albert McLeod Bethune, was born in 1899. The family moved to Florida, but the marriage foundered and the couple separated in 1907. She never remarried, and Albertus Bethune died in 1918.

In 1904, "with $1.50 and a prayer," Mary McLeod Bethune opened the school in Daytona Beach, Florida, that eventually became the prestigious Bethune-Cookman College, the only historically black college founded by a black woman that continues to thrive today. The initial student body consisted of five girls and her son; by 1923 the school had more than 300 students and a faculty and staff of twenty-five. Bethune was intimately involved with this institution—and by extension with the issue of providing

Mary McLeod Bethune
This 1943 painting by Betsy Graves Reyneau captures the strength and dignity of one of the twentieth century's most important African Americans. Behind Bethune is a picture of the first building at the Daytona Literary and Industrial School for Training of Negro Girls, which later became Bethune-Cookman College.
National Portrait Gallery, Smithsonian Institution/Art Resource, NY.

expanded educational opportunities for African Americans—for the rest of her life. Through her extensive civic involvement in Daytona Beach and the constant fundraising needed to keep her school afloat, she was quickly drawn into wider national networks, especially through the National Association of Colored Women (NACW)—the leading black women's organization in the first quarter of the twentieth century. Bethune served as president of that organization from 1924 to 1928. In 1935 she organized the National Council of Negro Women (NCNW), a coalition of the major national black women's associations, serving as its president until 1949.

Mary McLeod Bethune was a forceful personality and a born leader. The New Deal offered her a national platform through which to promote her agendas on race, education, women, and youth when she was named—at Eleanor Roosevelt's suggestion—to the advisory committee of the National Youth Administration in 1935. In the next year she was named director of the division of Negro Affairs in the NYA, where she served until 1944. One of her greatest contributions was the leadership she provided to the other black administrators who found opportunities in the New Deal. The Federal Council of Negro Affairs, known informally as the Black Cabinet, met on Sunday nights at her home in Washington. As the Washington correspondent for the Associated Negro Press noted, "Mrs. Bethune has gathered everything and everybody under her very ample wing since her arrival last June." Along with NAACP general secretary Walter White, she was the only ranking black administrator who had access to the White House.

Bethune recognized the limits of the New Deal's commitment to civil rights, but she remained a loyal supporter of Franklin Roosevelt, with whom she enjoyed an easy friendship. But it was Eleanor Roosevelt who became her staunchest political ally. When funding for a black housing project in Daytona Beach was stalled by bureaucratic red tape, local activists contacted Bethune, who in turn reached Eleanor Roosevelt, who with one call to the head of the Federal Housing Authority had the project back on track. On several occasions the first lady opened the White House to Bethune for conferences, thereby ensuring that they would receive national attention. Along the way the two women became personal friends as well as allies, although Roosevelt admitted that it took her a while to feel comfortable giving Bethune the customary peck on the cheek she bestowed when greeting white friends. Not until she kissed Mrs. Bethune without thinking about it, she told her daughter, did she feel that she had overcome the racial prejudice that was so much a part of Roosevelt's—and many white Americans'—background.

Bethune's basic strategy was to win policy-making positions for African Americans and then use those bases to work for more equitable treatment for blacks throughout the New Deal. Sometimes her small gestures were just as telling as her larger public stances. She always insisted on being called "Mrs. Bethune" as a term of respect, refusing to go down in history as "Mary from Florida." When a White House guard addressed her as "Auntie," a term whites often used indiscriminately for older black women, she looked at him sweetly and asked, "Which one of my brother's children are you?" Her entire adult life was devoted to improving conditions and access for her race. "The drums of Africa beat in my heart," she often said. "I cannot rest while there is a single Negro boy or girl lacking a chance to prove his worth."

There must have been many times when Bethune, a deeply religious woman, had to suppress personal feelings of disappointment or outright anger at the pace of change, but she always favored conciliation and compromise over confrontation. "I am diplomatic about certain things. I let people infer a great many things, but I am careful about what I say because I want to do certain things." But she also knew when to apply pressure, twist arms, appeal to publicity, and move a group toward concensus. As she once said forthrightly, "The White man has been thinking for us too long. We want him to think with us instead of for us."

When the National Youth Administration ceased operation in 1944, Bethune left government service but continued to be active in educational and charitable work. In 1952 she fulfilled a lifelong dream when she visited Liberia as an official U.S. representative at the inauguration of William Tubman as that country's president. She died of a heart attack in 1955 and was buried on the Bethune-Cookman campus. In 1974, on the ninety-ninth anniversary of her birth, the National Council of Negro Women dedicated the Mary McLeod Bethune Memorial Statue at Lincoln Park in Washington, D.C., just a short distance from the Capitol.

"Most people think I am a dreamer," Mary McLeod Bethune once said. "Through dreams many things come true." A dream come true was the 1938 gathering organized in conjunction with the National Council of Negro Women that brought sixty-seven black women leaders to the White House. Bethune recalled its significance soon thereafter:

> It certainly was history-making. . . . The pressure we have been making, the intercessions . . . they are finding their way. . . . The position I hold now—I give you that as an example. The first time in history that a Negro woman filled a national, federal position with the leeway, the opportunity . . . the contacts. Because one got in there, sixty-seven got in one day and many others are getting in here and there and there and there.

"A door has been sealed up for two hundred years," she concluded. "You can't open it overnight but little crevices are coming." Mary McLeod Bethune cracked open that door, and generations of African American activists, male and female, have been opening it wider and wider ever since.

filled the void created when the Supreme Court ruled the Agricultural Adjustment Act unconstitutional in January of that year. Under the new act, farmers received payments for cutting back the commercial production of crops such as wheat and cotton, which depleted the soil, and planting instead soil-building grasses and legumes such as clover and soybeans. Wheat and cotton were in fact major surplus commodities, and the law provided a way to cut production as well as encourage soil conservation. The Agricultural Adjustment Act of 1938 continued the policy of price supports and payments to farmers to limit production and established soil conservation as a permanent program.

Another priority of the Roosevelt administration was helping rural Americans stay on the land. The Rural Electrification Administration, established in 1935, brought power to farms in an attempt to improve the quality and productivity of rural life (see New Technology, "Rural Electrification," pp. 822–823). The New Deal also encouraged urban dwellers to return to rural areas. This "back to the land" motif animated many New Deal projects, especially those planned by the Resettlement

Administration under the direction of Rexford Tugwell. Some of the best-known examples were planned cooperative communities in rural areas, such as Arthurdale in West Virginia, and the "Greenbelt" residential towns outside Washington, Cincinnati, and Milwaukee.

Although the TVA, Shelterbelts, and Greenbelt towns were primarily environmental programs, they also put large numbers of the unemployed to work. The Civilian Conservation Corps—the so-called Tree Army—planted some 2 billion trees by 1941, a dozen for every American citizen at the time. Not only was this sound conservation, but it gave the 2.5 million CCC workers a job to do. Similarly, many WPA projects helped achieve conservation and recreational goals.

Today, New Deal projects affecting the natural environment can be seen throughout the country, artifacts from the depression era. CCC and WPA workers built the Blue Ridge Highway—the consummate parkway of the 1930s—connecting the Shenandoah National Park in Virginia with the Great Smoky Mountain National Park in North Carolina. In the West, government workers built the San Francisco Zoo,

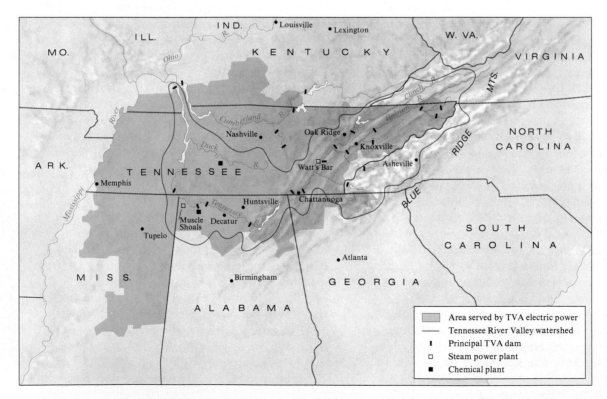

MAP 25.1
The Tennessee Valley Authority, 1933–1952
The Tennessee Valley Authority was one of the New Deal's most far-reaching environmental projects. Between 1933 and 1952 the TVA built twenty dams and improved five others. The cheap hydroelectric power generated by the dams brought electricity to hundreds of thousands of area residents.

ODETTE KEUN

A Foreigner Looks at the Tennessee Valley Authority

———————★———————

French writer Odette Keun visited the United States in 1936 and was so impressed by the TVA that she wrote a book about it. Among other observations, Keun felt that experiments like the TVA might help inhibit the development of an American variety of fascism.

The vital question before democracy is, therefore, not how to bring back an economic freedom which is irretrievably lost, but how to prevent the intellectual freedom, which is still our heritage, from being submerged. It is already threatened. It will be threatened more and more strongly in the years ahead—and the menace, of course, is dictatorship. But to fight dictatorship it is necessary first to understand in what circumstances it arises, and then to think out the counterattack which democracy can launch against its approaching force.

Dictatorship springs from two very clear causes. One is the total incapacity of parliamentary government: total, as in Germany in 1933 and in Spain in 1935. To such a breakdown neither the democratic nations of Europe nor America have yet been reduced, although everywhere there are very ominous creaks and cracks, and the authority and prestige of parliamentary institutions have greatly and perilously diminished. The other cause, infinitely closer to us and more dynamic, is the failure of the economic machine to function properly, and by functioning properly I mean ensuring a livelihood for the entire population. No system can survive if it cannot procure food and wages for the people who live under it. Man has to get subsistence from his rulers, for the most immediate and the most imperious law of our nature is that the belly must be filled. It is perfectly futile to orate on fine, high, and abstract principles to human beings who are permanently hungry, permanently harassed, permanently uncertain, who hear their wives begging for the rent and their children crying out for nourishment. . . .

One of the main tenets of liberalism—I reiterate this like a gramophone, but I must get it to sink in—is that all necessary overhauling and adjustment ought to be done in a manner which will minimize the shock to the greatest number, and soften as much as possible the unavoidable human suffering which these changes entail. This opposition to extremes, this practice of a graduated change, we can call "the middle of the road in time and space." But it is not nearly enough to conceive it and to bestow upon it a name. We must reach it. It is unutterably foolish to look at the middle of the road, to talk of the middle of the road, to hope for the middle of the road—and never get there.

Now I have tried to show that the middle of the road is already being laid down in America. The Tennessee Valley Authority is laying it down. Handicapped and restricted though it is in all sorts of ways, it is the noblest, the most intelligent, and the best attempt made in this country or in any other democratic country to economize, marshal, and integrate the actual assets of a region, plan its development and future, ameliorate its standards of living, establish it in a more enduring security, and render available to the people the benefits of the wealth of their district, and the results of science, discovery, invention, and disinterested forethought. In its inspiration and its goal there is goodness, for goodness is that which makes for unity of purpose with love, compassion, and respect for every life and every pattern of living. The economic machine, bad though it is, has not been smashed in the Tennessee Watershed; it is being very gradually, very carefully, very equitably reviewed and amended, and the citizens are being taught and directed, but not bullied, not coerced, not regimented, not frightened, within the constitutional frame the nation itself elected to build. It is not while the Tennessee Valley Authority has the valley in its keeping that despair or disintegration can prepare the ground for a dictatorship and the loss of freedom. The immortal contribution of the TVA to liberalism, not only in America but all over the world, is the blueprint it has drawn, and that it is now transforming into a living reality, of the road which liberals believe is the only road mankind should travel.

———————

Source: Odette Keun, *A Foreigner Looks at the TVA* (1937), in Oscar Handlin, ed., *This Was America* (Cambridge, MA: Harvard University Press, 1949), 547–549.

Rural Electrification

★

IN 1935 FEWER than one-tenth of the nation's 6.8 million farms had electricity. For millions of farm families that stark fact meant a life of unremitting toil made even harsher by the lack of simple conveniences. Farm families used an average of 200 gallons of water a day. Any chore requiring water—and most did—meant pumping the water from a distant well and carrying it to the house or barn in a pair of buckets that weighed as much as 30 pounds each. Water had to be heated on a wood-stove that required constant tending. Meeting a family's yearly water needs took 63 eight-hour days and involved carrying water a distance of 1,750 miles.

Rural women suffered especially from the lack of electricity. Canning, a necessity before refrigeration, kept women standing over steaming vats of fruit or vegetables, often in the worst summer heat, before the freshly harvested produce spoiled. Wash day, traditionally Monday, called for three large zinc washtubs for washing, rinsing, and bleaching. A week's wash consisted of four to eight loads, each requiring three washtubs of clean water hauled from the well. Few rural households could afford commercial soap,

"Blue Monday"
Laundry was one of women's hardest household chores. Although this woman did not have to haul water from an outdoor well, she still had to pump it by hand in order to do the wash because her home lacked electricity. She also had to wring out the wet clothes manually, another arduous task.
Corbis-Bettmann.

Berkeley's Tilden Park, and the canals of San Antonio. The CCC helped complete the East Coast's Appalachian Trail and the West Coast's Pacific Crest Trail through the Sierras. In state parks across the country, cabins, shelters, picnic areas, lodges, and observation towers were built in a style that has been called "government rustic." All those projects shared the New Deal ethos of leisure and recreation coexisting with conservation.

Although the New Deal was ahead of its time in its attention to conservation, its legacy to later environmental movements is mixed. Many of the tactics used in New Deal projects—damming rivers, blasting fire roads, altering the natural landscape with buildings and shelters—are now considered too intrusive. In the 1970s the TVA came under attack for its longstanding practice of strip mining (removing topsoil to get at outcrops of coal near the surface rather than mining in shafts underground) and the pollution caused by its

power plants and chemical factories. Because of environmental concerns, a project as massive as the TVA probably could never be undertaken today—an ironic conclusion to what was hailed at the time as an enlightened use of government power for the public good.

The New Deal and the Arts

In the arts, the depression had dried up traditional sources of private patronage, and like most Americans, creative artists had nowhere to turn except to Washington. The WPA project known as "Federal One" put unemployed artists, actors, and writers to work, but its spirit and purpose extended far beyond relief. New Deal administrators wanted to redefine the relationship between artists and the community so that art would no longer be the province of the elite. "Art for the millions" became a popular New Deal slogan.

so women used lye, which barely removed ground-in dirt from soiled clothes and was very harsh on hands. But if farm women dreaded Monday, they hated Tuesday even more. Tuesday meant ironing, another all-day job. The iron, a 6- or 7-pound wedge of metal, had to be heated on the stove, and because it did not retain heat for more than a few minutes, it took several irons to do a shirt. The women in Texas's hill country called them "sad irons."

A day that began in darkness and was given over to twelve hours of backbreaking toil brought few comforts in the evening. Reading by kerosene lamps strained the eyes. Children's eyes might be strong enough to read in the semidarkness, but few older people could read without squinting. The absence of electricity also meant no radios, which meant no contact with the outside world.

Studies showed that farmers would find many uses for electricity and would make good customers, but power companies balked at the prospect of bringing electricity to the countryside, claiming that it was not economically feasible to run lines to individual farms. In 1935 the federal government made a commitment to bring power to rural America. The Rural Electrification Administration, an independent agency, promoted the formation of nonprofit farm cooperatives to bring electricity to their regions. For a $5 down payment, local farmers could join an association and become eligible for low-interest federal loans covering the cost of installing power lines. Each household was committed to a monthly minimum usage, usually about $3, but as usage increased, the rates came down. By 1940, 40 percent of the nation's farms had electricity; in 1950, the rate reached 90 percent.

Electricity brought relief from the drudgery and isolation of farm life. An electric milking machine saved hours of manual labor, most of it previously done before dawn by the faint glow of a kerosene lamp so farmers could devote the daylight hours to outdoor chores. An electric water pump lightened many chores, especially the hauling of water. Electric irons, vacuum cleaners, and washing machines eased women's burdens.

People's responses to rural electrification were poignant. A small child told his mother, "I didn't realize how dark our house was until we got electric lights." One farm woman remembered, "I just turned on the light and kept looking at Paw. It was the first time I'd ever really seen him after dark." Another family, caught unaware by the timing of the hookup, saw their house from a distance and thought it was on fire. Schoolteachers noticed that children did better at school when they had light to do homework by at night. Along with the automobile, electricity probably did more than any other technological innovation to break down the barriers between urban and rural life in twentieth-century America.

The Federal Art Project (FAP) gave work to many of the twentieth century's leading painters, muralists, and sculptors at a point in their careers when the lack of private patronage might have prevented them from continuing their artistic production. Under the direction of Holger Cahill, an expert on American folk art, the FAP commissioned murals for public buildings and post offices across the country. Jackson Pollack, Alice Neel, Willem de Kooning, and Louise Nevelson all received support from the FAP.

The Federal Music Project employed 15,000 musicians under the direction of Nicholas Sokoloff, the conductor of the Cleveland Symphony Orchestra. Under this project, government-sponsored orchestras toured the country, presenting free concerts of classical and popular music. Like many New Deal programs, the Music Project emphasized American themes. The composer Aaron Copland wrote his ballets *Billy the Kid* (1938) and *Rodeo* (1942) for the WPA, basing them on western folk motifs. The federal government also employed the musicologist Charles Seeger and his wife, the composer Ruth Crawford Seeger, to catalog hundreds of American folk songs.

The former journalist Henry Alsberg headed the Federal Writers' Project (FWP), which at its height employed about 5,000 writers. Young FWP writers who would later achieve fame included Saul Bellow, Ralph Ellison, Tillie Olsen, Richard Wright, and John Cheever. The FWP produced more than a thousand publications. It collected oral histories of Americans from many walks of life, including a set of 2,000 narratives of former slaves. Its most ambitious project was a set of state guidebooks. Fifty-one state and territorial guides and twenty regional guides, including *U.S. One: Maine to Florida*, were published, mostly by commercial presses. Combining tourism, folklore, and history, the guides

New Deal Murals
The social-realist painter William Gropper (who also created the *"Gulliver's Travels"*
cartoon on p. 806) portrayed the contributions of labor to modern industry in the
heroic, dynamic style that was typical of public art during the depression. This mural,
Construction of a Dam, was commissioned in 1937 for the Department of the Interior
building in Washington, D.C.
National Museum of American Art/Art Resource.

reflected the resurgence of interest in everything American.

Of all the New Deal arts programs, the Federal Theatre Project (FTP) was the most ambitious. American drama thrived in the 1930s, the only time that the United States has had a federally supported national theater. (In contrast, most European countries have state-supported theater and arts companies.) Under the gifted direction of Hallie Flanagan, former head of Vassar College's Experimental Theater, the Theatre Project reached an audience of 25 to 30 million in the four years of its existence. Talented directors, playwrights, and actors, including Orson Welles, John Huston, and Arthur Miller, offered their talents and services. But the leftist leanings of many actors and productions left the FTP vulnerable to conservative attack, and Congress terminated the program in 1939. Federal One limped along under federal-state sponsorship until 1943, when wartime priorities dealt it a final blow.

The WPA arts projects were influenced by a broad artistic trend known as the *documentary impulse.* Combining social relevance with uniquely American themes, this approach—which presented actual facts and events in a way that aroused the interest and emotions of the audience—characterized artistic expression in the 1930s. The documentary, probably the decade's most distinctive genre, influenced practically every aspect of American culture: literature, photography, art, music, film, dance, theater, and radio.

The documentary impulse is evident in John Steinbeck's fiction and John Dos Passos's *USA* trilogy, which used actual newspaper clippings, dispatches, and headlines in its fictional story. The commercially produced *March of Time* newsreels, which movie audiences saw before the feature film, presented the news of the world for the pretelevision age. The filmmaker Pare Lorentz commissioned the composer Virgil Thompson to create music that set the mood for documentary movies such as *The Plow That Broke the Plains* (1936), about Midwestern farming, and *The River* (1936), a lyrical tribute to the Mississippi. The new photojournalism magazines, including *Life* and *Look* (founded in 1936 and 1937, respectively), also reflected this documentary approach. The New Deal institutionalized the trend by sending investigators such as journalists Lorena Hickok and Martha Gellhorn into the field to report on the conditions of people on relief.

Finally, the federal government played a leading role in compiling the photographic record of the 1930s. The Historical Section of the Resettlement Administration had a mandate to document and photograph the American scene for the government. Through their haunting images of sharecroppers, Dust Bowl migrants, and the urban homeless, photographers like Dorothea Lange, Walker Evans, Ben Shahn, and Margaret Bourke-White permanently shaped the popular image of the Great Depression. The government hired photographers solely for their professional skills—not to provide relief, as in Federal One's projects. Their photographs, collected by the Historical Section and, after 1937, the Farm Security Administration (FSA), rank as the best visual representation of life in the United States during the depression decade.

The Legacies of the New Deal

The New Deal set in motion far-reaching changes, notably the growth of a modern state of significant size.

For the first time people experienced the federal government as a concrete part of everyday life. During the 1930s more than one-third of the population received direct government assistance from new federal programs such as Social Security, farm loans, relief, and mortgage guarantees. Furthermore, the government had made a commitment to intervene in the economy when the private sector could not guarantee economic stability. New legislation regulated the stock market, reformed the Federal Reserve System by placing more power in the hands of Washington policy makers, and brought many practices of modern corporate life under federal regulation. The New Deal thus continued and accelerated the pattern begun during the Progressive Era of using federal regulation to bring order and regularity to economic life.

The New Deal also laid the foundations of America's welfare state—that is, the federal government's accep-

tance of primary responsibility for the individual and collective welfare of the people. Although the New Deal offered more benefits to American citizens than they had ever received before, its safety net had many holes, especially in comparison with the far more extensive welfare systems in Western Europe. Another serious defect of the emerging welfare system was its failure to reach a significant minority of American workers. For example, the Social Security program excluded domestic workers and farm workers for many years. And since state governments administered the programs, benefits varied widely, with southern states consistently providing the lowest amounts. Not until the Great Society programs of President Lyndon Johnson in the 1960s would social welfare programs reach significant numbers of America's poor.

To its credit, the New Deal recognized that poverty was a structural economic problem, not a matter of

Relief Blues
Between 1934 and 1939 O. Louis Guglielmi, an Italian immigrant, found work on the Federal Art Project of the WPA, to which he submitted this painting in 1938. Entitled *Relief Blues*, it represents the social concern and urban realism prominent in American painting during the 1930s. The starkness of the room and its occupants is intensified by the bright red slippers, the pink rose on the floor, and the red lipstick and nail polish of the woman on the left.
National Museum of American Art/Art Resource.

Life
Margaret Bourke-White's photograph of the Fort Peck Dam, with the two human figures in the foreground establishing its scale, graced the inaugural cover of *Life* magazine in 1936. Fort Peck was part of a series of dams the WPA was constructing in the Columbia River Basin for flood control. *Life*'s first issue also contained a photo essay about the town nearest to the Fort Peck Dam, which was named, appropriately, New Deal, Montana.
Margaret Bourke-White, *Life* Magazine. © 1936 Time, Inc.

relation to the economic benefits that poured into their communities. The Women's Division of the Democratic National Committee mobilized 80,000 women at the grass-roots level who supported what the New Deal had done for their communities. The unemployed also looked kindly on the Roosevelt administration. According to one of the earliest Gallup polls, 84 percent of those on relief voted the Democratic ticket in 1936.

The Democratic Party attracted more than the down-and-out. Roosevelt's charismatic personality and the dispersal of New Deal benefits to families throughout the social structure brought middle-class voters, many of them first- or second-generation immigrants, into the Democratic fold. The New Deal thus completed the transformation of the Democratic Party that had begun in the 1920s toward a coalition that reflected the

The Human Face of the Great Depression
Migrant Mother by Dorothea Lange is perhaps the most famous documentary photograph of the 1930s. Lange spent only ten minutes in the pea-picker's camp in California where she captured this image, and did not even get the name of the woman whose despair and resignation she so powerfully recorded. She was later identified as Florence Thompson, a full-blooded Cherokee from Oklahoma.
Library of Congress.

personal failure. But New Deal reformers assumed that once the depression was over, full employment and an active economy would take care of welfare needs, and poverty would wither away. It did not. When later administrations confronted the persistence of inequality and unemployment, they grafted welfare programs onto the jerry-built system left over from the New Deal. Thus, the American welfare system would always be marked by its birth during the crisis of the Great Depression.

But even if the early welfare system had serious flaws, it was brilliant politics. The Democratic Party courted the allegiance of citizens who benefited from New Deal programs. Organized labor aligned itself with the administration that had made it a legitimate force in modern industrial life. Blacks voted Democratic in direct

interests of ethnic groups, city dwellers, organized labor, blacks, and a broad cross-section of the middle class. Those voters provided the backbone of the Democratic coalition for decades to come.

Yet even in the 1930s the New Deal coalition contained potentially fatal contradictions, mainly involving the issue of race. Because Roosevelt depended on the support of southern white Democrats to pass New Deal legislation, he was unwilling to challenge the economic and political marginalization of blacks in the South. At the same time, New Deal programs were changing the face of southern agriculture by undermining the sharecropping tenant system and encouraging the migration of southern blacks to northern and western cities. Outside the South blacks were not prevented from voting, thus guaranteeing that civil rights would enter the national agenda. The resulting cracks would eventually weaken the coalition that had seemed so invincible at the height of Roosevelt's power.

America and an Insecure World Peace

———————★———————

Throughout the 1930s much of Franklin Roosevelt's, and the country's, attention was focused on the domestic crisis, but international events did not stand still. The rise of fascism in Europe and Asia in the 1930s threatened the fragile peace that had prevailed since the end of World War I. When the League of Nations proved too weak to deal with threats to world peace, President Roosevelt foresaw the possibility of America's participation in another war but bowed to the strong isolationist sentiment that predominated in the country. By 1939, however, the world—and the United States—was once again edging toward war.

Depression Diplomacy

During the early years of the New Deal, America's involvement in international affairs, especially in Europe, remained limited. Roosevelt put the national interest first, reasoning that only when the United States regained a stable economy could it act as an effective international leader. One of Roosevelt's few diplomatic initiatives in the early days of the New Deal was formal recognition of the Soviet Union in November 1933.

The Good Neighbor Policy. A significant development closer to home was the Good Neighbor Policy, under which the United States voluntarily renounced the use of military force and armed intervention in the

Western Hemisphere. At the core of this policy, which was developed by Roosevelt and Secretary of State Cordell Hull, was the recognition that the friendship of Latin American countries was essential to the security of the United States and that to win that trust the United States had to develop more equal partnerships with its neighbors. At the Pan American Conference in Montevideo, Uruguay, in December 1933 Hull proclaimed that "no state has the right to intervene in the internal or external affairs of another." In 1934 Congress repealed the Platt Amendment, a relic of the Spanish-American War, which had asserted the right of the United States to intervene in Cuba's internal affairs. Indicating the limits to the Good Neighbor Policy, however, the U.S. Navy kept (and still keeps) a major base at Cuba's Guantanamo Bay and continued to meddle in Cuban politics. And in numerous Latin American countries, U.S. diplomats frequently resorted to economic pressure to solidify the influence of the United States and benefit its multinational corporations.

Debates over Isolationism. An internationalist at heart, Franklin Roosevelt—like his predecessor, Woodrow Wilson—wanted the United States to play a prominent role in the international economic and political system. But FDR was hampered by the isolationism that had been building in both Congress and the nation throughout the 1920s, a product of growing disillusionment with American participation in World War I. In 1934 Gerald P. Nye, a Republican senator from North Dakota, began a congressional investigation into the profits of munitions makers during World War I, which then expanded into a wide investigation of the influence of economic interests on America's decision to declare war. Nye's committee concluded that war profiteers, whom it called "merchants of death," had maneuvered the nation into the war for financial gain.

Most of the committee's charges were dubious or simplistic, but they gave momentum to the isolationist movement and contributed to the passage of the Neutrality Act of 1935. Explicitly designed to prevent a recurrence of the events that had pulled the United States into World War I, the act imposed an embargo on trading arms with countries at war and declared that American citizens traveling on the ships of belligerent nations did so at their own risk. In 1936 Congress expanded the Neutrality Act to ban loans to belligerents, and in 1937 it adopted a "cash and carry" provision: if a country at war wanted to purchase nonmilitary goods from the United States, it had to pay for them in cash and pick them up in its own ships.

In that same year Congress explicitly reinforced earlier bans on sales of arms to Spain, where a bloody civil war had erupted in 1936. In Spain, army forces led by Generalissimo Francisco Franco, with strong support from the fascist regimes in Germany and Italy, were leading a rebellion against the elected republican coalition government. Only the Soviet Union and Mexico backed the Spanish government forces, called the Loyalists; the governments of the United States, Great Britain, and France sympathized with the Loyalists but remained neutral. Because Franco was receiving substantial military aid from Germany and Italy, the neutrality policy doomed the Loyalists.

Many American activists and intellectuals expressed shock at the policy of nonintervention. The Spanish Civil War was the most vital issue of their generation. "People of my sort," observed the writer Malcolm Cowley, "were more deeply stirred by the Spanish Civil War than by any other international event since the World War and the Russian Revolution." Ernest Hemingway immortalized the conflict in his novel *For Whom the Bell Tolls* (1940). Approximately 3,200 American men and women volunteered to fight on the Loyalist side. Calling themselves the Abraham Lincoln Brigade, they formed part of an international force of soldiers, ambulance drivers, and support personnel. Years later survivors recalled the struggle as the "good fight." Despite assistance from the Soviet Union, the Loyalists were outnumbered and inadequately supplied; more than half the American volunteers died in the carnage, which claimed over 700,000 lives altogether.

The Spanish Civil War
American volunteers who fought on the Loyalist side against Franco in the Spanish Civil War associated their fight against fascism with the figure of Abraham Lincoln, symbol of democracy and human rights. In a similar spirit, the American machine gun detachment of the Abraham Lincoln Brigade called itself the Tom Mooney Company in honor of the World War I labor activist imprisoned for his alleged role in planting a bomb during a preparedness parade in 1916.
Archive Photos.

Aggression and Appeasement

The Spanish Civil War was just one of several world crises that challenged the neutrality policy of the United States during the 1930s. Even more threatening were aggressive actions by Germany, Italy, and Japan, all determined to expand their borders and widen their influence. The first crisis was precipitated by Japan, a country with a militaristic regime intent on dominating the Pacific Basin. Japan needed raw materials and markets for its goods to become an imperial and industrial power. In 1931, desiring a buffer against its enemy, the Soviet Union, Japan occupied Manchuria, the northernmost province of China; in 1937 Japan launched a full-scale invasion of China. In both instances, the League of Nations condemned Japan's action but was helpless to stop the aggression.

Japan's defiance of the League gave encouragement to a fascist dictator half a world away. Italy's Benito Mussolini, who had come to power in 1922, had long been unhappy with the Versailles treaty, which had not awarded Italy any former German or Turkish colonies.

Nor had Italy ever forgotten its stinging defeat by Abyssinia (modern Ethiopia) in 1896, the first time Africans had successfully defended themselves against white imperialists. In 1935 Italy invaded Ethiopia, one of the few independent countries left in Africa. The Ethiopian emperor, Haile Selassie, appealed to the League of Nations, which condemned the invasion as aggression and this time imposed sanctions, but to little effect. By 1936 Italian subjugation of Ethiopia was complete.

The Rise of Hitler.   Not Italy, but Germany presented the gravest threat to the world order in the 1930s. The German Weimar Republic of the 1920s was fundamentally unstable, saddled with huge reparations payments and national passions inflamed by the guilt clause imposed by the Treaty of Versailles, in which Germany was made to take sole blame for World War I. Runaway inflation, fear of communism, labor unrest, and rising unemployment fueled the rise of Adolf Hitler and his National Socialist (Nazi) Party. On January 20, 1933, during the interregnum between the Hoover and

Roosevelt administrations, Hitler became chancellor of Germany and assumed dictatorial powers. Aiming at nothing short of world domination, as he made clear in his book *Mein Kampf* (My Struggle), Hitler sought to overturn the territorial settlements of the Versailles treaty, "restore" all the Germans of Central and Eastern Europe to a single greater German fatherland, and annex large areas of Eastern Europe. In his warped vision, "inferior races" such as Jews, Gypsies, and Slavs, as well as "undesirables" such as homosexuals and the mentally impaired, would have to make way for the "master race." In 1933 Hitler established the first concentration camp at Dachau in southeast Germany and opened a campaign of persecution against the Jews.

Hitler's strategy for gaining territory was to provoke a series of crises that gave Britain and France little alternative but to let him have his way. British prime minister Neville Chamberlain was a particularly insistent proponent of the policy that became known as "appeasement." In 1933 Germany withdrew from the League of Nations, and two years later Hitler announced that he planned to rearm Germany in violation of the Versailles treaty. No one stopped him. In 1936 Germany reoccupied the Rhineland, a region that had been declared a demilitarized zone under the treaty. Once again France and Britain took no action. Later that year Hitler and Mussolini joined forces in the Rome-Berlin Axis, a political and military alliance, and when the Spanish Civil War broke out, they supplied arms to the Spanish fascists. On November 26, 1936, Germany and Japan signed the Anti-Comintern Pact, a precursor to the military alliance between Japan and the Axis powers that was formalized in 1940.

As early as 1936, President Roosevelt had foreseen the possibility of U.S. participation in another European war, but he was determined to stay in line with public opinion. During the 1936 campaign, Roosevelt made a stirring antiwar statement that drew on his experience as assistant secretary of the navy during World War I: "I have seen blood running from the wounded. I have seen men coughing out their gassed lungs. . . . I have seen children starving. I have seen the agony of mothers and wives. I hate war." But in October 1937 Roosevelt seemed to take a small step away from isolationism when he denounced "the present reign of terror and international lawlessness" and called on peace-loving nations to oppose such aggression through a "quarantine." Roosevelt's statement reflected rhetorical opposition to militarism more than a specific call for collective security. In any case, at a time when Gallup polls showed that two-thirds of the American people believed the United States had made a mistake in entering World War I, there was no broad-based support for changing the isolationist course.

The Popular Front. Fearful of a world war set in motion by fascist aggression, the Soviet Union attempted to mobilize liberals in democratic countries into what was called a "popular front." In Europe and the United States, communist parties welcomed the cooperation of any group concerned about the threat of fascism to civil rights, organized labor, and world peace. The popular front coincided with the period of the Communist Party's greatest appeal in America, from 1935 to 1939, when party membership peaked at about 100,000, including many intellectuals and writers but also union organizers, working-class activists, and even a few New Deal administrators. The participation of the Abraham Lincoln Brigade on the Loyalist side in the Spanish Civil War was part of the popular front strategy, although these collective efforts could not keep the Spanish republic from falling to Franco's forces in March 1939.

The Failure of Appeasement. As persecution of the Jews and other minorities escalated in Germany, Hitler's ambitions grew. In 1938 he sent troops to annex Austria, while at the same time he schemed to seize part of Czechoslovakia, the keystone of Central Europe. Because Czechoslovakia had an alliance with France, war seemed imminent. But at the Munich Conference in September 1938, Britain and France capitulated, agreeing to let Germany annex the Sudetenland, the German-speaking border areas of Czechoslovakia, in return for Hitler's pledge to seek no more territory.

Within six months, however, Hitler's forces had overrun the rest of Czechoslovakia and threatened to march into Poland, exposing the folly of Neville Chamberlain's pronouncement that the Munich agreement had guaranteed "peace with honor . . . peace for our time." Britain and France prepared to take a stand. Then in August 1939 Hitler shocked the world by signing the Nonaggression Pact with the Soviet Union, allowing Germany to avoid waging war on two fronts. Just as shocked were supporters of the popular front, who were devastated by Stalin's willingness to strike a deal with the hated Hitler to stay out of war. The heyday of American communism ended abruptly.

With the signing of the Nazi-Soviet pact, the world again stood on the brink of war. Although most Americans hoped the United States would remain aloof from the coming European conflict, many began to realize that the nation faced a greater enemy than the economic problems that had gripped it for the past decade. Barely twenty years after the "war to end all wars," the United States prepared once again to enter a worldwide struggle for the survival of democracy.

Summary

★

The New Deal was the response of Franklin Roosevelt and the Democratic Party to the crisis of the Great Depression. The New Deal offered a broad-based program of political and economic reform, but its programs were hardly revolutionary. President Hoover had taken the first steps toward involving the federal government more actively in economic life, a trend that Roosevelt continued and expanded. The New Deal never cured the depression, but it restored confidence that Americans could overcome hard times. It provided a measure of economic security against the worst depression in American history by relieving many of its tragic effects. And legislation such as the Social Security Act of 1935 laid the foundation of the modern welfare state, bringing the United States more in line with other industrialized countries in its acceptance of responsibility for the collective welfare of its citizens.

The New Deal dramatically expanded the size and power of the federal government, continuing a trend that had begun in the late nineteenth and early twentieth centuries. Decisions made in Washington touched millions of individual lives. The New Deal provided new opportunities and a larger role in public life for blacks, women, Mexican Americans, and the labor movement. The collapse of the economy encouraged a reassertion of American values in literature and the arts. This artistic flowering was partly supported by a unique experiment in government patronage of the arts through the WPA. In politics the Democratic coalition of white southerners and the urban working class that had begun to emerge in the 1920s reached a climax in the landslide presidential victory of 1936. By 1938, however, the New Deal had run out of steam and hard times were far from over.

Although the attention of the country was focused on the domestic crisis throughout the decade, the rise of fascism in Germany, Italy, and Japan threatened the fragile world peace established by the Treaty of Versailles. American public opinion remained strongly isolationist, even as Europe stood on the edge of war in 1939, but President Roosevelt was already leading the nation toward participation in its second global war in a generation.

TIMELINE

1933   Emergency Banking Act

Glass-Steagall Act establishes FDIC

Agricultural Adjustment Act (AAA)

National Industrial Recovery Act (NIRA)

Tennessee Valley Authority (TVA)

United States abandons gold standard

Repeal of Prohibition

1934   Securities and Exchange Commission

Indian Reorganization Act

Platt Amendment repealed

1935   Supreme Court finds NIRA unconstitutional

National Union for Social Justice created, led by Father Coughlin

Resettlement Administration

National Labor Relations (Wagner) Act

Social Security Act

Works Progress Administration

Huey Long assassinated

Congress of Industrial Organizations (CIO) formed

Italy invades Ethiopia

1935–1937   Neutrality Acts

1936   Supreme Court finds AAA unconstitutional

Black Cabinet (Federal Council of Negro Affairs)

Roosevelt reelected

Life magazine founded

1936–1939   Spanish Civil War

1937   Sit-down strikes

Memorial Day Massacre

Supreme Court reorganization fails

Japan invades China

1937–1938   "Roosevelt recession"

1938   Fair Labor Standards Act

1939   Munich Conference

Federal Theatre Project terminated

Nazi-Soviet pact

World War II breaks out in Europe

Suggested Readings

★

Comprehensive introductions to the New Deal include Robert S. McElvaine, *The Great Depression* (1984); William E. Leuchtenburg, *Franklin D. Roosevelt and the New Deal* (1963); John A. Garraty, *The Great Depression* (1987); Roger Biles, *A New Deal for the American People* (1991); and Harvard Sitkoff, ed., *Fifty Years Later: The New Deal Evaluated* (1985).

The New Deal Takes Over, 1933–1935

The New Deal has inspired a voluminous bibliography. Frank Freidel, *Launching the New Deal* (1973), covers the first hundred days in detail. Monographs include Bernard Bellush, *The Failure of the NRA* (1975); Thomas K. McCraw, *TVA and the Power Fight* (1970); John Salmond, *The Civilian Conservation Corps* (1967); Roy Lubove, *The Struggle for Social Security* (1968); Mark Leff, *The Limits of Symbolic Reform: The New Deal and Taxation, 1933–1939* (1984); and Bonnie Fox Schwartz, *The Civilian Works Administration, 1933–1934* (1984). Ellis Hawley, *The New Deal and the Problem of Monopoly* (1966), provides a stimulating account of economic policy. Claire Bond Potter, *War on Crime* (1998), analyzes the Federal Bureau of Investigation and statebuilding in the 1930s. Agricultural developments are covered in Theodore Saloutos, *The American Farmer and the New Deal* (1982); and Sidney Baldwin, *Poverty and Politics: The Rise and Decline of the Farm Security Administration* (1968). Alan Brinkley, *Voices of Protest* (1982), covers the Coughlin and Long movements.

The Second New Deal, 1935–1938

Roosevelt's second term has drawn far less attention than has the 1933–1936 period. James MacGregor Burns, *Roosevelt: The Lion and the Fox* (1956), provides an overview, as does Barry Karl, *The Uneasy State* (1983). Alan Brinkley, *The End of Reform* (1995), discusses the New Deal and liberalism between 1937 and 1945. The growing opposition to the New Deal is treated in Clyde P. Weed, *The Nemesis of Reform: The Republican Party during the New Deal* (1994); and James T. Patterson, *Congressional Conservatism and the New Deal* (1967).

The New Deal's Impact on American Society

Katie Louchheim, ed., *The Making of the New Deal: The Insiders Speak* (1983), provides an engaging introduction to some of the men and women who shaped the New Deal. On women in the New Deal, see Susan Ware, *Beyond Suffrage* (1981). Blanche Cook, *Eleanor Roosevelt* (1991), takes the story to 1933; see also Lois Scharf, *Eleanor Roosevelt* (1987). Also of interest is Frances Perkins's memoir, *The Roosevelt I Knew* (1946).

On minorities and the New Deal, see Harvard Sitkoff, *A New Deal for Blacks* (1978); John B. Kirby, *Black Americans in the Roosevelt Era* (1980); Robert Zangrando, *The NAACP Crusade against Lynching, 1909–1950* (1980); and Nancy J. Weiss, *Farewell to the Party of Lincoln* (1983). For material on Mary McLeod Bethune, see Darlene Clark Hine, ed., *Black Women in America: An Historical Encyclopedia* (1993). George J. Sanchez, *Becoming Mexican American: Ethnicity, Culture and Identity in Chicano Los Angeles, 1900–1945* (1993), and David G. Gutierrez, *Walls and Mirrors: Mexican Americans, Mexican Immigrants, and the Politics of Ethnicity* (1995), describe the politicization of Mexican Americans in the 1930s.

Irving Bernstein, *The Turbulent Years* (1970) and *A Caring Society: The New Deal, the Worker, and the Great Depression* (1985), chronicle the story of the labor movement through 1941 in compelling detail. Additional studies include Ronald Schatz, *The Electrical Workers* (1983); Bruce Nelson, *Workers on the Waterfront* (1988); and Lizabeth Cohen, *Making a New Deal: Industrial Workers in Chicago, 1919–1939* (1990). Steven Fraser, *Labor Will Rule* (1991), is a fine biography of CIO leader Sidney Hillman. For women and the labor movement, see Annelise Orleck, *Common Sense and a Little Fire* (1995).

On Indian policy, see Donald Parman, *Navajos and the New Deal* (1976); Laurence Hauptman, *The Iroquois and the New Deal* (1981); and Laurence C. Kelly, *The Assault on Assimilation: John Collier and the Origins of Indian Policy Reform* (1983). For rural electrification, see D. Clayton Brown, *Electricity for Rural America* (1980).

The various New Deal programs have found historians in Jerry Mangione, *The Dream and the Deal: The Federal Writers' Project, 1935–1943* (1972); Richard McKinzie, *The New Deal for Artists* (1973); and Jane DeHart Mathews, *The Federal Theater, 1935–1939* (1967). Marlene Park and Gerald Markowitz, *Democratic Vistas* (1984), survey New Deal murals and art, and Barbara Melosh, *Engendering Culture* (1991), looks at New Deal public art and theater. General studies of cultural expression include William Stott, *Documentary Expression and Thirties America* (1973), and Richard Pells, *Radical Visions and American Dreams* (1973). The creation of the New Deal's welfare system is treated in James T. Patterson, *America's Struggle against Poverty* (1981), which carries the story through 1980. See also Michael Katz, *In the Shadow of the Poorhouse: A Social History of Welfare in America* (1986). For the enduring impact of Franklin Roosevelt on the political system, see William Leuchtenburg, *In the Shadow of FDR* (1983).

America and an Insecure World Peace

Robert Dallek, *Franklin Delano Roosevelt and American Foreign Policy, 1932–1945* (1979), and Wayne Cole, *Roosevelt and the Isolationists, 1932–1945* (1983), provide comprehensive overviews. See also Kenneth S. Davis, *FDR: Into the Storm, 1937–1940* (1993); Arnold Offner, *American Appeasement* (1976); and David Schmitz, *The United States and Fascist Italy, 1922–1940* (1988). On Latin America, see Walter LaFeber, *Inevitable Revolutions* (1983). Material on the relationship between American intellectuals and the Communist Party can be found in Harvey Klehr, *The Heyday of American Communism* (1984). Peter Carroll, *The Odyssey of the Abraham Lincoln Brigade* (1994), tells the story of Americans in the Spanish Civil War.

Back Him Up!

BUY WAR BONDS

The World at War,

1939–1945

O N A SUNDAY night in October 1938 the actor Orson Welles's "Mercury Theater of the Air" broadcast a modern version of *The War of the Worlds* (1898) by the British writer H. G. Wells. The fictional news bulletins, interspersed with simulated on-the-spot reports, convinced many people that Martians had landed near Princeton, New Jersey, and were invading the countryside. Even though the broadcast included four announcements that the radio program was a dramatization, some people fled their homes. No one doubted the power of radio anymore.

One reason that so many people believed in Orson Welles's fictional invasion may have been that in September 1938, radio programs had been interrupted repeatedly by ominous news bulletins about a possible European war. Even the September 30 reports of the Munich agreement among Britain, France, and Germany, which prevented war for another year, did not ease people's fears of imminent catastrophe. In the late 1930s popular culture reflected America's connection to international events, an involvement that the coming of World War II would intensify. When radios announced on December 7, 1941, that the Japanese had attacked Pearl Harbor, Americans realized that this news flash was not a hoax.

World War II ranks with the New Deal as a crucial period of political, social, and economic change in America. Mobilization for war pumped money and confidence into the economy, ending the Great Depression. The task of fighting a global war increased the government's influence on people's lives and caused dramatic social changes on the home front. But the most far-reaching

Mobilizing the Hearts and Minds of America
To offset the enormous cost of the war, the U.S. government sponsored a series of bond drives. This poster by Thomas Hart Benton, which the prominent artist donated in 1943 to the war effort, captured the spirit of unity and sacrifice needed to win World War II.
Library of Congress.

impact was international, as the United States accepted a leading—and continuing—role in world affairs. Within wartime strategies lay the seeds of the Cold War that would follow.

American Neutrality, 1939–1941

——————★——————

World War II officially began when German troops attacked Poland on September 1, 1939, and two days later Britain and France declared war on Germany. For more than two years the United States debated its course of action. Most Americans held two contradictory positions. The overwhelming majority supported the Allies. A 1939 poll showed that 84 percent wanted an Allied victory, 2 percent supported the Nazis, and 14 percent had no opinion. Even so, most Americans did not want to be drawn into another European war. This strong isolationist sentiment severely limited President Roosevelt's options.

The Road to War

Because the United States had become a major world power, whatever stand the country adopted after 1939 would affect the course of the European conflict. Two days after the outbreak of hostilities, the United States officially declared its neutrality. Roosevelt made no secret of his sympathies, however, pointedly rephrasing Woodrow Wilson's declaration of 1914: "This nation will remain a neutral nation, but I cannot ask that every American remain neutral in thought as well." So began what *Time* magazine would later call America's "thousand-step road to war."

At first the need for American intervention seemed remote. After the German conquest of Poland in September 1939, a false calm settled over Europe. This "phony war" lulled many Americans into believing that arming the Allies would be enough to defeat Germany. Hitler soon shattered that complacency. In a few hours on April 9, 1940, Nazi tanks overran Denmark. Norway fell to the Nazi *Blitzkrieg* ("lightning war") next, and the Netherlands, Belgium, and Luxembourg soon followed. Then the Germans stormed into France from the north, making short work of the combined British and French troops. On June 22, 1940, France fell. Only Britain stood between the United States and Hitler's plans for world domination.

Support for Intervention Grows.   During the summer and fall of 1940 German planes bombarded Britain mercilessly in the Battle of Britain, destroying the myth of its island invincibility. In America the debate over the nation's neutrality intensified. The journalist William Allen White and his Committee to Defend America by Aiding the Allies led the interventionists. Isolationists, including the aviator Charles Lindbergh, Senator Gerald Nye, and the former National Recovery Act administrator Hugh Johnson, formed the America First Committee in 1940 to keep the nation out of the war. They attracted the support of the *Chicago Tribune*, the Hearst chain of newspapers, and other conservative publications—especially those in the Midwest.

Despite the efforts of the America First Committee, in 1940 the United States moved closer to involvement in the war. In May, Roosevelt created the National Defense Advisory Commission and the Council of National Defense to advise on strategies for putting the economy and government on a defense footing. In June of that election year he brought two prominent Republicans, Henry Stimson and Frank Knox, into his cabinet as secretaries of war and the navy, respectively, to give a bipartisan character to the war preparations. During the summer the president traded fifty World War I destroyers to Great Britain in exchange for the right to build military bases on British possessions in the Atlantic, thereby circumventing the nation's neutrality laws by executive order. In October a bipartisan majority in Congress approved a large increase in defense spending and instituted the first peacetime draft registration and conscription in American history. Another draft law, which came up in August 1941, lengthening draftees' service from one year to two and a half years, passed by a single vote.

The 1940 Election.   While the war expanded in Europe, Asia, North Africa, and the Middle East, the United States prepared for the 1940 election. Would Roosevelt seek an unprecedented third term? He had not designated a successor, and the war in Europe convinced him that he should run. Roosevelt submitted to a "draft" at the Democratic National Convention in Chicago, but convention delegates balked at his choice for vice-president, liberal Secretary of Agriculture Henry A. Wallace, to replace John Nance Garner of Texas, a conservative who had long since broken with the New Deal. Wallace's nomination went through only after Eleanor Roosevelt, reminding delegates that this was "no ordinary time," asked them to put politics aside in a national crisis.

The Republicans nominated a political newcomer, Wendell Willkie of Indiana, a lawyer and the president of the Commonwealth and Southern Electric Utilities Company. Willkie, a former Democrat, supported many of the New Deal's domestic and international policies, including Roosevelt's trade of destroyers for military bases. The platforms of the two parties differed only slightly. Both pledged aid to the Allies but stopped short of calling for American participation in the war.

***The Debate over Intervention
Gets Personal***
Playing out the nationwide debate
between interventionists and isola-
tionists, a soldier grabs a picket sign
from a peace activist in front of the
White House in 1941.
T. McAvoy, *Life* Magazine. © Time, Inc.

Initially Willkie conducted his campaign in a bipartisan spirit, but as the election approached, Republican
leaders pressured him to go on the offensive. Charging
that Roosevelt was leading the country into war, Willkie
promised that he would not send "one American boy
into the shambles of another war." Roosevelt's reply on
October 28, 1940, probably clinched his victory: "I have
said this before, but I shall say it again and again and
again: Your boys are not going to be sent into foreign
wars." (Of course, if the United States was attacked, it
would no longer be a foreign war.) Willkie's spirited
campaign resulted in a closer election than those of
1932 and 1936, but Roosevelt and the vital Democratic
coalition won 55 percent of the popular vote and a
more lopsided victory in the electoral college.

The Lend-Lease Act. With the election behind him,
Roosevelt concentrated on persuading the American
people to increase aid to Britain, whose survival he
viewed as the key to American security. In November
1939 FDR had won a bitter battle in Congress to amend
the Neutrality Act of 1935 to allow the Allies to buy
weapons from the United States—but only on the cash-
and-carry basis established for nonmilitary goods in
1937. In March 1941, with German submarines sinking
British ships more rapidly than they could be replaced,
and Britain no longer able to afford to pay cash for
arms, Roosevelt convinced Congress to pass the Lend-

Lease Act. The legislation authorized the president to
"lease, lend, or otherwise dispose of" arms and other
equipment to any country whose defense was considered vital to the security of the United States. In a press
conference designed to build popular support for the
plan, Roosevelt had used the analogy of lending a
neighbor a garden hose to put out a fire: "I don't say to
him, . . . 'Neighbor, my garden hose cost me $15; you
have to pay me $15 for it.' . . . I don't want $15—I want
my garden hose back after the fire is over." To administer the program, Roosevelt turned to the former relief
administrator Harry Hopkins, who became one of his
most trusted advisors during the war years. After Germany invaded the Soviet Union in June 1941 (an abandonment of the Nazi-Soviet pact of two years earlier),
the United States extended lend-lease to the Soviet
Union, which became part of the Allied coalition.

In his State of the Union address to Congress in
January 1941, Roosevelt had connected lend-lease to
the defense of democracy at home as well as in
Europe. He spoke about what he called "four essential
human freedoms everywhere in the world"—freedom
of speech and expression, freedom of worship, freedom from want, and freedom from fear. Although
Roosevelt avoided stating explicitly that America had
to enter the war to protect those freedoms, he
intended to justify exactly that, for he now regarded
U.S. participation as inevitable. And, indeed, the

implementation of lend-lease marked the unofficial entrance of the United States into the European war.

The Atlantic Charter. The United States became even more involved in August 1941, when Roosevelt and the British prime minister, Winston Churchill, conferred secretly aboard a battleship off the Newfoundland coast to discuss goals and military strategy. It was the first time the two world leaders had met. Their joint press release, which became known as the Atlantic Charter, provided the ideological foundation of the Western cause and of the peace to follow. Like Wilson's Fourteen Points, the charter called for postwar economic collaboration and guarantees of political stability to ensure that "all men in all the lands may live out their lives in freedom from fear and want." The charter

also supported free trade, national self-determination, and the principle of collective security.

As in World War I, when Americans started supplying the Allies, Germany attacked American and Allied ships. By September 1941 Nazi submarines and American vessels were fighting an undeclared naval war in the Atlantic, unknown to the American public. Without an actual enemy attack, however, Roosevelt still hesitated to ask Congress for a declaration of war.

The Attack on Pearl Harbor

The final provocation came not from Germany but from Japan. Tensions between Japan and the United States had been building throughout the 1930s. Japanese military advances in China had upset the balance of

Pearl Harbor
The U.S. battleship *West Virginia* exploded into flames after receiving a direct hit during the surprise Japanese attack on Pearl Harbor on December 7, 1941. It was early Sunday morning, and many of the servicemen were still asleep. More than 2,400 Americans were killed; the Japanese suffered only light losses.
U.S. Navy.

political and economic power in the Pacific, where the United States had long enjoyed the economic benefits of the open-door policy, especially access to China's raw materials and large markets (see Chapter 21). It was the Japanese invasion of China in 1937 that caused Roosevelt to suggest that such aggressors should be "quarantined" by peace-loving nations. Despite such rhetoric, the United States avoided taking a stand, mainly because isolationism was still strong in the country. During the brutal sack of Nanking in 1937 the Japanese had sunk an American gunboat, the *Panay*, in the Yangtze River. In exchange for more than $2 million in damages, the United States allowed Japan to apologize and the incident was quickly smoothed over.

With the attention of the major powers focused on the war in Europe, Japan's imperial intentions became more expansionist. In 1940 Japan signed the Tri-Partite Pact, a defensive alliance with Germany and Italy that extended the Axis into Asia, and in the fall of 1940 Japanese troops occupied the northern part of French Indochina. The United States retaliated by effectively cutting off trade with Japan, including vital oil shipments that accounted for almost 80 percent of Japanese consumption. (At that time the United States was producing two-thirds of the world's oil.) Before its supplies ran down, Japan faced a choice: accept American demands that it cease its expansionism in Asia, or try to find alternative sources for those resources, most likely by seizing British and Dutch possessions in the Pacific. In July 1941 Japanese troops occupied the rest of Indochina; Roosevelt froze Japanese assets in the United States and instituted an embargo on trade with Japan.

In September 1941 the government of Prime Minister Hideki Tojo began secret preparations for war against the United States. Talks between the two nations continued without progress. By November American military intelligence knew that Japan was planning an attack but did not know where it would occur. Early on Sunday morning, December 7, 1941, Japanese bombers attacked the naval base at Pearl Harbor in Hawaii, killing more than 2,400 Americans. Eight battleships, three cruisers, three destroyers, and almost two hundred airplanes were destroyed or heavily damaged. Luckily for the United States, there were no aircraft carriers in port at the time—those vessels would be far more important in the war to come. The Japanese also failed to destroy Pearl Harbor's oil reserves, which would have stranded the navy in Hawaii until oil shipments arrived from the West Coast, thousands of miles away.

Although the attack was devastating, it united the American people in anger and a determination to fight. Pearl Harbor Day is still etched in the memories of millions of Americans who remember precisely what they were doing when they heard about the attack. The next day Roosevelt went before Congress. Calling December 7 "a date which will live in infamy," he asked for a declaration of war against Japan. The Senate unanimously voted for war, and the House concurred by a vote of 388 to 1. The lone dissenter was Jeannette Rankin of Montana, who had also opposed American entry into World War I. Three days later Germany and Italy declared war on the United States, and the United States in turn declared war on those nations.

Organizing for Victory

— ★ —

The task of fighting a global war accelerated the growing influence of the state on American life. Coordinating the changeover from civilian to war production, raising an army, and assembling the necessary work force taxed government agencies to the limit. Mobilization on such a scale demanded cooperation between business executives and political leaders in Washington, solidifying a partnership that had been growing since World War I. But the most dramatic expansion of power occurred at the presidential level when Congress passed the War Powers Act of December 18, 1941, giving Roosevelt unprecedented authority over all aspects of the conduct of the war.

Mobilizing for Defense

Defense mobilization had a powerful impact on the federal government's role in the economy (Figure 26.1). The federal budget of $95.2 billion in 1945 was ten times that of 1939, and the national debt grew sixfold, topping out at $258.6 billion in 1945. Along with huge federal budgets came greater acceptance of Keynesian economics, that is, the use of government fiscal policy to stimulate economic growth. The war also brought significant changes in the federal bureaucracy. The number of civilians employed by the government increased almost fourfold, to 3.8 million—a far more dramatic growth than the New Deal period had witnessed. At the height of wartime hiring the government gave the civil service exam two or three times a day.

Financing the War.   Taxes paid about half the cost of the war, compared with 30 percent of the cost of World War I. The Revenue Act of 1942 continued the income tax reform that had begun during World War I by taxing not just wealthy individuals and corporations but average citizens as well. The number of people paying income tax increased from 3.9 million in 1939 to 42.6 million in 1945; tax collections rose from $2.2 billion to $35.1 billion, facilitated by payroll deductions and tax

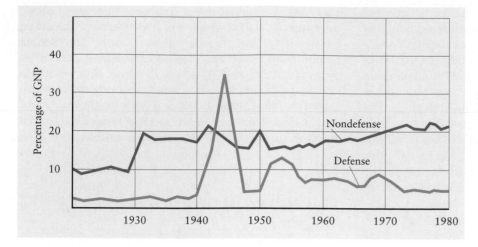

FIGURE 26.1
Government Spending as a Percentage of GNP
Government defense spending was a minuscule percentage of the gross national product in the 1930s, but it ballooned during World War II and rose again during the Korean War and, to a lesser degree, during the Vietnam War. Nondefense government spending did not display such wild fluctuations— just a steady, upward trend.

withholding, which were instituted in 1943. This mass-based tax system, a revolutionary change in the financing of the modern state, was sold to the taxpayers as a way to express their patriotism. War bond drives also gave people a patriotic opportunity to put their savings at the disposal of the government by buying long-term Treasury bonds, which financed the remaining cost of the war. War bonds had the additional benefit of withdrawing money from circulation, which helped hold down inflation.

Running the Economy. Like Woodrow Wilson during World War I, Roosevelt turned to business leaders to run the war economy. (Many of these executives became known as "dollar-a-year men" because they volunteered for government service while remaining on the corporate payroll.) Defense preparations had been under way since 1940; before Pearl Harbor 25 percent of the economy was already devoted to war production. In January 1941 Roosevelt established the Office of Production Management under William Knudsen, the president of General Motors. After the Japanese attack Roosevelt disbanded that agency and replaced it with the War Production Board (WPB), headed by Donald Nelson, a former Sears, Roebuck executive. The WPB awarded defense contracts, evaluated military and civilian requests for scarce resources, and oversaw the conversion of industries to military production. The WPB used the carrot more often than the stick. To encourage businesses to convert to war production, the board granted generous tax write-offs for plant construction and approved contracts with cost-plus provisions that guaranteed a profit and promised that businesses could keep the new factories after the war. As Secretary of War Henry Stimson put it, "you had better let business make money out of the process or business won't work."

In the interest of efficiency and maximum production, the WPB preferred to deal with large corporations

rather than with small businesses. The fifty-six largest corporations got three-fourths of the war contracts, with one-third going to the top ten. This system of allocating contracts, along with the suspension of antitrust prosecution during the war, hastened the trend toward large corporate structures. In 1940 the hundred largest companies manufactured 30 percent of the nation's industrial output; in 1945 their share was 70 percent. Those giant businesses would form the core of the military-industrial complex that came to link the federal government, corporations, and the military in an interdependent partnership in the postwar era (see Chapters 27 and 28).

The Office of Price Administration and Civilian Supply (OPA) supervised the domestic economy, allocating resources and trying to keep inflation down. By February 1942 retail prices were rising by 2 percent a month, as consumers had more income to spend than there were available goods and services. In April the OPA froze most prices and rents at their March 1942 levels. When loopholes, especially regarding food prices, undermined that effort, Congress passed the Anti-Inflation Act, which stabilized prices, wages, and salaries. The consumer price index rose by 28.3 percent between 1940 and 1945, but most of the inflation occurred before 1943.

Roosevelt remained unsatisfied with the mobilization effort; there were too many government agencies, and their actions often overlapped. In October 1942 he persuaded Justice James F. Byrnes to resign from the Supreme Court to head the Office of Economic Stabilization and, after 1943, the Office of War Mobilization. Byrnes soon became the second most powerful person in the administration and finally brought order to production goals for civilian and military needs. The results were remarkable.

The peak of mobilization occurred in late 1943, when two-thirds of the economy was directly involved

Why We Fight
This 1942 award-winning lithograph by Karl Koehler and Victor Ancona painted a sinister, menacing portrait of a Nazi officer, leaving little room for doubt as to why it was necessary to end Nazism.
National Museum of American Art, Smithsonian Institution, Washington, DC.

How We Fight
One way that America defeated the Axis powers was through war production. Government posters such as this 1942 litho-graph by Jean Carlu supported the home front effort.
National Museum of American Art, Smithsonian Institution, Washington, DC.

in the war effort, as opposed to only one-quarter in World War I. Shipbuilding showed that American productive capacity was at full strength. By 1941 the German navy had crippled transatlantic transport, sinking about 12 million tons of mostly U.S.-built Allied shipping in the North Atlantic. Producing replacement vessels became a high priority. By turning out clunky but easy-to-build Liberty ships, the United States produced 19 million tons of merchant shipping by 1943, up from 1 million tons two years earlier.

Henry J. Kaiser, a West Coast shipbuilder, performed shipyard production miracles. Using the mass-production techniques of the automobile industry, Kaiser cut the time needed to build a transport ship from 300 days to 17. He motivated workers through high pay and fringe benefits, including one of the country's first prepaid medical programs (see American

Lives, "Henry J. Kaiser: World War II's 'Miracle Man,'" pp. 840–841). Kaiser's name became synonymous with getting things done in a hurry.

Although not all industries could boast of freedom from *snafus* (an acronym coined during the war from the expression "situation normal, all fouled up"), business and government compiled an impressive record. As in World War I, industry played a significant role in the military victory. By 1945 the United States had turned out 86,000 tanks, 296,000 airplanes, 15 million rifles and machine guns, 64,000 landing craft, and 6,500 ships. Mobilization on this gigantic scale gave a tremendous boost to the economy, causing the gross national product to more than double. It rose from $99.7 billion in 1940 to $211 billion by the end of the war. After years of depression, Americans' faith in the capitalist system was restored. But it was a transformed economy that relied heavily on the government's participation.

Mobilizing the American Fighting Force

An expanded state presence was also evident in the government's mobilization of a fighting force. Under the chief of staff, George C. Marshall, the army grew from 200,000 soldiers in 1939 to over 8 million in 1945. By the end of World War II the U.S. armed forces numbered more than 15 million men and women. The army, including those who served in the Army Air Force, enlisted the most, but almost 4 million served in the navy, 600,000 in the marines, and 240,000 in the coast guard.

Henry J. Kaiser: World War II's "Miracle Man"

★

HENRY KAISER WAS a workaholic. His motto was "Find a Need and Fill It." He hated being alone and hated taking vacations. He worked twenty-hour days and expected his top managers to do the same. If ordinary mortals were trying to sleep in California, he made long-distance calls to associates in other time zones. "Whenever he had a new idea—and he commonly had a score or so daily—he reached for the telephone," noted his biographer, Mark Foster. As early as 1942 his company was running up then-extravagant phone bills of $250,000 a year.

Kaiser was one of the most widely known figures of the 1940s, a genuine folk hero to many for his ability to get things done. After shipyard triumphs such as the construction of an entire Liberty ship in four days, fifteen hours, and twenty-six minutes in November 1942, the press dubbed him the "Miracle Man." He was a special darling of media mogul Henry Luce: 40 percent of the popular articles on Kaiser between 1941 and 1943 appeared in *Time*, *Life*,

and *Fortune*, Luce's three major publications. Even the staid *Wall Street Journal* called him "Fabulous Mr. Kaiser." Franklin Roosevelt seriously considered the industrialist for the vice-presidential slot on the 1944 Democratic ticket and, according to FDR's cousin Margaret Suckley, even thought Kaiser could be the best man to succeed him if he chose not to run for reelection. A Roper poll in spring 1945 found that the public believed Henry Kaiser had done more than any other civilian to help the president win the war.

Kaiser's career and the rise of the modern American West went hand in hand. Born in upstate New York in 1882 to German immigrant parents, he left school at age thirteen to make his way in the world. In 1906 he headed west to Spokane, Washington, to establish himself in business so that he could marry his fiancée; in 1921 he and his family settled permanently in Oakland, California. From 1914 to 1931 Kaiser's contracting business built roads, trying to keep up with the West's insatiable demand for highways for the new cars rolling off the assembly lines in Detroit. In the 1930s Kaiser was part of a six-company partnership that successfully bid for massive engineering projects such as building the Hoover and Grand Coulee Dams, federally funded public works projects that permanently changed the western landscape. In the 1930s he also lobbied extensively in Washington, developing contacts with New Deal bureaucrats that would prove invaluable during the war years.

The Miracle Man
In November 1942, Henry Kaiser used an 81-piece, 14-foot-long model of the 10,400-ton Liberty freighter to show shipowners and navy representatives how it was built in the amazing time of 4 days, 15 hours, and 26 minutes.
Corbis-Bettmann.

Moved largely by wartime opportunities, Kaiser left construction to launch a career as an industrialist. He made his first big splash—literally—building Liberty ships faster and better than anyone else. Shipbuilding was an ideal choice for an inveterate self-promoter like Henry Kaiser. The World War II era boasted few photo opportunities better than a ship launching, and Kaiser invited Hollywood stars, members of the president's family, and a host of other celebrities to christen the ships, always with the newsreel cameras rolling and the photographers' flash bulbs popping. Thanks to his public relations machine, Kaiser's name was all over the news.

But before Kaiser could build ships he had to build shipyards. Drawing on the availability of vacant tracts of West Coast waterfront (something the older shipyards in the East did not have), he constructed work spaces large enough to accommodate the assembly of prefabricated ship components. Kaiser's shipyards in Richmond, California, were designed like a city grid, complete with numbered and lettered streets. "It was a city without houses," remembered one worker, "but the traffic was heavy. Cranes, trucks, trains noised by." Recalled a recent migrant from a small Iowa town, "It was such a huge place, something I had never been in. People from all walks of life, all coming and going and working, and the noise. The whole atmosphere was overwhelming to me."

Although Kaiser did not invent the subassembly technique, he was the most successful at applying mass production to shipbuilding. Previously, most jobs in shipbuilding had been skilled or semiskilled, requiring apprenticeship and training far too lengthy for the wartime emergency. To train new workers more quickly, the work process was broken down into small, specialized tasks, in effect de-skilling what had previously been a craft. As Kaiser put it, "production is not labor anymore, but a process."

The Kaiser shipyards were known as much for their corporate welfare programs as for their bureaucratized work climate. Kaiser offered his workers day care, financial and job counseling, subsidized housing, and especially health care, his most significant long-term contribution. The Kaiser Permanente Medical Care Program was founded in 1942, an outgrowth of prepaid health care plans first tried on remote federal construction projects in the 1930s. This health care system, the forerunner of today's health maintenance organizations (HMOs), was available to Kaiser workers for the nominal paycheck deduction of 50 cents a week. Almost 90 percent of his workers chose that option. Kaiser provided health care for both philanthropic and business reasons. The initial investment was quickly repaid in the form of healthier workers, lower absenteeism, and greater productivity. As a Permanente executive explained, "To the private physician, a sick person is an asset. To Permanente, a sick person is a liability. We'd go bankrupt if we didn't keep most of our members and their families well most of the time."

At the core of Kaiser's popularity was a dichotomy. The public saw him as a man who broke the rules for them, a self-made outsider who made things happen in wartime Washington despite the bureaucrats. Yet Kaiser could never have achieved his business miracles without a close working relationship with the federal government, which, for example, allowed him to borrow $300 million from the Reconstruction Finance Corporation during World War II to construct new plants. Noting the symbiotic relationship between business and government that increasingly characterized the twentieth century, historian Stephen B. Adams calls Henry Kaiser a *government entrepreneur*. But the public persisted in seeing him as an individualist, a symbol of a "can-do" age.

While many business executives faced the postwar period with caution, Kaiser looked forward to peacetime reconversion with the boundless optimism of a far-sighted entrepreneur. He was especially excited about opportunities for industrial expansion in the West. Between 1944 and 1946 he identified opportunities in areas such as steel, magnesium, and aluminum as well as foreseeing a demand for mass-produced suburban tract housing. In the 1950s he headed a multinational corporate empire that included many companies with assets close to $1 billion. In 1965 he became the first industrialist to win the AFL-CIO's highest honor, the Philip Murray–William Green Award.

To many Americans Henry Kaiser was a twentieth-century incarnation of Horatio Alger, even though he was a portly sixty years old in 1942 when he launched the Richmond shipyards. In terms of managerial style, he was more an old-style "seat-of-the-pants" entrepreneur than a modern corporate bureaucrat. He was a maverick, challenging traditional ways of doing business at every stage of his career at the same time that he seized the opportunities presented by the growth of the administrative state. He was a visionary in the role that he saw for an industrial West, a dream that was amply fulfilled during the postwar era. But he was also lucky, his success being the product of a highly favorable set of economic conditions both regionally in the West and globally during World War II and its aftermath. After his death in 1967 his industrial empire largely disappeared, but Kaiser Permanente lives on, one of the country's largest and most successful health maintenance organizations.

Draft boards registered about 31 million men between the ages of eighteen and forty-four and ordered physical examinations for about one-sixth of the male population. More than half the men failed to meet the physical standards, with defective teeth and poor vision causing the greatest number of rejections. The military also tried to screen out homosexuals, but its attempts were ineffectual. Once in military service, homosexuals found that the sex-segregated environment offered new possibilities for same-sex attraction. Wartime experiences also weakened patterns that traditionally channeled men and women toward heterosexuality: instead of going directly from parental homes into marriage, gay men and lesbians in the military lived away from kin in settings where they found opportunities to participate in a gay subculture that was more extensive than that found in civilian life.

Racial discrimination prevailed in the armed forces, mainly directed against the approximately 700,000 blacks in uniform. African Americans served in all branches of the armed forces but were assigned the most menial duties; a great number served as messboys on navy ships, for example. The army even segregated black and white blood banks, a policy that had no scientific merit. The National Association for the Advancement of Colored People (NAACP) and other civil rights groups chided the government with reminders such as "A Jim Crow army cannot fight for a free world," but the military refused to change its practices. In contrast, Mexican Americans were never officially segregated. Unlike blacks, they were welcomed into combat units, and seventeen Mexican Americans won the Congressional Medal of Honor.

Women found both opportunities and discrimination in the armed services. Approximately 350,000 American women enlisted in the armed services and achieved a permanent status in the military. There were about 140,000 WAC (Women's Army Corps) members, 100,000 naval WAVES (Women Accepted for Volunteer Emergency Service), 23,000 members of the Marine Corps Women's Reserve, and 13,000 SPARs (for Semper Paratus, or Always Ready, the coast guard's motto) in the coast guard. In addition, about 1,000 WASPs (Women's Airforce Service Pilots) ferried planes and supplies in noncombat areas. One-third of the nation's registered nurses, almost 75,000 overall, volunteered for military duty.

The armed forces limited the types of duty assigned to women, as it did with blacks. Women were barred from combat, although nurses and medical personnel sometimes served close to the front lines, risking capture or death. The social lives of women soldiers, most of whom were single, were more strictly regulated than those of their male counterparts, mainly out of fear of sexual impropriety. Most military jobs reflected stereotypes of women's roles in civilian life—clerical work,

The WACs Overseas
Not all military women were relegated to stateside duty. These eager WACs, members of the first Women's Army Corps unit to go overseas, have just arrived in North Africa in 1943 to begin their assignments.
Archive Photos.

communications, and health care. The widely distributed pinups of Betty Grable in a bathing suit, Rita Hayworth in a flimsy nightgown, and, for the black soldiers, the singer Lena Horne, were probably closer to the average GI's view of women than a WAC or a WAVE was.

Workers and the War Effort

When millions of citizens entered military service, a huge hole opened in the American work force. The backlog of depression-era unemployment quickly disappeared, and the United States faced a critical labor shortage. The nation's defense industries provided jobs for about 7 million new workers, including great numbers of women, blacks, and Mexican Americans who were given employment opportunities for the first time.

Rosie the Riveter.   Government planners "discovered" women while looking for workers to fill the jobs vacated by departing servicemen. The recruiting campaign drew on patriotism. One poster urged, "Longing won't bring him back sooner . . . GET A WAR JOB!" Recruiters promised that women would take to riveting machines and drill presses "as easily as to electric cake-mixers and vacuum cleaners." The artist Norman Rockwell supported the campaign by creating his famous "Rosie the Riveter" cover for the *Saturday Evening Post*.

Although the government directed its propaganda at housewives, women who were already employed gladly abandoned low-paying "women's" jobs as domestic servants or file clerks for higher-paying jobs in defense factories. Suddenly the nation's factories were full of women working as riveters, welders, blast furnace cleaners, and drill press operators. Women made up 36 percent of the labor force in 1945, compared with 24 percent at the beginning of the war.

Government planners and employers regarded women as just "filling in" while the men were away. Employers rarely offered day care or flexible hours, and government child care programs established by the 1940 Lanham Act reached only 10 percent of those who needed them. Because women were responsible for home care as well as their jobs, they had a higher absentee rate than did men. Often, the only way to get shopping done or take a child to the doctor was to skip work. Women war workers also faced discrimination on the job. In shipyards women with the most seniority and responsibility earned $6.95 a day, whereas the top men made as much as $22.

When the men came home from war and the plants returned to peacetime operations, Rosie the Riveter was out of a job. But many women refused to put on an apron and stay home. Women's participation in the labor force dropped temporarily when the war ended but rebounded steadily for the rest of the 1940s, especially among married women.

Organized Labor. Wartime mobilization also opened up opportunities to advance the labor movement and solidify the industrial breakthroughs of the 1930s. By the end of the war almost 15 million workers—one-third of the nonagricultural labor force, up from 9 million at the end of the previous decade—belonged to unions.

Organized labor responded to the war with an initial burst of patriotic unity. On December 23, 1941, representatives of major unions made a "no strike" pledge—although nonbinding—for the duration of the war. In January 1942 Roosevelt created the National War Labor Board (NWLB) composed of representatives of labor, management, and the public. The board established wages, hours, and working conditions and had the authority to order government seizure of plants that did not comply. Forty plants were seized during the war.

During its tenure the NWLB handled 17,650 disputes affecting 12 million workers. It resolved the controversial issue of union membership through a compromise. Under the principle of maintenance of membership, new hires did not have to join a union, but those who already belonged to a union had to maintain their membership over the life of the contract. Agitation for wage increases caused a more serious disagreement. Because managers wanted to keep production running smoothly and profitably, they were willing to pay higher wages. However, pay raises would conflict with OPA's attempt to combat inflation by stabilizing prices and salaries. In 1942 the NWLB established the "Little Steel Formula," which granted a 15 percent wage increase to match the increase in the cost of living since January 1, 1941, and another 24 percent by 1945. Actually, incomes rose by as much as 70 percent because workers earned overtime pay, which was not covered by wage ceilings. The tremendous increase in output during World War II occurred largely because people worked overtime.

Although incomes were now higher than anyone could have dreamed of during the depression, many union members felt cheated as they watched corporate profits soar in relation to wages. The high point of dissatisfaction came in 1943, when a nationwide railroad strike was narrowly averted. Then John L. Lewis led more than half a million United Mine Workers out on strike, demanding wages higher than the Little Steel Formula allowed. Although Lewis won concessions, he alienated Congress; because he had defied the government during wartime, he became one of the most disliked public figures of the 1940s.

Congress countered Lewis's action by overriding Roosevelt's veto of the Smith-Connally Labor Act of 1943, which required a thirty-day cooling-off period before a strike and prohibited strikes in defense industries entirely. Nevertheless, about 15,000 strikes occurred during the war. Though less than one-tenth of a percent of working hours were lost to strikes, the public perceived the disruptions as far more extensive. Labor unions won acceptance during the war years but also provoked significant public and congressional hostility, which would hamper the labor movement in the postwar years.

Civil Rights during Wartime

A new mood of militancy appeared among the nation's minorities during wartime. World War II disrupted a number of traditional patterns, and many barriers to racial equality tottered or fell. "A wind is rising throughout the world of free men everywhere," Eleanor Roosevelt wrote during the war, "and they will not be kept in bondage." Civil rights leaders pointed out parallels between anti-Semitism in Germany and racial discrimination in America and pledged themselves to a "Double V" campaign: victory over Nazism abroad and victory over racism and inequality at home.

Even before Pearl Harbor, activism was on the rise. In 1940 only 240 of the nation's 100,000 aircraft workers were black, and most of them were janitors. Black leaders demanded that the government require defense contractors to integrate their work forces. When the government took no action, A. Philip Randolph, head of the Brotherhood of Sleeping Car Porters, a black union,

Fighting for Freedom at Home and Abroad
This protester from the Negro Labor Relations League pointedly drew the parallel between blacks serving in the armed forces and a 1941 labor discrimination dispute at a Chicago dairy.
Library of Congress.

announced plans for a "March on Washington" in the summer of 1941. Roosevelt was not a strong supporter of civil rights, but he feared the embarrassment of a massive public protest. Even more, he worried about a disruption of war preparations.

In June 1941, in exchange for Randolph's cancellation of the march, Roosevelt issued Executive Order 8802, declaring "that there shall be no discrimination in the employment of workers in defense industries or government because of race, creed, color, or national origin." To oversee the policy, he established the Fair Employment Practices Committee (FEPC) in the Office of Production Management. Although this federal commitment to minority employment rights was unprecedented, it was limited in scope. For instance, it did not affect segregation in the armed forces. Moreover, the FEPC could not require compliance with its orders and often found that the needs of defense production took precedence over fair employment practices. The FEPC resolved only about one-third of the more than 8,000 complaints it received. Blacks made up 8 percent of defense workers in 1944, probably owing more to the labor shortage than to FEPC prodding.

Encouraged by the ideological climate of the war years, civil rights organizations increased in number and membership. Although the NAACP generally favored lobbying and legal strategies, the student chapter of the NAACP at Howard University used direct tactics. In 1944 it forced several restaurants in Washington, D.C., to serve blacks by picketing them with signs that read, "Are You for Hitler's Way or the American Way? Make Up Your Mind." In Chicago James Farmer helped found the Congress of Racial Equality (CORE), a group that became known nationwide for using direct action such as demonstrations and sit-ins.

An awareness of civil rights was heightened in other ways as well. The Swedish sociologist Gunnar Myrdal wrote an extensive analysis of race relations, *An American Dilemma: The Negro Problem and Modern Democracy* (1944), focusing many white Americans' attention on the issue for the first time. In 1944 the Supreme Court ruled in *Smith v. Allwright* that Texas's all-white primary election, commonly used to disfranchise blacks in southern states, was unconstitutional. These wartime developments laid the groundwork for the civil rights revolution of the 1950s and 1960s (see Voices from Abroad, "German POWs: American Race Relations," p. 845).

Mexican Americans also used the ideological climate of the war to press for change, building on their community's patriotic contributions to national defense and the armed services to challenge long-standing patterns of discrimination and exclusion. In Texas, where it was still common to see signs reading "No Dogs or Mexicans Allowed," community leaders protested segregation in schools and public facilities. In California, Mexican American labor activists argued that defense contractors' refusal to hire resident Mexican aliens violated Executive Order 8802's prohibition of discrimination on the basis of race, creed, color, or national origin.

The Sleepy Lagoon case of 1942 explicitly linked the experiences of Mexican Americans with the broader ideological underpinnings of the war effort. In the summer of 1942 a Mexican American youth was found dead near Sleepy Lagoon, a popular place to hang out in south-central Los Angeles. On exceedingly flimsy evidence, the police charged twenty-two members of a Mexican American gang called the 38th Street Club with murder and conspiracy, and in January 1943 an all-white jury convicted seventeen of the defendants. The Sleepy Lagoon Defense Committee, which one

GERMAN POWs

American Race Relations

———★———

During World War II, Nazi prisoners of war were assigned to various army camps throughout the United States, where their labor was often contracted out to help with the acute shortage of workers caused by war mobilization. German prisoners thus had a unique opportunity to observe American life. Here are some of their observations, mainly centered on the issue of race.

We picked cotton the length of the Mississippi. I'm an agriculturalist, and I know how to handle hard work, but there it was truly very, very hard. It was terribly hot, and we had to bend over all day. We had nothing to drink. . . . There were a great number of Blacks on the plantation. They required us to gather 100 lbs. of cotton a day; but of the Blacks, they demanded two or three times more. . . . For them it was worse than for us. And you have to see how they lived. Their farms: very ugly, very primitive. These people were so exploited. . . .

Me, I was in peas; picking and the canning factory. The farmers liked me, and wanted me to stay after the war, but I wasn't sure. . . . I met some old people of German origin one day, and these poor old people told me: "We feel alone here. It's sad. It's too big. If we could, we would walk back to Germany on foot. . . ." And the Blacks! They were always saying: "We are just like you: Prisoners; Oppressed; Second-class men. . . ."

There was a plumber who came to work in the camp. His name was Gutierrez, and he was Mexican. . . . He was a very nice guy. When he went to the barbershop, he stood in the corner, he did not move, and, as he was "colored," he had to wait until all the Whites were done. You know, things like that upset us very much. . . .

I was in a camp near Miami in Florida. I was one of the scavenger commandos; every morning we went to gather the garbage in the city. . . . People of German origin were the least nice to us. . . . Those who helped us the most, on the contrary, were the Jews. . . . Ah, the Jews and the Blacks.

———

Source: Arnold Krammer, *Nazi Prisoners of War in America* (New York: Stein and Day, 1979), 92–93.

---

scholar has called "the best known and most influential Mexican American–oriented advocacy organ to emerge in California in this period," eventually succeeded in getting the convictions overturned on appeal. The Defense Committee's premise was that the defendants had been deprived of their basic civil rights solely because of their ethnic background. As America fought to preserve democracy abroad, they argued, it must live up to democratic ideals at home.

In Los Angeles white hostility toward Mexican Americans had been smoldering for some time. Male Latino teenagers had organized *pachuco* (youth) gangs, sometimes also called *cholos*. Speaking a hybrid English-Spanish slang called *calo*, they sported slicked-down hair, tattoos, and a distinctive style of dress called the zoot suit, which featured padded shoulders, pegged trousers, clunky shoes, and broad-brimmed felt hats. The young women they escorted favored long coats, huarache sandals, and pompadour hairdos. Although zoot suits were most popular among Latinos, that style

was also taken up by blacks and by a few white working-class teenagers in Los Angeles, Detroit, New York, and Philadelphia as a symbol of alienation and self-assertion.

In July 1943 rumors that a *pachuco* gang had beaten a white sailor set off a four-day riot in Los Angeles, during which white servicemen entered Mexican American neighborhoods and attacked zoot suiters, taking special pleasure in slashing the pegged pants of their victims. The attacks occurred in full view of white police officers, who did nothing to stop the violence. Even as the war years opened new avenues for Mexican American participation in American life, they also brought ugly reminders of the persistence of racism and ethnic hostility.

Politics in Wartime

At a press conference late in 1943 Roosevelt playfully announced that "Dr. Win the War" had replaced "Dr. New Deal." In fact, business executives had already replaced many of the reformers and social activists who had staffed New Deal relief agencies in the 1930s. Although the federal government expanded dramatically during the war years, there was little attempt to use the state to promote social reform on the home front, as had occurred in World War I. An enlarged federal presence was justified only insofar as it assisted war aims.

During the early years of the war Roosevelt rarely pressed for social and economic change, in part because he was preoccupied with military matters but also because he faced certain political realities. The Republicans had picked up 10 seats in the Senate and 47 seats in the House in the 1940 elections, thus bolstering conservatives in Congress who sought to roll back New Deal measures. With little protest, Roosevelt agreed to drop several popular New Deal programs, including the Civilian Conservation Corps, the Works Progress Administration, and the National Youth Administration, which were deemed less necessary once war mobilization brought full employment. Severe budget cuts crippled the Farm Security Administration, which had represented the interests of poor farmers. The speed with which the government terminated those agencies suggested that they had been more a response to the crisis of the depression than a commitment to promoting the general welfare through federal programs. Programs with broad popular support such as Social Security were left untouched, however.

Later in the war Roosevelt began to promise new social welfare measures. In his State of the Union address in 1944 he called for a second bill of rights, which would serve as "a new basis of security and prosperity." This extension of the New Deal identified jobs, adequate food and clothing, decent homes, medical care, and education as basic rights. But the president's sweeping commitment remained largely rhetorical; congressional support for this vast extension of the welfare state did not exist in 1944. It was possible, however, to win some of those rights for a special group of American citizens: veterans. The Servicemen's Readjustment Act (1944), known as the GI Bill of Rights, provided education, job training, medical care, pensions, and mortgage loans for men and women who had served in the armed forces during the war.

Roosevelt's call for more social legislation was part of a plan to woo Democratic voters. In the 1942 election, Republicans picked up seats in both houses of Congress and increased their share of state governorships. The Democrats realized they would have to work hard to maintain the strength of their coalition in 1944. Once again Roosevelt headed the ticket, concluding that the continuation of the war made a fourth term necessary, but the years had taken their toll. Concern about Roosevelt's health and the need for a successor prompted the Democrats to drop Vice-President Henry Wallace, whose outspoken support for labor, civil rights, and domestic reform was too extreme for many party leaders. In Wallace's place they chose Senator Harry S Truman of Missouri. Truman, a World War I veteran and Kansas City haberdasher whose business had failed in the 1920–1921 recession, found more success in politics. Sponsored by Thomas Pendergast, the Democratic boss in Kansas City, he was elected to the Senate in 1934 and again in 1940. Truman became known for heading a Senate investigation of government waste and inefficiency in defense contracts during the war.

The Republicans nominated Governor Thomas E. Dewey of New York. Only forty-two years old, Dewey had won fame fighting organized crime as a U.S. attorney. He accepted the broad outlines of the welfare state and belonged to the internationalist wing of the Republican Party. The 1944 election was the closest since Woodrow Wilson had narrowly defeated Charles Evans Hughes in 1916: Roosevelt received 53.5 percent of the popular vote. The Democrats lost ground among farmers, but most ethnic groups remained solidly Democratic. Roosevelt got his customary support from the South, augmented by the overwhelming allegiance of members of the armed forces, who voted by absentee ballot. The party's margin of victory came from the cities. In urban areas with more than 100,000 people the president drew 60 percent of the vote.

Roosevelt also received strong support from organized labor. Under the prodding of CIO leaders Sidney Hillman and Philip Murray, labor contributed more than $1.5 million, or about 30 percent of the Democratic Party's election funds. The CIO's Political Action Committee canvassed door to door and conducted voter registration campaigns. Organized labor continued to play a significant role in the Democratic Party after the war.

Life on the Home Front

In contrast to World War I, once Congress declared war there was almost no domestic opposition to the nation's role in World War II. Americans fought for their way of life and to preserve democracy against Nazism and Japanese imperialism. Because the enemies seemed so evil and America's will to win was so strong, many remember it as the "good war." By the spring of 1945 soldiers who had completed their military duty, which averaged sixteen months, were beginning to return home. Fighting had been a dirty, bloody job—a far cry from their visions of saving democracy and stopping fascism. Dreams of marriage, a house in the suburbs, and a new car sustained many soldiers through the horror and tedium of the war. In 1947 veterans and their families made up one-fourth of the American population.

"For the Duration"

Although the United States did not suffer the physical devastation that ravaged much of Europe and the Pacific, the war affected the lives of those who stayed behind. Every time relatives of a loved one overseas saw the Western Union boy on his bicycle, they feared a telegram from the War department telling them that their son, husband, or father would not be coming home. Other Americans tolerated small deprivations daily. "Don't you know there's a war on?" became the standard reply to any request that could not be fulfilled. People accepted the fact that their lives would be different "for the duration."

Just like the soldiers in uniform, people on the home front had a job to do. They worked on civilian defense committees, donated blood, collected old newspapers and scrap material for recycling, and served on local rationing and draft boards. About 20 million home "Victory gardens" produced 40 percent of the vegetables grown in the United States. Advertising campaigns displaying the popular "V for Victory" slogan stressed patriotism, and all seven war bond drives were oversubscribed. These endeavors were encouraged by various federal agencies, especially the Office of War Information (OWI).

Perhaps the major source of American's high morale was wartime prosperity. Unemployment disappeared, and per capita income rose from $691 in 1939 to $1,515 in 1945. Despite geographical dislocations and shortages of many items, about 70 percent of Americans admitted midway through the war that they had personally experienced "no real sacrifices." A Red Cross worker put it bluntly: "The war was fun for America. I'm not talking about the poor souls who lost sons and daughters. But for the rest of us, the war was a hell of a good time."

During the war years demographic patterns rebounded from their depression-induced declines. Young people could afford to marry, and the imminent departure of men for military service induced many couples to take that step sooner rather than later. Not all those marriages survived the strain of separation or wartime relocation, and the divorce rate also rose. The birth rate went up, with many babies being conceived before their fathers went off to war. In effect, the wartime birth patterns marked the beginning of the "baby boom" that characterized American culture in the postwar period.

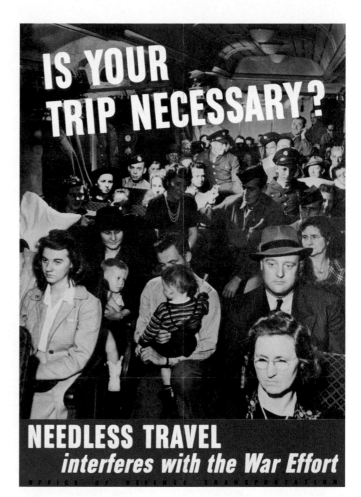

Please Stay Home
With the economy booming and most citizens reporting no great hardships or dislocations, Americans sometimes had to be reminded that there was a war on. A poster from the Office of Defense Transportation pointing out that needless travel interfered with the war effort jogged their memory.
Picture Research Consultants & Archives.

Popular Culture. Popular culture, especially the movies, reinforced the connection between the home front and the troops serving overseas. Average weekly movie attendance soared to over 100 million during the war. Demand was so high that many theaters operated around the clock to accommodate defense workers on the swing and night shifts. Hollywood escaped the restrictions and cutbacks that affected other industries, in part because studio heads argued that movies built morale. Popular actors like Jimmy Stewart and Clark Gable donned uniforms, and many Hollywood directors lent their services to the military. Director Frank Capra's "Why We Fight" films, a documentary series produced for the War department, explained war aims to new soldiers and sailors. John Huston provided an intense portrayal of men in combat in his documentary *The Battle of San Pietro* (1944).

Many movies, encouraged in part by the OWI, had patriotic themes. Stars such as John Wayne, Anthony Quinn, and Spencer Tracy portrayed the heroism of American fighting men in films like *Guadalcanal Diary* (1943), *Back to Bataan* (1945), and *Thirty Seconds over Tokyo* (1945). Other movies, such as *Watch on the Rhine* (1943) and Frank Capra's *Meet John Doe* (1943), warned of the danger of fascism at home and abroad, and the Academy Award–winning *Casablanca* (1943) demonstrated the heroism and patriotism of ordinary citizens. The box-office hit *Since You Went Away* (1943), starring Claudette Colbert as a housewife who took a war job after her husband left to fight, was one of many films that portrayed struggles on the home front. Newsreels accompanying feature films kept the public up to date on the war, as did on-the-spot radio broadcasts by commentators such as Edward R. Murrow. Thus, popular culture reflected America's new international responsibilities at the same time that it built up morale on the home front.

Entertaining the Troops
The original Stage Door Canteen opened in the basement of a Broadway theater in 1942. It provided servicemen with coffee, doughnuts, and big-time entertainment volunteered by Broadway and Hollywood stars. The canteen's popular weekly radio show was the inspiration for the 1943 movie *Stage Door Canteen*.
Lee Boltin Picture Library.

War correspondents such as John Hersey and Ernie Pyle (who was killed in a foxhole on Ie Shima by a Japanese bullet) reported on the GIs (short for "government issue") for readers back home. Reporters often portrayed the GIs as ordinary boys doing their patriotic duty. "When you looked into the eyes of those boys, you did not feel sorry for the Japs: you felt sorry for the boys," John Hersey wrote of the marines fighting in the Pacific battle of Guadalcanal in 1944. Another marine who fought there remembered it as simply a matter of survival: "The only way you could get it over with was to kill them off before they killed you. The war I knew was totally savage."

Throughout the war the Japanese were hated far more than the Germans, in part because Japan had attacked the United States but also because of the racism that was a constant undercurrent of World War II. Whereas Americans often differentiated between evil Nazi leaders and ordinary "good Germans" forced to go along with Nazi excesses, they lumped all Japanese together. Racial epithets such as "slant eyes" and "yellow monkeys" were widely used in conversation, and even respected magazines such as *Time*, *Life*, and *Newsweek* routinely referred to the enemy as "Japs."

Rationing.   For many Americans, the main inconveniences of the war were the limitations placed on consumption. In contrast to the largely voluntaristic approach used during World War I, federal agencies such as the Office of Price Administration subjected almost everything that Americans ate, wore, or used during World War II to rationing or regulation.

Rubber became the first scarce item. The Japanese conquest of Malaya and the Netherlands East Indies cut off 97 percent of America's imports of natural rubber, an essential raw material for war production. An entire new industry in synthetic rubber was born, and by late 1944 the United States was producing 762,000 tons of it a year, mostly for the war effort. Meanwhile, to conserve rubber, the government restricted the sale of tires, a difficult sacrifice for the nation's 30 million car owners, many of whom put their autos up on blocks for the duration. The government also rationed gasoline and fuel oil. Shortages of fuel oil forced schools and restaurants to shorten their hours, and home thermostats were lowered to 65 degrees. Gasoline rationing, introduced in December 1942, represented both a response to depleted domestic gasoline supplies and an attempt to save wear on precious rubber tires. To further discourage gasoline consumption, Congress imposed a nationwide speed limit of 35 miles per hour; as a result, highway death rates dropped dramatically.

By 1943 the amount of meat, butter, and other foods Americans could buy was regulated by a complicated system of rationing points and coupons. Most people cooperated with the restrictions, but almost one-fourth of the population occasionally bought items on the black market, especially meat, gasoline, and cigarettes. People found it especially hard to cut back on sugar. When sugar disappeared from grocery shelves, the government rationed it at a rate of 1 to 1½ cups per person a week. However, the manufacturers of products such as Coca-Cola and Wrigley's chewing gum received unlimited quantities of sugar by convincing the government that their products helped the morale of the men and women in the armed forces.

Shortages of other consumer products also hit the home front. People finally had enough money to buy refrigerators, cars, and radios, but the components of those items—including rubber, copper, and steel—were earmarked for war production. The last Ford rolled off the assembly line in 1942 as automobile plants converted to bomber production. To placate consumers, many companies ran advertisements promising delayed gratification: after the war, they told the public, you can buy that new house and fill it with all the appliances you want.

But some purchases could not wait. Among the most sought-after items on the black market were women's stockings. During the 1930s women had worn silk stockings, but when the war with Japan cut off imports of silk, they switched to nylon. Yet nylon was essential to war production: thirty-six pairs of nylons equaled one parachute. In a dramatic fashion change (and one associated with the image of Rosie the Riveter), many women began wearing slacks in public. The strict rationing of food and other items eased in the summer of 1944, when victory appeared on the horizon.

Migration and Family Life. The war not only affected what people ate, drank, and wore but also affected where they lived. People moved from one part of the country to another in unprecedented numbers. When men volunteered for or were drafted into the armed services, their families often followed them to training bases or points of debarkation. The lure of high-paying defense jobs encouraged others to move. About 15 million Americans changed residence during the war years, half of them by moving to another state. The pace of urbanization increased, but this movement was not simply an exodus from rural to urban areas. About 5.4 million people left farms, but 2.5 million moved onto them. The greatest number of people went west. The western states not only served as staging areas for the war in the Pacific but also had room for the new ship- and airplane-building industries. Their remote regions (for instance, Hanford, Washington, and Los Alamos, New Mexico) were ideal places to conduct top-secret research.

As a center of defense production California was affected by wartime migration more than any other state. "The Second Gold Rush Hits the West," headlined the *San Francisco Chronicle* in 1943. During the war one-tenth of all federal dollars went to California, and the state turned out one-sixth of total war production. California welcomed nearly 3 million new residents during the war, a 53 percent growth in population. They went where the defense jobs were—to Los Angeles, San Diego, and the San Francisco Bay area. Some towns grew practically overnight: just two years after the

A Family Effort
After migrating from the Midwest to Portland, Oregon, fifteen members of the family of John R. Brauckmiller (sixth from left) found jobs at Portland's Swan Island shipyard. A local newspaper pronounced them "the shipbuildingest family in America."
Ralph Vincent, *The Journal*, Portland, OR.

Kaiser Corporation opened a shipyard in Richmond, the population had quadrupled.

Migration and relocation often caused strains. In many towns with defense industries, housing was scarce and public transportation inadequate. Conflicts over public space and recreation erupted between old-timers and newcomers. Of special concern were the young people the war had set adrift from traditional community restraints. Newspapers were filled with stories of "latchkey" children who stayed home alone while their mothers worked in defense plants. Adolescents were even more of a problem. Teenage girls who hung around army bases looking for a good time were known as "victory girls." In 1942 and 1943 juvenile delinquency seemed to be reaching epidemic proportions.

Another significant result of the growth of war industries was the migration of more than a million African Americans to defense centers in California, Illinois, Michigan, Ohio, and Pennsylvania. The migrants'

need for jobs and housing led to racial conflict in several cities, with some of the worst racial violence taking place in the Detroit area. Early in 1942 black families encountered resistance and intimidation when they tried to move into the Sojourner Truth housing project in the Polish community of Hamtramck. In June 1943 a major race riot in Detroit itself left 34 people dead, including 25 blacks. Racial conflicts broke out in 47 cities across the country during 1943.

Although racial confrontations and zoot suit riots recalled the widespread racial tensions of World War I, the mood on the home front was generally calm in the 1940s. Leftists and communists faced little domestic repression, mainly because the Soviet Union became an ally of the United States after Pearl Harbor. German culture and German Americans did not come under suspicion, nor did most Italian Americans (unless they were fascist sympathizers), largely because there was little threat of either a German or Italian invasion.

Zoot Suits
Zoot suits gained wide popularity among American youth during the war. In 1943 this well-dressed teenager greased his hair in a ducktail and wore a loosely cut coat with padded shoulders ("fingertips") that reached midthigh, baggy pleated pants cut tight ("pegged") around the ankles, and a long gold watch chain. Corbis-Bettmann.

Japanese Relocation

The internment of Japanese Americans on the West Coast was a glaring exception to this record of tolerance. California had a long history of antagonism toward both Japanese and Chinese immigrants (see Chapters 16 and 21). The Japanese Americans, who clustered together in highly visible communities, were a small, politically impotent minority, numbering only about 112,000 in the three coastal states. Unlike German Americans and Italian Americans, the Japanese stood out. "A Jap's a Jap," General John DeWitt stated. "It makes no difference whether he is an American citizen or not." This sort of sentiment, coupled with fears of the West Coast's vulnerability to attack and the inflammatory rhetoric of newspapers and local politicians, fueled mounting demands that the region be rid of supposed Japanese spies.

In early 1942, in Executive Order 9022, Roosevelt approved a War department plan to intern Japanese Americans in relocation camps for the rest of the war. In March 1942 Milton Eisenhower, a career civil servant and the brother of General Dwight D. Eisenhower, took over the War Relocation Authority (WRA), a civilian agency created to carry out that policy. Despite the lack of evidence of disloyalty or sedition—no Japanese American was ever charged with espionage—few public leaders opposed the plan.

The relocation announcement shocked Japanese Americans, more than two-thirds of whom were native-born American citizens. (They were *Nisei*, the children of the foreign-born *Issei*.) The government gave families only a few days to dispose of their belongings and prepare for relocation. Businesses that had taken a lifetime to build were liquidated overnight, and speculators snapped up Japanese real estate for a fraction of its value.

Behind Barbed Wire
As part of the forced relocation of 120,000 Japanese Americans, Los Angeles photographer Toyo Miyatake and his family were sent to Manzanar, a camp in the California desert east of the Sierra Nevada. Miyatake secretly began shooting photographs of the camp, although he eventually received permission from the authorities to document life in the camp. This photograph of three young boys behind barbed wire with a watchtower in the distance must have been shot with official sanction because the photographer is on the other side of the barbed wire. It gives new meaning to the phrase "prisoners of war."
Toyo Miyatake.

A Japanese American music teacher got only $30 for her treasured piano. Another woman broke every piece of her family's heirloom porcelain rather than accept $17.50 from a secondhand dealer for it. But most Japanese Americans accepted the policy stoically. "*Shikata gu nai*," they said—it can't be helped, hardships must be borne.

Relocation took place in two stages. First the government sent Japanese Americans to temporary assembly centers such as the Santa Anita racetrack in Los Angeles, where they lived in stables that horses had occupied a few days earlier. Then they were moved to ten permanent camps away from the coast. Those internment camps in California, Arizona, Utah, Colorado, Wyoming, Idaho, and Arkansas "were in places where nobody had lived before and no one has lived since," a historian commented (Map 26.1). Milton Eisenhower had hoped the relocation camps would resemble the CCC youth camps of the New Deal, but the barbed wire and enforced communal living mocked his hopes. Although they were sometimes compared to Nazi concentration camps, the relocation centers more closely resembled Indian reservations (see American Voices, "Monica Sone: Japanese Relocation," p. 852).

All ten camps were in hot, dusty places, and their communal bathroom and dining facilities made family life nearly impossible. Eight people often lived in a space measuring 25 by 20 feet. No one had any privacy: when one baby cried, babies cried up and down the barracks. Boredom and generational differences between the *Issei*, with an average age of fifty-five, and the *Nisei*, with an average age of seventeen, added to the tensions.

Almost every Japanese American in California, Oregon, and Washington was involuntarily detained for some period during World War II. Ironically, the Japanese Americans who made up one-third of the population of Hawaii, and presumably posed a greater threat because of their numbers and proximity to Japan, were not affected. Less vulnerable to detention because of

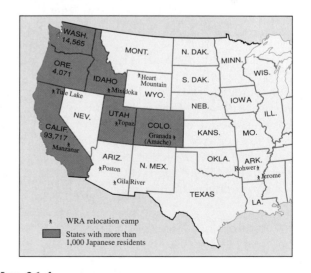

MAP 26.1
WRA Relocation Camps
In 1942 the government ordered 112,000 Japanese Americans living on the West Coast into internment camps in the nation's interior because of their supposed threat to public safety. Some of the camps were as far away as Arkansas.

MONICA SONE
Japanese Relocation

———————★———————

Monica (Itoi) Sone's autobiography, Nisei Daughter *(1953), tells the story of Japanese relocation from the perspective of a young woman in Seattle, Washington. Here she describes the Itoi family's forced evacuation to a temporary encampment called Camp Harmony; later they were moved to a settlement in Idaho. Although her parents spent the entire war in the camp, Monica Sone was allowed to leave in 1943 to attend college in Indiana.*

We felt fortunate to be assigned to a room at the end of the barracks because we had just one neighbor to worry about. The partition wall separating the rooms was only seven feet high with an opening of four feet at the top, so at night, Mrs. Funai next door could tell when Sumi was still sitting up in bed in the dark, putting her hair up. *"Mah,* Sumi-*chan,"* Mrs. Funai would say through the plank wall, "are you curling your hair tonight again? Do you put it up every night?" Sumi would put her hands on her hips and glare defiantly at the wall.

The block monitor, an impressive Nisei who looked like a star tackle with his crouching walk, came around the first night to tell us that we must all be inside our room by nine o'clock every night. At ten o'clock, he rapped at the door again, yelling, "Lights out!" and Mother rushed to turn the light off not a second later.

Throughout the barracks, there were a medley of creaking cots, whimpering infants and explosive night coughs. Our attention was riveted on the intense little wood stove which glowed so violently I feared it would melt right down to the floor. We soon learned that this condition lasted for only a short time, after which it suddenly turned into a deep freeze. Henry and Father took turns at the stove to produce the harrowing blast which all but singed our army blankets, but did not penetrate through them. As it grew quieter in the barracks, I could hear the light patter of rain. Soon I felt the "splat! splat!" of raindrops digging holes into my face. The dampness on my pillow spread like a mortal bleeding, and I finally had to get out and haul my cot toward the center of the room. In a short while Henry was up. "I've got multiple leaks, too. Have to complain to the landlord first thing in the morning."

All through the night I heard people getting up, dragging cots around. I stared at our little window, unable to sleep. I was glad Mother had put up a makeshift curtain on the window for I noticed a powerful beam of light sweeping across it every few seconds. The lights came from high towers placed around the camp where guards with Tommy guns kept a twenty-four hour vigil. I remembered the wire fence encircling us, and a knot of anger tightened in my breast. What was I doing behind a fence like a criminal? If there were accusations to be made, why hadn't I been given a fair trial? Maybe I wasn't considered an American anymore. My citizenship wasn't real, after all. Then what was I? I was certainly not a citizen of Japan as my parents were. On second thought, even Father and Mother were more alien residents of the United States than Japanese nationals for they had little tie with their mother country. In their twenty-five years in America, they had worked and paid their taxes to their adopted government as any other citizen.

Of one thing I was sure. The wire fence was real. I no longer had the right to walk out of it. It was because I had Japanese ancestors. It was also because some people had little faith in the ideas and ideals of democracy. They said that after all these were but words and could not possibly insure loyalty. New laws and camps were surer devices. I finally buried my face in my pillow to wipe out burning thoughts and snatch what sleep I could.

_____

Source: Monica Sone, *Nisei Daughter* (Boston: Little, Brown and Co., 1953), 176–178.

the islands' multiracial heritage, the Japanese also provided much of the unskilled labor on the islands. The Hawaiian economy could not function without them.

Cracks soon appeared in the relocation policy. Even with stepped-up recruitment of Mexican Americans through the *bracero* program, a labor shortage in farming led the government to furlough seasonal Japanese American agricultural workers from the camps as early as 1942. About 4,300 young people who had been in college when the relocation order came through were allowed to stay in school as long as they transferred out of the West Coast military zone. Another route out of the camps was enlistment in the armed services. The 442d Infantry Combat Team, a segregated unit serving in Europe and composed entirely of *Nisei* volunteers, was actually the most decorated unit in the armed forces.

The Supreme Court upheld the constitutionality of internment as a legitimate exercise of power during wartime in *Hirabayashi v. United States* (1943) and in *Korematsu v. United States* (1944). It was not until 1988, after years of lobbying by Japanese American groups, that Congress decided to issue a public apology and to give $20,000 in cash to each of the 60,000 surviving internees—small restitution indeed, but evidence that this shameful episode has been burned into the national conscience.

Fighting and Winning the War

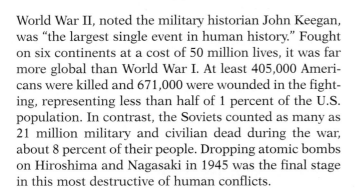

World War II, noted the military historian John Keegan, was "the largest single event in human history." Fought on six continents at a cost of 50 million lives, it was far more global than World War I. At least 405,000 Americans were killed and 671,000 were wounded in the fighting, representing less than half of 1 percent of the U.S. population. In contrast, the Soviets counted as many as 21 million military and civilian dead during the war, about 8 percent of their people. Dropping atomic bombs on Hiroshima and Nagasaki in 1945 was the final stage in this most destructive of human conflicts.

Wartime Aims and Strategies

The Allied coalition was composed mainly of Great Britain, the United States, and the Soviet Union, with other nations, notably China and France, playing lesser roles. Franklin Roosevelt, Britain's Winston Churchill, and Joseph Stalin, the premier of the Soviet Union, took the lead in setting overall strategy. The Atlantic Charter, drafted aboard ship during the Churchill-Roosevelt rendezvous off the Newfoundland coast in August 1941, formed the basis of the Allied vision of the postwar international order. However, Stalin had not been part of the agreement, and that would cause later disagreement over its goals.

Roosevelt's unswerving commitment to Britain's survival provided the basis for a strong, if not always smooth, relationship with Churchill. (Roosevelt's aide Harry Hopkins described his own role as that of a "catalytic agent between two prima donnas.") Stalin, however, was something of a mystery. He and Roosevelt did not meet until late in 1943. Although the United States and Great Britain disagreed on issues such as the postwar fate of colonial empires, the potential for conflict with the Soviet Union was far greater.

As far back as the lend-lease negotiations of early 1941, Churchill and Roosevelt had agreed that defeating Germany would be the first military priority because of that country's huge armies, massive industrial capacity, and mastery of technology. One way to wear down the Germans was to open a second front on the European continent, preferably in France. The Russians strongly argued for this strategy because it would draw German troops away from the Eastern Front and Russian soil. The issue came up so many times that the Soviet foreign minister, Vyacheslav Molotov, was said to know only four English words: *yes*, *no*, and *second front*.

Though Roosevelt assured Stalin informally that such a front would be opened in 1942, Churchill opposed the idea because he feared British troops would be trapped in a destructive ground war in France just as they had been during World War I. More practically, a second front was moot until American war production was raised to full capacity, since such a huge undertaking would depend primarily on American troops and supplies. As a result, for most of the war the Soviet Union bore the brunt of the land battle against Germany. Roosevelt and Churchill's foot-dragging infuriated Stalin, who was already suspicious about American and British intentions. His mistrust and bitterness carried over into the postwar world in the Cold War that followed the Allied victory.

At various points during the war the three leaders of the Grand Alliance met to discuss military strategy and plan the postwar peace. In January 1943 Roosevelt and Churchill met in Casablanca, Morocco; Stalin did not attend because the Battle of Stalingrad had reached a crucial point. The main outcome of the conference was the Allied demand for unconditional surrender of the Axis powers as a condition for peace. In November 1943 Roosevelt, Churchill, and the Chinese leader, Jiang Jieshi (Chiang Kai-shek), met in Cairo to discuss military operations in the Pacific theater; this conference was designed to keep China in the war. To Roosevelt's dismay, Jiang seemed more interested in fighting the communist revolution in his own country (see Chapter 27) than in mobilizing the Chinese people to expel the Japanese invaders.

Traveling directly from Cairo to Teheran, Iran, Roosevelt finally met Stalin late in November 1943. At the Teheran Conference Roosevelt and Churchill agreed to Stalin's demand for a second front within six months. In return, Stalin promised to join the fight against Japan after the war in Europe ended, a promise he kept. The three leaders also issued the Teheran Declaration, in which they welcomed the cooperation of all nations in the war and invited them to join the Big Three in a "world family of democratic nations." Churchill and Roosevelt also agreed tacitly to Stalin's demand that Poland's borders be redrawn to give the Soviet Union more territory. But the three leaders disagreed sharply about who should control the rest of Poland and the other Eastern European states. Roosevelt expressed confidence that the personal rapport he had developed with Stalin would aid postwar relations among the superpowers, but Stalin's territorial ambitions in Eastern Europe foreshadowed later divisions.

The War in Europe

During the first six months of 1942 the military news was so bad that it threatened to swamp the Grand Alliance. The Allies suffered severe defeats on land and sea throughout Europe and Asia. German armies pushed deeper into Soviet territory, reaching the outskirts of Moscow and Leningrad; simultaneously they started an offensive in North Africa aimed at seizing the Suez Canal, the critical transportation link to Africa and the Asian subcontinent. At sea German submarines were crippling American convoys carrying supplies to Europe. Since the United States was the main supplier of oil to the Allies, those attacks struck at the heart of the war effort, which was increasingly dependent on petroleum-based military equipment such as tanks and airplanes.

The turning point of the war in Europe occurred in the winter of 1942–1943, when the Soviets halted the German advance in the Battle of Stalingrad. By 1944, Stalin's forces had driven the German army out of the Soviet Union. Meanwhile the Allies launched a major offensive in North Africa, Churchill's substitute for a second front in France. Between November 1942 and May 1943 Allied troops under the leadership of Generals Dwight D. Eisenhower and George S. Patton defeated Germany's crack Afrika Korps led by General Erwin Rommel.

From Africa the Allied command followed Churchill's strategy of attacking the Axis powers through what he called its "soft underbelly": Sicily and the Italian peninsula. In July 1943 the fascist regime of Benito Mussolini fell, and Italy's new government joined the Allies. The Allied forces invaded Italy in the following fall, but the mountainous terrain and heavy resistance from German troops kept them from entering Rome until June 1944 (Map 26.2). The last German forces in Italy did not surrender until May 1945.

D-Day.   The long-awaited invasion of France to open the second front came on D-Day, the code name for the date of the Allied landing—June 6, 1944. That morning, after an agonizing delay caused by bad weather, the largest fleet ever assembled moved across the English Channel.

Hitting the Beach at Normandy
These American solidiers, part of almost 150,000 Allied troops, stormed the beaches of Normandy, France, on D-Day, June 6, 1944. More than a million Allied troops came ashore during the next month. Filmmaker Stephen Spielberg re-created the carnage and confusion of the landing in the opening scene of *Saving Private Ryan* (1998).
Library of Congress.

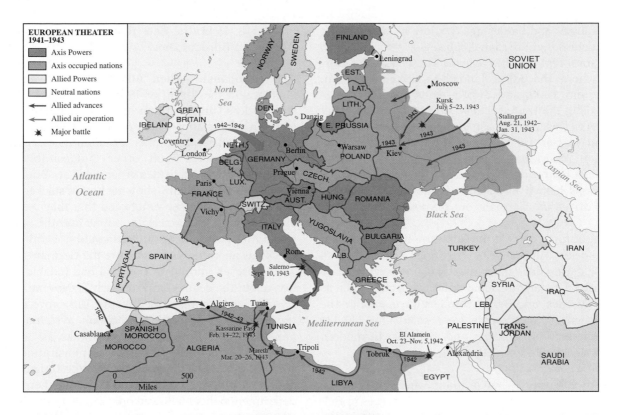

MAP 26.2
World War II in Europe
a. 1941–1943 Hitler's Germany reached its greatest extent in 1942, when Nazi forces stalled at Leningrad and Stalingrad. The tide of battle turned in the fall, when the Soviet army launched a massive counterattack at Stalingrad and Allied forces began to drive the Germans from North Africa. In 1943 the Allies invaded Sicily and the Italian mainland. **b. 1944–1945** On June 6, 1944 (D-Day), the Allies finally invaded France. It took almost a year for the Allied forces to close in on Berlin—the Soviets from the east and the Americans, British, and French from the west. Germany surrendered on May 8, 1945.

While airplanes and battleships offshore bombarded the German defenses, more than 4,000 vessels ferried troops, trucks, tanks, and supplies ashore. The beaches of Normandy where the Allies landed—code-named Utah, Omaha, Juno, Gold, and Sword—soon became household words in the United States, sites of great and quiet bravery as well as terrible casualties and death. Under the command of General Dwight Eisenhower, more than 1.5 million American, British, and Canadian soldiers crossed the Channel over the next few days. In August the Allied troops helped liberate Paris, and by September they had driven the Germans out of most of France and Belgium.

In the autumn of 1944 the German military situation looked hopeless. All that year, long-range Allied bombers had made daring daylight raids, damaging Nazi military and industrial installations and pulverizing cities such as Cologne, Dresden, and Berlin, the German capital. In the air campaign 305,000 people were killed and 780,000 were wounded, both soldiers and civilians. In modern war no one was safe from attack.

Victory in Europe. The Germans were not ready to give up, however. In December 1944 their forces in Belgium mounted an attack that began the Battle of the Bulge, so called because it made a dent in the Allied defenses. After ten days of heavy fighting in what was to be the final German offensive of the war, the Allies regained their momentum and pushed the Germans back across the Rhine River. Their goal was to take Berlin. American and British troops led the drive from the west, while Soviet troops advanced from the east through Poland, reaching Berlin first. On April 30, with much of Berlin in rubble from Allied bombing, Hitler committed suicide in his bunker. Germany surrendered

on May 8, 1945, the date that became known as V-E (Victory in Europe) Day.

The Holocaust. When Allied troops advanced into Germany in the spring of 1945, they came face to face with Hitler's "final solution of the Jewish question": the extermination camps where 6 million Jews had been put to death, along with another 6 million Poles, Slavs, Gypsies, homosexuals, and other "undesirables." Photographs from Nazi death camps at Buchenwald, Dachau, and Auschwitz, showing bodies stacked like firewood and survivors so emaciated that they were barely alive, horrified the American public and the rest of the world. But government officials could not claim that no one knew about the camps before the German surrender. The Roosevelt administration had had reliable information about the death camps as early as November 1942.

The lack of response by the U.S. government to the Holocaust—the Nazi regime's systematic near-annihilation of European Jewry—ranks as one of the gravest failures of the Roosevelt administration. So few Jews escaped the Holocaust because the United States—and the rest of the world—would not take them in. State department policies allowed only 21,000 refugees to enter this country during the war. The War Refugee Board, established in 1944 with little support from the Roosevelt administration, eventually helped save about 200,000 Jews. Several factors combined to inhibit U.S. action: anti-Semitism; fear of economic competition from a flood of refugees in a country just recovering from the depression; failure of the media to grasp the magnitude of the horror and publicize it accordingly; and failure of religious leaders, Jews and non-Jews alike, to speak out.

In justifying the American course of action, Roosevelt claimed that winning the war would be the strongest con-

The Living Dead
When Allied troops advanced into Germany in the spring of 1945, they came face to face with what had long been rumored—concentration camps, Adolf Hitler's "final solution of the Jewish question." Margaret Bourke-White was one of the first photographers on the scene. This haunting image from the Buchenwald death camp appeared in *Life* magazine.
Margaret Bourke-White, *Life* Magazine. © Time, Inc.

tribution America could make to liberating the camps. But it is hard to escape the conclusion that the United States could have done much more to lessen the Holocaust's terrible human toll.

The War in the Pacific

After the victory in Europe the Allies still had to defeat Japan. American forces bore the brunt of the fighting in the Pacific, just as the Russians had done in the land war in Europe. At the beginning of 1942 the news from the Pacific was uniformly grim. In the wake of Pearl Harbor, Japan had scored quickly with seaborne invasions of Hong Kong, Wake Island, and Guam. Japanese forces conquered much of Burma, Malaya, and the Philippines as well as the Solomon Islands and began to threaten Australia and India (see American Voices, "Anton Bilek: The War in the Pacific," p. 858). Japan achieved this huge territorial expansion in only three months. One of the few boosts for American morale came on April 18, 1942, when Colonel James H. Doolittle led sixteen American bombers on the first air raid on Tokyo, but the attack had little military value.

The more significant battles were far to the south. On May 7–8, 1942, in the Battle of the Coral Sea near southern New Guinea, American naval forces halted the Japanese offensive against Australia. In June, at the island of Midway, the Americans inflicted crucial damage on the Japanese fleet. For the first time, a major sea battle was waged—and decided—primarily by planes launched from aircraft carriers that never came within sight of each other. Submarines also played an important role in the naval battles, but the human cost was high: 22 percent of American submariners lost their lives during the war—the highest death rate in any branch of the armed services.

After the Battle of Midway the American military command, under General Douglas MacArthur and Admiral Chester W. Nimitz, took the offensive in the Pacific, adopting a plan of winning strategic positions essential for an eventual direct assault against Japan. For the next eighteen months American forces advanced arduously from one island to the next, winning major victories at Tulagi and Guadalcanal in the Solomon Islands and at Tarawa and Makin in the Gilberts. They reached the Marshall Islands in early 1944. In October 1944 the reconquest of the Philippines began with a victory in the Battle of Leyte Gulf, a massive naval encounter in which the Japanese lost practically their entire fleet whereas the Americans suffered only minimal losses (Map 26.3).

By early 1945 victory over Japan was in sight. The campaign in the Pacific moved slowly toward what military leaders anticipated would be a massive and costly invasion of Japan. To put U.S. planes within striking distance of Tokyo, Americans needed to capture Iwo Jima and Okinawa. In some of the fiercest fighting of the war, the marines sustained more than 20,000 casualties at Iwo Jima, including 6,000 dead; at Okinawa the toll reached 7,600 dead and 32,000 wounded. The closer U.S. forces got to the Japanese home islands, the more fiercely the Japanese fought. On Iwo Jima almost all of the 21,000 Japanese died.

By mid-1945 Japan's army, navy, and air force had suffered devastating losses. American bombing of the mainland had killed about 330,000 civilians and crippled the Japanese economy. In a last-ditch effort to stem the tide, Japanese pilots began suicidal kamikaze missions, crashing their planes and boats into American ships. This desperate action, combined with the Japanese military leadership's refusal to surrender, suggested that Japan would keep up the fight despite overwhelming losses. Based on the fighting at Okinawa and Iwo Jima, American military commanders grimly predicted millions of casualties in the upcoming invasion.

Planning the Postwar World

In February 1945 Roosevelt, Churchill, and Stalin held what would be their last conference at Yalta, a Black Sea resort. Victory in Europe and the Pacific was in sight, but no agreement had been reached on the peace to come. Roosevelt remained focused on maintaining Allied unity, which he saw as the key to postwar peace and stability. The fate of British colonies such as India, where an independence movement had already begun, caused friction between Roosevelt and Churchill. A more serious source of conflict was Stalin's desire for a band of Soviet-controlled satellite states to protect the Soviet Union's western border. With Soviet armies in control of much of Eastern Europe, Stalin had become increasingly inflexible on that issue, insisting that he needed friendly (that is, Soviet-dominated) governments there to provide a buffer zone to guarantee Soviet national security. Roosevelt acknowledged the legitimacy of that demand but, with the Atlantic Charter's principle of self-determination in mind, hoped for democratically elected governments in Poland and the neighboring countries. The two goals proved mutually exclusive.

At Yalta, Roosevelt and Churchill agreed in principle to the idea of a Soviet sphere of influence in Eastern Europe but deliberately left its dimensions vague. Stalin in return pledged to hold "free and unfettered elections" at an unspecified time. (Those elections never took place.) The compromise reached at Yalta was open to multiple interpretations. Admiral William D. Leahy, Roosevelt's chief military aide, described the agreement as "so elastic that the Russians can stretch it all the way from Yalta to Washington without technically breaking it."

Anton Bilek
The War in the Pacific

———————— ★ ————————

*A*nton Bilek grew up in Southern Illinois and enlisted in the army in 1939 at nineteen because jobs were hard to get. Sent to the Philippines in 1940, he was taken prisoner when the Japanese over-ran the Bataan peninsula in April 1942. He describes the infamous "Bataan Death March" and its aftermath.

The next morning, we got orders to get rid of all our arms and wait for the Japanese to come. General King had surrendered Bataan. They came in. First thing they did, they lined us up and started searchin' us. Anybody that had a ring or a wrist-watch or a pair of gold-rimmed spectacles, they took 'em. Glasses they'd throw on the floor and break 'em and put the gold rims in their pockets. If you had a ring, you handed it over. If you couldn't get it off, the guy'd put the bayonet right up against your neck. Fortunately I never wore a ring. I couldn't afford one.

They moved us about on the road. Here was a big stream of Americans and Filipinos marchin' by. They told us to get in the back of this column. This was the start of the Death March. (A long, deep sigh.) That was a sixty-mile walk. Here we were, three, four months on half-rations, less. The men were already thin, in shock. Undernourished, full of malaria. Dysentery is beginning to spread. This is even before the surrender. We had two hospitals chuck-full of men. Bataan peninsula was the worst malaria-infected province of the Philippines.

The Japanese emptied out the hospitals. Anybody that could walk, they forced 'em into line. You found all kinda bodies along the road. Some of 'em bloated, some had just been killed. If you fell out to the side, you were either shot by the guards or you were bayoneted and left there. We lost somewhere between six hundred and seven hundred Americans in the four days of the march. The Filipinos lost close to ten thousand. At San Fernando, we were stuffed into boxcars and taken about thirty-five miles further north. The cars were closed, you couldn't get air. In the hot sun, the temperature got up there. You couldn't fall down because you were held up by the guys stacked around you. You had a lot of guys blow their top, start screamin'. From there, they marched us another seven, eight miles to Camp O'Donnell, which was built hurriedly for the Philippine army. It was built like the huts were built, of native bamboo and *nipa* and grass. There must've been about nine thousand of us and about fifty thousand Filipinos. Americans in one camp, Filipinos in the other. We had to leave after a month and a half. The monsoon season was starting. A hurricane blew down two of the barracks. Eighty men were killed. Just crushed.

I went blind, momentarily. It scared the hell out of me. I was at the hospital for about two weeks, and the doctor, an American, said, "There's nothing I can do with you. Rest is the only thing. Eat all the rice you can get. That's your only medicine." That's the one thing that pulled me through. He said, "You won't have to go on details." The Japanese were comin' in and they'd take two, three hundred and start 'em repairing a bridge that was blown up. We were losin' a lot of men there. They couldn't work any more. They were dyin'. . . .

I'm back home. It's all over with. I'd like to forget it. I had nothin' against the Japanese. But I don't drive a Toyota or own a Sony. . . . A lotta friends I lost. We had 185 men in our squadron when the war started. Three and a half years later, when we were liberated from a prison camp in Japan, we were 39 left. It's them I think about. Men I played ball with, men I worked with, men I associated with. I miss 'em.

———————————

Source: Studs Terkel, *"The Good War": An Oral History of World War Two* (New York: Pantheon Books, 1984), 85, 90–91, 95–96.

At Yalta the three leaders also proceeded with plans to divide Germany into four zones to be controlled by the United States, Great Britain, France, and the Soviet Union. Berlin, the capital city that lay in the middle of the Soviet zone, would also be partitioned among the four powers. The divisive issue of German reparations remained unsettled.

The Big Three made further progress toward the establishment of a postwar international organization in the form of the United Nations. Roosevelt, determined to

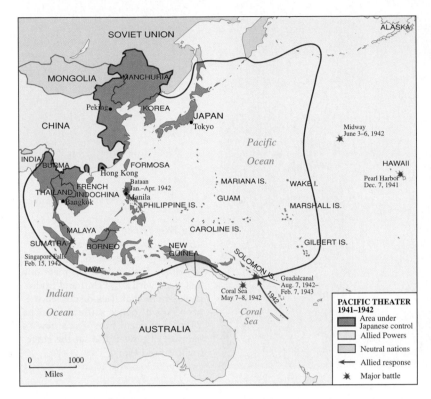

MAP 26.3
World War II in the Pacific
a. 1941–1942 After the attack on Pearl Harbor in December 1941 the Japanese rapidly extended their domination in the Pacific. The Japanese flag soon flew as far east as the Marshall and Gilbert Islands and as far south as the Solomon Islands and parts of New Guinea. Japan also controlled the Philippines, much of Southeast Asia, and parts of China, including Hong Kong. American naval victories at the Coral Sea and Midway stopped further Japanese expansion.

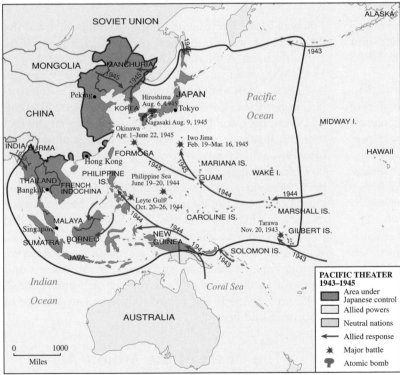

b. 1943–1945 Allied forces retook the islands in the Central Pacific in 1943 and 1944 and the Philippines early in 1945. The capture of Iwo Jima and Okinawa put U.S. bombers in position to attack Japan itself. The Japanese offered to surrender on August 10, after the United States dropped atomic bombs on Hiroshima and Nagasaki.

avoid Woodrow Wilson's mistakes in regard to the League of Nations, had already cultivated congressional backing; realizing that such an organization would be impotent without the Soviets' participation, he cultivated their support as well. British, American, and Soviet representatives had already met at Dumbarton Oaks, an estate in Washington, D.C., in September 1944 to begin

planning the structure of the organization. At Yalta the Big Three agreed that the Security Council of the United Nations would include the five major Allied powers—the United States, Britain, France, China, and the Soviet Union—plus six nations elected on a rotating basis. They also decided that the permanent members of the Security Council should have veto power over decisions of the

The Big Three at Yalta
With victory in Europe at hand, Roosevelt journeyed to Yalta, on the Black Sea, in 1945, to meet one last time with Churchill and Stalin. It was here that they discussed the problems of peace settlements. The Yalta agreement mirrored a new balance of power and set the stage for the Cold War.
Franklin D. Roosevelt Library.

General Assembly, in which all nations would be represented. Roosevelt, Churchill, and Stalin announced that the United Nations would convene in San Francisco on April 25, 1945.

Roosevelt returned to the United States in February, visibly exhausted by his 14,000-mile trip. He neglected to inform the American public of the concessions he had made to maintain the increasingly fragile wartime alliance. When he reported to Congress on the Yalta agreements, he made an unusual acknowledgment of his physical infirmity. Referring to the heavy steel braces he wore on his legs, he asked Congress to excuse him if he gave his speech sitting down. The sixty-three-year-old president was a very sick man, suffering from heart failure and high blood pressure. On April 12, 1945, during a short visit to his vacation home in Warm Springs, Georgia, Roosevelt suffered a cerebral hemorrhage and died.

Many Americans could not imagine any leader other than Franklin Roosevelt in the White House. Those who reached adulthood in the 1930s and 1940s had never known another president. In both depression and war he led the country through perilous times. As a global strategist he grasped America's predominant role and helped educate the country to accept its new international responsibilities. Roosevelt's model of leadership proved a difficult legacy for future presidents to match.

V-E Day came less than a month after Roosevelt died and Harry Truman succeeded to the presidency.

The war in the Pacific ended after Truman ordered the dropping of atomic bombs on two Japanese cities, Hiroshima on August 6 and Nagasaki on August 9, 1945. Many later questioned why the United States did not warn Japan about the attack or choose a noncivilian target; the rationale for dropping the second bomb was even less clear. Other critics suggested that the fact that the Japanese were a nonwhite race facilitated the momentous decision to drop the bombs. At the time, however, the belief that Japan's military leaders would never surrender unless their country was utterly devastated convinced policy makers that they had to deploy the devastating new weapon. The atomic bombs killed 100,000 people at Hiroshima and 60,000 at Nagasaki. Tens of thousands more died slowly of radiation poisoning. Japan offered to surrender on August 10 and signed a formal treaty of surrender on September 2, 1945. World War II had ended, but a new atomic age of insecurity had begun.

The Onset of the Atomic Age

The development of the atomic bomb was closely linked to wartime military strategy. In December 1938 German scientists had discovered that the nuclei of atoms could be split into smaller particles, a process called fission. With materials prepared from uranium, a chain reaction of nuclear fission would release tremendous amounts of energy. American scientists, including many refugees from fascist Italy and Nazi

Hiroshima
This was all that remained of Hiroshima after the dropping of an atomic bomb on August 6, 1945. The shell of Hiroshima's Museum of Science and Industry (visible in the photo), one of the few buildings left standing after the bomb, later became the center of a memorial to those who died in the blast.
National Archives.

Germany, produced the first controlled chain reaction on December 2, 1942, at the University of Chicago.

Scientists soon began working frantically to harness nuclear reactions for military purposes. Their goal was the development of an atomic bomb for use against Germany or, later, Japan. The secret research, called the Manhattan Project, cost $2 billion, employed 120,000 people, and involved the construction of thirty-seven installations in nineteen states under the direction of General Leslie R. Groves of the U.S. Army Corps of Engineers. In the final stages a team consisting of most of the country's top physicists assembled the bomb at an isolated desert site in Los Alamos, New Mexico. All this was hidden from Congress, the American people, and even Vice-President Truman. The secrecy and scope of this alliance between science and government constitute a dramatic example of how much the power of the state grew during wartime.

Roosevelt had followed the bomb's progress closely. He and his advisors had planned to deploy the bomb to end the war without the dreadful number of American casualties projected to result from an invasion of Japan. At the same time, policy makers hoped that the possession of such a powerful weapon—the "master card," in the words of Secretary of War Henry Stimson—might enhance American power in the postwar world. Instead, the new weapon became the first step in a deadly arms race between the United States and the Soviet Union.

Until the last moment the scientists did not know if the atomic bomb would work. On July 16, 1945, near Alamogordo, New Mexico, they watched in wonder as the test bomb exploded in a huge mushroom cloud. President Truman received news of the successful detonation in Potsdam, near Berlin, where he was about to meet with Churchill and Stalin in the final wartime conference about the shape of postwar Europe (see Chapter 27). Truman, who had not known about the bomb before he became president, was ecstatic about its potential, telling aides, "This is the greatest thing in history." Others were not so sure. J. Robert Oppenheimer, one of the leading scientists on the Manhattan Project, watched the test on that July morning in the New Mexico desert. Overwhelmed by its frightening power, he recalled the words from the Bhagavad Gita, a Hindu sacred text: "I am become Death, Destroyer of Worlds."

Franklin Roosevelt's death and the dropping of the atomic bomb came at a critical juncture in world affairs. Many questions had been left deliberately unresolved in the hopes of keeping the wartime alliance intact to guide the transition to peace. But as the war ended, issues such as the fate of Poland and Germany demanded action. The resulting compromises, not all of which were fully reported to the American people, tended to promote spheres of influence as the new basis of international power, rather than the ideals of national self-determination and economic cooperation laid out in the Atlantic Charter. Once the common enemies had been defeated, the wartime alliance became strained and then began to split apart in ways so fundamental that it is unlikely that Roosevelt could have kept it together if he had lived. Perhaps the greatest legacy of World War II was the Cold War that followed.

Summary

★

With the rise of fascism and imperialism in Germany, Italy, and Japan, the world was at war by 1939. Although most Americans clung to strong isolationist sentiment, President Roosevelt began mobilizing public opinion for intervention and converting the economy to war production. The Japanese attack on Pearl Harbor on December 7, 1941, brought the nation into World War II.

Defense mobilization ended the Great Depression and caused the economy to rebound. As with World War I, mobilization led to a dramatic expansion of the state. On the home front, the war resulted in rationing and shortages of many items but no serious hardships. Geographical mobility increased as labor shortages opened job opportunities for women, blacks, and Mexican Americans. The labor movement surged, and the ideological climate of fighting Nazism aided the cause of civil rights. However, Japanese Americans on the West Coast suffered a devastating denial of civil liberties when the government moved them into internment camps.

World War II was a global war, consisting of massive military campaigns in both Europe and the Pacific. The war news was bleak at first, but by 1943 the Allies had started to move toward victory, first in Europe and then in the Pacific. Soviet forces bore the brunt of the fighting in the European theater, while American forces primarily orchestrated the war effort in the Pacific. More than 15 million American men and women served in the armed forces, and at least 405,000 lost their lives.

While the Allied forces mobilized to defeat Germany and Japan, Roosevelt attempted to maintain harmony among the United States, Great Britain, and the Soviet Union. Many of the disagreements over wartime diplomacy would become serious problems in the postwar world, especially the fate of Eastern Europe and the intentions of the Soviet Union. Of all the major powers that fought in World War II, only the United States emerged physically unharmed. And at the end of the war, only the United States had a powerful new weapon, the atomic bomb. But the most enduring legacy of World War II was the onset of the Cold War, which would dominate American foreign policy for the next four decades.

TIMELINE

1938	Munich agreement
1939	Nazi-Soviet pact
	War breaks out in Europe
1940	Conscription reinstated
	America First Committee
	Roosevelt reelected to third term
1941	Roosevelt promulgates Four Freedoms
	Hitler invades Soviet Union
	Lend-Lease Act
	Fair Employment Practices Commission
	Atlantic Charter
	Japanese attack Pearl Harbor
1942	Battles of Coral Sea and Midway halt Japanese advance in the Pacific
	Women recruited for war industries
	Relocation of Japanese Americans
	Revenue Act of 1942
1942–1945	Rationing
1943	Race riots in Detroit and Los Angeles
	Fascism falls in Italy
	Teheran Conference
1944	Gunnar Myrdal, *An American Dilemma*
	D-Day invasion
	Reconquest of Philippines
	GI Bill of Rights
	Roosevelt reelected to fourth term
1945	Germany surrenders
	Battles of Iwo Jima and Okinawa
	Yalta Conference
	Harry Truman becomes president after Roosevelt's death
	United Nations convenes
	U.S. drops atomic bombs on Hiroshima and Nagasaki
	Japan surrenders

Suggested Readings

————————★————————

John Morton Blum, *V Was for Victory* (1976); William O'Neill, *A Democracy at War* (1993); Michael C. C. Adams, *The Best War Ever* (1994); and Geoffrey Perret, *Days of Sadness, Years of Triumph* (1973), offer good introductions to American politics and culture during the war years. A valuable collection of articles is found in Lewis A. Erenberg and Susan E. Hirsch, eds., *The War in American Culture* (1996). Studs Terkel, *"The Good War"* (1984), offers a powerful and provocative oral history of the war. John Keegan, *The Second World War* (1990), offers the best one-volume account of the battlefront aspects.

American Neutrality, 1939–1941

Depression and wartime diplomacy are covered in Robert Dallek, *Franklin D. Roosevelt and American Foreign Policy, 1932–1945* (1979), and Akira Iriye, *The Globalizing of America, 1913–1945* (1993). On American isolationism, see Wayne Cole, *Roosevelt and the Isolationists, 1932–1945* (1983). Warren T. Kimball, *The Most Unsordid Act* (1969), describes the lend-lease controversy of 1939–1941, whereas Kimball's *The Juggler: Franklin Roosevelt as Wartime Statesman* (1991), provides an overview of Roosevelt's leadership. Roberta Wohlstetter, *Pearl Harbor* (1962); Herbert Feis, *The Road to Pearl Harbor* (1950); and Gordon W. Prange, *At Dawn We Slept* (1981), describe the events that led to American entry into the war.

Organizing for Victory

George Flynn, *The Mess in Washington* (1979), and Harold G. Vatter, *The U.S. Economy in World War II* (1985), discuss America's economic mobilization. Mark S. Foster, *Henry J. Kaiser: Builder in the Modern American West* (1989), and Stephen B. Adams, *Mr. Kaiser Goes to Washington: The Rise of a Government Entrepreneur* (1997), are comprehensive accounts of Kaiser's career. Alan Winkler, *The Politics of Propaganda* (1978), covers the Office of War Information. On labor's role during war, see George Lipsitz, *Rainbow at Midnight: Labor and Culture in the 1940s* (1994); and Nelson Lichtenstein, *Labor's War at Home: The CIO in World War II* (1982). For more on politics in wartime, see James McGregor Burns, *Roosevelt: The Soldier of Freedom* (1970); Doris Kearns Goodwin, *No Ordinary Time* (1994); and Alan Brinkley, *The End of Reform* (1995).

Women's roles in wartime are covered by Susan Hartmann, *The Home Front and Beyond* (1982); Karen Anderson, *Wartime Women* (1980); D'Ann Campbell, *Women at War with America* (1984); Ruth Milkman, *Gender at Work* (1987); and Sherna B. Gluck, *Rosie the Riveter Revisited: Women, the War, and Social Change* (1987). Judy Barrett Litoff and David C. Smith, *We're in This War, Too* (1994), includes letters from American women in uniform, and Leisa D. Meyer, *Creating GI Jane* (1996), discusses the Women's Army Corps.

Life on the Home Front

William M. Tuttle Jr., *"Daddy's Gone to War"* (1993), describes World War II from the perspective of the nation's children. Alan Clive, *State of War* (1979), provides a case study of Michi-

gan during the war; Marilynn S. Johnson, *The Second Gold Rush* (1993), describes Oakland, California, and the East Bay. See also Gerald D. Nash, *The American West Transformed: The Impact of the Second World War* (1985). Clayton R. Koppes and Gregory D. Black, *Hollywood Goes to War* (1987), and Thomas Doherty, *Projections of War* (1993), cover the film industry. The experience of black Americans is treated in Albert Russell Buchanan, *Black Americans in World War II* (1977), and Neil Wynn, *The Afro-American and the Second World War* (1975). On racial tensions, see Dominic Capeci Jr., *Race Relations in Wartime Detroit* (1984), and Mauricio Mazan, *The Zoot Suit Riots* (1984). Richard Dalfiume, *Desegregation of the U.S. Armed Forces* (1969), covers black soldiers in the military, and Phillip McGuire, *Taps for a Jim Crow Army* (1993), offers a collection of letters from black soldiers. Alan Berube, *Coming Out under Fire* (1990), is an oral history of gay men and lesbians in the military; see also John D'Emilio, *Sexual Politics, Sexual Communities* (1983), for the impact of the war on gay Americans. Maurice Isserman, *Which Side Were You On?* (1982), analyzes the American Communist Party during the war. Two compelling accounts of Japanese relocation are Audre Girdner and Anne Loftus, *The Great Betrayal* (1969), and Roger Daniels, *Prisoners without Trial: Japanese-Americans in World War II* (1993). See also John Tateishi, ed., *And Justice For All: An Oral History of the Japanese-American Detention Camps* (1984); Peter Irons, *Justice at War: The Story of the Japanese-American Internment Cases* (1983); and Page Smith, *Democracy on Trial: The Japanese American Evacuation and Relocation in World War II* (1995).

Fighting and Winning the War

Extensive material chronicles the American military experience during World War II. Albert Russell Buchanan, *The United States and World War II* (1962), and Russell F. Weigley, *The American Way of War* (1973), provide overviews; Ronald Schaffer, *Wings of Judgement: American Bombing in World War II* (1985), and Bradley F. Smith, *The Shadow Warriors: OSS and the Origins of the CIA* (1983), are more specialized. Stephen Ambrose, *D-Day, June 6, 1944* (1994) and *Citizen Soldiers* (1997), describe the end of the fighting in Europe. David S. Wyman, *The Abandonment of the Jews* (1984), describes the lack of American response to the Holocaust from 1941 to 1945. On East Asia, see John W. Dower, *War without Mercy: Race and Power in the Pacific War* (1986); Ronald H. Spector, *Eagle against the Sun: The American War with Japan* (1984); and John Toland, *Rising Sun: The Decline and Fall of the Japanese Empire* (1970).

American diplomacy and the strategy of the Grand Alliance are surveyed in Lloyd Gardner, *Spheres of Influence* (1993). The relationship between the wartime conferences and the onset of the Cold War is treated in Walter LaFeber, *America, Russia, and the Cold War* (8th ed., 1996), and Stephen Ambrose and Douglas Brinkley, *Rise to Globalism* (8th ed., 1997). Richard Rhodes, *The Making of the Atomic Bomb* (1987), and Martin Sherwin, *A World Destroyed* (1975), provide compelling accounts of the development of the bomb. See also Gar Alperowitz, *The Decision to Use the Atomic Bomb* (1995); Ronald Takaki, *Hiroshima: Why America Dropped the Atomic Bomb* (1995); and Robert Jay Lifton and Greg Mitchell, *Hiroshima in America: Fifty Years of Denial* (1995).

Part Six

★

America and the World,
1945–1996

THEMATIC TIMELINE

	Diplomacy	Government	Economy	Society	Culture
	The Cold War Era— and After	**Redefining the Role of the State**	**Ups and Downs of U.S. Economic Dominance**	**Social Movements and Demographic Diversity**	**Consumer Culture and the Information Revolution**
1945	Truman Doctrine (1947) Marshall Plan (1948) NATO founded (1949)	Truman's Fair Deal liberalism Taft-Hartley Act (1947)	Bretton Woods system established: World Bank, IMF, GATT	Migration to cities accelerates Armed forces desegregated (1948)	End of wartime rationing Rise of television
1950	Permanent mobilization: NSC-68 (1950) Korean War (1950–1953)	Eisenhower's modern Republicanism Warren Court activism	Rise of military-industrial complex Service sector expands	*Brown v. Board of Education* (1954) Montgomery bus boycott (1955)	Growth of suburbia Baby boom
1960	Cuban missile crisis (1962) Nuclear test ban treaty (1963) Vietnam War escalates (1965)	High tide of liberalism: Great Society, War on Poverty Nixon ushers in conservative era	Kennedy-Johnson tax cut, military expenditures fuel economic growth	Student activism Civil Rights Act (1964); Voting Rights Act (1965) Revival of feminism	Shopping malls spread Baby boomers swell college enrollment Youth counterculture
1970	Nixon visits China (1972) SALT initiates détente (1972) Paris Peace Accords (1973)	Watergate scandal; Nixon resigns (1974) Deregulation begins under Ford and Carter	Arab oil embargo (1973–1974); inflation surges Deindustrialization brings unemployment to "Rustbelt" Income stagnation	*Roe v. Wade* (1973) Televangelists mobilize evangelical Protestants New Right urges conservative agenda	First Earth Day (1970) Gasoline shortages Apple introduces first personal computer (1977)
1980	Reagan arms buildup INF treaty (1988) Berlin Wall falls	Reagan Revolution Supreme Court conservatism	Reaganomics Budget and trade deficits soar Savings and loan bailout	New Hispanic and Asian immigration	MTV debuts AIDS epidemic
1990	War in the Persian Gulf USSR disintegrates; end of the Cold War U.S. peacekeeping forces in Bosnia	Democratic party adopts "moderate" policies Republican Congress shifts federal government tasks to states	Corporate downsizing NAFTA (1993) Asian economies decline	Third wave of feminism Affirmative action challenged Welfare reform	Health care crisis Information superhighway Biotech revolution

IN 1945 THE United States entered an era of unprecedented international power and influence. Unlike the period after World War I, American leaders did not avoid international commitments; instead, they aggressively pursued U.S. interests abroad, vowing to contain communism around the globe. The consequences of that struggle profoundly influenced the nation's domestic economy, political affairs, and social and cultural trends for the next half-century.

Diplomacy. First and most important, the United States took a leading, or hegemonic, role in global diplomatic and military affairs. When the Soviet Union challenged America's vision of postwar Europe, the Truman administration responded by crafting the policies and alliances that came to define the Cold War. That bipolar struggle lasted for more than forty years, spawned two "hot" wars in Korea and Vietnam, and fueled a terrifying and debilitating nuclear arms race. Although the moderate policy of détente pursued by Richard Nixon and later presidents helped ease tensions, the Cold War mentality prevailed until the collapse and disintegration of the Soviet Union in 1991.

Government. Second, America's global commitments had dramatic consequences for American government and politics. Until the national consensus fractured over the Vietnam War, liberals and conservatives agreed on keeping the country in a state of permanent mobilization and maintaining a large and well-equipped military establishment. The end of the Cold War brought modest cutbacks in defense spending, but an explosion of ethnic and religious conflicts in the former Yugoslavia, Africa, and other areas required U.S. military participation in several international peacekeeping missions in the 1990s. In the area of economic policy, all administrations, Republican and Democratic, were willing to intervene in the economy when private initiatives could not maintain steady growth. But liberals also pushed for a larger role for the federal government in the areas of social welfare and environmental protection. Under Harry S Truman, John F. Kennedy, and especially Lyndon B. Johnson, the government went beyond the New Deal by erecting an extensive federal and state apparatus to provide for the social well-being of the people. In subsequent years, particularly under the presidency of Ronald Reagan in the 1980s and the Republican control of Congress in the mid-1990s, conservatives cut back on many of the major programs and tried to delegate federal powers to the states.

Economy. Third, thanks to the growth of a military-industrial complex of enormous size and the expansion of consumer culture, the quarter-century after 1945 represented the heyday of American capitalism. Economic dominance abroad translated into unparalleled affluence at home. In the early 1970s, however, competition from other countries began to challenge America's economic supremacy, and for the next two decades many American workers experienced high unemployment, declining real wages, stagnant incomes, and a standard of living that could not match that of their parents. Following this period of global economic restructuring, the U.S. economy rebounded in the mid-1990s, reclaiming a position of undisputed dominance but sharing its leadership role with other industrial powers.

Society. Fourth, the victory over fascism in World War II led to renewed calls for America to make good on its promise of liberty and equality for all. In great waves of protests in the 1950s and 1960s, African Americans—and then women, Latinos, and other groups—challenged the political status quo. The resulting hard-won reforms brought concrete gains for many Americans, but since the late 1970s conservatives have challenged many of these initiatives. As the century drew to a close, the promise of true equality remained unfulfilled.

Culture. Fifth, American economic power in the postwar era accelerated the development of a consumer society based on suburbanization and technology. As millions of Americans migrated to new suburban developments after World War II, growing baby-boom families provided an expanded market for household products of all types. Among the most significant were new technological devices—television, video recorders, personal computers—that helped break down the isolation of suburban and rural living. Beginning in the 1960s, however, some people began to question the American obsession with material consumption and the environmental degradation it caused. In the 1990s the popularization of the Internet initiated an "information revolution," which both expanded and challenged the power of corporate-sponsored consumer culture.

Today, more than half a century after the end of World War II, Americans are living in an increasingly interwoven network of national and international forces. Outside events shape ordinary lives in ways that were inconceivable a century ago. As the Cold War era fades into history, the United States remains the sole military superpower, but it shares economic leadership in the new interdependent global system.

Cold War America, 1945–1960

WHEN HARRY TRUMAN arrived at the White House on April 12, 1945, after learning of Franklin D. Roosevelt's death, he asked the president's widow, "Is there anything I can do for you?" Eleanor Roosevelt responded, "Is there anything we can do for you? For you are the one in trouble now."

Truman inherited the presidency at a perilous time in modern American history. World War II had profoundly disrupted the global balance of power, leaving the United States and the Union of Soviet Socialist Republic (USSR) as the two most powerful nations. Each quickly moved to reshape the postwar world to serve its own national interests. Because the Soviet peoples had been victims of German aggression in both world wars, the USSR sought to create a buffer zone of friendly governments in Eastern Europe—a development that also advanced the Soviet agenda of promoting communist revolution. For its part, the Truman administration set out to contain communist influence in the region and to fortify noncommunist governments in Western Europe that shared America's commitment to a free-market system. Soon the two superpowers were locked in the confrontation known as the Cold War—a protracted economic, political, and military conflict that spread from Europe to Asia and around the world. The Cold War continued in the 1950s under the Republican presidency of Dwight Eisenhower, who modified some of Truman's initiatives but did little to ease tensions.

The Soviet-American conflict of the postwar years had important domestic repercussions for the United States. As World War II drew to a close, Americans

The Perils of the Cold War
In this detail of a 1948 Pulitzer Prize–winning cartoon, Rube Goldberg depicts the perilous nature of America's postwar peace—one that was based largely on atomic supremacy and the threat of nuclear annihilation.
University of California at Berkeley, Bancroft Library.

Postwar Devastation, 1945
Cologne, Germany, was one of many
European cities reduced to rubble during World War II. Here one of the
120,000 remaining inhabitants of
Cologne (from a prewar population of
780,000) sits homeless with all of her
belongings amid the ruins of this once
beautiful and prosperous city. United
States policy makers worried that physical devastation and economic disorder
would make many areas of Europe vulnerable to communist influence.
Johnny Florea, LIFE Magazine, © 1945
Time, Inc.

looked forward to reducing foreign and military spending, and many Republicans called for a return to prewar isolationism. But as U.S.-Soviet tensions escalated,
Cold War policies boosted military expenditures and
fueled an arms race. The Cold War also fostered a climate of fear and suspicion that led to a hunt for "subversives" in government, education, and the media. But
the economic benefits of international involvement also
gave rise to a period of unprecedented affluence and
prosperity. That prosperity helped to underwrite a continuation and, in some cases, an expansion of federal
power, perpetuating the New Deal in the postwar era.

The Early Cold War

★

When World War II ended, many parts of the world lay
devastated. Fifty million people had perished in the
conflict, and tens of millions were left homeless. Six
years of war unsettled the international system by creating power vacuums in Germany, Japan, and other
occupied countries, devastating Western Europe, and
dissolving colonial empires. Even before the war ended,
the United States and the Soviet Union were struggling
for advantage in those unstable areas; after the war
they engaged in a protracted global conflict. Hailed as

a battle between communism and capitalism, the Cold
War was in reality a more complex struggle over a
broad range of ideological, economic, and strategic
issues. As each side tried to protect its own national
security and way of life, its actions aroused fear in the
other, fueling a cycle of distrust and animosity that
would shape U.S.-Soviet relations for the next four
decades.

Sources of Conflict

Despite 400,000 American casualties, the United
States emerged from the war as the world's strongest,
wealthiest nation. Unscathed by bombing, U.S. industry and agriculture had grown rapidly during the war,
making America the world's leading manufacturer
and exporter. The nation's gross national product
soared, growing by 1945 to three times that of the
Soviet Union, its nearest competitor. The United
States also wielded enormous military power. American air and naval forces were the world's best, and the
United States alone possessed the atomic bomb. In
the postwar era U.S. policy makers tried to maintain
that supremacy and rebuild the world in America's
image.

The Soviet Union, in comparison, was relatively
weak. Sustaining the greatest casualties of any nation,
the USSR lost more than 20 million people—or one-

ninth of its total population—as a result of the war. The Soviet economy was devastated; more than 30,000 industrial plants had been destroyed, and the nation's agricultural output fell to half of what it had been in 1940. The Soviet Union's greatest asset was its army, including a vast force of troops occupying Eastern Europe and parts of Germany at the end of the war. Although the USSR hoped to preserve its influence in these areas, its dominance did not extend beyond the region.

The Soviet regional presence in Eastern Europe, however, raised serious concerns among U.S. policy makers, who feared the spread of communism across the European continent. With the defeat and dismantling of the Nazi government, American leaders worried that Soviet influence would expand across postwar Germany. Elsewhere in Europe economic chaos threatened to disrupt the political status quo, as did the growing popularity of communist and labor-led parties in Britain, Czechoslovakia, France, Greece, Italy, and Sweden. Although those parties generally remained independent of Moscow, American policy makers viewed them as sympathetic to Soviet initiatives and therefore as potential tools of the Kremlin. American security, those policy makers argued, required a strong, noncommunist Europe that could serve as a military and economic partner of the United States.

Political instability also characterized the "Third World," where World War II hastened the disintegration of colonial empires. Rising nationalist movements in developing regions and financial pressures on war-torn European countries after 1945 led to a severing of colonial ties and client-state relationships. American-Soviet rivalry for these areas was keen, for they provided essential markets for finished goods and had vital resources such as oil, tin, zinc, and manganese. In an air-age world where national defense stretched far beyond domestic borders, Third World nations also offered strategic sites for U.S. and Soviet military bases. The struggle for these economic and strategic benefits sparked a series of conflicts in Asia, the Middle East, and other regions.

Finally, the end of World War II marked the beginning of the nuclear age and the rise of atomic diplomacy. In 1945 the United States had sole possession of the atomic bomb and held it, as Secretary of War Henry Stimson explained, "rather ostentatiously on our hip." Emboldened by that monopoly, President Harry Truman decided to "get tough" with the Russians, a stance matched with equally stubborn resistance by the Soviet leader, Joseph Stalin. Both sides were inflexible in their demands and remained suspicious of each other's motives and actions. Stalin and Truman came to dislike each other so much that they refused to meet after the war. From 1945 to 1955, some of the most tense years of the Cold War, there were no summit meetings between Soviet and American heads of state. In this climate of mutual distrust, negotiation or compromise became virtually impossible.

Descent into Cold War, 1945–1946

During the war Franklin Roosevelt had worked effectively with Stalin, and he had intended to continue good relations with the Soviet Union in peacetime. In particular, he hoped that the United Nations would provide a forum for resolving postwar conflicts. Avoiding the disagreements that had doomed American membership in the League of Nations after World War I, the Senate approved America's participation in the United Nations in December 1945. A marked departure from earlier isolationist sentiment, the vote was a firm acknowledgment of the importance of American leadership in global affairs as well as a memorial to the late president's hopes for postwar peace.

Shortly before his death, however, Roosevelt had been disturbed by Soviet actions in Eastern Europe. As the Soviet army drove the Germans out of Russia and back through Eastern Europe, the USSR sponsored provisional governments in Poland, Romania, Hungary, and Bulgaria. At the Yalta Conference in February both America and Britain had agreed to recognize this Soviet "sphere of influence" with the condition that "free and unfettered elections" would be held as soon as possible. But in succeeding months the Soviets made no move to hold elections and rebuffed Western attempts to reorganize Soviet-installed governments.

When Truman assumed the presidency after Roosevelt's death, he quickly took a belligerent stance toward the Soviet Union. Recalling Britain's disastrous appeasement of Hitler in 1938, Truman decided that the United States had to stand up to the Soviet dictator. At a meeting a week after he took office, the new president berated the Soviet foreign minister, V. M. Molotov, for not honoring agreements on Poland. Truman used what he called "tough methods" again in July at the 1945 Potsdam Conference, which brought together the United States, Britain, and the Soviet Union. After learning of the successful test of America's atom bomb, Truman "told the Russians just where they got off and generally bossed the whole meeting," recalled British prime minister Winston Churchill. Negotiations on critical postwar issues deadlocked, revealing serious cracks in the Grand Alliance.

Policies governing the fate of occupied Germany were the only points of agreement between the United States and the Soviet Union at Potsdam. At Yalta the defeated German state had been divided into four occupation zones controlled by the United States, France, Britain, and the Soviet Union. At Potsdam the

Allies agreed to disarm the country, dismantle its military production facilities, and permit the occupying powers to extract reparations from the zones they controlled. Plans for future reunification stalled, however, as the United States and the Soviet Union each worried that a reunited German state would fall into the other's sphere. The economic base was thus laid for what would become the political division into East and West Germany four years later.

In March 1946 Winston Churchill issued an ominous warning to Americans about the deepening divide between Eastern and Western Europe. At the invitation of President Truman, Churchill delivered a major policy address in Fulton, Missouri. At Yalta, Churchill had gone along with plans for a Soviet sphere of influence in Eastern Europe, but now, out of office, he denounced the "expansive tendencies" of the Soviet Union: "From Stettin in the Baltic to Trieste in the Adriatic, an Iron Curtain has descended across the Continent." The former prime minister's widely publicized "Iron Curtain" speech helped convince many Americans that the Soviet Union posed a serious threat to national security.

As tensions over Europe divided the former allies, hopes of international cooperation in the control of atomic weapons also faded. In a plan that Truman's arms negotiator Bernard Baruch submitted to the United Nations in 1946, the United States proposed a system of international control that relied on manda-

tory inspection and supervision but preserved the American nuclear monopoly. The Soviets rejected the plan and concentrated efforts to complete their own bomb. The Truman administration likewise pursued its plans to develop more advanced nuclear energy and weapons systems. The failure of the Baruch Plan signaled the beginning of a frenzied nuclear arms race between the two superpowers.

Containing Communism

As tensions mounted between the superpowers, a new American policy, called *containment*, began to take shape. The most articulate and influential expression of the policy in 1946 and 1947 came from George F. Kennan, a scholarly diplomat who had devoted his career to studying the Soviet Union (see American Lives, "George F. Kennan: Architect of Containment," pp. 872–873). According to Kennan, the Soviets were moving "inexorably along the prescribed path, like a persistent toy automobile wound up and headed in a given direction, stopping only when it meets unanswerable force." To stop Soviet expansionism, Kennan argued, the United States should pursue a policy of "firm containment . . . at every point where [the Soviets] show signs of encroaching upon the interests of a peaceful and stable world."

Kennan's initial formulation recommended economic and diplomatic means to enforce containment, but the policy soon took on a military cast. In one version or another containment defined the foreign policy of every subsequent administration, both Democratic and Republican, well into the 1980s. In addition to the effort to stop the spread of communism, the containment doctrine served at least three other purposes: it provided a rallying cry for Americans of both parties to unite in fighting the Soviet threat; it justified the creation of a vast peacetime military machine; and it obscured other objectives of American foreign policy in the economic arena and the Third World.

The Truman Doctrine and the National Security Act. The emerging containment policy crystallized in 1947 over a crisis in Greece. In the spring of 1946, several thousand local communist guerrillas, who American advisors mistakenly believed were controlled by Moscow, launched a full-scale civil war against the government and the British occupation authorities. In February 1947 the British informed Truman that they could no longer afford to assist the Greek anticommunists. U.S. policy makers worried that Soviet influence in Greece threatened American and European interests in the eastern Mediterranean and the Middle East, especially in strategically located Turkey and the oil-rich state of Iran.

In response, the president announced what became known as the Truman Doctrine. In a speech to

The "Iron Curtain" Speech
At the invitation of President Truman, former British prime minister Winston Churchill delivered a historic address in Fulton, Missouri, on March 9, 1946, in which he warned Americans of the growing threat of Soviet expansion in Europe. It was during this speech that Churchill coined the expression "Iron Curtain," a metaphor that eerily foreshadowed the Soviet order in 1961 to build the Berlin Wall, dividing the Allied and Soviet sections of the city.
Winston Churchill Memorial and Library.

Congress on March 12 he requested large-scale military and economic assistance to Greece and Turkey and called for all Americans "to support free peoples who are resisting attempted subjugation by armed minorities or by outside pressures." To win popular support for the global fight against communism, and to squeeze money out of a Congress committed to reducing military spending, the president followed the advice of Republican senator Arthur Vandenberg. Chair of the Senate Foreign Relations Committee and a former isolationist, Vandenberg advised Truman to "scare hell" out of the American people—advice that the president apparently took to heart. If Greece fell to communism, Truman warned, the effects would be serious not only for Turkey but for the entire Middle East and even the world. Not just Greece but freedom itself was at issue, Truman declared: "If we falter in our leadership, we may endanger the peace of the world—and we shall surely endanger the welfare of our own nation." Despite the open-endedness of this military commitment, Congress quickly approved Truman's request for $300 million in aid to Greece and $100 million for Turkey. The appropriation reversed the postwar policy of sharp cuts in foreign spending and marked a new level of commitment to the emerging Cold War.

The Truman administration also worked with Congress to pass the National Security Act, which was designed to strengthen and streamline defense operations. Signed in July 1947, the act created three new bodies: a single Department of Defense to replace the previous Departments of War and the Navy; the National Security Council (NSC), an advisory body charged with helping the president set defense and military priorities; and the Central Intelligence Agency (CIA), a national intelligence-gathering operation that replaced the wartime Office of Strategic Services. The Atomic Energy Commission, established in 1946 under the executive branch, worked with the new agencies in the development of atomic energy and weapons. The establishment of these new bureaucratic structures marked the emergence of the national security state, a collection of powerful and highly secretive operations in the executive branch. Such structures accelerated the shift of policy-making initiative to the White House.

The Marshall Plan. As the president was promoting the Truman Doctrine, other members of his administration were busy devising the Marshall Plan, which Truman called "the other half of the walnut." A program of large-scale economic and military aid to Europe, the Marshall Plan—or European Recovery Program—was designed to complement the aggressive containment policy of the Truman Doctrine. Speaking at Harvard University's commencement in June 1947, Secretary of State George Marshall urged the nations

Charting a New Course for Europe with the Marshall Plan
Between 1948 and 1951 the European Recovery Program—popularly known as the Marshall Plan, after Secretary of State George C. Marshall—contributed over $12 billion toward its objective of "restoring the confidence of the European people in the economic future of their own countries and of Europe as a whole." This poster, targeted at Great Britain, stresses European cooperation in the rebuilding effort.
Courtesy Marshall Foundation.

of Europe to work out a comprehensive recovery program and then ask the United States for aid. By bolstering European economies devastated by the war, the United States could forestall the severe economic dislocation that might encourage the spread of communism. American economic self-interest was also a contributing factor—the legislation required that foreign aid dollars be spent on U.S. goods and services. A revitalized Europe centered on a strong West German economy would also provide a better market for American products.

Within Congress, however, there was significant opposition to Truman's pledge of economic aid to European economies. Isolationist Republicans attacked the Marshall Plan as a huge "international W.P.A." and a

George F. Kennan: Architect of Containment

————————★————————

O N FEBRUARY 22, 1946, A diplomatic advisor named George Kennan dictated an 8,000-word telegram from the U.S. embassy in Moscow. Responding to a Department of State request for an assessment of Soviet foreign policy, Kennan described the USSR as an insecure state intent on expansion, subversion, and the export of communist revolution. It was, he argued, "a political force committed fanatically to the belief that with the U.S. there can be no permanent modus vivendi." A preliminary blueprint of the containment theory, this "Long Telegram" was a confidential communiqué to President Harry Truman and Secretary of State James Byrnes. Within weeks, however, it became required reading for hundreds of U.S. military and diplomatic personnel around the world.

Kennan's Long Telegram found an enthusiastic audience among Washington policy makers who were eager to redefine U.S.-Soviet relations in the early postwar period. Its alarmist language helped convince the Truman administration to take a harder line against the Soviet Union and provided the ideological foundations for the emerging Cold War. Summoned back to Washington a few months later, Kennan became one of the most influential advisors in the Truman administration. Writing and lecturing continuously for the next forty years, he would also become one of the foremost foreign policy theorists of the twentieth century.

Kennan's containment theory was shaped by his many years of experience in the diplomatic corps. Born in Milwaukee in 1904, Kennan graduated from Princeton University in 1925 and entered the foreign service the following year. After holding minor positions in Switzerland and Germany, he was offered training as a Soviet specialist in 1929. Under the tutelage of anticommunist Russian émigrés in Berlin, Kennan studied Russian history, language, and literature and later served as a Soviet expert at the U.S. embassy in Latvia. In 1933, when Franklin Roosevelt

initiated diplomatic relations with the Soviet Union, Kennan helped open the new U.S. embassy in Moscow and joined the embassy staff. During his four years in the USSR, he witnessed the horrors of the Stalinist purges, an experience that fueled his animosity toward the Russian leader Joseph Stalin and the Soviet Communist regime. Between 1937 and 1944, Kennan occupied a variety of diplomatic posts in the United States and Europe, none of which truly satisfied him. When the new ambassador to the Soviet Union, Averell Harriman, requested him as an advisor in 1944, he jumped at the opportunity to return to Moscow.

Still deeply antagonistic toward the Soviet Union, Kennan disagreed with Roosevelt's wartime alliance with Stalin and issued a steady stream of anti-Soviet memoranda. During the war, most of these pronouncements fell on deaf years. With the end of the war and the rise of Soviet-American conflict over Poland, however, Harriman and other members of the Truman administration became more receptive to Kennan's views. Widespread praise for his Long Telegram won Kennan an offer to lecture at the National War College in Washington in April 1946. A year later, Secretary of State George Marshall appointed him director of the department's new Policy Planning Staff (PPS), which helped devise the Marshall Plan and other long-range foreign policy initiatives.

While serving as PPS director from 1947 to 1950, Kennan refined his ideas about containment. His best-known articulation of the theory appeared in a July 1947 article in *Foreign Affairs*, which he wrote anonymously as "Mr. X." Kennan's identity, however, was soon revealed, and his views of an antagonistic and deceitful Soviet state won wide currency. Conceding Soviet influence in Eastern Europe, he urged the United States and its allies to contain the Soviet threat through "the adroit and vigilant application of counter-force at a series of constantly shifting geographical and political points." By pursuing such a policy, Kennan speculated, Soviet power could be diminished since it "bears within it the seeds of its own decay."

As Kennan himself would later admit, his formulation of containment was ambiguous and imprecise. His use of the term *force* was vague; he failed to specify whether the United States should use political, economic, or military force to contain the Soviets. Nor did he place any geographical limits on Ameri-

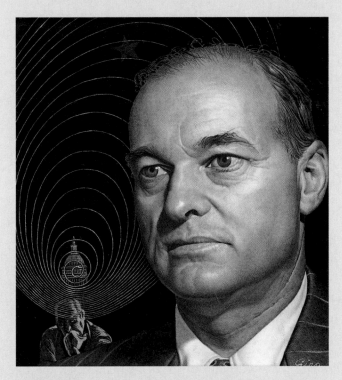

George F. Kennan
As a diplomat, foreign policy theorist, and historian, George F. Kennan has enjoyed a long and distinguished career spanning more than 70 years. This portrait by Guy Rowe dates from 1955.
National Portrait Gallery, Smithsonian Institution/Art Resource, NY.

can intervention. Although Kennan later claimed that containment was primarily a political/economic strategy intended to protect the world's key industrial areas, the ambiguity of the 1947 article invited American policy makers to interpret containment in the broadest possible fashion.

By 1950 Truman's increasingly hard-line approach toward the Soviet Union had alienated Kennan. He criticized the open-ended commitment of the Truman Doctrine, the militarization of containment under NSC-68, and the division of Europe under the NATO treaty. Increasingly marginalized by the new secretary of state, Dean Acheson, Kennan took a leave of absence to attend the Institute for Advanced Study at Princeton University. In 1952 he returned to the administration to serve as ambassador to the Soviet Union; within months, however, he was forced to resign after making disparaging remarks comparing Stalin's regime to Nazism.

With the election of Republican Dwight D. Eisenhower in 1952, Kennan's influence in Washington was further diminished. Eisenhower's secretary of state, the staunchly conservative John Foster Dulles, condemned containment as immoral and denounced Kennan for his "appeasement" of the Soviets in Eastern Europe. Kennan briefly returned to the diplomatic corps in 1961 as ambassador to Yugoslavia under President John F. Kennedy. Two years later, however, Congress revoked that country's most-favored-nation trading status, undermining Kennan's work and prompting his permanent retirement from government service.

As Kennan's diplomatic career waned, he became a renowned historian and theorist of American foreign relations. Working from his office at the Institute for Advanced Studies, he produced dozens of books and articles, including two Pulitzer Prize–winning works, *Russia Leaves the War* (1950) and his often-quoted *Memoirs* (1967). His popular historical text *American Diplomacy, 1900–1950* (1951) introduced millions of Americans to the "realist" critique of foreign policy—an approach that stresses national interests and power politics over the idealistic motives of both conservatives and liberals.

On numerous occasions, Kennan aired his realist views of controversial Cold War developments. During the 1950s he condemned McCarthyism and advocated Soviet and U.S. disengagement from Europe. Later he became an outspoken opponent of the Vietnam War, testifying before the Senate Foreign Relations Committee in 1966 that the containment doctrine was poorly suited to Indochina. Opposing moralistic foreign policy, he criticized Jimmy Carter's preoccupation with human rights in the 1970s and Ronald Reagan's dramatic arms buildup and anti-Soviet pronouncements in the 1980s. As an outspoken critic of the nuclear arms race, he called for "no first use" of nuclear weapons in 1984 and pressed for comprehensive arms control agreements.

The demise of the Soviet Union in 1991 seemed to fulfill Kennan's prophecy in the 1947 article and brought him renewed public attention. But historians continue to debate the usefulness of containment in ending the Cold War. During his long career, Kennan himself served as both chief architect and key critic of containment. His evolving views highlight the complexities and perils of Cold War policy making in the late twentieth century.

JEAN MONNET

Truman's Generous Proposal

———— ★ ————

Jean Monnet was an eminent French statesman and a tireless promoter of postwar European union. As head of a French postwar planning commission, he helped oversee the dispersal of Marshall Plan funds, the importance of which he described in his memoirs.

So we had at last concerted our efforts to halt France's economic decline; but now, once more, everything seemed to be at risk. Two years earlier [1947], we thought that we had plumbed the depths of material poverty. Now we were threatened with the loss of even basic essentials. . . . Our dollar resources were melting away at an alarming rate, because we were having to buy American wheat to replace the crops we had lost during the winter. This alone cost us $200m. instead of the $30m. we had expected to pay. In addition, we had to increase our coal imports at a time when prices had risen in the United States. In June, we met the cost with gold bullion from the Bank of France; in August, we cut off inessential imports. A further American loan was soon exhausted.

Nor was this grim situation confined to France. Britain too had come to the end of her resources. In February 1947 she had abruptly cancelled her aid to Greece and Turkey, whose burdens she had seemed able to assume in 1945. Overnight, this abrupt abdication gave the United States direct responsibility for part of Europe. Truman did not hesitate for a moment: with the decisiveness that was to mark his actions as President, he at once asked for credits and arms for both Turkey and Greece. . . . [Soon after], he announced the Truman Doctrine of March 12, 1947. Its significance was general: it meant that the United States would prevent Europe from becoming a depressed area at the mercy of Communist advance. On the very same day, the Four-Power Conference began in Moscow. There, for a whole month, George Marshall, Ernest Bevin, and Georges Bidault argued with Vyacheslav Molotov about all the problems of the peace, and above all about Germany.

When Marshall returned to Washington, he knew that for a long time there would be no further genuine dialogue with Stalin's Russia. The 'cold war', as it was soon to be known, had begun. . . . Information from a number of sources convinced Marshall and his Under-Secretary Dean Acheson that once again, as in 1941, the United States had a great historic duty. And once again there took place what I had witnessed in Washington a few years earlier: a small group of men brought to rapid maturity an idea which, when the Executive gave the word, turned into vigorous action. This time, it was done by five or six people, in total secrecy and at lightning speed. Marshall, Acheson, Clayton, Averell Harriman, and George Kennan worked out a proposal of unprecedented scope and generosity. It took us all by surprise when we read the speech that George Marshall made at Harvard on June 5, 1947. Chance had led him to choose the University's Commencement Day to launch something new in international relations: helping others to help themselves.

Source: Jean Monnet, *Memoirs*, trans. Richard Mayne (New York: Doubleday, 1978), 264–266.

"bold Socialist blue-print." But in the midst of this congressional stalemate, the Soviets staged a brutal coup in Czechoslovakia, one of the few Eastern European countries to have held free elections after the war and elected a coalition government that was widely admired in the West. When the Communists seized control of the country on February 25, 1948, and installed a new government, Congress rallied in support of the Marshall Plan. In March both houses voted overwhelmingly to approve funds for the program.

Historian Thomas J. McCormick calls the Marshall Plan "arguably the most innovative piece of foreign policy in American history." Over the next four years the United States contributed over $12 billion to a highly successful recovery effort (see Voices from Abroad, "Jean Monnet: Truman's Generous Proposal," above).

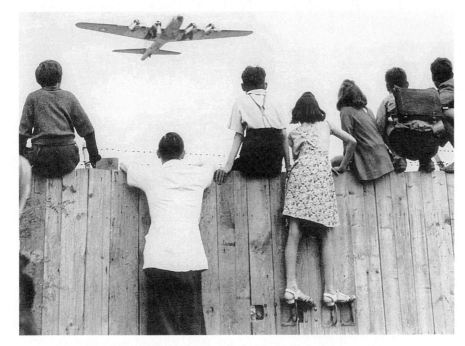

The Berlin Airlift
For 321 days American planes like this one flew 272,000 missions to bring food and other supplies to Berlin after the Soviet Union had blocked all surface routes into the former German capital. The blockade was finally lifted on May 12, 1949, after the Soviets conceded that it had been a failure.
Wide World Photos, Inc.

Western European economies revived and industrial production increased 64 percent, opening new areas for international trade. The Marshall Plan did not specifically exclude Eastern Europe or the Soviet Union, but it required that all participating nations exchange economic information and work toward the elimination of tariffs and other trade barriers. Soviet leaders denounced those conditions as attempts to draw Eastern Europe into the American orbit and forbade their satellite states of Czechoslovakia, Poland, and Hungary to participate.

The Berlin Airlift and the Creation of NATO. The Marshall Plan accelerated American and European efforts to rebuild and reunify the West German economy. In June 1948, after agreeing to fuse their zones of occupation, the United States, France, and Britain began a currency reform program in West Berlin. The economic revitalization of West Berlin, located deep within the Soviet zone of occupation (see Map 27.1), alarmed Soviet policy makers, who feared a resurgent Germany aligned with the West. To forestall that development, the Soviet Union imposed a blockade on all highway, rail, and river traffic to West Berlin. Truman responded with an airlift. For nearly a year American and British pilots, who had been dropping bombs on Berlin only four years earlier, flew in 2.5 million tons of food and fuel, nearly a ton for each West Berlin resident. On May 12, 1949, Stalin lifted the blockade, which by then had made the city a symbol of resistance to communism.

The coup in Czechoslovakia and the crisis in Berlin convinced U.S. policy makers of the need for a collective security pact. In April 1949, for the first time since the American Revolution, the United States entered into a peacetime military alliance, the North Atlantic Treaty Organization (NATO). To back up America's new stance, Truman asked Congress for $1.3 billion in military assistance to NATO and authorized the basing of four U.S. Army divisions in Western Europe. Under the NATO pact, twelve nations—the United States, Canada, Britain, France, Italy, Portugal, Belgium, the Netherlands, Luxembourg, Denmark, Norway, and Iceland—agreed that "an armed attack against one or more of them in Europe or North America shall be considered an attack against them all." In May 1949 those nations also agreed to the creation of the Federal Republic of Germany (West Germany), which joined NATO in 1955.

In response to the creation of NATO, the Soviet Union tightened its grip on Eastern Europe in October 1949 by creating a separate government for East Germany, which became the German Democratic Republic. The Soviets also organized an economic association, the Council for Mutual Economic Assistance (COMECON), in 1949 and a military alliance for Eastern Europe, the Warsaw Pact, in 1955. The postwar division of Europe was nearly complete (Map 27.1).

The "Fall" of China. As mutual suspicion between the United States and the Soviet Union deepened, Cold War doctrines began to influence the American position toward Asia as well. American policy there was

MAP 27.1
Cold War Europe, 1955
In 1949 the United States sponsored the creation of the North Atlantic Treaty Organization—an alliance of ten European nations, the United States, and Canada. West Germany was formally admitted to NATO in May 1955. A few days later the Soviet Union and seven other communist nations established a rival alliance, the Warsaw Pact.

based on Asia's importance in the world economy as much as on the desire to contain communism. At first, American plans for the region centered on a revitalized China, but political instability there prompted the Truman administration to focus instead on developing the Japanese economy. After dismantling Japan's military forces and weaponry, American occupation forces under General Douglas MacArthur began the job of transforming Japan into a bulwark of Asian capitalism. MacArthur drafted a democratic constitution and oversaw the rebuilding of the economy, paving the way for the restoration of Japanese sovereignty in 1951.

In China the situation was more precarious. Since the 1930s a civil war had been raging as Communist forces led by Mao Zedong (Mao Tse-tung) and Zhou Enlai (Chou En-lai) contended for power with conservative nationalist forces under Jiang Jieshi (Chiang Kai-shek). Although dissatisfied with the corrupt and inefficient Jiang regime, the Truman administration saw it as the only alternative to Mao and resigned itself to working with the nationalists. Between 1945 and 1949 the United States provided more than $2 billion to Jiang's forces, but to no avail. In 1947, Truman's key military advisor in China insisted that the nationalist government undertake "drastic political and economic reforms" in order to win the struggle against the Communists. When those reforms did not occur, the Truman administration cut off aid to the Nationalists in

August 1949, sealing their fate. The People's Republic of China was formally established on October 1, 1949, and what was left of Jiang's government fled to the island of Formosa (Taiwan).

Although nothing less than a massive U.S. military commitment could have stopped the Chinese Communists, many Americans viewed Mao's success as a defeat for the United States. Republican statesman John Foster Dulles, who would become secretary of state in the Eisenhower administration, assailed the communist victory in China as "the worst defeat the United States has suffered in its history." A pro-nationalist "China lobby," led by the powerful publisher Henry R. Luce (born in China to missionary parents) and Republican senators Karl Mundt of South Dakota and William S. Knowland of California, protested that the Department of State under the leadership of Truman's newly appointed secretary of state, Dean Acheson, was responsible for the "fall of China." As a result of pressure from the China lobby, most Department of State experts on East Asia were forced to resign. The loss of those experts created a critical knowledge gap that would handicap the United States for decades in dealing with Vietnam and other Asian trouble spots.

Although the Chinese Communists remained independent of Moscow, the United States refused to recognize what it called "Red China," instead giving diplomatic recognition to the exiled Nationalist government in Taiwan. The United States also used its influence to block China's admission to the United Nations. For almost twenty years, U.S. administrations treated the People's Republic of China, the world's most populous country, as a diplomatic nonentity.

Containment Militarized: NSC-68. New impetus for the policy of containment came in September 1949, when American military intelligence detected a rise in radioactivity in the atmosphere—proof that the Soviet Union had detonated an atomic bomb. The American atomic monopoly, which some military and political advisors had argued would last for decades, ended in only four years, forcing a major reassessment of the nation's foreign policy.

To devise a new diplomatic and military blueprint, Truman turned to the National Security Council. In April 1950 it delivered its report, known as NSC-68, to the president. Expressing alarm over the Soviet threat, the writers of the document made several specific recommendations, including the development of a hydrogen bomb, an advanced weapon that was a thousand times more destructive than the atomic bombs that had destroyed Hiroshima and Nagasaki. NSC-68 also supported increases in U.S. conventional forces and a strong system of alliances—reflections of the increasing militarization of the Cold War. Most important, it called for a tax hike to finance "a bold and massive program of rebuilding the West's defensive potential to surpass that of the Soviet world."

NSC-68 called for defense budgets totaling up to 20 percent of the gross national product, four times their level at that time. Now that the U.S. atomic monopoly had been broken, Truman's advisors also looked to build up conventional military forces to maintain American superiority. Truman, however, was reluctant to commit to a major defense buildup, fearing that it would overburden the budget. But the Korean War, which began just two months after NSC-68 was completed, helped transform the report's recommendations into reality.

The Cold War Heats Up: The Korean War

Although Truman acknowledged that communist success in China raised urgent questions for American foreign policy, he recognized the limits of American power in Asia. In December 1949 Secretary of State Dean Acheson clarified American policy. The United States, he said, would help Asian nations realize their aspirations but would consider itself bound to protect only a "defensive perimeter" extending from the Aleutian Islands in Alaska to Japan, the Ryukyus (a chain of

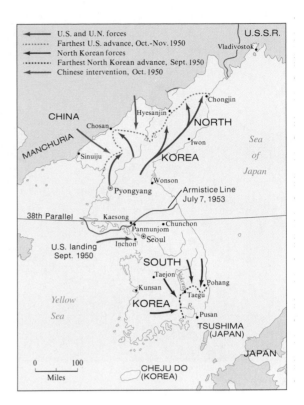

MAP 27.2
The Korean War, 1950–1953
The first months of the Korean War featured dramatic shifts in control up and down the 600-mile peninsula. From June to September 1950 North Korean troops overran most of the territory south of the 38th parallel. On September 15, U.N. forces under General Douglas MacArthur counterattacked behind enemy lines at Inchon and pushed north almost to the Chinese border. Massive Chinese intervention forced the U.N. troops to retreat to the 38th parallel in January 1951, and the war was a stalemate for the next two years.

small islands stretching from Japan to Taiwan), and the Philippines (a former American protectorate that had won its independence from the United States in 1946). If an attack occurred outside that perimeter—in Korea, Taiwan, or Southeast Asia, for example—"the initial reliance must be on the people attacked to resolve it and then upon . . . the United Nations."

A test of the new policy came quickly in Korea, a country whose artificial division after World War II contained the seeds for later conflict. Both the United States and the Soviet Union had troops in Korea at the end of the war, and neither side was willing to abandon its occupied territories. As a result, Korea was divided at the 38th parallel into competing spheres of influence (Map 27.2). The Soviets supported a communist government, led by Kim Il Sung, in North Korea; the United States backed Syngman Rhee, a longtime Korean nationalist, in South Korea. Soon sporadic fighting between North and South Koreans broke out along the 38th parallel, and a civil war began.

The Korean War
These men of the Second Infantry battalion, shown here in Korea in 1950, helped pave
the way for the formal integration of all U.S. Army units by 1954. The Korean War
marked the first time in the nation's history that all troops served in racially integrated
combat units.
National Archives.

On June 25, 1950, the North Koreans launched a surprise attack across the 38th parallel. The initiative for Korean reunification came from Kim Il Sung, but Stalin approved of the mission. Soviet and North Korean leaders may have expected Truman to ignore this armed challenge, but the president immediately asked the United Nations Security Council to authorize a "police action" against the invaders. Because the Soviet Union was temporarily boycotting the Security Council to protest the exclusion of the People's Republic of China from the United Nations, it could not veto Truman's request. Three days after the Security Council voted to send a peacekeeping force, Truman ordered U.S. troops to Korea.

The American intervention in Korea revealed the extent to which foreign policy formulation had been transferred from Congress to the president. When isolationist Republican senator Robert A. Taft of Ohio argued that the president should have obtained congressional approval before committing American troops to Korea, Truman boldly insisted that he already had the power he needed as commander in chief of the armed forces and executor of the treaty binding the United States to the United Nations. The Truman administration enjoyed widespread popular support for this action: in a July 1950 poll, 77 percent of the respondents approved of U.S. intervention. The Korean conflict—the first American combat effort to implement containment—thus became the first major American war undertaken without a formal declaration of war by Congress.

Fighting the War. Although fourteen other noncommunist members of the United Nations sent troops, the rapidly assembled United Nations army in Korea was overwhelmingly American. At the request of the Security Council, President Truman named General Douglas MacArthur, hero of the American victory in the Pacific and head of the postwar occupation of Japan, to lead the U.N. forces. At first the North Koreans held an overwhelming advantage, controlling practically the entire peninsula except the area around Pusan. But on September 15, 1950, MacArthur launched a surprise amphibious attack at Inchon, far behind the North Korean front line, while U.N. forces staged a breakout from Pusan. Within two weeks the U.N. forces controlled Seoul, the South Korean capital, and almost all the territory up to the 38th parallel (see Map 27.2).

Encouraged by this success, MacArthur sought the authority to lead his forces across the 38th parallel into North Korea. Truman's original plan had been to restore the 1945 border, but he managed to win U.N. support for the broader goal of creating "a unified, independent and democratic Korea." Although the Chinese government in

Beijing warned repeatedly that such a move would provoke its retaliation, American officials dismissed the warnings as a bluff. MacArthur's troops crossed the 38th parallel on October 9, reaching the Chinese border at the Yalu River by the end of the month. Just after Thanksgiving, a massive Chinese counterattack of almost 300,000 troops forced a retreat to the 38th parallel. On January 4, 1951, Communist troops reoccupied Seoul.

Two months later the American forces and their allies counterattacked, regained Seoul, and pushed back to the 38th parallel. Then stalemate set in. Public support for U.S. involvement dropped after Chinese intervention increased the likelihood of a long war. According to one poll in early January 1951, 66 percent of Americans thought the United States should withdraw, and 49 percent believed it was a mistake to have intervened at all. Given those domestic and international constraints, Truman and his advisors decided to work for a negotiated peace. They did not want to tie down large numbers of U.S. troops in Asia, far from what they considered more strategically important trouble spots in Europe and the Middle East. If the Korean War had become a larger war with China, General Omar N. Bradley, chairman of the Joint Chiefs of Staff, reasoned, it would have been "the wrong war, at the wrong place, at the wrong time, with the wrong enemy."

The Fate of Douglas MacArthur. MacArthur disagreed. Headstrong, arrogant, and brilliant, the general fervently believed that the nation's future opportunities lay in Asia, not in Europe. Disregarding Truman's instructions, MacArthur traveled to Taiwan and urged the nationalists to join in an attack on mainland China. He pleaded for U.S. permission to use the atomic bomb against targets in China. In an inflammatory letter to the House minority leader, the Republican Joseph J. Martin of Massachusetts, he denounced the Korean stalemate. "We must win," MacArthur declared. "There is no substitute for victory."

Martin released MacArthur's letter on April 6, 1951, as part of a concerted Republican campaign to challenge Truman's conduct of the war. The strategy backfired. On April 11 Truman relieved MacArthur of his command in Korea and Japan, accusing him of insubordination—a decision the Joint Chiefs of Staff supported. Truman's decision was nonetheless highly unpopular. The allure of decisive victory under a charismatic military leader temporarily pushed aside doubts about the war. Returning to tumultuous receptions in San Francisco, Chicago, and New York, MacArthur delivered an impassioned televised address to a joint session of Congress watched by millions of Americans. Although he failed to win the 1952 Republican presidential nomination, which he coveted, MacArthur's determination to roll back (rather than just contain) communist influence remained popular with many Americans.

The Korean War dragged on for more than two years after MacArthur's dismissal. Truce talks began in Korea in July 1951, but a final armistice was not signed until July 1953. Approximately 45 percent of American casualties were sustained in this period. The final settlement left Korea divided very near the original border at the 38th parallel and established a demilitarized zone between the two countries (see Map 27.2). North Korea remained firmly allied with the Soviet Union; South Korea signed a mutual defense treaty with the United States in 1954.

The Impact of the Korean War. The three-year conflict was costly for the United States: 54,200 American soldiers died, 103,000 were wounded, and military expenditures totaled $54 billion. Defense mobilization helped stimulate the American economy but did not foster the patriotic fervor that had characterized World War II. Struggling against heavy snow and subzero cold, American troops in Korea grew to hate the endless fighting that characterized the stalemate. "I'll fight for my country," a corporal from Chicago complained, "but I'm damned if I see why I'm fighting for this hell-hole." When the armistice was signed, there were few public celebrations.

The Korean War had a lasting impact on the conduct of American foreign policy. Truman's decision to commit troops to Korea without congressional approval set a precedent for future undeclared wars. The war also expanded American involvement in Asia, transforming containment into a truly global policy. During and after the war the United States stationed large numbers of troops in South Korea and increased military aid to French forces fighting communist insurgents in Indochina (see Chapter 29). Such commitments were costly. Overall defense expenditures grew from $13 billion in 1950, roughly one-third of the federal budget, to $50 billion in 1953, nearly two-thirds of the budget. Although military expenditures dropped briefly after the Korean War, defense spending remained at over $35 billion annually throughout the 1950s. American foreign policy had become more global, more militarized, and more costly. Even in times of peace, the United States now functioned in a state of permanent mobilization.

Harry Truman and the Cold War at Home

Harry S Truman brought a complex personality to the presidency. Alternately humble and cocky, he had none of Franklin D. Roosevelt's patrician ease and was a distinctly unpopular president. Yet he handled affairs with an assurance and crisp dispatch that have endeared him to later generations. "If you can't stand the heat, stay out of the kitchen," he liked to say of presidential responsibility. The major domestic issues that he faced were reconversion to a peacetime economy and fears of communist infiltration and subversion—fears that his administration played a part in fanning. Truman kept the New Deal coalition alive by proposing new federal programs to advance the interests of its constituencies, and his Fair Deal would influence the Democratic Party's agenda for the next twenty years.

The Challenge of Reconversion

When Truman became president in 1945, Americans welcomed him with an approval rating of 87 percent, according to Gallup polls. Within a year his popularity had dropped to 32 percent, and new phrases such as "To err is Truman" entered the political language. What had happened? New to the presidency, Truman had to oversee the complex conversion of a wartime economy to a peacetime one. In part because government planners had not known about the atomic bomb, they had assumed that reconversion could be phased in while the country went through the process of winning a land war in Japan that was expected to last through 1946. Instead World War II ended before adequate reconversion plans were in place.

The public's main fear in 1945 was that the depression would return once war production ended. To the relief of those who had lived through the hardships of the 1930s, the economy did not collapse. Despite a drop in government spending after the war, consumer spending increased because workers had amassed substantial wartime savings that they were eager to spend once wartime restrictions were lifted. The Servicemen's Readjustment Act of 1944, popularly known as the GI Bill, also put money into the economy by providing educational and economic assistance to returning veterans. Despite some temporary dislocations as war production shifted back to civilian uses and veterans were reabsorbed into the work force, unemployment did not increase significantly. The most visible layoffs involved the "Rosie the Riveters" who had taken high-paying defense jobs during the war and were now forced to find jobs in traditional areas of women's employment at much lower pay.

Economic Policy. But the transition was hardly trouble-free. The main domestic problem was inflation. Consumers wanted an end to wartime restrictions and price rationing, but Truman feared economic chaos if he lifted all controls immediately. In the summer of 1945 he eased industrial controls but retained the wartime Office of Price Administration (OPA). When

the OPA was disbanded and almost all controls were lifted in November 1946, prices soared. That year saw an annual inflation rate of 18.2 percent. The persistent shortages of food and products prompted by unfettered consumer spending also irritated many shoppers.

With the Employment Act of 1946, the federal government began developing mechanisms to pursue a more coherent economic policy. The legislation introduced federal fiscal planning on a permanent basis—not just in times of economic crisis—to achieve full employment. Besides supporting the Keynesian notion of government spending to spur economic growth, the act promoted the use of tax policy as a tool for managing the economy, using tax cuts to spur economic growth and tax increases to slow inflation. Yet the legislation was weak. It merely advocated rather than mandated such planning measures and gave the new three-member Council of Economic Advisors only an advisory role. It also failed to establish clear economic priorities, such as the proper relationship between the commitment to full employment and the need for a balanced budget. Nevertheless, the Employment Act of 1946 was an important milestone in establishing federal responsibility for the performance of the economy.

Postwar Strikes. The rapidly rising cost of living prompted demands for higher wages by the nation's workers. By 1945 the number of union members had swelled to more than 14 million—representing over one-third of the nonagricultural work force and two-thirds of all workers in the mining, manufacturing, construction, and transportation industries. Under government-sanctioned agreements the labor movement had held the line on wages during the war, but unions expressed frustration as postwar corporate profits doubled while real wages declined in the face of increasing inflation and the loss of wartime overtime pay. Determined to make up for their war-induced sacrifices, workers mounted strikes in major sectors of the economy, crippling the automobile, steel, and coal industries. By the end of the year 5 million workers had idled factories and mines for a total of 107,476,000 lost workdays.

Truman never doubted his course of action, even if it meant alienating organized labor, an important component of the Democratic coalition. "If you think I'm going to sit here and let you tie up this whole country, you're crazy as hell," he told the leaders of a nationwide railroad strike in the spring of 1946. Truman used his executive authority to place the nation's railroad system under federal control and asked Congress for the power to draft striking workers into the army, a move that infuriated labor but pressured strikers to go back to work. A few days later, on April 1, 1946, he seized control of the nation's coal mines to end a strike led by John L. Lewis and the United Mine Workers. Such actions won Truman support from Americans fed up with labor disruptions but angered organized labor.

These domestic upheavals did not bode well for the Democrats at the polls. In the 1946 congressional elections Republicans capitalized on popular dissatisfaction with reconversion with the simple slogan "Had enough?" Many voters answered in the affirmative, and the Republicans gained control of both houses of Congress for the first time since 1928. Truman and the Democrats seemed to have been thoroughly repudiated.

The Taft-Hartley Act. The Republican Congress elected in 1946 was determined to trim back several New Deal social welfare measures, and it singled out labor legislation as a special target. In 1947 Congress passed the Taft-Hartley Act, a rollback of several provisions of the 1935 National Labor Relations Act. Unions especially disliked section 14b, which allowed states to pass "right to work" laws that outlawed the *closed shop* (a workplace employing only union labor). The act also restricted the political power of unions by prohibiting the use of their dues for political activity, and it allowed the president to declare an eighty-day cooling-off period in strikes with a national impact. Truman issued a ringing veto of the Taft-Hartley bill in June 1947, calling it "bad for labor, bad for management, and bad for the country." Congress easily overrode the veto, but Truman's action brought labor back into the Democratic fold.

Truman Triumphant
In one of the most famous photographs in American political history, Harry S Truman gloats over an inaccurate headline in the Chicago *Tribune*. Pollsters had predicted an overwhelming victory for Thomas E. Dewey. Their primitive techniques, however, did not reflect the dramatic surge in support for Truman during the last days of the campaign.
Corbis-Bettmann.

The 1948 Election

Most observers believed that Truman faced an impossible task in the presidential campaign of 1948. The Republicans were united and well organized, maintaining the firm support of most white middle- and upper-income Protestant voters outside the South and that of many farmers and skilled workers. Eager to attract votes from traditional Democratic constituencies, the Republicans nominated Thomas E. Dewey, the politically moderate governor of New York who had demonstrated his attractiveness as a national candidate by garnering 46 percent of the popular vote in his 1944 campaign against Roosevelt. To increase their appeal in the West, the Republicans nominated Earl Warren, governor of California, for vice-president. Their brief platform promised to continue most New Deal reforms and supported a bipartisan foreign policy.

Truman, in contrast, led a party in disarray. Both the left and right wings of the Democratic Party split off and nominated their own candidates. Henry A. Wallace, a former New Deal liberal whom Truman had fired as secretary of commerce in 1946 because he was perceived as too "soft" on communism, ran as the candidate of the new Progressive Party. Wallace advocated increased government intervention in the economy, more power for labor unions, and cooperation with the Soviet Union.

Southern Democrats bolted the party over the issue of civil rights. At the Democratic national convention, northern liberals such as Mayor Hubert H. Humphrey of Minneapolis and gubernatorial candidate Adlai E. Stevenson of Illinois had pushed through a platform calling for the establishment of a permanent Fair Employment Practices Commission and federal antilynching and anti–poll tax legislation. Southern Democrats, unwilling to tolerate federal interference in race relations, walked out of the convention and created the States' Rights Party, popularly known as the Dixiecrats. They nominated Governor J. Strom Thurmond of South Carolina for president.

Truman responded to these challenges with one of the most effective presidential campaigns ever waged. He dramatically called Congress back into summer session to give the Republicans a chance to enact their platform into law. When they failed to do so, he launched a strenuous cross-country speaking tour, blasting the "do-nothing Republican Congress." He also hammered away at the Republicans' support for the antilabor Taft-Hartley Act and their opposition to legislation on housing, medical insurance, and civil

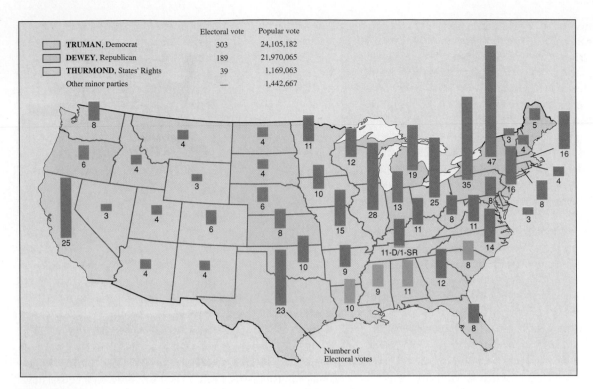

	Electoral vote	Popular vote
TRUMAN, Democrat	303	24,105,182
DEWEY, Republican	189	21,970,065
THURMOND, States' Rights	39	1,169,063
Other minor parties	—	1,442,667

MAP 27.3
The Election of 1948
Political advisor Clark Clifford planned Truman's electoral strategy in 1948, arguing that the president should concentrate his campaign in urban areas where the Democrats had their greatest strength. In an election with a low turnout Truman held onto enough support from the Roosevelt coalition of blacks, union members, and farmers to defeat Dewey by more than 2 million votes.

rights. By combining these domestic themes with attacks on the Soviet menace abroad, Truman revived his troubled campaign. At his rallies enthusiastic listeners took up the cry "Give 'em hell, Harry!"

Truman won a remarkable victory, receiving 49.6 percent of the vote to Dewey's 45.1 percent (Map 27.3). Strom Thurmond carried only four southern states, and Henry Wallace failed to win any electoral votes. The Democrats also regained control of both houses of Congress. Truman retained the support of organized labor and Jewish and Catholic voters in the big cities; the loyalty of northern black voters to the Democratic Party offset southern losses to the Dixiecrats. Most important, Truman appealed effectively to people like himself who hailed from the farms, towns, and small cities in the nation's heartland. He had grasped something the pollsters had missed: "Everybody's against me but the people."

Fair Deal Liberalism

Shortly after becoming president, Truman had proposed to Congress a twenty-one-point plan for expanded federal responsibilities. Anticipating a period of afflu-

ence rather than the austerity that had shaped the New Deal, Truman phrased his proposals in terms of the rights of individual citizens—the right to a "useful and remunerative" job, protection from monopoly, good housing, "adequate medical care," "protection from the economic fears of old age," and a "good education." Later Truman added support for civil rights and called his program the Fair Deal.

Truman's Fair Deal represented the essential aspects of postwar liberalism. Liberals believed in an activist federal government that would use its powers to stimulate economic growth, redress imbalances, and encourage social progress. With a rhetorical commitment to civil rights and economic abundance for all, liberalism called for the modern state to extend the benefits of capitalism to ever greater numbers of citizens. By expanding the welfare state at home while fighting communism abroad, Truman sought to steer a middle course between socialism on the left and fascism on the right. Historian Arthur Schlesinger Jr. dubbed this brand of liberalism "the Vital Center."

Truman's agenda ran up against a generally hostile Congress, despite its Democratic majority. The same conservative coalition that had blocked Roosevelt in his second term and had dismantled or cut popular New Deal programs during wartime continued to fight against Truman's proposals. Only parts of the Fair Deal won adoption: the minimum wage increased from 40 cents to 75 cents an hour, the Social Security system was extended to cover 10 million new workers, and Social Security benefits were raised by 75 percent. The National Housing Act of 1949 called for the construction of 810,000 units of low-income housing, although only half of that number was actually built under the program.

Truman's record on civil rights illustrates the opportunities and obstacles facing proponents of the Fair Deal. Although the struggle for civil rights had preoccupied African Americans since Reconstruction, it took on a new urgency in the 1940s. The callous treatment of black soldiers during World War II and the lynching of more than forty black men after the war—many of them veterans—sparked widespread anger. At the same time, black expectations had been raised by wartime opportunities and by symbolic victories such as Jackie Robinson's joining the Brooklyn Dodgers in 1947, breaking the color line in major league baseball. Truman's sympathies for civil rights were reinforced by the realization that black voters were playing an increasingly large role in the Democratic Party as they migrated from the South, where they were effectively disfranchised, to northern and western cities. Finally, Truman was sensitive to the world's view of America's treatment of blacks, especially since the Soviet Union often compared segregation of southern blacks with the Nazis' treatment of Jews.

Lacking a popular mandate on the civil rights issue, Truman turned to executive action. In 1946 he appointed a National Civil Rights Commission, whose 1947 report called for an expanded federal role that foreshadowed much of the civil rights legislation of the 1960s. He ordered the Justice department to prepare an *amicus curiae* ("friend of the court") brief in the Supreme Court case of *Shelley v. Kraemer* (1948), which struck down as unconstitutional restrictive covenants that enforced residential segregation by barring home buyers on the basis of race or religion. In the same year, Truman signed an executive order desegregating the armed forces. The Truman administration also proposed a federal antilynching law, federal protection of voting rights (such as an end to poll taxes), and a permanent federal agency to guarantee equal employment opportunities. A filibuster by southern conservatives, however, blocked such legislation in Congress.

Interest groups successfully opposed other key items on the Fair Deal agenda. The American Medical Association quashed a labor-backed movement for national health insurance by denouncing it as the first step toward "socialized medicine." Catholic groups successfully opposed legislation for aid to education because it did not include subsidies for parochial schools. Farmers, many of whom relied on unorga-

nized seasonal workers, refused to join labor in supporting repeal of the Taft-Hartley Act.

Two factors further limited the Fair Deal's chances for legislative success. One was the outbreak of the Korean War in 1950, which diverted national attention to foreign affairs. The other was the nation's growing fear of internal subversion. The anticommunist crusade was only one manifestation of the way the Cold War was increasingly permeating all facets of American life. Truman's administration played a significant role in heightening those domestic tensions.

The Great Fear

As American relations with the Soviet Union deteriorated in the late 1940s and early 1950s, fear of communism fueled a widespread campaign of domestic repression. Americans often call this phenomenon "McCarthyism," after Senator Joseph R. McCarthy of Wisconsin, the decade's most vocal anticommunist. But this "Great Fear" involved more than the work of just one man and was shared by many Americans who disagreed with McCarthy's vitriolic tactics. It built on the longstanding distrust of radicals and foreigners that had exploded in the Red Scare after World War I. Worsening Cold War tensions and partisan politics intersected with those deep-seated anxieties to spawn an obsessive concern with internal subversion. Ultimately, few Communists were found in positions of power; far more Americans became innocent victims of false accusations and innuendo. Although anticommunism also flourished in England, France, and other Western European nations, it took a particularly virulent form in the United States, where the term *communist* became synonymous with "un-American."

HUAC. The roots of postwar anticommunism date back to the late 1930s, when Democratic congressman Martin Dies of Texas and other conservatives launched the House Committee on Un-American Activities (HUAC) to investigate alleged fascist and communist subversion in labor unions and New Deal agencies. During America's World War II alliance with the Soviet Union, HUAC's visibility declined, but the committee reemerged after the war as Americans grew concerned over Soviet expansion in Eastern Europe. Revelations in 1946 of a Soviet spy ring operating in Canada and the United States accentuated American fears of Soviet subversion. Republicans in Congress capitalized on these fears, using accusations of communist subversion to discredit the Truman administration.

In 1947 HUAC helped launch the postwar red scare by holding widely publicized hearings on communist infiltration of the film industry. A group of writers and directors, soon dubbed the "Hollywood Ten," went to jail for contempt of Congress when they

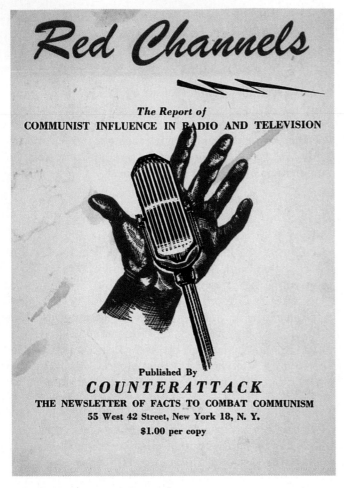

Red Channels

The Report of
COMMUNIST INFLUENCE IN RADIO AND TELEVISION

Published By
COUNTERATTACK
THE NEWSLETTER OF FACTS TO COMBAT COMMUNISM
55 West 42 Street, New York 18, N. Y.
$1.00 per copy

The Red Scare and the Media
After HUAC's 1947 investigation of the film industry, television and radio sponsors became wary of possible communist subversion on the airwaves. In 1950 three former FBI agents employed by a private consulting firm produced *Red Channels*, a booklet identifying 151 allegedly subversive entertainers. *Red Channels* was widely circulated among producers and was one of the key tools of the cultural Cold War.
The Michael Barson Collection/Past Perfect.

cited the First Amendment in refusing to testify about their past associations. Soon afterward former FBI agents in Hollywood circulated a list of actors, directors, and writers whose names had been mentioned in the HUAC investigation or whose associates and friends had been labeled as "reds." Industry executives denied the existence of a blacklist, but for ten years hundreds of people were shut out of work in the entertainment industry (see American Voices, "Mark Goodson Red Hunting on the Quiz Shows; or, What's My Party Line?" p. 885). The Weavers, a popular folk-singing group led by Pete Seeger, were blacklisted, and politically active actors such as Zero Mostel and John Garfield had difficulty finding work. One day the actress Jean Muir headlined the popular radio show

"The Aldrich Family"; the next she was out of a job—fired, according to the network, not because she was a Communist but because gossip about her alleged communist sympathies had made her too "controversial."

Anticommunism also emerged as a divisive force in the labor movement. In the 1930s and early 1940s Communists had been very active in labor organizing, and their contributions had been welcomed, if not openly acknowledged. But as conservatives charged that Soviet-led Communists were taking over American unions, the labor movement reversed itself in the late 1940s and purged Communists. The Taft-Hartley Act fueled this campaign by requiring labor leaders to take oaths swearing they were not Communists before their unions could participate in federally supervised elections. The president of the Congress of Industrial Organizations, Philip Murray, subsequently denounced communist sympathizers as "skulking cowards . . . apostles of hate." Eleven unions that refused to oust their communist or communist-sympathizing leaders were expelled from the CIO.

Truman's Loyalty Program. Attempting to protect himself against charges that he was "soft on communism" in the wake of the Soviet spy ring revelations, Truman fed the hysteria in March 1947 by issuing an executive order initiating a comprehensive investigation into the loyalty of all federal employees. More than 6 million individuals were subjected to security checks, 14,000 underwent intensive FBI investigation, and 2,000 were dismissed. The case of Dorothy Bailey reflects the experience of many of those who were dismissed. Bailey lost her job with the U.S. Employment Service, where she had worked for fourteen years, because an unidentified informer claimed that she was a Communist and associated with known Communists. Denying the charge, she was brought before the District of Columbia regional loyalty board, which introduced no evidence against her and called no witnesses to support its case. She was fired anyway.

Following Washington's lead, many state and local governments, universities, political organizations, churches, and businesses undertook their own antisubversion campaigns. Part of a broad-based "Popular Front" against fascism in the late 1930s and early 1940s, American Communists had worked in a wide variety of occupations and political organizations. In the chilling climate of the Cold War, however, many Americans began to fear these radicals, believing they would co-opt their political agendas or discredit their organizations. Loyalty programs and purges were seen as the solution. All 11,000 faculty members in the University of California system were required to take a loyalty oath; UCLA alone fired 157 who refused to do so. Many Catholic organizations became hotbeds of anticommunism, urging their members to combat "enemies" within the church. Because of the Communist

MARK GOODSON

Red Hunting on the Quiz Shows; or, What's My Party Line?

───────★───────

Active in the television industry from its earliest days, Mark Goodson was a highly successful producer whose game shows included "What's My Line?" "To Tell the Truth," "Password," and "Family Feud." In this interview, Goodson recalls his experience in the industry in the early 1950s when rampant anticommunism plagued the entertainment business.

I'm not sure when it began, but I believe it was early 1950. At that point I had no connection with the blacklisting that was going on, although I heard about it in the motion picture business and heard rumors about things that had happened on other shows, like *The Aldrich Family.* . . .

Soon afterwards, CBS installed a clearance division. There wasn't any discussion. We would just get the word—"drop that person"—and that was supposed to be it. Whenever I booked a guest or a panelist on *What's My Line?* or *I've Got a Secret*, one of our assistants would phone up and say, "We're going to use so-and-so." We'd either get the okay, or they'd call back and say. "Not clear," or "Sorry, we can't use them." Even advertising agencies—big ones, like Young & Rubicam and BBD&O—had their own clearance departments. They would never come out and say it. They would just write off somebody by saying, "He's a bad actor." You were never supposed to tell the person what it was about; you'd just

unbook them. They never admitted there was a blacklist. It just wasn't done. . . .

Anna Lee was an English actress on a later show of ours called *It's News to Me*. The sponsor was Sanka Coffee, a product of General Foods. The advertising agency was Young & Rubicam. One day, I received a call telling me we had to drop one of our panelists, Anna Lee, immediately. They said she was a radical, that she wrote a column for the *Daily Worker*. They couldn't allow that kind of stuff on the air. They claimed they were getting all kinds of mail. It seemed incongruous to me that this little English girl, someone who seemed very conservative, would be writing for a Communist newspaper. It just didn't sound right.

I took her out to lunch. After a little social conversation, I asked her about her politics. She told me that she wasn't political, except she voted Conservative in England. Her husband was a Republican from Texas.

I went to the agency and said, "You guys are really off your rocker. Anna Lee is nothing close to a liberal." They told me, "Oh, you're right. We checked on that. It's a different Anna Lee who writes for the *Daily Worker*." I remember being relieved and saying, "Well, that's good. You just made a mistake. Now we can forget this." But that wasn't the case. They told me, "We've still got to get rid of her, because the illusion is just as good as the reality. If our client continues to get the mail, no one is going to believe him when he says there's a second Anna Lee." At that point I lost it. I told them their demand was outrageous. They could cancel the show if they wanted to, but I would not drop somebody whose only crime was sharing a name. When I got back to my office, there was a phone call waiting for me. It was from a friend of mine at the agency. He said, "If I were you, I would not lose my temper like that. If you want to argue, do it quietly. After you left, somebody said, 'Is Goodson a pinko?'"

───────────

Source: Griffin Fariello, *Red Scare* (New York: Norton, 1995), 320–324.

Party's historic defense of racial equality, civil rights organizations such as the National Association for the Advancement of Colored People and the National Urban League were attacked as communist-influenced. To fend off such charges, civil rights groups subsequently purged themselves of Communists or sympathetic "fellow travelers." Some postwar liberals, such as Henry Wallace and his followers in the Progressive Party, continued to seek cooperation with the Soviet Union and defended the participation of Communists in their organizations. But many other liberals, most notably those in Americans for Democratic Action, founded in 1947, shunned potential left-wing allies and embraced a strident anticommunism.

The anticommunist crusade intensified in 1948 when HUAC began an investigation of Alger Hiss, a former New Dealer and State department official who had accompanied Franklin Roosevelt to Yalta. Republican congressman Richard M. Nixon of California orchestrated the HUAC investigation, an event that brought him national recognition and boosted his political career. The case against Hiss rested on the testimony of former Communist Whittaker Chambers, a senior editor at *Time* magazine. Chambers claimed that Hiss was a member of a secret communist cell in the government and had passed him classified documents in the 1930s. Hiss categorically denied the allegations and denied even knowing Chambers. Because the statute of limitations on espionage had expired by 1949, Hiss was charged with perjury for lying about his communist affiliations and acquaintance with Chambers. The first trial resulted in a hung jury; the second, in early 1950, found Hiss guilty and sentenced him to five years in federal prison. Even after Alger Hiss's death in 1996, the media continued to debate the question of his guilt or innocence. Recently released evidence from the Soviet archives suggests that he was in fact working with the Soviets at the time.

The Rise and Fall of McCarthy.   The conviction of Hiss increased paranoia about a communist conspiracy in the federal government and contributed to the meteoric rise of Senator Joseph McCarthy of Wisconsin. In February 1950, just a few weeks after the Hiss verdict, McCarthy delivered a bombshell during a speech in Wheeling, West Virginia: "I have here in my hand a list of the names of 205 men that were known to the Secretary of State as being members of the Communist Party and who nevertheless are still working and shaping the policy of the State Department." McCarthy never revealed the names on his list and later lowered the number to 81 and then to 57. Despite these inconsistencies, the public responded enthusiastically to his charges.

A Marine Air Corps veteran who had won a Senate seat in the 1946 Republican landslide, McCarthy discovered that anticommunist rhetoric could boost his political fortunes. Like other Republicans in the late 1940s, he leveled accusations of communist subversion

McCarthy's Assault on Civil Liberties
Senator Joseph McCarthy's reckless attacks on alleged Communists in the U.S. government stirred widespread public fears of Soviet subversion in the 1950s. His critics, such as cartoonist Al Hirschfeld, expressed alarm at what they saw as McCarthy's assault on American liberty.
© Al Hirschfeld. Drawing reproduced by special arrangement with The Margo Feiden Galleries, NY.

to embarrass Truman and the Democrats. Truman called McCarthy's charges "slander, lies, character assassination," but he could do nothing to curb them. McCarthy's political genius lay in his ability to make his name synonymous with the cause of uncovering subversives in government. Politicians who attacked him exposed themselves to charges of being "soft" on communism, the kiss of death in the postwar political climate. Because McCarthy charged that his critics themselves were part of "this conspiracy so immense," few political leaders challenged him. When Republican Dwight D. Eisenhower was elected president in 1952, he did not publicly challenge his party's most outspoken senator despite his personal dislike for McCarthy.

Although McCarthy never identified a single Communist in the federal government, a series of national and international events allowed him to retain credibility. Besides the Hiss case, the sensational 1951 espionage case of Julius and Ethel Rosenberg fueled McCarthy's allegations. Convicted of passing atomic secrets to the Soviet Union in a highly controversial trial, the Rosenbergs were executed in 1953. (As in the case of Alger Hiss, their convictions continue to be debated; the recent release of declassified documents from Project Venona, a top-secret intelligence mission during World War II, provided new evidence of Julius Rosenberg's guilt.) The Korean War, which embroiled the United States in a frustrating fight against communism in a faraway land, also made Americans susceptible to McCarthy's claims.

After four years of relentless red hunting, McCarthy overreached himself by launching an investigation into possible subversion in the U.S. Army in 1954. When lengthy televised hearings brought McCarthy's smear tactics and innuendos into the nation's living rooms, support for him declined. Joseph Welch, an attorney representing the army in the hearings, voiced the growing public disapproval of McCarthy when he burst out, "Senator, have you no decency?" Moreover, the end of the Korean War and the death of Stalin in 1953 also undercut public interest in McCarthy's anticommunist campaign. In December 1954 the Senate voted 67 to 22 to censure McCarthy for unbecoming conduct. He died from alcohol-related illness three years later at the age of forty-eight, his name forever attached to a period of political repression of which he was only the most flagrant manifestation.

"Modern Republicanism"

★

The 1952 election occurred in the middle of the Korean stalemate and at the height of the Great Fear. The newly elected president, Dwight D. Eisenhower, worked quickly to end the Korean War, but the grip of McCarthyism

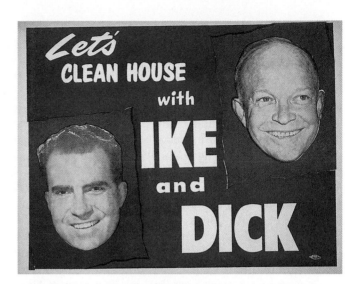

The 1952 Presidential Campaign
The 1952 Republican ticket of Dwight D. Eisenhower and Richard M. Nixon launched an effective attack on the Democratic leadership by stressing the Truman administration's involvement in bribery and influence-peddling scandals, and by capitalizing on Truman's failure to end the war in Korea. Collection of Janice L. and David J. Frent.

lasted longer. Eisenhower set the tone for what historians call "modern Republicanism"—an updated GOP approach that emphasized a slowdown, but not a dismantling, of federal responsibilities. Compared with their predecessors in the 1920s and their successors in the 1980s and 1990s, Eisenhower and other modern Republicans were more tolerant of the federal government's intervention in social and economic affairs, though they sought to limit its scope. More important to the average voter than Eisenhower's political philosophy, however, was his proven leadership in trying times; he seemed the right person to guide the nation through the perils of the continuing Cold War.

They Liked Ike

Eisenhower's status as a war hero was his greatest political asset. Born in 1890 and raised in Abilene, Kansas, he had graduated from the United States Military Academy at West Point in 1915. General Douglas MacArthur chose him as his aide in the early 1930s, and Eisenhower rose quickly through the ranks. After the Japanese attack on Pearl Harbor, he came to Washington under the sponsorship of a second mentor, General George C. Marshall. Eisenhower oversaw the Allied invasion of North Africa in 1942, and in 1944 became Supreme Commander of Allied Forces in Europe, where he had the mammoth task of coordinating the D-Day invasion of France. To hundreds of thousands of soldiers and to the millions who followed the war on newsreels, he was simply "Ike," the best known and most respected of the nation's military leaders.

A professional military man, Eisenhower claimed to stand "above politics." While in the army he had never voted, insisting that such political activity represented an intrusion of the military into civilian affairs. Many Democrats had hoped to make him their candidate for president in 1948 and again in 1952. Eisenhower wanted the office, but as a Republican. Resigning his position as commander of NATO forces in Europe, he quickly won several primaries and took delegates away from his rival, Senator Robert A. Taft of Ohio, in a tough fight at the Republican national convention. Eisenhower then asked Senator Richard M. Nixon of California to be his running mate. Young, tirelessly partisan, and sporting a strong anticommunist record from his crusade against Alger Hiss, Nixon brought regional balance and an aggressive campaign style to the ticket.

The Democrats never seriously considered renominating Harry Truman, who by 1952 was a thoroughly discredited leader. Lack of popular enthusiasm for the Korean War dealt the most severe blow to Truman's support, but a series of widely publicized scandals involving federal officials in bribery, kickbacks, and influence-peddling schemes caused voters to complain about the "mess in Washington." The Democrats turned instead to the popular governor of Illinois, Adlai E. Stevenson, who enjoyed the support of organized labor and respected liberals such as Eleanor Roosevelt. To appease southern voters who feared Stevenson's liberal agenda, the Democrats nominated Senator John A. Sparkman of Alabama for vice-president.

Throughout the 1952 campaign Stevenson advocated New Deal and Fair Deal policies with an almost literary eloquence, but Eisenhower's artfully unpretentious speeches were more effective with the voters. Eager to win the support of the broadest possible electorate, Eisenhower played down specific questions of policy. Instead, he attacked the Democrats with the "K1C2" formula—"Korea, Communism, and Corruption." In a campaign pledge that clinched the election he vowed, "I shall go to Korea," to end the stalemated war if elected.

The Republican campaign was temporarily set back by the revelation that wealthy Californians had set up a secret slush fund for Richard Nixon. Eisenhower contemplated dropping him from the ticket, but Nixon adroitly used a televised speech to convince voters that he had not misused campaign funds. Whereas Truman appointees had accepted mink coats from contractors— a reference to a widely reported case involving a loan examiner for the Reconstruction Finance Corporation— Nixon's wife wore a "respectable Republican cloth coat." Nixon did admit accepting one gift, a puppy his young daughters had named Checkers. That gift he would not give back, he declared earnestly. Nixon's televised pathos turned an embarrassing incident into an advantage, as sympathetic viewers flooded Republican headquarters with telegrams and phone calls. Outmaneuvered, Republican leaders had no choice but to keep Nixon on the ticket. The "Checkers speech" showed how politicians could use the powerful medium of television to their advantage.

That November Eisenhower won 55 percent of the popular vote, carrying all the northern and western states and four southern states as well. Republican candidates for Congress did not fare quite as well. They regained the Senate but won control of the House of Representatives by only a slender margin of four seats. In 1954 the Democrats would regain control of both houses, an advantage that they held even when the enormously popular Eisenhower won easy reelection in 1956.

The Hidden-Hand Presidency

Eisenhower offered modern Republicanism as an alternative to the Democrats' liberal agenda. He did his best to set a quieter national mood, hoping to decrease the need for federal intervention in social and economic issues. He refused to speak out publicly against Senator McCarthy and displayed little leadership in the emerging area of civil rights. As columnist Richard L. Strout observed in *The New Republic*, "The less he does the more they love him. Here is a man who doesn't rock the boat."

Yet Eisenhower was no stooge as president. Political scientist Fred Greenstein has characterized his style of leadership as the "hidden-hand presidency," pointing out that Eisenhower maneuvered deftly behind the scenes while not seeming to concern himself publicly with partisan questions. Others cite the president's skillful handling of the press. When his press secretary, James Hagerty, asked what he would say about a tricky foreign policy issue at a press conference, Eisenhower replied, "Don't worry, Jim. If that question comes up, I'll just confuse them."

Eisenhower presided cautiously over increases in federal activity. When the Soviet Union launched *Sputnik*, the first space satellite, in 1957, Eisenhower reluctantly approved a U.S. space program to catch up in this new Cold War competition. The National Aeronautics and Space Administration (NASA) was founded the following year. Arguing that the Cold War required more scientists and experts on foreign affairs, he persuaded Congress to appropriate additional money for college scholarships and to increase its support for research and development in universities and industry. Federal outlays for veterans' benefits, unemployment compensation, housing, and Social Security were increased, and the minimum wage was raised from

The* Sputnik *Crisis
The Soviet launching of the *Sputnik* space satellite in 1957 precipitated a crisis of confidence in American science and education. That sense of crisis was reflected in a 1950s "Space Race" card game, in which those dealt the *Sputnik* card would lose two turns.
The Michael Barson Collection/Past Perfect.

75 cents an hour to a dollar. The creation of the new Department of Health, Education and Welfare (HEW) in 1953 consolidated government control of social welfare programs.

The most extensive federal activity took place in the realm of transportation. In a move that drastically altered the American landscape and favored the trend toward privately owned automobiles, the Interstate Highway Act of 1956 authorized $26 billion over a ten-year period for the construction of a nationally integrated highway system. (This network of highways was also promoted to speed civilian evacuation in case of nuclear attack.) To link the Great Lakes with the Atlantic Ocean, the United States and Canada cosponsored in 1959 the construction of the St. Lawrence Sea-

way, a project that had been discussed since the 1930s. The interstate highway and the St. Lawrence Seaway projects were the largest public works programs to date, surpassing anything the New Deal had undertaken. They highlighted the vital role of federal spending in American life, even under a Republican administration.

Eisenhower realized that the vast federal budget, which reached almost 23 percent of the gross national product in the late 1950s, gave the government a major responsibility for the overall health of the nation's economy. The president made the fight against inflation, not full employment, his top economic priority. Eisenhower believed that a balanced budget and stable prices would encourage business confidence and lead to prosperity. His policies pleased investors: the economy grew 2.9 percent per year between 1953 and 1961, while inflation averaged only 1.5 percent annually. Periodic bouts of unemployment and recession continued (1953–1954, 1957–1958, and 1960–1961), but the unemployment rate stayed below 7 percent throughout the Eisenhower years.

Modern Republicanism, it turned out, resisted the unchecked expansion of the state but did not generally cut back federal power. Only in the area of natural resource development did the Eisenhower administration move to reduce federal activity—turning federal offshore oil contracting over to the states in 1953 and authorizing privately financed hydroelectric dams on the Snake River in 1955. In most other areas the responsibilities that the federal government had accepted—social welfare programs inherited from the New Deal, Keynesian intervention in the economy, and increased defense expenditures necessitated by the nation's growing role abroad—signaled an abandonment of the Republican style of limited government that had prevailed in the 1920s. When Eisenhower retired from public life in 1961, the federal government was an even greater presence in everyday life than it had been when he took office. Some of the most controversial federal initiatives occurred in the area of civil rights.

Emergence of Civil Rights as a National Issue

The civil rights movement was arguably the most important force for change in postwar America, and its accelerating momentum had profound implications for the federal government. Legal segregation of the races still governed the southern way of life in the early 1950s. In most states it was illegal for whites and blacks to eat in the same rooms in restaurants and luncheonettes, use the same waiting rooms and toilet facilities at bus and train stations, or ride in the same taxis.

All forms of public transportation were rigidly segregated by custom or by law. Even drinking fountains were labeled "White" and "Colored."

Brown v. Board of Education.

Unlike Harry Truman, Dwight Eisenhower showed little commitment to civil rights. In fact, he proved extremely reluctant to intervene in what was widely seen as a state issue. Inadvertently, though, he contributed to the advancement of the black cause by naming Governor Earl Warren of California as Chief Justice of the U.S. Supreme Court in September 1953. Warren's quiet persuasion convinced the Court to rule unanimously in *Brown v. Board of Education of Topeka* (1954) that racial segregation in the public schools was unconstitutional.

The 1954 decision was the culmination of a series of test cases challenging segregation in housing, transportation, and other areas that the NAACP had been litigating since the 1940s. The NAACP had filed the Topeka case on behalf of Linda Brown, a black student who attended a segregated school several miles from her home rather than the nearby white elementary school. The NAACP's chief counsel, Thurgood Marshall, argued that the legal segregation mandated by the Topeka, Kansas, Board of Education was inherently unconstitutional because it stigmatized an entire race and thereby denied it the "equal protection of the laws" guaranteed by the Fourteenth Amendment. In a unanimous decision announced on May 17, 1954, the Supreme Court agreed, overturning the "separate but equal" doctrine of *Plessy v. Ferguson* (see Chapter 18). Speaking for the Court, Chief Justice Earl Warren ruled:

> *To separate Negro children . . . solely because of their race generates a feeling of inferiority as to their status in the community that may affect their hearts and minds in a way unlikely ever to be undone. . . . We conclude that in the field of public education the doctrine of "separate but equal" has no place. Separate educational facilities are inherently unequal. . . . Any language in* Plessy v. Ferguson *contrary to these findings is rejected.*

Integration at Little Rock, Arkansas
With chants such as "Two-four-six-eight, we ain't gonna integrate," angry crowds taunted Elizabeth Eckford (shown here walking past white students and National Guardsmen) and eight other black students who tried to register at the previously all-white Central High School in Little Rock, Arkansas, on September 4, 1957. The court-ordered integration proceeded only after President Eisenhower reluctantly nationalized the Arkansas National Guard to protect the students.
Francis Miller, LIFE Magazine, © Time, Inc.

In response to NAACP suits over the next several years, the Supreme Court used the *Brown* precedent to overturn segregation in city parks, public beaches and golf courses, all forms of interstate and intrastate transportation, and public housing. Meanwhile, progress in desegregating schools was frustratingly slow. In a 1955 decision implementing the *Brown* decision, the Court declared that integration should proceed "with all deliberate speed." Many critics would later note that the deliberation was far more evident than the speed.

When it became clear that the Court was not going to back down on civil rights, white resistance solidified. In 1956, 101 members of Congress signed a "Southern Manifesto" denouncing the *Brown* decision as "a clear abuse of judicial power" and encouraging their constituents to defy it. In that year 500,000 southerners joined White Citizens' Councils dedicated to blocking school integration and other civil rights measures. Some whites revived the old tactics of violence and intimidation, swelling the ranks of the Ku Klux Klan to levels not seen since the 1920s.

Crisis in Little Rock. President Eisenhower was disturbed by the *Brown* decision, asserting, "I don't believe you can change the hearts of men with laws or decisions." (He later complained that his appointment of Earl Warren was "the biggest damn fool mistake I ever made.") While acknowledging *Brown* as the law of the land, he did not commit federal power to enforcing it. A crisis in Little Rock, Arkansas, finally forced him to intervene on the side of desegregation. In September 1957 nine black students attempted to enroll at the all-white Central High School after the local school board won a court order to implement a desegregation plan. Governor Orval Faubus called out the state National Guard to bar the children from entering the school, despite the court order. Then the mob took over. Every day a white crowd taunted the poised but obviously terrified black students with chants such as "Go back to the jungle." As the vicious scenes were replayed on television night after night, Eisenhower reluctantly decided to act. He sent 1,000 federal troops to Little Rock and nationalized 10,000 members of the Arkansas National Guard, ordering them to protect the students.

Eisenhower thus became the first president since Reconstruction to use federal troops to enforce the rights of blacks. He also signed the Civil Rights Act of 1957, a Democratic bill that created the U.S. Commission on Civil Rights to study federal laws and policies dealing with equal protection. Though admittedly weak, the act was the first national civil rights legislation passed since Reconstruction.

Montgomery Bus Boycott. White resistance to the *Brown* decision, as well as Eisenhower's hesitancy to act in Little Rock, showed that court victories were not enough to overthrow segregation. Black southerners had also grown alarmed with the rising level of white violence, particularly the brutal lynching of fourteen-year-old Emmett Till in Mississippi in 1955. Later that year, on December 1, a new strategy of nonviolent protest emerged when Rosa Parks, a seamstress and member of the NAACP in Montgomery, Alabama, refused to give up her seat on a city bus to a white man. She was promptly arrested and charged with violating a local segregation ordinance. "I felt it was just something I had to do," Parks stated. Although Parks was hardly the first black southerner to challenge Jim Crow laws, her upstanding social reputation and political connections with the civil rights movement soon made her case famous in the black community.

When local black residents met to discuss the proper response, they turned to the Reverend Martin Luther King Jr., who had become pastor of Dexter Street Baptist Church the year before. The son of a prominent black minister in Atlanta, King had received a B.A. from Morehouse College and a Ph.D. in theology from Boston University. King endorsed a plan by a local black women's organization to boycott Montgomery's bus system until it was integrated. For the next 381 days members of a united black community formed car pools or walked to work. The bus company neared bankruptcy, and downtown stores complained about the loss of business. But not until the Supreme Court ruled in November 1956 that bus segregation was unconstitutional did the city of Montgomery finally relent. "My feets is tired, but my soul is rested," said one woman boycotter.

The Montgomery bus boycott catapulted Martin Luther King to national prominence. In 1957, with the Reverend Ralph Abernathy and other southern black clergy, he founded the Southern Christian Leadership Conference (SCLC), based in Atlanta. The black church had long been the center of African American social and cultural life; now it lent its moral and organizational strength, as well as the voices of its most inspirational preachers, to the civil rights movement. Female black church members were one of the movement's strongest constituencies, transferring the skills that they had honed through years of church work to the fight for racial equality. The SCLC joined the NAACP as one of the main advocacy groups for racial justice. Even though these groups received little support from national political leaders in the 1950s, their limited victories laid the organizational groundwork for the dynamic civil rights movement that would emerge in the 1960s.

The Political Baptism of Martin Luther King Jr.
After the arrest of Rosa Parks in December 1955, the black community of Montgomery, Alabama, organized a citywide bus boycott with the help of Martin Luther King Jr., a local Baptist pastor. Many black women served as grass-roots organizers of the boycott, but it was King who rose to prominence as an eloquent and highly respected spokesperson for the emerging civil rights movement in the region. He is shown here in Montgomery, Alabama, in 1956 addressing a crowd during the bus boycott.
Dan Weiner, courtesy Sandra Weiner.

The "New Look" of Foreign Policy

Eisenhower felt far more comfortable exercising leadership in military and diplomatic affairs than in civil rights. One of his first acts as president was to negotiate an armistice in the Korean War. As he had pledged in the campaign, he visited Korea in December 1952. The final settlement was signed in July 1953 at Panmunjom (see Map 27.2) after the parties reached a compromise on the tricky issue of prisoner exchange. The war ended with both sides occupying the territory they had held at the start of the conflict in 1950.

Once the Korean War was settled, Eisenhower turned his attention to Europe and the Soviet Union. Stalin's death in March 1953 had precipitated an intra-party struggle that lasted until 1956, when Nikita S. Khrushchev emerged as Stalin's successor. Although Khrushchev surprised Westerners by calling for "peaceful coexistence" between communist and capitalist societies, he made certain that the Soviet Union's Eastern European satellites did not drift too far from the Soviet path. When nationalists revolted in Hungary in 1956 and moved to take the country out of the Warsaw Pact, Soviet tanks rapidly moved into Budapest—an action the United States could condemn but not realistically resist. Soviet repression of the Hungarian revolt showed that American policy makers had few, if any, options for rolling back Soviet power in Eastern Europe short of going to war with the USSR.

Although Eisenhower strongly opposed communism, as a fiscal conservative he hoped to keep the cost of containment at a manageable level. Under his New Look defense policy, the president sought to enhance American nuclear capabilities and encourage U.S. allies to bear greater military responsibility through increased foreign aid and an extensive system of defense alliances.

Massive Retaliation. Eisenhower and Secretary of State John Foster Dulles believed that the nation's main foreign enemy was a worldwide communist movement led by Moscow. They reasoned that the United States could economize by developing a massive nuclear arsenal as an alternative to more expensive conventional forces. Because nuclear weapons delivered "more bang for the buck" (in the words of Defense Secretary Charles E. Wilson), the Eisenhower administration relied on the threat of nuclear weapons to check Soviet expansion—a policy known as *massive retaliation.* The administration thus expanded its commitment to the hydrogen bomb, approving extensive atmospheric testing in the South Pacific and in western states such as Nevada, Colorado, and Utah beginning in 1952. To improve the nation's defenses against possible air attack from the Soviet Union, the administration supported research to develop the long-range bombing capabilities of the Strategic Air Command, and installed the Distant Early Warning line of radar stations in Alaska and Canada in 1958.

Those efforts, however, did not give the United States the military superiority it hoped for because the Soviets matched the United States weapon for weapon in an escalating arms race. The Soviet Union carried out its own atmospheric tests of hydrogen bombs between 1953 and 1958 and developed a fleet of long-range bombers. By 1958 both nations had intercontinental ballistic missiles (ICBMs). When an American nuclear submarine launched an atomic-tipped Polaris missile in 1960, Soviet leaders raced to produce an equivalent weapon. While boosting the military-industrial sectors of the United States and the Soviet Union, the arms race funneled immense resources into soon-to-be obsolete weapon systems.

The New Look policy also extended collective security agreements between the United States and its allies, encouraging the latter to take greater responsibility for their own military defense. To complement the NATO alliance in Europe, Secretary of State Dulles negotiated bilateral defense treaties with South Korea and the nationalist Chinese regime in Taiwan in 1954. In the same year, he orchestrated the creation of the Southeast Asia Treaty Organization (SEATO), linking America and its major European allies with Australia, Pakistan, Thailand, New Zealand, and the Philippines. This "pactomania," as some called it, required that the United States come to the defense of more than forty other countries. U.S. policy makers tended to support stable governments, no matter how repressive, as long as they were overtly anticommunist. Some of America's staunchest allies—the Philippines, Iran, Cuba, South Vietnam, and Nicaragua—were governed by military dictatorships or repressive right-wing civilian governments that lacked broad-based popular support.

CIA Activities. Secretary of State Dulles did not shrink from covert intervention against governments that were, in his opinion, too closely aligned with com-

Testing an Atomic Bomb
Throughout the 1950s the Atomic Energy Commission (AEC) conducted above-ground tests of atomic and hydrogen bombs. Thousands of soldiers were exposed to fallout during the tests, such as this one at Yucca Flats, Nevada, in April 1952. The AEC, ignoring or suppressing medical evidence to the contrary, mounted an extensive public relations campaign to convince local residents that the tests did not endanger their health.
FPG International.

munism. For such tasks he used the Central Intelligence Agency, which was headed by his brother, Allen Dulles. During the Eisenhower administration the CIA moved beyond its original mandate of intelligence gathering to active, albeit secret, involvement in the internal affairs of foreign countries.

In the 1950s the CIA successfully directed the overthrow of several foreign governments. When Iran's nationalist premier, Muhammad Mossadegh, seized British oil properties in 1953, CIA agents helped the young shah of Iran, Muhammad Reza Pahlavi, depose him. In 1954 the CIA supported a coup in Guatemala against the popularly elected Jacobo Arbenz Guzman, who had expropriated 250,000 uncultivated acres held by the American-owned United Fruit Company and accepted arms from the communist government of Czechoslovakia. The CIA also tried, unsuccessfully, to overthrow Achmed Sukarno of Indonesia in 1958 because of his tolerance for growing communist influence in that country's government. Eisenhower specifically approved those efforts. "Our traditional ideas of international sportsmanship," he wrote privately in 1955, "are scarcely applicable in the morass in which the world now flounders."

The Emerging Third World

American leaders had devised the containment policy in response to Soviet expansion in Eastern Europe, but they soon extended it to the new nations that were emerging in the Third World. Before World War II, nationalism, socialism, and religion had inspired powerful anticolonial movements; in the 1940s and 1950s those forces intensified and spread, especially in the Middle East, Africa, and Asia. Between 1947 and 1962 the British, French, Dutch, and Belgian empires all but disintegrated. Seeking to draw the newly created countries into an American-led world system, U.S. policy makers encouraged the development of stable market economies in those areas. They also sought to further the ideal of national self-determination. But under the growing East-West tensions of the Cold War, both the Truman and the Eisenhower administrations often failed to recognize that indigenous nationalist or socialist movements in emerging nations had their own goals and were not necessarily under the control of either local communists or the Soviet Union.

The Middle East.   The Middle East, an oil-rich area that was playing an increasingly central role in the strategic planning of both the United States and the Soviet Union, presented one of the most complicated challenges. Zionism, the Jewish nationalist movement, had long encouraged Jews to return to their ancient homeland of Israel (Palestine). After World War II many Jewish survivors of the Nazi extermination camps had resettled in Palestine, which was still controlled by Britain under a World War I mandate. On November 29, 1947, the U.N. General Assembly voted to partition Palestine into two states, Jewish and Arab—a decision that Egypt, Jordan, and other Arab League states resisted. On May 14, 1948, the British mandate ended, and Zionist leaders proclaimed the state of Israel. President Truman quickly recognized the new state, alienating the Arabs but winning crucial support from Jewish voters in the 1948 election.

The Birth of Israel, 1948
Prime Minister David Ben-Gurion reads Israel's Declaration of Independence to the new country's assembled officials. The photograph on the wall is of Theodor Herzl, one of the founders of Zionism.
Corbis-Bettmann.

Egypt was another site of conflict with the Arab nations, one that reflected the way in which Third World countries became embroiled in the Cold War. When Gamal Abdel Nasser came to power in Egypt in 1954, two years after independence from Britain, he pledged to lead not just his country but the entire Middle East out of its dependent, colonial relationship through a form of pan-Arab socialism. Nasser obtained arms and promises of economic assistance from the Soviet Union, including help in building the Aswan Dam on the Nile, a major water and energy development project. Secretary of State Dulles countered with an offer of American assistance, but Nasser refused to distance himself from the Soviets, declaring Egypt's neutrality in the Cold War. Unwilling to accept this stance of nonalignment, Dulles abruptly withdrew his offer in July 1956.

A week later Nasser retaliated against the withdrawal of Western financial aid by nationalizing the Suez Canal, over which Britain had retained administrative authority and through which three-quarters of Western Europe's oil was transported. Nasser said he would use the tolls from the canal to build the dam himself. After several months of fruitless negotiation, Britain and France, in alliance with Israel, attacked Egypt and retook the canal. Their attack occurred at the same time as the Soviet repression of the Hungarian revolt, placing the United States in the potentially awkward position of denouncing Soviet aggression while tolerating a similar action by its own allies. Eisenhower and the United Nations forced France and Britain to pull back. Egypt retook the Suez Canal and built the Aswan Dam with Soviet support. In the end the Suez crisis increased Soviet influence in the Third World, intensified anti-Western sentiment in Arab countries, and produced dissension among leading members of the NATO alliance.

The Eisenhower Doctrine. In early 1957, in the aftermath of the Suez crisis, the president persuaded Congress to approve the Eisenhower Doctrine. Addressing concerns over declining British influence in the Middle East, the policy stated that American forces would assist any nation in the region "requiring such aid, against overt armed aggression from any nation controlled by International Communism." Later that year Eisenhower invoked the doctrine when he sent the U.S. Sixth Fleet to the Mediterranean Sea to aid King Hussein against a Nasser-backed revolt in Jordan. A year later he landed 14,000 troops to back up a pro-U.S. government in Lebanon.

The attention that the Eisenhower administration paid to developments in the Middle East in the 1950s demonstrated how the desire for access to steady supplies of oil increasingly affected foreign policy. More broadly, attention to the Middle East confirmed the global scope of American interests. Just as the Korean War had stretched the application of containment from Europe to Asia, the Eisenhower Doctrine revealed U.S. intentions to influence events in the Middle East as well.

The Impact of the Cold War

★

The Cold War extended to the most distant areas of the globe, but it also had powerful effects on the domestic economy, politics, and cultural values of the United States. The Soviet-American conflict also affected Americans in a personal way: for the first time in the nation's history there was a peacetime draft. In the past the armed forces had shrunk to a skeleton volunteer force at the end of each war or foreign engagement. But when World War II ended, the draft was kept in place to meet the military commitments associated with the Cold War: occupation forces in defeated Axis countries, missile deployment operations in Europe, and counterinsurgency forces in the Third World. Sud-

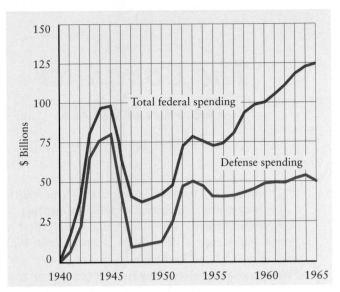

FIGURE 27.1
National Defense Spending, 1940–1965
In 1950 the defense budget was $13 billion, less than a third of total federal outlays. In 1961 defense spending reached $47 billion, fully half of the federal budget and almost 10 percent of the gross national product.

denly every neighborhood seemed to have a boy in the armed forces; many people made military service a career.

The postwar expansion of the military produced a dramatic shift in the country's economic priorities, as military spending took up a greater percentage of national income. Between 1900 and 1930, except for the two years that the United States fought in World War I, the country spent less than 1 percent of its GNP for military purposes. When Eisenhower left office in January 1961, the figure was closer to 10 percent, fully half of the federal budget (Figure 27.1). Even though the country was at peace during most of his administration, the economy and the government operated practically on a war footing.

The Military-Industrial Complex and Nuclear Proliferation

With its headquarters at the sprawling Pentagon in Arlington, Virginia, the Department of Defense had evolved into a massive bureaucracy that profoundly influenced the postwar economy. Aircraft companies such as Boeing and Lockheed did so much of their business with the government that they became dependent on Defense department orders. Federal money underwrote 90 percent of the cost of research on aviation and space, and also subsidized the scientific

The Computer Revolution

———————★———————

THE FIRST MODERN computers—information-processing machines capable of storing and manipulating data according to specified programs—appeared in the 1940s. During World War II engineers and mathematicians at the University of Pennsylvania developed a general-purpose, programmable electronic calculator called ENIAC (Electronic Numerical Integrator and Computer), which could add 5,000 ten-digit decimal numbers in one second. It stood 8 feet tall, measured 80 feet long, and weighed 30 tons; it used 18,000 vacuum tubes for computations. When it performed complex mathematical computations, one scientist noted, ENIAC sounded "like a roomful of ladies knitting." Although ENIAC lacked a central memory and could not store a program, it was the bridge to the modern computer revolution.

Six computers were under construction by 1947, including UNIVAC (Universal Automatic Computer), the first commercial computer system. To the general public in the 1950s, the word UNIVAC was synonymous with computer. UNIVAC was basically a data-processing system that could be tailored to an individual customer's needs. In 1951 the U.S. Census Bureau bought the first UNIVAC. Soon CBS-TV signed on, using a UNIVAC to predict the outcome of the 1952 presidential election. At 9 P.M., after only the East Coast polls had closed and with only 7 percent of the votes counted, UNIVAC predicted that Dwight D. Eisenhower would sweep the election with 438 electoral votes. CBS programmers and network executives, who had expected a closer election, got jittery and altered the program to give Eisenhower a far narrower margin. When the final tally gave him 442 electoral votes, only 4 votes off the original projection, commentator Edward R. Murrow observed, "The trouble with machines is people."

Computers are essentially collections of switches; the programs tell the machine which switches to turn on and off. The puzzle early computer scientists had to solve was how to increase the speed of this basic operation while lowering the cost. The first generation of computers needed vacuum tubes for computation power and used punched cards for writing programs and analyzing data. Computers such as ENIAC were room-size machines, and programming them could take several days because the programmers had to manually set thousands of switches in the on or off position. The vacuum tubes were the weakest part of early computers; the burnout of just a few of them could

instruments, automobile, and electronics industries. With the government paying part of the bill, corporations developed products with unprecedented speed. After the Pentagon backed IBM's investment in integrated circuits in the 1960s, these new devices—crucial to the computer revolution (see New Technology, "The Computer Revolution," above)—were in commercial production within three years. The impact of permanent mobilization was thus felt far beyond the defense industry.

The Cold War defense buildup brought mixed blessings. In positive terms, it created jobs: by the 1960s, perhaps as many as one in seven Americans owed his or her job to the military-industrial complex. In the South and West, where much of the new military activity was concentrated, dependence on federal defense spending was even greater (Map 27.4). That increased spending put money in the pockets of the millions of people working in defense-related industries, but it also limited the resources available for domestic needs. Moreover, the Cold War spurred a dangerous cycle of nuclear proliferation that would long outlive the Soviet-American conflict that spawned it.

The nuclear arms race affected all Americans by fostering a climate of fear and uncertainty. Bomb shelters and civil defense drills provided a daily reminder of the threat of nuclear war, and atomic research and testing had a devastating impact on human health. In the 1950s a small but growing number of citizens became concerned about the effects of radioactive fallout from above-ground bomb tests. In later years federal investigators documented a host of illnesses, deaths, and birth defects among families of veterans who had worked on weapons tests and among "downwinders"—residents near nuclear test sites and weapons facilities (see American Voices, "Isaac Nelson: Atomic Witness," p. 899).

An Early Computer Center
This computer–data-processing center featured an IBM 704 computer.

The invention of integrated circuits in 1959 ushered in the third computer generation, characterized by greater sophistication in miniaturization: the number of transistors that could be installed on a silicon chip increased dramatically, with a corresponding increase in computational power. The fourth computer generation arrived in 1971 with the development of the microprocessor, which placed the entire central processing unit (CPU) of a computer on a single silicon chip (about the size of the letter "O" on this page).

Miniaturization progressed so rapidly that by the mid-1970s a $1 chip provided as much processing power as had the ENIAC of thirty years earlier. Since then, transistor size has continued to shrink, resulting in chips with twice as many transistors roughly every eighteen months. The increased speed and memory of these chips, together with the immense data storage capabilities of the Internet (an online network first established by the Department of Defense in 1969), have made today's compact personal computers incredibly powerful tools. At the same time, scientists have been developing large-scale "supercomputers"—an integrated series of smaller computers that can be used to simulate complex natural and human phenomena such as weather, transportation systems, and genetics. Computers and computer technology have become so much a part of modern life that it is hard to remember how recent the origins of this technological revolution are.

shut down the entire system. Furthermore, the tubes gave off enormous amounts of heat, necessitating noisy and cumbersome air-conditioning units wherever computers operated. After a critical signal relay stopped one early program, scientists finally located the problem—a dead moth trapped in the apparatus, the origin of the term *debugging*.

The 1948 invention of the transistor revolutionized computers and the whole field of electronics, making the second generation of computers possible. Like vacuum tubes, transistors served as on-off switches, but they did not generate heat, burn out, or consume a lot of energy. They also were inexpensive to manufacture.

The most shocking revelations came to light in 1993 when the Department of Energy released millions of previously classified documents on human radiation experiments conducted under government auspices in the late 1940s and 1950s. The documents described over sixteen thousand cases involving the deliberate irradiation of human subjects, often without their consent or understanding. Some of the tests involved research for legitimate medical procedures, but others simply measured human tolerance of radioactive substances, some of which were known at the time to be extremely dangerous.

Arms Control

By the late 1950s, public concern over nuclear testing and fallout had become a high-profile issue, and new antinuclear groups such as SANE (the National Committee for a Sane Nuclear Policy) and Physicians for Social Responsibility called for an international test ban. Even Eisenhower, whose policies accelerated the arms race, had second thoughts about a nuclear policy—the aptly named MAD (Mutual Assured Destruction)—that was based on the premise of annihilating the enemy even if one's own country was destroyed. He also found spiraling arms expenditures a serious hindrance to balancing the federal budget, one of his chief fiscal goals. Consequently, Eisenhower tried to negotiate an arms limitation agreement with the Soviet Union. Laying the diplomatic groundwork for a possible arms treaty, Eisenhower and Khrushchev held a summit meeting in Geneva, Switzerland, in 1955—the first such meeting since the Potsdam Conference ten years before—and followed up with further disarmament talks over the next two years.

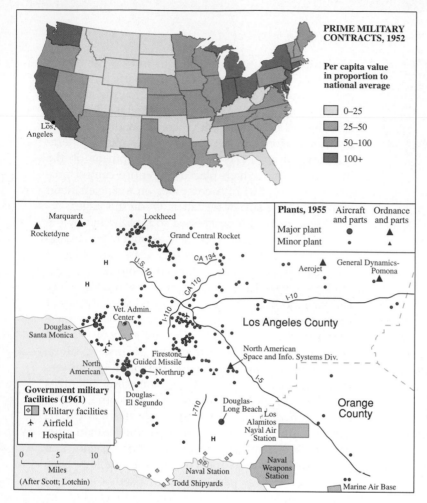

MAP 27.4
The Military-Industrial Complex in Los Angeles
The development and expansion of military facilities and defense contracting during the Cold War helped boost the populations and economies of Los Angeles and other Sun Belt cities and made the economies of California and other states highly dependent on defense expenditures.

Although those meetings did not yield the "open skies" mutual arms inspection treaty Eisenhower wanted, they did produce plans for another summit meeting in May 1960. Then, on May 5, the Soviets shot down an American U-2 spy plane over their territory and captured its pilot. Eisenhower at first denied that the plane was engaged in espionage but later admitted that he had authorized this and other secret flights over the USSR. In the midst of the dispute the summit meeting was canceled, and Eisenhower's last chance to negotiate an arms agreement evaporated.

Nuclear proliferation was not the only aspect of the Cold War that troubled Eisenhower. In his final address to the nation Eisenhower warned against the power of what he termed the "military-industrial com-

plex," which by then was employing 3.5 million Americans. Its pervasive influence, he said, "is felt in every city, every statehouse, every office of the federal government." Even though his administration had fostered this growth in the defense establishment to contain the Soviet threat, Eisenhower was gravely concerned about its implications for a democratic people: "We must guard against the acquisition of unwarranted influence, whether sought or unsought, by the military-industrial complex," he warned. "We must never let the weight of this combination endanger our liberties or democratic processes." With those words Dwight Eisenhower showed how well he understood the major transformations that the Cold War had brought to American life.

ISAAC NELSON
Atomic Witness

———★———

Isaac Nelson, a naval veteran of World War II, returned to his hometown of Cedar City, Utah, in 1945 and went to work for a nearby hardware company. Like many other residents of southern Utah, he and his wife Oleta lived downwind from the Nevada Test Site, where the U.S. government detonated 126 atomic bombs into the atmosphere between 1951 and 1963.

After 1951 they were going to start the testing in Nevada, and everybody was really excited, and thought maybe we'd get a part to play in it and show our patriotism. We wanted to help out what little we could. My wife and I and a hundred or so residents of Cedar drove out to see the first one. We huddled up, our blankets around us because it was cold, so early in the morning before daylight, and we were chattering like chipmunks, so excited! Pretty soon, why, the whole sky just flared up in an orange-red flash, and it was so brilliant that you could easily see the trees ten miles across the valley, and if you had a newspaper you could have easily read it, it was so bright. . . .

Later on in the day, you'd see these fallout clouds drifting down in Kanarraville, and up through Cedar, and if you'd ever seen one you'd never mistake it because it was definitely different from any rain cloud, kind of a pinkish-tan color strung out all down through the valley there for several miles. They'd float over the city and everyone would go out and ooh and aah just like a bunch of hicks. We was never warned that there was any danger involved in going out and being under these fallout clouds all the time I lived here. . . .

Along about 1955 a cloud came over Cedar, and my wife and I, the kids and the neighbors stood outside looking at it and talking about it. Later on towards evening, my wife, her skin, her hands, arms, neck, face, legs, anything that was exposed just turned a beet red. . . . She got a severe headache, and nausea, diarrhea, really miserable. We drove out to the hospital, and the doctor said, "Well it looks like sunburn, but then it doesn't." Her headache persisted for several months, and the diarrhea and nausea for a few weeks.

Four weeks after that I was sittin' in the front room reading the paper and she'd gone into the bathroom to wash her hair. All at once she let out the most ungodly scream, and I run in there and there's about half her hair layin' in the washbasin! You can imagine a woman with beautiful, raven-black hair, so black it would glint green in the sunlight just like a raven's wing. . . . She was in a state of panic. . . . After that she kept getting weaker, and listless, and she didn't even have any desire to go out in the garden to work with her flowers. . . . Finally [the doctors] said it looked like a large tumor in her brain, and they operated and removed a tumor about the size of a large orange or softball, but they couldn't get it all out, it was too embedded in the brain tissue. Oleta lived two years or so after that operation. She started going downhill from 1955 and died in 1965 at 41.

Source: Carole Gallagher, *American Ground Zero* (Cambridge, MA: MIT Press, 1993), 133–135.

Summary

★

Emerging from World War II as the world's most powerful nation, the United States soon became embroiled in a conflict with the Soviet Union over Eastern Europe. Twice a victim of German aggression, the Soviet Union used its occupation forces to establish a buffer zone of friendly governments in the region. The Truman administration, alarmed at what it saw as naked Soviet expansionism, set out to contain communist influence and to support noncommunist governments that shared America's commitment to a free-market system. Originally intended to curb the communist threat in Europe through economic and political aid, containment soon became a policy of military aid against communist and left-wing movements around the world.

Tension over communism abroad fostered a period of domestic repression and fear at home. Government, unions, schools, and other organizations instituted loyalty oaths as a requirement for employment; media organizations blacklisted suspected Communists; and congressional committees conducted sensationalized public investigations of alleged communist subversion. Red-hunting activities peaked during the anticommunist crusade of Senator Joseph McCarthy in the early 1950s, shattering the lives and careers of many innocent victims through false accusations and innuendo.

The Cold War also enhanced the power of the presidency and the national security state. With bipartisan support for the Cold War, the president gained greater latitude in foreign policy making and increasingly relied on covert operations of the Central Intelligence Agency to maintain friendly governments in the Third World. But these changes came at a price. The national security state required increased defense expenditures, which consumed an ever larger part of the gross national product. Americans now lived in a world where small foreign wars were a constant possibility and fear of a nuclear attack and radioactive fallout was part of daily life.

Under both Democratic and Republican presidents, New Deal reforms were modestly expanded during the postwar era. Harry Truman's Fair Deal proposed a sweeping program of social and economic reform but won only limited legislative victories in the areas of economic policy, social welfare, and civil rights. The Republican administration of Dwight Eisenhower did not roll back the New Deal and in fact presided over cautious increases in federal power through new initiatives in aerospace, education, and transportation. A growing civil rights movement in the South spurred federal activism on behalf of racial equality and put civil rights back on the national political agenda. Ultimately, the civil rights movement would usher in a broader wave of social activism in the 1960s, a development that was rooted in the affluence of the Cold War era.

T I M E L I N E

1945	Yalta and Potsdam conferences
	Harry S Truman succeeds Roosevelt as president
	End of World War II
1946	Kennan sends "Long Telegram" outlining containment policy
	Churchill's "Iron Curtain" speech
	Baruch Plan for international control of atomic weapons fails
	Employment Act
1947	Taft-Hartley Act
	Truman Doctrine
	National Security Act
	Marshall Plan
	House Un-American Activities Committee (HUAC) begins to investigate Hollywood
1948	Desegregation of U.S. armed forces
	Berlin airlift
1949	North Atlantic Treaty Organization (NATO) founded
	People's Republic of China established
	National Housing Act
	USSR detonates atomic bomb; U.S. atomic monopoly ends
1950	Senator Joseph McCarthy presents list of alleged Communists in government
	NSC-68 calls for permanent mobilization
1950– 1953	Korean War
1952	Dwight D. Eisenhower elected president
	U.S. detonates hydrogen bomb
1953	Joseph Stalin dies
1954	U.S. Army–McCarthy hearings
	Brown v. Board of Education of Topeka
1956	Suez crisis
	Interstate Highway Act
1957	Eisenhower Doctrine
	USSR launches *Sputnik*
	Eisenhower sends U.S. troops to Little Rock to ensure school integration
1958	NASA established
1960	American U-2 spy plane shot down over USSR

Suggested Readings

———————★———————

General works on the politics and diplomacy of the Cold War era include William Chafe, *The Unfinished Journey* (4th ed., 1999), and Paul Boyer, *Promises to Keep* (1995).

The Early Cold War

The best overviews of the Cold War are Walter LaFeber, *America, Russia, and the Cold War, 1945–1990* (8th ed., 1997); Thomas G. Paterson, *On Every Front: The Making and Unmaking of the Cold War* (rev. ed., 1992); and Stephen Ambrose and Douglas Brinkley, *Rise to Globalism* (8th ed., 1997). Melvyn P. Leffler presents a masterful and exhaustive synthesis of Truman's foreign policy in *A Preponderance of Power* (1992). For critical views of American aims, see H. W. Brands, *The Devil We Knew* (1993), and Richard Ned Lebow and Janice Gross Stein, *We All Lost the Cold War* (1994). John Lewis Gaddis blames the Cold War on both the United States and the Soviet Union in *Strategies of Containment* (1982), although his more recent works, *The Long Peace* (1987) and *The United States and the End of the Cold War* (1992), are more sympathetic to American policy making. For international perspectives on the Cold War, see Melvyn P. Leffler and David S. Painter, eds., *Origins of the Cold War: An International History* (1994), and Thomas J. McCormick, *America's Half-Century* (1989). Specialized studies include Ernest R. May, ed., *American Cold War Strategy: Interpreting NSC-68* (1993); Laurence S. Kaplan, *The United States and NATO* (1984); Michael Hogan, *The Marshall Plan* (1987); and Richard Freeland, *The Truman Doctrine and the Origins of McCarthyism* (1972).

The descent into the Cold War can also be viewed through the works of individual policy makers. Indispensable are Dean Acheson's modestly titled *Present at the Creation* (1970) and George F. Kennan's *American Diplomacy, 1900–1950* (1952), and *Memoirs, 1925–1950* (1967). Walter L. Hixson, *George F. Kennan: Cold War Iconoclast* (1989), presents a complex portrait of the architect of containment. Walter Lippmann, *The Cold War* (1947), offers a thoughtful critique of American foreign policy by a contemporary.

McGeorge Bundy, *Danger and Survival* (1989); Martin J. Sherwin, *A World Destroyed* (1975); and Gar Alperovitz, *Atomic Diplomacy* (2d ed., 1994), cover the impact of atomic weapons on American policy. For general discussions of America and nuclear weapons, see Paul Boyer, *By the Bomb's Early Light* (1985).

For developments in Asia, Akira Iriye, *The Cold War in Asia* (1974), is a good starting point. See also William Borden, *The Pacific Alliance* (1984); Warren I. Cohen, *America's Response to China* (2d ed., 1980); and Michael Schaller, *The United States and China in the Twentieth Century* (1979) and *The American Occupation of Japan* (1985).

There is an abundance of scholarship on the Korean War, including William Stueck, *The Korean War: An International History* (1995); Clay Blair, *The Forgotten War* (1988); Max Hastings, *The Korean War* (1987); Callum McDonald, *Korea: The War before Vietnam* (1987); Burton Kaufman, *The Korean War* (1986); and Rosemary Foot, *The Wrong War* (1985). Especially influential are the two volumes of *The Origins of the Korean War* by Bruce Cumings: *Liberation and the Emergence of*

Separate Regions, 1945–1947 (1981) and *The Roaring of the Cataract, 1947–1950* (1990). William Manchester, *American Caesar* (1979), and Michael Schaller, *Douglas MacArthur* (1989), offer stimulating biographies of a leading figure of the war.

Harry Truman and the Cold War at Home

Harry Truman, *Memoirs* (1952–1962), tells Truman's story in characteristically pointed language; see also Merle Miller's oral history, *Plain Speaking* (1980); David McCullough, *Truman* (1992), offers a generally sympathetic biography; Alonzo Hamby presents a more mixed view in *Man of the People: A Life of Harry S. Truman* (1995). General accounts of the Truman presidency can be found in Robert J. Donovan, *Tumultuous Years: The Presidency of Harry S. Truman, 1949–1953* (1982); Donald R. McCoy, *The Presidency of Harry S. Truman* (1984); and William Pemberton, *Harry S. Truman* (1989). Critical perspectives are presented in Barton J. Bernstein, ed., *Politics and Policies of the Truman Administration* (1970).

The literature on McCarthyism is voluminous. Recent works include Richard Gid Powers, *Not without Honor* (1996); Richard Fried, *Nightmare in Red: The McCarthy Era in Perspective* (1990); and Stephen J. Whitfield, *The Culture of the Cold War* (1991). David Caute, *The Great Fear* (1978), provides a detailed account, which can be supplemented by Victor Navasky, *Naming Names* (1980), and Athan Theoharis, *Spying on Americans* (1978). Two useful biographies are Thomas C. Reeves, *The Life and Times of Joe McCarthy* (1982), and David Oshinsky, *A Conspiracy So Immense* (1983).

"Modern Republicanism"

Two standard overviews of the Eisenhower administration, Herbert S. Parmet, *Eisenhower and the American Crusades* (1972), and Charles C. Alexander, *Holding the Line* (1975), can be supplemented by Fred I. Greenstein, *The Hidden-Hand Presidency* (1982), and Stephen Ambrose, *Eisenhower the President* (1984).

Robert F. Burk, *The Eisenhower Administration and Black Civil Rights* (1984), looks at what the administration did and did not do. Richard Kluger, *Simple Justice* (1975), and Mark Tushnet, *The NAACP's Legal Strategy against Segregated Education* (1987), analyze the *Brown* decision and its context. Martin Luther King Jr. recounts his experience in the Montgomery bus boycott in *Stride toward Freedom* (1958); and Taylor Branch, *Parting the Waters: America in the King Years, 1954–1963* (1988), provides a good account of King's early years.

The Impact of the Cold War

For the complex foreign policy of the 1950s, consult LaFeber, *America, Russia, and the Cold War*; Ambrose and Brinkley, *Rise to Globalism*; and McCormick, *America's Half-Century*. Gabriel Kolko, *Confronting the Third World, 1945–1980* (1988), offers a highly critical view of U.S. policy. On American involvement in the Middle East, see Bruce Kuniholm, *The Origins of the Cold War in the Near East* (1980), and Michael Stoff, *Oil, War, and American Security* (1980). On Latin America, see Stephen Rabe, *Eisenhower and Latin America: The Foreign Policy of Anticommunism* (1988).

Chapter 28

The Affluent Society and the Liberal Consensus,

1945–1965

I N 1959, VICE-PRESIDENT Richard Nixon traveled to Moscow to open the American National Exhibit, one of several efforts to reduce Cold War tensions in the late 1950s. After sipping Pepsi-Cola, Nixon and Soviet Premier Nikita Khrushchev got into a heated debate about the relative merits of Soviet and American societies. Instead of discussing rockets, submarines, and missiles, however, they talked dishwashers, toasters, and televisions. Both the subject of the animated conversation and its site—the kitchen of a model American home—led to its popular designation as the "kitchen debate." What was so striking about the Moscow exhibition was how its American planners enlisted affluence and mass consumption in the service of Cold War politics. The suburban life-style portrayed in the exhibit was intended to symbolize the superiority of capitalism over communism and imply that the American way of life would win the Cold War.

During the postwar era, millions of Americans pursued the promise of consumer society in the burgeoning suburbs, enjoying the highest standard of living in the nation's history. But this affluence was never as widespread as the Moscow exhibit implied. The middle-class suburban life-style was beyond the reach of many poor and nonwhite Americans, particularly those in the decaying central cities. Hoping to spread the abundance of a consumer society to greater numbers of Americans, the Democratic administrations of the early 1960s pressed for the expansion of New Deal social welfare programs. The administrations of John F. Kennedy and—to a much greater extent—Lyndon B. Johnson

The Growing Middle Class

Postwar affluence resulted in an unprecedented standard of living for the rapidly expanding middle class of the 1950s and 1960s. This 1951 photograph shows Du Pont worker Steve Czekalinski and his family amid a year's supply of food. Prior to the 1950s, most families relied on a diet of starches and smoked meats. The newfound prosperity of the growing middle class enabled families like the Czekalinskis to enrich their diets with fresh meats and vegetables and frozen food. The cost to the Czekalinskis in 1951 for a year's supply of food: $1,300.
Alexander Henderson/Hagley Museum and Library.

tried to use federal power to ensure the public welfare in areas such as health care, education, and civil rights. In the Great Society program—a burst of social legislation in 1964–1965 that marked the high tide of postwar liberalism—the Johnson administration attempted to use the fiscal powers of the state to redress the imbalances of the economy without directly challenging capitalism.

Liberal politicians also pursued an activist stance abroad. Continuing and in some cases expanding the Cold War policies of Truman and Eisenhower, the Kennedy and Johnson administrations took aggressive action against communist influence in Europe, the Caribbean, Vietnam (see Chapter 29), and other areas. The growing financial and political costs of that ambitious agenda, however, hampered further progress on the domestic front and revealed ominous cracks in the postwar liberal coalition.

The Affluent Society

★

By the end of 1945 war-induced prosperity had made the United States the richest country in the world. Because the government had curtailed new housing construction and rationed many consumer goods during the war, Americans in 1945 had accumulated savings of $140 billion, which they were eager to spend. Over the next two decades the gross national product (GNP) more than tripled, benefiting a wider segment of society than anyone would have dreamed possible in the dark days of the Great Depression. Millions of Americans, particularly working-class and middle-class whites, moved their families to new homes in the suburbs in a search for security and stability.

The Economic Record

The twenty-year period following World War II was the heyday of modern American capitalism. U.S. corporations and banking institutions so dominated the world economy that the period has been called the *Pax Americana* (American peace). U.S. military policy and foreign aid, as well as the absence of major economic competitors, were vital factors in extending the global reach of American corporate capitalism, which enjoyed remarkable growth in productivity and profits. American economic leadership abroad translated into affluence at home.

Corporate Strategies. The predominant thrust of modern corporate life was the consolidation of economic and financial resources by oligopolies, a few large producers who controlled the national and, increasingly, the world market. In 1970 the top four U.S. firms produced 91 percent of the motor vehicles sold in the domestic market and 90 percent of all breakfast cereal foods; the top four in tires produced 72 percent, in cigarettes 84 percent, and in detergents 70 percent. Despite laws restricting branch banking to a single state, in 1970 the four largest banks held 16 percent of the nation's banking assets; the top fifty banks held 48 percent.

Diversification—undertaking new activities and investments and moving into new markets—was the most important corporate strategy in the postwar era. By combining companies in unrelated industries, larger firms called conglomerates offered protection from instability in any single market, making them more effective international competitors. International Telephone and Telegraph became a diversified conglomerate by acquiring Continental Baking, Sheraton Hotels, Avis Rent-a-Car, Levitt and Sons (home builders), and Hartford Fire Insurance. Ling-Temco-Vought, another conglomerate, simultaneously produced steel, built ships, developed real estate, and brought cattle to market. These and other corporate acquisitions resulted in the nation's third great merger wave (the first two had taken place in the 1890s and the 1920s), which reached its peak in the 1960s.

The development of giant corporations was also based on the penetration of foreign markets. Unlike the Soviet Union, Western Europe, and Japan, America emerged physically unscathed from the war, with its defense industries eager to convert to consumer production. Soon American companies provided products and services for war-torn European and Asian markets, giving the nation a trade surplus close to $5 billion in 1960. International strategies enabled American business to enter these regions when domestic markets became saturated or when American recessions cut into sales. American products were considered the best in the world and were widely sought after abroad.

The Bretton Woods System. American global supremacy rested in part on decisions made at a United Nations economic conference held in Bretton Woods, New Hampshire, in July 1944, which established the U.S. dollar as the capitalist world's principal reserve currency. Two global institutions—the International Bank for Reconstruction and Development (commonly known as the World Bank) and the International Monetary Fund (IMF)—resulted from this meeting. The World Bank provided private loans for the reconstruction of war-torn Europe as well as for the development of Third World countries. The IMF was set up to stabilize the value of currencies, providing a secure and predictable monetary environment for trade. It did this by encouraging fixed exchange rates, which facilitated the

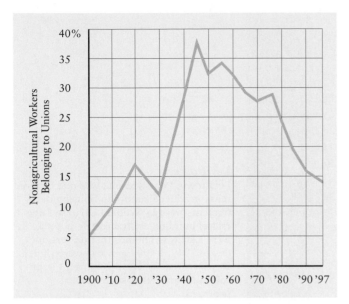

FIGURE 28.1
Labor Union Strength, 1900–1997
Labor unions reached their peak strength immediately after World War II. For the next thirty years they consistently represented more than a quarter of the nonfarm work force. After 1975, the influence of labor unions declined dramatically.
Source: AFL-CIO Information Bureau, Washington, DC.

free convertibility of currencies to gold or to the currencies of other trading nations; the strong U.S. dollar served as the benchmark. In 1947 multinational trade negotiations resulted in the first General Agreement on Tariffs and Trade (GATT), which led to the establishment of an international body to oversee trade rules and practices.

The World Bank, the IMF, and GATT were the cornerstones of the so-called Bretton Woods system, which guided the world economy after the war. The United States dominated the World Bank and the IMF because it contributed the most capital to them and because the U.S. dollar had a pivotal role in international currency exchange. Thus, these independent international organizations worked along lines that favored American-style internationalism over the economic nationalism that was traditional in most other countries. The World Bank, the IMF, and GATT encouraged stable prices, the liberalization of trade barriers and the reduction of tariffs, flexible domestic markets, and free trade based on fixed exchange rates. As long as the U.S. dollar remained the strongest currency, the Bretton Woods system would effectively serve America's global economic interests.

The Domestic Boom. U.S. economic supremacy abroad helped boost the domestic economy, creating millions of new jobs. One of the fastest-growing groups was salaried office workers, whose numbers increased

by 61 percent between 1947 and 1957. Growing corporate bureaucracies and increased access to a college education through the GI Bill helped expand the male white-collar ranks. These "organization men," as sociologist William Whyte called them, were joined by millions of women who moved into clerical work and other lower-paying service-sector occupations. Although the percentage of blue-collar manufacturing jobs declined slightly during this same period, the power of organized labor reached an all-time high (Figure 28.1). In 1955 the Congress of Industrial Organizations made a formal alliance with its old adversary, the American Federation of Labor. That merger created a single organization—the AFL-CIO—which represented more than 90 percent of the nation's 17.5 million union members. George Meany, a New York building-trades unionist, led this organization for the next twenty-four years with the goal of securing for labor its share of the record postwar profits. In exchange for labor peace and stability—that is, fewer strikes—corporate managers often cooperated with unions, agreeing to contracts that gave many workers secure, predictable, and steadily rising incomes.

As the income of many American workers grew, consumer spending soared. That spending, combined with federal outlays for defense and domestic programs, seemed to promise a continuously rising standard of living. The GNP grew from $213 billion in 1945 to more than $500 billion in 1960 (Figure 28.2). With the inflation rate under 3 percent in the 1950s, this steady economic growth meant a 25 percent rise in real income between 1946 and 1959. American homeownership rates reflected the rising standard of living: in 1940, 43 percent of American families owned their homes; by 1960, 62 percent did. The postwar boom was marred, however, by periodic bouts of recession and unemployment that particularly hurt low-income and nonwhite workers. Moreover, the rising standard of living was not accompanied by a redistribution of income: the top

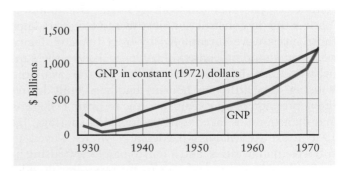

FIGURE 28.2
Gross National Product (GNP), 1929–1972
After a sharp dip during the Great Depression, the gross national product rose steadily in both real and constant dollars in the postwar period.

Levittown
Levittown, Pennsylvania, was one of three mass-produced suburban housing developments built by William Levitt, a Long Island building contractor. So popular were Levittown homes that on just one day in 1949, 1,400 contracts were signed. Homeowners especially enjoyed the privacy and space that such homes provided.
Van Bucher/Photo Researchers.

10 percent of Americans still earned more than the bottom half. Nevertheless, most Americans had more money to spend than ever before.

The Suburban Explosion

One of the most dynamic areas of the economy was the expanding suburban housing market. Although Americans had been gravitating toward urban areas throughout the twentieth century, the postwar period was characterized by two new patterns: one was a shift away from older cities in the Northeast and Midwest and toward newer urban centers in the South and West; the other, a mass defection from the cities to the suburbs. In the 1950s all but one of the nation's twelve most populous cities lost population. (The exception was Los Angeles, where vast tracts of undeveloped land allowed for suburban-style development.)

At the end of World War II many cities were surrounded by pastures and working farms. Due to a dramatic surge in construction, just five to ten years later those cities were surrounded by tract housing, factories, and shopping centers. People flocked to the suburbs in part because they followed the available housing. Very little new housing had been built during the depression or war years, and the returning veterans and their families faced a critical housing shortage. By 1960 more Americans—particularly whites—lived in suburbs than in cities, and a fourth of all the housing in the country had been built during the preceding decade, most of it single-family, owner-occupied homes.

The Housing Boom. William Levitt, an innovative Long Island building contractor, revolutionized the suburban housing market by applying mass-production

techniques to home construction. Levitt's company could build 150 homes per week, a rate of one house every sixteen minutes. A basic four-room house, complete with kitchen appliances and an attic that a handy homeowner could convert into two additional bedrooms, was priced at less than $10,000 in 1947. Levitt built planned communities in New York, New Jersey, and Pennsylvania—all named Levittown. Soon other developers were snapping up the cheap farmland surrounding urban areas. On the West Coast, the former shipbuilding magnate Henry Kaiser (see Chapter 26, American Lives, "Henry J. Kaiser: World War II's 'Miracle Man,'" pp. 840–841) moved into housing construction in the postwar era, building subdivisions in and around Los Angeles and San Francisco. Dozens of other developers followed suit, hastening the exodus from the farm and the central city.

Many families financed their homes with mortgages from the Federal Housing Administration and the Veterans Administration at rates dramatically lower than those offered by private lenders. In 1955 those two agencies wrote 41 percent of all nonfarm mortgages. Such lending demonstrated the quiet yet revolutionary way in which the federal government was entering and influencing daily life.

The new suburban homes—and much of the savings and loan and Veterans Administration money—were reserved almost exclusively for whites. Levittown homeowners had to sign a covenant prohibiting occupation "by members of other than the Caucasian Race"; Levitt did not sell houses directly to blacks until 1960. Other communities adopted similar covenants to exclude Jews or Asians. Although the Supreme Court had ruled in *Shelley v. Kraemer* (1948) that restrictive covenants were illegal, the custom continued infor-

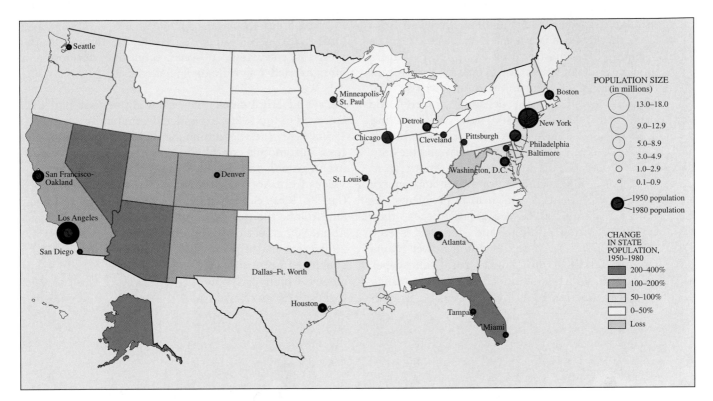

MAP 28.1
Metropolitan Growth, 1950–1980
A metropolitan area is generally defined as a central city that in combination with its surrounding territory forms an integrated economic and social unit. The U.S. Census Bureau introduced the Standard Metropolitan Statistical Area (SMSA) in 1950, but later changes in the definition of SMSA make it difficult to generalize from the 1950 figures. This map compares the population of central cities in 1950 with population figures for the more broadly defined metropolitan areas in 1980 to illustrate the extent and geographical distribution of metropolitan growth in the postwar period.

mally until the civil rights laws of the 1960s banned private discrimination.

Even though suburbia was often portrayed as a homogeneous, even bland, environment, there were strong cultural and class variations among suburbs. When less affluent firefighters, plasterers, machine-tool makers, and sales clerks moved to the suburbs, they were far more likely to settle in a modest Levittown than in an upper-middle-class suburb such as Winnetka, Illinois, or Shaker Heights, Ohio. Blacks shut out of white suburbs established their own communities, such as Lincoln Heights outside Cincinnati, Robbins on the edge of Chicago, and Kinloch near St. Louis. In well-equipped living quarters at bargain prices, working-class white and black families could share in the ultimate postwar suburban dream of giving "every kid an opportunity to grow up with grass stains on his pants."

The Sun Belt. The new patterns of growth and development were most striking in the South and West, where open space allowed for sprawling suburban-style expansion. Fueled by World War II defense spending,

the postwar development of the southern and western cities accelerated as industry took advantage of inexpensive land, unorganized labor, low taxes, and warm climates (now made livable through the new technology of air conditioning). Some of the most explosive growth occurred in Florida, Texas, and California—states that would become the industrial leaders of the emerging Sun Belt economy (Map 28.1). Between 1940 and 1970, Miami's metropolitan population increased by 79 percent with the addition of more than a million new residents, many of them older or retired. Texas cities, especially Houston and Dallas, grew as the petrochemical industry expanded rapidly after 1945. Spurred by massive defense spending, California grew the most rapidly, adding 2.6 million people in the 1940s and 3.1 million more in the 1950s. In 1970 California had about a tenth of the U.S. population, and in 1972 it replaced New York as the state with the largest number of electoral votes.

Business boosters in California and other Sun Belt states worked tirelessly to promote regional development. Local leaders lobbied for new defense installations and contracts, wooed scientific and artistic talent from the Northeast, and even purchased professional sports teams. In 1958 investors moved the Brooklyn Dodgers to Los Angeles and the New York Giants to San Francisco, allowing boosters to promote their towns as "big-league" cities. In subsequent decades, however, the success of Sun Belt cities raised new problems and challenges. Booming urban populations brought higher crime and poverty rates, making southern and western cities more like those in the Northeast. In the arid Southwest, increasing demands for water and energy resulted in environmental and health problems. As cities competed for scarce water resources, they depleted underground aquifers and dammed scenic rivers. The proliferation of coal-burning power plants increased air pollution and scarred rural landscapes through strip mining. The nuclear industry, which brought jobs and income to the West, also brought radi-

ation contamination to residents near atomic test sites, nuclear waste facilities, and uranium mines. In the West, as elsewhere, postwar economic development often carried a significant social cost.

Cars and Highways. The car culture that had first emerged in the 1920s expanded dramatically during the 1950s, with cars becoming symbols of status and success. Automobiles and highways were essential to suburban growth and the development of the Sun Belt (see Voices from Abroad, "Hanoch Bartov: 'Everyone Has a Car,'" p. 909). Suburbanites needed cars to get to work and to take their children to school and piano lessons. About 90 percent of suburban families owned cars, and 20 percent had more than one. With gas plentiful and cheap at 15 cents a gallon, no one cared about fuel efficiency, which was only 8 miles to the gallon for the biggest gas guzzlers. American cars became heavier

Highway Building
Federal funding of interstate transportation resulted in a burgeoning network of highways that transformed both urban and rural landscapes. This photograph shows the construction of the Congress (later renamed Eisenhower) Expressway in Chicago in 1950. The new expressway cut a wide swath through many West Side neighborhoods, forever altering the urban landscape and introducing city residents to traffic jams and air pollution.
Chicago Tribune.

HANOCH BARTOV

"Everyone Has a Car"

———————★———————

One of Israel's foremost writers and journalists, Hanoch Bartov spent two years in the United States working as a correspondent for the newspaper Lamerchav. As a newcomer to Los Angeles in the early 1960s, he was both fascinated and appalled by Americans' love affair with the automobile.

Our immediate decision to buy a car sprang from healthy instincts. Only later did I learn from bitter experience that in California, death was preferable to living without one. Neither the views from the plane nor the weird excursion that first evening hinted at what I would go through that first week.

Very simple—the nearest supermarket was about half a kilometer south of our apartment, the regional primary school two kilometers east, and my son's kindergarten even farther away. A trip to the post office—an undertaking, to the bank—an ordeal, to work—an impossibility.

Truth be told: the Los Angeles municipality . . . does have public transportation.

Buses go once an hour along the city's boulevards and avenues, gathering all the wretched of the earth, the poor and the needy, the old ladies forbidden by their grandchildren to drive, and other eccentric types. But few people can depend on buses, even should they swear never to deviate from the fixed routes. . . . There are no tramways. No one thought of a subway. Railroads—not now and not in the future.

Why? Because everyone has a car. A man invited me to his house, saying, "We are neighbors, within ten minutes of each other." After walking for an hour and a half I realized what he meant—"ten minute drive within the speed limit." Simply put, he

never thought I might interpret his remark to refer to the walking distance. The moment a baby sees the light of day in Los Angeles, a car is registered in his name in Detroit. . . .

At first perhaps people relished the freedom and independence a car provided. You get in, sit down, and grab the steering wheel, your mobility exceeding that of any other generation. No wonder people refuse to live downtown, where they can hear their neighbors, smell their cooking, and suffer frayed nerves as trains pass by bedroom windows. Instead, they get a piece of the desert, far from town, at half price, drag a water hose, grow grass, flowers, and trees, and build their dream house. . . .

The result? A widely scattered city, its houses far apart, its streets stretched in all directions. Olympic Boulevard from west to east, forty kilometers. Sepulveda Boulevard, from Long Beach in the south to the edge of the desert, forty kilometers. Altogether covering 1200 square kilometers. As of now.

Why "as of now"? Because greater distances mean more commuting, and more commuting leads to more cars. More cars means problems that push people even farther away from the city, which chases after them.

The urban sprawl is only one side effect. Two, some say three, million cars require an array of services. . . .

. . . Why bother parking, getting out, getting in, getting up and sitting down, when you can simply "drive in"? Mailboxes have their slots facing the road, at the level of the driver's hand. That is how dirty laundry is deposited, electricity and water bills paid. That is how love is made, how children are taken to school. That is how the anniversary wreath is laid on the graves of loved ones. There are drive-in movies. And, yes, we saw it with our own eyes: drive-in churches. Only in death is a man separated from his car and buried alone. . . .

———————

Source: Oscar and Lilian Handlin, eds., From the Outer World (Cambridge, MA: Harvard University Press, 1997), 293–296.

and bigger, creating a disparity in size with Japanese or European models that persists to this day, despite the downsizing of American vehicles since the 1970s.

More cars required more highways, which were funded largely by the federal government. In 1947 Congress authorized the construction of 37,000 miles of

highways; the National Interstate and Defense Highway Act of 1956 increased this commitment by another 42,500 miles. One of the largest civil engineering projects in world history, the new interstate system would link the entire country with roads at least four lanes wide. The interstate system changed both the cities and the countryside. It rerouted traffic through rural areas and created new communities of gas stations, fast-food outlets, and motels around highway exits. In urban areas new highways cut wide swaths through old neighborhoods and caused air pollution and traffic jams; critics complained about "autosclerosis," a hardening of the urban arteries.

The federally constructed highways also siphoned funding away from mass transit. With the support of the interstate trucking industry, Congress established the Highway Trust Fund in 1956 to collect fees to finance road building and maintenance; it specifically prohibited the use of its funds to promote urban mass transit. As municipal governments committed increasing resources to matching funds for federal highway construction, mass-transit systems languished. By 1960 two-thirds of Americans were driving to work each day. The percentage was even higher—between 80 and 95 percent—in Sun Belt cities like Los Angeles and Phoenix.

Highway construction had far-reaching effects on patterns of consumption and shopping. Instead of taking a train into the city or walking to a corner grocery store, people drove to suburban shopping malls and supermarkets. The first mall had appeared in Kansas City in the 1920s, and there were still only 8 in 1945; by 1960 the number had mushroomed to almost 4,000. When a 110-store complex at Roosevelt Field on suburban Long Island opened in 1956, it was conveniently situated at an expressway exit and had parking for 11,000 cars. Downtown retail areas and department stores soon declined.

Highways and suburbs also lured corporate business and manufacturing away from the cities. In the early 1950s, Stanford University in Palo Alto, California, built one of the nation's first *industrial parks*, a suburban, campuslike facility for light manufacturing. Exploiting its ties with university researchers, Stanford Industrial Park attracted Cold War defense contractors such as General Electric, Lockheed, and Hewlett-Packard. Those firms soon formed the nucleus of an electronic and high-tech region known as Silicon Valley. On the East Coast, a similar high-tech boom occurred outside Boston along Route 128, led by firms such as Polaroid and computer manufacturers Digital Equipment and Wang. In the Midwest the number of factories in suburban Chicago doubled between 1947 and 1954, and suburban Detroit saw a 220 percent increase.

The U.S. government's financing of highways and home building after World War II helped fuel a suburban explosion that was unique to North America. In war-ravaged European cities postwar housing construction was centered in high-density city neighborhoods or along mass-transit lines. Not until the 1960s and 1970s would Europeans experiment with low-density suburban housing, and their central cities never declined as precipitously as American cities did.

American Life during the Baby Boom

Hula-Hoops and poodle skirts, sock hops and rock 'n' roll, shiny cars and gleaming appliances—all signify the "fifties," a period that really stretched from 1945 through the early 1960s. The postwar years are remembered as a time of affluence and stability, a time when Americans enjoyed an optimistic faith in progress and technology and a serene family-centered culture enshrined in television sitcoms such as "Father Knows Best." This powerful myth, like many myths, has some truth to it, but there were other sides to the story. Focusing solely on affluence, popular culture, and consumption does not do justice to this complex period of economic and social transformation, which included challenges to the status quo as well as conformity.

Consumer Culture.   In some respects the consumer culture of the 1950s seemed like a return to the 1920s— a wealth of new gadgets and appliances, the expansion of consumer credit and advertising, more leisure time, the growing importance of the automobile, and the development of new types of mass media. Yet there was a significant difference: the postwar economy was far better balanced than that of the 1920s. By the 1950s consumption had become a hallmark of middle-class culture, but even blue-collar families had discretionary income to spend on consumer goods because of rising incomes.

As in the 1920s, though, prosperity was helped along by a dramatic increase in consumer credit, which enabled families to stretch their incomes. Between 1946 and 1958 short-term consumer credit rose from $8.4 billion to almost $45 billion. The Diners Club introduced the first credit card in 1950, followed by the American Express card and Bank Americard in 1959. By the 1970s the omnipresent plastic credit card had revolutionized personal and family finances.

Aggressive advertising contributed to the massive increase in consumer spending. In 1951 businesses spent more on advertising ($6.5 billion) than taxpayers did on primary and secondary education ($5 billion). The 1950s gave Americans the Marlboro man; M&Ms that "melt in your mouth, not in your hand"; Wonder Bread to "build strong bodies in twelve ways"; and the "Does she or doesn't she?" Clairol woman. Automobiles continued to be the most heavily advertised item in the 1950s, but advertising also promoted a variety of new consumer appliances to fill the suburban home. In 1946 automatic washing machines and electric dryers came on the market; commercial laundries across the country struggled to stay in business. The home freezer enabled families to eat seasonal foods, such as fruits and vegetables, all year long and encouraged the dramatic growth of the frozen-food industry. Partly because of the purchase of electrical appliances for the home, consumer use of electricity doubled during the 1950s.

Consumers had more free time in which to spend their money than ever before. In 1960 the average worker put in a five-day week, with eight paid holidays a year (double the 1946 standard) plus a paid two-week vacation. The travel industry grew rapidly during the 1950s, with Americans devoting a seventh of the GNP to spending on leisure and entertainment. Americans took to the interstate highway system by the millions, encouraging the dramatic growth of motel chains, roadside restaurants, and fast-food eateries. The first McDonald's restaurant opened in 1954 in San Bernardino, California; the Holiday Inn motel chain started in Memphis in 1952. Among the most popular destinations were national and state parks and Disneyland, which opened in Anaheim, California, in 1955. Aided by the strong U.S. dollar and the introduction of jet air travel in 1958, families flooded Europe each summer, earning the unflattering epithet of "ugly Americans" because many expected things to be just like home.

Television. Perhaps the most significant hallmark of postwar consumer culture was television. TV's leap to cultural prominence was swift and overpowering. There were only ten broadcasting stations in the country and a meager 7,000 sets in American homes in 1947. By 1960, 87 percent of American families had at least one television set. Viewers had only three or four channels to choose from, however; public television did not begin until 1967, and cable was a phenomenon of the 1980s.

Television developed as a government-controlled or subsidized service in other countries, but in the United States it emerged as private enterprise geared toward entertainment. Although stations were licensed by the Federal Communications Commission after 1941, television, like radio, depended entirely on advertising and corporate sponsorship for profits. Soon television supplanted radio as the chief diffuser of popular culture, its national programming promoting shared interests and tastes and reducing regional and ethnic differences. Movie attendance shrank throughout the postwar period, and studios increasingly relied on overseas distribution of American films to earn a profit.

Television encouraged the consumerism and advertising that have characterized mass culture since the 1920s. As in the golden era of radio in the 1920s and 1930s, corporations produced and sponsored major television shows such as "Texaco Star Theater" with Milton Berle and "General Electric Theater" hosted by Ronald Reagan. New products entered the home, such as frozen TV dinners, first introduced in 1954. *TV Guide*, founded in 1948, became the most successful new periodical of the 1950s. Television even affected city services. In 1954 the Toledo water commissioner wondered why water consumption rose dramatically during certain three-minute periods. The answer? All

Advertising in the TV Age
Aggressive advertising and the development of new products, such as color television, helped fuel the surge in consumer spending during the 1950s. Electricity usage more than doubled in the 1950s, as growing numbers of Americans purchased TVs and other appliances.
Courtesy Motorola Museum of Electronics. © 1999 Motorola Inc.

across Toledo, TV watchers flushed their toilets during commercials.

What Americans saw on television, besides the omnipresent commercials, was an overwhelmingly white, middle-class world of nuclear families living in suburban homes. "Leave It to Beaver," "Ozzie and Harriet," and similar sitcoms featured characters who adhered to clear-cut gender roles and plots based on small family crises that were always happily resolved by the end of the show. Programs such as "The Honeymooners," starring Jackie Gleason as a Brooklyn bus driver, and "Life of Reilly," a situation comedy featuring a California aircraft worker, were rare in their treatment of working-class lives. Nonwhite characters appeared mainly as servants, such as comedian Jack Benny's black "houseboy" Rochester or the Latino gardener with the anglicized name "Frank Smith" on "Father Knows Best."

The types of television programs developed in the 1950s built on older entertainment genres but also pioneered new ones. Taking over a popular radio and movie category, television offered some thirty westerns by 1959, including "Bonanza," the first color show.

National television coverage made professional sports big-time entertainment and big business—far exceeding the potential of radio. Programming geared to children, such as Walt Disney's "Mickey Mouse Club," "Howdy Doody," and "Captain Kangaroo," created the first generation of children to grow up glued to the tube. The appeal of popular quiz shows such as "Twenty-One" and "The $64,000 Question" was not diminished even when it was revealed in 1959 that contestants had received the questions in advance. Although the new medium did offer some serious programming, notably live theater and documentaries, Federal Communications Commissioner Newton Minow concluded in 1963 that television was "a vast wasteland." Its reassuring images of family life and postwar society, however, dovetailed with the social expectations of many Americans.

Religion and the Search for Security. The dislocations of the depression and war years made Americans yearn for security and a reaffirmation of traditional values. Some of this sentiment was expressed in a renewed emphasis on religion. Church membership rose from 49 percent of the population in 1940 to 69 percent in 1960. All the major denominations shared in the growth, which was accompanied by an ecumenical movement to bring Catholics, Protestants, and Jews together. The stress on religious harmony meshed with Cold War Americans' view of themselves as a righteous people opposed to "godless communism." In 1954 the phrase "under God" was inserted into the Pledge of Allegiance, and in 1956 Congress added "In God We Trust" to all U.S. coins.

Beyond patriotism, religion also served more deeply felt needs. In his popular television program Bishop Fulton Sheen asked, "Is life worth living?" He and countless others optimistically answered in the affirmative. None was more positive than Norman Vincent Peale, whose best-selling book *The Power of Positive Thinking* (1952) embodied the trend toward the therapeutic use of religion to assist men and women in coping with the stresses of modern life. Evangelical religion also experienced a resurgence, most evident in the dramatic rise to popularity of the Reverend Billy Graham, who used television, radio, advertising, and print media to spread the gospel. His nondenominational Evangelistic Association, founded in 1950, was a tremendous success. Although critics suggested that middle-class interest in religion stemmed less from spirituality than from the impulse toward conformity, the revival nonetheless spoke to Americans' search for spiritual meaning in uncertain times.

The Baby Boom. Even more dramatic testimony to the desire for stability in the postwar era was the emphasis Americans placed on the family and children.

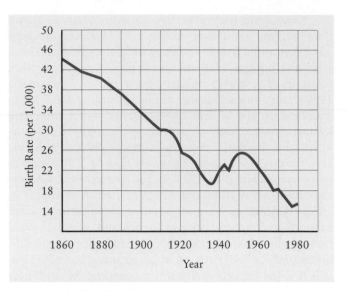

FIGURE 28.3
The Declining American Birth Rate, 1860–1980
When birth rates are viewed over more than a century, the postwar baby boom is clearly an aberration.

As one popular advice book put it, "The family is the center of your living. If it isn't, you've gone astray." Two things were noteworthy about the men and women who formed families between 1940 and 1960. First, their marriages were remarkably stable. Not until the mid-1960s did the divorce rate begin to rise sharply. Second, they were intent on having children.

After a century and a half of declining family size, the birth rate shot up: more babies were born between 1948 and 1953 than were born in the previous thirty years (Figure 28.3). Women who came of age in the 1930s had an average of 2.4 children; their counterparts in the 1950s averaged 3.2 children. As a result of this trend and a lengthened life expectancy due to improvements in diet, public health, and medicine, the American population rose dramatically from 140 million in 1945 to 179 million in 1960 and then to 203 million in 1970.

There are several reasons for this twenty-year upsurge that demographers call the *baby boom*, which peaked in 1957. Because a sustained rise in the birth rate did not occur in all the countries affected by World War II, it was not simply a response to the losses of war. More important was the drop in the average marriage age—to twenty-two for men and twenty for women—a trend that had begun during the war. The drop in the marriage age resulted in a surge of young married couples who produced a bumper crop of children.

To rear all those baby-boom children and keep them healthy, middle-class parents increasingly relied on the advice of experts. Accepting the advice of doctors and the federal government, they had their children inoculated with the Salk polio vaccine,

The Saturday Evening
POST
September 19, 1959 · 15¢

**Does it Help
to Swap Visits
With the Russians?**

A Woman's Dilemma in Postwar America
This 1959 cover of the *Saturday Evening Post* depicts some of the difficult choices facing women in the postwar era. Women's consignment to low-paid, dead-end jobs in the service sector encouraged many to become full-time homemakers. Once back in their suburban homes, however, many middle-class women felt isolated and trapped amid endless rounds of cooking, cleaning, and diaper changing. © The Curtis Publishing Company.

administered free in the nation's schools. The conquest of polio, which demonstrated the potential of government-sponsored public health programs, made the children of the 1950s one of the healthiest generations ever. Just as important was the widespread use of new "miracle drugs" such as penicillin (introduced in 1943), streptomycin (1945), and cortisone (1946).

Parents also embraced scientific child rearing, buying a million copies of Dr. Benjamin Spock's *Baby and Child Care* (1946) in the year it was published. New mothers found Spock's insistence that they abandon the rigid feeding and baby care schedules of an earlier generation liberating, though the book did not remove all their insecurities. Mothers who wanted to work outside the home felt guilty because Spock recommended that they be constantly available to respond to their children's needs. But if a mother was too protective of her children, Spock and others argued, she might hamper their adjustment to a normal adult life.

The baby boom had a broad and immediate impact on American society. It prompted a major expansion of the nation's educational system: by 1970 school expenditures were double those of the 1950 level. In addition, the consumer needs of all those babies fueled the economy as families bought food, diapers, toys, and clothing for their expanding broods. Together with federal expenditures on national security, family spending on consumer goods fueled the unparalleled prosperity and economic growth of the 1950s and 1960s.

The postwar baby boom would have a continuing impact on America for many decades. In the 1960s the baby-boom generation swelled college enrollments and, not coincidentally, the ranks of student protesters. By the 1970s, when the baby-boom generation entered the workplace, it had to compete for a limited number of

jobs in what had become a stagnant economy. The delayed marriages and later childbearing of the career-oriented baby boomers temporarily caused the birth rate to rise again in the 1980s. The 1990s produced the first baby-boom president (Bill Clinton) and widespread concern about the future viability of old-age assistance programs such as Social Security and Medicare as the baby boomers aged. The decisions made by many couples in the immediate postwar period to have large families would continue to affect American life well into the twenty-first century.

Contradictions in Women's Lives. The 1950s were characterized by a strong allegiance to traditional gender roles: a masculine ideal that emphasized men's roles as responsible breadwinners and a feminine ideal that pronounced that woman's place was in the home. What feminist Betty Friedan called the "feminine mystique" of the 1950s—that "the highest value and the only commitment for women is the fulfillment of their own femininity"—bore remarkable similarities to the nineteenth-century cult of true womanhood (see Chapter 19). However, the 1950s version of the cult of domesticity drew on twentieth-century science and culture, particularly psychology. Pronouncing motherhood the only "normal" female sex role, psychologists berated mothers who worked outside the home, charging that they damaged their children's development. Television, popular music, films, and advertising reinforced that notion by depicting career women as social and sexual misfits.

In her book *The Feminine Mystique* (1963) Betty Friedan identified "the problem that has no name"—the frustration and depression of many women who chafed under these narrowly prescribed gender roles (see

American Voices, "Joy Wilner: A Fifties Housewife," p. 915). Speaking from her own experience, Friedan described how she gave up a psychology fellowship and career in journalism to marry, move to the suburbs, and raise three children—only to find herself isolated and dissatisfied. Thousands of middle-class women responded enthusiastically to Friedan's theory, making her book a best seller. But not all housewives of the baby-boom era were unhappy or neurotic. Many working-class women embraced their new roles as housewives, delighted not to have to toil at low-paying jobs outside the home. Middle-class wives found constructive outlets for their energy in groups such as the League of Women Voters, the PTA, and the Junior League. And as in earlier periods, some women used the rhetoric of domesticity and maternalism to justify political activism, organizing around issues of community improvement, racial integration, and nuclear disarmament.

Another contradictory aspect of postwar culture was that despite the feminine mystique, more than one-third of American women held jobs outside the home. Many women took jobs to supplement family income and keep pace with rising standards of living, causing a dramatic rise in the number of older, married middle-class women in the labor force. At the turn of the twentieth century the typical female worker was a young recent immigrant who worked only until she married. By mid-century the typical female worker was in her forties, was married, and had children in school.

Occupational segmentation remained characteristic of women's work in the postwar period. Until 1964 the classified sections of most newspapers separated employment ads into columns headed "Help Wanted Male" and "Help Wanted Female." Staffing the expanding postwar service sector, more than 80 percent of all working women did stereotypical "women's work" as salespeople, health-care technicians, waitresses, flight attendants, servants, receptionists, telephone operators, and secretaries. In 1960 women represented only 3.5 percent of all lawyers and 6.1 percent of all physicians, but 97 percent of all nurses, 85 percent of all librarians, and 57 percent of all social workers. Along with women's jobs went women's pay, which averaged 60 percent of men's pay in 1963.

How could postwar society so steadfastly uphold the domestic ideal while an increasing number of wives and mothers took jobs? In many ways the women themselves kept the dramatic increase invisible. Fearing public disapproval of their decisions, such women usually justified their work in individual or family-oriented terms: "Of course I believe a woman's place is at home, but I took this job to save for college for our children." Moreover, when women took jobs outside the home, they retained full responsibility for child care and household management, which allowed families and society to avoid facing the implications of women's

new roles. As one overburdened woman noted, she now had "two full-time jobs instead of just one—underpaid clerical worker and unpaid housekeeper." The absence of an active feminist movement in the 1940s and 1950s meant most women had to cope on their own.

Youth Culture.   Beneath the surface of family togetherness and traditional gender roles lay other tensions—those between parents and children. Dating back to the 1920s, the emergence of a mass youth culture had its roots in the democratization of education, the growth of peer culture, and the growing consumer independence of teenagers in an age of affluence. Youth, eager to escape the climate of suburban conformity of their parents, had become a distinct new market that advertisers eagerly exploited. In 1956 advertisers projected an adolescent market of $9 billion for items such as transistor radios (introduced in 1952), clothing, and fads such as Silly Putty (1950) and Hula-Hoops (1958). Increasingly, advertisers targeted the young, both to capture their spending money and to exploit their influence on family spending patterns. Notice the changing slogans for Pepsi-Cola: "Twice as much for a nickel" (1935), "Be sociable—have a Pepsi" (1948), "Now it's Pepsi for those who think young" (1960), and finally "the Pepsi Generation" (1965).

Hollywood movies played a large role in fostering and legitimizing a teen culture separate from the safe and insulated suburban world that teenagers' parents had worked so hard to create. At a time when general movie attendance was declining because of competition from television, young people made up the largest audience for motion pictures. Hollywood studios catered to this market with films such as *The Wild One* (1951), starring Marlon Brando, and *Rebel without a Cause* (1955), starring James Dean, Natalie Wood, and Sal Mineo. "What are you rebelling against?" a waitress asks Brando in *The Wild One*. "Whattaya got?" he replies.

What really defined this generation, however, was its music. Rejecting the rigid boundaries of traditional popular music, teenagers in the 1950s discovered rock 'n' roll, an amalgam of white country and western music and the black urban music known as rhythm and blues. The Cleveland disc jockey Alan Freed played a major role in introducing white America to the new African American sound by playing rhythm and blues records on white radio stations beginning in 1954. Young white performers such as Bill Haley, Buddy Holly, and especially Elvis Presley incorporated the new mixture into their own music and capitalized on the new market (see American Lives, "Elvis Presley: Teen Idol of the 1950s," pp. 916–917). Between 1953 and 1959 record sales increased from $213 million to $603 million, with 45-rpm rock-'n'-roll records as the driving force. The new teen music shocked many white adults, who saw rock 'n' roll as an invitation to race-mixing, sexual promiscuity, and juvenile delinquency.

JOY WILNER
A Fifties Housewife

★

*L*ike millions of other middle-class women in the 1950s, Joy Wilner married an ambitious young professional and had children in quick succession. In this interview she recounts the joys and frustrations of her early years of marriage and motherhood and her struggle to accommodate herself to what Betty Friedan has termed the "feminine mystique."

I felt totally fulfilled, totally happy. We were the perfect couple—Ted was supportive of me and I was supportive of him and we never argued. Well, we didn't know how. We'd had no experience with conflict. Everything was fine. I had my next child sixteen months after the first. The second child was neither exactly planned nor unplanned. I didn't really intend to get pregnant again, but on the other hand, we weren't using birth control because, after all, we already had *one*. . . .

After the second baby, that was the first time I can remember conflict, feelings of being trapped, wondering what I was doing with my life. These weren't very distinct feelings, not like I wonder if this is the right man for me. Just uncomfortable feelings. At some point I expressed some of these feelings, in a very tentative way, to Ted and he said, "Well, if you feel that way, maybe we should get a divorce." I was terrified. The idea of divorce was inconceivable. I never mentioned the subject again.

At the same time, I got such pleasure, real physiological pleasure from my children—from playing with them, feeding them, watching them develop. Then we moved and Ted went into general practice, and at about the same time I had another child. I became his secretary, his nurse, and I was also handling the children, keeping them out of his hair. And of course, we were also establishing our identity as the doctor and his wife, so there was a lot of socializing. It was a busy time.

What amazes me now is that it never occurred to me not to do this. His career was just my life. There came a time when I felt I didn't have the strength for all this and I started breaking down. I can remember going into the shower and screaming—in the shower so that no one could hear me. Even then I didn't have conscious thoughts of "I hate this life"—I didn't think there was anything objectively wrong with the way I was living, just that I couldn't take it any more.

Source: Brett Harvey, ed., *The Fifties: An Oral History* (New York: HarperCollins, 1993), 103–104.

Cultural Dissenters. The youth rebellion was only one aspect of a broader undercurrent of discontent with the conformist culture of the 1950s. Postwar artists, jazz musicians, and writers also expressed their alienation from mainstream society through intensely personal, introspective art forms. In New York Jackson Pollock and other painters rejected the social realism of the 1930s for an unconventional style that became known as *abstract expressionism.* Swirling and splattering paint onto giant canvases, Pollock emphasized self-expression in the act of painting, capturing the chaotic atmosphere of the nuclear age. A similar trend developed in jazz, as black musicians originated a hard-driving improvisational style known as *bebop.* Whether the "hot" bebop of saxophonist Charlie Parker in the 1940s or the more subdued "cool" West Coast sound of the 1950s epitomized by Miles Davis, postwar jazz was cerebral, intimate, and individualistic.

Black jazz musicians found eager fans not only in the African American community but among young white Beats in New York and San Francisco. Disdaining the middle-class conformity, corporate capitalism, and suburban materialism of the 1950s, the Beats were a group of writers and poets who were both literary innovators and outspoken social critics. In his poem "Howl" (1956), which became a manifesto of the beat generation, Allen Ginsberg lamented: "I saw the best minds of my generation destroyed by madness, starving hysterical naked, dragging themselves through the angry streets at dawn looking for an angry fix." In works such as Jack Kerouac's novel *On the Road* (1957) the Beats glorified spontaneity, sexual adventurism, drug use, and spirituality. Although they were apolitical—their rebellion was strictly cultural—in the 1960s they inspired a new generation of rebels who would champion both political and cultural change.

Elvis Presley: Teen Idol of the 1950s

———————★———————

WHEN ELVIS PRESLEY performed on "The Ed Sullivan Show" in 1956, the television cameras zoomed in on his head and shoulders. The close-ups were inspired not by the young singer's good looks but by a desire to conceal his lower body. After several scandalous TV appearances earlier that season, CBS decided that Presley's sexually suggestive bumping and grinding were unsuitable for family viewing. Despite the censorship, Presley's performance was an unprecedented success, claiming over 80 percent of the television audience. His records sold 10 million copies that year alone and would account for a quarter of RCA's record sales over the next decade. More than any other recording artist of the 1950s Presley popularized the new hybrid music known as rock 'n' roll.

Born in East Tupelo, Mississippi, in 1935, Elvis Aron Presley grew up in a white working-class family that keenly felt the hardships of the Great Depression. Like many poor southerners, the Presleys moved frequently, in search of work as laborers and mill hands. When Elvis was thirteen, his father found a job at a paint factory in Memphis, and the Presleys settled in one of that city's new public-housing projects.

Elvis's earliest exposure to music came through gospel singing at the Pentecostal First Assembly of God Church, where his uncle was pastor. Later, when his family lived in or adjacent to the black districts of Tupelo and Memphis (as the South's poorest whites often did), Elvis gravitated toward local churches, bars, and clubs, where he gained a lifelong love of blues, gospel, and other black music.

Local radio was an equally powerful force in his musical education. In the late 1940s, commercial radio offered a diverse selection of musical programming, catering to the growing audience of rural migrants who had been moving to southern cities since World War II. Although there had always been significant cross-fertilization between white and black musical styles, industry promoters maintained an artificial distinction between "hillbilly" and "race" music. After World War II those derogatory labels gave way to the more respectable terms "country and western" and "rhythm and blues," but the programming remained rigidly segregated.

Young white southerners like Presley listened to both types of programs. They admired the traditional vocal styles and guitar picking they heard on "The Grand Ole Opry" and other country shows, and they developed a keen appreciation for the blues progressions and driving rhythms of black music. White youngsters' growing fascination with rhythm and blues was not generally acknowledged and was considered somewhat scandalous. But a small group of disc jockeys and record promoters spotted the potential of the new market. As Memphis record producer Sam Phillips once said, "If I could find a white man who had the Negro sound and the Negro feel, I could make a billion dollars."

Phillips found that man in Elvis Presley. In 1953 nineteen-year-old Presley was working as a truck driver and occasionally stopped by Phillips's Sun Studios to make sample recordings for his friends and family. Phillips remembered his unusual vocal style and later asked him to cut a record with a local band. The result was an eclectic mix of musical styles: on one side a white version of a black blues song, "That's All Right," on the other side a black-influenced interpretation of a bluegrass number, "Blue Moon of Kentucky." The record was an overnight local sensation and launched Presley into a national recording career the following year. Over the next decade he produced dozens of hits for RCA, including "Hound Dog," "Heartbreak Hotel," "Jailhouse Rock," and "Blue Suede Shoes."

Presley's success was based not only on his music but also on his stage presence and his relationship with the audience. With his slicked-back hair, long sideburns, and tight pants, Presley cultivated a lower-class "greaser" look that proved immensely popular with teenage fans. His quivering legs, gyrating pelvis, and playful sneer drove young female fans wild; they frequently mobbed the stage, grabbing at his clothes

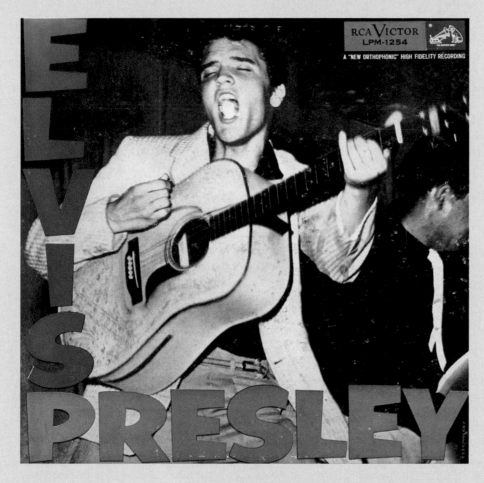

Elvis Presley
The young Elvis Presley, shown here on the cover of his first album in 1956, embodied cultural rebellion against the conservatism and triviality of adult life in the 1950s.
© 1956 BGM Music.

for souvenirs. Many adults, however, condemned such antics, associating them with juvenile delinquency, sexual immorality, and race-mixing. After his first television appearance, one critic described Presley's performance as "suggestive and vulgar, tinged with the kind of animalism that should be confined to dives and bordellos," and another critic called it "a strip-tease with clothes on." To many adults rock 'n' roll seemed an invitation to rebellion by the younger generation.

African Americans found Presley's success and notoriety somewhat ironic. Chuck Berry and other black musicians had been performing such music for years—but with little commercial success among white audiences. Many of them viewed the appropriation of black rhythm and blues by white artists as out-and-out theft. In the long run, however, the pop-

ularity of rock 'n' roll introduced black performers such as Little Richard, Fats Domino, and James Brown to white as well as black audiences.

Presley's musical popularity declined with his induction into the army in 1958 (the long arm of the state reached even the most popular stars). Afterward he headed for Hollywood, acting and singing in dozens of mostly mediocre teen-oriented movies. He enjoyed a comeback starting in 1968, but his career was hampered by personal problems. In 1977 he died of an accidental drug overdose. Since then he has become a cult figure, spawning hundreds of books and articles and a spate of Elvis impersonators. Graceland, his ornate home in Memphis, attracts more visitors per year than does George Washington's estate at Mount Vernon.

The Other America

As middle-class whites flocked to the suburbs, a diverse group of poor and working-class migrants, many of them nonwhite, moved into the central cities. With jobs and financial resources flowing to the suburbs, urban newcomers inherited a declining economy and a decaying environment. This "other America," as the social critic Michael Harrington called it, remained largely invisible to affluent white suburbanites.

Urban Migration

Newly arrived immigrants were one of several groups moving into the nation's cities in the postwar era. Although prior to 1965 U.S. immigration policy followed the restrictive national origins quota system set up in 1924 (see Chapter 23), Congress modified the law during and after World War II. The War Brides Act of 1945, permitting the entry and naturalization of the wives and children of Americans living abroad (mainly servicemen), brought thousands of new immigrants between 1950 and 1965, including some 17,000 Koreans. Three years later, the Displaced Persons Act admitted approximately 415,000 European refugees. The repeal of the Chinese Exclusion Act in 1943, made in deference to America's wartime alliance with China, and the passage of the McCarran-Walter Act in 1952 ended the exclusion of Chinese, Japanese, Korean, and Southeast Asian immigrants. Finally, in recognition of

the freeing of the Philippines from American control in 1946, Filipinos received their own quota (Figure 28.4).

Latino Immigration.   One of the largest groups of postwar migrants came from Mexico. Nearly 275,000 Mexicans came in the 1950s, and almost 444,000 in the 1960s. They moved primarily to western and southwestern cities such as Los Angeles, El Paso, and Phoenix, where they found jobs as migrant workers or in the expanding service sector. Large numbers of Mexican Americans also settled in Chicago, Detroit, Kansas City, and Denver. Before World War II, most Mexican Americans had lived in rural areas and engaged in agricultural work; by 1960, a majority were living in urban areas where they joined more settled communities of service and manufacturing workers.

Part of the stimulus for Mexican immigration came from the reinstitution of the *bracero* program from 1951 to 1964. Originally devised as a means of importing temporary labor during World War II, the *bracero* program brought 450,000 Mexican workers to the United States at its peak in 1959. But even as the federal government welcomed *braceros*, it deported those who stayed on illegally. In response to the recession of 1953–1954, which caused high unemployment throughout the nation, federal authorities deported nearly 4 million Mexicans in a program called "Operation Wetback." For a few years the level of illegal immigration was reduced, but it rose again after the *bracero* program ended.

Another group of Spanish-speaking migrants came from the American-controlled territory of Puerto Rico.

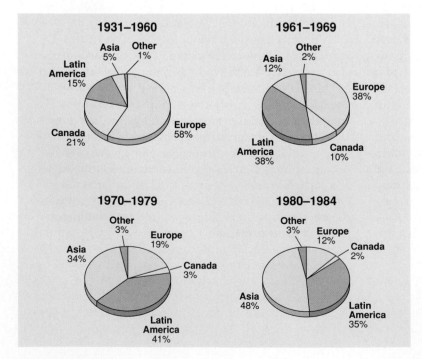

FIGURE 28.4
Legal Immigration to the United States by Region, 1931–1984
Source: Robert W. Gardner, Bryant Robie, and Peter C. Smith, "Asian Americans: Growth, Change, and Diversity," *Population Bulletin*, vol. 40, no. 4 (Washington, DC: Population Reference Bureau, 1985), 2.

Residents of that island had been American citizens since 1917, so their migration was not subject to immigration laws. The inflow from the island increased dramatically after World War II, when mechanization of the island's sugarcane industry pushed many rural Puerto Ricans off the land. When airlines began to offer cheap direct flights between San Juan and New York City (in the 1940s the fare was about $50, or two weeks' wages), Puerto Ricans became this country's first group to immigrate by air. Most Puerto Ricans went to New York, where they settled first in East ("Spanish") Harlem and then in other areas of the city. This massive migration, which grew from 70,000 in 1940 to 613,000 just twenty years later, transformed the ethnic composition of the city. More Puerto Ricans were living in New York City than in San Juan.

Cuban refugees constituted the third large group of Spanish-speaking immigrants. In the six years after Fidel Castro's seizure of power and institution of communist rule in 1959, an estimated 180,000 people fled Cuba for the United States. The Cuban refugee community grew so quickly that it turned Miami into a cosmopolitan, bilingual city almost overnight. Unlike most new immigrants, Miami's Cubans prospered, in large part because they had arrived with more resources. Cubans differed from most other Latino immigrants in that they were predominantly middle class and politically conservative.

Internal Migration.   Internal migration also brought large numbers of people to the cities, especially African Americans, continuing a trend that had begun during World War I (see Chapter 22). Black migration was hastened by the transformation of southern agriculture. New Deal agricultural policies and the development of synthetic fibers such as rayon and Dacron after World War II caused cotton acreage in the South to decline from 43 million acres in 1929 to less than 15 million in 1959. In addition, the ongoing mechanization of agriculture reduced the demand for farm labor. The mechanical cotton picker, introduced in 1944, could pick 1,000 pounds an hour compared with the 20 pounds picked by an experienced farmhand. As a result of these changes, the southern farm population fell from 16.2 million in 1930 to 5.9 million in 1960. Although both whites and blacks left the land, the starkest decline was among black farmers.

Some of the migrants settled in southern cities, where they found industrial jobs. White southerners from Appalachia moved north to "hillbilly" ghettos such as Cincinnati's Over the Rhine neighborhood and Chicago's Uptown. In the most dramatic population shift, as many as 3 million blacks headed to Chicago, New York, Washington, Detroit, Los Angeles, and other cities between 1940 and 1960. So pervasive were the migrants that certain sections of Chicago seemed like

Harlem in the Fifties
During and after World War II, thousands of African Americans left the rural South for northern and western cities, expanding the population of Harlem and other black neighborhoods. Ironically, the migrants arrived just as declining employment, deteriorating housing, and shrinking tax revenues were making life more difficult for inner-city residents.
Henry Hammond/Archive Photos.

the Mississippi Delta transplanted. By 1960 about half of the nation's black population was living outside the South, compared with only 23 percent before World War II.

In western cities, an influx of native Americans also contributed to the rise in the nonwhite urban population. Seeking to end federal involvement in Indian affairs, Congress in 1953 authorized a program to terminate the legal standing of native tribes and move their members off reservations. The program, which reflected a Cold War preoccupation with conformity and assimilation, enjoyed strong support from mining, timber, and agricultual interests that wanted to open reservation lands for private development. The Bureau of Indian Affairs encouraged voluntary migration to urban areas by subsidizing moving costs and establishing relocation centers in San Francisco, Denver, Chicago, and other cities. The relocation program proved problematic, however, as many Indians found it difficult to adjust to an urban environment and culture. Although the policy of forced termination was halted in 1958, by 1960 some 60,000 Indians had moved to the cities. Despite the program's stated goal of assimilation, most native American migrants settled together in poor urban neighborhoods alongside other nonwhite groups.

The Urban Crisis

American cities thus saw their nonwhite populations swell at the same time that whites were flocking to the suburbs. From 1950 to 1960 the nation's twelve largest cities lost 3.6 million whites and gained 4.5 million nonwhites. Tax revenues followed the more affluent whites out of the city and into the suburbs. A wealthy community such as Grosse Pointe, a suburb of Detroit, could far more easily fund first-rate schools and police and fire protection than could the city of Detroit, whose tax base shrank as businesses and middle-class residents relocated to the suburbs. The decay of urban services and infrastructure, coupled with growing racial fears, only accelerated white suburban flight in the 1960s.

By the time that blacks, Latinos, and native Americans moved into the inner cities, urban America was in poor shape. Housing continued to be a crucial problem. City planners, politicians, and real-estate developers responded with urban renewal programs, razing blighted city neighborhoods to make way for modern construction projects. Local residents were rarely consulted about whether they wanted their neighborhoods "renewed," and redevelopment programs often produced grim high-rise housing projects that destroyed community bonds and created anonymous open areas that were vulnerable to crime. Between 1949 and 1967 urban renewal demolished almost 400,000 buildings and displaced 1.4 million people. The 575,000 units of public housing built nationwide by 1964 came nowhere close to satisfying the need for affordable urban housing.

Urban renewal projects often benefited the wealthy at the expense of the poor. Many downtown "revitalization" projects replaced established racial-ethnic neighborhoods with expensive rental housing or office buildings where suburban commuters worked. Boston's West End, a poor but vibrant Italian American community, was razed by a private developer between 1958 and 1960 to build Charles River Park, an apartment complex whose rents were far too steep for the former residents. In San Francisco some 4,000 residents of the Western Addition, a predominantly black neighborhood, were displaced under an urban renewal program that built luxury housing, a shopping center, and an express boulevard. In both cities residents were forced into less desirable parts of the city, cut off from the vitality of their former neighborhoods.

The Other America
While many celebrated the "affluent society" of the postwar era, critics like Michael Harrington noted that thousands of Americans remained in poverty. Among them were many elderly people who struggled to survive on fixed incomes and without medical insurance.
Cincinnati Historical Society.

Despite pockets of "urban gentrification," postwar cities were increasingly becoming places of last resort for the nation's poor. Unlike earlier immigrants, for whom cities were gateways to social and economic betterment, inner-city residents in the postwar period faced diminishing hopes for improvement. Lured by the promise of plentiful jobs, migrants found that many of those opportunities had relocated to the suburban fringe, making steady employment out of reach for those who needed it most. The poor were also trapped in the cities because of racism. Migrants to the city, especially blacks, faced racial hostility and institutional barriers to mobility—biased school funding, hiring and promotion decisions, and credit practices. Two separate Americas were emerging: a largely white society in suburbs and peripheral areas, and an inner city populated by blacks, Latinos, and other disadvantaged groups.

The Fifties—The Way We Were?

Despite the contradictory developments of the postwar era, many Americans continue to view the 1950s as the historical norm—a time when families were close-knit and intact, children were happy, and the economy was growing. Despite the fear of nuclear annihilation, Americans were confident that theirs was the strongest country, both economically and morally, in the world. Changes in American family, political, and social life since then are often seen as declines from this ideal.

But perhaps the fifties should be regarded more as unique than as ideal—the result of a special combination of circumstances that could not be sustained on a permanent basis. In a 200-year trend toward smaller families, the postwar baby boom was certainly atypical, as was the remarkable stability of marriages. Scarred by memories of depression and World War II–era dislocations and scared by the ambiguities of living in the atomic age, the postwar generation embraced family life with a vengeance—a phenomenon that historian Elaine Tyler May calls "cold war, warm hearth." When social conditions changed in the 1960s, the profamily orientation gave way to the more individualistic ethos that characterized the rest of the century.

Our tendency to view the 1950s as the historical norm also fails to recognize that America's postwar affluence was based on international economic conditions that could not continue indefinitely. The war-devastated economies of Japan and West Germany would rebuild, taking advantage of new technology to compete with and eventually challenge American economic supremacy. So too would emerging industrial centers in the Pacific Rim such as South Korea, Hong Kong, and Singapore. For Americans who regard the economic dominance of the 1950s as the norm, any decline appears to be a disturbing loss of American power and economic strength rather than a return to a more balanced state of economic affairs.

The stereotypes of boundless affluence in the 1950s are also misleading, for they hide those persons who did not share equally in the American dream—displaced factory workers, destitute old people, female heads of households, blacks and other racial minority groups. Not until the publication of Michael Harrington's *The Other America* in 1962 did Americans begin to realize that in the richest country in the world more than a quarter of the population was poor. In the turbulent decade that followed, three contrasts—between suburban affluence and the "other America"; between the lure of the city for the poor and minorities and its grim, segregated reality; and between a heightened emphasis on domesticity and the widening opportunities for women—would spawn growing demands for social change that the nation's leaders could not ignore.

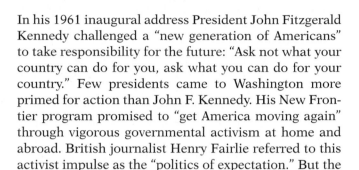

John F. Kennedy and the Politics of Expectation

———————★———————

In his 1961 inaugural address President John Fitzgerald Kennedy challenged a "new generation of Americans" to take responsibility for the future: "Ask not what your country can do for you, ask what you can do for your country." Few presidents came to Washington more primed for action than John F. Kennedy. His New Frontier program promised to "get America moving again" through vigorous governmental activism at home and abroad. British journalist Henry Fairlie referred to this activist impulse as the "politics of expectation." But the legislative achievements of Kennedy's New Frontier, particularly in domestic affairs, were modest.

The New Politics

The Republicans would have been happy to renominate Dwight D. Eisenhower for president, but the Twenty-second Amendment prevented them from doing so. Passed in 1951 by a Republican-controlled Congress to prevent a repetition of Franklin Roosevelt's four-term presidency, the amendment limited future presidents to two full terms. So in 1960 the Republicans turned to Vice-President Richard M. Nixon, who, like a good

The Kennedy Magnetism
John Kennedy, the Democratic candidate for president in 1960, used his youth and personality to attract voters. Here the Massachusetts senator draws an enthusiastic crowd on a campaign stop in Elgin, Illinois.
Wide World Photos, Inc.

1950s junior executive, had patiently waited for his turn at the top. Nixon campaigned for an updated version of Eisenhower's policies but was hampered by lukewarm support from the popular president. Asked by reporters whether Nixon had helped make any major policy decisions in his administration, Eisenhower replied, "If you give me a week I might think of one."

The Democrats chose Senator John Kennedy of Massachusetts, with the Senate majority leader, Lyndon B. Johnson of Texas, as the vice-presidential nominee. Kennedy, an alumnus of Harvard and a World War II hero, had inherited his love of politics from his grandfathers, both of whom had been colorful Irish-Catholic politicians in Boston. His wealthy father, Joseph P. Kennedy, had headed the Securities and Exchange Commission and served as ambassador to Great Britain under Roosevelt. First elected to Congress in 1946, John Kennedy moved to the Senate in 1952. Ambitious and hard-driven, Kennedy launched his campaign in 1960 with a platform calling for civil rights legislation, health care for the elderly, aid to education, urban

renewal, expanded military and space programs, and containment of communism abroad. With the country in the middle of a recession that had pushed unemployment to a postwar high, Kennedy vowed to "get America moving again."

At forty-three, Kennedy was poised to become the youngest man ever elected to the presidency and the nation's first Catholic chief executive. Turning his age into a powerful campaign asset, Kennedy practiced what came to be called the "new politics," an approach that emphasized youthful charisma, style, and personality rather than issues and platforms. Using the power of the media—particularly television—to reach voters directly, practitioners of the new politics relied on professional media consultants, political pollsters, and mass fundraising. Kennedy's family wealth and the contributions he raised from sources outside traditional party networks paid for his expensive campaign.

A series of four televised debates between the two principal candidates, a major innovation of the 1960 campaign, showed how important television was becoming to political life. Nixon, far less photogenic

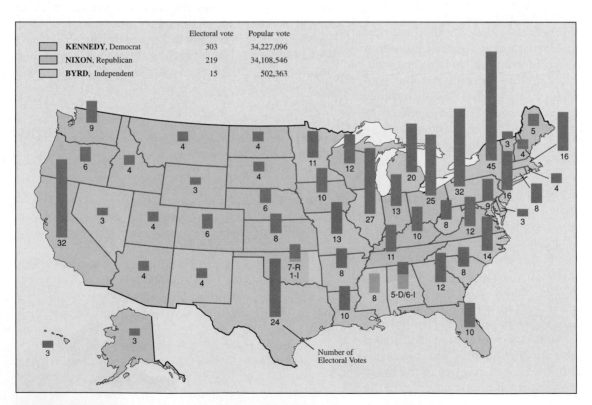

MAP 28.2
The Election of 1960
The Kennedy-Nixon contest was the closest since 1884. Kennedy won twelve states, including Illinois, by less than 2 percent of the two-party vote tally; he lost six others, including California, by a similarly small margin. Fifteen electors cast their votes for the Independent Democrat, Harry F. Byrd. Despite his razor-thin margin of victory, Kennedy won 303 electoral votes, the same number Truman had won in 1948, showing that the electoral college vote can be a misleading indicator of popular support.

than Kennedy, looked sallow and unshaven under the intense studio lights. Kennedy, in contrast, looked vigorous, cool, and self-confident on screen. Polls showed that television did sway political perceptions: voters who listened to the first debate on the radio concluded that Nixon had won, but those who viewed it on TV judged in Kennedy's favor.

Despite the edge Kennedy enjoyed in the debates, he won only the narrowest of electoral victories, receiving 49.7 percent of the popular vote to Nixon's 49.5 percent (Map 28.2). Kennedy successfully appealed to the diverse elements of the Democratic coalition, attracting large numbers of Catholic and black voters and a significant sector of the middle class; the vice-presidential nominee, Lyndon Johnson, brought in southern white Democrats. Yet only 120,000 votes separated the two candidates, and the shift of a few thousand votes in key states such as Illinois (where there were confirmed cases of voting fraud) would have reversed the outcome.

Activism Abroad

Although Kennedy's New Frontier platform included a long list of domestic social reforms, his greatest priority as president was foreign affairs. A resolute Cold Warrior, Kennedy took a hard line against communist expansionism. In contrast to Eisenhower, whose cost-saving New Look program had built up the American nuclear arsenal at the expense of conventional weapons, Kennedy proposed a new policy of *flexible response*, stating that the nation must be prepared "to deter all wars, general or limited, nuclear or conventional, large or small." Congress quickly granted Kennedy's military requests, and by 1963 the defense budget reached its highest level as a percentage of total federal expenditures in the Cold War era, greatly expanding the military-industrial complex (see Figure 27.1).

Flexible response measures were designed to deter direct attacks by the Soviet Union. To prepare for a new kind of warfare, evident in the wars of national liberation that had broken out in many Third World countries, Kennedy adopted a new military doctrine of *counterinsurgency*. Soon U.S. Army Special Forces, called Green Berets for their distinctive headgear, were receiving intensive training in repelling the random, small-scale attacks typical of guerrilla warfare. Vietnam would soon provide a testing ground for counterinsurgency techniques (see Chapter 29).

Peace Corps and Foreign Aid.   Another of Kennedy's projects, the Peace Corps (established in 1961 and headed by his brother-in-law, Sargent Shriver), embodied the commitment to public service that the president had called for in his inaugural address. Thousands of men and women, many of them recent college gradu-

The Peace Corps
The Peace Corps, a New Frontier program initiated in 1961, attracted thousands of idealistic young Americans, including these volunteers who worked in a vaccination program in Bolivia.
David S. Boyer/National Geographic Society Image Collection.

ates, agreed to devote two or more years to programs that had them teaching English to Filipino schoolchildren or helping African villagers obtain adequate supplies of water. Embodying the idealism of the early 1960s, the Peace Corps was also a Cold War weapon designed to bring Third World countries into the American orbit and away from communist influence.

For the same reason, Kennedy pushed for economic aid to developing countries. The State department's Agency for International Development coordinated foreign aid for the Third World, including surplus agricultural products distributed to developing nations through its Food for Peace program. In Latin America, the Alliance for Progress provided funds for food, education, medicine, and other services, although it did little to enhance economic growth or improve social conditions there.

Bay of Pigs Invasion. In April 1961 Kennedy undertook his first major initiative—an effort to overthrow the new Soviet-supported regime in Cuba. The United States had long maintained a naval base at Guantánamo Bay and exercised nearly total economic and political dominance of the island. But on New Year's Day in 1959 Fidel Castro overthrew the corrupt and unpopular dictator Fulgencio Batista and called for a revolution to reshape Cuban society. When Castro began agrarian reforms at odds with American interests, and nationalized American-owned banks and industries, relations with Washington deteriorated. By early 1961 the United States had declared an embargo on all exports to Cuba, cut back on imports of Cuban sugar, and broken off diplomatic relations with Castro's regime.

Isolated by the United States, Cuba turned increasingly toward the Soviet Union for economic and military support. Concerned about Castro's growing friendliness with the Soviets, in early 1961 Kennedy used plans originally drawn up by the Eisenhower administration to dispatch Cuban exiles living in Nicaragua to foment an anti-Castro uprising. The invaders had been trained by the Central Intelligence Agency (CIA) but were ill prepared for their task and

had little popular support. After landing at Cuba's Bay of Pigs on April 17, the tiny force of 1,400 men was crushed by Castro's troops (Map 28.3). Symptomatic of inept CIA planning, pilots taking off from Nicaragua to provide air cover for the landing forces forgot to set their watches ahead to Cuban time and arrived at the beach an hour late. The anticipated rebellion never occurred. The embarrassing failure of the Bay of Pigs invasion cast doubts on Kennedy's activist approach to international affairs.

U.S.-Soviet relations deteriorated further in June 1961, when Soviet premier Khrushchev deployed soldiers to sever communist-controlled East Berlin from the western sector of the city controlled by West Germany. Khrushchev took this action after the United States flatly rejected his proposal to withdraw both Soviet and Western occupation forces from the city. Determined to confront the Soviets publicly, Kennedy declared in a televised speech on July 25 that Berlin was the "great testing place of Western courage and will." With congressional approval, Kennedy added 300,000 troops to the armed forces and promptly dispatched 40,000 of them to Europe. In mid-August, to stop the exodus of East Germans to the West, the Sovi-

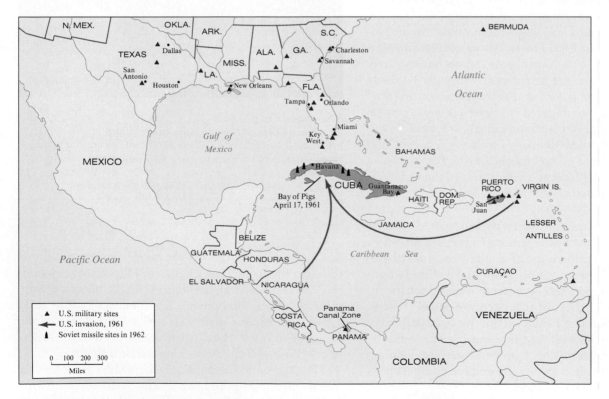

MAP 28.3
The United States and Cuba, 1961–1962
Fidel Castro's takeover in Cuba in 1959 brought Cold War tensions to the Caribbean. In 1961 the United States tried unsuccessfully to overthrow Castro's regime by supporting the Bay of Pigs invasion of Cuban exiles launched from Nicaragua and other points in the Caribbean. In 1962 a major confrontation with the Soviet Union occurred over Soviet missile sites in Cuba. The Soviets removed the missiles after President Kennedy ordered a naval blockade of the island, which lies just 90 miles south of Florida.

The Berlin Wall
In June 1962, President Kennedy traveled to West Berlin and delivered one of the most
memorable speeches of his career. Gazing into the communist sector of the city from a
podium beside the Berlin Wall, Kennedy affirmed the solidarity of the free world and
declared, "Let them come to Berlin."
Corbis-Bettmann.

ets ordered construction of the Berlin Wall, and East
German guards began policing the border. Visiting the
city in June 1963, Kennedy—standing beside the wall—
invoked the solidarity of the free world by declaring
"Ich bin ein Berliner" ("I am a Berliner") and
denounced the barrier as proof of the failure of communism. Until it was dismantled in 1989, the Berlin
Wall remained the supreme symbol of the Cold War.

Cuban Missile Crisis.   The climactic confrontation of
the Cold War came in October 1962. After the failed Bay
of Pigs invasion, the Kennedy administration increased
economic pressure against Cuba and resumed covert
efforts to overthrow the Castro regime. In response, the
Soviets stepped up military aid to Cuba, including the
installation of missiles (see Map 28.3). In early October,
American reconnaissance planes photographed Soviet-
built bases for intermediate-range ballistic missiles
(IRBMs), which could reach U.S. targets as far as 2,200
miles away. At least some of those nuclear weapons had
already been installed, and more were on the way.

Rather than work through Department of State or
diplomatic channels, Kennedy confronted the Soviet
Union publicly in a somber televised address on Mon-

day, October 22. Displaying the reconnaissance photos
as evidence, he announced that the United States would
impose a "quarantine on all offensive military equipment" intended for Cuba. As the two superpowers went
on full military alert, people around the world believed
that this long-dreaded direct confrontation between the
two superpowers would end in nuclear war. Americans
living in cities within range of the missiles restocked
their bomb shelters and calculated the fastest routes
out of town.

While the world held its breath, the Russian ships
halted their voyage. Khrushchev wrote to Kennedy that if
the United States agreed not to invade Cuba, the Soviets
would remove the missiles. In a second letter Khrushchev
demanded the removal of American missiles in Turkey as
a condition for resolving the crisis. On his brother
Robert's advice, the president publicly agreed to the
terms of the first letter but ignored the second one. (He
later secretly agreed to remove the missiles from Turkey,
a move that the United States had already planned.) On
the following Sunday, October 28, after the most harrowing week of the nuclear age, Kennedy and Khrushchev
both announced concessions: Kennedy pledged not to
invade Cuba, and Khrushchev promised to dismantle the

missile bases. "We're eyeball to eyeball," Secretary of State Dean Rusk observed, "and I think the other fellow just blinked."

Although the risk of nuclear war was greater during the Cuban missile crisis than it was at any other time in the postwar period, it led to a slight thaw in U.S.-Soviet relations. In the words of national security advisor McGeorge Bundy, "having come so close to the edge, the leaders of the two governments have since taken care to keep away from the cliff." Kennedy softened his Cold War rhetoric and began to strive for peaceful coexistence. Soviet leaders, similarly chastened, were willing to talk. In August 1963 the three nuclear powers—the United States, the Soviet Union, and Great Britain—agreed to ban the testing of nuclear weapons in the atmosphere, in space, and underwater. Underground testing, however, was allowed to continue. The new emphasis on peaceful coexistence also led to the establishment of a Washington-Moscow telecommunications "hot line" in 1963 so that leaders could contact each other quickly during potential crises.

But no matter how often American leaders talked about opening channels of communication with the Soviets, the preoccupation with the Soviet military threat to American security remained a cornerstone of U.S. policy. Nor did Soviet leaders moderate their concern over the threat that they believed the United States posed to the survival of the USSR. The Cold War, and the escalating arms race that accompanied it, would continue for another twenty-five years.

The New Frontier at Home

The expansive vision of presidential leadership that Kennedy and his advisors brought to the White House worked less well at home than it did abroad. Hampered by the lack of a popular mandate in the 1960 election, Kennedy could not mobilize public support for the domestic agenda of the New Frontier. A conservative coalition of southern Democrats and western and midwestern Republicans effectively stalled most liberal initiatives. More important, Kennedy was not nearly as impassioned about domestic reform as he was about foreign policy.

NASA. One program that did win both popular and congressional support was increased funding for the National Aeronautics and Space Administration (NASA), whose Mercury space program had begun in 1958. On May 5, 1961, just three months after Kennedy took office, Alan Shepard became the first American in space. (The Soviet cosmonaut Yuri Gagarin earned the distinction of being the first person in space when he made a 108-hour flight in April 1961.) The following year, American astronaut John Glenn manned the first space mission to orbit the earth. At the height of American fascination with space flight, Kennedy proposed that the nation commit itself to landing a man on the moon within the decade. To support this mission (accomplished in 1969), Kennedy persuaded Congress to greatly increase NASA's budget.

Economic Policy. Kennedy's most striking domestic achievement was his use of modern economic theory to shape government fiscal policy. New Dealers had gradually moved away from the ideal of a balanced budget, turning instead to deliberate deficit spending to stimulate economic growth. In addition to relying on federal spending to create the desired deficit, Kennedy and his advisors proposed a reduction in income taxes. A tax cut, they argued, would put more money in the hands of taxpayers, who would spend it, thereby creating more jobs. For a time federal expenditures would exceed federal income, but after a year or two the expanding economy would raise American incomes and generate higher tax revenues.

Congress balked at this unorthodox proposal, and the measure failed to pass. But Lyndon Johnson pressed for it after Kennedy's assassination, signing it into law in February 1964. The Kennedy-Johnson tax cut—the Tax Reduction Act (1964)—marked a milestone in the use of fiscal policy to encourage economic growth, an approach that Republicans and other fiscal conservatives would later embrace. Although an economic expansion started before the effects of the tax cut could be felt, Kennedy and his economic advisors got credit for it anyway. The gross national product grew at a rate of 5 percent during the 1960s, nearly twice the rate of the Eisenhower years. Much of the growth, however, was fueled by massive defense expenditures, especially spending for the escalating Vietnam War.

Kennedy's interest in stimulating economic growth did not include a commitment to spending for domestic social needs, although he did not entirely ignore the liberal legislative agenda of Franklin Roosevelt and Harry Truman. Kennedy managed to push through legislation raising the minimum wage and expanding Social Security benefits. But on other issues—federal aid to education, wilderness preservation, federal investment in mass transportation, and medical insurance for the elderly—he ran into determined congressional opposition from both Republicans and dissenters in his own party.

The Warren Court. Some of the most significant policies of the early 1960s came not from the Kennedy administration but from the Supreme Court. Much of the Court's judicial activism in these years was linked to Earl Warren, Chief Justice from 1953 to 1969. Warren's leadership had already influenced the Court's most important decision, *Brown v. Board of Education* (1954), requiring the desegregation of public schools (see Chapter 27). In the 1960s the Court continued to make landmark decisions. It reinforced defendants' rights in cases like *Miranda v. Arizona* (1966), which required arresting officers to notify a suspect that "he has a right to remain silent, that any statement he does make may be used in evidence against him, and that he has a right to the presence of an attorney, either retained or appointed." Tackling the issue of the reapportionment of state legislatures in *Baker v. Carr* (1962) and *Reynolds v. Sims* (1964), the Court put forth the doctrine of "one person, one vote," meaning that all citizens' votes should have equal weight, no matter where they lived. The ruling substantially increased the representation of both suburban and urban areas, with their concentrations of black and Spanish-speaking residents, at the expense of rural regions. One of the most controversial decisions was *Engel v. Vitale* (1962), which banned organized prayer in public schools as a violation of the First Amendment's injunction that "Congress shall make no law respecting an establishment of religion."

JFK and Civil Rights

Perhaps the gravest failure of the Kennedy administration was its reluctance to act on civil rights—the most important domestic issue of the 1960s. Building on the strategy of nonviolent direct action pioneered by Martin Luther King Jr. and the Montgomery bus boycotters in the 1950s, a younger generation of activists in the 1960s initiated new, more assertive tactics such as sit-ins, freedom rides, and voter registration campaigns.

Sit-Ins and Freedom Rides. This new phase of the civil rights movement began in Greensboro, North Carolina, on February 1, 1960, when four black college students took seats at the "whites only" lunch counter of a local Woolworth's, determined to "sit in" until they were served. Although the protesters were arrested, the sit-in tactic worked and quickly spread to other southern cities. A few months later Ella Baker, an administrator with the Southern Christian Leadership Conference and a lifelong activist, helped to organize the Student Non-Violent Coordinating Committee (SNCC, known as "Snick") to facilitate student sit-ins. By the end of the year, about 50,000 people had participated in sit-ins or other demonstrations, and 3,600 of them had been jailed, usually for disturbing the peace. But lunch counters had been desegregated in 126 cities throughout the South (see American Voices, "Anne Moody: 'We Would Like to Be Served,'" p. 928).

The success of SNCC's unorthodox tactics encouraged the Congress of Racial Equality (CORE), an interracial group founded in 1942, to adopt a more confrontational strategy. In 1961 CORE's executive director, James Farmer, organized a series of *freedom rides* on interstate bus lines throughout the South to call attention to the continuing segregation of public transportation despite the Supreme Court rulings. The bus-riding activists, mostly young, both black and white, were brutally attacked by white mobs. In Anniston, Alabama, club-wielding Ku Klux Klansmen attacked one of the buses with stones and set it on fire. Governor John Patterson refused to intervene, claiming, "I cannot guarantee protection for this bunch of rabble rousers."

Although the Kennedy administration generally opposed the freedom riders' activities, films of their beatings and the bus burning shown on the nightly news prompted Attorney General Robert Kennedy to send federal marshals to Alabama to restore order. Faced with Department of Justice intervention against those who defied the Interstate Commerce Commission's prohibition of segregation in interstate vehicles and facilities, most southern communities quietly acceded to the changes. And civil rights activists learned the lesson that nonviolent protest could succeed if it provoked vicious white resistance and generated publicity. Only when forced to, it appeared, would the federal authorities act.

Except for protecting the freedom riders, the Kennedy administration lent little support to the growing civil rights movement. Kennedy seemed to view civil rights protests as irritating political embarrassments that distracted him from more important domestic and international issues. Behind the scenes Kennedy even authorized clandestine FBI surveillance of Martin Luther King Jr. and a smear campaign against him.

Political realities, especially tensions within the Democratic coalition, also dampened Kennedy's enthusiasm for civil rights. Blacks had given Kennedy strong support in the 1960 election and he needed to keep them in the coalition, but Kennedy also needed the votes of southern Democrats to get his programs through Congress. Kennedy reached out to black constituencies by appointing former NAACP lawyer Thurgood Marshall to the U.S. Circuit Court of Appeals at the same time he appointed a number of white segregationist judges to southern benches. But as the civil rights movement became more confrontational, Kennedy could not maintain that delicate balancing act.

Birmingham. Events came to a head in 1963 in Birmingham, Alabama, when Martin Luther King Jr. and the Reverend Fred Shuttlesworth called for a protest against conditions in what King called "the most segregated city in the United States." In April thousands of black demonstrators marched downtown to picket Birmingham's department stores. They were met by Eugene "Bull" Connor, the city's commissioner of public safety, who used snarling dogs, electric cattle prods, and high-pressure fire hoses to break up the crowd. The hoses were so powerful that they ripped bark from trees and tore bricks from buildings, a scene captured for the evening news by television cameras. "The civil rights movement

ANNE MOODY
"We Would Like to Be Served"

─────★─────

Born in rural Mississippi in 1940, Anne Moody was one of thousands of black college students who joined the Student Non-Violent Coordinating Committee in the early 1960s. In her senior year, she participated in a sit-in at a Woolworth's lunch counter in Jackson, Mississippi, which she described in her autobiography.

At exactly 11 A.M., Pearlena, Memphis, and I entered Woolworth's from the rear entrance. We separated as soon as we stepped into the store, and made small purchases from various counters. . . .

Seconds before 11:15 we were occupying three seats at the previously segregated Woolworth's lunch counter. In the beginning the waitresses seemed to ignore us, as if they really didn't know what was going on. Our waitress walked past us a couple of times before she noticed we had started to write our own orders down and realized we wanted service. She asked us what we wanted. We began to read to her from our order slips. She told us that we would be served at the back counter, which was for Negroes.

"We would like to be served here," I said. . . .

At noon, students from a nearby white high school started pouring in to Woolworth's. When they first saw us they were sort of surprised. They didn't know how to react. A few started to heckle and the newsmen [who had arrived earlier] became interested again. Then the white students started chanting all kinds of anti-Negro slogans. We were called a little bit of everything. The rest of the seats except the three we were occupying had been roped off to prevent others from sitting down. A couple of the boys took one end of the rope and made it into a hangman's noose. Several attempts were made to put it around our necks. . . .

Memphis suggested that we pray. We bowed our heads, and all hell broke loose. A man rushed forward, threw Memphis from his seat, and slapped my face. Then another man who worked in the store threw me against an adjoining counter.

Down on my knees on the floor, I saw Memphis lying near the lunch counter with blood running out of the corners of his mouth. As he tried to protect his face, the man who'd thrown him down kept kicking him against the head. . . .

. . . The mob started smearing us with ketchup, mustard, sugar, pies, and everything on the counter. Soon Joan [Trumpauer, a white college student and NAACP member] and I were joined by John Salter, but the moment he sat down he was hit on the jaw with what appeared to be brass knuckles. Blood gushed from his face and someone threw salt into the open wound. . . .

. . . The mob took spray paint from the counter and sprayed it on the new demonstrators. The high school student had on a white shirt; the word "nigger" was written on his back with red spray paint.

We sat there for three hours taking a beating when the manager decided to close the store because the mob had begun to go wild with stuff from other counters. . . .

After the sit-in, all I could think of was how sick Mississippi whites were. They believed so much in the segregated Southern way of life, they would kill to preserve it. I sat there in the NAACP office and thought of how many times they had killed when this way of life was threatened. I knew that the killing had just begun. . . .

───────

Source: Anne Moody, *Coming of Age in Mississippi* (New York: Dell Publishing, Laurel Editions, 1968), 264–267.

should thank God for Bull Connor," President Kennedy noted. "He's helped it as much as Abraham Lincoln."

Realizing that he could no longer straddle the issue, Kennedy decided to step up the federal role in civil rights. On June 11, 1963, he went on television to promise major civil rights legislation banning discrimination in public accommodations and empowering the Department of Justice to seek desegregation on its own authority. Black leaders hailed the speech as a "Second Emancipation Proclamation," but for one person Kennedy's speech came too late. That night, Medgar Evers, president of the Mississippi chapter of the NAACP, was shot in the back and killed in his driveway in Jackson. The martyrdom of Evers became a spur to further action.

The March on Washington.   To rouse the conscience of the country and to marshal support for Kennedy's bill, civil rights leaders turned to a tactic that A. Phillip

Racial Violence in Birmingham
When thousands of blacks marched through downtown Birmingham, Alabama, to protest racial segregation in April 1963, they were met with fire hoses and attack dogs unleashed by Police Chief "Bull" Connor. The violence, which was televised on the national evening news, shocked many Americans and helped build sympathy for the civil rights movement among northern whites.
Bill Hudson/Wide World Photos, Inc.

Randolph had first suggested in 1941 (see Chapter 26): a massive march on Washington. Organized by Martin Luther King Jr. and other prominent black civil rights leaders, the march drew support from a broad coalition, including the National Council of Churches, the National Conference of Catholics for Interracial Justice, the American Jewish Congress, and the AFL-CIO's Industrial Union Department.

On August 28, 1963, about 250,000 black and white demonstrators—the largest demonstration up to that time—gathered at the Lincoln Memorial. The march culminated in a memorable speech delivered, indeed preached, by King in the evangelical style of the black church:

I have a dream that one day on the red hills of Georgia the sons of former slaves and the sons of former slaveowners will be able to sit down together at the table of brotherhood. I have a dream that one day even the state of Mississippi, a desert state sweltering with the heat of injustice and oppression, will be transformed into an oasis of freedom and justice. I have a

dream that my four little children will one day live in a nation where they will not be judged by the color of their skin but by the content of their character.

King ended with an exclamation from an old Negro spiritual: "Free at last! Free at last! Thank God almighty, we are free at last!"

King's eloquence and the sight of blacks and whites marching solemnly together did more than any other event to make the civil rights movement acceptable to white Americans. The March on Washington marked the climax of the nonviolent phase of the civil rights movement and confirmed King's position, especially among white liberals, as the leading speaker for the black cause. In 1964 King won the Nobel Peace Prize for his leadership.

Despite the impact of the march on public opinion, few congressional votes were changed by the event. Southern senators continued to block Kennedy's legislation by threatening a filibuster. Even more troubling was a new outbreak of violence by white extremists determined to oppose equality for

Martin Luther King Jr.
The Reverend Martin Luther King Jr. (1929–1968) was one of the most eloquent advocates of the civil rights movement. For many, his "I have a dream" speech at the 1963 March on Washington was the high point of the event.
Wide World Photos, Inc.

blacks at all costs. In September a Baptist church in Birmingham was bombed, and four black Sunday school students were killed. Two months later, President Kennedy was assassinated.

The Kennedy Assassination

Although the first two years of Kennedy's presidency had been plagued by foreign policy crises and domestic inaction, many political observers believed that by 1963 Kennedy was maturing as a national leader. On November 22, 1963, Kennedy went to Texas, a state he needed to win for reelection in 1964, to heal divisions in the party organization there. As he and his wife, Jacqueline, rode in an open car past the Texas School Book Depository in Dallas, he was shot through the head and neck by a sniper. Kennedy died a half hour later. (Whether accused killer Lee Harvey Oswald, a

twenty-four-year-old loner who had spent three years in the Soviet Union, was the sole gunman is still a matter of considerable controversy.) Before *Air Force One* left Dallas to take the president's body back to Washington, a grim-faced Lyndon Johnson was sworn in as president. Kennedy's stunned widow, still wearing her blood-stained pink suit, looked on.

By 1 P.M. Dallas time, just thirty minutes after the shooting, 68 percent of adults in the United States knew that Kennedy had been shot. By late afternoon, the proportion had risen to 99.8 percent, showing how the mass media could reach virtually every person in the nation within a few hours. As on Pearl Harbor Day in 1941, people never forgot what they were doing when they heard that Kennedy had been shot.

Kennedy's youthful image, the trauma of his assassination, and the collective sense that Americans had been robbed of a promising leader contributed to a powerful mystique. Only forty-six at the time of his death, he was the first president born in the twentieth century. The Kennedy myth had begun even before his tragic death. In June 1963 about 59 percent of the people surveyed claimed to have voted for Kennedy, a big jump over the 49.7 percent who actually had; after the assassination, that figure rose to 65 percent. A British journalist called it "a posthumous landslide."

The Kennedy mystique has overshadowed what most historians agree was at best a mixed record. Kennedy exercised bold presidential leadership in foreign affairs, but his initiatives in Cuba and Berlin marked the height of superpower confrontation during the Cold War. Moreover, his enthusiasm for fighting communism abroad had no domestic equivalent. Kennedy's proposals for educational aid, medical insurance, and other liberal reforms stalled, and his tax cut bill languished in Congress until after his death. Lyndon Johnson's decision to turn passage of civil rights legislation into a memorial to his slain predecessor provided an ironic climax to Kennedy's lukewarm support for the cause.

Lyndon B. Johnson and the Great Society

—————— ——————

Lyndon Baines Johnson, a seasoned politician who was best at negotiating in the backrooms of power, was no match for the Kennedy style, and he knew it. But less than a year after assuming office, Johnson won the 1964 presidential election in a landslide that far surpassed Kennedy's meager mandate in 1960. Johnson then used his astonishing energy and genius for compromise to bring to fruition many of Kennedy's stalled programs and more than a few of his own. Those legislative accomplishments are referred to as the "Great Society," Johnson's own phrase to describe his policies for ending poverty and racial injustice. It was the Great Society, not the much less ambitious New Frontier, that fulfilled and in many cases surpassed the New Deal liberal agenda of the 1930s (Table 28.1).

A Southern President and Civil Rights

Johnson brought to the presidency far more legislative experience than had any other modern president, and he used his talent to great effect. Born in the central Texas hill country in 1908, Johnson had served in government since 1932 as a congressional aide, New Deal administrator, congressman, senator, Senate majority leader, and finally vice-president. In his first year as president he used his powers of persuasion to push through the Kennedy-Johnson tax cut and a major piece of civil rights legislation.

Civil Rights Act of 1964. As a southerner, Johnson was eager to prove to the nation and to Kennedy's skeptical staff that he was a true liberal and a champion of racial equality. The Civil Rights Act, passed in June 1964 after a two-and-a-half-month filibuster by southern senators, was a landmark in the history of American race relations and one of the greatest achievements of the 1960s. Its keystone, Title VII, outlawed discrimination in employment on the basis of race, religion, sex, or national origin. Another section barred discrimination in public accommodations. The law gave integrationists two powerful new weapons: they could ask the U.S. attorney general to withhold federal funds from any government-run program that was not desegregated, and they could appeal discrimination in public accommodations and employment to the newly established Equal Employment Opportunity Commission. The Civil Rights Act resulted in the desegregation of public facilities throughout the South, including many public schools, but obstacles to black voting rights persisted.

Freedom Summer. In 1964, with the Civil Rights Act on the brink of passage, black organizations and churches mounted a major civil rights campaign in Mississippi known as Freedom Summer. Drawing on several thousand volunteers from across the country, including many idealistic white college students, Freedom Summer workers established freedom schools for black children, conducted a major voter registration drive, and organized the Mississippi Freedom Democratic Party, a political alternative to the all-white Mississippi Democratic organization.

White southerners reacted swiftly and violently to those efforts. In June, James Chaney, a CORE volunteer from Mississippi; Andrew Goodman, a student from New York; and Michael Schwerner, a New York social worker, disappeared from Philadelphia, Mississippi, and were presumed murdered. As public demand for an investigation grew, Rita Schwerner, Michael's wife, noted, "We all know that this search . . . is because Andrew Goodman and my husband are white. If only Chaney was involved, nothing would have been done." Six weeks later the FBI discovered the three bodies inside a newly constructed dam five miles away. Goodman and Schwerner had been killed by a single bullet each; Chaney had been brutally beaten with a chain and shot several times. An investigation later determined that members of the Ku Klux Klan had committed the crime. During Freedom Summer, fifteen civil rights workers were murdered, and only about twelve hundred black voters were registered.

The 1964 Election. If 1964 was a year of growing momentum in the civil rights movement and significant liberal legislative accomplishments in Congress, it was a year of conservative retrenchment in the Republican Party. The Republican nominee for president in 1964 was Senator Barry Goldwater of Arizona. Determined to offer "a choice, not an echo," Goldwater campaigned against the expansion of federal power in areas such as the economy and civil rights. Goldwater's crisp speeches rejected Republican efforts to build a moderate coalition. "Extremism in the defense of liberty is no vice," he stated in his acceptance speech at the Republican convention. "Moderation in the pursuit of justice is no virtue." On foreign affairs Goldwater was an aggressive anticommunist who once joked about "lobbing [a nuclear bomb] into the men's room of the Kremlin."

President Johnson easily won the Democratic nomination. Reaffirming his commitment to the party's liberal agenda but putting some distance between himself and the Kennedy clan, Johnson passed over Robert F. Kennedy for vice-president in favor of the Senator Hubert H. Humphrey of Minnesota, a well-known civil rights advocate. An attempt by the avowed segregationist George C. Wallace, governor of Alabama, to exploit a white backlash against civil rights showed early strength but then fizzled. Ironically, given his growing involvement in Vietnam, Johnson presented himself as the peace candidate. Using a frightening TV commercial showing a billowing mushroom cloud, Johnson campaigners exploited public fears about Goldwater's belligerent foreign policy. (The ad was pulled two days later in response to public outcries against fear mongering.) The Johnson-Humphrey ticket won by one of the largest margins in history, receiving 61.1 percent of the popular

TABLE 28.1

Major Great Society Legislation

Civil Rights

1964	Twenty-fourth Amendment	Outlawed poll tax in federal elections
	Civil Rights Act	Banned discrimination in employment and public accommodations on the basis of race, religion, sex, or national origin
1965	Voting Rights Act	Outlawed literacy tests for voting; provided federal supervision of registration in historically low-registration areas

Social Welfare

1964	Economic Opportunity Act	Created Office of Economic Opportunity (OEO) to administer War on Poverty programs such as Head Start, Job Corps, and Volunteers in Service to America (VISTA)
1965	Medical Care Act	Provided medical care for the poor (Medicaid) and the elderly (Medicare)
1966	Minimum Wage Act	Raised hourly minimum wage from $1.25 to $1.40 and expanded coverage to new groups

Education

1965	Elementary and Secondary Education Act	Granted federal aid for education of poor children
	National Endowment for the Arts and Humanities	Provided federal funding and support for artists and scholars
	Higher Education Act	Provided federal scholarships for postsecondary education

Housing and Urban Development

1964	Urban Mass Transportation Act	Provided federal aid to urban mass transit
	Omnibus Housing Act	Provided federal funds for public housing and rent subsidies for low-income families
1965	Housing and Urban Development Act	Created Department of Housing and Urban Development (HUD)
1966	Metropolitan Area Redevelopment and Demonstration Cities acts	Designated 150 "model cities" for combined programs of public housing, social services, and job training

Environment

| 1964 | Wilderness Preservation Act | Designated 9.1 million acres of federal lands as "wilderness areas," barring future roads, buildings, or commercial use |
| 1965 | Air and Water Quality acts | Set tougher air quality standards; required states to enforce water quality standards for interstate waters |

Miscellaneous

1964	Tax Reduction Act	Reduced personal and corporate income tax rates
1965	Immigration Act	Abandoned national quotas of 1924 law, allowing more non-European immigration
	Appalachian Regional Development Act	Provided federal funding for roads, health clinics, and other public works projects in economically depressed regions

vote and surpassing even the 1936 landslide of that great coalition builder Franklin D. Roosevelt, Johnson's political idol and mentor. And Johnson's coattails were long—his sweeping victory brought Democratic gains in both Congress and the state legislatures.

Enacting the Liberal Agenda

Like most New Deal liberals, Johnson took an expansive view of presidential leadership and the positive role of the federal government. The 1964 election gave him not only the popular mandate but, more important, the filibuster-proof Democratic Senate majority that he needed to push his programs forward. "Hurry boys, hurry," he urged his staff. "Get that legislation up to the Hill and out. Eighteen months from now ol' Landslide Lyndon will be Lame-Duck Lyndon." The Eighty-ninth Congress enacted more social reform measures than any session had since Franklin Roosevelt's first term, offering legislation for every important element of the Democratic coalition (see Table 28.1).

One of Johnson's first big successes was breaking the congressional deadlock on aid to education. Passed in April 1965, the Elementary and Secondary Education Act authorized $1 billion in federal funds to benefit impoverished children. By dispensing aid to schools on the basis of the number of needy children in attendance, the act sidestepped the religious issue by granting funds to public and parochial schools alike. That same year the Higher Education Act provided the first federal scholarships for college students and library grants to colleges and universities. The Eighty-ninth Congress also gave Johnson enough votes to enact the federal health insurance legislation first proposed by Truman. The result was two new programs: Medicare, a health plan for the elderly funded by a surcharge on Social Security payroll taxes, and Medicaid, a health plan for the poor paid for by general tax revenues. Because Congress did not impose a cap on medical expenses, which the medical industry opposed, federal expenditures for the two programs quickly escalated.

Although the Great Society is usually associated with programs for the disadvantaged, many of the Johnson administration's programs benefited more affluent Americans as well. Federal urban renewal and home mortgage assistance helped those who could afford to live in single-family homes or modern apartments. Medicare assistance went to every elderly person covered by Social Security, regardless of need. Federal aid for general public education programs benefited children of the middle class as well as the poor. Finally, the creation of the National Endowment for the Arts and the National Endowment for the Humanities in 1965 supported artists and scholars in their efforts to understand and interpret the nation's cultural heritage.

Another aspect of public welfare addressed by the Great Society was the environment. President Johnson pressed for the expansion of the national park system, improvement of air and water quality, and increased land-use planning. At the insistence of his wife, Lady Bird Johnson, he promoted the Highway Beautification Act of 1965. His approach marked a significant break with past conservation efforts, which had tended to concentrate on maintaining natural resources and national wealth. As Secretary of the Interior Stewart Udall explained, Great Society environmental programs emphasized quality of life, battling the problem "of vanishing beauty, of increasing ugliness, of shrinking open space, and of an overall environment that is diminished daily by pollution and noise and blight."

Taking advantage of the Great Society's reform climate, liberal Democrats also brought about significant changes in immigration policy. The Immigration Act of 1965 abandoned the quota system of the 1920s that had discriminated against Asians and southern and eastern Europeans, replacing it with more equitable numerical limits on immigration from Europe, Africa, Asia, and countries in the Western Hemisphere. Since close relatives of individuals who were already legal residents of the United States could be admitted over and above the numerical limits, the legislation led to an immigrant influx far greater than anticipated, with the heaviest volume coming from Asia and Latin America.

Voting Rights Act of 1965.   The federal government also stepped up its commitment to voting rights, although once again it took violence to provoke congressional action. During a voter registration march in February 1965, sheriff's deputies in Marion, Alabama, killed Jimmy Lee Jackson, a black voting rights advocate. In protest, King and other black leaders called for a massive march on Sunday, March 7, from nearby Selma to the state capital, Montgomery, 54 miles away. A staunch opponent of integration, Governor George Wallace banned the march, citing concern for public safety. As soon as the marchers left Selma, mounted state troopers attacked them in broad daylight with tear gas and clubs. Scenes from "Bloody Sunday" were shown on national television later that night; ironically, ABC interrupted *Judgment at Nuremberg*, a film about the Nazi war crimes trials, to show police officers attacking American citizens on the Pettus Bridge.

Lyndon Johnson called Bloody Sunday "an American tragedy" and redoubled his efforts to get Congress to pass his pending voting rights legislation. In a televised speech to a joint session of Congress on March 15 Johnson asserted, "It is wrong—deadly wrong, to deny any of your fellow Americans the right to vote in this country." Then, dramatically and repeatedly, Johnson invoked the best-known slogan of the civil rights movement, "We shall overcome." Watching the speech on television, Martin Luther King was moved to tears.

On August 6 Congress passed the Voting Rights Act of 1965, the second legislative landmark of the civil rights movement. The act suspended the literacy tests and other measures that most southern states had used to prevent blacks from registering to vote. It also authorized the attorney general to send federal examiners to register voters in any county where less than 50 percent of the voting-age population was registered, placing the entire registration and voting process under federal

to register in 1964, later declared, "It won't never go back where it was."

War on Poverty.   In the midst of his campaign for civil rights legislation, Johnson was also pursuing his ambitious goal of putting "an end to poverty in our time." During his presidency, those who lived below the poverty line—three-fourths of whom were white—made up about a quarter of the American population. They included isolated farmers and miners in Appalachia, blacks and Puerto Ricans in urban ghettos, Mexican Americans in migrant labor camps and urban *barrios,* native Americans on reservations, women raising families on their own, and the destitute elderly. Because programs such as Old Age Assistance, Aid to

Civil Rights Protesters in Selma
Protesting the killing of a black voting rights advocate, thousands of civil rights activists staged a 54-mile march from Selma to Montgomery, Alabama, on March 7, 1965. The men and women in this photograph, shown here singing songs of freedom, were part of the historic march. The peaceful protest turned violent when state troopers clubbed and tear-gassed demonstrators on the Pettus Bridge outside Selma. Public outrage over the violence on "Bloody Sunday," as the incident became known, helped Johnson push the Voting Rights Act through Congress that summer.
Bob Adelman/Magnum Photos, Inc.

Johnson's War on Poverty
During his five years in office, President Lyndon Johnson launched a political crusade against poverty and racial inequality. Here LBJ and his wife, Lady Bird, visit with the Fletcher family in Inez, Kentucky, a town in rural Appalachia—one of the regions targeted by Johnson's War on Poverty.
Corbis-Bettmann.

control. Together with the adoption in 1964 of the Twenty-fourth Amendment to the Constitution, which outlawed the federal poll tax, the Voting Rights Act allowed millions of blacks to register and vote for the first time. Congress reauthorized the Voting Rights Act in 1970, 1975, and 1982. The results in the South were stunning. In 1960 only 20 percent of eligible blacks were registered; by 1964 the figure had risen to 39 percent and by 1971 to 62 percent (Map 28.4). Hartman Turnbow, a Mississippi farmer who had risked his life

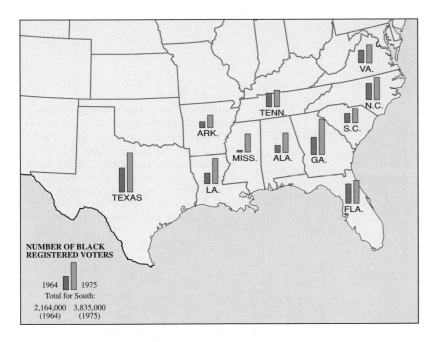

MAP 28.4
Black Voter Registration in the South, 1964 and 1975
After passage of the Voting Rights Act of 1965, black registration in the South increased dramatically. The bars show the number of blacks registered in 1964, before the act was passed, and in 1975, after it had been in effect for ten years. States in the Deep South, such as Mississippi, Alabama, and Georgia, had the biggest rises.

Dependent Children, and Aid to the Blind had strict eligibility restrictions, New Deal social welfare programs had failed to reach many of these people.

To reduce poverty, the Johnson administration expanded long-established social insurance, welfare, and public works programs. It broadened Social Security to include waiters and waitresses, domestic servants, farmworkers, and hospital employees. Social welfare expenditures increased rapidly, especially for Aid to Families with Dependent Children (AFDC), as did public housing and rent subsidy programs. Food Stamps, begun in 1964 largely to stabilize farm prices, grew into a major program of assistance to low-income families. The Appalachian Regional Development Act of 1965 provided federal funding for local roads, health clinics, and other public works projects in that poverty-stricken region. As during the New Deal, these social welfare programs developed in piecemeal fashion, without overall coordination.

The Office of Economic Opportunity (OEO), established by the Economic Opportunity Act of 1964, was the Great Society's showcase in the War on Poverty. Built around the twin strategies of equal opportunity and community action, OEO programs were so numerous and diverse that they recalled the alphabet agencies of the New Deal (see Table 28.1). Sargent Shriver, who moved from the Peace Corps to head the new agency, admitted, "It's like we went down to Cape Kennedy [the NASA space center in Florida] and launched a half dozen rockets at once."

OEO programs produced some of the most innovative measures of the Johnson administration. Head Start provided free nursery schools to prepare disadvantaged preschoolers for kindergarten. The Job Corps and the Neighborhood Youth Corps provided jobs and vocational training for young people. Upward Bound gave low-income teenagers the skills and motivation to go to college. Volunteers in Service to America (VISTA), modeled on the Peace Corps, promoted community service among youths in impoverished rural and urban areas. The Community Action Program encouraged the poor to demand "maximum feasible participation" in decisions that affected them. Community Action organizers worked closely with 2,000 lawyers employed by the Legal Services Program to provide the poor with free legal aid.

Cracks in the New Deal Coalition

By the end of 1965, the Johnson administration had compiled the most impressive legislative record of liberal reforms since the New Deal. It had put issues of poverty, justice, and access at the center of national political life, and it had expanded the federal government's role in protecting citizens' welfare. Yet the Great Society never quite measured up to the extravagant promises made for it, and by the end of the decade many of its programs were under attack.

In part, the political necessity of bowing to pressure from various interest groups hampered Great Society programs. For example, the American Medical Association used its influence to shape Medicare and Medicaid in ways that contributed to skyrocketing medical costs. And entrenched Democratic mayors such as Richard J. Daley of Chicago and Sam Yorty of Los Angeles vigorously resisted VISTA and Community

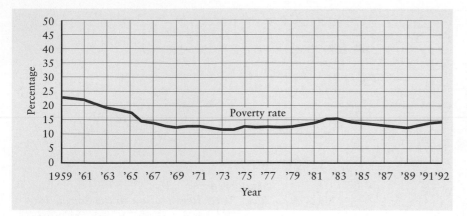

FIGURE 28.5
Americans in Poverty, 1960–1992
During the 1960s, the poverty rate among American families dropped from 20 percent to 13 percent, suggesting that the War on Poverty was bringing more Americans into the economic mainstream. Critics charged, however, that economic growth spurred by the Vietnam War accounted for the decrease.

Action Program agents who encouraged poor (and often nonwhite) people to demand the public services long withheld by unresponsive local governments. Many white working-class Democrats seconded these views, convinced that organized black and Latino groups were winning a disproportionate share of federal benefits. In response to such pressure, Johnson gradually phased out the Community Action Program and instead channeled spending for housing, social services, and other urban poverty programs through local municipal governments. That decision increased tensions between the Johnson administration and urban minority groups, while not fully mending the breach between the administration and its white working-class constituents—a rift that Republicans would later exploit.

Another inherent problem was the limited funding of Great Society programs. The annual budget for the War on Poverty, for example, was less than $2 billion. Still, the statistical decline in poverty during the 1960s suggests that the Great Society was successful on some levels. From 1963 to 1968, the proportion of Americans living below the poverty line dropped from 20 percent to 13 percent (Figure 28.5). Economic advancement of African Americans was even more marked: in the 1960s the black poverty rate was cut in half, and millions of blacks moved into the middle class, some through federal jobs in antipoverty programs. But critics charged that the reduction in the poverty rate was due to the decade's booming economy—fueled by defense spending for the Vietnam War—not to the War on Poverty. Moreover, although the overall standard of living increased, distribution of wealth was still uneven. The poor were better off in an absolute sense, but they remained far behind the middle class in a relative sense.

The implementation of the Great Society revealed deep contradictions in the New Deal coalition, which was torn among its diverse constituencies and their conflicting priorities. Those contradictions had been lurking in political life since Roosevelt and Truman had begun to expand the power of the federal government, but they surfaced forcefully in the climate fostered by the politics of expectation. Kennedy and Johnson had gathered an extraordinarily diverse set of groups into the New Deal coalition—middle-class and poor; white and nonwhite; Protestant, Jewish, and Catholic; urban and rural. For a brief period between 1964 and 1966 the coalition held together. But inevitably the claims of certain groups—such as the demand of blacks for civil rights and that of the urban poor for increased political power—conflicted with the interests of other Democratic supporters, such as white southerners and northern political bosses who wanted to maintain the status quo. In the end the New Deal coalition, which had fostered a vast expansion of federal power, could not sustain a consensus over the purposes that such a government ought to serve.

Democrats were also plagued by public disillusionment over the shortcomings of their reforms. In the early 1960s the lofty rhetoric of the New Frontier and the Great Society raised unprecedented expectations for social change. But competition for federal largesse was keen, and the shortage of funds for programs such as the War on Poverty left many promises unfulfilled, especially after 1965, when the escalation of the Vietnam War siphoned funding away from domestic programs. In 1966 the government spent $22 billion on the Vietnam War and only $1.2 billion on the War on Poverty. In the haunting phrase of Martin Luther King, the Great Society was "shot down on the battlefields of Vietnam."

Project Head Start
Project Head Start, which offered free early education programs for poor children,
was one of the most acclaimed programs of LBJ's War on Poverty. In 1965, folk singer
Tom Glazer staged a series of concerts for the more than 25,000 children enrolled in
Head Start throughout New York City.
Wide World Photos.

Summary

In the postwar era, American dominance of the global economy ensured an unprecedented level of domestic prosperity. Increased levels of spending on defense and consumer goods led to new economic development concentrated in the southern and western states and in the suburbs. Federal intervention in the economy, especially Cold War defense spending, boosted the economies and populations of California, Texas, Florida, and other emerging Sun Belt states. Federal home loan programs and highway construction spurred rapid suburban development, siphoning jobs and middle-class residents out of the central cities. At the same time, many blacks, Latinos, native Americans, and other low-income groups were migrating into these declining urban areas, where they encountered growing unemployment, rising crime, and deteriorating housing and education.

After years of depression and war-induced insecurity, Americans turned inward toward religion, home, and family. Postwar couples married young, had several children, and—if they were white and middle class—raised their children in a climate of suburban affluence and consumerism. The profamily orientation of the 1950s celebrated social conformity and traditional gender roles, even though millions of women entered the work force in those years. Many of the smoldering contradictions of the postwar period—unequally shared affluence, institutionalized racism, tensions in women's lives—helped spur the civil rights movement and other social reform efforts of the 1960s.

As Americans looked to Washington for solutions to the nation's social and economic ills, the Democrats offered a diverse array of federal programs designed to appeal to a broad range of constituencies. John F. Kennedy first set the agenda for this politics of expectation in his 1960 presidential bid, but the domestic accomplishments of his New Frontier were limited. Kennedy's activism was more evident in foreign policy, where he proved a resolute Cold Warrior. Following Kennedy's assassination in 1963, Lyndon Johnson played a critical role in pushing civil rights legislation through Congress. Moreover, Johnson used his formidable political skills to usher in the most ambitious legislative reform program since the New Deal. Congress funded an array of Great Society programs in education, medical care, social welfare, housing, transportation, and environmental protection. But although the Great Society raised hopes, it could not always deliver on its promises. Increasing military expenditures for the Vietnam conflict limited federal funds for domestic programs. And as federal functions and responsibilities grew, accommodating the diverse and often competing constituencies in the Democratic coalition became increasingly difficult. By the mid-1960s the liberal consensus was breaking apart.

TIMELINE

1944   Bretton Woods economic conference

World Bank and International Monetary Fund (IMF) founded

1947   Levittown, New York, built

1953–1958   Operation Wetback and Indian termination programs

1954   *Brown v. Board of Education of Topeka*

1955   AFL and CIO merge

Montgomery bus boycott

1956   National Interstate and Defense Highway Act

1957   Peak of postwar baby boom

School desegregation battle in Little Rock, Arkansas

Southern Christian Leadership Conference (SCLC) founded

1960   Sit-ins in Greensboro, North Carolina

John F. Kennedy elected president

1961   Peace Corps established

Freedom rides

Bay of Pigs invasion

Berlin Wall erected

1962   Michael Harrington's *The Other America*

Cuban missile crisis

1963   Betty Friedan, *The Feminine Mystique*

Civil rights protest in Birmingham, Alabama

March on Washington

Nuclear test-ban treaty

John F. Kennedy assassinated; Lyndon B. Johnson assumes presidency

1964   Freedom Summer

Civil Rights Act

Economic Opportunity Act inaugurates War on Poverty

Johnson elected president

1965   Immigration Act abolishes national quota system

Civil rights march from Selma to Montgomery

Voting Rights Act

Medicare and Medicaid programs established

Elementary and Secondary Education Act

Suggested Readings

General introductions to postwar society include Paul Boyer, *Promises to Keep* (1995); John Diggins, *The Proud Decades* (1988); and David Halberstam, *The Fifties* (1993).

The Affluent Society

For overviews of the economic changes of the postwar period see David P. Calleo, *The Imperious Economy* (1982). Herman P. Miller, *Rich Man, Poor Man* (1971), and Gabriel Kolko, *Wealth and Power in America* (1962), discuss inequality in income distribution. Michael Harrington, *The Other America* (1962), documents the persistence of poverty in the postwar era.

Kenneth Jackson, *Crabgrass Frontier* (1985), provides an overview of suburban development. Herbert Gans, *The Levittowners* (1967), and Bennett M. Berger, *Working-Class Suburb* (1960), are sociological studies of suburbia written by contemporaries. On postwar development in the South and West see Carl Abbott, *The Metropolitan Frontier: Cities in the Modern American West* (1993); Numan V. Bartley, *The New South, 1945–1980* (1995); and Richard Bernard and Bradley Rice, eds., *Sunbelt Cities* (1983).

Books that highlight the social and cultural history of the 1950s include Larry May, ed., *Recasting America* (1989), and Douglas T. Miller and Marion Nowak, *The Fifties* (1977). For popular culture, George Lipsitz, *Time Passages* (1991), surveys postwar television, music, film, and popular culture, and his *Rainbow at Midnight* (2d ed., 1994) looks at working-class culture and rock 'n' roll. Other treatments of the mass media include James L. Baughman, *The Republic of Mass Culture* (1992); Peter Biskind, *Seeing Is Believing* (1983); and Nora Sayre, *Running Time* (1982). Vance Packard's influential unmasking of the advertising industry, *The Hidden Persuaders* (1957), can be supplemented by Stephen Fox, *The Mirror Makers* (1984).

Richard Easterlin, *American Baby Boom in Historical Perspective* (1962), analyzes the demographic changes, as does Landon Y. Jones, *Great Expectations* (1980). Elaine May's *Homeward Bound* (1988) is the classic introduction to postwar family life, providing a historical corollary to Betty Friedan's *Feminine Mystique* (1963). Recent revisionist work challenging this view can be found in Joanne Meyerowitz, ed., *Not June Cleaver* (1994).

Youth culture is the subject of William Graeber's *Coming of Age in Buffalo* (1990). James Gilbert, *A Cycle of Outrage* (1986), looks at juvenile delinquency in the 1950s. Peter Guralnick, *Last Train to Memphis* (1994), is the definitive biography of Elvis Presley's early years. Discussions of cultural dissent in the 1950s can be found in Bruce Cook, *The Beat Generation* (1971), and Dan Wakefield, *New York in the Fifties* (1992).

The Other America

Reed Ueda, *Postwar Immigrant America* (1994), examines new trends in immigration since 1945. Jacqueline Jones compares black and white urban migrants in *The Dispossessed* (1992). Thomas Sugrue, *Origins of the Urban Crisis* (1996), analyzes the economic decline and racial antagonism that plagued postwar Detroit. Donald Fixico, *Termination and Relocation* (1986), looks at federal Indian policy from 1945 to 1970.

Jon C. Teaford, *Rough Road to Renaissance* (1990); John Mollenkopf, *The Contested City* (1983); and Kenneth Fox, *Metropolitan America* (1985), offer the most complete accounts of postwar urban development.

John F. Kennedy and the Politics of Expectation

The literature on the Kennedy years is voluminous. Among the best general accounts are Richard Reeves, *President Kennedy: Profile of Power* (1993); James Giglio, *The Presidency of JFK* (1991); David Burner, *JFK and a New Generation* (1988); and Jim F. Heath, *Decade of Disillusionment: The Kennedy-Johnson Years* (1975). Critical views appear in Seymour Hersh, *The Dark Side of Camelot* (1997); David Halberstam, *The Best and the Brightest* (1972); and Henry Fairlie, *The Kennedy Promise: The Politics of Expectation* (1973).

On foreign policy in the Kennedy years see Michael Beschloss, *The Crisis Years: Kennedy and Khrushchev, 1960–1963* (1990), and Thomas Paterson, *Kennedy's Quest for Victory* (1989). Ernest R. May and Philip D. Zelikow, eds., *The Kennedy Tapes: Inside the White House during the Cuban Missile Crisis* (1997), provide verbatim accounts of the Cuban missile crisis. Secondary treatments include James Nathan, *The Cuban Missile Crisis Revisited* (1992), and Thomas Paterson, *Contesting Castro* (1994). Gerald Posner, *Case Closed* (1993), provides the most definitive treatment of the Kennedy assassination.

The best overviews of the postwar civil rights movement are Robert Weisbrot, *Freedom Bound* (1990); Harvard Sitkoff, *The Struggle for Black Equality* (2d ed., 1993); and Clayborne Carson et al., *The Eyes on the Prize Civil Rights Reader* (1991). Histories of the major civil rights organizations include Carson's study of SNCC, *In Struggle* (1981), and August Meier and Elliot Rudwick, *CORE* (1973). Doug McAdam, *Freedom Summer* (1988), describes the experiences of northern volunteers during Freedom Summer. Two fine oral histories of the civil rights movement are Howell Raines, *My Soul Is Rested* (1977), and Henry Hampton and Steve Fayer, *Voices of Freedom* (1990).

Local accounts of grass-roots organizing include William H. Chafe's superb study of Greensboro, North Carolina, *Civilities and Civil Rights* (1980), and two recent studies of Mississippi: John Dittmer, *Local People* (1994), and Charles M. Payne, *I've Got the Light of Freedom* (1995). The role of women in the civil rights movement is examined in Vicki L. Crawford et al., *Women in the Civil Rights Movement: Trailblazers and Torchbearers, 1941–1965* (1990). Martin Luther King Jr. told his own story in *Why We Can't Wait* (1964). His biographers include David Garrow, *Bearing the Cross* (1986), and Taylor Branch, *Parting the Waters* (1988) and *Pillar of Fire* (1998).

Lyndon B. Johnson and the Great Society

Lyndon Johnson's account of his presidency can be found in *The Vantage Point* (1971). Doris Kearns, *Lyndon Johnson and the American Dream* (1976), and Merle Miller, *Lyndon: An Oral Biography* (1980), are based on extensive conversations with LBJ. Robert A. Caro focuses on Johnson's early career in *The Path to Power* (1982) and *Means of Ascent* (1989); Robert Dallek offers his own exhaustive account in *Lone Star Rising* (1991) and *Flawed Giant* (1998).

War Abroad and at Home: The Vietnam Era, 1961–1975

LYNDON JOHNSON, IN the crude language that characterized this tough-talking Texan, posed the trade-off starkly: "If I left the woman I really love—the Great Society—in order to get involved with that bitch of a war on the other side of the world, then I would lose everything at home. All my programs. All my hopes to feed the hungry and shelter the homeless. . . . But if I left that war and let the Communists take over South Vietnam, then I would be seen as a coward and my nation would be seen as an appeaser and we would both find it impossible to accomplish anything for anybody anywhere on the entire globe." In the end, his priorities were clear. "Losing the Great Society was a terrible thought, but not so terrible as the thought of being responsible for America's losing a war to the Communists. Nothing could possibly be worse than that."

Although most Americans first learned about Vietnam in the mid-1960s, the conflict occupied U.S. presidential administrations from Truman's to Ford's. U.S. troops fought in Vietnam for more than a decade—from the early 1960s to 1973—making it the nation's longest war. Moreover, as the country's first major military defeat, the war shook American confidence and damaged the international credibility it was supposed to uphold. The war took a toll at home, too. Defense spending temporarily boosted the economy but fueled inflation and diverted resources from domestic uses. As the war dragged on, antiwar sentiments spread across college campuses to the nation's streets, living rooms, and halls of state. Not since the Civil War was the nation so deeply and bitterly divided. Debates about the meaning and lessons of the war still resonate in American life.

The Longest War
American combat troops fought in Vietnam from 1965 to 1973, making it the longest war in the nation's history. Ambushed during a search-and-destroy mission, these soldiers await the arrival of a medical evacuation helicopter. More than 58,000 Americans lost their lives in the conflict, while another 300,000 were injured.
© Tim Page.

The "war at home" was part of a larger movement for social change in the 1960s. The postwar affluence of the middle class produced a self-assured generation of young whites who were optimistic about their ability to cure the nation's social ills. For young African Americans the affluence of the white middle class was a stark reminder of racial inequality. In the 1960s that same baby-boom generation swelled college enrollments, providing recruits for the civil rights campaign and other protest movements. Among women, increased access to education and greater participation in the work force in the postwar era sparked a revival of feminism. And the lofty Cold War rhetoric of international freedom and democracy prompted many to press for economic and racial justice at home.

Into the Quagmire, 1945–1968

────────★────────

Like many new nations that emerged from the dissolution of European empires after World War II, Vietnam was characterized by a volatile mix of nationalist sentiments, religious and cultural conflicts, economic need, and political turmoil. The rise of communism there was just one phase of that nation's larger struggle, which would eventually result in a bloody civil war. But American policy makers viewed these events singlemindedly through the lens of the Cold War, interpreting them as part of an internationally inspired communist movement toward global domination. Their failure to understand the complexity of Vietnam's internal conflicts led to a long and ultimately disastrous war.

The Roots of American Involvement

Vietnam, which had been part of the French colony of Indochina since the late nineteenth century, was occupied by Japan during World War II. Native resistance to the Japanese was led by Ho Chi Minh, a former schoolteacher and maritime worker, and the Vietnam Independence League, the Vietminh. First and foremost, the Vietminh were nationalists who wanted to end foreign rule in Vietnam. When the Japanese surrendered in 1945, Ho Chi Minh took advantage of the resulting power vacuum to proclaim—with words drawn from the American Declaration of Independence—the establishment of an independent republic of Vietnam. When France rejected his claim and reasserted control over the country the next year, an eight-year struggle that the Vietminh called the Anti-French War of Resistance ensued. Ho Chi Minh called on President Truman to support the struggle for Vietnamese independence, but Truman instead offered covert support to the French in

hopes of stabilizing a politically chaotic region and rebuilding the French economy.

By the end of the 1940s, American fears of communist expansion prompted the United States to step up its assistance to the French through the Marshall Plan and other Cold War measures. After the Chinese Revolution of 1949, the United States became concerned that China—along with the Soviet Union—might actively support anticolonial struggles in Asia and that newly independent countries would align themselves with the communists. At the same time, Republican charges that the Democrats had "lost" China influenced Truman to take a firmer stand against perceived communist aggression in both Korea and Vietnam. Truman also wanted to maintain good relations with France, whose support was crucial to the success of the new NATO alliance (see Chapter 27). Finally, Indochina played a strategic role in Secretary of State Dean Acheson's plans for an integrated Pacific Rim regional economy centered on a reindustrialized Japan.

When the Soviet Union and the new Chinese leaders recognized Ho Chi Minh's government early in 1950, the United States—along with Great Britain—recognized the noncommunist government of Bao Dai that the French had installed the previous year. Subsequently, the Truman and Eisenhower administrations provided substantial military support to the French—more than $2 billion by mid-1954. Eisenhower argued that such aid was essential to prevent the collapse of all the non-communist governments in the region in a chain reaction that he called the *domino effect*: "You have a row of dominoes set up, you knock over the first one, and what will happen to the last one is the certainty that it will go over very quickly."

Despite joint French-American efforts, Vietminh forces gained strength in northern Vietnam. In the spring of 1954, the French made a last stand at the isolated administrative fortress of Dienbienphu. France asked the United States to launch air strikes from nearby carriers to break the siege, but congressional opposition at home and Britain's refusal to join a pro-French coalition convinced Eisenhower to abstain from direct military intervention. Dienbienphu fell in May after a fifty-six-day siege.

The dramatic turn of events at Dienbienphu gave the Vietminh negotiating leverage at a conference in Geneva sponsored by Britain and the Soviet Union to discuss problems in Southeast Asia. The resulting 1954 Geneva Accords temporarily partitioned Vietnam at the 17th parallel and committed France to withdraw its forces from the area north of that line (Map 29.1). The accords also provided that within two years free elections would be held to choose a unified government for the entire nation. Eight of the nine national delegations in attendance signed the agreements, including China and the Vietminh, but the United States refused, instead issuing a separate protocol acknowledging the

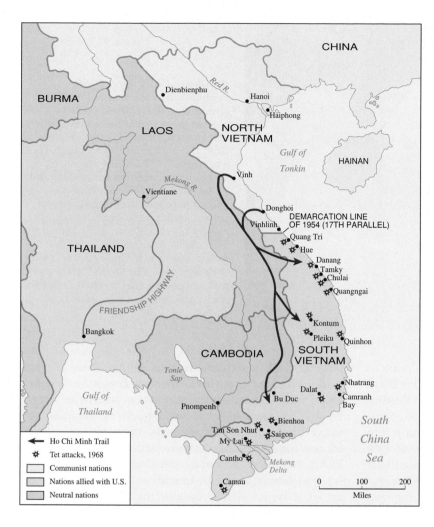

MAP 29.1
The Vietnam War, 1954–1975
The Vietnam War was a guerrilla war, fought in skirmishes and inconclusive encounters rather than decisive battles. Supporters of the National Liberation Front filtered into South Vietnam along the Ho Chi Minh Trail, which wound through Laos and Cambodia. In January 1968 Vietcong forces launched the Tet offensive, a surprise attack on several South Vietnamese cities and provincial centers. American vulnerability to these attacks served to undermine U.S. credibility and fueled opposition to the war.

agreements and promising to "refrain from the threat or use of force to disturb them."

Eisenhower had no intention of allowing a communist victory in Vietnam's upcoming election. With the help of CIA military operatives, he made sure that a pro-American government took power in South Vietnam in June 1954, just before the accords were signed. Ngo Dinh Diem, an anticommunist Catholic who had spent the previous eight years in the United States, returned to Vietnam as premier of the French-backed South Vietnamese government. The next year Diem, in a rigged election in which he won an unlikely 98.2 percent of the vote, became president of an independent South Vietnam. With the support of the United States, he then called off the reunification elections scheduled for 1956, mainly because everyone realized that the popular Ho Chi Minh would win easily in both the north and south.

From the perspective of the Vietnamese, the Geneva Accords marked only a brief interlude between two wars, one to end French colonial control and another to reunify Vietnam. In March 1956 the last French soldiers left Saigon, the capital of South Vietnam, and the United States replaced France as the dominant foreign power in that country. Diem's was just one in a long line

of U.S.-backed governments that failed to win the allegiance of the Vietnamese population.

Between 1955 and 1961 the Eisenhower administration viewed South Vietnam as vital to the security interests of the United States, sending Diem an average of $200 million a year in aid and stationing approximately 675 American military advisors in Saigon. But in reality, Vietnam was too small a country to play a significant role in the international balance of power. Furthermore, its communism was regional and intensely nationalistic, not expansionist. Nevertheless, the United States continued to see Vietnam as a critical battleground in the Cold War struggle to contain communism. Having stepped up U.S. involvement considerably, Eisenhower passed the Vietnam situation to his successor, John F. Kennedy.

The Kennedy Years

President Kennedy saw Vietnam as an ideal laboratory to try out the counterinsurgency techniques that were the centerpiece of his military policy (see Chapter 28). But first he had to prop up the faltering regime of Ngo Dinh Diem, who was highly unpopular because of his

Buddhist Protesters, 1966
Beginning in 1963, militant Buddhist monks staged a series of protests against the war that helped bring down the American-backed regime of Ngo Dinh Diem. Here, robed monks, part of a group of 250 Buddhist protesters, stage an antigovernment demonstration in Saigon. They are surrounded by barbed wire put there by government troops. Strongly nationalistic, the monks appealed for peace talks with the Vietcong and for free elections that would allow the Vietnamese to decide their own fate. The South Vietnamese military government arrested Buddhist leaders in 1966 and effectively crushed their movement.
Wide World Photos, Inc.

administration's corruption and brutality, aloofness from the peasantry, and greedy land policy. The Diem regime also faced a growing military threat. In December 1960, the Communist Party in North Vietnam organized most of Diem's opponents in South Vietnam into a revolutionary movement known as the National Liberation Front (NLF). To counter the threat, Kennedy increased the number of American military "advisors" (an elastic term that included helicopter units and special forces assigned to train the South Vietnamese in counterinsurgency techniques) to more than 16,000 by November 1963. To win the "hearts and minds" of Vietnamese peasants, he also sent economic development specialists. Kennedy refused, however, to send American combat troops to assist the South Vietnamese.

The American aid did little good. Diem's political inexperience and corruption, combined with his Catholicism in a predominantly Buddhist country, prevented him from creating a stable government. He enjoyed much more support in faraway America than he did in his native land, and he consistently misled his American allies about South Vietnamese military and social progress. The NLF's guerrilla forces—called the Vietcong by their opponents—made considerable headway against the Diem regime, using the revolutionary tactics of the Chinese leader Mao Zedong to blend into the South Vietnamese civilian population "like fish in the water." They found a receptive audience among peasants who had been alienated by Diem's strategic hamlet program, which uprooted families and whole villages and moved them into barbed-wire-enclosed compounds in a vain attempt to separate them from Ho Chi Minh's sympathizers.

Anti-Diem sentiment was also strong among Buddhists, who charged the government with religious persecution. Starting in May 1963, militant Buddhists

staged dramatic demonstrations against Diem. Several of the protesters set themselves on fire, and their suicides were recorded by American television crews. Diem's regime retaliated with raids on temples and mass arrests of Buddhist priests in August, prompting more antigovernment demonstrations. As opposition to Diem deepened, Kennedy decided that Diem would have to be removed. Ambassador Henry Cabot Lodge Jr. let it be known in Saigon that the United States would support a military coup that had "a good chance of succeeding." On November 1, 1963, Diem was driven from office and assassinated by officers of the South Vietnamese army.

Less than a month later, Kennedy himself was assassinated. Although historians continue to debate whether Kennedy would have withdrawn American forces from Vietnam had he lived, the actions of his administration clearly accelerated U.S. involvement. When Lyndon Johnson became president, he retained many of Kennedy's foreign policy advisors and quickly declared his intention to maintain support for South Vietnam. "I am not going to be the President who saw Southeast Asia go the way China went," Johnson asserted weeks after taking office. A new phase in the Americanization of the war was about to begin. When Johnson assumed the presidency in November 1963, 16,000 American troops were in Vietnam; when he left office in January 1969, there were more than 500,000.

Escalation under Johnson

The removal of Diem did not improve the efficiency or popularity of the Saigon government. Secretary of Defense Robert McNamara and other top advisors argued that only a rapid, full-scale deployment of U.S.

Aerial Bombing in Vietnam
The bombs dropped by U.S. forces in an attempt to root out Vietcong sympathizers inflicted heavy damage on the countryside and caused many civilian deaths. B-52 jets dropped most of the bombs.
Larry Burrows/LIFE Magazine © Time, Inc.

forces could prevent the imminent defeat of the South Vietnamese. But Johnson would need at least tacit congressional support, perhaps even a declaration of war, to commit U.S. forces to an offensive strategy. Originally Johnson wanted to wait until after the 1964 election to place this controversial request before Congress, but events gave him an opportunity to win authorization sooner.

The Gulf of Tonkin Resolution.   During the summer of 1964 American naval forces conducted surveillance missions off the North Vietnamese coast to aid amphibious attacks by the South Vietnamese. When the North Vietnamese resisted the attacks, President Johnson told the nation that on two separate occasions North Vietnamese torpedo boats had fired on American destroyers in international waters in the Gulf of Tonkin (see Map 29.1). At Johnson's request, Congress authorized him to "take all necessary measures to repel any armed attack against the forces of the United States and to prevent further aggression." On August 7 the Gulf of Tonkin Resolution passed by 88 to 2 votes in the Senate and 416 to 0 in the House. Only Senators Wayne Morse of Oregon and Ernest Gruening of Alaska opposed it as a "predated declaration of war" that further increased the president's ability to carry out foreign policy without consulting Congress.

Many questions were later raised about the resolution. A draft version had been ready for several months, awaiting just such an incident. The evidence of a North Vietnamese attack was sketchy at best. As the president admitted to his advisors soon afterward, "For all I know, our navy was shooting at whales out there." But this unverified attack got Johnson what he wanted—a sweeping mandate to conduct Vietnam operations as he

saw fit. It was the only formal approval of American intervention in Vietnam that Congress ever granted.

During the 1964 presidential campaign, Johnson declared, "We are not going to send American boys nine or ten thousand miles away from home to do what Asian boys ought to be doing for themselves." Yet plans were already being drawn up for a possible escalation of American efforts. With congressional support assured and the 1964 election safely over, the Johnson administration began the fateful move toward the total Americanization of the war. The escalation, which was accomplished during the first several months of 1965, took two forms: the initiation of direct bombing campaigns against North Vietnam and the deployment of ground troops.

Operation Rolling Thunder.   The first phase of escalation began on March 2, 1965, with Operation Rolling Thunder, a protracted campaign of bombing attacks against North Vietnam designed to cripple the economy and force the communists to the bargaining table. A special target was the Ho Chi Minh Trail, an elaborate network of paths, bridges, and shelters that stretched from North Vietnam through Cambodia and Laos into South Vietnam (see Map 29.1). By 1967 some 20,000 Vietnamese soldiers were moving southward along that route each month, along with the military equipment and other resources necessary to supply them.

Between 1965 and 1968 Operation Rolling Thunder (named for a Protestant hymn) dropped a million tons of bombs on North Vietnam, 800 tons a day for three and a half years. Each B-52 bombing sortie cost $30,000, and by early 1966, the direct costs of the air war had exceeded $1.7 billion. From 1965 to 1973 the United States dropped three times as many bombs on North Vietnam, a country roughly the size of Texas, as had fallen on Europe, Asia, and Africa during World War II. The several hundred captured American pilots downed in the raids then became pawns in negotiations with the North Vietnamese over the fate of prisoners of war.

To the amazement of American advisors, the bombing had little effect on the ability of the Vietnamese to wage war. Despite continuous sorties and the use of chemical defoliants to deny the Vietcong cover, the flow of troops and supplies to the south continued. The North Vietnamese quickly rebuilt roads and bridges, moved munitions plants underground, and constructed a network of tunnels and shelters. Instead of destroying enemy morale and bringing the North Vietnamese to the bargaining table, Operation Rolling Thunder intensified their will to fight. The bombing continued nevertheless.

The Arrival of U.S. Ground Troops.   A week after the launch of Operation Rolling Thunder, the United States sent its first official ground troops into combat duty when U.S. Marines waded ashore at Danang, South Vietnam's second largest city. Initially assigned to protect the nearby American air base, they were soon patrolling the countryside and skirmishing with the enemy. Beginning in the summer of 1965, combat operations shifted from a defensive stance to search-and-destroy missions designed to uncover and kill Vietcong forces. Fearing congressional opposition to this expanded military commitment, the Johnson administration did not reveal that a major change in policy had occurred.

Over the next three years the number of American troops in Vietnam grew dramatically. Although in 1965 U.S. troops were accompanied by military forces from Australia, New Zealand, and South Korea, the war increasingly became an American struggle, fought to achieve American aims. In 1966 more than 380,000 American soldiers were stationed in Vietnam; by 1968, there were 536,000 (Figure 29.1). The increasing demands of General William Westmoreland, commander of U.S. forces in Vietnam, confirmed a prediction made by presidential advisor George Ball in 1961 when

he warned an incredulous President Kennedy that if American ground troops were committed to Vietnam, 300,000 would be on the ground within five years. But as Kennedy observed before his death, requests for troops were like having a drink: "The effect wears off, and you have to take another."

The massive commitment of troops and air power threatened to destroy Vietnam's countryside and fragile resources. Taking to the extreme Johnson's call "to leave the footprints of America in Vietnam," the campaign of extensive defoliation and military bombardment made it difficult for peasants to practice the agriculture that provided the economic and cultural base of Vietnamese society. After one devastating but not unusual engagement the commanding U.S. officer remarked, "It became necessary to destroy the town in order to save it." Graffiti on a plane that dropped defoliants said, "Only you can prevent forests." (In later years chemicals such as Agent Orange were found to have highly toxic effects on humans and the environment.) The devastation was not limited to North Vietnam. South Vietnam, America's ally, absorbed more than twice the total bomb tonnage dropped on the north as U.S. forces tried to flush out Vietcong sympathizers. In Saigon and other South Vietnamese cities the influx of American soldiers and dollars distorted the local economy, spread corruption and prostitution, and triggered uncontrollable inflation and black-market activities.

Why did the dramatically increased American presence in Vietnam from 1965 on fail to turn the tide of the war? Certain advisors, such as former lieutenant colonel John Paul Vann, argued that military intervention would do little unless it was accompanied by reform of the Saigon government and increased popular support in the countryside. Other critics claimed that the United States never fully committed itself to total victory, although what total victory would have entailed remains in dispute. It is true, however, that military strategy was inextricably tied to political considerations. For domestic reasons, policy makers often searched for the elusive "middle ground" between an

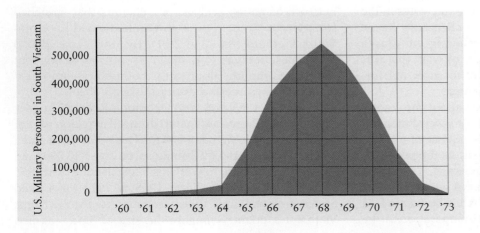

FIGURE 29.1
U.S. Troops in Vietnam, 1960–1973
When Lyndon Johnson escalated the Vietnam War, troop levels rose from 23,300 in December 1964 to 184,300 a year later. Troop levels eventually peaked at more than 543,000 personnel. Under Richard Nixon's Vietnamization program, beginning in the summer of 1969, levels drastically declined; the last U.S. military forces left South Vietnam on March 29, 1973.

all-out invasion (and the possibility of sparking a nuclear exchange between the superpowers) and the politically unacceptable alternative of disengagement. But this limited commitment was never enough to ensure victory, however defined.

The tremendous determination of the Vietnamese was a major factor. In the 1940s Ho Chi Minh had told his French imperialist foes, "You can kill ten of my men for every one I kill of yours, but even at those odds, you will lose and I will win." That same statement held true twenty years later against the Americans. The Vietcong were prepared to accept limitless casualties and to fight for as many years as necessary. North Vietnamese strategists astutely realized that the war did not have to be won on the battlefield, accurately predicting that American public opinion would not tolerate endless casualties and a long war of attrition. Time was on the Vietcong's side, although at an enormous cost to both sides.

The Combat Experience

Approximately 2.8 million Americans served in Vietnam. With an average age of only nineteen, this fighting force was one of the youngest in U.S. history. Most of those servicemen were too young to vote or drink (the voting age was twenty-one until the passage of the Twenty-sixth Amendment in 1971), but they were old enough to fight and die. They served for a variety of reasons. Some, including 7,000 women enlistees, were volunteers who joined out of a sense of patriotic duty or because they wanted to "see the world." But many more served because they were drafted. Until the country shifted to an all-volunteer force in 1973, the draft stood as a concrete reminder of the government's impact on the lives of ordinary Americans.

As troop needs increased, the draft reached deeper into the male population. In 1965 draftees accounted for 16 percent of total battle deaths; that figure rose to 34 percent in 1967 and 62 percent in 1969. Even more than in other recent wars, sons of the poor and the working class shouldered a disproportionate amount of the fighting, forming an estimated 80 percent of the enlisted ranks. Young men from more affluent backgrounds were more likely to avoid combat through student deferments, medical exemptions, and appointments to National Guard and reserve units—alternatives that made Johnson's Vietnam policy more palatable to the middle class.

At first many draftees and enlistees shared Cold War assumptions about the need to fight communism and the superiority of the American military. Service in Vietnam, however, quickly challenged simple notions of patriotism and the inevitability of victory (see American Voices, "Dave Cline: A Vietnam Vet Remembers," p. 948). The first thing new soldiers noticed when they got off the plane was the stench of napalm (a lethal incendiary substance), human waste, and death in this torrid jungle country. Sometimes they had to sprint from the plane to the safety of the base buildings because of mortar attacks, a sign of the boldness with which enemy forces operated throughout the country.

Unlike World War II soldiers who served "for the duration," Vietnam soldiers had a one-year tour of duty. For many it was simply a matter of getting through 365 days. For the first ninety days or so they were "cherries," slang for virgins, or inexperienced newcomers. Once they neared the end of the tour, soldiers might carry a "short-timer's stick," notched for the remaining days left; as each day passed, they would cut off a notch until only a small stub remained. Some soldiers longed for "million-dollar wounds"—serious but nonfatal injuries that would result in permanent removal from the battlefield. Some "grunts" (ordinary infantrymen) and "bloods" (a name that black draftees called themselves) deliberately avoided making close friends in case their buddies caught a grenade or triggered a booby trap on a routine patrol.

In "Nam" (soldiers' shorthand for Vietnam) days passed in boring menial work punctuated by flashes of intense fighting. "Most of the time, nothing happened," a soldier recalled, "but when something did, it happened instantaneously and without warning." The fighting had a surreal quality. Combat often intensified at night. Incoming and outgoing firepower lit up the sky while soldiers huddled sleeplessly on watch. There were rarely large-scale battles, only skirmishes; no front lines or conquering of territory, just operations during the day in areas that reverted to Vietcong control at night. Although some whole units were ambushed, casualties typically came in twos and threes.

A former marine captain recalled, "You never knew who was the enemy and who was the friend. They all looked alike. They all dressed alike. They were all Vietnamese. Some of them were Vietcong." He concluded graphically, "It wasn't like the San Francisco Forty-Niners on one side of the field and the Cincinnati Bengals on the other. The enemy was all around you." Because differentiating between friendly South Vietnamese and Vietcong sympathizers was difficult, many soldiers lumped them together as "gooks." A draftee noted of his indoctrination, "The only thing they told us about the Vietcong was they were gooks. They were to be killed."

Because territorial gains were often temporary and illusory, American success was measured in "body counts"—the number of enemy soldiers killed—and "kill ratios"—the ratio between enemy losses and U.S. casualties. "If it's dead and Vietnamese, it's VC [Vietcong]" was the rule of thumb in the bush. Casualty figures were often deliberately inflated. As a twenty-four-year-old army captain recalled, "I went out and killed one VC and liberated a prisoner. Next day the major called me in and told me that I'd killed fourteen VC and liberated six prisoners. You want to see the medal?"

AMERICAN VOICES

DAVE CLINE
A Vietnam Vet Remembers

———★———

Born in 1947, Dave Cline grew up in a working-class family outside Buffalo, New York. Drafted by the army in 1967, the twenty-year-old Cline was eager to help fight communist aggression in Vietnam. But after his arrival in Danang seven months later, his attitude toward the war quickly changed. Cline described this transformation in an interview conducted in 1992.

I went to basic training at Fort Dix. . . .

Down there, they used to give you basically two raps on why you were going to Vietnam. One was that rap about we're going to help the heroic South Vietnamese people. We're going to go fight for freedom [and repel] communist aggression. They'd show you the maps and stuff, the domino theory, the Red Chinese are trying to engulf all of southeast Asia. The other rap was: killing communists was your duty. . . .

The boat came into Danang, and then they flew us from Danang to Cu Chi. I remember it was humid and hot and smelled. First thing you do when you get in-country is, they give you these indoctrination classes and they say, "Forget all that shit they told; you can't trust any of these people. They're not really people anyway; they're gooks." . . . In other words: You see anyone with slant eyes, that's your potential enemy—don't trust them. That sort of blows away any "help the people" thing. . . .

I got wounded the last time out near the Cambodian border. This happened on December 20, 1967. Again, we were doing these sweeps and we were overrun about two in the morning. The North Vietnamese launched a massive human wave attack. We could hear them yelling orders maybe 25, 30 feet away, and these guys were charging. . . .

A guy came running up to my foxhole. We saw him coming from the next hole over and we didn't know if it was an American retreating over to us or a Vietnamese, because it was two in the morning. So we didn't shoot him.

I was sitting there with my rifle waiting to see, and all of a sudden he stuck his rifle in. I saw the front side of an AK-47 and a muzzle flash, and then I pulled my trigger. I shot him through his chest. I blacked out initially, but then I came to and found a round went right through my knee. They threw me in a foxhole and gave me a bottle of Darvons. I lay there until the battle ended. In the morning they medivaced me out.

They carried me over to this guy I had shot. He was sitting up against this tree stump. He was just sitting there with his rifle across his lap. He was dead. The sergeant started giving me this pep talk, "Here's the gook you killed!" In my unit they had a big thing about confirmed kills. If you had a confirmed kill and the person had an automatic weapon, then you were supposed to get a three-day in-country pass. . . .

This kid looked about the same age as me. The first thing I started thinking was, Why is he dead and I'm alive? . . .

Then after going into the hospital, I started thinking about that guy. I wonder if his mother knows he's dead? I wonder if he had a girlfriend? Looking back, I think I was retaining the sense that he was a human being.

Source: Richard Stacewicz, *Winter Soldiers: An Oral History of the Vietnam Veterans against the War* (New York: Twayne Publishers, 1997), 135–136, 140–141.

Fighting and surviving in such conditions took its toll. "Killing is the easiest part of the whole thing," one soldier recalled. "Sweating twenty-four hours a day, seeing guys drop all around you of heatstroke, not having food, not having water, sleeping only three hours a night for weeks at a time, that's what war is. Survival." Another veteran echoed that sentiment: "The hardest thing to come to grips with was the fact that making it through Vietnam—surviving—is probably the only worthwhile part of the experience. It wasn't going over there and saving the world from communism or defending the country." The pressure of waging war in those conditions drove many soldiers to seek escape in alcohol or cheap and readily available drugs.

The American women who served in Vietnam shared some of these experiences. As WACs, nurses, and civilian service workers with organizations such as the United Services Organization, women volunteers witnessed massive doses of death and mutilation, mainly inflicted on soldiers barely out of their teens. They tried not to get caught up in it emotionally, but as a navy nurse recalled, "It's pretty damn hard not getting involved when you see a nineteen- or twenty-year-old blond kid from the Midwest or California or the East Coast screaming and dying. A piece of my heart would go with each."

After the intensity and the boredom of the tour of duty, there remained one last hurdle. Unlike veterans of World War II or the Korean War, who usually came back home in groups by a long boat ride, Vietnam veterans were in Saigon one day and back on the American mainland the next. Soldiers returned home alone and received no deprogramming or counseling. As support for the war evaporated at home, veterans felt increasingly out of place.

The Consensus Unravels

During the Kennedy and early Johnson years most Americans supported the administration's conduct of foreign affairs, as they had throughout the Cold War period. But in the late 1960s public opinion began to turn against the war. In July 1967 a Gallup poll revealed that for the first time, a majority of Americans disapproved of Johnson's Vietnam policy and believed that the war had reached a stalemate.

The Television War. Television had much to do with shaping these attitudes. Vietnam was the first war in which television brought the fighting directly into the nation's living rooms. The escalation in Vietnam came just two years after the expansion of the nightly network news broadcasts from fifteen minutes to half an hour. By 1967 CBS and NBC were spending $5 million a year to cover the war from their expanded Saigon bureaus, an investment that guaranteed reports from Vietnam would appear on the news every night. Reporters soon learned that combat footage—what they called "shooting bloody"—had a better chance of airing than did reports about social reform or political developments. Every night Americans watched U.S. soldiers advancing steadily in the countryside and heard reporters detail staggering Vietcong losses and minimal U.S. casualties.

Despite the glowing reports that were fed to the American public about the progress of the war, a number of congressmen and administration officials grew pessimistic. In 1966, the Senate Foreign Relations Committee (chaired by J. William Fulbright, an outspoken critic of the war) conducted televised hearings that raised questions about the administration's Vietnam policies. In November of the following year, Secretary of Defense McNamara, one of the architects of the war, sent a memo to the president arguing that con-

A Televised War
This harrowing scene from Saigon during the Tet offensive in 1968 was broadcast on U.S. network news. The NBC bureau chief described the film in a terse telex message: "A VC officer was captured. The troops beat him. They bring him to [Brigadier General Nguyen Ngoc] Loan who is head of South Vietnamese national police. Loan pulls out his pistol, fires at the head of the VC, the VC falls, zoom on his head, blood spraying out. If he has it all it's startling stuff."
Wide World Photos, Inc.

tinued escalation "would be dangerous, costly in lives, and unsatisfactory to the American people." A few weeks later McNamara left the Defense department for the World Bank. "I do not know," he later wrote, "whether I quit or was fired." Pentagon analysts confirmed McNamara's doubts, estimating that the Vietcong could marshal 200,000 guerrillas a year indefinitely. But President Johnson continued to insist that victory was within reach. Journalists, especially those who had spent time in Vietnam, soon commented that the Johnson administration suffered from a "credibility gap."

Economic events put Johnson and his advisors even more on the defensive. In 1966 the federal deficit was $9.8 billion; in 1967, it jumped to $23 billion, with the Vietnam War costing the taxpayers $27 billion. Although the war was consuming only 3 percent of the gross national product, compared with 42 percent at the height of World War II and 12 percent during the Korean War, its costs became more evident as the growing federal deficit nudged the inflation rate upward. But only in the summer of 1967 did Johnson ask for a 10 percent surcharge on individual and corporate income, which Congress delayed approving until 1968. By then the inflationary spiral that would plague the American economy throughout the 1970s was already well under way.

The Rise of the Antiwar Movement.   Another major problem facing the Johnson administration was the growing strength and visibility of the antiwar movement. As in every American military conflict, a small group of dissenters opposed the war from the beginning, including pacifist organizations such as the War Resisters League and the Women's International League for Peace and Freedom, and religious groups such as the Quakers and the Fellowship for Reconciliation. Those groups were joined by a new generation of activists who had emerged in the 1950s in groups such as SANE (the National Committee for a Sane Nuclear Policy), Physicians for Social Responsibility, and Women Strike for Peace. These activists opposed the accelerating arms race in general and atmospheric testing in particular and lobbied successfully for the 1963 nuclear test-ban treaty between the United States and the Soviet Union (see Chapter 28).

Between 1963 and 1965, peace activists in both older and newer organizations staged protests, vigils, and letter-writing campaigns against U.S. involvement in the war. After the escalation in the spring of 1965, the antiwar movement was swelled by growing numbers of students, housewives, politicians, and artists, and a few elected officials. Critics of intervention argued that the war was morally wrong and antithetical to American ideals; that the goal of an independent, anticommunist South Vietnam was unattainable; and that American military involvement would not help the Vietnamese people. Though a diverse lot, all shared a common skepticism about the means and aims of U.S. policy.

Some Americans felt so strongly against the war that they adopted extreme methods of protest. In November 1965 Norman Morrison, a thirty-two-year-old Quaker activist—married and the father of an eighteen-month-old daughter—set himself on fire and burned to death near the gates of the Pentagon, 40 yards from Defense Secretary McNamara's office. Morrison undertook this protest after reading an account by a French priest who had despaired at seeing his Vietnamese parishioners burned by napalm during a bombing attack. Like the priest, Morrison was anguished about his inability to stop the carnage. To his wife he left this note: "Know that I love thee but must act for the children of the priest's village."

Morrison's suicide shocked the nation. Even McNamara later admitted that he was horrified by this "outcry against the killing that was destroying the lives of so many Vietnamese and American youth." Three weeks later an estimated 30,000 antiwar protesters converged on the White House, including a large contingent of college students. Over the next few years student protesters flocked to the antiwar movement, increasing its visibility and political clout. The fervor of this new generation drove not only the antiwar movement but a youthful rebellion that challenged authority on nearly every front.

The Challenge of Youth, 1962–1970

"There is everywhere protest, reevaluation, attack on the Establishment," social critic Paul Goodman asserted at the end of the 1960s. Novelist Norman Mailer agreed: "We're in a time that's divorced from the past. . . . There's utterly no tradition anymore." The civil rights movement had ignited the challenge to established institutions, teaching college students protest tactics such as marches, sit-ins, and mass confrontations. The idealism of Kennedy's New Frontier and Johnson's Great Society raised students' expectations of what they and their society could accomplish. Finally, the escalation of the Vietnam War in 1965 offered a compelling political cause to rally around, especially as the draft affected more and more college-age men. Vietnam would become the defining political issue of their generation.

Student Activism

The 1960s witnessed the first active student movement since the 1930s (see Chapter 24). Most of that depression-scarred generation had been unable to afford higher education, but its children—the baby boomers—flocked to colleges and universities in the postwar period. In addition, many soldiers who had served in World War II and the Korean War used the benefits of the GI Bill to finance higher education for themselves and later sent their children to college as well. In 1940 only 15 percent of all youth between the ages of eighteen and twenty-one attended college; in 1963 the proportion reached almost 50 percent.

The youthful rebelliousness so evident in 1950s popular culture infiltrated college campuses in the early 1960s, taking a distinctly political form. In June 1962 forty students from Big Ten and Ivy League universities met at a United Auto Workers conference center in Port Huron, Michigan, to found Students for a Democratic Society (SDS). Their manifesto, written by Tom Hayden, a University of Michigan student, drew heavily on the writings of the radical Columbia University sociologist C. Wright Mills. The Port Huron Statement expressed hostility toward bureaucracy, rejected Cold War ideology (including but not limited to the Vietnam conflict), emphasized participatory politics, and designated students as the major force for change in society. To distinguish themselves from the "Old Left"—communists, socialists, and other left-wing sectarians of the 1930s and 1940s—the founders of SDS referred to their movement as the "New Left." Consciously adopting the activist tactics pioneered by the civil rights movement, SDS devoted much of its early attention to grass-roots organizing in cities and on college campuses.

The Free Speech Movement. The first student protests broke out in the fall of 1964 at the University of California at Berkeley after the administration banned political activity near the Telegraph Avenue entrance to the campus, where student groups had traditionally distributed leaflets and recruited volunteers. In response, all the major student organizations, from SDS to the conservative Youth for Goldwater, formed a coalition called the Free Speech Movement and organized a sit-in at the main administration building. The university agreed to drop the ban.

The Free Speech Movement owed a strong debt to the civil rights movement. Berkeley had sent more volunteers to Freedom Summer in Mississippi in 1964 than had any other campus, and the students had been radicalized by the experience. Mario Savio spoke for many of them:

> *Last summer I went to Mississippi to join the struggle there for civil rights. This fall I am engaged in another phase of the same struggle, this time in Berkeley. The two battlefields may seem quite different to some observers, but this is not the case. The same rights are at stake in both places—the right to participate as citizens in a democratic society and to struggle against the same enemy. In Mississippi an autocratic and powerful minority rules, through organized violence, to suppress the vast, virtually powerless majority. In California, the privileged minority manipulates the university bureaucracy to suppress the students' political expression.*

On a deeper level Berkeley students were challenging a university that in their view had grown too big, too impersonal, and too insulated from the major social issues of the day. The largest universities, like the largest corporations, had grown the fastest in the postwar era. In 1940 only two campuses had as many as 20,000 students; in 1969 thirty-nine "multiversities" were at least that large. Emboldened by the Berkeley experience, college students across the country were soon protesting everything from dress codes to course requirements, tenure decisions, and academic grading systems.

Students also protested their universities' complicity in the problems of the ghettos that surrounded many urban campuses. Columbia, for example, was a major property owner in Harlem, which bordered its campus. When the university announced plans in 1968 to build a new gymnasium, displacing local stores and housing, students chanting "Gym Crow must go" tore down the fence at the construction site and took over several university buildings. At Berkeley, students and administrators

Free Speech at Berkeley, 1964
Students at the University of California's Berkeley campus protested the administration's decision to ban political activity in the school plaza. Free speech demonstrators, many of them active in the civil rights movement, relied on tactics and arguments that they learned during that struggle.
University of California at Berkeley, Bancroft Library.

clashed in 1969 over a parcel of vacant land near the campus that a coalition of students and residents had turned into a "People's Park." When the university asserted its right to the land, a violent confrontation broke out and an onlooker was killed. At both Columbia and Berkeley, administration decisions to use local police officers to break up the demonstrations radicalized many more students than had originally supported the protests. As campus disturbances spread, more and more university buildings were blocked, occupied, or picketed, and classes were frequently dismissed or canceled.

The Antiwar Movement. No issue provoked more impassioned and sustained protest than the Vietnam War. A strong spur to activism was a change in the Selective Service System. In the past, young men could use deferments for college, graduate school, teaching, and parenthood to avoid the draft until they reached the cutoff age of twenty-six; a disproportionate number of deferments went to affluent whites. In response to criticism of the class and racial bias inherent in the system, automatic student deferments were abolished in January 1966. To avoid the draft, some young men enlisted in the National Guard or the reserves; others declared themselves conscientious objectors. Several thousand ignored

Columbia University Protests, 1968
At the height of the Vietnam War in 1968, Columbia University students launched a
series of protests against military research contracts, university governance, and the
construction of a gymnasium in a nearby Harlem neighborhood.
Steve Schapiro/Black Star.

their induction notices entirely, risking prosecution for draft evasion. Others left the country, most often for Canada or Sweden. Opponents of the war burned their draft cards in public acts of civil disobedience, closed down induction centers, and on a few occasions broke into Selective Service offices to destroy or mutilate files.

As antiwar and draft protests multiplied, students realized that their universities were deeply implicated in the war effort. In some cases as much as 60 percent of a university's research budget came from government contracts, especially from the Department of Defense. Protesters blocked campus recruitment by Dow Chemical Company because it produced napalm and Agent Orange. Arguing that universities should not train students for war, protesters demanded that the Reserve Officer Training Corps (ROTC) be removed from campus.

Mass demonstrations against the war consumed much of the energy of the student movement in the late 1960s as students became part of the larger antiwar movement. Rallies, "teach-ins," and student strikes became commonplace, and in October 1967 more than 100,000 antiwar demonstrators, many of them students, marched on Washington as part of "Stop the Draft Week." Criticism of American policy also came from abroad. Cuban revolutionary leader Che Guevara denounced the war as an imperialist struggle, a view embraced by a growing number of young American radicals (see Voices from Abroad, "Che Guevara: Viet-

nam and the World Freedom Struggle," p. 953). Lyndon Johnson, who had earlier dismissed antiwar protesters as "nervous Nellies" or communist dupes, now faced large-scale public opposition to his policies. The administration thus waged a two-front offensive: a military operation in Vietnam and a war for public opinion at home.

The Rise of the Counterculture

The antiwar movement accelerated the erosion of confidence in established American institutions and values. While the New Left took to the streets in protest, a growing number of young Americans undertook their own revolution against authority and middle-class respectability. Building on the cultural rebellion articulated by the Beat generation in the 1950s, the *counterculture* (so-called because it challenged so many established values) encouraged personal liberation through new musical and clothing styles, spiritual exploration, and experimentation with sex and drugs.

The impact of the counterculture was soon evident even to the uninitiated. For one thing, young people's clothing and hairstyles changed radically. At Berkeley's free speech demonstrations in 1964, young men wore coats and ties and women wore skirts and sweaters. At antiwar protests just three or four years later, youths defiantly dressed in unisex ragged blue jeans, tie-dyed

CHE GUEVARA

Vietnam and the World Freedom Struggle

———★———

*C*he Guevara, a leader of the Cuban Revolution, later worked with revolutionary nationalist movements in Africa and Latin America. Between his departure from Cuba in 1965 and his death in Bolivia in 1967, he made only one public statement. His message, "Vietnam and the World Freedom Struggle," helped convince some young American radicals of the necessity of armed struggle at home and abroad.

This is the painful reality: Vietnam, a nation representing the aspirations and the hopes for victory of the entire world of the disinherited, is tragically alone. . . .

And—what grandeur has been shown by this people! What stoicism and valor in this people! And what a lesson for the world their struggle holds!

It will be a long time before we know if President Johnson ever seriously thought of initiating some of the popular reforms necessary to soften the sharpness of the class contradictions that are appearing with explosive force and more and more frequently.

What is certain is that the improvements announced under the pompous label of the Great Society have gone down the drain in Vietnam.

The greatest of the imperialist powers feels in its own heart the drain caused by a poor, backward country; and its fabulous economy feels the effect of the war. . . .

And for us, the exploited of the world, what should our role be in this? . . .

Our part, the responsibility of the exploited and backward areas of the world, is to eliminate the bases sustaining imperialism—our oppressed peoples, from whom capital, raw materials, technicians and cheap labor are extracted, and to whom new capital, means of domination, arms and all kinds of goods are exported, submerging us in absolute dependence.

The fundamental element of this strategic goal will be, then, the real liberation of the peoples, a liberation that will be obtained through armed struggle in the majority of cases, and which, in the Americas, will have almost unfailingly the property of becoming converted into a socialist revolution.

In focusing on the destruction of imperialism, it is necessary to identify its head, which is none other than the United States of North America. . . .

The adversary must not be underestimated; the North American soldier has technical ability and is backed by means of such magnitude as to make him formidable. He lacks the essential ideological motivation which his most hated rivals of today have to the highest degree—the Vietnamese soldiers. . . .

Over there, the imperialist troops encounter the discomforts of those accustomed to the standard of living which the North American nation boasts. They have to confront a hostile land, the insecurity of those who cannot move without feeling that they are walking on enemy territory; death for those who go outside of fortified redoubts; the permanent hostility of the entire population.

All this continues to provoke repercussions inside the United States; it is going to arouse a factor that was attenuated in the days of the full vigor of imperialism—the class struggle inside its own territory.

Source: Ernesto C. Guevara, *Che Guevara Speaks* (New York: Pathfinder Press, 1967), 144–159.

T-shirts, beads, and army fatigues. Unorthodox clothes and long, unkempt hair identified a new phenomenon of American youth culture: the hippie. The uncomprehending older generation often had a simple response: "Get a haircut."

Popular music mirrored changing political moods. Folksinger Pete Seeger set the tone for the era with idealistic songs such as the antiwar ballad "Where Have All the Flowers Gone?" Joan Baez gained national prominence singing "We Shall Overcome" and other political anthems at protest rallies. In 1963, the year of the Birmingham demonstrations and President Kennedy's assassination, Bob Dylan's "Blowin' in the Wind" reflected the impatience of people whose faith in liberalism was wearing thin.

Other winds of change came from abroad. Early in 1964 the Beatles, four working-class youths from Liverpool, England, burst onto the American scene. As Elvis

Sgt. Pepper's Lonely Hearts Club Band
The colorful collage on the cover of this 1967 Beatles album allowed fans to debate (occasionally under the influence of marijuana or LSD) the symbolism of those depicted. Can you identify Mae West, Karl Marx, Bob Dylan, Albert Einstein, Lenny Bruce, and Marilyn Monroe, as well as the "Fab Four" in their various disguises?
© Apple Corps Ltd.

Presley had done eight years earlier, they thrust their way into the national consciousness through a series of television appearances on "The Ed Sullivan Show." The Beatles' music, by turns lyrical and driving, was phenomenally successful, spawning a commercial and cultural phenomenon called Beatlemania that deepened the generational divide begun by rock 'n' roll in the 1950s. After the Beatles came the angrier, more rebellious music of other British groups, notably the Rolling Stones, whose raunchy 1965 hit "(I Can't Get No) Satisfaction" signaled a new openness about sexuality.

Drugs were almost as important as rock music in the youth culture of the 1960s. Drugs were hardly new to the American scene: the Beats had experimented with mind-altering drugs, and many jazz musicians had used heroin and cocaine for decades. But the recreational use of drugs—especially marijuana and the hallucinogen lysergic acid diethylamide, popularly known as LSD or "acid"—had never been so widespread, or so celebrated in popular music. San Francisco bands such as the Grateful Dead and the Jefferson Airplane and musicians like the Seattle-born guitarist Jimi Hendrix developed a style of music known as "acid rock," characterized by long, heavily amplified guitar solos and psychedelic lighting effects. The Beatles, whose early songs had simply stated "I want to hold your hand,"

now celebrated the new drug-induced consciousness of "tangerine trees and marmalade skies" in hits such as "Lucy in the Sky with Diamonds" (1967).

For a brief time adherents of the counterculture believed that a new age was dawning. In 1967 the "world's first Human Be-In" drew 20,000 people to Golden Gate Park in San Francisco. The Beat poet Allen Ginsberg "purified" the site with a Buddhist ritual, political activists embraced "drug freaks," and the LSD advocate Timothy Leary, a former Harvard psychology instructor, urged the gathering to "turn on to the scene, tune in to what is happening, and drop out." That summer—dubbed the "Summer of Love"—San Francisco's Haight-Ashbury, New York's East Village, and Chicago's Uptown neighborhoods swelled with "flower children." Their faith in instant love and peace was soon tested, however, as dropouts, drifters, and teenage runaways coped with bad drug trips, venereal disease, and violence. In 1967 seventeen murders and more than a hundred rapes were reported in Haight-Ashbury alone.

Meanwhile, the appeal of rock music and drugs continued to spread. In August 1969 more than 400,000 people journeyed to Bethel, New York, to "get high" on music, drugs, and sex at the three-day Woodstock Music and Art Fair. Despite torrential rain and numerous drug overdoses, most enjoyed the festival, which was heralded as the birth of the "Woodstock nation." A few months later, however, an outdoor concert by the Rolling Stones at Altamont Speedway near San Francisco degenerated into a near riot, leaving four dead and hundreds injured.

Rejecting both the mainstream culture and the growing anarchy of the counterculture, some young people headed for rural communes located in areas such as the mountains between Santa Cruz and San Francisco, the wide-open spaces of New Mexico, and the pastoral solitude of Vermont. Following in the tradition of earlier American utopian communities, communes provided economic and sexual alternatives to nuclear families and were removed from the watchful eye of mainstream America (and local drug enforcement agents). Members grew their own food, baked their own bread, and rejected materialism and commercialism in favor of rural self-sufficiency. But the communes of the 1960s did not just look backward. Their advocacy of organic farming—growing food without chemicals or pesticides—anticipated and influenced the environmental concerns that would emerge in the 1970s (see Chapter 30).

The Widening Struggle for Civil Rights

The counterculture and the antiwar movement were not the only social movements to challenge the status quo in the 1960s. Black frustration and anger fueled a new racial militance as the civil rights struggle moved outside the South to take on the more stubborn problems of entrenched poverty and racism. The rhetoric and tactics of the emerging black power movement shattered the existing civil rights coalition and galvanized white opposition. At the same time, the tactics that the civil rights movement had pioneered—legislative and judicial challenges, nonviolent direct action, and mobilization of public opinion—were adopted by women, Mexican Americans, native Americans, and other groups to press their demands. As a civil rights worker observed, "What started out as an identity crisis for Negroes turned out to be an identity crisis for the nation."

Rising Militance.   Once the system of legal, or *de jure*, segregation had fallen, the civil rights movement turned to the more difficult task of eliminating the *de facto* segregation, enforced by custom, that made blacks second-class citizens throughout the nation. Outside the South, racial discrimination was less flagrant, but it was pervasive, especially in education, housing, and employment. Although the *Brown* decision outlawed separate schools, it did nothing to change educational systems in areas where schools were all-black or all-white because of residential segregation. Not until 1973 did federal judges begin to extend the desegregation that had begun in the South two decades earlier to schools in the rest of the country.

As civil rights leaders took on the new target of northern racism, the movement fractured along generational lines. Students who had risked assault to sit in at lunch counters or to register to vote grew impatient with the gradualism of their elders. Some younger black activists, eager for confrontation and faster change, questioned the very goal of integration into white society. Black separatism, espoused by earlier black leaders such as Marcus Garvey in the 1920s (see Chapter 23), was revived in the 1960s by the Nation of Islam, which had more than 10,000 members and many more sympathizers. Popularly known as the Black Muslims, the Nation of Islam was extremely hostile to whites, whom its leader Elijah Muhammad called "blue-eyed devils." Forcefully promoting black nationalism, the group stressed black pride, unity, and self-help.

The Black Muslims' most charismatic figure was Malcolm X. Born Malcolm Little in Omaha in 1925, he converted to the Nation of Islam while serving time in prison for attempted burglary. Replacing his "slave name" with an X to signify his lost African name, Malcolm X was a brilliant debater and spellbinding speaker who preached a philosophy quite different from Martin Luther King's. Malcolm X advocated militant protest and separatism and condoned the use of violence for self-defense and self-assertion. He was hostile to the traditional civil rights organizations, caustically referring to the 1963 march as the "Farce on Washington."

In 1964, after a power struggle with Elijah Muhammad, Malcolm X broke with the Nation of Islam. He then made a pilgrimage to Mecca, the holiest site of traditional Islam, and toured Africa, where he embraced the liberation struggles of all colonized peoples. On his return to the United States, Malcolm X moved away from antiwhite rhetoric toward an internationalist vision of the black future. On February 21, 1965, he was assassinated while giving a speech at the Audubon Ballroom in Harlem. Three Black Muslims were later convicted for the murder. Malcolm X's autobiography, cowritten by Alex Haley and published soon after his death, became one of the decade's most influential books.

Black Power.   Although Malcolm X's call for black cultural and political independence appealed to young black activists in SNCC and CORE, many balked at the idea of converting to Islam, preferring a secular black nationalist movement. In 1966 SNCC leader Stokely Carmichael christened a new era in the black struggle when he called for black self-reliance and racial pride under the banner of "black power." Amid growing distrust of white domination, SNCC embraced black power and effectively ejected its white members. In the same year Huey Newton and Bobby Seale, two college students in Oakland, California, founded the Black Panthers as a militant self-defense organization to protect local blacks from police violence. The Panthers undertook a wide range of community-organizing projects in several cities, but their affinity for Third World revolutionary movements and armed struggle became their most publicized attribute.

Among the most significant legacies of black power was the assertion of racial pride. Many young blacks insisted on being called Afro-American rather than Negro, a term they found demeaning because of its historical association with slavery and racism. Rejecting white tastes and standards, blacks wore African clothing and Afro hairstyles and helped awaken interest in black history, art, and literature. Black students demanded courses in African American history and culture, the forerunners of the Afro-American or black studies departments established by many universities in the late 1960s and early 1970s. By acknowledging race as a key factor in American life, these new courses and programs had an enduring impact on the way American history was taught and written.

The new black assertiveness alarmed many white Americans. They had been willing to go along with the moderate reforms of the 1950s and early 1960s but became wary when blacks started demanding higher-paying jobs, housing in white neighborhoods, integrated schools, and increased political power. In 1966, 84 percent of all whites thought blacks were demanding too much change, up from 34 percent five years earlier. White backlash soon became a powerful force in both political parties.

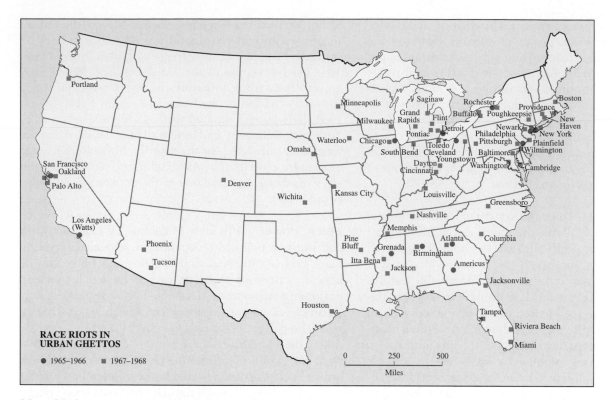

MAP 29.2
Racial Unrest in America's Cities, 1965–1968
American cities suffered through four "long hot summers" of rioting in the mid-1960s. In 1967, the worst year, riots broke out across the United States, including the South and West. Major riots did not usually occur in the same city two years in a row.

Summer in the City.   A major reason for the erosion of white support was a wave of riots that struck the nation's cities. Every summer from 1964 to 1968 images of defiant black youths and burning buildings filled the nightly TV news. Mired in declining urban neighborhoods with high unemployment, dilapidated housing, and substandard education and services, black residents angrily denounced the racism of white employers, landlords, shopkeepers, and labor unions. Many blacks especially resented the police, whose violent presence in black neighborhoods made them seem like "an occupying army." Stimulated by the successes of southern blacks who had challenged whites and gotten results, young urban blacks expressed their grievances through their own brand of direct action.

The first "long hot summer" began in July 1964 in New York City, when police shot a young black criminal suspect in Harlem. Angry youths looted and rioted for a week. The volatile issue of police brutality would set off riots in a number of cities over the next four years (Map 29.2). In August 1965 the arrest of a young black motorist in the Watts section of Los Angeles sparked six days of rioting that left thirty-four blacks dead. Ironically, Watts erupted only five days after President Johnson hailed the passage of the Voting Rights Act of 1965 as the

next great step toward racial equality. For many young urban blacks the legal gains of the civil rights movement were irrelevant to their daily experience of poverty and economic exploitation. Instead of singing "We shall overcome," Watts rioters shouted "Burn, baby, burn."

The riots of 1967 were the most serious of all, engulfing twenty-two cities in July and August. The most devastating outbreaks occurred in Newark and Detroit. Forty-three people were killed in Detroit alone, nearly all of them black, and $50 million of property was destroyed; federal paratroopers, some just back from service in Vietnam, were sent in to restore order. As in most of the riots, the arson and looting in Detroit targeted white-owned stores and property, though there was little physical violence against white people.

On July 29, 1967, President Johnson appointed a special commission to investigate the riots. The final report of the National Advisory Commission on Civil Disorders (also known as the Kerner Commission), released in March 1968, detailed the continuing inequality and racism of urban life. It also issued a warning: "Our nation is moving toward two societies, one black, one white—separate and unequal. . . . What white Americans have never fully understood—but what the Negro can never forget—is that white society is deeply implicated in the ghetto. White institutions created it, white institutions maintain it, and white society condones it."

The Assassination of Martin Luther King Jr. On April 4, 1968, barely a month after the Kerner Commission released its report, Martin Luther King was assassinated in Memphis, Tennessee, where he had gone to support a strike by predominantly black sanitation workers. King's death set off an explosion of urban rioting, with major violence breaking out in more than a hundred cities.

With King's assassination the civil rights movement lost the black leader best able to stir the conscience of white America. At the time of his death, King was only thirty-nine years old. During the last years of his life he had moved toward a broader view of the structural problems of poverty and racism faced by blacks in contemporary America. He spoke out eloquently against the Vietnam War, and in 1968 he was planning a poor people's campaign to raise issues of economic injustice and inequality. How successful King would have been in those endeavors will never be known, but his death marked the passing of an important national leader and symbolized the troubled course of the civil rights movement.

The Legacy of the Civil Rights Movement

The 1960s brought permanent, indeed revolutionary, changes in American race relations. Jim Crow segregation was overturned in less than a decade, and federal legislation was passed to ensure protection of black Americans' most basic civil rights. The enfranchisement of blacks in southern states ended political control there by a lily-white Democratic Party and allowed black candidates to enter the political arena. White candidates who had once been ardent segregationists now courted the black vote. In time Martin Luther King's

Mourning Martin Luther King Jr.
Thousands of African Americans mourned the death of the country's foremost civil rights leader, Martin Luther King, who had been assassinated in Memphis, Tennessee, on April 4, 1968. Among those who marched alongside King's casket, borne by a simple farm wagon pulled by mules, were future presidential candidate Jesse Jackson (in green) and future U.N. ambassador Andrew Young (at the left corner of the casket). During that week racial uprisings broke out in more than a hundred cities.
Wide World Photos, Inc.

greatness was recognized even among whites in the South; in 1986 his birthday became a national holiday.

Yet much remained undone. The more entrenched forms of segregation and discrimination persisted despite the legal reforms of the 1960s. African Americans, particularly those in the central cities, continued to make up a disproportionate number of the poor, unemployed, and undereducated. As the civil rights movement gradually disintegrated, its agenda remained unfinished.

The Chicano Movement.   Despite its limitations, the civil rights movement provided a fresh and innovative model for social change. Although Mexican Americans had been actively working for civil rights since the 1930s (see Chapter 24), poverty, an uncertain legal status, and language barriers made political mobilization difficult. That situation began to change when the Mexican-American Political Association (MAPA) mobilized support for Kennedy in 1960; in return Kennedy appointed several Mexican American leaders to posts in Washington. Over the next four years, MAPA and other political organizations successfully worked to elect Mexican American candidates to Congress, including Edward Roybal of California and Henry Gonzalez and Elizo de la Garza of Texas in the House, and Joseph Montoya of New Mexico in the Senate.

Younger Mexican Americans quickly grew impatient with MAPA, however. The *barrios* of Los Angeles and other western cities produced the militant Brown Berets, who modeled themselves on the Black Panthers (who wore black berets). Rejecting the assimilationist approach of their elders, 1,500 Mexican American students met in Denver in 1969 to hammer out a new nationalist political and cultural agenda. They proclaimed a new term, *Chicano*, to replace *Mexican American* and subsequently organized a political party, La Raza Unida (The United Race), to promote Mexican American interests and candidates. In California and other southwestern states, students staged demonstrations and boycotts to press for bilingual education, the hiring of more Chicano teachers, and the creation of programs in Chicano studies. By the 1970s dozens of universities in the region were offering such programs.

Chicano strategists also pursued economic objectives. Working in the fields around Delano, California, labor leader César Chávez organized the United Farm Workers (UFW), the first union to represent migrant workers successfully. A 1965 grape pickers' strike and a nationwide boycott of table grapes brought Chávez and his union national publicity and won support from the AFL-CIO and Senator Robert F. Kennedy of New York. Chávez was soon receiving almost as much media attention as Martin Luther King Jr. Victory came in 1970, when California grape growers signed contracts recognizing the UFW.

The Native American Movement.   North American Indians also found a model in the civil rights movement.

Native Americans, who numbered nearly 800,000 in the 1960s, were an exceedingly diverse group, divided by language, tribal history, region, and degree of integration into mainstream American life. Moreover, the termination policy that had begun in the 1950s had accelerated the breakdown of tribal life and the dispersal of native American populations. But native Americans also shared an unemployment rate ten times the national average, as well as the worst poverty, the most inadequate housing, the highest disease rates, and the least access to education of any group in the United States.

As early as World War II, the National Council of American Indians had lobbied for the improvement of those conditions, but now some Indian groups became more assertive. Like the young militants in other movements, they challenged the accommodationist approach of their elders. Proposing a new name for themselves—native Americans—they organized protests and demonstrations to build support for their cause. In 1968 several Chipewyan from Minnesota organized the militant American Indian Movement (AIM), which modeled itself on the black power movement and drew its strength from the third of the native American population that lived in "red ghettos" in cities throughout the West.

In November 1969 AIM seized the deserted federal penitentiary on Alcatraz Island in San Francisco Bay, offering the government $24 worth of trinkets to pay for it, supposedly the sum the Dutch had paid the native inhabitants for Manhattan Island in 1626. The occupation of Alcatraz lasted until the summer of 1971. A year later, a thousand protesters occupied the headquarters of the Federal Bureau of Indian Affairs in Washington, D.C., which was to many native Americans a hated symbol of the inconsistent federal policy on tribal welfare (see American Voices, "Mary Crow Dog: The Trail of Broken Treaties," p. 960).

In February 1973, a group of Sioux organized by AIM leaders began an occupation of the tiny village of Wounded Knee, South Dakota, the site of the army massacre of the Sioux in 1890 (see Chapter 16). They were protesting the light sentences given to a group of white men convicted of killing a Sioux in 1972. To dramatize their cause, the protesters took eleven hostages and occupied several buildings. But when a gun battle with the FBI left one protester dead and another wounded, the seventy-one-day siege collapsed. Although the new native American activism alienated many whites, it helped spur government action on tribal issues (see Chapter 31).

Identity Politics.   Civil rights, once seen as a movement exclusively for the rights of black people, also sparked a new awareness among some predominantly white groups. Americans of Polish, Italian, Greek, and Slavic descent, most of them working class and Catholic, proudly embraced their ethnic identity. Through groups like the Grey Panthers, elderly Americans organized to demand better health, social security, and other benefits.

Wounded Knee Revisited
In 1973 members of the American Indian Movement staged a seventy-one-day protest at Wounded Knee, South Dakota, the site of the 1890 massacre of two hundred Sioux by U.S. soldiers. The takeover was sparked by the murder of a local Sioux by a group of whites but quickly expanded to include demands for basic reforms in federal Indian policy and tribal governance.
Corbis-Bettmann.

Similarly, homosexual men and women banded together to protest legal and social oppression based on sexual orientation. Going beyond an older legalistic approach to homosexual rights, the gay liberation movement was born in 1969 in the Stonewall riot in New York City, in which patrons of a gay bar in Greenwich Village fought back against police harassment. Activists took the new name *gay* rather than *homosexual;* founded advocacy groups, newspapers, and political organizations to challenge discrimination and prejudice; and provided emotional support for those who "came out" by publicly affirming their homosexual identity.

For many gays and members of various ethnic and cultural groups, political activism based on heightened group identity represented one of the most significant legacies of the African American struggle. It also posed dilemmas for those who had multiple social identities (such as gay or elderly nonwhites) and were pressured to choose one primary identity over others.

The Revival of Feminism

The civil rights movement also helped reactivate feminism, a movement that had been languishing since the 1920s. Just as the abolition movement had been the training ground for an earlier generation of women's rights advocates in the nineteenth century, the black struggle inspired and influenced young feminists in the 1960s. But the revival of feminism also grew out of postwar social and demographic changes that affected younger and older women alike. More women were attending college and working outside the home than ever before, the birth rate was falling again after its baby-boom high, and divorce rates were skyrocketing—all developments that undercut traditional gender expectations. Those changing social realities created a major constituency for the emerging women's movement.

Throughout the 1960s, older, politically active professional women sought change by working through the political system. Many of them came together in the President's Commission on the Status of Women, a group appointed by John F. Kennedy to counter criticism about his administration's poor record on women's issues. In 1963 the commission issued a report that documented the employment and educational discrimination faced by women. More important than the report's conservative recommendations was the nationwide network of women in public life that formed during the course of the commission's work.

Another spark that ignited the revival of feminism was Betty Friedan's best-selling book, *The Feminine Mystique*, published in 1963. A pointed indictment of women's suburban domesticity that grew out of Friedan's experiences as a housewife in the 1950s, the book explored what she called "the problem that has no name": "As she made the beds, shopped for groceries, matched slipcover material, ate peanut butter sandwiches with her children, chauffeured Cub Scouts and Brownies, lay beside her husband at night—she was afraid to ask even of herself the silent question—'Is this all?'" Women responded enthusiastically to Friedan's story, especially white, college-educated women whose backgrounds resembled the author's. *The Feminine Mystique* gave women a vocabulary for their dissatisfaction and introduced many of them to the powerful ideas of modern feminism.

Like so many constituencies in postwar America, women's rights activists looked to the federal government for help. The first step occurred in 1963 when Congress passed the Equal Pay Act, which directed that men and women be paid the same wages for doing the same job. Even more important was the Civil Rights Act of 1964, which had as great an impact on women as it did on blacks and other minorities. Title VII, which barred discrimination in employment on the basis of race, color, religion, national origin, or sex, eventually became a powerful tool in the fight against sex discrimination. Initially, however, the Equal Employment Opportunity Commission avoided implementing it.

MARY CROW DOG
The Trail of Broken Treaties

———— ★ ————

In November 1972, 19-year old Mary Crow Dog traveled to Washington, D.C., with several hundred other Sioux from the Rosebud and Pine Ridge reservations in South Dakota. As she explains in her autobiography, their group was one of several caravans participating in a protest known as the Trail of Broken Treaties, which ended in a six-day occupation of the Bureau of Indian Affairs headquarters.

When we arrived in Washington we got lost. We had been promised food and accommodation, but due to government pressure many church groups which had offered to put us up and feed us got scared and backed off. . . .

Somebody suggested, "Let's all go to the BIA." It seemed the natural thing to do, to go to the Bureau of Indian Affairs building on Constitution Avenue. They would have to put us up. It was "our" building after all. Besides, that was what we had come for, to complain about the treatment the bureau was dishing out to us. . . . Next thing I knew we were in it. We spilled into the building like a great avalanche. Some people put up a tipi on the front lawn. . . . The building finally belonged to us and we lost no time turning it into a tribal village. . . .

We pushed the police and guards out of the building. Some did not wait to be pushed but jumped out of the ground-floor windows like so many frogs. We had formulated twenty Indian demands. These were all rejected by the few bureaucrats sent to negotiate with us. . . . Soon we listened to other voices as the occupation turned into a siege. I heard somebody yelling, "The pigs are here." I could see from the window that it was true. The whole building was surrounded by helmeted police armed with all kinds of guns. A fight broke out between the police and our security. Some of our young men got hit over the head with police clubs and we saw the blood streaming down their faces. . . .

We barricaded all doors and the lowest windows with document boxes, Xerox machines, tables, file cabinets, anything we could lay our hands on. . . .

From then on, every morning we were given a court order to get out by six P.M. Come six o'clock and we would be standing there ready to join battle. I think many brothers and sisters were prepared to die right on the steps of the BIA building. . . .

In the end a compromise was reached. The government said . . . they would appoint two high administration officials to seriously consider our twenty demands. Our expenses to get home would be paid. Nobody would be prosecuted. Of course, our twenty points were never gone into afterward. From the practical point of view, nothing had been achieved. . . . But morally it had been a great victory. We had faced White America collectively, not as individual tribes. We had stood up to the government and gone through our baptism of fire. We had not run.

———————

Source: Mary Crow Dog, *Lakota Woman* (New York: Grove Weidenfeld, 1990), 84–85, 88–91.

Dissatisfied with the commission's reluctance to promote women's rights, Friedan and others founded the National Organization for Women (NOW) in 1966. Modeling itself on groups such as the NAACP, NOW aimed to be a civil rights organization for women. "The purpose of NOW," its statement of purpose declared, "is to take action to bring women into full participation in the mainstream of American society now, exercising all the privileges and responsibilities thereof in truly equal partnership with men." Under Friedan, who served as NOW's first president, its membership grew from 1,000 in 1967 to 15,000 in 1971. Men made up a fourth of NOW's early membership. It is still the largest feminist organization in the United States.

Under the banner "women's liberation," a younger generation of women came to feminism by a different path. White women had made up about half of the students who went south with SNCC in the 1964 Freedom Summer project. College women developed self-confidence and organizational skills working in the South and found role models in older women, both black and white, who were prominent in the movement. Yet women volunteers also found that they were expected to do all the cleaning and cooking at the Freedom Houses where SNCC volunteers lived. "We didn't come down here to work as maids this summer," one complained.

After 1965 black power militancy made white women as well as white men unwelcome in the civil

Women's Liberation
Arguing that beauty contests were degrading to women, members of the National Women's Liberation Party staged a protest against the Miss America pageant held in Atlantic City, New Jersey, in September 1968.
Wide World Photos, Inc.

rights movement. But when these women transferred their energies to the student and antiwar groups that were emerging, they found the New Left groups equally male dominated and unsupportive. When the antiwar movement adopted draft resistance as its central strategy, women found themselves relegated to roles as sex objects. "Girls say yes to guys who say no" was a popular slogan. Women who tried to raise feminist issues at conventions were shouted off the platform with jeers such as "Move on, little girl, we have more important issues to talk about here than women's liberation."

Around 1967 the contradiction between the New Left's lip service to egalitarianism and women's treatment by male leaders caused radical women to found their own movement. In contrast to women's rights groups such as NOW, which had traditional organizational structures and dues-paying members, radical women formed loose collectives whose shifting memberships often lacked any coordinating structure. The women's liberation movement (or "women's lib," as it was dubbed by the media) went public in 1968 when it staged a protest at the Miss America pageant. The demonstration included a "freedom trash can" into which women were encouraged to throw false eyelashes, hair curlers, brassieres, and girdles—all considered symbols of female oppression. The media quickly labeled the radical feminists "bra burners." The derisive name stuck, although no brassieres were actually burned.

An activity with a more lasting impact was *consciousness raising*, group sessions in which women shared their experiences of being female. Swapping stories about being passed over for promotion, needing a husband's signature on a credit card application, or enduring the humiliation of whistles and leers while walking down the street helped participants realize that their individual problems were part of a wider pattern of oppression. The slogan "The personal is political" became a rallying cry of the movement.

Feminism's potential as a mass movement was demonstrated on August 26, 1970, when thousands of women throughout the country marched to celebrate the fiftieth anniversary of the Nineteenth Amendment. A flood of new converts broke down the barriers between radical and more traditional activists, as did a growing convergence of interests. Radical women realized that key feminist goals—child care, equal pay, abortion rights—could best be achieved in the political arena. At the same time, more traditional feminists developed a broader view of women's oppression, including tentative support for divisive issues such as abortion and lesbian rights. Although the movement remained largely white and middle class, feminists were beginning to think of themselves as part of a broad and increasingly influential social movement that would continue to grow.

The Long Road Home, 1968–1975

———————★———————

The United States in 1968 was deeply polarized. Riots in the cities, black and Chicano power, campus unrest, and a host of protests and challenges were in the eyes of many citizens tearing the country in two. But Vietnam remained the central domestic and foreign policy issue. Although the Johnson administration insisted that there was "light at the end of the tunnel," the reality was otherwise. The war would continue, at home and in Vietnam, for another five years.

1968: A Year of Shocks

By 1968, as Lyndon Johnson planned his reelection campaign, antiwar protests and rising battlefield casualties had eroded public support for the war. Since the assassination of Diem in 1963, South Vietnam had undergone a series of military coups and counter-coups. In the spring of 1966, the Johnson administration pressured the South Vietnamese government to adopt democratic reforms, including a new constitution and popular elections. In September 1967, U.S. officials helped elect Nguyen Van Thieu president of South Vietnam. Thieu's regime, the administration hoped, would broaden its support at home, legitimize the South Vietnamese government in the eyes of the American public, and advance the military struggle against the communists.

The Tet Offensive. Those hopes were quickly shattered on January 30, 1968, when the Vietcong unleashed a massive, well-coordinated assault on major urban areas in the south. Known as the Tet offensive, the assault was timed to coincide with the Vietnamese holiday of Tet, celebrating the lunar New Year. Vietcong forces struck thirty-six of the forty-four provincial capitals and five of the six major cities, including Saigon, where they raided the supposedly impregnable U.S. embassy (see Map 29.1). Once again the United States and South Vietnamese forces had seriously underestimated the capabilities of their foes, who had been planning the attack since the previous fall. "Even had I known exactly what was to take place," an intelligence officer explained, "it was so preposterous that I probably would have been unable to sell it to anybody."

In strictly military terms the Tet offensive was a failure for the Vietcong, for it did not bring about the collapse of the South Vietnamese government. But its effect on American morale was devastating. With congressional support already slipping, the Tet offensive convinced many of Johnson's advisors that the war was unwinnable. When General Westmoreland asked for 206,000 additional troops, a deployment that would have required the politically explosive course of calling up the reserves, Johnson turned him down.

Covered extensively by the media, the Tet offensive made a mockery of official pronouncements that the United States was winning in Vietnam and helped swing American public opinion more clearly against the war. Just before Tet, a Gallup poll found that 56 percent of Americans considered themselves "hawks" (supporters of the war) and only 28 percent identified themselves as "doves" (opponents). Women and blacks consistently opposed the war more than white men did,

and younger people more than older. Three months after the Tet offensive, doves outnumbered hawks by 42 to 41 percent. This turnaround, however, did not mean that a majority supported the peace movement. Many who called themselves doves had concluded that the war was unwinnable and opposed it on pragmatic, rather than moral, grounds. As one housewife told a pollster, "I want to get out, but I don't want to give up."

Political Turmoil. The growing opposition to the war spilled over into the 1968 presidential campaign. Senator Eugene J. McCarthy of Minnesota had already entered the Democratic primaries as an antiwar alternative to Lyndon Johnson. A core of student activists went "clean for Gene" by cutting their hair and putting away their blue jeans to avoid alienating voters. In March President Johnson won the first state primary election in New Hampshire, but McCarthy received a stunning 42.2 percent of the vote. His strong showing against an incumbent president reflected profound dissatisfaction with the course of the war, even among those who were hawks. Sensing the president's vulnerability, Senator Robert Kennedy of New York, who had earlier decided against entering the race, announced his candidacy.

Johnson realized that his political support was evaporating. On March 31, at the end of an otherwise mundane televised address, he stunned the nation by announcing that he would not seek reelection. Johnson had already reversed his policy of incremental escalation of the war when he turned down Westmoreland's request for more troops. Now he called a partial bombing halt and vowed to devote his remaining months in office to the search for peace. On May 10, 1968, preliminary peace talks between the United States and North Vietnam began in Paris.

Just four days after Johnson's withdrawal from the presidential race, Martin Luther King Jr. was assassinated in Memphis. Soon afterward, a major student confrontation at Columbia University ended only when police forcibly removed protesters from the administration buildings they had occupied, beating and injuring dozens of demonstrators in the process. Student unrest seemed likely to become a worldwide phenomenon in May, when a massive strike by students and labor unions toppled the French government in protest over working conditions, university policies, and other issues.

Then came another tragedy. As Robert Kennedy celebrated his California primary victory over Eugene McCarthy on June 5, 1968, he was shot dead by Sirhan Sirhan, a young Palestinian who was thought to oppose Kennedy's pro-Israel stance. Once again the nation went through the ritual of burying a Kennedy. In two strokes—the assassinations of Martin Luther King and Robert Kennedy—liberalism, as the student leader Tom Hayden put it, was "decapitated."

Robert Kennedy's assassination shattered the dreams of many who hoped that social change could be achieved through the political system. In his brief but dramatic campaign Robert Kennedy had energized the traditional components of the New Deal coalition, including blue-collar workers and black voters, in a way that the more cerebral Eugene McCarthy never did. So widespread was Kennedy's appeal that election-day exit polls in Indiana found that many voters who had supported him in the primary voted for the conservative candidate George Wallace in November.

Kennedy's death also weakened the Democratic Party, which had not fully recovered from Johnson's withdrawal. McCarthy proceeded listlessly through the rest of his campaign, and Senator George S. McGovern of South Dakota entered the Democratic race in an effort to keep the Kennedy forces together. Meanwhile, Vice-President Hubert H. Humphrey lined up pledges from the traditional Democratic constituencies—unions, city machines, and state political organizations. The Democrats thus found themselves on the verge of nominating not an antiwar candidate but a public figure closely associated with Johnson's war policies. The stage was set for the Democratic National Convention in Chicago in August.

The Siege of Chicago. With Vietnam emerging as the central campaign issue in the 1968 elections, the political divisions generated by the war consumed the Democratic Party. Most of the drama at the national convention occurred not in the main hall but outside, on the streets of Chicago. Led by "Yippie" (Youth International Party) activists Jerry Rubin and Abbie Hoffman, approximately ten thousand protesters descended on Chicago. With theatrics geared toward maximum media exposure, they called for an end to the war, the legalization of marijuana, and the abolition of money. To mock the "pigs" who ruled America, they nominated a live pig for president, which was promptly confiscated by Chicago's humane society. Their stunts diverted attention from the more serious, and far more numerous, antiwar activists who had come to Chicago as convention delegates or volunteers.

Chicago's old-line Democratic mayor, Richard J. Daley, had little tolerance for antiwar protesters and called out the police to break up the demonstrations. Several nights of skirmishes between protesters and police culminated on the evening of the nominations in what an official report later described as a "police riot." Officers dispersed protesters with Mace, tear gas, and clubs. While protesters chanted "The whole world is watching," the television networks ran film of the riot during the nominating speeches. In one memorable moment, Senator Abraham Ribicoff of Connecticut interrupted his nominating speech for Senator McGovern to interject, "With George McGovern we wouldn't have Gestapo tactics on the streets of

RFK
Bobby Kennedy inspired strong passions during his 1968 campaign. Followers often tore off his cuff links as they tried to touch him or shake his hand.
Steve Schapiro/Black Star.

Chicago." The cameras panned to Mayor Daley, livid with rage and clearly mouthing obscenities.

Television coverage of the riots was hardly excessive—about 32 minutes on CBS and less than 14 minutes on NBC—but it cemented an impression of the Democrats as the party of disorder. The Democrats dispiritedly gave the nomination to Hubert H. Humphrey, who chose Senator Edmund S. Muskie of Maine as his running mate. The convention approved a middle-of-the-road platform that endorsed Johnson's policy of continuing the fighting in Vietnam while exploring diplomatic means to end the conflict.

Backlash. Among the general public, the turmoil at the Democratic convention unleashed a backlash against antiwar protesters and strengthened support for proponents of "law and order," which became the conservative catch phrase of the next several years. Many Americans, though opposed to the war, were fed up with protest and dissent. Governor George C. Wallace of Alabama, who left the Democrats to head a third-party ticket called the American Independent Party, skillfully exploited their growing hostility by making student protests and urban riots his chief campaign issues. But Wallace, who in 1963 had promised to enforce "segregation now . . . segregation tomorrow . . . and segregation forever," also exploited the mounting backlash against the civil rights movement. Articulating the resentments of many working-class whites, he delivered a populist message that combined attacks on liberal intellectuals and government elites with strident denunciations of school desegregation and forced busing.

Even more than George Wallace, Richard Nixon effectively tapped the growing conservative mood of the electorate. After his unsuccessful presidential campaign in 1960 and his loss in the California gubernatorial race in 1962, Nixon engineered an amazing political comeback. In 1968 the "new" Nixon easily beat back primary challenges by three governors—Ronald Reagan of California, George Romney of Michigan, and Nelson Rockefeller of New York—to win the Republican nomination. He chose Spiro Agnew, the conservative governor of Maryland, as his running mate to attract southern voters, especially Wallace supporters, who opposed Democratic civil rights initiatives. In what his campaign advisor Kevin Phillips called the "southern strategy," Nixon hoped to make impressive inroads in the once solidly Democratic South. He also used traditional populist appeals, pledging to represent the "quiet voice" of the "great majority of Americans, the forgotten Americans, the nonshouters, the nondemonstrators."

Despite the Democratic debacle in Chicago, the election was closely contested. Humphrey rallied in the last weeks of the campaign by gingerly disassociating himself from Johnson's war policies. Then, in a televised address on October 31, President Johnson announced a complete halt of the bombing of North Vietnam. Nixon countered by intimating that he had his own plan for ending the war, although in reality no such plan existed. On election day Nixon received 43.4 percent of the popular vote to Humphrey's 42.7 percent, defeating Humphrey by a scant 510,000 votes out of the 73 million cast (Map 29.3). Wallace finished with 13.5 percent of the popular vote, becoming the most successful third-party candidate since the Progressive Party's Robert M. La Follette in 1924. Nixon owed his election largely to the split in the Democratic coalition, but his southern strategy produced a decisive victory in the electoral college and hinted at the future emergence of a new Republican majority. In the meantime, however, the Democrats retained a majority in both houses of Congress.

The 1968 election revealed the growing polarization of American society over the Vietnam War and other events of the 1960s. Nixon appealed to a segment of society that came to be known as the "silent majority"—hardworking, nonprotesting, and generally white Amer-icans. According to social scientists Ben J. Wattenberg and Richard Scammon in their influential book *The Real Majority* (1970), the typical American was a white forty-seven-year-old machinist's wife from Dayton, Ohio, and this was what she was concerned about:

> To know that the lady in Dayton is afraid to walk the streets alone at night, to know that she has a mixed view about blacks and civil rights because before moving to the suburbs she lived in a neighborhood that became all black, to know that her brother-in-law is a policeman, to know that she does not have the money to move if her new neighborhood deteriorates, to know that she is deeply distressed that her son is going to a community junior college where LSD was found on campus—to know all this is the beginning of contemporary political wisdom.

Although Nixon's victory suggested a growing national consensus around the law-and-order perspective of the silent majority, heated protest and controversy would persist until the war ended.

Nixon's War

Long Lyndon Johnson's war, Vietnam now became Richard Nixon's and would drag on for another four years. At first Nixon sought to end the war by expanding its scope as a means of pressuring the North Vietnamese to negotiate. But Nixon and his national security advisor, Henry Kissinger, soon realized that the public would not support such an approach. So shortly after taking office, Nixon sent a letter to North Vietnamese leaders proposing mutual troop withdrawals, an offer they flatly refused. In March 1969, to convince Hanoi that the United States meant business, Nixon ordered secret bombing raids on the neighboring country of Cambodia, through which the North Vietnamese transported supplies and reinforcements. To keep Congress and the public ignorant about those sorties, the air force officials in charge of the bombings fed accurate information about the raids into one Defense department computer while placing data omitting the Cambodian targets into another. The faulty projections from the second computer were the ones given to Congress.

Vietnamization and Its Critics.   When the intensified bombing failed to end the war, Nixon and Kissinger adopted a policy of *Vietnamization.* On June 8, 1969, Nixon announced that 25,000 American troops would be withdrawn by August and replaced by South Vietnamese forces. Antiwar protesters denounced the new policy, which protected American lives at the expense of the Vietnamese and would not end the war. Even the U.S. ambassador to Vietnam, Ellsworth Bunker, noted that it was just a matter of changing "the color of the bodies." On October 15, 1969, millions of people in cities across the country joined a one-day "moratorium" to protest

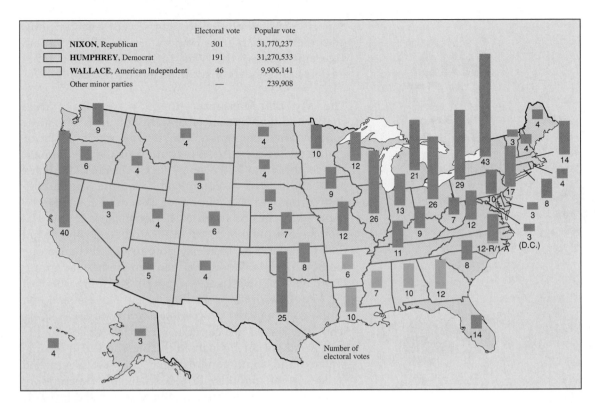

		Electoral vote	Popular vote
	NIXON, Republican	301	31,770,237
	HUMPHREY, Democrat	191	31,270,533
	WALLACE, American Independent	46	9,906,141
	Other minor parties	—	239,908

MAP 29.3
The Election of 1968
As late as mid-September the third-party candidate George C. Wallace of Alabama had
the support of 21 percent of the voters. But in November he received only 13.5 percent of
the vote, winning five states and showing that the South was no longer solidly Democratic. The Republican Richard M. Nixon defeated Hubert H. Humphrey with only 43.4 percent of the popular vote.

the war. A month later, more than a quarter of a million people mobilized in Washington to call for an end to the fighting, the largest antiwar demonstration to date.

Nixon staunchly insisted that he would not be swayed by the mounting protests against the war, stating that "North Vietnam cannot defeat or humiliate the United States; only Americans can do that." Vice-President Spiro Agnew attacked dissenters as "ideological eunuchs" and "nattering nabobs of negativism." During the November 1969 march on Washington the president closeted himself in the White House and watched football on television.

On April 30, 1970, the previously secret bombing of Cambodia culminated in an "incursion" into that country by American ground forces to destroy enemy havens there. The invasion proved only a short-term setback for the North Vietnamese, who continued to boycott the Paris peace talks. More critically, the American action— along with the ongoing North Vietnamese intervention there—destabilized the country, exposing it to a takeover by the ruthless Khmer Rouge later in the 1970s.

Nixon's televised address announcing the invasion, followed by *New York Times* revelations of the earlier U.S. bombing campaign in Cambodia, prompted antiwar leaders to organize a national student strike. On May 4, at

Kent State University outside Cleveland, panicky National Guardsmen fired into a crowd of students at a noontime antiwar rally on May 4. Four people were killed, eleven wounded. Only two of those killed, Jeffrey Miller and Alison Krause, had participated in the demonstration; William Shroeder and Sandra Scheur were passing by on their way to class. Soon afterward, amid campus protests over Vietnam and other issues, National Guardsmen stormed a dormitory at Jackson State College in Mississippi, killing two black students. Over the next few months, more than 450 colleges closed because of strikes, and 80 percent of all American college campuses experienced some kind of protest. In June 1970, soon after the Kent State slayings, a Gallup poll reported that campus unrest—either student protests or the violent responses to them—was the main issue troubling Americans.

At the same time, dissatisfaction with the war continued to spread. Congressional opposition intensified with the invasion of Cambodia, and in June 1970 the Senate voted to repeal the Gulf of Tonkin Resolution and cut off funding for operations in Cambodia. Even American troops in Vietnam showed mounting opposition to their mission. From 1969 to 1971 the number of troops refusing combat orders steadily increased, and thousands of U.S. soldiers deserted. Many among the

WHO LOST VIET NAM?

"NOT I," SAID IKE. "I JUST SENT MONEY."

"NOT I," SAID JACK. "I JUST SENT ADVISORS."

"NOT I," SAID LYNDON. "I JUST FOLLOWED JACK."

"NOT I," SAID DICK. "I JUST HONORED JACK AND LYNDON'S COMMITMENTS."

"NOT I," SAID JERRY. "WHAT WAS THE QUESTION?"

"**YOU** LOST VIETNAM," SAID HENRY, "BECAUSE YOU DIDN'T TRUST YOUR LEADERS."

Passing the Buck
Highlighting the long and tortured history of the war, Jules Feiffer's 1975 cartoon offered a biting commentary on the lack of presidential accountability for U.S. policies in Vietnam.

majority who continued to fight sewed peace symbols onto their uniforms. At home a group called Vietnam Veterans against the War turned in their combat medals at mass demonstrations at the U.S. Capitol.

The My Lai Massacre. In 1971 Americans were confronted with the sheer brutality of the Vietnamese conflict when Lieutenant William L. Calley was court-martialed for atrocities committed in the Vietnamese village of My Lai (see Map 29.1). In March 1968 Calley had commanded a platoon on a routine search-and-destroy mission. Retaliating for casualties sustained by their fellow troops in an earlier engagement, the platoon apparently murdered 350 Vietnamese villagers on Calley's order. The incident came to light because one member of the platoon refused to go along with a military cover-up; investigative reporter Seymour Hersh of the *New York Times* broke the story in November 1969. In the court-martial proceedings, a jury of six soldiers who had served in Vietnam sentenced Calley to life imprisonment for his part in the massacre. Yet George Wallace and some congressional conservatives called Calley a hero, and after President Nixon's intervention, his sentence was reduced, and he was paroled in 1974.

The Decline of Antiwar Protest. After the outbreak of protest and violence following Kent State, antiwar activism began to ebb. Student strikes in the spring of 1971 and 1972, though large in number, never approached the emotional intensity of earlier demonstrations. SDS and other antiwar groups fell victim to police harassment, and FBI and CIA agents infiltrated and disrupted radical organizations. After 1968 the New Left splintered into factions, its energy spent. One radical faction formed the Weathermen, a tiny band of self-styled revolutionaries who embraced terrorist tactics—such as the destruction of the Army Math building at the University of Wisconsin at Madison in 1970—that alienated more moderate activists.

Nixon's Vietnamization policy also played a role in the decline of antiwar protest by dramatically reducing the number of U.S. soldiers in combat. When Nixon took office, more than 543,000 American soldiers were serving in Vietnam; by the end of 1970, 334,000; two years later, 24,200 (see Figure 29.1). Nixon's promise to continue troop withdrawals, end the draft, and institute an all-volunteer army by 1973 deprived the antiwar movement of important organizing issues, particularly on college campuses. Some students simply "burned

Kent State
The shootings by National Guardsmen of four students at Kent State University in Ohio on May 4, 1970, set off campus demonstrations and protests across the country. The protester shown here holds a placard memorializing the slain students as well as the two black students killed soon afterward at Jackson State College in Mississippi. The president of Columbia University called May 1970 "the most disastrous month . . . in the history of American higher education."
Michael Abramson/Black Star.

out," but commitment to social causes did not disappear altogether. In the early 1970s many student activists refocused their energies on causes such as feminism and environmentalism.

Détente. While Nixon was prosecuting the war in Vietnam to halt the spread of communism, he and Henry Kissinger were formulating a new policy toward the Soviet Union and China. Known as *détente* (the French word for a relaxation of tensions), Nixon's policy was to seek peaceful coexistence with the two communist powers and to link those overtures with his plan to end the Vietnam War. Nixon encouraged the Soviet and Chinese leaders to reduce military aid to North Vietnam as a means of pressuring the North Vietnamese to the negotiating table.

As a lifelong anticommunist crusader, Nixon was better able than a Democratic president would have been to seek accommodation with the two communist superpowers. After all, no one could accuse Richard Nixon of being soft on communism. Since the Chinese Revolution of 1949 the United States had refused to recognize the government of the People's Republic of China, instead giving unconditional support to the Nationalist Chinese government in Taiwan. Nixon moved away from that policy, reasoning that the United States could exploit the growing rift between the People's Republic of

China and the Soviet Union. In February 1972, Nixon journeyed to China, walked along the Great Wall, and toasted Chinese leaders in Beijing. Nixon's visit set the stage for the formal establishment of diplomatic relations, which took place in 1979.

In a similar spirit of détente Nixon journeyed to Moscow in May 1972 to sign the Strategic Arms Limitations Treaty (SALT I) between the United States and the Soviet Union. Although SALT I fell far short of ending the arms race, it did limit the production and deployment of intercontinental ballistic missiles (ICBMs) and antiballistic missile systems (ABMs). Yet the treaty was also an acknowledgment that the United States was unwilling to shoulder the massive military spending that would have been necessary to regain the nuclear and military superiority it had enjoyed immediately after World War II. Most critically, Nixon hoped that rapprochement with the Soviets would help resolve the prolonged crisis in Vietnam.

American Withdrawal from Vietnam. The Paris peace talks had been stalemated since 1968. The war had been "Vietnamized" and American casualties had decreased, but the South Vietnamese military was unable to hold its own. In late 1971, as American troops withdrew from the region, communist forces stepped up their attacks on Laos, Cambodia, and South Vietnam. The next spring North Vietnamese forces launched a major new offensive against South Vietnamese targets south of the demilitarized zone, in Binh Long province and in the Central Highlands (see American Lives, "John Paul Vann: Dissident Patriot," pp. 970–971). As the fighting intensified, Nixon ordered B-52 bombing raids against North Vietnam in April and the mining of all North Vietnamese ports a month later.

Increased combat activity in the spring of 1972 helped revive the Paris peace talks. Anxious to advance détente, Soviet and Chinese leaders pressured Hanoi back to the negotiating table. With the fall presidential election looming in the United States, Nixon hoped to undercut his antiwar critics by making concessions to the North Vietnamese. That October Henry Kissinger and North Vietnamese negotiator Le Duc Tho reached a cease-fire agreement calling for the withdrawal of the remaining U.S. troops, the return of all American prisoners of war, and the continued presence of North Vietnamese troops in South Vietnam (a major sticking point in earlier negotiations). Nixon and Kissinger also promised the North Vietnamese substantial aid for postwar reconstruction. On the eve of the 1972 presidential election Kissinger announced that "peace is at hand." With serious negotiations under way, Nixon returned to the White House with a resounding electoral victory (see Chapter 30).

The peace initiative, however, stalled once more when the South Vietnamese rejected the provision concerning

North Vietnamese troop positions, and the North declined to compromise further. With negotiations deadlocked, Nixon stepped up military action again. In a final destructive demonstration of American military strength—the "Christmas bombings" from December 17 to December 30, 1972—North Vietnamese civilian and military targets in Hanoi and Haiphong were subjected to the most devastating bombing of the war. Finally, on January 27, 1973, a cease-fire was signed in Paris by representatives of the United States, North and South Vietnam, and the Vietcong. The Paris Peace Accords differed little from the proposal of the previous October, and they failed to deliver on Nixon's often-repeated promise of "peace with honor." Basically, they mandated the unilateral withdrawal of American troops in exchange for the return of American prisoners of war held in North Vietnam. For most Americans, that amount of face-saving was enough.

The 1973 cease-fire did not resolve Vietnam's civil war. Without massive U.S. military and economic aid and with North Vietnamese guerrillas operating freely throughout the countryside, it was only a matter of time before the South Vietnamese government of General Nguyen Van Thieu fell to the more disciplined and popular communist forces. In March 1975 North Vietnamese forces launched a final offensive. Horrified American viewers watched on television as South Vietnamese officials and soldiers struggled with American embassy personnel for space on the last helicopters that flew out of Saigon before North Vietnamese troops entered the city. On April 29, 1975, Vietnam was reunited; Saigon was renamed Ho Chi Minh City in honor of the communist leader, who had died in 1969.

The Legacy of Vietnam

The Vietnam War exacted an enormous cost from America in human terms. Some 58,000 U.S. soldiers died, and another 300,000 were wounded. Even those who came back unharmed returned to an often hostile or indifferent reception. As one vet recalled, "Bringing up the Nam was like farting at the dinner table. Everybody looks away embarrassed and acts like nothing happened. Well, pardon me." The psychological tensions of serving in Vietnam and the abrupt transition back to America sowed the seeds of what is now recognized as post-traumatic stress disorder—recurring physical and psychological problems, often leading to higher than average rates of divorce, unemployment, and suicide. Only in the 1980s did America begin to make its peace with those who had served in the nation's most unpopular war.

In Southeast Asia the damage was even greater. The war claimed an estimated 1.5 million Vietnamese lives and devastated the country's physical and economic infrastructure. Neighboring Laos and Cambodia also suffered, particularly Cambodia, where the Khmer Rouge killed an estimated 2 million Cambodians (25 percent of the population) in a brutal "relocation" campaign between 1975 and 1979. All told, the war pro-

Hanoi Devastated
The North Vietnamese capital of Hanoi sustained heavy damage from bombing raids by American B-52 jets. The most devastating raids occurred during the "Christmas bombings" in December 1972, just weeks before the Paris Peace Accords were signed.
Marc Riboud/Magnum Photos, Inc.

duced nearly 10 million Southeast Asian refugees, many of whom immigrated to the United States. Among the refugees were thousands of Amerasians, the offspring of American soldiers and Vietnamese women. Spurned by their fathers and most Vietnamese, more than 30,000 Amerasians immigrated to the United States in the 1990s.

The defeat in Vietnam prompted Americans to think differently about foreign affairs and acknowledge the limits of U.S. power abroad. The United States became less willing to plunge into overseas military commitments, a controversial development that conservatives dubbed the "Vietnam syndrome." In 1973 Congress expressed its hostility to undeclared wars like those in Vietnam and Korea by passing the War Powers Act, which required the president to report any use of military force within forty-eight hours and directed hostilities to cease within sixty days unless Congress declared war. On those occasions when Congress did agree to foreign intervention, as in the Persian Gulf

War of 1990–1991, American leaders would insist on obtainable military objectives and careful handling of the media—elements often lacking in Vietnam. Perhaps most important, any future foreign entanglement would be evaluated in terms of its potential for becoming "another Vietnam."

The Vietnam War also distorted American economic and social life. At a total price of over $150 billion, the war siphoned economic resources from domestic needs, added to the deficit, and fueled inflation. The war critically shattered the liberal consensus that had supported the Democratic coalition. Even more serious, the conduct of the war—the lies about American successes on the battlefield, the questionable representation of events in the Gulf of Tonkin, the secret war on Cambodia—spawned deep distrust of government among American citizens. The discrediting of liberalism, the increased cynicism about government, and the growing social turmoil that accompanied the war paved the way for a new era of conservatism.

The Vietnam Veterans' Memorial
Conceived and funded by a small group of veterans, the Vietnam Veterans' Memorial was dedicated in Washington, D.C., in November 1982. The memorial, designed by Maya Ling Lin, a Yale architecture student, consists of two walls of black granite inscribed with the names of 58,183 men and women who died in the war. The wall of names has tremendous emotional impact on viewers and has become one of the most popular tourist destinations in the nation's capital.
Peter Marlow/Magnum Photos, Inc.

John Paul Vann: Dissident Patriot

———— ★ ————

THE DIVISIONS CAUSED by the Vietnam War haunted Arlington National Cemetery on June 16, 1972, when three hundred mourners assembled for the funeral of John Paul Vann. "The soldier of the war in Vietnam," Vann had been killed in a helicopter crash in the Central Highlands the week before. Politicians and military leaders closely associated with the war effort were very much in evidence—General William Westmoreland, CIA Director William Colby, the conservative journalist Joseph Alsop, and Secretary of State William Rogers. But so were Daniel Ellsberg, a former Pentagon official who had publicly turned against the war, and Senator Edward Kennedy, another war opponent who had shared Vann's concern about the plight of Vietnamese refugees. In a time of intense polarization over a war that was still going on, this assemblage of hawks and doves was an exceptional sight.

Vann's family also showed the rifts over Vietnam that day. His wife of twenty-six years, Mary Jane, had requested two pieces of music: the upbeat "Colonel Bogie March" from the film *The Bridge on the River Kwai*, one of her husband's favorites, and the haunting antiwar ballad "Where Have All the Flowers Gone?" to express her opposition to the war. One of Vann's sons, twenty-one-year-old Jesse, hated the war so profoundly that he tore his draft card in two at the funeral, placing half of it on his father's casket. He planned to give the other half to President Richard Nixon at the White House ceremony after the funeral, where his father would be presented posthumously with the Presidential Medal of Freedom. Only at the last moment was Jesse talked out of his act of defiance, agreeing that this was, after all, his father's day.

Also at the funeral was *New York Times* reporter Neil Sheehan, who decided at that moment to write a biography of Vann, which he published sixteen years later, *A Bright and Shining Lie*. Sheehan, along with David Halberstam and other reporters, had fallen under Vann's spell during his first tour of duty in Vietnam in 1963, when Vann seemed to be the only American official who was willing to admit that the war was not going well. Sheehan had continued to rely on Vann's outspoken assessments for the rest of the war. "In this war without heroes, this man had been the one compelling figure," Sheehan concluded. "By an obsession, by an unyielding dedication to the war, he had come to personify the American endeavor in Vietnam."

John Paul Vann was an enormously complicated person—a born leader, a visionary, a man who knew no physical fear, but most of all a true believer in America's mission to share democracy with countries "less fortunate" than the United States. His early years were shaped by poverty and lack of opportunity. Born in 1924 to a working-class family in Norfolk, Virginia, he grew up poor during the Great Depression. A colleague later remembered him as a "cocky little red-necked guy with a rural Virginia twang." World War II offered a ticket out; when Vann turned eighteen in 1943, he enlisted and made the army his career. He served with distinction in the Korean War and then took assignments in West Germany and the United States. But in 1959 his service record was stained by accusations of the statutory rape of a fifteen-year-old girl. Even though the army eventually dropped the charges, the scandal effectively prevented him from moving up in the military bureaucracy. Neil Sheehan later concluded that Vann's "moral heroism" in speaking out against the conduct of the war to the seeming detriment of his career was rooted in his awareness that he had nothing to lose, although reporters did not know the full story at the time.

In 1963 the thirty-nine-year-old Lieutenant Colonel Vann was sent to Vietnam, where he served as a senior advisor to a South Vietnamese infantry division in the Mekong Delta. At the battle of Ap Bac he watched his South Vietnamese counterpart purposely refuse to fight the battle the way it had been planned and let the enemy escape. In a moment of epiphany Vann realized that the rosy reports being fed to Saigon and Washington were false, that Saigon suffered from "an institutionalized unwillingness to fight." After unsuccessful attempts to enlighten his superiors, he leaked his meticulously documented assessments to reporters such as Halberstam and Sheehan. His candor won him few friends in the military, and at the end of his tour of duty he was reassigned to the Pentagon. He tried to alert the Joint Chiefs of Staff that the war was not being won, but at the last moment the scheduled briefing was canceled, in large part because the Joint Chiefs did not want to

Planning Strategy
Lieutenant Colonel John P. Vann
(left) shown during his tour of duty
in Vietnam in 1963, discussing a
tactical decision.
U.S. Army Photo/U.S. Department of
Defense, Still Media Records Center,
Washington, DC.

hear his version of the problem. Frustrated and disillusioned, Vann resigned from the army soon afterward and went to work for a civilian defense contractor.

Before long, however, Vann grew restless with stateside life and tried to rejoin the military. Wary of Vann's public criticism of the war, the army refused to accept him. In 1965 Vann found civilian employment with the Agency for International Development in a pacification program to win over the peasants to the South Vietnamese side rather than the National Liberation Front. Arriving just as the major escalation of the war was getting under way, Vann would stay in Vietnam (except for brief trips home) until his death. His honesty and unmatched familiarity with conditions in the countryside led him to conclude that the communists were doing a far better job at appealing to the local population than was the corrupt Saigon government. As he wrote to a friend in 1965, "If I were a lad of eighteen faced with the same choice—whether to support the GVN [Government of Vietnam] or the NLF—and a member of a rural community, I would surely choose the NLF." His concern for winning over the local peasantry made him an outspoken opponent of the heavy bombing inflicted on the Vietnamese countryside to roust Vietcong sympathizers. He also strongly criticized General Westmoreland's strategy of sending in more American troops to wear down the Vietcong in a war

of attrition, arguing that this would be useless without major reforms in the Saigon government.

Despite his role as a gadfly and even though he was now a civilian, Vann assumed more and more responsibility in the day-to-day conduct of the war. In 1971 he was given authority over all the U.S. military forces in the Central Highlands, the equivalent of the position of major general. But by then, according to Sheehan, Vann had "lost his compass." He was no longer able to assess realistically the ability or will of the South Vietnamese to fight without American aid. He continued to insist that the war could be won through pacification and reform in Saigon despite evidence of growing Vietcong strength. When his helicopter went down at Kontum in 1972, he had almost single-handedly saved the Central Highlands from a North Vietnamese offensive. Within six months the United States formally ended its involvement. Two years later Vietnam was reunited under communist rule.

John Paul Vann never wavered in his belief that in Vietnam America's cause was just and its intentions good. He had no quarrel with the war itself, just with the way it was fought. Vann thought he knew the answers, but Saigon and Washington chose not to listen. His life and death serve as a reminder of the complexities of the Vietnam experience: could it ever really have been "won," and what would "winning" have meant? Neil Sheehan is convinced that Vann "died believing he had won his war."

Summary

★

America's involvement in Vietnam lasted nearly thirty years, growing incrementally from one administration to the next. Under Truman, Eisenhower, and Kennedy, the United States threw its support behind the French and later the South Vietnamese government in an effort to contain the communist threat in Asia. Lyndon Johnson escalated the war in 1965 from an ostensibly defensive action to an offensive combat mission. Between 1965 and 1968 sustained bombing attacks on North Vietnam were accompanied by ever larger infusions of U.S. ground troops. But the Tet offensive of January 1968 highlighted the discrepancy between the administration's glowing accounts of the war and its tortuous reality, and marked the beginning of U.S. efforts to disengage from the conflict. Richard Nixon spent another five years trying to end the war, promising Americans "peace with honor." Under his program of Vietnamization Nixon gradually withdrew U.S. troops while secretly bombing and later invading Cambodia in a futile attempt to destroy enemy havens. The final withdrawal of American troops took place in 1973 under the terms of the Paris Peace Accords. The war marked a turning point in U.S. foreign relations, revealing the limitations of American military power in a complex postwar world.

The war also had serious consequences at home, as Americans turned against one another in bitter conflict. Galvanized by opposition to military escalation and the draft, the antiwar movement spread rapidly among college students and other young people who staged a series of mass protests between 1967 and 1971. The spirit of rebellion was not limited to the antiwar movement. The New Left challenged university policies and corporate dominance of society, while the more apolitical counterculture preached personal liberation through sex, drugs, music, and spirituality. As the civil rights struggle moved beyond the South, rising militancy and racial strife divided the movement and fueled white opposition to change. At the same time, however, the new black power movement encouraged racial pride and assertiveness, serving as a model for Mexican Americans, native Americans, and other ethnic groups. The civil rights movement also helped inspire a resurgence of feminism and the birth of the gay liberation movement.

The domestic struggle over the war and other issues divided the Democratic Party, resulting in a Democratic National Convention riven with protest and violence in the summer of 1968. The assassinations of Martin Luther King and Robert Kennedy and a series of urban riots that year further shocked the nation and fueled a growing public desire for law and order. Although antiwar protests continued into the early 1970s, a new mood of conservatism took hold in the country, contributing to the resurgence of the Republican Party under Richard Nixon.

TIMELINE

1946	War begins between French and Vietminh
1950	China and Soviet Union recognize Ho Chi Minh's government
	United States recognizes French-backed government of Bao Dai and sends military aid
1954	French defeat at Dienbienphu
	Geneva Accords partition Vietnam at 17th parallel
1962	Students for a Democratic Society (SDS) founded
1963	Coup ousts Ngo Dinh Diem in South Vietnam
1964	Free Speech Movement at Berkeley
	Gulf of Tonkin Resolution authorizes military action in Vietnam
1965	Malcolm X assassinated
	Operation Rolling Thunder escalates war through mass bombing campaigns
	First U.S. combat troops arrive in Vietnam
	Race riot in the Watts district of Los Angeles
1966	National Organization for Women (NOW) founded
	Stokely Carmichael proclaims black power
1967	Hippie counterculture's "Summer of Love"
	Race riots in Detroit and Newark
1968	Tet offensive dashes American hopes of victory
	Martin Luther King Jr. assassinated
	Robert F. Kennedy assassinated
	Riot at Democratic National Convention in Chicago
	Women's liberation movement emerges
1969	Stonewall riot leads to gay liberation movement
	Vietnam moratorium
	American Indian Movement seizes Alcatraz
1970	Nixon orders invasion of Cambodia; renewed antiwar protests
	Killings at Kent State and Jackson State
1972	Nixon visits People's Republic of China
	SALT I Treaty with Soviet Union
	Christmas bombings of Hanoi and Haiphong
1973	Paris Peace Accords
	War Powers Act
1975	Fall of Saigon

Suggested Readings

Among the best general accounts of the Vietnam War are George Herring, *America's Longest War* (3rd ed., 1996); Stanley Karnow, *Vietnam: A History* (rev. ed., 1991); and Marilyn Young, *The Vietnam Wars, 1945–1990* (1991). Guenter Lewy offers a controversial defense of American involvement in *America in Vietnam* (1978).

Into the Quagmire, 1945–1968

The origins of American involvement in Vietnam are covered in Loren Baritz, *Backfire: A History of How American Culture Led Us into Vietnam* (1985); Larry Berman, *Planning a Tragedy* (1982) and *Lyndon Johnson's War* (1989); Robert Buzzanco, *Masters of War* (1996); Lloyd Gardner, *Approaching Vietnam* (1988); David Halberstam, *The Making of a Quagmire* (rev. ed., 1988); and Brian VanDeMark, *Into the Quagmire* (1991). A fascinating insight into Vietnam policy making in the 1960s can be found in Neil Sheehan, *The Pentagon Papers* (1971). Secretary of Defense Robert McNamara offers an insider's view and belated apologia in *In Retrospect* (1995).

For a sense of what the war felt like to the soldiers who fought it, see Mark Baker, *Nam* (1982); Philip Caputo, *Rumor of War* (1977); Michael Herr, *Dispatches* (1977); Tim O'Brien, *If I Die in a Combat Zone* (1973); and Ron Kovic, *Born on the Fourth of July* (1976). Wallace Terry, *Bloods* (1984), surveys the experiences of black veterans, and Keith Walker, *A Piece of My Heart* (1985), introduces the often forgotten stories of the women who served in Vietnam. Christian G. Appy offers a class analysis of the Vietnam experience in *Working-Class War* (1993). Neil Sheehan surveys the entire Vietnam experience through the life of career soldier John Paul Vann in *A Bright and Shining Lie* (1988).

The Challenge of Youth, 1962–1970

There are a growing number of survey works on the 1960s, including David Steigerwald, *The Sixties and the End of Modern America* (1995); Terry Anderson, *The Movement and the Sixties* (1994); David Farber, *The Age of Great Dreams: America in the 1960s* (1994); Todd Gitlin, *The Sixties: Years of Hope, Days of Rage* (1987); and Allen J. Matusow, *The Unraveling of America* (1984).

The student activism of the 1960s is the subject of dozens of eyewitness accounts and scholarly works. See Kenneth Keniston, *The Uncommitted* (1965) and *Young Radicals* (1969); Nathan Glazer, *Remembering the Answers* (1970); and Philip Slater, *The Pursuit of Loneliness* (1970). On student revolt see W. J. Rorabaugh, *Berkeley at War* (1989); Kirkpatrick Sale, *SDS* (1973); Wini Breines, *Community and Organization in the New Left, 1962–1968* (1982); and James Miller, *Democracy Is in the Streets* (1987). The definitive book on the antiwar movement is Charles DeBenedetti, with Charles Chatfield, *An American Ordeal* (1990).

Morris Dickstein, *Gates of Eden* (1977), is an excellent account of cultural developments in the 1960s. Other sources include Theodore Roszak, *The Making of a Counter-Culture* (1969); and Charles Reich, *The Greening of America* (1970). Gerald Howard, ed., *The Sixties* (1982), is a good anthology of the decade's art, politics, and culture. Philip Norman, *Shout! The Beatles in Their Generation* (1981), and Jon Weiner, *Come Together: John Lennon in His Times* (1984), cover developments in popular music.

Major texts of the black power movement include Stokely Carmichael and Charles Hamilton, *Black Power* (1967); James Baldwin, *The Fire Next Time* (1963); and Eldridge Cleaver, *Soul on Ice* (1968). *The Autobiography of Malcolm X* (cowritten with Alex Haley, 1966) has become a black literary classic; it can be supplemented by Michael Eric Dyson, *Making Malcolm: The Myth and Meaning of Malcolm X* (1995). William L. Van Deburg, *New Day in Babylon* (1992), provides a general historical account of the black power movement.

Report of the National Advisory Commission on Civil Disorders (1968) analyzes the decade's major race riots. See also Joe R. Feagin and Harlan Hahn, *Ghetto Revolts* (1973), and Robert Fogelson, *Violence as Protest* (1971). Sidney Fine's book on the Detroit riot, *Violence in the Model City* (1989), provides the most thorough historical treatment of race rioting in this period.

Carlos Muñoz Jr., *Youth, Identity and Power: The Chicano Movement* (1989), and Juan Gomez-Quiñones, *Chicano Politics* (1990), examine the rise of the Chicano movement in the 1960s. Peter Matthiessen, *In the Spirit of Crazy Horse* (1983), chronicles the American Indian Movement's ongoing conflict with the FBI and the federal government. Martin Duberman, *Stonewall* (1993), looks at the birth of the gay movement in the late 1960s.

General histories of women's activism in the 1960s include Cynthia Harrison, *On Account of Sex: The Politics of Women's Issues, 1945–1968* (1988), and Susan M. Hartmann, *From Margin to Mainstream: American Women and Politics since 1960* (1989). The revival of feminism is examined in Jo Freeman, *The Politics of Women's Liberation* (1975), and Judith Hole and Ellen Levine, *The Rebirth of Feminism* (1971). Sara Evans, *Personal Politics* (1979), traces the roots of feminism in the civil rights movement and the New Left.

The Long Road Home, 1968–1975

The Tet offensive is the subject of Don Oberdoffer's *Tet! The Turning Point in the Vietnam War* (1971). The domestic events of 1968 are covered in David Caute, *The Year of the Barricades* (1968), and David Farber, *Chicago '68* (1988). Norman Mailer provides a contemporary view of the national political conventions in *Miami and the Siege of Chicago* (1968). William C. Berman, *America's Right Turn* (2nd ed., 1998), chronicles the rightward shift in politics. Kevin Phillips, *The Emerging Republican Majority* (1969), and Richard Scammon and Ben J. Wattenberg, *The Real Majority* (1970), describe the voters Richard Nixon tried to reach. Dan Carter, *The Politics of Rage* (1996), examines the political career of George Wallace.

William Bundy, *The Tangled Web* (1998), and Robert S. Litwak, *Détente and the Nixon Doctrine* (1984), are overviews of Nixon's foreign policy. On his Vietnam policy see the general works on Vietnam listed above as well as the highly critical study by William Shawcross, *Sideshow: Kissinger, Nixon, and the Destruction of Cambodia* (1979). An account of the My Lai massacre can be found in Seymour Hersh, *Cover-Up* (1972). Robert Jay Lifton, *Home from the War* (1973); Paul Starr, *The Discarded Army* (1973); and Lawrence Baskir and William A. Strauss, *Chance and Circumstance*, discuss the problems of returning Vietnam veterans.

Chapter 30

---★---

The Lean Years,
1969–1980

The Nixon Years
The Republican Domestic Agenda
The 1972 Election
Watergate

The Economic Downturn
The Energy Crisis
Economic Woes

Reform and Reaction in the 1970s
The New Activism: Environmental and Consumer
  Movements
Challenges to Tradition: The Women's Movement
  and Gay Rights
Racial Minorities
The Politics of Resentment

From Ford to Reagan
Ford's Caretaker Presidency
Jimmy Carter: The Outsider as President
The Reagan Revolution

AS THE VIETNAM War ended, Americans turned inward to attend to their own needs and interests, just as they had done in the years after World Wars I and II. But the 1970s, unlike the 1920s and 1950s, were not a time of postwar prosperity and optimism. To many Americans the withdrawal from Vietnam represented a humiliating defeat that underscored the diminished role of U.S. power in the international arena. Growing economic problems in the early 1970s—rising oil prices, runaway inflation, declining productivity, and stagnating incomes—compounded that sense of disillusionment. In the mid-1970s industrial competition abroad, together with the newly asserted independence of the oil-producing Arab nations, produced a severe economic crisis at home. As the dollar plummeted on the world market and the trade deficit soared, the overwhelming postwar economic superiority of the United States came to an end.

Americans also grew disenchanted with political leadership in the 1970s as one public official after another resigned for misconduct, including (for the first time in history) the president, Richard Nixon. The Watergate scandal, which forced Nixon's resignation, became the defining experience of the decade, a symbol of the growing cynicism and lack of confidence that pervaded the nation in the 1970s. In the wake of Watergate, the lackluster administrations of Gerald Ford and Jimmy Carter contributed to Americans' growing skepticism about government and its capacity to improve people's lives.

Earth Day
One of the most dynamic areas of social activism in the 1960s and 1970s was the environmental movement, which addressed issues such as wilderness preservation, energy policy, and toxic dumping. The growing significance of this movement was demonstrated on Earth Day, May 4, 1970, when thousands gathered in New York (shown here) and in other cities and towns across the country to register their concern for the endangered planet.
Ken Regan.

But the 1970s was a paradoxical decade: in the midst of growing disaffection with national politics was ongoing commitment to social change. Social movements such as feminism and environmentalism had their greatest impact in the 1970s. But like the civil rights and anti-war movements of the 1960s, social activism in the 1970s stirred fears and uncertainty among some blue-collar and middle-class Americans. Furthermore, the darkening economic climate undercut the sense of social generosity that had characterized the 1960s and fueled what political commentator Alan Crawford called a "politics of resentment." The 1970s was thus a complex and transitional decade in which expanding social activism helped spur a conservative reaction that would influence the nation for the next several decades.

The Nixon Years

——————★——————

With his election to the presidency in 1968, Richard Nixon set the stage for the new conservatism. His policies heralded a long-term Republican effort to trim back the Great Society, shifting a number of federal responsibilities back to the states. But unlike his Republican successors, Nixon actively embraced the use of federal power—within limits—to uphold government responsibility for social welfare, environmental protection, and economic stability. While maintaining a strong federal government, he hoped to reduce governmental inefficiency through better management. Ultimately, however, Nixon's suspicion of his political opponents and his ruthless efforts in the 1972 campaign led to his downfall in the Watergate scandal, a political drama that consumed the nation.

The Republican Domestic Agenda

In a 1968 campaign pledge to "the average American," Nixon vowed to "reverse the flow of power and resources from the states and communities to Washington and start power and resources flowing back . . . to the people." Nixon's New Federalism marked a retreat from the long-term consolidation of federal power that had characterized American political life since the New Deal. One of its hallmarks was the 1972 program of *revenue sharing*, which distributed a portion of federal tax revenues to the states as block grants to be spent as state officials saw fit. In subsequent years revenue sharing would become a key Republican strategy for reducing federal social programs and bureaucracy.

Nixon also worked to scale down certain government programs that had grown dramatically during the Johnson administration. Viewing many Democratic social programs as bloated and inefficient, he reduced funding for most of the War on Poverty and dismantled the Office of Economic Opportunity altogether in 1971. Nixon also *impounded* (refused to spend) billions of dollars appropriated by Congress for urban renewal, pollution control, and other environmental initiatives. Although his administration claimed to support civil rights, Nixon adopted a cautious approach toward racial issues so as not to alienate southern white voters. In a leaked 1970 memo, presidential advisor Daniel Patrick Moynihan, a Democrat who had joined the Nixon White House, suggested that "the issue of race could benefit from a period of benign neglect"—a revelation that scandalized liberals and embarrassed the administration. Nixon also vetoed a 1971 bill to establish a comprehensive national child-care system, fearing that such "communal approaches to child rearing" would "Sovietize" American children.

As an alternative to Democratic social legislation, the administration put forward its own antipoverty program in an ambitious attempt to overhaul the jerry-built welfare system. In 1969, following the advice of Moynihan, Nixon proposed a Family Assistance Plan that would provide a family of four a small but guaranteed annual income. The appeal of this proposal lay in its simplicity: it would eliminate the multiple layers of bureaucrats (caseworkers, local and state officials, and federal employees) who administered Aid to Families with Dependent Children (AFDC), the nation's largest welfare program. But the bill floundered in the Senate: conservatives attacked it for putting the federal government too deeply into the welfare business, and liberals and social welfare activists opposed it for not going far enough. Welfare reform would remain a contentious political issue for the next twenty-five years.

Although Nixon sought to streamline or scale back certain antipoverty programs, he actively expanded federal entitlement programs and the regulatory apparatus. Facing Democratic majorities in both houses of Congress, Nixon agreed to the growth of major entitlement programs such as Medicare, Medicaid, and Social Security. In 1970, he signed a bill establishing the Environmental Protection Agency (EPA) to coordinate the growing federal responsibilities for environmental action. In 1972, to monitor the health and safety of workers and consumers, Nixon approved legislation creating the Occupational Safety and Health Administration (OSHA) and the Consumer Products Safety Commission. As inflation spiraled upward in 1971, he also made use of the federal powers granted under the Economic Stabilization Act of 1970 to institute wage and price controls, the first such measures since World War II. Although Nixon offered only lukewarm support for much of this legislation, his administration generally continued the expansion of federal power that had been under way since the New Deal.

Nixon demonstrated his commitment to conservative social values most clearly with his appointments to the Supreme Court. One of his first acts was to nominate the conservative Warren Burger to replace retired Chief Justice Earl Warren in the spring of 1969. Over the next five years, Nixon named three more Supreme Court justices—Harry Blackmun, Lewis F. Powell Jr., and William Rehnquist—the last becoming the leading conservative force on the Court through the 1990s.

Conservative judges did not always give Nixon the decisions he wanted. Despite attempts by the Justice Department to halt further desegregation in the face of determined white opposition, the Court ordered busing to achieve racial balance in the case of *Swann v. Charlotte-Mecklenburg Board of Education* (1971). In *Furman v. Georgia* (1972) the Supreme Court issued strict guidelines restricting the implementation of capital punishment, although it did not rule the death penalty unconstitutional. And in the controversial 1973 case of *Roe v. Wade*, Justice Harry Blackmun wrote the decision striking down Texas and Georgia laws prohibiting abortion.

The 1972 Election

Nixon's reelection in 1972 was never much in doubt. In May, the threat of a conservative third-party challenge from Alabama's governor, George Wallace, ended abruptly when an assailant in a suburban Maryland shopping mall shot Wallace, paralyzing him from the waist down. With Wallace out of the picture, Nixon's strategy of wooing southern white voters away from the Democrats got a boost. Nixon also benefited from the disarray in the Democratic Party, which was deeply divided over Vietnam and civil rights. After the 1968 Chicago convention the party had changed its way of selecting delegates and candidates, pledging to include "minority groups, young people and women in reasonable relationship to their presence in the population." The ratification of the Twenty-sixth Amendment in 1971, lowering the national voting age to eighteen, reinforced the power of the youth vote. Tensions soon arose between those groups and the old-line Democratic officeholders and labor union leaders who had formerly dominated the party.

Senator George McGovern of South Dakota, a noted liberal and an outspoken opponent of the Vietnam War, reaped the greatest benefit from the new Democratic guidelines. By 1972 he was supported by an army of antiwar activists who blitzed precinct caucuses and won delegate commitments far beyond his support among voters. In the past, an alliance of party bosses and union leaders almost certainly would have rejected an upstart candidate such as McGovern, but few old-line leaders qualified as delegates to the nominating convention under the changed rules. Typical of the new

Richard Nixon on the Campaign Trail
One of the most resilient political figures in American history, Richard Nixon won the presidential elections of 1968 and 1972 after losing campaigns for president in 1960 and for governor of California in 1962. Even after his resignation in 1974, Nixon reemerged as an elder statesman and was frequently consulted for his views on foreign affairs.
Charles Moore/Black Star.

Democratic look, the black minister and civil rights veteran Jesse Jackson replaced Mayor Richard Daley of Chicago as head of the Illinois delegation.

McGovern's campaign against Nixon was an unrelieved disaster. Surprised to learn that his running mate, Senator Thomas F. Eagleton of Missouri, had undergone electroshock therapy for depression some years earlier, McGovern first supported him "1,000 percent," then abruptly insisted that he quit the ticket. Sargent Shriver, the former head of the Peace Corps and the Office of Economic Opportunity, replaced Eagleton, but McGovern's waffling made him appear weak and indecisive. Moreover, he was far too liberal for many traditional Democrats, who rejected his ill-defined proposals for welfare reform, did not rally around his calls for unilateral withdrawal from Vietnam, and ignored his charges that the Nixon administration had corruptly abused its power.

Nixon's campaign took full advantage of McGovern's weaknesses. Although the war in Vietnam dragged on, Nixon's Vietnamization policy had reduced weekly American combat deaths from three hundred in 1968 to almost none in 1972. Henry Kissinger's premature declaration that "peace is at hand" raised hopes for a negotiated settlement (see Chapter 29). Not only did those initiatives rob the Democrats of their greatest appeal—their antiwar stance—but an improving economy further favored the Republicans.

Nixon won handily, receiving nearly 61 percent of the popular vote and carrying every state except Massachusetts and the District of Columbia. The Democrats maintained control of both houses of Congress, but McGovern's showing pointed to a significant erosion of the traditional Democratic coalition: he received only 18 percent of the southern white Protestant vote and 38 percent of the big-city Catholic vote. Only blacks, Jews, and low-income voters remained loyal.

Watergate

Watergate, the great constitutional crisis of the early 1970s, was a direct result of Nixon's ruthless political tactics, his secretive style of governing, and his obsession with the antiwar movement. Many Americans saw Watergate as consisting of only the evil deeds of one person (Richard Nixon) and one unlawful act (obstruction of justice). But Watergate was not an isolated incident; it was part of a broad pattern of illegality and misuse of power that flourished in the crisis atmosphere of the Vietnam War.

Before the Break-In. The new administration began to stretch the boundaries of the law under the guise of national security just four months into Nixon's first term. In the spring of 1969, after the *New York Times* reported the secret bombing of Cambodia, the White House asked the FBI to find out who had leaked the story. Without seeking a warrant, the FBI illegally tapped the phone conversations of several journalists and low-level staffers on the National Security Council. The source of the leak was never found, but the precedent for warrantless surveillance had been set.

Over the next several years the Nixon administration would repeatedly invoke supposed domestic threats to national security to justify its actions. In 1970 the White House asked Tom Huston, a former army intelligence officer, to draw up an extensive plan for secret domestic counterintelligence—opening mail, tapping phones, and arranging break-ins—to discredit the antiwar movement. President Nixon approved the scheme, which involved coordinated efforts by the FBI, CIA, and Justice Department. FBI director J. Edgar Hoover, however, refused to cooperate with other government agencies in activities that he interpreted as being exclusively within the domain of the FBI.

Nixon's obsession with the antiwar movement grew in June 1971, when Daniel Ellsberg, a former Defense department analyst who had become disillusioned with the war, leaked the so-called Pentagon Papers to the *New York Times.* Commissioned by Secretary of Defense Robert McNamara in 1967, the Pentagon Papers was a classified study of American involvement in Vietnam that included hundreds of government documents from the Kennedy and Johnson years. The report detailed so many American blunders and misjudgments that McNamara had commented on first reading it, "You know, they could hang people for what is in there." In a subsequent court challenge the Nixon administration attempted to block publication of the Pentagon Papers. In an effort to discredit Ellsberg, White House underlings broke into his psychiatrist's office to look for damaging information. The burglars failed to turn up anything embarrassing on Ellsberg, and the judge dismissed the pending case against him when the break-in was revealed.

In another abuse of presidential power committed prior to the 1972 campaign, the White House established a clandestine intelligence group led by former CIA agents G. Gordon Liddy and Howard Hunt. Known as the "plumbers" because they were supposed to plug leaks of government information, they relied on tactics such as using the Internal Revenue Service and other agencies to harass opponents of the administration named on an "enemies list" drawn up by the presidential counsel John Dean. A major target of the plumbers was the Democratic Party, whose front-running candidate, Senator Edmund Muskie of Maine, was the object of several "dirty tricks" during the primaries. For example, white New Hampshire voters were awakened in the middle of the night by callers from the "Harlem for Muskie" committee, and posters appeared in Florida saying "Help Muskie in Busing More Children Now." Most damaging was a letter to a New Hampshire newspaper forged by one of Nixon's campaign aides accusing Muskie of ethnic insensitivity to French Canadians. Together those dirty tricks derailed Muskie's primary campaign.

These secret and highly questionable activities were financed by massive illegal fundraising efforts by the Committee to Re-Elect the President (known as CREEP), which was headed by Attorney General John Mitchell. In soliciting funds from major corporations, Nixon's fundraisers used high-pressure tactics that included implied threats of federal tax audits and other punitive measures for companies that failed to contribute. CREEP subsequently raised over $20 million, a portion of which was used to finance various dirty tricks, including the break-in that led to the Watergate scandal.

The Break-In. Early on the morning of June 17, 1972, an alert security guard noticed something amiss at the headquarters of the Democratic National Committee at the Watergate apartment complex in Washington. Five men carrying cameras, wiretapping equipment, and a large amount of cash were arrested; two accomplices were apprehended soon afterward. Three of the accused men had ties either to the White House or to CREEP; the remaining four, all from Miami, had been involved in CIA-linked anti-Castro activities. Nixon's press secretary, Ronald Ziegler, promptly dismissed the break-in as a "third-rate burglary attempt." Nixon soon claimed that White House counsel John Dean had conducted a full investigation of the incident (no such investigation ever took place) and stated categorically that "no one on the White House staff, no one in this administration, presently employed, was involved in this very bizarre incident." The cover-up had begun.

Subsequent investigations revealed that six days after the break-in the president had ordered his chief of staff, H. R. Haldeman, to instruct the CIA to tell the FBI not to probe too deeply into connections between the White House and the burglars. That action constituted obstruction of justice. Nixon apparently feared that the Watergate burglary would lead to an investigation of the dubious fundraising methods and political sabotage practiced by his reelection committee.

The Watergate burglars were convicted in January 1973. With Nixon's approval, John Dean tried to buy their continued silence with $400,000 in hush money and hints of presidential pardons. However, prodded by the presiding judge, John Sirica, one of the convicted burglars began to talk. Two tenacious investigative reporters at the *Washington Post,* Carl Bernstein and Bob Woodward, exposed the attempted cover-up and traced it back to the White House. In February the Senate voted 77 to 0 to establish a select committee to investigate the scandal. Dean started to get nervous, and in March 1973 he warned Nixon, referring to the cover-up, that "there is a cancer within, close to the presidency, that is growing." In April Nixon accepted the resignations of Haldeman, Assistant Secretary of Commerce Jeb Stuart Magruder, and Chief Domestic Advisor John Ehrlichman, all of whom had been implicated in the cover-up. He also fired Dean, who had agreed to testify in the case in exchange for immunity from prosecution. As evidence mounted linking the scandal directly with the White House, press secretary Ziegler declared all previous statements on Watergate "inoperative."

In May the Senate Watergate Committee, chaired by Senator Sam Ervin of North Carolina, began nationally televised hearings that riveted the nation for the next six months. On June 14 Magruder testified before the committee, confessing his guilt and implicating Attorney General John Mitchell, Dean, and others in the Water-

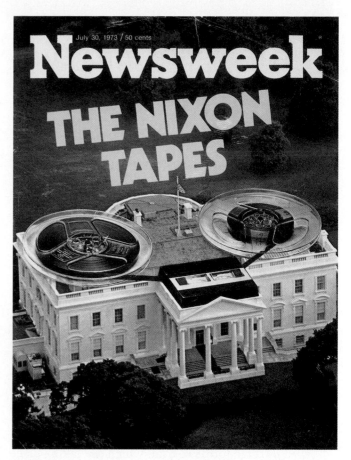

Watergate
In July 1973, White House aide Alexander Butterfield testified before the Senate Watergate Committee that all oval office telephone communications had been recorded on a secret taping system. Although Nixon tried in vain to suppress the tapes by claiming executive privilege, their eventual release—including statements directly implicating the president in the Watergate cover-up—led to Nixon's resignation in August of 1974.
©1973 Wally McNamee & Matt Sultan/Newsweek Inc. All rights reserved. Reprinted with permission.

gate affair. In five days of riveting testimony in late June, Dean implicated Nixon in the cover-up (see Voices from Abroad, "Watergate and Due Process," p. 980). Even more startling testimony came from an aide who revealed that Nixon had a secret taping system in the Oval Office. "I was hoping you fellows wouldn't ask me about that," Alexander Butterfield sheepishly told the committee. Until the existence of the tapes was disclosed, it had been Dean's word against Nixon's; now finding out what had actually been said seemed possible.

The president steadfastly "stonewalled" the committee's demand that he surrender the tapes, citing executive privilege and national security. Archibald Cox, a special prosecutor appointed by Nixon to investigate the Watergate events, successfully petitioned a lower federal court to order the president to hand over the tapes. Still Nixon refused to comply, ordering Attorney General Elliott Richardson to fire Cox. Richardson

Watergate and Due Process

━━━━━━━★━━━━━━━

Foreign reaction to the Watergate scandal included both praise and condemnation of America's handling of the crisis. One of the sharpest criticisms came from the venerable British daily newspaper the Times (London), which ran an editorial in 1973 attacking the American press for publishing highly prejudicial material, including damaging testimony before the Senate investigating committee by White House counsel John Dean.

The President of the United States is in the unenviable position of being tried by his fellow countrymen in three different forums, each of which has its own particular deficiencies. . . . What Mr. Nixon is now receiving is a Washington variant of lynch law, and that while he may or may not be innocent, he may never be proved guilty by a process so clearly lacking in justice.

The three forms of trial, which are taking place simultaneously, are the Ervin Committee in the Senate . . . the Grand Jury, and the media, including *The New York Times* and the *Washington Post*.

The Ervin Committee is investigating precisely because the Senate thought that the due process of law was working too slowly. The Senators are trying to ask fair and relevant questions. . . . Yet Senate committees are not courts: they do not have an adversary procedure; they do not have cross examination by Counsel for the accused; they can take and certainly do take hearsay evidence. . . . The enormous publicity given to hearsay evidence in televised hearings is so prejudicial that it alone would seem to preclude the possibility of fair trial for any accused, even including the President himself if there were impeachment proceedings.

The second tribunal is the Grand Jury. No student of British law will forget that we abandoned the Grand Jury procedure because of its notorious weaknesses as an instrument of justice. Grand Jury proceedings provide the prosecutor with opportunities to introduce prejudicial evidence, which would not be admissible in a trial. The Watergate Grand Jury proceedings have been held in camera but have been widely leaked. The public has therefore a partial and unreliable account of these proceedings; that must be more damaging to the administration of justice than if there were a full account or no account at all. . . .

The third tribunal is the press, with television. . . . The American press, and particularly the *Washington Post*, deserve their full credit for forcing the Watergate affair into the open. They are however now publishing vast quantities of prejudicial matter, that would be contempt under British law, which again must tend to prejudice the fair trial of any accused, or, if it came to that, of the President. . . .

What the President is accused of that really matters is to have interfered with the course of justice. That would be as grave an offence as a President could commit. Yet are not the Senate committee who are taking and publishing hearsay evidence to the whole country also interfering with the course of justice? . . .

And what about the press? . . . How can one justify the decision to publish the Dean leak? . . . Here is a piece of wholly suspect evidence—unsworn, unverified, not cross-examined, contradicting previous evidence, subject to none of the safeguards of due process, given by a man who may be bargaining for his freedom. How can the newspapers defend themselves from the very charge that they are bringing against the President, the charge of making a fair trial impossible, if they now publish evidence so damning and so doubtful with all the weight of authority that their publication gives?

───────────

Source: Times (London) editorial, June 5, 1973, 17.

refused and resigned in protest, as did Assistant Attorney General William Ruckelshaus. Solicitor General Robert Bork, third in command in the Justice department, finally carried out his order, but the action backfired. The "Saturday Night Massacre" sparked public outrage and renewed demands for release of the tapes.

After additional federal subpoenas the following spring, Nixon released heavily edited transcripts of the tapes, whose most frequent words seemed to be "expletive deleted," a phrase necessitated by the extensive profanity on the tapes. Senate Republican leader Hugh Scott called the edited transcripts "deplorable, disgusting, shabby, immoral." Most suspicious was an eighteen-minute gap in the tape of a crucial meeting of Nixon, Haldeman, and Ehrlichman on June 20, 1972, three days after the break-in.

The Final Days. The Watergate affair moved into its final phase in the summer of 1974, when a committee of the House of Representatives convened impeachment hearings. On July 30 seven Republicans joined the Democratic majority to vote three articles of impeachment against Richard Nixon: obstruction of justice, abuse of power, and subverting the Constitution. Two days later the Supreme Court ruled unanimously that Nixon had no right to claim executive privilege as a justification for refusing to turn over additional tapes. Under pressure, on August 5 Nixon released the unexpurgated tapes, which contained shocking evidence (the so-called smoking gun) that he had ordered the cover-up as early as six days after the break-in. In effect, the president had been lying to the American people since that time. A delegation of the most senior members of Congress, led by Senator Barry Goldwater, informed the president that no more than fifteen senators still supported him. Facing certain conviction in a Senate trial, on August 9, 1974, Nixon became the first U.S. president to resign.

The next day Vice-President Gerald Ford was sworn in as president. Ford, a former Michigan congressman and House minority leader, had replaced Spiro Agnew in 1973 after Agnew resigned under indictment for accepting kickbacks on construction contracts while serving as governor of Maryland and vice-president. The transfer of power from Nixon to Ford went remarkably smoothly. A month later, however, Ford stunned the nation by granting a "full, free, and absolute" pardon of Nixon "for all offenses he had committed or might have committed during his presidency." Ford took that action, he said, to spare the country the agony of reliving Watergate. While Nixon retired to his estate in San Clemente, California, twenty-five members of his administration went to prison, including Nixon's closest advisors, H. R. Haldeman, John Ehrlichman, and John Mitchell. Named only as an "unindicted co-conspirator" in their trials, Nixon refused to admit guilt for what had happened, conceding only that Watergate represented an error of judgment.

The Aftermath. In response to the abuses of the Nixon administration, Congress adopted several reforms to contain the power of what historian Arthur M. Schlesinger Jr. called "the imperial presidency." In 1974 a strengthened Freedom of Information Act gave citizens greater access to files that federal government agencies had amassed on them. The 1974 Congressional Budget and Impoundment Control Act restricted the president's authority to impound federal funds (that is, to refuse to spend money appropriated by Congress for programs opposed by the White House). The Fair Campaign Practices Act of 1974 limited campaign contributions and provided for stricter accountability and public financing of presidential campaigns. Finally, in cases of alleged criminal activity in the executive branch, the Independent Counsel Act of 1978 required the attorney general to call on a panel of three federal judges to appoint a special prosecutor—thus precluding future "Saturday Night Massacres."

Perhaps the most significant legacy of Watergate, however, was the wave of cynicism that swept the country in its wake. Beginning with Lyndon Johnson's "credibility gap" in the Vietnam War, public distrust of government had risen steadily with the disclosure of Nixon's secret bombing of Cambodia and the illegal surveillance and harassment of antiwar protesters and other political opponents. The saga of Watergate seemed to confirm the suspicions of many Americans that politicians were hopelessly corrupt and that the federal government was out of control. Ironically, some of the post-Watergate legislation intended to curb political abuses ended up further undermining public confidence. In the case of the Fair Campaign Practices Act, which allowed an unlimited number of political action committees (PACs) to donate up to $5,000 per candidate, corporations and lobbying groups found they could actually increase their political influence by making multiple donations. By the end of the decade close to 3,000 PACs were playing an increasingly pivotal—and some would argue unethical—role in national elections. The Independent Counsel Act, which would be invoked twenty-one times between 1978 and 1999, revealed a string of political scandals in both parties and raised doubts about the political "independence" of some of the appointed prosecutors. Such measures fueled public cynicism about politics for the foreseeable future.

The Economic Downturn

Economic difficulties compounded Americans' political disillusionment. After twenty-five years of world leadership, the economic dominance of the United States had begun to fade. Growing international demands for natural resources, particularly oil, and unstable access to foreign supplies wreaked havoc with the domestic economy. At the same time, foreign competitors were successfully expanding their share of the world market, edging out American-made products. The result was a sharp downturn in the economy that marked the end of America's overwhelming economic superiority in the postwar era.

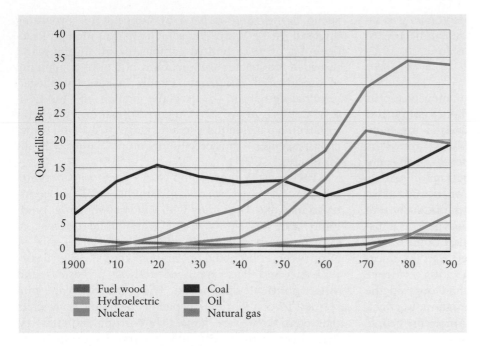

FIGURE 30.1
U.S. Energy Consumption,
1900–1990
Coal was the nation's primary source of
energy until the 1950s, when oil and natural gas became the dominant fuels. The
use of nuclear and hydroelectric power
also rose substantially in the postwar era.
Since the late 1970s fuel-efficient
automobiles and conservation measures
have reduced total energy use.

The Energy Crisis

"Without oil," Interior Secretary Harold Ickes had
noted back in 1933, "American civilization as we know
it could not exist." That continues to be true today,
when not only the United States but the entire modern
world lives in a hydrocarbon age, dependent on petroleum and its by-products. In the twentieth century, oil
supplanted coal as the main energy source for the
industrial world because it was cheaper, cleaner, and
more abundant (Figure 30.1). Between 1949 and 1972,
world energy consumption more than tripled, and the
demand for oil increased more than five and a half
times. Access to oil, especially at the low prices that
prevailed in the 1950s and 1960s, fostered rapid economic growth and rising standards of living in most of
the world, especially in the United States.

Until well into the twentieth century, the United
States was the world's leading producer and consumer
of oil. During World War II, America still produced
two-thirds of the world's oil, but by 1972 its share had
fallen to only 22 percent, even though domestic production continued to rise. By the late 1960s the United
States was buying more and more oil on the world market to keep up with shrinking domestic reserves and
growing demand.

The imported oil came primarily from the Middle
East, where production increased a stupendous 1,500
percent in the twenty-five years after World War II. The
rise of nationalism and the corresponding decline of
colonialism in the postwar era had encouraged Persian
Gulf nations to wrest control of the industry from the
European and American oil companies that had previously dominated petroleum exploration and production

in that region, reaping enormous profits along the way.
In 1960 oil-producing countries in the Third World
formed the Organization of Petroleum Exporting Countries (OPEC) in an attempt to exercise more control over
the world oil market. Five of the founding countries—
the Middle Eastern states of Saudi Arabia, Kuwait, Iran,
and Iraq, plus Venezuela—were the source of more than
80 percent of the world's crude oil exports. In 1960 the
oil industry was in the middle of a twenty-year period of
surplus capacity, and prices stayed low.

In the early 1970s, however, the balance shifted.
Several trends—a sharp increase in worldwide demand,
the end of excess capacity, political instability in the
Middle East, the shift of the United States from a net
exporter to a net importer of oil—came together to set
the stage for what would soon be OPEC's "golden age."
The year 1973 was the turning point. Between 1973 and
1975 OPEC deliberately raised the price of a barrel of
oil from $3 to $12. By the end of the decade the price
had peaked at $34 a barrel. Because the United States
depended heavily on Middle Eastern oil, the price rise
set off furious inflation.

OPEC members also found that oil could be used as
a weapon in global politics. In 1973 OPEC instituted an
oil embargo against the United States, Western Europe,
and Japan, in retaliation for their aid to Israel during
the Yom Kippur War. (The conflict had begun earlier
that year on October 6, Yom Kippur—the holiest day in
Judaism—when Egypt and Syria invaded Israel in an
attempt to retake lands occupied by Israel in the Six
Day War of 1967.) The embargo, which lasted until
1974, forced the United States to scramble to meet its
domestic energy needs. Americans either had to curtail
their driving or had to spend long hours in line at the

pumps; gas prices climbed 40 percent in a matter of months. A national speed limit of 55 miles per hour was instituted to conserve fuel.

Drivers wanted to buy more fuel-efficient cars, but the U.S. automobile industry had little to offer except "gas-guzzlers" built to run on cheap gasoline. Soon the domestic auto industry was in a slump as Americans bought cheaper, more fuel-efficient foreign cars, primarily those manufactured in Japan and West Germany. Since the United States owed much of its twentieth-century prosperity to the automobile (one in six jobs was tied directly or indirectly to the auto industry in the 1970s), this downturn had profound implications for the American economy. Moreover, the energy crisis was an enormous shock to the American psyche. Suddenly Americans felt like hostages to economic forces beyond their control.

Economic Woes

While the energy crisis dealt a swift blow to the U.S. economy, a series of long-term economic developments had equally damaging results. The high cost of the Vietnam War and the Great Society had contributed to a steadily growing federal deficit and spiraling inflation. In the industrial sector growing competition from the reviving economies of West Germany and Japan reduced demand for American goods worldwide. In 1955 American-made goods had accounted for 32 percent of all imports by major capitalist countries; by 1970 U.S. products accounted for only 18 percent of the total, and the percentage continued to decline in the 1970s. As a result, in 1971 the dollar fell to its lowest level on the world market since 1949, and the United States posted its first trade deficit in almost a century.

Nixon's Remedies. That year, with the 1972 election looming, Nixon took several bold steps to turn the economy around and avoid a recession. To stem the decline in currency and trade, he suspended the 1944 Bretton Woods system, one of the pillars of the postwar economic order (see Chapter 28). Once again, the dollar would fluctuate in relation to the price of an ounce of gold, which increased from its former set price of $35 to as much as $800 on the international market during the 1970s. The abandonment of Bretton Woods, which effectively devalued the dollar in hopes of encouraging foreign trade, represented a frank acknowledgment that America's currency was no longer the world's strongest. Nixon also instituted wage and price controls to curb inflation and offered a "full employment" budget for 1972, including $11 billion in deficit spending to boost the sluggish economy.

These measures brought a temporary improvement in the economy, but the general decline persisted. Overall economic growth as measured by the gross national

No Gas
During the energy crisis of 1973–1974, American motorists faced widespread gasoline shortages for the first time since World War II. Although gas was not rationed, gas stations were closed on Sundays, air travel was cut by 10 percent, and a national speed limit of 55 miles per hour was imposed.
Tony Korody/Sygma.

product (GNP) had averaged 4.1 percent per year in the 1960s; in the 1970s, this measure dropped to only 2.9 percent. Tellingly, all the real growth occurred before 1973, the year the OPEC oil embargo began. By 1980 nine Western European countries had surpassed the United States in per capita GNP. Between 1973 and the mid-1990s, most American workers saw their real incomes drop and maintained their family income levels only by working longer hours or by having additional family members join the paid work force.

Many of these new workers were women employed in the expanding service sector. Women in particular entered the clerical work force, where jobs dominated by narrow and repetitive tasks did not allow for control and autonomy. In most cases their salaries were lower than the hourly wages of unionized blue-collar workers. Millions of other women entered blue-collar service

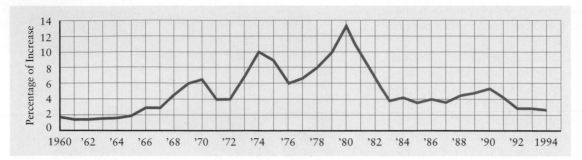

FIGURE 30.2
The Consumer Price Index, 1960–1994
The annual inflation rate peaked in 1980, the last year of Carter's presidency.
Source: U.S. Statistical Abstract, 1995.

occupations, performing manual labor for hourly wages under factory-like conditions in laundries, restaurants, warehouses, and other businesses. For nonwhite and working-class women, a "pink-collar" ghetto offered minimum-wage jobs in hotels, hospitals, and beauty salons.

Stagnating wages and the growth of the low-paying service sector produced a noticeable decline in most Americans' standard of living. Discretionary income per worker dropped 18 percent between 1973 and the early 1980s. At the same time, galloping inflation forced consumer prices upward. The Consumer Price Index (CPI) reached double-digit peaks of around 10 percent in 1974 and over 13 percent in 1980 (Figure 30.2). Housing prices rose even more rapidly, with the average cost of a single-family home more than doubling in the 1970s. Homeownership thus became less accessible to many working-class and middle-class Americans, including many baby boomers who were entering adulthood.

Young adults also faced a constricted job market in the late 1970s as a record number of baby-boom job seekers competed for a limited number of positions. Unemployment peaked at around 9 percent in 1975, declined briefly, and then edged upward again to around 6 to 7 percent in the late 1970s. The devastating combination of inflation and unemployment—dubbed *stagflation*—was resistant to traditional government remedies such as deficit spending and tax reduction and bedeviled presidential administrations from Nixon to Reagan.

Deindustrialization. American economic woes were most acute in the industrial sector, which entered a prolonged period of decline. The economists Barry Bluestone and Bennett Harrison estimate that the United States lost between 32 million and 38 million jobs in the 1970s as a direct result of deindustrialization, "the widespread, systematic disinvestment in the nation's productive capacity." Investors who had for-

merly bought stock in basic U.S. industries began to speculate on risky new ventures in the stock market or put their money into foreign companies or mergers (that often resulted in job layoffs). Many U.S. firms relocated overseas, partly to take advantage of cheaper labor and production costs and partly because federal tax law permitted corporations to deduct foreign expenses from their domestic profits. By the end of the 1970s the hundred largest multinational corporations and banks were earning more than a third of their overall profits abroad.

The most dramatic consequences of deindustrialization occurred in the older northeastern and midwestern industrial regions, which came to be known as the Rust Belt. Nightly newscasts were full of stories of the closings of unprofitable plants. The dominant images of American industry in the mid-twentieth century—huge factories such as Ford's River Rouge plant outside Detroit; the General Electric plant in Lynn, Massachusetts; and the United States Steel Corporation compound in Gary, Indiana—were becoming relics of a past stage of industrial development.

When a community's major employer closed up shop and left town, the effect was devastating. In 1977 the Lykes Corporation shut the Campbell Works of the Youngstown Sheet and Tube Company, laying off 4,100 Ohio steelworkers. Two years later Youngstown was still reeling. A third of the displaced workers, considered too old to retrain for new positions, had been forced to take early retirement at half of their previous salaries. Ten percent had moved, many of them to nonunion jobs in the Sun Belt, where the economy continued its dramatic postwar growth. Another 15 percent were still looking for work, their unemployment compensation long since exhausted. Among the 40 percent who were the "success stories" (those who had found other jobs), many had taken huge wage cuts. A former rigger, for instance, was selling women's shoes for $2.37 an hour. The impact of such plant closings rippled through communities across America's heartland.

Deindustrialization
Scores of industrial plants closed in the 1970s, putting many American workers out of work. At the same time, more Americans were buying cheaper imported cars, fueling anger toward foreign competitors. David Helfferich of Greenburg, Pennsylvania, bashed this Japanese-made Honda Civic and urged others to "buy American" as a means of protecting U.S. jobs.
Wide World Photos, Inc.

The changing economic conditions that fostered foreign investment and plant closings posed critical problems for the labor movement. As foreign competition cut into American corporate profits in the 1970s, industry was less willing to treat labor as a partner in making economic decisions. Union leaders often learned about a plant closing from the TV news at the same time that ordinary workers and the general public learned about it. Under such conditions, the power of organized labor declined in the 1970s, with a drop in union membership from 28 percent to 23 percent of the work force. Labor's bargaining position was increasingly vulnerable in the face of multinational conglomerates with vast international resources and mobility. Some employers facing strikes or labor problems simply closed their domestic operations and turned to a cheaper, more compliant work force abroad. In a competitive global environment, labor's prospects for regaining its earlier strength were dim, and union leaders shifted their priorities to holding on to gains they had already won.

Reform and Reaction in the 1970s

———————★———————

The nation's economic problems and growing cynicism about government led to deep public anxiety and resentment, and caused many Americans to turn inward to private satisfactions. The journalist Tom Wolfe labeled the 1970s the "Me Decade" because of its widespread obsession with life-styles and personal well-being, and the historian Christopher Lasch referred derisively to the decade's "culture of narcissism." But those labels hardly do justice to a decade in which environmentalism, feminism, lesbian and gay rights, and other social movements blossomed. Furthermore, such characterizations neglect the growing social conservatism that was in part a response to such movements. In the transitional decade of the 1970s, all these trends coexisted in a complex pattern of shifting crosscurrents.

The New Activism: Environmental and Consumer Movements

After 1970, many baby boomers left the counterculture behind and settled down to pursue careers and material success. But these young adults sought personal fulfillment as well. In a quest for physical and spiritual well-being, millions of Americans began jogging, riding bicycles, or working out at the gym. The fitness craze coincided with heightened environmental awareness, which spurred demands for pesticide-free foods and vegetarian cookbooks. Some young people embraced the spiritual and self-help techniques of the human potential, or New Age, movement, while others turned to new religious movements such as the Hare Krishna, the Church of Scientology, and the Unification Church of the Reverend Sun Myung Moon.

A few baby boomers continued to pursue the unfinished social and political agendas of the 1960s. Moving into law, education, social work, medicine, and other

Rachel Carson
A pioneer of the modern environmental movement, biologist Rachel Carson documented the adverse effects of DDT and other pesticides in her 1962 best seller, *Silent Spring.* This photograph, taken in 1961, shows Carson conducting fieldwork.
Alfred Eisenstadt/LIFE Magazine © Time, Inc.

fields, former radicals practiced their activism at a grass-roots level. Some moved into the left wing of the Democratic Party, while others helped establish a host of community-based organizations such as health clinics, food co-ops, and day-care centers. On the local level, the progressive spirit of the 1960s lived on.

Environmental Awareness. One of the most dynamic sources of activism in the 1970s was the environmental movement. The birth of America's modern environmental movement can be dated to the 1962 publication of Rachel Carson's *Silent Spring,* a powerful analysis of the impact of pesticides, especially DDT, on the food chain. Other issues that galvanized public opinion included a huge oil spill in January 1969 off the coast of Santa Barbara, California, which devastated beaches and sea life along the Pacific coast, and the environmental impact of projects such as the Alaska pipeline and a proposed airport in the Florida Everglades. New scientific research also revealed the harmful effects of chlorofluorocarbons and other fossil fuel by-products on the ozone layer of the earth's atmosphere, potentially destroying its protective properties and causing global warming. Environmentalism became a mass movement on the first Earth Day, April 22, 1970, when 20 million citizens gathered across the country to show their support for their endangered planet.

The United States had long consumed vast quantities of natural resources and had built a vigorous economy based on resource exploitation. Even as Americans became increasingly aware of the possible exhaustion of the earth's resources, the idea that there were limits to growth was revolutionary and difficult to accept, but so too were unhealthy air and polluted water. Concern about environmental quality and ecological values may be seen as an offshoot of the advanced consumer economy that defined the postwar period. Moving beyond basic necessities, many Americans demanded an even higher standard of living that included a healthy environment and corresponding life-styles. That desire led to new demands on the state, as citizens expected the federal government to take responsibility for environmental issues.

Many of the new environmentalists had been 1960s-style activists, and they brought their radical political sensibilities to environmental issues. For example, environmental activists talked about the "rights of nature" just as they talked about the rights of women or blacks. They construed the search for alternative technologies (especially solar power) as a political statement against a corporate structure that seemed increasingly hostile to human-scale technology—and to humans as well. Activists used sit-ins and other protest tactics developed in the civil rights and antiwar movements to mobilize mass support for specific issues or pieces of legislation. Like those movements, environmentalism was characterized by its decentralized nature and local orientation.

The environmental movement also raised public awareness of the dangers resulting from the dumping or release into the environment of toxic wastes. In 1978, outside Niagara Falls, New York, the Love Canal housing development made headlines when local residents discovered that it had been built over an underground chemical waste-disposal site. Lois Gibbs and other residents became aware of abnormally high rates of illness, miscarriages, and birth defects among Love Canal families. In 1980 a state of emergency was declared, and the New York State government paid homeowners to relocate (see American Lives, "Lois Marie Gibbs: Environmental Activist," pp. 988–989).

One of the worst offenders was the federal government itself. In the Cold War rush to produce bombs and weapons for national security, nuclear weapons plants carelessly released billions of gallons of radioactive waste into the environment. For example, the uranium-processing plant built in 1954 at Fernald, Ohio, dumped liquid wastes into open-air waste-storage pits, which then leaked into regional waterways. At the Hanford Nuclear Reservation near Richland, Washington, plutonium waste and toxic chemicals contaminated the soil and seeped into the Columbia River. Environmentalists called on the federal government to clean up this chemical legacy of the Cold War, but with only limited success.

Nuclear Power. Nuclear energy also became a subject of citizen action in the 1970s, when rising oil prices and shortages pitted environmental concerns against the need for alternative energy sources. To reduce the nation's dependence on foreign oil, some politicians and utility companies promoted the expansion of nuclear power. By January 1974, forty-two nuclear power plants were in operation, and over a hundred more were planned. The construction of nuclear power plants and reactors had gone largely unchallenged in the 1950s and 1960s, but it suddenly became controversial in the 1970s. Community activists protested plans for new reactors, citing inadequate disaster evacuation plans and the unresolved problem of disposing of radioactive waste. The mass protests of the Clamshell Alliance and other antinuclear groups helped to prevent or delay the start-up of nuclear reactors in Seabrook, New Hampshire, and Shoreham, New York.

Public fears about nuclear safety seemed to be confirmed in March 1979 when the central core reactor of a nuclear plant at Three Mile Island near Harrisburg, Pennsylvania, came critically close to a meltdown. Nearly a hundred thousand residents were evacuated as a precaution. A prompt shutdown brought the problem under control before any radioactive material was released into the environment, but a member of the panel investigating the accident admitted, "We were damn lucky." Ultimately, Three Mile Island made Americans reassess whether nuclear power could be a viable solution to the nation's energy needs. Grass-roots activism, combined with public fears about the potential dangers of nuclear energy, convinced many utility companies to abandon nuclear power despite its short-term economic advantages.

Environmental Legislation. Citizens' concerns over nuclear power, chemical contamination, pesticide poisoning, and other environmental issues created bipartisan support for an array of new federal legislation. In 1969 Congress passed the National Environmental Policy Act, requiring the developers of public projects to file an environmental impact statement (EIS) to assess the consequences of changing use patterns on a particular ecosystem. The EIS soon became a useful tool for citizens' groups trying to block unwanted development by private industry or government. The next year Nixon established the EPA and signed the Clean Air Act, which toughened standards for auto emissions to reduce smog and air pollution. Two years later Congress banned the use of DDT. And in 1973 the Endangered Species Act expanded the Endangered Animals Act of 1964, granting species such as snail darters and spotted owls protected status. Environmental protection thus joined social welfare, defense, and national security as areas for federal intervention in the postwar era.

But the environmental movement did not go uncontested. EPA-mandated fuel economy standards for cars, for example, provoked criticism for threatening the health of the auto industry as it struggled to keep up with foreign competitors. Corporations resented environmental regulations, but so did many of their workers, who believed that tightened standards threatened their jobs and placed nature over human beings. "If you're hungry and out of work, eat an environmentalist" read one labor union's bumper sticker. In a time of rising unemployment and deindustrialization, activists clashed head-on with proponents of economic development, full employment, and global competitiveness.

The Consumer Movement. Paralleling the rise of environmentalism was a growing consumer protection movement to eliminate harmful consumer products and curb dangerous practices by American corporations. The consumer movement had originated in the Progressive Era with the founding of government agencies such as the Food and Drug Administration (see Chapter 20). After decades of inertia, the consumer movement reemerged in the 1960s under the leadership of Ralph Nader, a young Harvard-educated lawyer whose book *Unsafe at Any Speed* (1965) attacked General Motors for putting flashy style ahead of safe handling and fuel economy in its engineering of the Chevrolet Corvair.

In 1969 Nader launched a Washington-based consumer protection organization that gave rise to the Public Interest Research Group, a national network of consumer groups that focused on issues ranging from product safety to consumer fraud and environmental pollution. Staffed by a handful of lawyers and hundreds of student volunteers known as "Nader's Raiders," the organization pioneered legal tactics such as the class-action suit, which allowed people with common grievances to sue as a group. Nader's organization became a model for dozens of other groups that emerged in the 1970s and afterward to combat the health hazards of smoking, unethical insurance and credit practices, and other consumer problems. The establishment of the federal Consumer Products Safety Commission in 1972 reflected the growing importance of consumer protection in American life.

Challenges to Tradition: The Women's Movement and Gay Rights

Along with environmentalism, feminism proved to be the most enduring movement to emerge from the 1960s. In the next decade the women's movement grew more sophisticated, generating an array of women-oriented services and organizations, from rape crisis centers and battered women's shelters to feminist health collectives and women's bookstores. *Our Bodies, Ourselves,* a

Lois Marie Gibbs: Environmental Activist

★

IN 1978 LOIS GIBBS was a twenty-seven-year-old housewife living in Niagara Falls, New York. A chemical worker's wife and the mother of two children, Gibbs spent her days cooking, shopping, and cleaning the family's modest three-bedroom home. Two years later Gibbs was a nationally known figure. As leader of the fight against toxic waste at Love Canal, she organized hundreds of local families, squared off with the governor of New York State, testified before Congress, appeared on national television, and was recognized by President Jimmy Carter for her efforts. She was, as she liked to put it, "the housewife who went to Washington."

Born in Grand Island, New York, in 1951, Lois Conn was one of six children in a blue-collar family in the industrial region surrounding Buffalo. After graduating from high school in 1969, she worked as a nurse's aide at a convalescent home and married Harry Gibbs, a worker at a local chemical plant. After the birth of their first child, Michael, they purchased a home in a quiet, tree-lined neighborhood. Lois quit her job to stay at home and in 1975 gave birth to a daughter. With no inkling of what lay beneath them, the Gibbses finished their basement, tended their garden, and enjoyed a peaceful suburban existence.

The first sign of trouble came in 1977, when their son Michael entered kindergarten at the neighborhood school. Within three months, he developed epilepsy and soon contracted asthma and chronic urinary and ear infections. The following spring Gibbs read newspaper reports about toxic chemicals buried beneath the school and tried to have her son transferred. When school officials rejected her request, insisting that the school was safe, Gibbs launched a petition drive to have the school closed.

At first Gibbs was reticent about approaching her neighbors, afraid of having doors slammed in her face. But what she found surprised her. Not only were people interested in and concerned about the dangers of chemicals, but many of them had health problems of their own, including respiratory ailments, cancer,

miscarriages, and birth defects. "The more I heard, the more frightened I became," said Gibbs. "The entire community seemed to be sick."

Gibbs set out to educate herself about the area's history. Consulting local newspaper files, she learned about Love Canal, a six-mile-long canal project developed by William T. Love in the 1890s to connect the upper and lower branches of the Niagara River. Construction had been under way when the depression of 1893 doomed the project, leaving a partially dug trench. The land later became a dump site used mainly by the Hooker Chemical Corporation, which disposed of 22,000 tons of chemical wastes there between 1942 and 1953. (Health officials eventually identified over 200 different compounds at the site, including highly toxic substances such as dioxin—used in the herbicide Agent Orange—toluene, and benzene.) After filling and covering over the site in 1953, Hooker sold the land to the Board of Education for one dollar, stipulating that the company not be held responsible for any future injury or death. Housing subdivisions soon sprang up around the site, and a new elementary school near the corner of the canal opened in 1955.

By the time Gibbs began meeting with her neighbors in 1978, rusted metal drums were surfacing in backyards, chemical sludge was seeping into basements, and residents were complaining about dead trees, burned feet, and a recurring stench. In June of that year the New York State Health Department began collecting air, soil, and blood samples from households closest to the canal. After finding abnormally high rates of birth defects and miscarriages, the health department issued an order on August 2 for reconstruction of the canal site and recommended the evacuation of all pregnant women and children under age two. Soon afterward concerned residents established the Love Canal Homeowners Association (LCHA) to fight for permanent relocation of Love Canal families and elected Lois Gibbs as LCHA president. Under pressure from Gibbs and the LCHA, New York's governor, Hugh Carey, agreed a few days later to relocate the 239 families closest to the canal, purchasing their homes at the replacement value.

While Gibbs and the LCHA applauded Carey's action, they worried about the other 810 families remaining in the neighborhood, many of whose homes also showed dangerous levels of chemicals. Gibbs appealed to federal and local officials for further action but encountered repeated delays, denials, and rebuffs. The mayor of Niagara Falls denounced Gibbs's efforts, claiming that the adverse publicity would destroy the city's tourist industry. Meanwhile,

Lois Marie Gibbs
A twenty-seven-year-old housewife in Niagara Falls, New York, Lois Gibbs became the leader of a campaign against toxic waste in her neighborhood in 1978. As president of the Love Canal Homeowners Association, Gibbs fought successfully for the permanent relocation of more than a thousand Love Canal families.
Corbis-Bettmann.

the state health department refused to relocate more families until it could complete further studies. At one point in 1979 the department claimed to have lost the residents' health records and instructed them to start the lengthy documentation process all over again.

Faced with bureaucratic inertia, Gibbs sought out sympathetic scientists to help the residents conduct their own studies. Their most important finding came from a neighborhood survey showing health problems clustered around swales—underground drainage ditches that led away from the canal—and suggesting more widespread contamination. The LCHA promptly released the findings to the media. Gibbs got publicity in other ways as well: she appeared on talk shows, organized picketing at the canal construction site, and was arrested for blocking truck traffic. When state officials still failed to take action, Gibbs led a group of citizens to the state capitol in Albany, bearing cardboard coffins symbolizing Love Canal victims. Throughout the Love Canal crisis

Gibbs made frequent trips to Albany and Washington to negotiate with state officials, the governor's office, Senator Daniel Patrick Moynihan, and other federal representatives.

Like other housewives involved in the crisis, Gibbs gained a new independence through her activities outside the home. Those activities, however, also caused tension in her marriage. "My husband was getting upset with me," she recalled. "I was never home . . . dinner was never on time." She and her husband divorced in 1980.

In May of that year events at Love Canal came to a head when the U.S. Environmental Protection Agency released a study showing abnormally high levels of chromosome breakage in Love Canal residents (suggesting increased risks of cancer, miscarriage, and birth defects). In an act of desperation Gibbs and two other housewives took two EPA officials hostage in the LCHA office while hundreds of angry residents surrounded the building, demanding federal relocation of Love Canal families. Coming in the middle of the Iranian hostage crisis, the women's ploy brought national media coverage but also a threat of reprisal from the FBI. To avoid violence, Gibbs released the officials, but she also demanded a response from President Jimmy Carter within forty-eight hours. Two days later, on May 21, Carter declared a health emergency at Love Canal, authorizing the temporary relocation of the remaining 810 families. Later that year he signed a bill permitting the permanent relocation of those families and the purchase of their homes; he also signed a bill establishing a "Superfund" to clean up Love Canal and thousands of other toxic waste sites identified by the EPA.

Using part of the $30,000 the state paid for her home, Gibbs and her children moved to Washington, D.C., in 1981. There she founded the Citizens Clearinghouse for Hazardous Waste, a consulting group for grass-roots organizations working on problems related to pesticides, solid waste, asbestos, and other toxic substances. She married a toxicologist, gave birth to two more children, and continues to work as director of the Citizens Clearinghouse.

One of the communities the Citizens Clearinghouse has been watching is Love Canal. In 1990 the EPA declared Love Canal habitable again after a twelve-year, $250 million cleanup. The elementary school and the 239 houses closest to the canal had been demolished, but 236 other homes were rehabilitated and sold at discount prices to eager buyers. Public officials insist the new containment system has safely and permanently sealed off the dump. Lois Gibbs is not so sure.

The Expanding Women's Movement
By the late 1970s the feminist movement had broadened its base, attracting women of all ages and backgrounds, such as this delegate to the 1977 National Women's Conference in Houston, Texas. As the slogan on her hat implies, though, the movement was already on the defensive against right-wing claims that it undermined traditional values.
Bettye Lane.

observance of the United Nations' International Women's Year. Their "National Plan of Action" represented a hard-won consensus on topics ranging from violence against women to homemakers' rights, the needs of older women, health, and, most controversial, abortion rights and other reproductive issues.

Women's political mobilization resulted in significant legislative and administrative gains. With the passage of Title IX of the Educational Amendments Act of 1972, which broadened the 1964 Civil Rights Act to include educational institutions, Congress prohibited colleges and universities that received federal funds from discriminating on the basis of sex, a change that particularly benefited women athletes. In 1972 Congress authorized child-care deductions for working parents; in 1974 it passed the Equal Credit Opportunity Act, which significantly improved women's access to credit, including charge cards and mortgages, in their own names and on the basis of their own (not their husbands') incomes.

Abortion Rights. The Supreme Court also significantly advanced the cause of women's rights. In several rulings the Court read a right of privacy into the Ninth and Fourteenth Amendments' concept of personal liberty to give women more control over their reproductive lives. In 1965 *Griswold v. Connecticut* had overturned state laws against the sale of contraceptive devices to married adults, a protection that was extended to single persons in 1972. In 1973 *Roe v. Wade* struck down Texas and Georgia statutes that allowed abortions only if the mother's life was in danger. According to this 7-to-2 decision, states could no longer outlaw abortions performed during the first trimester, or three months, of pregnancy. Rather than addressing the issue in feminist terms, such as women's right to control their own bodies, the justices interpreted abortion as a medical issue, basing their controversial decision on the confidentiality of the doctor-patient relationship as well as the individual's right to privacy.

Roe v. Wade nationalized the liberalization of state abortion laws that had begun in New York in 1970, but it also fueled the development of a powerful anti-abortion movement. Believing that the "right to life" of the unborn took precedence over a woman's right to choose whether to terminate a pregnancy, abortion opponents attempted to overturn *Roe v. Wade*. In 1976 they convinced Congress to deny Medicaid funds for abortions for poor women, one of the opening rounds in a protracted legislative and judicial campaign to chip away at the *Roe* decision.

The Equal Rights Amendment. In the 1970s the women's movement increasingly united around the proposed Equal Rights Amendment (ERA) to the Constitution. The ERA, first introduced in Congress in 1923

women's health manual published by a group of Boston women in 1973, quickly became a best seller. In 1972 Gloria Steinem and other journalists founded *Ms.* magazine, the first consumer magazine aimed at a feminist audience. Formerly all-male bastions, such as Yale, Princeton, and the U.S. Military Academy at West Point, admitted women undergraduates for the first time, and hundreds of colleges started women's studies programs. By 1977 the National Organization for Women (NOW) had sixty-five thousand members.

Women were also increasingly visible in politics and public life. The National Women's Political Caucus, founded in 1971, actively promoted the election of women to public office. Among the women to enter Congress were Bella Abzug and Geraldine Ferraro from New York and Patricia Schroeder from Colorado. Ella Grasso won election as Connecticut's governor in 1974, and Dixie Lee Ray as Washington's in 1976. In November 1977 twenty thousand women came to Houston for the first National Women's Conference, part of the

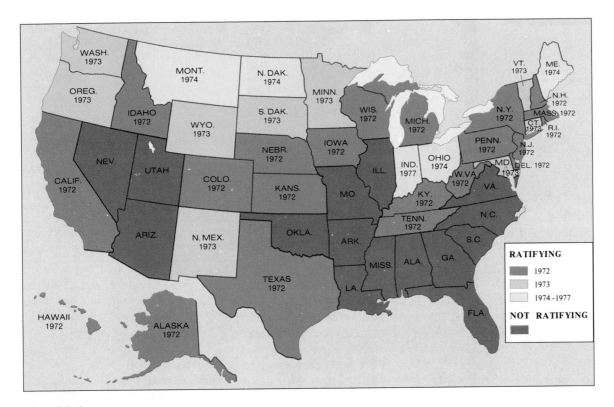

MAP 30.1
States Ratifying the Equal Rights Amendment
The Equal Rights Amendment quickly won support in 1972 and 1973 but then stalled.
ERAmerica, a coalition of women's groups formed in 1976, lobbied extensively, particu-
larly in Florida, North Carolina, and Illinois, but failed to sway the conservative legisla-
tures in those states. Efforts to revive the ERA in the 1980s were unsuccessful.

by the National Woman's Party, stated in its entirety,
"Equality of rights under the law shall not be denied or
abridged by the United States or any State on the basis
of sex." In 1970 feminists revived the amendment,
which passed the House but died in the Senate. In the
next session it passed in both houses of Congress and
was submitted to the states for ratification.

Thirty-four states quickly passed the ERA between
1972 and the end of 1974, but then the momentum
stopped (Map 30.1). Only Indiana ratified after that
point, leaving the amendment three states short of the
necessary three-fourths' majority. Most of the nonrati-
fying states were in the South and the West; Illinois also
held out despite spirited campaigns there by ERA supporters. Congress extended the deadline for ratification
until June 30, 1982, but the Equal Rights Amendment
still fell short.

Stalemate.   The fate of the ERA and the battle over
abortion rights show that by the mid-1970s the momentum of the women's movement was beginning to slow.
The contradictions of identity politics created internal
divisions within the feminist movement based on race,
class, age, and sexual orientation. Most critically, for
many nonwhite and working-class women, feminism

seemed to represent the interests only of self-seeking
white career women. The ERA, for example, promised
to open certain high-paying occupations to individual
women but also to eliminate gender-specific protective
legislation such as maximum hours laws considered
essential to many women workers. The feminist movement also faced growing social conservatism among
Americans generally. Although 63 percent of the
women polled in 1975 said that they favored "efforts to
strengthen and change women's status in society," a
growing number of men and women expressed concern
over what seemed to be revolutionary changes in
women's traditional roles. Especially disturbing to
many women were attitudes that seemed to denigrate
those who chose to be full-time housewives.

Phyllis Schlafly, long active in conservative causes,
led the antifeminist backlash. Notwithstanding her law
degree and active career while raising five children,
Schlafly advocated traditional roles for women.
Schlafly's STOP ERA organization claimed that the
amendment would create an unnatural "unisex society,"
permit women to be drafted, and prohibit separate toilets for men and women. (Feminists argued that those
charges were groundless.) Grass-roots networks of conservative women showed up at statehouses with home-

The Income Gap
Although the feminist movement helped create greater opportunities for women, it could not redress the longstanding economic inequalities between men and women. Cartoonist Doug Marlette offered this satirical look at the income gap in 1982, when women earned only fifty-nine cents for every dollar men earned.
Doug Marlette. © The Charlotte Observer.

baked bread and apple pies, symbols of their traditional domestic roles. Their message, that women would lose more than they would gain if the ERA passed, found favor among many men and women, especially those troubled by the rapid pace of social change.

Although the feminist movement was on the defensive by the mid-1970s, women's lives showed no signs of returning to the patterns of the 1950s. Because of increasing economic pressures, the proportion of women in the paid work force continued to rise, from 44 percent in 1970 to 51 percent in 1980. Easier access to birth control permitted women to enjoy greater sexual freedom, although they also became more vulnerable to male sexual pressures. With a growing number of career options available to them, many women, particularly educated white women, stayed single or delayed marriage and child rearing. The birth rate continued its postwar decline, reaching an all-time low in the mid-1970s (see Figure 28.5). At the same time, the divorce rate rose 82 percent in the 1970s, as more men and women chose to leave unhappy marriages.

Such changes brought increased autonomy for many women, but they also caused new hardships, particularly in poor and working-class families. Divorce left many women with low-paying jobs and inadequate child care. More tolerant attitudes toward premarital sex, along with other social and economic factors, contributed to rising teenage pregnancy rates. Increasing rates of divorce and adolescent pregnancy produced a sharp rise in the number of female-headed families, which in turn resulted in a "feminization" of poverty. By 1980 women accounted for 66 percent of the nation's adults living below the poverty line. Such developments made many Americans uneasy and fueled a growing wave of social reaction.

Gays and Lesbians.   Like the women's movement, the gay liberation movement achieved greater visibility in the 1970s. Thousands of gay men and lesbians "came out" in those years, publicly—and proudly—proclaiming their sexual orientation and often embracing alternative gender roles (see American Voices, "David Kopay: The Real Score: A Gay Athlete Comes Out," p. 993). Growing gay communities in New York's Greenwich Village, San Francisco's Castro, and other urban enclaves gave rise to hundreds of new gay and lesbian clubs, churches, businesses, and political organizations. In 1973 the National Gay Task Force launched a campaign to include gay men and lesbians as a protected group under civil rights laws covering employment and housing. Such efforts were most successful on the local level; during the 1970s Detroit, Boston, Los Angeles, Miami, San Francisco, and other cities passed laws barring discrimination on the basis of sexual orientation.

Like abortion and the ERA, gay rights came under attack from conservatives who defended traditional gender roles and believed that protecting gay people's rights would encourage immoral behavior. When the Miami city council passed a measure banning discrimination against gay men and lesbians in 1977, the singer Anita Bryant led a campaign to repeal the law by popular referendum. Later that year voters overturned the measure by a two-to-one majority, prompting similar anti–gay rights campaigns around the country.

Racial Minorities

Although the civil rights movement was in disarray by the late 1960s, minority group protests over the next decade continued to win social and economic gains. Native Americans saw some of the most significant changes. In

David Kopay

The Real Score: A Gay Athlete Comes Out

————— ★ —————

For ten years, David Kopay played professional football for the San Francisco Forty-Niners, the Detroit Lions, the Washington Redskins, the New Orleans Saints, and the Green Bay Packers. In 1975, at the end of his playing career, Kopay publicly acknowledged his homosexuality, creating a national furor in the sports world.

I always knew I was a bit different, but I kept it kind of quiet. I didn't think of myself as queer. In fact I couldn't even say that word for years and years. . . .

When I thought about the future, I assumed I'd be able to get a job in coaching because I was a player-coach my last few years playing. I was always working behind the scenes with the young ballplayers, coaching them. But I wasn't getting any interviews. There were all kinds of rumors about me being gay. . . .

By the time I spoke out, I really had nothing left to lose. It felt like I didn't have a choice—I just had to do it. Then one morning in 1975 I saw an article in the *Washington Star* about homosexual athletes and why they had everything to lose. There was an interview in the article with Jerry Smith [Washington Redskins tight end who died of AIDS in 1986]. . . .

. . . I was at a time and place in my own coming out where I felt that if I was going to survive, I had to speak out. It was do that or maybe go crazy.

So I called Lynn Rosellini, who was the reporter for the article that quoted Jerry Smith. Lynn was doing an entire series on gay athletes. . . .

Everybody said there was going to be a terrible backlash against me when Lynn's article was published. But there wasn't a backlash against me personally: There was a backlash against all the television shows and radio stations that I went on. And the newspapers. The *Washington Star* said they had never received more negative mail for anything they'd ever done—hundreds of horrible hate letters. Only two or three were addressed to me directly; the rest were addressed to the *Washington Star* editor and Lynn Rosellini for doing the series on gay athletes. The letters said things like, "It doesn't belong on the sports page as a model for our young boys and girls." "How could the *Washington Star* run an article like this?" I got letters that said, "I hope you never get a coaching job. Yours in Christ. Love. . . ." Just horrible things.

I never did get a coaching job. I was really quite frightened because I didn't know what I was going to do. No one would hire me to be a coach, I think, because of the image problem. They didn't think I could fill the role of the coach as guardian of the morals of the young students—the father figure. I also knew that I probably wouldn't get that really good sales-rep job that a lot of the other guys got. I had to make a spot for myself somehow, so I wound up working with Perry Young for a year on my book, *The Dave Kopay Story.*

I think we knew we were doing something good. . . .

A lot of kids still write. They say that the book meant so much to them. They remember that it changed them a lot or made a difference.

———————

Source: Eric Marcus, *Making History* (New York: Harper Collins, 1992), 275–277.

1971 the Alaska Native Land Claims Act restored 40 million acres to Eskimos, Aleuts, and other native peoples, along with $960 million in compensation. Smaller settlements were made with tribes in Maine, New Mexico, South Dakota, and Washington State. Most important, the federal government abandoned the tribal termination program that it had begun in the 1950s (see Chapter 28). Under the Indian Self-Determination Act of 1974, Congress restored the legal status of tribes to govern themselves and gave them authority over federal programs on their reservations (Map 30.2).

Busing. The court-mandated busing of children to achieve school desegregation proved to be the most disruptive social issue of the 1970s. Progress in achieving the desegregation mandated by *Brown v. Board of Education of Topeka* had been slow. In the 1970s both the courts and the Justice department pushed for more

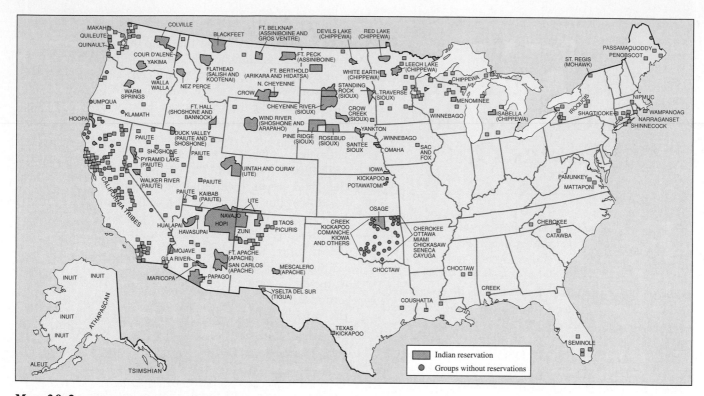

MAP 30.2
American Indian Reservations
Although native Americans have been able to preserve small enclaves in the northeastern
states, most Indian reservations are in the West. Beginning in the 1970s, various nations
filed land claims against federal and state governments.

action, first in the South, which grudgingly complied, and then in the rest of the country. In *Millicent v. Bradley* (1974), for example, the Court ordered cities with deeply ingrained patterns of residential segregation to use busing within municipal boundaries to integrate their classrooms. The decision sparked both race-based and class-based resentments; many white working-class city dwellers objected to busing not only because they opposed racial integration but because such schemes had been devised by affluent suburbanites whose school districts were unaffected by the plans.

The most violent opposition occurred in Boston in 1974–1975. The strongly Irish-Catholic working-class neighborhood of South Boston responded to the arrival of black students from the Roxbury section with mob scenes reminiscent of Little Rock in 1957 (see American Voices, "Phyllis Ellison: Busing in Boston," p. 996). Armed riot police were needed to keep South Boston High School open. Threatened by court-ordered busing, many white parents transferred their children to private schools; the resulting "white flight" increased the racial imbalance that busing was intended to redress. Some black parents also opposed busing, calling instead for better schools in predominantly black neighborhoods. By the late 1970s federal courts were backing away from their earlier insistence on busing to achieve racial balance.

Affirmative Action. Almost as divisive as busing was the implementation of *affirmative action*—procedures designed to redress historical patterns of race and sex discrimination in employment and education. First put forward by Lyndon Johnson's administration in 1965, affirmative action programs such as hiring and enrollment goals and recruitment and training programs expanded opportunities for blacks and Latinos. The number of black students enrolled in colleges and universities doubled between 1970 and 1977 to 1.1 million, or 9.3 percent of the total student enrollment. A small but growing number of black graduates moved into white-collar professions in corporations, banks, universities, and law firms. Others found new opportunities in civil service occupations such as law enforcement and firefighting or entered apprenticeships in the skilled construction trades. Latinos experienced similar gains in education and employment. On the whole, however, both groups experienced only marginal economic improvement, since poor and working-class nonwhites bore the brunt of job loss and unemployment in the 1970s.

Nevertheless, many whites, who were also feeling the economic pinch, came to resent affirmative action programs as infringements on their rights. A growing number of white men raised the cry of "reverse discrimination," claiming that they had been passed over

in favor of less qualified minority group members or women. In 1978 a white man named Allan Bakke sued the University of California Medical School at Davis for rejecting him while admitting minority candidates with lesser qualifications. The Supreme Court ruling in *Bakke v. University of California* was inconclusive. Though it branded the medical school's strict quota illegal and ordered Bakke admitted, it stated that racial factors could be considered in making hiring and admission decisions, thus upholding the principle of affirmative action. But the *Bakke* decision was clearly a setback for the proponents of affirmative action, and it set the stage for subsequent efforts to eliminate those programs in the 1990s.

The Politics of Resentment

The often vociferous opposition to busing, affirmative action, gay-rights ordinances, and the Equal Rights Amendment, along with the rapidly growing anti-abortion movement, constituted a broad backlash against the social changes of the previous decade. The economic changes of the 1970s, which left many working-class and middle-class Americans with lower disposable incomes, rising prices, and higher taxes, further fueled what conservative writer Alan Crawford has termed the "politics of resentment"—a grass-roots revolt against "special-interest groups" (such as women, minorities, and gays) and growing expenditures on social welfare. Special groups and programs, conservatives believed, robbed other Americans of educational and employment opportunities and created a fiscal burden on the working and middle classes.

Although the politics of resentment most often centered on socioeconomic issues, it also took the form of local taxpayers' revolts. In 1978 California voters passed Proposition 13, a measure that reduced prop-erty taxes and eventually undercut local governments' ability to maintain schools and other public services. Promising tax relief to middle-class homeowners and reduced funding for busing and other programs benefiting the urban poor (who were invariably viewed as nonwhite), Proposition 13 became the model for similar tax-cutting measures around the country in the late 1970s and 1980s.

Evangelical Religion. The rising popularity of evangelical religion also fueled the conservative resurgence of the 1970s. Evangelicalism, a conservative Protestant movement that emphasized strict moral codes based on the Bible and an emotional "born-again" experience, had been growing steadily since World War II under the leadership of charismatic preachers such as Billy Graham. Soon evangelical groups set up their own school systems, newspapers, and broadcasting networks. A new breed of televangelist, such as Jerry Falwell, built vast television ministries through religious programs aired on the new Christian Broadcasting Network founded by the Virginia preacher Pat Robertson.

In the 1970s, while membership in the liberal mainstream Protestant churches declined, evangelical denominations showed energetic growth. According to a Gallup poll conducted in 1976, some 50 million Americans, about a quarter of the population, were affiliated with evangelical churches. President Jimmy Carter, a member of the evangelical Southern Baptist Church, proudly proclaimed the influence of Jesus Christ in his life, as did the singers Pat Boone and Johnny Cash, the former Watergate convicts Jeb Magruder and Charles Colson, and the black-power activist Eldridge Cleaver.

The New Right. Addressing a broad range of social and cultural issues, a growing number of evangelicals

PHYLLIS ELLISON
Busing in Boston
————————★————————

Nowhere in the North was busing more divisive than in Boston in 1974–1975. Phyllis Ellison was one of fifty-six black students from the predominantly black neighborhoods of Columbia Point and Roxbury who were assigned to South Boston High School. In this interview she describes incidents from her sophomore year, including the day a white student was stabbed by a black student during a melee at the school. The student's wound was not fatal, but the incident led to heightened resistance and recriminations.

I remember my first day going on the bus to South Boston High School. I wasn't afraid because I felt important. I didn't know what to expect, what was waiting for me up the hill. We had police escorts. I think there was three motorcycle cops and then two police cruisers in front of the bus, and so I felt really important at that time, not knowing what was on the other side of the hill.

Well, when we started up the hill you could hear people saying, "Niggers go home." There were signs, they had made a sign saying, "Black people stay out. We don't want any niggers in our school." And there were people on the corners holding bananas like we were apes, monkeys. "Monkeys get out, get them out of our neighborhood. We don't want you in our schools." . . .

You can't imagine how tense it was inside the classroom. A teacher was almost afraid to say the wrong thing, because they knew that that would excite the whole class, a disturbance in the class-room. The black students sat on one side of the classes. The white students sat on the other side of the classes. . . . In the lunchrooms . . . [it] was the same thing. . . . So really, it was separate, I mean, we attended the same school, but we really never did anything together. . . .

I remember the day Michael Faith got stabbed vividly, because I was in the principal's office and all of a sudden you heard a lot of commotion and you heard kids screaming and yelling and saying, "He's dead, he's dead. That black nigger killed him. He's dead, he's dead." And then the principal running out of the office. There was a lot of commotion and screaming, yelling, hollering, "Get the niggers at Southie." I was really afraid. And the principal came back into the office and said, Call the ambulance and tell all the black students that were in the office to stay there. A police officer was in there and they were trying to get the white students out of the building, because they had just gone on a rampage and they were just going to hurt the first black stu-dent that they saw. . . . The black students were locked in their rooms and all the white students were let go out of their classrooms. I remember us going into a room, and outside you just saw a crowd of people, I mean, just so many people, I can't even count. . . . I remember the police cars coming up the street, attempting to, and people turning over the police cars, and I was just amazed that they could do something like that. The police tried to get horses up. They wouldn't let the horses get up. They stoned the horses. They stoned the cars. And I thought that day that we would never get out of South Boston High School. . . .

Source: Henry Hampton and Steve Fayer, *Voices of Freedom: An Oral History of the Civil Rights Movement from the 1950s through the 1980s* (New York: Bantam, 1990), 600, 610, 612–613.

spoke out against abortion, busing, sex education, pornography, feminism, and gay rights. Hoping to bring these religious views to a wider public, Jerry Falwell founded the Moral Majority in 1979, a politi-cal pressure group that promoted staunch anticom-munism and Christian "family values"—traditional gender roles, heterosexuality, family cohesion. Soon the extensive media and fundraising networks of the Christian right became the organizational base for a larger conservative movement known as the New Right. Using computerized mass mailing campaigns that targeted evangelical constituencies, New Right political groups such as the National Conservative Political Action Committee and the American Conser-vative Union mobilized thousands of followers and millions of dollars to support conservative candidates and causes.

During the 1970s conservatives were most active at the local level, building from the ground up a move-ment that would help elect Ronald Reagan in 1980. Lib-

Jerry Falwell
The resurgence of evangelical religion in the 1970s was accompanied by a conservative movement in politics known as the New Right. Founded in 1979 by televangelist Jerry Falwell, the Moral Majority was one of the earliest New Right groups, committed to promoting "family values" in American society and politics.
Dennis Brack/Black Star.

eral activists shared this grass-roots approach but were less effective in using modern technological tools to sustain a mass following. Among both liberals and conservatives, the dynamism of local organizing developed in the absence of effective political leadership on the national level.

From Ford to Reagan

In the wake of Watergate many citizens became cynical about the federal government and politicians in general. "Don't vote. It only encourages them" read one bumper sticker for the 1976 presidential campaign. Indeed, political leaders proved unable to deal with the rising inflation, stagnant growth, and declining productivity that plagued the U.S. economy in the 1970s. The fall of Saigon in 1975 reminded Americans of the failure of the nation's Vietnam policy. The world was changing, and Americans grappled with the unsettling idea that perhaps the United States would not continue to be the all-powerful country it had been for much of the postwar era. As Americans approached the 1980 election, this growing sense of impotence erupted in fury over the Iranian hostage crisis.

Ford's Caretaker Presidency

During the two years Gerald Ford held the nation's highest office, he failed to establish his legitimacy as president. His pardon of Nixon a month after taking office hurt his political credibility. Moreover, he was a less activist executive than Nixon, preferring voluntary action by the private sector over federal initiatives. Ford's hostility to government activism often put him at odds with the Democrats, who, in the wake of Watergate, increased their majorities in both houses of Congress in the 1974 elections.

Ford's biggest problem was the economy, which was reeling from inflation set in motion by the Vietnam War, rising OPEC prices, and the growing trade deficit. In an attempt to curtail prices, the Federal Reserve Board in 1974 tightened the money supply and drove up interest rates. The following year the economy entered its deepest downturn since the Great Depression. Production declined more than 10 percent, and nearly 9 percent of the work force was unemployed. Though many of the nation's economic problems were beyond the president's control, Ford's failure to take vigorous action made him appear timid and ineffective.

In foreign policy Ford was equally lacking in presidential leadership. He maintained Nixon's initiatives toward détente by asking Henry Kissinger to stay on as secretary of state, a position he had held since 1973. Ford met with Soviet leaders hoping to hammer out the details of a SALT II (Strategic Arms Limitation Talks) agreement, but he made little progress. Ford and Kissinger also continued Nixon's policy of increasing American support for the shah of Iran, ignoring the bitter opposition and anti-Western sentiment that the shah's policy of rapid modernization was provoking among Iran's growing Muslim fundamentalist population.

After the abuses of the Nixon era, Ford's genial style and candor were refreshing, but he failed to convey the assurance and competence needed in a time of mounting economic and international problems. "Gerald Ford is an awfully nice man who isn't up to the presidency," *The New Republic* concluded, and voters agreed.

Jimmy Carter: The Outsider as President

Only in the skewed political atmosphere of post-Watergate America could the Democrats have chosen their 1976 nominee, James E. Carter Jr. "Jimmy Who?" the media scoffed about this engineer and former entrepreneur in agricultural commodities from Plains, Georgia, popularly portrayed as a peanut farmer. But they soon changed their tune. Avoiding issues and controversy, Carter played up his role as a Washington outsider, pledging to restore morality to government. "I will never lie to you," he piously told voters. President Ford staved off a conservative challenge from Governor Ronald Reagan of California; then he dumped his moderate vice-president, Nelson Rockefeller, in favor of the more conservative Senator Robert J. Dole of Kansas. Carter chose as his running mate Senator Walter F. Mondale of Minnesota, who had ties to the traditional Democratic constituencies of labor, liberals, blacks, and big-city machines. Carter won the election with 50 percent of the popular vote to Ford's 48 percent.

Carter immediately tried to set a different tone for his administration. On Inauguration Day he renounced formal wear in favor of a business suit; instead of riding in a limousine, he and his wife, Rosalynn, walked from the Capitol to the White House. Throughout his term he relied heavily on symbolic gestures—staying in the homes of ordinary citizens, holding town meetings, and dressing in an informal cardigan sweater for fireside chats to the nation. But Carter's homespun approach soon wore thin as people looked for substance behind the symbols.

Ultimately Carter failed to develop an effective style of domestic leadership, a task made more difficult by the post-Watergate climate of skepticism and apathy. His outsider strategy distanced him from traditional sources of power in Washington, and he did little to heal the breach. After three years in office, Carter's chief domestic aide, Hamilton Jordan, still had not introduced himself to Thomas ("Tip") O'Neill, the Speaker of the House of Representatives and the most powerful Democrat on Capitol Hill. Shying away from established Democratic leaders, Carter turned to advisors and friends who had worked with him in Georgia, none of whom had Washington experience. When his budget director, Bert Lance, was questioned about financial irregularities at his Atlanta bank, the case undercut Carter's pledges to restore integrity and morality to the government.

Inflation was Carter's major domestic challenge. When he took office, the nation was still recovering from the severe 1975–1976 recession. Carter called for increased government spending and lower taxes, but when those actions provoked renewed inflation, he called for spending cuts and a delay in the tax reductions. This zigzag fiscal policy eroded both business

and consumer confidence. Unemployment hovered between 6 and 7 percent, and inflation rose from 6.5 percent in 1977 to 13.4 percent in 1980 (see Figure 30.2). To counter inflation, the Federal Reserve Board repeatedly raised interest rates; in 1980 they topped 20 percent, a historic high. A deep recession finally broke the inflationary spiral in 1982, a year after Carter left office.

The Carter administration expanded the federal bureaucracy in some cases while limiting its reach in others. Carter created the separate cabinet-level departments of energy and education and approved new environmental protection measures, such as a $1.6 billion "Superfund" to clean up chemical pollution sites. Through an executive order in 1978, he set aside 56 million acres in Alaska as national park and forest lands. But Carter also reformed the civil service system to streamline the federal bureaucracy, and he presided over the deregulation of the airline, trucking, and railroad industries. With deregulation, prices often dropped, but the resulting cutthroat competition drove many firms out of business and encouraged corporate consolidation. The president also unsuccessfully supported gradual decontrol of oil and natural gas prices as a spur to domestic production and conservation.

Overall, Carter's attempt to provide leadership during the energy crisis failed. He called efforts for energy conservation "the moral equivalent of war" (borrowing a phrase from the nineteenth-century philosopher William James). The media, unable to find the substance behind the rhetoric, reduced the phrase to "MEOW." In early 1979 a revolution in Iran spurred higher oil prices, and gas lines again reminded Americans of their dependence on foreign oil. That summer Carter's approval rating dropped to 26 percent, lower than Richard Nixon's at the height of the Watergate scandal.

Foreign Policy and Diplomacy. Jimmy Carter's commitment to human rights was the centerpiece of his new direction in foreign affairs. He criticized the suppression of dissent in the Soviet Union and withdrew economic and military aid from Argentina, Uruguay, Ethiopia, and other countries that violated human rights. He also established an Office of Human Rights within the State department. Unable to change the abusive policies of the Philippines, South Korea, South Africa, and other longtime U.S. allies, he did manage to raise public awareness of human rights, making it an issue that future administrations would have to address.

In Latin America, Carter's most important contribution was the resolution of the lingering dispute over control of the Panama Canal. In a treaty signed on September 7, 1977, the United States agreed to turn over control of the canal to Panama on December 31, 1999. In return, the United States retained the right to send its ships through the canal in case of war, even though

A Framework for Peace
President Jimmy Carter's greatest foreign-policy achievement was the personal diplomacy he exerted to persuade President Anwar Sadat of Egypt (left) and Prime Minister Menachem Begin of Israel (right) to sign a peace treaty in 1978. The signing of the Camp David accords marked an important first step in constructing a framework for peace in the Middle East.
Jimmy Carter Presidential Library.

the canal itself would be declared neutral territory. Despite conservatives' outcry that the United States was giving away more than it got, the Senate narrowly approved the treaty.

Although Carter had campaigned to free the United States from its "inordinate fear of Communism," relations with the Soviet Union soon became tense, largely because of problems surrounding arms limitation talks. Soviet leader Leonid Brezhnev signed SALT II in 1979, but hopes for Senate ratification of the arms control treaty collapsed when the Soviet Union invaded Afghanistan in December. In retaliation for this aggression, which Carter viewed as a threat to Middle Eastern oil supplies, the United States curtailed grain sales to the USSR and boycotted the 1980 summer Olympic Games in Moscow. (The Soviets returned the gesture by boycotting the 1984 summer games in Los Angeles.) When Carter left office in 1981, relations with the Soviet Union were worse than they had been since the 1960s.

President Carter achieved both his most stunning success and his greatest failure in the Middle East. Relations between Egypt and Israel had remained tense since the 1973 Yom Kippur War. In 1978 President Carter helped to break the stalemate by inviting Israel's prime minister, Menachem Begin, and Egyptian president Anwar Sadat to Camp David, the presidential retreat in Maryland. Two weeks of discussions and Carter's promise of significant additional foreign aid to Egypt persuaded Sadat and Begin to agree on a "framework for peace." The framework outlined in the Camp David peace accords included Egypt's recognition of Israel's right to exist and Israel's return of the Sinai peninsula, which it had occupied since 1967. The transfer of Sinai territory took place from 1979 to 1982.

The Iranian Hostage Crisis. Dramatically less successful was U.S. policy toward Iran. Ever since the CIA had helped install Muhammad Reza Pahlavi on the throne in 1953, the United States had counted on Iran as a faithful ally in the troubled Middle East. The shah was a major customer for American arms, using "petrodollars" from the sale of oil to the United States to purchase close to $20 billion worth of weapons between 1972 and 1979. Visiting Iran in late 1977, President Carter declared it "an island of stability in one of the more troubled areas of the world." Overlooking the repressive tactics of Iran's CIA-trained secret police, SAVAK, Carter followed the lead of previous Cold War policy makers for whom access to oil reserves and the shah's consistently anticommunist stance outweighed all other considerations.

Early in 1979, however, a revolution led by a fundamentalist Muslim leader, Ayatollah Ruhollah Khomeini, overthrew the shah's government and drove him into exile. The United States had ignored warning signs that the shah's efforts to westernize Iran had offended fundamentalist Islamic leaders; the CIA had also downplayed the extent to which hatred of the United States had helped coalesce opposition to the shah. In late October 1979 the Carter administration made a controversial decision to admit the deposed shah, who was suffering from incurable cancer, into the United States for medical treatment. Iran's new leaders had warned that such an action would provoke retaliation, but Henry Kissinger and other foreign policy leaders argued that the United States should assist the shah, both for humanitarian reasons and in return for his years of support for American policy. In response, on November 4, 1979, fundamentalist Muslim students under Khomeini's direction seized the U.S. Embassy in Teheran, taking American hostages in a flagrant violation of the principle of diplomatic immunity. The hostage takers demanded that the shah be returned to Iran for trial and punishment, but the United States refused. Instead President Carter suspended arms sales to Iran, froze Iranian assets in American banks, and

American Hostages in Iran
Images of blindfolded, handcuffed American hostages seized
by Iranian militants at the American embassy in Teheran in
November 1979 shocked the nation and created a foreign-
policy crisis that eventually cost Jimmy Carter the presidency.
Mingam/Liaison.

threatened to deport Iranian students in the United
States. Fifty-two hostages remained in captivity.

For the next fourteen months the Iranian hostage
crisis paralyzed the presidency of Jimmy Carter. Night
after night humiliating pictures of blindfolded hostages
appeared on television newscasts. (Media-conscious
Iranian students printed their anti-American placards
in English.) The late-night television news program
Nightline, featuring the journalist Ted Koppel, originated as "America Held Hostage," a nightly update on
the news from Iran that provided an unexpected way
for ABC to compete with Johnny Carson's *Tonight
Show*. The extensive media coverage and Carter's insistence that the hostages' safe return was his top priority
enhanced their value to their captors, but he could do
little to win their release until the Iranian government
was willing to negotiate. An attempt to mount a military rescue of the hostages failed miserably in April
1980, six months into the crisis, because of helicopter
equipment failures in the desert. Secretary of State
Cyrus Vance, who had not been informed about the rescue attempt, resigned in protest, claiming that it had
further endangered the lives of the hostages. The
abortive rescue mission reinforced the view of Carter as
bumbling and ineffective.

The Reagan Revolution

With Carter embroiled in the hostage crisis on the eve
of the 1980 presidential election, the Republicans

gained momentum by nominating former California
governor Ronald Reagan. Born in Tampico, Illinois, in
1911, Reagan won a modest reputation as a Hollywood
actor in the late 1930s and early 1940s. As president of
the Screen Actors Guild in the early 1950s, he was
deeply affected by the anticommunist crusade in Hollywood, which hastened his political metamorphosis
from New Deal Democrat to conservative Republican.
After endorsing Barry Goldwater in 1964, Reagan
entered politics, serving as governor of California from
1967 to 1975. After losing a bid for the presidency in
1976, Reagan secured the nomination easily in 1980,
choosing former CIA director George Bush as his running mate.

In the final months of the campaign, Carter took on
an embattled and defensive tone while Reagan
remained upbeat and decisive. Exploiting the hostage
issue, Reagan called the Iranians "barbarians" and
"common criminals" and hinted that he would take
strong action to win the hostages' return. At the same
time, Reagan effectively appealed to the politics of
resentment that flourished during the lean years of the
1970s. In a televised debate between the candidates,
Reagan emphasized the economic plight of working-
and middle-class Americans when he posed the rhetorical question, "Are you better off today than you were
four years ago?" Battered by inflation, unemployment,
and income stagnation, many viewers answered no.

In November, Reagan won in a landslide, with
51 percent of the popular vote to Carter's 41 percent
(Map 30.3). Riding his coattails, the Republicans won
control of the Senate for the first time since 1954,
although the Democrats maintained their hold on the
House. Voter turnout, however, was at its lowest level
since the 1920s; only 53 percent of those eligible went
to the polls, and many poor and working-class voters
stayed away. Nevertheless, the election confirmed the
growth in the power of the Republican Party since
Richard Nixon's victory in 1968.

Superior financial resources and a realignment of
the electorate contributed to the Republican resurgence of the 1970s. The political action committees that
had proliferated under the Fair Campaign Practices Act
of 1974 collected large sums for both parties, but particularly for the Republicans. While the Democratic
Party saw its key constituency—organized labor—
dwindle, the GOP's financial superiority enabled it to
make sophisticated and effective use of television and
direct mail to reach voters directly. This aggressive out-
reach helped bring about a realignment of the electorate. The core of the Republican Party that elected
Ronald Reagan remained the upper-middle-class white
Protestant voters who supported balanced budgets, disliked government activism, feared crime and communism, and believed in a strong national defense. Those
values had been the essence of postwar conservatism.
But now new groups gravitated toward the Republican

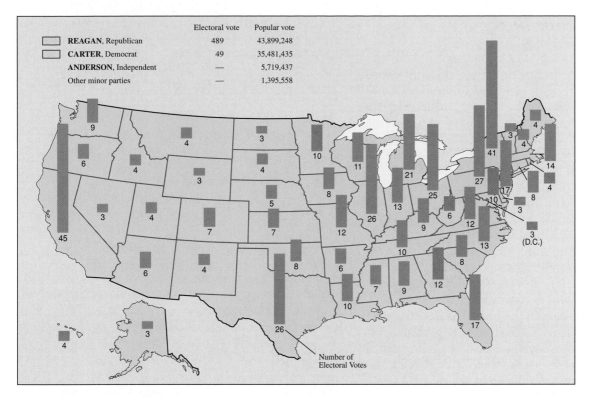

		Electoral vote	Popular vote
	REAGAN, Republican	489	43,899,248
	CARTER, Democrat	49	35,481,435
	ANDERSON, Independent	—	5,719,437
	Other minor parties	—	1,395,558

Number of Electoral Votes

MAP 30.3
The Election of 1980
Ronald Reagan defeated Democratic incumbent Jimmy Carter, winning all but six states and the District of Columbia. Winning 51 percent of the popular vote, Reagan cut deeply into the traditional Democratic coalition by wooing many southern whites, urban ethnics, and blue-collar workers. Republicans also won control of the Senate for the first time since 1954.

vision: southern whites disaffected by big government and black civil rights gains; urban ethnics who had moved to the suburbs; blue-collar workers, especially Catholics; young voters who identified themselves as conservatives; and voters in the West who had become increasingly unhappy with Jimmy Carter's policies on the environment and energy development. With the wooing of these "Reagan Democrats," the Republican Party made deep inroads into Democratic territory, eroding that party's traditional coalition of southerners, blacks, laborers, and urban ethnics.

Perhaps the most significant constituency in the Republican Party was the New Right, whose emphasis on traditional values and fundamentalist Christian morality dovetailed well with conservative Republican ideology. In 1980 New Right concerns formed the basis for the party's platform, which called for a constitutional ban on abortion, voluntary prayer in the public schools, and a mandatory death penalty for certain crimes. The Republicans also demanded an end to court-mandated busing and, for the first time in forty years, opposed the Equal Rights Amendment. A key factor in the 1980 election, the emergence of the New Right contributed to the conservative rebirth of the Republican Party under Ronald Reagan.

On January 20, 1981, at the exact moment when Carter turned over the presidency to Reagan, the Iranian government released the American hostages. After 444 days of captivity, the hostages returned home to an ecstatic patriotic welcome, a reflection of the public's frustration over their long ordeal. While most Americans continued to maintain that "We're Number One," the hostage crisis in Iran came to symbolize the loss of America's power to control world affairs. Its psychological impact was magnified because it came at the end of the decade that had witnessed Watergate, the American defeat in Vietnam, and the OPEC embargo.

To a great extent this decline in influence was magnified by the unusual predominance the United States had enjoyed after World War II, an advantage that could not realistically last forever. The return to economic and political power by Japan and Western Europe, the control of vital oil resources by Middle Eastern countries, and the industrialization of some Third World nations had widened the cast of international actors. Still, many Americans were unable to accept anything less than the economic and political supremacy of the postwar years. Ronald Reagan rode their frustrations and their hopes to victory in 1980.

Summary

★

With his election to the presidency in 1968, Richard Nixon became a harbinger of more conservative times in American social and political life. During his five years in the White House Nixon sought to trim back the welfare state through federal revenue sharing, cutbacks in Great Society antipoverty programs, and a reduced commitment to civil rights. But Nixon did not shrink from the use of executive power; he implemented wage and price controls to fight inflation, periodically impounded federal funds, and expanded the role of the government in environmental and consumer affairs. Nixon's plans, however, were cut short after his administration took part in a series of illegal acts during his campaign for reelection in 1972. The resulting Watergate scandal forced him to resign in 1974.

For much of the decade the United States struggled with economic problems, including high inflation, skyrocketing energy costs, stagnation of income, and a diminished position in world trade. A series of gas shortages during the Arab oil embargo of 1973–1974 and the Iranian revolution in 1979 had a devastating impact on American society and caused many people to question the country's voracious pattern of energy consumption.

Although many Americans became cynical about politics after Watergate and Vietnam, some continued to pursue the unfinished social agendas of the 1960s. Most notably, the environmental and women's movements showed dynamic growth and activism at the grass-roots level. Movements for consumer protection, gay and lesbian rights, and racial equality also continued to make modest gains. By the late 1970s, however, a new, more conservative social mood—based in part on the resurgence of evangelical Christianity—limited further progress on issues such as abortion rights, the Equal Rights Amendment, gay and lesbian rights, busing, and affirmative action.

On the national level ineffective political leadership by Gerald Ford led to his defeat in 1976 by Jimmy Carter of Georgia, who campaigned as a Washington outsider. Taking a high moral tone, Carter made human rights a priority of his administration and helped negotiate the Camp David peace accords between Egypt and Israel in 1978. But his own inexperience, mounting economic problems, and growing troubles abroad plagued his administration. The end of the decade was dominated by the Iranian hostage crisis, as Islamic fundamentalists held fifty-two hostages at the U.S. embassy in Teheran for 444 days. The hostage crisis virtually paralyzed Carter's presidency, helping Ronald Reagan win election in 1980.

T I M E L I N E

1968	Richard Nixon elected president
1970	Earth Day first observed
	Environmental Protection Agency established
1971	Pentagon Papers published
	Nixon suspends Bretton Woods system
	Swann v. Charlotte-Mecklenburg institutes busing
1972	Revenue sharing begins
	Watergate break-in; Nixon reelected
	Congress passes Equal Rights Amendment
1973	Spiro Agnew resigns; Gerald Ford appointed vice-president
	Roe v. Wade legalizes abortion
1973–1974	Arab oil embargo; gas shortages
1974	Nixon resigns; Ford becomes president and pardons Nixon
1974–1975	Busing controversy in Boston
1975–1976	Recession
1976	Jimmy Carter elected president
1978	Carter brokers Camp David accords
	Bakke v. University of California limits affirmative action
	Love Canal crisis begins
1979	Second oil crisis
	Three Mile Island nuclear accident
	Hostages seized at American embassy in Teheran, Iran
	USSR invades Afghanistan
1980	"Superfund" created to clean up chemical pollution
	Ronald Reagan elected president

Suggested Readings

─────────★─────────

A definitive scholarly history of the 1970s has yet to be written. Peter N. Carroll's popular history, *It Seemed Like Nothing Happened* (1982), provides a general overview of the period, as do Paul Boyer's chapters on the 1970s in *Promises to Keep* (1995).

The Nixon Years

Jonathan Schell, *The Time of Illusion* (1976), offers an insightful discussion of the Nixon administration. Herbert Parmet's *Richard Nixon and His America* (1990) and Stephen Ambrose's three-volume *Nixon* (1987, 1991) are two of many biographies of a complex political leader. Kim McQuaid, *The Anxious Years: America in the Vietnam-Watergate Era* (1989), is an overview of the Nixon era. See also Garry Wills, *Nixon Agonistes* (rev. ed., 1990), and Nixon's own recollections in *RN: The Memoirs of Richard Nixon* (1978).

Stanley Kutler, *The Wars of Watergate* (1990); Anthony Lukas, *Nightmare: The Underside of the Nixon Years* (1976); and Theodore H. White, *Breach of Faith* (1975), are comprehensive accounts of the Watergate scandal. Also of interest are the books by the *Washington Post* journalists who broke the story, Carl Bernstein and Bob Woodward: *All the President's Men* (1974) and *The Final Days* (1976). Stanley Kutler, *Abuse of Power: The New Nixon Tapes* (1997), is a collection of transcripts from the White House tapes relating to Watergate and other Nixon-era scandals.

The Economic Downturn

Barry Commoner, *The Closing Circle* (1971) and *The Poverty of Power* (1976), and Robert Heilbroner, *An Inquiry into the Human Prospect* (1974), cogently assess the origins of the energy crisis and the prospects for the future. See also Lester C. Thurow, *The Zero-Sum Society* (1980), and Robert Stobaugh and Daniel Yergin, *Energy Future* (1980). Daniel Yergin, *The Prize* (1991), and John M. Blair, *The Control of Oil* (1976), treat OPEC developments.

General introductions to the economic developments of the decade are Barry Bluestone and Bennett Harrison, *The Deindustrialization of America* (1982); Richard J. Barnet and Ronald E. Muller, *Global Reach* (1974); Richard J. Barnet, *The Lean Years* (1980); John P. Hoerr, *And the Wolf Finally Came: The Decline of the Steel Industry* (1988); Robert Calleo, *The Imperious Economy* (1982); and Gardner Means et al., *The Roots of Inflation* (1975).

Reform and Reaction in the 1970s

Tom Wolfe gave the decade its name in "The Me Decade and the Third Great Awakening," *New York Magazine* (August 23, 1976). Influential books include Christopher Lasch, *The Culture of Narcissism* (1978), and Gail Sheehy, *Passages* (1976).

For a general overview of the environmental movement, see Samuel P. Hays, *Beauty, Health, and Permanence: Environmental Politics in the United States, 1955–1985* (1987). Roderick Nash provides a history of environmental ethics in *The Rights of Nature* (1989). Books that were influential in shaping public awareness of ecological issues include Rachel Carson, *Silent Spring* (1962); Paul R. Ehrlich, *The Population Bomb* (1968); Frances Moore Lappé, *Diet for a Small Planet* (1971); and Philip Slater, *Earthwalk* (1974). Lois Marie Gibbs describes her experience with the Love Canal crisis in *Love Canal: My Story* (1982). Charles McCarry chronicles Ralph Nader's crusade for consumer protection in *Citizen Nader* (1972).

On women and feminism in the 1970s, see Alice Echols, *Daring to Be Bad* (1989); Susan M. Hartmann, *From Margin to Mainstream: American Women and Politics Since 1960* (1989); and Winifred D. Wandersee, *On the Move: American Women in the 1970s* (1988). Donald G. Mathews and Jane S. De Hart analyze the struggle over the ERA in *Sex, Gender, and the Politics of ERA* (1990), and Carol Felsenthal examines the life of the ERA opponent Phyllis Schlafly in *The Sweetheart of the Silent Majority* (1981). David Garrow, *Liberty and Sexuality: The Right to Privacy and the Making of* Roe v. Wade (1994), is an in-depth examination of the 1973 abortion decision. On the public abortion debate, see Faye Ginsberg, *Contested Lives* (1989), and Kristen Luker, *Abortion and the Politics of Motherhood* (1984).

Leigh W. Rutledge surveys the gay and lesbian movement in *The Gay Decades: From Stonewall to the Present* (1992). Thomas Byrne Edsall with Mary D. Edsall, *Chain Reaction: The Impact of Race, Rights and Taxes on American Politics* (1991), examines some of the divisive social issues of the 1970s. J. Anthony Lukas, *Common Ground* (1985), tells the story of the Boston busing crisis through the biographies of three families. Paul Moreno, *From Direct Action to Affirmative Action* (1997); Robert J. Weiss, *We Want Jobs* (1997); and Lydia Chavez, *The Color Bind* (1998), treat the controversial topic of affirmative action.

Alan Crawford, *Thunder on the Right* (1980), and Peter Steinfels, *The Neo-Conservatives* (1979), survey the new conservatism. John Woodridge, *The Evangelicals* (1975), analyzes the rise of evangelical religion, and Quentin J. Schultze looks at evangelicals' use of the media in *Televangelism and American Culture* (1991). On the political role of the Christian right, see Michael Liensch, *Redeeming America: Piety and Politics in the New Christian Right* (1993).

From Ford to Reagan

John R. Greene examines the Ford administration in *The Presidency of Gerald R. Ford* (1995), as do James Cannon, *Time and Chance: Gerald Ford's Appointment with History* (1993), and Richard Reeves, *A Ford, Not a Lincoln* (1975).

Peter G. Bourne, *Jimmy Carter* (1997), is a comprehensive biography. Generally unfavorable portraits of the Carter presidency are found in Burton Kaufman, *The Presidency of James Earl Carter Jr.* (1993); Robert Shogan, *Promises to Keep* (1977); Haynes Johnson, *In the Absence of Power* (1980); and Clark Mollenhoff, *The President Who Failed* (1980). See also Erwin Hargrove, *Jimmy Carter as President* (1989); Charles Jones, *The Trusteeship Presidency* (1988); and Jimmy Carter's presidential memoirs, *Keeping Faith* (rev. ed., 1995). James Fallows, *National Defense* (1981), provides an incisive overview of defense developments. See also A. Glenn Mower Jr., *Human Rights and American Foreign Policy: The Carter and Reagan Experiences* (1987). Gary Sick, *All Fall Down: America's Tragic Encounter with Iran* (1986), provides an account of the Iranian hostage crisis, and Jack Germond, *Blue Smoke and Mirrors* (1981), examines the presidential election of 1980.

Chapter 31

A New Domestic and World Order,

1981–1996

The Reagan-Bush Years, 1981–1993
Reaganomics
Reagan's Second Term
The Bush Presidency

Foreign Relations under Reagan and Bush
Third World Interventions and a Soviet Thaw
The End of the Cold War
War in the Persian Gulf, 1990–1991

Uncertain Times
The Economy
An Increasingly Pluralistic Society
Culture Wars
The Environmental Movement at Twenty-five
Popular Culture and Popular Technology

Restructuring the Domestic Order: Public Life, 1992–1996
Clinton's First Term
"The Era of Big Government Is Over"

O N NOVEMBER 9, 1989, millions of television viewers worldwide watched jubilant Germans swarm through the Berlin Wall after the East German government lifted all restrictions on passage between the eastern and western sectors of the city. The Berlin Wall, which had divided the city since 1961, was the foremost symbol of communist repression and the Cold War division of Europe. Over the years more than four hundred East Germans had lost their lives trying to escape to the freedom of the other side. Now East and West Berliners, young and old, danced and mingled on what remained of the structure. When the Berlin Wall came down, it brought communism's grip over Eastern Europe down with it. Soon the Soviet Union would fall to the forces of change. In 1956 Soviet premier Nikita Khrushchev had told the United States, "We will bury you." Now the tombstone read, "The Soviet Union, 1917–1991."

Just as Americans had been drawn into a web of shared national experience in the 1920s, globalization linked Americans with the rest of the world in the 1980s and 1990s. Political choices made in Washington had international economic implications, but so did decisions made in Tokyo, Beijing, Bonn, and Brussels, as the United States increasingly shared power and influence with other nations in an interconnected global economy. Paradoxically, with the collapse of the Soviet Union, the United States achieved military dominance as the world's only remaining superpower. During the Persian Gulf crisis of 1990–1991 President George Bush called for a "new world order . . . in which nations recognize the shared responsibility for freedom and injustice."

The Wall Comes Tumbling Down
The destruction of the Berlin Wall in November 1989 symbolized the end of the Cold War.
Alexandra Avakian/Woodfin Camp & Associates.

Festive Times at the Reagan White House
Since Ronald and Nancy Reagan were both former actors, perhaps they thought of Fred Astaire and Ginger Rogers (see
p. 783) when they struck this pose at a White House state dinner in May 1985. Some former White House staffers now suspect that Reagan was already showing signs of early
Alzheimer's disease by that point.
Photo by Harry Benson. Cover courtesy VANITY FAIR. © 1985 by Condé-
Nast Publications, Inc.

As the United States struggled to redefine its role in
the post–Cold War world, it faced critical challenges at
home. Americans grappled with racial, ethnic, and cultural conflict; fears about the economy; and a growing
disenchantment with the failure of political leaders to
solve many of the nation's pressing problems. But the
most far-reaching debate was over the role of the federal government in public life. The rise of the state, one
of the most important developments in twentieth-
century American history, was slowed and even partially reversed by Ronald Reagan's election in 1980, the
presidency of George Bush, and the election of a
Republican Congress in 1994. New Deal liberalism and
an activist federal government were in retreat, despite
the Democratic capture of the White House in 1992. In
his 1996 State of the Union address, President Clinton
acknowledged this new domestic order by declaring,
"The era of big government is over."

The Reagan-Bush Years, 1981–1993

★

George Bush's one term as president often seems indis-
tinguishable from the two terms of his predecessor
Ronald Reagan, in part because Bush followed the
basic policies of the previous administration. But Bush
was also overshadowed because Reagan, though not a
particularly capable president, possessed extraordinary
charisma. First elected at sixty-nine, he was the oldest
person ever to serve as president, yet he conveyed a
sense of physical vigor. By capitalizing on his skills as
an actor and a public speaker, winning the support of
the emerging New Right within the Republican Party,
and appealing to core American values such as family,
liberty, and economic freedom, Reagan became one of
the most popular presidents of the twentieth century.

Reaganomics

Since the New Deal programs of the 1930s, Americans
had generally assumed that federal action could best
solve the nation's social and economic problems. The
election of Ronald Reagan called into question almost
half a century of activism. "Government is not the solution to our problem," he declared. "Government is the
problem."

Reagan's first priority was to reshape the nation's
fiscal and tax policies. The term *Reaganomics* came to
stand for the tax cuts and domestic budget reductions
enacted in 1981 and 1982 and the controversial supply-
side economic theory that lay behind them. According
to this theory, high taxes siphoned capital that would
otherwise be invested, stimulating economic growth.
Tax cuts therefore would promote investment, causing
an economic expansion that would increase tax revenues. Together with cuts in government spending,
especially on entitlement programs, tax cuts would also
shrink the federal budget deficit. Critics charged that
conservative Republicans deliberately cut taxes to force
reductions in federal funding for the social programs
that they abhorred.

The first part of this economic policy—tax cuts—
was enacted in the Economic Recovery Tax Act of 1981,
arguably the most significant legislation of the Reagan
years. This across-the-board tax cut reduced basic personal income tax rates 25 percent over three years and
introduced the indexation of tax brackets, which kept
tax rates constant when incomes rose solely because of
inflation. The reductions were supposed to be linked to
drastic cutbacks in federal expenditures. But while cuts
were made in food stamps, unemployment compensation, and welfare programs such as Aid to Families with

Dependent Children (AFDC), congressional resistance kept intact the Medicare and Social Security programs, which consumed a far greater proportion of the budget.

All the money saved from the cuts in government spending—and far more—was plowed into a five-year, $1.2 trillion defense buildup. This huge increase fulfilled Reagan's campaign pledge to "make America Number One again." The B-1 bomber, which Carter had canceled, was resurrected, and the development of a new missile system, the MX, was begun. Reagan's most ambitious, and controversial, weapons plan was the 1983 Strategic Defense Initiative (SDI), popularly known as "Star Wars" from the movie of that name. SDI would be a satellite and laser shield to detect and intercept incoming missiles. Reagan supporters claimed that SDI would render nuclear war obsolete, but scientists doubted its feasibility.

Another basic tenet of Reaganomics was that many federal regulations impeded growth and productivity because of the high cost of compliance. The administration moved to abolish or reduce federal regulation of the workplace, health care, consumer protection, and the environment. Much of the responsibility, and the cost, of those activities was transferred to the states.

Meanwhile, the Federal Reserve Board chose to combat inflation, which had been high since the mid–1970s, with *monetary policy*—that is, setting interest rates and controlling the amount of money in circulation to stimulate or slow the economy as needed. By raising the interest rate for corporate borrowers, the Federal Reserve reduced inflation from 12.4 percent in 1980 to 4 percent in 1982. Unfortunately, the Fed's tightening of the money supply also brought on the "Reagan Recession" of 1981–1982, which threw some 10 million Americans out of work. The recession bottomed out in early 1983, however, and the economy began to grow. For the rest of the decade inflation stayed low, aided by a worldwide drop in energy costs. Despite limited growth of the gross national product, the Reagan administration presided over the longest peacetime economic expansion in American history to date.

If all had gone according to the administration's plan, the budget should have been balanced by 1984, but that did not happen. The increased revenue from economic growth promised by supply-side economics fell far short of expectations. Furthermore, despite what seemed like wrenching cuts in federal programs, the drop in revenues from the tax cuts was far steeper than the amount pruned from the budget, mainly because of the military buildup. Federal deficits began to balloon alarmingly.

Reagan's Second Term

During the 1984 presidential campaign, Reagan ran on the theme "It's Morning in America," suggesting that a new day of prosperity and pride was dawning. The Democrats nominated Walter Mondale, Carter's vice-president and a former Minnesota senator, to run against Ronald Reagan. With strong ties to labor unions, minority groups, and party leaders, Mondale epitomized the New Deal coalition. To appeal to women voters, he selected Representative Geraldine Ferraro of New York as his running mate, the first woman on a major party ticket. Reagan won a landslide victory, carrying the entire country except Minnesota and the District of Columbia. He did especially well among young (eighteen-to twenty-one-year-old) voters, receiving 62 percent of their support.

After a string of administrations that had ended in discord (Johnson and Vietnam), disgrace (Nixon and Watergate), or frustration (Carter and Iran), many Americans responded warmly to Reagan's confident leadership. He became known as the "Great Communicator" because of his ability to establish a rapport with the American people through the medium of television. Reagan's enormous personal popularity brought to mind that of Dwight Eisenhower in the 1950s. Also like Eisenhower's, his coattails were short: Democrats maintained control of the House and picked up two seats in the Senate; they would regain control of the Senate in 1986.

The Iran-Contra Affair. A major scandal marred Reagan's second term. In 1986 news leaked out that the administration had negotiated an arms-for-hostages deal with the revolutionary government of Iran, the same government Reagan had denounced during the 1980 hostage crisis. In an attempt to gain Iran's help in freeing American hostages held by pro-Iranian forces in Lebanon, the United States had covertly sold arms to Iran. Some of the profits generated by the arms sales were diverted by the Central Intelligence Agency as military aid to the Contras, counterrevolutionaries in Nicaragua, whom the administration supported over the popularly elected communist regime of the Sandinistas.

The covert diversion of funds, an action both illegal and unconstitutional, was the brainstorm of Marine Lieutenant Colonel Oliver North, a National Security Council aide at the time. After the American press picked up the story, North shredded hundreds of documents but missed a key memo that linked the White House to the plan. Congress investigated the mounting scandal in 1986 and 1987, but White House officials testifed that the president knew nothing about the diversion. Ronald Reagan's defense remained simple and consistent: "I don't remember."

The scandal bore many similarities to Watergate, including the possibility that the president had acted illegally and unconstitutionally, but this time there were no significant calls for impeachment. Early in Reagan's administration, one of his critics had coined the phrase "Teflon presidency" to describe Reagan—bad news didn't stick; it just rolled off. Reagan weathered "Iran-Contragate," but the scandal did weaken his presidency.

Reagan Legacies. The president proposed no bold domestic policy initiatives in his last two years in office. Reagan had come into office promising to dismantle an intrusive federal bureaucracy, reduce federal entitlement programs, and give free-market forces greater scope in the economy. During his two terms Reagan reordered the priorities of the federal government but failed to reduce its size or scope. Although spending for most poverty programs was cut, Social Security and other entitlement programs remained untouched. Despite Reagan's failure to achieve his goals, his spending cuts and antigovernment rhetoric shaped the terms of political debate for the rest of the century.

One of Reagan's most significant legacies was his conservative judicial appointments, the area where the New Right had the greatest impact on his administration. In 1981 he nominated Sandra Day O'Connor to the Supreme Court, the first woman ever to serve, and in his second term he appointed two more justices, Antonin Scalia and Anthony Kennedy. Justice William Rehnquist, a noted conservative appointed by Nixon, was elevated to Chief Justice in 1986. Under Rehnquist's leadership the Court, often by a 5-to-4 mar-

Patriotism and Politics
At a confetti parade for the 1988 Summer Olympic team held at Disneyland, California, in September 1988, Republican presidential candidate George Bush and his wife Barbara bask in the glow of America's success.
Cynthia Johnson. © TIME Magazine.

Another Barrier Falls
In 1981 Sandra Day O'Connor (shown here with Chief Justice Warren Burger) became the first woman appointed to the Supreme Court. In 1993 she was joined by Ruth Bader Ginsburg.
Fred Ward/Black Star.

gin, chipped away at the Warren Court's legacy in decisions on individual liberties, affirmative action, and the rights of criminal defendants.

Ironically, for a president who had promised to balance the budget by 1984, Reagan's largest legacy was the national debt, which tripled during his two terms from the combined effects of increased military spending, tax reductions for high-income taxpayers, and Congress's refusal to approve deep cuts in domestic programs (Figure 31.1). In 1989 the national debt stood at $2.8 trillion, more than $11,000 for every American citizen.

The nation was also running an annual deficit in its trade with other nations. Exports had been falling since the 1970s, when American products began to encounter increasing competition in world markets. In the early 1980s the high exchange rate for dollars made U.S. goods more expensive for foreign buyers and imports more affordable for Americans. The budget and trade deficits contributed to a major shift in 1985: for the first time since 1915 the United States was a debtor rather than a creditor nation. Since then, with phenomenal speed, the United States has accumulated the world's largest foreign debt.

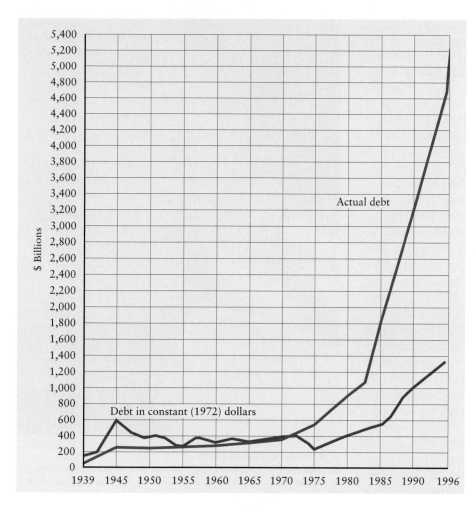

FIGURE 31.1
The Escalating Federal Debt,
1939–1996
The federal debt, which soared during World War II, remained fairly stable until the huge annual deficits of the 1980s. Deficits remained high in the 1990s, but political pressure to balance the budget promised reductions in the national debt.
Source: U.S. Statistical Abstract, 1997.

The Bush Presidency

George Herbert Walker Bush was a loyal vice-president but did not share all of Reagan's conservative views. Bush won the Republican nomination in 1988 by beating back challenges from Senate minority leader Robert Dole, television evangelist Pat Robertson, and congressional representative Jack Kemp. Bush's choice for vice-president, young conservative Indiana senator Dan Quayle, who had used family connections to avoid service in Vietnam, added little to the ticket. In the Democratic primaries, the contest was between Governor Michael Dukakis of Massachusetts and the charismatic civil rights leader Jesse Jackson, whose populist Rainbow Coalition embraced the diversity of Democratic constituencies. Dukakis, a somewhat bland figure known for a technocratic approach to state government, received the party's nomination and chose Senator Lloyd Bentsen of Texas as his running mate.

The 1988 campaign had a harsh cast to it, with negative commercials and televised "sound bites" replacing meaningful discussion of the issues. The sound bite "Read My Lips: No New Taxes," drawn from Bush's acceptance speech at the Republican convention, became that party's campaign mantra. In a television ad featuring a mug shot of Willie Horton, a black man convicted of murder who had killed again while on parole from a Massachusetts prison, Republicans pandered to voters' racist fears and implied that Dukakis was soft on crime. Forced on the defensive, Dukakis failed to mount an effective counterattack. Bush carried thirty-eight states, winning the popular vote 53.4 percent to 45.6 percent.

Domestic and Economic Policy. A key issue during Bush's four years as president was the economy. His campaign promise of a "kinder, gentler administration" was doomed by his predecessor's economic policies, especially the budget deficit, which had peaked at $221 billion in 1986 before leveling off. The Gramm-Rudman Balanced Budget Act, passed in 1985, had mandated automatic cuts if budget targets were not met in 1991. Facing the prospect of a halt in nonessential government services and the layoff of thousands of government employees, Congress froze annual outlays for discretionary spending and initiated one of the largest tax increases in history. Bush's failure to keep his "no new taxes" promise earned him the undying enmity of Republican conservatives, who saw it as a betrayal of Reaganomics, and dramatically hurt his chances for reelection in 1992. In the long run, however, the 1990 budget deal laid the groundwork for the balanced budgets of the late 1990s.

Changing federal spending priorities had a direct impact on state and local governments. Under Reagan's New Federalism, states and localities had been forced to take over some federal programs entirely and cope with cuts in federal grants for many others, including housing, education, transportation, public works, and social services. Federal-state programs such as Medicaid, whose costs soared in the 1970s and 1980s as a result of inflation and higher demand, accounted for increasingly large parts of state budgets, as did spending for welfare, education, and prisons. State and local governments could balance their budgets only by finding new sources of revenue (thus risking taxpayer revolts) or by reducing spending and services. Fiscal conditions were especially bad in the Northeast, but California and several midwestern states also faced severe shortfalls.

A recession that began in 1990 further eroded state and local tax revenues. Incomes decreased, and poverty increased sharply. In 1991 unemployment approached 7 percent nationwide; state and local governments laid off workers to save money even as they faced greater demands for social services and unemployment compensation. Industrial and white-collar layoffs spread, and in many American families someone had already lost a job or feared that a layoff might happen soon. Recovery was slowed by the massive federal debt, overburdened state and local governments, and decreasing consumer confidence.

The Savings and Loan Crisis.   Another drag on the economy was the collapse of the savings and loan industry. The scandal had its roots in decisions made during the Reagan administration, but its full impact was felt only after Bush took office.

Savings and loan associations (S & Ls), also called "thrifts," invested depositors' savings in home mortgages. Since 1934 deposits in S & Ls had been insured by the Federal Savings and Loan Insurance Corporation (FSLIC). After S & Ls complained in 1982 that high inflation and soaring interest rates were reducing their profits, Reagan's deregulation program permitted them to invest in commercial real estate and businesses. The real-estate market boomed for most of the 1980s, so the loans and investments were profitable. But when construction and the oil boom in the Southwest slowed and the stock market tumbled sharply in 1987, savings and loan associations' losses mounted, and the value of their assets plummeted. Some S & Ls were taken over by commercial banks, but many simply went bankrupt, forcing the federal government to make good its guarantee to depositors. To recoup some of the massive losses, the Bush administration set up a temporary agency in 1989 to sell the remaining assets—primarily defaulted real estate. It took the Resolution Trust Cor-

A Woman of Conscience
Accusations by University of Oklahoma law professor Anita Hill that Supreme Court nominee Clarence Thomas had sexually harassed her sparked fierce debate. Many felt that had there been more women in the Senate, Hill's charges would have been treated more seriously. After the 1992 election, women's representation did in fact increase to six women in the Senate and forty-seven in the House of Representatives. Markel/Gamma Liaison.

poration six years to clean up the mess, at a total cost to American taxpayers of $150 billion.

Supreme Court Conservatism.   During the Bush administration, the Supreme Court continued to move away from liberal activism toward a more conservative stance, especially on the issue of abortion. The 1989 *Webster v. Reproductive Health Services* decision permitted states to restrict abortion, and the next year, in *Rust v. Sullivan*, the Court upheld a federal regulation barring personnel at federally funded health clinics from discussing abortion with their clients. In 1992, in *Planned Parenthood v. Casey*, the Court upheld a Pennsylvania law mandating informed consent and a twenty-four-hour waiting period before an abortion could be performed. But the justices also reaffirmed the "essential holding" of *Roe v. Wade:* women had a constitutional right to abortion.

In 1990 David Souter, a little known federal judge from New Hampshire who appealed to Bush because he had not taken a stand on abortion, easily won confirmation to the Supreme Court. But the next year a major controversy erupted over Bush's nomination of Clarence Thomas, a black conservative with little judicial experience. Just as Thomas's confirmation hearings were drawing to a close, a former colleague, Anita Hill, testified publicly that Thomas had sexually harassed her in the early 1980s. After widely watched (and widely debated) televised testimony by both Thomas and Hill before the all-male Senate Judiciary Committee, the Senate confirmed Thomas by a narrow margin. In the wake of the hearings, national polls confirmed the pervasiveness of sexual harassment on the job: four out of ten women said they had been the object of unwanted sexual advances from men in the workplace.

Foreign Relations under Reagan and Bush

————————★————————

The collapse of détente late in the Carter administration, after the Soviet Union's invasion of Afghanistan, underlay Ronald Reagan's confrontational approach toward the Soviet Union and inspired the major defense buildup that occurred during his first term. Backed by Republican hard-liners, and determined to reduce communist influence in developing nations, Reagan articulated some of the harshest anti-Soviet rhetoric since the 1950s. In 1983 he went so far as to call the Soviet Union an "evil empire." The collapse of the Soviet Union in 1991 removed that nation as a credible threat, but new post–Cold War challenges quickly appeared.

Third World Interventions and a Soviet Thaw

Despite Reagan's rhetoric, not all of his international problems involved U.S.-Soviet confrontations. In 1983, after Israel invaded Lebanon, anti-Israeli Muslim fundamentalists bombed the U.S. Embassy in Beirut. A second bombing killed 239 U.S. Marine peacekeepers barracked in the city. Around the world, terrorist assassins struck down Prime Minister Indira Gandhi in India and President Anwar Sadat in Egypt. But it was airplane hijackings and countless terrorist incidents in the Middle East that led Reagan to order air strikes against one highly visible source of terrorism, Muammar Khadafy of Libya.

The administration reserved its most concerted attention for Central America, however. Halting what was seen as the spread of communism in that region became practically an obsession. In El Salvador it supported a repressive right-wing regime that was fighting against leftists. In 1983 Reagan ordered U.S. Marines to

Sightseeing in Moscow
Just five years after calling the Soviet Union an "evil empire," Ronald Reagan poses for a photo with Soviet premier Mikhail Gorbachev in front of Moscow's St. Basil Cathedral in May 1988. The incongruity of consummate cold warrior Ronald Reagan in Red Square was on a par with the sight of Richard Nixon strolling along the Great Wall of China in 1972.
Joe Marquette.

invade the tiny Caribbean island of Grenada, claiming that its Cuban-supported communist regime posed a threat to other states in the region.

Reagan's top priority, however, was to overthrow the communist-led Sandinista government in Nicaragua. In 1981 the United States suspended aid to Nicaragua, charging that the Sandinistas, along with Cuba and the Soviet Union, were supplying arms to the rebels in El Salvador, which the Sandinistas denied. At the same time, the CIA began to provide extensive covert support to Nicaragua's opposition forces, known as the Contras, whom Reagan called "freedom fighters." Wary of the assumption of unconstitutional powers by the executive branch, Congress responded in 1984 by passing the Boland Amendment, which banned the CIA or any other intelligence agency from providing military support to the Contras—a provision violated in the Iran-Contra affair, the greatest crisis of Reagan's presidency.

Surprisingly, given Reagan's rhetoric, his second term brought a reduction in tension with the Soviet Union. In 1985 Reagan met the new Soviet premier, Mikhail Gorbachev, in Geneva in the first superpower

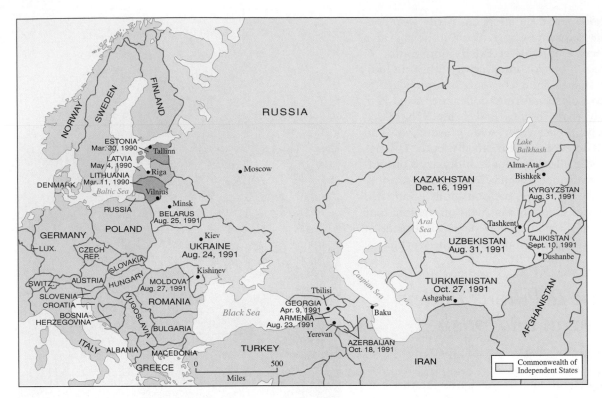

MAP 31.1

The Collapse of Communism in Eastern Europe and the Soviet Union
The end of the Soviet empire in Eastern Europe and the collapse of communism in the
Soviet Union itself dramatically changed the borders of Europe and Central Asia. West
and East Germany reunited, while the nations of Czechoslovakia and Yugoslavia, created
by the 1919 Versailles treaty, divided into smaller states. The old Soviet Union produced
fifteen new countries, of which eleven remained loosely bound in the Commonwealth of
Independent States (CIS).

summit meeting since 1979. They met again the following year in Reykjavik, Iceland. In December 1987
Reagan and Gorbachev agreed at a Washington summit
to eliminate all intermediate-range missiles based in
Europe. The agreement marked the first time an existing
category of weapons was scrapped, and it was the most
significant postwar disarmament decision since the 1972
SALT I agreement. Although a fourth summit in Moscow
in April 1988 produced no further cuts in nuclear arms,
the sight of the two first families attending the Bolshoi
Ballet together and strolling amiably in Red Square
demonstrated the new cordial relationship between the
former rivals. When the Soviets announced soon afterward that they were withdrawing from Afghanistan,
prospects for cooperation appeared to be even brighter.

The End of the Cold War

For years American policy makers had warned about the
"domino" effect of countries falling to communism. Now
the domino effect was unexpectedly working in the opposite direction. In 1989 the grip of communism on Eastern
Europe loosened and then let go completely in a series of

mostly nonviolent "velvet revolutions" (the phrase came
from Czech leader Vaclav Havel) that climaxed in the
destruction of the Berlin Wall in November. Soon the
Soviet Union itself succumbed to the forces of change.

The background for those dramatic upheavals lay in
changes set in motion by the Soviet leader Mikhail Gorbachev after 1985. His policies of *glasnost* (openness)
and *perestroika* (economic restructuring) signaled a willingness to tolerate significant changes in the Soviet bloc
and in Soviet relationships with the rest of the world.
But the Soviet leader, always more popular outside his
country than at home, found it easier to call for the dismantling of the old system than to build something new.

On August 19, 1991, alarmed Soviet military leaders seized Gorbachev and attempted unsuccessfully to
oust him. The failure of the coup broke the grip of the
Communist Party over the Soviet Union. Lithuania had
declared its independence in March 1990, and now the
Baltic republics of Latvia and Estonia followed suit. In
December the Union of Soviet Socialist Republics formally dissolved itself to make way for the eleven-
member Commonwealth of Independent States (CIS)
(Map 31.1). Gorbachev resigned, and the charismatic

reform leader Boris Yeltsin, president of the new state of Russia—the largest and most populous republic—became the preeminent leader in the region.

The suddenness of the collapse of the Soviet Union and the end of the Cold War stunned America and the rest of the world. For more than forty years the United States had been locked in an ideological battle with its archenemy, the Soviet Union. American citizens had endured fear of nuclear annihilation, anticommunist witch-hunts, and secret radiation experiments. During the Cold War the United States spent some $4 trillion on nuclear weapons alone. Republicans claimed that Reagan's military buildup had caused the Soviet Union to collapse, but George Kennan—the only original architect of containment still alive—disagreed: "Nobody—no country, no party, no person—'won' the cold war." According to Kennan (and many other observers), both sides paid a heavy price.

The director of the Central Intelligence Agency summed up the dilemma of forging a post–Cold War foreign policy: "We have slain a large dragon, but we live now in a jungle filled with a bewildering variety of poisonous snakes. And in many ways, the dragon was easier to keep track of." Instead of superpower confrontations, violence often arose from regional conflicts over ethnicity, religion, and nationalism, such as in Bosnia, the former Yugoslavia, after 1991. As the only military superpower, the United States was often asked to wield its still enormous influence in the void left by the collapse of communism. Far from receding as the Cold War ended, American military and political leadership seemed even more necessary in the new world order.

War in the Persian Gulf, 1990–1991

The first new challenge arose in the Middle East. On August 2, 1990, Iraq invaded Kuwait. Saddam Hussein's brutal conquest of his oil-rich neighbor took American policy makers by surprise (see Voices from Abroad, "Saddam Hussein: Calling for a Holy War against the United States," p. 1014). President Bush orchestrated broad international support for a series of United Nations Security Council resolutions condemning Iraq, calling for its withdrawal from Kuwait, and imposing an embargo and trade sanctions. The United Nations was finally working the way its Dumbarton Oaks planners had hoped, in large part because superpower tensions had abated with the end of the Cold War.

When Saddam Hussein showed no signs of complying with the resolutions, Bush prodded the United Nations to create a legal framework for an international military offensive against the man he repeatedly called "the butcher of Baghdad." In November the Security Council voted to use force if Iraq did not withdraw from Kuwait by January 15. In early January, Congress debated whether to give sanctions more time

Women at War
Women played key and visible roles in the Persian Gulf War, comprising approximately 10 percent of the American troops. Increasing numbers of women are choosing military careers, despite widespread reports of sexual harassment and other forms of discrimination.
Luc Delahaye/SIPA Press.

to work, and then, in a 52-to-48 vote, the Senate authorized military action. On January 16, President Bush announced to the nation that "the liberation of Kuwait has begun."

The American commitment of 540,000 troops matched the number at the height of the Vietnam War in 1968. But this was a new, all-volunteer military that included thousands of reservists called up from civilian jobs. Blacks and members of other minorities, many attracted to military service by benefits such as education and health care, made up a third of the force. Women, accounting for approximately 10 percent of the troops, were a far greater presence than in Vietnam, although they served in support, not direct combat, positions.

The forty-two-day war was a resounding success for the coalition forces, which, as in the Korean War, were predominantly American. In a series of well-orchestrated briefings, General Colin Powell, chairman of the Joint Chiefs of Staff, and the commanding general, H. Norman Schwarzkopf, projected a confident new image for the post-Vietnam military. The air-land strategy of "Operation Desert Storm" began with a month of air strikes to crush communications, destroy armaments, and pummel the morale of the Iraqi troops, followed by a ground offensive against Iraqi troops in Kuwait and southern Iraq. The ground phase

SADDAM HUSSEIN

Calling for a Holy War against the United States

———————★———————

After Iraq invaded Kuwait in August 1990, President Saddam Hussein of Iraq justified the action in the language of Jihad, Muslim holy war. Hussein's call for a holy war against the United States suggested the ways in which Islamic fundamentalism had become part of the larger political discourse of the Arab world, particularly in political relations with Western nations.

This great crisis started on the 2d of August, between the faithful rulers and presidents of these nations— the unjust rulers who have abused everything that is noble and holy until they are now standing in a position which enables the devil to manipulate them. This is the great crisis of this age in this great part of the world where the material side of life has surpassed the spiritual one and the moral one. . . . This is the war of right against wrong and is a crisis between Allah's teachings and the devil.

Allah the Almighty has made his choice—the choice for the fighters and the strugglers who are in favor of principles, God has chosen the arena for this crisis to be the Arab World, and has put the Arabs in a progressive position in which the Iraqis are among the foremost. And to confirm once more the meaning that God taught us ever since the first light of faith and belief, which is that the arena of the Arab world is the arena of the first belief and Arabs have always been an example and a model for belief and faith in God Almighty and are the ones who are worthy of true happiness.

It is now your turn, Arabs, to save all humanity and not just save yourselves, and to show the principles and meanings of the message of Islam, of which you are all believers and of which you are all leaders.

It is now your turn to save humanity from the unjust powers who are corrupt and exploit us and are so proud of their positions, and these are led by the United States of America. . . .

For, as we know out of a story from the Holy Koran, the rulers, the corrupt rulers, have always been ousted by their people for it is a right on all of us to carry out the holy jihad, the holy war of Islam, to liberate the holy shrines of Islam. While the ruler of Saudi Arabia called himself the custodian of the two holy shrines, while in fact he is an agent, for he has given away his land to the foreigners.

We call upon all Arabs, each according to his potentials and capabilities within the teachings of Allah and according to the Muslim holy war of jihad, to fight this U.S. presence of non-believers and to fight the stance taken by the Arab agents who have followed these foreigners. And we hail the people of Saudi Arabia who are being fooled by their rulers, as well as the people of dear Egypt, as well as all the people of the Arab nations who are not of the same position as their leaders, and they believe in their pride and their sovereignty over their land. We call on them to revolt against their traitors, their rulers, and to fight foreign presence in the holy lands. And we support them, and more important, that God is with them.

———————

Source: New York Times, September 6, 1990, A19.

of the war was launched on February 23; within days thousands of Iraqi troops fled or surrendered, and the fighting quickly ended (Map 31.2). Saddam Hussein remained firmly in power, however, with his arsenal of weapons of mass destruction intact, despite his promise to remove all biological, chemical, and nuclear arms and allow United Nations inspectors to verify their destruction.

The rapid success of the ground war and relief at the amazingly low number of U.S. casualties (145 Americans killed in action, a stark contrast to the high Iraqi civilian and military casualties) produced a euphoric reaction at home. For many, the stellar performance of American troops banished the ghost of Vietnam, the antimilitary malaise resulting from that prolonged, inconclusive, and divisive war. "By God,

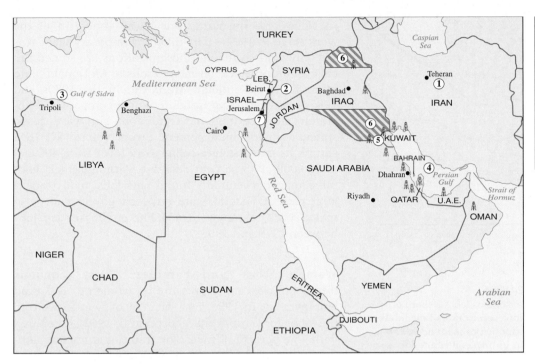

1. Teheran hostage taking, Nov.1979–Jan.1981
2. 241 U.S. peacekeeping troops die in bombing, Oct. 1983.
3. U.S. air strikes, Mar.–Apr. 1986.
4. U.S. Navy shoots down Iranian airliner, July 1988.
5. Operation Desert Storm (Gulf War) Jan.-Feb. 1991.
6. U.S. declares "no-fly zones" in northern and southern Iraq, 1992.
7. U.S. brokers Israeli-Palestinian peace treaty, May 1994.

⚒ Oil fields

MAP 31.2
U.S. Involvement in the Middle East, 1980–1994
The United States has long played an active role in the Middle East, pursuing the twin goals of protecting Israel's security and ensuring a reliable supply of low-cost oil from the Persian Gulf states. By far the largest intervention came in 1991, when, under United Nations auspices, President Bush sent 540,000 American troops to liberate Kuwait from Iraq. The United States also played a major role in the 1994 agreement allowing for Palestinian self-rule in the Gaza Strip and parts of the West Bank.

we've kicked the Vietnam Syndrome once and for all," gloated George Bush. The president's approval rating shot up precipitously, but it declined almost as quickly when the continuing recession showed that the easy victory had masked the country's serious economic problems. One consumer observed, "The country is feeling good about the war, I'm feeling good about it, but I still can't afford a new car."

Uncertain Times

Opinion polls taken in the early 1990s showed that Americans were deeply concerned about the future— their own and their children's. Americans were also concerned about crime in the streets, terrorism from abroad, increases in poverty and homelessness, the decline of the inner cities, illegal immigration, the environment, the failure of public schools, the unresolved abortion issue, and AIDS. But above all they worried about their own economic security and

whether they would be able to keep their jobs in an era of global competition. These fears persisted despite the fact, which became increasingly clear as the 1990s progressed, that the U.S. economy remained the strongest in the world.

The Economy

Slow growth in productivity and growing inequality in income distribution were the most salient economic trends in the 1980s and 1990s. From the late nineteenth century through World War II, productivity grew at an average of about 1.8 percent per year, enough to double living standards every forty years. From 1945 to 1973 productivity grew 2.8 percent annually, allowing the standard of living to double in one generation. In the quarter-century since 1973, however, productivity increased less than 1 percent annually, barely enough to double the standard of living in eighty years.

Along with slowed productivity went stagnating real income (Figure 31.2). Adjusted for inflation, the wages of the typical, or median, family basically stayed the same. In 1991 the typical family's real income was

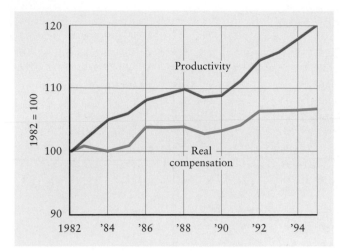

FIGURE 31.2
Productivity and Wages, 1982–1995
Usually as productivity increases, so does labor's share of
national income. In the 1990s, however, workers failed to reap
the rewards of the increased productivity shown here. Labor's
relative loss in real compensation in turn contributed to a rise
in corporate profits.
Source: New York Times, January 2, 1996, C20. Copyright © 1996 by The
New York Times Co. Reprinted by permission.

only 5 percent higher than it had been in 1973, and that
increase was achieved mainly because Americans were
working more hours and because multiple members of
a household were employed.

At the same time that wage stagnation was squeez-
ing the middle class, economic inequality increased:
the rich got richer, the poor got poorer, and the middle
class shrank. By 1996 the United States was the most
economically stratified industrial nation in the world.
Instead of the broadly based prosperity of the immediate postwar years, statistics from the Congressional
Budget Office showed that the richest 1 percent of
American families reaped most of the gains of
Reaganomics. This trend continued in the 1990s: in
1996, according to a *Business Week* study, the pay of top
executives was 209 times that of a factory employee, a
pay gap double what it had been five years earlier. Even
relatively well-advantaged Americans felt a sense of
diminished expectations. Earlier generations had
aspired to doing better than their parents financially;
now many young adults wondered whether they could
achieve even a modest middle-class life-style.

These diminished expectations stemmed in part
from changes in the job market. By the end of the twentieth century, the average employee could typically
expect to make several job or career shifts over the
course of a lifetime. Following an established pattern,
the number of minimum-wage service jobs continued to
grow, while the number of union-protected manufactur-

ing jobs kept shrinking. For many—one-fifth of the
work force in 1994—part-time or temporary work was
the only work available (these positions are sometimes
called "McJobs," a reference to jobs at McDonald's and
other fast-food outlets). Moreover, in the 1980s and
1990s the downsizing trend, in which companies deliberately shed permanent workers to cut wage costs,
spread to middle management. From 1980 to 1995 IBM
shrank its mostly white-collar work force from 400,000
to 220,000, a 45 percent decrease. Although most laid-
off managers eventually found new jobs, many took a
large pay cut. Federal, state, and local governments also
scaled back, eliminating 454,000 public service jobs
between 1979 and 1993.

Women, Work, and Families. These economic
trends put even more pressure on women to seek paid
employment. In 1996, 59.1 percent of women were in
the labor force (up from 38 percent in 1962), compared
with 75.8 percent of men. The traditional nuclear family of employed father, homemaker wife, and children
was found in less than 15 percent of U.S. households.
Married working women and single or divorced working women with children continued to bear the major
share of household and child-care responsibilities. For
working parents with children, family schedules were
often as intricate as time-and-motion studies.

While business leaders and the media often focused
on the breakthroughs made by women near the top of
the corporate ladder, one of every five working women
still held a clerical or secretarial job—the same proportion as in 1950. Women's pay lagged behind men's, and
the gap was especially wide for black and Latino
women. Yet women continued to make inroads in male-
dominated fields. Among all workers under age thirty-
five, women accounted for one in three doctors, four in
ten mail carriers, and a majority of purchasing agents.

Corporate Strategies. Another major cause of diminished economic expectations in the 1980s and early 1990s
was the widespread fear that American corporations
were no longer competitive in the global marketplace.
Americans viewed with alarm the economic success of
Germany and Japan, the growing U.S. trade deficit, and
the infusion of foreign investment money into the United
States. In order to compete, American corporations
adopted new technologies, including microelectronics,
biotechnology (see New Technology, "The Biotech Revolution," pp. 1018–1019), computers, and robots, and by
the mid-1990s they saw their former competitiveness
begin to return. For example, Bethlehem Steel, which
invested $6 billion to modernize its operations between
1989 and 1997, doubled its productivity.

Other firms retooled their corporate vision. In
1980–1981 Ford Motor Company lost $2.5 billion,

despite laying off 150,000 workers. In the face of this desperate situation, Ford shifted its focus from maximizing output to improving quality and consumer satisfaction, making assembly-line workers more involved in the company and its products by giving them more responsibility. The popular Ford Taurus, introduced in 1986, typified the new focus on quality.

While management struggled to improve productivity, the labor movement—hurt by downsizing, foreign competition, fear of layoffs, government hostility during the Reagan-Bush years, and its own failure to organize unskilled workers—continued to decline. The number of union members dropped from 20 million in 1978 to 16.3 million in 1996, representing only 14.5 percent of the labor force. Although union membership was more than one-third female and one-fifth black, union leadership remained overwhelmingly white and male.

An Increasingly Pluralistic Society

The 1990 census counted 246.9 million Americans, an increase of over 22 million people since the 1980 census. In 1996, the United States had a population of 265.5 million people, one-fourth of whom claimed African, Asian, Hispanic, or American Indian ancestry. The main reason for the growth in population was increased immigration, especially from Latin America and Asia (Maps 31.3 and 31.4). In 1994, 8.7 percent of the U.S. population was foreign-born, almost double the 4.8 percent of 1970 and the highest proportion since World War II. This level, however, was still far below its modern historic high of 14.7 percent in 1910, after the great tide of early twentieth-century immigration.

In the 1980s over 7 million immigrants entered the country, accounting for more than a third of the population growth in that decade. LAX and JFK, the Los Angeles and New York international airports, were the main points of entry, replacing Ellis Island, which, after decades of abandonment and decay, was turned into a museum and tourist attraction. The first major immigration legislation since 1965, the 1986 Immigration Reform and Control Act (Simpson-Mazzoli Act), attempted to establish a fair entry process. It also granted legal status to some illegal aliens, primarily Mexicans and other Latinos, who had entered the United States before 1982. Revisions to the law in 1990 expanded the quota of immigrants to 700,000 per year and gave priority to skilled workers and relatives of current residents.

Hispanic Immigration. Much of the new immigration came from Latin America and the Caribbean. In 1950 there were 4 million Hispanics in the United States; in 1996 the number was 28.3 million. The terms *Hispanic* and *Latino*, which include Spanish-speaking people from Mexico, Cuba, Puerto Rico, El Salvador,

and other Latin American countries, refer to a variety of distinctive heritages. Hispanics are the second largest minority group after blacks and the second fastest growing after Asians. Western states such as California, Texas, and New Mexico, which border Mexico, originally contained the most immigrants, but in the postwar period new arrivals from Puerto Rico and Central and South America increasingly settled on the East Coast. Latinos now live in urban areas throughout the country, making up more than one-tenth of the populations of Florida and New York, for example.

Asian Americans. Asia was the other major source of immigrants. This migration, which increased almost 108 percent from 1980 to 1990, consisted mainly of people from China, the Philippines, Vietnam, Laos, Cambodia, Korea, India, and Pakistan. Chinese Americans are still the dominant Asian group in the United States, followed by Filipinos. In 1990 California had more Asian Americans—almost 10 percent of the population—than did any other state.

Some of this immigration was traceable to upheavals in Southeast Asia. More than 700,000 Indochinese refugees entered the country in the decade after American involvement in Vietnam ended in 1975. The first arrivals were highly educated people, who, after a few years, generally achieved economic success. Many of the later refugees came with less education

New Immigrants
In the 1980s many Korean immigrants got their start by opening small grocery stores in urban neighborhoods. Their success sometimes led to conflicts with other racial groups, such as blacks and Hispanics, who were often their customers as well as competitors.
Kay Chernush/The Image Bank.

The Biotech Revolution

★

WAS ZACHARY TAYLOR poisoned? Did Abraham Lincoln have a rare disease called Marfan's syndrome? Were Tzar Nicholas II and his family executed during the Bolshevik Revolution in 1918? Was the Vietnam serviceman buried in Arlington Cemetery's Tomb of the Unknowns really Air Force Lieutenant Michael Blassie? Recent advances in DNA testing, part of the dramatic growth in biotechnology in the 1980s and 1990s, mean that these historical questions, plus a host of contemporary ones, can be answered. With promises of breakthroughs in medicine (gene therapy and cancer research), the environment (genetically altered microorganisms for pollution cleanup), and agriculture (genetically engineered foods), biotechnology offers the possibility not just to understand but also to manipulate the processes of life.

The essence of biotechnology is exploiting genes, a process revolutionized by the 1953 discovery of DNA by scientists James Watson and Francis Crick. DNA (deoxyribonucleic acid) is the molecule that carries the genetic blueprint of all living things; genes are DNA chains made up of hundreds or some-

Cracking the Genetic Code
A researcher enters DNA sequences into a computer as part of the effort to map the human genome.
© J. Griffin/The Image Works.

and fewer skills and struggled for a foothold. When the Cambodian population in the former textile town of Lowell, Massachusetts, increased from 3,500 in 1985 to 20,000 just three years later, the school system struggled to find bilingual teachers fluent in Khmer, the Cambodian language.

The new immigrants' impact on the social, economic, and cultural landscape of the country has been tremendous. In many places they have created thriving ethnic communities, such as Little Saigon in Orange County, California; Little Havana in Miami; and Koreatown in Los Angeles. Tens of thousands of Soviet Jews fleeing religious and political persecution in the 1980s created Little Odessa in Brooklyn, New York. Ethnic restaurants and shops have sprung up across the country, and at least three hundred specialized periodicals serve immigrant readers. But demographers noted another pattern in major metropolitan areas with heavy immigration: for every immigrant who moved in, a native-born (usually white) person left.

Anti-Immigrant Sentiment.   Ethnic and racial diversity, always a source of conflict in American culture, became a defining theme of the 1990s as new immigrants often became scapegoats for all that was wrong in the United States. Even though economists gener-

times thousands of simple molecules. Like finger-prints, no two people (other than identical twins) have the same genetic characteristics. Once DNA's structure was understood, it became theoretically possible to isolate the genetic codes that control everything from hair color to height to inherited diseases and certain cancers. In the 1980s laboratory advances such as PCR (polymerase chain reaction, polymerase being the enzyme that triggers the replication of DNA) made it possible to take a single fragment of DNA and copy it infinitely. In the past, DNA samples had often been too meager to work with. One immediate result of PCR was the introduction of the most sensitive test yet for the AIDS virus.

One of the earliest applications of DNA research was in criminal justice cases. From blood, saliva, semen, or hair samples, it became possible to show whether the genetic profile of a suspect matched the DNA information gathered at the crime scene. By 1995, DNA testing had been used in more than twenty-four thousand criminal cases. Some of its most dramatic results proved the innocence of individuals convicted before this technology was available; DNA testing established that their genetic makeup was so markedly different from the surviving evidence that they could not possibly have committed the crimes for which they were imprisoned. Even so, as the 1995 murder trial and acquittal of former football star O.J. Simpson showed, DNA testing remained controversial. Simpson's defense team was able to raise doubts about possible contamination of Simpson's blood samples by faulty laboratory procedures and to counter seemingly overwhelming DNA-based medical evidence that linked bloodstains on Simpson's socks, gloves, and car to the victims.

DNA testing was just one of many promising medical and scientific discoveries to emerge in the 1980s and 1990s. Biotech companies such as Genentech, Amgen, and Biogen pioneered in finding practical—and potentially profitable—applications for the new technology, making biotech companies hot tickets for investors. Nowhere was the promise of this research more evident than in medical technology, where biotechnology became the driving force in the creation of genetically engineered drugs and vaccines, the identification of specific genes that cause cystic fibrosis and sickle-cell anemia, and the transplantation of either healthy or genetically altered cells to treat cancer. But initial excitement palled as companies found it difficult to translate this new understanding of the cell's nucleus into products that could actually be shown in clinical trials to benefit humans. So volatile has the biotech business been that one analyst called it "free fall" rather than free enterprise—bungee jumping without the bungee.

One of the most ambitious projects undertaken to date is the Human Genome Project, launched in 1988 with the goal of deciphering the entire human genetic code (the entirety of the DNA in an organism is called its genome). If completed as planned early in the twenty-first century, this genetic blueprint would serve a purpose not unlike the periodic table of elements, the basis for twentieth-century research in chemistry. Given that there are approximately 3 billion nucleic acid base pairs in just one set of human chromosomes, the success of this project is intricately linked to the expanding capacities of modern computers. Biochemistry, medical research, and computer science are increasingly intertwined as earlier technological revolutions spawn new ones.

ally believe that immigrants give more than they take, providing a fresh source of predominantly youthful and highly motivated workers who take jobs that are not wanted by other people or move into new jobs in the growing service sector, many American-born workers still feared that immigrants would adversely affect their job prospects in a time of diminished economic opportunity. Immigrants, both legal and illegal, provided inviting targets when budgetary crises on the state and local levels mandated cutbacks (see American Voices, "Cuauhtémoc Menendez: The Undocumented Worker," p. 1022). Polls showed strong public support for denying government assistance to all immigrants, regardless of their legal status, on the unproven assumption that immigrants were lured here by generous public services.

The most dramatic challenges to immigrants have emerged on the state level. In the 1980s California absorbed far more immigrants than any other state: more than a third of its growth in that decade came from foreign immigration. In 1994 California voters (including a majority of Hispanic voters) overwhelmingly approved a ballot initiative provocatively called "Save Our State," also known as Proposition 187. This initiative barred undocumented aliens from public schools, nonemergency care at public health clinics,

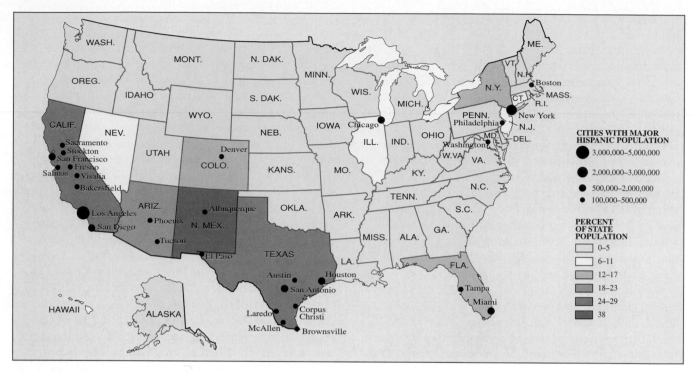

MAP 31.3
Hispanic American Population, 1990
The Hispanic population of the United States is concentrated in California, New York,
Texas, Florida, and Illinois, mainly in urban areas. Demographers predict that Hispanic
Americans will overtake African Americans as the largest minority group early in the
twenty-first century and that by the year 2050 non-Hispanic whites will constitute only
about half of the U.S. population.

and all other state social services. It also required law
enforcement officers, school administrators, and social
workers to report suspected illegal immigrants to the
federal Immigration and Naturalization Service.
Though opponents challenged the constitutionality of
the ballot referendum, anti-immigrant feeling soon
spread to other parts of the country.

The Plight of Urban America. One by-product of
this increased immigration was that black Americans
constituted a comparatively smaller percentage of the
minority population in 1990 than they had earlier in
the century. (Black immigration from the Caribbean
and Africa has been too small to affect this trend.)
Demographers predict that Latinos will outnumber
blacks in the U.S. population early in the twenty-first
century. Although a 1997 National Academy of Sciences report found that "some black workers have lost
their jobs to immigrants," for the most part African
Americans were not adversely affected by the new
immigration. But economic necessity and entrenched
segregation patterns forced urban blacks and new
immigrants to fight for space in decaying, crime-
ridden ghettos, where unemployment rates sometimes

hit 60 percent and overcrowded and underfunded inner
city schools struggled to provide a proper education.

In the 1980s the historical tide of black migration
to the cities that had begun before World War I started
to recede. Southern blacks who learned about the poor
job prospects were less likely to seek new lives in urban
areas; quite the contrary, almost anyone who could
leave was moving out of the inner cities, usually for a
more stable urban neighborhood or the suburbs. In Los
Angeles, as Asians and Latinos moved in, middle-class
blacks moved out, usually to neighboring counties such
as Riverside, San Bernardino, and Ventura. Some
blacks even made a reverse migration back to the
South. Compared with the crime-ridden and dilapidated housing projects in Chicago or South-Central Los
Angeles, the post–civil rights South seemed attractive.
Atlanta was one of the most popular destinations.

In April 1992 the frustration and anger of impoverished urban Americans erupted in five days of riots in
Los Angeles, the worst civil disorder since the 1960s.
The violence took sixty lives and caused $850 million in
damage. The rioting was set off by the acquittal on all
but one charge of four white Los Angeles police officers
accused of using excessive force while arresting a black

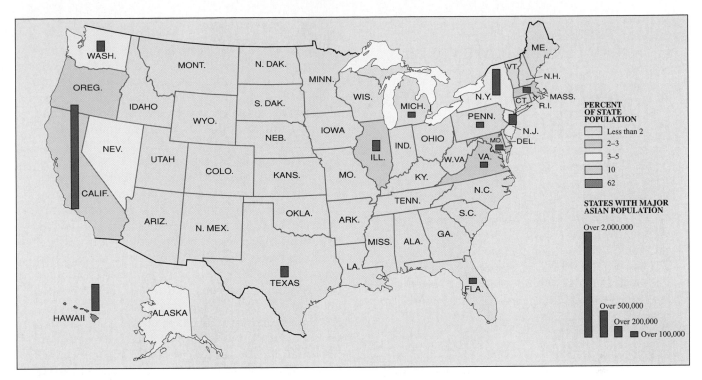

MAP 31.4
Asian American Population, 1990
In 1990 Asian Americans made up just under 3 percent of the total U.S. population. Asian population is concentrated on the East and West coasts, especially in California, and in major cities.

motorist, Rodney King, on March 3, 1991. The predominantly white jury was not swayed by a graphic 81-second amateur video of the arrest that showed the officers kicking, clubbing, and beating King. The video, shown repeatedly on television, brought renewed attention to the issue of police brutality and the harassment of minorities. Three of the officers were later convicted on federal charges of violating King's civil rights.

The Los Angeles riots exposed the cleavages in urban neighborhoods. Trapped in the nation's inner cities, many blacks resented recent immigrants who were struggling to get ahead—and often succeeding. As a result some blacks targeted Korean-owned stores for arson and looting. Latinos also felt frustrated about high unemployment and crowded housing conditions. According to the Los Angeles Police Department, Latinos accounted for more than half of those arrested and a third of those killed during the rioting.

The Debate over Affirmative Action. One of the ways federal and state governments had tried to help blacks and Latinos was through the establishment of affirmative action programs in government hiring, contracts, and university admissions. From the inception of affirmative action programs in 1965 and their extension to women in 1967, many Americans, often white men, had viewed

To Live and Die in L.A.
The images from South-Central Los Angeles in the wake of the 1992 riots looked eerily similar to those from Watts in 1965. The underlying causes of both riots were similar as well—police brutality, racism, and frustration about lack of jobs and opportunity.
Sylvie Kreiss/Liaison.

CUAUHTÉMOC MENENDEZ

The Undocumented Worker

──────★──────

In this oral history, Cuauhtémoc Menendez, an immigrant construction worker, reflects on the controversial issue of undocumented Mexican workers—an issue that helped feed anti-immigrant sentiment in the 1980s and 1990s. After working for ten years in the United States, Menendez returned to Guadalajara, Mexico, for good.

In the United States, to get rid of all the illegals, you don't need a border or the Immigration. Simply, if there is no work, what would the illegals do there? Really, I don't see the reason to form groups and lines at the border like in the thirties. The United States is an advanced industrial society, the same in the city as it is in the agricultural areas. It's logical that there is the need for workers. For the United States it is a great advantage, because Mexican labor is very cheap. The illegal produces his product much cheaper, and they can sell it cheaper to the American people. In this sense the illegal helps the United States.

He also helps Mexico. All of the *mojados* bring money back. We don't take money out of Mexico. Those of us who work in the United States help our country more than the rich who send their Mexican money out. We support our country.

Normally the Mexican who goes to the United States goes to work in jobs that many Americans don't want. In the first place, it's hard work. I'm not going to say that they can't do the work, but they don't want to work for the same price as the Mexican. It's clear that there is this contradiction, this antipathy toward the Mexican who is there illegally. They look at the *mojados* as scabs. The Chicanos and Mexican-Americans look at us from this perspective because they think we are the reason they don't have jobs. But it's not true. We are there at the convenience of the owners and bosses who want cheap labor, cheaper than they can get there. It isn't our fault. We have the necessity to work. I don't think it's a sin to subsist in another country that offers the opportunity to live a little better than is possible for us in Mexico.

Some Americans think they are going to take away our work, but it isn't certain, because it's an important factor to the economy of the United States. What I want to say is that I didn't take work away from any North American. What happened was, there was a competition for the work. I'm not saying I was better, but I worked harder, and they paid for the work. My boss always accepted me because my work was good; he knew it was good. I worked faster and harder. For this my work was accepted. You know, an American boss doesn't pay someone for his good looks, no matter where you're from, nor for friendships or *compadrazgo*. It's for the skill. If a Mexican can demonstrate that he's a good worker, they will pay him.

Source: Marilyn P. Davis, *Mexican Voices, American Dreams: An Oral History of Mexican Immigration to the United States* (New York: Henry Holt, 1990), 410–411.

---

them as unfair and discriminatory. Some, like Allen Bakke, even took their cases to court (see Chapter 30). But affirmative action remained official government policy until the 1990s, when arguments over minority and immigrant rights as well as the shrinking economy and white resentment fueled a renewed debate on the issue.

The impact of affirmative action was most evident in college admissions. The University of California system had undertaken one of the most far-reaching plans. As late as 1984 whites had made up about two-thirds of the undergraduate student body. In 1994, as a result of the implementation of affirmative action, students at the Berkeley campus were 39 percent Asian, 32 percent white, 14 percent Latino, 6 percent black, and 1 percent native American (8 percent of the students did not identify their race). In 1996 California voters banned consideration of race, ethnicity, or gender in college admissions, public employment, and contracting. The next year the number of blacks admitted to Berkeley dropped 57 percent, and admissions of Hispanics declined 40 percent. Minority enrollments dropped in the rest of the California system as well, though not to the same extreme.

Culture Wars

One reason affirmative action became a political issue in the 1990s was that many—including prominent conservatives like George F. Will, William Bennett, and Patrick Buchanan—saw it as a threat to core American values. Linking affirmative action with multiculturalism—the attempt to represent the diversity of American society and its peoples—critics feared that all this counting by race, gender, sexual preference, and age would lead to the fragmentation of American society. Attempts to revise American history textbooks along multicultural lines were especially contentious, as were efforts by Stanford and other universities to revise college curricula to include non-European cultures in the study of Western civilization.

Culture wars broke out on other fronts as well. Conservatives in Congress led an effort to eliminate federal funding for the arts, humanities, and public television, arguing that the federal government should not be in the business of supporting works that many found offensive or antithetical to traditional American values. The National Endowments for the Arts and the Humanities survived, but with drastically reduced budgets. Conservatives also took aim at the speech codes that many colleges adopted to ban racist or sexist comments from everyday language.

Backlash against Feminism. The women's movement also became a target of conservative critics. In the widely read *Backlash: The Undeclared War on American Women* (1991), journalist Susan Faludi described a powerful reaction against the gains American women had won in the 1960s and 1970s. Spearheaded by New Right leaders, the media, and organizations such as Concerned Women for America, an increasing number of conservatives held the women's movement responsible for every ill afflicting modern women—from infertility to eating disorders to rising divorce rates. Yet polls showed strong support for many feminist demands, such as pay equity, increased access to jobs, reproductive rights, and more equitable sharing of household and child-care responsibilities.

Feminism was also weakened by racial and generational fault lines. Despite the attempts of prominent feminist organizations such as the National Organization for Women (NOW) to focus on racial and ethnic differences among women, African Americans and other women of color often felt themselves to be tokens in a predominantly white movement. Many young women felt that the movement had become too obsessed with women as passive victims (of date rape, discrimination, sexual harassment, the media's beauty myth, and so forth) rather than offering women models of empowerment. But other young women, influenced by women's studies programs and the explosion of feminist scholarship, forged a third wave of feminism in the 1990s (see American Voices, "Laurie Ouellette: A Third-Wave Feminist," p. 1024).

The deep national divide over abortion, one of the main issues associated with feminism, continued to polarize the country. In the 1980s and 1990s harassment and violence toward those who sought or provided abortion became increasingly common. In 1994 four workers were killed, including two receptionists at Boston clinics. Although only a fraction of anti-abortion activists supported such extreme acts, disruptive confrontational tactics made it more dangerous for women to exercise their legal right to an abortion. In May 1994 Congress passed the Freedom of Access to Clinic Entrances Act (FACE), which imposed federal fines and prison terms on those who used physical obstruction or intimidation to interfere with access to reproductive health services.

Gays and American Society. Gay rights was another field of battle. Gay activists used their political clout in more than a hundred communities across the country to win civil rights legislation protecting gay men and lesbians from discrimination in public housing, education, real estate, public accommodations, and employment. Certain cities, including New York City, Washington, D.C., and San Francisco, allowed same-sex couples to register as domestic partners.

To conservatives, especially the Christian Right and its sympathizers in Congress, a gay life-style was an affront to traditional family values. Pat Robertson, Jesse Helms, and others denounced civil rights protections for gays as undeserved "special rights." Such tactics helped antigay forces win a 1992 Colorado referendum to add a state constitutional amendment barring local jurisdictions from passing laws protecting gays and lesbians from discrimination. The U.S. Supreme Court overturned the Colorado provision in 1996, but this decision had little or no effect on the rising incidence of antigay harassment and violence. Twenty-five years after Stonewall, gay people were more visible in American society but were not universally accepted.

A grim backdrop to gay men's struggles against discrimination was the AIDS epidemic. Physicians first recognized acquired immune deficiency syndrome (AIDS) in 1981, and its cause was identified as the human immunodeficiency virus (HIV). At first little government funding was directed toward AIDS research or treatment; critics charged that this lack of attention reflected society's antipathy toward gay men, the earliest victims of the disease in the United States. The 1985 death from AIDS of Rock Hudson, a film star who had hidden his sexual orientation to maintain his Hollywood career, finally broke through the barrier of public apathy. But AIDS began to gain public attention only when it became clear that heterosexuals, such as hemophiliacs and others who received the virus through blood transfusions, were affected as well. A galvanizing moment was the 1991

LAURIE OUELLETTE

A Third-Wave Feminist

★

Born in 1966 and educated at the University of Minnesota, Laurie Ouellette represents the generation of women who benefited from the changes set in motion by the revival of feminism but who are confused about what feminism means. She calls on the movement to broaden its vision.

As a member of the first generation of women to benefit from the gains of the '70s women's movement without participating in its struggles, I grew up on the sidelines of feminism—too young to take part in those moments, debates, and events that would define the women's movement but old enough to experience firsthand the societal changes it had wrought.

Ironically, it is due to the modest success of feminism that many young women like myself were raised with an illusion of equality. Like most women my age, I never really thought much about feminism while I was growing up. Looking back, though, I believe it has always influenced me. Growing up with divorced parents, especially a father who was ambivalent about parental responsibilities, probably has much to do with this fact. I was only five when my parents separated in 1971, and I couldn't possibly have imagined or understood the ERA marches or the triumphal result of *Roe v. Wade* that would make history in just a few short years. Certainly I couldn't have defined the word *feminism*. Still, watching my mother struggle emotionally and financially as a single parent made the concept of gender injustice painfully clear. . . .

It was at the University of Minnesota that I first took an interest in feminist classics like *The Feminine Mystique, Sisterhood Is Powerful,* and *Sexual Politics.* They expressed the anger of an earlier generation that simultaneously captivated me and excluded me. Reading them so long after the excitement of their publication made my own consciousness-raising seem anticlimactic. Like many of my white middle-class friends, I believed that we wouldn't have to worry about issues like discrimination, oppression, and getting stuck in the housewife role. We wondered why we should join forces with a battle for women's equality that the media repeatedly declared was already "won."

My experiences after college made me think again about feminism. A public television internship where I was expected to perform menial secretarial tasks while my male (and, I might add, less experienced) co-interns worked on interesting and challenging projects shocked me into realizing the difficulties facing women in the workplace. Likewise, living in an inner-city neighborhood and being involved in community issues there showed me the dire need for feminism in the lives of the poor women, elderly women, and women of color who were my neighbors. Watching these women, many of them single mothers, struggle daily to find shelter, child care, and food made me realize that they had not been touched at all by the women's movement gains of the '70s. . . .

My 24-year-old sister stands out as an example of other routes that feminism must move toward. Whereas I have focused my energies on attending graduate school and working toward a professional career, she has chosen to forfeit similar plans, for now, in favor of marrying young, moving to the country, and raising a family. Does she signify a regression into the homemaker role of the 1950s? On the contrary. For her, issues such as getting midwifery legalized and insured, providing information about breast-feeding to rural mothers, countering the male-dominated medical establishment by using and recommending natural and alternative healing methods, and raising her own daughter with positive gender esteem are central to a feminist agenda.

Only by recognizing and helping to provide choices—both lifestyle and reproductive—for women of all races, economic levels, and ages, as well as supporting all women in their struggles to make those choices, will the women of my generation, the first to be raised in the shadow of feminism and witness its successes and failures, be able to build a successful third wave of the feminist movement.

Source: Laurie Ouellette, "Our Turn Now: Reflections of a 26-Year-Old Feminist," *Utne Reader* (July–August 1992), 118–120.

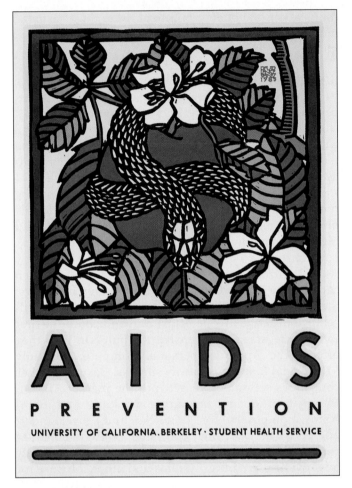

AIDS Awareness
This poster by David Lance Goines uses the image of the Garden of Eden to warn of the dangers of AIDS. By 1985, the year this poster appeared, 12,500 Americans had already died of AIDS, and the country began to confront the epidemic's human and medical costs.
David Lance Goines.

announcement by basketball great Earvin ("Magic") Johnson that he was HIV-positive. Since the mid-1980s, however, AIDS cases had been increasing among heterosexuals, especially intravenous drug users and their sex partners, as well as bisexuals. At the end of the twentieth century, women constituted the group with the fastest growing incidence of HIV infection in the United States. Some people lived for years symptom-free while being HIV-positive, and new treatment strategies using "cocktails" of several powerful drugs were leading to cautious optimism about controlling the disease, although scientists warned that the drugs were not effective for between 30 and 50 percent of patients. To date, more Americans have died of AIDS than were killed in the Korean and Vietnam Wars combined.

The Environmental Movement at Twenty-five

On April 26, 1995, when Americans came together for the twenty-fifth anniversary of Earth Day, they had much to celebrate. The nation's rivers and waterways were cleaner; air pollution had been reduced by a third; and lead emissions from fuel, a cause of retardation in children, had been cut by an astounding 98 percent. The bald eagle and the California condor had come back from the brink of extinction. More than six thousand communities across the country had recycling programs. Activists realized there was still much to be done, however. Despite efforts to reduce urban smog, two of five Americans lived in areas with unhealthy air. Many rivers and lakes were still unsafe for fishing and swimming. One of four Americans lived within four miles of a toxic waste dump, and this trend, which activists termed *environmental racism*, disproportionally affected lower-income communities.

In addition to addressing problems in their own communities, Americans were becoming increasingly aware that the environment required action not just from the United States but from the global community as a whole. Three pressing environmental problems crossed national boundaries and demanded international action: the depletion of the ozone layer, acid rain, and global warming. An important precedent for international action on environmental issues was set by the 1987 Montreal protocol, in which thirty-four nations agreed to phase out ozone-damaging chlorofluorocarbons (CFCs) by 1999. In June 1992 delegates from 170 countries to the United Nations Earth Summit in Rio de Janeiro adopted a treaty on global warming, and in 1994 the United States joined sixty-three other countries in signing the Basel Convention, which banned the export of hazardous wastes from industrialized to developing countries. In the future, U.S. environmental policy, like so much else of modern life, would operate more and more within an international framework.

Popular Culture and Popular Technology

Image was everything in the 1980s and 1990s, or so commentators said, pointing to the flamboyant rock stars Michael Jackson and Madonna and even to the genial, charismatic President Reagan. One strong influence on popular culture was MTV, which premiered in 1981. With its creative choreography, flashy colors, and rapid cuts, it seemed a perfect fit to the short attention span of a TV generation raised on programs such as *Sesame Street*. The MTV style soon showed up in mainstream media and even political campaigns, which adapted the 30-second sound bites common on television news

Be Kind to Your Mother (Earth)
This poster, created by Jennifer Morla to commemorate the twenty-fifth anniversary of Earth Day in 1995, urges people to celebrate the event by "making everyday [sic] Earth Day." Simple things that ordinary citizens can do to save the earth include stopping junk mail, recycling cans and bottles, carpooling, taking shorter showers, and recharging batteries rather than throwing them away.
© 1995 Morla Design, San Francisco.

shows to their own purposes. The national newspaper *USA Today*, which debuted in 1982, also adapted the style, featuring eye-catching graphics, color photographs, and short, easy-to-read articles. Soon more staid newspapers followed suit.

New technology, especially satellite transmission and live "minicam" broadcasting, reshaped the television industry. Also new was the increased availability of cable channels. By the mid-1990s viewers could choose from over a hundred channels, including upstarts such as Ted Turner's all-news CNN (Cable News Network), the ESPN all-sports channel, and the Fox network, which were all challenging the three major networks for viewers and profits. Media, com-

munications, and entertainment were big business, increasingly drawn into global financial networks, markets, and mergers.

Technology also reshaped the home. The 1980s saw the introduction of videocassette recorders (VCRs), compact disc (CD) players, cellular phones, and inexpensive fax machines. By 1995 eight out of ten American households had a VCR. At first Hollywood feared decreasing box-office admissions, but it soon found that VCRs created a large new market for recent films as well as for vintage movies. Video was everywhere—stores, elevators, airplanes, tennis courts, operating rooms. With the introduction of camcorders, the family photo album could be supplemented by a video of a high school graduation, a marriage, or a birth.

But it was the personal computer (PC) that truly revolutionized home and office. The big breakthrough came from Apple Computer. Two young hobbyists, Steve Jobs and Steve Wozniak, operating from a bedroom and garage in Palo Alto, California, built the first easy-to-use, small, inexpensive computer. In 1977 they offered the Apple II personal computer for only $1,195, and it was a runaway success. Belatedly, other companies scrambled to get into the market. IBM, a leader in producing tabulating machines and mainframe computers for business and government, offered its first personal computer in 1981. Software companies such as Microsoft and Lotus grew rapidly by providing operating systems and other software for this expanding market (see American Lives, "Bill Gates: Microsoft's Leader in the Computer Revolution," pp. 1028–1029). In January 1983 *Time* magazine broke with fifty-five years of tradition by naming the personal computer its "machine of the year." In 1995, 37 percent of American households had at least one personal computer.

The impact of the personal computer on business was nearly universal. More than any other technological advance, the computer created the modern electronic office. Even the smallest business could keep all its records, do all its correspondence and billing, and run its own direct-mail advertising campaigns on a single desktop machine. The very concept of the office was changing as a new category of telecommuters were able to work at home by means of computer, modem, electronic mail, and fax machine.

Today new technologies utilizing fiber optics, microwave relays, and satellites can transmit massive quantities of information to and from almost any place on earth, and even in outer space, via the *information superhighway*, or Internet. By 1996, 40 million people in the United States alone used the Internet, and experts predicted that by the year 2000 more than 250 million people in over 170 countries would have access to cyberspace—that place behind the computer screen that you can't see but you know is there.

Honey, Where's the Remote?
How many channels can you watch? How many websites can you visit? In the 1990s
Americans began to complain of information overload. This image of a person viewing
500 cable TV stations simultaneously was created by photographer Louis Psihoyos for
an article on technology that appeared in *National Geographic*.
© 1995 Louis Psihoyos-Matrix.

The Internet had Cold War roots, originating in a 1969 effort by the Pentagon to create a communications network that could survive a nuclear war. The Pentagon gave up control of the Internet in 1984, and the subsequent rapid spread of personal computers, modems, and networked computing made the Internet attractive (some would say addictive) to average citizens and commercial enterprises. At first the Internet was used mainly by scientists and other professionals to communicate with their peers through electronic mail (e-mail); then the arrival of the World Wide Web in 1991 enhanced its commercial possibilities. The Web allowed companies, organizations, political campaigns, and even the White House to create their own websites of visual and textual information for consumers to click on to at their discretion. Businesses and entrepreneurs began to use the Internet to sell their products and services, leading critics to fear that the Net would become a big shopping mall. But many economists and business analysts thought that cyberspace would be one of the driving forces for economic growth in the twenty-first century.

Theoretically available to all, at the close of the twentieth century cyberspace was still mostly available to those who could afford it, and the gap between information haves and have-nots was wide and getting wider. In 1995 only 10 percent of American households (generally those with incomes above $50,000) had the computers, modems, telephone connections, and gateway software necessary to participate in this revolution. According to a 1993 Census Bureau study, the gap was racial as well as economic: 37.5 percent of whites had computers at home, work, or school, compared with 25 percent of blacks and 22 percent of Hispanics. Who was going to get on the information superhighway and who was going to be left by the wayside was one of the most troubling issues for the twenty-first century. Critics warned against "information apartheid" or "electronic redlining" (the latter term derived from the banking practice of refusing loans to people in low-income areas).

Popular writers Alvin and Heidi Toffler used the term *Third Wave* for the new computing and telecommunications technologies and predicted that they would transform the global economy as dramatically as did the first wave (the agricultural revolution) and the second (the Industrial Revolution). The Tofflers suggested that if the wave of the future is indeed information, individuals who are not highly educated and computer-literate will find themselves greatly disadvantaged as they try to compete in the twenty-first-century workplace.

Bill Gates: Microsoft's Leader in the Computer Revolution

————★————

IN THE ELEVENTH grade Bill Gates told a friend that he would be a millionaire by the time he was thirty. When Gates went to Harvard two years later, he revised his prediction downward to twenty-five. He was being far too modest. At the age of thirty-one Bill Gates became the youngest self-made billionaire ever. In 1992 *Forbes* magazine named him the richest person in America. What was the source of all this wealth? Microsoft Corporation, whose software runs on nine of every ten personal computers sold in the United States. Microsoft is the most successful start-up company in the history of American business.

This is no Horatio Alger, rags-to-riches story. William Henry Gates III was born into a wealthy Seattle family on October 28, 1955. His father, William Gates Jr., is a successful corporate lawyer and former president of the Washington State Bar Association; his mother, Mary, was a prominent United Way volunteer who also served as a regent of the University of Washington. Gates attended the exclusive Lakeside School, one of the first schools in the country to offer students computer access, thanks to a time-sharing arrangement paid for by the school's mothers' club. The eighth-grader was hooked. Another Lakeside classmate and computer whiz was tenth-grader Paul Allen, who joined Gates in 1972 to found a company called Traf-O-Data, which counted vehicles at busy intersections by using a rudimentary computer device. In 1975 these two former classmates founded Microsoft. Allen was twenty-one; Gates, who would soon drop out of Harvard, all of nineteen.

Gates looked even younger. When Miriam Lubow became Microsoft's office manager in 1977, she was appalled when some "kid" whipped by her desk into the office of "Mr. Gates" and began playing with the computer terminal. That kid was Bill Gates. In the early days of Microsoft, Gates was too young to rent a car or have a drink with prospective clients on a business trip. His smudged glasses and unkempt hair became trademarks. But looks can be deceiving, as competitors have found out ever since.

In certain ways Gates and Allen were classic hackers—nerdy, mathematically inclined, and fascinated by the possibilities for computation (and mischief) that early computers provided. But most hackers saw computers as a hobby or a game. Back then the thought of owning one's own computer seemed as far-fetched as owning a nuclear submarine. But right from the start Gates and Allen saw commercial possibilities in the new field, long before the personal computer revolution of the 1980s. They anticipated that there would be money to be made writing, and especially marketing, software for the new machines. Microsoft's domination has resulted less from developing innovative products than from anticipating trends in the industry, getting products quickly into the marketplace, and then using its market share to bludgeon the competition. The phenomenal success of products such as MS-DOS and Windows was due as much to Microsoft's relentless marketing barrage as to any inherent technological superiority of its products. One Microsoft veteran described the corporate strategy in this way: "See where everybody's headed then catch up and go past them."

In the early days Microsoft was more like a college dorm than the billion-dollar business it later became. The "Microkids" were barely out of their teens, and some were still in high school. Nobody kept regular hours (in fact, the walls lacked clocks), and they existed on junk food, rock music, and free Coke, a tradition that Microsoft still maintains. A married employee was an oddity, and almost all the programmers were men. Parking slots were unnumbered as a way to reward early arrivals. Gates's competitive and confrontational managerial style set the tone: "That's the stupidest thing I ever heard" was a frequently heard comment.

Gates literally could not sit still, and Seattle-based Microsoft continued to grow at a fantastic rate. Gates had once thought it might employ 20 people; by 1982, Microsoft had 200 employees and sales of $32 million. In 1985, when the company went public, Gates, Allen (who had left the company in

Microsoft Employees, 1978
This group portrait shows eleven of Microsoft's thirteen employees as the company was about to relocate from Albuquerque, New Mexico, to Seattle, Washington. Bill Gates is in the front row, far left; Paul Allen is in the front row, far right. They may look geeky or weird, but they built Microsoft into a multibillion dollar corporation.
Photo Courtesy Bob Wallace.

1983 after a bout with Hodgkin's disease), and many Microsoft employees became overnight millionaires. Allen later cashed in some of his stock to buy the Portland Trailblazers. Gates used some of his personal wealth to build a $53 million house on Lake Washington outside Seattle, whose property taxes alone (estimated at $620,000 in 1998) would buy a luxury home in most U.S. cities. The house is a series of interconnected pavilions set deep into a hillside, with its own salmon estuary, a twenty-car subterranean garage, a trampoline room, and video "walls" in every room to display changing electronic images of art (for which Gates has bought the rights from major museums). "Working for Bill, you design for change," said the architect. That sums up Gates's approach to business as well.

The next step for Gates and Microsoft was onto the information superhighway. Internet commerce is projected to generate $180 billion of business a year by the beginning of the twenty-first century, and Gates wants Microsoft to be part of that connection. But if Microsoft is able to use its market share to force consumers to use its applications and links to the World Wide Web rather than competitors' browsers, thereby controlling access to the information, entertainment, shopping, real estate, and travel services that the Web provides, its dominance will increase even more. When the Justice department took Microsoft to court in 1998 for violating the antitrust laws, Gates brashly replied that he was simply giving consumers what they wanted. The fact that Attorney General Janet Reno did not even use a personal computer seemed to confirm Microsoft's view that the Department of Justice was out of touch with the importance of computers to modern life.

Friends note Bill Gates's "extraordinary bandwidth"—that is, the amount of information he can absorb—but it is his insights into business rather than technology that set Gates apart. His entrepreneurial streak would have made Henry Ford or John D. Rockefeller proud. The future, however, comes quickly in the computer field, and Gates keenly worries about being left behind in the next stage of the revolution: "It's a little scary that as computer technology has moved ahead there's never been a leader from one era who was also a leader in the next." He takes this as a warning and a challenge: "I want to defy historical tradition."

"Software is cool," Gates told CNN's Larry King to explain the hoopla surrounding the release of Microsoft's Windows 95. To the computer crowd, cool is the opposite of random, which means out of it, wrong, or inane. No one, especially not his competitors, has ever accused Bill Gates of being random.

Passing the Torch to a New Generation
Baby boomer Bill Clinton, shown here campaigning in 1992, and his running mate Al
Gore billed themselves as representing a "new generation of leadership." Born in 1946
and 1948, respectively, they came of age in the turbulent 1960s. Vietnam, not World
War II or Korea, was the war that defined their generation.
Ira Wyman/Sygma.

Restructuring the Domestic Order: Public Life, 1992–1996

— ★ —

To make progress on the environment, on the faltering economy, and on the deep social cleavages surrounding race, gender, and sexual orientation, Americans needed forceful leadership. But the strong showing of independent candidate Ross Perot and low voter turnout in the 1992 presidential election signaled deep dissatisfaction with the American political system. As if using a remote control device, Americans were clicking off politics as usual. After sixty years of supporting federal activism to combat social ills, the Democratic Party found that its core ideology was out of step with a country more concerned with cutting taxes, scaling back government, and balancing the budget. As Democrats abandoned many of their long-held liberal beliefs, the Republican Party moved even farther to the right. Looming over all their political debates was the federal deficit.

Clinton's First Term

With the end of the Cold War, domestic affairs returned to their normal place at the center of American politics. As the campaign for the 1992 presidential election got under way, the economy was the overriding issue because the recession that had begun in 1990 showed no signs of abating. Bush easily won renomination, overwhelming his lone opponent, the conservative columnist Pat Buchanan. To solidify the support of the New Right, Vice-President Dan Quayle spoke out strongly for "family values" and other conservative social agendas. Bush responded to criticism that he lacked a vision for domestic affairs by blaming the Democratic Congress for thwarting his initiatives.

Bill Clinton, the longtime governor of Arkansas, one of the nation's poorest states, emerged as the Democratic front-runner. He survived charges of marital infidelity and draft dodging and questions about a dubious Arkansas real-estate deal dubbed "Whitewater" to win the Democratic nomination. For his running mate he chose Al Gore, a second-term senator from Tennessee, widely known for his environmental best seller, *Earth in the Balance.* At age forty-four, Gore was a year and a half younger than Clinton, making them the first baby-boom national ticket.

In the middle of the primary season, the Texas billionaire H. Ross Perot capitalized on voters' desire for change by announcing on CNN's "Larry King Live" that he would run as an independent candidate. Although Perot dropped out of the race on the last day of the Democratic convention, he reentered it less than five weeks before the election, adding a well-financed wild card in an unusual election year.

The Democrats mounted an aggressive, effective campaign that focused on Clinton's plans to solve domestic problems, especially education, health care, and the economy. Gore added expertise on defense and environmental issues. Bush was hurt by the weak economy, his continued focus on foreign over domestic policy, and especially his reneging on the "no new taxes" pledge. On election day Clinton received 43 percent of the popular vote to Bush's 38 percent and Perot's 19 percent (Map 31.5). Although Perot did not win a single state, his popular vote was the highest for an independent candidate since Theodore Roosevelt in 1912. The Democrats retained control of both houses of Congress, ending twelve years of divided government. But the narrowness of Clinton's victory and the public's perception that he waffled on the issues did not bode well for his ability to lead the country.

Early Administrative and Legislative Record. As William Jefferson Clinton was sworn into office in January 1993, the liberals who had supported him hoped that a Democratic presidency could erase the Reagan-Bush legacy and oversee the creation of a new democratic social agenda. At first, Clinton seemed to fulfill that promise. In 1993 he nominated the liberal Ruth Bader Ginsburg for a seat on the Supreme Court. The president also appointed Janet Reno as attorney general, the first woman to hold that post. Other trailblazing cabinet appointments included Secretary of Health and Human Services Donna E. Shalala and, in Clinton's second term, Secretary of State Madeleine K. Albright. Clinton chose an African American, Ron Brown, as secretary of commerce, and two Latinos, Henry Cisneros and Frederico Peña, to head the Department of Housing and Urban Development (HUD) and the Department of Transportation, respectively.

Clinton's early legislative record was mixed. In early 1993 he signed into law the Family and Medical Leave Act, twice vetoed by Bush. It provided workers with up to twelve weeks of unpaid leave to tend to a newborn or an adopted child or a family medical emergency. In May, Congress passed the so-called motor-voter bill, which required states to allow citizens to register to vote when they applied for or renewed a driver's license. But when Clinton tried to implement his campaign promise to lift the ban on gays serving in the armed forces, he ran into such fierce opposition that he backed off. His compromise policy of "don't ask, don't tell, don't pursue" satisfied no one, and the bungled handling of this emotionally charged issue called into question his willingness to stand firm on issues of principle.

By the time Clinton took office, the economy had pulled out of the 1990 recession, so he was able to focus on other economic issues, especially the opening of foreign markets to U.S. goods. In 1992 President Bush had signed the North American Free Trade Agreement (NAFTA), in which the United States, Canada, and Mexico agreed to create a free-trade zone covering all of North America, the largest such zone in the world. Strongly supported by the business community, NAFTA was bitterly opposed by labor unions worried about losing jobs to lower-paid Mexican workers, and by environmentalists concerned about weak enforcement of antipollution laws south of the border. Nonetheless, with Clinton's support, Congress narrowly passed NAFTA in November 1993.

Another major development in international trade was the revision in 1994 of the General Agreement on Tariffs and Trade (GATT), the treaty governing most international trade that was part of the Bretton Woods system created at the end of World War II (see Chapter 28). This new round of revisions, the eighth since the 1940s, cut tariffs on many manufactured products and for the first time established regulations protecting intellectual property such as patents, copyrights, and trademarks for software, entertainment, and pharmaceuticals. The U.S. Senate ratified the treaty in December 1994.

With the recession over but crime rates on the rise, crime replaced the economy as a major concern among voters. In 1993, despite the opposition of the National

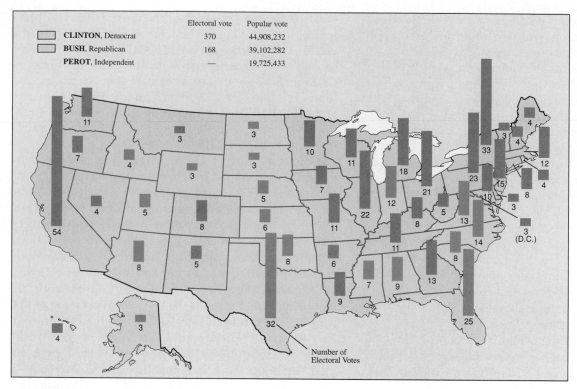

		Electoral vote	Popular vote
	CLINTON, Democrat	370	44,908,232
	BUSH, Republican	168	39,102,282
	PEROT, Independent	—	19,725,433

Number of
Electoral Votes

MAP 31.5
The Election of 1992
The first national election since the end of the Cold War was dominated by concern over the economy. The first-ever all-southerner Democratic ticket of Bill Clinton and Al Gore won broad support across the country, cutting into Republican strongholds in the South and West. The independent candidate, H. Ross Perot, won no electoral votes but polled an impressive 19 percent of the popular vote.

Rifle Association, Congress passed the Brady Handgun Violence Prevention Act, named for James Brady, the White House press secretary who was crippled in a 1981 attempted assassination of President Reagan. A much more wide-ranging piece of legislation was the Omnibus Violent Crime Control and Prevention Act (1994), which authorized $30.2 billion for stepped-up law enforcement, crime prevention, and prison construction and administration. The act also expanded the death penalty to more than fifty federal crimes and banned the sale and possession of certain kinds of assault weapons. One result was a dramatic increase in the federal and state prison population, from 774,000 in 1990 to almost 1.2 million in 1996. The U.S. incarceration rate was six to ten times higher than the rate in most industrial nations, and only Russia had a larger share of its citizens behind bars.

Health Care Reform. Responding to the deep anxieties Americans had about their economic security and despite his slender electoral mandate, Clinton staked his political fortunes on his campaign promise of uni-

versal health care. Though the United States spent more on health care than any other country ($843 billion in 1992, up 9.5 percent from the year before), it remained the only major industrialized country not to provide national health insurance. Spiraling medical costs (double the rate of inflation since 1970), rising premiums, and the large number of Americans without health insurance (one-sixth of the population in 1992) had brought the health care system to a crisis.

The president chose his wife, Hillary Rodham Clinton, to head the task force that would draft the legislation, a controversial move since no first lady had ever played such a formal role in policy making. The resulting proposal was based on the idea of managed competition: market forces, not the government, would control health care costs and expand citizens' access to health care. But even this mild form of social engineering ran into intense opposition from the well-financed pharmaceutical and insurance industries. In August 1994 the Senate failed to act on the plan, and by September congressional leaders admitted that health care reform was dead.

A Forceful and Controversial First Lady
Drawing inspiration from Eleanor Roosevelt, Hillary Rodham Clinton hoped the country would be ready for a first lady who could play a role in shaping health care policy. It wasn't.
Robert Trippet/SIPA Press.

While the political system dithered, private market forces were already transforming the nation's medical system, replacing the traditional "fee for service" system with managed care plans that limited consumers' choice of doctors and treatments to cut costs. Medical care was rapidly becoming the domain of Wall Street and big business, and growing numbers of Americans joined health maintenance organizations (HMOs) or looser "preferred provider" networks. While managed care succeeded in curbing the cost of health care premiums, private sector initiatives did nothing to help the unemployed and workers without health insurance, whose numbers continued to grow. An estimated 43.4 million Americans had no health insurance in 1995, over 17 percent of the population under the age of sixty-five, and experts predicted that these statistics would climb.

Post–Cold War Foreign Policy. One reason why health care reform failed was that President Clinton was never able to devote his full attention to building a consensus for the plan and shepherding it through Congress. In October 1993, for example, just after he had announced the plan, twelve American soldiers were killed on a United Nations peacekeeping mission

in Somalia. Then Clinton had to turn his attention to divisive issues such as the closely contested NAFTA vote, Haiti, and the worsening situation in Bosnia. This patchwork approach to foreign policy added to the perception of Clinton as vacillating, indecisive, and lacking a central vision. Not until 1996 did Clinton's foreign policy team begin to articulate a clear policy on when the United States should intervene in crises overseas.

In the former Soviet Union the increasing unpopularity of Russian president Boris Yeltsin's efforts to bring about fundamental market reforms and the mounting evidence of rampant corruption made American leaders less optimistic about the emergence of democracy in Russia. Yeltsin's harsh repression of dissent in the breakaway region of Chechnya strained the already difficult relationship with the United States.

Nothing seemed more intractable than the problems engulfing the former state of Yugoslavia, which typified the localized conflicts based on ethnicity, religion, and nationality that increasingly replaced the superpower conflicts of the Cold War era. In what military analysts call "postmodern" or "future" wars, there is no distinction between armies and people—anybody who gets in the way gets killed. Unlike the Persian Gulf War, these conflicts do not rely on highly sophisticated technology and massive armies but still can be incredibly destructive.

The roots of the Bosnian conflict went back at least as far as the outbreak of World War I, but the immediate backdrop was the breakup of the state of Yugoslavia in 1991 into five independent states in the wake of the collapse of communism in Eastern Europe (see Map 31.1). The province of Bosnia and Herzegovina, made up largely of Muslims and committed to a multiethnic (Serb, Croat, and Muslim) state, had declared its independence in 1992. But Bosnian Serbs, supported financially and militarily by what remained of Yugoslavia, formed their own breakaway state and began a siege of Sarajevo, the Bosnian capital, which was the site of the 1984 Winter Olympics. In the countryside the Serbs launched a ruthless campaign of "ethnic cleansing," driving Bosnian Muslims and Croats from their homes and into concentration camps or shooting them in mass executions. More than 250,000 people were killed or reported missing after war broke out in April 1992.

After three years of unsuccessful efforts by the European powers to stop the carnage, the world's only superpower, the United States, exercised some leadership—backed by military force—to end the worst conflict in Europe since World War II. In November 1995 Secretary of State Warren Christopher and chief negotiator Richard Holbrooke brokered the Dayton Peace Accords, which ended the war at least temporarily. To implement the peace, the United States sent troops to

Clinton in Bosnia
In his role as commander in chief, President Clinton visited
Bosnia in January 1996 to show his support for the peacekeep-
ing mission. Here he salutes American troops in the Bosnian
town of Tuzla.
Peterson/Gamma Liaison.

Bosnia as part of a NATO-led force, although a major
goal of American policy—a viable and unified Bosnia—
remained unfulfilled.

At the same time, the end of Cold War superpower
rivalry presented unexpected opportunities to resolve
other longstanding regional, ethnic, and religious conflicts. In Haiti, the threat of a U.S. invasion in October
1993 led to the restoration of the exiled president, Jean-
Bertrand Aristide, who had been ousted by a military
coup in 1991. In South Africa, the end of the fifty-year
policy of racial separation was capped in May 1994 by
the election of Nelson Mandela, who had spent twenty-
seven years in prison for challenging apartheid, as the
country's first black president. And in a move that was
seen as a symbolic end to the American experience in
Vietnam, the United States established diplomatic relations with Hanoi in July 1995, two decades after the fall
of Saigon.

With the end of the Cold War, many citizens had
hoped for a peace dividend, redirecting money from
defense to domestic programs. But America's global
responsibilities had not declined. Given the new
budget-cutting consciousness in Washington, the
Department of Defense entered a period of retrench-

ment. By closing military bases around the country,
cutting total personnel by 20 percent from 1900 to
1994, and making cutbacks in research and development for new weapons systems, the post–Cold War
defense budget leveled off at around $250 billion, down
from a peak in 1989 of $346 billion (in 1994 dollars).
This small peace dividend was swallowed up by the
huge deficit.

Scandals and Independent Counsels.   In June 1994
President Clinton signed a little-noticed piece of legislation that reauthorized the independent counsel
statute, which had lapsed in late 1992. The law, which
applied to approximately seventy top Washington officials, gave the attorney general the authority to request
a three-judge court to appoint an independent counsel
if there were "reasonable grounds" to believe investigation of official misconduct was warranted. A legacy of
Watergate originally passed in 1978, the law was
intended to remove the potential for conflict of interest
that would arise if the attorney general investigated
members of the administration of which he or she was
a member. It replaced special prosecutors, who had
been part of the Justice department and (as Archibald
Cox found out in 1973) subject to firing, with independent counsels, who could not be fired and who were
given unlimited budgets and time to complete their
investigations.

Five weeks after Clinton reactivated the law and at
the request of Attorney General Janet Reno, a panel of
federal judges named Kenneth Starr to investigate a set
of allegations involving the defunct Whitewater Development Corporation and a bankrupt S & L called
Madison Guaranty in Arkansas with which Bill and
Hillary Clinton had been involved. In the initial stage of
his Whitewater investigations Starr produced three
convictions and ten guilty pleas, some from Clinton's
close associates. The independent counsel statute, however, empowered the independent counsel to pursue
"related matters," and Starr's case steadily widened into
a probe that included investigating the 1993 suicide of
a White House aide and former Arkansas colleague of
the Clintons named Vincent Foster, staff firings at the
White House travel office, and finally, four years and
$40 million later, allegations that President Clinton had
a sexual affair with a White House intern named
Monica Lewinsky.

President Clinton was not the only member of his
administration to be the target of an independent counsel. In 1994 agriculture secretary Mike Espy was investigated for accepting illegal gratuities. In 1995 independent
counsels looked into charges that HUD Secretary Henry
Cisneros had made false statements during confirmation,
and into Commerce Secretary Ron Brown's personal
finances. Later, independent counsels were appointed to

investigate allegations surrounding Interior Secretary Bruce Babbitt and Labor Secretary Alexis Herman.

Despite the good intentions of the original statute, the breadth of its scope (one Justice department insider called it an "unguided missile"), its vulnerability to partisan politics, and the fact that the vast majority of its investigations ended without the filing of any criminal charges led many to question its usefulness. Instead of increasing public trust, the independent counsel statute tended to encourage citizens' cynicism with government, an unfortunate side effect in already cynical times.

"The Era of Big Government Is Over"

The 1994 midterm election produced one of the most significant sea changes in recent political history—the culmination of the shift that had begun with Ronald Reagan's election in 1980. Republicans gained 52 seats in the House, giving them control for the first time in forty years; they also retook the Senate for the first time since 1986. In the House the centerpiece of the new Republican majority was the "Contract with America," a list of legislation that Newt Gingrich of Georgia, the new Speaker, vowed would be voted on in the first one hundred days of the session. The contract included constitutional amendments to balance the budget and term limits for congressional office; $245 billion in tax cuts for individuals and incentives for small businesses; cuts in welfare and other entitlement programs; anticrime initiatives; and cutbacks in federal regulations. Initially portrayed as ideological revolutionaries determined to shake Congress to its core, the members of the GOP "Class of '94" became more pragmatic as they settled into Congress. Said Mississippi congressman Roger Wicker, "I didn't come to Washington to burn all the buildings down."

Balancing the Budget. A balanced budget and reducing the national debt, key Republican goals, were endorsed by many Democrats as well. Both practical and political considerations made these difficult to achieve, especially since the Republicans also wanted to cut taxes. Interest on the debt had to be paid. Defense spending in the post–Cold War world had declined only slightly. That left Medicare and Medicaid, Social Security, and all other government programs as targets for savings. Since Social Security was considered untouchable, Congress looked to health care and discretionary spending for savings.

Despite the failure of Clinton's health care reform bill, by 1995 wide public agreement supported the notion that it was essential to bring health care costs under control. Medicare, signed into law by President Johnson in 1965, had cost almost $160 billion in 1994, almost 10 percent of the entire federal budget. As new medical technologies proliferated and the number of elderly people increased, expenses were rising at a rate of 10 percent a year. In the fall of 1995 Congress passed a budget cutting $270 billion from projected spending on Medicare and $170 billion from Medicaid over seven years. Other savings came from cuts in various discretionary programs, including education and the environment.

Clinton accepted Congress's resolve to balance the budget in seven years but, vowing to protect the nation from an "extremist" Congress, vetoed the budget itself. In the standoff that followed, nonessential departments of the government were forced to shut down twice for lack of funds, but polls showed that a majority of Americans held Congress, not the president, responsible. The budget that Clinton finally signed in April 1996 left Medicare and Social Security intact, though it did meet the Republicans' goal of cutting $23 billion in discretionary spending. In 1997 Clinton and congressional leaders announced a historic balanced budget agreement, and in January 1998, aided by a strong economy swelling the U.S. Treasury, Clinton submitted the first balanced budget in nearly thirty years.

Welfare Reform. Since the Reagan Era, the long-accepted argument that the federal government had an obligation to the poor was supplanted by rhetoric about cost-effectiveness, personal responsibility, and turning programs over to the states. Although Clinton promised in the 1992 campaign to "end welfare as we know it," serious debate on the issue did not begin until the Republicans took over Congress in 1995. Welfare, a joint federal-state program, represented a fairly small part of the budget, but to Republicans it was the prime example of misguided government priorities. The benefits of the main welfare program, AFDC, were far from generous: the average annual welfare payment to families (including food stamps) was $7,740, well below the 1995 poverty line of $12,188. In the 1990s both Democratic and Republican statehouses adopted various financial incentives to try to change welfare beneficiaries' behavior, including setting time limits, imposing work requirements, and denying benefits for additional children born to women on AFDC.

In August 1996, after vetoing two Republican-authored bills, President Clinton signed into law the Personal Responsibility and Work Opportunity Act, mandating a historic overhaul of federal entitlements. The law ended the federal guarantee of cash assistance to poor children by abolishing AFDC, required most adult recipients to find work within two years, set a five-

A Bipartisan Balanced Budget
On August 5, 1997, a smiling President Clinton signs the balanced budget bill, surrounded by congressional leaders including House Speaker Newt Gingrich of Georgia
(second from right) and House Budget Committee chairman John Kasich of Ohio (far
right). Also looking on with satisfaction is Vice-President Al Gore, who already had
hopes for the presidency in 2000.
Ron Edmonds/Wide World Photos, Inc.

year limit on payments to any family, and gave states
wide discretion in running their welfare programs.

The 1996 Election.   The Republican takeover of Congress had one unintended consequence—it united the
usually fractious Democrats behind Bill Clinton.
Unopposed in the primaries, Clinton was able to
burnish his image as a moderate "New Democrat." His
political fortunes were aided by the unpopularity of the
Republican Congress since the government shutdowns.

He also benefited from the strong state of the economy.
Economic indicators released shortly before election
day showed that the "misery index"—a combination of
the unemployment rate and inflation—was the lowest it
had been in twenty-seven years.

In the Republican primaries, voters flirted with
conservative commentator Pat Buchanan and magazine publisher Steve Forbes before settling on Senate
Majority Leader Bob Dole of Kansas as their presidential candidate. Dole was acceptable to both conserva-

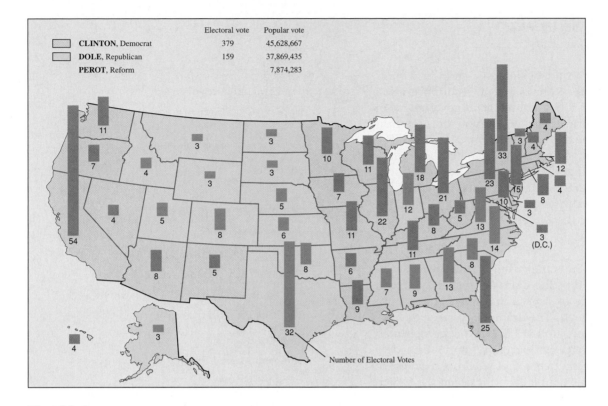

		Electoral vote	Popular vote
	CLINTON, Democrat	379	45,628,667
	DOLE, Republican	159	37,869,435
	PEROT, Reform		7,874,283

Number of Electoral Votes

MAP 31.6
The Election of 1996
Clinton and Gore broadened their electoral base from 1992, picking up traditional
Republican strongholds like Florida and dominating all regions of the country except the
South and the Great Plains. But with Republicans still in control of both houses of
Congress, Clinton faced uncertain prospects in his second term.

tive and moderate wings of the party, though his detached campaign style failed to generate much enthusiasm. He made a 15 percent across-the-board tax cut the centerpiece of his campaign, and selected former representative Jack Kemp, a leading proponent of supply-side economics, as his running mate.

Americans seemed to make up their minds early about the candidates, so the campaign was rather lackluster. Clinton emphasized his success in reducing the budget deficit, raising the minimum wage to $5.15 an hour, and reforming welfare, and he took credit for the 10 million new jobs created during his first term. In November, Clinton became the first Democratic president since Franklin Roosevelt to win reelection (Map 31.6). However, voter turnout was the lowest since Calvin Coolidge won in 1924. Despite fears of Democratic coattails, Republicans retained control of the House of Representatives and increased their majority in the Senate; they also maintained control of the majority of statehouses. The main lesson of the election

was voters' endorsement of the status quo of divided government, with the hope that cooperation, rather than gridlock and paralysis, would characterize the final years of the twentieth century.

The period from 1981 to 1996 brought enormous changes to the United States: the end of the four-decade Cold War; a dramatic rethinking of the role of the state in modern American life; the ongoing globalization of political and economic life; and growing diversity in American culture and public life. Those fifteen years seemed likely to be as important a period of realignment as the 1930s and 1940s, when the New Deal state was formed and the United States took on its global responsibilities in World War II and its aftermath. The period was certainly as dramatic as the 1890s, when the country completed the process of industrialization, absorbed a huge wave of immigrants, and secured an overseas empire. But given all the challenges the nation faced at home and abroad, it was too soon to declare an end to the activist American state.

Summary

★

In the 1980s and 1990s a new domestic and world order shaped American life. Ronald Reagan's administration advocated a smaller role for the federal government in domestic programs and the restoration of American prestige abroad through a massive military buildup. The term *Reaganomics* stood for tax cuts and budget reductions enacted in 1981 and 1982. Reagan's economic policies, notably deregulation and tax cuts, added to the concentration of wealth in the 1980s. Reagan remained enormously popular throughout his two terms but left large budget deficits to his successor, Vice-President George Bush.

The most important change during the Bush administration was the end of the Cold War, which had been the guiding principle of American foreign policy since the end of World War II. The dramatic collapse of communism in the Soviet Union in 1991 further complicated the old truisms. The post–Cold War future seemed to promise a fragile world peace that would be vulnerable to regional and ethnic conflicts but in which the United States, as the world's only remaining superpower, would still play the dominant leadership role. The United States also played a leading role in an increasingly global economy but no longer dominated the world economy as it had done during the Pax Americana of the immediate postwar world.

American society in the 1980s and 1990s continued to turn inward to address its own needs. Increased immigration, notably from Latin America and Asia, changed the demographic balance of many areas, especially the cities, and the strains of an increasingly diverse society were reflected in debates over affirmative action and multiculturalism. Slow productivity growth, wage stagnation, and growing inequality in income were the major domestic economic trends. Meanwhile, American businesses struggled to compete in an increasingly competitive global marketplace. The information superhighway and cyberspace pointed to a high-tech future.

Soon after the Democrats regained the White House with the election of Bill Clinton in 1992, the Republican landslide of 1994 reshaped politics dramatically by emphasizing a balanced budget, tax cuts, and shrinking the federal government by turning programs over to the states. In January 1996 even President Clinton admitted, "The era of big government is over." In August he signed a welfare reform bill that ended the federal guarantee of cash assistance to the poor. Clinton won reelection to a second term, but continued Republican control of Congress suggested that the long-term trend of federal activism had been slowed, if not reversed.

TIMELINE

1981	Economic Recovery Tax Act
	Sandra Day O'Connor nominated to Supreme Court
	Beginning of AIDS epidemic
1981–1983	Recession
1983	Star Wars proposed
1984	Geraldine Ferraro becomes first woman on major party ticket
1985	Gramm-Rudman Balanced Budget Act
	United States becomes a debtor nation
	Mikhail Gorbachev takes power in USSR
1986	Iran-Contra affair
	Simpson-Mazzoli Immigration Act
1987	Montreal environmental protocol
1988	George Bush elected president
1989	Savings and loan crisis
	Political revolutions in Eastern Europe
	Webster v. Reproductive Health Services
1990–1991	Persian Gulf crisis
1990–1992	Recession
1991	Dissolution of Soviet Union ends Cold War
	Clarence Thomas–Anita Hill hearings
1992	Los Angeles riots
	Earth Summit at Rio de Janeiro
	Bill Clinton elected president
1993	Family and Medical Leave Act
	NAFTA ratified
1994	Omnibus Violent Crime Control and Prevention Act
	Health care reform fails
	Republicans gain control of Congress
1995	United States establishes diplomatic relations with Vietnam
	Twenty-fifth anniversary of Earth Day
	U.S. troops enforce peace in Bosnia
1996	Personal Responsibility and Work Opportunity Act
	Clinton reelected

Suggested Readings

Few historians have turned their attention to the period after 1980, leaving the field to journalists, economists, and political scientists. The Bureau of the Census offers a fine introduction to the period in its *Statistical Abstract of the United States* (117th ed., 1997). Essays on important issues are available in the *Congressional Quarterly Researcher*.

The Reagan-Bush Years, 1981–1993

Haynes Johnson, *Sleepwalking through History* (1991), provides an excellent overview of America in the Reagan years. See also Michael Rogin, *Ronald Reagan: The Movie* (1987); Lou Cannon, *President Reagan: A Role of a Lifetime* (1991); Michael Schaller, *Reckoning with Reagan: America and Its President in the 1980s* (1992); and Peggy Noonan, *What I Saw at the Revolution* (1990).

On Reaganomics, George Gilder's *Wealth and Poverty* (1981) represents the views held by many in the Reagan administration, but David Stockman's memoir, *The Triumph of Politics* (1986), is more revealing. See also Benjamin Friedman, *Day of Reckoning: The Consequences of American Economic Policy under Reagan and After* (1988).

On the Bush administration, see James A. Baker, *The Politics of Diplomacy* (1995), and Stephen R. Graubard, *Mr. Bush's War: Adventures in the Politics of Illusion* (1992). On politics, see E. J. Dionne, *Why Americans Hate Politics* (1992); William Greider, *Who Will Tell the People?* (1992); and Kevin Phillips, *The Politics of Rich and Poor: Wealth and the American Electorate in the Reagan Aftermath* (1990).

Foreign Relations under Reagan and Bush

For foreign policy, Stephen Ambrose and Douglas Brinkley, *Rise to Globalism* (8th ed., 1997), provide a comprehensive overview of the Reagan and Bush years. The Iran-Contra scandal is covered in Jane Hunter et al., *The Iran-Contra Connection* (1987). Good introductions to U.S. foreign relations with Central and South America include Walter LaFeber, *Inevitable Revolutions* (1984), and Thomas Carothers, *In the Name of Democracy: U.S. Policy toward Latin America in the Reagan Years* (1991).

The emergence of a new world order has provoked commentary from economists, journalists, and historians, including Paul Kennedy, *The Rise and Fall of the Great Powers* (1987); Joseph Nye, *Bound to Lead: The Changing Nature of American Power* (1990); Robert Kuttner, *The End of Laissez Faire* (1991); and Henry R. Nau, *The Myth of America's Decline* (1990). See also Michael Beschloss and Strobe Talbott, *At the Highest Levels: The Inside Story of the End of the Cold War* (1994), and Michael J. Hugan, ed., *The End of the Cold War: Its Meanings and Implications* (1992).

Uncertain Times

Paul Krugman, *Peddling Prosperity: Economic Sense and Nonsense in the Age of Diminished Expectations* (1994), and Jeffrey Madrick, *The End of Affluence* (1995), provide overviews of economic trends since the 1970s. Lester C. Thurow offers an insightful analysis of the world economic changes accompanying the collapse of communism in *The Future of Capitalism*

(1996). For overviews of U.S. competitiveness in the global marketplace, see Daniel Yergin and Joseph Stanislaw, *The Commanding Heights* (1998); Hedrick Smith, *Rethinking America* (1995); and Robert B. Reich, *The Work of Nations: Preparing Ourselves for 21st Century Capitalism* (1991). Books that address the growing inequality in American life include William J. Wilson, *The Truly Disadvantaged* (1987); Nicholas Lemann, *The Promised Land* (1989); and Andrew Hacker, *Two Nations: Black and White, Separate, Hostile, Unequal* (1992).

On women, work, and families, see Hilda Scott, *Working Your Way to the Bottom: The Feminization of Poverty* (1985), and Arlie Hochschild, *The Second Shift: Working Parents and the Revolution at Home* (1989). For feminism and its critics, see Susan Faludi, *Backlash: The Undeclared War on American Women* (1991). Toni Morrison, ed., *Race-ing Justice, En-gendering Power* (1992), covers the Clarence Thomas–Anita Hill hearings.

David Reimers, *Still the Golden Door* (2nd ed., 1992), covers immigration policy in the postwar period. Roberto Suro, *Strangers among Us* (1998), shows how Latino immigration is transforming America. Ronald Takaki, *Strangers from a Different Shore* (1989), covers Asian Americans. On race and politics in California since 1978, see Peter Schrag, *Paradise Lost* (1998).

Randy Shilts, *And the Band Played On: Politics, People, and the AIDS Epidemic* (1987), is a controversial critique of inaction in the early years of the AIDS epidemic. Allan Bloom, *The Closing of the American Mind* (1987), and E. D. Hirsch Jr., *Cultural Literacy* (1988), deal with issues of curriculum, learning, and literacy. Lawrence W. Levine, *The Opening of the American Mind* (1996), challenges many of their assumptions. For differing views on affirmative action, see Stephen L. Carter, *Reflections of an Affirmative Action Baby* (1991), and Gertrude Ezorsky, *Racism and Justice: The Case for Affirmative Action* (1991). Gregg Easterbrook provides a general overview of the environment in *A Moment on the Earth* (1995). Daniel Yergin, *The Prize* (1991), chronicles how oil dominates modern life, with both economic and environmental consequences.

For the story of Bill Gates and Microsoft, see Steven Manes, *Gates* (1993), and James Wallace, *Hard Drive* (1992). Also of interest is Joshua Quittner and Michelle Slatalla, *Speeding the Net: The Inside Story of Netscape and How It Challenged Microsoft* (1998). For biotechnology, see Robert Cook-Deegan, *The Gene Wars* (1994); Arthur Kornberg, *The Golden Helix: Inside Biotech Ventures* (1996); and Eric S. Grace, *Biotechnology Unzipped* (1997).

Restructuring the Domestic Order: Public Life, 1992–1996

For an excellent overview of the Clinton administration's first year, see Elizabeth Drew, *Finding His Voice* (1994). Other sources include Bob Woodward, *The Agenda* (1994), and Roger Morris, *Partners in Power: The Clintons and Their America* (1996). James B. Stewart, *Blood Sport: The President and His Adversaries* (1996), analyzes Whitewater. Richard Holbrooke, *To End a War* (1998), provides a compelling insider's account of the Dayton peace talks on Bosnia. William Greider, *Fortress America* (1998), examines the American military in the post–Cold War era. On the Republican agenda, see Newt Gingrich, *To Renew America* (1995). See also Dan Balz and Ronald Brownstein, *Storming the Gates: Protest Politics and the Republican Revival* (1996), and Ralph Reed, *Active Faith: How Christians Are Changing the Soul of American Politics* (1996).

Epilogue

★

America and the World at 2000:

How Historians Interpret Contemporary Events and Their Legacy for the Future

IT IS THE year 2000. Here, courtesy of one of those catchy communications that circulate on the Internet from time to time, are some verbal snapshots of what a person born in 1980—for example, a college student reading this textbook—remembers about the events of the past twenty years. (If you were born before 1980, be forewarned that this will make you feel old, perhaps very old.)

- You have never been afraid of nuclear war. To you, "the day after" means a pill, not a movie about the aftermath of nuclear conflagration.
- You were nine years old when the Berlin Wall fell and eleven years old when the former Soviet Union broke up, and therefore you do not remember the Cold War.
- The Vietnam War seems as distant as World War II or the Civil War, and you have only preadolescent memories of the Persian Gulf War.
- You are too young to remember the space shuttle *Challenger* blowing up in 1986 or the Chinese uprising at Tiananmen Square in 1989.
- You have no recollections of the Reagan era and do not know that he was once shot.
- You have always had an answering machine and cable television, and you cannot imagine not having a remote control.
- Your lifetime has always included awareness of AIDS.

Many, but by no means all, of these topics are covered in the last chapter of *America's History,* including the end of the Cold War, new technology, Operation Desert Storm, and the AIDS epidemic. These topics rep-resent a sample of what historians currently think is important to include in a comprehensive survey of late twentieth-century American life. In contrast, the 1981 Reagan assassination attempt, the nuclear freeze movement of the early 1980s, the *Challenger* disaster, and Tiananmen Square didn't make the cut.

Writing history is about making choices, about deciding what to include and what to leave out; and nowhere is this process more difficult than in writing the history of recent events. The key question for future editions of *America's History* is what contemporary events will emerge as truly significant historically (and thus warrant inclusion in a broad synthesis of American history and culture) and what events will be judged mere blips on the historical consciousness (things that seemed all-encompassing at the time but whose long-term significance subsequently paled). What the historian's knowledge can add is some sense from the past about how to think about the present, when all of us are bombarded daily with headlines and breaking stories and when our own memories and reactions to stories and events can cloud or influence our ability to regard them objectively. Today's headlines do not always become tomorrow's history.

In a 1992 interview former president Richard M. Nixon stated bluntly, "In my view, history is never worth reading until it's fifty years old. It takes fifty years before you're able to come back and evaluate a man or a period of time." The mere passage of time does often help participants understand events and place them in a broad historical context. For example, historians know much more about the origins of the Cold War now that documents are surfacing from the former

The Original Webmaster
Tim Berners-Lee, here represented in a mosaic composed of 2,304 websites, was the brains behind the World Wide Web.
PhotomosaicTM by Robert Silvers/www.photomosaic.com.

Soviet Union and other formerly communist states that present their side of the global conflict. Fifty years after the fact, Swiss banks are now coming up with an accounting of what happened to money deposited there by Jews later killed in Hitler's concentration camps.

Yet if textbook writers took Nixon's advice literally, they would end their books just after World War II and the onset of the Cold War. Of course this isn't possible or desirable, and the enormous outpouring of excellent scholarship that informs Part Six of *America's History* demonstrates that it is indeed possible to assess and interpret historically events of the fairly recent past such as the Cold War, the civil rights movement, the growth of suburbia, and the changing contours of the global economy. But the closer the past gets to the present, the harder the task becomes. That does not mean, however, that historians have to cede the recent past, or even contemporary events, to journalists and television analysts.

What follows is an overview of the key areas in modern American life that have been traced throughout this book—politics, society and culture, the economy, and diplomacy—at the historical moment when the twentieth century turns into the twenty-first. Thinking about the range of topics covered reinforces the point that reading a textbook like *America's History* is just the first step toward mastering the history of the enormously complex world we inhabit. Just as in earlier chapters, we examine the larger themes, shifting perspectives, and emerging syntheses in these key areas, but with a more tentative and open-ended perspective. Think of this part of *America's History* as a historical document: how a group of American historians saw the challenges and promises of writing the contemporary history of their society as the year 2000 approached. Look at the choice of issues and mode of analysis to discover how historians gather and evaluate evidence, how they link individual events to larger patterns and themes, and yes, how they are often forced to revise their earlier conclusions or change their minds entirely.

Readers of this last part have an advantage over its authors: you know how certain stories have turned out by 2000, something that historians writing about them in 1999 do not. Maybe fifty years from now you will pass along an old copy of this college textbook to your grandchildren, and future generations, like Richard Nixon said, will be able to tell us how we did.

Politics. Although most recent textbooks seek to replace a "presidential synthesis"—that is, a narrative and analysis structured around specific administrations—with an organization that treats social and cultural history as fully as political developments, it is certainly true that the importance of the office and the power of the president require every textbook to men-

tion all, or almost all, presidential elections. The last chapter of *America's History* ended, for example, with the 1996 election, and the next edition will certainly give a prominent place to the results of the election in 2000. But which accomplishments and failures historians will choose to write about for Bill Clinton's second term is far less clear. In fact, Clinton's impeachment by the House and subsequent trial in the Senate raised the possibility that the popular president, whose approval ratings remained high throughout the crisis, might not even serve out his second term. As journalist R. W. Apple observed, "In the toxic politics of century's end in Washington, the inconceivable has become the commonplace."

The political fallout from President Clinton's affair with White House intern Monica Lewinsky is an excellent example of the difficulties of writing contemporary history when the story is literally unfolding on a day-to-day basis. Indeed, we sympathized with a journalist in the *Washington Post* writing about December 19, 1998, the historic day when the House of Representatives voted two articles of impeachment—obstruction of justice and perjury—against President Clinton: "So this is what history feels like before the historians get hold of it. Before they choose, interpret, compress, highlight and elide. History feels awfully confusing."

As historians, we attempt no assessment here about the nature of the scandal or the political maneuvering surrounding impeachment and the subsequent Senate trial. Instead, we try to step back and think about the implications of the political crisis for the institution of the presidency and the country as a whole. For example, will the presidency be permanently undermined by the impeachment process (Clinton's case was only the second time in America's history that a president was impeached), or will the institution and the country prove as resilient as they did in 1974 in the aftermath of Richard Nixon's resignation to avoid imminent removal from office? Has the historic balance of power between the three branches of government been permanently upset by a partisan Congress pursuing an open-ended investigation of a sitting president of the opposite political party? What will be the effects of the impeachment proceedings on citizens' attitudes toward their elected representatives and the system of government in Washington in general? These are some of the larger questions that will concern historians who evaluate this era in the years to come.

One striking aspect of the political crisis on which historians will no doubt focus is the role that the Internet and cable news (whose extensive coverage spawned the slogan "All Monica, all the time") played in spreading the story. In the past, information about the unfolding story would have filtered through journalistic or congressional sources, or it would have remained secret entirely. Think how different the Watergate

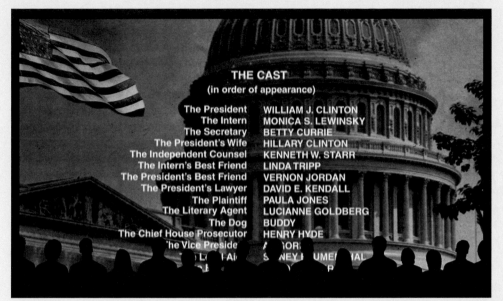

THE CAST
(in order of appearance)

The President	WILLIAM J. CLINTON
The Intern	MONICA S. LEWINSKY
The Secretary	BETTY CURRIE
The President's Wife	HILLARY CLINTON
The Independent Counsel	KENNETH W. STARR
The Intern's Best Friend	LINDA TRIPP
The President's Best Friend	VERNON JORDAN
The President's Lawyer	DAVID E. KENDALL
The Plaintiff	PAULA JONES
The Literary Agent	LUCIANNE GOLDBERG
The Dog	BUDDY
The Chief House Prosecutor	HENRY HYDE

The Impeachment Players
For more than a year the Monica Lewinsky story dominated the news, making household names of major and minor characters. Then, like a movie, it ended. Most Americans seemed relieved that the ordeal was over, telling pollsters that they were ready for Clinton and the country to move on.
Jesse Gordon/The New York Times. Reprinted with permission.

impeachment hearings would have been if ordinary citizens had had direct access in 1974 to the masses of detail and evidence that were available to the public at century's end. The Internet, barely a factor in public life until the mid-1990s, is challenging more traditional sources of news information, such as television or newspapers, as a major purveyor of information about contemporary events. The downside to such instant information is that much of it is circulated with minimal editorial controls or checks, leading to unsubstantiated statements and more than a few rumors. One of the tasks for future historians will be to sift fact from fiction in this proliferation of new sources of information.

Another factor that turned the Clinton-Lewinsky scandal into an even bigger story than it might have been otherwise was the way in which the media has turned the world into a global village: anyone, anywhere in the world, could tune in and watch the story unfolding live. (CNN's on-the-spot coverage of the Persian Gulf War in 1990–1991 was a turning point in such media coverage.) This explosion of information access coincided with what one critic has called the "growing tabloidization of American culture," a frenzy for gossip that has blurred the lines between public and private. What does it say about contemporary American culture that we know more about the intimate details of the president's sexual habits than about nearly anyone else's but our own? These trends, building in the late twentieth century, will be hard to derail in the twenty-first.

Yet it is quite possible that when historians draw up their assessment of the Clinton presidency and the politics of governance in the 1990s, the impeachment scandal, in hindsight, will not be seen as the most serious or important issue of President Clinton's eight years in office. Writing in the heat of the moment robs historians of the ability to step back, gather evidence, and listen to and weigh different viewpoints—essential to the historian's craft. But it is not always necessary to wait fifty years in order to get a better historical perspective on events; sometimes just a few years will do.

A good case in point is the 1994 congressional election, in which Republicans won control of the House of Representatives for the first time in forty years with a campaign organized around an antigovernment theme spelled out in their "Contract with America." When the previous edition of *America's History* was being written, the congressional election had just occurred, and as historians and authors we interpreted the electoral results as a potential watershed in twentieth-century political history, perhaps (although we intentionally fudged a bit here) one that signaled the end of the rise of the state. Four years later, in the wake of the results of the 1998 congressional election in which Democrats picked up five seats in the House (unprecedented for a party in power in an off-year election) instead of losing seats in an anti-Clinton stampede, it was the architect of the 1994 Republican victory, Speaker of the House Newt Gingrich, who resigned, not Bill Clinton. Not a single Washington pundit had predicted this startling turn of events. Suddenly the "Republican revolution" of 1994 looked less like a history-altering turning point than a minor political realignment.

History will always have to take account of these sudden, unexpected turns of events—the election upsets, the assassinations, the natural disasters—that can seem to change the course of history overnight. But historians need not place themselves at the mercy of fast-breaking news; instead, they can attempt to place

Part of the Problem, Part of the Solution
Since Bill Clinton is part of the baby-boom generation that will put pressure on the ailing social security system in the twenty-first century, he has a personal stake in the issue. His political investment is stronger: a successful overhaul of Social Security could be a major legacy of his administration.
Chick Harrity for USN & WR.

events in the broader historical context of the country's national history and promise to revisit their assessment later to see if it has weathered the test of time and evidence. In other cases, historians can draw on their knowledge of the past to identify contemporary issues likely to emerge as defining moments when they write about this period in the future. Please excuse us if the details are a bit hazy as we gaze into our crystal balls.

One such issue is Social Security. Perhaps when we look back at the Clinton years, one of the most important critical markers will be whether the budget surplus that began in 1997 was used to shore up the ailing Social Security system. A driving concern at the close of the century is what will happen when the baby boomers (Americans born between 1945 and 1963) begin to retire and collect Social Security. Current projections show Social Security running short of money to pay all promised benefits by 2032. As a result of these gloomy predictions, many Americans are losing confidence that government pensions, one of the cornerstones of the American welfare state, will actually be available for them when they retire. The historical problem has been identified, but not the solution.

Another political issue that historians will be writing about in the future is health care. As we discussed in the last chapter of *America's History*, Clinton's 1994 plan for reform of the health care system was considered overly sweeping. An incremental, market-driven approach featuring managed care seemed to better suit the needs of the country at the time, with the result that by 1998 almost two-thirds of the population (61%) belonged to some kind of health maintenance organization (HMO). But no sooner had managed care become the predominant method of dispensing health

care than doubts set in. Complaints about restrictions on the kinds of care and services available, often fueled by heart-wrenching stories of patients denied access to potentially lifesaving treatments by their cost-conscious HMOs, became so widespread that health care advocates and politicians proposed a "Patient's Bill of Rights" to expand patient choice and make HMOs accountable for the quality of care provided. Furthermore, managed care had failed to reach the growing proportion of Americans (more than one-sixth of the population) who had no access to health insurance at all.

Another puzzle of contemporary politics that history must address is what happened to the welfare system and its beneficiaries after Congress and the states passed sweeping changes in the 1990s, especially the 1996 federal law placing a five-year lifetime limit on assistance for single mothers and a two-year limit for adults without dependent children. Welfare recipients affected by these changes would theoretically reach the end of their benefits at various points between 1998 and 2001, but welfare rolls were already dropping precipitously before the federal deadlines kicked in. For example, Wisconsin, which had developed an ambitious "workfare" program to get people off welfare, saw its number of cases drop from almost 80,000 in 1994 to just over 10,000 four years later.

Yet there was no consensus on what this drop meant or what had happened to the former welfare recipients. Were they able to use state employment services to develop skills and find jobs, or did they find jobs simply because the economy was booming? What will happen if the economy slows down, becoming unable to absorb all those who want to work and possi-

Proud New Citizens
The many faces of America are reflected in this group of newly naturalized citizens in Brooklyn, New York. Behind each of these smiles is a story that is part of America's history at the end of the twentieth century.
Lynn Johnson.

bly throwing them back on welfare? Is the goal of workfare to help people find jobs in the private sector, or merely to discourage the poor from applying for public assistance in the first place? Some answers will emerge when the time limits are reached; others will take longer. Only with the completion of substantive studies of what actually happened to former welfare recipients will historians have the data to mount an assessment of the success or failure of attempts, in President Clinton's words, to "end welfare as we know it." As with Social Security and health care, this task will be crucial to understanding the evolution of the commitment of the state to public welfare, one of the major themes of the twentieth century.

Society and Culture. There are no accurate data at the time this book goes to press to predict the future of welfare, but there are much more reliable projections about the changing racial makeup of American society. The U.S. Census Bureau predicts that in the year 2050 whites will make up 52.7 percent of the American population (down from 75.7% in 1990), with Hispanics accounting for 21.1 percent, blacks 15 percent, and Asians 10.1 percent. If any level of intermarriage had been factored in (studies show Hispanics and Asians marry outside their racial groups much more often than do blacks), the projected white "majority" would probably have slipped to a white "minority." At the close of the twentieth century, already one out of twenty-five married couples is interracial, and there are at least three million children of mixed-race parentage in the country. (This latter figure does not even include the millions of Hispanic mestizos, as well as black Americans who have either European or American

Indian ancestors.) Probably the best known example of the country's increasingly multi-racial heritage is golfer Tiger Woods, who likes to call himself a "Cablinasian" to reflect his multiracial background of Caucasian, black, native American, and Asian heritages.

It won't be necessary to wait until 2050 for another demographic milestone: around the year 2005, according to Census Bureau projections, Hispanics will surpass blacks as the country's largest minority group. This is a development of great historical import. For most of the country's history, racial issues have been seen literally as "black and white." The rising numbers of Hispanics and Asians will push the United States to reframe the American discourse on race. Whether or not Hispanics and Asians join forces with blacks will have significant implications for civil rights organizations and divisive national issues such as affirmative action. By contrast, if Hispanics and Asians are seen more as "honorary whites" in a mostly white mixed-race majority, then the historic black-nonblack dichotomy may continue or even intensify. Americans have often talked about their society as a melting pot, and the twentieth century witnessed a broadened acceptance of a wider range of cultures and skin colors. Deep divisions accompanied the shift, however, and such acrimony (which died down temporarily in the late 1990s after flaring up earlier in the decade) is likely to return periodically in the next century, especially during periods of economic or social conflict.

The changing nature of the American population is also having a decided impact on America's religious life. In a trend that will likely continue into the next century, mainline (and often liberal) Protestant denominations

Southern Baptists Reach Out
In 1995, as part of their effort to reach
out to African Americans (who currently account for about 500,000 of the
Southern Baptist Convention's 15.5 million members), Southern Baptist leaders officially repudiated racism and
asked for forgiveness for their role in
defending segregation.
Alan S. Weiner/Gamma Liaison.

such as Episcopalians, Methodists, and Presbyterians
have been losing members since their peak during the
baby-boom era in the mid-1960s. The greatest growth
for Protestants since the 1970s has been in the more
conservative Southern Baptist Convention, which
became the largest religious organization in the United
States after the Roman Catholic Church. At the same
time, changes in immigration laws have increased the
ranks of Catholics as well as believers of other faiths,
including larger numbers of American Muslims, Buddhists, and Hindus—religions that had not previously
been well represented in the United States. A multiracial society is also increasingly a multireligious one.

In a trend with wide-reaching implications, some
American-based faiths have become so multinational
that they no longer depend solely on American believers. The most striking example of that trend is the
Church of Jesus Christ of Latter-day Saints, or Mormons. In 1980 three-quarters of Mormonism's 4.6 million believers lived in the United States; by 1997 the
church had 10 million followers, the majority of them
overseas. The Assemblies of God, a pentecostal denom-
ination founded in Arkansas in 1914 whose believers
seek to be filled with the Holy Spirit, also had more followers abroad than in the United States, especially in
Brazil. Reflecting this new complexity of American religious life, one scholar observed, "It's a fun time to be a
student of religion, because there are a lot of interesting changes going on. We don't know where they're
going to end up." That sums up the challenge of writing
the history of contemporary America.

Another contemporary trend worth watching is the
nation's energy use at the turn of the century, a phenomenon that calls into question how significant a
realignment actually occurred as a result of the energy
crisis of the 1970s. By the late 1990s Americans were
using almost as much energy per capita as they had in
1973, wiping out practically all the savings that had
occurred through conservation and efficiency after the
energy crisis. At century's end, Americans consume
more than twice as much energy per person as Europeans or Japanese. (Only Canadians, with a larger percentage of heavy industry and a colder climate,
consume more worldwide.) The short-term reason for
the turnaround is clear: a worldwide decline in oil
prices, which made it cheaper and easier for Americans
to live more energy-intensive life-styles. Two symptoms
of the shift: the growing popularity of sports utility
vehicles, and the trend toward larger, more appliance-
laden houses. To meet these energy needs, the United
States now imports about 50 percent of its oil, up from
35 percent in 1973. Even though energy experts warn
that a tightening of oil supplies and higher prices are
inevitable, few are heeding the message. This change in
mentality also threatens to undercut the international
progress made in the 1980s and 1990s on pressing environmental issues such as global warming, acid rain,
and depletion of the ozone layer.

As befits *America's History*'s overarching interpretation of the twentieth century—globalization—many of
the issues that face the United States at 2000 are global
issues. The environment is one; the AIDS epidemic is

Los Angeles by Night
The vast expanse that is the Los Angeles metropolitan area is especially striking at night, as captured by artist Peter Alexander. Yet think of the vast amounts of energy being consumed by those city lights.
James Corcoran Gallery, Santa Monica, CA.

another. According to a United Nations study conducted in 1997, more than 30 million people worldwide suffered from AIDS or were infected with HIV, the virus that causes AIDS. The problem was especially acute in Africa, where 21 million were infected; in the country of Zimbabwe, the rate was one in four. Rates were lower in Asia, Eastern Europe, and South America, but the disease was spreading there as well. In the United States, by contrast, the number of AIDS deaths dropped from 31,256 in 1995 to 16,685 just two years later, the result of potent—and expensive—drugs that allowed certain infected people to manage their disease. But even after extensive public health campaigns were launched, the number of new infections was not dropping in the United States. The worldwide impact of AIDS puts it on a comparable basis to the Black Death, the bubonic plague epidemic that swept through fourteenth-century Europe and killed 20 million people (one-quarter of Europe's population), and the influenza pandemic of 1918–1919 that killed 20 million people worldwide. With an AIDS vaccine a distant hope, there is no end in sight to this terrible scourge.

According to *USA Today,* 75 percent of Americans believe that another major and deadly disease will appear by 2025. In other ways, however, Americans seem to expect miracles from medical science in the next century. Fueled by consumer demands for health information and a desire to live longer, healthier lives, the news media routinely treat advances in science and medicine as front-page news. When the *New York Times* ran a feature story about a possible breakthrough in cancer research in 1998, hopes soared that cancer might once and for all be conquered. "OUR BEST HOPE" proclaimed one headline, with an accompanying article by a cancer-stricken journalist that stated, "Maybe we don't have to die." Doctors often learn about new drugs and procedures right along with their patients through newspaper accounts and drug company–sponsored advertisements; patients also surf the Internet for information about clinical trials of new treatments or experimental drugs for specific diseases. This democratization of medical knowledge empowers some consumers, but at the cost of inflating hopes about untested drugs and procedures that are years away from marketability. Yet Americans' hope for a cure—for breast cancer, for AIDS, for Alzheimer's disease—continues unabated.

The Economy. Nowhere has it been harder for historians to use the past to make predictions about the future than in the field of economics. Past mistakes can be embarrassing. Here is what the authors of *America's*

Health Care
Throughout the 1990s, America grappled with how to provide affordable health care
for its citizens. First lady Hillary Rodham Clinton took part in this protest against
Medicare and Medicaid cuts in New York City in 1995.
Stephan Ferry/Gamma Liaison.

History said at the conclusion of the second edition (1993): "The early twenty-first century will likely be most favorable to Pacific Rim and EC [European Community] countries. . . . The strongest individual economies will likely continue to be those of Japan and Germany." By the publication of the third edition (1997) our tone had shifted a bit, with the United States emerging as the dominant player in the new world order but sharing global economic and political influence with Japan, China, Singapore, Hong Kong, and other Pacific Rim countries; Canada and Mexico in North America; and the newly revitalized EC. We concluded, "Temporarily on the sidelines are the nations of the former Soviet Union and Eastern Europe."

At least we were right about Russia: in the summer of 1998 the Russian economy essentially went bankrupt, defaulting on loans and devaluing the ruble. All the other countries mentioned—with the exception of Canada, Mexico, and Germany—were engulfed in a global economic slowdown that started in 1997. The change in fortunes was especially acute in Asia, where the picture went from miracle to meltdown, with nine of Asia's thirteen major economies either in recession or depression by 1998. Especially hard hit was Japan, the world's second largest economy after the United States and the one country that just a few years earlier had seemed poised to dominate the global economy.

As the world's economic troubles deepened, the new buzzword among politicians and economists was an updated version of the domino theory called *contagion*—the idea that if one country's economy was allowed to implode, it might set in motion an uncontrollable sequence of events around the world. The International Monetary Fund (IMF) and the World Bank, set up in the wake of World War II to ensure financial stability in world markets, responded by making one costly rescue bailout of a shaky economy after another—Thailand, Indonesia, South Korea, and Rus-

Multinational McChicken
The proliferation of McDonald's franchises worldwide symbolizes the multinational nature of modern economic life. However, reaching new markets often necessitates a certain amount of cultural adaptation, as these McDonald's workers in traditional Muslim dress demonstrate in Jakarta, Indonesia.
Wide World Photos, Inc.

sia. Fears were raised that Brazil, Venezuela, or Mexico might be next.

How could things change so quickly? In 1989 it was widely accepted that Japan was rising and America was declining, or, as the scholar Chalmers Johnson put it, "The cold war is over, and Japan won." Now the opposite appears to be true: the U.S. economy looks strong, almost invincible, and the Asian economies are in serious trouble. One conclusion that seems likely is that when an economy is performing well, as was Japan's in the late 1980s and America's in the late 1990s, it temporarily hides all sorts of problems. As economist Laura D'Andrea Tyson observes, "In prosperous times we overstate the good and understate the bad." One of the most troubling "bad" trends is the growing disparity in wealth and opportunity that characterizes the American economy at the end of the century, with the very rich profiting the most from the recent period of prosperity.

As historians struggle to make sense of the global economic picture, they are hampered not just by the dramatic turn of events in Asia but also by the fact that many economic tenets no longer seem as reliable as they once did. For example, since 1960 a widely accepted economic principle called the Phillips Curve posited that there could be low inflation or low unemployment, but not both. Yet the boom of the 1990s has seen inflation *and* unemployment drop to their lowest levels in generations. Another long-held economic tenet claimed that measures to lower the deficit would act as a drag on the economy, thereby slowing economic growth. Yet in the 1990s the United States has experienced both significant deficit reduction and a period of sustained economic growth. No longer does world economic growth automatically lead to higher oil prices: oil prices have fallen steadily since the early 1980s as a result of new sources of oil flooding the market. In other words, many of the principles and tenets on

Chemical Warfare
The threat of chemical and biological warfare posed new challenges for American security. Here soldiers engage in chemical warfare training at Fort Drum, New York.
© M. Greenlar/The Image Works.

which economists—and historians who rely on those economists—depend seem to have broken down. Perhaps the ups and downs of the past ten years will lead to the emergence of new economic laws, but for now we are all struggling to make sense of a complex and deeply interconnected world economy.

Diplomacy. Just as complicated are the emerging contours of the post–Cold War world. Note that historians are still using the Cold War as the organizing concept for the late twentieth century, even though it ended a decade earlier. Future textbooks will probably recognize the events of 1989–1991 in Eastern Europe and the Soviet Union as *the* defining watershed in the late twentieth century; certainly the years 1945–1991 would provide a logical periodization for Part Six in a future edition of *America's History*. Events since then—the last part of Chapter 31 and this epilogue—would in effect be the opening of a new Part Seven, as yet unnamed and (with apologies to the sports world) with themes and "players" to be announced later.

Despite the end of the Cold War, much of American foreign policy is still directed toward the goals that have shaped much of the twentieth century, such as the desire to contain powerful or potentially powerful nations that might appear as rivals. Thus the United States supported the expansion of NATO to include former Communist bloc members Poland, Hungary, and the Czech Republic as a hedge against a resurgent Russia. As to policy toward China, the world's most populous country, the United States promoted its version of free-market capitalism and democracy at the same time as it worried about China's nuclear capabilities and

human rights violations. Protecting U.S. access to oil reserves worldwide remained a high priority, with the oil-rich Caspian region (wedged between Russia and Iran) emerging as the newest stage for superpower maneuvering.

On the eve of the twenty-first century, terrorism emerged as a central concern of U.S. foreign policy. A series of terrorist attacks, often directed at American citizens or embassies abroad but occasionally at targets in the United States (such as the 1993 bombing of New York City's World Trade Center), heightened America's sense of vulnerability. Even though the number of lives lost was relatively small (98 Americans were killed in foreign terrorist attacks between 1989 and 1998, less than are killed on average each year by lightning), driving the fear was the perception that terrorists pose a continuous, deadly, and invisible threat to American interests and installations throughout the world. Like the Cold War fears of nuclear annihilation that sent schoolchildren ducking and cowering under their desks, no one is ever safe in a world where terrorists reign.

But unlike the Cold War, a period during which the Soviet Union was identified as America's primary enemy, terrorist attacks cannot necessarily be traced to a single state or a single leader. Instead of having a central headquarters like the Kremlin, loose organizations are dispersed throughout many countries. At the end of the twentieth century, the strongest threats to American interests come from militant Islamic sects committed to a messianic vision of the end of Western influence in the Arab world and the ultimate destruction of the United States. Responsibility for attacks is often difficult to pin down—was it Hezbollah, Islamic Jihad, or

Crisis in Kosovo
In 1999 violence broke out in the Yugoslavian province of Kosovo, spearheaded by
Yugoslav president Slobodan Milosevic's attempts to "cleanse" the province of ethnic
Albanians. Here a group of ethnic Albanian refugees weep as they leave their homes in
Kosovo.
Wide World Photos, Inc.

Osama bin Laden's followers?—and bringing terrorists
to international justice is even harder to carry out.
Retaliation can sometimes be effective, but at other
times it simply provokes further terrorism in a war of
attrition.

Although there are few rules or guidelines for a
coming war against terrorism, the world was beginning to feel confident that nuclear proliferation had
been slowed or even halted as the century drew to an
end. Then, in 1998, India and Pakistan each defied
world opinion by testing a nuclear device. In the immediate aftermath of World War II, only the largest and
most advanced countries could realistically hope to

develop nuclear weapons; but fifty years later, the
capacity is spread much more broadly. Until India and
Pakistan conducted their tests, only five countries had
declared nuclear-weapons capability: the United
States, Russia, Britain, France, and China (although
most observers believe that Israel had such capacity as
well). In addition, Iran, Iraq, North Korea, and Libya
were suspected of having secret nuclear-weapons programs. What was especially worrisome about the
Indian and Pakistani tests was that these neighboring
countries had a long history of acrimony in one of the
world's most dangerous regions. While the world
talked gravely about nuclear proliferation, India and

A Hero for Our Jaded Times

Nelson Mandela is that rare contemporary hero whose stature seems destined to be confirmed posthumously by history. In a valedictory address to the United Nations in 1998, Mandela spoke of his long personal journey:

> Born as the First World War came to a close and departing from public life as the world marks half a century of the Universal Declaration of Human Rights, I have reached that part of the long walk when the opportunity is granted, as it should be to all men and women, to retire to some rest and tranquility in the village of my birth.
>
> As I sit in Qunu and grow as ancient as its hills . . . I will continue to hope that Africa's renaissance will strike deep roots and blossom forever, without regard to the changing seasons. . . .
>
> Then would history and the billions throughout the world proclaim that it was right that we dreamed and that we toiled to give life to a workable dream.

Louise Gubb/The Image Works.

Pakistan talked about national pride, national security, and self-defense. This new round of nuclear testing confirms how profoundly the detonation of the atomic bomb in 1945 affected the subsequent history of the world. It may be possible to manage and contain nuclear capacities and to discourage their use, but they will never be halted entirely.

Small countries as well as terrorist organizations realize that they do not require a nuclear bomb to be taken seriously: short-range nuclear missiles, germ warfare, and poison gas can be just as effective, and far cheaper. (This threat is sometimes abbreviated as "NBC"—nuclear, biological, and chemical weapons; or alternatively, weapons of mass destruction.) Much of the basic material and technology is available for purchase on the thriving world arms market, in which countries like the United States, the former states of the Soviet Union, France, and Britain are large dealers. Given this traffic in arms, it is fairly easy for inter-

mediaries in the Middle East and the Third World to buy what they need. It is said that highly destructive Cruise missiles can be bought for approximately $10,000 apiece, making them in some ways the "poor man's nukes." Obviously their potential danger increases when combined with the capacity for chemical and biological warfare. Unlike policing who has and who doesn't have the bomb, the containment of arms proliferation and suspected chemical and biological warfare is an even more complex task, as the United States has discovered in its dealings with Iraq and Saddam Hussein in the aftermath of the 1990–1991 Gulf War.

At the same time, incredibly destructive conflicts that have little to do with high-tech weaponry and everything to do with ethnicity, religion, and territory have flared up periodically in the aftermath of the Cold War and threaten to do so for the foreseeable future. The Balkans especially continue to challenge U.S. pol-

Facing the Millennium
Until the sixteenth century, maps of the world were flat. On the eve of the twenty-first
century, our vision of the world is practically infinite.
CORBIS/Randy Faris.

icy makers, NATO leaders, and United Nations peace-keeping forces. Would the Yugoslavian province of Kosovo, which U.S. peace envoy Richard Holbrooke in 1998 called "the most dangerous place in Europe," become the next Bosnia? Or would it be the Yugosla-vian republic of Montenegro? Can genocides such as occurred in Bosnia and Rwanda be prevented in the future?

The contemporary world can be a scary place indeed, but there are rays of hope at the end of the twentieth century, especially the possible resolutions of problems that have long defied peaceful solutions: the hope that the 1998 Good Friday accords may finally bring peace to Ireland, that U.S.–Cuban relations might improve in the wake of Pope John Paul II's visit to Cuba in 1998, even that Palestinians and Israelis may work out a mutually acceptable framework for the West Bank. The end of apartheid in South Africa and that country's determination to come to grips with its past is surely one of the twentieth century's most inspiring developments, as are the emergence of democratic countries from the former Soviet satellites in Eastern Europe. Along with globalization and the challenge of forging a post–Cold War foreign policy, these potential breakthroughs are part of the story of America and the world in 2000.

★ ★ ★

As the world counted down the days until the new century, millennial fever gripped the nation. That is, of course, if the world did not shut down because of a computer glitch on January 1, 2000. Despite billions of dollars spent worldwide to upgrade old systems, even computer scientists could not predict whether computers would boot up, whether planes would be able to fly safely, whether the microchip in the coffee machine would perk on that morning. That cup of coffee might be especially necessary after the New Year's Eve celebrations planned to ring in the new century. Never mind that technically the millennium doesn't begin until January 1, 2001.

By the time you read this textbook, the Y2K problem will have turned out to be a huge hoax, a massive disaster, or some of both. You know what happened and we don't, a perfect example of the pitfalls of writing the history of contemporary America and the world. Welcome to the new millennium!

The Declaration of Independence

In Congress, July 4, 1776, The Unanimous Declaration of the Thirteen United States of America

When in the Course of human events, it becomes necessary for one people to dissolve the political bands which have connected them with another, and to assume among the Powers of the earth, the separate and equal station to which the Laws of Nature and of Nature's God entitle them, a decent respect to the opinions of mankind requires that they should declare the causes which impel them to the separation.

We hold these truths to be self-evident, that all men are created equal, that they are endowed by their Creator with certain unalienable rights, that among these are Life, Liberty, and the pursuit of Happiness. That to secure these rights, Governments are instituted among Men, deriving their just powers from the consent of the governed. That whenever any Form of Government becomes destructive of these ends, it is the Right of the People to alter or to abolish it, and to institute new Government, laying its foundation on such principles and organizing its powers in such form, as to them shall seem most likely to effect their Safety and Happiness. Prudence, indeed, will dictate that Governments long established should not be changed for light and transient causes; and accordingly all experience hath shown, that mankind are more disposed to suffer, while evils are sufferable, than to right themselves by abolishing the forms to which they are accustomed. But when a long train of abuses and usurpations, pursuing invariably the same Object evinces a design to reduce them under absolute Despotism, it is their right, it is their duty, to throw off such Government, and to provide new Guards for their future security.—Such has been the patient sufferance of these Colonies; and such is now the necessity which constrains them to alter their former Systems of Government. The history of the present King of Great Britain is a history of repeated injuries and usurpations, all having in direct object the establishment of an absolute Tyranny over these States. To prove this, let Facts be submitted to a candid world.

He has refused his Assent to Laws, the most wholesome and necessary for the public good.

He has forbidden his Governors to pass Laws of immediate and pressing importance, unless suspended in their operation till his Assent should be obtained; and, when so suspended, he has utterly neglected to attend to them.

He has refused to pass other Laws for the accommodation of large districts of people, unless those people would relinquish the right of Representation in the Legislature, a right inestimable to them and formidable to tyrants only.

He has called together legislative bodies at places unusual, uncomfortable, and distant from the depository of their public Records, for the sole purpose of fatiguing them into compliance with his measures.

He has dissolved Representative Houses repeatedly, for opposing with manly firmness his invasions on the rights of the people.

He has refused for a long time, after such dissolutions, to cause others to be elected; whereby the Legislative powers, incapable of Annihilation, have returned to the People at large for their exercise; the State remaining in the mean time exposed to all the dangers of invasion from without and convulsions within.

He has endeavoured to prevent the population of these States; for that purpose obstructing the Laws of Naturalization of Foreigners; refusing to pass others to encourage their migrations hither, and raising the conditions of new Appropriations of Lands.

He has obstructed the Administration of Justice, by refusing his Assent to Laws for establishing Judiciary powers.

He has made Judges dependent on his Will alone, for the tenure of their offices, and the amount and payment of their salaries.

He has erected a multitude of New Offices, and sent hither swarms of Officers to harass our People, and eat out their substance.

He has kept among us, in times of peace, Standing Armies without the Consent of our legislature.

He has combined with others to subject us to a jurisdiction foreign to our constitution, and unacknowledged by our laws; giving his Assent to their Acts of pretended Legislation:

For quartering large bodies of armed troops among us:

For protecting them, by a mock Trial, from Punishment for any Murders which they should commit on the Inhabitants of these States:

For cutting off our Trade with all parts of the world:

For imposing taxes on us without our Consent:

For depriving us, in many cases, of the benefits of Trial by jury:

For transporting us beyond Seas to be tried for pretended offences:

For abolishing the free System of English Laws in a neighbouring Province, establishing therein an Arbitrary government, and enlarging its Boundaries so as to render it at once an example and fit instrument for introducing the same absolute rule into these Colonies:

For taking away our Charters, abolishing our most valuable Laws, and altering fundamentally the Forms of our Governments:

For suspending our own Legislatures, and declaring themselves invested with Power to legislate for us in all cases whatsoever.

He has abdicated Government here, by declaring us out of his Protection and waging War against us.

He has plundered our seas, ravaged our Coasts, burnt our towns, and destroyed the lives of our people.

He is at this time transporting large armies of foreign mercenaries to compleat the works of death, desolation, and tyranny, already begun with circumstances of Cruelty & perfidy scarcely paralleled in the most barbarous ages, and totally unworthy the Head of a civilized nation.

He has constrained our fellow Citizens taken Captive on the high Seas to bear Arms against their Country, to become the executioners of their friends and Brethren, or to fall themselves by their Hands.

He has excited domestic insurrections amongst us, and has endeavoured to bring on the inhabitants of our frontiers, the merciless Indian Savages, whose known rule of warfare, is an undistinguished destruction of all ages, sexes, and conditions.

In every stage of these Oppressions We have Petitioned for Redress in the most humble terms: Our repeated Petitions have been answered only by repeated injury. A Prince, whose character is thus marked by every act which may define a Tyrant, is unfit to be the ruler of a free people.

Nor have We been wanting in attention to our British brethren. We have warned them from time to time of attempts by their legislature to extend an unwarrantable jurisdiction over us. We have reminded them of the circumstances of our emigration and settlement here. We have appealed to their native justice and magnanimity, and we have conjured them by the ties of our common kindred to disavow these usurpations, which, would inevitably interrupt our connections and correspondence. They too have been deaf to the voice of justice and of consanguinity. We must, therefore, acquiesce in the necessity, which denounces our Separation, and hold them, as we hold the rest of mankind, Enemies in War, in Peace Friends.

We, therefore, the Representatives of the United States of America, in General Congress, Assembled, appealing to the Supreme Judge of the world for the rectitude of our intentions, do, in the Name, and by Authority of the good People of these Colonies, solemnly publish and declare, That these United Colonies are, and of Right ought to be FREE AND INDEPENDENT STATES; that they are Absolved from all Allegiance to the British Crown, and that all political connection between them and the State of Great Britain, is and ought to be totally dissolved; and that as Free and Independent States, they have full Power to levy War, conclude Peace, contract Alliances, establish Commerce, and to do all other Acts and Things which Independent States may of right do. And for the support of this Declaration, with a firm reliance on the Protection of Divine Providence, we mutually pledge to each other our Lives, our Fortunes, and our sacred Honor.

John Hancock

Button Gwinnett	George Wythe	James Wilson	Josiah Bartlett
Lyman Hall	Richard Henry Lee	Geo. Ross	Wm. Whipple
Geo. Walton	Th. Jefferson	Caesar Rodney	Matthew Thornton
Wm. Hooper	Benja. Harrison	Geo. Read	Saml. Adams
Joseph Hewes	Thos. Nelson, Jr.	Thos. M'Kean	John Adams
John Penn	Francis Lightfoot Lee	Wm. Floyd	Robt. Treat Paine
Edward Rutledge	Carter Braxton	Phil. Livingston	Elbridge Gerry
Thos. Heyward, Junr.	Robt. Morris	Frans. Lewis	Step. Hopkins
Thomas Lynch, Junr.	Benjamin Rush	Lewis Morris	William Ellery
Arthur Middleton	Benja. Franklin	Richd. Stockton	Roger Sherman
Samuel Chase	John Morton	John Witherspoon	Sam'el Huntington
Wm. Paca	Geo. Clymer	Fras. Hopkinson	Wm. Williams
Thos. Stone	Jas. Smith	John Hart	Oliver Wolcott
Charles Carroll of Carrollton	Geo. Taylor	Abra. Clark	

The Articles of Confederation and Perpetual Union

Agreed to in Congress,
November 15, 1777
Ratified March 1781

BETWEEN THE STATES OF NEW HAMPSHIRE, MASSACHUSETTS BAY, RHODE ISLAND AND PROVIDENCE PLANTATIONS, CONNECTICUT, NEW YORK, NEW JERSEY, PENNSYLVANIA, DELAWARE, MARYLAND, VIRGINIA, NORTH CAROLINA, SOUTH CAROLINA, GEORGIA.*

Article 1.

The stile of this confederacy shall be "The United States of America."

Article 2.

Each State retains its sovereignty, freedom and independence, and every power, jurisdiction, and right, which is not by this confederation expressly delegated to the United States, in Congress assembled.

Article 3.

The said states hereby severally enter into a firm league of friendship with each other for their common defence, the security of their liberties and their mutual and general welfare; binding themselves to assist each other against all force offered to, or attacks made upon them, or any of them, on account of religion, sovereignty, trade, or any other pretence whatever.

Article 4.

The better to secure and perpetuate mutual friendship and intercourse among the people of the different states in this union, the free inhabitants of each of these states, paupers, vagabonds, and fugitives from justice excepted, shall be entitled to all privileges and immunities of free citizens in the several states; and the people of each State shall have free ingress and regress to and from any other State, and shall enjoy therein all the privileges of trade and commerce, subject to the same duties, impositions, and restrictions, as the inhabitants thereof respectively; provided, that such restrictions shall not extend so far as to prevent the removal of property, imported into any State, to any other State of which the owner is an inhabitant; provided also, that no imposition, duties, or restriction, shall be laid by any State on the property of the United States, or either of them.

If any person guilty of, or charged with treason, felony, or other high misdemeanor in any State, shall flee from justice and be found in any of the United States, he shall, upon demand of the governor or executive power of the State from which he fled, be delivered up and removed to the State having jurisdiction of his offence.

Full faith and credit shall be given in each of these states to the records, acts, and judicial proceedings of the courts and magistrates of every other State.

Article 5.

For the more convenient management of the general interests of the United States, delegates shall be annually appointed, in such manner as the legislature of each State shall direct, to meet in Congress, on the 1st Monday in November in every year, with a power reserved to each State to recal its delegates, or any of them, at any time within the year, and to send others in their stead for the remainder of the year.

No State shall be represented in Congress by less than two, nor by more than seven members; and no person shall be capable of being a delegate for more than three years in any term of six years; nor shall any person, being a delegate, be capable of holding any office under the United States, for which he, or any other for his benefit, receives any salary, fees, or emolument of any kind.

Each State shall maintain its own delegates in a meeting of the states, and while they act as members of the committee of the states.

In determining questions in the United States, in Congress assembled, each State shall have one vote.

Freedom of speech and debate in Congress shall not be impeached or questioned in any court or place out of Congress: and the members of Congress shall be protected in their persons from arrests and imprisonments, during the time of their going to and from, and attendance on Congress, except for treason, felony, or breach of the peace.

*This copy of the final draft of the Articles of Confederation is taken from the Journals, 9:907–925, November 15, 1777.

Article 6.

No State, without the consent of the United States, in Congress assembled, shall send any embassy to, or receive any embassy from, or enter into any conference, agreement, alliance, or treaty with any king, prince, or state; nor shall any person, holding any office of profit or trust under the United States, or any of them, accept of any present, emolument, office or title, of any kind whatever, from any king, prince, or foreign state; nor shall the United States, in Congress assembled, or any of them, grant any title of nobility.

No two or more states shall enter into any treaty, confederation, or alliance, whatever, between them, without the consent of the United States, in Congress assembled, specifying accurately the purposes for which the same is to be entered into, and how long it shall continue.

No state shall lay any imposts or duties which may interfere with any stipulations in treaties entered into by the United States, in Congress assembled, with any king, prince, or state, in pursuance of any treaties already proposed by Congress to the courts of France and Spain.

No vessels of war shall be kept up in time of peace by any State, except such number only as shall be deemed necessary by the United States, in Congress assembled, for the defence of such State or its trade; nor shall any body of forces be kept up by any State, in time of peace, except such number only as, in the judgment of the United States, in Congress assembled, shall be deemed requisite to garrison the forts necessary for the defence of such State; but every State shall always keep up a well regulated and disciplined militia, sufficiently armed and accoutred, and shall provide, and constantly have ready for use, in public stores, a due number of field pieces and tents, and a proper quantity of arms, ammunition and camp equipage.

No State shall engage in any war without the consent of the United States, in Congress assembled, unless such State be actually invaded by enemies, or shall have received certain advice of a resolution being formed by some nation of Indians to invade such State, and the danger is so imminent as not to admit of a delay till the United States, in Congress assembled, can be consulted; nor shall any State grant commissions to any ships or vessels of war, nor letters of marque or reprisal, except it be after a declaration of war by the United States, in Congress assembled, and then only against the kingdom or state, and the subjects thereof, against which war has been so declared, and under such regulations as shall be established by the United States, in Congress assembled, unless such State be infested by pirates, in which case vessels of war may be fitted out for that occasion, and kept so long as the danger shall continue, or until the United States, in Congress assembled, shall determine otherwise.

Article 7.

When land forces are raised by any State for the common defence, all officers of or under the rank of colonel, shall be appointed by the legislature of each State respectively, by whom such forces shall be raised, or in such manner as such State shall direct; and all vacancies shall be filled up by the State which first made the appointment.

Article 8.

All charges of war and all other expences, that shall be incurred for the common defence or general welfare, and allowed by the United States, in Congress assembled, shall be defrayed out of a common treasury, which shall be supplied by the several states, in proportion to the value of all land within each State, granted to or surveyed for any person, as such land and the buildings and improvements thereon shall be estimated according to such mode as the United States, in Congress assembled, shall, from time to time, direct and appoint.

The taxes for paying that proportion shall be laid and levied by the authority and direction of the legislatures of the several states, within the time agreed upon by the United States, in Congress assembled.

Article 9.

The United States, in Congress assembled, shall have the sole and exclusive right and power of determining on peace and war, except in the cases mentioned in the 6th article; of sending and receiving ambassadors; entering into treaties and alliances, provided that no treaty of commerce shall be made, whereby the legislative power of the respective states shall be restrained from imposing such imposts and duties on foreigners as their own people are subjected to, or from prohibiting the exportation or importation of any species of goods or commodities whatsoever; of establishing rules for deciding, in all cases, what captures on land or water shall be legal, and in what manner prizes, taken by land or naval forces in the service of the United States, shall be divided or appropriated; of granting letters of marque and reprisal in times of peace; appointing courts for the trial of piracies and felonies committed on the high seas, and establishing courts for receiving and determining, finally, appeals in all cases of captures; provided, that no member of Congress shall be appointed a judge of any of the said courts.

The United States, in Congress assembled, shall also be the last resort on appeal in all disputes and differences now subsisting, or that hereafter may arise between two or more states concerning boundary, jurisdiction or any other cause whatever; which authority shall always be exercised in the manner following: whenever the legislative or executive authority, or lawful agent of any State, in controversy with another, shall present a petition to Congress, stating the matter in question, and praying for a hearing, notice thereof shall be given, by order of Congress, to the legislative or executive authority of the other State in controversy, and a day assigned for the appearance of the parties by their lawful agents, who shall then be directed to appoint, by joint consent, commissioners or judges to constitute a court for hearing and determining the matter in question; but, if they cannot agree,

Congress shall name three persons out of each of the United States, and from the list of such persons each party shall alternately strike out one, the petitioners beginning, until the number shall be reduced to thirteen; and from that number not less than seven, nor more than nine names, as Congress shall direct, shall, in the presence of Congress, be drawn out by lot; and the persons whose names shall be so drawn, or any five of them, shall be commissioners or judges to hear and finally determine the controversy, so always as a major part of the judges who shall hear the cause shall agree in the determination; and if either party shall neglect to attend at the day appointed, without shewing reasons which Congress shall judge sufficient, or, being present, shall refuse to strike, the Congress shall proceed to nominate three persons out of each State, and the secretary of Congress shall strike in behalf of such party absent or refusing; and the judgment and sentence of the court to be appointed, in the manner before prescribed, shall be final and conclusive; and if any of the parties shall refuse to submit to the authority of such court, or to appear or defend their claim or cause, the court shall nevertheless proceed to pronounce sentence or judgment, which shall, in like manner, be final and decisive, the judgment or sentence and other proceedings begin, in either case, transmitted to Congress, and lodged among the acts of Congress for the security of the parties concerned: provided, that every commissioner, before he sits in judgment, shall take an oath, to be administered by one of the judges of the supreme or superior court of the State where the cause shall be tried, "well and truly to hear and determine the matter in question, according to the best of his judgment, without favour, affection, or hope of reward:" provided, also, that no State shall be deprived of territory for the benefit of the United States.

All controversies concerning the private right of soil, claimed under different grants of two or more states, whose jurisdictions, as they may respect such lands and the states which passed such grants, are adjusted, the said grants, or either of them, being at the same time claimed to have originated antecedent to such settlement of jurisdiction, shall, on the petition of either party to the Congress of the United States, be finally determined, as near as may be, in the same manner as is before prescribed for deciding disputes respecting territorial jurisdiction between different states.

The United States, in Congress assembled, shall also have the sole and exclusive right and power of regulating the alloy and value of coin struck by their own authority, or by that of the respective states; fixing the standard of weights and measures throughout the United States; regulating the trade and managing all affairs with the Indians not members of any of the states; provided that the legislative right of any State within its own limits be not infringed or violated; establishing and regulating post offices from one State to another throughout all the United States, and exacting such postage on the papers passing through the same as may be requisite to defray the expences of the said office; appointing all officers of the land forces in the service of the United States, excepting regimental officers; appointing all the officers of the naval forces, and commissioning all officers whatever in the service of the United States; making rules for the government and regulation of the said land and naval forces, and directing their operations.

The United States, in Congress assembled, shall have authority to appoint a committee to sit in the recess of Congress, to be denominated "a Committee of the States," and to consist of one delegate from each State, and to appoint such other committees and civil officers as may be necessary for managing the general affairs of the United States, under their direction; to appoint one of their number to preside; provided that no person be allowed to serve in the office of president more than one year in any term of three years; to ascertain the necessary sums of money to be raised for the service of the United States, and to appropriate and apply the same for defraying the public expences; to borrow money or emit bills on the credit of the United States, transmitting, every half year, to the respective states, an account of the sums of money so borrowed or emitted; to build and equip a navy; to agree upon the number of land forces, and to make requisitions from each State for its quota, in proportion to the number of white inhabitants in such State; which requisitions shall be binding; and thereupon, the legislature of each State shall appoint the regimental officers, raise the men, and cloathe, arm, and equip them in a soldier-like manner, at the expence of the United States; and the officers and men so cloathed, armed, and equipped, shall march to the place appointed and within the time agreed on by the United States, in Congress assembled; but if the United States, in Congress assembled, shall, on consideration of circumstances, judge proper that any State should not raise men, or should raise a smaller number than its quota, and that any other State should raise a greater number of men than the quota thereof, such extra number shall be raised, officered, cloathed, armed, and equipped in the same manner as the quota of such State, unless the legislature of such State shall judge that such extra number cannot be safely spared out of the same, in which case they shall raise, officer, cloathe, arm, and equip as many of such extra number as they judge can be safely spared. And the officers and men so cloathed, armed, and equipped, shall march to the place appointed and within the time agreed on by the United States, in Congress assembled.

The United States, in Congress assembled, shall never engage in a war, nor grant letters of marque and reprisal in time of peace, nor enter into any treaties or alliances, nor coin money, nor regulate the value thereof, nor ascertain the sums and expences necessary for the defence and welfare of the United States, or any of them: nor emit bills, nor borrow money on the credit of the United States, nor appropriate money, nor agree upon the number of vessels of war to be built or purchased, or the number of land or sea forces to be raised, nor appoint a commander in chief of the army or navy, unless nine states assent to the same; nor shall a question on any other point, except for adjourning from day to day, be determined, unless by the votes of a majority of the United States, in Congress assembled.

The Congress of the United States shall have power to adjourn to any time within the year, and to any place within the United States, so that no period of adjournment be for a longer duration than the space of six months, and shall publish the journal of their proceedings monthly, except such parts thereof, relating to treaties, alliances or military operations, as, in their judgment, require secrecy; and the yeas and nays of the delegates of each State on any question shall be entered on the journal, when it is desired by any delegate; and the delegates of a State, or any of them, at his, or their request, shall be furnished with a transcript of the said journal, except such parts as are above excepted, to lay before the legislatures of the several states.

Article 10.

The committee of the states, or any nine of them, shall be authorized to execute, in the recess of Congress, such of the powers of Congress as the United States, in Congress assembled, by the consent of nine states, shall, from time to time, think expedient to vest them with; provided, that no power be delegated to the said committee, for the exercise of which, by the articles of confederation, the voice of nine states, in the Congress of the United States assembled, is requisite.

Article 11.

Canada acceding to this confederation, and joining in the measures of the United States, shall be admitted into and entitled to all the advantages of this union; but no other colony shall be admitted into the same, unless such admission be agreed to by nine states.

Article 12.

All bills of credit emitted, monies borrowed and debts contracted by, or under the authority of Congress before the assembling of the United States, in pursuance of the present confederation, shall be deemed and considered as a charge against the United States, for payment and satisfaction whereof the said United States and the public faith are hereby solemnly pledged.

Article 13.

Every State shall abide by the determinations of the United States, in Congress assembled, on all questions which, by this confederation, are submitted to them. And the articles of this confederation shall be inviolably observed by every State, and the union shall be perpetual; nor shall any alteration at any time hereafter be made in any of them, unless such alteration be agreed to in a Congress of the United States, and be afterwards confirmed by the legislatures of every State.

These articles shall be proposed to the legislatures of all the United States, to be considered, and if approved of by them, they are advised to authorize their delegates to ratify the same in the Congress of the United States; which being done, the same shall become conclusive.

The Constitution of the United States of America

Agreed to by Philadelphia Convention, September 17, 1787
Implemented March 4, 1789

We the People of the United States, in Order to form a more perfect Union, establish Justice, insure domestic Tranquility, provide for the common defence, promote the general Welfare, and secure the Blessings of Liberty to ourselves and our Posterity, do ordain and establish this Constitution for the United States of America.

Article I

SECTION 1 All legislative Powers herein granted shall be vested in a Congress of the United States, which shall consist of a Senate and a House of Representatives.

SECTION 2 The House of Representatives shall be composed of Members chosen every second Year by the People of the several States, and the Electors in each State shall have the Qualifications requisite for Electors of the most numerous Branch of the State Legislature.

No Person shall be a Representative who shall not have attained to the Age of twenty-five Years, and been seven Years a Citizen of the United States, and who shall not, when elected, be an Inhabitant of that State in which he shall be chosen.

Representatives and direct Taxes shall be apportioned among the several States which may be included within this Union, according to their respective Numbers, *which shall be determined by adding to the whole Number of free Persons, including those bound to Service for a Term of Years, and excluding Indians not taxed, three fifths of all other Persons.** The actual Enumeration shall be made within three Years after the first Meeting of the Congress of the United States, and within every subsequent Term of ten Years, in such Manner as they shall by Law direct. The Number of Representatives shall not exceed one for every thirty Thousand, but each State shall have at Least one Representative; and *until such enumeration shall be made, the State of New Hampshire shall be entitled to chuse three, Massachusetts eight, Rhode Island and Providence Plantations one, Connecticut five, New-York six, New Jersey four, Pennsylvania eight, Delaware one, Maryland six, Virginia ten, North Carolina five, South Carolina five, and Georgia three.*

When vacancies happen in the Representation from any State, the Executive Authority thereof shall issue Writs of Election to fill such Vacancies.

The House of Representatives shall chuse their Speaker and other Officers; and shall have the sole Power of Impeachment.

SECTION 3 The Senate of the United States shall be composed of two Senators from each State, *chosen by the Legislature thereof,*† for six Years; and each Senator shall have one Vote.

Immediately after they shall be assembled in Consequence of the first Election, they shall be divided as equally as may be into three Classes. The Seats of the Senators of the first Class shall be vacated at the Expiration of the second Year, of the second Class at the Expiration of the fourth Year, and of the third Class at the Expiration of the sixth Year, so that one-third may be chosen every second Year; *and if Vacancies happen by Resignation, or otherwise, during the Recess of the Legislature of any State, the Executive thereof may make temporary Appointments until the next Meeting of the Legislature, which shall then fill such Vacancies.*‡

No person shall be a Senator who shall not have attained to the Age of thirty Years, and been nine Years a Citizen of the United States, and who shall not, when elected, be an Inhabitant of that State for which he shall be chosen.

The Vice President of the United States shall be President of the Senate, but shall have no Vote, unless they be equally divided.

The Senate shall chuse their other Officers, and also a President pro tempore, in the absence of the Vice President, or when he shall exercise the Office of President of the United States.

The Senate shall have the sole Power to try all Impeachments. When sitting for that Purpose, they shall be on Oath or Affirmation. When the President of the United States is tried, the Chief Justice shall preside: And no Person shall be convicted without the Concurrence of two thirds of the Members present.

Judgment in Cases of Impeachment shall not extend further than to removal from Office, and disqualification to hold and enjoy any Office of honor, Trust or Profit under the United States: but the Party convicted shall nevertheless be liable and subject to Indictment, Trial, Judgment and Punishment, according to Law.

Note: The Constitution became effective March 4, 1789. Provisions in italics are no longer relevant or have been changed by constitutional amendment.
*Changed by Section 2 of the Fourteenth Amendment.

†Changed by Section 1 of the Seventeenth Amendment.
‡Changed by Clause 2 of the Seventeenth Amendment.

SECTION 4 The Times, Places and Manner of holding Elections for Senators and Representatives, shall be prescribed in each State by the Legislature thereof; but the Congress may at any time by Law make or alter such Regulations, except as to the Places of Chusing Senators.

The Congress shall assemble at least once in every Year, and such Meeting *shall be on the first Monday in December, unless they shall by Law appoint a different Day.**

SECTION 5 Each House shall be the Judge of the Elections, Returns and Qualifications of its own Members, and a Majority of each shall constitute a Quorum to do Business; but a smaller number may adjourn from day to day, and may be authorized to compel the Attendance of absent Members, in such Manner, and under such Penalties, as each House may provide.

Each House may determine the Rules of its Proceedings, punish its Members for disorderly Behavior, and, with the Concurrence of two thirds, expel a Member.

Each House shall keep a Journal of its Proceedings, and from time to time publish the same, excepting such Parts as may in their Judgment require Secrecy; and the Yeas and Nays of the Members of either House on any question shall, at the Desire of one-fifth of those Present, be entered on the Journal.

Neither House, during the Session of Congress, shall, without the Consent of the other, adjourn for more than three days, nor to any other Place than that in which the two Houses shall be sitting.

SECTION 6 The Senators and Representatives shall receive a Compensation for their Services, to be ascertained by Law, and paid out of the Treasury of the United States. They shall in all Cases, except Treason, Felony and Breach of the Peace, be privileged from Arrest during their Attendance at the Session of their respective Houses, and in going to and returning from the same; and for any Speech or Debate in either House, they shall not be questioned in any other Place.

No Senator or Representative shall, during the Time for which he was elected, be appointed to any civil Office under the Authority of the United States, which shall have been created, or the Emoluments whereof shall have been increased, during such time; and no Person holding any Office under the United States, shall be a Member of either House during his Continuance in Office.

SECTION 7 All Bills for raising Revenue shall originate in the House of Representatives; but the Senate may propose or concur with Amendments as on other Bills.

Every Bill which shall have passed the House of Representatives and the Senate, shall, before it becomes a Law, be presented to the President of the United States; If he approve he shall sign it, but if not he shall return it, with his Objections to that House in which it shall have originated, who shall enter the Objections at large on their Journal, and proceed to reconsider it. If after such Reconsideration two thirds of that House shall agree to pass the Bill, it shall be sent, together with the Objections, to the other House, by which it shall likewise be reconsidered, and if approved by two thirds of that House, it shall become a Law. But in all such Cases the Votes of both Houses shall be determined by Yeas and Nays, and the Names of the Persons voting for and against the Bill shall be entered on the Journal of each House respectively. If any Bill shall not be returned by the President within ten Days (Sundays excepted) after it shall have been presented to him, the Same shall be a Law, in like Manner as if he had signed it, unless the Congress by their Adjournment prevent its Return, in which Case it shall not be a Law.

Every Order, Resolution, or Vote to which the Concurrence of the Senate and the House of Representatives may be necessary (except on a question of Adjournment) shall be presented to the President of the United States; and before the Same shall take Effect, shall be approved by him, or being disapproved by him, shall be repassed by two thirds of the Senate and House of Representatives, according to the Rules and Limitations prescribed in the Case of a Bill.

SECTION 8 The Congress shall have Power To lay and collect Taxes, Duties, Imposts and Excises, to pay the Debts and provide for the common Defence and general Welfare of the United States; but all Duties, Imposts and Excises shall be uniform throughout the United States;

To borrow money on the credit of the United States;

To regulate Commerce with foreign Nations, and among the several States, and with the Indian Tribes;

To establish an uniform Rule of Naturalization, and uniform Laws on the subject of Bankruptcies throughout the United States;

To coin Money, regulate the Value thereof, and of foreign Coin, and fix the Standard of Weights and Measures;

To provide for the Punishment of counterfeiting the Securities and current Coin of the United States;

To establish Post Offices and post Roads;

To promote the Progress of Science and useful Arts, by securing for limited Times to Authors and Inventors the exclusive Right to their respective Writings and Discoveries;

To constitute Tribunals inferior to the supreme Court;

To define and punish Piracies and Felonies committed on the high Seas, and Offenses against the Law of Nations;

To declare War, grant Letters of Marque and Reprisal, and make Rules concerning Captures on Land and Water;

To raise and support Armies, but no Appropriation of Money to that Use shall be for a longer Term than two Years;

To provide and maintain a Navy;

To make Rules for the Government and Regulation of the land and naval Forces;

To provide for calling forth the Militia to execute the Laws of the Union, suppress Insurrections and repel Invasions;

To provide for organizing, arming, and disciplining the Militia, and for governing such Part of them as may be employed in the Service of the United States, reserving to the States respectively, the Appointment of the Officers, and the Authority of training the Militia according to the discipline prescribed by Congress;

To exercise exclusive Legislation in all Cases whatsoever, over such District (not exceeding ten Miles square) as may, by Cession of particular States, and the acceptance of Congress, become the Seat of Government of the United States, and to

*Changed by Section 2 of the Twentieth Amendment.

exercise like Authority over all Places purchased by the Consent of the Legislature of the State in which the Same shall be, for the Erection of Forts, Magazines, Arsenals, dock-Yards, and other needful Buildings;—And

To make all Laws which shall be necessary and proper for carrying into Execution the foregoing Powers, and all other Powers vested by this Constitution in the Government of the United States, or in any Department or Officer thereof.

SECTION 9 The Migration or Importation of such Persons as any of the States now existing shall think proper to admit, shall not be prohibited by the Congress prior to the Year one thousand eight hundred and eight but a tax or duty may be imposed on such Importation, not exceeding ten dollars for each Person.

The privilege of the Writ of Habeas Corpus shall not be suspended, unless when in Cases of Rebellion or Invasion the public Safety may require it.

No Bill of Attainder or ex post facto Law shall be passed.

No capitation, or other direct, Tax shall be laid, unless in Proportion to the Census or Enumeration herein before directed to be taken. *

No Tax or Duty shall be laid on Articles exported from any State.

No Preference shall be given by any Regulation of Commerce or Revenue to the Ports of one State over those of another: nor shall Vessels bound to, or from, one State, be obliged to enter, clear, or pay Duties in another.

No Money shall be drawn from the Treasury, but in Consequence of Appropriations made by law; and a regular Statement and Account of the Receipts and Expenditures of all public Money shall be published from time to time.

No Title of Nobility shall be granted by the United States: And no Person holding any Office of Profit or Trust under them, shall, without the Consent of the Congress, accept of any present, Emolument, Office, or Title, of any kind whatever, from any King, Prince, or foreign State.

SECTION 10 No State shall enter into any Treaty, Alliance, or Confederation; grant Letters of Marque and Reprisal; coin Money; emit Bills of Credit; make any Thing but gold and silver Coin a Tender in Payment of Debts; pass any Bill of Attainder, ex post facto Law, or Law impairing the Obligation of Contracts, or grant any Title of Nobility.

No State shall, without the Consent of the Congress, lay any Imposts or Duties on Imports or Exports, except what may be absolutely necessary for executing its inspection Laws: and the net Produce of all Duties and Imposts, laid by any State on Imports or Exports, shall be for the Use of the Treasury of the United States; and all such Laws shall be subject to the Revision and Control of the Congress.

No State shall, without the Consent of the Congress, lay any duty of Tonnage, keep Troops, or Ships of War in time of Peace, enter into any Agreement or Compact with another State, or with a foreign Power, or engage in War, unless actually invaded, or in such imminent Danger as will not admit of delay.

Article II

SECTION 1 The executive Power shall be vested in a President of the United States of America. He shall hold his Office during the Term of four Years, and, together with the Vice President, chosen for the same Term, be elected, as follows:

Each State shall appoint, in such Manner as the Legislature thereof may direct, a Number of Electors, equal to the whole Number of Senators and Representatives to which the State may be entitled in the Congress; but no Senator or Representative, or Person holding an Office of Trust or Profit under the United States, shall be appointed an Elector.

The Electors shall meet in their respective States, and vote by Ballot for two Persons, of whom one at least shall not be an Inhabitant of the same State with themselves. And they shall make a List of all the Persons voted for, and of the Number of Votes for each; which List they shall sign and certify, and transmit sealed to the Seat of the Government of the United States, directed to the President of the Senate. The President of the Senate shall, in the Presence of the Senate and House of Representatives, open all the Certificates, and the Votes shall then be counted. The Person having the greatest Number of Votes shall be the President, if such Number be a Majority of the whole Number of Electors appointed; and if there be more than one who have such Majority, and have an equal Number of Votes, then the House of Representatives shall immediately chuse by Ballot one of them for President; and if no Person have a Majority, then from the five highest on the List the said House shall in like Manner chuse the President. But in chusing the President, the Votes shall be taken by States, the Representation from each State having one Vote; a quorum for this Purpose shall consist of a Member or Members from two thirds of the States, and a Majority of all the States shall be necessary to a Choice. In every Case, after the Choice of the President, the Person having the greatest Number of Votes of the Electors shall be the Vice President. But if there should remain two or more who have equal Votes, the Senate shall chuse from them by Ballot the Vice President.†

The Congress may determine the Time of chusing the Electors, and the Day on which they shall give their Votes; which Day shall be the same throughout the United States.

No Person except a natural born Citizen, or a Citizen of the United States, at the time of the Adoption of this Constitution, shall be eligible to the Office of President; neither shall any Person be eligible to that Office who shall not have attained to the Age of thirty five Years, and been fourteen Years a Resident within the United States.

In Case of the Removal of the President from Office, or of his Death, Resignation, or Inability to discharge the Powers and Duties of the said Office, the same shall devolve on the Vice President, *and the Congress may by Law provide for the Case of Removal, Death, Resignation, or Inability, both of the President and Vice President, declaring what Officer shall then act as President, and such Officer shall act accordingly, until the Disability be removed, or a President shall be elected.*‡

The President shall, at stated Times, receive for his Services a Compensation, which shall neither be increased nor

*Changed by the Sixteenth Amendment.

†Superseded by the Twelfth Amendment.
‡Modified by the Twenty-fifth Amendment.

diminished during the Period for which he shall have been elected, and he shall not receive within that Period any other Emolument from the United States, or any of them.

Before he enter on the Execution of his Office, he shall take the following Oath or Affirmation:—"I do solemnly swear (or affirm) that I will faithfully execute the Office of President of the United States, and will to the best of my Ability, preserve, protect and defend the Constitution of the United States."

SECTION 2 The President shall be Commander in Chief of the Army and Navy of the United States, and of the Militia of the several States, when called into the actual Service of the United States; he may require the Opinion, in writing, of the principal Officer in each of the executive Departments, upon any Subject relating to the Duties of their respective Offices, and he shall have Power to Grant Reprieves and Pardons for Offences against the United States, except in Cases of Impeachment.

He shall have Power, by and with the Advice and Consent of the Senate, to make Treaties, provided two thirds of the Senators present concur; and he shall nominate, and by and with the Advice and Consent of the Senate, shall appoint Ambassadors, other public Ministers and Consuls, Judges of the supreme Court, and all other Officers of the United States, whose Appointments are not herein otherwise provided for, and which shall be established by Law: but the Congress may by Law vest the Appointment of such inferior Officers, as they think proper, in the President alone, in the Courts of Law, or in the Heads of Departments.

The President shall have Power to fill up all Vacancies that may happen during the Recess of the Senate, by granting Commissions which shall expire at the End of their next Session.

SECTION 3 He shall from time to time give to the Congress Information of the State of the Union, and recommend to their Consideration such Measures as he shall judge necessary and expedient; he may, on extraordinary Occasions, convene both Houses, or either of them, and in Case of Disagreement between them, with Respect to the Time of Adjournment, he may adjourn them to such Time as he shall think proper; he shall receive Ambassadors and other public Ministers; he shall take Care that the Laws be faithfully executed, and shall Commission all the Officers of the United States.

SECTION 4 The President, Vice President and all civil Officers of the United States, shall be removed from Office on Impeachment for, and Conviction of, Treason, Bribery, or other high Crimes and Misdemeanors.

Article III

SECTION 1 The judicial Power of the United States, shall be vested in one supreme Court, and in such inferior Courts as the Congress may from time to time ordain and establish. The Judges, both of the supreme and inferior Courts, shall hold their Offices during good Behaviour, and shall, at stated Times, receive for their Services a Compensation, which shall not be diminished during their Continuance in Office.

SECTION 2 The judicial Power shall extend to all Cases, in Law and Equity, arising under this Constitution, the Laws of the United States, and Treaties made, or which shall be made, under their Authority;—to all Cases affecting Ambassadors, other public Ministers and Consuls;—to all Cases of admiralty and maritime Jurisdiction;—to Controversies to which the United States shall be a Party;—to Controversies between two or more States;—*between a State and Citizens of another State;**—between Citizens of different States;—between Citizens of the same State claiming Lands under Grants of different States, and between a State, or the Citizens thereof, and foreign States, Citizens or Subjects.

In all Cases affecting Ambassadors, other public Ministers and Consuls, and those in which a State shall be Party, the supreme Court shall have original Jurisdiction. In all the other Cases before mentioned, the supreme Court shall have appellate Jurisdiction, both as to Law and Fact, with such Exceptions, and under such Regulations as the Congress shall make.

The trial of all Crimes, except in Cases of Impeachment, shall be by Jury; and such Trial shall be held in the State where said Crimes shall have been committed; but when not committed within any State, the Trial shall be at such Place or Places as the Congress may by Law have directed.

SECTION 3 Treason against the United States, shall consist only in levying War against them, or in adhering to their Enemies, giving them Aid and Comfort. No Person shall be convicted of Treason unless on the Testimony of two Witnesses to the same overt Act, or on Confession in open Court.

The Congress shall have Power to declare the Punishment of Treason, but no Attainder of Treason shall work Corruption of Blood, or Forefeiture except during the Life of the Person attainted.

Article IV

SECTION 1 Full Faith and Credit shall be given in each State to the public Acts, Records, and judicial Proceedings of every other State. And the Congress may by general Laws prescribe the Manner in which such Acts, Records, and Proceedings shall be proved, and the Effect thereof.

SECTION 2 The Citizens of each State shall be entitled to all Privileges and Immunities of Citizens in the several States.

A Person charged in any State with Treason, Felony, or other Crime, who shall flee from Justice, and be found in another State, shall on demand of the executive Authority of the State from which he fled, be delivered up, to be removed to the State having Jurisdiction of the Crime.

No Person held to Service or Labour in one State, under the Laws thereof, escaping into another, shall, in Consequence of any Law or Regulation therein, be discharged from such Service or Labour, but shall be delivered up on Claim of the Party to whom such Service or Labour may be due.†

---

*Restricted by the Eleventh Amendment.
†Superseded by the Thirteenth Amendment.

SECTION 3 New States may be admitted by the Congress into this Union; but no new State shall be formed or erected within the Jurisdiction of any other State; nor any State be formed by the Junction of two or more States, or parts of States, without the Consent of the Legislatures of the States concerned as well as of the Congress.

The Congress shall have Power to dispose of and make all needful Rules and Regulations respecting the Territory or other Property belonging to the United States; and nothing in this Constitution shall be so construed as to Prejudice any Claims of the United States, or of any particular State.

SECTION 4 The United States shall guarantee to every State in this Union a Republican Form of Government, and shall protect each of them against Invasion; and on Application of the Legislature, or of the Executive (when the Legislature cannot be convened) against domestic Violence.

Article V

The Congress, whenever two thirds of both Houses shall deem it necessary, shall propose Amendments to this Constitution, or, on the Application of the Legislatures of two thirds of the several States, shall call a Convention for proposing Amendments, which, in either Case, shall be valid to all Intents and Purposes, as Part of this Constitution, when ratified by the Legislatures of three fourths of the several States, or by Conventions in three fourths thereof, as the one or the other Mode of Ratification may be proposed by the Congress; Provided that no Amendment which may be made prior to the Year One thousand eight hundred and eight shall in any Manner affect the first and fourth Clauses in the Ninth Section of the first Article; and that no State, without its Consent, shall be deprived of its equal Suffrage in the Senate.

Article VI

All Debts contracted and Engagements entered into, before the Adoption of this Constitution, shall be as valid against the United States under this Constitution, as under the Confederation.

This Constitution, and the Laws of the United States which shall be made in Pursuance thereof; and all Treaties made, or which shall be made, under the Authority of the United States, shall be the supreme Law of the Land; and the Judges in every State shall be bound thereby, any Thing in the Constitution or Laws of any State to the Contrary notwithstanding.

The Senators and Representatives before mentioned, and the Members of the several State Legislatures, and all executive and judicial Officers, both of the United States and of the several States, shall be bound by Oath or Affirmation, to support this Constitution; but no religious Test shall ever be required as a Qualification to any Office or public Trust under the United States.

Article VII

The Ratification of the Conventions of nine States shall be sufficient for the Establishment of this Constitution between the States so ratifying the Same.

Done in Convention by the Unanimous Consent of the States present the Seventeenth Day of September in the Year of our Lord one thousand seven hundred and Eighty seven and of the Independence of the United States of America the Twelfth. In Witness whereof We have hereunto subscribed our Names.

Go. Washington
President and deputy from Virginia

New Hampshire
John Langdon
Nicholas Gilman

Massachusetts
Nathaniel Gorham
Rufus King

Connecticut
Wm. Saml. Johnson
Roger Sherman

New York
Alexander Hamilton

New Jersey
Wil. Livingston
David Brearley
Wm. Paterson
Jona. Dayton

Pennsylvania
B. Franklin
Thomas Mifflin
Robt. Morris
Geo. Clymer
Thos. FitzSimons
Jared Ingersoll
James Wilson
Gouv. Morris

Delaware
Geo. Read
Gunning Bedford jun
John Dickinson
Richard Bassett
Jaco. Broom

Maryland
James McHenry
Dan. of St. Thos. Jenifer
Danl. Carroll

Virginia
John Blair
James Madison, Jr.

North Carolina
Wm. Blount
Richd. Dobbs Spaight
Hu Williamson

South Carolina
J. Rutledge
Charles Cotesworth Pinckney
Pierce Butler

Georgia
William Few
Abr. Baldwin

Amendments to the Constitution with Annotations (Including the Six Unratified Amendments)

In their effort to gain Antifederalists' support for the Constitution, Federalists frequently pointed to the inclusion of Article 5, which provides an orderly method of amending the Constitution. In contrast, the Articles of Confederation, which were universally recognized as seriously flawed, offered no means of amendment. For their part, Antifederalists argued that the amendment process was so "intricate" that one might as easily roll "sixes an hundred times in succession" as change the Constitution.

The system for amendment laid out in the Constitution requires that two-thirds of both houses of Congress agree to a proposed amendment, which must then be ratified by three-quarters of the legislatures of the states. Alternatively, an amendment may be proposed by a convention called by the legislatures of two-thirds of the states. Since 1789, members of Congress have proposed thousands of amendments. Besides the seventeen amendments added since 1791, only the six "unratified" ones included here were approved by two-thirds of both houses but not ratified by the states.

Among the many amendments that never made it out of Congress have been proposals to declare dueling, divorce, and interracial marriage unconstitutional as well as proposals to establish a national university, to acknowledge the sovereignty of Jesus Christ, and to prohibit any person from possessing wealth in excess of $10 million.*

Among the issues facing Americans today that might lead to constitutional amendment are efforts to balance the federal budget, to limit the number of terms elected officials may serve, to limit access to or prohibit abortion, to establish English as the official language of the United States, and to prohibit flag burning. None of these proposed amendments has yet garnered enough support in Congress to be sent to the states for ratification.

Although the first ten amendments to the Constitution are commonly known as the Bill of Rights, only Amendments 1–8 actually provide guarantees of individual rights. Amendments 9 and 10 deal with the structure of power within the constitutional system. The Bill of Rights was promised to appease Antifederalists who refused to ratify the Constitution without guarantees of individual liberties and limitations to federal power. After studying more than two hundred amendments recommended by the ratifying con-

ventions of the states, Federalist James Madison presented a list of seventeen to Congress, which used Madison's list as the foundation for the twelve amendments that were sent to the states for ratification. Ten of the twelve were adopted in 1791. The first on the list of twelve, known as the Reapportionment Amendment, was never adopted (see p. D-15). The second proposed amendment was adopted in 1992 as Amendment 27 (see p. D-23).

Amendment I [1791]†

Congress shall make no law respecting an establishment of religion, or prohibiting the free exercise thereof; or abridging the freedom of speech, or of the press; or the right of the people peaceably to assemble, and to petition the government for a redress of grievances.

The First Amendment is a potent symbol for many Americans. Most are well aware of their rights to free speech, freedom of the press, and freedom of religion and their rights to assemble and to petition, even if they cannot cite the exact words of this amendment.

The First Amendment guarantee of freedom of religion has two clauses: the "free exercise clause," which allows individuals to practice or not practice any religion, and the "establishment clause," which prevents the federal government from discriminating against or favoring any particular religion. This clause was designed to create what Thomas Jefferson referred to as "a wall of separation between church and state." In the 1960s, the Supreme Court ruled that the First Amendment prohibits prayer and Bible reading in public schools.

Although the rights to free speech and freedom of the press are established in the First Amendment, it was not until the twentieth century that the Supreme Court began to explore the full meaning of these guarantees. In 1919, the Court ruled in Schenck v. United States *that the government could suppress free expression only where it could cite a "clear and present danger." In a decision that continues to raise controversies, the Court ruled in 1990, in* Texas v. Johnson, *that flag burning is a form of symbolic speech protected by the First Amendment.*

---

*Richard B. Bernstein, *Amending America* (New York: Times Books, 1993), 177–181.

†The dates in brackets indicate when the amendment was ratified.

Amendment II [1791]

A well-regulated militia being necessary to the security of a free State, the right of the people to keep and bear arms shall not be infringed.

★ ★ ★

Fear of a standing army under the control of a hostile government made the Second Amendment an important part of the Bill of Rights. Advocates of gun ownership claim that the amendment prevents the government from regulating firearms. Proponents of gun control argue that the amendment is designed only to protect the right of the states to maintain militia units.

In 1939, the Supreme Court ruled in United States v. Miller *that the Second Amendment did not protect the right of an individual to own a sawed-off shotgun, which it argued was not ordinary militia equipment. Since then, the Supreme Court has refused to hear Second Amendment cases, whereas lower courts have upheld firearm regulations. Several justices currently on the bench seem to favor a narrow interpretation of the Second Amendment, which would allow gun control legislation. The controversy over the impact of the Second Amendment on gun owners and gun control legislation will certainly continue.*

Amendment III [1791]

No soldier shall, in time of peace, be quartered in any house without the consent of the owner, nor in time of war, but in a manner to be prescribed by law.

★ ★ ★

The Third Amendment was extremely important to the framers of the Constitution, but today it is nearly forgotten. American colonists were especially outraged that they were forced to quarter British troops in the years before and during the American Revolution. The philosophy of the Third Amendment has been viewed by some justices and scholars as the foundation of the modern constitutional right to privacy.

Amendment IV [1791]

The right of the people to be secure in their persons, houses, papers, and effects, against unreasonable searches and seizures, shall not be violated, and no warrants shall issue but upon probable cause, supported by oath or affirmation, and particularly describing the place to be searched, and the persons or things to be seized.

★ ★ ★

In the years before the Revolution, the houses, barns, stores, and warehouses of American colonists were ransacked by British authorities under "writs of assistance" or general warrants. The British, thus empowered, searched for seditious material or smuggled goods that could then be used as evidence against colonists who were charged with a crime only after the items were found.

The first part of the Fourth Amendment protects citizens from "unreasonable" searches and seizures. The Supreme Court has interpreted this protection as well as the words search *and* seizure *in different ways at different times. At one time, the Court did not recognize electronic eavesdropping as a form of search and seizure, although it does today. At times, an "unreasonable" search has been almost any search carried out without a warrant, but in the two decades before 1969 the Court sometimes sanctioned warrantless searches that it considered reasonable based on "the total atmosphere of the case."*

The second part of the Fourth Amendment defines the procedure for issuing a search warrant and states the requirement of "probable cause," which is generally viewed as evidence indicating that a suspect has committed an offense.

The Fourth Amendment has been controversial because the Court has sometimes excluded evidence that has been seized in violation of constitutional standards. The justification is that excluding such evidence deters violations of the amendment, but doing so may allow a guilty person to escape punishment.

Amendment V [1791]

No person shall be held to answer for a capital, or otherwise infamous crime, unless on a presentment or indictment of a grand jury, except in cases arising in the land or naval forces, or in the militia, when in actual service in time of war or public danger; nor shall any person be subject for the same offence to be twice put in jeopardy of life or limb; nor shall be compelled in any criminal case to be a witness against himself, nor be deprived of life, liberty, or property, without due process of law; nor shall private property be taken for public use without just compensation.

★ ★ ★

The Fifth Amendment protects people against government authority in the prosecution of criminal offenses. It prohibits the state, first, from charging a person with a serious crime without a grand jury hearing to decide whether there is sufficient evidence to support the charge and, second, from charging a person with the same crime twice. The best-known aspect of the Fifth Amendment is that it prevents a person from being "compelled . . . to be a witness against himself." The last clause, the "takings clause," limits the power of the government to seize property.

Although invoking the Fifth Amendment is popularly viewed as a confession of guilt, a person may be innocent yet still fear prosecution. For example, during the Cold War era of the late 1940s and 1950s, many people who had participated in legal activities that were associated with the Communist Party claimed the Fifth Amendment privilege rather than testify before the House Un-American Activities Committee because the mood of the times cast those activities in a negative light. Because "taking the Fifth" was viewed as an admission of guilt, those people often lost their jobs or became unemployable. Nonetheless, the right to protect oneself against self-incrimination plays an important role in guarding against the collective power of the state.

Amendment VI [1791]

In all criminal prosecutions, the accused shall enjoy the right to a speedy and public trial, by an impartial jury of the State and district wherein the crime shall have been committed, which district shall have been previously ascertained by law, and to be informed of the nature and cause of the accusation; to be confronted with the witnesses against him; to have compulsory process for obtaining witnesses in his favor, and to have the assistance of counsel for his defence.

The original Constitution put few limits on the government's power to investigate, prosecute, and punish crime. This process was of great concern to the early Americans, however, and of the twenty-eight rights specified in the first eight amendments, fifteen have to do with it. Seven rights are specified in the Sixth Amendment. These include the right to a speedy trial, a public trial, a jury trial, a notice of accusation, confrontation by opposing witnesses, testimony by favorable witnesses, and the assistance of counsel.

Amendment VII [1791]

In suits at common law, where the value in controversy shall exceed twenty dollars, the right of trial by jury shall be preserved, and no fact tried by a jury shall be otherwise reexamined in any court of the United States, than according to the rules of the common law.

This amendment guarantees people the same right to a trial by jury as was guaranteed by English common law in 1791. Under common law, in civil trials (those involving money damages) the role of the judge was to settle questions of law and that of the jury was to settle questions of fact. The amendment does not specify the size of the jury or its role in a trial, however. The Supreme Court has generally held that those issues be determined by English common law of 1791, which stated that a jury consists of twelve people, that a trial must be conducted before a judge who instructs the jury on the law and advises it on facts, and that a verdict must be unanimous.

Amendment VIII [1791]

Excessive bail shall not be required, nor excessive fines imposed, nor cruel and unusual punishments inflicted.

The language used to guarantee the three rights in this amendment was inspired by the English Bill of Rights of 1689. The Supreme Court has not had a lot to say about "excessive fines." In recent years it has agreed that despite the provision against "excessive bail," persons who are believed to be dangerous to others can be held without bail even before they have been convicted.

Although opponents of the death penalty have not succeeded in using the Eighth Amendment to achieve the end of

capital punishment, the clause regarding "cruel and unusual punishments" has been used to prohibit capital punishment in certain cases.

Amendment IX [1791]

The enumeration in the Constitution, of certain rights, shall not be construed to deny or disparage others retained by the people.

Some Federalists feared that inclusion of the Bill of Rights in the Constitution would allow later generations of interpreters to claim that the people had surrendered any rights not specifically enumerated there. To guard against this, Madison added language that became the Ninth Amendment. Interest in this heretofore largely ignored amendment revived in 1965 when it was used in a concurring opinion in Griswold v. Connecticut *(1965). While Justice William O. Douglas called on the Third Amendment to support the right to privacy in deciding that case, Justice Arthur Goldberg, in the concurring opinion, argued that the right to privacy regarding contraception was an unenumerated right that was protected by the Ninth Amendment.*

In 1980, the Court ruled that the right of the press to attend a public trial was protected by the Ninth Amendment. Although some scholars argue that modern judges cannot identify the unenumerated rights that the framers were trying to protect, others argue that the Ninth Amendment should be read as providing a constitutional "presumption of liberty" that allows people to act in any way that does not violate the rights of others.

Amendment X [1791]

The powers not delegated to the United States by the Constitution, nor prohibited by it to the States, are reserved to the States respectively, or to the people.

The Antifederalists were especially eager to see a "reserved powers clause" explicitly guaranteeing the states control over their internal affairs. Not surprisingly, the Tenth Amendment has been a frequent battleground in the struggle over states' rights and federal supremacy. Prior to the Civil War, the Jeffersonian Republican Party and Jacksonian Democrats invoked the Tenth Amendment to prohibit the federal government from making decisions about whether people in individual states could own slaves. The Tenth Amendment was virtually suspended during Reconstruction following the Civil War. In 1883, however, the Supreme Court declared the Civil Rights Act of 1875 unconstitutional on the grounds that it violated the Tenth Amendment. Business interests also called on the amendment to block efforts at federal regulation.

The Court was inconsistent over the next several decades as it attempted to resolve the tension between the restrictions of the Tenth Amendment and the powers the Constitution granted to Congress to regulate interstate commerce and levy taxes. The

Court upheld the Pure Food and Drug Act (1906), the Meat Inspection Acts (1906 and 1907), and the White Slave Traffic Act (1910), all of which affected the states, but it struck down an act prohibiting interstate shipment of goods produced through child labor. Between 1934 and 1935, a number of New Deal programs created by Franklin D. Roosevelt were declared unconstitutional on the grounds that they violated the Tenth Amendment. As Roosevelt appointees changed the composition of the Court, the Tenth Amendment was declared to have no substantive meaning. Generally, the amendment is held to protect the rights of states to regulate internal matters such as local government, education, commerce, labor, and business, as well as matters involving families such as marriage, divorce, and inheritance within the state.

Unratified Amendment

Reapportionment Amendment (proposed by Congress September 25, 1789, along with the Bill of Rights)

After the first enumeration required by the first article of the Constitution, there shall be one Representative for every thirty thousand, until the number shall amount to one hundred, after which the proportion shall be so regulated by Congress, that there shall be not less than one hundred Representatives, nor less than one Representative for every forty thousand persons, until the number of Representatives shall amount to two hundred; after which the proportion shall be so regulated by Congress, that there shall not be less than two hundred Representatives, nor more than one Representative for every fifty thousand persons.

If the Reapportionment Amendment had passed and remained in effect, the House of Representatives today would have more than 5,000 members rather than 435 to reflect the current U.S. population.

Amendment XI [1798]

The judicial power of the United States shall not be construed to extend to any suit in law or equity, commenced or prosecuted against one of the United States by citizens of another State, or by citizens or subjects of any foreign state.

In 1793, the Supreme Court ruled in favor of Alexander Chisholm, executor of the estate of a deceased South Carolina merchant. Chisholm was suing the state of Georgia because the merchant had never been paid for provisions he had supplied during the Revolution. Many regarded this Court decision as an error that violated the intent of the Constitution.

Antifederalists and many other Americans feared a powerful federal court system because they worried that it would become like the British courts of this period, which were accountable only to the monarch. Furthermore, Chisholm v. Georgia prompted a series of suits against state governments by creditors and suppliers who had made loans during the war.

In addition, state legislators and Congress feared that the shaky economies of the new states, as well as the country as a whole, would be destroyed, especially if Loyalists who had fled to other countries sought reimbursement for land and property that had been seized. The day after the Supreme Court announced its decision, a resolution proposing the Eleventh Amendment, which overturned the decision in Chisholm v. Georgia, was introduced in the U.S. Senate.

Amendment XII [1804]

The electors shall meet in their respective States, and vote by ballot for President and Vice-President, one of whom, at least, shall not be an inhabitant of the same State with themselves; they shall name in their ballots the person voted for as President, and in distinct ballots the person voted for as Vice-President, and they shall make distinct lists of all persons voted for as President, and of all persons voted for as Vice-President, and of the number of votes for each, which lists they shall sign and certify, and transmit sealed to the seat of government of the United States, directed to the President of the Senate;—the President of the Senate shall, in the presence of the Senate and House of Representatives, open all the certificates and the votes shall then be counted;—the person having the greatest number of votes for President shall be the President, if such number be a majority of the whole number of electors appointed; and if no person have such majority, then from the persons having the highest numbers not exceeding three on the list of those voted for as President, the House of Representatives shall choose immediately, by ballot, the President. But in choosing the President, the votes shall be taken by States, the representation from each State having one vote; a quorum for this purpose shall consist of a member or members from two-thirds of the States, and a majority of all the States shall be necessary to a choice. And if the House of Representatives shall not choose a President whenever the right of choice shall devolve upon them, before *the fourth day of March* next following, then the Vice-President shall act as President, as in the case of the death or other constitutional disability of the President.

The person having the greatest number of votes as Vice-President shall be the Vice-President, if such number be a majority of the whole number of electors appointed; and if no person have a majority, then from the two highest numbers on the list the Senate shall choose the Vice-President; a quorum for the purpose shall consist of two-thirds of the whole number of Senators, and a majority of the whole number shall be necessary to a choice. But no person constitutionally ineligible to the office of President shall be eligible to that of Vice-President of the United States.

The framers of the Constitution disliked political parties and assumed that none would ever form. Under the original system, electors chosen by the states would each vote for two candidates. The candidate who won the most votes would become president, and the person who won the second-highest number of votes would become vice-president. Rivalries between Federalists and Republicans led to the formation of political parties, however,

even before George Washington had left office. In 1796, Federalist John Adams was chosen as president, and his great rival, Thomas Jefferson (whose party was called the Republican Party), became his vice-president. In 1800, all the electors cast their two votes as one of two party blocs. Jefferson and his fellow Republican nominee, Aaron Burr, were tied with seventy-three votes each. The contest went to the House of Representatives, which finally elected Jefferson after thirty-six ballots. The Twelfth Amendment prevents these problems by requiring electors to vote separately for the president and vice-president.

Unratified Amendment

Titles of Nobility Amendment
(proposed by Congress May 1, 1810)

If any citizen of the United States shall accept, claim, receive or retain any title of nobility or honor or shall, without the consent of Congress, accept and retain any present, pension, office or emolument of any kind whatever, from any emperor, king, prince or foreign power, such person shall cease to be a citizen of the United States, and shall be incapable of holding any office of trust or profit under them, or either of them.

This amendment would have extended Article 1, section 9, clause 8 of the Constitution, which prevents the awarding of titles by the United States and the acceptance of such awards from foreign powers without congressional consent. Historians speculate that general nervousness about the power of the Emperor Napoleon, who was at that time extending France's empire throughout Europe, may have prompted the proposal. Though it fell one vote short of ratification, Congress and the American people thought the proposal had been ratified, and it was included in many nineteenth-century editions of the Constitution.

The Civil War and Reconstruction Amendments (Thirteenth, Fourteenth, and Fifteenth Amendments)

In the four months between the election of Abraham Lincoln and his inauguration, more than two hundred proposed constitutional amendments were presented to Congress as part of a desperate attempt to hold the rapidly dissolving Union together. Most of these were efforts to appease the southern states by protecting the right to own slaves or by disfranchising African Americans through constitutional amendment. None were able to win the votes required from Congress to send them to the states. Ultimately, the Corwin Amendment seemed to be the only hope for preserving the Union by amending the Constitution.

The northern victors in the Civil War tried to restructure the Constitution just as the war had restructured the nation. Yet they were often divided in their goals. Some wanted to end slavery; others hoped for social and economic equality regardless of race; others hoped that extending the power of the ballot box to former slaves would help create a new political order. The debates over the Thirteenth, Fourteenth, and Fif-

teenth Amendments were bitter. Few of those who fought for these changes were satisfied with the amendments themselves; fewer still were satisfied with their interpretation. Although the amendments put an end to the legal status of slavery, it was nearly a hundred years after the amendments' passage before most of the descendants of former slaves could begin to experience the economic, social, and political equality the amendments were intended to provide.

Unratified Amendment

Corwin Amendment (proposed by Congress March 2, 1861)

No amendment shall be made to the Constitution which will authorize or give to Congress the power to abolish or interfere, within any State, with the domestic institutions thereof, including that of persons held to labor or service by the laws of said State.

Following the election of Abraham Lincoln, Congress scrambled to try to prevent the secession of the slaveholding states. House member Thomas Corwin of Ohio proposed the "unamendable" amendment in the hope that by protecting slavery where it existed, Congress would keep the southern states in the Union. Lincoln indicated his support for the proposed amendment in his first inaugural address. Only Ohio and Maryland ratified the Corwin Amendment before it was forgotten.

Amendment XIII [1865]

SECTION 1 Neither slavery nor involuntary servitude, except as a punishment for crime whereof the party shall have been duly convicted, shall exist within the United States, or any place subject to their jurisdiction.

SECTION 2 Congress shall have power to enforce this article by appropriate legislation.

Because the Emancipation Proclamation of 1863 abolished slavery only in the parts of the Confederacy still in rebellion, Republicans proposed a Thirteenth Amendment that would extend abolition to the entire South. In February 1865, when the proposal was approved by the House, the gallery of the House was newly opened to black Americans who had a chance at last to see their government at work. Passage of the proposal was greeted by wild cheers from the gallery as well as tears on the House floor, where congressional representatives openly embraced one another.

The problem of ratification remained, however. The Union position was that the Confederate states were part of the country of thirty-six states. Therefore, twenty-seven states were needed to ratify the amendment. When Kentucky and Delaware rejected it, backers realized that without approval from at least four former Confederate states, the amendment would fail. Lincoln's successor, President Andrew Johnson, made ratification of the Thirteenth Amendment a condition for southern states to rejoin the Union. Under those terms, all the former Confederate states except Mississippi accepted the Thirteenth Amendment, and by the end of 1865 the amendment had become part of the Constitution and slavery had been prohibited in the United States.

Amendment XIV [1868]

SECTION 1 All persons born or naturalized in the United States, and subject to the jurisdiction thereof, are citizens of the United States and of the State wherein they reside. No State shall make or enforce any law which shall abridge the privileges or immunities of citizens of the United States; nor shall any State deprive any person of life, liberty, or property, without due process of law; nor deny to any person within its jurisdiction the equal protection of the laws.

SECTION 2 Representatives shall be appointed among the several States according to their respective numbers, counting the whole number of persons in each State, excluding Indians not taxed. But when the right to vote at any election for the choice of electors for President and Vice-President of the United States, Representatives in Congress, the executive and judicial officers of a State, or the members of the legislature thereof, is denied to any of the male inhabitants of such State, being twenty-one years of age and citizens of the United States, or in any way abridged, except for participation in rebellion, or other crime, the basis of representation therein shall be reduced in the proportion which the number of such male citizens shall bear to the whole number of male citizens twenty-one years of age in such State.

SECTION 3 No person shall be a Senator or Representative in Congress, or Elector of President and Vice-President, or hold any office, civil or military, under the United States, or under any State, who, having previously taken an oath, as a member of Congress, or as an officer of the United States, or as a member of any State legislature, or as an executive or judicial officer of any State, to support the Constitution of the United States, shall have engaged in insurrection or rebellion against the same, or given aid or comfort to the enemies thereof. Congress may, by a vote of two-thirds of each house, remove such disability.

SECTION 4 The validity of the public debt of the United States, authorized by law, including debts incurred for payment of pensions and bounties for services in suppressing insurrection or rebellion, shall not be questioned. But neither the United States nor any State shall assume or pay any debt or obligation incurred in aid of insurrection or rebellion against the United States, or any claim for the loss or emancipation of any slave; but all such debts, obligations, and claims shall be held illegal and void.

SECTION 5 The Congress shall have power to enforce, by appropriate legislation, the provisions of this article.

★ ★ ★

Without Lincoln's leadership in the reconstruction of the nation following the Civil War, it soon became clear that the Thirteenth Amendment needed additional constitutional support. Less than a year after Lincoln's assassination, Andrew Johnson was ready to bring the former Confederate states back into the Union with few changes in their governments or politics. Anxious Republicans drafted the Fourteenth Amendment to prevent that from happening. The most important provisions of this complex amendment made all native-born or naturalized persons American citizens and prohibited states from abridging the "privileges or immunities" of citizens; depriving them of "life, liberty, or property, without due process of law"; and denying them "equal protection of the laws." In essence, it made all former slaves citizens and protected the rights of all citizens against violation by their own state governments.

As occurred in the case of the Thirteenth Amendment, former Confederate states were forced to ratify the amendment as a condition of representation in the House and the Senate. The intentions of the Fourteenth Amendment, and how those intentions should be enforced, have been the most debated point of constitutional history. The terms due process and equal protection have been especially troublesome. Was the amendment designed to outlaw racial segregation? Or was the goal simply to prevent the leaders of the rebellious South from gaining political power?

The framers of the Fourteenth Amendment hoped section 2 would produce black voters who would increase the power of the Republican Party. The federal government, however, never used its power to punish states for denying blacks their right to vote. Although the Fourteenth Amendment had an immediate impact in giving black Americans citizenship, it did nothing to protect blacks from the vengeance of whites once Reconstruction ended. In the late nineteenth and early twentieth centuries, section 1 of the Fourteenth Amendment was often used to protect business interests and strike down laws protecting workers on the grounds that the rights of "persons," that is, corporations, were protected by "due process." More recently, the Fourteenth Amendment has been used to justify school desegregation and affirmative action programs, as well as to dismantle such programs.

Amendment XV [1870]

SECTION 1 The right of citizens of the United States to vote shall not be denied or abridged by the United States or by any State on account of race, color, or previous condition of servitude.

SECTION 2 The Congress shall have power to enforce this article by appropriate legislation.

★ ★ ★

The Fifteenth Amendment was the last major piece of Reconstruction legislation. Although earlier Reconstruction acts had already required black suffrage in the South, the Fifteenth Amendment extended black voting rights to the entire nation. Some Republicans felt morally obligated to do away with the double standard between North and South because many northern states had stubbornly refused to enfranchise blacks.

Others believed that the freedman's ballot required the extra protection of a constitutional amendment to shield it from white counterattack. But partisan advantage also played an important role in the amendment's passage, because Republicans hoped that by giving the ballot to northern blacks, they could lessen their party's political vulnerability.

Many women's rights advocates had fought for the amendment. They had felt betrayed by the inclusion of the word male *in section 2 of the Fourteenth Amendment and were further angered when the proposed Fifteenth Amendment failed to prohibit denial of the right to vote on the grounds of sex as well as "race, color, or previous condition of servitude." In this amendment, for the first time, the federal government claimed the power to regulate the franchise, or vote. It was also the first time the Constitution placed limits on the power of the states to regulate access to the franchise. Although ratified in 1870, however, the amendment was not enforced until the twentieth century.*

The Progressive Amendments (Sixteenth–Nineteenth Amendments)

No amendments were added to the Constitution between the Civil War and the Progressive Era. America was changing, however, in fundamental ways. The rapid industrialization of the United States after the Civil War led to many social and economic problems. Hundreds of amendments were proposed, but none received enough support in Congress to be sent to the states. Some scholars believe that regional differences and rivalries were so strong during this period that it was almost impossible to gain a consensus on a constitutional amendment. During the Progressive Era, however, the Constitution was amended four times in seven years.

Amendment XVI [1913]

The Congress shall have power to lay and collect taxes on incomes, from whatever source derived, without apportionment among the several States, and without regard to any census or enumeration.

★ ★ ★

Until passage of the Sixteenth Amendment, most of the money used to run the federal government came from customs duties and taxes on specific items, such as liquor. During the Civil War, the federal government taxed incomes as an emergency measure. Pressure to enact an income tax came from those who were concerned about the growing gap between rich and poor in the United States. The Populist Party began campaigning for a graduated income tax in 1892, and support continued to grow. By 1909 thirty-three proposed income tax amendments had been presented in Congress, but lobbying by corporate and other special interests had defeated them all. In June 1909 the growing pressure for an income tax, which had been endorsed by Presidents Roosevelt and Taft, finally pushed an amendment through the Senate. The required thirty-six states had ratified the amendment by February 1913.

Amendment XVII [1913]

SECTION 1 The Senate of the United States shall be composed of two Senators from each State, elected by the people thereof, for six years; and each Senator shall have one vote. The electors in each State shall have the qualifications requisite for electors of [voters for] the most numerous branch of the State legislatures.

SECTION 2 When vacancies happen in the representation of any State in the Senate, the executive authority of such State shall issue writs of election to fill such vacancies: Provided, that the Legislature of any State may empower the executive thereof to make temporary appointments until the people fill the vacancies by election as the Legislature may direct.

SECTION 3 This amendment shall not be so construed as to affect the election or term of any Senator chosen before it becomes valid as part of the Constitution.

★ ★ ★

The framers of the Constitution saw the members of the House as the representatives of the people and the members of the Senate as the representatives of the states. Originally senators were to be chosen by the state legislators. According to reform advocates, however, the growth of private industry and transportation conglomerates during the late nineteenth century had created a network of corruption in which wealth and power were exchanged for influence and votes in the Senate. Senator Nelson Aldrich, who represented Rhode Island in this period, for example, was known as "the senator from Standard Oil" because of his open support of special business interests.

Efforts to amend the Constitution to allow direct election of senators had begun in 1826, but because any proposal had to be approved by the Senate, reform seemed impossible. Progressives tried to gain influence in the Senate by instituting party caucuses and primary elections, which gave citizens the chance to express their choice of a senator who could then be officially elected by the state legislature. By 1910 fourteen of the country's thirty senators received popular votes through a state primary before the state legislature made its selection. Despairing of getting a proposal through the Senate, supporters of a direct-election amendment had begun in 1893 to seek a convention of representatives from two-thirds of the states to propose an amendment that could then be ratified. By 1905 thirty-one of forty-five states had endorsed such an amendment. Finally, in 1911, despite extraordinary opposition, a proposed amendment passed the Senate; by 1913 it had been ratified.

Amendment XVIII [1919; repealed 1933 by Amendment XXI]

SECTION 1 After one year from the ratification of this article the manufacture, sale, or transportation of intoxicating liquors within, the importation thereof into, or the exportation thereof from the United States and all territory subject to the jurisdiction thereof, for beverage purposes, is hereby prohibited.

Section 2 The Congress and the several States shall have concurrent power to enforce this article by appropriate legislation.

Section 3 This article shall be inoperative unless it shall have been ratified as an amendment to the Constitution by the legislatures of the several States, as provided by the Constitution, within seven years from the date of the submission thereof to the States by the Congress.

The Prohibition Party, formed in 1869, began calling for a constitutional amendment to outlaw alcoholic beverages in 1872. A prohibition amendment was first proposed in the Senate in 1876 and was revived eighteen times before 1913. Between 1913 and 1919, another thirty-nine attempts were made to prohibit liquor in the United States through a constitutional amendment. Prohibition became a key element of the Progressive agenda as reformers linked alcohol and drunkenness to numerous social problems, including the corruption of immigrant voters. Whereas opponents of such an amendment argued that it was undemocratic, supporters claimed that their efforts had widespread public support. The admission of twelve "dry" western states to the Union in the early twentieth century and the spirit of sacrifice during World War I laid the groundwork for passage and ratification of the Eighteenth Amendment in 1919. Opponents added a time limit to the amendment in the hope that they could thereby block ratification, but this effort failed. (See also Amendment XXI.)

Amendment XIX [1920]

Section 1 The right of citizens of the United States to vote shall not be denied or abridged by the United States or by any State on account of sex.

Section 2 Congress shall have the power to enforce this article by appropriate legislation.

Advocates of women's rights tried and failed to link woman suffrage to the Fourteenth and Fifteenth Amendments. Nonetheless, the effort for woman suffrage continued. Between 1878 and 1912, at least one and sometimes as many as four proposed amendments were introduced in Congress each year to grant women the right to vote. Although over time women won very limited voting rights in some states, at both the state and federal levels opposition to an amendment for woman suffrage remained very strong. President Woodrow Wilson and other officials felt that the federal government should not interfere with the power of the states in this matter. And many people were concerned that giving women the vote would result in their abandoning traditional gender roles. In 1919, following a protracted and often bitter campaign of protest in which women went on hunger strikes and chained themselves to fences, an amendment was introduced with the backing of President Wilson. It narrowly passed the Senate (after efforts to limit the suffrage to white women failed) and was adopted in 1920 after Tennessee became the thirty-sixth state to ratify it.

Unratified Amendment

Child Labor Amendment
(proposed by Congress June 2, 1924)

Section 1 The Congress shall have power to limit, regulate, and prohibit the labor of persons under eighteen years of age.

Section 2 The power of the several States is unimpaired by this article except that the operation of State laws shall be suspended to the extent necessary to give effect to legislation enacted by Congress.

Throughout the late nineteenth and early twentieth centuries, alarm over the condition of child workers grew. Opponents of child labor argued that children worked in dangerous and unhealthy conditions, that they took jobs from adult workers, that they depressed wages in certain industries, and that states that allowed child labor had an economic advantage over those that did not. Defenders of child labor claimed that children provided needed income in many families, that working at a young age helped to develop character, and that the effort to prohibit the practice constituted an invasion of family privacy.

In 1916, Congress passed a law that made it illegal to sell through interstate commerce goods made by children. The Supreme Court, however, ruled that the law violated the limits on the power of Congress to regulate interstate commerce. Congress then tried to penalize industries that used child labor by taxing such goods. This measure was also thrown out by the courts. In response, reformers set out to amend the Constitution. The proposed amendment was ratified by twenty-eight states, but by 1925 thirteen states had rejected it. Passage of the Fair Labor Standards Act in 1938, which was upheld by the Supreme Court in 1941, made the amendment irrelevant.

Amendment XX [1933]

Section 1 The terms of the President and Vice-President shall end at noon on the twentieth day of January, and the terms of Senators and Representatives at noon on the third day of January, of the years in which such terms would have ended if this article had not been ratified; and the terms of their successors shall then began.

Section 2 The Congress shall assemble at least once in every year, and such meeting shall begin at noon on the third day of January, unless they shall by law appoint a different day.

Section 3 If, at the time fixed for the beginning of the term of the President, the President-elect shall have died, the Vice-President-elect shall become President. If a President shall not have been chosen before the time fixed for the beginning of his term, or if the President-elect shall have failed to qualify, then the Vice-President-elect shall act as President until a President shall have qualified; and the Congress may by law provide for the case wherein neither a President-elect nor a Vice-President-elect shall have qualified, declaring who shall then act as President, or the manner in which one who is to act shall be selected, and such person shall act accordingly until a President or Vice-President shall have qualified.

SECTION 4 The Congress may by law provide for the case of the death of any of the persons from whom the House of Representatives may choose a President whenever the right of choice shall have devolved upon them, and for the case of the death of any of the persons from whom the Senate may choose a Vice-President whenever the right of choice shall have devolved upon them.

SECTION 5 Sections 1 and 2 shall take effect on the 15th day of October following the ratification of this article.

SECTION 6 This article shall be inoperative unless it shall have been ratified as an amendment to the Constitution by the Legislatures of three-fourths of the several States within seven years from the date of its submission.

Until 1933, presidents took office on March 4. Because elections are held in early November and electoral votes are counted in mid-December, this meant that more than three months passed between the time a new president was elected and when he took office. Moving the inauguration to January shortened the transition period and allowed Congress to begin its term closer to the time of the president's inauguration. Although this seems like a minor change, an amendment was required because the Constitution specifies terms of office. This amendment also deals with questions of succession in the event that a president- or vice-president-elect dies before assuming office. Section 3 also clarifies a method for resolving a deadlock in the electoral college.

Amendment XXI [1933]

SECTION 1 The eighteenth article of amendment to the Constitution of the United States is hereby repealed.

SECTION 2 The transportation or importation into any State, Territory, or Possession of the United States for delivery or use therein of intoxicating liquors, in violation of the laws thereof, is hereby prohibited.

SECTION 3 This article shall be inoperative unless it shall have been ratified as an amendment to the Constitution by conventions in the several States, as provided in the Constitution, within seven years from the date of the submission thereof to the States by the Congress.

Widespread violation of the Volstead Act, the law enacted to enforce prohibition, made the United States a nation of law-breakers. Prohibition caused more problems than it solved by encouraging crime, bribery, and corruption. Further, a coalition of liquor and beer manufacturers, personal liberty advocates, and constitutional scholars joined forces to challenge the amendment. By 1929 thirty proposed repeal amendments had

been introduced in Congress, and the Democratic Party made repeal part of its platform in the 1932 presidential campaign. The Twenty-first Amendment was proposed in February 1933 and ratified less than a year later. The failure of the effort to enforce prohibition through a constitutional amendment has often been cited by opponents of subsequent efforts to shape public virtue and private morality.

Amendment XXII [1951]

SECTION 1 No person shall be elected to the office of the President more than twice, and no person who has held the office of President, or acted as President, for more than two years of a term to which some other person was elected President shall be elected to the office of President more than once. But this article shall not apply to any person holding the office of President when this Article was proposed by the Congress, and shall not prevent any person who may be holding the office of President, or acting as President, during the term within which this Article becomes operative from holding the office of President or acting as President during the remainder of such term.

SECTION 2 This article shall be inoperative unless it shall have been ratified as an amendment to the Constitution by the legislatures of three-fourths of the several States within seven years from the date of its submission to the States by the Congress.

George Washington's refusal to seek a third term of office set a precedent that stood until 1912, when former president Theodore Roosevelt sought, without success, another term as an independent candidate. Democrat Franklin Roosevelt was the only president to seek and win a fourth term, though he did so amid great controversy. Roosevelt died in April 1945, a few months after the beginning of his fourth term. In 1946 Republicans won control of the House and the Senate, and early in 1947 a proposal for an amendment to limit future presidents to two four-year terms was offered to the states for ratification. Democratic critics of the Twenty-second Amendment charged that it was a partisan posthumous jab at Roosevelt.

Since the Twenty-second Amendment was adopted, however, the only presidents who might have been able to seek a third term, had it not existed, were Republicans Dwight Eisenhower and Ronald Reagan. Since 1826, Congress has entertained 160 proposed amendments to limit the president to one six-year term. Such amendments have been backed by fifteen presidents, including Gerald Ford and Jimmy Carter.

Amendment XXIII [1961]

SECTION 1 The District constituting the seat of Government of the United States shall appoint in such manner as the Congress may direct: A number of electors of President and Vice-President equal to the whole number of Senators and Representatives in Congress to which the District would be entitled if it were a State, but in no event more than the least populous State; they shall be in addition to those appointed by the States, but they shall be considered for the purposes of the election of President and Vice-President, to be electors appointed by a State; and they shall meet in the District and perform such duties as provided by the twelfth article of amendment.

SECTION 2 The Congress shall have the power to enforce this article by appropriate legislation.

★ ★ ★

When Washington, D.C., was established as a federal district, no one expected that a significant number of people would make it their permanent and primary residence. A proposal to allow citizens of the district to vote in presidential elections was approved by Congress in June 1960 and was ratified on March 29, 1961.

Amendment XXIV [1964]

SECTION 1 The right of citizens of the United States to vote in any primary or other election for President or Vice-President, for electors for President or Vice-President, or for Senator or Representative in Congress, shall not be denied or abridged by the United States or any State by reason of failure to pay any poll tax or other tax.

SECTION 2 The Congress shall have the power to enforce this article by appropriate legislation.

★ ★ ★

In the colonial and Revolutionary eras, financial independence was seen as necessary to political independence, and the poll tax was used as a requirement for voting. By the twentieth century, however, the poll tax was used mostly to bar poor people, especially southern blacks, from voting. Although conservatives complained that the amendment interfered with states' rights, liberals thought that the amendment did not go far enough because it barred the poll tax only in national elections and not in state or local elections. The amendment was ratified in 1964, however, and two years later the Supreme Court ruled that poll taxes in state and local elections also violated the equal protection clause of the Fourteenth Amendment.

Amendment XXV [1967]

SECTION 1 In case of the removal of the President from office or of his death or resignation, the Vice-President shall become President.

SECTION 2 Whenever there is a vacancy in the office of the Vice-President, the President shall nominate a Vice-President who shall take office upon confirmation by a majority vote of both Houses of Congress.

SECTION 3 Whenever the President transmits to the President pro tempore of the Senate and the Speaker of the House of Representatives his written declaration that he is unable to discharge the powers and duties of his office, and until he transmits to them a written declaration to the contrary, such powers and duties shall be discharged by the Vice-President as Acting President.

SECTION 4 Whenever the Vice-President and a majority of either the principal officers of the executive departments or of such other body as Congress may by law provide, transmit to the President pro tempore of the Senate and the Speaker of the House of Representatives their written declaration that the President is unable to discharge the powers and duties of his office, the Vice-President shall immediately assume the powers and duties of the office as Acting President.

Thereafter, when the President transmits to the President pro tempore of the Senate and the Speaker of the House of Representatives his written declaration that no inability exists, he shall resume the powers and duties of his office unless the Vice-President and a majority of either the principal officers of the executive department[s] or of such other body as Congress may by law provide, transmit within four days to the President pro tempore of the Senate and the Speaker of the House of Representatives their written declaration that the President is unable to discharge the powers and duties of his office. Thereupon Congress shall decide the issue, assembling within forty-eight hours for that purpose if not in session. If the Congress, within twenty-one days after receipt of the latter written declaration, or, if Congress is not in session, within twenty-one days after Congress is required to assemble, determines by two-thirds vote of both Houses that the President is unable to discharge the powers and duties of his office, the Vice-President shall continue to discharge the same as Acting President; otherwise, the President shall resume the powers and duties of his office.

★ ★ ★

The framers of the Constitution established the office of vice-president because someone was needed to preside over the Senate. The first president to die in office was William Henry Harrison, in 1841. Vice-President John Tyler had himself sworn in as president, setting a precedent that was followed when seven later presidents died in office. The assassination of President James A. Garfield in 1881 posed a new problem, however. After he was shot, the president was incapacitated for two months before he died; he was unable to lead the country, and his vice-president, Chester A. Arthur, was unable to assume leadership. Efforts to resolve questions of succession in the event of a presidential disability thus began with the death of Garfield.

In 1963 the assassination of President John F. Kennedy galvanized Congress to action. Vice-President Lyndon Johnson was a chain smoker with a history of heart trouble. According to the 1947 Presidential Succession Act, the two men who stood in line to succeed him were the seventy-two-year-old Speaker of the House and the eighty-six-year-old president of the Senate. There were serious concerns that any of these men might become incapacitated while serving as chief executive. The first time the Twenty-fifth Amendment was used, however, was not in the case of presidential death or illness, but during the Watergate crisis. When Vice-President Spiro T. Agnew was forced to resign following allegations of bribery and tax violations, President Richard M. Nixon appointed House Minority

Leader Gerald R. Ford vice-president. Ford became president following Nixon's resignation eight months later and named Nelson A. Rockefeller as his vice-president. Thus, for more than two years, the two highest offices in the country were held by people who had not been elected to them.

Amendment XXVI [1971]

SECTION 1 The right of citizens of the United States, who are eighteen years of age or older, to vote shall not be denied or abridged by the United States or by any State on account of age.

SECTION 2 The Congress shall have power to enforce this article by appropriate legislation.

Efforts to lower the voting age from twenty-one to eighteen began during World War II. Recognizing that those who were old enough to fight a war should have some say in the government policies that involved them in the war, Presidents Eisenhower, Johnson, and Nixon endorsed the idea. In 1970, the combined pressure of the antiwar movement and the demographic pressure of the baby-boom generation led to a Voting Rights Act lowering the voting age in federal, state, and local elections.

In Oregon v. Mitchell *(1970), the state of Oregon challenged the right of Congress to determine the age at which people could vote in state or local elections. The Supreme Court agreed with Oregon. Because the Voting Rights Act was ruled unconstitutional, the Constitution had to be amended to allow passage of a law that would lower the voting age. The amendment was ratified in a little more than three months, making it the most rapidly ratified amendment in U.S. history.*

Unratified Amendment

Equal Rights Amendment (proposed by Congress March 22, 1972; seven-year deadline for ratification extended, June 30, 1982)

SECTION 1 Equality of rights under the law shall not be denied or abridged by the United States or by any State on account of sex.

SECTION 2 The Congress shall have the power to enforce, by appropriate legislation, the provisions of this article.

SECTION 3 This amendment shall take effect two years after the date of ratification.

In 1923, soon after women had won the right to vote, Alice Paul, a leading activist in the woman suffrage movement, proposed an amendment requiring equal treatment of men and women. Opponents of the proposal argued that such an amendment would invalidate laws that protected women and would make women subject to the military draft. After the 1964 Civil Rights Act was adopted, protective workplace legislation was removed anyway.

The renewal of the women's movement, as a byproduct of the civil rights and antiwar movements, led to a revival of the Equal Rights Amendment (ERA) in Congress. Disagreements over language held up congressional passage of the proposed amendment, but on March 22, 1972, the Senate approved the ERA by a vote of eighty-four to eight, and it was sent to the states. Six states ratified the amendment within two days, and by the middle of 1973 the amendment seemed well on its way to adoption, with thirty of the needed thirty-eight states having ratified it. In the mid-1970s, however, a powerful "Stop ERA" campaign developed. The campaign portrayed the ERA as a threat to "family values" and traditional relationships between men and women. Although thirty-five states ratified the ERA, five of those state legislatures voted to rescind ratification, and the amendment was never adopted.

Unratified Amendment

D.C. Statehood Amendment (proposed by Congress August 22, 1978)

SECTION 1 For purposes of representation in the Congress, election of the President and Vice President, and article V of this Constitution, the District constituting the seat of government of the United States shall be treated as though it were a State.

SECTION 2 The exercise of the rights and powers conferred under this article shall be by the people of the District constituting the seat of government, and as shall be provided by Congress.

SECTION 3 The twenty-third article of amendment to the Constitution of the United States is hereby repealed.

SECTION 4 This article shall be inoperative, unless it shall have been ratified as an amendment to the Constitution by the legislatures of three-fourths of the several states within seven years from the date of its submission.

The 1961 ratification of the Twenty-third Amendment, giving residents of the District of Columbia the right to vote for a president and vice-president, inspired an effort to give residents of the district full voting rights. In 1966, President Lyndon Johnson appointed a mayor and city council; in 1971, D.C. residents were allowed to name a nonvoting delegate to the House; and in 1981, residents were allowed to elect the mayor and city council. Congress retained the right to overrule laws that might affect commuters, the height of federal buildings, and selection of judges and prosecutors. The district's nonvoting delegate to Congress, Walter Fauntroy, lobbied fiercely for a congressional amendment granting statehood to the district. In 1978 a proposed amendment was approved and sent to the states. A number of states quickly ratified the

amendment, but, like the ERA, the D.C. Statehood Amendment ran into trouble. Opponents argued that section 2 created a separate category of "nominal" statehood. They argued that the federal district should be eliminated and that the territory should be reabsorbed into the state of Maryland. Although these theoretical arguments were strong, some scholars believe that racist attitudes toward the predominantly black population of the city also constituted a factor leading to the defeat of the amendment.

Amendment XXVII [1992]

No law, varying the compensation for the services of the Senators and Representatives, shall take effect, until an election of Representatives shall have intervened.

Whereas the Twenty-sixth Amendment was the most rapidly ratified amendment in U.S. history, the Twenty-seventh Amendment had the longest journey to ratification. First proposed by James Madison in 1789 as part of the package that included the Bill of Rights, this amendment had been ratified by only six states by 1791. In 1873, however, it was ratified by Ohio to protest a massive retroactive salary increase by the federal government. Unlike later proposed amendments, this one came with no time limit on ratification. In the early 1980s, Gregory D. Watson, a University of Texas economics major, discovered the "lost" amendment and began a single-handed campaign to get state legislators to introduce it for ratification. In 1983 it was accepted by Maine. In 1984 it passed the Colorado legislature. Ratifications trickled in slowly until May 1992, when Michigan and New Jersey became the thirty-eighth and thirty-ninth states, respectively, to ratify. This amendment prevents members of Congress from raising their own salaries without giving voters a chance to vote them out of office before they can benefit from the raises.

The American Nation

Admission of States into the Union

State	Date of Admission	State	Date of Admission	State	Date of Admission
1. Delaware	December 7, 1787	18. Louisiana	April 30, 1812	35. West Virginia	June 20, 1863
2. Pennsylvania	December 12, 1787	19. Indiana	December 11, 1816	36. Nevada	October 31, 1864
3. New Jersey	December 18, 1787	20. Mississippi	December 10, 1817	37. Nebraska	March 1, 1867
4. Georgia	January 2, 1788	21. Illinois	December 3, 1818	38. Colorado	August 1, 1876
5. Connecticut	January 9, 1788	22. Alabama	December 14, 1819	39. North Dakota	November 2, 1889
6. Massachusetts	February 6, 1788	23. Maine	March 15, 1820	40. South Dakota	November 2, 1889
7. Maryland	April 28, 1788	24. Missouri	August 10, 1821	41. Montana	November 8, 1889
8. South Carolina	May 23, 1788	25. Arkansas	June 15, 1836	42. Washington	November 11, 1889
9. New Hampshire	June 21, 1788	26. Michigan	January 26, 1837	43. Idaho	July 3, 1890
10. Virginia	June 25, 1788	27. Florida	March 3, 1845	44. Wyoming	July 10, 1890
11. New York	July 26, 1788	28. Texas	December 29, 1845	45. Utah	January 4, 1896
12. North Carolina	November 21, 1789	29. Iowa	December 28, 1846	46. Oklahoma	November 16, 1907
13. Rhode Island	May 29, 1790	30. Wisconsin	May 29, 1848	47. New Mexico	January 6, 1912
14. Vermont	March 4, 1791	31. California	September 9, 1850	48. Arizona	February 14, 1912
15. Kentucky	June 1, 1792	32. Minnesota	May 11, 1858	49. Alaska	January 3, 1959
16. Tennessee	June 1, 1796	33. Oregon	February 14, 1859	50. Hawaii	August 21, 1959
17. Ohio	March 1, 1803	34. Kansas	January 29, 1861		

Territorial Expansion

Territory	Date Acquired	Square Miles	How Acquired
Original states and territories	1783	888,685	Treaty of Paris
Louisiana Purchase	1803	827,192	Purchased from France
Florida	1819	72,003	Adams-Onís Treaty
Texas	1845	390,143	Annexation of independent country
Oregon	1846	285,580	Oregon Boundary Treaty
Mexican cession	1848	529,017	Treaty of Guadalupe Hidalgo
Gadsden Purchase	1853	29,640	Purchased from Mexico
Midway Islands	1867	2	Annexation of uninhabited islands
Alaska	1867	589,757	Purchased from Russia
Hawaii	1898	6,450	Annexation of independent country
Wake Island	1898	3	Annexation of uninhabited island
Puerto Rico	1899	3,435	Treaty of Paris
Guam	1899	212	Treaty of Paris
The Philippines	1899–1946	115,600	Treaty of Paris; granted independence
American Samoa	1900	76	Treaty with Germany and Great Britain
Panama Canal Zone	1904–1978	553	Hay–Bunau-Varilla Treaty
U.S. Virgin Islands	1917	133	Purchased from Denmark
Trust Territory of the Pacific Islands*	1947	717	United Nations Trusteeship

*A number of these islands have recently been granted independence: Federated States of Micronesia, 1990; Marshall Islands, 1991; Palau, 1994.

Presidential Elections

Year	Candidates	Parties	Percentage of Popular Vote	Electoral Vote	Percentage of Voter Participation
1789	**George Washington**	No party designations	*	69	
	John Adams†			34	
	Other candidates			35	
1792	**George Washington**	No party designations		132	
	John Adams			77	
	George Clinton			50	
	Other candidates			5	
1796	**John Adams**	Federalist		71	
	Thomas Jefferson	Democratic-Republican		68	
	Thomas Pinckney	Federalist		59	
	Aaron Burr	Democratic-Republican		30	
	Other candidates			48	
1800	**Thomas Jefferson**	Democratic-Republican		73	
	Aaron Burr	Democratic-Republican		73	
	John Adams	Federalist		65	
	Charles C. Pinckney	Federalist		64	
	John Jay	Federalist		1	
1804	**Thomas Jefferson**	Democratic-Republican		162	
	Charles C. Pinckney	Federalist		14	
1808	**James Madison**	Democratic-Republican		122	
	Charles C. Pinckney	Federalist		47	
	George Clinton	Democratic-Republican		6	
1812	**James Madison**	Democratic-Republican		128	
	De Witt Clinton	Federalist		89	
1816	**James Monroe**	Democratic-Republican		183	
	Rufus King	Federalist		34	
1820	**James Monroe**	Democratic-Republican		231	
	John Quincy Adams	Independent Republican		1	
1824	**John Quincy Adams**	Democratic-Republican	30.5	84	26.9
	Andrew Jackson	Democratic-Republican	43.1	99	
	Henry Clay	Democratic-Republican	13.2	37	
	William H. Crawford	Democratic-Republican	13.1	41	
1828	**Andrew Jackson**	Democratic	56.0	178	57.6
	John Quincy Adams	National Republican	44.0	83	
1832	**Andrew Jackson**	Democratic	54.5	219	55.4
	Henry Clay	National Republican	37.5	49	
	William Wirt	Anti-Masonic	8.0	7	
	John Floyd	Democratic	‡	11	
1836	**Martin Van Buren**	Democratic	50.9	170	57.8
	William H. Harrison	Whig		73	
	Hugh L. White	Whig		26	
	Daniel Webster	Whig	49.1	14	
	W. P. Mangum	Whig		11	
1840	**William H. Harrison**	Whig	53.1	234	80.2
	Martin Van Buren	Democratic	46.9	60	

*Prior to 1824, most presidential electors were chosen by state legislators rather than by popular vote.
†Before the Twelfth Amendment was passed in 1804, the electoral college voted for two presidential candidates; the runner-up became vice-president.
‡Percentages below 2.5 have been omitted. Hence the percentage of popular vote might not total 100 percent.

Year	Candidates	Parties	Percentage of Popular Vote	Electoral Vote	Percentage of Voter Participation
1844	**James K. Polk**	Democratic	49.6	170	78.9
	Henry Clay	Whig	48.1	105	
	James G. Birney	Liberty	2.3		
1848	**Zachary Taylor**	Whig	47.4	163	72.7
	Lewis Cass	Democratic	42.5	127	
	Martin Van Buren	Free Soil	10.1		
1852	**Franklin Pierce**	Democratic	50.9	254	69.6
	Winfield Scott	Whig	44.1	42	
	John P. Hale	Free Soil	5.0		
1856	**James Buchanan**	Democratic	45.3	174	78.9
	John C. Frémont	Republican	33.1	114	
	Millard Fillmore	American	21.6	8	
1860	**Abraham Lincoln**	Republican	39.8	180	81.2
	Stephen A. Douglas	Democratic	29.5	12	
	John C. Breckinridge	Democratic	18.1	72	
	John Bell	Constitutional Union	12.6	39	
1864	**Abraham Lincoln**	Republican	55.0	212	73.8
	George B. McClellan	Democratic	45.0	21	
1868	**Ulysses S. Grant**	Republican	52.7	214	78.1
	Horatio Seymour	Democratic	47.3	80	
1872	**Ulysses S. Grant**	Republican	55.6	286	71.3
	Horace Greeley	Democratic	43.9		
1876	**Rutherford B. Hayes**	Republican	48.0	185	81.8
	Samuel J. Tilden	Democratic	51.0	184	
1880	**James A. Garfield**	Republican	48.5	214	79.4
	Winfield S. Hancock	Democratic	48.1	155	
	James B. Weaver	Greenback-Labor	3.4		
1884	**Grover Cleveland**	Democratic	48.5	219	77.5
	James G. Blaine	Republican	48.2	182	
1888	**Benjamin Harrison**	Republican	47.9	233	79.3
	Grover Cleveland	Democratic	48.6	168	
1892	**Grover Cleveland**	Democratic	46.1	277	74.7
	Benjamin Harrison	Republican	43.0	145	
	James B. Weaver	People's	8.5	22	
1896	**William McKinley**	Republican	51.1	271	79.3
	William J. Bryan	Democratic	47.7	176	
1900	**William McKinley**	Republican	51.7	292	73.2
	William J. Bryan	Democratic; Populist	45.5	155	
1904	**Theodore Roosevelt**	Republican	57.4	336	65.2
	Alton B. Parker	Democratic	37.6	140	
	Eugene V. Debs	Socialist	3.0		
1908	**William H. Taft**	Republican	51.6	321	65.4
	William J. Bryan	Democratic	43.1	162	
	Eugene V. Debs	Socialist	2.8		
1912	**Woodrow Wilson**	Democratic	41.9	435	58.8
	Theodore Roosevelt	Progressive	27.4	88	
	William H. Taft	Republican	23.2	8	
	Eugene V. Debs	Socialist	6.0		

Year	Candidates	Parties	Percentage of Popular Vote	Electoral Vote	Percentage of Voter Participation
1916	**Woodrow Wilson**	Democratic	49.4	277	61.6
	Charles E. Hughes	Republican	46.2	254	
	A. L. Benson	Socialist	3.2		
1920	**Warren G. Harding**	Republican	60.4	404	49.2
	James M. Cox	Democratic	34.2	127	
	Eugene V. Debs	Socialist	3.4		
1924	**Calvin Coolidge**	Republican	54.0	382	48.9
	John W. Davis	Democratic	28.8	136	
	Robert M. La Follette	Progressive	16.6	13	
1928	**Herbert C. Hoover**	Republican	58.2	444	56.9
	Alfred E. Smith	Democratic	40.9	87	
1932	**Franklin D. Roosevelt**	Democratic	57.4	472	56.9
	Herbert C. Hoover	Republican	39.7	59	
1936	**Franklin D. Roosevelt**	Democratic	60.8	523	61.0
	Alfred M. Landon	Republican	36.5	8	
1940	**Franklin D. Roosevelt**	Democratic	54.8	449	62.5
	Wendell L. Willkie	Republican	44.8	82	
1944	**Franklin D. Roosevelt**	Democratic	53.5	432	55.9
	Thomas E. Dewey	Republican	46.0	99	
1948	**Harry S Truman**	Democratic	49.6	303	53.0
	Thomas E. Dewey	Republican	45.1	189	
1952	**Dwight D. Eisenhower**	Republican	55.1	442	63.3
	Adlai E. Stevenson	Democratic	44.4	89	
1956	**Dwight D. Eisenhower**	Republican	57.6	457	60.6
	Adlai E. Stevenson	Democratic	42.1	73	
1960	**John F. Kennedy**	Democratic	49.7	303	64.0
	Richard M. Nixon	Republican	49.5	219	
1964	**Lyndon B. Johnson**	Democratic	61.1	486	61.7
	Barry M. Goldwater	Republican	38.5	52	
1968	**Richard M. Nixon**	Republican	43.4	301	60.6
	Hubert H. Humphrey	Democratic	42.7	191	
	George C. Wallace	American Independent	13.5	46	
1972	**Richard M. Nixon**	Republican	60.7	520	55.5
	George S. McGovern	Democratic	37.5	17	
1976	**Jimmy Carter**	Democratic	50.1	297	54.3
	Gerald R. Ford	Republican	48.0	240	
1980	**Ronald W. Reagan**	Republican	50.7	489	53.0
	Jimmy Carter	Democratic	41.0	49	
	John B. Anderson	Independent	6.6	0	
1984	**Ronald W. Reagan**	Republican	58.4	525	52.9
	Walter F. Mondale	Democratic	41.6	13	
1988	**George H. W. Bush**	Republican	53.4	426	50.3
	Michael Dukakis	Democratic	45.6	111*	
1992	**Bill Clinton**	Democratic	43.7	370	55.1
	George H. W. Bush	Republican	38.0	168	
	H. Ross Perot	Independent	19.0	0	
1996	**Bill Clinton**	Democratic	49	379	49.0
	Robert J. Dole	Republican	41	159	
	H. Ross Perot	Reform	8	0	

*One Dukakis elector cast a vote for Lloyd Bentsen.

Supreme Court Justices

Name	Terms of Service	Appointed by	Name	Terms of Service	Appointed by
John Jay*, N.Y.	1789–1795	Washington	Joseph McKenna, Cal.	1898–1925	McKinley
James Wilson, Pa.	1789–1798	Washington	Oliver W. Holmes, Mass.	1902–1932	T. Roosevelt
John Rutledge, S.C.	1790–1791	Washington	William R. Day, Ohio	1903–1922	T. Roosevelt
William Cushing, Mass.	1790–1810	Washington	William H. Moody, Mass.	1906–1910	T. Roosevelt
John Blair, Va.	1790–1796	Washington	Horace H. Lurton, Tenn.	1910–1914	Taft
James Iredell, N.C.	1790–1799	Washington	Charles E. Hughes, N.Y.	1910–1916	Taft
Thomas Johnson, Md.	1792–1793	Washington	**Edward D. White,** La.	1910–1921	Taft
William Paterson, N.J.	1793–1806	Washington	Willis Van Devanter, Wy.	1911–1937	Taft
John Rutledge, S.C.	1795	Washington	Joseph R. Lamar, Ga.	1911–1916	Taft
Samuel Chase, Md.	1796–1811	Washington	Mahlon Pitney, N.J.	1912–1922	Taft
Oliver Ellsworth, Conn.	1796–1800	Washington	James C. McReynolds, Tenn.	1914–1941	Wilson
Bushrod Washington, Va.	1799–1829	J. Adams	Louis D. Brandeis, Mass.	1916–1939	Wilson
Alfred Moore, N.C.	1800–1804	J. Adams	John H. Clarke, Ohio	1916–1922	Wilson
John Marshall, Va.	1801–1835	J. Adams	**William H. Taft,** Conn.	1921–1930	Harding
William Johnson, S.C.	1804–1834	Jefferson	George Sutherland, Utah	1922–1938	Harding
Brockholst Livingston, N.Y.	1807–1823	Jefferson	Pierce Butler, Minn.	1923–1939	Harding
Thomas Todd, Ky.	1807–1826	Jefferson	Edward T. Sanford, Tenn.	1923–1930	Harding
Gabriel Duvall, Md.	1811–1835	Madison	Harlan F. Stone, N.Y.	1925–1941	Coolidge
Joseph Story, Mass.	1812–1845	Madison	**Charles E. Hughes,** N.Y.	1930–1941	Hoover
Smith Thompson, N.Y.	1823–1843	Monroe	Owen J. Roberts, Pa.	1930–1945	Hoover
Robert Trimble, Ky.	1826–1828	J. Q. Adams	Benjamin N. Cardozo, N.Y.	1932–1938	Hoover
John McLean, Ohio	1830–1861	Jackson	Hugo L. Black, Ala.	1937–1971	F. Roosevelt
Henry Baldwin, Pa.	1830–1844	Jackson	Stanley F. Reed, Ky.	1938–1957	F. Roosevelt
James M. Wayne, Ga.	1835–1867	Jackson	Felix Frankfurter, Mass.	1939–1962	F. Roosevelt
Roger B. Taney, Md.	1836–1864	Jackson	William O. Douglas, Conn.	1939–1975	F. Roosevelt
Philip P. Barbour, Va.	1836–1841	Jackson	Frank Murphy, Mich.	1940–1949	F. Roosevelt
John Cartron, Tenn.	1837–1865	Van Buren	**Harlan F. Stone,** N.Y.	1941–1946	F. Roosevelt
John McKinley, Ala.	1838–1852	Van Buren	James R. Byrnes, S.C.	1941–1942	F. Roosevelt
Peter V. Daniel, Va.	1842–1860	Van Buren	Robert H. Jackson, N.Y.	1941–1954	F. Roosevelt
Samuel Nelson, N.Y.	1845–1872	Tyler	Wiley B. Rutledge, Iowa	1943–1949	F. Roosevelt
Levi Woodbury, N.H.	1845–1851	Polk	Harold H. Burton, Ohio	1945–1958	Truman
Robert C. Grier, Pa.	1846–1870	Polk	**Frederick M. Vinson,** Ky.	1946–1953	Truman
Benjamin R. Curtis, Mass.	1851–1857	Fillmore	Tom C. Clark, Texas	1949–1967	Truman
John A. Campbell, Ala.	1853–1861	Pierce	Sherman Minton, Ind.	1949–1956	Truman
Nathan Clifford, Me.	1858–1881	Buchanan	**Earl Warren,** Cal.	1953–1969	Eisenhower
Noah H. Swayne, Ohio	1862–1881	Lincoln	John Marshall Harlan, N.Y.	1955–1971	Eisenhower
Samuel F. Miller, Iowa	1862–1890	Lincoln	William J. Brennan Jr., N.J.	1956–1990	Eisenhower
David Davis, Ill.	1862–1877	Lincoln	Charles E. Whittaker, Mo.	1957–1962	Eisenhower
Stephen J. Field, Cal.	1863–1897	Lincoln	Potter Stewart, Ohio	1958–1981	Eisenhower
Salmon P. Chase, Ohio	1864–1873	Lincoln	Bryon R. White, Colo.	1962–1993	Kennedy
William Strong, Pa.	1870–1880	Grant	Arthur J. Goldberg, Ill.	1962–1965	Kennedy
Joseph P. Bradley, N.J.	1870–1892	Grant	Abe Fortas, Tenn.	1965–1969	Johnson
Ward Hunt, N.Y.	1873–1882	Grant	Thurgood Marshall, Md.	1967–1991	Johnson
Morrison R. Waite, Ohio	1874–1888	Grant	**Warren E. Burger,** Minn.	1969–1986	Nixon
John M. Harlan, Ky.	1877–1911	Hayes	Harry A. Blackmun, Minn.	1970–1994	Nixon
William B. Woods, Ga.	1881–1887	Hayes	Lewis F. Powell Jr., Va.	1971–1987	Nixon
Stanley Matthews, Ohio	1881–1889	Garfield	William H. Rehnquist, Ariz.	1971–1986	Nixon
Horace Gray, Mass.	1882–1902	Arthur	John Paul Stevens, Ill.	1975–	Ford
Samuel Blatchford, N.Y.	1882–1893	Arthur	Sandra Day O'Connor, Ariz.	1981–	Reagan
Lucius Q. C. Lamar, Miss.	1888–1893	Cleveland	**William H. Rehnquist,** Ariz.	1986–	Reagan
Melville W. Fuller, Ill.	1888–1910	Cleveland	Antonin Scalia, Va.	1986–	Reagan
David J. Brewer, Kan.	1890–1910	B. Harrison	Anthony M. Kennedy, Cal.	1988–	Reagan
Henry B. Brown, Mich.	1891–1906	B. Harrison	David H. Souter, N.H.	1990–	Bush
George Shiras Jr., Pa.	1892–1903	B. Harrison	Clarence Thomas, Ga.	1991–	Bush
Howell E. Jackson, Tenn.	1893–1895	B. Harrison	Ruth Bader Ginsburg, N.Y.	1993–	Clinton
Edward D. White, La.	1894–1910	Cleveland	Stephen G. Breyer, Mass.	1994–	Clinton
Rufus W. Peckham, N.Y.	1896–1909	Cleveland			

*Chief Justices are printed in bold type.

The American People:
A Demographic Survey

A Demographic Profile of the American People

Year	Life Expectancy from Birth		Average Age at First Marriage		Number of Children Under 5 (per 1,000 Women Aged 20–44)	Percentage of Women in Paid Employment	Percentage of Paid Workers Who Are Women
	White	Black	Men	Women			
1820					1,295	6.2	7.3
1830					1,145	6.4	7.4
1840					1,085	8.4	9.6
1850					923	10.1	10.8
1860					929	9.7	10.2
1870					839	13.7	14.8
1880					822	14.7	15.2
1890			26.1	22.0	716	18.2	17.0
1900	47.6	33.0	25.9	21.9	688	21.2	18.1
1910	50.3	35.6	25.1	21.6	643	24.8	20.0
1920	54.9	45.3	24.6	21.2	604	23.9	20.4
1930	61.4	48.1	24.3	21.3	511	24.4	21.9
1940	64.2	53.1	24.3	21.5	429	25.4	24.6
1950	69.1	60.8	22.8	20.3	589	29.1	27.8
1960	70.6	63.6	22.8	20.3	737	34.8	32.3
1970	71.7	65.3	22.5	20.6	530	43.3	38.0
1980	74.4	68.1	24.7	22.0	440	51.5	42.6
1990	76.2	71.4	26.1	23.9	377	57.4	45.2
1996	76.8	71.9	26.3	24.3	339	59.8	46.1

Source: Historical Statistics of the United States, Colonial Times to 1970 (1975); Statistical Abstract of the United States, 1998.

American Population

Year	Population	Percentage Increase	Year	Population	Percentage Increase
1610	350	—	1810	7,239,881	36.4
1620	2,300	557.1	1820	9,638,453	33.1
1630	4,600	100.0	1830	12,866,020	33.5
1640	26,600	478.3	1840	17,069,453	32.7
1650	50,400	90.8	1850	23,191,876	35.9
1660	75,100	49.0	1860	31,443,321	35.6
1670	111,900	49.0	1870	39,818,449	26.6
1680	151,500	35.4	1880	50,155,783	26.0
1690	210,400	38.9	1890	62,947,714	25.5
1700	250,900	19.2	1900	75,994,575	20.7
1710	331,700	32.2	1910	91,972,266	21.0
1720	466,200	40.5	1920	105,710,620	14.9
1730	629,400	35.0	1930	122,775,046	16.1
1740	905,600	43.9	1940	131,669,275	7.2
1750	1,170,800	29.3	1950	150,697,361	14.5
1760	1,593,600	36.1	1960	179,323,175	19.0
1770	2,148,100	34.8	1970	203,235,298	13.3
1780	2,780,400	29.4	1980	226,545,805	11.5
1790	3,929,214	41.3	1990	248,709,873	9.8
1800	5,308,483	35.1	1997	267,901,000	7.7

Note: These figures largely ignore the native American population. Census takers never made any effort to count the native American population that lived outside their political jurisdictions and compiled only casual and incomplete enumerations of those living within their jurisdictions until 1890. In that year the federal government attempted a full count of the Indian population: the Census found 125,719 Indians in 1890, compared with only 12,543 in 1870 and 33,985 in 1880.

Source: Historical Statistics of the United States, Colonial Times to 1970 (1975); *Statistical Abstract of the United States, 1998.*

White/Nonwhite Population

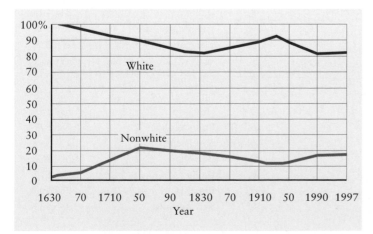

Urban/Rural Population

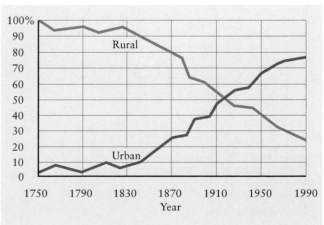

The Ten Largest Cities by Population, 1700–1990

		City	Population			City	Population
1700	1.	Boston	6,700	1910	1.	New York	4,766,883
	2.	New York	4,937*		2.	Chicago	2,185,283
	3.	Philadelphia	4,400†		3.	Philadelphia	1,549,008
1790	1.	Philadelphia	42,520		4.	St. Louis	687,029
	2.	New York	33,131		5.	Boston	670,585
	3.	Boston	18,038		6.	Cleveland	560,663
	4.	Charleston, S.C.	16,359		7.	Baltimore	558,485
	5.	Baltimore	13,503		8.	Pittsburgh	533,905
	6.	Salem, Mass.	7,921		9.	Detroit	465,766
	7.	Newport, R.I.	6,716		10.	Buffalo	423,715
	8.	Providence, R.I.	6,380	1930	1.	New York	6,930,446
	9.	Marblehead, Mass.	5,661		2.	Chicago	3,376,438
	10.	Portsmouth, N.H.	4,720		3.	Philadelphia	1,950,961
1830	1.	New York	197,112		4.	Detroit	1,568,662
	2.	Philadelphia	161,410		5.	Los Angeles	1,238,048
	3.	Baltimore	80,620		6.	Cleveland	900,429
	4.	Boston	61,392		7.	St. Louis	821,960
	5.	Charleston, S.C.	30,289		8.	Baltimore	804,874
	6.	New Orleans	29,737		9.	Boston	781,188
	7.	Cincinnati	24,831		10.	Pittsburgh	669,817
	8.	Albany, N.Y.	24,209	1950	1.	New York	7,891,957
	9.	Brooklyn, N.Y.	20,535		2.	Chicago	3,620,962
	10.	Washington, D.C.	18,826		3.	Philadelphia	2,071,605
1850	1.	New York	515,547		4.	Los Angeles	1,970,358
	2.	Philadelphia	340,045		5.	Detroit	1,849,568
	3.	Baltimore	169,054		6.	Baltimore	949,708
	4.	Boston	136,881		7.	Cleveland	914,808
	5.	New Orleans	116,375		8.	St. Louis	856,796
	6.	Cincinnati	115,435		9.	Washington, D.C.	802,178
	7.	Brooklyn, N.Y.	96,838		10.	Boston	801,444
	8.	St. Louis	77,860	1970	1.	New York	7,895,563
	9.	Albany, N.Y.	50,763		2.	Chicago	3,369,357
	10.	Pittsburgh	46,601		3.	Los Angeles	2,811,801
1870	1.	New York	942,292		4.	Philadelphia	1,949,996
	2.	Philadelphia	674,022		5.	Detroit	1,514,063
	3.	Brooklyn, N.Y.	419,921‡		6.	Houston	1,233,535
	4.	St. Louis	310,864		7.	Baltimore	905,787
	5.	Chicago	298,977		8.	Dallas	844,401
	6.	Baltimore	267,354		9.	Washington, D.C.	756,668
	7.	Boston	250,526		10.	Cleveland	750,879
	8.	Cincinnati	216,239	1990	1.	New York	7,322,564
	9.	New Orleans	191,418		2.	Los Angeles	3,485,398
	10.	San Francisco	149,473		3.	Chicago	2,783,726
					4.	Houston	1,630,553
					5.	Philadelphia	1,585,577
					6.	San Diego	1,110,549

*Figure from a census taken in 1698.
†Philadelphia figures include suburbs.
‡Annexed to New York in 1898.
Source: U.S. Census data.

	7.	Detroit	1,027,974
	8.	Dallas	1,006,877
	9.	Phoenix	983,403
	10.	San Antonio	935,933

Immigration by Decade

Year	Number	Percentage of Total Population	Year	Number	Percentage of Total Population
1821–1830	151,824	1.6	1921–1930	4,107,209	3.9
1831–1840	599,125	4.6	1931–1940	528,431	0.4
1841–1850	1,713,251	10.0	1941–1950	1,035,039	0.7
1851–1860	2,598,214	11.2	1951–1960	2,515,479	1.6
1861–1870	2,314,824	7.4	1961–1970	3,321,677	1.8
1871–1880	2,812,191	7.1	1971–1980	4,493,000	2.2
1881–1890	5,246,613	10.5	1981–1990	7,338,000	3.0
1891–1900	3,687,546	5.8	1991–1996	6,146,300	2.3
1901–1910	8,795,386	11.6	Total	29,485,135	
1911–1920	5,735,811	6.2			
Total	33,654,785		1821–1996		
			Grand Total	63,139,920	

Source: U.S. Bureau of the Census, *Historical Statistics of the United States, Colonial Times to 1970* (1975), part 1, 105–106; *Statistical Abstract of the United States, 1998.*

Regional Origins

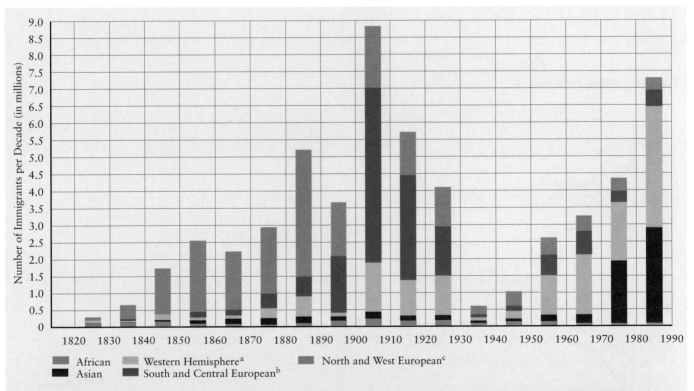

Legend:
- African
- Asian
- Western Hemisphere[a]
- South and Central European[b]
- North and West European[c]

[a] Canada and all countries in South America and Central America.
[b] Italy, Spain, Portugal, Greece, Germany (Austria included, 1938–1945), Poland, Czechoslovakia (since 1920), Yugoslavia (since 1920), Hungary (since 1861), Austria (since 1861, except 1938–1945), former USSR (excludes Asian USSR between 1931 and 1963), Latvia, Estonia, Lithuania, Finland, Romania, Bulgaria, Turkey (in Europe), and other European countries not classified elsewhere.
[c] Great Britain, Ireland, Norway, Sweden, Denmark, Iceland, Netherlands, Belgium, Luxembourg, Switzerland, France.
Source: Stephan Thernstrom, ed., *Harvard Encyclopedia of American Ethnic Groups* (1980), 480; U.S. Bureau of the Census, *Statistical Abstract of the United States, 1991.*

The Labor Force (Thousands of Workers)

Year	Agriculture	Mining	Manufacturing	Construction	Trade	Other	Total
1810	1,950	11	75	—	—	294	2,330
1840	3,570	32	500	290	350	918	5,660
1850	4,520	102	1,200	410	530	1,488	8,250
1860	5,880	176	1,530	520	890	2,114	11,110
1870	6,790	180	2,470	780	1,310	1,400	12,930
1880	8,920	280	3,290	900	1,930	2,070	17,390
1890	9,960	440	4,390	1,510	2,960	4,060	23,320
1900	11,680	637	5,895	1,665	3,970	5,223	29,070
1910	11,770	1,068	8,332	1,949	5,320	9,041	37,480
1920	10,790	1,180	11,190	1,233	5,845	11,372	41,610
1930	10,560	1,009	9,884	1,988	8,122	17,267	48,830
1940	9,575	925	11,309	1,876	9,328	23,277	56,290
1950	7,870	901	15,648	3,029	12,152	25,870	65,470
1960	5,970	709	17,145	3,640	14,051	32,545	74,060
1970	3,463	516	20,746	4,818	15,008	34,127	78,678
1980	3,364	979	21,942	6,215	20,191	46,612	99,303
1990	3,223	724	21,346	7,764	24,622	60,849	117,914
1997	3,399	634	20,835	8,302	26,777	69,611	129,558

Source: Historical Statistics of the United States, Colonial Times to 1970 (1975), 139; Statistical Abstract of the United States, 1998, table 675.

Changing Labor Patterns

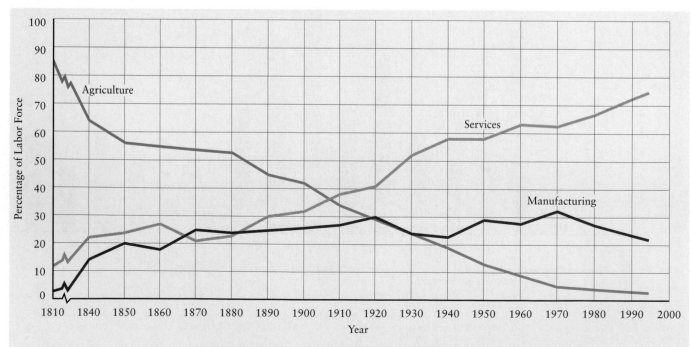

Source: Historical Statistics of the United States, Colonial Times to 1970 (1975), 139; Statistical Abstract of the United States, 1998, table 675.

Birth Rate, 1820–2000

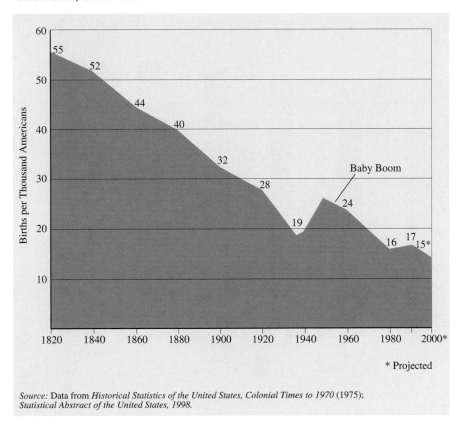

Source: Data from *Historical Statistics of the United States, Colonial Times to 1970* (1975);
Statistical Abstract of the United States, 1998.

Death Rate, 1900–2000

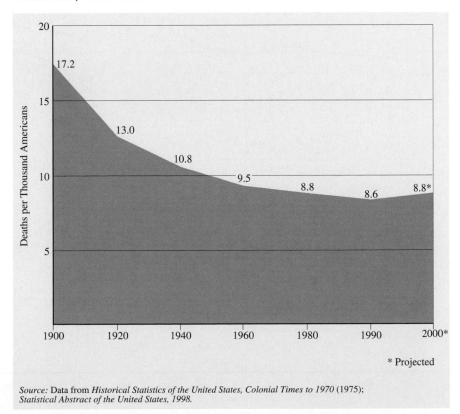

Source: Data from *Historical Statistics of the United States, Colonial Times to 1970* (1975);
Statistical Abstract of the United States, 1998.

Life Expectancy (at birth), 1900–2000

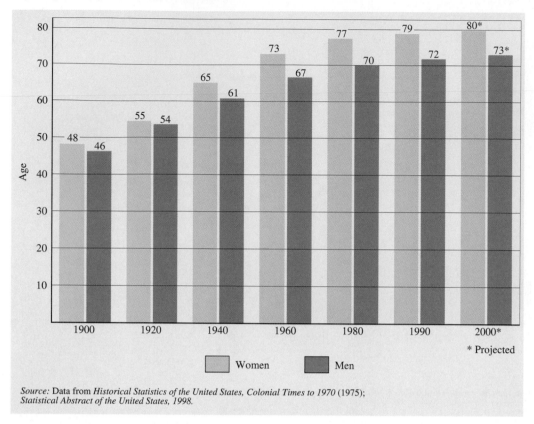

Source: Data from *Historical Statistics of the United States, Colonial Times to 1970* (1975); *Statistical Abstract of the United States, 1998.*

The Aging of the U.S. Population, 1850–1997

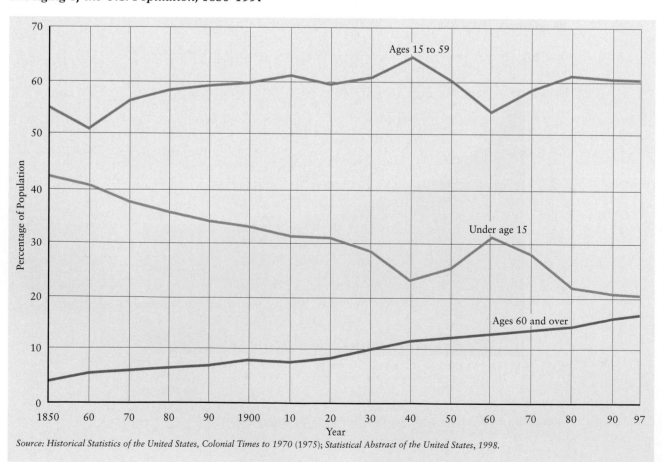

Source: Historical Statistics of the United States, Colonial Times to 1970 (1975); *Statistical Abstract of the United States, 1998.*

The American Government and Economy

The Growth of the Federal Government

	Employees (millions)		Receipts and Outlays ($ millions)	
Year	Civilian	Military	Receipts	Outlays
1900	0.23	0.12	567	521
1910	0.38	0.13	676	694
1920	0.65	0.34	6,649	6,358
1930	0.61	0.25	4,058	3,320
1940	1.04	0.45	6,900	9,600
1950	1.96	1.46	40,900	43,100
1960	2.38	2.47	92,500	92,200
1970	3.00	3.06	193,700	196,600
1980	2.99	2.05	517,112	590,920
1990	3.13	2.07	1,031,321	1,252,705
1997	2.78	1.43	1,579,292	1,601,235

Source: Statistical Profile of the United States, 1900–1980; Statistical Abstract of the United States, 1998.

Gross National Product, 1840–1990

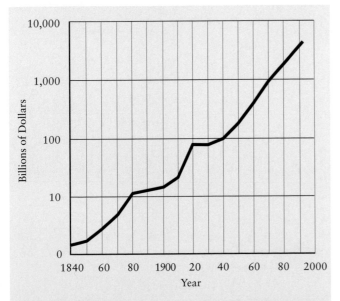

Note: GNP values have not been adjusted for inflation or deflation. GNP is plotted here on a logarithmic scale.
Source: Statistical Abstract of the United States, 1995.

GNP per Capita, 1840–1990

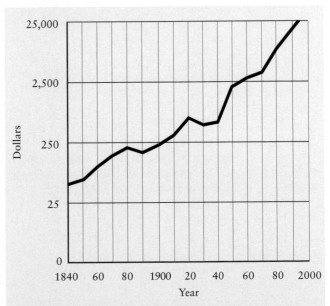

Note: GNP values have not been adjusted for inflation or deflation. GNP is plotted here on a logarithmic scale.

A-13

Main Sectors of the U.S. Economy: 1849, 1899, 1950, 1990

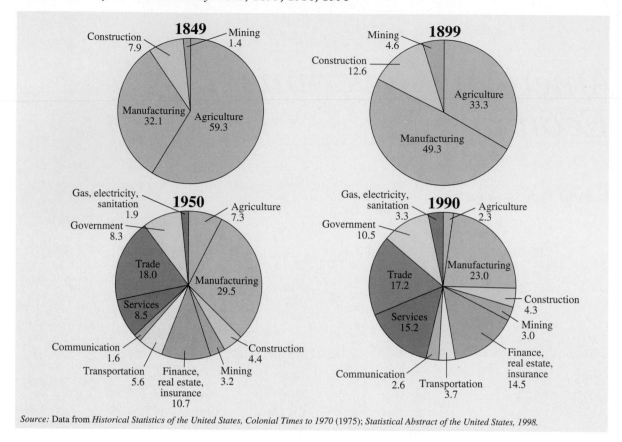

Source: Data from *Historical Statistics of the United States, Colonial Times to 1970* (1975); *Statistical Abstract of the United States, 1998.*

This index estimates how consumer prices changed on the average over ten-year intervals. Such estimates are highly uncertain, particularly when they are used to make comparisons over long periods of time.

To convert £ (pounds Sterling, until 1770) or $ (U.S. dollars, beginning in 1780) from any date in the past to the equivalent in 1990 dollars, multiply the historical price by the appropriate conversion multiplier. For example, £10 Sterling in 1730 would equal about $867 in 1990 (£10 × 86.7 = $867), or $10 in 1870 would equal about $99 in 1990 ($10 × 9.9 = $99). Then add another 20 percent to account for the rise in prices between 1990 and 1997.

Consumer Price Index and Conversion Table

Year	Price Index (1860 = 100)	Conversion Multiplier
1700	130	53.3
1710	100	69.3
1720	76	91.3
1730	80	86.7
1740	66	105.1
1750	84	82.6
1760	96	72.3
1770	100	69.3
1780	165	9.5
1790	148	10.6
1800	151	10.4
1810	148	10.6
1820	141	11.1
1830	111	14.1
1840	104	15.1
1850	94	16.6
1860	100	15.6
1870	157	9.9
1880	123	12.7
1890	109	14.3
1900	101	15.5
1910	114	13.7
1920	240	6.5
1930	200	7.8
1940	168	9.3
1950	288	5.4
1960	354	4.4
1970	464	3.4
1980	985	1.6
1990	1563	1.0
1997	1950	0.8

Source: Adapted from John J. McCusker, "How Much Is That in Real Money? A Historical Price Index for Use as a Deflator of Money Value in the Economy of the United States," *Proceedings of the American Antiquarian Society,* vol. 101, pt. 2 (1991), 297–390; *Statistical Abstract of the United States,* 1998, table 772.

Seattle
Olympia
WASHINGTON
Spokane
Columbia R.
Portland
Salem
OREGON
Boise
IDAHO
Snake R.
Great Falls
Helena
MONTANA
Missouri R.
Yellowstone R.
Billings
NORTH DAKOTA
Bismarck
SOUTH DAKOTA
Pierre
Reno
NEVADA
Carson City
Sacramento
San Francisco Oakland
San Jose
SIERRA NEVADA
Fresno
CALIFORNIA
San Joaquin R.
Sacramento R.
Great Salt Lake
Salt Lake City
UTAH
Green R.
WYOMING
ROCKY MOUNTAINS
Cheyenne
North Platte
NEBRASKA
South Platte
Denver
COLORADO
Colorado Springs
Platte R.
KANSAS
Wi
Las Vegas
Pacific Ocean
Los Angeles
San Diego
ARIZONA
Colorado R.
Phoenix
Tucson
Santa Fe
Albuquerque
NEW MEXICO
El Paso
Rio Grande
Pecos R.
Amarillo
OKLAHOM
TEXA
Nueces R.
San Antonio
Aus

45°
45°
40°
35°
30°

Pacific Ocean
Honolulu
HAWAII
22°
20°
160°
155°
0   100
Miles

RUSSIA
70°
BROOKS RANGE
Yukon R.
CANADA
International Date Line
60°
Bering Sea
ALASKA
ALASKA RANGE
Anchorage
Juneau
Gulf of Alaska
MEXICO
50°
175°   175°   165°   155°   145°   135°
0   500
Miles

CANADA

MINNESOTA
Duluth

St. Paul
Minneapolis

WISCONSIN
Milwaukee
Madison ★

L. Superior

MICHIGAN

L. Huron

L. Michigan

Lansing ★
Detroit
Chicago
Gary

IOWA
Des Moines

ILLINOIS
Springfield ★

INDIANA
Indianapolis ★

Cleveland
OHIO
Columbus ★

L. Ontario
Buffalo

L. Erie

Wheeling

Pittsburgh

PENNSYLVANIA

Allegheny R.

Harrisburg ★

St. Lawrence R.

MAINE
Augusta ★
Portland
Burlington
Montpelier ★ N.H.
VT. Concord ★
Manchester ★
Albany ★
NEW YORK
MASS.
Hartford ★ Boston
CONN. Providence ★
R.I.
Newark New York
Trenton ★
NEW JERSEY
Philadelphia

Omaha
Lincoln

Kansas City
Jefferson City ★
St. Louis

MISSOURI

Missouri R.

Illinois R.

Wabash R.

Ohio R.

Cincinnati
Louisville
Frankfort ★

KENTUCKY

Cumberland R.

WEST
VIRGINIA
Charleston ★

APPALACHIAN MOUNTAINS

Potomac

Baltimore
MD. ★
Annapolis ★

Richmond ★
VIRGINIA

Dover
DELAWARE

WASHINGTON D.C.

Norfolk

Roanoke R.

Kansas R.

Oklahoma City

Canadian R.

ARKANSAS
Little Rock ★

Memphis

Tennessee R.

Mississippi R.

Nashville ★

TENNESSEE

Knoxville

Raleigh ★

NORTH CAROLINA

Charlotte

Cape Fear R.

Dallas

Sabine R.

Trinity R.

LOUISIANA

Red R.

Jackson ★
MISSISSIPPI

Birmingham
Montgomery ★
ALABAMA

Alabama R.

Chattahoochee R.

Atlanta ★

GEORGIA

Altamaha R.

SOUTH
CAROLINA
Columbia ★

Santee R.

Charleston

Houston

Baton Rouge ★
New Orleans

Tallahassee ★

Jacksonville

FLORIDA

Miami

Atlantic Ocean

BAHAMAS

CUBA

Gulf of Mexico

Atlantic
Ocean
67° 66°

San Juan ★
PUERTO RICO
Ponce
18°

Caribbean Sea

0   50
Miles

Elevation

Feet	Meters
9,843	3,000
6,562	2,000
3,281	1,000
1,640	500
656	200
0	0
Below sea level	Below sea level

200   400
Miles

95°   90°   85°   80°   75°

Political divisions as of September 1999

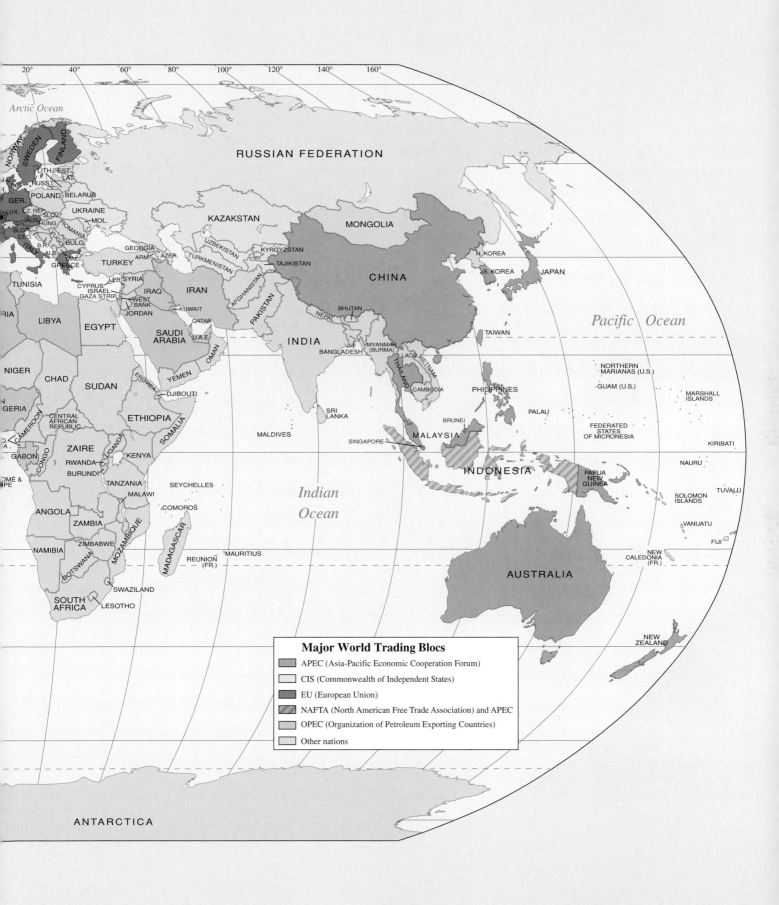

20° 40° 60° 80° 100° 120° 140° 160°

Arctic Ocean

RUSSIAN FEDERATION

NORWAY
SWEDEN
FINLAND
LITH. EST.
LAT.
RUSS.
GER. POLAND BELARUS
LUX. CZ. REP. UKRAINE
AUS. SLOV. HUNG.
SLO. ROMANIA
CRO. YUGO. MOL.
ITALY B.H. BULG.
ALB. MAC.
GREECE

KAZAKSTAN

MONGOLIA

GEORGIA
ARM. AZER. UZBEKISTAN KYRGYZSTAN
TURKEY TURKMENISTAN TAJIKISTAN
CYPRUS LEB. SYRIA
ISRAEL IRAQ IRAN AFGHANISTAN
GAZA STRIP WEST JORDAN PAKISTAN
BANK KUWAIT
QATAR
U.A.E.

CHINA

N. KOREA
S. KOREA JAPAN

TAIWAN

Pacific Ocean

TUNISIA

LIBYA EGYPT SAUDI
ARABIA OMAN INDIA

NEPAL BHUTAN
BANGLADESH
MYANMAR
(BURMA)

NIGER CHAD SUDAN YEMEN
ERITREA DJIBOUTI

LAOS VIETNAM
THAILAND
CAMBODIA

PHILIPPINES

NORTHERN
MARIANAS (U.S.)

GUAM (U.S.)

MARSHALL
ISLANDS

GERIA CENTRAL
AFRICAN
REPUBLIC ETHIOPIA

SRI
LANKA

PALAU

CAMEROON
GABON CONGO ZAIRE UGANDA KENYA
RWANDA
BURUNDI SOMALIA

MALDIVES

SINGAPORE MALAYSIA

BRUNEI

FEDERATED
STATES
OF MICRONESIA

KIRIBATI

OMÉ &
PE TANZANIA
MALAWI

SEYCHELLES

NAURU

INDONESIA

PAPUA
NEW
GUINEA

TUVALU

ANGOLA ZAMBIA MOZAMBIQUE
COMOROS

Indian
Ocean

SOLOMON
ISLANDS

NAMIBIA ZIMBABWE MADAGASCAR
BOTSWANA

REUNION
(FR.) MAURITIUS

VANUATU

NEW
CALEDONIA
(FR.)

FIJI

SWAZILAND
SOUTH
AFRICA LESOTHO

AUSTRALIA

NEW
ZEALAND

ANTARCTICA

Major World Trading Blocs

APEC (Asia-Pacific Economic Cooperation Forum)

CIS (Commonwealth of Independent States)

EU (European Union)

NAFTA (North American Free Trade Association) and APEC

OPEC (Organization of Petroleum Exporting Countries)

Other nations

Internet Resources

★

The Internet has been a useful place for scholars to communicate and publish information in recent years. Electronic discussion lists, electronic journals, and primary texts are among the resources available for historians on the Internet. The following sources are good places to find historical information. You can also search for information on the World Wide Web using any of a number of search engines. However, bear in mind that there is no board of editors screening Internet sites for accuracy or usefulness, and the search engines generally rely on free-text searches rather than subject headings. Be critical of all of your sources, particularly those found on the Internet.

American Memory: Historical Collection from the National Digital Library Program. <http://rs6.loc.gov/amhome.html> An Internet site that features digitized primary source materials from the Library of Congress, among them African American pamphlets, Civil War photographs, documents from the Continental Congress and the Constitutional Convention of 1774–1790, materials on woman suffrage, and oral histories.

Decisions of the U.S. Supreme Court. <http://supct.law.cornell.edu/supct/#historic> This database can be used to search for information on various Supreme Court cases. Although the site primarily covers cases that occurred after 1990, there is information on some earlier historic cases. The justices' opinions, as originally written, are also included.

Directory of Scholarly and Professional Electronic Conferences. <http://n2h2.com/KOVAKS/> A good place to find out what electronic conversations are going on in a scholarly discipline. Includes a good search facility and instructions on how to connect to e-mail discussion lists, newsgroups, and interactive chat sites with academic content. Once identified, these conferences are good places to raise questions, find out what controversies are currently stirring the profession, and even find out about grants and jobs.

Douglass Archives of American Public Addresses. <http://douglass.speech.nwu.edu/> An electronic archive of American speeches and documents by a variety of people from Jane Addams to Jonathan Edwards to Theodore Roosevelt.

Historical Text Archive. <http://www.msstate.edu/Archives/History> A Web interface for the oldest and largest Internet site for historical documents. Includes sections on native American, African American, and U.S. history, in which can be found texts of the Declaration of Independence, the U.S. Constitution, the Constitution of Iroquois Nations, World War II surrender documents, photograph collections, and a great deal more. These can be used online or saved as files.

History Links from Yahoo. <http://www.yahoo.com/Humanities/History/> A categorically arranged and fre-

quently updated site list for all types of history. Some of the sources are more useful than others, but this can be a helpful gateway to some good information.

Index of Civil War Information. <http://www.cwc.lsu.edu/cwc/civlink.html> Compiled by the United States Civil War Center, this index lists everything from diaries to historic battlefields to reenactments.

Index of Native American Resources on the Internet. <http://hanksville.phast.umass.edu/misc/Naresources.html> A vast index of native American resources organized by category. Within the history category, links are organized under subcategories: oral history, written history, geographical areas, timelines, and photographs and photographic archives. A central place to come in the search for information on native American history.

Index of Resources for Historians. <http://kuhttp.cc.ukans.edu/history/index.html> A vast list of more than 1,700 links to sites of interest to historians, arranged alphabetically by general topic. Some links are to sources for general reference information, but most are on historical topics. A good place to start an exploration of Internet resources.

Internet Archives of Texts and Documents. <http://history.hanover.edu/texts.html> As stated on its home page, the purpose of this site is to make primary sources available to students and faculty. Arranged chronologically, geographically, and by subject, the site lists speeches, reports, and other primary-document links. It also includes some secondary sources on each subject.

Internet Resources for Students of Afro-American History. <http://www.libraries.rutgers.edu/rulib/socsci/hist/afrores.html> A good place to begin research on topics in African American history. The site is indexed and linked to a wide variety of sources, including primary documents, text collections, and archival sources on African American history. Individual documents such as slave narratives and petitions; the Fugitive Slave Acts; and speeches by W. E. B. Du Bois, Booker T. Washington, and Martin Luther King Jr. are categorized by century.

The Martin Luther King Jr. Papers Project. <http://www.stanford.edu/group/King/> Organized by Stanford University, this site gives information about Martin Luther King Jr. and offers some of his writings.

Native Web. <http://www.nativeweb.org> One of the best organized and most accessible sites available on native American issues, *Native Web* combines an events calendar and message board with history, statistics, a list of news sources, archives, new and updated related sites each week, and documents. The text is indexed and can be searched by subject, nation, and geographic region.

Perry-Castañeda Library Map Collection. <http://www.lib.utexas.edu/Libs/PCL/MAP_collection.html> The University of

Texas at Austin Library has put over seven hundred U.S. maps on the Web for viewing by students and professors alike.

Smithsonian Institution. <http://www.si.edu> Organized by subject, such as military history or Hispanic/Latino American resources, this site offers selected links to sites hosted by Smithsonian Institution museums and organizations. Content includes graphics of museum pieces and relevant textual information, book suggestions, maps, and links.

United States History Index. <http://www.ukans.edu/~usa /index.html> Maintained by a history professor and arranged by subject, such as women's history, labor history, and agricultural history, this index provides links to a variety of other sites. Although the list is extensive, it does not include a synopsis of each site, which makes finding specific information a time-consuming process.

United States History Resources by Period. <http://www .cms.ccsd.k12.co.us/SONY/Intrecs/byperiod.html> This list of links to a variety of history sites is arranged chronologically and updated periodically.

United States Holocaust Museum. <http://www.ushmm .org/learn.html> This site contains information about the Holocaust Museum in Washington, D.C., as well as information on the Holocaust in general, and it lists links to related sites.

Women's History Resources. <http://www.mcps.k12 .md.us/curriculum/socialstd/Women_Bookmarks.html> An extensive listing of women's history sources available on the Internet. The site indexes resources on subjects as diverse as woman suffrage, women in the workplace, and celebrated women writers. Some of the links are to equally vast indexes, providing an overwhelming wealth of information.

Credits

Chapter 15

"David Macrae: The Devastated South." Excerpt from pages 345–347 in *America through British Eyes*, edited by Allan Nevins. Copyright © 1968 by Peter Nevins. Reprinted by permission of Peter Smith Publisher, Inc., Gloucester, MA.

Chapter 16

"Baron Joseph Alexander von Hübner: A Western Boom Town." Excerpt from pages 313–315 in *This Was America*, edited by Oscar Handlin. Copyright © 1949 by the President and Fellows of Harvard College. Copyright © 1960 by Oscar Handlin. Reprinted by permission of the author.

"Black Elk: Wounded Knee: Something Terrible Happened..." Excerpt from pages 254–257, 260–262 in *Black Elk Speaks* by John G. Neihardt. Copyright 1932, 1959, 1972 by John G. Neihardt. Copyright © 1961 by the John G. Neihardt Trust. Reprinted by permission of the University of Nebraska Press.

"Ida Lindgren: Swedish Emigrant in Frontier Kansas." Excerpt from pages 143–144, 153–154, 156 in *Letters from the Promised Land: Swedes in America, 1840–1914* by H. Arnold Barton, editor. Copyright © 1975 by H. Arnold Barton. Reprinted by permission of the University of Minnesota Press.

Chapter 17

"John Brophy: A Miner's Son." Excerpt from pages 44–48 in *American Labor: The Twentieth Century* by Jerold S. Auerbach, editor. Reprinted by permission.

"Count Vay de Vaya und Luskod: Pittsburgh Inferno." Excerpt from pages 407–410 in *This Was America* by Oscar Handlin, editor. Copyright © 1949 by the President and Fellows of Harvard College. Copyright © 1960 by Oscar Handlin. Reprinted by permission of the author.

Table 17.1: "Freight Rates for Transporting Crops." Adapted from p. 352 in *The Nation Transformed* by Sigmund Diamond, editor. Copyright © 1963 by Sigmund Diamond. Reprinted by permission of George Braziller, Inc.

Table 17.2: "Comparison of South and Non-South Value Added per Worker, 1910." Adapted from page 163 in *Old South, New South: Revolutions in the Southern Economy since the Civil War* by Gavin Wright. Copyright © 1986 by Gavin Wright. Reprinted by permission of BasicBooks, a division of Harper-Collins Publishers, Inc.

Chapter 18

"Charles Boissevain: Touring the South, 1880." Excerpt from pages 337–342 in *This Was America* by Oscar Handlin, editor. Copyright © 1949 by the President and Fellows of Harvard College. Copyright © 1960 by Oscar Handlin. Reprinted by permission of the author.

Figure 18.2: "Distributions of Weekly Wages for Black and White Workers in Virginia 1907." Adapted from page 184 in *Old South, New South: Revolutions in the Southern Economy since the Civil War* by Gavin Wright. Copyright © 1986 by Gavin Wright. Reprinted by permission of BasicBooks, a division of Harper-Collins Publishers, Inc.

Chapter 19

Excerpt from *A Bintel Brief*, edited by Isaac Metzger. Copyright © 1971 by Isaac Metzger. Reprinted by permission.

"M. Carey Thomas: Women's America Speech." Excerpt from pages 273–275 in *Women's America: Refocusing the Past*, Fourth Edition, by Linda K. Kerber and Jane De Hart, editors. Reprinted by permission of Oxford University Press.

Table 19.2: "Foreign-Born Population of Philadelphia, 1870 and 1910." Adapted from page 205 in *The Peoples of Philadelphia* edited by Allen F. Davis and Mark Haller. Copyright © 1973 by Temple University. Reprinted by permission of Temple University Press. All rights reserved.

Chapter 20

"Pauline Newman: Working for the Triangle Shirtwaist Company." Excerpt from *American Mosaic: The Immigrant Experience in the Words of Those Who Lived It*, edited by Joan Morrison and Charlotte Fox Zabusky. Copyright © 1980 by Joan Morrison and Charlotte Fox Zabusky. Currently available from the University of Pittsburgh Press.

"Charles Edward Russell: Muckraking." Excerpt from pages 135–139 in *Bare Hands and Stone Walls* by Charles Edward Russell. Copyright © 1933 by Charles Scribner's Sons; copyright renewed © 1961 by Charles Edward Russell. Reprinted with the permission of Scribner, a Division of Simon & Schuster.

Chapter 21

"George W. Prioleau: Black Soldiers in a White Man's War." Excerpt from pages 27–29 in *"Smoked Yankees" and the Struggle for Empire, 1898–1902* by Willard B. Gatewood. Copyright © 1987 by the Board of Trustees of the University of Arkansas. Reprinted by permission of the University of Arkansas Press.

Chapter 22

"Frederick A. Pottle: Mustard Gas." Excerpt from pages 117–118 in *Stretchers: The Story of a Hospital on the Western Front* by Frederick A. Pottle. Copyright © 1929 by Frederick A. Pottle. Reprinted by permission of Yale University Press.

Chapter 27

"Mark Goodson: Red Hunting on the Quiz Shows; or, What's My Party Line?" Excerpt from pages 320–324 in *Memories of the American Inquisition: An Oral History* by Griffin Fariello. Copyright © 1995 by Griffin Fariello. Reprinted by permission of W.W. Norton & Company, Inc.

"Isaac Nelson: Atomic Witness." Excerpt from pages 133–135 in *American Ground Zero: The Secret Nuclear War* by Carole Gallagher. Copyright © 1993 Carole Gallagher. Reprinted by permission of the author.

"Jean Monnet: Truman's Generous Proposal." Excerpt from pages 264–265 in *Memoirs* by Jean Monnet, translated by Richard Mayne. Translation copyright © 1978 by Doubleday, a division of Bantam Doubleday Dell Publishing Group, Inc. Used by permission of Doubleday, a division of Random House, Inc.

Chapter 28

"Joy Wilner: A Fifties Housewife." Excerpt from pages 103–104 in *The Fifties: An Oral History* by Brett Harvey, editor. Copyright © 1993 by Brett Harvey. Reprinted by permission of HarperCollins Publishers, Inc.

"Ann Moody: 'We Would Like to Be Served.'" Excerpt from pages 264–267 in *Coming of Age in Mississippi* by Anne Moody. Copyright © 1968 by Anne Moody. Used by permission of Doubleday, a division of Random House, Inc.

"Hanoch Bartov: 'Everyone Has a Car.'" Excerpt from *Arbaah Israelim Vekhol America (Four Israelis and the Whole of America)* by Hanoch Bartov. © Hanoch Bartov, Acum House, Israel. Reprinted by permission of the author and Acum House.

Chapter 29

"Mary Crow Dog: The Trail of Broken Treaties." Excerpt from pages 86–91 in *Lakota Woman* by Mary Crow Dog and Richard Erdos. Copyright © 1990 by Mary Crow Dog and Richard Erdos. Reprinted by permission of Grove Atlantic, Inc.

"Dave Cline: A Vietnam Vet Remembers." Excerpt from pages 135–141 in *Winter Soldiers: An Oral History of the Vietnam Veterans against the War* by Richard Stacewicz. Copyright © 1997 by Richard Stacewicz. Reprinted by permission of Macmillan, a division of Simon & Schuster.

"Che Guevara: Vietnam and the World Freedom Struggle." Excerpt from pages 144–159 of *Ernesto Che Guevara Speaks: Selected Speeches & Writings*. Copyright © Pathfinder Press. Reprinted by permission.

Chapter 30

"Phyllis Ellison: Busing in Boston." Excerpt from pages 600, 610, 612–613 in *Voices of Freedom: An Oral History of the Civil Rights Movement from the 1950s through the 1980s* by Henry Hampton and Steve Fayer. Copyright © 1990 by Blackside, Inc. Used by permission of Bantam Books, a division of Bantam Doubleday Dell Publishing Group, Inc.

"Watergate and Due Process." Excerpt from *The London Times*, Editorial, June 5, 1973, page 17. © Times Newspapers Limited, London, 1973. Reprinted by permission of News International Syndication.

"David Kopay: The Real Score: A Gay Athlete Comes Out." Excerpt from *The David Kopay Story: An Extraordinary Self-Revelation* by David Kopay & Perry D. Young. Copyright © 1988 by David Kopay & Perry D. Young. Reprinted by permission of Donald I. Fine, an imprint of Dutton/Plume, a division of Penguin Putnam, Inc.

Chapter 31

"Saddam Hussein: Calling for a Holy War against the United States." From *The New York Times*, September 6, 1990, page A19. Copyright © 1990 by The New York Times Company. Reprinted by permission.

"Cuauhtémoc Menendez: The Undocumented Worker." Excerpt from pages 410–411 in *Mexican Voices, American Dreams: An Oral History of Mexican Immigration to the United States* by Marilyn P. Davis. Copyright © 1990 by Marilyn P. Davis. Reprinted by permission of Henry Holt & Company, Inc.

Figure 31.2: "Productivity and Wages, 1982–1995." From *The New York Times*, January 2, 1996, page C20. Copyright © 1996 by The New York Times Company. Reprinted by permission.

Index